Field of sunflowers, a common crop in central and southern France

Leaning Tower of Pisa rising behind the Baptistry *(see p411)*

The spectacular hilltop Monestir de Montserrat in Catalonia *(see pp316–17)*

HOW TO USE THIS GUIDE

This Dorling Kindersley travel guide helps you to get the most from your visit to Europe. *Visiting Europe* maps the continent, and gives tips on practical considerations and travel. *Europe at a Glance* gives an overview of some of the main attractions and a brief history. The book is divided into seven sections, each covering a group of two, three, or four countries. The chapter on each country starts with a historical portrait and a map of the country. The main sightseeing section then follows, with maps of the major cities. For each country there is a section of practical and travel information, followed by listings of recommended hotels and restaurants.

EUROPE MAP
The colored areas shown on the map on the inside front cover indicate the 19 country chapters in this guide.

1 At a Glance
The map here highlights the most interesting cities, towns, and regions in the countries covered in the section (in this example Italy and Greece).

Each country chapter has color-coded thumb tabs.

2 Introduction to a Country
This section gives the reader an insight into the country's geography, historical background, politics, and the character of the people. A chart lists the key dates and events in the country's history.

3 Country Map
For easy reference, sights in each country are numbered and plotted on a map. The black bullet numbers (e.g. ❸) also indicate the order in which the sights are covered in the chapter.

Sights at a Glance lists the numbered sights in alphabetical order.

For the larger countries there is an index of the practical and listings pages at the end of the chapter.

EYEWITNESS TRAVEL

EUROPE

LONDON, NEW YORK,
MELBOURNE, MUNICH AND DELHI
www.dk.com

PROJECT EDITOR Ferdie McDonald, Claire Marsden
ART EDITOR Paul Jackson
EDITORS Sam Atkinson, Simon Hall, Andrew Szudek
DESIGNERS Anthony Limerick, Sue Metcalfe-Megginson,
Rebecca Milner
PICTURE RESEARCHERS Katherine Mesquita, Alex Pepper, Lily Sellar
MAP CO-ORDINATOR Casper Morris
DTP DESIGNER Maite Lantaron

MAPS
Ben Bowles, Rob Clynes, James Macdonald
(Colourmap Scanning Ltd)

PHOTOGRAPHERS
Max Alexander, Demetrio Carrasco, Kim Sayer, Linda Whitwam

Printed and bound by South China Printing Co. Ltd., China

12 13 14 15 10 9 8 7 6 5 4 3 2 1

First published in Great Britain in 2001
by Dorling Kindersley Limited
80 Strand, London WC2R 0RL

Reprinted with revisions 2002, 2003, 2004, 2006, 2008, 2010, 2012

Copyright © 2001, 2012 Dorling Kindersley Limited, London
A Penguin Company

A CIP CATALOGUE RECORD IS AVAILABLE FROM THE BRITISH LIBRARY.

ISBN 978-1-4053-7065-3

FLOORS ARE REFERRED TO THROUGHOUT IN ACCORDANCE WITH EUROPEAN
USAGE; IE THE "FIRST FLOOR" IS THE FLOOR ABOVE GROUND LEVEL.

Front cover main image: Castlenaud-la-Chapelle, Aquitaine

MIX
Paper from
responsible sources
FSC
www.fsc.org   FSC™ C018179

**The information in this
DK Eyewitness Travel Guide is checked regularly.**
Every effort has been made to ensure that this book is as up-to-date
as possible at the time of going to press. Some details, however,
such as telephone numbers, opening hours, prices, gallery hanging
arrangements and travel information are liable to change. The
publishers cannot accept responsibility for any consequences arising
from the use of this book, nor for any material on third party
websites, and cannot guarantee that any website address in this
book will be a suitable source of travel information. We value the
views and suggestions of our readers very highly. Please write to:
Publisher, DK Eyewitness Travel Guides, Dorling Kindersley, 80 Strand,
London WC2R 0RL, Great Britain, or email: travelguides@dk.com.

Enjoying the evening sunshine in a
café overlooking a Greek harbor

CONTENTS

**Punting on the Cam beside Queens'
College, Cambridge *(see p73)***

◁ La Maison du Roi, Brussels' magnificent town hall *(see pp224–5)*

4 City Map
This plots individual sights within the most important cities. The sights within a city such as Rome are indicated with clear bullet numbers (e.g. ③), in contrast to the black bullets used on the country maps.

Visitors' Checklist gives all the practical information needed to plan your visit.

Sights at a Glance lists the numbered sights within the city.

5 Major Sights
Historic buildings are dissected to reveal their interiors, while museums and galleries have color-coded floor plans to help you find the most important exhibits.

Stars indicate the features that no visitor should miss.

6 Detailed Information
Cities, towns and other sights are described individually. Their entries appear in the same order as the numbering on the country map at the beginning of the section.

Each entry begins with essential practical information, including the address and telephone number of the local tourist information office. Opening times are given for major sights and museums.

7 Practical Information
This section covers subjects such as visas, security, travel, shopping, and entertainment. The larger countries are covered in greater detail.

Directory boxes give contact information for the services and venues mentioned in the text.

Climate charts *(see p13)* are provided for each country.

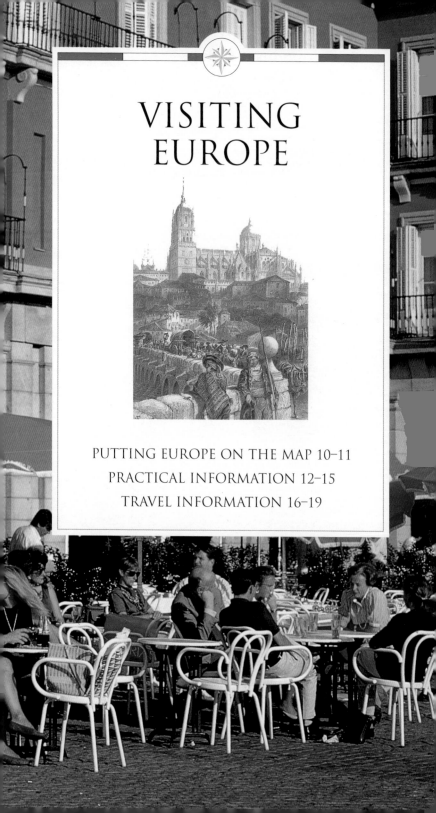

VISITING
EUROPE

Putting Europe on the Map

The continent of Europe stretches as far east as Russia's Ural Mountains, a total surface area of 10.4 million sq km (4 million sq miles). However, the 20 countries covered in this guide occupy a much smaller area, being concentrated in the northwestern and central parts of the continent and along the Mediterranean coast in the south. These countries are shown on this map in dark green. They include 18 of the nations that make up the European Union, the political association of European states based in Brussels *(see p228)*. The map also shows the principal international airports and the major road links. Europe's rail network is shown on the map on the inside back cover.

Satellite Photograph of Europe
This image shows the range of landscapes on the European continent, from the frozen coast of northern Scandinavia, through fertile plains on either side of the Alps and Pyrenees, to the balmy regions of the Mediterranean.

0 kilometers 250

0 miles   250

KEY

✈ International airport

— Highway

— Major road

--- Ferry route

▬▬ International boundary

◁ **Café life in Plaza Mayor, Madrid**

DISTANCE CHART

ATHENS

2564 1593	BERLIN							
3023 1878	**782** 486	BRUSSELS						
3227 2005	**1057** 657	**327** 203	LONDON					
3883 2413	**2342** 1455	**1568** 974	**1732** 1076	MADRID				
2967 1844	**1076** 669	**302** 188	**415** 258	**1267** 787	PARIS			
1902 1182	**1520** 945	**1501** 933	**1802** 1120	**2093** 1301	**1460** 907	ROME		
3650 2268	**1035** 643	**1594** 991	**1820** 1131	**3222** 2002	**1861** 1156	**2622** 1629	STOCKHOLM	
2188 1360	**589** 366	**1335** 830	**1838** 1142	**2932** 1822	**1623** 1009	**1834** 1140	**1601** 995	WARSAW

Distance by road in kilometers
Distance by road in miles

PRACTICAL INFORMATION

Millions of visitors travel to Europe for reasons many Europeans take for granted – the rich diversity of history, architecture, art, and landscape. In Western Europe tourist facilities are generally of a high standard, while in the former Communist countries of Eastern Europe their scope and quality have improved significantly over the past

The European Union Flag

decade. As a result, the whole of Europe is more accessible. This section gives information on practical matters such as passport formalities and how to get around. Many countries are members of the European Union, with certain laws in common, but there are also notable differences. In each country chapter a *Practical Information* section gives specific details for visitors.

WHEN TO GO

The best time to visit Europe depends on your itinerary, but most people prefer the summer months, between May and September. Due to the diverse geography of Europe, the weather has wide variations. Summers in northwestern Europe can be cool and rainy, while in the east they can be unbearably hot. The Mediterranean, with its hot, dry summers and relatively mild winters, has the balmiest climate, but crowds are a major drawback, particularly in July and August, making May and June better times to visit. August is the busiest month because this is when most French, Italian, and Spanish citizens take their vacations.

The climate of parts of Scandinavia is extreme: in winter in the north the sun rises only for a few hours and the roads can be blocked by snow, while summertime attracts many visitors, drawn by the prospect of enjoying the "midnight sun".

The mountainous areas of Europe have unique climates. The Pyrenees, Alps, and Apennines all have short summers and long winters with heavy snowfall. Consequently, these regions offer wonderful opportunities for skiing.

EUROPEAN TIME ZONES

The 20 countries covered in this guide fall across three time zones. Great Britain, Ireland, and Portugal are on GMT (Greenwich Mean Time), while the other European countries are one hour ahead

(+1), except for Greece, which is two hours ahead (+2). So, for example, London, Dublin, and Lisbon are five hours ahead of New York, while Paris and Budapest are six hours ahead, and Athens is seven hours ahead.

In Europe the clocks go forward by one hour in March (Daylight Saving), and go back in the fall, usually in October.

PASSPORTS AND VISAS

Most western European countries belong to the European Union. Based in Brussels, this European authority has the power to pass certain laws affecting all member states. There are currently 27 member states.

There are no passport controls between the following EU members: Germany, France, Spain, Portugal, Belgium, Luxembourg, the Netherlands, Italy, and Austria. In theory it is sufficient to carry an identity card when traveling between these countries, but it is worth carrying your passport just in case. The other EU countries have yet to sign up to this agreement, and so passports are needed by everyone entering or leaving.

If you are arriving in Europe from a non-EU country, a passport is required. However, visitors from the United States, Canada, Japan, Australia, New Zealand, Norway, and Switzerland, amongst others, no longer require visas for visits under three months to countries in the EU. Check this with the embassy of the country you

plan to visit. If you have a visa for one of the Schengen countries, you are permitted to visit all of the countries in the agreement (Austria, Estonia, Greece, Latvia, The Netherlands, Slovakia, Belgium, Finland, Hungary, Lithuania, Norway, Slovenia, Czech Republic, France, Iceland, Luxembourg, Poland, Spain, Denmark, Germany, Italy, Malta, Portugal, Sweden and Switzerland).

Some countries require a visa regardless of your length of stay; refer to the individual *Practical Information* sections in each chapter for full details.

STUDENT CARDS

As well as various bus and rail tickets that offer discounts on European travel *(see p18)*, students with a recognized student card may be eligible for a wider range of discounts. The best card is the International Student Identity Card (ISIC), which gives discounts on all kinds of goods and transport, as well as cheap admission to many museums, galleries, and other sights. Most students can obtain this card from their educational establishment at home but it can also be obtained abroad from an ISIC issuing office or from branches of STA Travel *(see p17)*. For US students, this card also includes some medical cover.

CUSTOMS AND DUTY-FREE

Duty-free goods are not available for purchase when traveling between EU countries;

these goods can only be bought on entry to or exit from the European Union as a whole. The allowances are as follows: tobacco (200 cigarettes, 50 cigars, or 250g of loose tobacco); alcohol (1 liter of strong spirits, 2 liters of alcohol under 22 percent proof, and 4 liters of wine); coffee (500g), and perfume (60ml).

When entering a country you will be asked to declare certain items from abroad and pay duty on any amount that exceeds that country's allowance; the nature of these goods will vary from country to country. This process applies on returning to your home country with goods acquired in Europe.

VALUE ADDED TAX

In the EU, all goods and services (except certain items such as food and children's clothes) are subject to a Value Added Tax, known as VAT in the UK, which is included in most prices. If you are not a European Union citizen, you may get a refund of this tax, but it can be a lengthy process.

The easiest way to do this is to shop where you see the "Euro Free Tax" sign, although the stores that offer this service may be expensive or sell only luxury goods. After showing your passport to the shop assistant and completing a form, the VAT will be deducted from your bill.

In certain countries you need to keep your receipts and VAT forms and present them at the Tax Refund desk with your unopened purchases when you leave the country. These forms are processed and a refund will eventually be sent to your home address.

PERSONAL SECURITY

Europe is one of the safest places to travel, but you should always take certain safety measures. If you are traveling alone and especially at night, it is best to avoid deserted and poorly lit buildings, and places such as back streets and parking lots. If you should be a victim of an attack or robbery, report it

immediately to the local police. Pickpockets are common throughout Europe, but certain crimes are worse in certain countries – specific information is given in the *Practical Information* section of each country chapter.

By far the safest way of carrying money is in the form of traveler's checks *(see p14)*, which allow you to keep your hard cash to a minimum. Never leave your belongings unattended, and make sure they are adequately insured before you leave home. Keep your valuables well concealed, especially in crowds. It is advisable to wear minimal jewelry when going out; leave it in your hotel safe instead.

INSURANCE AND MEDICAL TREATMENT

Travel insurance is essential to cover any loss or damage to your possessions and for unexpected medical and dental treatment. Many major credit cards (including American Express) offer some insurance if you purchase your flights or vacation package with them, so check this before buying a separate policy. If possible, buy one which pays for medical treatment on the spot, rather than a policy

which reimburses you later. Most general insurance policies do not cover potentially dangerous activities such as climbing, skiing, and scuba diving – these cost extra. If you plan to do any of these, check that you will be covered.

CONVERSION CHART

Officially the metric system is used throughout Europe, but Imperial measures are commonly used in Britain. British pints and gallons are 20 percent larger than US measures.

Imperial to Metric
1 inch = 2.54 centimeters
1 foot = 30 centimeters
1 mile = 1.6 kilometers
1 ounce = 28 grams
1 pound = 454 grams
1 US pint = 0.47 liter
1 UK pint = 0.55 liter
1 US gallon = 3.8 liters
1 UK gallon = 4.6 liters

Metric to Imperial
1 millimeter = 0.04 inch
1 centimeter = 0.4 inch
1 meter = 3 feet 3 inches
1 kilometer = 0.6 mile
1 gram = 0.035 ounce
1 kilogram = 2.2 pounds
1 liter = 2.1 US pints
1 liter = 1.76 UK pints

THE CLIMATE OF EUROPE

As a continent that ranges south from the Arctic Circle to just north of the tropics, Europe experiences a diversity of climates, yet because it is influenced by the warm Gulf Stream its climate is overall much more temperate than other areas at the same latitudes. The *Practical Information* section for each country contains a panel like the one below giving details of average temperatures, rainfall, and sunshine for each season of the year.

ROME

° C/F	29/84		
18/64 19/66	22/72		
9/48	13/55	12/54
0°C 32°F		4/40

Average daily maximum temperature

Average daily minimum temperature

	6 hrs	10 hrs	7 hrs	5 hrs

Average daily hours of sunshine

	51 mm	21 mm	95 mm	87 mm
month	Apr	Jul	Oct	Jan

Average monthly rainfall

Communications and Money

In the 21st century communications are developing quickly so that few places in Europe remain completely out of touch. With the advent of cell phones, e-mail access on computers, and Internet cafés, ways to communicate are now more numerous, easy, and relatively cheap. Many hotels and restaurants readily accept most credit cards, so cash is normally only needed for smaller transactions or in remote spots. The introduction of the euro in some countries has also made life much easier for travelers touring Europe.

TELEPHONES

These days, when more and more people have a cell or mobile phone, the need for a public telephone may be less urgent. However, be aware that not all cell phones work everywhere. If you want to use your cell phone abroad you need to arrange this with your service provider. Also, most US cell phones do not work in Europe (except AT&T and T-Mobile) and vice versa – but you can now buy phones that work in both continents. US companies will also rent cell phones for use while in Europe. If you have a GSM phone that is compatible in Europe check with your service provider that it has been set up for roaming. If your home operator does not offer coverage in another country you will be able to make calls as your phone will roam into a host operator's network, usually automatically. However, it can be very costly to make and receive calls this way.

Most European countries have excellent public telephones in towns and cities. In the more isolated regions, it is less likely that you will come across a telephone kiosk where you can make international calls.

MAIL SERVICES

Mail services are generally fast and efficient, with letters and cards typically taking five days to reach North America, or a week to get to Australasia. The mail service does vary across the continent, however, and in some areas, such as Eastern Europe and in remote parts of Greece the service may be much slower.

INTERNET ACCESS

Internet and email services are widely available in every major city across Europe. There are also growing numbers of Internet cafés in towns and resorts, so it

should not be difficult to access email accounts or connect to the web. In Internet cafés you normally pay a fee for a fixed amount of time, which varies according to local use and rates.

VoIP (Voice over Internet Protocol) is a way of communicating telephonically via your computer. Most Internet cafés will have at least one such system installed. In order to use it, you will need a Skype account (free to set up), a set of headphones and a microphone (these are often but not always provided by the café). Calls are free between Skype users but there is a charge to land lines and cell phones.

Many hotels have Wi-Fi (wireless) Internet access, so travelers with their own laptop can have easy access. Check in advance if there is a charge for this.

CHANGING MONEY

Now that 23 countries take the euro, there is no need to change money so frequently. Check within each area chapter of this guide to see which countries participate.

Currency exchanges *(bureaux de change)* can be found in most towns – particularly within banks or post offices. Banks usually tend to offer the best rates. Most airports, central train stations, large hotels, and border posts also have currency exchanges.

Many visitors use traveler's checks when abroad because, unlike cash, they can be replaced by the bank if they are lost or stolen. However, if you have a plastic card with a pin number for your bank account or credit card, and as long as you belong to a global network such as Plus/Visa, or Cirrus/Mastercard, ATM machines can provide instant access to your funds. Be aware that credit cards charge interest if you take out cash. You can find ATM machines in banks, shopping malls, and stations. When paying by card, note that many European countries use "chip and pin" so swipe debit/credit cards may be refused.

INTERNATIONAL DIALING CODES

The list below gives the international dialing codes for the countries covered in this guide. When calling from the US and Canada prefix all numbers by "011;" from Australia by "0011;" from New Zealand by "00." When calling from within Europe, use the "00" prefix. If you are unsure, call international directory inquiries.

• Austria	43	• Luxembourg	352
• Belgium	32	• Netherlands	31
• Czech Republic	420	• Norway	47
• Denmark	45	• Poland	48
• Finland	358	• Portugal	351
• France	33	• Spain	34
• Germany	49	• Switzerland	41
• Greece	30	• Sweden	46
• Hungary	36	• United Kingdom	44
• Ireland (Republic)	353	(Great Britain and	
• Italy	39	Northern Ireland)	

THE EURO

The Euro (€) is the common currency of the European Union (EU). It went into general circulation on January 1, 2002, initially for 12 participating countries. The old currencies were phased out, leaving the Euro as the sole currency. EU members using the Euro as sole official currency are known as the Eurozone. Several EU members have opted out of joining this common currency. Euro notes are identical throughout the Eurozone countries, each one including designs of fictional architectural structures. The coins, however, have one side identical (the value side), and one side with an image unique to each country. Both notes and coins are exchangeable in each of the participating Euro countries.

Bank Notes

Euro bank notes have seven denominations. The €5 note (grey in color) is the smallest, followed by the €10 note (pink), €20 note (blue), €50 note (orange), €100 note (green), €200 note (yellow), and €500 note (purple). All notes show the stars of the European Union.

€5 note

€10 note

€20 note

€50 note

€100 note

€200 note

€500 note

€2 coin   €1 coin   50 cents   20 cents   10 cents

Coins

The euro has eight coin denominations: €1 and €2; 50 cents, 20 cents, 10 cents, 5 cents, 2 cents, and 1 cent. The €1 and €2 coins are both silver and gold in color. The 50-, 20-, and 10-cent coins are gold. The 5-, 2-, and 1-cent coins are bronze.

5 cents   2 cents   1 cent

Europe by Air

With its network of international flights, Europe is one of the most accessible parts of the world to reach by air. Compared with North America and Australasia, European flights are a relatively cheap, quick and convenient way to get to and around Europe. In an industry previously dominated by state-run carriers and major private airlines, the recent rise of budget airlines offering "no-frills" flights has opened up many new destinations and made air travel more affordable.

FLYING TO EUROPE

If you are traveling from a major international airport, you will usually be able to find a direct flight to many European cities. Main destinations include London, Paris, Amsterdam, Rome, Milan, and Frankfurt. Most of the major North American airlines such as Delta, Air Canada, American, and Continental have frequent flights to all parts of Europe, as does Qantas from Australia. For more details on flights to specific destinations, see the *Travel Information* sections for individual countries.

Although most major airports are based on the outskirts of European capitals and other big cities, all can be reached by efficient train, bus, taxi, and sometimes subway services. Many of the smaller airlines use less convenient airports, with a longer transfer time but this is reflected in their cheaper fares.

EUROPEAN NATIONAL AIRLINES

Most European countries have a national carrier which serves international destinations, and these usually offer frequent flights per day to their home countries at convenient times.

Scheduled flights on national airlines usually provide more legroom (essential on long flights) and a better quality of in-flight service than charter airlines, with complimentary items such as headphones and drinks. Fares can be more expensive but it is worth shopping around for the best deals. The largest national carriers include **British Airways, Air France,** Iberia (Spain), **KLM** (the Netherlands), **Lufthansa** (Germany), *Alitalia* (Italy), and **SAS** (Scandinavia).

FLIGHT TIMES

As a rough guide, flights from New York to London take about 6 hours 30 minutes, to Paris and Frankfurt 7 hours 30 minutes, and to Rome 8 hours 30 minutes. Flights from Sydney to London take around 23 hours via Bangkok, to Paris 23 hours via Singapore, to Frankfurt 22 hours via Singapore, and to Rome 25 hours via Bangkok. Flights from Auckland to London take about 24 hours, and to Frankfurt 23 hours.

KEEPING COSTS DOWN

As a rule, European air fares are cheaper between November and March (with the exception of Christmas and Easter weeks), while the high season is from June to mid-September. A "shoulder season" of moderate prices exists between these months. Try, if you can, to travel mid-week, because tickets are cheaper and airports are less busy.

Whatever season you travel, there are ways of saving money on air fares. A good way to start is to contact a travel agent that specializes in budget travel, such as **STA Travel** in the US. If you are young (under 25), a student, or a senior citizen, you will usually find special reduced-fare air tickets. Otherwise, you save money when you book in advance. If you can book 14 to 21 days ahead, APEX (Advanced Purchase Excursion) or Super APEX tickets are available direct from the airlines and are much cheaper. With these there is a minimum stay requirement of 7 days but they can still be good value. It is cheaper still to buy air tickets through a travel agent. Be aware, however, that the cheaper the ticket, the more inflexible it usually is. You may not be able to alter, transfer, or cancel your flight, or if you do there may be stiff penalties, so check the conditions beforehand.

It is always cheaper to book a return (round-trip) ticket with fixed dates rather than an "open" return. You can also get an "open jaw" return, which allows you to enter via one city and exit via another (not necessarily in the same country). This is useful if you are doing a grand tour, but "open jaw" tickets are often more expensive than regular returns. Companies such as **Trailfinders** in the UK, and **STA Travel** in the US, offer their own versions of these.

Depending on how far you have to travel, round-the-world (RTW) tickets can also work out cheaper than the standard long-haul returns. These enable you to fly around the world on specified routes, as long as you don't backtrack on yourself.

Look out for good deals from established travel agents and package operators that are advertised in newspapers and travel magazines. Airlines will quote you the regular price for a ticket, but they can often reduce this if they have unsold seats. Consolidators, or "bucket shops", buy unsold tickets in bulk (often for off-season travel) and sell them at cheaper rates.

Standby tickets are also economical, but you have to be flexible about your date and time of departure; be aware that you sometimes have to wait (possibly for days) for a cancellation.

CHARTER FLIGHTS

It is always worth investigating charter flight fares. There are quite a few companies that book whole planes or blocks of seats in advance, then resell the tickets at more competitive rates. The main drawback with these tickets is that they are usually non-refundable. They also tend to land at remote airports and at wildly unsocial hours. The level of in-flight service and comfort is usually lower, too.

PACKAGE DEALS

One of the easiest ways to arrange your visit to Europe is to book a package vacation. These are offered by all the major airlines, as well as various reputable independent companies, such as **Central Holidays** and **American Express**. They normally include flights, transfers, and accommodations, and sometimes side trips and food, and the cost is sometimes far less than if you were to buy these separately. While an excellent way of reducing the strain of organizing your vacation, the downside with a package tour is that it usually involves traveling in large numbers on specific flights to a hotel which, because the price has been pared to the bone, may not offer a high standard of food or facilities. On the other hand, there are specialist package tour operators that do offer top quality hotels and use scheduled flights.

FLY-DRIVE

Many airlines, as well as numerous travel companies, offer fly-drive packages, which combine air fares and car rental. These deals are often worth considering, as they give you flexibility and offer a saving over arranging the two parts separately.

INTERNET BOOKING

The Internet is becoming a popular way of booking tickets. Two of the best sites for this are **Expedia and Opodo**. Expedia has a system called a "Fare Tracker" whereby you fill in a form online and they e-mail you information when tickets become available. The US company **Europebyair** also provides excellent deals on flights to Europe. It offers a Flight Pass for non-European citizens, valid for 62 European cities and one-way flights between these destinations for a very reasonable price.

FLIGHTS WITHIN EUROPE

There is an extensive flight network serving most major cities, making it quick and easy to fly within Europe. If you are traveling some distance, and especially between Great Britain and other parts of Europe, flying can be the least expensive way to go. Indeed, if you want to get to destinations such as Portugal or Greece quickly, flying is almost the only option. However, between major cities, such as Berlin and Paris, you could go by train, which is almost as quick and cheap, and saves the trouble of getting to an airport *(see p18)*.

It is best to avoid flying between major cities on Friday evenings and early Monday mornings because these flights can be crowded with European commuters.

As with transatlantic flights, you can get cheaper tickets by booking early. The best cities for finding good deals from "bucket shops" are London, Athens, and Amsterdam.

LOW-COST AIRLINES

Recent years have seen the emergence of so-called "no frills" airlines in Europe, such as **Ryanair, easyJet, Air Berlin** and **Eurowings**, which offer very competitive prices. A return flight from London to Berlin, for example, can cost as little as £50 ($70). To keep prices down, there is usually less legroom, onboard catering and checked luggage costs extra, and outlying airports may be used, but unless you must have these benefits, the price justifies the inconvenience.

DIRECTORY

EUROPEAN NATIONAL AIRLINES

Air France
Tel 800-237 2747 (US).
Tel 1-300 39 01 90 (Aus).
www.airfrance.com

Alitalia
Tel 800-223 5730 (US).
www.alitalia.com

British Airways
Tel 800-AIRWAYS (US).
Tel 1-300 767 177 (Aus).
www.britishairways.com

Iberia
Tel 800-772 4642 (US).
www.iberia.com

KLM
Tel 1-800-618 0104 (US).
Tel 01300 392 192 (Aus).
www.klm.com

Lufthansa
Tel 800-645 3880 (US).
Tel 1-300 655 727 (Aus).
www.lufthansa.com

SAS
Tel 800-221 2350 (US).
Tel 300 727 707 (Aus).
www.flysas.com

TRAVEL AGENTS

STA Travel
30 3rd Avenue, New York, NY 10003, US.
Tel 212-473 6100.
www.statravel.com

Trailfinders
194 Kensington High St, London W8, UK.
Tel 020-7938 3939
(for long-haul travel).
Tel 0845 050 5945 (for European travel).
www.trailfinders.com

PACKAGE DEALS

American Express
Tel 1800-297 2977 (US).
www.americanexpress.com/travel

Central Holidays
Tel 800-539 7098.
www.centralholidays.com

INTERNET BOOKING

Europebyair
www.europebyair.com

Expedia
www.expedia.com

Opodo
www.opodo.com

LOW-COST AIRLINES

Air Berlin
www.airberlin.com

easyJet
www.easyjet.com

Eurowings
www.eurowings.com

Ryanair
www.ryanair.com

Europe by Train

Trains are generally a popular, reliable, and comfortable means of travel, which also gives visitors the chance to enjoy the passing countryside. With the Channel Tunnel in operation between Britain and France, it is now possible to travel all the way from Scotland to mainland Greece by rail, and the number of passes and discounts on offer ensure that costs need not be high.

TYPES OF TRAIN

All kinds of train serve the rail network in Europe, from the slow local lines of remote regions, to fast diesel-powered intercity expresses. For the latter, such as the French TGV *(Train à Grande Vitesse)*, the Spanish AVE *(Alta Velocidad Española)*, and the German ICE (InterCity Express), you usually need to reserve a seat in advance, and they are more expensive.

A pan-European rail system is still a dream of the European Union, but there has been some progress. The French operate TGV trains to Zürich, Bern, Turin, and Milan, where they link up with Italy's Pendolino trains; Brussels is connected to Paris, Amsterdam, Cologne, and Geneva by the high-speed Thalys network, while Germany's ICE system also runs to Bern, Switzerland.

Overnight trains are popular, offering couchettes, or bunks (usually four or six per compartment), or the more desirable sleepers (usually two or three beds per compartment). The price of a sleeper tends to be higher (three times the couchette price), but it is worth it if comfort is important.

RAIL PASSES FOR NON-EUROPEANS

The cheapest way of seeing Europe by rail is to buy one of the many passes available. For non-Europeans the most popular of these is the Eurailpass from **Eurail**, or if you are under 26, the Eurail Youthpass. It is best to buy these tickets in the US or Australia before traveling because they can be 10 percent cheaper than if you wait and buy them in Europe. You can also buy these on the Internet through Eurail and **Rail Europe**. These passes do not include the supplements payable on many of the faster trains: the EC (EuroCity), IC (InterCity), and EN (EuroNight) trains. You must pay these before boarding – if you don't and are caught by a conductor you will then have to pay the supplement plus a fine.

The Eurailpass offers unlimited travel in 22 European countries. These include Austria, Belgium, Bulgaria, Croatia, Czech Republic, Denmark, Finland, France, Germany, Greece, Hungary, Ireland, Italy, Luxembourg, the Netherlands, Norway, Portugal, Romania, Slovenia, Spain, Sweden, and Switzerland. It is available as a consecutive-day pass if you want to make frequent short hops by train, or as a flexi-pass if you are on a trip with extended stop-overs. It is also valid for some ferries.

Other variations on the Eurailpass include the Saver Flexipass, which gives at least a 15 percent reduction per person when two or more people are traveling together. The Youth Flexipass is an option for those under 26 years of age.

For further information on national train services and passes in individual countries see the *Travel Information* section for each country.

PASSES FOR EUROPEANS

For Europeans the best pass is the Inter-Rail, which is also available from Rail Europe or from main train operators in individual countries. The Inter-Rail pass divides 28 countries in Europe into eight zones and is for anyone under 26 years old who has been resident in a European country for at least six months. For those over 26 years, there is the Inter-Rail 26-Plus. What you pay depends on the number of zones you want to travel in and the length of your stay.

EUROSTAR/EUROTUNNEL

Connecting London's St. Pancras International Station to Lille and the Gare du Nord in Paris the **Eurostar** foot passenger train service provides the fastest link between the two capitals. It also operates to Brussels' Gare du Midi. These journeys take less than two and a half hours.

The **Eurotunnel** company operates a service between Folkestone in Great Britain and Calais in France that has drive-in compartments for vehicles. For a day trip it costs a set price per car with passengers (the more passengers, the cheaper the cost per person). Daytime journeys are more expensive than those departing after 10pm.

DIRECTORY

RAIL PASSES

Eurail
www.eurail.com
Official US website.
www.railpass.com
Tel 877-RAILPASS (US).
Booking and information.

Rail Europe
1 Regent Street,
London SW1Y 4XT.
Tel 0844-848 4064 (US: 1-800-622 8600).
◻ 10am–6pm Mon–Fri, 10am–5pm Sat.
www.raileurope.com
For Eurailpasses.
www.raileurope.co.uk
For Inter-Rail passes.

EUROSTAR/EUROTUNNEL

Eurostar
Tel 08432-186 186 (UK).
Tel 01233-617 575 (outside UK).
www.eurostar.com
For foot passengers.

Eurotunnel
Tel 08443-353 535 (UK).
Tel 0810-63 03 04 (France).
www.eurotunnel.com
For cars & buses.

Europe by Road and Ferry

While many prefer the ease of traveling by train when they want to get somewhere fast, traveling by car gives you the chance to stop at will and explore many areas of Europe on the way. Car ferries and the Channel Tunnel have extended Europe's boundaries into the Scottish Hebrides and down to the Aegean.

DRIVING PERMITS

Many non-European licenses can be used in Europe, but an international driving permit is worth having, if only to make life easier when renting or leasing a vehicle (you have to be at least 21 years of age when renting). Be aware that it is mandatory to have an international permit in parts of Eastern Europe. The permit lasts for one year.

DRIVING IN EUROPE

In Great Britain, Northern Ireland, the Republic of Ireland, Cyprus, Malta, and Gibraltar people drive on the left-hand side of the road. The rest of Europe drives on the right. Remember that in most of Europe distances are measured in kilometers (1 km equals 0.6 miles). The exceptions are Great Britain and Ireland, which work in both metric and Imperial measurements. Most highways have a speed limit of around 100–135 km/h (60–80 mph). The fastest roads are in Germany where the speed limit is 210 km/h (130 mph) on the *Autobahnen*. Roads are very congested during August, the vacation month, especially during the first and last weekends and on routes to the coast.

The cost of driving in Europe varies from country to country. Italian *autostrade*, French *autoroutes*, and Spanish *autopistas* are regularly punctuated by toll booths, while a one-time fee must be paid on entering Switzerland and Austria. However, the vast majority of roads are free in the Netherlands, Great Britain, and Germany, although tolls are charged on certain bridges.

Fuel prices vary enormously across Europe. Gibraltar, Andorra, and Luxembourg are by far the cheapest, while France, Italy, and the Netherlands are the most expensive, with Spain, Great Britain, and Switzerland somewhere in between. The difference in price can be up to 30 percent. Unleaded gas is used almost exclusively in Scandinavia and Western Europe, but it is rarely available in the east.

CAR RENTAL

Car rental is a competitive business in Europe, so prices are generally quite affordable. The biggest car rental companies in Europe are Europcar, Avis, Hertz, Sixt, and Budget, all of which offer an excellent level of service. Local contact details are given in the *Travel Information* section for each country. There are also US companies that specialize in European car rentals. These include firms such as **Europcar, Kemwel, Europe by Car**, and **Auto Europe**.

TRAVELING BY BUS

Domestic bus services provide an alternative to the rail network throughout Europe, and while these are cheaper, they are also generally much slower and offer less in terms of comfort and amenities. The exceptions are Portugal, Greece, and parts of Spain, where buses have superseded trains, and Hungary, which has a bus system that is as good as the rail network. In most European countries, buses are best used as extensions of the railway, affording access to villages and remoter regions. Advance bookings for these are rarely needed.

International buses are also a second-best to express trains, but the tour options are worth considering. One example, **Eurolines**, offers passes that allow you to visit 43 European capitals over a 15- or 30-day period.

TRAVELING BY FERRY

Once in Europe you may need to go by boat to get to the more outlying areas. Many of the islands of Greece and Scotland, for example, are only accessible by sea. Or, if you start your trip to Europe by flying into Great Britain, it is possible to continue by ferry, catamaran, or hydrofoil to Ireland, France, Belgium, the Netherlands, and Spain. Companies operating regular ferries from Great Britain are **P&O** and **DFDS Seaways**.

It can also be easier and cheaper to travel by sea than by air from Spain to the Balearic Islands, from Italy to Sardinia and Sicily, and to Greece from Italy. For further details, see the *Travel Information* section of the individual countries.

DIRECTORY

CAR RENTAL

Auto Europe
Tel 888-223 5555 (US).
www.autoeurope.com

Europcar
Tel 877-940 6900 (US).
www.europcar.com

Europe by Car
Tel 800-223 1516 (US).
www.europebycarblog.com

Kemwel
Tel 877-820 0668 (US).
www.kemwel.com

TRAVELING BY BUS

Eurolines
Tel 08717-818 181 (UK).
www.eurolines.co.uk

FERRY SERVICES

DFDS Seaways
Tel 0871-522 3883 (UK).
www.dfdsseaways.co.uk

P&O
Tel 08716-642 121 (UK).
www.poferries.com

EUROPE AT
A GLANCE

The Landscapes of Europe

A wide range of climatic and geological conditions
has forged an impressive variety of landscapes in
Europe. Although the appearance of much of the
land has changed dramatically since mankind began
to cultivate it around 7,000 years ago, there are still
many remote and wild regions, such as the
spectacular peaks of the Alps and the Pyrenees.
As well as being simply beautiful in their own right,
Europe's diverse landscapes offer endless
opportunities for outdoor activities.

Norway
*Indenting the country's west
coast, the wild and rugged
Norwegian fjords are a truly
spectacular sight, offering
some of the most breathtaking
scenery in Scandinavia.*

Great Britain
*Dartmoor in southwest England is a wilderness
of great natural beauty. The windswept open
moorland at the area's bleak and isolated
heart has inspired many romantic tales.*

ATLANTIC
OCEAN

NORTH
SEA

IRELAND   GREAT
            BRITAIN

NETHERLA

BELGIUM &
LUXEMBOUR

France
*The wine-producing
regions of France, such
as Champagne, boast
lush, fertile vegetation,
with row upon row of
neatly planted vines.*

Bay
of
Biscay

FRANCE

PORTUGAL

SPAIN

MEDITERRANEAN SE

Portugal
*The interior of southern Portugal is
largely characterized by parched plains,
dotted with cork oaks and olive trees,
and vast dusty wheat fields stretching
uninterrupted to the horizon.*

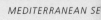
0 km   250

0 miles   250

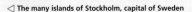
◁ The many islands of Stockholm, capital of Sweden

Hungary
North of the Hungarian capital, the Danube flows through a verdant landscape of vineyards, orchards, and thickly wooded hills. Known as the Danube Bend, this is one of the river's most beautiful stretches.

Switzerland
Switzerland's landscape is dominated by the Alps, Europe's highest mountain range. Dramatic, snow-covered peaks, stunning vistas, and a range of first-class winter sports facilities draw millions of visitors to this part of Europe every year.

Greece
The Greek mainland and islands have some of Europe's finest coastal scenery. There are thousands of beaches, ranging from small rocky coves backed by pine-clad cliffs to broad swathes of golden sand.

SWEDEN

FINLAND

BALTIC
SEA

RK

POLAND

MANY

CZECH
REPUBLIC

AUSTRIA   HUNGARY

ITALY

GREECE

Great Museums and Galleries

The museums and galleries of Europe include
national collections, the former collections of
Europe's royal and noble families, and a whole host
of smaller local institutions. The museums highlighted
here are those with the largest and richest collections,
which ought to be included in the itinerary of every
visitor to Europe. Between them they contain many of
the world's best-known and best-loved artistic
treasures. These range from archaeological
finds from the early civilizations of the
Middle East, through pieces from Egyptian,
Greek, and Roman times, to masterpieces
of the Renaissance and other great
periods of European art.

Rijksmuseum, Amsterdam
*The Rijksmuseum (see pp256–8)
is known for its Rembrandts
and other great Dutch paintings
of the 17th century. Frans Hals'*
Wedding Portrait *is a joyful
celebration of Dutch life.*

British Museum, London
*A vast collection of
antiquities and other
artifacts from all over the
world is is housed inside
Britain's national museum
(see pp52–3). There is a
fascinating display of
mummies and other
exhibits from Ancient Egypt.*

Louvre, Paris
*The celebrated
home of the*
Mona Lisa *and the*
Venus de Milo, *the
Louvre also houses
Jean Watteau's
melancholy study*
Gilles or Pierrot
*(c.1717), one of
many French
works on display
(see pp158–60).*

*ATLANTIC
OCEAN*

NORTH
SEA

IRELAND

GREAT
BRITAIN

NETHE

BELGI
LUXEMB

*Bay
of
Biscay*

FRANCE

PORTUGAL

SPAIN

MEDITERRANEA

Prado, Madrid
*The former royal collection in
Madrid (see pp288–90) contains
the finest assembly of Spanish
paintings in the world. Of many
highly individual works, Goya's*
Saturn Devouring His Son *is one
of the most powerful.*

| 0 km | 250 |
| 0 miles | 250 |

Pergamon Museum, Berlin
This fabulous collection of antiquities includes the famous blue-tiled Ishtar Gate from Babylon, dating from the 6th century BC (see p532).

The Hermitage, St. Petersburg
The Hermitage (see p696) *houses an impressive collection of Impressionist paintings, such as* Woman Combing her Hair *(c.1885) by Edgar Degas.*

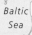

Kunsthistorisches Museum, Vienna
Based on the imperial collections of the Habsburgs, the museum (see p596) *houses archaeology, paintings, and sculpture, such as this woodcarving of the Madonna (c.1495) by Tilman Riemenschneider.*

Uffizi, Florence
The Uffizi (see pp422–4) *was built originally as the "offices" of the Medici rulers of Florence. Transformed into a gallery in 1581, the building now displays such masterpieces as* The Annunciation *by da Vinci.*

Vatican Museums, Rome
Classical and Early Christian statues excavated in Rome over the centuries include this charming Good Shepherd *(4th century AD). The vast papal museum* (see pp396–8) *also holds great paintings by Michelangelo and Raphael commissioned during the Renaissance.*

The History of Europe

In this timeline of European history, important political and social events appear on the upper half of the page, while the lower half charts contemporary developments in art and architecture. In the art and architecture section the emphasis is on structures and works of art that both illustrate major historical trends and can still be seen today. They are described in more detail in the main sightseeing section of the book.

451–429 BC The great general Perikles presides as uncrowned king of Athens. He establishes democracy in the city and commissions great buildings such as the Parthenon (*see pp478–80*). However, he also involves Athens in Peloponnesian Wars (431–404), in which Sparta and its allies defeat Athens

FROM PREHISTORY TO THE EARLY MIDDLE AGES

From prehistoric times Europe saw a succession of civilizations that flourished then collapsed. Much of our knowledge of the period comes only from archaeological remains, although the Mycenaeans did leave written inscriptions. Later periods are chronicled in Greek and Roman histories. However, many of these were written long after the events they describe and tend to be a blend of legend and fact.

c.1500 BC Mycenaean culture dominates mainland Greece This gold death mask from Mycenae, known as the "Mask of Agamemnon," is on display at the National Museum of Archaeology in Athens (*see p476*)

750–600 BC Greek colonists spread to Sicily, southern Italy, Marseille, and Spain

c.800 BC Rise of Etruscans in Italy

509 BC Romans expel Etruscan kings and found republic

c.2300 BC Start of Bronze Age in Europe

2000–1100 BC Series of Minoan civilizations in Crete

c.1000 BC Iron-working reaches central Europe from the Near East

PREHISTORY				CLASSICAL
2500 BC	2000 BC	1500 BC	1000 BC	500 BC
MINOAN AND MYCENAEAN				GREEK AND ETRUSCAN

c.1200 BC Collapse of Mycenaean culture

6th century BC Etruscan sarcophagi topped with lifelike terra-cotta sculptures of the deceased (*see p405*)

c.1450 BC Mycenaeans (*see p491*) take over palace of Knossos. Palaces in mainland Greece start to exhibit pillared, frescoed halls, ideas borrowed from the Minoans

447 BC Work begins on the Parthenon, the great temple dedicated to Athena on the Acropolis in Athens (*see pp478–80*)

4th century BC Magnificent Greek theater built at Epidaurus (*see p491*)

c.1700 BC First Minoan palace at Knossos on Crete destroyed. A new palace was immediately built to replace it. This colorful scene is one of many fine Minoan frescoes in the Irákleio Archaeological Museum in Crete (*see p500*)

6th century BC Greek vases of the red-figure type start to appear. The figures are left in the color of the clay, silhouetted against a black glaze. They often show scenes of myth and legend, such as the Trojan War

ART AND ARCHITECTURE

Artistic styles in prehistoric Minoan and Mycenaean cultures were strongly influenced by Egyptian and Middle Eastern models. However, during the Hellenistic period the trend was reversed. Following Alexander the Great's conquests, Greek styles of sculpture, temple architecture, and ceramics were exported to Egypt and as far east as Afghanistan. The Romans were great admirers of the Greeks and the growth of the Roman Empire helped spread the Greek aesthetic throughout western Europe.

27 BC Augustus becomes first Roman emperor. This sculpture in the Vatican Museums (*see pp396–8*) shows him in a traditional Greek heroic pose

5th century AD Visigoths take control of Iberian Peninsula. The Roman aqueduct at Segovia (*see p294*) survived both the Visigothic and the subsequent Moorish invasion of Spain

201 BC Rome defeats Carthaginians and expands rapidly to dominate Mediterranean

AD 476 Fall of Western Roman Empire

c.AD 481–511 Franks under Clovis conquer much of present-day France

AD 493–526 Kingdom of Italy ruled by Theodoric the Ostrogoth from Ravenna

338 BC Philip II defeats Greeks, making Macedon great power

323 BC Death of Alexander the Great. His empire stretches from Macedon to northern India

AD 117 Roman Empire at greatest extent on death of Emperor Trajan

AD 395 Division of Roman Empire into eastern and western halves

AD 313 Edict of Milan: Christianity favored by Roman emperor Constantine

6th century AD Byzantines reconquer much of Italy, but then lose most of their gains to the Lombards

AD 711 Moorish invasion of Spain

GREECE	ROMAN EMPIRE		AFTER THE FALL OF ROME	
250 BC	AD 1	AD 250	500	750
HELLENISTIC AND ROMAN			BYZANTINE	

AD 30 Amphitheater built at Verona (*see p430*)

AD 118 Building of magnificent domed temple, the Pantheon in Rome (*see p400*)

8th–10th centuries AD Churches in distinctive pre-Romanesque style built in Asturias, part of northern Spain never conquered by the Moors. Examples survive in Oviedo (*see p303*)

AD 72 Work starts on the Colosseum in Rome (*see p403*)

4th century AD Christian motifs start to appear in Roman art; building of St. Peter's and other Christian basilicas in Rome

7th century AD Sutton Hoo ship burial. Over much of Europe relics from this era are rare. One exception is the treasure found buried with an Anglo-Saxon leader, who died c.625. The hoard can be seen at the British Museum (*see p52*)

AD 81 Arch of Titus (*see p402*) erected in Rome to commemorate crushing of Jewish Revolt in AD 70. It served as a model for later triumphal arches

5th century AD Apse mosaics in church of Santa Maria Maggiore, Rome (*see p404*)

c.330 BC Start of Hellenistic period. *The Dying Galatian* was a famous Greek sculpture dating from the 3rd century BC. It was frequently copied in the Hellenistic period. This Roman copy is in the Capitoline Museums in Rome (*see p401*)

6th century AD Byzantine mosaics in church of Sant'Apollinare Nuovo in Ravenna (*see p443*). Ravenna remained an outpost of the Byzantine Empire until AD 752

FROM THE MIDDLE AGES TO THE 18TH CENTURY

During this period many of the states of present-day Europe gradually took shape, with powerful centralized kingdoms, notably Spain, Portugal, France, and England, emerging from the medieval feudal system. The Middle Ages were marked by wars between kings and nobles and even between popes and emperors. The Catholic church owned extensive lands and was a powerful political force. However, its influence over much of northern Europe was lost in the Reformation of the 16th century with the emergence of Protestantism.

1096–9 First Crusade; knights of northern Europe capture Jerusalem

1066 Norman conquest of England

12th and 13th centuries Emperors and popes fight for control of Germany and Italy. Frederick I Barbarossa, Holy Roman Emperor, quarreled frequently with the pope but set off on the Third Crusade, only to drown in 1190 before he reached the Holy Land

9th century Vikings terrorize Europe, gaining control of much of England, Scotland, Ireland, and northern France. The Isle of Lewis chessmen (11th century) give a striking picture of the members of a Viking court. Carved of walrus ivory, they can be seen in the British Museum (see pp52–3)

896 Magyars reach eastern Europe, laying foundation of present-day Hungary

1054 East-West Schism: Roman Church splits definitively with Eastern Orthodox Church

12th and 13th centuries Gradual reconquest of Spain and Portugal from the Moors

800 The Frankish king, Charlemagne, is crowned Holy Roman Emperor

955 Saxon king Otto defeats Magyars

12th century Venice grows rich supplying the crusades and trading with the east

EARLY MIDDLE AGES			MIDDLE AGES	
800	900	1000	1100	1200
BYZANTINE AND ROMANESQUE				GOTHIC

c.800 Book of Kells, the greatest of the Irish illuminated copies of the Bible (see p125)

1064 Work begins on Pisa's Duomo (see p411), a magnificent example of Italian Romanesque

1071 Completion of St. Mark's, Venice's great Byzantine basilica (see pp434–5)

10th century Beginnings of Romanesque architecture, characterized by rounded Roman arches, delicate arcades, and tall bell towers

c.1194 Chartres Cathedral, France (see pp180–81) rebuilt in new Gothic style. Pointed arches and ribbed vaulting create possibility of soaring height in church design

9th and 10th centuries Irish High Crosses (see p125)

11th century Christianity reaches Norway – building of striking wooden "stave" churches (see p656)

c.785 Start of building of the Mezquita in Córdoba, capital of the Moorish Caliphate in Spain (see pp326–7). The mibrab (prayer niche) is framed by a beautiful horseshoe arch. Spanish buildings retained Moorish features like this even after the completion of the reconquest of Spain in 1492

late 11th century Building of Durham Cathedral (see p77), England's finest Norman (Romanesque) church

ART AND ARCHITECTURE

The Middle Ages in Europe produced remarkable ecclesiastical architecture: first in the Romanesque style, then the even more spectacular Gothic. The Renaissance turned its back on the Gothic with the rediscovery of Classical principles, while Renaissance art was based on scientific understanding of perspective and anatomy, and also on the idealism of Classical sculpture.

c.1267–1336 Life of Giotto, who introduces a new realism to Italian painting. St. Francis appears to the Monks at Arles is one of a series of magnificent frescoes he painted for the Basilica di San Francesco in Assisi (see pp406–7)

1618–48 Thirty Years' War: religious differences and territorial ambitions embroil most of northern Europe

1386 Union of crowns of Poland and Lithuania, which together form largest state in Europe

1517 Martin Luther condemns church in his 95 Theses, sparking Reformation. Protestantism sweeps across much of northern Europe

1347–51 Black Death kills perhaps a third of the population of Europe

1492 Spanish expel Moors from Granada; Columbus's first voyage to America

1458–90 Hungary at its height in reign of Matthias Corvinus

1520s Charles V, Holy Roman Emperor, defeats François I of France in war for control of Italy

1683 Defeat of Turks at siege of Vienna allows expansion of Austrian Habsburg empire

1715 Death of Louis XIV. The "Sun King" made France the most powerful state in Europe and presided over the great age of French Classical culture. However, his expansionist policies were largely thwarted by the British, Austrians, and Dutch

1337–1453 Hundred Years' War between England and France

1453 Collapse of Byzantine Empire increases Turkish threat to eastern Europe

1609 Dutch gain effective independence from Spain

1622 Battle of Mohács; Kingdom of Hungary falls to Turks

1740–86 Rise of Prussia under Frederick II "the Great"

LATE MIDDLE AGES	REFORMATION	AGE OF ENLIGHTENMENT
1300 1400	1500 1600	1700
	RENAISSANCE	BAROQUE ROCOCO

1436 Completion of dome of Florence Cathedral *(see pp416–17)*

1441 Death of great Flemish painter Van Eyck, who perfected oil-painting technique

1519 Château de Chambord, François I's magnificent Renaissance château in the Loire Valley *(see p179)*

1730s Light decorative Rococo style, most popular in France, southern Germany, and Austria

1483–1520 Life of Raphael, painter of the Raphael Rooms in the Vatican *(see p398)*

1704 Start of building of Blenheim Palace, grandest of the stately homes of 18th-century Britain *(see pp74–5)*

1598–1680 Life of Gian Lorenzo Bernini, leading architect and sculptor of the Roman Baroque

1606–69 Life of Rembrandt, greatest of the 17th-century Dutch masters

1452–1519 Life of Leonardo da Vinci, multi-talented Renaissance genius. There are two versions of his *Virgin of the Rocks*, one in the Louvre, Paris *(see pp158–60)*, and one in the British Museum, London *(see pp52–3)*

1661 Enlargement of French royal palace at Versailles *(see pp168–9)* begins

1475–1564 Life of painter, sculptor, and architect Michelangelo

1675–1710 Building of Christopher Wren's St. Paul's Cathedral in London *(see p58)*

THE FRENCH REVOLUTION TO THE PRESENT

The French Revolution established a supposedly democratic republic, but the need for a central authority allowed the brilliant general Napoleon to take power and proclaim himself Emperor. The Old Regime died hard and after Napoleon's defeat, many of the old rulers of Europe were restored to their thrones. In time, however, birthright and tradition had to give way to technological progress, the growth of capitalism, the rising power of the bourgeoisie, and the spread of workers' movements. Greater democracy gave the vote to more and more of the population, but wherever democracy broke down, there was the danger it would be replaced by a totalitarian regime, such as the Nazis in Germany and the Communist regimes of the old Soviet Bloc.

1901 First award of Nobel prizes in Sweden and Norway

1830–40 George Stephenson's *Rocket* becomes the prototype for steam locomotives. Following the success of the Liverpool–Manchester line, opened in 1930, the spread of railroads speeds the Industrial Revolution in Britain

1804 Napoleon crowns himself Emperor of the French

1789 French Revolution leads to execution by guillotine of Louis XVI and reign of of terror in in 1793.

1805 Napoleon defeats Austrians at Austerlitz; by 1807 he controls most of western and central Europe

1812 Defeats in Peninsular War and Russia weaken French hold on Europe

1815 Napoleon defeated at Waterloo; Congress of Vienna more or less restores status quo in Europe

1831 Creation of Kingdom of Belgium

1838–1901 Reign of Queen Victoria: apogee of British Empire

1848 Year of revolutions throughout Europe

1852 Napoleon III becomes Emperor of France

1860 Unification of most of Italy

1870 Franco-Prussian War; German victory allows Bismarck to achieve unification of Germany

AGE OF ENLIGHTENMENT		INDUSTRIAL REVOLUTION			AGE
1775	1800	1825	1850	1875	19
NEOCLASSICAL	EMPIRE	REGENCY	REALISM	IMPRESSIONISM	

1785 *The Oath of the Horatii* by Jacques Louis David, French Neoclassical painter. This incident from early Roman history extols the republican spirit that would inspire the French Revolution.

c.1814 Goya's paintings recording atrocities in the Peninsular War, *May 2, 1808* and *May 3, 1808*. They hang in the Prado, Madrid *(see pp288–90)*

c.1800 Empire style in fashion and furnishings. Many aspects of design in Europe influenced by Napoleon's Egyptian expedition

1841–1919 Life of Pierre Auguste Renoir, one of the greatest of the artists associated with the Impressionist movement

1852–70 Second Empire style; rebuilding of Paris by Haussmann *(see p164)*

1857–65 The Ringstrasse built in Vienna, an example of grand 19th-century city planning

1874 Claude Monet uses the word "Impression" in title of a painting, giving rise to the term Impressionism

1883 Gaudí begins work on la Sagrada Família cathedral in Barcelona *(see pp312–13)*

1890 Suicide of Dutch painter Van Gogh, unrecognized in his lifetime, now the most sought-after of Post-Impressionist painters *(see p259)*

ART AND ARCHITECTURE

Revivalist styles dominated 19th-century architecture, with imitations of Classical, Gothic, and Renaissance buildings. In contrast, painting evolved radically following the example of the French Impressionists. In the 20th century new building materials – steel, concrete, and glass – were the inspiration of Modernism. Modern art meanwhile experimented with every conceivable form of expression from Surrealism to Conceptual Art.

1890s Era of Art Nouveau. The posters of Czech-born Alfons Mucha typify the style, also known as Jugendstil or Secession. Many artists break away from the official academy of their country, notably in Vienna and Berlin

1907 First exhibition of Cubist works by Picasso and others

1914 Outbreak of World War I. Millions die as trench warfare along Western Front reaches stalemate

1989 Collapse of Communism in Eastern Europe. Poland, Hungary, Czechoslovakia, and other countries oust Communist rulers. Reopening of Berlin Wall leads to reunification of Germany in 1990

1939 Outbreak of World War II. Germany overruns Poland, then, in 1940, France

1944 Normandy Landings. Allied forces create second front, which leads to eventual defeat of Germany in 1945

1995 Membership of European Union reaches 15, with entry of Sweden, Finland, and Austria

1949 Berlin Air Lift stops Russian blockade of West Berlin

1918 Defeat of Germany, following American entry into war in 1917

1956 Hungarian uprising against Communist rule crushed by Russian tanks

2002 Introduction of common currency, the euro, in 12 countries of the European Union

1936–9 Spanish Civil War

1957 Treaty of Rome: European Economic Community marks beginning of European Union

2004 Ten more countries join the European Union

1933 Hitler comes to power in Germany

1968 Student protests in France and many other parts of Europe

2007 Bulgaria and Romania join the European Union

1919 Treaty of Versailles (1919) creates new states, including Poland, Czechoslovakia, Hungary, and Finland

1973 Carnation Revolution in Portugal

2013 Croatia set to join the European Union

...ERIALISM			THE EUROPEAN UNION		
1925	1950	1975	2000	2025
...VEAU ART DECO AND MODERNISM			POST-MODERNISM	

2012 The Shard opens in London, the tallest building in the European Union

1999 Sir Norman Foster's striking additions to the old Reichstag building in Berlin *(see p530)*

1937 *Guernica* painted by Pablo Picasso in reaction to bombing of Basque civilians in Spanish Civil War. The painting is currently on show at the Centro de Arte Reina Sofía, Madrid *(see p291)*

1997 Astonishing sculptural forms used by American architect Frank Gehry for new Guggenheim Museum in Bilbao *(see p304)*

1992 Barcelona Olympics. The city's glorious 20th-century buildings by Gaudí and others are restored and the old port is transformed *(see pp306–15)*

1920s and 1930s The term Art Deco is given to design and architecture using modern materials and clean, geometrical shapes

1977 Opening of the Centre Pompidou in Paris *(see p153)*. The design by Renzo Piano, Richard Rogers, and Gianfranco Franchini places service ducts and escalators on the outside of the building

1919 Foundation of Bauhaus in Weimar *(see p543)*, which exerts worldwide influence on architecture

BRITAIN AND IRELAND

Britain and Ireland at a Glance

The islands of Great Britain and Ireland lie to the northwest of continental Europe and have remained relatively isolated throughout their history. Great Britain consists of three countries, England, Scotland, and Wales, each with a distinctive way of life and traditions. These three, together with Northern Ireland, form the United Kingdom. In the south of Ireland, the Republic of Ireland is a separate country. London, one of Europe's liveliest cities, offers the greatest range of cultural attractions. The islands have a rich variety of landscapes, from rolling green hills to windswept moors and craggy mountains in the Scottish Highlands.

The Highlands (see p87) *is an area prized for its beauty and diversity of wildlife. This region of mountains and glens is home to many animal species rarely found living wild elsewhere in the British Isles.*

Inverness

Fort William

Glasgow

Belfast

IRELAND
(See pp108–39)

Galway

DUBLIN

Caernarfon

Dublin (see pp112–21), *Ireland's capital, has a lively atmosphere. Many of its finest public buildings, such as the Custom House, date from the 18th century.*

Killarney   Cork

Killarney (see p127) *is a typical friendly Irish town in County Kerry. The surrounding area is renowned for its spectacular scenery, with three huge lakes, waterfalls, and some of the country's highest mountains.*

Plymou

◁ **A tranquil corner of England's Lake District**

Edinburgh
(see pp82–6) *is the administrative and cultural capital of Scotland. Its castle, which dates back to the 12th century, gives spectacular views of the entire city.*

LOCATOR MAP

York (see pp78–9) *is a city of historical treasures, with many relics from the Roman and Viking ages. Its magnificent minster has the largest collection of medieval stained glass in Britain, and the city walls are well preserved.*

London (see pp42–63) *was founded by the Romans in the 1st century AD. The oldest part of the capital is the City, where Sir Christopher Wren's masterpiece, St. Paul's Cathedral, stands.*

Aberdeen

EDINBURGH

Carlisle

York

Manchester
Liverpool

GREAT BRITAIN
(See pp32–107)

Birmingham

Cambridge

Oxford

iff
Bristol
Bath

LONDON

Brighton

Exeter

| 0 km | 75 |
| 0 miles | 75 |

Bath (see pp70–71) *is named after the Roman baths that stand at the heart of the old town, next to the splendid medieval abbey. The city is full of elegant Georgian terraces, built in local honey-colored limestone.*

GREAT BRITAIN

*S*eparated from the rest of Europe by the English Channel, Britain has been assiduous in preserving its traditions. However, the island can offer the visitor much more than stately castles and pretty villages. A diversity of landscape, culture, literature, art, and architecture, as well as a unique heritage, results in a nation balancing the needs of the present with those of the past.

Britain's character has been shaped by its geographical position as an island. Never successfully invaded since 1066, its people have developed their own distinctive traditions, and although today a member of the European Union, Britain continues to delight in its nonconformity. Britain's heritage can be seen in its ancient castles, cathedrals, and stately homes with their gardens and parklands. It is also evident in the many age-old customs played out across the nation throughout the year.

For a small island, Great Britain encompasses a surprising variety in its regions, whose inhabitants maintain distinct identities. Scotland and Wales are separate countries from England with their own legislative assemblies. They also have their own surviving Gaelic languages and unique traditions.

The landscape is varied, too, from the mountains of Wales, Scotland, and the north, through the flat expanses of the Midlands and eastern England, to the soft, rolling hills of the south and west. The long, broad beaches of East Anglia contrast with the rocky inlets along much of the west coast.

Despite the spread of towns and cities over the last two centuries, rural Britain still flourishes. The countryside is dotted with farms and charming villages, with picturesque cottages and lovingly tended gardens. The most prosperous and densely populated part of the nation is the Southeast, close to London, where modern office buildings bear witness to the growth of service and high-tech industries.

HISTORY

Britain began to assume a cohesive character as early as the 7th century AD, as Anglo-Saxon tribes migrating from the continent absorbed existing Celtic and Roman influences and finally achieved supremacy in England.

Punting on the River Cherwell, Oxford

◁ **St. Martin-in-the-Fields church and the fountains of London's Trafalgar Square**

However, they suffered repeated Viking incursions and were overcome by the Normans at the Battle of Hastings in 1066, when William the Conqueror founded the royal lineage which still rules the country today. The disparate cultures of the Normans and Anglo-Saxons combined to form the English nation, a process nurtured by Britain's position as an island. Scotland's four divided kingdoms had also unified under one monarch by this time, with the crowning of Duncan I in 1034.

The next 400 years saw English kings extend their domain at home as well as abroad. Wales was conquered in 1282, and by 1296 control was also gained over Scotland. The Scots rose up again, however, winning back their independence under Robert the Bruce in 1314. The Tudor monarchs consolidated England's strength and laid the foundations for Britain's future

**Queen Elizabeth I
(reigned 1558–1603)**

commercial success. Henry VIII recognized the importance of sea power and, under his daughter, Elizabeth I, English sailors ranged far across the world. The total defeat of the Spanish Armada in 1588 confirmed Britain's position as a major maritime power.

The Stuart period saw the English and Scottish crowns unite, but internal struggles eventually led to the Civil War in 1642. By the time of the Act of Union with Scotland in 1707, however, the whole island was united and the foundations for representative government had been laid. The combination of internal security and maritime strength allowed Britain to seek wealth overseas. By the end of the Napoleonic Wars in 1815, Britain was the world's leading trading nation. The opportunities offered by industrialization were seized, and by the reign of Queen Victoria (1837–1901), a colossal empire had been established across the globe. Challenged by Europe and the rise of the US, and drained by its role in two world wars, Britain's influence waned after 1945. By the 1970s almost all its former colonies had become independent Commonwealth nations.

KEY DATES IN BRITISH HISTORY

AD 43–410 Roman occupation of Britain

440–50 Start of Angle, Saxon, and Jute invasions

1034 Duncan I becomes first king of all Scotland

1066 William the Conqueror defeats King Harold and becomes the first Norman king of England

1256 First Parliament to include ordinary citizens

1533–4 Henry VIII forms Church of England

1535 Act of Union with Wales

1558–1603 Reign of Elizabeth I

1603 Union of English and Scottish crowns; James VI of Scotland becomes James I of England

1642 Civil War breaks out

1649 Charles I executed. Commonwealth declared by Parliament

1707 Act of Union with Scotland

1721 Robert Walpole becomes Britain's first Prime Minister

1837–1901 Reign of Queen Victoria. Industrial Revolution leads to growth of British Empire

1924 First Labour government

1948 National Health Service introduced

1973 Britain joins European Community

1999 Formation of Scottish Parliament and Welsh Assembly

2005 52 killed and hundreds injured in terrorist bomb attacks on public transport in London

SOCIETY AND POLITICS

British cities are melting-pots for people not just from different parts of the country but also from overseas. Irish immigration has long ensured a flow of labor into the country, and since the 1950s hundreds of thousands have come

The colorful costumes of Notting Hill Carnival, an annual multicultural celebration held in London

The Eden Project, Cornwall, an entertaining educational center devoted to mankind's relationship with plants

from former colonies in Africa, Asia, and the Caribbean, many of which are members of the Commonwealth. Nearly five percent of Britain's 62 million inhabitants are from non-white ethnic groups – and about half of these were born in Britain. The result is a multicultural society that can boast a wide range of music, art, food, and religions.

Britain's class structure is based on a subtle mixture of heredity and wealth. Even though many of the great inherited fortunes no longer exist, some old landed families still live on their estates, and many now open them to the public. The monarchy's position highlights the dilemma of a people seeking to preserve its most potent symbol of national unity in an age suspicious of inherited privilege. Without real political power, although still head of the Church of England, the Queen and her family are subject to increasing public scrutiny.

Democracy has deep foundations in Britain. With the exception of the 17th-century Civil War, power has passed gradually from the Crown to the people's elected representatives. During the 20th and 21st centuries, the Labour (left wing) and Conservative (right wing) parties have, during their periods in office, favored a mix of public and private ownership for industry and ample funding for the state health and welfare systems.

A cricketing pub sign showing the 18th-century version of the game

CULTURE AND THE ARTS

Britain has a famous theatrical tradition stretching back to the 16th century and William Shakespeare. His plays have been performed on stage almost continuously since they were written, and the works of 17th- and 18th-century writers are also frequently revived. Modern British playwrights, such as Tom Stoppard, draw on this long tradition with their vivid language and by using comedy to illustrate serious themes.

In the visual arts, Britain has a strong tradition in portraiture, landscape, and watercolor. In modern times David Hockney and Francis Bacon, and sculptors Henry Moore and Barbara Hepworth have enjoyed worldwide recognition. Britain has also become famous for its innovative fashion designers, such as Vivienne Westwood and the late Alexander McQueen.

The indigenous film industry produces occasional international hits such as *Four Weddings and a Funeral* and *The King's Speech*. British television is famous for the high quality of its news, current affairs, and nature programs, as well as for its drama.

The British are great sports fans. Soccer, rugby, cricket, and lawn tennis are popular. An instantly recognizable English image is that of the cricket match on a village green. The British also make use of their national parks as enthusiastic walkers and hikers.

Exploring Great Britain

Britain's main attraction is its capital, London, but there are many other noteworthy towns to explore throughout the country. Highlights include the university cities of Cambridge and Oxford, the historic centers of York and Bath, and Edinburgh, the capital of Scotland. In the sparsely populated regions of Northern England, Wales, and Scotland, the land itself becomes the center of attention – the Lake District, Snowdonia, and the Isle of Skye are all areas of outstanding natural beauty.

SIGHTS AT A GLANCE

Aberdeen **28**
Bath pp70–71 **9**
Blenheim Palace pp74–5 **15**
Brighton **3**
Bristol **10**
Caernarfon **13**
Cairngorms **29**
Cambridge **17**
Canterbury **2**
Cardiff **11**
Chester **18**
Devon and Cornwall **8**
Durham **23**
Edinburgh pp82–6 **24**
Glasgow **25**
Inverness **30**

Isle of Skye **31**
Lake District **22**
Liverpool **19**
LONDON pp42–63 **1**
Manchester **20**
Oxford **14**
St. Andrews **27**
Salisbury **6**
Snowdonia **12**
Stirling **26**
Stonehenge **7**
Stratford-upon-Avon **16**
Winchester **5**
Windsor Castle pp66–7 **4**
York pp78–9 **21**

Brighton's Palace Pier viewed from the promenade

KEY

✈ Airport
⛴ Ferry port
— Highway
— Major road
— Railroad
···· Channel Tunnel
▬▬▬ International border
– – Administrative border

For additional map symbols *see back flap*

DISTANCE CHART

LONDON

Distance in kilometers
Distance in miles

LONDON								
179 111	BIRMINGHAM							
241 150	**164** 102	CARDIFF						
599 372	**466** 290	**600** 373	EDINBURGH					
626 389	**470** 292	**602** 374	**72** 45	GLASGOW				
851 529	**721** 448	**853** 530	**254** 158	**269** 167	INVERNESS			
296 184	**130** 81	**278** 173	**343** 213	**344** 214	**597** 371	MANCHESTER		
341 212	**332** 206	**261** 152	**784** 427	**785** 426	**1038** 545	**451** 250	PLYMOUTH	
333 207	**208** 129	**381** 237	**301** 187	**344** 214	**550** 342	**106** 66	**532** 331	YORK

The haunting landscape of the Isle of Skye

A98

A96

Orkney Isles
Shetland Isles

28 Aberdeen

St. Andrews

Tweed

A1

A696

Newcastle-
upon-Tyne
Tynemouth
Sunderland
Durham 23

Bergen, Stavanger

NORTH
SEA

A66
A1(M)
Middlesbrough

ndal
Swale
A19
A65
Scarborough
A64

Leeds &
Bradford
Bradford
Leeds 21 York
ston M62 M62
Huddersfield
Kingston upon Hull
20 Manchester
Sheffield
Grimsby
A16
Chester
Stoke-on-Trent
A6
Lincoln
Derby
M1
Nottingham

Rotterdam, Zeebrugge

E N G L A N D A47
M54 M6 Leicester Peterborough Norwich
Birmingham A11
Warwick Northampton A14
16 Stratford- 17 Cambridge
upon-Avon Ipswich
Blenheim M40 Luton A1(M) Stansted Harwich
Palace 15 M1 M11
cester Oxford 14 Chelmsford M25
Swindon Thames
Bristol Windsor 4 1 LONDON
9 Bath Castle Heathrow Canterbury 2
Stonehenge 7 M3 M2 Ramsgate
alisbury 6 5 Winchester Gatwick Dover
Southampton Brighton Folkestone
Portsmouth A23 3 Newhaven Calais
Bournemouth A27
Weymouth Isle of Wight Boulogne

NETHERLANDS

AMSTERDAM
The Hague A12 Utrecht
Arnhem
Hoek van Rotterdam
Holland Eindhoven

Groningen

A4

Hamburg, Göteborg, Esbjerg

Zeebrugge
Ostend Antwerp
Dunkerque A10 BRUSSELS
BELGIUM Liège
Lille

Channel

English

FRANCE N1

St-Malo
Cherbourg Caen, Le Havre
Dieppe Amiens
Rouen Paris

0 kilometers	75
0 miles	75

London ❶

The largest city in Europe, London is home to over
seven million people. Founded by the Romans in the first
century AD as an administrative center and trading
port, the capital is the principal residence of British
monarchs, as well as the center of government and
business, and is rich in historic buildings. In addition
to its many museums and galleries, London is an exciting
city, with a vast array of entertainments. In 2012 London
hosted the Olympic Games. Developments completed
for the event such as the Aquatics Centre, designed by
Zaha Hadid, have added to the city's attractions.

**Millennium Foot Bridge leading
to the Tate Modern on Bankside**

**Summer relaxation along the banks
of the Thames at Richmond**

SIGHTS AT A GLANCE

British Museum pp52–3 ⑩
Buckingham Palace ④
Covent Garden ⑨
Houses of Parliament ②
Hyde Park ⑬
London Eye ③
Madame Tussaud's ⑪
Museum of London ⑱
National Gallery ⑥
Natural History Museum ⑮

Piccadilly ⑧
Regent's Park ⑫
St. Paul's Cathedral ⑰
Science Museum ⑭
Shakespeare's Globe ⑳
Tate Britain ⑤
Tate Modern ⑲
Tower Bridge ㉒
Tower of London pp60–61 ㉑
Trafalgar Square ⑦

Victoria and Albert Museum ⑯
Westminster Abbey pp46–7 ①

Greater London *(see inset map)*

Greenwich ㉓
Hampton Court ㉖
Notting Hill and
  Portobello Road ㉔
Richmond and Kew ㉕

A   B   C

GETTING AROUND

London's subway system – the "tube" or "underground" – runs from about 5:30am until just after midnight. Overground rail services are useful for trips farther afield. London's buses are now much quicker, since the introduction of the Congestion Charge (£10 a day) to enter central London with a car. The well-known black cabs are a safe and convenient way to travel from door to door.

SEE ALSO

• **Where to Stay** pp96–8

• **Where to Eat** pp102–4

GREATER LONDON

KEY

Area of main map

Viewing Big Ben and Westminster Abbey from the capsules of the London Eye

KEY

	Sight / Place of interest
✈	Airport
🚉	Train station
⊖	Underground station
🚌	Bus station
	Riverboat boarding point
P	Parking
i	Tourist information
	Pedestrian street

Street-by-Street: Whitehall and Westminster

Westminster has been at the center of political and religious power in England since the 11th century, when King Canute built a palace here and Edward the Confessor founded Westminster Abbey. Whitehall is synonymous with the ministries concentrated around it. On weekdays the streets are crowded with civil servants going about their business, replaced at weekends by a steady flow of tourists.

Downing Street
No. 10 has been the prime minister's official residence since 1732, when Sir Robert Walpole was given the house by George II.

The Cabinet War Rooms, now open to the public, were Winston Churchill's World War II headquarters.

St. Margaret's Church is a favorite venue for political and society weddings.

★ Westminster Abbey
The abbey (see pp46–7) is London's oldest and most important church. The north façade is a Victorian addition.

Central Hall was built in 1911 as a Methodist meeting hall. In 1946 it hosted the first General Assembly of the United Nations.

Dean's Yard
This secluded grassy square is surrounded by picturesque buildings from different periods, many used by Westminster School.

Statue of Richard the Lion-Heart (1860)

The Burghers of Calais is a cast of Auguste Rodin's 1886 original sculpture in France.

For hotels and restaurants in this region see pp96–8 and pp102–4

Entrance to Horse Guards

Trafalgar Square

The Cenotaph (1920) is a war memorial by Sir Edwin Lutyens.

The Norman Shaw Buidings were the site of the original Scotland Yard, headquarters of the Metropolitan Police.

Westminster Pier is the main starting point for river trips.

Westminster station

★ **Houses of Parliament**
The seat of government is dominated by the clock tower, holding the 14-ton bell Big Ben, hung in 1858. Its deep chimes are broadcast daily on BBC radio.

Banqueting House
Inigo Jones designed this elegant Palladian building in 1622. It is famous for this ceiling painted by Rubens for Charles I.

KEY

– – – Suggested route

0 meters	100
0 yards	100

STAR SIGHTS

★ Westminster Abbey

★ Houses of Parliament

Westminster Abbey ①

See pp46–7.

Houses of Parliament ②

SW1. **Tel** 020-7219 3000. ⊖ Westminster. 🚌 3, 11, 12, 24, 53, 88, 148, 159, 211, 453. 🎫 call 0844-847 1672 to book tour tickets. Guided tours to UK residents free via your MP or with adm charge through www.ticketmaster.co.uk. Overseas visitors must purchase a ticket. **www**.parliament.uk

Since the 16th century this site has been the seat of the two Houses of Parliament: the House of Commons, made up of elected Members of Parliament (MPs) and the upper house, the House of Lords. The latter, formerly filled with hereditary peers, bishops, and life peers, was reformed in 2000.

The present Neo-Gothic building replaced the original palace, which was destroyed by fire in 1834.

To hear debates in either of the houses from the visitors' galleries, you can purchase a ticket on the day from next to the Jewel Tower in Abingdon Green. To attend Prime Minister's Question Time, apply for tickets to your local MP or to your embassy well ahead.

London Eye ③

South Bank SE1. **Tel** 0871-781 3000. ⊖ Waterloo, Westminster. 🚌 77, RV1, 381. ◯ daily. ● Dec 25, Jan 8–21. 🎫 (pick up tickets at County Hall, next to the Eye, at least 30 mins before boarding time). 🎫 ♿ **www**.londoneye.co.uk

Reaching to a height of 135 m (443 ft) above the Thames river, this is the world's highest Ferris wheel, and was installed to mark the Millennium. Its capsules offer a gentle, 30-minute ride as the wheel makes a full turn, with breathtaking views over the city and for up to 42 km (26 miles) around. "Flights" are on the hour or half-hour and need to be booked as the wheel is very popular.

Westminster Abbey ①

Westminster Abbey has been the burial place of Britain's monarchs since the 11th century and the setting for many coronations and royal weddings, including the marriage of the Duke and Duchess of Cambridge in 2011. It has an exceptionally diverse array of architectural styles, ranging from the austere French Gothic of the nave to the astonishing complexity of Henry VII's chapel. Half national church, half national museum, the abbey is crammed with an extraordinary collection of tombs and monuments honoring some of Britain's greatest public figures, from politicians to poets.

North/Main Entrance
The mock-medieval stonework, like this carved dragon, is Victorian.

Statesmen's Aisle contains monuments to some of the country's greatest political leaders.

The Cloisters, built mainly in the 13th and 14th centuries, link the abbey church with the other buildings.

★ Nave
Built under the direction of master mason Henry Yevele, the nave reaches to a height of 31 m (102 ft), and is the highest in England. The ratio of height to width is 3:1.

CORONATION
The coronation ceremony is over 1,000 years old and since 1066, with the crowning of William the Conqueror on Christmas Day, the abbey has been its sumptuous setting. The coronation of Queen Elizabeth II in 1953 was the first to be televised.

Flying Buttresses
The massive flying buttresses help transfer the great weight of the 31-m (102-ft) high nave.

STAR FEATURES

★ Nave

★ Henry VII Chapel

★ Chapter House

★ **Henry VII Chapel**
The Chapel, built in 1503–19, has superb late Perpendicular vaultings and choir stalls dating from 1512.

WILLIAM SHAKESPEARE 1564–1616
ROYAL AT STRATFORD-ON-AVON

Poets' Corner
Among the great poets honored here are Shakespeare (above), Chaucer, and T.S. Eliot.

The Sanctuary, built by Henry III, has been the scene of 38 coronations.

VISITORS' CHECKLIST

Broad Sanctuary SW1.
Tel 020-7222 5152. ⊖ St.
James's Park, Westminster.
🚌 3, 11, 12, 24, 53, 88, 148,
159, 211, 453.
🚢 Westminster Pier.
Cloisters ☐ 8am–6pm daily.
**Royal Chapels, Poets' Corner,
Chapter House, Choir,
Statesmen's Aisle & Nave**
☐ 9:30am–4:30pm Mon–Fri
(until 7pm Wed), 9:30am–2pm
Sat. **Museum** ☐ 10:30am–4pm
daily. 🎫 free to cloisters, College
Garden and St. Margaret's
Church; the rest has an admission
charge. 🎫 ♿ limited. ✝
Evensong: 5pm Mon–Fri,
3pm Sat & Sun. ♫ ♿
www.westminster-abbey.org

★ **Chapter House**
This beautiful octagonal room, remarkable for its 13th-century tiled floor, is lit by six huge stained-glass windows showing scenes from the abbey's history.

The museum has many of the abbey's treasures, including wood, plaster, and wax effigies of monarchs.

The Pyx Chamber is where the coinage was tested in medieval times.

HISTORICAL PLAN OF THE ABBEY

The first abbey church was established as early as the 10th century, but the present French-influenced Gothic structure was begun in 1245 at the behest of Henry III. Because of its unique role as the coronation church, the abbey escaped Henry VIII's dissolution of Britain's monastic buildings (1536–9) during the Protestant Reformation.

KEY

▨	Built before 1400
▨	Built in 1503–19
▨	Completed by 1745
▨	Completed after 1850

The Chapel of St. Edward the Confessor
The Coronation Chair is housed here, with the tombs of medieval monarchs.

The Victoria Monument, Buckingham Palace

Valuable works of art, such as *The Music Lesson* (c.1660) by Dutch master Jan Vermeer, are on display in the Picture Gallery. A selection of works from the monarch's art collection, one of the finest and most valuable in the world, is displayed in the **Queen's Gallery**, a small building located to one side of the palace. The famous Changing of the Guard takes place on the palace forecourt. Crowds gather to watch the colorful half-hour parade of guards, dressed in red jackets and tall, furry hats called bearskins, exchanging the palace keys.

State coaches and other official vehicles may be viewed at the Royal Mews nearby. The star exhibit is the gold state coach built for George III in 1761, with fine panels by Giovanni Cipriani.

Overlooking the forecourt, the East Wing façade of the palace was redesigned by Aston Webb in 1913. He also created the spacious, tree-lined avenue known as the Mall, which leads from the palace to Trafalgar Square. Used for royal processions on special occasions, the Mall is closed to traffic on Sundays. The national flags of foreign heads of state fly from its flagpoles during official visits.

The avenue follows the edge of St. James's Park, a reserve for wildfowl, and popular picnic spot in the heart of the city. Originally a marsh, the park was drained by Henry VIII and incorporated into his hunting grounds. Later, Charles II redesigned it as a fashionable promenade, with an aviary along its southern edge (from which Birdcage Walk takes its name). In summer, concerts are held on the park bandstand.

Buckingham Palace ④

SW1. **Tel** *020-7766 7300.* ⊖ *St. James's Park, Victoria, Green Park.* 🚌 *C1, C10, 11, 16, 36, 38, 52, 73, 211.* **State Rooms** ◯ *Aug–end Sep: daily.* 🎟 📷 ♿ *phone first.* **Queen's Gallery** 🎟 **Changing of the Guard** *11:30am on alternate days (subject to change).* **Tel** *020-7321 2233.* **www.**royalcollection.org.uk

The Queen's official London home is a very popular attraction. Conversion of the 18th-century Buckingham House was begun for George IV in 1826, but the first monarch to occupy the palace was Queen Victoria, in 1837. When the monarch is in residence the Royal Standard flag is flown.

The palace tour takes visitors up the grand staircase and through the splendor of the state rooms. The royal family's private apartments are not open to the public.

In the Music Room royal babies are christened, and state guests presented. The Queen carries out many formal ceremonies in the richly gilded Throne Room, and the Ballroom is used for state banquets and investitures.

Tate Britain ⑤

Millbank SW1. **Tel** *020-7887 8888.* ⊖ *Pimlico.* 🚌 *77a, 88, 507, C10.* 🚤 *between Tate Britain and Tate Modern.* ◯ *10am–6pm daily.* ● *Dec 24–26.* 🎟 *for major exhibitions.* ♿ 📷 🍴 🛍 📷 **www.**tate.org.uk

Founded in 1897, the Tate Gallery, now called Tate Britain, focuses primarily on British art. Many of the modern works formerly kept here have been moved to the Tate Modern (*see p59*), further down the Thames river.

Tate Britain shows the world's largest display of British art, ranging from Tudor times to the present day, in line with the original intention of the gallery's sponsor, sugar magnate Sir Henry Tate.

One of the most exquisite early works is a portrait of a bejeweled Elizabeth I (c.1575), by Nicholas Hilliard. The influence of the 17th-century Flemish artist Sir Anthony van Dyck on English painters can be seen in William Dobson's *Endymion Porter* (1642–5) and the works of Thomas Gainsborough (1727–88).

Among the collection are some fine examples of William Hogarth's sharply satirical pictures. The famed horse paintings of George Stubbs include *Mares and Foals in a Landscape* (1760).

Tate Britain holds a large number of paintings by the visionary poet and artist William Blake (1757–1827).

The portico of the Tate Britain building, dating from 1897

The Trafalgar Square façade of the National Gallery

His work was imbued with a mystical intensity, a typical example being *Satan Smiting Job with Sore Boils* (c.1826). England's great 19th-century landscape artists, Constable and Turner, are also well represented. John Constable's famous *Flatford Mill*, painted in 1816–17, is one of his many depictions of the Essex countryside. The Clore Galleries, open since 1987, house the works of J.M.W. Turner (1775–1851), whose paintings were left to the nation some years after his death on condition that they were kept together. His watercolor *A City on a River at Sunset* (1832) is a highlight.

The Tate also has on display many works by the 19th-century Pre-Raphaelites, including J.E. Millais' *Ophelia* (1851–2), as well as the works of several modern and contemporary artists, such as Henry Moore and David Hockney. The Tate's exhibitions change frequently to explore as much of the collection as possible.

National Gallery ⑥

Trafalgar Sq WC2. **Tel** 020-7747 2885. 🚇 *Charing Cross, Leicester Sq, Piccadilly Circus.* 🚌 *3, 6, 9, 11 & many others.* ⏰ *10am–6pm daily (to 9pm Fri).* ⏸ *Jan 1, Dec 24–26.* ♿ *via Sainsbury Wing entrance.* 📷 🖥
www.nationalgallery.org.uk

London's leading art museum, the National Gallery has over 2,300 paintings, most on permanent display. The collection was started in 1824 when the House of Commons agreed to purchase 38 major paintings. These became the core of a national collection of European art that now ranges from Giotto in the 13th century to the 19th-century Impressionists. The gallery's particular strengths are in Dutch, Italian Renaissance, and 17th-century Spanish painting.

The gallery's paintings are hung in chronological order. In 1991 the modern Sainsbury Wing was added to the main Neoclassical building (1834–8) to house the impressive Early Renaissance collection (1260–1510). *The Leonardo Cartoon* (c.1500), a chalk drawing by Leonardo da Vinci of the Virgin and Child, St. Anne, and John the Baptist, has been moved from here to a more prominent position near the Trafalgar Square entrance. Other Italian painters represented include Masaccio, Piero della Francesca, and Botticelli.

Perhaps the most famous of the Northern European works is *The Arnolfini Marriage* by Jan van Eyck (1434).

Most of the gallery's other exhibits are housed on the first floor of the main building. Among the 16th-century paintings, *The Adoration of the Kings* (1564) by Flemish artist Pieter Brueghel the Elder is notable. *Christ Mocked* (1490–1500) by Hieronymus Bosch is included in the Netherlandish and German section. The superb Dutch collection gives two rooms to Rembrandt. Annibale Carracci and Caravaggio are strongly represented among Italian painters. Spanish artist Diego Velázquez's only surviving female nude, *The Rokeby Venus* (1647–51), is one of the most popular and well-known of the 17th-century works of art. The great age of 19th-century landscape painting is perhaps best represented by Constable's *The Hay Wain* (1821), a masterpiece of changing light and shadow.

In the Impressionist section, Renoir's *Boating on the Seine* (1879–80) demonstrates the free, flickering touch used by the movement's artists to capture the fleeting moment. Other 19th-century highlights include Van Gogh's *Sunflowers*, Monet's *Waterlilies*, Rousseau's *Tropical Storm with Tiger*, and Seurat's *Bathers at Asnières*.

Lesser paintings of all periods are displayed on the lower floor of the main building. The better of the gallery's two restaurants is located in the Sainsbury Wing.

Bathers at Asnières (1884) by Georges Seurat, in the National Gallery

The West End

The West End is the city's social and cultural center, right next to the London home of the royal family. Stretching from the edge of Hyde Park to Covent Garden, the district bustles all day and late into the night. Whether you are looking for art, history, street- or café-life, it is the most rewarding area in which to begin an exploration of the city. Monuments, shops, cinemas, and restaurants radiate out from Trafalgar Square, and the entertainment scene is at its liveliest in the busy streets around Chinatown, Soho, and Leicester Square. From the garish lights of boisterous Piccadilly Circus to genteel St. James's Square, the West End embraces all aspects of London life, and caters to every budget.

Trafalgar Square by night with Nelson's Column in the foreground

Trafalgar Square ⑦

WC2. 🔁 Charing Cross. 🚌 3, 6, 9, 11, 12, 13, 15, 23, 24, 29, 53, 88, 91, 139, 159, 176, 453.

London's main venue for rallies and outdoor public meetings, Trafalgar Square was conceived by John Nash and mostly constructed during the 1830s. The 50-m (165-ft) tall column commemorates Admiral Lord Nelson, Britain's most famous sea lord, and dates from 1842. Edwin Landseer's four lions were added 25 years later. Today the square is very popular with tourists.

Admiralty Arch, designed in 1911, separates courtly London from the hurly-burly of Trafalgar Square. The central gate is opened only for royal processions. The restored buildings on the square's south side were built in 1880 as the Grand Hotel. The north side is now taken up by the National Gallery

and its Sainsbury Wing (see p49). In the northeast corner stands **St. Martin-in-the-Fields**. This 18th-century church by James Gibbs became a model for the Colonial style of church-building in the US.

Adjoining the National Gallery, the **National Portrait Gallery** depicts Britain's history through portraits, photographs, and sculptures. Subjects range from Elizabeth I to photographs of politicians, actors, and rock stars.

Further north, Leicester Square is at the heart of the West End entertainment district with the city's leading cinemas and lively nightclubs, while London's Chinatown attracts a steady throng of diners and shoppers. Bordering it, Shaftesbury Avenue is the main artery of London's theaterland.

🏛 **National Portrait Gallery**
2 St. Martin's Place WC2. **Tel** 020-7306 0055. ◯ daily. ⬤ Dec 24–26. 🖼 for special exhibitions. 🖢 🔲 🔳 🎧 audio guide. **www**.npg.org.uk

Piccadilly ⑧

W1. 🔁 Piccadilly Circus, Green Park. 🚌 9, 14, 19, 22, 38.

The thoroughfare called Piccadilly links Hyde Park Corner with Piccadilly Circus, but the name also refers to the surrounding area. Today Piccadilly has two contrasting faces: a bustling commercial district full of shopping arcades, eateries, and cinemas; and St. James's, to the south, which still focuses on a wealthy, glamorous clientele.

Piccadilly Circus, with its dazzling neon lights, is a focal point of the West End. It began as an early 19th-century crossroads between Piccadilly and John Nash's Regent Street. Briefly an elegant space, edged by curving stucco facades, by 1910 the first electric advertisements had been installed.

Crowds congregate beneath the delicately poised figure of Eros, the Greek god of love. Erected in 1892 as a memorial to the Earl of Shaftesbury, a Victorian philanthropist, the statue was originally intended to represent an angel of mercy.

Among the many notable sights along Piccadilly, the **Royal Academy**, founded in 1768, houses a permanent art collection, including a Michelangelo relief of the Madonna and Child (1505). Its annual summer exhibition is renowned for clever juxtaposition of new and established works.

The tranquil **St. James's Church** was designed by Sir Christopher Wren in 1684,

Alfred Gilbert's 1892 statue of Eros in Piccadilly Circus

A street performer in front of crowds at Covent Garden's Piazza

and the 18th-century **Spencer House** contains fine period furniture and paintings. This Palladian palace was built for an ancestor of Princess Diana.

Shopping in and around Piccadilly is very expensive, especially in Bond Street, where many famous designer labels have stores, and in the Burlington Arcade, which is patrolled by beadles. On Piccadilly itself, Fortnum and Mason, founded in 1707, is one of London's most prestigious food stores, while the grand Ritz hotel is a popular afternoon tea venue for the suitably dressed. Jermyn Street is renowned for high quality men's clothing.

South of Piccadilly is St. James's Square, laid out in the 1670s and dominated by a statue of William III. It has long been the most fashionable address in London. Pall Mall, named after the 17th-century game of *palle-maille* (a cross between croquet and golf) once played here, is lined with gentlemen's clubs, which admit only members and their guests. It leads to the 16th-century **St. James's Palace**, built for Henry VIII. The palace is still the official headquarters of the Court of St. James. Opposite is the **Queen's Chapel**, the first Classical church in England.

🏛 **Royal Academy**
Burlington House, Piccadilly W1.
Tel 020-7300 8000. ☐ daily. ●
Good Fri, Dec 24 & 25. 🎫 for
exhibitions. 🎫 reserve in advance.
🅰 www.royalacademy.org.uk

🏛 **Spencer House**
27 St. James's Pl SW1. *Tel* 020-7499
8620. ☐ Sun. ● Jan & Aug. 🎫
compulsory (call 020-7514 1958).
🅰 www.spencerhouse.co.uk

Covent Garden ⑨

WC2. ⊖ *Covent Garden.* 🚌 *1, 6,
9, 13, 15, 23, 59, 68, 87, 91, 168,
171, 176.* 🎫 *daily.*

Open-air cafés, street entertainers, stylish shops, and markets make Covent Garden a magnet for visitors. The name derives from a medieval convent garden which supplied Westminster Abbey with produce.

At its center is the Piazza, designed by 17th-century architect Inigo Jones as an elegant residential square, after an example from the Tuscan town of Livorno. For a time, houses around the Piazza were highly sought-after, but decline accelerated when a fruit and vegetable market developed. In 1973 the market moved to a new site and Covent Garden was revamped. Today only **St. Paul's Church** remains of Inigo Jones's buildings. Samuel Pepys saw a Punch and Judy show under the portico in 1662, and street entertainment has been a tradition here ever since.

The **Royal Opera House** (*see p95*), designed in 1858 by E.M. Barry, but totally renovated in 1997–9, is home to the Royal Opera and Royal Ballet Companies. Many of the world's greatest dance performers have appeared on its stage.

Covent Garden has many theatrical associations. The site of the **Theatre Royal**, completed in 1812, has been occupied by a theater since 1663. **St. Martin's Theatre** is home to the world's longest running play, *The Mousetrap*.

Other attractions include the **London Transport Museum** and an area of "alternative" shops around Neal Street and Neal's Yard. The **Lamb and Flag** (1623) in Rose Street is one of London's oldest pubs.

🏛 **London Transport Museum**
Covent Garden WC2. *Tel* 020-7379
6344. ☐ daily. ● Dec 24–26. 🎫
🎫 🅰 www.ltmuseum.co.uk

Statue of a resting ballerina, facing the Royal Opera House

British Museum ⑩

The oldest public museum in the world, the British Museum was established in 1753 to house the collections of the physician Sir Hans Sloane (1660–1753). Sloane's artifacts have been added to by gifts and purchases from all over the world, and the museum now contains innumerable items stretching from the present day to prehistory. Robert Smirke designed the main part of the building (1823–50), but the architectural highlight is the modern Great Court, with the world-famous Reading Room at its center, opened by the Queen in 2000. The 94 galleries which run for more than 2 miles (4 km), cover civilizations from ancient Assyria to modern Japan.

PREHISTORIC AND ROMAN BRITAIN

Relics of prehistoric Britain are on display in six separate galleries. The most impressive items include the Mold gold cape made from a sheet of decorated gold; an antlered headdress worn by hunter-gatherers some 9,000 years ago; and "Lindow Man," a 1st-century AD sacrificial victim who lay preserved in a bog until 1984. Some superb Celtic metalwork is also on show, alongside the silver Mildenhall Treasure and other notable Roman pieces. The Hinton St. Mary mosaic (4th century AD) features a roundel containing the earliest known British depiction of Christ.

MEDIEVAL, RENAISSANCE, AND MODERN OBJECTS

The spectacular Sutton Hoo ship treasure, the burial hoard of a 7th-century Anglo-Saxon king, is on display in Room 41. This superb find, made in 1939, revolutionized scholars' understanding of Anglo-Saxon life and ritual. The artifacts uncovered include a helmet and shield, Celtic hanging bowls, the remains of a lyre, and gold and garnet jewelry.

Adjacent galleries contain a collection of clocks, watches, and scientific instruments. Some exquisite timepieces are on view, including a 400-year-old clock from Prague, designed as a model galleon; in its day it pitched, played

Reconstruction of the ceremonial helmet found at Sutton Hoo

music, and even fired a cannon. Also nearby are the famous 12th-century Lewis chessmen, and a gallery housing Baron Ferdinand Rothschild's (1839–98) remarkably varied treasures. The most spectacular of these is a gold enameled reliquary of the Holy Thorn (Christ's Crown of Thorns), dating from the 15th century.

The museum's modern collection includes Wedgwood pottery, illustrated books, glassware, and a series of Russian revolutionary plates.

WESTERN ASIA

Numerous galleries at the museum are devoted to the Western Asian collections, covering 7,000 years of history. The most famous items are the 7th-century BC Assyrian reliefs from King Ashurbanipal's palace at Nineveh, but of equal interest are two large human-headed bulls from 7th-century BC Khorsabad, and an inscribed Black Obelisk of Assyrian King Shalmaneser III. Rooms 51–59 on the upper floor contain pieces from ancient Sumeria, part of the Oxus Treasure (which lay buried for over 2,000 years), and the museum's collection of clay cuneiform tablets. The earliest of these are inscribed with the oldest known pictographs (c.3300 BC).

ANCIENT EGYPT

Egyptian sculptures can be found in Room 4 on the main floor. These include a fine red granite head of a king, thought to be Amenophis III, and a colossal statue of king Ramses II. Also on show is the Rosetta Stone, which was used by Jean-François Champollion (1790–1832) as a primer for deciphering Egyptian hieroglyphs. An extraordinary array of mummies, jewelry, and Coptic art can also be found in rooms 61–66 upstairs, including a famous bronze cat with a gold nose-ring. The various instruments used by embalmers to preserve bodies before entombment are all displayed.

Ancient Egyptian tomb painting, *The Festival of Sekhtet* (1410 BC)

The Portland Vase, depicting the betrothal of Peleus and Thetis

GREECE AND ROME

The Greek and Roman collections include the museum's most famous treasure, the Elgin Marbles. These 5th-century BC reliefs from the Parthenon once comprised a marble frieze which decorated Athena's temple at the Acropolis in Athens. Much of it was ruined in battle in 1687, and most of what survived was removed between 1801 and 1804 by the British diplomat Lord Elgin, and sold to the British nation. Other highlights include the Nereid Monument, and sculptures and friezes from the Mausoleum at Halicarnassus. The beautiful 1st-century BC cameo-glass Portland Vase is located in the Roman Empire section.

ORIENTAL ART

Fine porcelain and ancient Shang bronzes (c.1500–1050 BC) are highlights of the museum's Chinese collection. Particularly impressive are the ceremonial ancient Chinese bronze vessels, with their enigmatic animal-head shapes. The fine Chinese ceramics range from delicate tea bowls to a model pond which is almost a thousand years old. Adjacent to these is one of the finest collections of Asian religious sculpture outside India. These include an assortment of sculpted

The Young Prince with his Parents (c.1600), an Indian miniature

reliefs which once covered the walls of the Buddhist temple at Amarati, and which recount stories from the life of the Buddha. A Korean section contains some gigantic works of Buddhist art.

Islamic art, including a stunning jade terrapin found in a water tank, can be found in Room 34. Rooms 90–94 house temporary exhibitions for prints and drawings from Asia and Japan.

AFRICA

An interesting collection of African sculptures, textiles, and graphic art can be found in Room 25, located in the basement. Famous bronzes from the Kingdom of Benin stand alongside modern African prints, paintings, and drawings, plus an array of colorful fabrics.

THE GREAT COURT AND THE OLD READING ROOM

Surrounding the Reading Room of the former British Library, the £100-million Great Court opened to coincide with the new millennium. Designed by Sir Norman Foster, the Court is covered by a wide-span, lightweight roof, creating London's first ever indoor public square. The Reading Room itself has been restored to its original design, so visitors can sample the atmosphere which Karl Marx, Mahatma Gandhi, and George Bernard Shaw found so agreeable. From the outside, however, it is scarcely recognizable; it is housed in a multi-level construction which partly supports the roof, and which also contains a Center for Education, temporary exhibition galleries, bookshops, cafés, and restaurants. Part of the Reading Room also serves as a study suite where those wishing to learn more about the Museum's collections have access to information.

The Great Court and Reading Room of the British Museum

Madame Tussaud's ⑪

Marylebone Rd NW1. **Tel** 0871-894 3000. ◎ Baker St. ◯ 9:30am–5:30pm daily. ● Dec 24 (afternoon) & Dec 25. 🎟 🔒 🖥 ♿ www.madame-tussauds.com

Madame Tussaud began her wax-modeling career making death masks of victims of the French Revolution. In 1835, after moving to England, she set up an exhibition of her work in Baker Street, near the museum's present site.

Traditional techniques are still used to create the figures of royalty, politicians, actors, pop stars, and sporting heroes.

In the renowned Chamber of Horrors some of the original French Revolution death masks are displayed, and vivid scenes of murders are recreated: the murderer Dr Crippen, Vlad the impaler; and the chill gloom of an east London Victorian street during Jack the Ripper's time in the late 19th century.

In the final section – the Spirit of London – visitors travel in stylized taxi-cabs and participate in momentous events in the city's history, from the Great Fire of 1666 to the Swinging Sixties.

Making a model of singer Luciano Pavarotti at Madame Tussaud's

Regent's Park ⑫

NW1. **Tel** 020-7486 7905. ◎ Regent's Park, Great Portland St, Camden Town. ◯ daily. ♿ **London Zoo Tel** 0844-225 1826. ◯ daily. ● Dec 25. 🎟

This area of land was enclosed as a park in 1812. John Nash designed the scheme and originally envisaged a kind of

Wooden rowboats available to rent on Regent's Park boating lake

garden suburb, dotted with 56 villas in a variety of Classical styles. Eight villas were eventually built inside the park (three survive round the edge of the Inner Circle).

The boating lake boasts many varieties of water birds. In summer Queen Mary's Gardens are full of flowers and Shakespeare productions are staged at the Open Air Theater nearby. Musical performances are also held at the bandstand on the weekend. Broad Walk provides a picturesque stroll north from Park Square towards Primrose Hill.

London Zoo, with its vast animal enclosures, borders the park, and is also an important center of wildlife research and conservation work.

Statue of Peter Pan in Kensington Gardens

Hyde Park ⑬

W2. **Tel** 020-7298 2100. ◎ Hyde Park Corner, Knightsbridge, Lancaster Gate, Marble Arch. ◯ dawn–11pm daily. ♿

The ancient manor of Hyde was part of the lands of Westminster Abbey seized by Henry VIII at the Dissolution of the Monasteries in 1536. James I opened the park to the public in the early 17th century, and it was soon one of the city's most fashionable public spaces. Unfortunately it also became popular with duelists and highwaymen, prompting William III to have 300 lights hung along Rotten Row, the first street in

England to be lit at night. Today Rotten Row is used for horseback riding.

In 1730 the Westbourne River was dammed by Queen Caroline to create an artificial lake – the Serpentine. Today cafés, restaurants, and the Serpentine Gallery, which has exhibitions of modern art, dot the fringes of the lake, which is a popular venue for boating and swimming.

At the southeast corner of Hyde Park stands Apsley House, the grand former home of the Duke of Wellington. Now a museum of memorabilia to the great politician and soldier, the lavish interiors designed by Robert Adam are also worth seeing.

A law passed in 1872 made it legal to assemble an audience and address it on whatever topic you chose. Since then, Speaker's Corner, at the northeast corner of the park, has been the established venue for budding orators. Crowds gather on Sundays to listen to lively speeches.

Adjoining Hyde Park are Kensington Gardens, the former grounds of Kensington Palace, which were opened to the public in 1841. A royal residence for centuries, the palace was Princess Diana's home until her untimely death.

Attractions in the gardens include the bronze statue of J. M. Barrie's fictional Peter Pan (1912), by George Frampton, and the Round Pond where model boats are sailed. The dignified Orangery (1704) is now an upscale café.

For hotels and restaurants in this region see pp96–8 and pp102–4

Street-by-Street: South Kensington

The numerous museums and colleges created in the wake of the Great Exhibition of 1851 *(see pp56–7)* continue to give this neighbourhood its dignified character. Visited as much by Londoners as tourists, the museum area is liveliest on Sundays and on summer evenings during the Royal Albert Hall's famous season of classical "Prom" concerts *(see p126).*

to Kensington Gardens

The Royal Albert Hall
Opened in 1870 and modeled on a Roman amphitheater, this magnificent concert hall hosts a range of events.

The Memorial to the Great Exhibition is surmounted by a bronze statue of its instigator, Prince Albert.

The Royal College of Music, founded in 1882, exhibits historic musical instruments from around the world.

PRINCE CONSORT ROAD

ALBERT COURT

Imperial College, part of London University, is one of the country's leading scientific institutions.

★ Natural History Museum
This pterodactyl is part of a menagerie of sculptures that adorn the facade of the great museum (see p56).

IMPERIAL COLLEGE ROAD

EXHIBITION ROAD

★ Science Museum
Fascinating exhibits, such as this 18th-century steam engine, celebrate the history of science and technology (see p56).

CROMWELL ROAD

KEY

— — — Suggested route

STAR SIGHTS

★ Science Museum

★ Natural History Museum

★ Victoria and Albert Museum

South Kensington station (two entrances on Exhibition Road)

0 meters 100
0 yards 100

★ Victoria and Albert Museum
The museum has a fine collection of decorative arts from around the world (see p57).

Children exploring the "Pattern Pod" at the Science Museum

Science Museum ⑭

Exhibition Rd SW7. ⊖ *South Kensington.* 🚌 *14, 49, 70, 74, 345, 360, 414, 430, C1.* **Tel** *0870-870 4868.* ◯ *daily.* ⬤ *Dec 24–26.* 🎟 *for special exhibitions only.* ♿ www.sciencemuseum.org.uk

Centuries of scientific and technological development are illustrated and explained at the Science Museum – from Ancient Greek and Roman medicine to space exploration and nuclear fission.

The massive and impressive collection, exhibited on five floors, includes steam engines, spacecraft, and early mechanical computers. The museum aims to bring entertainment to the process of learning, with numerous interactive displays for children and staff on hand to provide explanations. Of equal importance is the social context of science: how inventions have transformed day-to-day life, and the process of discovery itself.

The best of the displays are "Flight," which gives visitors the opportunity to experiment with aeronautical concepts, and "Launch Pad," designed to give 7- to 13-year-olds a knowledge of basic scientific principles.

"The Exploration of Space" exhibits the scarred Apollo 10 spacecraft which carried three astronauts to the moon and back in May 1969. There is also a video of the Apollo 11 moon landing a few weeks later.

More down-to-earth, but just as absorbing, is "Food for Thought," which reveals the impact of science and technology on every aspect of diet, explored through demonstrations and historic reconstructions, such as an 18th-century kitchen.

Other popular sections include "Optics," which has holograms, lasers, and color-mixing experiments, and "Power and Land Transport," which displays working steam engines, vintage trains, cars, and motorbikes.

The Wellcome Wing is devoted to contemporary science and technology. "Antenna" is a constantly updated exhibition devoted to the latest scientific breakthroughs. "Pattern Pod" introduces younger children to the patterns of science in a fun and colorful way. "Digitopolis" explores our relationship with digital technology, including virtual reality. "In Future" is a multi-user game in which participants decide how current scientific research could affect the future. Our understanding of human identity is the subject of "Who Am I?", where visitors can learn about genetics and current biomedical discoveries. The wing also contains an IMAX® cinema, a SimEx simulator ride, and a café.

Natural History Museum ⑮

Cromwell Rd SW7. ⊖ *South Kensington.* 🚌 *14, 49, 70, 74, 345, 360, 414, 430, C1.* **Tel** *020-7942 5000.* ◯ *daily.* ⬤ *Dec 24–26.* 🎟 ♿ www.nhm.ac.uk

This vast building, designed by Alfred Waterhouse, is the most architecturally flamboyant of the South Kensington museums. Its richly sculpted stonework conceals an iron and steel frame. This building technique was revolutionary when the museum first opened in 1881. The imaginative displays tackle fundamental issues such as the ecology and evolution of the planet, the origin of species, and the development of human beings – all explained through a dynamic combination of the latest technology, interactive displays, and traditional exhibits.

Triceratops skull, Natural History Museum

The museum is divided into three sections: the Life and Earth Galleries and the Darwin Centre. In the Life Galleries, the Ecology exhibition begins its exploration of the complex web of the natural world, and man's role in it, through a convincing replica of a rainforest. The most popular exhibits are in the Dinosaur section which has real dinosaur skeletons and life-like animatronics. "Creepy Crawlies," with specimens from the insect and spider world, and the Mammals exhibition, enable visitors to see endangered and dangerous creatures.

The Earth Galleries explore the history of Earth and its wealth of natural resources,

The colorful "Antenna" section in the Science Museum Wellcome Wing

and offer the opportunity to experience the rumblings of an earthquake. The second phase of the Darwin Centre's development – a state-of-the-art, eight-story scientific research and education facility – opened in September 2009. An interactive journey into a vast concrete cocoon enables visitors to see into the museum's collections and laboratories, and to observe how museum scientists work.

Victoria and Albert Museum ⑯

Cromwell Rd SW7. ⊖ *South Kensington.* ▥ *14, 74, C1.* **Tel** *020-7942 2000.* ◯ *10am–5:45pm daily.* ◯ *Dec 24–26.* ▨ *for special exhibitions.* ☑ ☒ **www.vam.ac.uk**

Originally founded in 1852 as a Museum of Manufacturing – to inspire and raise standards among students of design – the V&A, as it is popularly known, has 11 km (7 miles) of galleries on four floors. The museum was renamed by Queen Victoria in 1899, in memory of her late husband, and contains one of the world's richest collections of fine and applied arts.

Since 1909 the museum has been housed in a building designed by Sir Aston Webb. The museum has undergone a dramatic restructuring of much of its collection and gallery spaces, alongside a grand development of the central Pirelli Garden.

Donatello's marble relief of *The Ascension* is included in the sculpture collection along with sculptures from India and the Middle and Far East. Craftsmanship in porcelain, glass, and pottery is displayed on levels 4 and 6, with rare pieces by Picasso and Bernard Leach, intricate Near Eastern tiles, and a wide selection of Chinese pieces.

The most celebrated item in the vast array of furniture is

Facade of the Victoria and Albert Museum

18th-century wooden doll, Victoria and Albert Museum

the *Great Bed of Ware*, made around 1590. The Victorian designers who decorated the plush Morris, Gamble, and Poynter Rooms recreated historic styles with newer industrial materials. The fully furnished interiors offer a vivid picture of social life through their displays of furniture and other domestic objects. Among exhibits in the 20th-Century Gallery is Daniel Weil's painting *Radio in a Bag* (1983). The V&A has a wide collection of musical instruments and metalwork, including a 16th-century salt cellar, the *Burghley Nef*. The Silver gallery also explores the history and techniques of silvermaking. Gallery III is devoted to the making of sculpture, ranging from medieval ivories to modern bronzes.

Among the textiles, weapons, jewelry, metalwork, glass, and paintings of the South Asia gallery is the automated *Tippoo's Tiger* (c.1790), which mauls a European soldier when activated. Eight galleries, devoted to the arts of the Far East, display rare jade and ceramics, a giant Buddha's head from AD 700–900, and a Ming canopied bed. Among exhibits in the China gallery is a watercolor on silk from the Qing Dynasty (1644–1912). The Toshiba Gallery focuses on Japanese art, including Samurai armor and woodblock prints. The world-renowned Fashion Court is displayed on level 1. It is devoted to fashionable clothing from the mid-1500s to the present day. The figures here are fully dressed, complete with contemporary accessories.

The museum also houses valuable illustrated documents in the National Art Library and the national collection of photographs with images from 1856 to the present.

The City and Southwark

Dominated by gleaming office blocks, befitting its status as London's financial and business center, the City is also the oldest part of the capital. The Great Fire of 1666 obliterated many of its buildings, and much of the reconstruction was undertaken by Sir Christopher Wren. St. Paul's Cathedral is the most magnificent of his surviving works. Humming with activity in business hours, the City empties at night. Southwark, on the south bank of the Thames, was a refuge for prostitutes and gamblers in the Middle Ages. Theaters, including the Globe, where many of Shakespeare's plays were performed, and other places of entertainment were built along the waterfront in the second half of the 16th century.

Spacious interior of St. Paul's Cathedral in the City

St. Paul's Cathedral ⑰

Ludgate Hill EC4. *Tel 020-7246 8350.* 🚇 *City Thames Link.* 🚇 *St. Paul's, Mansion House.* 🚌 *4, 11, 15, 17, 23, 25, 76 & 172.* 🕐 *9:30am–4pm Mon–Sat; for services only Sun, Dec 25 & Good Fri. Check website for partial or full closures.* 🎧 *www.stpauls.co.uk*

Rebuilt on the site of a medieval cathedral after the Great Fire of 1666, this magnificent Baroque building, designed by Sir Christopher Wren, was completed in 1710.

St. Paul's has been the setting for great ceremonial events, including the funeral of Sir Winston Churchill in 1965 and the wedding of Prince Charles and Lady Diana in 1981.

At 110 m (360 ft) high, the dome is the second largest in the world, after that of St. Peter's in Rome. Supported by a brick cone, the lantern weighs a massive 850 tonnes. The dome's gallery affords a splendid view over London.

Modifications to Wren's original plan include the towers of the west front, the double colonnade of the west portico, and the balustrade – added against his wishes in 1718. Pediment carvings on the west portico show the Conversion of St. Paul.

Wren created a cool and majestic interior. The nave, transepts, and choir are arranged in the traditional shape of a cross. Its climax is in the great open space of the crossing, below the main dome, which is decorated with monochrome frescoes by Sir James Thornhill, a leading architectural painter

of the time. From the south aisle, 259 steps ascend to the circular Whispering Gallery, so-called because of the unusual acoustics.

Much of the fine wrought ironwork was created by Jean Tijou, a Huguenot refugee. The intricate carvings of cherubs, fruits, and garlands on the choir stalls are the work of Grinling Gibbons.

Memorials to famous figures, such as Lawrence of Arabia and Lord Nelson, can be seen in the crypt. The inscription on Wren's tomb is fitting: "Reader, if you seek a monument, look all around you."

Museum of London ⑱

150 London Wall EC2. *Tel 0207-0019 844.* 🚇 *Barbican, St. Paul's.* 🕐 *10am–6pm daily.* 🚫 *Dec 24–26.* 🎧 *www.museumoflondon.org.uk*

This fascinating museum traces life in London from prehistoric times to the 20th century, through nine permanent galleries.

Objects from Roman London include a brightly colored 2nd-century fresco, while from the Tudor city an example of an early English delft plate, made in 1602 at Aldgate, bears an inscription praising Elizabeth I.

The 17th-century section contains the shirt Charles I wore on the scaffold, and an audio-visual display recreating the Great Fire of 1666. A dress in Spitalfields silk, dating from 1753, is among the many fine costumes on display.

One of the most popular exhibits is the lavishly gilded Lord Mayor's State Coach, built in 1757 and still used for the Lord Mayor's Show held in November each year.

The Victorian Walk takes visitors back to the time of Charles Dickens, vividly recreating the atmosphere of 19th-century London with authentic shop interiors.

Roman wall painting in the Museum of London

Sculpture from inaugural exhibition in the vast Turbine Hall, Tate Modern

Tate Modern ⑲

Bankside SE1. **Tel** 020-7887 8888.
⊖ Southwark, Blackfriars, Waterloo.
🚌 45, 63, 100, 381, 344, RV1. 🚤
from Tate Britain. 🕐 10am–6pm
Sun–Thu, 10am–10pm Fri & Sat. ●
Dec 24–26. 🎫 special exhibitions.
🚹 📷 www.tate.org.uk/modern

One of the world's most important collections of 20th-century art now has a worthy home in this imposing former power station with its vast, cathedral-like spaces.

Originally designed by Sir Giles Gilbert Scott, the architect of London's red telephone kiosks, the huge Bankside building had been disused since 1981, when it was acquired by the Tate Gallery in 2000. Swiss architects were responsible for the building's redesign, which allows the works of art to be displayed in a dynamic style.

Unusually, the permanent collection is exhibited in four themed groups: poetry and dream, idea and object, states of flux and material gestures. The paintings and sculptures embrace Surrealism, Abstract Expressionism, Pop Art, Minimal and Conceptual Art.

Major works include Picasso's *The Three Dancers*, Dalí's *The Metamorphosis of*
Narcissus, and Andy Warhol's *Marilyn Diptych*. There are also temporary exhibitions of works by lesser-known artists, and by more controversial newcomers. At the top of the building are two floors enclosed in glass. One is a restaurant with superb views. Natural light filters down to the upper galleries.

Shakespeare's Globe ⑳

214 New Globe Walk SE1. **Tel** 020-
7401 9919. ⊖ London Bridge,
Mansion House, Southwark. 🕐 daily.
● Dec 24, 25. **Performances** May–
Oct. 🎫 🚹 📷 every 30 mins.
www.shakespeares-globe.org

A detailed reproduction of an Elizabethan theater has been built on the riverside close to the site of the original Globe, Shakespeare's "wooden O" where many of his plays were first performed. Open to the elements, the theater operates only in the summer. Seeing a play here can be a lively experience, with "groundlings" (those with cheap standing-room tickets) in front of the stage encouraged to cheer or jeer. An informative tour of the theater is offered by "resting"
Globe actors, and visitors can enjoy seeing center stage among them. Beneath the theater is the Underglobe, where every aspect of Shakespeare's work is vividly brought to life through the use of modern technology and traditional crafts.

Tower of London ㉑

See pp60–61.

Tower Bridge ㉒

SE1. **Tel** 020-7403 3761. ⊖ Tower
Hill, London Bridge. **The Tower
Bridge Exhibition** 🕐 daily.
● Dec 24–26. 🎫 🚹 📷
www.towerbridge.org.uk

This flamboyant piece of Victorian engineering, completed in 1894, soon became a symbol of London. Its two Gothic towers contain the mechanism for raising the roadway to permit large ships to pass through. The towers are made of a supporting steel framework clad in stone. When raised, the roadway creates a space 40 m (135 ft) high and 60 m (200 ft) wide. In its heyday it was raised and lowered five times a day.

The bridge now houses **The Tower Bridge Exhibition**, with displays which bring its history to life. There are fine river views from the walkways between the towers, and the steam engine room which was in use until 1976 can be visited.

Tower Bridge, a symbol of Victorian London

Tower of London ㉑

Tower of London raven

Soon after he became king in 1066, William the Conqueror built a fortress here to guard the entrance to London from the Thames Estuary. In 1097 the White Tower, which today occupies the center of the complex, was completed in stone; other fine buildings have been added over the centuries. The Tower has served as a royal residence, armory, treasury, and most famously as a prison for enemies of the Crown. Some were tortured and among those who met their death here were the "Princes in the Tower," the sons and heirs of Edward IV. Today the Tower is a popular attraction, housing the Crown Jewels and other fine exhibits. Thirty seven Yeoman Warders, known as "Beefeaters," guard the complex and live here. Its most celebrated residents are seven ravens. Legend claims that the kingdom will fall if they desert the Tower.

Beauchamp Tower
Many high-ranking prisoners were held here, often with their own servants. The tower was built by Edward I around 1281.

Tower Green was the execution site for aristocratic prisoners, away from crowds on Tower Hill, where many had to submit to public execution. Seven people died here, including two of Henry VIII's six wives, Anne Boleyn and Catherine Howard.

Two 13th-century curtain walls protect the tower.

Queen's House
This Tudor building is the sovereign's official residence at the Tower.

Main entrance from Tower Hill (Middle Tower)

THE CROWN JEWELS

The world's best-known collection of precious objects, now displayed in a splendid exhibition room, includes the gorgeous regalia of crowns, scepters, orbs, and swords used at coronations and other state occasions. Most date from 1661, when Charles II commissioned replacements for regalia destroyed by Parliament after the execution of Charles I. Only a few older pieces survived, hidden by royalist clergymen until the Restoration. These included Edward the Confessor's sapphire ring, now incorporated into the Imperial State Crown. The crown was made for Queen Victoria in 1837 and has been used at the coronation of every monarch since.

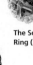

The Sovereign's Ring (1831)

The Sovereign's Orb (1661), a hollow gold sphere encrusted with jewels

★ **Jewel House**
Among the magnificent Crown Jewels is the Scepter with the Cross (1660), which contains the world's largest diamond.

★ **White Tower**
When the tower was finished in 1097, it was London's tallest building at 27 m (90 ft) high.

VISITORS' CHECKLIST

Tower Hill EC3. **Tel** 0870-756 7070. 🚇 Tower Hill; Docklands Light Railway to Tower Gateway; London Bridge; Fenchurch St. 🚌 15, 42, 78, 100. 🚢 from Westminster to Tower Pier. 🕐 10am–5:30pm Sun & Mon; 9am–5:30pm Tue–Sat; closes 4:30pm in winter. Last adm: 30 mins before closing.
🚫 Jan 1, Dec 24–26. 📷 ♿ limited, except Jewel House.
Ceremony of the Keys:
9:30pm daily. **www**.hrp.org.uk

★ **Chapel of St. John**
This austere yet beautiful Romanesque chapel is a particularly fine example of Norman architecture.

Thames

Traitors' Gate
The infamous entrance was used for prisoners brought from trial in Westminster Hall.

Bloody Tower
Explored in a display here, Edward IV's two sons were put in the Bloody Tower by their uncle, Richard of Gloucester, in 1483. The princes, depicted here by John Millais (1829–96), disappeared mysteriously and their uncle became King Richard III later that year. In 1674 the skeletons of two children were found nearby.

STAR SIGHTS

★ Jewel House

★ White Tower

★ Chapel of St. John

London: Farther Afield

Over the centuries, London has steadily expanded to embrace the scores of villages that surrounded it. Although now linked in an almost unbroken urban sprawl, many of these areas have managed to retain a strong individual character. Portobello Road has hosted a market since 1837, while Notting Hill, once farmland, is now covered with townhouses. Greenwich and Richmond recall the days when the Thames was an important artery for transport and commerce. The riverside around Richmond and Kew to the southwest of London was a favorite site for the great country retreats of the aristocracy. Perhaps the grandest riverside residence of all is the royal palace of Hampton Court, set in elaborate, luxurious gardens.

View from the hill at Greenwich of the 17th-century Queen's House

Greenwich ㉓

SE10. 🚆 *Greenwich, Maze Hill, & Docklands Light Railway to Cutty Sark, Greenwich.* 🚢 *from Westminster.*

Best known as the place from which the world's time is measured, Greenwich also marks the historic eastern approach to London by land and water. The area is steeped in maritime and royal history.

The meridian line that divides the earth's eastern and western hemispheres passes through the **Royal Observatory Greenwich** (now housing a museum). Designed by Christopher Wren, the building is topped by a ball on a rod, dropped at 1pm every day since 1833 so that ships' chronometers could be set by it. The Observatory also boasts the **Peter Harrison Planetarium**, the only one of its kind in London.

Because of its links with time, Greenwich was chosen as the site for Britain's year 2000 exhibition. Formerly the Millennium Dome, the **O₂**

Arena is now used as an entertainment complex. The exquisite **Queen's House**, has been restored to how it looked in the late 17th century. Highlights are the unusually-shaped main hall and the intriguing spiral "tulip staircase".

The adjoining **National Maritime Museum** has exhibits ranging from primitive canoes, through Elizabethan galleons, to modern ships. Nearby, the **Old Royal Naval College** was designed in two halves so the Queen's House could retain its river view. The chapel and the Painted Hall are open to the public.

The **Cutty Sark** is a 19th-century clipper ship. The ship is undergoing restoration, due for completion in 2012, with

A rare 24-hour clock at the Old Royal Observatory, Greenwich

new exhibitions on board and alongside the ship.

🏛 **Royal Observatory Greenwich**
Blackheath Ave. **Tel** 020-8858 4422. ◯ *daily.* ● *Dec 24–26.* ♿ 🔋
www.rog.nmm.ac.uk

🏛 **Queen's House and National Maritime Museum**
Romney Rd SE10. **Tel** 020-8312 6608. ◯ *daily.* ● *Dec 24–26.* ♿ *limited.* 📷 **www.nmm.ac.uk**

A colorful antique shop on London's Portobello Road

Notting Hill and Portobello Road ㉔

W11. 🚇 *Notting Hill Gate, Ladbroke Grove.* 🏪 *Fri & Sat.*

Notting Hill and Portobello Road have been a focus for the Caribbean community since the peak years of immigration in the 1950s and 1960s. Today this is a trendy residential district, whose vibrant cosmopolitan spirit is captured in the 1999 film starring Julia Roberts and Hugh Grant.

The West Indian flavor is best experienced during Europe's largest street carnival. First held in 1966, it takes over the entire area on the August bank holiday weekend. For three days costumed parades flood through the crowded streets.

Portobello Road market has a bustling atmosphere with hundreds of stands and shops selling a variety of collectables. The southern end consists almost exclusively of stands selling antiques, jewelry, and souvenirs popular with tourists.

Richmond and Kew ㉕

SW15. ⊖ *Kew Gardens, Richmond.* 🚃 *to Kew Bridge, Richmond.*

The attractive village of Richmond took its name from a palace built in 1500 by Henry VII (formerly the Earl of Richmond), the remains of which can be seen off the green. The vast **Richmond Park** was once Charles I's royal hunting ground. In summer, boats sail from central London to Richmond and Kew.

The nobility continued to favor Richmond after royalty had left, and some of their mansions have survived. The Palladian villa, **Marble Hill House**, was completed in 1729 for the mistress of George II.

On the opposite side of the Thames, **Ham House**, built in 1610 for Sir Thomas Vavasour (Knight Marshal to James I), had its heyday later that century when the aristocratic Lauderdale family moved in. Ham was extended and refurbished as a palatial villa, reflecting the Duke of Lauderdale's status as one of Charles II's most powerful ministers. Much of this luxurious interior decor remains.

On the riverbank to the south, **Kew Gardens**, the most complete botanic gardens in the world, is flawlessly maintained, with examples of nearly every plant that can be grown in Britain. Highlights are the Palm House, with thousands of exotic tropical blooms, and the delicate plants of the Temperate House. The Gardens became a UNESCO World Heritage Site in 2003. Near the river, **Kew Bridge Steam Museum** is housed in an old water pumping station.

An aerial view of the impressive Hampton Court Palace

🏛 **Ham House**
Ham St, Ham. **Tel** 020-940 1950.
◻ Apr–Oct: Sat–Thu. **Gardens, shop & café** ◻ daily. 📷 📷

🌿 **Kew Gardens**
Kew. **Tel** 020-8332 5655. ⊖ *Kew Gardens.* 🚌 65, 237, 267, 391, 419.
◻ daily. ● Dec 24, 25. 📷 ♿ 🍴

Deer grazing in Richmond Park, a former royal hunting ground

Hampton Court ㉖

East Molesey, Surrey. **Tel** 0844-482 7777. 🚇 🚃 *Hampton Court.* 🚌 111, 216, 411, 451, 461, R68. ◻ daily. ● Dec 24–26. 📷 ♿ 🍴 📷 www.hrp.org.uk

Cardinal Wolsey, chief minister to Henry VIII, began building Hampton Court in 1514. A few years later, in the hope of retaining royal favor, he gave

it to the king. The palace was extended first by Henry, and again at the end of the 17th century by William III and Mary II, with the help of Christopher Wren.

From the outside the palace is a harmonious blend of Tudor and English Baroque. A remarkable feature is the Astronomical Clock, created for Henry VIII in 1540.

Inside, Wren's Classical royal rooms, such as the King's Apartments, contrast with Tudor architecture, such as the Great Hall. The stained-glass window here shows Henry VIII flanked by the coats of arms of his six wives. Superb woodwork in the Chapel Royal, including the massive reredos by Grinling Gibbons, dates from a major refurbishment by Queen Anne (c.1711). In the Queen's Gallery, where entertainments were often staged, the marble chimneypiece is by John Nost. Many of the state apartments are decorated with furniture, paintings, and tapestries from the Royal Collection. The King's Staircase has wall paintings by Antonio Verrio. Nine canvases depicting the Triumph of Julius Caesar (1490) are housed in the Mantegna Gallery.

The restored Baroque privy garden, originally created for William and Mary, features radiating avenues of majestic limes and formal flowerbeds. The Fountain Garden still has a few yews planted during their reign. Other attractions are the maze and the Great Vine, planted in 1768.

The distinctive Palm House at London's famous Kew Gardens

Canterbury ❷

Kent. 🏛 50,000. 🚆 🚌
🛈 The Buttermarket, Sun Street
(01227-378 100). 🏴 Wed & Fri.

Canterbury was an important
Roman town even before St.
Augustine arrived in 597, sent
by the pope to convert the
Anglo-Saxons to Christianity.
The town rose in importance,
soon becoming the center of
Christianity in England.

Under the Normans, the city
maintained its position as the
country's leading archbishopric.
A new cathedral was built on
the ruins of the Anglo-Saxon
cathedral in 1070. It was
enlarged and rebuilt many
times; as a result it embraces
examples of all styles of
medieval architecture.

The most poignant moment
in the cathedral's history
came in 1170 when Thomas
Becket, the Archbishop of
Canterbury and enemy of King
Henry II, was murdered here.
Trinity Chapel was built to
house Becket's remains.

Until the Dissolution the
cathedral was one of the chief
places of pilgrimage in all
Christendom. The Canterbury
Tales by Geoffrey Chaucer
(c.1345–1400), one of the
greatest works of early English
literature, tells of a group of
pilgrims who are traveling
from London to Becket's
shrine in 1387.

Adjacent to the ruins of
St. Augustine's Abbey is
St. Martin's Church, one of
the oldest in England.

The domes and minarets of the Royal Pavilion, Brighton

Beneath Canterbury's streets
lies the **Roman Museum**, the
highlight of which are the
foundations of a Roman house.

🏛 **Cathedral**
Christ Church Gate. **Tel** 01227-762
862. ⭕ daily. ⭕ during services &
concerts, Good Fri, Dec 25. 📷 ♿
🌐 www.canterbury-cathedral.org

Brighton ❸

🏛 249,000. 🚆 🚌 🛈 5 Pavilion
Bldgs (01273-290 337). 🏴 Mon–Sat.
🎭 International Arts Festival (May).

As the nearest south coast
city to London, Brighton is
perennially popular.

The spirit of the Prince
Regent (later George IV) lives
on in the magnificence of the
Royal Pavilion, originally a
farmhouse where the prince
resided with the Catholic
widow Mrs. Fitzherbert after
their secret marriage. As his

parties became more lavish,
George needed a suitably
extravagant setting. In 1815 he
employed architect John Nash
to transform the house into the
fantastic Oriental palace that
we see today. Completed in
1822, the exterior remains
largely unaltered.

Traditional seaside fun is
centered around Brighton's
pebble beach. **Brighton Pier**,
a late-Victorian pleasure
ground, is now filled with
amusement arcades. Also
worth visiting is the maze
of shops and winding alleys
from the original village
of Brighthelmstone, called
The Lanes.

🎪 **Royal Pavilion**
Old Steine. **Tel** 03000-290 900. ⭕
daily. ⭕ Dec 25 & 26. 📷 📷 📷
♿ limited. www.royalpavilion.org.uk

Windsor Castle ❹

See pp66–7.

Winchester ❺

Hampshire. 🏛 36,000. 🚆 🚌
🛈 Guildhall, The Broadway
(01962-840 500). 🏴 Wed–Sat.

The capital of the ancient
kingdom of Wessex, the city
of Winchester was also the
headquarters of England's
Anglo-Saxon kings.

William the Conqueror built
one of his first English castles
here. The only surviving part
is the **Great Hall**, erected in
1235 to replace the original. It
is now home to the legendary
Round Table of King Arthur,

Canterbury Cathedral dominating the skyline

said to have been built by the wizard Merlin but actually made in the 13th century.

The **Westgate Museum** is one of two surviving 12th-century gatehouses in the city wall. The room (once a prison) above the gate has a glorious 16th-century painted ceiling.

Winchester has been an ecclesiastical center for many centuries. Its fine **cathedral** was begun in 1079. Originally a Benedictine monastery, it has preserved much of its Norman architecture despite numerous modifications. The writer Jane Austin is buried here. Built around 1110, **Wolvesey Castle**, once home of the bishops of Winchester, now lies in ruins.

♜ Great Hall
Castle Ave. **Tel** 01962-846 476. ⏾ 10am–5pm daily. ● Dec 25, 26. ♿

The 13th-century Round Table in the Great Hall, Winchester

Salisbury ❻

Wiltshire. 👥 40,000. 🚆 🚌 ⓘ Fish Row (01722-334 956). ⌚ Tue & Sat. 🎪 Salisbury Festival (end May–mid-Jun).

Salisbury was founded in 1220, when the Norman hilltop settlement of Old Sarum was abandoned in favor of a site amid lush water meadows, where the Nadder, Bourne, Avon, Ebble, and Wylye meet.

A **cathedral** was built here in the early 13th century. It is a fine example of the Early English style of Gothic architecture, typified by tall, pointed lancet windows. The magnificent landmark spire is the tallest in England.

The spacious and tranquil **Close**, with its schools, alm-

The awe-inspiring megaliths of Stonehenge, Salisbury Plain

shouses, and clergy housing, makes a fine setting for Salisbury's cathedral. In the medieval King's House, **the Salisbury and South Wiltshire Museum** has displays on early man, Stonehenge, and Old Sarum.

Beyond the walls of the Cathedral Close, Salisbury developed its chessboard layout, with areas devoted to different trades, perpetuated in street names such as Fish Row and Butcher Row.

The busy High Street leads to the 13th-century **Church of St. Thomas**, which has a lovely carved timber roof (1450). Nearby on Silver Street, **Poultry Cross** was built in the 15th century as a covered poultry market. In the bustling **Market Place** many of the brick and tile-hung Georgian facades conceal medieval houses.

🔒 Cathedral
The Close. **Tel** 01722-555 120. ⏾ daily. 🎟 donation. 📷 ♿

🏛 Salisbury and South Wiltshire Museum
The Close. **Tel** 01722-332 151. ⏾ Mon–Sat (Jun–Sep: Sun pm). ● Dec 23–31. 🎟 ♿ limited

Stonehenge ❼

Off A303, Wiltshire. **Tel** 01722-334 956. 🚌 3 from Salisbury. ⏾ daily. ● Dec 24 & 25. 🎟 📷 ♿

Built in several stages from about 3000 BC onward, Stonehenge is Europe's most famous prehistoric monument. We can only guess at the rituals that took place here, but the alignment of the stones leaves little doubt that the circle reflects the changing trajectory of the sun through the sky and the passing of the seasons.

Stonehenge's monumental scale is all the more impressive given that the only available tools were made of stone, wood, and bone. To quarry, transport, and erect the huge stones, its builders must have had the command of immense resources and pools of labor. Stonehenge was completed in about 1250 BC; despite popular belief, it was not built by the Druids, who flourished in Britain 1,000 years later.

A collection of ceremonial bronze weapons, jewelry, and other finds excavated at Stonehenge can be seen in the museum in Salisbury.

Sculpture by Elisabeth Frink (1930–93) in Cathedral Close, Salisbury

Windsor Castle ❹

The oldest continuously inhabited royal residence in Britain, the castle, originally made of wood, was founded by William the Conqueror in the late 11th century to guard the western approaches to London. He chose the site because it was on high ground and just a day's journey from the Tower of London. Successive monarchs have made alterations that render it a remarkable monument to royalty's changing tastes. King George V's affection for it was shown when he chose Windsor for his family surname in 1917. The castle is an official residence of the present queen, who often stays here at weekends.

Albert Memorial Chapel
First built in the 1240s, it was rebuilt in 1485 and finally converted into a memorial for Prince Albert in 1863.

King Henry VIII Gate

Castle Hill and main entrance

★ **St. George's Chapel**
The architectural highlight of the castle, this chapel was built between 1475 and 1528 and is an outstanding Late Gothic work. Ten monarchs are buried here.

The Round Tower
was first built in wood by William the Conqueror. In 1170 it was rebuilt in stone by Henry II. It now houses the Royal Archives and Photographic Collection.

Statue of Charles II

Albert Memorial
Chapel (1485)

The Round
Tower
(1080)

Waterloo
Chamber (1820s)

St. George's
Hall (1357–68)

Lower Ward

**Middle
Ward**

St. George's Chapel (1475–1528)

Upper Ward

KEY

☐	11th–13th centuries
☐	14th century
☐	15th–18th centuries
☐	19th–20th centuries

**WINDSOR
CASTLE'S HISTORY**
Most of the work on the castle – founded in 1080 as a motte and bailey – was carried out by Henry II and Edward III, before it was remodeled by George IV in 1823.

Drawing Gallery
This chalk etching of Christ by Michelangelo is part of the Resurrection *Series. It belongs to the Royal Collection, a small selection of which is shown here at any one time.*

VISITORS' CHECKLIST

Castle Hill. *Tel* 020-7766 7304.
◯ 9:45am–5:15pm (Nov–Feb: 4:15pm) daily (last adm: 1 hr 15 mins before closing). ● 12, 13 & 27 Jun; 25 & 26 Dec. 🈲 ♿ ✝
St. George's Chapel 5:15pm Mon–Sat; Sun (for worshippers).

The Audience Chamber is where the Queen greets her guests.

The Queen's Ballroom

Queen Mary's Dolls' House was designed by Sir Edwin Lutyens in 1924. Nearly every item was built on a 1:12 ratio. The wine cellar contains genuine vintage wine.

Waterloo Chamber
Created as part of Charles Long's brief for remodeling the castle in 1823, the Waterloo Chamber was previously a mere space between curtain walls.

Brunswick Tower

The East Terrace Garden was created by Sir Jeffry Wyatville for King George IV in the 1820s.

★ **State Apartments**
These rooms hold many treasures, including this late 18th-century state bed in the King's State Bedchamber, used for the visit in 1855 of Napoleon III.

STAR FEATURES

★ St. George's Chapel

★ State Apartments

The Fire of 1992
A devastating blaze began during maintenance work on the State Apartments. St. George's Hall was damaged but has been rebuilt.

West front of the Cathedral Church of St. Peter in Exeter, Devon

Devon and Cornwall ❽

🚉 🚌 *Truro (Cornwall), Exeter (Devon).* 🛈 *Boscawen Street, Truro (01872-274 555); Dix's Field, Exeter (01392-665 700).*

Miles of stunning coastline dominate this magical corner of Britain. Busy seaside resorts alternate with secluded coves and fishing villages rich in maritime history. Inland, lush pastures contrast with stark and treeless moorland.

Britain's most westerly point, **Land's End**, is noted for its remote and wild landscape. Nearby, the former Benedictine monastery of **St. Michael's Mount** rises dramatically from the waters of Mount Bay off Cornwall's southern coast. On the north coast, **St. Ives**, with its crescent of golden sands, is internationally renowned for its two art museums, the Barbara Hepworth Museum and the Tate Gallery St. Ives.

The **Eden Project** in St. Austell was built in 1998–2000 in an old Cornish china clay pit. The aim of this vast educational and research center is to teach visitors about the vital relationship between plants, people, and resources in an informative and fun way. Two bulbous "greenhouses," huge segmented geodesic domes known as biomes, dominate the site, which holds some 4,500 species of plants.

The administrative capital of Cornwall is **Truro**, a city of gracious Georgian buildings and cobbled streets. Here, the Royal Cornwall Museum has displays on mining, smuggling, and Methodism.

Devon's capital is **Exeter**, a lively city with fine Roman and medieval relics. The mainly 14th-century Cathedral Church of St. Peter is one of the most superbly ornamented cathedrals in Britain.

Devon's most popular recreation area is **Dartmoor National Park**. At its heart is a bleak and windswept landscape, dotted with tors – outcrops of granite rock – and grazed by herds of wild ponies.

❌ **Eden Project**
St. Austell. **Tel** *01726-811 911.*
🚉 🚌 *St. Austell, then local bus.*
⭕ *daily.* ⬤ *Dec 24 & 25.* 🈲 🚻
www.edenproject.com

❌ **Dartmoor National Park**
Devon. 🚉 🚌 *to Exeter, Plymouth, Totnes then local bus.* 🛈 *Visitor Centre, Princetown (01822-890414).*

Bath ❾

See pp70–71.

A wild Dartmoor pony, a familiar sight in Devon's national park

Bristol ❿

Avon. 🚶 *450,000.* ✈ 🚉 🚌
🛈 *E Shed, 1 Canon's Road (0906-711 2191).* 🛒 *daily.* 🎭 *Harbor Festival (Jul–Aug), International Balloon Fiesta (Aug).*

The city of Bristol, at the mouth of the Avon, was once the main British port for transatlantic trade, pioneering the era of the steam liner. The city grew rich on the transportation of wine, tobacco, and, in the 17th century, slaves.

There is a covered market in the city center, part of which occupies the **Corn Exchange**, built by John Wood the Elder in 1743. **St. John's Gate** has colorful statues of Bristol's mythical founders, King Brennus and King Benilus.

Bristol's **cathedral** took an unusually long time to build. The choir was begun in 1298, the transepts and tower were finished in 1515, but the nave took another 350 years to build.

Designed by Isambard Kingdom Brunel, the **SS Great Britain** was the world's first large iron passenger ship. Launched in 1843, it traveled 32 times round the world. The ship now stands in the dock where it was originally built, undergoing restoration.

The **British Empire and Commonwealth Museum**, in the 19th-century rail station at Temple Meads, is the first major museum to chart the 500-year history of the British Empire.

The **Arnolfini Gallery** is a showcase for contemporary art, dance, drama, and film. It is on the harborside, which is lined with cafés, bars, and galleries. .

Cornwall's wild and rugged southern coastline

Wales

Wales is a country of outstanding natural beauty, with varied landscapes. Visitors come to climb dramatic mountain peaks, walk in the forests, fish in the broad rivers, and enjoy the miles of untainted coastline. The country's many seaside towns have long been popular with British vacationers. As well as outdoor pursuits, there is the vibrancy of Welsh culture, with its strong Celtic roots, to be experienced. The Welsh have their own language, which has survived despite the pervasive use of the English tongue.

Snowdonia, famous for dangerous peaks and popular with climbers

Cardiff Castle's clock tower, a 19th-century addition by Burges

Cardiff ⓫

Glamorgan. 🏠 310,000. 🛬 🚉 🚌
🛈 The Hayes (029-2087 3573).
🎪 Cardiff Festival (Jul/Aug).

Cardiff was first occupied by the Romans, who built a fort here in AD 75. In the 1830s the town began to develop as a port, and by 1913 it was the world's leading coal exporter. Confirmed as the Welsh capital in 1955, it is now devoted to commerce and administration.
Cardiff Castle began as a Roman fort. It was renovated in the 19th century by William Burges, who created an ornate mansion rich in medieval images and romantic detail.
Cardiff's civic center is set around Alexandra Gardens. The Neoclassical **City Hall** (1905) is dominated by its huge dome and clock tower. The **Crown Building** now houses the Welsh Office, responsible for Welsh government affairs.
To the south of the center, the docklands are being transformed by the creation of a marina and waterfront. Here, the **Pier Head Building**, constructed in 1896, is a reminder of the city's heyday.

⚜ **Cardiff Castle**
Castle St. **Tel** 029-2087 8100. ☐ daily.
⬤ Jan 1, Dec 25–26. 🎫 📷 📹
grounds only. www.cardiffcastle.com

Snowdonia ⓬

Gwynedd. 🚉 Betws-y-Coed.
🛈 Station Road, Barmouth (01341-280 787).

The scenery of Snowdonia National Park ranges from rugged mountain country to moors and beaches. The area is well known as a destination for hikers, and villages such as **Betws-y-Coed** and **Llanberis** are busy hill-walking centers.
The main focus of this vast area is **Snowdon**, which at 1,085 m (3,560 ft) is the highest peak in Wales. Hikers wishing to explore Snowdonia's peaks should be wary of sudden weather changes. In summer, less intrepid visitors can take the Snowdon Mountain Railway from Llanberis to Snowdon's summit.

Caernarfon ⓭

Gwynedd. 🏠 10,000. 🚌 🛈 Castle St (01286-672 232). 🛒 Sat.

One of the most famous castles in Wales looms over this busy town, created after Edward I's defeat of the last native Welsh prince, Llywelyn ap Gruffydd, in 1283. The town walls merge with modern streets that spread beyond the medieval center and open into a market square.
Caernarfon Castle was built as a seat of government for North Wales. It contains several interesting displays, including the **Royal Welsh Fusiliers Museum** and an exhibition tracing the history of the Princes of Wales.
On the hill above the town are the ruins of **Segontium**, a Roman fort built around AD 78.

⚜ **Caernarfon Castle**
Y Maes. **Tel** 01286-677 617.
☐ daily. ⬤ Jan 1, Dec 24–26. 🎫 📷

Caernarfon Castle, one of the forbidding fortresses built by Edward I

Street-by-Street: Bath ❾

Bath owes its magnificent Georgian town-scape to the bubbling pool of water at the heart of the Roman baths. The Romans transformed Bath into England's first spa resort and it regained fame as a spa town in the 18th century. At this time the two brilliant John Woods (Elder and Younger) designed the city's fine Palladian-style buildings. Today, the traffic-free heart of this lively town is full of street musicians, museums, and enticing shops.

The Circus
This is a daring departure from the typical Georgian square, by John Wood the Elder (1704–54)

No. 1 Royal Crescent is a museum which provides a glimpse of 18th-century aristocratic life.

No. 17 is where the 18th-century painter Thomas Gainsborough lived.

Assembly Rooms and Fashion Museum

★ Royal Crescent
Hailed as the most majestic street in Britain, this graceful arc of 30 houses (1769–75) is the masterpiece of John Wood the Younger. West of Royal Crescent, Royal Victoria Park (1830) is the city's largest open space.

Jane Austen
(1775–1817), the writer, stayed at No. 13 Queen Square on one of many visits to Bath in her youth.

Milsom Street and New Bond Street contain some of Bath's most elegant shops.

Theatre Royal (1805)

KEY

– – – Suggested route

| 0 meters | 100 |
| 0 yards | 100 |

STAR SIGHTS

★ Royal Crescent
★ Roman Baths
★ Bath Abbey

Pump Room
These tearooms once formed the social hub of the 18th-century spa community. They contain this decorative drinking fountain.

THE KING'S SPRING

Pulteney Bridge
This charming bridge (1769–74), designed by Robert Adam, is lined with shops and links the center with the magnificent Great Pulteney Street.

The Building of Bath Collection shows how, in the 18th century, the city was transformed from a medieval wool town into one of Europe's most elegant spas.

VISITORS' CHECKLIST

Avon. 85,000. Bristol Airport, 32 km (20 miles) W. Dorchester St. Manvers St. Abbey Chambers, Abbey Church Yard (0906-711 2000). daily. International Music Festival (May–Jun). **Roman Baths Museum** daily. Dec 25 & 26. limited.

★ Bath Abbey
The splendid abbey stands at the heart of the old city in the Abbey Church Yard, a paved piazza enlivened by buskers. Its unique facade features stone angels climbing Jacob's Ladder to heaven.

★ Roman Baths
Built in the 1st century, this bathing complex is one of Britain's greatest memorials to the Roman era.

Great Pulteney Street

Parade Gardens
Courting couples came to this pretty riverside park for secret liaisons in the 18th century.

Sally Lunn's House (1482) is one of Bath's oldest houses.

Train station

The massive dining hall at Christ Church College, Oxford University

Oxford ⑭

Oxfordshire. 🏛 134,000. 🚉 🚌
ℹ 15–16 Broad St (01865-252 200).
🏪 Wed, Thu. 🎡 St. Giles Fair (Sep).

Oxford has long been a strategic point on the western routes into London – its name describes its position as a convenient spot for crossing the river (a ford for oxen).

English students expelled from Paris founded the university in 1167. The development of England's first university created the spectacular skyline of tall towers and "dreaming spires."

Many of the 36 colleges that make up **Oxford University** were founded between the 13th and 16th centuries and cluster around the city center. The colleges were designed along the lines of monastic buildings but were surrounded by gardens.

Christ Church, the largest of the Oxford colleges, dates from 1525 when Cardinal Wolsey founded it as an ecclesiastical college. It has produced 13 British prime ministers in the last 200 years. Other colleges worth visiting are **All Souls**, **Magdalen**, **Merton**, **Lincoln**, and **Corpus Christi**.

The university's library, the **Bodleian**, was founded in 1320. One of its most famous rooms is the Divinity School (1488), which has a beautiful Gothic vaulted ceiling. The Baroque rotunda named the **Radcliffe Camera** (1748) is a reading room.

Oxford is more than just a university town and there is a wealth of interesting sights aside from the colleges.

One of the best British museums outside London, the **Ashmolean Museum** was opened in 1683. The museum's exceptional art collection includes works by Bellini, Raphael, Turner, Rembrandt, Michelangelo, Picasso, and a large group of Pre-Raphaelites. There is also the Alfred Jewel,

Radcliffe Camera, Bodleian Library, Oxford

a ring that is more than 1,000 years old.

Carfax Tower is all that remains of the 14th-century Church of St. Martin, demolished in 1896. Watch the clock strike the quarter hours, and climb to the top for a panoramic view of the city.

The **Martyrs' Memorial** commemorates the three Protestants burned at the stake on Broad Street – Bishops Latimer and Ridley in 1555, and Archbishop Cranmer in 1556 – during the reign of Catholic Queen Mary.

St. Mary the Virgin Church is the official church of the university, and is said to be the most visited parish church in England.

Two of Oxford's most interesting museums adjoin each other. The **University Museum of Natural History** contains relics of dinosaurs as well as a stuffed dodo. The **Pitt Rivers Museum** has one of the world's most extensive ethnographic collections – masks and tribal totems from Africa and the Far East – and archaeological displays.

Completed in 1669, the **Sheldonian Theatre** was the first building designed by Christopher Wren and was built as a place to hold university degree ceremonies. The ceiling depicts the triumph of religion, art, and science over envy, hatred, and malice.

🏛 **Ashmolean Museum**
Beaumont St. **Tel** 01865-278 002.
⭘ Tue–Sat, Sun pm & public hols.
⬤ Jan 1, Good Fri, Dec 25–28.
🎟 Tue, Fri, Sat. ♿

🏛 **University Museum and Pitt Rivers Museum**
Parks Rd. **Tel** 01865-272 950 /270 927
⭘ University: daily; Pitt Rivers: 10am–4:30pm daily. ⬤ Easter, Dec 24–26. ♿ limited.

The Great Quadrangle of All Souls College, Oxford University

Blenheim Palace ⑮

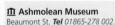
See pp74–5.

Stratford-upon-Avon **⓰**

Warwickshire. 🏠 22,000. 🚇 🚌 ℹ️
Bridge Foot (0870-160 7930). 🅿️ Fri.
📅 Shakespeare's Birthday (late Apr).

Situated on the west bank of the River Avon, Stratford-upon-Avon attracts hordes of tourists eager to see buildings connected with William Shakespeare, born here in 1564. The town is also the provincial home of the Royal Shakespeare Company, whose performances are staged at the **Royal Shakespeare Theatre**.

The High Street turns into Chapel Street, the site of **New Place**. Shakespeare died here in 1616, and it is now a herb garden. The playwright is buried at **Holy Trinity Church**. Bought for the nation in 1847, **Shakespeare's Birthplace** was restored to Elizabethan style. It is regarded by many as a shrine to the great man, who lived here for many years, and offers a fascinating insight into his life.

Shakespeare monument at Holy Trinity Church, Stratford

Another Stratford native, John Harvard, emigrated to America and in 1638 left his estate to a new college, later renamed Harvard University. **Harvard House** displays family mementos.

No tour of Stratford would be complete without a visit to **Anne Hathaway's Cottage**. Before her marriage to Shakespeare Anne lived here, 1 mile (1.5 km) from the town. Despite fire damage, the cottage is still impressive, with some original 16th-century furniture.

Cambridge **⓱**

Cambridgeshire. 🏠 120,000. 🚇
🚌 ℹ️ Wheeler St (0871-226 8006).
🅿️ daily. 📅 Folk Festival (July).

Cambridge has been an important town since Roman times, being located at the first navigable point on the River Cam. When, in 1209, a group of religious scholars broke away from Oxford University after academic and religious disputes, they came here. Student life dominates the city, but it is also a thriving market center serving a rich agricultural region.

Cambridge University has 31 colleges, the oldest being **Peterhouse** (1284) and the newest **Robinson** (1979). Many of the older colleges have peaceful gardens backing onto the River Cam, which are known as "Backs." An enjoyable way to view these is to rent a punt (a long narrow boat propelled by using a pole) from one of the boatyards along the river – with a "chauffeur" if required. The layout of the older colleges, as at Oxford, derives from their early connections with religious institutions, although few escaped heavy-handed alterations in the Victorian era.

Henry VI founded **King's College** in 1441. Work on the chapel – one of the most important examples of late medieval English architecture – began five years later, took 90 years to complete. Henry himself decided that the building should dominate the city and gave specific instructions about its dimensions. He also stipulated that a choir of six lay clerks and 16 boy choristers – educated at the College school – should sing daily at services.

The awe-inspiring choir of King's College Chapel, Cambridge

This still happens in term time but today the choir also gives concerts all over the world.

St. John's College, whose alumni include the Romantic poet William Wordsworth, spans the Cam and boasts one of the town's most beautiful bridges. Known as the Bridge of Sighs, it was named after its Venetian counterpart.

One of Britain's oldest public museums, the **Fitzwilliam Museum** has works of exceptional quality and rarity, especially antiquities, ceramics, paintings, and manuscripts. These include paintings by Titian and the 17th-century Dutch masters, an impressive collection of works by the French Impressionists, and most of the important British artists of the past 300 years.

🏛️ **Fitzwilliam Museum**
Trumpington St. **Tel** 01223-332
900. 🕐 Tue–Sun & public hols. 🔴
Jan 1, Good Fri, Dec 24–26, 31.
💷 donation. ♿ limited.

Bridge of Sighs, St. John's College, Cambridge University

Blenheim Palace ⑮

After John Churchill, the 1st Duke of Marlborough, defeated the French at the Battle of Blenheim in 1704, Queen Anne gave him the manor of Woodstock and had this palatial house built for him in gratitude. Designed by Nicholas Hawksmoor and Sir John Vanbrugh, it is one of the country's most outstanding examples of English Baroque. The magnificent palace grounds, at the center of which is a huge lake, owe their present appearance to the great 18th-century landscape designer, Lancelot (Capability) Brown. Blenheim Palace was the birthplace, in 1874, of the wartime British prime minister, Winston Churchill. Today the palace is the home of the 11th Duke and Duchess of Marlborough.

★ **Long Library**
This 55-m (183-ft) long room was designed by Vanbrugh as a picture gallery. The stucco work on the ceiling is by Isaac Mansfield (1725).

The Grand Bridge was built in 1708. It has a 31-m (101-ft) main span and contains rooms within its structure.

The Chapel holds a marble monument to the 1st Duke of Marlborough, sculpted in 1733.

★ **Water Terrace Gardens**
These splendid gardens were laid out in the 1920s by French architect Achille Duchêne in 17th-century style, with detailed patterned beds and fountains.

STAR SIGHTS

- ★ Long Library
- ★ Saloon
- ★ Water Terrace Gardens

Great Hall
The hall's magnificent ceiling, painted by Sir James Thornhill in 1716, shows Marlborough presenting his plan for the Battle of Blenheim to Britannia.

The lion sculptures (1709), which overlook the Great Court, are by Grinling Gibbons.

The Untold Story

East Gate

The Italian Garden contains the Mermaid Fountain, dating from the late 19th century.

Entrance

The Green Drawing Room has a full-length portrait of the 4th Duke of Marlborough by George Romney (1734–1802).

Red Drawing Room

OTHER NOTABLE STATELY HOMES

Burghley House
Lincolnshire. **Tel** 01780-752 451. 🚉 Stamford. ◯ Apr–Oct: daily. 🎦 🍴 📶
Built by Queen Elizabeth I's adviser, William Cecil, 1st Lord Burghley (1520–98).

Castle Howard
Yorkshire. **Tel** 01653-648 333. 🚉 York, then bus. ◯ mid-Mar–Oct, end Nov–mid-Dec: daily. 🎦 🍴 📷 📶
Baroque mansion (1699–1712) by John Vanbrugh and Nicholas Hawksmoor.

Chatsworth House
Derbyshire. **Tel** 01246-582 204. 🚉 Chesterfield. ◯ mid-Mar–Dec: daily. 🎦 📷 🍴 📶 limited.
Splendid Baroque palace built in 1687–1707 by the 4th Earl of Devonshire.

Hardwick Hall
Derbyshire. **Tel** 01246-850 430. 🚉 Chesterfield. ◯ Apr–Oct: Wed, Thu, Sat, Sun. 🎦 📷 🍴 📶 limited.
Fine Tudor mansion begun in 1591 by Bess of Hardwick, Countess of Shrewsbury.

★ Saloon
The murals and painted ceiling of the state dining room are by French artist Louis Laguerre (1663–1721). The room is used once a year on Christmas Day.

EIGHTEENTH-CENTURY GARDENS

Styles of gardening in Britain expanded alongside architecture and other fashions. The 18th century brought a taste for large-scale "natural" landscapes, characterized by woods, lakes, and a seeming lack of boundaries. The pioneer of this new style was the famous landscape designer Lancelot (Capability) Brown (1715–83). His nickname came from his habit of telling clients that their land had "great capabilities." In 1764 he re-landscaped the grounds of Blenheim Palace, creating the magnificent, huge lake. Today his reputation is controversial, because in creating his idyllic landscapes he swept away many of the beautiful formal gardens previously in vogue.

Capability Brown (1715–83)

Detail of a carving on the façade of Bishop Lloyd's House, Chester

Chester ⑱

Cheshire. 🏘 125,000. 🚌 🚇
ℹ️ Town Hall, Northgate St (01244-402 111). 🏛 Mon–Sat.

First settled by the Romans in AD 79, the main streets of Chester are now lined with timber buildings, many dating from the 13th and 14th centuries. These are the **Chester Rows**, which, with their two tiers of stores and continuous upper gallery, anticipate today's multistory shops by several centuries. Their oriel windows and decorative timber-work are mostly 19th century. The facade of the 16th-century **Bishop Lloyd's House** in Watergate Street is the most richly carved in Chester. The Rows are at their most attractive where Eastgate Street meets Bridge Street.

A town crier calls the hour and announces news from the Cross – a reconstruction of a 15th-century stone crucifix. South of here, the **Grosvenor Museum** explains Chester's history. To the north is the **cathedral**. The choir stalls have splendid misericords and delicate spirelets on the canopies. The cathedral is surrounded on two sides by high city walls, originally Roman but rebuilt at intervals. Also worth seeing is the **Roman amphitheater** just outside town, built in AD 100.

🏛 **Grosvenor Museum**
Grosvenor St. **Tel** 01244-402 033.
⬭ Mon–Sat, Sun pm. ⬤ Jan 1,
Good Fri, Dec 24–26. ⬥ limited. 🖼

Liverpool ⑲

Liverpool. 🏘 450,000. ✈ 11 km (7 miles) SE. 🚢 🚇 🚌 ℹ️ Albert Dock (0151-707 0729).
🏛 Sun. **www**.visitliverpool.com

During the 17th and 18th centuries, Liverpool's westerly seaboard gave it a leading role in the Caribbean slave trade. After the city's first ocean steamer set sail from here in 1840, would-be emigrants to the New World poured into the city, including a large number of Irish refugees of the potato famine.

Liverpool's waterfront is overlooked by the well-known **Royal Liver Building**. The 19th-century warehouses around Albert Dock have been redeveloped as museums, galleries, restaurants, and shops. Among these, the **Maritime Museum** and the **Tate Liverpool**, which houses one of the best collections of contemporary art in England outside of London, are well worth visiting. Liverpool is famous as the home town of the phenomenally successful Beatles. The **Beatles Story** is a walk-through exhibition which charts their meteoric rise to fame in the 1960s.

Clock tower of the Royal Liver Building, Liverpool

One of the most prestigious art galleries in the city is **The Walker**. Paintings range from early Italian and Flemish works to 20th-century art.

Liverpool's Gothic-style **Anglican Cathedral**, completed in 1978 by Sir Giles Gilbert Scott, is the world's largest. The Roman Catholic **Metropolitan Cathedral of Christ the King** (1962–7) is a striking circular building surmounted by a stylized crown of thorns 88 m (290 ft) high.

🏛 **Tate Liverpool**
Albert Dock. **Tel** 0151-702 7400.
⬭ Tue–Sun (Jun–Oct: Mon). ⬤ Jan 1, Good Friday, Dec 24–26. 🖼 ⬥

🏛 **The Walker**
William Brown St. **Tel** 0151-478 4199. ⬭ daily. ⬤ Good Friday, Dec 25 & 26. 🖼 by appt. ⬥

Manchester ⑳

Manchester. 🏘 2.5 million. ✈ 18 km (11 miles) S. 🚇 🚌 ℹ️ Lloyd St (0871-222 8223). 🏛 daily.

Manchester is famous as a pioneer of the industrial age, with its cotton spinning machines and early railways.

Among the city's many fine 19th-century buildings are the Neo-Gothic **cathedral**, the **Royal Exchange**, now a theater and restaurant, and the **Free Trade Hall**, now the Radisson Edwardian Hotel, with only the original facade remaining. The **Manchester Ship Canal**, opened in 1894, is a magnificent engineering feat.

The **Museum of Science and Industry in Manchester** captures the city's spirit of industrial might with a display of working steam engines and

Modern city blocks on the banks of the Manchester Ship Canal

Lush, green fields below the Skiddaw fells in the Lake District

an exhibition on the Liverpool and Manchester Railway. Another museum of note is the **Whitworth Art Gallery**, with its splendid collection of contemporary art, textiles, and prints. The Turner watercolors are a highlight. Housed in a 19th-century porticoed building, the **City Art Galleries** contain an excellent selection of British art, as well as early Italian, Flemish, and French paintings.

The Lakeland poet William Wordsworth

🏛 **Whitworth Art Gallery**
University of Manchester, Oxford Rd.
Tel 0161-275 7450. ⬛ 10am–5pm
Mon–Sat & Sun pm. ⬤ Dec 24–
Jan 2, Good Fri. ♿ ▯

York ㉑

See pp78–9.

Lake District ㉒

Cumbria. 🚊 Kendal; Windermere.
🚌 Kendal; Keswick; Windermere.
🛈 Town Hall, Highgate, Kendal
(01539-725 758); Moot Hall, Market
Sq, Keswick (01768-772 645).

The Lake District boasts some of the country's most spectacular scenery, with high peaks, lonely fells, and beautiful lakes. The area constitutes Britain's largest national park and offers a range of outdoor activities, from hill walking to boating.

Kendal is the southern gateway to the Lake District. Of interest here is the Museum of Lakeland Life and Industry, housed in the stable block of the 18th-century Abbot Hall. The nearest lake to Kendal is Windermere, over 16 km (10 miles) long. A year-round car ferry connects the lake's east and west shores, and summer steamers link the main towns on the north-south axis. Among these, one of the most popular is **Bowness**, where the Windermere Steamboat Museum has a collection of superbly restored watercraft.

Ambleside, another attractive lakeside town, is a good base for walkers and climbers. Nearby is Hill Top, the 17th-century farmhouse where the author Beatrix Potter wrote many of her famous children's stories.

The Lake District's most famous son, the Romantic poet William Wordsworth (1770–1850), lived for a while at **Grasmere**, on the shores of the lake of the same name, north of Ambleside. His home, Dove Cottage, contains a museum dedicated to his life.

To the west of Windermere lie Coniston Water and picturesque **Duddon Valley**, popular walking country.

In the northern part of the Lake District **Keswick**, with its lake, Derwent Water, has been a busy vacation destination since Victorian days. The Keswick Museum and Art Gallery holds original manuscripts of Lakeland writers such as Robert Southey (1774–1843) and Wordsworth. To the east of the town lies the ancient stone circle of Castlerigg. North of Keswick is Skiddaw, England's fourth highest peak and a straightforward climb for anyone reasonably fit.

Durham ㉓

County Durham. 🚊 🚌 🛈 Millenium
Place (0191-384 3720). ⬛ Sat.

Durham was built on a rocky peninsula in 995. The site was chosen as the last resting place for the remains of St. Cuthbert. The relics of the Venerable Bede were brought here 27 years later, adding to the town's attraction to pilgrims.

Durham's **cathedral**, built between 1093 and 1274, is a striking Norman structure. The vast dimensions of the 900-year-old columns, piers, and vaults, and the lozenge, chevron, and dogtooth patterns carved into them, are its main innovative features. The exotic Galilee Chapel, begun in 1170, was inspired by the mosque at Córdoba, Spain (see pp326–7).

The Norman **castle**, begun in 1072, served as an Episcopal Palace until 1832, when Bishop William van Mildert gave it away to found Britain's third university here. In the castle grounds, Tunstal's Chapel was built around 1542 and has some particularly fine woodwork, including a unicorn misericord. The castle keep, sited on a mound, is now part of the university.

♜ **Durham Castle**
Tel 0191-334 3800. ⬛ univ hols:
daily; term: daily (pm); call ahead for
special closures. ▯

Moorish-style arches in the 12th-century Galilee Chapel, Durham Cathedral

Street-by-Street: York ㉑

The city of York has retained so much of its medieval structure that walking into its center is like entering a living museum. Many of the ancient timbered houses, which overhang narrow, winding streets such as the Shambles, are protected by a conservation order. Cars are banned from the center, so there are always student bikes bouncing over cobbled streets. The chief glory of York is its cathedral, the Minster. The city also has 18 medieval churches, 5 km (3 miles) of medieval city walls, and many elegant Jacobean and Georgian buildings.

York's medieval city walls still encircle the old city. It is possible to walk round them, although there are large gaps. The gates are known as "bars."

At Monk Bar the gatehouse retains a working portcullis.

★ York Minster
The 15th-century choir screen is lined with statues of the kings of England from William I to Henry VI.

Thirsk

St. Mary's Abbey

The Yorkshire Museum contains a fine collection of fossils, discovered at Whitby in the 19th century.

Lendal Bridge

Train station, bus station, National Railway Museum, and Leeds

Ye Old Starre Inne is one of the oldest pubs in York.

In Coffee Yard, look out for the carved figure of a red devil, relic of a medieval print shop.

Guildhall
This two-headed medieval roof boss is on the 15th-century Guildhall, situated beside the River Ouse and restored after bomb damage during World War II.

St. Olave's Church
The 11th-century church, next to the gatehouse of St. Mary's Abbey, was founded by the Earl of Northumbria in memory of St. Olaf, King of Norway. To the left is the Chapel of St. Mary on the Walls.

★ Jorvik Viking Center
The many artifacts on show here illustrate the time when York was a strategic Viking town.

VISITORS' CHECKLIST

🏠 120,000. 🚉 🚌 Station Rd.
ℹ️ 1 Museum St (01904-550 099). 🍴 daily. 🎭 Jorvik Festival (Feb); St. Nicholas Fair (Nov). **York Minster** Deangate. **Tel** 01904-557 216. ◯ daily. **Jorvik Viking Center** Coppergate Walk. **Tel** 01904-543 400. ◯ daily. ⬤ Dec 25. **www**.visityork.org

Whip-Ma-Whop-Ma-Gate is York's tiniest street. The name means "neither one thing nor the other street."

Merchant Adventurers' Hall

★ York Castle Museum
Converted from two 18th-century prisons, the museum features reconstructions of old York and the cell of the notorious highwayman Dick Turpin (1706–39).

St. Mary's Church

Clifford's Tower (c.1250)

→ Hull

🅿️

| 0 meters | 100 |
| 0 yards | 100 |

KEY

- - - Suggested route

STAR SIGHTS

★ York Minster

★ Jorvik Viking Center

★ York Castle Museum

Exploring York

To the Romans the city of York was Eboracum, to the Saxons it was Eoforwic, and to the Vikings Jorvik. Danish street names are a reminder that from 867 York was a major Viking settlement. **Jorvik Viking Center**, the Viking museum, is built underground on an archaeological site excavated at Coppergate. The latest technology brings the sights and smells of 10th-century York dramatically to life.

Between 1100 and 1500 York was England's second city. **York Minster**, the largest Gothic church in northern Europe, was begun in 1220. It has a remarkable collection of medieval stained glass. The vast Great East Window (1405–8) depicts the Creation. In 1984 a disastrous fire in the south transept destroyed the roof and shattered its magnificent rose window. This has since been restored.

Much of York's wealth in the late Middle Ages came from the cloth trade. The **Merchant Adventurers' Hall**, the headquarters of a powerful guild of traders, is a beautifully preserved timber-framed building that dates from the mid-14th century.

In the 19th century York's position on the route to Scotland made it a major rail center. Train enthusiasts should head for the **National Railway Museum**, the largest of its kind in the world, where the rolling stock on show includes Queen Victoria's royal carriage.

🏛 **National Railway Museum**
Leeman Rd. **Tel** 08448-153 139.
◯ daily. ⬤ Dec 24–26. ♿

The square central tower of York Minster rising above the city

Scotland

Scotland's landscape is breathtaking, with sparkling lochs, awesome mountains, and windswept isles. The ruggedness of its climate and natural environment has helped to forge a tough, self-reliant nation, whose history has been characterized by resistance to English domination. Castles, many in ruins, are found all over the country – a legacy of its turbulent past. Culturally, Edinburgh has always been the country's chief attraction, but the rival city of Glasgow, despite the collapse of its traditional heavy industries, has much to offer too.

The imposing City Chambers in George Square, Glasgow

Edinburgh ㉔

See pp82–6.

Glasgow ㉕

🏃 *735,000.* ✈ 🚉 🚌 ℹ *11 George Square (0141-566 4064).* 📅 *Sat, Sun.* 🎷 *Jazz Festival (Jul).* **www.**seeglasgow.com

Glasgow's era of great prosperity was the industrial 19th century. Coal seams in Lanarkshire fueled the city's cotton mills and ironworks, belying its Celtic name, *Glas cu*, meaning "dear green place." Relics of this

manufacturing past contrast starkly with the glossy image of modern Glasgow, renowned for its galleries and museums. The deprived East End stands side by side with the restored 18th-century Merchant City and Victorian George Square.

Glasgow's **cathedral** was one of the few to escape destruction during the Scottish Reformation and is a rare example of an almost complete 13th-century church. The crypt holds the tomb of St. Mungo. In the cathedral precinct, the **St. Mungo Museum of Religious Life and Art** is the first of its kind in the world, illustrating religious themes with a superb range of artifacts.

It is in the more affluent West End, to where merchants retreated from industrial Clydeside, that Glasgow's most important galleries and museums can be found. The **Kelvingrove Art Gallery and Museum**, housed in a striking red sandstone building dating to 1901, is home to a splendid collection of art, with works by Botticelli, Giorgione, Rembrandt, Degas, Millet, and Monet, while the Scottish Gallery contains the

Stained glass by Charles Rennie Mackintosh

famous *Massacre of Glencoe* by James Hamilton (1853–94). Other highlights include dinosaur skeletons, Egyptian artifacts and a real spitfire suspended in the main hall.

The **Hunterian Art Gallery** houses Scotland's largest print collection and paintings by major European artists from the 16th century to the present. A display of works by Glasgow's most celebrated designer, Charles Rennie Mackintosh (1868–1928), is supplemented by a reconstruction of No. 6 Florentine Terrace, where he lived from 1906 to 1914.

South of the river, the Pollok Country Park is the site of the **Burrell Collection**, star of Glasgow's renaissance. Highlights include examples of 15th-century stained glass and tapestries, a bronze bull's head (7th century BC) from Turkey, Matthijs Maris' *The Sisters* (1875), and a self-portrait by Rembrandt (1632). On the same site, Pollok House is an attractive Georgian building. It holds one of Britain's best collections of 16th- to 19th-century Spanish paintings.

Other sights worth visiting are the **Tenement House**, a modest apartment in a tenement block preserved from Edwardian times, and **Provand's Lordship** (1471), the city's oldest surviving house. The **House for an Art Lover** is a showcase for the work of Charles Rennie Mackintosh. For a social history of the city from the 12th to the 20th century, visit the **People's Palace**, a cultural museum located in the city's East End.

🏛 **Kelvingrove Art Gallery and Museum**
Argyle St, Kelvingrove. *Tel* 0141-276 9599. ⭘ *daily.* ● *Jan 1–2, Dec 25–26.* 📷 ♿

🏛 **Hunterian Art Gallery**
82 Hillhead St. *Tel* 0141-330 5431. ⭘ *Mon–Sat.* ● *Dec 24–Jan 5 & public hols.* ♿ *restricted.*

🏛 **Burrell Collection**
Pollok Country Park. *Tel* 0141-287 2550. ⭘ *daily.* ● *Jan 1–2, Dec 25–26 & 31.* 📷 ♿ 🖥 📷

The Burrell Collection in Pollok Country Park on Glasgow's outskirts

The 15th-century Stirling Castle, atop its rocky crag

Stirling ㉖

🏯 28,000. 🚉 🚌 🛈 41 Dunbarton Rd (01786-475 019). **www**.visitscotland.com

Located between the Ochil Hills and the Campsie Fells, Stirling grew up around its castle, historically one of Scotland's most important fortresses. **Stirling Castle** is one of the finest examples of Renaissance architecture in the country. Dating from the 15th century, it was last defended, against the Jacobites, in 1746, and stands within sight of no fewer than seven battlefields. One of these – Bannockburn – was where Robert the Bruce defeated the English in 1314.

Stirling's Old Town is still protected by the original 16th-century walls, built to keep out Henry VIII. Two buildings stand out among a number of historic monuments in the town: the medieval **Church of the Holy Rude** and **Mar's Wark**, with its ornate facade.

♣ **Stirling Castle**
Castle Wynd. **Tel** 01786-450 000. 🕐 daily. 🔴 Dec 25 & 26. 🎫 💳 ♿ limited. 🔲 🛈

St.Andrews ㉗

Fife. 🏯 14,000. 🚉 Leuchars. 🚌 🛈 70 Market St (01334-472 021). **www**.standrews.co.uk

Scotland's oldest university town and one-time ecclesiastical capital, St. Andrews is now a shrine for golfers from all over the world. Its main streets and cobbled alleys, lined with university buildings and medieval churches, converge on the ruined 12th-century **cathedral**. Once the largest in Scotland, it was later pillaged for stones to build the town. **St. Andrew's Castle** was built for the bishops of the town in 1200.

The Royal and Ancient Golf Club, founded in 1754, has a magnificent links course and is the ruling arbiter of the game. The city has other golf courses, open to the public for a modest fee, and is home to the **British Golf Museum**.

🏛 **British Golf Museum**
Bruce Embankment. **Tel** 01334-460 046. 🕐 9:30am–5:30pm daily (Nov–Mar: 10am–4pm daily). 🎫 ♿ 🛈

An old railway poster illustrating the lure of St. Andrews for golfing enthusiasts

GOLF

Scotland's national game was pioneered on the sandy links around St. Andrews. The earliest record dates from 1457, when golf was banned by James II on the grounds that it was interfering with his subjects' archery practice. Mary, Queen of Scots enjoyed the game and was berated in 1568 for playing straight after the murder of her husband Darnley. Scotland has several other world-class golf courses, including Royal Troon, Gleneagles, and Carnoustie.

Victorian engraving of Mary, Queen of Scots at St. Andrews

Aberdeen ㉘

🏯 220,000. ✈ 13 km (8 miles) NW. 🚉 🚌 🛈 23 Union St (01224-288 828). 🔷 Thu, Fri, Sat.

Europe's offshore oil capital, Aberdeen is also one of Britain's most important fishing ports, and hosts Scotland's largest fish market.

Among its fine buildings is the 16th-century home of a former provost (mayor) of the city. Period rooms inside **Provost Skene's House** span 200 years of design and include the 17th-century Great Hall, a Regency Room, and a Georgian Dining Room. The Painted Gallery holds one of Scotland's most important cycles of religious art, dating from the 17th century.

Founded in 1495, **King's College** was the city's first university. The chapel has stained-glass windows by Douglas Strachan.

St. Andrew's Cathedral is the Mother Church of the Episcopal Communion in the United States. Coats of arms on the ceiling depict the American states.

Housed in a historic building overlooking the harbor, **Aberdeen Maritime Museum** traces the city's long seafaring tradition.

🏚 **Provost Skene's House**
Guestrow. **Tel** 01224-641 086. 🕐 Mon–Sat. 🔴 Jan 1–2, Dec 25–31. **www**.aagm.co.uk

Edinburgh ㉔

It was not until the reign of James IV (1488–1513) that Edinburgh gained the status of Scotland's capital. Overcrowding made the Old Town a difficult place to live, and led to the construction of a Georgian New Town in the late 1700s. Today, Edinburgh is second only to London as a financial center in the British Isles, and houses the new Scottish parliament building, situated next to the old Palace of Holyroodhouse. Edinburgh hosts a celebrated annual International Festival every August. One of the world's premier arts jamborees, it features drama, dance, opera, music, and ballet. The more eclectic "Fringe" developed in parallel with the official event, but has now exceeded it in terms of size. It is estimated that the population of the city doubles from 400,000 to 800,000 every August.

View of Princes Street from the top of Calton Hill

GETTING AROUND

Central Edinburgh is compact, so walking or cycling is an excellent way to explore the city. Other options include a comprehensive bus service and a multitude of black taxis. Avoid exploring the center by car, because the streets tend to be congested with traffic, and parking may be difficult. Car use is actively discouraged.

SEE ALSO

• *Where to Stay* p101

• *Where to Eat* p107

SIGHTS AT A GLANCE

Calton Hill ⑧
Edinburgh Castle ①
Greyfriars Kirk ⑤
Palace of Holyroodhouse ⑨
National Gallery of Scotland ④
New Town ②
Royal Mile ③
Royal Museum and
  Museum of Scotland ⑥
Scottish National Portrait
  Gallery ⑦

An audience of thousands at the Military Tattoo in Edinburgh Castle, held during August each year

KEY

▢	Sight / Place of interest
🚉	Train station
🚌	Bus station
🅿	Parking
ℹ	Tourist information
✚	Church
▬	Pedestrian street

Entrance to the Fringe information office, located on the Royal Mile

The battlements of Edinburgh Castle rising above Princes Street Gardens

Edinburgh Castle ①

Castle Hill. **Tel** 0131-225 9846. ◻
summer: 9:30am–6pm daily; winter:
9:30am–5pm daily. ● Dec 25 & 26.
▨ ▣ ◾ www.historic-scotland.
gov.uk

Standing on the basalt core
of an extinct volcano, the
castle is an assemblage of
buildings dating from the 12th
to the 20th centuries, reflecting
its changing role as fortress,
palace, military garrison, and
state prison. The castle was a
favorite royal residence until
the Union of 1603, after which
monarchs resided in England.

The Scottish regalia are
displayed in the 15th-century
palace where Mary, Queen of
Scots gave birth to James VI.
The castle also holds the Stone
of Destiny, a relic of ancient
Scottish kings seized by the
English, and returned in 1996.
The castle's oldest existing
building is the 12th-century
St. Margaret's Chapel. A
stained-glass window depicts
the queen of Malcolm III,
after whom it is named.

Other important buildings
include the 15th-century **Great
Hall**, meeting place of the Scottish parliament until 1639, and
the **Governor's House** (1742).
A 15th-century Burgundian
siege gun, known as Mons
Meg, is kept in the vaults,
where French graffiti recall
the prisoners held here in the
18th- and 19th-century wars.

New Town ②

The first phase of the "New
Town," to the north of Princes
Street, was built in the 18th
century to relieve the
congested and unsanitary
conditions of the old town.
Charlotte Square, with its
lavish town houses, was the
climax of this phase. On the
north side, the **Georgian
House**, owned by the National
Trust of Scotland, has been
furnished to show the lifestyle
of its 18th-century residents.

The most magnificent of
the later developments is the
Moray Estate, by James
Gillespie Graham, where a

linked series of large houses
forms a crescent, an oval, and
a twelve-sided circus.

🏛 **Georgian House**
7 Charlotte Sq. **Tel** 0844-493 2117.
◻ Mar–Dec: daily. ▨ ◾ limited.

Royal Mile ③

Composed of four ancient
streets which formed the main
thoroughfare of medieval
Edinburgh, the Royal Mile
linked the castle to Holyrood
Palace. A walk starting from
the castle takes you past
many of the city's oldest
buildings and a number of
interesting museums.

The lower floors of the
**Tartan Weaving Mill &
Exhibition** date from the early
17th century and were once
the home of the Laird of
Cockpen. Its 19th-century
Camera Obscura remains a
popular attraction. A little
further on, **Gladstone's Land**
is a carefully restored 17th-
century merchant's house.
Another fine mansion, built in
1622, has been converted into
a **Writers' Museum**, housing
memorabilia of Robert Burns,
Sir Walter Scott, and Robert
Louis Stevenson.

St. Giles Cathedral, properly
known as the High Kirk of
Edinburgh, was the base from
which Protestant minister
John Knox led the Scottish
Reformation. His house, also
on the Royal Mile, is open to
the public. The cathedral's
Thistle Chapel has impressive
rib-vaulting and carved heraldic
canopies. It honors the knights
of the Most Ancient and Most

Charlotte Square in the New Town

For hotels and restaurants in this region see pp96–101 and pp102–7

Noble Order of the Thistle. Just past St. Giles, the Italianate **Parliament House**, built in the 1630s, has housed the Scottish Courts since the 1707 Act of Union with England and Wales.

Farther east, opposite **John Knox's House** (1450), there is a good **Museum of Childhood**, while **The People's Story** (1591) tells the social history of Edinburgh – from plagues to punk rock.

Thistle Chapel, St. Giles Cathedral, Royal Mile

🏠 **Gladstone's Land**
477B Lawnmarket. **Tel** 0844 493 2120. ☐ Apr–Oct: 10am–5pm daily (Jul–Aug: 10am–6:30pm daily). 📷

National Gallery of Scotland ④

The Mound. **Tel** 0131-624 6200.
☐ daily. 📷 by appt. ♿
www.nationalgalleries.org

One of Scotland's finest art galleries, the National Gallery of Scotland has an impressive collection of British and European paintings. Designed by William Henry Playfair, it was opened in 1859. Many of the works of art are still exhibited as they were in the 19th century. Serried ranks of paintings hang on deep red walls behind a profusion of statues and period furniture.

Some of the highlights among the Scottish works are the society portraits by Allan Ramsay and Henry Raeburn, including the latter's *Reverend Robert Walker Skating on Duddingston Loch* (c.1800), an image reproduced annually on thousands of Christmas cards.

German works include Gerard David's almost comic-strip treatment of the *Three Legends of St. Nicholas*, dating from the early 16th century. Italian paintings include a fine *Madonna* by Raphael, as well as works by Titian and Tintoretto. From Spain there is a delightful genre painting of *An Old Woman Cooking Eggs* by Velázquez (c.1620).

An entire room is devoted to *The Seven Sacraments* by Nicholas Poussin, dating from around 1640. Dutch and Flemish painters represented include Rembrandt, Van Dyck, and Rubens, while among the British offerings are important works by Reynolds and Gainsborough.

Greyfriars Kirk ⑤

Greyfriars Place. **Tel** 0131-225 1900.
☐ Apr–Oct: Mon–Sat; Nov–Mar: Thu pm. 📷 ♿

Greyfriars Kirk played a key role in Scotland's history. In 1638 the National Covenant was signed here, marking the Protestant stand against Charles I's imposition of an episcopal church. Throughout the wars of the 17th century, the kirkyard was used as a mass grave for executed Covenanters. The Martyrs' Monument is a sobering reminder of the many Scots who lost their lives. Greyfriars is also known for its association with a faithful dog, Bobby, who lived beside his master's grave from 1858 to 1872. Greyfriars Bobby's statue stands outside Greyfriars Kirk.

Greyfriars Bobby

Royal Museum and Museum of Scotland ⑥

Chambers St. **Tel** 0300-123 6789.
☐ 10am–5pm daily. 📷 ♿ 📱 📷
www.nms.ac.uk

A great Victorian glass palace, completed in 1888, houses the **Royal Museum of Scotland**. It started life as an industrial museum, but over time acquired an eclectic array of exhibits, ranging from stuffed animals to ethnographic artifacts.

In 1993 work began on a site next door, to display Scotland's impressive array of antiquities. The resulting **Museum of Scotland**, opened in 1998, tells the story of the country, starting with its geology and natural history, through to later industrial developments. Among its many stunning exhibits is St. Fillan's Crozier, said to have been carried at the head of the Scottish army at Bannockburn in 1314.

An Old Woman Cooking Eggs by Velázquez, National Gallery of Scotland

The view from Duncan's Monument at the top of Calton Hill, Edinburgh

Scottish National Portrait Gallery ⑦

1 Queen St. **Tel** 0131-624 6200.
◻ 10am–5pm daily. ● Dec 25 &
26. ♿ 📷 🚻
www.nationalgalleries.org

The Portrait Gallery is housed in a red sandstone Gothic revival building, which was restored between 2009 and 2011. It owns a wonderful collection of paintings that details the history of 12 generations of Stuarts, from the time of Robert the Bruce to Queen Anne. It also houses portraits of famous Scots, including one of the country's best-loved poet Robert Burns (1759–96) by Alexander Nasmyth. Others portrayed include Flora MacDonald, who helped Bonnie Prince Charlie escape after his defeat by the English in 1745, and Ramsay MacDonald, who became Britain's first Labour prime minister in 1924.

The building also holds the Scottish National Photography collection, which has over 30,000 images dating from the 1840s to the present day.

Calton Hill ⑧

City center east, via Waterloo Pl.

Calton Hill, at the east end of Princes Street, is a large open space dotted with Neo-classical monuments. It has one of Edinburgh's more memorable landmarks – a half-finished "Parthenon".

Conceived as the National Monument to the dead of the Napoleonic Wars, building began in 1822 but funds ran out and it was never finished. Nearby, the **Nelson Monument** commemorates the British victory at Trafalgar, providing a fine vantage point over the city. The Classical theme continues with Duncan's Monument and the old **City Observatory**, designed by William Playfair in 1818 and based on Athens' Tower of the Winds. Tours and free lectures are arranged here by the Astro-nomical Society of Edinburgh.

Palace of Holyroodhouse ⑨

East end of the Royal Mile. **Tel** 0131-556 5100. ◻ daily. ● check for seasonal closures. 📷 ♿ limited.

Queen Elizabeth II's official Scottish residence, the palace was built by James IV in the grounds of an abbey in 1498. It was later the home of

James V and his wife, Mary of Guise, and was remodeled in the 1670s for Charles II. The Royal Apartments (including the Throne Room and Royal Dining Room) are used for investiture and for banquets whenever the Queen visits. A chamber in the so-called James V tower is believed to have been the scene of David Rizzio's murder in 1566. He was the Italian secretary of Mary, Queen of Scots. She witnessed the grisly act, which was authorized by her jealous husband, Lord Darnley. Bonnie Prince Charlie, last of the Stuart pretenders to the English throne, also held court at Holyrood Palace, in 1745.

The adjacent Holyrood Park, a former royal hunting ground, is home to three lochs, a large number of wildfowl, and the Salisbury Crags. Its high point is the hill known as Arthur's Seat, an extinct volcano and well-known Edinburgh landmark. The name is probably a corruption of Archer's Seat.

The grand 17th-century façade of Holyrood Palace

The Highlands

Stock images of Scottishness – clans and tartans, whisky and porridge, bagpipes and heather – originate in the Highlands. Gaelic-speaking Celts arrived from Ireland before the 7th century, establishing small fishing and cattle-raising communities. Nowadays the region has oil and tourist industries. Inverness, the Highland capital, makes a good starting point for exploring Loch Ness and the Cairngorms. The Isle of Skye has some of Britain's most dramatic scenery.

Sea lochs on the Isle of Skye, dominated by the Cuillin peaks

Snow-covered peaks of the Cairngorms, viewed from Aviemore

Cairngorms ㉙

🚃 🚌 *Aviemore.* ℹ️ *Grampian Rd, Aviemore (01479-810 363).*

Rising to a height of 1,309 m (4,296 ft), the Cairngorm mountains form the highest landmass in Britain.

Cairn Gorm itself is the site of one of Britain's first ski centers. Transportation to the 28 ski runs is provided daily from **Aviemore**. The chairlift that climbs Cairn Gorm affords superb views over the Spey Valley. **Rothiemurchus Estate** has a visitor center offering guided walks.

The **Cairngorm Reindeer Center** organizes walks in the hills among Britain's only herd of reindeer, and ospreys can be observed at the **Loch Garten Nature Reserve**.

Drivers can see bison, bears, wolves, and boar in the **Kincraig Highland Wildlife Park**.

Inverness ㉚

🏠 *60,000.* 🚃 🚌
ℹ️ *Castle Wynd (01463-234 353).*
www.visithighlands.com

Inverness is the center of communication, commerce, and administration for the Highlands. Dominating the high ground above the town is **Inverness Castle**, a Victorian building of red sandstone. Below the castle, the **Inverness Museum and Art Gallery** provides a good introduction to the region's history. Its exhibits include a fine collection of Inverness silver. The **Scottish Kiltmaker Visitor Centre** offers an insight into the history, culture, and tradition of the kilt.

In summer **Jacobite Cruises** (call 01463-233 999 for information) runs regular boat trips along the Caledonian Canal and on the famous **Loch Ness**, southwest of Inverness. The Loch is 39 km (24 miles) long and up to 305 m (1,000 ft) deep. On the western shore, the ruins of the 16th-century **Urquhart Castle** can be seen. The **Official Loch Ness Exhibition Centre** provides information about the Loch and its mythical monster.

🏛 **Museum and Art Gallery**
1 Castle Wynd. **Tel** 01463-237 114.
◯ Mon–Sat. ● Jan 1–2, Dec 25–26. ♿

Isle of Skye ㉛

🏠 *11,500.* 🚢 *from Mallaig or Glenelg.* 🚌 ℹ️ *Bayfield House, Portree (01478-612 137).*

Skye, the largest of the Inner Hebrides, can be reached by the bridge linking Kyle of Lochalsh and Kyleakin. The coast is shaped by a series of dramatic sea lochs, while the landscape, from Quiraing, a plateau of volcanic towers and spikes in the north, to the Cuillins, one of Britain's most spectacular mountain ranges, is majestic. Bonnie Prince Charlie (1720–88) escaped here from the mainland disguised as a maidservant following the defeat of his army at Culloden.

Skye's main settlement is **Portree**, with its colorful harbor. **Dunvegan Castle** on the island's northwest coast has been the seat of the Clan MacLeod chiefs for over seven centuries. South of here, the **Talisker distillery** produces one of the best Highland malts.

The ruins of Urquhart Castle on the western shore of Loch Ness

Practical Information

Colorful pageantry, ancient history, and a varied countryside attract millions of tourists to Britain each year. Facilities for visitors have improved considerably in recent years, with major urban centers offering a good variety of restaurants and hotels. The affluent southern region is more expensive than the rest of Britain. Telephone and postal systems are efficient, and violent crime is uncommon.

WHEN TO VISIT

Britain's temperate maritime climate does not produce extremes of heat or cold, but weather patterns shift constantly, and the climate can differ widely in places only a short distance apart. The southeast is generally drier than elsewhere. Be sure to pack a mix of warm and light clothing and an umbrella. Walkers can be surprised by bad weather.

Britain's towns and cities are all-year destinations, but many attractions open only between Easter and October. Some hotels are crammed at Christmas and New Year. The main family holiday months, July and August, and public holidays, are always busy. Spring and fall offer a good compromise: fewer crowds and relatively fine weather.

TOURIST INFORMATION

The **British Tourist Authority (BTA)** has offices in a number of major cities worldwide. In Britain, tourist information is available in many towns and public places, including airports, main train and bus stations, and at some sites of

historical interest. These bureaux offer general tourist advice and will also reserve accommodations.

Both the regional and national tourist boards have comprehensive lists of local attractions and registered accommodations. The monthly magazine of **VisitBritain**, *In Britain*, available in tourist offices, contains articles about worthwhile places to visit and also includes an events diary. A charge may be made for more detailed maps and books.

For route planning, road atlases and local maps and guidebooks are available in most bookstores.

OPENING HOURS

Many businesses and shops are closed on Sundays, though trading is now legal. Museums and galleries are generally open from 10am to 5 or 6pm, with many opening later in the day on Sundays. Those outside the capital are normally closed for one day or one afternoon a week. On public holidays, known as bank holidays in Britain, banks, offices, most shops, and some restaurants will be closed.

VISA REQUIREMENTS AND CUSTOMS

A valid passport is needed to enter Britain. Visitors from the European Union (EU), the United States, Canada, New Zealand, and Australia do not require a visa to enter the country. Anyone who arrives in Britain from a member country of the EU can pass through a special channel at customs, but random checks are still made to detect any prohibited goods.

When entering from outside the EU go through the green customs channel if you have nothing to declare, and the red channel if you have goods which exceed allowances.

PERSONAL SECURITY

Britain is not a dangerous place for visitors, and it is most unlikely that your stay will be blighted by crime. Due to past terrorist attacks, there are occasional security alerts, notably on the underground, but these are mainly false alarms, often due to people accidentally leaving a bag or parcel lying around.

POLICE

The sight of a traditional British "bobby" patrolling the streets in a tall hat is now less common than the police patrol car with flashing lights and sirens. However, policemen on foot can still be found, and are courteous and helpful. If you have anything stolen, you should report the theft at the nearest police station.

THE CLIMATE OF GREAT BRITAIN

The moderate British climate rarely sees winter nights colder than -15 °C (5 °F), even in the far north, or summer days warmer than 30 °C (86 °F) in the south. Despite the country's reputation, annual rainfall is quite low – less than 100 cm (40 in) – and heavy rain is rare. The Atlantic coast, warmed by the Gulf Stream, gives the west a warmer, wetter climate than the east.

LONDON

°C/F	Apr	Jul	Oct	Jan
high	13/55	22/72	16/60	7/45
		14/58	10/50	
low	7/44			3/38
sun (hrs)	5	6	3.5	1.5
rain (mm)	39	45	50	44

0°C / 32°F

EDINBURGH

°C/F	Apr	Jul	Oct	Jan
high	11/52	18/62	13/56	16/61
		11/52	7/44	
low	4/39			0/32
sun (hrs)	2.5	5.5	3	1.5
rain (mm)	38	70	58	47

0°C / 32°F

EMERGENCY SERVICES

In an emergency, dial 999 to reach police, fire, and ambulance services, which are on call 24-hours a day. Calls are free. In coastal areas this number also applies for calls to the voluntary coastguard rescue service. You can also turn up at a hospital emergency room at any time. Emergency medical treatment in a British National Health Service (NHS) emergency room is free, but any kind of additional medical care could prove to be very expensive if you don't have insurance or your country does not have a reciprocal agreement.

HEALTH ISSUES

You can buy a wide range of medicines from pharmacies, which in Britain are known as chemists. Boots is the best-known chain store. If you are likely to need prescription drugs, either bring your own or get your doctor to write out the generic name of the drug (as opposed to the brand name). Some pharmacies are open until midnight, whilst doctors' offices (known as surgeries) are normally open during the day only.

FACILITIES FOR THE DISABLED

The facilities on offer for disabled visitors to Britain are improving: new buildings offer elevators and ramps for wheelchair access, and adapted toilets. Many banks, theaters, and museums provide aids for the visually or hearing impaired. Given advance notice, rail, ferry, and bus personnel will help disabled passengers. The Disabled Person's Railcard provides discounted rail fares. Hertz offers hand-controlled vehicles for rental at no extra cost. For more information contact **RADAR**, **Mobility International** or **Tourism For All**.

BANKING AND CURRENCY

Britain's currency is the pound sterling (£), which is divided into 100 pence (p). Scottish banknotes are also legal tender in England and Wales, but not all stores take them.

Banking hours vary, but most are open from 9am to 5pm, Monday to Friday. Most banks cash traveler's checks, and have cash machines (ATMs) that accept most cards. You can also change money at private bureaux de change, which are located in tourist areas and operate longer hours than banks. Exchange rates and commission charges can vary.

Although credit cards are widely accepted in Britain, smaller stores, guesthouses, and cafés may not have the facilities for card transactions. Britain uses the "chip and PIN" system instead of a signature on a credit slip. You will need a four-digit PIN, so ask your bank for one before you leave.

COMMUNICATIONS

Public telephone booths are available throughout Britain and may be card- or coin-operated. In major towns, some booths are able to accept credit cards and offer internet access. It is cheaper to telephone in the evenings and at weekends.

Post offices are usually open from 9am to 5:30pm Monday to Friday, and until 12:30pm on Saturday. Sub-post offices are located in local stores. Stamps can be purchased from any outlet which displays the sign "Stamps sold here." Mail boxes are always painted red.

DIRECTORY

TOURIST INFORMATION

Enjoy England Ireland
www.enjoyengland.ie

VisitBritain
www.visitbritain.com

VisitBritain Australia
Level 3, Suite 2, 32 Walker St, North Sydney, NSW 2060.
www.visitbritain.com

VisitBritain Canada
160 Bloor St East, Suite 905, Toronto, M4W 1B9.
www.visitbritain.com

VisitBritain New Zealand
www.visitbritain.com

VisitBritain United States
Suite 701, 551 Fifth Ave, New York, NY 10176.
www.visitbritain.com

REGIONAL TOURIST BOARDS

Britain/England
1 Regent St, London W1.
www.visitbritain.com

London
1 Regent St, London W1.
www.visitlondon.com

Scotland
Tel 0131-472 2222.
www.visitscotland.com

Wales
Tel 0870-830 0306.
www.visitwales.com

EMBASSIES

Australian High Commission
Australia House, Strand, London WC2.
Tel 020-7379 4334.
www.australia.org.uk

Canadian High Commission
MacDonald House, 1 Grosvenor Square, London W1K.
Tel 020-7258 6600.
www.canada.org.uk

New Zealand High Commission
80 Haymarket, London SW1.
Tel 020-7930 8422.
www.nzembassy.com

US Embassy
24 Grosvenor Sq, London W1.
Tel 020-7499 9000.
www.usembassy.org.uk

EMERGENCY NUMBERS

Police, Ambulance, Coastguard, and Fire services
Tel 999.

FACILITIES FOR THE DISABLED

Disabled Living Foundation
Tel 0845-130 9177.

Mobility International
North America
Tel 541-343 1284.
www.miusa.org

RADAR
Tel 020-7250 3222.
www.radar.org.uk

Tourism For All
Tel 0845-124 9971.

Travel Information

Since it is an international gateway for air and sea traffic, traveling to Britain poses few problems. By air, visitors have a large choice of carriers serving Europe, Australasia, and North America. Bus travel is an inexpensive form of transportation from Europe, while traveling by train has been transformed by the advent of the Channel Tunnel. Traveling within Britain itself is fairly easy. There is an extensive road network reaching all parts of the country. The national rail network is improving and services to the smaller towns are good. Bus travel is the least expensive option; it serves most areas but can be slow.

FLYING TO GREAT BRITAIN

Britain has about 130 airports but only a handful of these are equipped for long-distance travel. The largest is London's Heathrow, which is served by many of the world's leading airlines, with direct flights from most major cities. Other international airports include London Gatwick, London Stansted, Manchester, Birmingham, Newcastle, Glasgow, and Edinburgh.

British Airways has flights to destinations across the world. Other British airlines include **Virgin Atlantic**, with routes to the US and Far East, and **bmi british midland international**, which flies to the US and Western Europe. Several no-frills airlines, such as Ryanair and easyJet, offer low-cost flights to destinations all over Europe.

American airlines offering services to Britain include **American Airlines**, **Delta Air Lines**, and United, while from Canada, the main carrier is **Air Canada**. From Australasia, **Qantas** and **Air New Zealand** vie for passengers with many Far Eastern rivals.

CHARTERS AND PACKAGE DEALS

Charter flights offer relatively inexpensive seats, but have less flexible departure times than standard scheduled flights. Packages are also worth considering, as airlines and tour operators can put together a great range of flexible deals to suit your needs. These can include car rental or rail travel.

DOMESTIC FLIGHTS

Britain's size means that internal air travel only makes sense over long distances, such as from London to Scotland, or to one of the offshore islands.

The **British Airways** shuttle flights between London and cities such as Glasgow, Edinburgh, and Manchester are popular with business travelers. At peak times, flights leave every hour, while at other times there is usually a flight every two hours.

TRAVELING IN LONDON

In London, daily, weekly, and monthly tickets called Travelcards are valid on all public transportation as are pre-pay Oyster cards, which you can credit before your journey. If you are only using buses, it is better to buy a daily or weekly bus pass. Passes are available at most newsagents and train or underground stations.

Fares in London are based on six train zones and two bus zones; there is a standard charge for travel within each zone and between zones, regardless of the distance traveled. The area covered by each zone varies slightly between buses and trains.

If you are in London for four days or more, a two-zone weekly Travelcard is advisable; for more than ten days, it is worth buying an Oyster card.

London also has express train services to Britain's two busiest airports, Heathrow and Gatwick, which leave from Paddington and Victoria stations respectively at regular intervals. The journey time is 15 minutes to Heathrow, and 30 minutes to Gatwick.

When traveling by bus, you must purchase a ticket before boarding. The sightseeing buses that drive past many of London's historic sights are often run by private companies and will not accept bus passes or Travelcards.

All-night bus services are available in London from about 11pm until early morning. You can use Travelcards and bus passes on these. Night buses carry the letter N before the route number, and most pass through Trafalgar Square.

Taxis are available at major train stations, as well as at ranks near hotels and all over central London. All licensed cabs must carry a "For Hire" sign, which is lit up whenever they are free. The famous black cabs are the safest taxis to use in London since all the drivers are licensed. Most cab drivers expect a tip.

Sometimes, the best way to see London is on foot, but however you choose to get around, try to avoid the rush hours from 8 to 9:30am, and 4:30 to 6:30pm.

LONDON UNDERGROUND

The underground in London, known as the tube, is one of the largest systems of its kind in the world. London tube trains run every day, except December 25, from about 5:30am until after midnight. Fewer trains run on Sundays. The 12 tube lines are color-coded and maps are available at every station, while maps of the central section are displayed on each train.

RAIL TRAVEL

Britain has a privatized rail network that covers the whole of the country. It consists of several regional services, such as Great North Eastern Railways and Great Western Trains. **Virgin Trains**, which runs many cross-country routes, operates two other networks – West Coast Trains and Cross Country Trains. The system is generally quite reliable.

The main stations in London all serve different areas of the country; Euston serves the Midlands and northwest, King's Cross serves the northeast and Scotland, Liverpool Street serves East Anglia, Waterloo and Paddington serve the West Country and Wales, and Victoria and Charing Cross serve the South Coast.

First-class tickets for most journeys are available, and roundtrip fares are less costly than two one-way tickets. There are four discount fare types for adults: Apex and Superapex tickets must be booked at least a week or 14 days in advance; Savers and Supersavers cannot be used during peak hours.

If you plan to do much traveling by train around Britain, buy a rail pass. These can be bought from BR agents abroad, such as **Rail Europe** and **CIE Tours International**. The All Line Rail Rover allows unlimited travel within Great Britain. Passes are available for families and young persons.

LONG-DISTANCE BUSES

In Britain, long-distance express buses and ones used for sightseeing excursions are usually referred to as coaches. Coach services are generally less expensive than rail travel. Journey times, however, are longer and much less predictable on crowded roads. Tickets can be purchased at major international airports, **Victoria Coach Station** – the main terminal for journeys into and out of London – and most large travel agents. The largest British coach operator is **National Express**. Another major operator is **Scottish Citylink**, with services between London, the North, and Scotland.

TRAVELING BY ROAD

The most startling difference for many foreign motorists in Britain is that one drives on the left, with corresponding adjustments at traffic circles and junctions. Distances are measured in miles. Traffic density in towns and at busy holiday times can cause long delays. Parking is a particular problem in towns and cities.

Renting a car in Britain can be expensive. One of the most competitive national companies is **Autos Abroad**, but small local firms may undercut even these rates. International car rental companies such as **Avis**, **Budget**, and **Hertz** also operate in Britain. You need a valid driver's license and a passport when you rent. Most companies will not rent to novice drivers, and set age limits (usually 21–70).

FERRY SERVICES

About 20 car and passenger services travel regularly across the Channel and the North and Irish seas, the major ones including **DFDS Seaways** and **P&O**. Fares vary greatly according to the season, time of travel, and duration of stay.

Brittany Ferries run longer (often overnight) services between Plymouth, Poole and Portsmouth to the west coast of France as well as one 20-hour service outside the winter months between Plymouth and Santander in Spain.

CHANNEL TUNNEL

The Channel Tunnel offers a nonstop rail link between Britain and Europe. **Eurostar** services (for foot passengers) run from St. Pancras station in London to Lille and Paris in France, and Brussels in Belgium. Traveling from London direct to Brussels or Paris takes 2–2½ hours.

The **Eurotunnel** service (commonly known as the Shuttle) transports vehicles between Folkestone and Calais in about half an hour.

DIRECTORY

AIRLINES

Air Canada
Tel 0871-220 1111 (UK).
Tel 1800-372 4190 (US and Canada).

Air New Zealand
Tel 0800-028 4149 (UK).
Tel 0800-737 000 (NZ).

American Airlines
Tel 0844-499 7300 (UK).
Tel 800-433 7300 (US).

bmi british midland international
Tel 0844-8484 888 (UK).

British Airways
Tel 0844-493 0787 (UK).
Tel 1-800-AIRWAYS (US).

Delta Air Lines
Tel 0845-600 0950 (UK).
Tel 800-241 4141 (US).

Qantas
Tel 0845-774 7767 (UK).
Tel 13 13 13 (Australia).

Virgin Atlantic
Tel 0844-209 7777 (UK).
Tel 800-821 5438 (US).

RAIL TRAVEL

CIE Tours International
Tel 353-1-703 1888 (IRL).

National Rail Inquiries
Tel 0845-748 49 50.

Rail Europe
Tel 08448-484 064.
www.raileurope.co.uk

Virgin Trains
Tel 08719-774 222.

BUS COMPANIES

National Express
Tel 08717-818 181.
www.nationalexpress.com

Scottish Citylink
Tel 0871-266 3333.
www.citylink.co.uk

CAR RENTAL

Autos Abroad
Tel 0844-826 6536.
www.autosabroad.com

Avis
Tel 0844-581 0147.
www.avis.co.uk

Budget
Tel 0844-544 3470.
www.budget.co.uk

Hertz
Tel 0870-844 8844.
www.hertz.co.uk

FERRY SERVICES

Brittany Ferries
Tel 0871-244 0744.

DFDS Seaways
Tel 0871-522 3883.

P&O
Tel 08716-642 121.

CHANNEL TUNNEL SERVICES

Eurostar
Tel 08432-186 186.
www.eurostar.com
(for foot passengers).

Eurotunnel
Tel 0844-353 535
(for cars & buses).

Shopping

While the West End of London is undeniably Britain's most exciting place to shop, many regional centers offer nearly as wide a range of goods. Moreover, regional shopping can be less stressful, less expensive, and remarkably varied, with craft studios, farm shops, street markets, and factory showrooms adding to the enjoyment of bargain-hunting. Britain is famous for its country clothing: wool, tartan, waxed cotton, and tweed are all popular, along with classic prints such as Liberty or Laura Ashley. Other particularly British goods include antiques, floral soaps and scents, porcelain, glass, and local crafts.

OPENING HOURS

In general, you can assume most stores in Britain will open during the week from 9am or 10am until 5pm or 6pm. Hours on Saturdays may be shorter. Some town-center stores now open on Sundays, but more often when it is near Christmas. Some stores open late for one evening a week – usually Thursday – while in villages the shops may close at lunchtime for an hour, or for one afternoon each week. Market days vary from town to town; some markets are held on Sundays.

OUT-OF-TOWN SHOPPING CENTERS

These large complexes, similar to American malls, are rapidly increasing around Britain. The advantages of car access and easy, cheap parking are undeniable, and most centers are accessible by public transportation. The centers usually feature clusters of popular upscale stores, with many services offered, such as toilets, cafés, nurseries, restaurants, and movies.

DEPARTMENT STORES

Certain big department stores are only found in London, but others have provincial branches. **John Lewis**, for example, has shops in 37 locations. It sells a huge range of fabrics, clothing, and household items, combining quality service with good value. **Marks & Spencer**, with branches throughout Britain, is even more of a household name, famed for its good-value clothing and prepared food. The sizes of all chain stores, and the range of stock they carry, will differ from region to region.

The most famous of London's many department stores is **Harrods**, with 300 departments, 4,000 employees, and a spectacular Edwardian food hall. Nearby, **Harvey Nichols** stocks designer clothing and boasts the city's most stylish food hall. Gourmets should make a pilgrimage to **Fortnum and Mason**, which has stocked high-quality food for nearly 300 years. **Selfridges** sells virtually everything, from fine cashmeres to household gadgets. **Liberty**, the West End's last privately owned department store, still sells the hand-blocked silks and Oriental goods for which it was famous when it first opened in 1875.

CLOTHING STORES

Once again, London has the widest range, from *haute couture* to cheap and cheerful ready-made items. Shopping for clothing in the regions, however, can often be less tiring. Many towns popular with tourists – Oxford, Bath, and York for instance – have independently-owned clothing stores where you receive more personal service. Or you could try one of the chain stores found throughout the country for stylish, reasonably priced clothes, as well as younger and less expensive fashions.

Traditional British clothing – waxed Barbour jackets and Burberry trench coats – are found in outlets such as **The Scotch House, Burberry,** and **Gieves and Hawkes**, while **Laura Ashley** is renowned for its floral print dresses. For kilts and tartans, the best place is **Hector Russell**, found in both Edinburgh and Glasgow.

London is the place for designer fashions, however, as many designers have specialized outlets here. **Vivienne Westwood**, doyenne of the punkish avant-garde, uses London as her British base.

MARKETS

Large towns and cities usually have a central covered market that operates most weekdays, selling everything from fresh produce to pots and pans. Many towns hold weekly markets in the main square.

The fashionable markets of London are **Covent Garden, Portobello Road,** and **Camden Lock**, where you can find an assortment of secondhand clothes, handmade crafts, and antiques. **Spitalfields** is a burgeoning East End market.

FOOD AND DRINK

Supermarkets are a good place to shop for food. The range and quality of items in stock is usually excellent. Several large chains compete for market share and as a result, prices are generally lower than smaller shops. However, the smaller town-center stores such as local bakeries, greengrocers, or markets, may give you a more interesting choice of fresh regional produce, and more personal service.

Alcoholic beverages are available in a huge variety of shops around Britain, many of them wine merchants, such as the chain store **Oddbins**. For whisky, Scotland is the place to go; **Cadenheads** and **The Whisky Shop** both have a wide variety of rare scotches.

BOOKS AND MAGAZINES

The capital is the hub of Britain's book trade, as many of the country's leading publishers are located within central London. Charing Cross

Road is the focal point for those searching for new, antiquarian, and secondhand volumes, and it is the home of **Foyle's**, with its massive but notoriously badly organized stock. Large branches of such chains as **Waterstone's** and **WH Smith** (which also sells magazines) are here, although they can also be found in most cities and major towns.

GIFTS AND SOUVENIRS

Most reputable large stores can arrange to ship expensive items back home for you. If you want to buy things that you can carry in a suitcase, the choice is wide. You can purchase attractive, well-made, portable craft items all

over the country, especially in those areas that are popular with tourists. For slightly more unusual presents, have a look in museum shops and at the range of items available in National Trust and English Heritage properties.

Some chain stores are very convenient places to pick up attractive gifts and souvenirs. **The Body Shop** sells natural cosmetics and toiletries in recyclable plastic packaging, while **Past Times** sells modern reproductions of ancient British jewelry designs, including Celtic, Roman, and Tudor pieces. For designer gifts, try the **Conran Shop** in London, which sells stylish accessories for the home.

ART AND ANTIQUES

Britain's long history means there are many interesting artifacts to be found. Many towns, such as Brighton, have dozens of antique shops. You might also like to visit a jumble or flea market in the hope of picking up a bargain.

The largest collection of original photographs for sale in the country is at the **Photographers' Gallery** in London. For paintings, **Maas Gallery** in London's Mayfair district excels in Victorian masters. In Scotland, **The Scottish Gallery** has everything from jewelry to pieces by well-known Scottish artists, while **Finnie Antiques** is a treasure trove of antiques.

DIRECTORY

DEPARTMENT STORES

Fortnum and Mason
181 Piccadilly,
London W1.
Tel 020-7734 8040.

Harrods
87–135 Brompton Rd,
London SW1.
Tel 020-7730 1234.

Harvey Nichols
109–125 Knightsbridge,
London SW1.
Tel 020-7235 5000.

John Lewis
69 St. James Centre,
Edinburgh EH1.
Tel 0131-556 9121.
One of many branches.

Liberty
210–220 Regent St,
London W1.
Tel 020-7734 1234.

Marks & Spencer
173 & 458 Oxford St,
London W1.
Tel 020-7935 7954.
Two of many branches.

Selfridges
400 Oxford St,
London W1.
Tel 0800-123 400.

CLOTHING STORES

Burberry
21–23 Bond Street,
London W1.
Tel 020-7839 5222.

2 Brompton Rd,
London SW1.
Tel 020-7581 2151.

Gieves & Hawkes
1 Savile Row,
London W1.
Tel 020-7432 6403.

Hector Russell
110 Buchanan St,
Glasgow G1.
Tel 0800 980 4010.

Laura Ashley
At House of Fraser,
318 Oxford St,
London W1.
Tel 0871-230 2301.
One of many branches.

Vivienne Westwood
44 Conduit St, London
W1. *Tel 020-7439 1109.*

MARKETS

Camden Lock
Chalk Farm Rd,
London NW1.
🕐 9:30am–5:30pm Mon–Fri, 10am–6pm Sat & Sun.

Covent Garden
The Piazza, London WC2.
🕐 9am–5pm daily.

Portobello Road
Portobello Rd,
London W10.
🕐 7am–5:30pm Sat.

Spitalfields
Commercial St, London E1.
🕐 9am–5pm daily.

FOOD AND DRINK

Cadenheads
172 Canongate,
Edinburgh EH8.
Tel 0131-556 5864.

Oddbins
7 Borough High St,
London SE1 9SU.
Tel 020-7407 5957.
One of many branches.

The Whisky Shop
Unit L2/O2, Buchanan
Galleries, 220 Buchanan
Street, Glasgow G1.
Tel 0141-331 0022.

BOOKS AND MAGAZINES

Foyle's
113–119 Charing Cross
Rd, London WC2.
Tel 020-7437 5660.

Waterstone's
128 Princes St, Edinburgh.
Tel 0843 290 8313.
One of many branches.

WH Smith
124 Holborn, London
EC1N 2QX.
Tel 020-7379 7313.
One of many branches.

GIFTS AND SOUVENIRS

The Body Shop
374 Oxford St,
London W1.
Tel 020-7409 7868.
One of many branches.

Conran Shop
Michelin House, 81
Fulham Rd, London SW3.
Tel 020-7589 7401.

Past Times
Unit 44, Lower Level,
Cribb's Causeway,
Bristol BS34.
Tel 0117-959 2423.
One of many branches.

ART AND ANTIQUES

Finnie Antiques
The Red House, Croftamie,
Lanarkshire G63.
Tel 01360-661 166.

Maas Gallery
15a Clifford St,
London W1.
Tel 020-7734 2302.

Photographers' Gallery
16–18 Ramilies St,
London W1F.
Tel 0845-262 1618.

The Scottish Gallery
16 Dundas St,
Edinburgh EH3.
Tel 0131-558 1200.

Entertainment

London is the entertainment capital of Britain, with an array of world-class cultural and sporting events. Around the country, theaters, opera houses, concert halls, and other venues host a wide range of performing and dramatic arts programs. The summer months also see numerous open-air arts festivals. Ticket prices are often less expensive outside the capital. Britain offers hundreds of special interest holidays for those wanting to acquire a new skill or learn a new sport. Walking, sailing, skiing, pony-trekking, and golfing holidays are popular. Soccer, rugby, and cricket are favorite sports.

ENTERTAINMENT LISTINGS

For information about what's on in London, check the *Evening Standard* or the listings magazine *Time Out* (published every Wednesday). All the quality broadsheet newspapers have detailed arts reviews and listings of cultural events in London and throughout the country. Local newspapers, libraries, and tourist offices can supply details of regional events.

TICKETS

Ticket availability varies from show to show. You may be able to buy a ticket at the door, especially for a mid-week matinee, but for the more popular West End shows seats may have to be reserved weeks or even months in advance through agencies – ubiquitous in central London – or by telephone or in person at theater box offices. Half-price tickets for some same-day shows can be obtained from Leicester Square. Beware of counterfeit tickets offered by touts.

THEATER

Britain has an enduring theatrical tradition dating back to Shakespeare. London is the place to enjoy theater at its most varied and glamorous. The West End alone has more than 50 theaters. The **Barbican** and the **National Theatre** stage a mixture of classics and challenging new productions. The major commercial theaters, showing more popular plays and musicals, are located along Shaftesbury Avenue and the Haymarket, and around Covent Garden and Charing Cross Road.

Outside the capital, at Stratford-upon-Avon, the **Royal Shakespeare Theatre** presents a year-round program of the great bard's works. Bristol's **Theatre Royal** is the oldest working theater in Britain. Good productions are staged at the Manchester **Royal Exchange**, and the **Traverse** in Edinburgh.

Open-air theater is a feature of city life in the summer with street entertainers at London's Covent Garden and other urban centers. London's Globe theater (*see pp58–9*) stages performances of Shakespeare's plays, and open-air theaters at Regent's Park and Holland Park also have a summer program.

Perhaps the liveliest theatrical festival in Britain is the two-week **Edinburgh Festival** held in late summer. Many seaside resorts also have a summer theater season.

MUSIC

A diverse musical repertoire can be found in a variety of venues across Great Britain. London, in particular, is one of the world's great centers for music, and home to several world-class orchestras and chamber groups. As well as classical concerts, there are dozens of rock, reggae, soul, folk, country, jazz, and Latin concerts taking place on every day of the week. There are also numerous nightclubs that play everything from 70s disco to the very latest house-music beats.

Major pop-concert venues in the capital include **Wembley Arena** and **Carling Apollo**. The **Royal Albert Hall** hosts a range of concerts, including the popular classical Proms. The **Wigmore Hall**, the **Barbican Concert Hall**, and the **Royal Festival Hall** are also notable classical venues. The **Royal Opera House** is a world-class venue, and is home to the Royal Opera. English National Opera performs at the **London Coliseum**. Classical open-air concerts are also held at Marble Hill House and **Kenwood House** during the summer.

A wide range of musical events is staged in towns and cities across Great Britain. Liverpool and Manchester have excellent orchestras and are also centers for modern music, while **Glyndebourne** hosts an annual opera festival. Wales has a very strong choral tradition, while northern England is renowned for booming brass bands. Scotland, of course, is famous for its bagpipers.

DANCE

Classical ballet is performed at the **Royal Opera House**, home of the Royal Ballet, and the **London Coliseum** where the English National Ballet usually performs. The **Place Theatre, Sadler's Wells**, and the **Institute for Contemporary Art** (**ICA**) are major venues for contemporary dance.

Birmingham is home to the Birmingham Royal Ballet and is the best place to see performances outside London. Traditional English Morris dancing or the Scottish Highland fling and Celtic dancing (*ceilidhs*) can be enjoyed at local festivals.

CINEMA

The latest movies can be seen in any large town. Premieres with international film stars are usually held at London's Leicester Square cinemas. The capital now has a 3D cinema, the **BFI London IMAX**. Young children may see films graded U (universal) or PG (parental guidance). Cinema prices vary widely; some are less expensive at off-peak times, such as Mondays or afternoons. For first nights of new releases it is advisable to book in advance.

SPECIAL INTEREST VACATIONS

Hundreds of options are available for any kind of sport, to arts and crafts, such as painting, calligraphy, and jewelry-making, and a wide range of educational courses to suit all levels.

Reservations can be made with organizers or through a travel agent. The English and Scottish Tourist Boards have pamphlets on some of these activities.

OUTDOOR ACTIVITIES

Britain has an extensive network of long-distance footpaths and shorter trail routes for walkers, together with designated cycle routes and bridle paths.

There are 2,000 golf courses in Britain and many clubs welcome visiting players (bring confirmation of your handicap). Green fees vary widely. Tennis courts can be found in every town and many hotels.

Sailing is popular in the Lake District, and the south coast resorts have plenty of pleasure craft. Boating on the Thames and on Britain's network of canals is a common summer pursuit. Surfers and windsurfers head for the West Country and South Wales.

The best game fishing (trout and salmon) is in the West Country, Wales, and Scotland. Soccer, rugby, cricket, and horse-racing are all popular sports in Britain. Details of matches and meetings can be found in national newspapers. During the last week of June and the first week of July, the Wimbledon tournament attracts many visitors to the **All England Lawn Tennis and Croquet Club**.

Among adventure sport options are rock-climbing and mountaineering, aeronautical sports and gliding. Skiing and other winter sports are possible in Scotland. Ice-skating rinks are located in major cities and horse-riding centers are found throughout the country, with pony-trekking in tourist areas.

DIRECTORY

THEATER

Barbican
Silk St, London EC2.
Tel 020-7638 4141.

Bristol Old Vic
King St
Bristol BS1.
Tel 0117-987 7877.

Edinburgh Festival
The Hub, Castlehill,
Edinburgh EH1.
Tel 0131-473 2015.

National Theatre
Southbank Centre,
London SE1.
Tel 020-7452 3400.

Royal Exchange
St. Anne's Square,
Manchester M2.
Tel 0161-833 9833.

Royal Shakespeare Theatre
Stratford-upon-Avon
CV37.
Tel 0844-800 1110.

Traverse
Cambridge St,
Edinburgh EH1.
Tel 0131-228 1404.

MUSIC

Glyndebourne
Lewes, East Sussex BN8.
Tel 01273-812 321.

Kenwood House
Hampstead Lane,
London NW3.
Tel 020-8348 1286.

Carling Apollo
Queen Caroline St,
London W6.
Tel 0871-971 5892.

London Coliseum
St. Martin's Lane,
London WC2.
Tel 0871-472 4088.

Philharmonic Hall
Hope St, Liverpool L1 9BP.
Tel 0151-709 3789.

Royal Albert Hall
Kensington Gore,
London SW7.
Tel 020-7589 8212.

Royal Festival Hall
Southbank Centre,
London SE1.
Tel 0844 875 0073.

Royal Opera House
Bow St, London WC2.
Tel 020-7304 4000.

Symphony Hall
International Convention
Centre, Broad St,
Birmingham B1 2EA.
Tel 0121-780 3333.

Wembley Arena
Empire Way, Wembley,
Middlesex HA9.
Tel 0870-060 0870.

Wigmore Hall
36 Wigmore St,
London W1.
Tel 020-7935 2141.

DANCE

ICA
Nash House, Carlton
House Terrace,
The Mall, London SW1.
Tel 020-7930 3647.

Sadler's Wells
Rosebery Ave,
London EC1.
Tel 0844-412 4300.

The Place
17 Duke's Road,
London WC1.
Tel 020-7121 1100.

CINEMA

BFI London IMAX
Waterloo Rd,
London SE1.
Tel 020-7199 6000.

OUTDOOR ACTIVITIES

All England Lawn Tennis and Croquet Club
Church Road, Wimbledon,
London SW19.
Tel 020-8946 2244.

Association of Pleasure Craft Operators
Marine House, Thorpe Lea
Rd, Egham, Surrey.
Tel 01784-223603.

British Activity Holiday Association
The Hollies, Oak Bank
Lane, Hoole Village,
Chester CH1.
Tel 01244-301 342.
www.baha.org.uk

British Mountaineering Council
177–179 Burton Rd,
Manchester M20.
Tel 0161-445 6111.

British Waterways
64 Clarendon Rd,
Watford, WD17.
Tel 01923-201 120.

English Golf Union
National Golf Centre,
The Broadway,
Woodhall Spa, Lincs LN10.
Tel 01526-354 500.

Outward Bound
Hackthorpe Hall,
Hackthorpe, Cumbria
CA10 2HX.
Tel 01931-740 000.

Ski Club of Great Britain
57–63 Church Road,
London SW19.
Tel 020-8410 2000.

Where to Stay in Great Britain

The range of accommodations available in Britain is extensive, and whatever your budget you should find something to suit you. London is much more expensive than the rest of the country, but even here there are affordable yet comfortable hotels. Out in the country, B&Bs (offering bed and breakfast) are economical.

PRICE CATEGORIES
For a standard double room per night, inclusive of service charge and any additional taxes such as VAT:

£ under £65
££ £65–£100
£££ £100–£150
££££ £150–£200
£££££ over £200

LONDON

WEST END AND WESTMINSTER Dover Hotel   W   £

42–44 Belgrave Rd, SW1 **Tel** *020-7821 9085* **Fax** *020-7834 6425* **Rooms** *34*   **Map** *C4*

This well-maintained hotel is terrific value for money. It may not be luxurious once past the grand stucco facade, but the decor is refreshingly modern and every room has satellite TV and pristine en suite shower and WC. It's handy for Victoria Station and Pimlico's many pubs and cafés. **www.dover-hotel.co.uk**

WEST END AND WESTMINSTER Citadines Covent Garden/Holborn   £££

94–99 High Holborn, WC1 **Tel** *020-7395 8800* **Fax** *020-7395 8799* **Rooms** *192*   **Map** *D3*

This centrally located branch of the French apart'hotel chain offers pleasant, good-value accommodations for up to four people. Studios or one-bedroom apartments have kitchenettes, dining tables, satellite TVs, and hi-fis. There are also handy business facilities and an on-site breakfast room. **www.citadines.com**

WEST END AND WESTMINSTER Elizabeth Hotel and Apartments   £££

37 Eccleston Square, SW1 **Tel** *020-7828 6812* **Fax** *020-7828 6814* **Rooms** *37 & 5 apartments*   **Map** *C4*

The rates are surprisingly reasonable in this elegant town house hotel on a grand garden square. Winston Churchill used to live a couple of doors down. Rooms are simple yet tastefully furnished and guests have access to the private gardens and stately drawing room with newspapers, tea, coffee, and biscuits. **www.elizabethhotel.com**

WEST END AND WESTMINSTER Claridges   £££££

Brook St, W1 **Tel** *020-7107 8862* **Fax** *020-7499 2210* **Rooms** *203*   **Map** *C3*

Favored by the European aristocracy in the 19th century, Empress Eugènie wintered here. Nowadays it attracts show business *glitterati* and business clients alike. Rooms range from Victorian to contemporary by way of fabulous Art Deco suites. Gordon Ramsay's fêted restaurant and a smart bar are further draws. **www.claridges.co.uk**

WEST END AND WESTMINSTER Covent Garden Hotel   £££££

10 Monmouth St, WC2 **Tel** *020-7806 1000* **Fax** *020-7806 1100* **Rooms** *58*   **Map** *D3*

This exquisite hotel's Covent Garden location is one reason why it is popular with thespians. Part of the Firmdale chain, it is decorated in contemporary-English style with antiques and fresh fabrics. Brasserie Max is a popular meeting spot and films are shown in the luxurious screening room at weekends. **www.firmdalehotels.com**

WEST END AND WESTMINSTER One Aldwych   £££££

1 Aldwych, WC2 **Tel** *020-7300 0501* **Fax** *020-7300 1001* **Rooms** *105*   **Map** *D3*

A grand modern hotel in former Edwardian newspaper offices. Impressive details include original art and tarazzo-stone bathrooms with heated floors and mini TVs. There is a spacious health club with a swimming pool, several trendy restaurants, and the buzzing, high-ceilinged Lobby Bar. **www.onealdwych.com**

WEST END AND WESTMINSTER Ritz   £££££

150 Piccadilly, W1 **Tel** *020-7493 8181* **Fax** *020-7493 2687* **Rooms** *136*   **Map** *C3*

There are two staff for every room in this famous grand hotel on the edge of Green Park. You can even have your luggage unpacked for you. Rooms are in lavish Louis XVI style with antique furnishings and gold leaf, plus all modern conveniences. The Rivoli Bar has been restored to its Art Deco splendor. **www.theritzlondon.com**

WEST END AND WESTMINSTER Savoy   £££££

Strand, WC2 **Tel** *020-7836 4343* **Fax** *020-7240 6040* **Rooms** *263*   **Map** *D3*

This legendary hotel was an afterthought, Richard D'Oyly Carte capitalized on the success of his Savoy Theatre by providing a place to stay. The rest is history. Monet painted the Thames view from his window, Elton John flooded a bathroom, and the dry martini was made popular in the bar. There's a rooftop pool as well. **www.fairmont.com/savoy**

WEST END AND WESTMINSTER The Connaught   £££££

Carlos Place, W1 **Tel** *020-7499 7070* **Fax** *020-7495 3262* **Rooms** *92*   **Map** *C3*

The Connaught maintains its traditional charm while moving with the times. Facilities include butler service and a state-of-the-art gym. The interior feels less stuffy since many of the public rooms, including the Grill and the Connaught Bar, were restyled by renowned designer Nina Campbell. **www.theconnaught.com**

Key to Symbols *see back cover flap*

WEST END AND WESTMINSTER The Dorchester

Park Lane, W1 **Tel** *020-7629 8888* **Fax** *020-7629 8080* **Rooms** *250*　　　　　　　　　　　　**Map** *B3*

The epitome of the glamorous luxury hotel, with an outrageously lavish lobby and a star-studded history, the Dorchester was revamped in 2007 but maintains its tasteful floral bedrooms. The Art Deco-style marble bathtubs are probably the deepest in London. For even more pampering, pop down to the fabulous Art Deco spa. **www.thedorchester.com**

SOUTH KENSINGTON AND HYDE PARK Edward Lear

28–30 Seymour St, W1 **Tel** *020-7402 5401* **Fax** *020-7706 3766* **Rooms** *31*　　　　　　　　　　**Map** *B3*

This characterful small hotel is in the former home of Victorian poet and artist Edward Lear. Rooms are tidy and spacious with satellite TVs. Opt for en suite or shared facilities to keep the cost down. There's a computer with free Internet access and leather seating in the pleasant guests' lounge. **www.edlear.co.uk**

SOUTH KENSINGTON AND HYDE PARK Knightsbridge Green Hotel

159 Knightsbridge, SW1 **Tel** *020-7584 6274* **Fax** *020-7225 1635* **Rooms** *30*　　　　　　　　**Map** *B4*

A shopaholic's dream, this well-kept hotel is right on Knightsbridge and rates are reasonable for more spending power in Harrods and Harvey Nichols. The tidy, modern rooms are regularly upgraded and feature air conditioning, satellite TVs, and wireless Internet access. There's also a small business center on-site. **www.thekghotel.com**

SOUTH KENSINGTON AND HYDE PARK Blakes Hotel

33 Roland Gardens, SW7 **Tel** *020-7370 6701* **Fax** *020-7373 0442* **Rooms** *45*　　　　　　　　**Map** *B4*

Blakes is the original "boutique hotel", created by designer Anouska Hempel in 1978. Rooms range in style from baronial manor to opulent Oriental and contain pieces collected on her travels. The discreet residential location has made it a favorite celebrity hideaway. Only some suites are air conditioned. **www.blakeshotels.com**

SOUTH KENSINGTON AND HYDE PARK The Capital Hotel

22–24 Basil St, SW3 **Tel** *020-7589 5171* **Fax** *020-7225 0011* **Rooms** *50*　　　　　　　　　　**Map** *B4*

Situated between Harrods and Harvey Nichols, this service-oriented hotel even offers personal shoppers and jogging partners. Its Michelin two-starred restaurant has been refurbished in 1940s-influenced style. Bedrooms feature king-size beds, designer fabrics, and the latest technology. **www.capitalhotel.co.uk**

SOUTH KENSINGTON AND HYDE PARK The Gore

190 Queen's Gate, SW7 **Tel** *020-7584 6601* **Fax** *020-7589 8127* **Rooms** *50*　　　　　　　　　　**Map** *A4*

The Gore has been in operation for more than 110 years and, while it has been refurbished, it still preserves the atmosphere of a bygone age. Rooms feature four-poster beds, framed pictures, luxurious draperies, and opulent fabrics. There's a paneled bar and casual bistro as well. **www.gorehotel.co.uk**

SOUTH KENSINGTON AND HYDE PARK The Halkin

5 Halkin St, SW1 **Tel** *020-7333 1000* **Fax** *020-7333 1100* **Rooms** *41*　　　　　　　　　　　　**Map** *B4*

Modern comforts meet Eastern serenity at this gracious luxury hotel. Warm wood tones, curved lines, and creamy bed linen are accented by southeast Asian art handpicked by the Singaporean owner. Be sure to have a meal at Nahm, it is the only Michelin-starred Thai restaurant outside Thailand. **www.halkin.como.bz**

REGENT'S PARK AND BLOOMSBURY Crescent Hotel

49–50 Cartwright Gardens, WC1 **Tel** *020-7387 1515* **Fax** *020-7383 2054* **Rooms** *27*　　　　**Map** *D2*

One of several hotels in this striking Regency Street, the Crescent has been run by the same family since the 1950s. Most of the well-kept bedrooms have en suite facilities. Soft drinks and snacks are served in the lounge, and guests can use the tennis courts in the private gardens. **www.crescenthoteloflondon.com**

REGENT'S PARK AND BLOOMSBURY Hotel Cavendish

75 Gower St, WC1 **Tel** *020-7636 9079* **Fax** *020-7580 3609* **Rooms** *31*　　　　　　　　　　　**Map** *C2*

This characterful B&B near London University has a fascinating history, D.H. Lawrence and the Beatles have stayed here. Rooms are simple yet comfortably furnished, and some have original fireplaces. Original artworks brighten up the breakfast room and there's a pretty garden as well. Shared facilities available. **www.hotelcavendish.com**

REGENT'S PARK AND BLOOMSBURY 22 York Street

22 York St, W1 **Tel** *020-7224 2990* **Fax** *020-7224 1990* **Rooms** *10*　　　　　　　　　　　　**Map** *B3*

This beautiful property is a cut above most B&Bs. Liz and Michael Callis ensure that rooms in these two immaculately preserved Georgian houses are spotless and stylishly furnished with antiques and French quilts. A gourmet continental breakfast is served in the rustic kitchen. Non-smoking throughout. **www.22yorkstreet.co.uk**

REGENT'S PARK AND BLOOMSBURY Charlotte Street Hotel

15 Charlotte St, W1 **Tel** *020-7806 2000* **Fax** *020-7806 2002* **Rooms** *52*　　　　　　　　　　**Map** *C2*

The ground floor bar is always buzzing with local workers as well as guests in this exquisitely designed hotel in a street full of restaurants. Reflecting the area's history, its decor nods to the Bloomsbury Set period with original artworks by Vanessa Bell and others. Weekend films in the screening room. **www.charlottestreethotel.com**

REGENT'S PARK AND BLOOMSBURY The Langham London

1C Portland Place, W1 **Tel** *020-7636 1000* **Fax** *020-7323 2340* **Rooms** *382*　　　　　　　　**Map** *C2*

The Langham was Europe's first grand hotel when it opened in 1865 and still offers an ultra-luxurious experience behind its sprawling Victorian facade. Rooms achieve a tasteful middle ground between modern and traditional and there are extensive spa facilities including a swimming pool. Near Regent's Park. **www.langhamhotels.com**

Map References *see map of London pp42–3*

REGENT'S PARK AND BLOOMSBURY Sanderson

🖥 P 👬 ᵭ 📺 🗐 ᵭ 🆆   €€€€€

50 Berners St, W1 **Tel** *020-7300 1400* **Fax** *020-7300 1401* **Rooms** *150*   **Map** *C3*

The Sanderson's witty decor, including a red lips sofa and framed portrait that seems to hang in mid-air, is like a surreal stage set. Rooms have every comfort, and the Malaysian restaurant, Suki, and two sophisticated cocktail bars are destinations in their own right. The Agua spa offers holistic pampering. **www.sandersonlondon.com**

THE CITY AND SOUTHWARK The Zetter

🖥 👬 ᵭ 📺 🗐 ᵭ 🆆   €€€

86–88 Clerkenwell Rd, EC1 **Tel** *020-7324 4444* **Fax** *020-7324 4445* **Rooms** *59*   **Map** *E3*

In an area known for its loft apartments, this is a loft hotel in a 19th-century warehouse. Rooms have exposed brick, quirky 1970s furniture, old Penguin books, hot-water bottles, and high-tech extras, while vending machines on each floor dispense necessities. Hip contemporary restaurant at street level. **www.thezetter.com**

THE CITY AND SOUTHWARK Andaz

🖥 P 👬 ᵭ 📺 🗐 ᵭ 🆆   €€€€€

40 Liverpool St, EC2 **Tel** *020-7961 1234* **Fax** *020-7961 1235* **Rooms** *267*   **Map** *F3*

Part of the Hyatt group, Andaz is housed in one of London's original railway hotels, a beautiful red-brick Victorian building dating back to 1884. The hotel has five bars and five restaurants on the premises. Cutting-edge art is displayed throughout and bedrooms are furnished with Eames and Jacobson pieces. **www.andaz.com**

NOTTING HILL The Portobello Hotel

🖥 👬 ᵭ 🆆   €€€€€

22 Stanley Gardens, W11 **Tel** *020-7727 2777* **Fax** *020-7792 9641* **Rooms** *24*

This divinely decadent Notting Hill mansion has lured rock royalty for over 30 years with its hip location and extravagantly decorated rooms. Choose from such exotic retreats as the serene Japanese room with private grotto garden and the notorious "Round Bed Room", with its freestanding Victorian bath. **www.portobello-hotel.co.uk**

SOUTHERN ENGLAND

BRIGHTON The Grand Brighton

🖥 👬 ᵭ 📺   €€

97-99 Kings Rd, Brighton, East Sussex, BN1 2FW **Tel** *01273-224300* **Fax** *01273-720 613* **Rooms** *201*

Brighton's only five-star hotel, this is arguably the nation's finest big seaside hotel. The iconic Victorian building sits on the bustling seafront. Its magnificent dining room and bar serve a classic British menu and Sussex cream teas. Price includes breakfast. **www.devere-hotels.com**

BRIGHTON Hotel Du Vin Brighton

👬 ᵭ 🗐   €€€

2–6 Ship St, Brighton, East Sussex, BN1 1AD **Tel** *01273-718588* **Fax** *01273-718599* **Rooms** *49*

Set in the Lanes conservation area, a stone's throw from the seafront, this cutting-edge hotel and bistro is housed in a collection of eccentric, Gothic Revival and mock-Tudor buildings. All the bedrooms are elegantly decorated with Egyptian linen and handsprung mattresses. A "Pub du Vin" is next door. **www.hotelduvin.com**

CANTERBURY The Falstaff

P 👬 ᵭ   €€€

8–10 St Dunstans St., Canterbury, Kent, CT2 8AF **Tel** *01227-462138* **Fax** *01227-463525* **Rooms** *46*

The Falstaff, at the heart of one of England's most historic cities, celebrated its 600th year in 2005. The one-time coaching inn has been extended to incorporate a restored wooden mill. All rooms are en suite, and have TV and hot drink facilities. It stands next to the imposing Westgate Tower. **www.thefalstaffincanterbury.com**

CANTERBURY The Abode

🖥 👬 📺   €€€€

30–33 High St, Canterbury, Kent, CT1 2RX **Tel** *01227-766266* **Fax** *01227-451512* **Rooms** *72*

Located on the pedestrianized High Street in Canterbury, The Abode dates from the 16th century and has many original features. All the bedrooms, some furnished in Tudor or Georgian style, have satellite TV. Enjoy food and drinks at the champagne bar, fine dining restaurant, or the Old Brewery. Price includes breakfast. **www.abodehotels.co.uk**

WINCHESTER Lainston House

👬 📺 ᵭ   €€€€

Sparsholt, Winchester, Hampshire, S021 2LT **Tel** *01962-776088* **Fax** *01962-776672* **Rooms** *50*

One of England's most handsome hotels, Lainston House has country style yet is just minutes from the center of Winchester. Behind the imposing Queen Anne red-brick frontage is a friendly welcome. There are 63 acres to wander in, a gourmet restaurant, and you can always order a DVD from room service. **www.exclusivehotels.co.uk**

THE WEST COUNTRY AND WALES

BATH Royal Crescent

🖥 👬 ≋ ᵭ 📺   €€€€€

16 Royal Crescent, Bath, Somerset, BA1 2LS **Tel** *01225-823333* **Fax** *01225-339401* **Rooms** *45*

Located at the center of Bath's glorious semi-circle of Georgian grandiosity. The simple but imposing Bath stone façade is the first glimpse of one of Britain's great hotels. Rooms brim with antiques, beds are luxuriant, there's a spa, and the restaurant is elegance personified. **www.royalcrescent.co.uk**

Key to Price Guide *see p96* **Map References** *see map of London pp42–3*

BEDDGELERT Sygun Fawr Country House ⏐⏐ 🚶 �🅦 £££

Beddgelert, Gwynedd, LL55 4NE **Tel & Fax** *01766-890258* **Rooms** *12*

Set in a truly rural setting, this four-star, country-house hotel sits amid a vast expanse of mountains and gardens. The rooms at this former 17th-century manor feature exposed stone work, oak beams, and inglenook fireplaces. The dining room is in the oldest part of the building and has antique furniture. Breakfast included. **www.sygunfawr.co.uk**

BRECON Castle of Brecon 🍽️ 🚶 ⛱️ �🅦 £££

The Castle Square, Brecon, Powys, LD3 9DB **Tel** *01874-624611* **Fax** *01874-623737* **Rooms** *40*

The oldest hotel in Wales and located in the town center, this outstanding family-run establishment occupies the remains of Brecon castle. The rooms are spacious, with en suite facilities; the south-facing rooms have breathtaking views over Brecon Beacons National Park. Ideally located for walking and horse riding. **www.breconcastle.co.uk**

BRISTOL Lodge on the Park 📺 P 🍽️ ⛱️ £

Aztec West, Almondsbury, Bristol, Somerset, BS32 4TS **Tel** *01454-201 777* **Rooms** *36*

The Lodge on the Park is a stylish alternative to a budget hotel. It has a non-descript exterior, but rooms are clean, modern, and offer good value for money. There is a Starbucks on site, and a bistro serving pizzas and pasta dishes. Amenities in the rooms include flatscreen TVs. **www.lodgeonthepark.com**

CARDIFF St David's Hotel & Spa 📺 🍽️ 🏊 📺 ⛱️ £££££

Havannah St, Cardiff, CF10 5SD **Tel** *02920-454045* **Fax** *02920-487056* **Rooms** *132*

Overlooking Cardiff's trendy waterfront bay, this five-star hotel and spa is one of Wales's most luxurious hotels. Offers plush rooms and state-of-the-art leisure amenities. Each room has a private, deck-style balcony with views across the bay. Tailormade spa packages are available, as are conference facilities. **www.thestdavidshotel.com**

EXETER Nobody Inn 🍽️ £

Doddiscombsleigh, Exeter, Devon, EX6 7PS **Tel** *01647-252394* **Fax** *01647-252978* **Rooms** *5*

This 16th-century inn is set in the rolling Devon countryside, 6 miles (9 km) southwest of Exeter. The inn is renowned for its excellent restaurant, which has a good whisky and wine list, and local cheeses on the menu. The rooms are all ensuite and exude an old-world charm. **www.nobodyinn.co.uk**

PENZANCE Summer House 🍽️ £££

Cornwall Terrace, Penzance, Cornwall, TR18 4HL **Tel** *01736-363744* **Fax** *01736-360959* **Rooms** *5*

This charming Grade II listed Regency house has been converted into a delightfully intimate hotel and lies very close to the sea. Tropical walled garden, fresh-cut flowers, polished wooden floors and inventive Mediterranean inspired cuisine await. All the bedrooms are individually styled. Price includes breakfast. **www.summerhouse-cornwall.com**

PORTHKERRY Egerton Grey P 🍽️ 🚶 £££

Porthkerry, Barry, South Glamorgan, CF62 3BZ **Tel** *01446-711666* **Fax** *01446-711690* **Rooms** *10*

Refined Victorian country-house hotel boasting a vast collection of antiques. The rooms are furnished with a wealth of period furnishings, original brasswork, open fireplaces, ornate mouldings, and oak paneling – even the food in the restaurant is served on antique china. The huge grounds include a croquet lawn. **www.egertongrey.co.uk**

PORTMEIRION Portmeirion P 🍽️ 🏊 🚶 ⛱️ £££

Portmeirion, Gwynedd, LL48 6ET **Tel** *01766-770000* **Fax** *01766-771331* **Rooms** *68*

This village-like complex, built initially by Clough Williams-Ellis as a private peninsula, is now a holiday retreat with a popular hotel, self-catering cottages, shops, and restaurants. The lavish rooms and suites are furnished in a contemporary style, and are well-equipped with modern facilities. **www.portmeirion-village.com**

ST IVES The Garrack Hotel 🍽️ 🏊 🚶 📺 ⛱️ £££

Burthallam Lane, St Ives, Cornwall, TR26 3AA **Tel** *01736-796199* **Fax** *01736-798955* **Rooms** *18*

Unusually for the busy little artists' haunt of St Ives, the Garrack has its own on-site car parking, as well as delightfully themed subtropical gardens. All rooms have private bathrooms and TV while some have jacuzzi or spa baths. Dine on seafood, meat, and vegetarian specialties. Includes breakfast. **www.garrack.com**

CENTRAL ENGLAND

BIRMINGHAM Malmaison 📺 🍽️ 🚶 📺 ⛱️ �🅦 £££

1 Wharfside St, Birmingham, B1 1RD **Tel** *0121-2465000* **Fax** *0121-2465002* **Rooms** *189*

A stylish, award-winning hotel in a former 1960s Royal Mail sorting office, Malmaison sits amid designer stores and within walking distance of the city center. The rooms are furnished in chocolate and cream tones, with soft lighting, and CD libraries. Also has a spa with sauna, Jacuzzi, and choice of treatments. **www.malmaison-birmingham.com**

CAMBRIDGE Arundel House Hotel P 🍽️ 🚶 ££

Chesterton Rd, Cambridge, Cambridgeshire, CB4 3AN **Tel** *01223-367701* **Fax** *01223-367721* **Rooms** *103*

This hotel, created from a terrace of late 19th-century Victorian houses, overlooks the River Cam and is a short walk from the city center. The historic façade and gracefully decorated rooms have been retained while providing all the latest amenities. Parking is available. Price includes continental breakfast. **www.arundelhousehotels.co.uk**

CAMBRIDGE The Old Bridge Hotel

1 High Street, Huntingdon, Cambridgeshire, PE29 3TQ Tel 01480-424300 Fax 01480-411017 Rooms 24

At this handsome, ivy-clad 18th-century building on the banks of the river Onse, the rooms are all individually designed and have comfortable beds, wool or silk duvet covers, and power showers. The restaurant uses both local and seasonal produce and is popular with residents nearby. **www.huntsbridge.com**

OXFORD The Old Parsonage Hotel

1 Banbury Rd, Oxford, Oxfordshire, OX2 6NN Tel 01865-310210 Fax 01865-311262 Rooms 30

Walls of Cotswold stone screen the Old Parsonage from Oxford's passing hubbub, creating the pleasing illusion of a country retreat. The luxurious bedrooms are air conditioned and have broadband Internet. Fresh Jersey lobsters are served in the restaurant from May through September. **www.oldparsonage-hotel.co.uk**

OXFORD Macdonald Randolph Hotel

Beaumont St, Oxford, Oxfordshire, OX1 2LN Tel 01865-256400 Fax 01865-791678 Rooms 151

The refined Randolph has starred in the TV series *Inspector Morse* and numerous movies, including *Shadowlands*. It's the veritable heart of Oxford, and a favorite for students' parents, American tourists, and the business community. Rooms are tastefully decorated. Dining is in classical silver-service mode. **www.macdonaldhotels.co.uk**

STRATFORD-UPON-AVON Victoria Spa Lodge

Bishopton Lane, Bishopton, Stratford-upon-Avon, Warwickshire, CV37 9QY Tel 01789-267985 Rooms 7

Built in 1837, this non-smoking Victorian spa hotel was visited by Queen Victoria, hence its name and the appearance of her coat of arms in the hotel gables. The bedrooms face forward onto the hotel grounds; some overlook Stratford-upon-Avon's canal. Serves a generous breakfast, and has a helpful staff. **www.stratford-upon-avon.co.uk/victoriaspa**

WILMCOTE Pear Tree Cottage

7 Church Rd, Wilmcote, Stratford-upon-Avon, CV37 9UX Tel 01789-205889 Fax 01789-262862 Rooms 2

Perfectly located for exploring Shakespeare country, these two self-catering apartments are just a short walk from Mary Arden's House – the home of Shakespeare's mother. Guests are free to make use of the peaceful garden, and the owners are happy to advise on local attractions and restaurants. **www.peartreecot.co.uk**

NORTHERN ENGLAND

DURHAM Whitworth Hall Country Park Hotel

Brancepeth, Durham, County Durham, DL16 7QX Tel 01388-811772 Fax 01388-818669 Rooms 29

A Grade II listed building set amid several acres of lovely gardens. Offers stately en suite rooms; some with great views. The deer grazing in the surrounding grounds enhance the hotel's tranquil and relaxing ambiance. An idyllic location for weddings. Also provides conference facilities. **www.bw-whitworthhall.co.uk**

GRASMERE Howfoot Lodge

Town End, Grasmere, Cumbria, LA22 9SQ Tel 015394-35366 Fax 015394-35268 Rooms 7

This Victorian guesthouse is owned by the Wordsworth Trust. It stands in landscaped gardens and has pleasant, spacious rooms, two of which are deluxe standard. An excellent place for outdoor activities such as walks and bicycling. **www.howfoot.co.uk**

LEEDS 42 The Calls

42 The Call, Leeds, West Yorkshire, LS2 7EW Tel 0113-2440099 Fax 0113-2344100 Rooms 41

A refreshingly different town-house hotel that manages to be trendy without becoming a cliché. This converted cornmill, set beside River Aire, features beamed ceilings, original mill mechanisms, modern handmade beds, and a collection of original works of art. Offers luxurious rooms. **www.42thecalls.co.uk**

LIVERPOOL Hope Street Hotel

40 Hope St, Liverpool L1 9DA Tel 0151-7093000 Fax 0151-7092454 Rooms 89

Built in 1860 in the style of a Venetian palazzo, Liverpool's first boutique hotel is set in the city's beautiful Georgian quarter. The contemporary rooms are individually designed and feature solid wood floors, large beds, and Egyptian cotton sheets. A good base from which to explore this World Heritage city. **www.hopestreethotel.co.uk**

MANCHESTER The Midland Hotel

Peter St, Manchester, Lancashire, M60 2DS Tel 0161-2363333 Fax 0161-9324100 Rooms 312

This imposing, red sandstone hotel has been one of Manchester's most familiar landmarks since it opened in 1903. Elegance, luxury, and high standards of service, comfort, and cuisine are on offer. Also has an indoor pool and a spa. Price includes breakfast. Free Internet. **www.qhotels.co.uk**

PENRITH North Lakes Hotel & Spa

Ullswater Rd, Penrith, Cumbria, CA11 8QT Tel 01768-868111 Fax 01768-868291 Rooms 84

The use of local stone, natural wood, and open log fires create a genuine "away from it all" mood at this delightful family resort. Features a children's activity program, massive indoor pool, and a spa. This contemporary hotel is a Shire Hotels property. Price includes breakfast. **www.northlakeshotel.com**

Key to Price Guide *see p96* **Key to Symbols** *see back cover flap*

WINDERMERE Holbeck Ghyll ☒☒☒☒ £££££

Holbeck Lane, Windermere, Cumbria, LA23 1LU **Tel** *01539-432375* **Fax** *01539-434743* **Rooms** *23*

An oasis of calm, perfect for relaxing on the terrace and soaking up fantastic views across Lake Windermere to the rugged fells beyond. Food is mouthwateringly good, and the plush armchairs and open fire of the lounge encourage relaxation. Holbeck Ghyll also has a spa and sauna, and a Michelin-starred restaurant. **www.holbeckghyll.com**

YORK Middlethorpe Hall ☒☒☒☒☒☒☒ ££££

Bishopthorpe Rd, York, Yorkshire, YO23 2GB **Tel** *01904-641241* **Fax** *01904-620176* **Rooms** *29*

One of the selective Historic House Hotels chain and, arguably, its finest. Set on 20 acres of outstanding gardens and parkland, this country-house hotel is filled with antiques and works of art. Built in 1699, it offers elegant accommodations in the main house and the adjacent mews cottages. **www.middlethorpe.com**

SCOTLAND

ABERDEEN Ardoe House Hotel ☒☒☒☒☒☒ ££

S Deeside Rd, Aberdeen, Aberdeenshire, AB12 5YP **Tel** *08701-942104* **Fax** *01224-861283* **Rooms** *109*

Located 5 km (3 miles) from the city center, this is one of Aberdeen's best hotels. The rooms at this luxurious retreat are lavish and tastefully decorated. The suites have four-poster beds. All rooms offer striking views of the countryside. Also has amenities such as Jacuzzi, tennis courts, and beauty salons. **www.mercure.com**

EDINBURGH The Robertson Guesthouse ☒☒ £

5 Hartingdon Gardens, Edinburgh, EH10 4LD **Tel** *0131-2292652* **Fax** *0131-2210130* **Rooms** *6*

This charming Victorian house in a quiet cul de sac is situated within walking distance of the city center so it is well placed for visiting the sights. Ensuite rooms are clean, comfortably furnished, and equipped with tea and coffee, TV, and wireless Internet access. There's a comprehensive breakfast menu. **www.robertson-guesthouse.com**

EDINBURGH The Scotsman ☒☒☒☒☒ ££££

20 N Bridge, Edinburgh, EH1 1TR **Tel** *0131-5565565* **Fax** *0131-6523652* **Rooms** *69*

This stylish hotel is housed in the converted former offices of *The Scotsman* newspaper, and offers great views of the city. The luxurious rooms and suites are decorated with authentic Scottish estate tweeds, and feature amenities such as DVD and CD players, TVs, Internet access, coffee makers, and more. **www.thescotsmanhotel.co.uk**

EDINBURGH The Balmoral ☒☒☒☒☒ £££££

1 Princes St, Edinburgh, EH2 2EQ **Tel** *0131-5562414* **Fax** *0131-5573747* **Rooms** *188*

Boasting the best known address in Edinburgh, The Balmoral is favored by those who are accustomed to the very best in life. This elegant hotel has luxurious, tastefully furnished suites and rooms, with Internet access, TVs, and more. Also offers conference facilities, a spa, and a Michelin-starred restaurant. **www.roccofortecollection.com**

GLASGOW Premier Inn ☒☒☒☒☒☒ £

80 Ballater St, Glasgow, G5 0TW **Tel** *0870-4236452* **Fax** *0870-4236453* **Rooms** *114*

This city-center budget hotel offers modern, spacious, and well-equipped rooms with facilities such as satellite TV, walk-in shower rooms, and trouser presses. Families are well catered for here, and children under 16 stay for free. Full Scottish breakfast is served in the trendy hotel bistro. **www.premierinn.com**

GLASGOW Radisson SAS ☒☒☒☒ ££££

301 Argyle St, Glasgow, G2 8DL **Tel** *0141-2043333* **Fax** *0141-2043344* **Rooms** *247*

This contemporary, award-winning hotel is mainly recognized for its innovative design. Boasts lavishly furnished rooms, suites, and an apartment, well-equipped with many innovative features. Also has conference rooms, a popular bar, and a good restaurant. A definite choice for those who appreciate modern surroundings. **www.radisson.com**

INVERNESS Glenmoriston Town House ☒☒ £££

20 Ness Bank, Inverness, Inverness-shire, IV2 4SF **Tel** *0463-223777* **Fax** *01463-712378* **Rooms** *30*

A traditional town-house hotel that has been tastefully and luxuriously upgraded. The hotel overlooks the River Ness and is only minutes from the town center. The rooms are furnished in a contemporary style, with modern amenities. Boasts an award-winning French restaurant and brasserie. **www.glenmoristontownhouse.com**

ISLE OF SKYE Duisdale ☒ ££

Isle Ornsay, Sleat, Isle of Skye, Inverness-shire, IV43 8QW **Tel** *01471-833202* **Fax** *01471-833404* **Rooms** *17*

Friendly Victorian house set on a hill, with magnificent views of the Sound of Sleat. This small hotel has been flamboyantly decorated and has lots of character. The rooms are spacious and comfortably furnished. Also offers delicious food and lovely gardens. **www.duisdale.com**

ISLE OF SKYE Three Chimneys ☒☒☒ £££££

Colbost, Dunvegan, Isle of Skye, Inverness-shire, IV55 8ZT **Tel** *01470-511258* **Fax** *01470-511358* **Rooms** *6*

Arguably the finest restaurant-with-rooms in Scotland, this intimate hotel is recognized for the excellence of its cooking and hospitality of the owners. Features modern and luxurious accommodations. The spectacular location makes for a memorable visit. **www.threechimneys.co.uk**

Where to Eat in Great Britain

The British restaurant scene has moved far from its once dismal reputation. This is partly due to an influx of foreign chefs and cooking styles, but home-grown restaurateurs have risen to the challenge of redeeming British food, too, and the indigenous cooking has improved out of all recognition since the early 1990s.

PRICE CATEGORIES
Include a three-course meal for one, half a bottle of house wine, and all unavoidable extra charges such as cover, service, and VAT:

£ under £20
££ £20–£35
£££ £35–£45
££££ £45–£55
£££££ over £55

LONDON

WEST END AND WESTMINSTER Belgo Centraal
££

50 Earlham St, WC2H 9LJ **Tel** 020-7813 2233 **Map** D3

Nice and handy for Neal Street, Belgo Centraal remains popular every night. The cool young staff whip up a great variety of Belgian cuisine, from *moules marinières* to more exotic creations featuring Belgium's famous beers. Meat-eaters are also catered for. Eat at the long refectory tables and enjoy the fun.

WEST END AND WESTMINSTER Elena's L'Etoile
££

30 Charlotte St, W1T 2NA **Tel** 020-7636 7189 **Map** C2

This long-standing local eatery is extremely busy at lunchtime, with media people from surrounding ad agencies and TV companies. The time-tested menu delivers classic French bistro food under the gaze of celebrity pictures that cover the walls. It's not cheap but guarantees quality and that indefinable extra – real atmosphere.

WEST END AND WESTMINSTER Gay Hussar
££

2 Greek St, W1D 4NB **Tel** 020-7437 0973 **Map** D3

Once the place of choice for old journalists to meet, gossip, and enjoy second-rate food that reminded them of their private schools. Now, however, it provides a proper insight into authentic Hungarian cuisine, wines, and spirits. Good value for money.

WEST END AND WESTMINSTER Bertorelli
£££

37 St Martin's Lane, WC2N 4ER **Tel** 020-7836 5837 **Map** D3

An Italian institution, Bertorelli's Roman empire now has a number of branches. The first restaurant opened in 1913, and the menu is still based on simple Italian dishes; freshly prepared and flavorful home cooking is served in a friendly ambiance. Sensible prices are an extra bonus.

WEST END AND WESTMINSTER Langan's Brasserie
£££

Stratton St, W1J 8LB **Tel** 020-7491 8822 **Map** C3

The original and perhaps still the best in this chain of restaurants, Langan's faithfully adheres to the style of its late eponymous owner. Service is discreetly attentive and the staff are friendly. Try the house specialty, Langan's bangers and mash with white onion sauce, or the fabulous soufflé with anchovy sauce.

WEST END AND WESTMINSTER L'Escargot Marco Pierre White
£££

48 Greek St, W1D 4EF **Tel** 020-7439 7474 **Map** D3

Another Soho institution, this restaurant is now run by Marco Pierre White, a legendary chef. Expect high standards but be surprised by the very reasonable prices. In the Picasso Room you can look at some of the master's works while eating artistically crafted fine food. Try the parfait of foie gras *en gelée* with toasted Poilâne bread. Closed Sat lunch and Sun.

WEST END AND WESTMINSTER Loch Fyne
£££

2–4 Catherine St, WC2B 5YJ **Tel** 020-7240 4999 **Map** D3

At Loch Fyne, a seafood restaurant, the fish and shellfish are brought in fresh from Scotland. The wine list is suitably chosen to match the crustaceans and other edible sea creatures on offer. Portions are generous whether you choose a platter of oysters or a large plate of poached smoked haddock. There's a second branch at Grace Church St, EC3V.

WEST END AND WESTMINSTER Porter's English Restaurant
£££

17 Henrietta St, WC2E 8QH **Tel** 020-7836 6466 **Map** D3

A great place for proper fish and chips, Porter's is known for serving hearty British "grub" with tasty pie dishes such as steak and Guinness, cod, salmon, and prawn. Desserts are equally large and not for those on a diet. Prices are good for the location. Cheerful staff. Special lunch deal includes a ticket for the London Eye.

WEST END AND WESTMINSTER Sofra
£££

36 Tavistock St, WC2E 7PB **Tel** 020-7240 3773 **Map** D3

A reputed London institution, Sofra has been serving superior Turkish food for many years. The specialty is the healthy option involving a variety of little dishes to share. Bread and olives come free throughout the meal, while dips such as hummous and *tzatziki* always taste fresh and clean.

Key to Symbols *see back cover flap*

WEST END AND WESTMINSTER The Gaucho Grill

125 Chancery Lane, WC2A 1PU **Tel** *020-7242 7727*

Map D3

There are a few branches of the Gaucho around London and they remain of consistent value. The star attraction is still its delicious steak. A large wine list helps wash down an enormous meal and the cocktails are good too. Ideal for pleasant, no-frills dining, it's a well-priced place in a reasonably expensive area. Closed Sundays.

WEST END AND WESTMINSTER Hakkasan

8 Hanway Place, W1T 1HD **Tel** *020-7927 7000*

Map C3

An expensive Chinese restaurant, Hakkasan has maintained a consistently high turnover. The decor is superb, and the food even more so. No windows mean you can't peer in to check it out before entering. Although busy, it's a great choice for gourmets who can afford it. Don't miss the dim sum.

WEST END AND WESTMINSTER Umu

14–16 Bruton Place, W1J 6L **Tel** *020-7499 8881*

Map C3

Seriously expensive, Michelin-starred, and extremely stylish, Umu has a futuristic front door that will make you gasp. The beautiful interior and friendly service by great staff are impressive too. With a remarkable sake list, this is one of the few places in London where you can find genuine Japanese *kaiseki*. Good tasting menu. Closed Sun and Dec 24–early Jan.

SOUTH KENSINGTON AND HYDE PARK Racine

239 Brompton Rd, SW3 2EP **Tel** *020-7584 4477*

Map B4

Racine sets out to showcase French cuisine and succeeds very well. Genuine French food, French waiters, and great atmosphere all combine to keep locals coming back for more. The venison, when in season, is excellent and the menu changes regularly. The service is good.

SOUTH KENSINGTON AND HYDE PARK Nahm

The Halkin, 5 Halkin St, SW1X 7DJ **Tel** *020-7333 1234*

Map C4

This remarkable Thai restaurant has a Michelin star so you can arrive with high expectations. The set menu doesn't disappoint. A recommended appetizer is *ma hor* (minced prawns and chicken simmered in palm sugar with deep fried shallots, garlic, and peanuts, served on pineapple and mandarin orange). Not cheap but worth the price.

SOUTH KENSINGTON AND HYDE PARK Zafferano

15 Lowndes St, SW1X 9EY **Tel** *020-7235 5800*

Map B4

Zafferano has long been recognized as one of the capital's premier Italian restaurants. It's a discreet place, where the emphasis is firmly on the quality of the food. Dishes such as risotto with white truffle and char-grilled lamb with aubergine (eggplant) allow the quality of the ingredients to shine through.

SOUTH KENSINGTON AND HYDE PARK Restaurant Gordon Ramsay

68 Royal Hospital Rd, SW3 4HP **Tel** *020-7352 4441*

Map B4

Awarded with three Michelin stars, this restaurant strives for perfection in everything from place settings to service. Expensive, yet reputedly the best restaurant in London, this dining experience promises to be unforgettable. As a souvenir of London, meal memories here will last a lifetime.

SOUTH KENSINGTON AND HYDE PARK Tom Aikens

43 Elystan St, SW3 3NT **Tel** *020-7584 2003*

Map B4

Top chef, Tom Aikens is often praised by other chefs for his lovingly constructed and beautifully plated dishes. A practitioner of classic cuisine, his flavors are finely balanced and the overall eating experience is highly memorable. A very popular restaurant, so book ahead. Closed Sundays.

REGENT'S PARK AND BLOOMSBURY Mushu

53 Warren St, W1T 5NL **Tel** *020-7388 3629*

This contemporary, casual restaurant serves fast and fresh Oriental food from an open view kitchen. The water dumplings, Beijing dumplings, and ramen noodle soups are authentic and come highly recommended. In the evening, the place transforms into a more formal, yet relaxed, bar and restaurant, serving Oriental tapas. Closed Sat & Sun.

REGENT'S PARK AND BLOOMSBURY Orrery

55 Marylebone High Street, W1U 5RB **Tel** *020-7616 8000*

Map C2

Housed in an old stable block, the dining room is a calm oasis offering stylish dining and contemporary French cuisine. Head for the summer roof terrace for al fresco dining and choose from the *menu du jour* or the à la carte. The intimate bar area is a good place to sample fine Cuban cigars.

THE CITY AND SOUTHWARK Bengal Cuisine

12 Brick Lane, E1 6RF **Tel** *020-7377 8405*

Just about every building in Brick Lane is an Indian restaurant, but the quality varies. Bengal Cuisine is certainly a lot more modern than most of them. The food is very good value and the cook goes easy on the chilli to suit the Western palate. Staff are happy to advise on dishes if asked. There's a good Sunday buffet as well.

THE CITY AND SOUTHWARK Baltic

74 Blackfriars Rd, SE1 8HA **Tel** *020-7928 1111*

Map D4

Located inside a former coach house with high ceilings, Baltic exudes charm. The eastern European influence is noticeable in Baltic's beetroot and vodka cured salmon. There's a massive range of vodkas and the food constantly surprises with dishes such as roast saddle of wild boar. The kitchen is on show and there's often live jazz.

Map References see map of London pp42–3

THE CITY AND SOUTHWARK Silka

€€

6–8 Southwark St, London Bridge, SE1 1TL **Tel** 020-7378 6161

Map E4

Ayurvedic food is a specialty here, which is essentially food balanced for body and soul, and is particularly good for vegetarians. Of course, there are also all the usual Indian dishes too. There is some reluctance on the staff's part to write down your order so do check that what arrives is actually what you asked for. Closed Sundays.

THE CITY AND SOUTHWARK The Spitz

€€

109 Commercial St, Old Spitalfields Market, E1 6BG

The Spitz, a combination of music venue, gallery, bar and bistro, is a friendly place, with live background music setting the ideal tone. The location near Spitalfields Market attracts a mixed crowd. Food is diverse and imaginative: goat's cheese and walnut salad is a specialty. The live jazz is only on Fridays and Saturdays.

THE CITY AND SOUTHWARK Moro

€€€

34–36 Exmouth Market, EC1R 4QE **Tel** 020-7833 8336

Moro is well known for its Spanish-Moroccan cuisine and serves up consistently good food to regulars. Courgette (zucchini) and mint tortilla is an example of light, flavorsome food and there are some very good breads. Buy ingredients next door and take their famous cookbook home with you. Closed Sundays.

GREENWICH Rivington Grill

€€€

178 Greenwich High Rd, Greenwich, SE10 8NN **Tel** 020-8293 9270

Located next to a cinema, Rivington is a great spot for lunch, dinner, or drinks before or after a movie or tour around historic Greenwich. Hearty British cuisine including regional dishes is served in a modern dining room with exposed brick-work, crisp white linen tablecloths, and low lighting. The Market Breakfast is good. Closed dinner Mon & Tue morning.

SOUTHERN ENGLAND

BRIGHTON Seven Dials

€€

1, Buckingham Place, Seven Dials, Brighton, East Sussex, BN1 3TD **Tel** 01273-885555

A bustling eatery much beloved by Brighton's Sunday supplement set, Seven Dials is housed in a converted bank. The menu makes good use of local organic produce. Private dining is provided in the downstairs Vault, while a summer terrace offers the perfect spot for al fresco people-watching.

BRIGHTON La Fourchette

€€€

105 Western Rd, Brighton, East Sussex, BN1 2AA **Tel** 01273-722556

Lauded as one of Brighton's best restaurants, this handsome bistro is a relaxed showcase for regional and classic French cooking. The odd Moroccan twist spices up proceedings. An excellent wine list to match, while the choice of desserts will test the strongest resolve.

CANTERBURY The Goods Shed

€€

Station Road West, Canterbury, Kent, CT2 8AN **Tel** 01227-459153

At this farmers' market diner-cum-café, there's a blackboard menu offering well-constructed treats. The simple home cooking uses the best of the day's produce from the myriad of stalls. As it is increasingly popular with local foodies, seating can be a problem during peak times. Closed Mondays; lunch only Sundays.

SALISBURY Gastro Bistro at the Pheasant Inn

€€

19 Salt Lane, Salisbury, Wiltshire, SP1 1DT **Tel** 01722-322866

Situated in the town center, Gastro Bistro occupies part of the Pheasant Inn, which dates from 1638. Inside there are traditional beams, while outside there's a pretty courtyard for summer dining. Home-cooked Mediterranean dishes include *bouillabaisse*, *cassoulet*, and *tarte Tatin*. The menu also includes roasts, salads, and seafood.

WINDSOR The Mango Lounge

€€

9 Datchet Rd, Windsor, Berkshire, SL4 1QB **Tel** 01753-855576

With views across to Windsor Castle, this contemporary Indian restaurant's mouthwatering menu lives up to its promise. Innovative cooking blends a wide variety of flavors and textures to create such dishes as Old Delhi style chicken. Refreshing mango and passion fruit brûlée is a great way to end a meal. Excellent service. Closed Dec 25.

THE WEST COUNTRY AND WALES

BATH Moon and Sixpence

€€

27 Milsom Place, Bath, Somerset, BA1 1BZ **Tel** 01225-320088

A well-kept secret, Moon and Sixpence is a favorite with locals and discerning visitors. Slightly hidden up a cobbled path, it offers quiet dining right in the bustling city center. The reasonably priced food is loosely termed modern international. Particularly pleasant in summer when table service is provided in the downstairs conservatory or outside terrace.

BATH The Bath Priory

Weston Road, Bath, Somerset, BA1 2XT **Tel** *01225-331922*

Not the original Priory, this top-notch establishment stands in a vast 19th-century Bath property, surrounded by four acres of award-winning gardens. The views are outstanding, and the food is pretty spectacular too. Chef Michael Caines has two Michelin stars and is renowned for innovative modern European cuisine. Try the seasonal tasting menu.

BRISTOL Riverstation

The Grove, Bristol, BS1 4RB **Tel** *0117-9144434*

Formerly a harborside police station left in decline, Riverstation has fully exploited its potential to become one of the city's top restaurants offering modern European cuisine. Of its two floors, the dock floor has a bar and kitchen which is busy all day long. The other floor is a light and airy restaurant. Closed Sun evenings.

CARDIFF The Armless Dragon

97 Wyeverne Road, Cathays, Cardiff, CF24 4BG **Tel** *02920-382357*

At the Armless Dragon, one of Cardiff's most popular dining venues, contemporary Welsh cuisine is served in a smart, but laid-back setting. The menu is arranged by theme, using local produce from Wales, such as chicken from Monmouthshire, ham from Carmarthen, spider crab from Pembrokeshire, and lamb from Brecon.

CHAGFORD Gidleigh Park

Gidleigh Park, Chagford Devon, TQ13 8HH **Tel** *01647-432367*

Officially one of the best restaurants this country has to offer, Gidleigh Park has won several awards and accolades. The attention to detail is what sets it apart. Menus change according to the season, but expect fine quality whatever the month. The wine choice is also among the nation's best. Perfect for special occasions.

DARTMOUTH Angélique

2 South Embankment, Dartmouth, Devon, TQ6 9BH **Tel** *01803-839425*

The Angélique overlooks the River Dart in the attractive regatta town of Dartmouth. The ground floor boasts a warm and lively feel, where guests can enjoy their meal while watching Michelin-starred head chef Darren Brown work in an open kitchen. Upstairs is more intimate and calm with stunning views. Rooms also available. Closed Mon & Sun evenings.

EXETER Thai Orchid

5 Cathedral Yard, Exeter, Devon, EX1 1HJ **Tel** *01392-214215*

Very friendly and welcoming service greets you as soon as you step inside this pleasing Oriental establishment. Authentic Thai cuisine is on offer in the 16th-century building, where the stone-masons who built Exeter's glorious cathedral originally boarded. Fresh orchids on each table are a thoughtful finishing touch.

LLANBERIS The Gwynedd Inn & Restaurant

Llanberis, Snowdonia, Gwynedd, LL55 4SU **Tel** *01286-870203*

Fabulously situated at the foot of Mount Snowdon, this restaurant prides itself on the varied menu of local and seasonal cuisine. The owners, Mark and Dita Bartlett, pay meticulous attention to every detail. Dinner and lunch come complete with sightseeing information.

PENZANCE Harris's

46 New St, Penzance, Cornwall, TR18 2LZ **Tel** *01736-364408*

Run by the Harris family for over 30 years, this small restaurant wins acclaim for freshly made dishes served with local produce and fish from nearby Newlyn market. There are excellent-value fixed-price menus for both lunch and dinner, where you can choose one, two, or three courses. The crab Florentine comes highly recommended.

ST IVES Alba

Old Lifeboat House, Wharf Rd, St Ives, Cornwall, TR26 1LT **Tel** *01736-797222*

With spectacular views of the bay, mesmerizing Alba is housed in the old lifeboat building. Equally breathtaking is the double AA Rosette cuisine, predominantly seafood, all sourced locally. The accompanying wine list is as impressive. The restaurant is split between two floors.

CENTRAL ENGLAND

BIRMINGHAM Purnell's

55 Cornwall St, Birmingham, B3 2DH **Tel** *0121-2129799*

Reservations are essential at Purnell's, where Michelin-starred chef Glynn Purnell creates highly innovative, beautifully presented dishes with a wide variety of flavors and a strong influence of Asian spices. The seven-course tasting menu is a great way to try several dishes, or there are fixed price and à la carte menus. Closed Mon, Sat lunch, and Sun.

CAMBRIDGE Restaurant 22

22 Chesterton Rd, Cambridge, Cambridgeshire, CB4 3AX **Tel** *01223-351880*

Small but perfectly formed, Restaurant 22 is set in a smart Victorian town house that serves British and French favorites, with the odd Asian twist added for extra interest. The decent wine list is predominantly French, but does travel farther afield to good effect.

CAMBRIDGE Midsummer House   ⟨symbols⟩   ⓔⓔⓔⓔⓔ

Midsummer Common, Cambridge, Cambridgeshire, CB4 1HA **Tel** *01223-369299*

On the banks of the River Cam, Midsummer House is a plush restaurant that boasts an array of awards, including two Michelin stars. The elegant ambiance is well-served by a kitchen with a heavy French accent. A slate floor and warm shades give a distinctly Mediterranean feel to proceedings. Closed Mon, Tue lunch, Sun.

OXFORD Browns   ⟨symbols⟩   ⓔⓔ

5–11 Woodstock Rd, Oxford, Oxfordshire, OX2 6HA **Tel** *01865-511995*

A branch of the booming brasserie chain, Browns is a firm favorite with business folk and weekend lunchers. The menu has sharing platters, along with more contemporary dishes, such as asparagus and wild mushroom risotto, to complement snacks and salads, sandwiches, and steaks. Pretty seating spills out onto the sidewalk in summer.

OXFORD Cherwell Boathouse   ⟨symbols⟩   ⓔⓔⓔ

Bardwell Rd, Oxford, Oxfordshire, OX2 6SR **Tel** *01865-552746*

With a riverfront location at a punting station, Cherwell Boathouse is a favorite with wine buffs and romantics. Simple, but flawless, modern European cooking is enhanced by a well-priced and famously good wine selection. Try the honed-to-perfection goat's cheese or adventurous dishes such as pan-fried pollock. There's an al fresco terrace.

STRATFORD-UPON-AVON Marlowe's Restaurant   ⓔⓔⓔ

18 High St, Stratford-upon-Avon, Warwickshire, CV37 6AU **Tel** *01789-204999*

Two restaurants housed in an Elizabethan town house, in the heart of Stratford. Serves both as a silver-service formal restaurant, perfect for business clients and posh events, and as a more informal and lower priced bistro with patio dining. Autographed pictures of visiting glitterati such as Vanessa Redgrave and Sir Alec Guinness line the bar. Closed Sun.

NORTHERN ENGLAND

AMBLESIDE The Log House   ⓔ

Lake Rd, Ambleside, Cumbria, LA22 0DN **Tel** *01539-431077*

Nestled on Lake Road for nearly a century, Log House offers a relaxed dining experience, and the menu features high quality, seasonal produce. The building was imported from Norway by the artist Alfred Heaton for use as a studio. Three ensuite double bedrooms make this an ideal destination for a gourmet weekend. Open for dinner Tue–Sun.

COCKERMOUTH Quince and Medlar   ⟨symbols⟩   ⓔⓔ

11–13 Castlegate, Cockermouth, Cumbria, CA13 9EU **Tel** *01900-823579*

A historic, Georgian building near Cockermouth Castle is home to this family-run, vegetarian restaurant. The stylish surroundings enhance the intimate candlelit dinners. Since 1989, this eatery has been serving imaginative dishes, exploiting modern vegetarian cuisine to the full and drawing inspiration from around the world. Closed Sun & Mon.

DURHAM Bistro 21   ⟨symbols⟩   ⓔⓔⓔ

Aykley Heads House, Aykley Heads, Durham, County Durham, DH1 5TS **Tel** *0191-3844354*

Set within an early 18th-century building, originally a farmhouse, this popular bistro retains a distinct bucolic feel and, in summer, tables appear in the courtyard for al fresco dining. The cuisine is modern British with overtones of the Mediterranean and there's an ever-changing list of special dishes exploiting seasonal fresh produce. Closed Sundays.

LIVERPOOL 60 Hope Street   ⟨symbols⟩   ⓔⓔⓔⓔ

60 Hope St, Liverpool, Merseyside, L1 9BZ **Tel** *0151-7076060*

Ideal for a casual meal, the Café Bar in the basement serves a range of light meals, from sandwiches and salads to more substantial dishes. For a formal setting, choose the restaurant, which offers modern European cuisine within relaxed and unpretentious surroundings. The wine selection complements the food.

MANCHESTER Stock   ⟨symbols⟩   ⓔⓔⓔ

The Stock Exchange, 4 Norfolk Street, Manchester, Lancashire, M2 1DW **Tel** *0161-8396644*

Housed in the city's former Edwardian stock exchange building, this Italian restaurant serves classic antipasti and home-made gnocchi. The steak Fiorentina and mixed seafood platter are excellent. Vegetarians are well catered for and there's a very good winelist too. Closed Sundays.

WINDERMERE Holbeck Ghyll Country House Hotel   ⟨symbols⟩   ⓔⓔⓔⓔ

Holbeck Lane, Windermere, Cumbria, LA23 1LU **Tel** *01539-432375*

Set in a 19th-century hunting lodge, this intimate, Michelin-star restaurant (voted Cumbrian Restaurant of the Year) has good views across the lake. Serves English cuisine which reflects just a hint of France. The set dinner offers a tempting range of choices at each course, such as scallops or langoustine followed by beef, pigeon, or venison with a port-based sauce.

WINDERMERE The Samling   ⟨symbols⟩   ⓔⓔⓔⓔ

Ambleside Rd, Windermere, Cumbria, LA23 1LR **Tel** *01539-431922*

This delightful, award-winning restaurant offers dining in unashamed comfort. Line-caught sea bass, hand-dived scallops, and succulent Herdwick lamb are some of the dishes on the gourmet menu. The well-stocked cellar holds choice wines from across the world, plus some fine old whiskies.

Key to Price Guide *see p102* **Key to Symbols** *see back cover flap*

YORK Melton's Too ⚐♿ ££

25 Walmgate, York, North Yorkshire, YO1 9TX **Tel** *01904-629222*

Located in a former saddler's, this open plan bistro retains many original features, but has a distinctively modern feel. While losing nothing of the original Melton's dedication to good cooking, this place has a more informal appeal; an ideal venue whether you want just a light bite or a full dinner. The bar has a good range of specialty beers.

YORK The Blue Bicycle Restaurant ⚐♪♟ £££

34 Fossgate, York, North Yorkshire, YO1 9TA **Tel** *01904-658147*

Seafood and modern European dishes are the specialties at this atmospheric restaurant. Situated beside River Foss, in a building that housed a 19th-century brothel, it still retains some of the original booths in the cellar. A guitarist provides an added attraction on Saturday evenings. Closed Mon–Wed lunch.

SCOTLAND

ABERDEEN Silver Darling ⚐♟ ££££

N. Pier, Pocra Quay, Footdee, Aberdeen, Aberdeenshire, AB11 5DQ **Tel** *01224-576229*

A superb seafood bistro restaurant located on the north side of Aberdeen harbor. This well-established venue is one of the best places to enjoy the daily catch, which has been carefully cooked and presented. Try and get a table by the window to make the most of the splendid coastline views. Closed Sat lunch & all day Sun.

EDINBURGH Dubh Prais Restaurant ⚐♟ £££

123b High St, Royal Mile, Edinburgh, EH1 1SG **Tel** *0131-557 5732*

Pronounced "Doo Prash" which means "Black Cooking Pot" in Gaelic, this romantic cellar restaurant offers a complete Scottish dining experience. The best of Scotland's produce, including Highland game, smoked salmon, and Aberdeen Angus beef, are used in a contemporary take on traditional dishes. Closed Sun & Mon.

EDINBURGH The Grain Store ♟ ££££

30 Victoria St, Edinburgh, EH1 2JW **Tel** *0131-2257635*

All dishes are individually cooked to order, including sauces, and use quality Scottish produce. Bread is freshly baked on the premises, and desserts are created by an in-house pastry chef. There's an excellent winelist featuring both European and New World wines. Views from the restaurant include Victoria Street and the historic West Bow district.

EDINBURGH Restaurant Martin Wishart ♿♟ £££££

54 The Shore, Edinburgh, EH6 6RA **Tel** *0131-5533557*

Possibly the finest dining experience in all of Scotland. Chef Martin Wishart's creative and innovative cuisine is in great demand by lovers of fine food, and justifiably so. Serves modern French fare, using the best produce available. The service is excellent, the ambiance welcoming, and the experience truly memorable.

GLASGOW Brian Maule at Chardon d'Or ♟ ££££

176 W Regent St, Glasgow, G2 4RL **Tel** *0141-2483801*

One of the finest restaurants in the city. Highly acclaimed chef Brian Maule provides an innovative menu of French cuisine, using locally sourced Scottish ingredients. Serves a variety of fish, poultry, and game. The stylish, yet unpretentious, ambiance and the friendly and efficient staff complete the experience. Closed Sat lunch & Sun.

GLASGOW Ubiquitous Chip ⚐♿♟ ££££

12 Ashton Lane, Glasgow, G12 8SJ **Tel** *0141-3345007*

A Glasgow West End institution, this prestigious restaurant serves traditional Scottish cuisine, made with fresh local ingredients, and has been a home of culinary excellence for over 30 years. Great atmosphere and a friendly staff make this a notable dining spot. There's a bar and roof terrace.

INVERNESS Culloden House ⚐♟ ££££

Culloden, Inverness, Inverness-shire, IV2 7BZ **Tel** *01463-790461*

A historic building with loads of character, set in lovely grounds, close to the Culloden Visitor Center. Offers Scottish country house-style food, with sauces, jellies, sorbets, and mousses interspersing a wide variety of hearty and appetizing meat, game, and fish dishes. Accommodations are also available.

OBAN The Knipoch Hotel ⚐♿♟ £££

On A816, nr Oban, Argyll, PA34 4QT **Tel** *01852-316251*

Situated on the outskirts of Oban, this traditional country hotel has been a popular stopping place for many years. The bar meals here are excellent, while the dinners range from three to five courses. In addition, the huge array of vegetables and flamboyant puddings are as eyecatching as they are tasty.

ST. ANDREWS The Peat Inn ♿♟ ££££

On B940, Cupar, nr St Andrews, Fife, KY15 5LH **Tel** *01334-840206*

Highly accomplished modern cooking, using regional produce and seasonal vegetables, has established this smart hotel-restaurant as one of Britain's best. The innovative cuisine is prepared by renowned chef David Wilson, whose passion for good Scottish fare is evident in his creations. Lunch is particularly good value. Closed first two weeks Jan.

IRELAND

I *t is easy to see Ireland as a lush, green island dotted with quaint, thatched cottages and friendly pubs filled with music, wit, and poetry. Despite the contrasting reality of rapid economic growth and fundamental political change, the tourist industry helps sustain this image of rural bliss, and the genuine good humor of the people invariably makes Ireland a most welcoming place to visit.*

History and religion have created two communities in Ireland, with the Protestant majority in the North determined to remain part of the United Kingdom. Bombings and shootings in Northern Ireland tarnished the world's view of the country, but the Good Friday Agreement of 1998 brought new hopes for peace.

Despite the Troubles of the past, the Irish retain a positive attitude. Both parts of the island have young, highly educated populations. The Republic of Ireland, formerly among the poorer countries of the European Union, became one of its success stories during the economic boom known as the "Celtic Tiger" years. Between 1990 and 2007, the economy saw growth of between 7 and 11 percent annually. But in 2007 it became evident that the inflated economy was built on an unsustainable property bubble. Worldwide recession prompted a crisis in the Irish banking system, which had been lending recklessly to developers. The EU and IMF provided a €85 billion bailout in 2010, but unemployment and emigration remains high. Agriculture remains a mainstay of the economy, with dairy cattle feeding on rich meadowlands and sheep grazing on the poorer upland pastures. The traditional Irish talent for breeding and training racehorses is undiminished. Tourism thrives with more than 5.5 million visitors to the Republic each year and Dublin is one of Europe's hotspots for a weekend break.

HISTORY

In the past Ireland's isolation cut it off from many of the major events of European history. Roman legions never invaded and the country's early history is shrouded in myths of warring gods and heroic High Kings.

Dingle, a lively, friendly fishing harbor in southwest Ireland

◁ The ruined Rock of Cashel, once a fortress of the kings of Munster, then seat of a medieval bishopric

O'Connell Street in Dublin just after the Easter Rising of 1916

The bellicose Celtic tribes were quick to embrace Christianity in the 5th century AD. Until the Viking invasions of the 9th century, Ireland enjoyed an era of relative peace. Huge monasteries were founded, where scholarship and the arts flourished. The Vikings never succeeded in gaining control of the island, but in 1169 the English arrived with greater ambitions. Many Irish chiefs submitted to Henry II of England, and his Anglo-Norman knights carved out large fiefdoms for themselves.

Direct English control was usually limited to the "Pale", the well-defended area around Dublin. Matters changed when in 1532 Henry VIII broke with the Catholic church. Ireland became a battleground between Irish Catholics and English armies dispatched to crush resistance. Irish lands were confiscated and granted to Protestants from England and Scotland. England's conquest was completed with William of Orange's victory over James II in 1690. During the English Ascendancy, repressive Penal Laws denied Irish Catholics the most basic freedoms, but opposition to English rule was never totally quashed.

The Famine of 1845–8 was the bleakest period of Irish history. Over two million either died or were forced to emigrate. A campaign for Home Rule gathered strength, but it took the war of 1919–21 to force the issue. The Treaty of 1921 divided the island in two. The South became the Irish Free State, gaining full independence in 1937. The Catholic minority in Northern Ireland suffered under Protestant rule and in the late 1960s began to stage civil rights protests. The situation quickly got out of hand. The British sent in troops and acts of terrorism and sectarian violence took the place of reasoned dialogue.

KEY DATES IN IRISH HISTORY

8th century BC Humans first inhabit Ireland

600 BC Arrival of Celts from Europe and Britain

AD 432 St. Patrick brings Christianity to Ireland

795 First Viking invasion

999 Viking king of Dublin defeated by Irish High King, Brian Boru

1169 Anglo-Norman invasion; Henry II of England proclaims himself overlord of Ireland

1541 Henry VIII declared King of Ireland

1690 William of Orange defeats James II at Battle of the Boyne

1695 Penal Laws restrict civil rights of Catholics

1801 Act of Union with Britain

1828 Catholic Emancipation Act

1845–8 Potato Famine leaves one million dead

1916 Easter Rising

1921 Anglo-Irish treaty divides Ireland into the Irish Free State and Northern Ireland

1937 The Irish Free State becomes entirely independent of Britain and is renamed Éire

1969 British troops sent to Northern Ireland

1998 Good Friday Agreement sets out framework for self-government in Northern Ireland

2005 Provisional IRA announces full ceasefire

2008 Crisis in the banking system ends boom

2010 EU and IMF approve an €85 bn bailout

LANGUAGE AND CULTURE

Ireland was a Gaelic-speaking nation until the 16th century, when English rule sent the language into decline. The Republic today is officially bilingual and 35 percent of adults claim to know some Gaelic. Many speak it fluently, but perhaps only 3 percent use it regularly. Some degree of knowledge is needed for careers in the public sector. Irish culture, on the other hand, is in no danger of being eroded. The people have a genuine love of legends, literature, and songs, and festivals play an important part in community life. Traditional and modern music flourishes, whether at well-attended concerts or impromptu sessions in the local pub.

Traditional Irish dance

Jaunting car for hire in Killarney

Exploring Ireland

Dublin is Ireland's chief attraction, a small, friendly capital with most of its sights and lively nightlife concentrated in the center. Elsewhere the pace of life is less hectic and the country's great appeal is in its landscape: from the lush green pastures, bogs, and lakes of the center of the island to dramatic mountains and bleak, rocky headlands in the southwest. Touring by car is the most convenient way to explore Ireland, and the quality of the roads on both sides of the border have improved dramatically.

SIGHTS AT A GLANCE

KEY

✈ Airport

⛴ Ferry port

— Highway

- - Highway under construction

— Major road

— Railroad

▬▬ International border

Dublin ❶

Although it is a fairly small city, Ireland's capital is famous for its many pubs, and its rich cultural heritage attracts millions of visitors each year. The Liffey river runs through the middle of the city, and is the original source of its prosperity. The first harbor in Dublin was established in the early 9th century, when Vikings founded one of their largest settlements outside Scandinavia on the site of the present city. Since then, it has suffered wars and conflict over many centuries. In the 20th century Dublin established its own identity and today it is a thriving, modern city, rich in history and proud of its past. Dublin and its surrounding county have a population of just over one million.

SIGHTS AT A GLANCE

Christ Church Cathedral ⑨
Dublin Castle ⑦
Dublinia and the Viking World ⑩
Grafton Street ⑤
The Liffey ⑪
Merrion Square ②
National Gallery of Ireland ③
National Museum of Ireland – Archaeology ④
O'Connell Street ⑫
Parnell Square ⑬
St. Patrick's Cathedral ⑧
Temple Bar ⑥
Trinity College ①

Greater Dublin
(see inset map)
Guinness Store House ⑭
Phoenix Park ⑮

KEY

■	Sight / Place of interest
✈	International airport
⚓	Ferry port
🚉	Train station
🚌	Bus station
🚊	Tram stop
P	Parking
i	Tourist information
✝	Church
=	Pedestrian street

SEE ALSO

- *Where to Stay* p136
- *Where to Eat* p138

GREATER DUBLIN

0 km 5

0 miles 5

Drogheda
Swords
Malahide
Irish Sea
Dublin Airport
Finglas
Royal Canal
Galway   Liffey
Glasnevin
Marino
Howth
Lucan
Grand Canal
Kilmainham
Dublin
Dublin Bay
Douglas, Holyhead
Clondalkin
Ballsbridge
Rathmines
Limerick
Blackrock
Holyhead
Dundrum
Dun Laoghaire
Wicklow

KEY

Area of main map

GETTING AROUND

Dublin is fairly easy to get around. The
suburban train service DART serves
three stations in the city center –
Connolly, Tara Street, and Pearse – and
run out along the coast to the north
and south of the city. Bus services run
every 20–40 minutes and the Nitelink
departs every half hour on selected
routes on Friday and Saturday nights,
midnight–4am. The Luas Light Rail network travels between the city center
and inland suburbs. Dublin Bikes is a
self-service bike rental with 44 hire stations around the city.

James Joyce Cultural Centre

St Mary's Pro-Cathedral

Abbey Theatre

Custom House

Busáras

Connolly Station

Tara Street

Bank of Ireland

College Green

College Park

National Library

St Ann's Church

Mansion House

Shelbourne Hotel

Leinster House

National Museum of Ireland-Natural History

Government Buildings

St Stephen's Green

Newman House

Iveagh House

0 meters 300

0 yards 300

Street-by-Street: Southeast Dublin

The area around College Green, dominated by the façades of the Bank of Ireland and Trinity College, is very much the heart of Dublin. The alleys and malls cutting across busy pedestrianized Grafton Street boast many of Dublin's better stores, hotels, and restaurants. Just off Kildare Street are the Irish Parliament, the National Library, and the National Museum of Ireland – Archaeology. To escape the city bustle many head for sanctuary in St. Stephen's Green.

Dublin Castle ←

The Bank of Ireland is a grand Georgian edifice, originally built as the Irish Parliament.

Statue of Molly Malone (1988)

Grafton Street
This popular pedestrian street is home to many of Dublin's best shops, such as Brown Thomas (see p117).

St. Ann's Church
This striking façade of the 18th-century church was added in 1868. The interior features lovely stained-glass windows.

The Mansion House has been the offical residence of Dublin's Lord Mayor since 1715.

Fusiliers' Arch (1907)

St. Stephen's Green
This relaxing city park is surrounded by many fine buildings. In summer, lunchtime concerts attract tourists and workers alike.

For hotels and restaurants in this region see pp136–7 and pp138–9

O'Connell
Bridge

★ Trinity College
*The focal point of
Parliament Square,
the largest of Trinity's
spacious quadrangles,
is the elegant Italianate
bell tower known as the
"Campanile". Designed
by Sir Charles Lanyon,
it was erected in 1853*
(see p116).

National Library
*Saintly cherubs appear on the frieze
around the library's magnificent
old reading room, once a hangout
of novelist James Joyce.*

Leinster House
was taken over
as the seat
of the Irish
Parliament
in 1922.

**★ National Museum of
Ireland – Archaeology**
*The collection of Irish
antiquities includes this
bronze object from the 2nd
century AD, known as the
Petrie Crown* (see p117).

NASSAU STREET

FREDERICK STREET

OLESWORTH STREET

KILDARE STREET

The Shelbourne Hotel
*Built in 1867, the hotel dominates
the north side of St. Stephen's
Green. It is popular with tourists
and locals for afternoon tea.*

STAR SIGHTS

★ Trinity College

★ National Museum

| 0 meters | 50 |
| 0 yards | 50 |

KEY

– – – Suggested route

View down the central aisle of
Trinity College's Old Library

Trinity College ①

College Green. *Tel* 01-896 2320.
🚇 *DART to Pearse.* 🚌 *7, 10, 14, 15,
45, 46, 48 & many others.* **Old
Library and Treasury** ◻ *daily.*
● *10 days at Christmas.* 🏷 ♿
www.bookofkells.ie

Trinity was founded in 1592
by Elizabeth I on the site of
an Augustinian monastery as
a bastion of Protestantism. It
was not until the 1970s that
Catholics started entering the
university. Its cobbled quads
and lawns still have a monastic
feel, providing a pleasant
haven in the heart of the city.
In front of the main entrance
on College Green are statues
of two of Trinity's most famous
18th-century students, playwright Oliver Goldsmith and

political writer Edmund Burke.
Literary alumni of more recent
times include the playwrights
Oscar Wilde (1854–1900) and
Samuel Beckett (1906–89).

The oldest surviving part of
the college is the red-brick
building (the Rubrics) on the
east side of Library Square,
built around 1700. The Old
Library itself dates from 1732.
Its spectacular Long Room
measures 64 m (210 ft) from
end to end. It houses 200,000
antiquarian texts,
marble busts of
scholars and the
oldest harp in
Ireland. Below
the Library is the
Treasury, where
the college's
most precious
volumes – the
beautifully
illuminated
manuscripts
produced in
Ireland from the
7th to the 9th
century – are
kept. The most
famous, the *Book of Kells (see
p125)*, may have been created
by monks from Iona, who fled
to Kells in 806 after a Viking
raid. The scribes embellished
the text with intricate patterns
as well as human figures and
animals. Almost as fine is the
Book of Durrow, which dates
from the late 7th century.

**Portrait of St. Matthew
from the Book of Kells**

Merrion Square ②

🚇 *DART to Pearse.* 🚌 *5, 7A, 8, 10,
45 & many others.*

Merrion Square is one of
Dublin's largest and grandest
Georgian squares. Covering
about 5 ha (12 acres), the
square was laid out by John
Ensor around 1762.

On the west side are the
impressive façades of the
Natural History Museum, the
National Gallery
of Ireland and
the front garden
of Leinster House,
seat of the Dáil
and the Seanad
(the two houses
of the Irish Par-
liament). The
other three sides
of the square are
lined with lovely
Georgian town
houses. Many
have brightly
painted doors
and original
features such as
wrought-iron balconies,
ornate doorknockers and fan-
lights. The oldest and finest
houses are on the north side.

Many of the houses – now
predominantly used as office
space – have plaques detailing
famous former occupants,
such as Catholic emancipation
leader Daniel O'Connell, who

Facade of Trinity College, Dublin, the Republic's most prestigious university

Georgian town houses overlooking Merrion Square gardens

lived at No. 58, and poet W.B. Yeats (No. 82). Oscar Wilde spent his childhood at No. 1.

The attractive central park has colorful flower and shrub beds. In the 1840s it served a grim function as a soup kitchen, feeding the hungry during the Great Famine.

National Gallery of Ireland ③

Merrion Square West & Clare St. *Tel* 01-661 5133. 🚊 DART to Pearse. 🚌 5, 7, 45 & 48A. ⬭ daily (pm only Sun). Parts of the gallery will close during extensive refurbishment until 2013. ⬭ Good Fri & Dec 24–26. 🎫 🚫 ♿ ⬭ 🍴 www.nationalgallery.ie

This purpose-built gallery was opened to the public in 1864. More than 700 works are on display and, although there is a strong emphasis on Irish land-scapes and portraits, all major schools of European painting are represented. The ground-floor rooms show Irish and British art, including a whole section dedicated to the works of Jack B. Yeats (1871–1957).

Over the years the gallery has benefited from many generous bequests. Playwright George Bernard Shaw left a third of his estate to it. The Shaw Fund Gallery is lined with full-length por-traits, dating from the 17th century onward, and lit by magnificent Waterford Crystal chandeliers.

On the first floor works are hung according to nation. The Italian, French, Flemish and Dutch

collections dominate. Caravag-gio's *The Taking of Christ,* a major attraction, hung unrecog-nized for years in the Dublin Jesuit House of Study, until rediscovered in 1990.

National Museum of Ireland – Archaeology ④

Kildare St. *Tel* 01-677 7444. 🚊 DART to Pearse. 🚋 Luas green line to St. Stephen's Green. 🚌 10, 11, 13 and many others. ⬭ Tue–Sat & 2–5pm Sun. ⬤ Good Fri & Dec 25. 🎫 🚫 ⬭ 🍴 ♿ ground floor only. www.museum.ie

The National Museum of Ireland – Archaeology was built in the 1880s to the design of Sir Thomas Deane. Its splendid domed rotunda features marble pillars and a zodiac mosaic floor. The ground floor holds *Or – Ireland's Gold,* a collection of Bronze Age finds, includ-ing many beautiful pieces of jewelry. Objects from the later Iron Age Celtic period are on display in the Treasury. There are also many well-known treasures from the era of Irish Christianity (see pp124–5).

The Taking of Christ by Caravaggio (1602), one of the highlights of the National Gallery

The first floor houses Viking artifacts and the Ancient Egypt gallery. The Viking exhibition features coins, pottery, and swords excavated in the 1970s from the Viking settlement, discovered beside the Liffey at Wood Quay near Christ Church Cathedral *(see p119).*

The Museum has another branch at Benburb Street, west of the city center. Housed in the vast Collins Barracks, established in 1700 by William III, is the National Museum of Ireland – Decorative Arts & History. The principal exhibits are the museum's collections of furniture, silver, weaponry, and scientific instruments, as well as an exhibition on the 1916 Easter Rising and events that occurred in the decade 1913–1923.

7th-century plaque depicting the Crucifixion, National Museum

Grafton Street ⑤

🚌 14, 15, 46 & many others.

The spine of Dublin's most stylish shopping district runs south from College Green to the glass St. Stephen's Green Shopping Centre. This busy pedestrianized strip, with its energetic buskers and talented street theater artists, boasts one of Dublin's best department stores, Brown Thomas, and popular traditional pubs hidden along the side streets.

At the junction with Nassau Street is a statue by Jean Rynhart of *Molly Malone* (1988), the celebrated "cockles and mussels" street trader of the well-known Irish folk song.

Shoppers in Temple Bar

Temple Bar ⑥

🚌 11, 16A, 19A. 🚶 St. Andrews church (01-605 7700). **Project Arts Centre** 39 East Essex Street. **Tel** 01-881 9613. 🕐 11am–7pm Mon–Sat; shows nightly. 🖥 ♿

The area of cobbled streets between Dame Street and the Liffey are named after Sir William Temple who acquired the land in the early 1600s. The term "bar" meant a riverside path. In the 1800s it was home to small businesses, but over the years went into decline. In the early 1960s the land was bought up with plans for redevelopment. Artists and retailers took short-term leases but stayed on when the plans were scrapped and Temple Bar prospered. Today it is an exciting place, with restaurants, bars, clubs, shops, and galleries. Organizations based here include the **Irish Film Institute**, which has two screens, as well as a bookshop and café, **Project Arts Centre**, a contemporary arts center for theater, dance, film, music, and visual art, and the **Gallery of Photography**, the only Irish art gallery devoted solely to photographs.

Jonathan Swift, Dean of St. Patrick's from 1713

St. Patrick's Cathedral ⑧

St. Patrick's Close. **Tel** 01-453 9472. 🚌 49A, 49B, 54A, 65A, 65B, 123. 🕐 daily. 📷 ♿

Ireland's largest church was founded beside a sacred well where St. Patrick is said to have baptized converts around AD 450. It was originally just a wooden chapel, but in 1192 Archbishop John Comyn commissioned a magnificent new stone structure.

The cathedral is 91 m (300 ft) long; at the western end is a 43-m (141-ft) tower, restored by Archbishop Minot in 1370 and now known as the Minot Tower. Much of the present building dates back to work completed between 1254 and 1270. Thanks to the generosity of Sir Benjamin

Dublin Castle ⑦

For seven centuries Dublin Castle was a symbol of English rule, ever since the Anglo-Normans built a fortress here in the 13th century. Nothing remains of the original structure except the much-modified Record Tower and the butt of the Powder Tower. After a fire in 1684, the Surveyor-General, Sir William Robinson, laid down the plans for the Upper and Lower Castle Yards in their present form. On the first floor of the south side of the Upper Yard are the luxurious State Apartments. The Chester Beatty Library has artistic and religious treasures from around the world.

Picture Gallery

Entrance to State Apartm

Octagonal Tower (c. 1812)

Record Tower

Bermingham Tower can be viewed at Ship St Gate. It served as a prison and as a storage place for administration records.

St. Patrick's Hall
This grand hall is hung with banners of the Knights of St. Patrick. The 18th-century ceiling paintings are allegories of the relationship between Britain and Ireland.

The Throne Room dates from 1740. The throne itself is said to have been built for King George IV in 1821.

Guinness, the cathedral underwent extensive restoration during the 1860s.

The interior is dotted with memorials. The most elaborate is the one erected in 1632 by Richard Boyle, Earl of Cork, in memory of his second wife Katherine. It is decorated with painted carvings of members of the Boyle family. Others remembered in the church include the harpist Turlough O'Carolan (1670–1738) and Douglas Hyde (1860–1949), Ireland's first President.

Many visitors come to see the memorials associated with Jonathan Swift (1667–1745), Dean of St. Patrick's and a scathing satirist, best known as the author of *Gulliver's Travels*. In the south aisle is "Swift's Corner," which has various memorabilia such as an altar table and a bookcase holding his death mask. On the southwest side of the nave, two brass plates mark his grave and that of his beloved "Stella", Ester Johnson.

Christ Church Cathedral ⑨

Christchurch Place. **Tel** 01-677 8099. 🚌 49A, 49B, 50, 54A, 65A, 65B, 66, 77, 123. ◯ daily. ● Dec 26 & 27. 📷 🔥 limited. **www**.cccdub.ie

The cathedral was commissioned in 1172 by Richard de Clare, known as Strongbow, the Anglo-Norman conqueror of Dublin, and by Archbishop Laurence O'Toole. It replaced an earlier wooden church built by the Vikings. At the Reformation, the cathedral passed to the Protestant Church of Ireland. It was remodeled by architect George Street in the 1870s. Even so, the north wall, the one closest to the river, still leans out alarmingly as a result of subsidence. As part of the remodeling, the Old Synod Hall was built and linked to the cathedral by an

Christ Church Cathedral viewed from the east, with the Old Synod Hall behind

attractive covered bridge.

In the atmospheric crypt are fragments removed from the cathedral during its restoration. There are also the mummified bodies of a cat and a rat found in an organ pipe in the 1860s. There is a permanent exhibition of the cathedral's treasures as well.

The nave has some fine early Gothic arches. At the west end is a memorial known as the Strongbow Monument. The large effigy in chain armor is probably not Strongbow, but the curious half-figure beside it may be part of his original tomb. The Chapel of St. Laud houses a casket containing the heart of St. Laurence O'Toole.

Dublinia and the Viking World ⑩

St. Michael's Hill. **Tel** 01-679 4611. 🚌 49A, 49B, 54A, 123. ◯ daily. ● Mar 17, Dec 23–26. 📷 🔥 **www**.dublinia.ie

Housed in the Neo-Gothic Synod Hall, which is linked by a bridge to Christ Church Cathedral, this heritage center covers this period of Dublin's history from the arrival of the Anglo-Normans in 1170 to the closure of the monasteries in the 1540s. An audio tour takes visitors through lifesize reconstructions of the medieval city. An interactive archaeology exhibition opened in 2009.

Bedford Tower (1760)

Entrance to Upper Yard

Lower Yard

Chapel Royal (1814)

Government offices

Figure of Justice
Cynical Dubliners have joked that this statue above the castle entrance appears to be turning her back on the city.

VISITORS' CHECKLIST

Off Dame St. **Tel** 01-645 8813. 🚌 49, 77, 77A, 123. **State Apartments** ◯ daily (Sun pm only). ● Jan 1, Good Fri, Dec 24–28. 📷 🔥 obligatory. **Chester Beatty Library** ◯ 10am–5pm Mon–Fri. ● Jan 1, Good Fri, Dec 24–26, public hols. **www**.dublincastle.ie

James Gandon's Four Courts overlooking the River Liffey

The Liffey ⑪

🚌 25, 25A, 51, 66, 66A, 67, 67A, 68, 69 and many others.

Though modest in size compared with the rivers of other capital cities, the Liffey features strongly in Dubliners' everyday lives and holds a special place in their affections. The handiest pedestrian link between Temple Bar (see p118) and the north of the city is **Ha'penny Bridge**. This attractive, cast-iron bridge, originally called Wellington Bridge, was opened in 1816. Its official name now is the Liffey Bridge. Its better-known nickname comes from the toll of a halfpenny levied on it up until 1919.

The two most impressive buildings on the Liffey are the **Custom House** and the **Four Courts**, both designed by

Carved head representing the River Liffey on the Custom House

James Gandon at the end of the 18th century. In 1921, supporters of Sinn Fein celebrated their election victory by setting light to the Custom House, seen as a symbol of British imperialism. The building was not fully restored until 1991, when it reopened as government offices. A series of 14 magnificent heads by Edward Smyth, personifying Ireland's rivers and the Atlantic Ocean, form the keystones of arches and entrances.

The Four Courts suffered a similar fate during the Irish Civil War of 1921–2, when it was bombarded by government troops after being seized by anti-Treaty rebels. Here too, the buildings were restored to their original design. A copper-covered lantern dome rises above a Corinthian portico crowned with the figures of Moses, Justice and Mercy.

O'Connell Street ⑫

🚌 3, 10, 11, 13, 16A, and many others.

Dublin's main thoroughfare, formerly called Sackville Street, was renamed in 1922 after Daniel O'Connell, who was known as the "Liberator"

for his tireless campaigns for Catholic rights in the 19th century. The street was laid out in the 18th century as an elegant residential parade, but the construction of Carlisle (now O'Connell) Bridge in 1790 turned it into the city's principal north-south route. As a result, little remains of its intended grandeur.

A few venerable buildings survive, including the **General Post Office**, which became a symbol of the 1916 Easter Rising. Members of the Irish Volunteers and Irish Citizen Army seized the building on Easter Monday,

The monument to Daniel O'Connell

and Patrick Pearse read out the Proclamation of the Irish Republic from its steps. The rebels remained inside for a week, but shelling from the British eventually forced them out. During the following weeks, 14 of the leaders were caught and shot. Inside the building is a sculpture of the mythical Irish hero Cuchulainn, dedicated to those who died, and a small museum tells the history of the postal service.

A walk up the central mall is the best way to inspect the series of sculptures lining the route. At the south end stands a massive memorial to Daniel O'Connell, unveiled in 1882. In the middle is an elegant spire and at the north end is the monument to Charles Stewart Parnell (1846–91).

Parnell Square ⑬

🚌 *3, 10, 11A, 13, 16A, 19A.*
Dublin Writers Museum 18 Parnell Sq North. *Tel 01-872 2077.* 🔲 *daily.*
🌑 *Dec 25 & 26.* 🖼 **Dublin City Gallery, The Hugh Lane** Charlemont House. *Tel 01-222 5550.* 🔲 *Tue–Sun.* 🌑 *Dec 24–27 & public hols.*

The square at the top of O'Connell Street looks sadly neglected. Even so, it contains a number of noteworthy sights, including the **Rotunda Hospital**, Europe's first purpose-built maternity hospital, opened in 1757. Its chapel has some fine Rococo stuccowork. The former grand supper room of the hospital is now the **Gate Theatre**, famous for producing new plays.

On the north side of the square, two grand 18th-century townhouses have been converted into museums: the **Dublin Writers Museum**, devoted to Irish literature, and the **Dublin City Gallery, The Hugh Lane**. The latter houses the Impressionist paintings bequeathed to Dublin Corporation by Sir Hugh Lane, who died on the torpedoed liner *Lusitania* in 1915. The square also contains a **Garden of Remembrance** opened in 1966 on the 50th anniversary of the Easter Rising.

Arthur Guinness

Guinness Storehouse ⑭

St. James's Gate, Dublin 8. *Tel 01-408 4800.* 🚌 *51B, 78A, 123.*
🔲 *daily.* 🌑 *Good Fri, Dec 24–26, Jan 1.* 🖼 🔧 🖥 🍴 🛍
www.guinness-storehouse.com

Guinness is a black beer, known as "stout," renowned for its distinctive malty flavor and smooth creamy head. The Guinness brewery site at St James's Gate is the largest brewery in Europe and exports beers to more than 120 countries.

The World of Guinness exhibition is housed in a 19th-century warehouse, used for hop storage until the 1950s. It chronicles 200 years of brewing at St James's Gate. The tour starts in a Victorian kieve (or mash filter), and goes on to examine all other stages of the brewing process.

Displays show how production methods have changed over the years since 1759, when Arthur Guinness took over the backstreet brewery. Guinness started brewing ale, but was more of a black beer called "porter," popular in London's markets. He developed a new recipe for porter (the word "stout" was not used until the 1920s). So successful was the switch that he made his first export shipment in 1769.

The tour ends with a complimentary pint of Guinness in the Granty Bar, where visitors can also enjoy 360° views of the city.

The Phoenix Column

Phoenix Park ⑮

Park Gate, Conyngham Rd, Dublin 8.
🚌 *25, 26, 51, 66, 67, 68.* 🔲 *daily.*
Visitor Center *Tel 01-677 0095.*
🔲 *Mar–Oct: daily; Nov–Feb: Wed–Sun.* 🔧 *limited.* **Zoo** *Tel 01-474 8900.* 🔲 *daily.* 🖼 🛍 🖥 🍴 🔧
www.dublinzoo.ie

Just to the west of the city center, ringed by an 11-km (7-mile) wall, is Europe's largest enclosed city park. The name "Phoenix" is said to be a corruption of the Gaelic Fionn Uisce, or "clear water." The Phoenix Column is crowned by a statue of the mythical bird. The park originated in 1662, when the Duke of Ormonde turned the land into a deer park. It was opened to the public in 1745.

Near Park Gate is the lakeside People's Garden. A little further on are the Zoological Gardens, which are renowned for the breeding of lions, including the one that introduces MGM movies.

The park has two very conspicuous monuments. The Wellington Testimonial is a 63-m (204-ft) obelisk, begun in 1817 and completed in 1861. Its bronze bas-reliefs were made from captured French cannons. The 27-m (90-ft) steel Papal Cross marks the spot where the pope said Mass in front of one million people in 1979. Buildings within the park include two 18th-century houses: Áras an Uachtaráin, the Irish President's official residence, for which 525 tickets are issued every Saturday for a free guided tour, and Deerfield, home of the US ambassador. Ashtown Castle is a restored 17th-century tower house, now the Phoenix Park Visitor Centre.

The Gallery of Writers at the Dublin Writers Museum, Parnell Square

Southeast Ireland

Enjoying the warmest climate in Ireland, the Southeast has always presented an attractive prospect for invaders and settlers. Its highlights include the Neolithic tombs in the Valley of the Boyne, early Christian monastic sites, and towns such as Waterford that grew from Viking settlements. It is also the setting for many great 18th-century houses built by the ruling English aristocracy. The wildest landscapes of the region are to be found in the forested hills and desolate moorland of the Wicklow Mountains south of Dublin.

Elegant stuccoed hall and staircase in Castletown House

Castletown House ❷

Celbridge, Co. Kildare. **Tel** 01-628 8252. 🚌 67, 67A from Dublin. ⏰ mid-Mar–Oct: 10am–6pm Tue–Sun; winter programme: see website. 🔴 Mon (except public hols). 🎫 obligatory. 📷 🅿 ♿ limited. **www**.castletownhouse.ie

Built in 1722–32 for William Conolly, Speaker of the Irish Parliament, Castletown was Ireland's first grand Palladian-style country house. Most of the interiors were commissioned by Lady Louisa Lennox, wife of Conolly's great-nephew, Tom, who lived here in the late 18th century. It was she who added the magnificent long gallery at the top of the house, with its Pompeiian-style friezes, cobalt-blue walls and niches framing Classical

statuary. From the long gallery visitors can admire the curious obelisk-topped memorial to Speaker Conolly erected by his widow in 1740.

A portrait of Lady Louisa is incorporated in the superb Rococo stuccowork by the Francini brothers in the staircase hall. Another personal reminder of Lady Louisa is the print room, the last surviving, intact example of its kind. In the 18th century, ladies pasted prints directly on to the wall and framed them with elaborate festoons.

Newgrange ❸

8 km (5 miles) E of Slane, Co. Meath. 🚆 to Drogheda. 🚌 to visitor centre via Drogheda. **Brú na Bóinne Interpretive Centre Tel** 041-988 0300. ⏰ daily. 🔴 Dec 24–27. 🎫 📷 obligatory. 🚫 in tomb. 🅿 ♿

The origins of Newgrange, one of the most important passage graves in Europe, are steeped in mystery. Built around 3200 BC, the grave was rediscovered in 1699. When it was excavated in the 1960s, archaeologists realized that at dawn on the winter

solstice (December 21) a beam of sunlight shines through the roof box, a rectangular opening above the entrance to the tomb and a feature unique to Newgrange. The light travels along the 19-m (62-ft) passage and hits the central recess in the burial chamber. It is thus the world's oldest solar observatory.

Between 1962 and 1975 the grave and the mound, or cairn, covering it were restored. The retaining wall at the front of the cairn was rebuilt using white quartz and granite stones found scattered around the site. It is estimated that the original tomb, created by people who had neither the wheel nor metal tools, may have taken up to 70 years to build. About 200,000 tons of loose stones were transported to build the cairn. Larger slabs were used to make the circle around the cairn and the retaining kerb. Many of the kerbstones and the slabs lining the passage and chamber are decorated with zigzags, spirals, and other geometric motifs.

Each of the three recesses in the central chamber contained a chiseled "basin stone" that held funerary offerings and the bones of the dead. The chamber's corbeled ceiling has proved completely water-proof for 5,000 years.

Newgrange is very popular, especially in summer, so queues are likely and you have to wait your turn at the **Brú na Bóinne Interpretive Centre**. This has displays on the area's Stone Age heritage. The tour includes the nearby tomb at Knowth. The last one starts at 3:15pm in winter and at 5:15pm in midsummer.

Aerial view of Newgrange, showing the cairn and circle of standing stones

Round tower at Glendalough

Glendalough ❹

Co. Wicklow. 🚌 St. Kevin's Bus from Dublin. **Ruins** ◯ daily. 🌿 in summer. **Visitor Center** *Tel* 0404-45352. ◯ daily. ● Dec 23–30. 🌿 limited. **www**.glendalough.ie

The steep, wooded slopes of Glendalough, the "valley of the two lakes," harbor one of Ireland's most atmospheric ruined monasteries. Founded by St. Kevin in the 6th century, it functioned as a monastic center until the Dissolution of the Monasteries in 1539.

Most of the buildings date from the 10th to 12th centuries. The reconstruction (*see pp124–5*) shows how the monastery may have looked in its heyday. The main ruins lie near the smaller Lower Lake. You enter the monastery through the double stone arch of the gatehouse, from where a short walk leads to a graveyard with a restored round tower in one corner. Other ruins include the roofless cathedral, the tiny Priest's House and St. Kevin's Cross. Below, nestled in the lush valley, stands a small oratory. It is popularly known as St. Kevin's Kitchen, because its belfry resembles a chimney.

A path along the south bank of the river leads to the Upper Lake and some of the other buildings associated with St. Kevin. Here, the scenery is wilder and you are better able to enjoy the tranquillity of Glendalough.

Kilkenny ❺

Co. Kilkenny. 🚶 26,000. 🚃 🚌 ℹ️ *Shee Almshouse, Rose Inn St (056-775 1500).* 🎭 *Kilkenny Arts Festival (Aug).*

In a lovely setting beside the River Nore, Kilkenny is Ireland's most attractive inland city. Many of its houses feature the local black limestone, known as Kilkenny marble. The city is proud of its heritage and hosts a major arts festival. It is also a brewery city, filled with atmospheric old pubs.

Kilkenny Castle is a 12th-century castle that was remodeled in Victorian times. It is set in extensive parkland, and was the seat of the Butler family for almost 600 years from around 1391 until 1967, when it was presented to the people of Kilkenny. Two wings of the castle have been restored to their 19th-century splendor and include a library, a drawing room, and the magnificent Long Gallery. The River Wing houses the Butler Gallery of Contemporary Art.

The area known, in the days of segregation, as Englishtown boasts the city's grandest buildings, such as Rothe House, a fine Tudor merchant's house, built around two courtyards. The area of narrow alleyways or "slips" is part of Kilkenny's medieval heritage.

The Irishtown district is dominated by **St. Canice's Cathedral** and a round tower that you can climb for a good view of the city. The Gothic cathedral dates from the 13th century. It has a finely sculpted west door and an array of 16th-century tombs with beautiful effigies of the Butler family in the south transept.

♦ Kilkenny Castle
The Parade. *Tel* 056-772 1450. ◯ daily. ● Good Fri, Christmas (see website). 🌿 📷 obligatory. 🚫 🌿 limited. **www**.kilkennycastle.ie

Waterford ❻

Co. Waterford. 🚶 49,000. 🚃 🚌 🚌 ℹ️ *The Granary, Merchant's Quay (051-875 823).* 🛒 Sat. 🎭 *International Festival of Light Opera (Sep).*

Ireland's oldest city, Waterford was founded by the Vikings in 914, and later extended by the Anglo-Normans. Its commanding position on the Suir estuary made it southeast Ireland's main port. The 18th century saw the establishment of local industries, including the world-famous glassworks.

The remains of the city walls define the area fortified by the Normans. The largest surviving structure is **Reginald's Tower**, overlooking the river. Although the city retains its medieval layout, most of the finest buildings are Georgian, including **Christchurch Cathedral**, designed in the 1770s by local architect John Roberts. From June to August you can admire the waterfront by taking a pleasure cruise on the river.

Waterford Crystal decanter

The **Waterford Crystal Factory** lies 2.5 km (1.5 miles) south of the center. The original factory was founded in 1783, but closed in 1851. A new factory opened in 1947.

🏛 Waterford Crystal Factory
Kilbarry. *Tel* 051-317 0000. ◯ Mar–Oct: 9am–4:15pm daily; Nov–Feb: 9am–3:15pm Mon–Fri. 🌿 📷 🌿 **www**.waterfordvisitorcentre.com

Tomb of 2nd Marquess of Ormonde in St. Canice's Cathedral, Kilkenny

Early Celtic Christianity

Ireland became Christian in the 5th century, following the missions of St. Patrick and others. The situation was soon reversed, with many Irish missionaries, such as St. Columba and St. Columbanus, sailing to Great Britain, France, and beyond. The Irish church developed more or less free from the control of Rome, but nevertheless had strong links with the east. As in Egypt, the Christian faith inspired a proliferation of hermitages and remote monasteries. Decorative motifs in illuminated manuscripts reflect Egyptian Christian imagery, and materials used in making the inks came from the Middle East. The advent of the Vikings in the 9th century forced the monasteries to take defensive measures, but they continued to flourish despite frequent raids.

Conical roof

Lookout window

Wooden floor

Movable ladder

Round towers, *first built in the 10th century, were bell houses, store houses, and landmarks for approaching visitors. The entrance could be 4 m (13 ft) above ground and was reached by a ladder.*

CELTIC MONASTERY

This reconstruction shows Glendalough in about 1100. Monasteries were probably the largest centers of population in Ireland before the Vikings started to found towns.

Refectory and kitchen

Abbot's house

Craftsmen's dwellings

St. Mary's Church

The watermill

The Magnus Domus

St. Kevin's Church

IRELAND'S HIGH CROSSES

High Crosses are found in parts of Britain as well as Ireland, yet in their profusion and craftsmanship, Irish crosses are exceptional. The ringed cross has become a symbol of Irish Christianity and is still imitated today. The medieval High Crosses were carved between the 8th and 12th centuries. Early ones, such as the 8th-century cross at Ahenny, bore spirals and interlacing patterns, but in the 9th and 10th centuries a new style emerged with sculpted scenes from the bible, "sermons in stone," aimed at educating a largely illiterate population.

Muiredach's Cross *at Monasterboice is the finest surviving example of a cross carved with biblical scenes. This panel shows the Fall of Man: Eve offering Adam the apple in the Garden of Eden and Cain slaying Abel.*

Ornamental High Cross at Ahenny

Cross of the Scriptures, Clonmacnoise

THE BOOK OF KELLS

The most richly decorated of all the Irish illuminated manuscripts dating from the 8th–10th centuries, the Book of Kells contains the four gospels in Latin, copied onto leaves of high-quality vellum. It is remarkable both for the beauty of the script and for the inspired fantasy of the illumination. There is no record of its existence before the early 11th century, but it was probably created in about 800. It would have taken many years of work by the

Page of the Genealogy of Christ from the Book of Kells

scriptorium of a monastery. It may have been brought to Kells by monks from Iona who fled to Ireland after a Viking raid in 806. The manuscript was moved to Trinity College *(see p116)* in the 17th century for safe-keeping.

WHERE TO SEE EARLY CHRISTIAN SITES IN IRELAND

Important early Christian sites besides Glendalough include Clonmacnoise, the Rock of Cashel *(see p126)*, Clonfert, Kells, and Devenish Island. Though most of the monastic buildings are ruins, they have usually continued to be used as cemeteries right up to modern times. Monasteries were built on the Aran Islands *(see p129)* and even on the remote rocky Skellig Michael off the Kerry Coast. Round towers and High Crosses are pre-served all over Ireland, often standing beside churches of much more recent construction.

Gatehouse

Guesthouse and stable

Monks' dwellings and barns

The cathedral was the largest of the many churches built in and around the monastery.

The Crozier of the Abbots of Clonmacnoise *dates from the 11th century. The incised patterns on the ornate silver casing show the strong influence of Viking designs.*

The Voyage of St. Brendan *is a fantastic legend of early medieval Irish Christianity. The 6th-century saint and his followers set sail into the Atlantic in a small boat, sighting volcanic islands, ice floes, whales, and even, some say, America.*

Clonmacnoise *was founded in the 6th century. The monastery was noted for its piety and scholarship. Now it is an atmospheric collection of ruins in a remote spot on the Shannon. This carved Romanesque doorway is part of the Nun's Church.*

Devenish Island *has a fine restored round tower and enjoys a peaceful setting on Lower Lough Erne. Lake islands were popular as monastic sites.*

Southwest Ireland

Magnificent scenery has attracted visitors to this region since Victorian times. Killarney and its romantic lakes are a powerful magnet for tourists, as is the attractive coastline of Cork and Kerry, where rocky headlands jut out into the Atlantic and colorful fishing villages nestle in the bays. Yet much of the southwest remains unspoiled, with a friendly atmosphere and authentic culture still alive in Irish-speaking pockets.

The Rock of Cashel

Cashel ❼

Co. Tipperary. 🏃 11,400. 🚌 🅸
Heritage Centre, Main St (062- 62511).
Rock Tel *062-61437.* ◯ *daily.* ●
Dec 24–26. 🅰 🅲 🅶 *limited.*

The town's great attraction is the magnificent medieval Rock of Cashel. Many people stay overnight to enjoy eerie floodlit views of the rocky stronghold rising dramatically out of the Tipperary plain. The Rock was a symbol of royal and ecclesiastical power for more than a thousand years. From the 5th century AD it was the seat of the Kings of Munster, rulers of southwest Ireland. In 1101, they handed Cashel over to the Church, and it flourished as a religious center until a siege by a Cromwellian army in 1647 ended in the massacre of its 3,000 occupants.

A good proportion of the medieval complex still stands, though the main building, the Gothic cathedral, is roofless. The earlier Cormac's Chapel is an outstanding example of Romanesque architecture. Other prominent features of the Rock are a restored round tower and the weatherbeaten St. Patrick's Cross. The carved figure on the east face of the cross is said to be St. Patrick.

Cork ❽

Co. Cork. 🏃 123,000. 🚆 🚌
🅸 *Tourist House, Grand Parade (0214-255 100).* 🎷 *Jazz Festival (Oct); Film Festival (Oct).*

Cork city derives its name from the marshy banks of the River Lee – its Irish name Corcaigh means marsh – where St. Finbarr founded a monastery around AD 650. The center of Cork today occupies an island between two arms of the river. Its waterways, bridges, and narrow alleys, combined with the Georgian architecture of the old Quays, give Cork a continental feel. In the 18th century many of today's streets were waterways lined with warehouses and merchants' residences.

Noted for its chic bars, ethnic restaurants, bookshops, and boutiques, Paul Street is the hub of the liveliest district in town. The nearby **Crawford Art Gallery** has some fine Irish works of art.

A prominent landmark is the steeple of **St. Anne Shandon** on a hill in the north of the city. It is topped by a weather vane in the shape of a salmon. Visitors can climb up and ring the famous Shandon bells.

🏛 **Crawford Art Gallery**
Emmet Place. **Tel** *0214-805 042.*
◯ *10am–5pm Mon–Sat.* ● *public hols, Dec 24–Jan 3.* 🍴 🖥 🛍 🅶

The battlemented keep and other ruined towers of Blarney Castle

Environs
Beautiful countryside surrounds Cork, especially along the valley of the Lee river. Popular outings include a tour of the whiskey-making **Old Midleton Distillery**, and a trip to **Blarney Castle** and the legendary stone that bestows magical eloquence on all who kiss it. There are also plenty of opportunities for walking and fishing.

🏛 **Old Midleton Distillery**
Midleton, Co. Cork. **Tel** *0214-613 594.* ◯ *daily.* ● *Dec 24–26, Dec 31–Jan 1.* 🅰 🅲 🛍 🖥 🅶

♣ **Blarney Castle**
Blarney, Co. Cork. **Tel** *0214- 385252.* ◯ *daily.* ● *Dec 24 & 25.* 🅸 🅶 *grounds only.*

South channel of the Lee river flowing through the city of Cork

For hotels and restaurants in this region see pp136–7 and pp138–9

Newman's Mall in the quaint village of Kinsale

Kinsale ❾

Co. Cork. 🏛 *3,400*. 🚌 ℹ *Pier Road (0214-772 234).* 🎫 *Regatta (Aug); Festival of Fine Food (Oct).*

For many visitors to Ireland, Kinsale heads the list of places to see. One of the prettiest small towns in Ireland, it has had a long and checkered history. The defeat of the Irish forces and their Spanish allies at the Battle of Kinsale in 1601 signalled the end of the old Gaelic order.

An important naval base in the 17th and 18th centuries, Kinsale today is a popular yachting center. It is also famous for the quality of its cuisine and has a popular annual Festival of Fine Food.

Charles Fort, a fine example of a star-shaped bastion fort, was built by the English in the 1670s to protect Kinsale against foreign naval forces. To reach it take the signposted coastal walk from the quayside.

⚓ **Charles Fort**
3 km (2 miles) E of Kinsale.
Tel *0214-772 263.* ⏰ *mid-Mar–Oct: 10am–6pm daily; Nov–mid-Mar: 10am–5pm daily. Last adm: 1 hr before closing.* ⏺ *Christmas week.* ♿🎫📷💺 *limited.*

Killarney ❿

Co. Kerry. 🏛 *13,500.* 🚉 🚌 ℹ *Beech Road (064-6631633).*

Killarney is often derided as "a tourist town" but this does not detract from its cheerful atmosphere. The infectious Kerry humor is personified by the wise-cracking "jarveys," whose families have run jaunting cars (pony and trap rides) here for generations. The town does get very crowded in the summer but this is inevitable, given the lure of the **Lakes of Killarney**. The three lakes and many of the heather-covered hills surrounding them lie within **Killarney National Park**. Although the landscape is dotted with ruined castles and abbeys, the lakes are the focus of attention: the moody watery scenery is subject to subtle shifts of light and color. Well-known beauty spots include the Meeting of the Waters, the Ladies' View, so called because it delighted Queen Victoria's ladies-in-waiting in 1861, and the Gap of Dunloe, a dramatic mountain pass. The largest of the lakes, Lough Leane, is dotted with uninhabited islands. Boat trips across the lake run from Ross Castle on the shore nearest Killarney.

Overlooking the lakes is **Muckross House**, an imposing mansion built in 1843 in Elizabethan style, set in beautiful gardens. It houses the Museum of Kerry Folklife. Next door is the Walled Garden Centre, which incorporates the garden, a restaurant, and a craft center.

The town is also the starting point for the popular **Ring of Kerry** tour around the Iveragh Peninsula. Allow a day's drive to enjoy its captivating scenery.

🚇 **Muckross House**
4 km (2.5 miles) S of Killarney.
Tel *064-6670144.* ⏰ *daily.* ⏺ *Jan 1, Dec 24–26.* 🎫📷📹📷💺

Dingle ⓫

Co. Kerry. 🏛 *2,100.* 🚌 ℹ *Apr–Oct: Strand St (06691-51188).* 🛒 *Fri.*

This once remote Irish-speaking town is today a thriving fishing port and popular tourist center. Brightly painted – often fairly hippy – craft shops and cafés abound. Along the quayside are lively bars offering music and seafood. The harbor is home to Dingle's biggest star, Fungi the dolphin, who has been a permanent resident since 1983 and can be visited by boat or on swimming trips.

Gallarus Oratory, a tiny dry-stone Early Christian church

Environs

Dingle is a good base for exploring the scattered archaeological remains of the Dingle Peninsula. The most fascinating is the **Gallarus Oratory**, northwest of Dingle. This miniature dry-stone church, shaped like an upturned boat, was built from the 6th to the 9th centuries. West of Dingle, along the coast road, are the Iron Age fort of Dunbeg and Early Christian beehive huts.

The Upper Lake, smallest and most remote of the Lakes of Killarney

Bunratty Castle ⑫

This formidable 15th-century castle is one of Ireland's major tourist attractions. Its most important residents were the O'Briens, Earls of Thomond, who lived here from the early 16th century until the 1640s. The interior has been restored to look as it did under the so-called "Great Earl," who died in 1624. The adjacent Folk Park and the mock medieval banquets held in the castle attract many visitors, but despite its commercialization, Bunratty is well worth a visit. The Folk Park recreates rural and urban life at the end of the 19th century, with a village, complete with stores, a school, and dwellings ranging from a laborer's cottage to an elegant Georgian house.

VISITORS' CHECKLIST

Bunratty, Co. Clare. *Tel 061-360 788.* ▣ from Limerick, Ennis & Shannon Airport. **Castle & Folk Park** ◯ 9am–5:30pm daily (Jun–Aug: 9am–6pm). Last entry to castle 4pm all year. ● Good Fri, Dec 24–26. ▨ ▮▮ ৬ to Folk Park. **www**.shannonheritage.com

Great Hall
The castle's grandest room served as banqueting hall and audience chamber. Among the furnishings bought by the owner, Lord Gort, when he set about restoring the castle in the 1950s was this Tudor standard.

South Solar
The carved ceiling here is partly a reconstruction in late Tudor style.

The North Solar was the Great Earl's private apartment.

The Murder Hole was designed for pouring boiling water or pitch onto the heads of attackers.

Entrance

The Earl's Robing Room also served as a private audience chamber.

North Front
The entrance, raised well above ground level to deter invaders, is typical of castles of the period.

Main Guard
This was where the castle's soldiers ate, slept, and listened to music from the Minstrels' Gallery.

The imposing Kylemore Abbey on the shores of Kylemore Lough, Connemara

Galway ⑬

Co. Galway. 🏃 60,000. 🚂 🚌
ℹ *The Fairgreen, Foster St (091-537 700).* 🚢 *Sat & Sun.* 🎭 *Arts Festival (mid-Jul); Galway Races (late Jul/Aug); Oyster Festivals (early & late Sep).*

Galway is the center for the Irish-speaking regions in the West of Ireland and a lively university city. In the 15th and 16th centuries it was a prosperous trading port, controlled by 14 merchant families, or "tribes." Its allegiance to the English Crown cost the city dear when, in 1652, it was sacked by Cromwell's forces. In the 18th century Galway fell into decline, but in recent years, its fortunes have revived through high-tech industries.

The city stands on the banks of the Corrib river. Many of the best stores, pubs, theaters, and historic sights are packed into the narrow lanes of the "Latin Quarter" around Quay

Colorful shopfronts lining Quay Street in Galway's "Latin Quarter"

Street. Nearby is the Collegiate Church of St. Nicholas, the city's finest medieval building. To the south stands the 16th-century Spanish Arch, where ships from Spain unloaded their cargoes. Across the Corrib, facing the arch, is the Claddagh. The only remnants of this once close-knit, Gaelic-speaking community are its friendly pubs and Claddagh rings – betrothal rings that are traditionally handed down from mother to daughter.

Connemara ⑭

Co. Galway. 🚌 *to Clifden or Letterfrack.* ℹ *Mar–Oct: Galway Road, Clifden (095-21163).* **National Park Visitors' Center** *Tel 095-41 054.* 🕐 *Mar–Oct: daily.* 🖥 🚻

This wild region to the west of Galway encompasses bogs, mountains, and rugged Atlantic coastline. The small market town of Clifden is a convenient and popular base for exploring. Starting from Clifden, the **Sky Road** is an 11-km (7-mile) circular route with spectacular ocean views. South of Clifden, the coast road to Roundstone skirts a massive bog, impromptu landing site of the first transatlantic flight made by Alcock and Brown in 1919.

Connemara National Park near Letterfrack includes some spectacular scenery, dominated by the mountains known as the Twelve Bens. Here visitors have a chance to spot red deer and the famous Connemara ponies.

Nearby **Kylemore Abbey** is a 19th-century romantic, battlemented fantasy. It became an abbey when Benedictine nuns, fleeing from Belgium during World War I, sought refuge here. The building is now a select girls' boarding school, but its gardens, with restaurant, shop, and spectacular lakeside setting make it a popular destination.

Aran Islands ⑮

Co. Galway. 🏃 900. 🛫 *from Connemara (091-593 034).* 🚢 *from Rossaveal (091-568 903); from Doolin (Easter–Sep: 065-707 4455).* ℹ *Kilronan, Inishmore (099-61263).* **Heritage Center** 🕐 *daily.* 🖥 🚻 🚻

Inishmore, Inishmaan, and Inisheer, the three Aran Islands, are formed from a limestone ridge. The largest, Inishmore, is 13 km (8 miles) long and 3 km (2 miles) wide. The attractions of the islands include the austere landscape crisscrossed with dry-stone walls, stunning coastal views, and prehistoric stone forts. The islands are a bastion of traditional Irish culture with most of the islanders engaged in fishing, farming, or tourism. Ferries sail at least once a day in winter and several times daily in summer. Cars cannot be taken to the islands.

At Kilronan on Inishmore, jaunting cars (ponies and traps) and minibuses wait by the pier to give tours; bicycles can also be hired. Nearby, the **Aran Heritage Center** is dedicated to the disappearing Aran way of life. The islands are famous for their distinctive knitwear and traditional costumes.

Northern Ireland

The province of Northern Ireland was created after the partition of the island in 1921. Its six counties (plus Donegal, Monaghan, and Cavan, which became part of the Republic) were part of Ulster, one of Ireland's four traditional kingdoms. Though densely populated and industrialized around Belfast, away from the capital the region is primarily agricultural. It also has areas of outstanding natural beauty, notably the rugged Antrim coastline around the Giant's Causeway.

Mosaic of St. Patrick's journey to Ireland in Belfast Cathedral

Belfast ⑯

Co. Antrim. 🏙 500,000. ✈ 🚉 🚌 🛈 47 Donegall Place (028-9024 6609). 🎪 Royal Ulster Agricultural Show & Lord Mayor's Show (May); Belfast Festival at Queen's (late Oct–Nov).

Belfast was the only city in Ireland to experience the full force of the Industrial Revolution. Its shipbuilding, linen, rope-making, and tobacco industries caused the population to rise to almost 400,000 by the end of World War I. The wealth it enjoyed is still evident in its imposing banks, churches, and other public buildings. The Troubles and the decline of traditional industries have since damaged economic life, but Belfast remains a handsome city and most visitors are agreeably surprised by the genuine friendliness of the people.

Most of Belfast's main streets (and bus routes) radiate out from the hub of Donegall Square. In its center stands the vast Portland stone bulk of the 1906 **City Hall** with its huge central copper dome. Statues around the building include Queen Victoria at the front and, on the east side, Sir Edward Harland, founder of the Harland and Wolff shipyard, which built the *Titanic*. A memorial to those who died when the ship sank in 1912 stands close by.

Sights in and around the square include the **Linen Hall Library**, the late-Victorian **Grand Opera House** in Great Victoria Street, and Belfast's most famous pub, the **Crown Liquor Saloon**, which dates back to the 1880s.

The Neo-Romanesque **Belfast Cathedral** in Donegall Street is the Protestant cathedral, consecrated in 1904. The interior is remarkable for the vast mosaics added by the two Misses Martin in the 1920s. Lord Carson (1854–1935), implacable opponent of Home Rule, is buried in the south aisle.

Away from the center, Belfast has pleasant suburbs unaffected by the civil strife of the Troubles. The area around **Queen's University** to the south of the city has two major attractions in the **Ulster Museum** and the **Botanic Gardens**. The museum covers all aspects of Ulster, from archaeology to technology. Its treasures include jewelry from the *Girona*, a Spanish Armada ship that sank off the Giant's Causeway in 1588.

Detail of Titanic Memorial outside Belfast City Hall

🏛 **Ulster Museum**
Botanic Gardens. **Tel** 0845-608 000. 🕐 10am–5pm Tue–Sun. 🎫 📷 🛗 🔗 www.ulstermuseum.org.uk

Giant's Causeway ⑰

Co. Antrim. 🚉 to Portrush. 🚌 from Portrush, Bushmills, or Coleraine. **Visitors' Center** (028-2073 1855). 🕐 daily. 🅿️ 📷 on request. 🛗 limited. www.giantscausewaycentre.com

The sheer strangeness of the Giant's Causeway and the bizarre regularity of its basalt columns has made it the subject of numerous legends. The most popular tells how the giant, Finn MacCool, laid the causeway to provide a path across the sea to Scotland so he could do battle with a rival Scottish giant called Benandonner. The geological explanation is that 61 million years ago, in a series of volcanic eruptions, molten lava poured from narrow fissures in the ground, filling in the valleys and

The ornate Victorian interior of the Crown Liquor Saloon

For hotels and restaurants in this region see pp136–7 and pp138–9

The extraordinarily regular columns of the Giant's Causeway exposed at low tide

burning the vegetation that grew here. The basalt lava cooled rapidly. In the process it shrank and cracked evenly into polygonal blocks. Towards the end of the Ice Age, erosion by sea ice exposed the rocks and shaped the Causeway. Most of the columns are hexagonal, but some have four, five, eight, or even ten sides. They are generally about 30 cm (12 in) across. There are in fact three causeways, the Grand, Middle, and Little. Distinctive features have been given poetic names, such as the "Honeycomb" and the "Wishing Chair."

Tourists arrive by the busload from the visitors' center. Nothing, however, can destroy the magic of the place, and it is easy to escape the crowds by taking one of the coastal paths.

Old Bushmills Distillery ⑱

Bushmills, Co. Antrim. **Tel** 028-2073 3218. 🚌 from Giant's Causeway & Coleraine. ◯ Mar–Oct: daily; Nov–Feb: daily (pm Sat & Sun). ◯ Good Fri pm, Jul 12, 2 weeks at Christmas. 🎫 🏠 🎥 obligatory. 🍽 ♿ limited.

Bushmills has an attractive square and an excellent river for salmon and trout fishing,

but its main claim to fame is whiskey. The Old Bushmills plant prides itself on being the oldest distillery in the world, its "Grant to Distil" dating from 1608.

In 1974 Bushmills joined the Irish Distillers Group based at the Midleton plant near Cork *(see p126)*, but its brands have retained their distinctive character. "Old Bushmills" is unusual in that it is made from a blend of single malt and a single grain. The tour of the distillery, which features audio-visual displays, ends with a sampling session in the "1608 Bar," which is housed in the former malt kilns.

Whiskey barrel at Old Bushmills

Ulster-American Folk Park ⑲

Co. Tyrone. **Tel** 028-8224 3292. 🚌 from Omagh. ◯ Mar–Sep: 10am–5pm Tue–Sun; Oct–Feb: 10am–4pm Tue–Sun. 🎫 🏠 🍽 ♿ **www**.folkpark.com

One of the best open-air museums of its kind, the Folk Park grew up around the restored boyhood home of Judge Thomas Mellon (founder of the Pittsburgh banking dynasty). The park's permanent exhibition, called "Emigrants," examines why two million people left Ulster

for America during the 18th and 19th centuries. It also shows what became of them, following stories of both fortune and failure.

The park has more than 30 historic buildings, some of them original, some replicas. There are settler homesteads, a mass house, a post office, a schoolhouse, and a forge, some with craft displays, all with costumed interpretative guides. There's also an Ulster streetscape, a reconstructed emigrant ship, and a Pennsylvania farmstead, complete with log barn, corn crib, and smokehouse. The six-roomed farmhouse is based on one built by Thomas Mellon and his father in the early years of their new life in America.

The Centre for Migration Studies assists the descendants of emigrants in tracing their family roots. Popular American festivals, such as Halloween and Independence Day, are celebrated at the park.

Pennsylvania log farmhouse at the Ulster-American Folk Park

Practical & Travel Information

Ireland's capital cities compare favorably to any in Europe for ease of transportation and communications, but in remoter areas the pace of life is slower. In the most isolated parts, public transportation can be infrequent. The division of Ireland into the Republic and Northern Ireland, with separate currencies and communication systems, complicates matters further. Travel in Ireland is best enjoyed if you adopt the Irish approach and just take your time.

TOURIST INFORMATION

Before leaving for Ireland you can get information from **Fáilte Ireland** (Irish Tourist Board) or **Northern Ireland Tourist Board** (NITB) offices. Regional tourist offices provide more detailed information, including accommodations.

In summer, all the sights are open but crowds are naturally at their biggest. In winter many sights keep shorter hours or open only at the weekend and some close down completely.

VISA REQUIREMENTS

Visitors from EU member states, the US, Canada, Australia, and New Zealand need a valid passport but not a visa for entry into the Republic or Northern Ireland. UK nationals do not need a passport to enter the Republic, but may find one useful as proof of identity.

SAFETY AND EMERGENCIES

Ireland is one of the safest places to travel in Europe. Petty theft, such as pickpocketing, is seldom a problem outside certain parts of Dublin and a few other large towns. Tourist offices and hoteliers will gladly point out the areas to be avoided. In Northern Ireland, the main security risk in the recent past has been the threat of bombings, though even at the height of the Troubles this hardly ever affected tourists. Visitors may find, on the rare occasion, they are confronted by a police checkpoint. If you see a sign indicating a checkpoint ahead, slow down and use low beams. Have your passport handy as proof of identity.

Travel insurance for the UK will not cover you for the Republic, so make sure you purchase an adequate insurance policy.

The police are called the Gardaí in the Republic and the Police Service of Northern Ireland (PSNI) in the north.

BANKING AND CURRENCY

The unit of currency in the Republic since 2002 has been the euro (see p15). All euro notes and coins are exchangeable in each of the participating Eurozone countries.

Northern Ireland uses British currency – pounds sterling (£). These currencies are not inter-changeable. Alongside the Bank of England currency in the North, four provincial banks issue their own notes, for use only in the province.

Banking hours are from 10am to 4pm, although some banks close for lunch from 12:30 to 1:30pm.

COMMUNICATIONS

Main post offices in the Republic and Northern Ireland are usually open from 9am to 5:30pm during the week and from 9am to 1pm on Saturdays. The postal service in Northern Ireland is much faster than that in the Republic, where it can take at least five days for a letter to reach the United States.

Most phones in the Republic are operated by Eircom, and in Northern Ireland by British Telecom. Both offer efficient, up-to-date card- and coin-operated public phones.

FLYING TO IRELAND

Flights from most of the large European cities arrive at Dublin Airport. The major airlines operating between Britain and the Republic are **Aer Lingus** and budget rival **Ryanair**, which is based in Ireland. Aer Lingus and **Continental Airlines** fly direct from the US to Shannon Airport, 16 km (10 miles) outside Limerick, as well as to Dublin Airport. Aeroflot flies from Shannon to Moscow via Amsterdam or via Dublin.

There are flights for pilgrims to Knock International Airport from Dublin, London Stansted, Manchester Airport, and others.

Cork airport is served by flights from London (Heathrow and Stansted), Paris, Birmingham, Manchester, and Bristol airports amongst others.

bmi British Midland flies to Belfast International Airport from Cardiff, Manchester, and Birmingham. **easyjet** have flights to Britain, France, Spain, Portugal, Poland, Malta, the Netherlands, and Switzerland from Belfast.

THE CLIMATE OF IRELAND

Rain can be the scourge of a holiday in Ireland, especially on the west coast. However, strong winds off the Atlantic mean that the weather often changes with astonishing speed. Though the rainfall is heavy, winters are mild and there is little snowfall except on the higher mountains. Dublin and the sheltered east coast have the warmest climate and least rainfall.

DUBLIN			
°C/F		19/67	
	12/53	11/51	13/56
0°C	3/38		7/45	7/45
32°F			2/35
☀ 5 hrs	5 hrs	3 hrs	2 hrs
☂ 46 mm	52 mm	67 mm	69 mm
month	Apr	Jul	Oct	Jan

ARRIVING BY SEA

Ferries from ports in Britain and France are a popular way of getting to Ireland, especially with groups or families intending to tour the country by car. There are large seasonal variations in fares, but discounts may be available on internet bookings.

Irish Ferries and **Stena Line** operate regular crossings from Holyhead, Pembroke, and Fishguard in Wales to Dublin Port, Dun Laoghaire, and Rosslare. The fastest routes take about 1 hour 40 minutes. There are also Irish Ferries services from Holyhead to Dublin and to Rosslare from Cherbourg and Roscoff.

The fastest crossing to Belfast is the 1 hour 45 minute Stena Line service from Stranraer in Scotland. **P&O Irish Sea** cross to Larne (north of Belfast) from Cairnryan in Scotland, and **Norfolkline** runs a regular service from Liverpool to Dublin and Belfast.

You can buy combined coach/ferry and rail/ferry tickets from coach offices or train stations all over Britain.

RAIL TRAVEL

Although the more rural areas in the Republic are not served by rail, **Irish Rail** (Iarnród Éireann) operates a service to most large towns. Dublin has two main train stations: Connolly serves the north and the line south along the coast to Rosslare; Heuston serves Cork and the southwest, and Galway and the west. Dublin's local rail service, the DART (Dublin Area Rapid Transit), links towns between Malahide (County Dublin) and Greystones (County Wicklow) with the center. The Luas tramline runs within Dublin city center.

There are two main routes out of Belfast: a line westward to Londonderry, and Ireland's only cross-border service, a high-speed service linking Belfast and Dublin.

BUSES AND TAXIS

The Republic's national bus company, **Bus Éireann**, runs routes to all cities and most towns. **Ulsterbus** runs a service in Northern Ireland, with express links between all major towns. A "Rambler" ticket allows a period of unlimited bus travel in the Republic. In the North, a "Freedom of Northern Ireland" ticket offers the same benefits.

Taxis in Ireland range from saloon cars to people carriers. The most likely places to find taxis are at train and bus stations, hotels, and taxi stands.

CAR RENTAL

Car rental firms do good business, so in summer it is wise to book ahead. Car rental – particularly in the Republic – can be expensive and the best rates are often obtained by reserving in advance online. Broker companies, such as **Holiday Autos** in the UK, will shop around to get the best deal. If you intend to cross the border in either direction, you must inform the rental company, as there may be an additional insurance premium.

In both the Republic and in Northern Ireland, motorists drive on the left as in Great Britain (see p91).

DIRECTORY

TOURIST BOARDS

Fáilte Ireland
In Ireland:
Baggot St Bridge,
Dublin 2.
Tel 01-602 4000.
www.failteireland.ie
In the US:
345 Park Avenue,
New York,
NY 10154.
Tel 1800-223 6470.

Northern Ireland Tourist Board
In Northern Ireland:
St. Anne's Court,
59 North St, Belfast BT1
1NB. **Tel** 028-9023 1221.
www.discovernorthern
ireland.com
In the UK:
103 Wigmore St,
London W1U 1QS.
Tel 020-7518 0800.
www.discoverireland.com

EMBASSIES

Australia
7th Floor, Fitzwilton
House, Wilton Terrace,
Dublin 2.
Tel 01-664 5300.

Canada
7–8 Wilton Terrace,
Dublin 2.
Tel 01-234 4000.

UK
29 Merrion Rd, Dublin 4.
Tel 01-234 4000.

US
42 Elgin Rd, Ballsbridge,
Dublin 4.
Tel 01-668 8777.

EMERGENCY SERVICES

**Police, Ambulance,
and Fire services**
Tel 999 (Republic and NI).

AIRLINES

Aer Lingus
Tel 0818 365 000
(Dublin).
Tel 0870-876 5000 (UK).
Tel 1800-474 7424 (US).
www.aerlingus.com

bmi British Midland
Tel 01-283 0700 (Dublin).
Tel 0870-607 0555 (UK).
www.flybmi.com

Continental Airlines
Tel 1890 925 252
(Dublin).
Tel 1800-523 3273 (US).
www.continental.com

easyjet
Tel 0870-6000 000 (UK).
www.easyjet.com

Ryanair
Tel 0818-303 030
(Dublin).
Tel 0871-246 000 (UK).
www.ryanair.com

FERRY COMPANIES

Irish Ferries
Tel 0818-300 400 (Dublin).
Tel 0870-517 1717 (UK).

Norfolkline
Tel 01-819 2999 (Dublin).
Tel 0844-499 0007 (UK).

P&O Irish Sea
Tel 0140-73434 (Dublin).
Tel 0871-664 4999 (UK).

Stena Line
Tel 01-204 7777 (Dublin).
Tel 0844-770 7070 (UK).

RAIL TRAVEL

Irish Rail (Iarnród Éireann)
Tel 01-836 6222.
www.irishrail.ie

Northern Ireland Railways
Tel 028-9066 6630.
www.translink.co.uk

BUS COMPANIES

Bus Éireann
Tel 01-836 6111.

Ulsterbus/Translink
Tel 028-9066 6630.

CAR RENTAL

Holiday Autos
Tel 0871-472 5229 (UK).

Shopping & Entertainment

Ireland offers a wide range of quality handmade goods, including Aran sweaters, Waterford crystal, fine Irish linen, and Donegal tweed. As with its produce, the best entertainment is local and highly individual. Ireland's cities are well served by theaters, cinemas, and concert venues, but there are many other local events including arts festivals with traditional music and dance. Not to be overlooked is the entertainment provided by a night in an Irish pub. Finally, the beautiful countryside offers the chance to unwind by walking, riding, fishing, or playing a round of golf.

WHERE TO SHOP

The choice of places to shop in Ireland ranges from tiny workshops to large factory outlets, and from chic boutiques to high-street chain stores.

In Dublin, the Temple Bar area contains a number of fashionable craft shops. One of the largest shopping centers in the city is St. Stephen's Green Shopping Centre, full of clothes and craft shops. Near Grafton Street is the Powerscourt Townhouse Shopping Centre.

CRAFTS

Crafts are a flourishing way of life in rural Ireland. The Crafts Council of Ireland, which has branches in Kilkenny and Dublin, can recommend good small-scale specialist stores. Outlets particularly worth visiting include the **Kilkenny Design Centre** and **Bricín**, which sell a wide selection of items.

Established in 19th-century Ulster, the **Belleek Pottery** produces creamy china with intricately worked decorative motifs, such as shamrocks and flowers. **Royal Tara China**, in Galway, is Ireland's leading fine bone china manufacturer, with designs inspired by Celtic themes.

Waterford Crystal is undoubtedly the most famous name in Irish glass-making but there are many other names of similar quality. **Galway Irish Crystal** is an excellent make, available as elegant ornaments and gifts. Jerpoint Abbey in County Kilkenny inspires stylish local designs by **Jerpoint Glass**. With a tradition that dates

back to Celtic times, distinctive jewelry is produced all over Ireland. The Claddagh ring of Galway is the most famous. It is a symbol of friendship, love, and loyalty, and features two hands cradling a crowned heart.

Aran sweaters are sold all over Ireland, but particularly in County Galway and on the Aran Islands. A well-known outlet for these and other knitwear products is **Blarney Woollen Mills**. Donegal tweed is a byword for quality, noted for its texture and subtle colors. It can be bought at **Magee of Donegal**.

Damask linen was brought to Northern Ireland in the late 17th century by Huguenot refugees. The North is still the place for linen, with sheets and table linen on sale in Belfast at **Smyth's Irish Linen**.

Smoked salmon, farmhouse cheeses, handmade preserves, and, of course, Irish whiskey make perfect last-minute gifts.

ENTERTAINMENT LISTINGS AND TICKETS

The tourist board for the Republic, **Fáilte Ireland**, and the **Northern Ireland Tourist Board** (see p133) both publish a yearly *Calendar of Events* that lists major fixtures and events around the country. The regional tourist offices also provide local information.

Tickets are often available on the night but it is safer to book in advance. Most venues will accept credit card bookings. Look at www.dublin.ie for information about the city's nightlife. The free *Dublin Event Guide* is available from pubs and cafés.

ENTERTAINMENT VENUES

In many Irish cities, the main theaters host a wide range of concerts, events, and plays. In central Belfast, the **Grand Opera House** and **Lyric Theatre** put on an interesting program. Dublin's two most famous theaters the **Abbey** and the **Gate Theatre** are renowned for their productions of Irish and international plays, as is the **Cork Opera House**.

Keep an eye out for smaller theater groups around the country. The **Druid Theatre** in Galway puts on an original repertoire and Waterford boasts a resident drama company at the **Garter Lane Arts Centre**.

Other venues for classical music include Dublin's great auditorium, the **National Concert Hall**, the **Crawford Art Gallery** in Cork, and the **Ulster Hall** in Belfast.

The **Waterford Festival of Light Opera** and the **Wexford Festival of Opera** attract opera lovers from around the world. Wexford revives neglected operas while Waterford puts on more mainstream operas and musicals. Dublin's main opera venue is the 19th-century **Gaiety Theatre**.

Rock concerts are held in the **O₂ Dublin** or at the many outdoor sites during the summer. Die-hard rock and jazz fans should search out the musical pubs for Irish bands.

IRISH MUSIC AND DANCE

The Irish pub has helped keep traditional music alive and provided the setting for the musical revival that began in the 1960s. Nights of Irish music and song are scheduled in pubs such as Johnnie Fox's in Dublin, and The Laurels in Killarney. However, sessions of informal or impromptu music are commonplace. Wherever you are, the locals will advise you of the nearest musical pubs.

Popular dance spectaculars have raised the profile, if not the understanding, of real Irish country dance. Visit **Comhaltas Ceoltóirí Éireann**, in Monkstown near Dublin, or any of its branches around the country for genuine traditional music and dance nights all year.

IRISH FESTIVALS

The Irish are expert festival organizers, staging a week of street entertainment, theater, music, and dance to celebrate almost everything under the sun *(see Directory for listings)*.

IRISH PUBS

The Irish pub is known for its convivial atmosphere and the "crack" – the Irish expression for fun. Wit is washed down with the national drinks of whiskey or Guinness.

City pubs often have grand interiors, a testament to the importance of the brewing and distilling industries in Victorian times. In the countryside, pubs provide an important focus for far-flung rural communities and some even double as shops.

Pubs vary greatly throughout the country, so be sure to try out a few wherever you visit. Dublin is famed for its literary pubs; the **Dublin Literary Pub Crawl** is an entertaining way to get a feel for the city's booze-fuelled literary heritage. Spontaneous music sessions are common in the many pubs of Kilkenny and County Clare. Some of the most picturesque establishments are in Cork and Kerry. Galway's tourists and student population guarantee a lively pub atmosphere.

OUTDOOR ACTIVITES

No matter where you are in Ireland, the countryside is never far away. Horses thrive on the green turf and racing is a national passion. A day at the track during

Galway Race Week in July is a great social event. Those who want to do more than just watch should try horse-back riding through the unspoiled countryside.

Another way to experience the countryside is to take a river or canal cruise. **Emerald Star** has a fleet of cruisers for use on the waterways. Alternatively you may want to play golf at one of Ireland's beautiful golf courses, or try some fishing. Maps and locations for fishing are available from the **Central Fisheries Board**. The **Golfing Union of Ireland** can advise on golf courses.

Detailed information on a wide range of outdoor activities is available from **Fáilte Ireland** *(see p133)*, and local tourist offices.

DIRECTORY

CRAFTS

Belleek Pottery
Belleek, Co. Fermanagh.
Tel 028-6865 8501.

Blarney Woollen Mills
Blarney, Co. Cork.
Tel 021-451 6111.

Bricín
26 High Street, Killarney, Co. Kerry.
Tel 064-663 4902.

Galway Irish Crystal
Merlin Park, Galway.
Tel 091-757 311.

Jerpoint Glass
Stoneyford, Co. Kilkenny.
Tel 056-772 4350.

Kilkenny Design Centre
Castle Yard, Kilkenny.
Tel 056-22118.

Magee of Donegal
The Diamond, Donegal.
Tel 073-22660.

Royal Tara China
Tara Hall, Mervue, Galway.
Tel 091-705 602.

Smyth's Irish Linen
65 Royal Ave, Belfast.
Tel 028-9024 2232.

Waterford Crystal
Kilbarry, Waterford.
Tel 051-373 311.

ENTERTAINMENT VENUES

Abbey Theatre
Abbey St Lower, Dublin 1.
Tel 01-878 7222.

Cork Opera House
Emmet Place, Cork.
Tel 021-427 0022.

Crawford Art Gallery
Emmet Place, Cork.
Tel 0214-805 024.

Druid Theatre
Flood St, Galway.
Tel 091-568 660.

Gaiety Theatre
South King St, Dublin 2.
Tel 01-677 1717.

Garter Lane Arts Centre
22A O'Connell St, Waterford.
Tel 051-855 038.

Gate Theatre
Cavendish Row, Dublin 1.
Tel 01-874 4045.

Grand Opera House
Great Victoria St, Belfast.
Tel 028-9024 1919.

Lyric Theatre
Tel 028-9038 5685.
www.lyrictheatre.co.uk

National Concert Hall
Earlsfort Terrace, Dublin 2.
Tel 01-417 0000.

O₂ Dublin
North Wall Quay, Dublin 1.
Tel 01-819 8888.

Ulster Hall
Bedford St, Belfast.
Tel 028-9032 3900.

MUSIC, DANCE, AND FESTIVALS

Comhaltas Ceoltóirí Éireann
32 Belgrave Sq, Monkstown, Co. Dublin.
Tel 01-280 0295.

Dublin Theatre Festival
Assorted drama (Sep/Oct).
44 East Essex St, Dublin 2.
Tel 01-677 8439.

Galway Arts Festival
Theater, music, and dance (Jul). Black Box Theatre, Dyke Rd, Galway.
Tel 091-566 577.

Kilkenny Arts Festival
Visual art, literature, theater, and dance (Aug).
9–10 Abbey Business Centre, Kilkenny.
Tel 056-775 2175.

Waterford Festival of Light Opera
Light opera (late Sep–Oct).
For information contact the Theatre Royal.
Tel 051-874 402.

Wexford Festival of Opera
Opera (Oct–Nov).
Wexford Opera House, High St, Wexford.
Tel 053-912 2144.

IRISH PUBS

Dublin Literary Pub Crawl
1 Suffolk St.
Tel 01-670 5602.

OUTDOOR ACTIVITIES

Central Fisheries Board
Balheary Rd, Swords, County Dublin.
Tel 01-884 2600.
www.cfb.ie

Emerald Star
The Marina, Carrick-on-Shannon, Co. Leitrim.
Tel 071-962 7633.

Golfing Union of Ireland
www.gui.ie

Where to Stay in Ireland

The choice of accommodations in Ireland is enormous: you can stay in an elegant 18th-century country house, a luxurious (or slightly run-down) castle, a Victorian town house, an old-fashioned commercial hotel, or a cozy village inn. Whichever you choose, you can be certain you'll receive a warm welcome.

PRICE CATEGORIES
Price categories for a standard double room per night, including tax, service and breakfast. Prices for Belfast are in pounds sterling.
€ under €65 (£50)
€€ €65–€130 (£50–£100)
€€€ €130–€190 (£100–£150)
€€€€ €190–€260 (£150–£200)
€€€€€ over €260 (£200)

DUBLIN

SOUTHEAST DUBLIN Baggot Court Townhouse
€€   Map F5
92 Baggot St Lower, Dublin 2 **Tel** *01-661 2819* **Fax** *01-661 0253* **Rooms** *16*

Warm and friendly, Baggot Court Townhouse is located in the heart of Georgian Dublin, near the Grand Canal and only a short walk from St. Stephen's Green. All rooms are comfortable, featuring en suite bathrooms, flat-screen TVs, and tea- and coffee-making facilities. Award-winning Irish and continental breakfasts. **www.baggotcourt.com**

SOUTHEAST DUBLIN Buswells
€€€   Map E4
25 Molesworth St, Dublin 2 **Tel** *01-614 6500* **Fax** *01-676 2090* **Rooms** *67*

Comprising five Georgian town houses, this slightly old-fashioned hotel has been in operation since 1882. It has a central location beside government buildings and on a street renowned for high-level commercial art galleries. The sophisticated interior is done in warm colors. Frequented by political figures. **www.quinnhotels.com**

SOUTHEAST DUBLIN Number 31
€€€   Map E5
31 Leeson Close, Leeson St Lower, Dublin 2 **Tel** *01-676 5011* **Fax** *01-676 2929* **Rooms** *20*

Reputedly the most stylish guesthouse in the city, this elegant Georgian house is more of a boutique hotel than a B&B, with individually decorated, luxurious bedrooms. The Coach House features a collection of original art and a sunken seating area. Award-winning breakfasts are served in the plant-filled conservatory. **www.number31.ie**

SOUTHEAST DUBLIN Davenport
€€€€   Map F4
Merrion Square, Dublin 2 **Tel** *01-607 3500* **Fax** *01-661 5663* **Rooms** *115*

Close to the National Gallery, this hotel lies in the heart of Georgian Dublin. The Neo-Classical facade dates from 1863. Mahogany, brass and marble furnishings give it the feel of a gentleman's club. Ample bedrooms are well appointed with warmly colored decor. There's a fitness suite. **www.ocallaghanhotels.com**

SOUTHWEST DUBLIN Avalon House
€   Map C4
55 Aungier St, Dublin 2 **Tel** *01-475 0001* **Fax** *01-475 0303* **Rooms** *70*

One of the longest established hostels in the city, the centrally located Avalon House provides cheap and cheerful accommodations in a restored redbrick Victorian building. Rooms are clean, with pine and tile floors, high ceilings, and an open fire. Popular with young, independent travelers. There's a café in the front. **www.avalon-house.ie**

SOUTHWEST DUBLIN Jury's Christchurch Inn
€€   Map B4
Christ Church Place, Dublin 8 **Tel** *01-454 0000* **Fax** *01-454 0012* **Rooms** *182*

Opposite Christ Church Cathedral, in the old Viking center of Dublin, this modern hotel lies within walking distance of Temple Bar and the city centre. Rooms are neat and well equipped. Bathrooms are adequate, if a little on the small side. Prices charged per room prove particularly good value for families. **www.jurysinn.com**

SOUTHWEST DUBLIN Clarence Hotel
€€€€   Map C3
6–8 Wellington Quay, Dublin 2 **Tel** *01-407 0800* **Fax** *01-407 0820* **Rooms** *49*

Overlooking the River Liffey, this 1852 Dublin landmark was bought by the rock band U2 in 1992 and has acquired cult status. With original wood-paneling in Arts and Crafts style, and luxuriously furnished rooms, this old establishment successfully combines contemporary cool and comfort. **www.theclarence.ie**

NORTH OF THE LIFFEY Gresham Hotel
€€€   Map D2
23 O'Connell St Upper, Dublin 1 **Tel** *01-874 6881* **Fax** *01-878 7175* **Rooms** *288*

One of Dublin's oldest and best-known hotels, the Gresham is a popular rendezvous spot with ever-lively public areas. It has pleasant furnishings that combine classic and contemporary styles, and the well-equipped bedrooms are cheerfully decorated. A good business hotel. **www.gresham-hotels.com**

FARTHER AFIELD Glenogra Guesthouse
€€
64 Merrion Road, Ballsbridge, Dublin 4 **Tel** *01-668 3661* **Fax** *01-668 3698* **Rooms** *12*

This stylish and award-winning guesthouse provides pleasant and good-value B&B accommodations in this leafy, up-market area of Dublin. The owners create a welcoming atmosphere for their guests. Bedrooms are well-appointed and the breakfast is good. **www.glenogra.com**

Map References *see map of Dublin pp112–3*

REST OF IRELAND

BELFAST Europa Hotel

Great Victoria St, Co Antrim, BT2 7AP **Tel** *028-9027 1066* **Fax** *028-9032 7800* **Rooms** *265*

An imposing building in the heart of the Golden Mile, Europa is one of Belfast's best hotels, ideal for business people and tourists. Bill Clinton stayed here during his visits to the city. Standard rooms offer en suite facilities and all other expected amenities. The Grand Opera House and Waterfront Hall are nearby. **www.hastingshotels.com**

CASHEL Cashel Palace Hotel

Main St, Co Tipperary **Tel** *062-62707* **Fax** *062-61521* **Rooms** *23*

Originally a bishop's palace, this beautiful Queen Anne-style house, dating from 1730, is set in its own grounds in the centre of Cashel town. The large, elegant rooms overlook tranquil gardens to the rear and the famed Rock of Cashel. The Bishop's Buttery restaurant serves lunch and dinner. A peaceful retreat. **www.cashel-palace.ie**

CLIFDEN Dolphin Beach Country House

Lower Sky Rd, Co Galway **Tel** *095-21204* **Fax** *095-22935* **Rooms** *9*

This charming beachside house, with its own private cove, is bright and stylish, with a friendly atmosphere. Bedrooms are spacious, with antique furniture and crisp bed linen and there is delicious home cooking in the dining room overlooking the bay. **www.dolphinbeachhouse.com**

CORK Hayfield Manor Hotel

Perrott Ave, College Rd, Co Cork **Tel** *021-484 5900* **Fax** *021-431 6839* **Rooms** *88*

A member of the Small Luxury Hotels of the World, this delightful place is set amid gardens. Though opened in 1996, it has the feel of a fine period house. Elegant furnishings are of a high standard. Generously proportioned and thoughtfully designed bedrooms come with good bathrooms. Excellent leisure facilities. **www.hayfieldmanor.ie**

DINGLE Emlagh House

Dingle, Co Kerry **Tel** *066-915 2345* **Fax** *066-915 2369* **Rooms** *10*

A few minutes' walk from the heart of Dingle, this luxurious guesthouse is set in peaceful landscaped gardens. It is furnished in a tasteful country-house style with Irish art, though a contemporary feel prevails. Bedrooms are cosy, ample and decorated with flowers. Most have harbor views. Closed mid-Nov–Mar. **www.emlaghhouse.com**

GALWAY Galway Bay Hotel

The Promenade, Salthill, Co Galway **Tel** *091-520 520* **Fax** *091-520 530* **Rooms** *153*

The four-star Galway Bay Hotel is located 2 km (1 mile) from Galway city center, overlooking the promenade at Salthill. Rooms are stylishly furnished, and the best ones have views of Galway Bay. There's a choice of both formal and informal dining options, including the award-winning Lobster Pot restaurant. **www.galwaybayhotel.net**

KILKENNY Butler House

16 Patrick St, Co Kilkenny **Tel** *056-776 5707* **Fax** *056-776 5626* **Rooms** *13*

This gracious Georgian town house is an integral part of the Kilkenny Castle estate. Decor is contemporary, with period features such as marble fireplaces and plasterwork ceilings. Bedrooms are large and relatively snug. Excellent breakfasts in the refurbished stables of the castle, which now houses the Kilkenny Design Centre. **www.butler.ie**

KILLARNEY Hotel Dunloe Castle

Killarney, Co Kerry **Tel** *064-664 4111* **Fax** *064-44583* **Rooms** *110*

This modern hotel stands in lovely subtropical gardens, with its award-winning collection of rare plants and flowers, by the ruins of the 13th-century castle. Rooms are large and well appointed. Facilities feature an on-site equestrian centre, indoor tennis courts and fishing on the River Laune. Closed during the winter. **www.thedunloe.com**

KINSALE Old Bank House

11 Pearse St, Co Cork **Tel** *021-477 4075* **Fax** *021-477 4296* **Rooms** *17*

Situated right in the center of town, this used to be a working branch of the Munster and Leinster Bank. Now it is a well-run guesthouse, offering excellent accommodations. Bedrooms are spacious and decorated in a country-house style with good bathrooms. Some enjoy picturesque views of the town. **www.oldbankhousekinsale.com**

LETTERFRACK Rosleague Manor House Hotel

Letterfrack, Co Galway **Tel** *095-41101* **Fax** *095-41168* **Rooms** *20*

This wonderful, 200-year-old Regency Manor is a tranquil retreat. Gardens planted with exotic plants and shrubs sweep down to Ballinakill Bay. Elegantly furnished, it holds great charm and character and provides relaxed luxury and panoramic views. Country house cuisine is superbly executed. Closed during the winter. **www.rosleague.com**

WATERFORD Waterford Castle

The Island, Ballinakill, Co Waterford **Tel** *051-878 203* **Fax** *051-879 316* **Rooms** *19*

Dating from the 15th century, this luxury hotel lies on a private 310-acre island, 5 km (3 miles) outside Waterford city. Reached by a private car ferry, the Castle mixes old-world elegance with modern comfort. Good fine-dining choices as well as an 18-hole golf course and tennis. Non-smoking property. **www.waterfordcastle.com**

Key to Symbols *see back cover flap*

Where to Eat in Ireland

Thanks to the island's high-quality fish and other fresh produce, Irish cooking now ranks among the best in Europe; the town of Kinsale in County Cork has established itself as "Gourmet Capital of Ireland." If your budget is small, it is still possible to eat well, with a wealth of options in both city and rural locations.

PRICE CATEGORIES
Price categories for a three-course meal for one, including half a bottle of house wine, and all extra charges. Prices for Belfast are in pounds sterling:
€ under €25 (£15)
€€ €25–€35 (£15–£25)
€€€ €35–€50 (£25–£35)
€€€€ €50–€70 (£35–£50)
€€€€€ over €70 (£50)

DUBLIN

SOUTHEAST DUBLIN Avoca Café   €

11–13 Suffolk St, Dublin 2 **Tel** *01-672 6019*   **Map** E4

Climb to the top floor of the renowned Irish craft shop, Avoca, and be rewarded with creative, wholesome, and colorful cooking in a bright and airy room. Its popularity is testament to the delicious salads, quiches, tarts, and desserts on offer. There's also a self-service café in the basement offering similar fare for half the price.

SOUTHEAST DUBLIN Trocadero   €€€

3–4 Andrew St, Dublin 2 **Tel** *01-677 5545*   **Map** D3

This much-loved restaurant has been in operation since 1956. A haunt of actors and the literati, it has deep-red walls lined with black-and-white images of the notables who have passed through its doors. Traditional classics include rack of lamb, steak, Dublin Bay prawns, and tempting desserts. Service is intimate and welcoming. Early bird menu.

SOUTHEAST DUBLIN Bang Café   €€€€

11 Merrion Row, Dublin 2 **Tel** *01-676 0898*   **Map** E5

Across the road from the Shelbourne Hotel, this hip restaurant is the essence of stylish minimalism, reflected in its food as well as the decor of natural tones and dark wood furnishings. Contemporary cuisine includes good fish dishes, mouthwatering scallops, and excellent sausages and mash. Service is professional.

SOUTHEAST DUBLIN L'Ecrivain   €€€€€

109a Lower Baggot St, Dublin 2 **Tel** *01-661 1919*   **Map** F5

One of the best restaurants in the city, L'Ecrivain combines classic formality with contemporary cool. Authentic French cuisine with an Irish flavor. Seasonal game and seafood as well as tasty desserts and cheeses also figure on the menu. Service is great.

SOUTHWEST DUBLIN Leo Burdock's   €

2 Werburgh St, Dublin 8 **Tel** *01-454 0306*   **Map** B4

The patrons of Leo Burdock's, the oldest fish-and-chip takeaway in Dublin, include the ordinary folk of Dublin and the stars. Fresh fish and chips made from top-grade Irish potatoes. There's a wide choice of fish including scampi, smoked cod, haddock, and lemon sole goujon. Service is efficient. There's another branch on Liffey Street.

SOUTHWEST DUBLIN Lord Edward   €€€

23 Christchurch Place, Dublin 8 **Tel** *01-454 2420*   **Map** B4

The oldest seafood restaurant in the city, Lord Edward is located above a cosy and traditional pub, which serves lunch downstairs. It has changed little over the years and maintains an old-fashioned feel. Long-established waiters are known for their charming service.

SOUTHWEST DUBLIN The Tea Room   €€€€

The Clarence Hotel, 6–8 Wellington Quay, Dublin 2 **Tel** *01-407 0813*   **Map** C3

The Clarence Hotel is owned by rock band U2. Come in by the Essex Street entrance, opposite the Project Theatre, and savor excellent cuisine served in this stylish dining room. High ceilings and large windows create a bright and airy atmosphere. Menus are innovative and seasonal – try the market menu. The lunch menu is particularly good value.

NORTH OF THE LIFFEY Chapter One   €€€€€

18–19 Parnell Sq, Dublin 1 **Tel** *01-873 2266*   **Map** C1

In the cellar of the Dublin Writers' Museum, Chapter One is often cited by critics as the best restaurant north of the Liffey. Relish the imaginative European cuisine, with an Irish twist, in a dining room of character and comfort. The pre-theater menu is a favorite among regulars who frequent the nearby Gate theater.

FARTHER AFIELD The Lobster Pot   €€€€

9 Ballsbridge Terrace, Ballsbridge, Dublin 4 **Tel** *01-660 9170*

This long-established upstairs restaurant deservedly commands a loyal following. High-quality food is well presented by professional, charming waiters. Specialities feature dressed Kilmore crab, Dublin Bay prawns in Provençal sauce, generously-sized sole on the bone, delicious steaks, chicken, and game dishes.

Map References *see map of Dublin pp138–9*

REST OF IRELAND

BELFAST Cayenne

7 Ascot House, Shaftesbury Sq, Co Antrim, BT2 7DB **Tel** *028-90331532*

Celebrity chef owners Paul and Jeanne Rankin serve a delicious mix of Thai, Japanese, and other Asian-influenced dishes. Exotic and innovative mains, such as spiced breast of duck with Shanghai noodles, sprouting broccoli, oyster mushrooms, and black bean sauce are typical.

BLARNEY Blair's Inn

Cloghroe, Co Cork **Tel** *021-4381470*

Immaculately maintained and very inviting, this pretty whitewashed riverside pub has hanging flower baskets and a lovely garden outside. Inside, open fires and a charming interior are complemented by reliably good, award-winning food. Traditional dishes include casserole of beef and stout, and corned beef.

CASHEL Chez Hans Restaurant

Moore Lane, Co Tipperary **Tel** *062-61177*

Since 1968, patrons have been traveling from all over the county to savor the excellent cooking here. Housed in a converted church, it has become a veritable temple for food-lovers. Dishes showcase succulent Tipperary beef and lamb. Sole on the bone is particularly good. The early-bird dinner is good value. Reservations advised.

CLIFDEN Ardagh Hotel & Restaurant

Ballyconneely Rd, Co Galway **Tel** *095-21384*

This award-winning restaurant, situated on the first floor of the hotel, has lovely views of the sea, particularly at sunset. The modern dining room is welcoming, with linen tablecloths, candles, fresh flowers, and an open fire. On the menu are lobsters from the on-site sea tank, locally caught seafood, and prime meats. Closed during the winter.

CORK Jacobs on the Mall

30a South Mall, Co Cork **Tel** *021-4251530*

This highly acclaimed restaurant, with one of the country's leading chefs, is set in the former Turkish baths. Decorated in a charming contemporary style, it has a unique ambience. Creative and colorful dishes include scallops and crab cakes with mango salad, and a hot-and-sour dressing. Home-made ice creams are irresistible.

DINGLE Lord Baker's Restaurant & Bar

Main St, Co Kerry **Tel** *066-9151277*

Believed to be the oldest bar in Dingle, this welcoming hostelry, with an open fire, serves delicious bar food such as home-made soups, crab claws in garlic butter, and smoked salmon with capers. The restaurant is more formal. Specialties include classic seafood mornay and monkfish wrapped in bacon. Early bird menu available.

GALWAY The Park Room Restaurant

Park House Hotel, Co Galway **Tel** *091-564924*

Located within the pleasant Park House hotel, this restaurant offers Irish and international cuisine of a very good standard. Linen-clad tablecloths and fresh flowers create a relaxed, welcoming atmosphere. Sample dishes include pan-fried fillet of John Dory and ostrich fillet with garlic potato and grilled shallots. Just off Eyre Square.

KILKENNY Zuni

26 Patrick St, Co Kilkenny **Tel** *056-7723999*

Also offering stylish accommodations, Zuni has become a by-word for contemporary chic and superb food in this delightful medieval town. A well-designed restaurant, it has a great atmosphere and tasteful furnishings. The cuisine is worldly in style. Try the tasty risotto, salads, and pasta. Early bird menu available.

KILLARNEY Gaby's Seafood Restaurant

27 High St, Co Kerry **Tel** *064-32519*

A member of the World Master Chefs Society and one of Ireland's longest established seafood restaurants, Gaby's reputedly offers the best seafood in town. Cooking is imaginative and of a high standard with a carefully chosen wine list. A real treat is the lobster "Gaby" with cognac and cream. Desserts are exquisite.

KINSALE Man Friday

Scilly, Co Cork **Tel** *021-4772260*

The oldest restaurant in Kinsale, Man Friday is nationally regarded for its excellent cuisine, unique atmosphere, and friendly service. A recipient of numerous awards, it comprises a number of adjoining rooms of character and a garden terrace, lovely on a summer's evening. There's a great choice of comfort food and a superb seafood platter.

WATERFORD Fitzpatrick's Restaurant

Manor Court Lodge, Cork Rd, Co Waterford **Tel** *051-378851*

In a listed stone building on the outskirts of the city, this bright and colorful fine-dining restaurant is reputed for its classical cuisine with a French influence. Linen-clad tables with fresh flowers and candles create a welcoming atmosphere. Try the roasted sea bass. Staff are courteous and attentive. Reservations are recommended.

Key to Symbols *see back cover flap*

FRANCE AND THE
LOW COUNTRIES

France and the Low Countries at a Glance

France dominates the northwest of continental Europe. To the northeast of France lie Belgium and the Netherlands, known as the Low Countries because they occupy flat plains and land reclaimed from the sea. South of Belgium is the tiny state of Luxembourg. France has some of Europe's greatest attractions, notably the culture and nightlife of Paris. Visitors often choose to tour just one or two of the country's regions: the mountains of the Alps or the Pyrenees, one of the historic wine-growing areas, or the warm south. Belgium and the Netherlands have many historic cities full of fine museums and art galleries. Visiting these countries can be rewarding because all the major sights lie within easy reach of each other.

Paris (see pp150–71), *France's capital, is a city of distinctive districts. Montmartre, the hilltop artists' quarter, is dominated by the Sacré Coeur.*

The Loire Valley (see pp176–9) *is one of France's most popular regions for touring. It is dotted with magnificent châteaux, built by kings and nobles during the Renaissance. One of the finest is Chenonceau.*

- Cherbourg
- St. Malo
- Rennes
- Nantes
- PAR
- Chartres
- Orléa

FRANCE
(See pp144–217)

- Limoges

Southwest France (see pp188–9) *has a huge variety of attractions, from the peaks of the Pyrenees to Atlantic seaside resorts such as Biarritz and the world-famous vineyards of Bordeaux (see p186).*

- Bordeaux
- Biarritz
- Toulouse

0 km   75

0 miles   75

◁ A field of poppies in northeast France, where the battles of World War I were fought

LOCATOR MAP

Amsterdam (see pp248–59) *is a unique city, criss-crossed by canals, its relaxed atmosphere a refreshing change from Europe's other traffic-clogged capital cities.*

Brussels (see pp222–9), *the capital of Belgium, thrives as the headquarters of the European Union. The Grand Place, with its soaring Gothic town hall, is one of Europe's most spectacular squares.*

Dijon (see pp184–5) *flourished in the Middle Ages under the powerful dukes of Burgundy. The former palace where the dukes held court now houses the prestigious Musée des Beaux Arts, with its rich collection of art and sculpture.*

The South of France (see pp190–97) *is one of the traditional playgrounds of Europe's rich and famous, where grand hotels, luxury yachts, and pristine beaches contrast with picturesque old fishing ports.*

Amsterdam

Brussels

Luxembourg City

Reims

Nancy

Strasbourg

Troyes

Dijon

Besançon

Lyon

Grenoble

Marseille

Cannes

FRANCE

The best advocates for visiting France are the French themselves, convinced as they are that their way of life is best, and their country the most civilized on earth. The food and wine are justly celebrated, while French literature, art, cinema, and architecture can be both profound and provocative. France is a country that stimulates the intellect and gratifies the senses.

France belongs to both northern and southern Europe, encompassing regions ranging from Brittany, with its Celtic maritime heritage, and Germanic Alsace-Lorraine, to the Mediterranean sunbelt and the peaks of the Alps and Pyrenees. The capital, Paris, is the country's linchpin, with its intellectual excitement, intense tempo of life, and notoriously brusque citizens.

Strangely, as life in France becomes more city-based and industrialized, so the desire grows to safeguard the old, traditional ways and to value rural life. The idea of life in the country – *douceur de vivre* (the Good Life), long tables set in the sun for the wine and anecdotes to flow – is as seductive as ever for residents and visitors alike. Nevertheless, the rural way of life has been changing. Whereas in 1945 one person in three worked in farming, today it is only one in 20. France's main exports used to be luxury goods such as perfumes, Champagne, and Cognac; today, these have been overtaken by cars, telecommunications equipment, and fighter aircraft. The French remain firmly committed to their roots, however, and often keep a place in the country for vacations or their retirement.

HISTORY

Though famous for the rootedness of its peasant population, France has also been a European melting pot, from the arrival of the Celtic Gauls in the 1st millennium BC, through to the Mediterranean immigrations of the 20th century. Roman conquest by Julius Caesar had an enduring impact but, from the 4th and 5th centuries AD, Germanic invaders destroyed much of the Roman legacy. The Franks provided political leadership in the following centuries, but when their line died out in the late 10th century, France was politically fragmented.

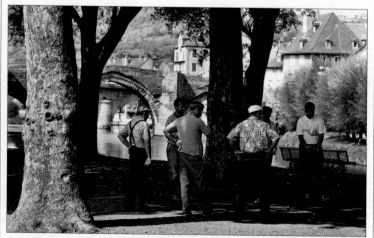

The traditional game of *boules or pétanque*, still a popular pastime – especially in the south

◁ The Château de Saumur, one of the many fairy-tale castles of the Loire Valley

The Capetian dynasty gradually pieced France together over the Middle Ages, a period of economic prosperity and cultural vitality. The Black Death and the Hundred Years' War brought setbacks, and French power was seriously threatened by the dukes of Burgundy and the English crown. In the Renaissance period, François I (reigned 1515–47) dreamt of making France a major power, but was thwarted by the Habsburg Emperor Charles V. The Reformation then plunged the country into religious conflict. However, the 17th century saw France, under Louis XIV, rise to dominate Europe militarily and intellectually.

Napoleon, the brilliant general who rose to be Emperor of France

In the Age of Enlightenment French culture and institutions were the envy of Europe. The ideas of Voltaire and Rousseau undermined the authority of the Church and the state, nowhere more than in France itself. The Revolution of 1789 ended the absolute monarchy and introduced major social and institutional reforms, many of which were endorsed by Napoleon, whose empire dominated Europe at the start of the 19th century. Yet the Revolution also inaugurated the instability that has remained a hallmark of French politics: since 1789, France has seen three forms of monarchy, two empires, and five republics.

Throughout the political turmoil of the 19th century, France remained a leading source of literary and artistic movements. In painting, the French Impressionists were the inspiration for the development of modern art and would-be painters began to flock to Paris instead of Rome. France also retained its position as the arbiter of taste in fashion, food, wine, and good manners.

Rivalry with Germany dominated French politics for most of the late 19th and early 20th centuries. The population losses in World War I were traumatic for France, while during 1940–44 the country was occupied by Germany. Yet since 1955, the two countries have proved the backbone of the developing European Union.

KEY DATES IN FRENCH HISTORY

1200–700 BC Arrival of the Celts during Bronze and Iron Ages

51 BC Romans complete conquest of Gaul

AD 481 Frankish leader Clovis becomes first Merovingian king

800 Coronation of Charlemagne, greatest of the Carolingians, as Holy Roman Emperor

1180–1223 Reign of Philip Augustus

1337–1453 Hundred Years' War with England

1562–93 Wars of Religion

1660–1715 Reign of Louis XIV

1789 French Revolution

1804 Napoleon crowned emperor

1815 Defeat of Napoleon: monarchy restored

1848 Revolution; short-lived Second Republic

1852–70 Second Empire under Napoleon III

1919 Treaty of Versailles after World War I

1940 Germans overrun France

1958 Fifth Republic with president Charles de Gaulle

1968 Student uprising and de Gaulle's downfall

1994 Channel Tunnel opens

2002 Euro replaces Franc as legal tender

2010 Henry IV's skull found; burial ceremony at Basilica St Denis in 2011

2012 New TGV line extends to Barcelona, Spain

MODERN POLITICS

For much of the 20th century, domestic politics was marked by confrontations between Left and Right. In 1958 the problems of governing the country led to the introduction of a new constitution – the Fifth Republic – with Charles de Gaulle as president. However, in 1968

The student uprising of May 1968, which challenged all the old assumptions of the French ruling elite

Avant-garde art and literature and modern architecture enjoy strong patronage in France. Exciting architectural projects range from new buildings in Paris – the Louvre pyramid and La Grande Arche at La Défense – to the post-modern housing projects of Nîmes and Marseille in the south.

CONTEMPORARY SOCIETY

Social change has resulted from the decline in the influence of the Catholic Church. Parental authoritarianism has waned and there is a much freer ambiance in schools – two trends resulting from the May 1968 uprising.

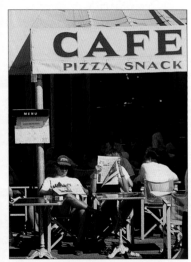

Relaxing in the sun at a traditional French café

protesting students and striking workers combined to paralyse the country and de Gaulle resigned the following year.

The old divide between Left and Right has given way to a more center-focused consensus fostered by François Mitterrand, Socialist President from 1981 to 1995, and forced on the Conservative Jacques Chirac, who succeeded him, by the election of Socialist Lionel Jospin as Prime Minister in 1997. In 2002, however, a landslide victory for the center-right coalition ousted Jospin. The election of Nicolas Sarkozy as President in 2007 confirmed the center-right politics. The Republican spirit lives on in strikes and mass demonstrations. Unemployment has led to growing racism against Arab immigrants.

French social life, except between close friends, has always been marked by formality – handshaking, and the use of titles and the formal *vous* rather than the intimate *tu*. However, this is changing, especially among the young, who now call you by your first name, and use *tu* even in an office context. Standards of dress have become more informal too, though the French are still very concerned to dress well.

Tempting display of *charcuterie* and cheeses on a Lyon market stall

France is a country where tradition and progress are found side by side. The Euro has taken over, yet some people still calculate in old Francs, replaced back in 1960. France's agribusiness is one of the most modern in the world, but the peasant farmer is deeply revered. France has Europe's largest hypermarkets, which have been ousting local grocers. Although American in inspiration, they are French in what they sell, with wonderful displays of cheeses and a huge range of fresh vegetables, fruit, and herbs.

LANGUAGE AND CULTURE

Culture is taken seriously in France: writers, intellectuals, artists, and fashion designers are held in high esteem. The French remain justly proud of their cinema, and are determined to defend it against pressures from Hollywood. Other activities – from the music industry to the French language itself – are subject to the same protectionist attitudes.

The TGV, France's impressive high-speed train

Exploring France

France is a large country and, although it has over 60 million inhabitants, is less densely populated than most of its western European neighbors. Paris belongs to northern Europe, while the south is Mediterranean in climate and lifestyle. Distances limit the amount of the country you can visit, though train services are good and there is an extensive network of highways. Popular tourist destinations include the châteaux of the Loire, the mountains of the Alps and Pyrenees, historic wine-growing regions *(see pp186–7)*, and the resorts of the Côte d'Azur.

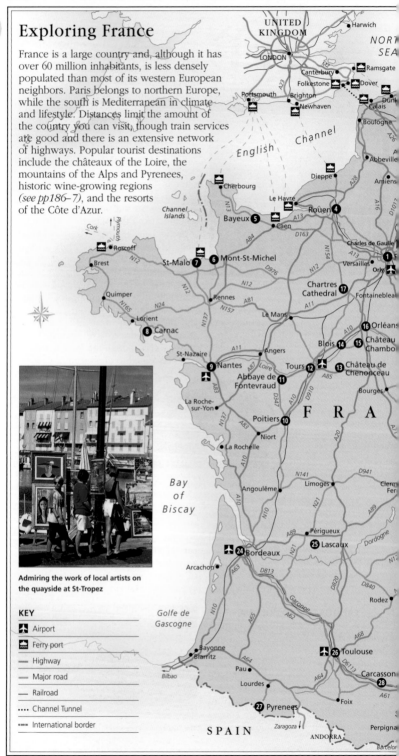

Admiring the work of local artists on the quayside at St-Tropez

KEY

✈	Airport
⛴	Ferry port
—	Highway
—	Major road
—	Railroad
....	Channel Tunnel
-··-	International border

Map labels:

UNITED KINGDOM · Harwich · LONDON · Canterbury · Ramsgate · Folkestone · Dover · Portsmouth · Brighton · Dunk · Calais · Newhaven · Boulogne · NORTH SEA · Channel · English Channel · Abbeville · Dieppe · Amiens · Cherbourg · Le Havre · Rouen ④ · Bayeux ⑤ · Caen · Channel Islands · Charles de Gaulle · Versailles · Orly · Roscoff · Brest · St-Malo ⑦ · Mont-St-Michel ⑥ · Chartres Cathedral ⑰ · Fontainebleau · Quimper · Rennes · Le Mans · Orléans ⑯ · Lorient · Carnac ⑧ · Angers · Blois ⑭ · Château Chambo ⑮ · St-Nazaire · Nantes ⑨ · Abbaye de Fontevraud ⑪ · Tours ⑫ · Château de Chenonceau ⑬ · Bourges · La Roche-sur-Yon · Poitiers ⑩ · Niort · La Rochelle · F R A · Angoulême · Limoges · Clerm Fer · Périgueux · Lascaux ㉕ · Dordogne · Bordeaux ㉔ · Arcachon · Rodez · Bay of Biscay · Golfe de Gascogne · Bayonne · Biarritz · Bilbao · Pau · Toulouse ㉖ · Carcassor ㉘ · Lourdes · Foix · Pyrenees ㉗ · Zaragoza · ANDORRA · Perpigna · SPAIN · Barcel

For additional map symbols *see back flap*

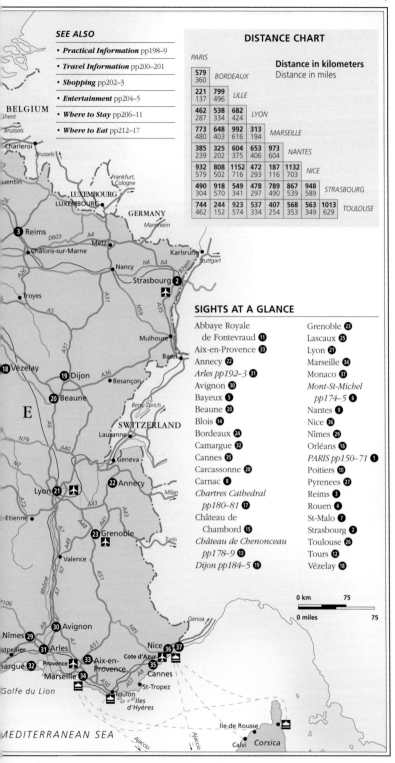

DISTANCE CHART

Distance in kilometers
Distance in miles

PARIS								
579 / 360	BORDEAUX							
221 / 137	799 / 496	LILLE						
462 / 287	538 / 334	682 / 424	LYON					
773 / 480	648 / 403	992 / 616	313 / 194	MARSEILLE				
385 / 239	325 / 202	604 / 375	653 / 406	973 / 604	NANTES			
932 / 579	808 / 502	1152 / 716	472 / 293	187 / 116	1132 / 703	NICE		
490 / 304	918 / 570	549 / 341	478 / 297	789 / 490	867 / 539	948 / 589	STRASBOURG	
744 / 462	244 / 152	923 / 574	537 / 334	407 / 254	568 / 353	563 / 349	1013 / 629	TOULOUSE

SIGHTS AT A GLANCE

Abbaye Royale
  de Fontevraud ⑪
Aix-en-Provence ㉝
Annecy ㉒
Arles pp192–3 ㉛
Avignon ㉚
Bayeux ⑤
Beaune ⑳
Blois ⑭
Bordeaux ㉔
Camargue ㉜
Cannes ㉟
Carcassonne ㉘
Carnac ⑧
Chartres Cathedral
  pp180–81 ⑰
Château de
  Chambord ⑮
Château de Chenonceau
  pp178–9 ⑬
Dijon pp184–5 ⑲

Grenoble ㉓
Lascaux ㉕
Lyon ㉑
Marseille ㉞
Monaco ㉗
Mont-St-Michel
  pp174–5 ⑥
Nantes ⑨
Nice ㊱
Nîmes ㉙
Orléans ⑯
PARIS pp150–71 ①
Poitiers ⑩
Pyrenees ㉗
Reims ③
Rouen ④
St-Malo ⑦
Strasbourg ②
Toulouse ㉖
Tours ⑫
Vézelay ⑱

0 km   75
0 miles   75

Paris ❶

Paris is a city of over two million people, and has been the economic, political, and artistic hub of France since Roman times. During the medieval and Renaissance periods, Paris dominated northern Europe as a religious and cultural center. The city was rejuvenated in the mid-19th century, when its slums were replaced with the elegant avenues and boulevards that make modern Paris a delight to stroll around. Today the city strives to be at the heart of a unified Europe. Chic cafés, gourmet restaurants, and fashionable shopping are the major attractions for many visitors.

Notre-Dame viewed from the tranquil setting of Square Jean XXIII

SEE ALSO

- *Where to Stay* pp206–8

- *Where to Eat* pp212–13

SIGHTS AT A GLANCE

Arc de Triomphe ㉑
Centre Pompidou ④
Champs-Elysées ㉒
Eiffel Tower ⑱
Ile de la Cité ①
Les Invalides ⑰
Jardin du Luxembourg ⑨
Jardin des Tuileries ⑫
Musée du Louvre pp158–60 ⑪
Musée de l'Orangerie ⑬
Musée d'Orsay ⑮

Musée Picasso ⑤
Musée du Quai Branly ⑲
Musée Rodin ⑯
Notre-Dame pp154–5 ②
Palais de Chaillot ⑳
Panthéon ⑧
Place de la Bastille ⑦
Place de la Concorde ⑭
Place des Vosges ⑥
St-Germain-des-Prés ⑩
Sainte-Chapelle ③

Greater Paris *(see inset map)*

Basilique St-Denis ㉙
Bois de Boulogne ㉗
Château de Fontainebleau ㉜
Château de Vaux-le-Vicomte ㉛
Château de Versailles pp168–9 ㉘
Cimetière du Père Lachaise ㉕
La Défense ㉖
Disneyland Paris ㉚
Montmartre ㉓
Parc de la Villette ㉔

GETTING AROUND

The Parisian subway consists of 16 metro lines, referred to by their number and terminus names. In central Paris, these lines overlap the routes of the RER commuter trains, which reach outlying areas. Buses are often the fastest way to travel short distances. The city's night buses are called Noctiliens. Taxis are expensive, but handy after the metro shuts down. A self-service bike system, Vélib, operates in central Paris.

GREATER PARIS

Lille
Charles de Gaulle Airport
Pontoise
Enghien
Le Bourget Airport
St Denis
Bobigny
Disneyland (10 km)
Nanterre
St Germain
Montreuil
Boulogne
Rouen
Versailles
Sceaux
Créteil
Fontainebleau (40 km)
Orly Airport
Vaux-le-Vicomte (20 km)
Reims

0 km   10
0 miles   10

KEY

	Area of main map

KEY

	Sight / Place of interest
✈	Airport
Ⓜ	Metro station
RER	RER station
Ⓟ	Parking
i	Tourist information
✝	Church
✡	Synagogue

0 meters   750
0 yards   750

MARAIS

LATIN QUARTER

ILE ST LOUIS

Western end of the Ile de la Cité, where the island is crossed by the Pont Neuf

Ile de la Cité ①

Ⓜ *Châtelet, Cité*. **Conciergerie** 2 Blvd du Palais. **Tel** *01-53 40 60 80.*
⭘ *daily.* ⬤ *Jan 1, May 1, Dec 25.*
🎦 🎫 *(phone to check).*
www.monuments-nationaux.fr

This boat-shaped island on the Seine is the nucleus of Paris. The capital's name derives from the Parisii, one of the Celtic tribes who lived here in the 3rd century BC. The settlement was later expanded by the Romans, the Franks, and the Capetian kings.

Remains of the earliest buildings can be seen in the **Crypte Archéologique** (closed Monday), below the square in front of the mighty Notre-Dame cathedral, which stands at one end of the island. At the other end is another Gothic masterpiece: the Sainte-Chapelle church, surrounded by the huge complex of buildings forming the **Palais de Justice**. One of these, the sinister-looking **Conciergerie**, was a prison from 1391 until 1914. During the French Revolution the prison filled to overflowing, and Marie-Antoinette was held in a tiny cell here until her execution in 1793. The Conciergerie has a superb Gothic Hall and a 14th-century clock tower.

Crossing the western end of the island is the oldest bridge in Paris, the oddly named **Pont Neuf** (new bridge), which dates back to 1578.

The colorful Marché aux Fleurs et Oiseaux takes place daily in the Place Louis Lépine and is the city's most famous flower market. On Sundays caged birds are also sold.

Notre-Dame ②

See pp154–5.

Sainte-Chapelle ③

4 Boulevard du Palais. **Tel** *01-53 40 60 80.* Ⓜ *Cité.* ⭘ *daily.* ⬤ *Jan 1, May 1, Dec 25.* 🎦 🎫 ♿

Hailed as one of the great architectural masterpieces of the Western world, in the Middle Ages this church was likened to "a gateway to heaven." Sainte-Chapelle was built in 1248 to house sacred relics, including Christ's Crown of Thorns, purchased from the Byzantine emperor at great expense by the devout King Louis IX.

The church consists of two chapels. The lower chapel was used by servants and minor officials, while the exquisite upper chapel, reached by means of a narrow, spiral staircase, was reserved for the royal family and courtiers. This chapel has many

glorious stained-glass windows, separated by pencil-like columns soaring 15 m (50 ft) to the star-studded roof. Over 1,100 biblical scenes from the Old and New Testaments are depicted, as well as the story of how the relics were brought to Sainte-Chapelle. The 86 panels of the circular Rose Window, which are best seen at sunset, tell the story of the Apocalypse.

Badly damaged during the Revolution, and converted into a flour warehouse, the church was renovated a century later by architect Viollet-le-Duc. The spire, erected in 1853, rises 75 m (245 ft) into the air.

The Gothic Sainte-Chapelle church

For hotels and restaurants in this region see pp206–8 and pp212–13

Centre Pompidou ④

Pl G Pompidou. **Tel** 01-44 78 12 33.
Ⓜ *Rambuteau, Châtelet, Hôtel de Ville.* Ⓡ *Châtelet-Les-Halles.*
🚌 *21, 29, 38, 47 & many others.*
Musée National d'Art Moderne
🕐 *11am–9pm Wed–Mon.*
⬤ *May 1.* 🎫 ✔ ♿
www.centrepompidou.fr

With its skeleton of struts, ducts, and elevators scaling the outside of the building, and offering fine views of the city, this famous cultural center has room for a vast exhibition area inside.

Among the artists featured in the Musée National d'Art Moderne are Matisse, Picasso, Miró, and Pollock, representing such schools as Fauvism, Cubism, and Surrealism. Star attractions are *Sorrow of the King* (1952) by Matisse, and Georges Braque's *The Duo* (1937). A library is housed on the first, second, and third floors, while temporary exhibitions are held on the first and sixth floors.

Outside, the Piazza is usually full of crowds watching the street performers. On one side of the square, the Atelier Brancusi is a reconstruction of the workshop of Romanian-born artist Constantin Brancusi (1876–1957), who left his entire *oeuvre* to the nation.

Musée Picasso ⑤

Hôtel Salé, 5 Rue de Thorigny.
Tel 01-42 71 25 21. Ⓜ *St-Sébastien Froissart, St-Paul.* ⬤ *for renovations until 2013.* 🎫 ✔ 📷 ♿ **www**. musee-picasso.fr

The Spanish-born artist Pablo Picasso (1881–1973) spent most of his life in France. On his death, the French state inherited many of his works in lieu of death duties, opening a museum to display them in 1986. Housed in a 17th-century mansion originally built for a salt tax collector, the collection comprises over 200 paintings, 158 sculptures, 100 ceramic works, and some 3,000 sketches and engravings. The full extent of Picasso's artistic development is presented, from the somber

Pipes and ducts on the outside of the Centre Pompidou

Blue period *Self-Portrait* (1901) to Cubist collages and Neoclassical works such as *Pipes of Pan*. Highlights include *The Two Brothers* (1906), *The Kiss* (1969), and *Two Women Running on the Beach* (1922). There is also a sculpture garden. The museum closed at the end of 2009 while a programme of renovations is carried out.

Place des Vosges ⑥

Ⓜ *Bastille, St-Paul.*

This perfectly symmetrical square, laid out in 1605 by Henri IV, and known as Place Royale, was once the residence of the aristocracy. Considered among the most beautiful in the world by Parisians and visitors alike, the square is surrounded by 36 houses, nine on each side. Built of brick and stone, with dormer windows over arcades, they have survived intact for almost 400 years. Today, the historic houses accommodate antiques shops and fashionable cafés.

The square has been the scene of many historical events over the centuries, including a three-day tournament in celebration of the marriage of Louis XIII to Anne of Austria in 1615. Among the square's famous former residents are the literary hostess, Madame de Sévigné, born here in 1626, Cardinal Richelieu, pillar of the monarchy, and Victor Hugo, who lived in one of the houses for 16 years.

Place de la Bastille ⑦

Ⓜ *Bastille.*

Nothing remains of the infamous prison stormed by the revolutionary mob on July 14, 1789, the event that sparked the French Revolution. A row of paving stones from No. 5 to No. 49 Boulevard Henri IV traces the line of former fortifications.

The 52-m (170-ft) hollow bronze Colonne de Juillet stands in the middle of the traffic-clogged square to honor the victims of the July Revolution of 1830. On the south side of the square (at 120 Rue de Lyon) is the 2,700-seat **Opéra Bastille**, completed in 1989, the bicentennial of the French Revolution.

Central fountain and fine Renaissance houses in the Place des Vosges

Notre-Dame ②

No other building embodies the history of Paris more than Notre-Dame. It stands majestically on the Ile de la Cité, cradle of the city. Built on the site of a Roman temple, the cathedral was commissioned by Bishop de Sully in 1160. The first stone was laid in 1163, marking the start of two centuries of toil by armies of medieval architects and craftsmen. It has been witness to great events of French history ever since, including the coronation of Napoleon Bonaparte (1804) and the state funeral of Charles de Gaulle (1970). During the Revolution, the building was desecrated and rechristened the Temple of Reason. Extensive renovations (including the addition of the spire and gargoyles) were carried out in the 19th century by architect Viollet-le-Duc.

★ West Front
Three main portals with superb statuary, a central rose window, and an openwork gallery are the outstanding features of the cathedral's facade.

The South Tower houses Emmanuel, the cathedral's most sonorous bell.

★ Galerie des Chimières
The cathedral's grotesque gargoyles (chimières) perch menacingly around ledges high on the facade.

The West Rose Window depicts the Virgin in a medallion of rich reds and blues.

STAR FEATURES

- ★ West Front and Portals
- ★ Flying Buttresses
- ★ Rose Windows
- ★ Galerie des Chimières

The Kings' Gallery features 28 kings of Judah gazing down from above the main door.

★ Portal of the Virgin
A statue of the Virgin surrounded by kings decorates this massive 13th-century portal.

★ **Flying Buttresses**
Jean Ravy's spectacular flying buttresses at the east end of the cathedral have a span of 15 m (50 ft).

VISITORS' CHECKLIST

6 Place du Parvis-Notre-Dame.
Tel 01-42 34 56 10. **M** Cité.
21, 38, 47, 85, 96 to Ile de la Cité.
8am–6:45pm daily, to 7:15pm
Sat & Sun (Treasury: 9:30am–6pm
Mon–Fri, to 6:30pm Sat; from
1:30pm Sun); towers: daily.)
8am, 9am, noon, 6:15pm Mon–
Fri; 8am, 9am, noon, 6:30pm Sat;
8:30am, 10am, 11:30am,
12:45pm, 6:30pm Sun. for
Treasury and towers.

The Spire, designed by Viollet-le-Duc, soars to a height of 90 m (295 ft).

★ **South Rose Window**
The south facade window, with its central depiction of Christ, is an impressive 13 m (43 ft) in diameter.

The Treasury houses the cathedral's religious treasures, including ancient manuscripts and reliquaries.

The transept was completed during the reign of Louis IX, in the 13th century.

Statue of Virgin and Child
Against the southeast pillar of the crossing stands the 14th-century statue of the Virgin and Child. It was brought to the cathedral from the chapel of St. Aignan and is known as Notre-Dame de Paris (Our Lady of Paris).

The Cathedral from the Left Bank
Notre-Dame's spectacular island setting is enhanced by the trees of Square Jean XXIII, a formal garden laid out at the eastern end of the Ile de la Cité.

Street-by-Street: Latin Quarter

Since the Middle Ages this riverside quarter has been dominated by the Sorbonne – it acquired its name from early Latin-speaking students. The area is generally associated with artists, intellectuals, and a bohemian way of life, and has a history of political unrest. In 1871 the Place St-Michel became the center of the Paris Commune, and in May 1968 it was one of the sites of the student uprisings that briefly engulfed the city.

St-Séverin
Begun in the 13th century, this beautiful church took three centuries to build and is a fine example of the Flamboyant Gothic style.

St-Michel Ⓜ

★ Boulevard St-Michel
The northern end of the Boul'Mich, as it is affectionately known, is a lively mélange of cafés, bookshops, and clothes stores, with nightclubs and experimental film houses nearby.

QUAI ST MICHEL

RUE DE LA HARPE

RUE DU PETIT P

BLVD ST MICHEL

Ⓜ

BLVD ST GERMAIN

Cluny-
La Sorbonne

BLVD ST JACQUES

Little Athens
takes its name from the many Greek restaurants situated in its picturesque streets.

RUE THENARD

BLVD ST

RUE DES ECOLES

★ Musée National du Moyen Age
The museum holds a fine collection of medieval art, with many beautiful tapestries. This detail is from the late 15th-century series of tapestries The Lady with the Unicorn.

| 0 meters | 100 |
| 0 yards | 100 |

For hotels and restaurants in this region see pp206–8 and pp212–13

LA SORBONNE

Seat of the University of Paris until 1969, the Sorbonne was established in 1257 by Robert de Sorbon, confessor to Louis IX, to enable poor scholars to study theology. It achieved fame as a center of learning in the late Middle Ages. The first printing house in France was founded here in 1469. Suppressed during the Revolution for opposition to liberal, 18th-century philosophical ideas, and re-established by Napoleon in 1806, the Sorbonne split into 13 separate universities in 1971. Lectures are still held on the original site.

St-Julien-le-Pauvre, one of the oldest churches in Paris, dates back to the 12th century.

Maubert-Mutualité

KEY

– – – Suggested route

STAR SIGHTS

★ Musée National du Moyen Age

★ Boulevard St-Michel

View of the Panthéon from the Jardin du Luxembourg

Panthéon ⑧

Place du Panthéon. **Tel** 01-44 32 18 00 Ⓜ Place Monge, Cardinal-Lemoine. ◯ daily. ● Jan 1, May 1, Jul 14, Dec 25. 🖼 🚻

Famous as the last resting place of some of France's greatest citizens, this magnificent church was built between 1764 and 1790 to honor Sainte Geneviève, patron saint of Paris. During the Revolution it was turned into a pantheon, to house the tombs of the illustrious.

Based on Rome's pantheon, the temple portico has 22 Corinthian columns, while the tall dome was inspired by that of St. Paul's in London (see p58). Geneviève's life is celebrated in a series of 19th-century nave murals. Many French notables rest in the crypt, including Voltaire, Rousseau, and Victor Hugo. The ashes of Pierre and Marie Curie are also held here.

De Médicis fountain in the Jardin du Luxembourg

Jardin du Luxembourg ⑨

Ⓜ Odéon. ⒭ⒺⓇ Luxembourg. ◯ daily.

This graceful and historic area offers a peaceful haven in the heart of Paris. The gardens, which cover 25 ha (60 acres), were opened to the public in the 19th century by their then owner, the Comte de Provence. They are centered around the Luxembourg Palace, which was built for Marie de Médicis, the widow of Henri IV, and is now the home of the French Senate. Dominating the gardens is an octagonal lake surrounded by formal terraces, where sunbathers gather on fine summer days.

St-Germain-des-Prés ⑩

3 Place St-Germain-des-Prés. **Tel** 01-55 42 81 33. Ⓜ St-Germain-des-Prés. ◯ daily. 🚻 (reserve in advance)

Originating in 558 as a basilica to house holy relics, this is the oldest church in Paris. St-Germain had become a powerful Benedictine abbey by the Middle Ages, but was largely destroyed by fire in 1794. Major restoration took place in the 19th century. A single tower survives from the original tower, housing one of the most ancient belfries in France. Famous tombs include that of 17th-century philosopher, René Descartes.

After World War II, the area attracted writers and artists, including one of the leading figures of the Existentialist movement, Jean-Paul Sartre, and writer Simone de Beauvoir. Bars and cafés, such as *Les Deux Magots* and the *Café de Flore*, which were their daily haunts, are now popular with tourists.

Musée du Louvre ⑪

The Musée du Louvre, containing one of the world's most important art collections, has a history dating back to medieval times. First built as a fortress in 1190 by King Philippe-Auguste, it lost its dungeon and keep in the reign of François I, who commissioned a Renaissance-style building. Thereafter, four centuries of kings and emperors improved and enlarged the palace. It was first opened as a museum in 1793 under the First Republic. Work on new collections is due to finish in 2015.

The Louvre's east facade, added in the 17th century

Pyramid entrance

The Jardin du Carrousel was once the grand approach to the Tuileries Palace, which was set ablaze in 1871 by insurgents of the Paris Commune.

The Carrousel du Louvre underground visitors' complex (1993), with galleries, shops, restrooms, parking, and an information desk, lies beneath the Arc de Triomphe du Carrousel.

Denon Wing

Cour Visconti

The inverted glass pyramid brings light to the subterranean complex, echoing the new main entrance to the museum in the Cour Napoléon.

BUILDING THE LOUVRE

Over many centuries the Louvre was enlarged by a succession of French rulers and latterly by the state, shown below with their dates.

MAJOR ALTERATIONS

▪	Reign of François I (1515–47)
▫	Catherine de' Médici (about 1560)
▪	Reign of Henri IV (1589–1610)
▪	Reign of Louis XIII (1610–43)
▫	Reign of Louis XIV (1643–1715)
▪	Reign of Napoleon I (1804–15)
▪	Reign of Napoleon III (1852–70)
▫	François Mitterrand (1981–95)

★ **Arc de Triomphe du Carrousel**
This triumphal arch was built to celebrate Napoleon's military victories in 1806.

STAR FEATURES

★ Perrault Colonnade

★ Medieval Moats

★ Arc de Triomphe du Carrousel

For hotels and restaurants in this region see pp206–8 and pp212–13

THE GLASS PYRAMID

Plans for the modernization and expansion of the Louvre were first conceived in 1981. These included the transfer of the Ministry of Finance from the Richelieu wing to offices elsewhere and a new main entrance.

This took the form of a metal and glass pyramid designed by architect I.M. Pei. Opened in 1989, the pyramid enables the visitor to see the surrounding buildings, while allowing light down into the underground visitors' reception area.

VISITORS' CHECKLIST

Entrance through Pyramid or directly from metro. **Tel** *01 40 20 53 17.* [M] *Palais-Royal, Louvre Rivoli, Musée du Louvre.* [=] *21, 24, 27, 39, 49, 68, 69, 72, 81, 95.* [RER] *Châtelet-les-Halles.* [P] *Carrousel du Louvre (entrance via Ave du Général Lemmonnier); Place du Louvre, Rue St-Honoré.* **Museum** [ ] *9am–6pm Wed–Sun.* [ ] *Jan 1, May 1, Aug 15, Dec 25.* **Hall Napoléon** *(including History of the Louvre, Medieval Louvre, temporary exhibitions, restaurants, bookshop.)* [ ] *9am–10pm (6pm for exhibitions) Wed–Mon.* [ ] *same as museum.* [ ] *(reduced after 6pm)* [ ] *partial.* [ ] *phone 01 40 20 55 55.* **www.louvre.fr**

Cour Marly is a glass-roofed courtyard that houses the famous *Marly Horses*, sculpted by Antoine Coysevox (1706) and Guillaume Coustou (1745) for the royal château at Marly.

Richelieu Wing

The Hall Napoléon, where temporary exhibitions are held, is situated under the pyramid.

Sully Wing

Cour Carrée

★ **Perrault's Colonnade**
The east façade, with its majestic rows of columns, was built by Claude Perrault, who worked on the Louvre with Louis Le Vau in the mid-17th century.

The Salle des Caryatides is named after the four monumental statues created by Jean Goujon in 1550 to support the upper gallery. Built for Henri II, it is the oldest room in the palace.

The Cour Napoléon dates mostly from the 19th century.

Philippe-Auguste's old fortress, with its distinctive tower and keep, was transformed into a royal residence by Charles V in about 1365.

★ **Medieval Moats**
The base of the twin towers and the drawbridge support of Philippe-Auguste's fortress can be seen in the excavated area.

Exploring the Louvre's Collection

Owing to the vast size of the Louvre's collection, it is useful to set a few viewing priorities before starting. The collection of European paintings (1400–1848) is comprehensive, with over half the works by French artists. The extensively renovated departments of Oriental, Egyptian, Greek, Etruscan, and Roman antiquities are of world renown and feature numerous new acquisitions and rare treasures. The hugely varied display of *objets d'art* includes furniture, jewelry, scientific instruments, and armor.

The famously enigmatic *Mona Lisa* (c.1504) by Leonardo da Vinci

EUROPEAN PAINTING: 1400 TO 1848

Notable Flemish paintings include Jan van Eyck's *Madonna of the Chancellor Rolin* (c.1435). The fine Dutch collection features *Self-portrait* and *Bathsheba* (1654), both by Rembrandt. Among important German works are a *Venus* (1529) by Lucas Cranach and a portrait of Erasmus by Hans Holbein.

Italian paintings are arranged chronologically, and include Fra Angelico's *Coronation of the Virgin* (1435) and the celebrated *Mona Lisa* (1504) by Leonardo da Vinci.

Outstanding French works are represented by Enguerrand Quarton's *Villeneuve-lès-Avignon Pietà* (1455) and the delightfully frivolous *The Bathers* (1770) by Fragonard.

Among English artists featured are Gainsborough, Reynolds, and Turner, while the Spanish collection has portraits by Goya and works by El Greco and Zurbarán.

EUROPEAN SCULPTURE: 1100 TO 1848

The French section opens with a 12th-century figure of Christ and a head of St. Peter. Several works by French sculptor Pierre Puget (1620–94) are assembled in a glass-covered courtyard. Other masterpieces of French sculpture, including Jean-Antoine Houdon's busts of Diderot and Voltaire, stand in the Cour Marly. A notable Flemish sculpture is Adrian de Vries's long-limbed *Mercury and Psyche* (1593). Michelangelo's *Slaves* and Benvenuto Cellini's *Fontainebleau Nymph* are among the many splendid Italian works.

ORIENTAL AND EGYPTIAN ANTIQUITIES

Important works of Mesopotamian art include one of the world's oldest documents, a basalt block, bearing a proclamation of laws by Babylonian King Hammurabi, from about 1750 BC.

The warlike Assyrians are represented by delicate carvings, and a fine example of Persian art is the enameled brickwork depicting the king's archers (5th century BC).

Egyptian art on display, dating from between 2500 and 1400 BC, and mostly produced for the dead, includes lifelike funeral portraits, such as the *Squatting Scribe*, and several sculptures of married couples.

GREEK, ETRUSCAN, AND ROMAN ANTIQUITIES

The famous Greek marble statues here, the *Winged Victory of Samothrace* and the *Venus de Milo*, both date from the Hellenistic period (late 3rd to 2nd century BC). A highlight of the Roman section is a 2nd-century AD bronze head of the Emperor Hadrian. Other fine pieces include a bust of Agrippa and a basalt head of Livia. The star of the Etruscan collection is the terra-cotta sarcophagus of a married couple. Among the vast array of earlier fragments, a geometric head from the Cyclades (2700 BC) and a swan-necked bowl hammered out of a gold sheet (2500 BC) are noteworthy.

OBJETS D'ART

More than 8,000 items feature in this collection, many of which came from the Abbey of St-Denis, where the kings of France were crowned. Treasures include a serpentine plate from the 1st century AD and a golden scepter made for King Charles V in about 1380. The French crown jewels include the splendid coronation crowns of Louis XV and Napoleon, scepters, and swords. The Regent, one of the purest diamonds in the world, worn by Louis XV at his coronation in 1722, is also on show.

Venus de Milo

An entire room is taken up with a series of tapestries, the *Hunts of Maximilian*, executed for Emperor Charles V in 1530. The large collection of French furniture ranges from the 16th to the 19th centuries, and includes pieces by exceptional furniture-maker André Charles Boulle. He is particularly noted for his technique of inlaying copper and tortoiseshell. Among more unusual items is Marie-Antoinette's inlaid steel and bronze writing desk.

Neoclassical statues and urns
in the Jardin des Tuileries

Jardin des Tuileries ⑫

M *Tuileries, Concorde.* ☐ *Apr–Sep:
7am–9pm daily; Oct–Mar: 7:30am–
7pm daily.*

These gardens once belonged
to the Palais des Tuileries,
a palace which was razed to
the ground during the time of
the Paris Commune in 1871.

The gardens were laid out in
the 17th century by André Le
Nôtre, royal gardener to Louis
XIV. He created a Neoclassical
garden with a broad central
avenue, regularly spaced
terraces, and topiary arranged
in geometric designs. A project
which started in 1998 created a
garden with lime and chestnut
trees and striking modern
sculptures. Also in the gardens,

Entrance to the great collection of Impressionist
and other paintings at the Musée de l'Orangerie

two royal tennis courts built in
1851 and known as the *Jeu de
Paume* – literally "game of the
palm" – now host exhibitions
of contemporary art.

Musée de l'Orangerie ⑬

*Jardin des Tuileries, Place de la
Concorde.* **Tel** *01-44 77 80 07.*
M *Concorde.* 🚌 *24, 42, 52, 72,
73, 84, 94.* ☐ *9am–6pm
Wed–Mon.* ● *May 1, Dec 25.*
🎫 🖥 🛇 ♿
www.musee-orangerie.fr

The museum reopened in
2006 following a long closure
for restructuring. Claude
Monet's crowning work, his
celebrated water lily series,
still takes pride of place here.
Known as the *Nymphéas*, most
of the canvases were painted
between 1899 and 1921 in the
garden at Giverny, Normandy,
where Monet lived from 1883
until his death at the age of 86.

This superb work is com-
plemented by the Walter-
Guillaume collection of artists
of the Ecole de Paris, from
the late Impressionist era to
the inter-war period. Among a
number of paintings by
Cézanne are still lifes,
portraits such as *Madame
Cézanne*, and landscapes.
The collection also features
The Red Rock. There are 24
canvases by Renoir,
one the most
notable of which
is *Les Jeunes Filles
au Piano*. Picasso
is represented by
early works such
as *The Female
Bathers*. Henri
Rousseau has nine
paintings, including
*The Wedding and
Le Carriole du Père
Junier*. Among
outstanding
portraits is that of
by Modigliano.
Works by Sisley,
Derain, and Utrillo
are also featured.
All the works are
bathed in the
natural light that
filters through the
windows of
the museum.

Place de la Concorde ⑭

M *Concorde.*

One of Europe's most
magnificent and historic
squares, covering over 8 ha
(20 acres), the Place de la
Concorde was a swamp until
the mid-18th century. It
became the Place Louis XV in
1763 when royal architect
Jacques-Ange Gabriel was
asked by the king to design a
suitable setting for an
equestrian statue of himself.
He created an open octagon,
with only the north side
containing mansions.

The statue, which lasted
here less than 20 years,
was replaced by the
guillotine (the Black
Widow, as it came to
be known), and the
square was renamed
Place de la Révolution.
On January 21, 1793,
Louis XVI was
beheaded here,
followed by over
1,300 other victims,
including Marie
Antoinette, Madame
du Barry, Charlotte
Corday (Marat's
assassin), and
revolutionary
leaders Danton
and Robespierre.
The blood-soaked
square was
optimistically
renamed Place de
la Concorde after
the Reign of Terror
finally came to an
end in 1794.

The grandeur
of the square was
enhanced a few
decades later when
the 3,200-year-old Luxor
obelisk was presented to King
Louis-Philippe as a gift from
the viceroy of Egypt (who
also donated Cleopatra's
Needle in London). Two
fountains and eight statues
personifying French cities
were also installed.

Flanking the Rue Royale on
the north side of the square
are two of Gabriel's
Neoclassical mansions, the
Hôtel de la Marine and the
exclusive Hôtel Crillon.

**Obelisk in Place
de la Concorde**

Interior of the Musée d'Orsay, showing original station architecture

Musée d'Orsay ⑮

Rue de la Légion d'Honneur. **Tel** 01-40 49 49 78. **M** Solférino. **RER** Musée d'Orsay. 24, 68, 69, 84 & many others. ◯ Tue–Sun. ● Jan 1, May 1, Dec 25. 🎫 🎥 ♿ **www**.musee-orsay.fr

Originally built as a rail terminus in the heart of Paris, Victor Laloux's superb building, completed in 1900, narrowly avoided demolition in the 1970s. In 1986 it reopened as the Musée d'Orsay, with much of the original architecture preserved. The majority of the exhibits are paintings and sculptures dating from between 1848 and 1914, but there are also displays of furniture, the decorative arts, and cinema. The social, political, and technological context in which these diverse visual arts were created is explained.

Paintings from before 1870 are on the ground floor, presided over by Thomas Couture's massive *Romans in the Age of Decadence* (1847). Neoclassical masterpieces, such as Ingres' *La Source*, hang near Romantic works like Delacroix's turbulent *Tiger Hunt* (1854), and canvases by Degas and Manet, including the latter's *Le Déjeuner sur l'Herbe* and *Olympia* (1863).

The museum's central aisle overflows with sculpture, from Daumier's satirical busts of members of parliament to Carpeaux's exuberant *The Dance* (1868). Decorative arts and architecture are on the middle level, where there is

also a display of Art Nouveau, including Lalique glassware. Impressionist works on the upper level include Renoir's *Bal du Moulin de la Galette* (1876). Matisse's *Luxe, Calme et Volupté* is among highlights of the post-1900 collection.

Musée Rodin ⑯

79 Rue de Varenne. **Tel** 01-44 18 61 10. **M** Varenne. **RER** Invalides. 6, 9, 82, 87, 92. ◯ Tue–Sun. ● Jan 1, May 1, Dec 25. ♿ restricted. **www**.musee-rodin.fr

Auguste Rodin (1840–1917), widely regarded as one of France's greatest sculptors, lived and worked here in the Hôtel Biron, an elegant 18th-century mansion, from 1908 until his death. In return for a state-owned flat and studio, Rodin left his work to the nation, and it is now exhibited here. Some of his most celebrated sculptures are on display in the attractive garden and include *The Burghers of Calais, The Thinker, The Gates of Hell,* and *Balzac.*

The indoor exhibits are arranged in chronological order, spanning the whole of Rodin's career. Major works in the collection include *The Kiss* and *Eve.*

Rodin's The Kiss (1886) at the Musée Rodin

Les Invalides ⑰

M La Tour-Maubourg, Varenne. **RER** Invalides. 28, 63, 69 & many others. **Hôtel des Invalides Tel** 08-10 11 33 99. ◯ daily. ● Jan 1, May 1, Nov 1, Dec 25. **St-Louis-des-Invalides Tel** 01-44 42 37 72. ◯ daily. **Dôme Church Tel** 01-44 42 37 72. ◯ daily. ● Jan 1, May 1, Jun 17, Nov 1, Dec 25, first Mon of each month (except Jul & Aug). 🎫 🎥 ♿ restricted.

This vast ensemble of monumental buildings is one of the most impressive architectural sights in Paris. The imposing **Hôtel des Invalides**, from which the area takes its name, was commissioned by Louis XIV in 1671 for his wounded and homeless veterans. Designed by Libéral Bruand, it was completed in 1676 by Jules Hardouin-Mansart. Nearly 6,000 soldiers once resided here; today there are fewer than 100. Behind the Hôtel's harmonious Classical facade – a masterpiece of French 17th-century architecture – are several museums.

The **Musée de l'Armée** is one of the most comprehensive museums of military history in the world, with exhibits covering all periods from the Stone Age to World War II. Among items on display are François I's ivory hunting horns and a selection of arms from China, Japan, and India. The **Musée de l'Ordre de la Libération** was set up to honor feats of heroism during World War II, while the **Musée des Plans-Reliefs** has an extensive collection of detailed models of French forts and fortified towns, considered top secret until as late as the 1950s.

St-Louis-des-Invalides, the chapel of the Hôtel des Invalides, is also known as the "soldiers' church." It was built from 1679 to 1708 by Jules Hardouin-Mansart, to Bruand's design. The stark, Classical interior is designed in the shape of a Greek cross and has a fine 17th-century organ by Alexandre Thierry.

The **Dôme Church** was begun in 1676 to complement the existing buildings of Les Invalides, and to reflect the splendor of Louis XIV's reign. Reserved for the exclusive use of the Sun King himself, the resulting masterpiece is one of the greatest examples of *grand siècle* architecture and a monument to Bourbon glory. The crypt houses the tomb of Napoleon – six coffins with an enormous red sarcophagus on a pedestal of green granite. Marshal Foch, the World War I hero, is also buried here.

Facade of the Hôtel des Invalides, showing the splendid gilded dome

Eiffel Tower ⑱

Built for the Universal Exhibition of 1889, and to commemorate the centennial of the Revolution, the 324-m (1,063-ft) Eiffel Tower (Tour Eiffel) was meant to be a temporary addition to the Paris skyline. Designed by Gustave Eiffel, it was fiercely decried by 19th-century aesthetes. It was the world's tallest building until 1931, when New York's Empire State Building was completed. A number of crazy stunts have been attempted here. In 1912 a local tailor launched himself from the tower using a cape as wings. He plunged to his death.

Double-decker elevators take visitors to the top level, which can hold up to 400 people at a time.

The Jules Verne Restaurant is one of the best in Paris, offering excellent food and panoramic views.

VISITORS' CHECKLIST

Champ-de-Mars. **Tel** *08-92 70 12 39*. Ⓜ *Bir Hakeim*. 🚇 *Champ-de-Mars, Trocadéro*. 🚌 *42, 69, 82, 87*. ⬜ *daily*. 🅿 🅰 *limited*. 🅿 🍴 www.tour-eiffel.fr

The third level, 276 m (905 ft) above the ground, offers superb views. On a clear day it is possible to see for 72 km (45 miles) – as far as Chartres Cathedral *(see pp180–81)*.

The second level, at 115 m (376 ft), is reached either by elevator or by 359 steps from the first level.

THE EIFFEL TOWER IN FIGURES

- There are a total of 1,665 steps from bottom to top
- The tower is held together by a total of 2.5 million rivets
- It never sways more than 7 cm (2.5 in)
- The tower weighs 10,100 tons
- 50 tons of paint are used every seven years

The Eiffel Tower at night

The first level, at 57 m (187 ft), can be reached by elevator or by 345 steps. There is a restaurant here.

Trocadéro fountains in front of the Palais de Chaillot

Musée du Quai Branly ⑲

22 Rue de l'Université. **Tel** 01-56 61 70 00. **M** Alma-Marceau. **RER** Pont de l'Alma. ☐ Tue–Sun. 🦽 ⫙ 🛗 **www**.quaibranly.fr

Built to give the arts of Africa, Asia, Oceania, and the Americas a platform as shining as that reserved for Western art, this museum boasts a collection of more than 3,000 objects. It is particularly strong on Africa, with stone, wooden, and ivory masks, as well as

ceremonial tools. The Jean Nouvel-designed building, raised on stilts, is a sight in itself: the ingenious use of glass allows the surrounding greenery to act as a natural backdrop for the collection.

Palais de Chaillot ⑳

Place du Trocadéro 17. **M** Trocadéro. **RER** Trocadéro. 🚌 27, 30, 32, 63, 72, 82. **Museums** ☐ Wed–Mon. 🦽 ⫙

With its curved colonnaded wings, each culminating in a vast pavilion, this palace was

designed in Neoclassical style for the 1937 Paris Exhibition by Azéma, Louis-Hippolyte Boileau, and Jacques Carlu. It is adorned with sculptures and bas-reliefs, and the pavilion walls are inscribed in gold with words composed by the poet Paul Valéry. The square between the two pavilions is highly decorated with bronze sculptures, ornamental pools, and shooting fountains. Steps lead down from here to the **Théâtre National de Chaillot**, famous for its avant-garde productions.

The **Cité de l'Architecture et du Patrimoine** is a vast complex and information center incorporating Viollet-le-Duc's original Musée des Monuments Français (1882).

The **Musée de l'Homme** in the west wing (closed for renovation until 2014) traces human evolution through a series of anthropological, archaeological, and ethnological displays. Next door is the **Musée National de la Marine**, devoted to French naval history.

The centerpiece of the lovely Jardins de Trocadéro is a long rectangular ornamental pool, bordered by statues. The gardens themselves are perfect for a quiet evening stroll.

BARON HAUSSMANN

A lawyer by training and civil servant by profession, Georges-Eugène Haussmann (1809–91) was appointed Prefect of the Seine in 1853 by Napoleon III. For 17 years Haussmann was responsible for the urban modernization of Paris. With a team of the best architects and engineers, he demolished the chaotic, insanitary streets of the medieval city and created a well-ventilated and ordered capital in a geometrical grid. He also increased the number of street-lights and sidewalks, giving rise to the cafés that enliven modern Parisian street life. The plan involved redesigning the area at one end of the Champs-Elysées and creating a star of 12 avenues centered around the new Arc de Triomphe.

The east facade of the Arc de Triomphe

Arc de Triomphe ㉑

Place Charles de Gaulle. *Tel* 01-55 37
73 77. **M** **RER** *Charles de Gaulle–
Etoile.* 22, 30, 31, 73, 92. daily.
Jan 1, May 1, May 8 (am), Jul 14
(am), Nov 11 (am), Dec 25.
www.monuments-nationaux.fr

After his greatest victory,
the Battle of Austerlitz in
1805, Napoleon promised his
men they would "go home
beneath triumphal arches."
The first stone of what was
to become the world's most
famous triumphal arch was
laid the following year. But
disruptions to architect Jean
Chalgrin's plans – combined
with the demise of Napoleonic
power – delayed completion
until 1836. Standing 50 m
(164 ft) high, the Arc is
encrusted with flamboyant
reliefs, shields, and sculptures,
depicting military scenes such
as the Napoleonic battles of
Austerlitz and Aboukir.

On Armistice Day, 1921, the
body of the Unknown Soldier
was placed beneath the arch
to commemorate the dead of
World War I. The flame of
remembrance which burns
above the tomb is rekindled by
various veterans organizations
each evening. Today, the Arc

de Triomphe is the customary
rallying point for many victory
celebrations and parades.

The viewing platform on top
of the Arc overlooks the length
of the Champs-Elysées. Inside
the Arc, a museum documents
its history and construction.

Champs-Elysées ㉒

M *Franklin D. Roosevelt, George V,
Champs-Elysées Clemenceau.* **Grand
Palais** Porte A, Ave Eisenhower.
Tel 01-44 13 17 17. *Wed–Mon
(only for exhibitions).* **Palais de la
Découverte** *Tel* 01-56 43 20 21.
Tue–Sun. **Petit Palais** Ave
Winston Churchill. *Tel* 01-53 43 40
00. *Tue–Sun.* public hols.
for temporary exhibitions.

Paris's most famous and
popular thoroughfare had its
beginnings in about 1667,
when landscape gardener
André Le Nôtre extended the
royal view from the Tuileries
by creating a tree-lined avenue.
The Champs-Elysées (Elysian
Fields) has also been known
as the "triumphal way" since
the homecoming of Napoleon's
body from St. Helena in 1840.
With the addition of cafés and
restaurants in the late 19th
century, the Champs-Elysées

became the most fashionable
boulevard in Paris.

The formal gardens that line
the Champs-Elysées from Place
de la Concorde to the Rond-
Point have changed little since
they were laid out by architect
Jacques Hittorff in 1838, and
were used as the setting for the
1855 World's Fair. The Grand
Palais and the Petit Palais
were also built here for the
Universal Exhibition of 1900.

The exterior of the massive
Grand Palais combines an
imposing Neoclassical facade
with Art Nouveau ironwork. A
splendid glass roof is decorated with colossal bronze statues of flying horses and
chariots at its four corners.
Inside is a science exhibition
(Le Palais de la Découverte)
and the Galeries Nationales
du Grand Palais, which holds
frequent temporary exhibitions.

Facing the Grand Palais,
the **Petit Palais** houses the
Musée des Beaux-Arts de la
Ville de Paris. Arranged
around a semicircular courtyard and garden, the palace is
similar in style to the Grand
Palais, with Ionic columns, a
grand porch, and a dome
echoing that of the Invalides
across the river. The exhibits
are divided into medieval and
Renaissance *objets d'art*,
paintings, and drawings; 18th-
century furniture and *objets
d'art;* and works by the French
artists Gustave Courbet, Jean
Ingres, and Eugène Delacroix.

**Musée des Beaux-Arts de la Ville de
Paris, in the Petit Palais**

The deceptively rustic exterior of Au Lapin Agile, one of the best known nightspots in Paris

Montmartre ㉓

Ⓜ Abbesses, Anvers. 🚌 30, 54, 80, 85. **Sacré-Coeur** 35 Rue du Chevalier de la Barre. **Tel** 01-53 41 89 00. ◯ daily. 📷 for crypt and dome. ♿ restricted. **www**.sacre-coeur-montmartre.com

The steep hill of Montmartre has been associated with artists for 200 years. Théodore Géricault and Camille Corot came here at the start of the 19th century, and in the early 20th century Maurice Utrillo immortalized the streets in his works. Today, street artists of varying talents exhibit their work in the Place du Tertre, and thrive on the tourist trade. Exhibitions at the **Musée de Mont-martre** usually feature works of artists associated with the area, while the **Musée d'Art Naïf Max Fourny** houses almost 600 examples of naive art. The **Espace Montmartre Salvador Dalí** displays over 300 works by the Surrealist painter and sculptor. Much of the area

still preserves its rather louche, prewar atmosphere. Former literary haunt **Au Lapin Agile**, or "Agile Rabbit," is now a club. The celebrated **Moulin Rouge** nightclub is also in the vicinity.

The name Montmartre, thought to derive from martyrs tortured and killed here around AD 250, is also associated with the grandiose **Sacré-Coeur**. Dedicated to the Sacred Heart of Christ, the basilica was built as a result of a vow made at the outbreak of the Franco-Prussian War in 1870. Businessmen Alexandre

Facade of the Romano-Byzantine Sacré-Coeur

Legentil and Hubert Rohault de Fleury promised to finance its construction should France be spared from the impending Prussian onslaught. Despite the war and the Siege of Paris, invasion was averted and work began in 1876 to Paul Abadie's designs. The basilica, completed in 1914, is one of France's most important Roman Catholic shrines. It contains many treasures, including a figure of the *Virgin Mary and Child* (1896) by Brunet.

Below the forecourt, Square Willette is laid out on the side of a hill in a series of descending terraces. A funicular railway takes visitors up from the bottom of the gardens to the foot of the steps of the basilica.

Parc de la Villette ㉔

30 Ave Corentin-Cariou. Ⓜ Porte de la Villette. 🚌 75, 139, 150, 152, 250A. **Cité des Sciences Tel** 01-40 05 80 00. ◯ Tue–Sun. 📷 ♿

The old slaughterhouses and livestock market of Paris have been transformed into this massive urban park, designed by Bernard Tschumi.

The major attraction of the site is the **Cité des Sciences et de l'Industrie**, a hugely popular science and technology museum. Architect Adrien Fainsilber has created an imaginative interplay of light, vegetation, and water in the high-tech, five-floor building, which soars to a height of 40 m (133 ft). At the museum's heart is the Explora exhibit, a fascinating guide to the worlds of science and technology. The Géode, a giant entertainment sphere, houses a huge hemispherical cinema screen. In the auditorium of the Planetarium, special effects projectors create exciting images of the stars and planets.

Also in the park, the **Grande Halle** was the old cattle hall, and has been turned into a huge exhibition space. The **Cité de la Musique** is a quirky but elegant complex that holds a music conservatory – home of the world-famous Paris *conservatoire* since 1990 – and a concert hall. Built as a venue for pop concerts, the **Zénith theater** seats over 6,000 spectators.

Cimetière du Père Lachaise ㉕

16 Rue du Repos. Ⓜ *Père-Lachaise, A Dumas.* **Tel** 01-55 25 82 10. ◯ *daily.*

Paris's most prestigious cemetery is set on a wooded hill overlooking the city. The land was once owned by Père de la Chaise, Louis XIV's confessor, but it was bought by order of Napoleon in 1803 to create a completely new cemetery. This became so popular with the Parisian bourgeoisie that its boundaries were extended six times during the 19th century. Here are buried celebrities such as the writer Honoré de Balzac, the famous playwright Molière, the composer Frédéric Chopin, singer Edith Piaf, and actors Simone Signoret and Yves Montand. Famous foreigners interred in the cemetery include Oscar Wilde and the singer Jim Morrison. The Columbarium, built at the end of the 19th century, houses the ashes of American dancer Isadora

Monument to Oscar Wilde in the Père Lachaise Cemetery

Duncan, among others. The equally charismatic Sarah Bernhardt, famous for her portrayal of Racine heroines, also reposes at Père Lachaise. Striking funerary sculpture and famous graves make this a pleasant place for a leisurely, nostalgic stroll.

La Défense ㉖

ⓇⒺⓇ *La Défense.* **La Grande Arche** **Tel** 01-46 93 19 00. ◯ *daily.*

This still-expanding skyscraper business city on the western edge of Paris is one of the largest office developments in Europe and covers 80 ha (198 acres). It was launched in 1957 to create a new home for leading French and foreign companies. **La Grande Arche**

is an enormous hollow cube, spacious enough to contain Notre-Dame cathedral. Designed by Danish architect Otto von Spreckelsen, the arch houses an exhibition gallery and museum, and offers superb views over the city.

Bois de Boulogne ㉗

Ⓜ *Porte Maillot, Porte Dauphine, Porte d'Auteuil, Sablons.* ◯ *24 hrs daily.* to specialist gardens and museum.

Located between the river Seine and the western edges of Paris, this 865-ha (2,137-acre) park offers a vast belt of greenery for strolling, cycling, riding, boating, picnicking, or spending a day at the races. The Bois de Boulogne was once part of the immense Forêt du Rouvre. In the mid-19th century Napoleon III had the area redesigned and landscaped by Baron Haussmann along the lines of Hyde Park in London *(see p54)*. A number of self-contained parks include the Pré Catelan, which has the widest beech tree in Paris, and the Bagatelle gardens, with architectural follies and an 18th-century villa famous for its rose garden. The villa was built in just 64 days as the result of a bet between the Comte d'Artois and Marie-Antoinette.

By day the Bois is busy with families, joggers, and walkers, but after dark it is notoriously seedy – and best avoided.

Kiosque de l'Empereur, on an island in the Grand Lac, Bois de Boulogne

Château de Versailles ㉘

Visitors passing through the dazzling state rooms of this colossal palace, or strolling in its vast gardens, will soon understand why it was the glory of the Sun King's reign. Started by Louis XIV in 1668, the palace grew from a modest hunting lodge built for his father, Louis XIII, to become the largest palace in Europe, housing some 20,000 people. Architect Louis Le Vau built the first section, which expanded into an enlarged courtyard. From 1678, Jules Hardouin-Mansart added the north and south wings and the superb Hall of Mirrors. He also designed the chapel, completed in 1710. The interiors were largely the work of Charles Le Brun, and the great landscape gardener, André Le Nôtre, redesigned the gardens with their monumental fountains.

★ **Hall of Mirrors**
This magnificent room, 70 m (233 ft) long, was the setting for great state occasions. It was here that the Treaty of Versailles was ratified at the end of World War I.

Marble Courtyard
The courtyard is decorated with marble paving, urns, and busts. Above the gilded central balcony, the figures of Hercules and Mars flank the clock on the pediment.

The South Wing
originally housed the apartments of great nobles. It is now a history museum.

Ministers' Courtyard

Royal Courtyard

The ornate main gate, designed by Mansart, is crowned by the royal coat of arms.

★ **Chapelle Royale**
Mansart's last great work, this Baroque chapel was Louis XIV's final addition to Versailles. The beautiful interior is decorated with Corinthian columns and superb Baroque murals.

STAR FEATURES

★ Chapelle Royale

★ Hall of Mirrors

VISITORS' CHECKLIST

Versailles, Yvelines. **Tel** 01-30 83
78 00. � Versailles Chantiers,
Versailles Rive Droite. **RER** Versailles
Rive Gauche. 🚌 171 from Paris.
Château ◻ 9am–6:30pm Tue–
Sun (5:30pm in winter). ◻ some
public hols. 🎟 **Grand & Petit
Trianon** ◻ pm daily. ◻ Jan 1,
Dec 25. 🎟 📷 ♿ **Musée des
Carrosses** ◻ some public hols.
🎟 📷 Grands Eaux Nocturnes
(Jul–Aug: Sat eve).

The 17th-century Fountain of Neptune by Le Nôtre and Mansart

North Wing
*The chapel, Opera House,
and picture galleries occupy
this wing, which originally
housed royal apartments.*

Parterres
(flowerbeds)

The Opera House in the
North Wing was completed
for the 1770 marriage of
the future Louis XVI and
Marie-Antoinette.

Exploring the Palace
The main rooms of the palace
are on the first floor. Around
the Marble Courtyard are the
private apartments of the king
and queen. Visitors can see
the King's Bedroom, where
Louis XIV died, aged 77, in
1715. The room next door, the
Cabinet du Conseil, was where
the monarch would receive
ministers and family members.

On the garden side, the state
apartments are richly decorated
with colored marbles, carvings
in stone and wood, murals,
and gilded furniture. Each is
dedicated to an Olympian
deity. Louis XIV's throne room,
the Salon d'Apollon, designed
by Le Brun, is dedicated to
the god Apollo. A copy
of the famous portrait of
Louis by Hyacinthe
Rigaud hangs above the
fireplace. The war theme
of the Salon de la Guerre
is reinforced by a stucco
relief of Louis XIV riding
to victory. The high point
of the tour is the Hall of
Mirrors, with its 17 great
mirrors reflecting the light
from tall arched windows.

Among the other major
attractions are the Chapelle
Royale and the **Musée des
Carrosses** (coach museum)
opposite the palace.

The Gardens of Versailles
The gardens are a fitting
counterpart to the colossal
palace. Immediately in front
of the palace is the Water
Parterre, decorated with superb
bronze statues. Paths lead
through the formal gardens,
with their regularly patterned
flowerbeds and hedges, to
groves, lakes, fountains, and
architectural features such as
the Colonnade (1685), a circle
of marble arches designed by
Mansart. The largest stretch
of water is the Grand Canal,
where Louis XIV held
spectacular boating parties.

The gardens contain two
smaller palaces. The **Grand
Trianon**, built of stone and
pink marble, was designed by
Mansart in 1687 as a discreet
hideaway for Louis XIV and
his mistress, Madame de
Maintenon. The nearby **Petit
Trianon** (1762) was built for
Madame de Pompadour,
Louis XV's
mistress. It later
became a favorite
retreat of Marie-
Antoinette.
Behind it is the
Hameau, a mini-
village where the
queen would
dress up as a
shepherdess and
play with a flock
of groomed and
perfumed lambs.

Marie-Antoinette's beloved Petit Trianon

Basilique St-Denis ㉙

1 Rue de la Légion d'Honneur. **M**
St-Denis-Basilique. **RER** *St-Denis.* **Tel**
01-48 09 83 54. ☐ *daily.* ● *Jan 1,
May 1, Dec 25.* 📷 ✔ ♿ *restricted.*

Constructed between 1137 and
1281, the basilica is on the site
of the tomb of St. Denis, the
first bishop of Paris, who was
beheaded in Montmartre in
AD 250. According to legend,
his decapitated figure, clutching
his head, was seen here, and
an abbey was erected to
commemorate the martyred
bishop. The basilica was the
first church to be built in the
Gothic style of architecture.

From as early as the 7th
century St-Denis was a burial
place for French rulers, and
all the queens of France were
crowned here. During the
Revolution many tombs were
desecrated and scattered, but
the best were stored, and now
represent a fine collection of
funerary art. Memorials
include those of Henri II (died
1559) and Catherine de' Medici
(died 1589), and Louis XVI and
Marie-Antoinette (died 1793).

Of the medieval effigies, the
most impressive are of Charles
V (1364) and a 12th-century
likeness of Blanche de France
with her dog. Their mask-like
serenity contrasts with the
realistic Renaissance portrayal
of agony in the sculptures of
the mausoleum of Louis XII
and Anne de Bretagne.

In 2011 the skull of Henry IV
was buried here, having been
in the possession of a private
collector since the 1950s.

Disneyland Paris ㉚

Marne-la-Vallée, Seine-et-Marne. 🚗
*TGV from several major cities to Marne
la Vallée/Chessy.* **RER** *Marne-la-Vallée-
Chessy.* ✈ *from CDG & Orly airports.*
Tel *08-25 30 02 22.* ☐ *daily.* 📷 ♿
www.disneylandparis.com

The theme park, which lies
32 km (20 miles) east of Paris,
covers 60 ha (150 acres). It is
divided into five themed areas.
Although these rely heavily on
Hollywood nostalgia, Disneyland Paris has tried to give the
park a European touch.

"Frontierland," inspired by
the Wild West of 19th-century
America, can be explored on
paddlewheel steamboats. A
roller coaster trundles through
mountain scenery.

In "Adventureland" visitors
encounter characters and tales
from adventure fiction,
including Caribbean pirates
and the Swiss Family Robinson.

Small-town America at the
turn of the century is evoked
in "Main Street." Authentic
details include horse-drawn
vehicles and a traditional
barber's shop.

Young children will enjoy
"Fantasyland," devoted to
Disney characters and tales,
where they can fly with Peter
Pan or search the Alice in
Wonderland maze for the
Queen of Hearts' castle.

"Discoveryland" has futuristic
architecture and sophisticated
technology. Here, visitors can
choose to be miniaturized by
a hapless inventor or sent on
a thrilling space trip.

Château de Vaux-le-Vicomte ㉛

Maincy, Seine-et-Marne. 🚗 **RER**
*Melun, then taxi or shuttle bus (Apr–
Sep: Sat & Sun).* **Tel** *01-64 14 41 90.*
☐ *mid-Mar–mid-Oct: daily.* 📷 ♿

Located 64 km (40 miles)
southeast of Paris, just north
of Melun, the château enjoys a
peaceful rural setting. Nicolas
Fouquet, a powerful court
financier to Louis XIV,
challenged architect Le Vau and
decorator Le Brun to create the
most sumptuous palace of
the day. The result was one
of the greatest 17th-century
French châteaux. However,
it also led to his downfall.
Louis was so enraged –
because its luxury cast the
royal palaces into the shade –
that he had Fouquet arrested
and confiscated all his estates.

As befits Fouquet's grand
tastes, the interior is a gilded
banquet of frescoes, stucco,
caryatids, and giant busts.
The Salon des Muses boasts

The tomb of Louis XII and Anne de Bretagne in the Basilique St-Denis

Château de Vaux-le-Vicomte seen across the formal gardens designed by Le Nôtre

Le Brun's magnificent frescoed ceiling of dancing nymphs and poetic sphinxes. La Grande Chambre Carrée is decorated in Louis XIII style with paneled walls and an impressive triumphal frieze, evoking Rome.

Much of Vaux-le-Vicomte's fame is due to landscape gardener André Le Nôtre (1613–1700). At Vaux he perfected the concept of the *jardin à la française*: avenues framed by statues and box hedges, water gardens with ornate pools, and geometrical parterres "embroidered" with floral motifs.

Château de Fontainebleau ㉜

Seine-et-Marne. 🚇 **Tel** 01-60 71 50 70. ◯ *Wed–Mon.* 📷 🎫 ♿
www.musee-chateau-fontainebleau.fr

Fontainebleau was a favorite royal residence from the 12th to the mid-19th century. Its charm lies in its relative informality and its spectacular setting in a forest 65 km (40 miles) south of Paris. The present château dates back to François I. Drawn to the area by the local hunting, the Renaissance king created a decorative château modeled on Florentine and Roman styles. Subsequent rulers enlarged and embellished the château, creating a cluster of buildings

in various styles from different periods. During the Revolution the apartments were looted by a mob, and remained bare until the 1800s when Napoleon refurbished the whole interior.

The Cour du Cheval Blanc, once a simple enclosed courtyard, was transformed by Napoleon into the main approach to the château. At one end is the Escalier du Fer-à-Cheval (1634), an imposing horseshoe-shaped staircase.

The interior suites showcase the château's history as a royal residence. The Galerie François I has a superb collection of Renaissance art. The Salle de Bal, a Renaissance ballroom designed by Primaticcio (1552), features emblems of Henri II on the walnut coffered ceiling

and reflected in the parquet floor. The apartments of Napoleon I house his grandiose throne, in the former Chambre du Roi. The complex of buildings also contains the Musée Napoléon, in which eight rooms recreate different scenes from the Emperor's life.

Nearby is the Chapelle de la Sainte Trinité, designed for Henri II in 1550. The chapel acquired its vaulted and frescoed ceiling under Henri IV, and was completed during the reign of Louis XIII.

The gardens are also worth exploring. The Jardin Anglais is a romantic "English" garden planted with cypresses and exotic species. The Jardin de Diana features a bronze fountain of Diana the huntress.

The Salle de Bal of Henri II, Château de Fontainebleau

Northern France

Northern France's main sights span thousands of years of history, from the awesome megaliths of Carnac, through the 18th-century grandeur of Nancy's town architecture, to Strasbourg's futuristic Palais de l'Europe, seat of the European Parliament. Its cities boast some of the country's greatest cathedrals, such as those of Reims and Rouen. The region's most famous religious monument is Mont-St-Michel, whose evocative silhouette has welcomed pilgrims since the 11th century.

Strasbourg's fine Gothic cathedral surrounded by historic buildings

Strasbourg ❷

Bas Rhin. 🏛 450,000. ✈ 15 km (8 miles) SW. 🚇 🚌 🛈 17 Place de la Cathédrale (03-88 52 28 28). 🎄 Christmas market (Dec). **www**.otstrasbourg.fr

Located halfway between Paris and Prague, this cosmopolitan city is often known as "the crossroads of Europe." It is also home to the European Parliament.

A boat trip along the waterways that encircle Strasbourg's Old Town takes in the **Ponts-Couverts** – bridges with medieval watchtowers – and the old tanners' district, dotted with attractive half-timbered houses.

Dating from the late 11th century, the **Cathédrale Notre-Dame** dominates the city. There are wonderful views from the top of its spire.

The grand Classical **Palais Rohan** houses three museums: the Musée des Beaux Arts, the Musée Archéologique, and the Musée des Arts Décoratifs, which has one of the finest displays of ceramics in France.

Also worth visiting is the **Musée d'Art Moderne et Contemporain**, **Le Vaisseau**, a scientific discovery center for children aged 3–15, and the **Musée Alsacien**, which contains exhibits on local traditions, arts, and crafts.

Reims ❸

Marne. 🏛 210,000. 🚇 🚌 🛈 2 Rue Guillaume de Machault (08-92 70 13 51). **www**.reims-tourisme.com

Renowned throughout the world from countless champagne labels, Reims has a rich historical legacy.

The city's most famous monument is the magnificent Gothic **Cathédrale Notre-Dame**, begun in 1211. For several centuries the cathedral was the setting for the coronation of French kings. Highlights are the 13th-century Great Rose Window and the west facade, decorated with over 2,300 statues.

On the eve of a coronation, the future king spent the night in the **Palais du Tau** (1690), the archbishops' palace adjoining the cathedral.

Its 15th-century banqueting hall, the Salle du Tau, with its barrel-vaulted ceiling and Arras tapestries, is a star attraction.

Among other fine historic buildings are the 17th-century **Ancien Collège des Jésuites**, which is now a school, and the **Basilique St-Remi**, Reims' oldest church.

Relics of the town's Roman past include the **Cryptoportique**, part of the former forum, and the **Porte Mars**, a triumphal Augustan arch.

The **Musée de la Reddition** occupies the building that served as Eisenhower's French headquarters during World War II. It was here, in 1945, that the general received the Germans' surrender, which ended the war.

🏰 **Cathédrale Notre-Dame**
Place du Cardinal Luçon. ◯ daily.
🎫 &

Environs
A short drive south of Reims is **Epernay**. Here you can visit the cellars of a number of distinguished champagne "houses," including those of Moët et Chandon.

Rouen ❹

Seine Maritime. 🏛 138,000. ✈ 11 km (7 miles) SE. 🚇 🚌 🛈 25 Place de la Cathédrale (02-32 08 32 40). **www**.rouenvalleedeseine.com

Formerly a Celtic trading post, Roman garrison, and Viking colony, Rouen became the capital of the Norman Duchy in 911. Today it is a rich and cultured city that boasts a wealth of splendid

Statuary on the west facade of Reims' Cathédrale Notre-Dame

Detail from the 11th-century Bayeux Tapestry

historical monuments. Rouen's Gothic cathedral, the **Cathédrale Notre-Dame**, has an impressive west facade, made famous by the great Impressionist painter Claude Monet (1840–1926), who made almost 30 paintings of it. A number of these can be seen in the city's excellent **Musée des Beaux Arts**.

From the cathedral, the Rue du Gros Horloge leads west, passing under the city's Great Clock, to the Place du Vieux Marché, where Joan of Arc was burnt at the stake in 1431.

The Flamboyant Gothic **Eglise St-Maclou** and the Gothic **Eglise St-Ouen** are two of Rouen's finest churches. The Eglise St-Ouen is noted for its restored 14th-century stained-glass windows.

The **Musée de la Céramique** displays around 1,000 pieces of Rouen faïence – colorful glazed earthenware – as well as other pieces of French and foreign china.

The former family home of Gustave Flaubert (1821–80) has been converted into a museum containing memorabilia from this famous French novelist's life.

🏛 **Musée des Beaux Arts**
Square Verdrel. *Tel* 02-35 71 28 40. ⬜ Wed–Mon. ⬤ public hols. 🔲 &

Bayeux ❺

Calvados. 🔼 15,000. 🚊 🚌 🛈 Pont-St-Jean (02-31 51 28). **www**.bessin-normandie.com

The main reason for making a stop at this small town in Normandy is to see the world-renowned Bayeux Tapestry. This incredible work of art depicts William the Conqueror's invasion of England and

the Battle of Hastings in the 11th century from the Norman perspective. It was probably commissioned by Bishop Odo of Bayeux, William's half-brother. The 70-m (230-ft) long embroidered hanging is displayed in a renovated seminary, the **Centre Guillaume-le-Conquérant**, which also gives a detailed audio-visual account of the events leading up to the Norman conquest.

Apart from its tapestry, a cluster of 15th–19th-century buildings and the Gothic **Cathédrale Notre-Dame** are Bayeux's principal attractions.

Bayeux was the first town in Nazi-occupied France to be liberated by the Allies following the D-Day landings in 1944. On the southwest side of the town's ring road, the **Musée Mémorial de la Bataille de Normandie** traces the events of the Battle of Normandy in World War II.

🏛 **Centre Guillaume-le-Conquérant**
Rue de Nesmond. *Tel* 02-31 51 25 50. ⬜ daily. ⬤ Jan 1 & 2, second week in Jan, Dec 25 & 26. 🔲 &

Mont-St-Michel ❻

See pp174–5.

St-Malo ❼

Ille-et-Vilaine. 🔼 53,000. ✈ 🚊 🚌 🛈 Esplanade St-Vincent (08-25 13 52 00). 🛒 Tue, Fri (Old Town). **www**.saint-malo-tourisme.com

Once a fortified island, St-Malo stands in a commanding position at the mouth of the river Rance. In the 16th–19th centuries the port won prosperity and power through the exploits of its seafaring

population. Intra-muros, the old walled city, is encircled by ramparts that provide fine views of St-Malo and its off-shore islands. Within the city walls is a web of narrow, cobbled streets with tall 18th-century buildings housing many souvenir shops, seafood restaurants, and creperies.

St-Malo's castle, the **Château de St-Malo** dates from the 14th and 15th centuries. The great keep today houses an interesting museum charting the city's history. In the three-towered fortification known as the **Tour Solidor**, to the west of St-Malo, is a museum devoted to the ships and sailors that rounded Cape Horn.

Carnac ❽

Morbihan. 🔼 4,600. 🚌 🛈 74 Avenue des Druides (02-97 52 13 52).

This popular town is probably most famous as one of the world's great prehistoric sites. As long ago as 4000 BC thousands of ancient granite rocks were arranged in mysterious lines and patterns in the country-side around Carnac by Mega-lithic tribes. Their original purpose is uncertain, though they are thought to have religious significance or to be related to an early astronomical calendar. Celts, Romans, and Christians have since adapted them to their own beliefs.

You can see some of the menhirs at the Kermario site, on the town outskirts, while in the center, the **Musée de Préhistoire** gives an insight into the area's ancient history.

Menhirs (prehistoric standing stones) in a field near Carnac

Mont-St-Michel ❻

Shrouded by mist, the silhouette of Mont-St-Michel is one of the most enchanting sights in France. Now linked to the mainland by a causeway, the island of Mont-Tombe (Tomb on the Hill) stands at the mouth of the river Couesnon, crowned by a fortified abbey that almost doubles its height. Lying strategically on the frontier between Normandy and Brittany, Mont-St-Michel grew from a humble 8th-century oratory to become a Benedictine monastery that had its greatest influence in the 12th and 13th centuries. Pilgrims known as *miquelots* journeyed from afar to honor the cult of St. Michael, and the monastery was a renowned center of medieval learning. After the French Revolution the abbey became a prison. It is now a national monument that draws some 850,000 visitors a year. Work on a bridge to link the island to the mainland is due to finish in 2015.

★ **Abbey Church**
Four bays of the Romanesque nave in the abbey church survive. Three were pulled down in 1776, creating the West Terrace.

Gautier's Leap
Situated at the top of the Inner Staircase, this terrace is named after a prisoner who leaped to his death here.

The ramparts – a series of fortified walls with imposing towers – were built following attacks by the English during the Hundred Years' War.

St. Aubert's Chapel, built on an outcrop of rock, dates from the 15th-century and is dedicated to Aubert, the founder of Mont-St-Michel.

Gabriel Tower

Entrance

VISITING THE ABBEY

The abbey is built on three levels, which reflect the monastic hierarchy. The monks lived on the highest level *(shown here)*, in an enclosed world of church, cloister, and refectory. The abbot entertained his noble guests on the middle level. Soldiers and pilgrims further down on the social scale were received at the lowest level. Guided tours begin at the West Terrace at the church (highest) level and end on the lowest level in the almonry, where alms were distributed to the poor.

La Merveille is the name given to the buildings on the north side of the church.

Cloisters

Refectory

Abbey Church

West Terrace

Gautier's Leap

Great Inner Staircase

★ Cloisters
With their elegant English Purbeck marble
columns, the cloisters are a beautiful example
of early 13th-century Anglo-Norman style.

★ La Merveille
The main three-story monastic
complex, added to the church's
north side in the early 13th
century, is known as La
Merveille (The Miracle). The
Knights' Room, on the middle
floor, has magnificent Gothic
rib-vaulting and finely
decorated capitals.

Eglise
St-Pierre

Liberty Tower

Tour du
Roy

The Arcade Tower
provided lodgings for
the abbot's soldiers.

★ Grande Rue
Now crowded with tourists
and souvenir shops, the pilgrims' route,
followed since the 12th century, climbs up
past the Eglise St-Pierre to
the abbey gates.

VISITORS' CHECKLIST

🚍 to Pontorson, then bus.
ℹ️ Boulevard de l'Avancée
(02-33 60 14 30).
www.ot-montsaintmichel.com
Abbey Tel 02-33 89 80 00.
🕐 May–Aug: 9am–7pm;
Sep–Apr: 9:30am– 6pm.
Night visits during summer.
🔴 Jan 1, May 1, Dec 25. 🈲
✝️ 12:15pm Tue–Sat; 11:30am
Sun. 🎦 🛈 **www**.monuments-
nationaux.fr

STAR FEATURES

★ Abbey Church

★ La Merveille

★ Cloisters

★ Grande Rue

The Loire Valley

Renowned for its sumptuous chateaux, the relics of royal days gone by, the glorious valley of the Loire is rich in both history and architecture. As the Loire runs through the heart of France, so the region embodies the essence of the French way of life. Its sophisticated cities, luxuriant landscape, and magnificent food and wine add up to a modern paradise. The Loire has long been described as exemplifying *la douceur de vivre*: it combines a leisurely pace of life, a mild climate, and the gentle ways of its inhabitants. The overall impression is one of an unostentatious taste for the good things in life.

Tomb of François II in Cathédrale St-Pierre et St-Paul, Nantes

Nantes ❾

Loire-Atlantique. 🏠 *270,000.* ✈ 🚉
🚌 ℹ *3 Cours Olivier de Clisson
(08-92 46 40 44).* 🕑 *Tue–Sun.*
www.nantes-tourisme.com

The ancient port of Nantes was the ducal capital of Brittany for 600 years, but is now considered a part of the Pays de la Loire. Many of its fine 18th- and 19th-century buildings were built on profits from maritime trade. Modern-day Nantes is a lively city, with good museums, chic bars and shops, and wide open spaces.

The **Cathédrale St-Pierre et St-Paul** was begun in 1434, but not completed until 1893. It is notable for its sculpted Gothic portals and Renaissance tomb of François II (1435–88), the last duke of Brittany.

The **Château des Ducs de Bretagne**, now with a museum documenting the town's history, was the birthplace of Anne of Brittany, who irrevocably joined her fiercely independent duchy to France by her successive marriages to Charles VIII and Louis XII. A smaller royal lodging lies to the west of it. It was here, in Brittany's Catholic bastion, that Henri IV signed the 1598 Edict of Nantes, which granted all Protestants freedom of worship.

The **Musée des Beaux-Arts** has a splendid array of paintings representing key movements from the 15th to the 20th centuries. Packed with mementos, books, and maps, the **Musée Jules Verne** is dedicated to the life and works of the famous writer (1828–1905).

🏛 **Musée des Beaux-Arts**
10 Rue Georges Clemenceau.
Tel 02-51 17 45 00. 🕑 closed for
restoration until 2013. 📷 👍 🖥 📷

Poitiers ❿

Vienne. 🏠 *85,000.* ✈ 🚉 🚌
ℹ *45 Place Charles de Gaulle
(05-49 41 21 24).* 🕑 *Tue–Sun.*
www.ot-poitiers.fr

Three of the greatest battles in French history were fought around Poitiers, the most famous in 732 when Charles Martel halted the Arab invasion. Today the town is a dynamic regional capital with a rich architectural heritage.

Behind the Renaissance façade of the **Palais de Justice** is the 12th-century great hall of the palace of Henry II and Richard the Lion-Heart. This is thought to be the scene of Joan of Arc's examination by a council of theologians in 1429.

Notre-Dame-la-Grande, whose west front is covered with superb 12th-century Poitevin sculpture, stands out among the city's churches, as does the 4th-century **Baptistère St-Jean**, one of the oldest Christian buildings in France. The latter contains Romanesque frescoes.

The **Musée Sainte-Croix** has archaeological exhibits, as well as paintings and sculpture.

Environs

Just 7 km (4.5 miles) north of Poitiers, **Futuroscope** is a theme park dedicated to state-of-the-art visual technology, including the largest cinema screen in Europe.

🏛 **Futuroscope**
Jaunay-Clan. **Tel** 05-49 49 11 12.
🕑 check calendar on website. 🕑
Jan. 📷 👍 www.futuroscope.com

The high-tech Kinemax cinema at Futuroscope, near Poitiers

Abbaye Royale de Fontevraud ⑪

Maine-et-Loire. ▦ **Tel** 02-41 51 73 52. ◯ daily. ● Jan, Feb–mid-Apr: Mon, Dec 25. ▨ ☑ & restricted. **www**.abbaye-fontevraud.com

Fontevraud Royal Abbey, founded in 1101, was the largest of its kind in France. It now hosts concerts and exhibitions. The abbey's nuns lived around the Renaissance Grand Moûtier cloisters, and the leper colony's nurses were housed in the St-Lazare priory, now the abbey's hotel. Little remains of the monastic quarters, but the St-Benoît hospital survives. Most impressive is the octagonal kitchen in the Tour Evraud, a rare example of secular Romanesque architecture.

In the nave of the abbey church, the painted effigy of Henry Plantagenet (1133– 1189), Count of Anjou and King of England, lies by those of his wife Eleanor of Aquitaine, who died here in 1204, and their son, Richard the Lion-Heart (1157–1199).

Tours ⑫

Indre-et-Loire. 🏠 140,000. ✈ ▦ ▦ ▯ 78 Rue Bernard Palissy (02-47 70 37 37). ▤ Tue–Sun.

The pleasant cathedral city of Tours is built on the site of a Roman town, and became an important center of Christianity in the 4th century under St. Martin. In 1461 Louis XI made the city the French capital. However, during Henri IV's reign, the city lost favor with the monarchy and the capital left Tours for Paris.

The medieval old town, Le Vieux Tours, is full of narrow streets lined with beautiful half-timbered houses. St. Martin's tomb lies in the crypt of the New Basilica, built on the site of the medieval Old Basilica. Two towers, the **Tour Charlemagne** and the **Tour de l'Horloge**, survive from the earlier building.

Nearby, the vaulted cellars of the 13th-century **Eglise St-Julien** now form the **Musée des Vins de Touraine**, where exhibits include a Renaissance winepress and displays on early viticultural history.

The foundation stone of the **Cathédrale St-Gatien** was laid in the early 13th century. Building work continued until the mid-16th century, and the cathedral provides an illustration of how the Gothic style developed over time.

The **Château Royal de Tours**, a royal residence between the 13th and 15th centuries, houses modern art exhibitions and exhibits, which explain the history of Tours.

Château de Chenonceau ⑬

See pp178–9.

Blois ⑭

Loir-et-Cher. 🏠 60,000. ▦ ▦ ▯ Place du Château (02-54 90 41 41). ▤ Sat.

A powerful feudal stronghold in the 12th century, Blois rose to glory under Louis XII, who established his court here in 1498. The town remained at the center of French royal and political life for much of the next century. Today, Blois is the quintessential Loire town. The partly pedestrianized old quarter is full of romantic courtyards and fine mansions.

François I's staircase, Château de Blois

Home to kings Louis XII, François I, and Henri III, no other Loire château has such a sensational history as the **Château de Blois**. It was here, in 1588, that the ambitious Duc de Guise, leader of the Catholic Holy League, was murdered on the orders of Henri III. The building itself juxtaposes four distinct architectural styles, reflecting its varied history.

Among Blois' most impressive religious monuments are the beautiful three-spired **Eglise St-Nicolas**, formerly part of a 12th-century Benedictine abbey, and the **Cathédrale St-Louis**, which dominates the eastern half of the city. The cathedral is a 17th-century reconstruction of a Gothic church that was almost destroyed in 1678.

♠ **Château de Blois**
Place du Château. **Tel** 02-54 90 33 33. ◯ daily. ● Jan 1, Dec 25. ▨ ☑

The historic town of Blois, viewed from across the Loire

Château de Chenonceau ⑬

Chenonceau, stretching romantically across the River Cher, is considered by many to be the loveliest of the Loire châteaux. Surrounded by elegant formal gardens and wooded grounds, this pure Renaissance building began life as a modest manor and water mill. Over the centuries it was transformed by the wives and mistresses of its successive owners into a palace designed solely for pleasure. On July and August evenings, the *Promenade Nocturne* allows visitors to stroll about the gardens accompanied by classical music.

Chambre de Catherine de' Medici
Henri II's wife Catherine made her own mark on Chenonceau's design, with this sumptuous bedchamber.

Louise de Lorraine's room was painted black and decorated with monograms, tears, and knots in white after the assassination of her husband, Henri III.

Formal Gardens
The current designs of the formal gardens created by Diane de Poitiers and Catherine de' Medici date from the 19th century.

The Cabinet Vert was originally covered with green velvet.

The Tour des Marques survives from the 15th-century castle of the Marques family.

Chapel
The chapel has a vaulted ceiling and sculpted pilasters. The stained glass, destroyed by a bomb in 1944, was replaced in 1953.

Grande Galerie
The elegant gallery is Florentine in style. It was created by Catherine de' Medici in 1570–76 as an addition to the bridge built for Diane de Poitiers.

The arched bridge
over the Cher was
designed by Philibert
de l'Orme in 1559 for
Diane de Poitiers. It
was built on the site
of the old water mill.

DIANE DE POITIERS

Diane de Poitiers was
Henry II's lifelong mistress,
holding court as queen of
France in all but name. Her
beauty inspired many
French artists, who often
depicted her in the role
of Diana, the Classical
goddess of the hunt.

In 1547 Henry offered the
Château de Chenonceau
to Diane, who improved
the palace by creating
stunning formal gardens
and an arched bridge over
the River Cher.

After Henry's accidental
death in 1559, Diane was
forced to leave Chenon-
ceau by his widow
Catherine de' Medici, in
exchange for the fortress-
like Château de Chaumont.
Diane retired to Anet, and
remained there until her
death in 1566.

The Château de Chambord on the banks of the Closson

Château de Chambord ⓯

Loir-et-Cher. 🚌 *to Blois, then taxi or*
bus. **Tel** *02-54 50 40 00.* ⬤ *daily.*
⬤ *Jan 1, May 1, Dec 25.* 📷 📷

The brainchild of the extra
vagant François I, the
château began as a hunting
lodge in the Forêt de Boulogne. In 1519 the original
building was razed and
Chambord begun, to a design
probably initiated by Leonardo
da Vinci. By 1537 the keep,
with its towers and terraces,
had been completed by 1,800
men and three master masons.
The following year, François I
began building a private royal
pavilion on the northeast
corner, with a connecting
two-story gallery. His son,
Henri II, continued the west
wing with the chapel, and
Louis XIV completed the 440-
roomed edifice in 1685.

The innovative double-helix
Grand Staircase was supposedly designed by Leonardo
da Vinci. The two flights of
stairs ensure that the person
going up and the person
going down cannot meet.

Orléans ⓰

Loiret. 🏘 *113,000.* 🚐 🚊 🚌 🛈 *2*
Place de l'Etape (02-38 24 05 05). 🛒
Tue–Sun. 🎭 *Fête Jeanne d'Arc (May*
7 & 8). **www**.tourisme-orleans.com

Orléans was the capital of
medieval France, and it was
here that Joan of Arc battled

the English in 1429, during
the Hundred Years' War.
Later captured by the enemy
and accused of witch-craft,
she was burned at the stake
in Rouen at the age of 19.
Since her martyrdom, Joan
has become a pervasive
presence in Orléans.

A faded grandeur lingers in
Vieil Orléans, the old quarter
bounded by the imposing
Cathédrale Sainte-Croix, the
Loire, and the Place du Martroi.
The **Maison de Jeanne d'Arc**
was rebuilt in 1961 on the site
where Joan lodged in 1429.
Inside, audiovisual exhibits
recreate her life.

A selection of European art
of the 16th to early 20th
centuries is on display at the
Musée des Beaux-Arts.

🏛 **Maison de Jeanne d'Arc**
3 Place du Général de Gaulle. **Tel**
02-38 52 99 89. ⬤ *closed for*
renovations during 2012. 📷

The lofty interior of the Cathédrale
Sainte-Croix, Orléans

Chartres Cathedral ⑰

According to art historian Emile Male, "Chartres is the mind of the Middle Ages manifest." Begun in 1020, the Romanesque cathedral was destroyed by a devastating fire in 1194. Only the north and south towers, south steeple, west portal, and crypt remained. Inside, the sacred *Veil of the Virgin* relic was the sole treasure to survive. Peasant and lord alike labored to rebuild the church in just 25 years. Few alterations were made after 1250 and, fortunately, Chartres was left unscathed by the Wars of Religion and the French Revolution. The result is an authentic Gothic cathedral with a true "Bible in stone and glass" reputation.

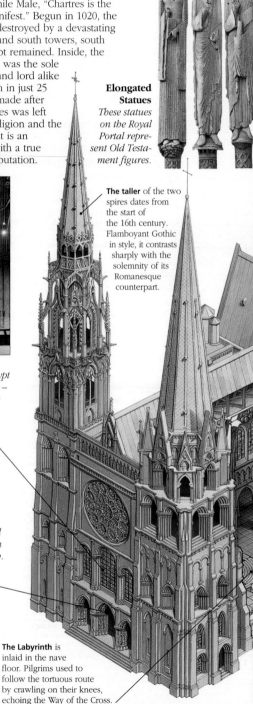

Elongated Statues
These statues on the Royal Portal represent Old Testament figures.

The taller of the two spires dates from the start of the 16th century. Flamboyant Gothic in style, it contrasts sharply with the solemnity of its Romanesque counterpart.

Gothic Nave
As wide as the Romanesque crypt below it – the largest in France – the Gothic nave reaches a lofty height of 37 m (121 ft).

★ Stained-Glass Windows
The three 12th-century lancet windows on the west front, celebrated for their rare blue color, are among the oldest of their kind in the world.

★ Royal Portal
The Royal Portal (1145–55) and part of the west front survive from the original Romanesque church. The central tympanum has a carving of Christ in Majesty.

STAR FEATURES

★ South Porch

★ Royal Portal

★ Stained-Glass Windows

The Labyrinth is inlaid in the nave floor. Pilgrims used to follow the tortuous route by crawling on their knees, echoing the Way of the Cross.

CHARTRES' STAINED GLASS

Over 150 stained-glass windows in the cathedral illustrate biblical stories and daily life in the 13th century (bring binoculars if you can). During both World Wars the windows were dismantled piece by piece and removed for safety. Some windows were restored and releaded in the 1970s, and in 2006 further restoration work commenced. Each window is divided into panels, which are usually read from left to right, bottom to top (earth to heaven). The number of figures or abstract shapes used is symbolic: three stands for the Church; squares and the number four symbolize the material world or the four elements; circles represent eternal life.

VISITORS' CHECKLIST

Place de la Cathédrale, Chartres, Eure-et-Loir. 🚉 🚌 from Paris. **Tel** 02-37 21 75 02. ◯ 8:30am–7:30pm daily. ✝ 11:45am & 6pm Mon–Sat (9am Tue, Fri); 9:15 (Latin) & 11am Sun. 🚻 📷 **www**.cathedrale-chartres.org

Our Lady of the Pillar
Carved from dark pear wood, this 16th-century replica of a 13th-century statue is a striking shrine that is often surrounded by candles.

The vaulted ceiling is supported by a network of ribs.

The St. Piat Chapel was built between 1324 and 1353.

South Rose Window
The cathedral has three massive rose windows. That on the south front (c.1225) illustrates the Apocalypse, *with Christ in Majesty.*

★ South Porch
Sculpture on the massive South Porch (1197–1209) reflects a selection of New Testament teaching.

Burgundy and the French Alps

Burgundy is France's richest province, historically, culturally, and gastronomically. The region's fine wines have inspired awe for centuries, and every year the historic town of Beaune hosts one of the most famous wine auctions in the world. Dijon is a splendid city, filled with the great palaces of the old Burgundian nobility. The majestic French Alps attract visitors for winter sports, and, in summer, walking and a host of water sports on the glittering mountain lakes.

Tympanum sculpture showing Christ and the apostles at Basilique Ste-Madeleine, Vézelay

Vézelay ⓘ

Yonne. 🏠 400. 🚌 **Basilique Ste-Madeleine** *Tel* 03-86 33 39 50. 🚉 Sermizelles, then bus. ◯ daily. 📷

Tourists come to Vézelay to visit the picturesque **Basilique Ste-Madeleine**. In the 12th century, at the height of its glory, the abbey claimed to house the relics of Mary Magdalene, and it was a starting point for the pilgrim-age to Santiago de Compostela in Spain *(see p302)*.

The star attractions of the Romanesque church are the tympanum sculpture (1120–35) above the central doorway, the exquisitely carved capitals in the nave and narthex, and the immense Gothic choir.

Dijon ⓘ

See pp184–5.

Beaune ⓘ

Côte D'Or. 🏠 23,000. 🚉 🚌 ℹ *Boulevard Pepreuil (03-80 26 21 30).* 🎵 *Baroque Music (Jul).*

The indisputable highlight of the old center of Beaune is the **Hôtel-Dieu**. The hospice was founded in 1443 for the town's inhabitants, many of whom were left poverty-stricken after the Hundred Years' War. Today it is considered a medieval jewel, with its superb multicolored Burgundian roof tiles. It houses many treasures, including the religious masterpiece, Rogier van der Weyden's *Last Judgement* polyptych.

The Hôtel des Ducs de Bourgogne, built in the 14th–16th centuries, houses the **Musée du Vin de Bourgogne**, with displays of traditional winemaking equipment.

Further to the north is the 12th-century Romanesque church, the **Collégiale Notre-Dame**, which has a collection of fine 15th-century tapestries.

🏛 Hôtel-Dieu
Rue de l'Hôtel-Dieu. *Tel* 03-80 24 45 00. ◯ daily. ● Dec–Mar: 11:30am–2pm daily. 📷 📷 ♿

Lyon ⓘ

Rhône. 🏠 453,000. ✈ 25 km (16 miles) E. 🚉 🚌 ℹ Place Belle-cour (04-72 77 69 69). ● daily.
www.lyon-france.com

Dramatically situated on the banks of the Rhône and Saône rivers, Lyon has been a vital gateway between the north and south since ancient times. Vieux Lyon, the oldest part of the city, is the site of the Roman settlement of Lugdunum, the commercial and military capital of Gaul founded by Julius Caesar in 44 BC. Vestiges of this prosperous city can be seen in the superb **Musée de la Civilisation Gallo-Romaine**. There are also two excavated Roman amphitheaters: the **Grand Théâtre**, built in 15 BC to seat 30,000 spectators, and the smaller **Odéon**.

Other major sights are the 19th-century mock-Byzantine **Basilique Notre-Dame de Fourvière**, and the **Cathédrale St-Jean**, begun in the 12th century. Vieux Lyon's fine Renaissance mansions are the former homes of bankers and silk merchants.

THE DUKES OF BURGUNDY

In the 14th and 15th centuries the dukes of Burgundy built up one of the most powerful states in Europe, which in-cluded Flanders and parts of Holland. From the time of Philip the Bold (1342–1404) the ducal court became a center of art, chivalry, and immense wealth. The duchy's demise came with the death of Charles the Bold in 1477.

Tomb of Philip the Bold in Dijon's Musée des Beaux Arts *(see p184)*

Cathédrale St-Jean at the foot of the slopes of Vieux Lyon

The excellent **Musée des Beaux Arts** showcases the country's largest and most important collection of fine arts after the Louvre. The modern works, dating from after the mid-1900s, have found a new home in the **Musée d'Art Contemporain** in the north of the city. An exquisite display of silks and tapestries, some dating back to early Christian times, can be seen in the **Musée des Tissus**.

🏛 **Musée de la Civilisation Gallo-Romaine**
17 Rue Cléberg. *Tel* 04-72 38 49 30.
◻ *Tue–Sun.* ● *public hols.* 🎟 ♿

Annecy ㉒

Annecy. 🏙 *51,000.* 🚉 🚌 🛈 *1 Rue Jean Jaurès (04-50 45 00 33).* ☀ *Tue, Fri–Sun.* **www**.lac-annecy.com

Annecy is one of the most beautiful towns in the Alps, set at the northern tip of Lac d'Annecy and surrounded by snow-capped mountains.

A stroll around the town's small medieval quarter, with its canals, flower-covered bridges, and arcaded streets,

is one of the main attractions of a stay here. Look out for the formidable **Palais de l'Isle**, a 12th-century prison in the middle of the Thiou canal.

The turreted **Château d'Annecy**, perched high on a hill, affords fine panoramic views. The clear waters of the lake are perfect for swimming and water sports. Boat trips leave from the Quai Thiou.

Environs
One way to enjoy the area's spectacular scenery is to take a boat to **Talloires**, a tiny lakeside village, noted for its hotels and restaurants.

Grenoble ㉓

Isère. 🏙 *165,000.* ✈ 🚉 🚌
🛈 *14 Rue de la République (04-76 42 41 41).* ☀ *Tue–Sun.*

Ancient capital of Dauphiné, Grenoble is a busy and thriving city, attractively located at the confluence of the Drac and Isère rivers, in the shadow of the mighty Vercors and Chartreuse massifs.

A cable car from the Quai Stéphane-Jay on the north bank of the Isère takes you up to the 16th-century **Fort de la Bastille**, where you are rewarded with magnificent views of the city and surrounding mountains. From here, paths lead down through pretty gardens to the excellent **Musée Dauphinois** at the foot of the hill. Housed in a 17th-century convent, the museum contains displays on local history, arts, and crafts.

On the other side of the river, the focus of life is the Place Grenette, a lively square lined with sidewalk cafés. Nearby, the Place St-André is the heart of the medieval city, overlooked by Grenoble's oldest buildings, including the 13th-century **Eglise St-André** and the 15th-century **Palais de Justice**.

Also worth visiting is the **Musée de Grenoble**, the city's principal art museum. With works by Chagall, Picasso, and Matisse, the modern collection is especially good.

🏛 **Musée de Grenoble**
5 Place de Lavalette. *Tel* 04-76 63 44 44. ◻ *Wed–Mon.* ● *Jan 1, May 1, Dec 25.* 🎟 📷 ♿

Annecy's 12th-century Palais de l'Isle on the Thiou canal

Street by Street: Dijon ⑲

The center of Dijon is noted for its architectural splendor – a legacy from the dukes of Burgundy *(see p182)*. Wealthy parliament members also had elegant *hôtels particuliers* (private mansions) built in the 17th and 18th centuries. The capital of Burgundy, Dijon today has a rich cultural life and a renowned university. The city's great art treasures are housed in the Palais des Ducs. Dijon is also famous for its mustard and *pain d'épice* (gingerbread), a reminder of the town's position on the medieval spice route. A major rail hub during the 19th century, it now has a TGV link to Paris.

Hôtel de Voguë
This elegant 17th-century mansion is decorated with Burgundian cabbages and fruit garlands by Hugues Sambin.

★ **Notre-Dame**
This magnificent 13th-century Gothic church is best known for its many gargoyles, the Jacquemart clock, and, on the north wall, the sculpted owl (chouette), said to bring good luck when touched.

Train and bus stations

RUE ODEBERT

RUE QUENTIN

RUE DE LA PREFECTURE

RUE MUSETTE

RUE DES FORGES

RUE DE LA LIBERTE

RUE DU BOURG

RUE J. MERCIER

R. VAUBAN

PL DE LIBERAT

Musée des Beaux Arts
The collection of Flemish masters here includes this 14th-century triptych by Jacques de Baerze and Melchior Broederlam.

Place de la Libération
was created by Mansart in the 17th century.

★ **Palais des Ducs**
The dukes of Burgundy held court here, but the building seen today was mainly built in the 17th century for the parliament. It now houses the Musée des Beaux Arts.

Rue Verrerie

This cobbled street in the old merchants' quarter is lined with medieval half-timbered houses. Some, such as Nos. 8, 10, and 12, have fine wood carvings.

VISITORS' CHECKLIST

Côte d'Or. 🏠 153,000. ✈ 5 km (3 miles) SSE. 🚃 🚌 Cours de la Gare. 🛈 11 rue des Forges (08-92 70 05 58). 🏛 Tue, Fri, Sat. 🎵 Festival de Musique (Jun); Fêtes de la Vigne (Sep). **Musée des Beaux Arts Tel** 03-80 74 52 09. ◯ Wed–Mon. ● main public hols. 🎟 ♿ **Musée Magnin Tel** 03-80 67 11 10. ◯ Tue–Sun. ● some public hols. 🎟 ♿ limited.

★ St-Michel

Begun in the 15th century and completed in the 17th century, St-Michel's facade combines Flamboyant Gothic with Renaissance details. On the richly carved porch, angels and biblical motifs mingle with mythological themes.

Musée Magnin

A collection of French and foreign 16th–19th-century paintings is displayed among period furniture in this 17th-century mansion.

The Eglise St-Etienne
dates from the 11th century but has been rebuilt many times. Its characteristic lantern was added in 1686.

STAR SIGHTS

★ Palais des Ducs

★ Notre-Dame

★ St-Michel

KEY

– – – Suggested route

0 meters   100

0 yards   100

The Wines of France

Winemaking in France dates back to pre-Roman times, although it was the Romans who disseminated the culture of the vine and the practise of wine-making throughout the country. The range, quality, and reputation of the fine wines of Bordeaux, Burgundy, and Champagne in particular have made them role models the world over. France's everyday wines can be highly enjoyable too, with plenty of good-value *IGP (Indication Géographique Protegée)* and *vins de France* now emerging from the southern regions. Many wine producers offer tours and have their own tasting rooms, where visitors can try a selection of wines without feeling pressurized to buy.

Château Cos d'Estournel, *in the Bordeaux region, produces a rich and fruity Cabernet Sauvignon. The grandeur of its exotic design is typical of château architecture.*

THE WINE REGIONS OF FRANCE

Each of the 10 principal wine-producing regions has its own identity, based on grape varieties, climate and soil, and local culture. Around 40 percent of all French wines are included in the *appellation d'origine contrôlée* system, which guarantees their style and geographic origin, though not their quality.

BORDEAUX WINES

Bordeaux is the world's largest fine wine region, and, for its red wines, certainly the most familiar outside France. The great wine-producing areas lie close to the banks of the rivers Gironde, Garonne, and Dordogne. These rivers, and the river port of Bordeaux itself, have been crucial to the region's wine trade; some of the prettiest châteaux line the river banks, enabling easy transportation. Grape varieties used include Cabernet Sauvignon, Merlot, and Petit Verdot (red); Sémillon and Sauvignon Blanc (white).

Château Pitray

Château Thieuley

HOW TO READ A WINE LABEL

Even the simplest label will provide a key to the wine's flavor and quality. It will bear the name of the wine and its producer, its vintage if there is one, and whether it comes from a strictly defined area (*appellation contrôlée* or is a more general *IGP* or *vin de France*. It may also have a regional grading, as with the *crus classés* in Bordeaux. The shape and color of the bottle are also guides. Most good-quality wine is bottled in green glass, which helps to protect it from light.

The property or producer

Château-bottled, rather than a wine from a grower's cooperative or a merchant

NIS EN BOUTEILLE AU CH...EAU
CHÂTEAU MARGAUX
GRAND VIN

PREMIER GRAND CRU CLASSÉ
MARGAUX

Capacity of the bottle

The vintage, from the French word *vendange*, or harvest

The wine's *appellation contrôlée*

Domaine François Raveneau **Domaine Michel Lafarge**

BURGUNDY WINES

The tiny vineyards in each of Burgundy's wine-producing regions, from Chablis in the north to Beaujolais in the south, can produce wines that, at their best, are unequalled anywhere else. This is unmissable territory for the "serious" wine-lover, with its time-honored traditions and dazzling *grands crus*. Grape varieties used include Pinot Noir, Gamay, and César (red); Pinot Blanc and Chardonnay (white).

TOURS OF MAJOR WINERIES

Winemakers are usually happy to welcome tourists in summer, but try not to visit at harvest time (Sep–Oct). Whatever time of year you visit, be sure to make an appointment in advance.

Bordeaux
Château Figeac
Saint Emilion. *Tel 05-57 24 72 26.*
www.chateau-figeac.com

Château Haut-Brion
Pessac. *Tel 05-56 00 29 30.*
www.haut-brion.com

Château Margaux
Margaux. *Tel 05-57 88 83 83.*
www.chateau-margaux.com

Château Lafite Rothschild
Pauillac. *Tel 05-56 73 18 18.*
www.lafite.com

Burgundy
Domaine Brocard
Préhy, near Chablis. *Tel 03-86 41 49 00.* www.brocard.fr

Maison Louis Latour
18 Rue des Tonneliers, Beaune.
Tel 03-80 24 81 00.
www.louislatour.com

Champagne
Moët & Chandon
20 Avenue de Champagne, Epernay. *Tel 03-26 51 20 00.*
www.moet.com

Piper Heidsieck
51 Boulevard Henry Vasnier, Reims. *Tel 03-26 84 43 00.*
www.piper-heidsieck.com

Tattinger
9 Place Nicaise, Reims.
Tel 03-26 85 45 35.
www.tattinger.fr

Champagne *is a region synonymous with the finest sparkling wines. The skill of the blenders, using reserves of older wines, creates consistency and excellence year on year. Champagne bubbles are produced by fermenting yeast inside the bottle – traditional methods are still used all over the region. In a process called remuage, bottles are gradually rotated in order to loosen the sediment, which is ultimately removed from the wine.*

KEY

- Alsace and Lorraine
- Bordeaux
- Burgundy
- Champagne
- Jura and Savoie
- Languedoc-Roussillon
- The Loire Valley
- Provence
- The Rhône Valley
- Southwest France

Chardonnay vines *in the grand cru vineyard of Corton-Charlemagne produce some of the greatest white Burgundies of all. The Chardonnay grape is now cultivated not only in Burgundy and Champagne, but all over the world.*

Southwest France

The southwest is farming France, a green and peaceful land nurturing crops from sunflowers to walnuts. Other key country products include forest timber, Bordeaux wines, and wild mushrooms. Major modern industries, including aerospace, are focused on the two chief cities, Bordeaux and Toulouse. Visitors are mainly drawn to the wine chateaux, the ski slopes of the Pyrenees, and the prehistoric caves of the Dordogne. The major sights of this favored region include some of France's most celebrated Romanesque buildings.

Monument aux Girondins, Place des Quinconces, Bordeaux

Bordeaux ㉔

Gironde. 👥 220,000. ✈ 🚋 🚌
🅸 12 Cours du 30 Juillet (05-56 00 66 00). 🔄 daily. 🎭 Fête du Vin (Jun every two years from 2012).
www.bordeaux-tourisme.com

Built on a curve of the Garonne river, Bordeaux has been a major port since pre-Roman times and for centuries a focus and crossroads of European trade. The export of wine has always been the basis of the city's prosperity, and today the Bordeaux region produces over 70 million cases of wine per year.

Along the waterfront, a long sweep of Classical façades is broken by the Esplanade des Quinconces, with its statues and fountains. At one end, the Monument aux Girondins (1804–1902) commemorates the Girondists sent to the guillotine by Robespierre

during the Terror (1793–5). Buildings of architectural interest include the massive **Basilique St-Michel**, begun in 1350, which took 200 years to complete, and the 18th-century **Grand Théâtre**, a magnificent example of the French Neoclassical style. The **Musée des Beaux Arts** holds an excellent collection of paintings, ranging from the Renaissance to our time.

🏛 **Musée des Beaux Arts**
20 Cours d'Albret. **Tel** 05-56 10 20 56. ⭕ Wed–Mon. ⬤ public hols.
🖼

Environs
The tourist office in Bordeaux organizes tours to various wine châteaux (see pp186–7).

Lascaux ㉕

Montignac. **Tel** 05-53 51 95 03. ⭕ mid-Feb–Mar & Nov–Dec: Tue–Sun; Easter– Oct: daily. ⬤ Jan–mid-Feb, Dec 25. 🖼 ✔

Lascaux is the most famous of the prehistoric sites in the Dordogne region. Four young boys and their dog came

across the caves and their astounding Palaeolithic paintings in 1940, and the importance of their discovery was swiftly recognized.

Lascaux has been closed to the public since 1963 because of deterioration due to carbon dioxide caused by breathing. An exact copy, Lascaux II, has been created a few minutes' walk down the hillside, using the same materials. The replica is beautiful and should not be spurned: high-antlered elk, bison, and plump horses cover the walls, moving in herds or files, surrounded by arrows and geometric symbols thought to have had ritual significance.

Toulouse ㉖

Haute-Garonne. 👥 390,000. ✈ 🚋 🚌
🚆 🅸 Donjon du Capitole (08-92 18 01 80). 🔄 Tue–Sun. 🎭 Piano (Sep), Contemporary dance (end Jan–early Feb). www.toulouse-tourisme.com

Toulouse, the most important town in southwest France, is the country's fourth largest metropolis, and a major industrial and university city.

The area is also famous for its aerospace industry; Concorde, Airbus, and the Ariane space rocket all originated here. Airbus tours can be booked at www.taxiway.fr. **Cité de l'Espace** has a planetarium and interactive exhibits on space exploration.

The church known as **Les Jacobins** was begun in 1229 and took over two centuries to finish. The Gothic masterpiece features a soaring, 22-branched palm tree vault in the apse.

Palm vaulting in the apse of Les Jacobins, Toulouse

A picturesque village set in a lush valley among the foothills of the Pyrenees mountains

The bell tower (1294) is much imitated in southwest France. Toulouse became a center of Romanesque art in Europe due to its position on the route to Santiago de Compostela *(see p302)*. The largest Romanesque basilica in Europe, the **Basilique de St-Sernin**, was built in the 11th–12th centuries to accommodate pilgrims. The **Musée des Augustins** has sculptures from the period, and incorporates cloisters from a 14th-century Augustinian priory. Also featured are French, Italian, and Flemish paintings.

The 16th-century palace known as the **Hôtel d'Assézat** now houses the Fondation Bemberg, named after local art lover Georges Bemberg, with Renaissance art and 19th- and 20th-century French work.

🏛 **Musée des Augustins**
21 Rue de Metz. *Tel* 05-61 22 21 82. ◯ daily. ● Jan 1, May 1, Dec 25. ◻ ☑ ☒ ☒ www.augustins.org

Pyrenees ㉗

✕ Pau. ☐ ▭ Bayonne & Pau.
ℹ Place des Basques, Bayonne (08-20 42 64 64); Place Royale, Pau (05-59 27 27 08).

The mountains dominate life in the French Pyrenees. A region in many ways closer to Spain than France, over the centuries its remote terrain and tenacious people have given heretics a hiding place and refugees an escape route.

The **Parc National des Pyrénées** extends 100 km (62 miles) along the French–Spanish frontier. It boasts some of the most splendid alpine scenery in Europe, and is rich in flora and fauna. Within the park are 350 km (217 miles) of footpaths.

The region's oldest inhabitants, the Basque people, have maintained their own language and culture. **Bayonne** on the Atlantic coast is the capital of the French Basque country, and has been an important town since Roman times. **Biarritz**, west of Bayonne, has two casinos and three good beaches, with the best surfing in Europe. A short distance south, **St-Jean-de-Luz** is a sleepy fishing village that explodes into life in summer. A main attraction is the Eglise St-Jean Baptiste, where Louis XIV married the Infanta Maria Teresa of Spain in 1660.

A lively university town with elegant architecture, **Pau** is the most interesting large town in the central Pyrenees. It has long been a favorite resort of affluent foreigners.

Other places of interest include the many mountain ski resorts, the shrine at **Lourdes**, and the pretty hilltop town of **St-Bertrand-de-Comminges**.

THE MIRACLE OF LOURDES

In 1858, a 14-year-old girl named Bernadette Soubirous experienced 18 visions of the Virgin at the Grotte Massabielle near the town of Lourdes. Despite being told to keep away from the cave by her mother – and the local magistrate – she was guided to a spring with miraculous healing powers. The

Pilgrims at an open-air mass in Lourdes

church endorsed the miracles in the 1860s, and since then many people claim to have been cured by the holy water. A huge city of shrines, churches, and hospices has since grown up around the spring, with a dynamic tourist industry to match.

The South of France

The south is France's most popular holiday region, drawing millions of visitors each year to the resorts of the Riviera and the Côte d'Azur, and to the vivid landscape and historic villages of Provence. Painters such as Cézanne, van Gogh, and Picasso, have been inspired by the luminous light and brilliant colors of the region. Agriculture is still a mainstay of the economy, but the high-tech industries of Nice also make a significant contribution to the region's prosperity.

Château Comtal in the restored citadel of Carcassonne

Carcassonne ㉘

Aude. 🏠 46,000. 🚗 🚌 ✈ 🚶 ℹ 28 Rue de Verdun (04-68 10 24 30). 🛒 Tue, Thu & Sat. 🎭 Festival de la Cité (all of Jul), Medieval fête (Aug). **www**.carcassonne-tourisme.com

The citadel of Carcassonne is a perfectly restored medieval town. It crowns a steep bank above the Aude river, a fairy-tale sight of turrets and ramparts overlooking the Basse Ville below.

The strategic position of the citadel between the Atlantic and the Mediterranean led to its original settlement, consolidated by the Romans in the 2nd century BC.

At its zenith in the 12th century the town was ruled by the Trencavels, who built the château and cathedral. The Cathars, a persecuted Christian sect, were given sanctuary here in 1209 but, after a two-week siege, the town fell to the Crusaders sent to eradicate them. The attentions of architectural historian Viollet-le-Duc led to Carcassonne's restoration in the 19th century.

Flanked by sandstone towers, the defenses of the **Porte Narbonnaise** included two portcullises, two iron doors, a moat, and a draw-bridge. A fortress within a fortress, the **Château Comtal** has a surrounding moat and five defensive towers.

Within the Romanesque and Gothic **Basilique St-Nazaire** is the famous Siege Stone, inscribed with scenes said to depict the siege of 1209.

Nîmes ㉙

Gard. 🏠 145,000. ✈ 🚶 🚌 ℹ 6 Rue Auguste (04-66 58 38 00). 🛒 daily. **www**.ot-nimes.fr

An important crossroads in the ancient world, Nîmes is well known for its bullfights and Roman antiquities. The city has had a turbulent history, and suffered particularly in the 16th-century Wars of Religion, when the Romanesque **Cathédrale Notre-Dame et St-Castor** was badly damaged. In the 17th and 18th centuries the town prospered from textile manufacturing, one of the most enduring products being denim or serge de Nîmes.

All roads in the city lead to the amphitheater, **Les Arènes**. Built at the end of the 1st century AD, it is still in use today as a venue for concerts, sporting events, and bullfights.

The **Maison Carrée** is an elegant Roman temple, the pride of Nîmes. Built by Augustus' son-in-law Marcus Agrippa, it is one of the best preserved in the world, with finely fluted Corinthian columns and a sculpted frieze.

Set in the Roman wall is the **Porte d'Auguste**, a gateway built for travelers on the Domitian Way, which passed through the center of Nîmes. Nearby is the **Castellum**, a tower used for storing water brought in by aqueduct. The water was distributed around the town by a canal system. A display of Roman statues and mosaics can be seen at the **Musée Archéologique**.

Five floors of Nîmes' controversial arts complex, the **Carré d'Art**, which stands opposite the Maison Carrée, lie underground. The complex incorporates a library, a roof-terrace restaurant around a huge glass atrium, and the Musée d'Art Contemporain.

🏛 **Musée Archéologique**
13 bis Boulevard Amiral Courbet. **Tel** 04-66 76 74 80. ⬤ Tue–Sun. ⬤ Jan 1, May 1, Nov 1, Dec 25.

Environs

To the northeast of the city lies the **Pont du Gard**, a 2,000-year-old aqueduct. The Romans considered this to be the best testimony to the greatness of their empire, and at 49 m (160 ft) it was the highest bridge they ever built.

The Pont du Gard, outside Nîmes, a major feat of Roman engineering

Avignon 🟥

Vaucluse. 🏢 100,000. ✈ 🚉 🚌
ℹ 41 Cours Jean Jaurès (04-32 74
32 74). 🏪 Tue–Sun. 🎭 Le Festival
d'Avignon (mid-Jul–mid-Aug).
www.avignon-tourisme.com

Massive ramparts enclose this
fascinating town. The huge
Palais des Papes is the
dominant feature, but
Avignon contains other riches.
To the north of the Palais is
the 13th-century **Musée du
Petit Palais**, once the Archbishop of Avignon's residence.
It has received such notorious
guests as Cesare Borgia and
Louis XIV. Now a museum,
it displays Romanesque
and Gothic sculpture and
paintings of the Avignon and
Italian Schools, with works by
Botticelli and Carpaccio.

Avignon boasts some fine
churches, such as the 12th-
century **Cathédrale de Notre-**

**Open-air performance at
the annual Avignon Festival**

Dame-des-Doms, with its
Romanesque cupola and
papal tombs, and the 14th-
century **Eglise St-Didier**.

The **Musée Lapidaire**
contains statues, mosaics,
and carvings from pre-Roman
Provence. The **Musée Calvet**
features a superb array of
exhibits, including Roman
finds. It also gives an overview
of French art during the past
500 years, with works by

Rodin, Manet, and Dufy.
The Place de l'Horloge is the
center of Avignon's social life.
Under the town hall's Gothic
clock tower stands a merry-
go-round from 1900. Until the
19th century, brightly-patterned
calicoes called *indiennes* were
printed nearby. These inspired
today's Provençal patterns.

From mid-July until mid-
August, the Avignon Festival
takes place at the Palais des
Papes. France's largest festival,
it includes ballet, drama, and
classical concerts. The "Off"
festival has street theater and
music from folk to jazz.

The **Pont St-Bénézet**, built
from 1171–1185, once had 22
arches, but most were destroyed by floods in 1668. One
of the remaining arches bears
the tiny Chapelle St-Nicolas.

> ⛪ **Palais des Papes**
> Place du Palais-des-Papes. **Tel** 04-90
> 27 50 00. ⭘ daily. 🈲 🎫

PALAIS DES PAPES

Pope Clement V moved the papal court to Avignon
in 1309. Here it remained until 1377, during which
time his successors transformed the modest episcopal building into the present magnificent palace.

The **Consistory Hall**
contains frescoes
(1340) by Simone
Martini.

Bell tower

Grand Tinel
*This vast banqueting hall was used
for celebrating religious festivals.*

The **Stag Room**, Clement
VI's study, is covered in
14th-century hunting
frescoes and ceramic tiles.

**Pope's
Chamber**

Benedict XII's cloister
incorporates the guest
and staff wings, and the
Benedictine chapel.

The Great Audience Hall is
divided into two naves by
five sculpted columns.

The Great Chapel was
once covered in green
tapestries ornamented
with red roses.

Street-by-Street: Arles ❸

Few other towns in Provence combine all the region's charms so well as Arles. Its position on the Rhône makes it a natural gateway to the Camargue *(see p195)*. Its Roman remains, such as Constantine's baths and the amphitheater, are complemented by the ocher walls and Roman-tiled roofs of later buildings. Van Gogh spent time here in 1888–9, but Arles is no longer the industrial town he painted. Visitors are now its main business, and entertainment ranges from the Arles Festival to bullfights. A bastion of Provençal tradition and culture, its museums are among the best in the region. For enthusiasts, an inclusive ticket is available giving access to all museums and monuments. All the tourist sites in Arles are within walking distance of the central Place de la République.

The Musée Réattu houses 18th-century and modern art, including Picasso sketches, paintings by local artist Jacques Réattu (1760–1833), sculptures by Russian-born Ossip Zadkine (1890–1967), and photography.

View of Arles from the opposite bank of the Rhône

The Palais Constantine was once a grand imperial palace. Now only its vast Roman baths remain, dating from the 4th century AD.

The Museon Arlaten was founded in 1904 by the Provençal poet Frédéric Mistral with his Nobel Prize money. It is currently closed for renovations, and is due to reopen in 2014.

The Hôtel de Ville, the town hall, has an impressive vaulted ceiling.

★ Eglise St-Trophime
This fine Romanesque church has an ornate 12th-century portal carved with saints and apostles.

L'Espace Van Gogh is dedicated to the famous artist's life and works.

STAR SIGHTS

- ★ Les Arènes
- ★ Théâtre Antique
- ★ Eglise St-Trophime

Roman Obelisk
This ancient obelisk with fountains at its base (one of which is shown here) came from the Roman circus across the Rhône.

★ **Les Arènes**
*The amphitheater is
one of the best-
preserved Roman sites
in Provence. The top
tier provides an
excellent panoramic
view of Arles.*

★ **Théâtre Antique**
*Once a Roman theater, its
stones were later used for
other buildings. These last
remaining columns
are called the
"two widows".*

RUE DE GRILLE
RUE BARBES
RUE ARISTIDE BRIAND
ROND-POINT DES ARÈNES
RUE A TARDIEU
RUE DE LA BASTILLE
RUE DIDEROT
CALADE
PLACE DE
LA MAJOR
RUE GRAND COUVENT
RUE DE LA MADELEINE
CLOITRE
RUE PORTE-DE-LAURE
MONTEE VAUBAN
EVARD DES LICES

**Notre-Dame-de-la-
Major** is dedicated to
St. George, patron
saint of the Camargue
gardians (cowboys).

**Cloisters of
St-Trophime**
*This sculpted
capital is a fine
example of the
Romanesque beauty
of the cloisters.*

AMPHITHEATER

The most impressive of the
surviving Roman monuments,
the amphitheater was the
largest of the Roman buildings
in Gaul. Slightly oval, it measures 136 m (446 ft) by 107 m
(351 ft) and could seat 21,000.
The floors of some of the
internal rooms were decorated
with mosaics, the better to
wash down after bloody
affrays. Today bullfights, bull
races, and other events are
held regularly in the arena.

Rodeo-style games in the arena

KEY

– – – Suggested route

0 meters ————— 100

0 yards ————— 100

Camargue ❷

Bouches-du-Rhône. 🚃 🚌 🛈 5
Ave Van Gogh, Stes-Maries-de-la-Mer
(04-90 97 82 55). 🎭 Pèlerinage des
Gitans (end May & end Oct).
www.saintesmaries.com

This flat, sparsely populated land is one of Europe's major wetland regions and natural history sites. Extensive areas of salt marsh, lakes, pastures, and sand dunes cover a vast 140,000 ha (346,000 acres). The native white horses and black bulls are tended by the region's cowboys, or *gardians*. Numerous seabirds and wildfowl also occupy the region.

Bullfights are advertised in **Saintes-Maries-de-la-Mer**, the region's main tourist center, which has a sandy beach with water sports and boat trips.

A few kilometers inland, the information center at **Pont-de-Gau** offers wonderful views over the flat lagoon. Photographs and documents chronicle the history of the Camargue and its diverse flora and fauna. Most of the birds that live in or migrate within the region, including thousands of flamingoes which come here to breed, can be seen at the nearby **Parc Ornithologique du Pont-de-Gau**.

Camargue
gardian

In the north of the region, a traditional Provençal *mas* or farmhouse, Mas du Pont de Rousty, has been converted to accommodate the fascinating **Musée Camarguais**. Displays here provide an introduction to the customs and traditions of the Camargue.

🦅 Parc Ornithologique du Pont-de-Gau
Pont-de-Gau. **Tel** 04-90 97 82 62.
◯ daily. ⬤ Dec 25. 🎫 ⚫

🏛 Musée Camarguais
Parc Naturel Régional de Camargue,
Mas du Pont de Rousty. **Tel** 04-90 97
10 82. ◯ Wed–Mon. ⬤ public
hols. 🎫 ⚫

Impressionist painter Cézanne's studio in Aix-en-Provence

Aix-en-Provence ❸

Bouches-du-Rhône. 🏘 140,000. 🚃
🚌 🛈 2 Place Général de Gaulle
(04-42 16 11 61). 🅿 daily.
www.aixenprovencetourism.com

Provence's former capital is an international students' town, with a university that dates back to 1409. The city was transformed in the 17th century, when ramparts, first raised by the Romans in their town of Aquae Sextiae, were pulled down, and the mansion-lined Cours Mirabeau was built.

North of the Cours Mirabeau lies the town's old quarter. **Cathédrale St-Sauveur** creaks with history. The jewel of the church is the triptych of *The Burning Bush* (1476) by Nicolas Froment. The modest **Atelier Paul Cézanne**, a studio designed by Cézanne himself, is much as he left it when he died in 1906.

The main museum is the **Musée Granet**. François Granet (1775–1849) left his collection of French, Italian, and Flemish paintings to Aix. Work by Provençal artists is also shown, some by Granet.

🏛 Musée Granet
13 Rue Cardinale. **Tel** 04-42 52 88
32. ◯ Tue–Sun. 🎫 ⚫

Marseille ❹

Bouches-du-Rhône. 🏘 1,000,000.
✈ 25 km NW. 🚃 🚌 🛈 4 La
Canebière (08-26 50 05 00). 🅿
daily. **www**.marseille-tourisme.com

France's most important port and oldest major city is centered on the surprisingly attractive Vieux Port. On the north side are the commercial docks and the old town, rebuilt after World War II.

The old town's finest building is the **Vieille Charité**, a large, well-restored 17th-century hospice. The first floor has a small but rich collection of ancient Egyptian artifacts.

The Neo-Byzantine **Notre-Dame-de-la-Garde** dominates the city but Marseille's finest piece of religious architecture is the **Abbaye de St-Victor**, founded in the 5th century, with crypts containing catacombs, sarcophagi, and the cave of the martyr St. Victor.

During postwar rebuilding the Roman docks were uncovered. The **Musée des Docks Romains** mainly displays large storage urns once used for wine, grain, and oil. In the Centre Bourse shopping center is the **Musée d'Histoire de Marseille** (closed for renovations until 2013). Reconstructions of the city at the height of the Greek period make this a good starting point for a tour.

Old harbor of Marseille, looking towards the Quai de Rive Neuve

Flavors of the South of France

It's a heady experience just to stand, look, and sniff in a Provençal market. Tables sag under piles of braided pink garlic, colorful fresh peppers, tomatoes, eggplants, zucchini, and asparagus. In the fall and winter an earthy scent fills the air, with wild mushrooms, Swiss chard, walnuts, and quinces crowding the stalls. The waters of Coastal Provence provide a bountiful sea harvest, including plump mussels, oysters, and *tellines* (tiny clams). The area is especially famous for its fish dishes, notably *bouillabaisse*. Lamb is the most common meat in Provence; the best comes from the Camargue, where lambs graze on herbs and salt-marsh grass. The South supplies France with the first of the season's peaches, cherries, and apricots.

Rosemary

Fish liquor

Red snapper

Bouillabaisse, *a fish soup originating in Marseille, is a luxury today. It consists of an assortment of local seafood including monkfish, mullet, snapper, scorpion fish, and conger eel, flavoured with tomatoes, saffron, and olive oil. Traditionally, the fish liquor is served first with croutons spread with rouille, a spicy mayonnaise. The fish is eaten afterwards.*

Croutons

Rouille (meaning "rust"), a mayonnaise with chillies and garlic

Monkfish

Conger eel **Red mullet**

OLIVES AND OLIVE OIL
Most of the olive crop is crushed for oil. Ripe olives are black and the unripe ones are green; both can be preserved in brine or oil. At the end of the olive harvest *tapenade* is popular, a paste of black olives, capers, anchovies, and olive oil eaten with bread.

Fougasse *is a flattish, lattice-like bread variously studded with black olives, anchovies, onions, and spices. The sweet version is flavoured with almonds.*

HUILE D'OLIVE VIERGE

Black olives **Tapenade** **Olive oil**

Aïoli *is a sauce made of egg yolks, garlic, and olive oil. It is served with salt cod, boiled eggs, snails, or raw vegetables.*

Ratatouille *is a stew of onions, eggplants, zucchini, tomatoes, and peppers, cooked in olive oil and garlic.*

Salade Niçoise *comes in many versions but always includes lettuce, green beans, tomatoes, black olives, eggs, and anchovies.*

The Côte d'Azur

The Côte d'Azur is, without doubt, the most celebrated seaside in Europe. Almost everybody who has been anybody for the past 100 years has succumbed to its glittering allure. Today the Côte d'Azur is busy all year round; expect heavy traffic around Cannes and St-Tropez in summer. Between Cannes and Menton, the coast forms the glamorous French Riviera, playground of the rich and famous. The bustling city of Nice lies at the area's heart, richly deserving the title "capital of the Côte d'Azur."

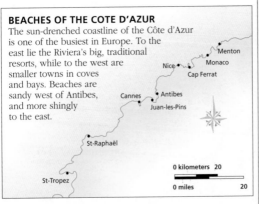

BEACHES OF THE COTE D'AZUR

The sun-drenched coastline of the Côte d'Azur is one of the busiest in Europe. To the east lie the Riviera's big, traditional resorts, while to the west are smaller towns in coves and bays. Beaches are sandy west of Antibes, and more shingly to the east.

Menton
Monaco
Nice
Cap Ferrat
Cannes   Antibes
Juan-les-Pins

St-Raphaël

0 kilometers 20
0 miles   20

St-Tropez

Exploring the Côte d'Azur

The Côte d'Azur is the most popular destination in France for sun-worshipers, with its seaside vacation towns and long, golden beaches. **St-Tropez** is currently the trendiest resort; Tahini-Plage is the coast's showcase for fun, sun, fashion, and glamor. By contrast, the family resort of **St-Raphaël** is peaceful, with excellent tourist facilities.

East of **Cannes**, at the western edge of the Riviera, **Juan-les-Pins** is a lively resort. Its all-night bars, nightclubs, and cafés make it popular with teenagers and young adults.

Founded by the Greeks, **Antibes** is one of the oldest towns along this stretch of coast, and home to a large museum of Picasso's work, donated by the artist himself.

Clifftop walks replace seafront promenades around the wooded peninsula of **Cap Ferrat**, where grand villas and private beaches can be glimpsed between the trees.

At the eastern edge of the Riviera, past the glitz of the casinos and hotels of **Monaco**, the beaches of **Menton** are the warmest along the coast; sunbathers enjoy a beach climate all year round.

Harborside at St-Tropez on the Côte d'Azur

For hotels and restaurants in this region see pp206–11 and pp212–17

Uma Thurman arriving at the Cannes Film Festival

Cannes ③⑤

Alpes-Maritimes. 🏙 70,000. ✈ 🚇 🚌 ℹ *Palais des Festivals, 1 La Croisette (04-92 99 84 22).* 🔄 *daily.*

The first thing that most people associate with Cannes is its many festivals, especially the International Film Festival held each May. The first Cannes Film Festival took place in 1946 and, for a while, it remained a small and exclusive affair. The mid-1950s marked the change from artistic event to media circus, but Cannes remains the international marketplace for moviemakers and distributors. The annual festival is held in the huge **Palais des Festivals**.

There is, however, more to the city than this glittering event. The Old Town is centered in the Le Suquet district, which is dominated by the church of **Notre-Dame de l'Espérance**, built in the 16th and 17th centuries in the Provençal Gothic style. The famed **Boulevard de la Croisette** is lined with palm trees. Luxury stores and hotels look out over fine sandy beaches.

Nice ③⑥

Alpes-Maritimes. 🏙 346,000. ✈ 🚇 🚌 ℹ *5 Promenade des Anglais (08-92 70 74 07).* 🔄 *Tue–Sun.* 🎭 *Carnival (Feb).* **www**.nicetourisme.com

The largest resort on the Mediterranean coast, Nice has the second busiest airport in France. Its temperate winter climate and verdant subtropical vegetation have long attracted visitors, and today it is also a center for business conferences and package travelers.

There are many art museums in Nice, two of which devote themselves to the works of particular artists. The **Musée Matisse** displays drawings, paintings, bronzes, fabrics, and artifacts. The **Musée Chagall** holds the largest collection of works by Marc Chagall, with paintings, drawings, sculpture, stained glass, and mosaics.

A strikingly original complex of four marble-faced towers linked by glass passageways houses the **Musée d'Art Contemporain**. The collection is particularly strong in Neo-Realism and Pop Art. The **Musée des Beaux Arts** displays works by Dufy, Monet, Renoir, and Sisley.

A 19th-century palace, the **Palais Masséna** is filled with paintings of the Nice school, works by the Impressionists, Provençal ceramics, folk art, and a gold cloak once worn by Napoleon's beloved Josephine.

The onion domes of the **Cathédrale Orthodoxe Russe St-Nicolas**, completed in 1912, make this Nice's most distinctive landmark.

🏛 **Musée Matisse**
164 Ave des Arènes de Cimiez.
Tel 04-93 81 08 08. 🕐 Wed–Mon.
◑ some public hols. &

🏛 **Musée Chagall**
36 Ave du Docteur Ménard. **Tel** 04-93 53 87 20. 🕐 Wed–Mon. ◑ Jan 1, May 1, Dec 25. 📷 &

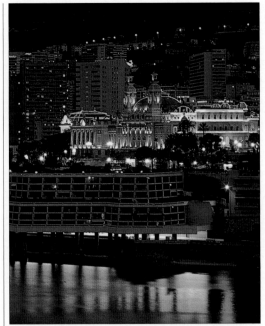

Skyscrapers and apartment blocks of modern Monte Carlo in Monaco

Monaco ③⑦

Monaco. 🏘 34,000. ✈ (Nice).
🚆 ℹ 2a Boulevard des Moulins (092-16 61 16). 🗓 daily. 🎪 International Circus Festival (Jan–Feb). **www**.visitmonaco.com

Arriving among the towering skyscrapers of Monaco today, it is hard to envisage the turbulence of its history. At first a Greek settlement, later taken by the Romans, it was bought from the Genoese in 1297 by the Grimaldis who, in spite of bitter family feuds, still rule as the world's oldest monarchy. Monaco covers 1.9 sq km (0.74 sq miles) and, although its size has increased by one-third in the form of landfills, it still occupies an area smaller than New York's Central Park.

The best-known section of Monaco is Monte Carlo. People flock to the annual car rally held here in January, but the area owes its renown mainly to its **Grand Casino**. Source of countless legends, it was instituted by Charles III to save himself from bankruptcy in 1856. So successful was this money-making venture that, by 1870, he was able to

abolish taxation for his people. Designed in 1878 and set in formal gardens, the casino gives a splendid view over Monaco. Even the most exclusive of the gaming rooms can be visited.

Across the harbor lies Monaco-Ville, the seat of government. The interior of the 13th-century **Palais Princier**, with its priceless furniture and magnificent frescoes, is open to the public from April to September.

The aquarium of the **Musée Océanographique** holds rare species of marine plants and animals. Marine explorer Jacques Cousteau established his research center here.

A quiet stretch along Nice's 5 km (3 miles) of beachfront

The lavish surroundings of the Belle Epoque Grand Casino

Practical Information

France is justifiably proud of its many attractions, for which it has good tourist information facilities. Both in France and abroad, French Government Tourist Offices are an invaluable source of reference for practical aspects of your stay, especially for those with special needs. If you are unfortunate enough to need medical or emergency assistance, France has excellent hospitals, ambulance, fire, and police services. The country also has a modern communications network, making it easy to keep in touch by telephone, post, or e-mail.

VISA REQUIREMENTS AND CUSTOMS

Currently there are no visa requirements for EU nationals or visitors from the United States, Canada, Australia or New Zealand who plan to stay in France for under three months. Visitors from most other countries require a tourist visa. Non-EU visitors can, with some exceptions, reclaim the French sales tax (TVA) on goods if they spend over a certain amount in one shop and get a *détaxe* receipt.

TOURIST INFORMATION

All major cities and large towns have *offices de tourisme*. Small towns and even villages have *syndicats d'initiative*. Both will give you town plans, advice on accommodations, and information on regional recreational and cultural activities.

You can also get information before you leave for France from **French Government Tourist Offices**, or by contacting local tourist offices (see

individual town headings in this guide) or the appropriate CRT (Comité Régional de Tourisme) – ask the FGTO for the address.

PERSONAL SECURITY

Violent crime is rare in France – even a major city such as Paris is surprisingly safe. However, muggings and brawls do occur, so avoid isolated or poorly lit places, especially at night. Women should take extra care, especially when traveling alone. Also beware of pickpockets, who are active in large cities.

POLICE

There are two types of police in France. The *Police Nationale* look after large towns and cities. If you need to contact them, find the *Commissariat de Police* (police headquarters). Small towns, villages, and country areas are policed by the *Gendarmerie Nationale*. If you need to report a crime in these places, go to the nearest local *gendarmerie*.

OPENING HOURS

Generally, opening hours for tourist sights are from 10am–5:40pm with one late evening per week. Most close on public holidays.

National museums and sights are normally closed on Tuesdays, with a few exceptions which close on Mondays. Municipal museums normally close on Mondays. Churches are open every day but sometimes shut at lunchtime.

FACILITIES FOR THE DISABLED

Facilities for the disabled vary in France. Details of services in most towns can be obtained from the **GIHP** (Groupement pour l'Insertion des Personnes Handicapées Physiques). The **Association des Paralysés de France** provides information on wheelchair access.

MEDICAL TREATMENT

All European Union Nationals are entitled to French social security coverage. However, treatment must be paid for at the time, and hospital rates vary widely. Reimbursements may be obtained if you have the correct documents before you travel, but the process is long and complicated.

All travelers, particularly non-EU nationals, should, therefore, consider purchasing travel insurance before they arrive. In the case of a medical emergency call **SAMU** (*Service d'Aide Médicale Urgence*). However, it is often faster to call **Sapeurs Pompiers** (the fire

THE CLIMATE OF FRANCE

Set on Europe's western edge, France has a varied, temperate climate. An Atlantic influence prevails in the northwest, with westerly sea winds bringing humidity and warm winters. The east experiences Continental temperature extremes with frosty, clear winters and often stormy summers. The south enjoys a Mediterranean climate, with hot, dry summers and mild winters.

PARIS
°C/F

month	Apr	Jul	Oct	Jan
°C/F high	14/58	24/75 15/59	16/61	
	7/44		9/49	7/44
°C/F low 0°C 32°F				2/35
sun	6 hrs	8 hrs	4.5 hrs	2 hrs
rain	50 mm	58 mm	55 mm	55 mm

NICE
°C/F

month	Apr	Jul	Oct	Jan
°C/F high	17/63	27/80 19/67	21/70	
	10/50		13/55	13/55
°C/F low 0°C 32°F				5/41
sun	7.5 hrs	11 hrs	6.5 hrs	5 hrs
rain	62 mm	16 mm	108 mm	83 mm

service), who offer a first aid and ambulance service. This is particularly true in rural areas.

Casualty departments (service des urgences) in public hospitals can deal with most medical problems. Your consulate should be able to provide you with details of an English-speaking doctor in the area. Pharmacists can also suggest treatments for many health problems. Look for the green cross sign outside pharmacies.

BANKING AND CURRENCY

The French unit of currency is the euro (see p15).

Most credit cards are widely accepted in France, but, because of the high commissions charged, American Express is often not. The most commonly used credit card is Carte Bleue/Visa. Eurocard/ MasterCard (Access in UK) is also often accepted. Credit cards issued in France contain a microchip and are called "smart cards," but many machines can also read cards with magnetic strips. If you find your conventional card cannot be read in the smart card slot get the cashier to swipe the card through the magnetic reader. You will be asked to tap in your PIN code (code confidentiel) on a small keypad.

You can also use credit cards in most banks to withdraw cash; either from an ATM (automatic teller machine), which should have an English language option, or from a cash desk. Most banks will cash traveler's checks. Opening hours are usually Mon–Fri, from 9am–4:30 or 5:15pm, with some banks also open on Saturday morning. Many close for lunch, and many, especially in the south, are closed on Monday.

You can also exchange money at bureaux de change offices, which operate longer hours than banks. Exchange rates and commission charges can vary.

COMMUNICATIONS

Payphones in France take mainly plastic telephone cards (télécartes). Only a few take coins. Cards are cheaper and more convenient to use than coins. They are sold in 50 or 120 units and can be bought at post offices, tobacconists (tabacs), and newsagents. For local calls, a unit lasts up to six minutes. Many phones also accept credit cards (with a PIN number). Some post offices have telephone booths (cabines) where you can call first and pay afterwards. This

is cheaper than making long-distance calls from hotels.

La Poste (the Post Office) used to be called the P.T.T. (postes, télégraphes, téléphones), and some road signs still give directions to the P.T.T. The postal service in France is fast and reliable. However, it is not cheap, especially when sending a parcel abroad.

At La Poste, postage stamps (timbres) are sold singly or in carnets of seven or ten. They are also sold at tabacs, although you need to go to the post office for international stamps. At post offices you can also use telephone directories (annuaires), buy phonecards, cash or buy money orders (mandats), and make international calls.

Post offices usually open from 9am–5pm Mon–Fri, often with a break for lunch, and 9am–noon on Saturdays. Mail boxes are yellow, and often have separate slots for the town you are in, the département, and other destinations (autres destinations).

Although the Internet is widely used in France, Internet cafés have not proved to be successful. However, there are usually a few in the major cities and resorts. In Paris there are free Wi-Fi spots in many metro stations.

DIRECTORY

EMBASSIES

Australia
4 Rue Jean Rey, 75015 Paris. **Tel** 01-40 59 33 06. **www**.france.embassy. gov.au

Canada
35 Ave Montaigne, 75008 Paris. **Tel** 01-44 43 29 00. **www**.canada international.gc.ca

UK
Consulate:
18bis Rue d'Anjou, 75008 Paris. **Tel** 01-44 51 31 00. **http://**ukinfrance.fco.gov. uk

US
2 Ave Gabriel, 75008 Paris. **Tel** 01-43 12 22 22. **http://**usembassy.gov

TOURIST INFORMATION

Paris Convention & Visitors Bureau Headquarters
25–27 Rue des Pyramides, 75001 Paris.
Tel 01495-24263.
www.franceguide.com

In Australia:
French Tourist Bureau, Level 22, 25 Bligh Street, Sydney, NSW 2000. **Tel** 612-9321 5244.

In Canada:
1800 Ave McGill College, Suite 1010, Montréal, Québec H3A 3J6. **Tel** 288-2026.

In the UK:
Lincoln House, 300 High Holborn, London WC1V 7JH. **Tel** 0906-824 4123.

In the US:
444 Madison Ave, New York, NY 10022. **Tel** 212-838 7800.

FACILITIES FOR THE DISABLED

Association des Paralysés de France
17 Bld August Blanqui, 75013 Paris.
Tel 01-45 89 40 57. **www**.apf.asso.fr

GIHP
32 Rue Paradis, 75010 Paris. **Tel** 01-43 95 66 36.

EMERGENCY NUMBERS

Ambulance (SAMU)
Tel 15 or 18 (Sapeurs Pompiers).

Fire (Sapeurs Pompiers)
Tel 18 or 112.

Police and Gendarmerie
Tel 17.

BANKING

American Express
11 Rue Scribe, 75009 Paris.
Tel 01-47 77 70 00.

Travelex
Tel 0800 908 330.

Travel Information

France has highly advanced transportation systems, with Paris at the hub of its air, rail, and road networks. Paris's two main airports have direct flights to North America, Africa, Japan, and the rest of Europe. The city's six major railway stations connect it to some 6,000 destinations in France, and provide links to the whole of Europe. An extensive, well-developed road network makes it easy to reach all parts of the country by car or bus. France is also well connected by sea, with frequent ferry crossings from the UK to ports on the Channel.

FLYING TO FRANCE

France is served by nearly all international airlines. Paris is the major airline destination in France, but there are a number of other international airports across the country. Some airports near the border, such as Geneva, Basle, and Luxembourg, can also be used for destinations in France.

The main French airline is **Air France**, which has services to major cities across the world. The main British airlines with regular flights to France are **British Airways** and **British Midland**. Inexpensive flights from the UK to various French destinations are available from carriers such as **easyJet** and **Ryanair**. Major airlines including **American Airlines**, **Delta**, and **United** operate flights from the United States. **Air Canada** flies from several cities in Canada, and **Qantas** provides flights from Australia and New Zealand.

AIR FARES

Airline fares are at their highest during the peak summer season in France, usually from July to September. Fierce competition between airlines, however, means there are often discounts on offer.

APEX fares are booked in advance. They cannot be changed or cancelled without penalty and there are also minimum and maximum stay requirements. Packages are also worth considering, as airlines and tour operators can put together a great range of flexible deals to suit your needs. These can include car rental and rail travel, enabling you to continue overland.

DOMESTIC FLIGHTS

There are a number of domestic airlines that fly between the cities of France, some of which only operate within one region; others also fly to French-speaking countries, with Air France offering the largest number of routes. However, unless you are eligible for discounts, you may find it cheaper and faster to travel on the high-speed trains, given the time it can take to reach the airports.

FERRY SERVICES

There are several crossings between the UK and French ports. **P&O Ferries** operates between Dover and Calais, with frequent crossings (75–90 minutes).

Brittany Ferries runs a nine-hour service from Portsmouth to St-Malo, a six-hour service from Portsmouth to Caen, a three-hour service from Poole to Cherbourg, and a six-hour service from Plymouth to Roscoff.

LD Lines runs an eight-hour overnight service from Portsmouth to Le Havre. **Transmanche Ferries**, a sister company of LD Lines, runs a route between Newhaven and Dieppe, which takes about four hours. **Norfolkline** has a two-hour crossing from Dover to Dunkerque.

CHANNEL TUNNEL

The Channel Tunnel (Tunnel sous La Manche) was inaugurated in 1994. A car-carrying shuttle service, which is operated by **Eurotunnel**, runs between Folkestone and Calais. The passenger service, **Eurostar**, links London and Paris (2.5 hrs).

GETTING AROUND PARIS

Central Paris is compact, and the best way to get around is often to walk. Public transportation in the city is good, however, with an efficient metro (subway) system, frequent buses, and a commuter train service (RER). These are all operated by the Paris transportation company, RATP.

There are many types of ticket available, sold at metro and RER stations, and most can be used on any RATP service, including buses. Single bus tickets can also be bought from the driver when boarding. All tickets used on buses must be stamped in the machine on board.

Single RATP tickets are valid in metro/RER zones 1 or 2, or for any bus journey. *Carnets* (books of ten single tickets), are more economical if you plan to make a number of journeys. Various passes are also available, which entitle you to unlimited travel in certain zones for a set number of days.

Vélib is a self-service bike hire scheme in Paris. Users can hire a bike from one station and return it to another.

RAIL TRAVEL

France has always been known for the punctuality of its trains. The French state railway, the **Société Nationale des Chemins de Fer (SNCF)**, provides an excellent rail network which covers nearly all of France. The fastest services are provided by the high-speed TGV *(Trains à Grande Vitesse)* trains, which link most major cities.

Overnight services are popular in France, and most long-distance trains have *couchettes* (bunks), which you must reserve for a fee. Reservations are also compulsory for all TGV services, trains on public holidays, and for a *siège inclinable* (reclinable seat). Information on the various rail services and fares is available from the **Rail Europe** office in London. In France, leaflets are available at most stations. There are a number of special tickets available, including ones for over 60s, families, and under 26s. There are also special tickets for those doing a lot of train travel.

Automatic ticket and reservation machines *(billetterie automatique)* are found at main stations. They take credit cards or coins. You can also check train times, fares, and make reservations by phoning **SNCF**. Both reservations and tickets must be validated in one of the orange *composteur* machines near the platforms before boarding the train.

TRAVELING BY ROAD

France has one of the densest road networks in Europe, with modern motorways which allow quick and easy access to all parts of the country. However, you can save money on tolls and explore France in a more leisurely way by using some of the other high-quality roads, such as RN *(route nationale)* and D *(départe- mentale)* routes.

Most motorways in France have a toll system *(autoroutes à péage)*, which can be quite expensive, especially over long distances. There are some short sections which are free, however, usually close to major centers. Tolls can be paid with either credit cards or cash. Where only small sums are involved, you throw coins into a large receptacle and the change is given automatically.

Speed limits in France are shown in km/h. The limit in all towns, unless shown otherwise, is 50 km/h (30 mph). On major roads, higher limits are usually shown. On the *autoroutes* the usual limit is 130 km/h (80 mph), but this is reduced to 110 km/h (70 mph) when it is raining. On-the-spot fines may be demanded for speeding offences, and there are severe penalties for drink-driving.

Sunday is usually a good time to travel in France, as there are very few trucks on the road. Try to avoid traveling at the French holiday rush periods known as the *grands départs*. The worst times are weekends in July, and at the beginning and end of August.

All the main international car-rental companies operate in France. It is worth ringing around before you leave for France as there are many special offers for rentals booked and prepaid in the UK or US. Good deals are often available from **Autos Abroad**, brokers who use cars owned by other car rental companies. Booking in this way may work out at half the price of the standard rental.

BUSES

Long-distance buses generally operate only where there is not a good train service in operation (for example, between Geneva and Nice). SNCF (the state railway) operates some bus routes and issues regional TER *(Transports Express Régionaux)* timetables and tickets. **Eurolines** serves a wider range of destinations within France, as well as providing services to hundreds of major cities across Europe. They also offer excursions and arrange accommodations.

There are also many local buses, which run from the town's *Gare Routière*.

DIRECTORY

AIRLINES

Air Canada
Tel 08-26 88 08 81.
Tel 888-247 2262 (Can).
www.aircanada.com

Air France
Tel 3654.
Tel 020-7734 7879 (UK).
Tel 800-237 2747 (US).
www.airfrance.com

American Airlines
Tel 08-26 46 09 50 (France).
Tel 800-433 7300 (US).
www.aa.com

British Airways
Tel 08-25 82 54 00.
Tel 0844-490 0787 (UK).
www.britishairways.com

British Midland
Tel 0844-8484 888 (UK).
www.flybmi.com

Delta Air Lines
Tel 08-11 64 00 05.
Tel 800-221 12 12 (US).
www.delta.com

easyJet
Tel 0871-244 2366 (UK).
www.easyjet.com

Qantas
Tel 0208-600 4300 (UK).
Tel 13 13 13 (Aus).
www.qantas.com

Ryanair
Tel 0871-246 0000 (UK).
Tel 0892-780 210 (France).
www.ryanair.com

United Airlines
Tel 0845-8444 777 (UK).
Tel 800-864 8331 (US).
www.united.com

FERRY SERVICES

Brittany Ferries
Tel 08-25 82 88 28.
Tel 0871-244 0744 (UK).
www.brittanyferries.com

Norfolkline
Tel 0871-574 7235 (UK).
www.norfolkline.com

LD Lines
Tel 0844-576 8836 (UK).

P&O Ferries
Tel 0871-664 5645 (UK).
www.poferries.com

Transmanche Ferries
Tel 0825 304 304 .
Tel 0800 917 1201 (UK).

CHANNEL TUNNEL

Eurostar
Tel 08-92 35 35 39.
Tel 0870-518 6186 (UK).
www.eurostar.com

Eurotunnel
Tel 810-630 304.
Tel 0870-535 3535 (UK).
www.eurotunnel.com

RAIL TRAVEL

Rail Europe
Tel 0870-5848 848.
Tel 0844-848 4064 (UK).
www.raileurope.co.uk

SNCF, Paris
Tel 3635.
www.voyages-sncf.com

CAR RENTAL

Autos Abroad
Tel 0844-826 6536 (UK).
www.autosabroad.com

Avis
Tel 0844-581 8181 (UK).
Tel 08-20 05 05 05 (Paris).
www.avis.fr

Europcar
Tel 0871-384 0235 (UK).
Tel 08-25 35 83 58 (Paris).
www.europcar.com

Hertz
Tel 0870-844 8844 (UK).
Tel 0825-86 18 61 (Paris).
www.hertz.com

BUSES

Eurolines
Tel 08-92 89 90 91.
www.eurolines.fr

Shopping

Shopping in France is a delight. Whether you go to the hypermarkets and department stores, or seek out the many small specialist stores and markets, you will be tempted by the stylish presentation and high quality of the goods on offer. France is especially renowned for its wine, with a vast selection available, from cheap table wines to classic vintages. French food is also excellent, in particular the cheeses, cured meats, patés, cakes, and pastries. France also offers world-famous fashion, pottery and porcelain, crystal, and fine-quality antiques.

OPENING HOURS

Food shops open at about 7am and close around noon for lunch. After lunch most are open until 7pm or later. Bakeries often stay open until 1pm or later.

Shops that do not close at lunchtime include some supermarkets, department stores, and most hypermarkets.

General opening hours for non-food shops are around 9am–7pm Mon–Sat, often with a break for lunch. Many are closed on Mondays.

Food shops (and newsagents) are open on Sunday mornings. Virtually every shop in France is closed on Sunday afternoon, except for the last weeks before Christmas when hypermarkets remain open all day. Smaller shops may be closed one day of the week, usually Monday. However, those in tourist regions are often open every day in the high season.

LARGER SHOPS

Hypermarkets *(hypermarchés* or *grandes surfaces)* can be found on the outskirts of every sizeable town: look for signs indicating *centre commercial.* Among the biggest are Carrefour, Casino, Auchan, and Continent. Discount petrol is often included, and most, but not all, now have pumps which take credit cards.

Department stores *(grands magasins)*, such as the cheap and cheerful Monoprix and Prisunic, are often found in town centers. Others, like the more upscale **Au Printemps** and **Galeries Lafayette**, can be found both in town and out-of-town centers.

SPECIALIST SHOPS

One of the pleasures of shopping in France is that specialist shops for food still flourish despite the new large supermarkets. The *boulangerie,* for bread, is frequently combined with a *pâtisserie* selling cakes and pastries. The *traiteur* sells prepared foods. Cheese shops *(fromagerie)* and other shops specializing in dairy products *(laiterie)* may also be combined, while the *boucherie* (butcher's) and *charcuterie* (pork butcher's/delicatessen) are often separate shops. For general groceries go to an *épicerie.* An *épicerie fine* is a delicatessen.

MARKETS

Markets are found in towns and villages all over France. To find out where the market is, ask a passerby for *le marché.* Markets usually finish promptly at noon and do not reopen in the afternoon.

Look for local producers, including those with only one or two special items to sell, as their goods are often cheaper and of better quality.

By law, price tags include the origin of all produce: *pays* means local. Chickens from Bresse are marketed wearing a red, white, and blue badge giving the name of the producer as proof of authenticity. If you are visiting markets over several weeks, look for items just coming into season, such as fresh walnuts, the first wild asparagus, truffles, early artichokes, or wild strawberries. The special seasonal markets held throughout France are the best places to find these

items, and there are often *foires artisanales* held at the same time, which sell local produce, arts, and crafts.

REGIONAL PRODUCE

French regional specialties can be bought outside their area of origin, although it is interesting to buy them locally. Provence, in the south, prides itself on the quality of its olive oil, while the southwest is notable for its patés. Central France is famous for snails, cured meats, and Roquefort cheese. Cheese is also an important product of the temperate north, the best-known varieties being Brie and Camembert.

Popular drinks are also associated with particular regions. Pastis, made from aniseed, is popular in the south, while Calvados, made from apples, is from the north.

Location also determines quality. Lyon's culinary importance stems from the many locally produced cheeses, the proximity of Bresse for chickens, Charolais for beef, and the Alsace region for sausages.

WINE

In wine-producing areas, follow the *dégustation* (tasting) signs to vineyards *(domaines)* where you can taste the wine. You will be expected to buy at least one bottle. Wine cooperatives sell the wine of small producers. Here you can buy wine in five- and ten-liter containers *(en vrac)*, as well as in bottles. The wine is often rated AOC, *appellation d'origine contrôlée,* selling at less than 2 euros a liter. As wine sold *en vrac* is "duty-free," customers receive a *laissez-passer* (permit) indicating their destination. Bottled wine sold by co-ops is duty-paid.

CLOTHING

France is famous for its fashion, and elegant clothes can be found even in quite small towns. Paris, however, is the home of *haute couture.* There are 23 couture houses listed with the Fédération

Française de la Couture, and most of these are concentrated on the Right Bank around Rue du Faubourg-St-Honoré and Avenue Montaigne. Famous names include **Yves Saint Laurent**, **Chanel**, **Guy Laroche**, **Gucci**, **Nina Ricci**, and **Christian Dior**. Other top designers include **Hermès** and **Giorgio Armani**.

Men don't have the luxury of *haute couture* dressing: their choice is limited to ready-to-wear, but most of the big name womenswear designers also produce a range for men. A good example is **Gianni Versace**, with his classic Italian clothes for men. On the Right Bank, the household name designers include **Giorgio Armani**, the stylish **Pierre Cardin**, **Yves Saint Laurent**, and **Lanvin**, who is particularly popular for his beautifully made leather accessories. If time is short and you want to make all your purchases under one roof, try the *grands magasins*. These stores offer a wide choice of fashions, and prices will be more within most people's budgets. **Au Printemps**, for example, is huge, with separate buildings for menswear, household goods, and womens' and children's clothes. The beauty department, with its vast perfume selection, is definitely worth a visit. **Le Bon Marché**, on the Left Bank, was the first department store in Paris, and is the most chic, with an excellent food hall. **Galeries Lafayette** has a wide range of clothes at all price levels. There are also homewares, and the branch in Boulevard Haussmann has Paris's biggest souvenir shop.

ART AND ANTIQUES

You can buy fabulous art and antiques from stores, galleries, and flea-markets all over France. The best places to visit in Paris are **Le Louvre des Antiquaires**, a huge building containing around 250 antique dealers, and the famous **Marché aux Puces de St-Ouen** flea market (open Saturday to Monday). To avoid paying duty, you will need a certificate of authenticity when exporting objets d'art over 20 years old and any goods over a century old that are worth more than €150,000. Seek professional advice and declare them at customs if in doubt.

TAX-FREE SHOPPING

Visitors resident outside the European Union can reclaim the sales tax, TVA, on French goods if they spend more than €305 in one shop, get a *détaxe* receipt, and take the goods out of the country within six months. The form should be handed in at customs when leaving the country, and the reimbursement will be sent to you.

Exceptions for *détaxe* rebates are food and drink, medicines, tobacco, cars, and motorbikes. More information is available from the **Centre des Renseignements des Douanes**, but this is usually in French.

DIRECTORY

CLOTHING

Chanel
42 Ave Montaigne,
75008 Paris.
Tel 01-47 23 74 12.
5 Bld de la Croisette,
06400 Cannes.
Tel 04-93 38 55 05.

Christian Dior
30 Ave Montaigne,
75008 Paris.
Tel 01-40 73 73 73.
38 Bld de la Croisette,
06400 Cannes.
Tel 04-92 98 98 00.

Gianni Versace
45 Ave Montaigne,
75008 Paris.
Tel 01-47 42 88 02.

Giorgio Armani
2 Avenue Montaigne,
75008 Paris.
Tel 01-56 89 01 19.

Gucci
60 Ave Montaigne,
75008 Paris.
Tel 01-56 69 80 80.

Guy Laroche
35 Rue François 1er,
75008 Paris.
Tel 01-40 69 68 00.

Hermès
24 Rue du Faubourg
St-Honoré,
75008 Paris.
Tel 01-40 17 47 17.

Lanvin
22 Rue de Faubourg St-
Honoré,
75008 Paris.
Tel 01-44 71 33 33.

Nina Ricci
39 Ave Montaigne,
75008 Paris.
Tel 01-40 88 64 51.

Pierre Cardin
9 Rue Duras,
75008 Paris.
Tel 01-42 66 14 92.

Yves Saint Laurent
6 Place St Sulpice, 75006
Paris (women's fashion).
Tel 01-43 29 43 00.

32 Rue Faubourg St
Honoré,
75008 Paris
(men's fashion).
Tel 01-53 05 80 80.
65 Bld Croisette,
06400 Cannes.
Tel 04-93 46 99 17.

DEPARTMENT STORES

Le Bon Marché
24 Rue de Sèvres,
75007 Paris.
Tel 01 44 39 80 00.

Galeries Lafayette
40 Bld Haussmann,
75009 Paris.
Tel 08 25 85 40 00.
11 Rue Ste Catherine,
33000 Bordeaux.
Tel 05-56 90 92 71.
6 Rue Maréchal Foch,
06400 Cannes.
Tel 04-97 06 25 00.

Au Printemps
64 Bld Haussman,
75009 Paris.
Tel 01-42 82 50 00.

ART AND ANTIQUES

Le Louvre des Antiquaires
2 Place du Palais-Royal,
75001 Paris.
Tel 01-42 97 27 27.

Marché aux Puces de St-Ouen
Av Porte de Clignancourt,
75018 Paris.

TAX-FREE SHOPPING

Centre des Renseignements des Douanes
Direction Générale,
11 Rue des Deux
Communes,
93558 Montreuil.
Tel 08-11 20 44 44.
www.douane-gouv.fr

Entertainment

The entertainment center of France is Paris. Whether your preference is for drama, ballet, opera, jazz, cinema, or dancing the night away, Paris has it all. Across the rest of the country the arts are also well represented, and there are a number of internationally renowned arts festivals throughout the year. With a varied physical, as well as cultural, landscape, there are also many possibilities for outdoor sports and activities, including golf, tennis, walking, and skiing. Specialist holidays cater to those interested in French language, food, and wine.

ENTERTAINMENT LISTINGS

Two of the best listings magazines in Paris are *Pariscope* and *L'Officiel des Spectacles*. Published every Wednesday, you can pick them up at any newsstand. Local newspapers and *offices de tourisme* are the best places to find entertainment listings for the regions.

BOOKING TICKETS

Depending on the event, tickets can often be bought at the door, but for popular events it is wiser to purchase tickets in advance, at the box office or at **FNAC** chains. Theater box offices open daily from about 11am–7pm. Most accept credit card bookings by telephone. You can also purchase tickets from **Virgin Megastore** and other commercial centers in large towns.

THEATER

From the grandeur of the **Comédie Française** to slapstick farce and avant-garde drama, theater is flourishing in Paris. Founded in 1680 by royal decree, the Comédie Française is the bastion of French theater, aiming to keep classical drama in the public eye. In an underground auditorium in the Art Deco Palais de Chaillot, the **Théâtre National de Chaillot** stages lively productions of mainstream European classics. The **Théâtre National de la Colline** specializes in contemporary drama. Among the most important of the independents is the **Comédie des Champs-Elysées**, while for

over 100 years the **Palais Royal** has been the temple of risqué farce.

Excellent theaters and productions are also to be found in major cities across France, and there are big theater festivals held in Nancy (June) and Avignon (July; *see p191*).

MUSIC

The music scene in Paris has never been so busy, especially with the emergence of many internationally successful contemporary French groups. There are numerous first-class venues in the city, with excellent jazz, opera, contemporary, and classical music concerts.

Opened in 1989, the ultra-modern 2,700-seat **Opéra de Paris Bastille** stages classic and modern operas. Productions from outside France are staged at the **Opéra Comique**. The **Salle Pleyel** is Paris's principal concert hall and home of the Orchestre de Paris. Paris's newest venue is the **Cité de la Musique** in the Parc de la Villette.

Top international and pop acts are usually to be found at huge arenas such as the **Palais Omnisports de Paris-Bercy** or the **Zénith**. A more intimate atmosphere is found at the legendary **Olympia**.

Paris is, perhaps, most renowned for its jazz, and the best talent in the world can be heard here on any evening, especially throughout October during the jazz festival. All the great jazz musicians have performed at **New Morning**, which also hosts African, Brazilian, and other sounds. For Dixieland go to **Le Petit Journal St-Michel**.

Jazz is also popular across France, and big international jazz festivals are held right through the year, in Cannes (February; *see p196*), Antibes and Juan-le-Pins (July), and Le Mans (April). Opera and classical music are also widely performed, notably at the Aix festival during July (*see p195*).

CLUBS AND CABARET

Music in Paris nightclubs tends to follow the trends set in the US and Britain, although home-grown groups, especially those playing garage, are popular and influential both here and abroad.

Balajo, once frequented by Edith Piaf, and the ultra-hip **Folies Clubbing**, once a strip joint, are particularly up-to-the-minute with their music. For a more Latin touch, try **La Java**. The dance floor of this club, where Edith Piaf once performed, now sways to the sounds of Cuban and Brazilian music.

When it comes to picking a cabaret, the rule of thumb is simple: the better-known places are best. The **Folies-Bergère** is the oldest music hall in Paris and probably the most famous in the world. It is closely rivaled by the **Lido** and the **Moulin Rouge**, birthplace of the cancan.

CINEMA

Paris is the world's capital of film appreciation. There are now more than 300 screens within the city limits, distributed among 100 cinemas. Most are concentrated in cinema belts, which enjoy the added appeal of nearby restaurants and shops. The Champs-Elysées has the densest cinema strip in town, where you can see the latest Hollywood smash or French *auteur* triumph, as well as some classic re-issues.

The cinemas on the Grands Boulevards include two notable architectural landmarks: the 2,800-seat **Le Grand Rex**, with its Baroque decor, and the **Max Linder Panorama**, which was refurbished in the 1980s.

The largest screen in France is the **La Géode** flagship in the 19th *arrondissement*. On the Left Bank, the area around Odéon-St-Germain-des-Prés has taken over from the Latin Quarter as the city's heartland for art and repertory cinemas.

OUTDOOR ACTIVITIES

A country as richly diverse in culture and geography as France offers an amazing variety of sport and leisure activities. Information on current leisure and sporting activities in a particular region is available from the tourist offices listed for each town in this guide.

Golf is popular in France, especially along the north and south coasts and in Aquitaine. You will need to take your handicap certificate with you if you want to play. Tennis is also a favorite sport, and there are courts to rent in almost every town.

More than 30,000 km (19,000 miles) of *Grandes Randonnés* (long distance tracks) and shorter *Petites Randonnés* cover France. The routes are clearly way-marked, and vary in difficulty, including long pilgrim routes, alpine crossings, and tracks through national parks. Some routes are open to mountain bikes and horses.

The mountains provide for excellent skiing and mountaineering. The Atlantic coast around Biarritz offers some of the best surfing and windsurfing in Europe. Sailing and waterskiing are popular all round France, and swimming facilities are generally good, although beaches in the south can be crowded in August.

SPECIALIST VACATIONS

French government Tourist Offices (*see p199*) have extensive information on travel companies offering special interest vacations. Send off

or download from a selection of brochures. Vacations are based on subjects such as the French language, wine appreciation, and cooking, as well as craft activities and organized nature trips.

SPECTATOR SPORT

The main sporting action in France revolves largely around soccer, rugby, tennis, and horse racing. There are various stadia and circuits all over the country; the best are near major cities, particularly Paris. Here, the **Stade de France** and the **Palais Omnisports de Paris-Bercy** host all the major events. **Parc des Princes** is home to the top Paris soccer team Paris St-Germain.

Cycling is also a very popular sport in France, and there is racing action across the country. The most famous event is the annual Tour de France held during July.

DIRECTORY

BOOKING TICKETS

FNAC
Forum Les Halles,
1 Rue Pierre Lescot,
75001 Paris.
Tel 08-25 02 00 20.

Virgin Megastore
52–60 Av des Champs-
Elysées, 75008 Paris.
Tel 01-49 53 50 00.

THEATER

Comédie des Champs-Elysées
15 Ave Montaigne,
75008 Paris.
Tel 01-53 23 99 19.

Comédie Française
1 Pl Colette,
75001 Paris.
Tel 08-25 10 16 80.

Palais Royal
38 Rue Montpensier,
75001 Paris.
Tel 01-42 97 40 00.

Théâtre National de Chaillot
Place du Trocadéro,
75016 Paris.
Tel 01-53 65 30 00.

Théâtre National de la Colline
15 Rue Malte-Brun, 75020
Paris. **Tel** 01-44 62 52 52.

MUSIC

Cité de la Musique
221 Ave Jean-Jaurès,
75019 Paris.
Tel 01-44 84 44 84.

Opéra Comique
(Salle Favart) 5 Rue Favart,
75002 Paris.
Tel 01-42 44 45 40.

Opéra de Paris Bastille
120 Rue de Lyon, 75012
Paris. **Tel** 01-40 01 17 89.

New Morning
7–9 Rue des Petites-
Ecuries, 75010 Paris.
Tel 01-45 23 51 41.

Olympia
28 Bld des Capucines,
75009 Paris.
Tel 08-92 68 33 68.

Palais Omnisports de Paris-Bercy
8 Bld de Bercy 75012.
Tel 08-92 69 23 00.

Le Petit Journal St-Michel
71 Bld St-Michel, 75005
Paris. **Tel** 01-43 26 28 59.

Salle Pleyel
252 Rue du Faubourg
St-Honoré, 75008 Paris.
Tel 01-42 56 13 13.

Zénith
211 Ave Jean-Jaurès,
75019 Paris.
Tel 08-90 71 02 07.

CLUBS AND CABARET

Balajo
9 Rue de Lappe, 75011
Paris. **Tel** 09-54 94 54 09.

Folies-Bergère
32 Rue Richer, 75009
Paris. **Tel** 08-92 68 16 50.

Folies Clubbing
11 Pl Pigalle, 75009 Paris.
Tel 01-48 78 55 25.

La Java
105 Rue du Faubourg-du-
Temple, 75010 Paris.
Tel 01-42 02 20 52.

Lido
116 bis Ave Champs-
Elysées, 75008 Paris.
Tel 01-40 76 56 10.

Moulin Rouge
82 Bld de Clichy, 75018
Paris. **Tel** 01-53 09 82 82.

CINEMA

La Géode
26 Ave Corentin-Cariou,
75019 Paris.
Tel 08-92 68 45 40.

Le Grand Rex
1 Bld Poissonnière, 75002
Paris. **Tel** 01-45 08 93 89.

Max Linder Panorama
24 Bld Poissonnière,
75009 Paris.
Tel 01 48 24 00 47.

SPECTATOR SPORT

Palais Omnisports de Paris-Bercy
8 Bld de Bercy, 75012
Paris. **Tel** 08-92 69 23 00.

Parc des Princes
24 Rue du Commandant-
Guilbaud, 75016 Paris.
Tel 01 42 30 32 75.

Stade de France
La Plaine St-Denis,
93210 Paris.
Tel 08-92 70 09 00.

Where to Stay in France

French hotels are graded from one to a maximum of five stars. They range from historic châteaux with magnificent furnishings and food to informal family-run hotels. In high season some will offer only full *pension* (all meals) or *demi-pension* (breakfast and dinner). A popular option for a self-catering vacation is a rural *gîte*.

PRICE CATEGORIES
Price categories for a standard double room per night during the high season, including tax and service. Breakfast is not included, unless specified:

€ under €80
€€ €80–€130
€€€ €130–€180
€€€€ €180–€250
€€€€€ €250

PARIS

BEAUBOURG AND LES HALLES Hôtel Brittanique
€€€€   Map E3
20 av Victoria, 75001 **Tel** 01-42 33 74 59 **Fax** 01-42 33 83 65 **Rooms** 39

The Brittanique has a convenient, central location on a calm side street just a few steps away from the Châtelet. British charm meets French chic in the decor, and the staff are very helpful and friendly. There's a buffet breakfast, and also a range of *boulangeries* and restaurants nearby. **www.hotelbrittanique.fr**

CHAILLOT QUARTER Hôtel du Bois
€€€€   Map B2
11 rue du Dôme, 75016 **Tel** 01-45 00 31 96 **Fax** 01-45 00 90 05 **Rooms** 39

Two minutes from the Arc de Triomphe and the Champs Elysées, Hôtel du Bois is ideal for haute-couture boutique lovers. Behind a typically Parisian facade is a contemporary interior – chic furniture in the lounge, thick patterned carpets, and fine prints in the guest rooms. **www.hoteldubois.com**

CHAILLOT QUARTER Hôtel Keppler
€€€€€   Map B2
10 rue Keppler, 75016 **Tel** 01-47 20 65 05 **Fax** 01-47 23 02 29 **Rooms** 44

This sophisticated hotel has bold black and white decor designed by Pierre Yves Rochon, and is located just steps away from the Champs Elysées. Set on a quiet street, the rooms here are simple but clean, spacious and comfortable. High ceilings throughout add to the sense of space. **www.hotelkeppler.fr**

CHAILLOT QUARTER Raphaël
€€€€€   Map B2
17 av Kléber, 75016 **Tel** 01-53 64 32 00 **Fax** 01-53 64 32 01 **Rooms** 83

This hotel is the epitome of discreet elegance, where film stars come to be sheltered from the paparazzi. The decor is opulent, and the roof terrace bar is the loveliest in Paris, popular with the jet set. There are amazing views of the city, especially at night when the monuments are illuminated. **www.raphael-hotel.com**

CHAMPS-ELYSEES Résidence Lord Byron
€€€€   Map B2
5 rue Chateaubriand, 75008 **Tel** 01-43 59 89 98 **Fax** 01-42 89 46 04 **Rooms** 31

Close to the Etoile, the Résidence Lord Byron is a small, discreet hotel with a courtyard garden for breakfast. Its bright guest rooms are quiet but small; if you want more space, ask for a salon room or a ground-floor room. **www.hotel-lordbyron.fr**

CHAMPS-ELYSEES Four Seasons George V
€€€€€   Map B2
31 av George V, 75008 **Tel** 01-49 52 70 00 **Fax** 01-49 52 70 10 **Rooms** 246

This legendary hotel, dotted with salons, old furniture, and art, lost a little of its charm when it was renovated. But it gained a stunning restaurant, Le Cinq, which boasts the world's top sommelier and an award-winning chef. There is also a great spa. Sheer opulence. Parking is available for guests. **www.fourseasons.com/paris**

CHAMPS-ELYSEES Le Bristol
€€€€€   Map B2
112 rue du Faubourg-St-Honoré, 75008 **Tel** 01-53 43 43 00 **Fax** 01-53 43 43 01 **Rooms** 162

One of Paris's finest hotels, the Bristol's large rooms are sumptuously decorated with antiques and magnificent marble bathrooms. The period dining room, with its Flemish tapestries and glittering crystal chandeliers, has been given rave reviews. There is a wonderful swimming pool. **www.lebristolparis.com**

INVALIDES AND EIFFEL TOWER QUARTER Grand Hôtel Levêque
€€   Map B3
29 rue Cler, 75007 **Tel** 01-47 05 49 15 **Fax** 01-45 50 49 36 **Rooms** 50

The Levêque lies between the Eiffel Tower and the Invalides on a pedestrianized street with a quaint fruit-and-vegetable market. The great location isn't the only attraction – guest rooms are simple and well kept, and the hotel also provides a buffet breakfast. **www.hotel-leveque.com**

INVALIDES AND EIFFEL TOWER QUARTER Hôtel de Suède St-Germain
€€€€   Map C4
31 rue Vaneau, 75007 **Tel** 01-47 05 00 08 **Fax** 01-47 05 69 27 **Rooms** 39

Located near the Orsay and Rodin museums, Hôtel de Suède St-Germain offers elegant rooms, decorated in late 18th-century style with pale colors. Guests receive an exceptionally warm welcome. The deluxe rooms offer a view over the park. A lovely little garden to breakfast in completes the picture. **www.hoteldesuede.com**

Key to Symbols *see back cover flap*

LATIN QUARTER Hôtel Esmeralda
4 rue St-Julien-le-Pauvre, 75005 **Tel** *01-43 54 19 20* **Fax** *01-40 51 00 68* **Rooms** *16*
€€
Map *E4*

The much-loved bohemian Hôtel Esmeralda lies in the heart of the Latin Quarter. With old stone walls and beamed ceilings, its charm has seduced the likes of Terence Stamp and Serge Gainsbourg. The best rooms overlook Notre-Dame cathedral. **www.hotel-esmeralda.fr**

LATIN QUARTER Hôtel des Grandes Ecoles
75 rue Cardinal Lemoine, 75005 **Tel** *01-43 26 79 23* **Fax** *01-43 25 28 15* **Rooms** *51*
€€€
Map *D4*

This hotel is a cluster of three small houses around a beautiful garden, where you can breakfast in good weather. The rooms are all comfortable and furnished with traditional 18th-century-style floral wallpaper; some open on to the courtyard. Parking is available for an additional fee. **www.hotel-grandes-ecoles.com**

LATIN QUARTER Hôtel des Grands Hommes
17 pl du Panthéon, 75005 **Tel** *01-46 34 19 60* **Fax** *01-43 26 67 32* **Rooms** *31*
€€€€
Map *E4*

Teachers at the Sorbonne frequent this quiet family hotel close to the Jardin du Luxembourg. It boasts a great view of the Panthéon from the attic rooms on the upper floor. The guest rooms are comfortable. **www.hoteldesgrandshommes.com**

LUXEMBOURG QUARTER Hôtel Aviatic
105 Rue de Vaugirard, 75006 **Tel** *01-53 63 25 50* **Fax** *01-53 63 25 55* **Rooms** *43*
€€€€
Map *D4*

A hotel of character situated between St-Germain and the Luxembourg Quarter, the much-loved Aviatic combines elegant style with modern amenities. The spacious rooms are individually decorated in a contemporary style. Parking is available for an additional fee. **www.aviatic.fr**

MONTMARTRE Regyn's Montmartre
18 pl des Abbesses, 75018 **Tel** *01-42 54 45 21* **Fax** *01-42 23 76 69* **Rooms** *22*
€

Near Sacré-Cœur, this is an impeccably kept budget hotel. The top-floor guest rooms have views of the Eiffel Tower. Around the corner is Tabac des Deux Moulins at 15 rue le Pic, where the 2001 film *Amélie* was set. **www.paris-hotels-montmartre.com/regyns**

MONTMARTRE Terrass Hôtel
12–14 rue Joseph-de-Maistre, 75018 **Tel** *01-46 06 72 85* **Fax** *01-44 92 34 30* **Rooms** *98*
€€€€€

Montmartre's most luxurious hotel, the rooms here are comfortably, if unremarkably, furnished. A few rooms retain the original Art-Deco woodwork. The big draw is the rooftop restaurant, where in the summer fashionable Parisians take in a world-class view. **www.terrass-hotel.com**

MONTPARNASSE Villa des Artistes
9 rue de la Grande Chaumière, 75006 **Tel** *01-43 26 60 86* **Fax** *01-43 54 73 70* **Rooms** *55*
€€€

The Villa des Artistes aims to recreate Montparnasse's artistic heyday when Modigliani, Beckett, and Fitzgerald were all visitors here. The guest rooms are clean, but the main draw is the large patio garden and fountain, where you can breakfast in peace. **www.villa-artistes.com**

OPERA QUARTER Ambassador
16 bd Haussmann, 75009 **Tel** *01-44 83 40 40* **Fax** *01-44 83 40 57* **Rooms** *297*
€€€€€
Map *D2*

One of Paris's best Art Deco hotels, the Ambassador has been restored to its former glory with plush carpeting and antique furniture. The ground floor has pink marble columns, Baccarat crystal chandeliers, and Aubusson tapestries. The restaurant, "16 Haussmann", is popular with Parisian gourmets. **www.radissonblu.com/ambassadorhotel-paris**

ST-GERMAIN-DES-PRES Grand Hôtel des Balcons
3 rue Casimir Delavigne, 75006 **Tel** *01-46 34 78 50* **Fax** *01-46 34 06 27* **Rooms** *50*
€€
Map *D4*

Embellished with Art Nouveau features, this hotel has a beautiful hall with stained-glass windows and striking 19th-century-style lamps and wood paneling. Most guest rooms, quiet and well-decorated, enjoy a balcony. **www.balcons.com**

ST-GERMAIN-DES-PRES Hôtel du Quai Voltaire
19 quai Voltaire, 75007 **Tel** *01-42 61 50 91* **Fax** *01-42 61 62 26* **Rooms** *33*
€€€
Map *D3*

Overlooking the river, this hotel was once the favorite of Blondin, Baudelaire, and Pissarro, and has featured in several films. It is best to avoid the rooms facing the quay, as they suffer from traffic noise. Higher floors are quieter, though, and the views are superb. **www.quaivoltaire.com**

ST-GERMAIN-DES-PRES Hôtel de l'Abbaye St-Germain
10 rue Cassette, 75006 **Tel** *01-45 44 38 11* **Fax** *01-45 48 07 86* **Rooms** *44*
€€€€€
Map *D4*

A 17th-century convent, just steps from the Jardin du Luxembourg, this charming hotel has a history as a preferred hideout for artists and writers. Its finely furnished guest rooms and apartments have been tastefully done up and provided with modern facilities. **www.hotelabbayeparis.com**

ST-GERMAIN-DES-PRES Relais Christine
3 rue Christine, 75006 **Tel** *01-40 51 60 80* **Fax** *01-40 51 60 81* **Rooms** *51*
€€€€€
Map *D4*

Always full, the Relais Christine is the epitome of the hôtel de charme. Part of a cloister from a 16th-century abbey, the hotel is a romantic, peaceful haven. The guest rooms, especially the deluxe rooms, are bright and spacious. Marvelous spa and beauty treatments are available. Reserve in advance. **www.relais-christine.com**

Map References *see map of Paris pp150–51*

THE MARAIS Hôtel de la Bretonnerie

🛏 ⓦ €€

22 rue Ste-Croix de la Bretonnerie, 75004 **Tel** *01-48 87 77 63* **Fax** *01-42 77 26 78* **Rooms** *29*   **Map** *D3*

Carved stone walls and an arched dining room in the basement are some of the charming features of Hôtel de la Bretonnerie, housed in a 17th-century mansion. Its spacious rooms, with beams and antique furniture, are each decorated differently. Service is warm and friendly. **www.bretonnerie.com**

THE MARAIS Pavillon de la Reine

🛏 ▤ 🅿 ⓦ €€€€€

28 pl des Vosges, 75003 **Tel** *01-40 29 19 19* **Fax** *01-40 29 19 20* **Rooms** *54*   **Map** *F4*

Set back from the marvelous place des Vosges, the Pavillon de la Reine is the best hotel in the Marais. Incredibly romantic, the hotel has a peaceful courtyard and sumptuous guest rooms, furnished with excellent reproduction antiques. **www.pavillon-de-la-reine.com**

TUILERIES QUARTER Brighton

🛏 ▤ ♿ ⓦ €€€

218 rue de Rivoli, 75001 **Tel** *01-47 03 61 61* **Fax** *01-42 60 31 78* **Rooms** *61*   **Map** *D3*

A real insiders' location, the Brighton provides a much-sought-after Rivoli address without the sky-high prices. The guest rooms have beautiful, high ceilings and large windows that look out either over the Jardin des Tuileries or over the courtyard. **www.esprit-de-france.com**

TUILERIES QUARTER Ritz

🛏 🍴 ♨ 🏋 📺 ▤ 🅿 ⓦ €€€€€

15 pl Vendôme, 75001 **Tel** *01-43 16 30 30* **Fax** *01-43 16 45 38* **Rooms** *161*   **Map** *D3*

A legendary address, the Ritz still lives up to its reputation, combining elegance and decadence. The Louis XVI furniture and chandeliers are all original, and the floral arrangements are works of art. The Hemingway Bar is home to the glitterati. **www.ritzparis.com**

VERSAILLES Hôtel de Clagny

ⓦ €

6 impasse de Clagny, 78000 **Tel** *01-39 50 18 09* **Fax** *01-39 50 85 17* **Rooms** *21*

The welcome in this quiet hotel near the train station is genuinely friendly. The rooms are simply furnished and clean, but unremarkable. There are numerous restaurants in the vicinity, and the owners of the Hôtel de Clagny are only too pleased to offer guidance.

FONTAINEBLEAU Grand Hôtel de l'Aigle Noir

🛏 ♿ ♨ 🏋 📺 ▤ 🅿 ⓦ €€€

27 pl de Napoléon Bonaparte, 77300 **Tel** *01-60 74 60 00* **Fax** *01-60 74 60 01* **Rooms** *18*

This prestigious mansion overlooks Fontainebleau château and its vast park. The elegant rooms are decorated in styles ranging from Louis XIII to Napoléon III. The conciergerie can organize a host of activities in the area and the bar serves snacks all day. **www.hotelaiglenoir.com**

NORTHERN FRANCE

CARNAC Hôtel Tumulus

🛏 🍴 ♨ 🅿 ⓦ €€

Route de la Tumulus, 56340 **Tel** *02-97 85 08 21* **Fax** *02-97 52 81 88* **Rooms** *13*

This hotel is located near the prehistoric sights that have made Carnac world famous. The rooms are elegantly furnished, some come with a terrace overlooking the hotel gardens and others have fine views of the Quiberon Bay. A pool, spa, and hammam all add to the appeal. **www.hotel-tumulus.com**

REIMS Château Les Crayères

🛏 🍴 🏋 ▤ 🅿 ⓦ €€€€€

64 bd Henry Vasnier, 51100 **Tel** *03-26 24 90 00* **Fax** *03-26 24 90 01* **Rooms** *20*

Superbly aristocratic château with every luxury set in an English-style park next to the Roman crayères – the wine cellars of the Champagne houses which have been cut into the chalk. There is a superb restaurant, one of the best in France. **www.lescrayeres.com**

ROUEN Le Vieux Carré

ⓦ €

34 rue Ganterie, 76000 **Tel** *02-35 71 67 70* **Fax** *02-35 71 19 17* **Rooms** *13*

City-center hotel near the Musée des Beaux Arts and a short walk from the cathedral. This charming timbered 18th-century building hides prettily decorated, intimate guest rooms. Cozy atmosphere and attentive service. There is a shaded cobbled courtyard and tearoom. **www.vieux-carre.fr**

ST MALO Hôtel Elizabeth

🏋 🅿 ⓦ €€

2 rue des Cordiers, 35400 **Tel** *02-99 56 24 98* **Fax** *02-99 56 39 24* **Rooms** *17*

This hotel is located within the ramparts of the old town, just 2 minutes' drive from the ferry terminal. The building has a 16th-century stone façade. The interior is classic in style, if a little somber. Rooms are comfortable and well equipped. Friendly owners, and private garage. Closed Jan–Feb. **www.hotel-elizabeth.fr**

STRASBOURG Au Cerf d'Or

🛏 🍴 ♨ 🏋 ▤ ⓦ €

6 pl de l'Hôpital, 67000 **Tel** *03-88 36 20 05* **Fax** *03-88 36 68 67* **Rooms** *43*

An inexpensive base for visiting the sights of old Strasbourg, this old-style half-timbered Alsace hotel has refurbished rooms throughout. The main hotel has more charming rooms, but the annex has a small pool and a sauna. There are several restaurants on the nearby waterfront. **www.cerf-dor.com**

THE LOIRE VALLEY

AZAY LE RIDEAU Le Grand Monarque

🔒 P W €

3 Place de la République, 37190 **Tel** *02-47 45 40 08* **Fax** *02-47 45 46 25* **Rooms** 24

In a peaceful setting, this hotel comprises two buildings, one an ancient staging post, the other a large house, separated by a tree-lined courtyard. The rooms are traditionally furnished and bathrooms functional. An attractive terrace overlooking the park is the ideal spot for summer breakfasts. **www.legrandmonarque.com**

CHARTRES Le Grand Monarque

€€

22 place des Epars, 28005 **Tel** *02-37 18 15 15* **Fax** *02-37 36 34 18* **Rooms** 55

This converted 16th-century staging post, with massively thick stone walls, has been managed by the same family since the 1960s; part of the Best Western network. The rooms are simple. There is a pleasant bistro, and a gastronomic restaurant, "Le Georges". **www.bw-grand-monarque.com**

CHENONCEAUX Hostel du Roy

€

9 rue du Dr Bretonneau, 37150 **Tel** *02-47 23 90 17* **Fax** *02-47 23 89 81* **Rooms** 32

A sprawling hotel-restaurant, with a 16th-century fireplace and a dining room hung with hunting trophies. The well-equipped rooms are simple and appealing, and the atmosphere relaxing. There is a garden and pretty terrace. The restaurant serves classic dishes, including game in season. **www.hostelduroy.com**

CHINON Château de Marçay

€€€€

Le Château, 37500 **Tel** *02-47 93 03 47* **Fax** *02-47 93 45 33* **Rooms** 34

Elegant hotel in this restored 15th-century fortified château. Enjoy the lovely views over the surrounding parkland and vineyards from the well-appointed bedrooms. Refined and aristocratic atmosphere, impeccable service and cuisine. **www.chateaudemarcay.com**

FONTEVRAUD-L'ABBAYE Le Prieuré St-Lazare

€€

38 rte St Jean de l'Habit, 49590 **Tel** *02-41 51 73 16* **Fax** *02-41 51 75 50* **Rooms** 52

The surroundings of this hotel, housed in the former St-Lazare priory within the famous royal abbey complex, are stunning. The rooms are elegantly decorated in a modern, contemporary style. The restaurant, in the ancient cloister, is a gourmet's delight. Closed mid-Nov–mid-Mar. **www.hotelfp-fontevraud.com**

NANTES Hôtel La Pérouse

€€

3 allée Duquesne, 44000 **Tel** *02-40 89 75 00* **Fax** *02-40 89 76 00* **Rooms** 46

Named after a French navigator, this chic hotel with its zen atmosphere opened in 1993. The rooms have glossy wooden flooring and crisp, contemporary furniture. Reasonably quiet. The breakfast buffet is good. Free access to nearby gym for guests. **www.hotel-laperouse.fr**

TOURS Hôtel de l'Univers

€€€

5 bd Heurteloup, 37000 **Tel** *02-47 05 37 12* **Fax** *02-47 61 51 80* **Rooms** 87

Statesmen and royals have stayed at this luxurious hotel. A picture gallery depicts the famous guests since 1846. Elegant architecture, right in the city center, with large, prettily furnished bedrooms. The restaurant serves classic gourmet cuisine. Private garage. **www.oceaniahotels.com**

BURGUNDY AND THE FRENCH ALPS

ANNECY Hôtel Palais de l'Isle

€

13 rue Perriére, 74000 **Tel** *04-50 45 86 87* **Fax** *04-50 51 87 15* **Rooms** 33

Opposite the Palais de l'Isle is this hotel, which sits like a Venetian palazzo on the edge of the Thounin canal. The 18th-century house has comfortable rooms with modern amenities. The best rooms overlook the canal; the rooms overlooking the courtyard are rather small. **www.hoteldupalaisdelisle.com**

BEAUNE Hôtel Le Cep

€€€

27 rue Maufoux, 21200 **Tel** *03-80 22 35 48* **Fax** *03-80 22 76 80* **Rooms** 64

In the heart of the old town is this elegant hotel, renovated in a Renaissance style. Legend has it that Louis XIV preferred to stay here rather than at the hospice. The rooms, some with Baroque decor, are ornately furnished with antiques. Each is named after a local wine. **www.hotel-cep-beaune.com**

DIJON Hostellerie le Sauvage

€

64 rue Monge, 21000 **Tel** *03-80 41 31 21* **Fax** *03-80 42 06 07* **Rooms** 22

This attractive half-timbered hotel was a staging post in the 15th century. Located in the city center near the historic sites, it can be noisy – the quietest rooms overlook a lovely interior cobbled courtyard, where meals can be taken in fine weather. Excellent service. Good breakfast. **www.hotellesauvage.com**

Key to Symbols *see back cover flap*

GEVREY-CHAMBERTIN Hôtel les Grands Crus
📋 P W   €€

Route des Grands Crus, 21220 **Tel** *03-80 34 34 15* **Fax** *03-80 51 89 07* **Rooms** *24*

A light, airy hotel with wonderful views over the *grands crus* vineyards. Located in the heart of the Côte de Nuits, this country house built in a typical Burgundian style has traditionally furnished rooms that overlook the garden. The comfy lounge centers around an open fireplace. Closed Dec–Easter. **www.hoteldesgrandscrus.com**

GRENOBLE Splendid Hôtel
🛏 👥 📋 P W   €

22 rue Thiers, 38000 **Tel** *04-76 46 33 12* **Fax** *04-76 46 35 24* **Rooms** *45*

Smart, centrally located hotel in a quiet location, with a walled garden. The guest rooms range from classical to modern, with gaily painted frescoes. Efficient service and amenities. Continental and à la carte breakfast served in the dining room, or garden terrace. **www.splendid-hotel.com**

VEZELAY L'Espérance
🍴 👥 👥 📋 P W   €€€€€

St-Père-sous-Vézelay, 89450 **Tel** *03-86 33 39 10* **Fax** *03-86 33 26 15* **Rooms** *34*

The guest rooms here are in three buildings: the main building has classic furnishings, Moulin has rustic charm, and Pré des Marguerites is contemporary, with terraces overlooking the garden. Wonderful restaurant, excellent but expensive wines, and impeccable service. Closed mid-Jan–Mar. **www.marc-meneau-esperance.com**

SOUTHWEST FRANCE

BIARRITZ Hôtel du Palais
🛏 👥 👥 🍴 📋 P W   €€€€€

1 av de l'Impératrice, 64200 **Tel** *05-59 41 64 00* **Fax** *05-59 41 67 99* **Rooms** *132*

The grande dame of Biarritz's hotel scene, with an ambiance harking back to the resort's Belle Epoque heyday. A magnificent heated seawater pool, direct beach access, a putting green, a playground, and kids' pool complement the lovely rooms and outstanding restaurants. **www.hotel-du-palais.com**

BORDEAUX Best Western Bayonne Etche-Ona
🛏 📋 W   €€€

4 rue Martignac, 33000 **Tel** *05-56 48 00 88* **Rooms** *63*

This is two hotels in one: the contemporary Bayonne and (just round the corner) the more atmospheric Etche-Ona with its Basque-inspired decor. Both occupy elegant 18th-century mansions in the heart of the Golden Triangle and offer comfortable rooms and top-notch service. **www.bordeaux-hotel.com**

MARGAUX Le Pavillon de Margaux
🍴 👥 📋 P W   €€

3 rue Georges-Mandel, 33460 **Tel** *05-57 88 77 54* **Fax** *05-57 88 77 73* **Rooms** *14*

In the center of Margaux village, this handsome hotel provides a comfortable base for exploring the Médoc vineyards. Guest rooms, which are "sponsored" by local wine châteaux, are individually styled. Some have antiques and four-posters, others rattan and floral fabrics. **www.pavillonmargaux.com**

PAU Hôtel du Parc Beaumont
🛏 🍴 📋 P W   €€€€

1 av Edouard VII, 64000 **Tel** *05-59 11 84 00* **Fax** *05-59 11 85 00* **Rooms** *80*

This luxurious modern hotel, part of the Concorde group, stands in beautiful grounds next to Pau's casino and palm-lined boulevard with great views of the Pyrenees. Rooms are lavishly furnished, and there is a heated pool, whirlpool, sauna, and hammam (Turkish bath). **www.hotel-parc-beaumont.com**

ST JEAN-DE-LUZ La Devinière
P W   €€€

5 rue Loquin, 64500 **Tel** *05-59 26 05 51* **Fax** *05-59 51 26 38* **Rooms** *10*

The bedrooms in this charming 18th-century building are all different, prettily decorated and furnished with antiques, artworks, and rare books. There is a cozy lounge-library with an open fireplace and a grand piano, and a breakfast-tea room. Tiny garden. No restaurant. **www.hotel-la-deviniere.com**

TOULOUSE Hôtel des Beaux Arts
🛏 🍴 📋 P W   €€€

1 pl du Pont Neuf, 31000 **Tel** *05-34 45 42 42* **Fax** *05-34 45 42 43* **Rooms** *20*

Behind a beautiful Belle Epoque façade, beside the Pont Neuf, lies a chic hotel with modern comforts. The less expensive rooms are on the small side – better to upgrade for river views and more space. For a special occasion, opt for room 42 with its own tiny terrace among the roof tiles. **www.hotelsdesbeauxarts.com**

THE SOUTH OF FRANCE

AIGUES-MORTES Hôtel St Louis
🍴 P W   €

10 rue Amiral Courbet, 30220 **Tel** *04-66 53 72 68* **Fax** *04-66 53 75 92* **Rooms** *22*

Spacious rooms with modern comforts and a location next to the famous Constant Tower make this friendly hotel in an 18th-century building one of the better places to stay in Aigues-Mortes. Good restaurant, pretty patio, and garage parking available for a fee. Closed mid-Oct–Easter. **www.lesaintlouis.fr**

Key to Price Guide *see p206* **Key to Symbols** *see back cover flap*

AIX EN PROVENCE Hôtel des Augustins

3 rue Masse, 13100 **Tel** *04-42 27 28 59* **Fax** *04-42 26 74 87* **Rooms** *29*

In a converted 12th-century convent, with the reception housed in a 15th-century chapel, the Hôtel des Augustins offers a haven of peace in the heart of bustling Aix. The rooms are large and comfortable in traditional Provençal style. No restaurant, but places to eat nearby. **www.hotel-augustins.com**

ANTIBES Mas Djoliba

29 av Provence, 06600 **Tel** *04-93 34 02 48* **Fax** *04-93 34 05 81* **Rooms** *13*

Mas Djoliba is a big, old-fashioned farmhouse set among lots of greenery, with palm trees surrounding the pool terrace. Convenient for old Antibes and the beaches nearby, it is perfect for a romantic weekend or a longer stay. Closed Nov–Feb. **www.hotel-djoliba.com**

ARLES Hôtel d'Arlatan

26 rue du Sauvage, 13200 **Tel** *04-90 93 56 66* **Fax** *04-90 49 68 45* **Rooms** *47*

The former 15th-century town residence of the Comtes d'Arlatan, this is one of the most beautiful historic hotels in the region. The rooms are furnished with antiques. Glass panels in the salon floor reveal 4th-century Roman foundations. Walled garden and stone terrace. **www.hotel-arlatan.fr**

CANNES Hôtel Molière

5-7 rue Molière, 06400 **Tel** *04-93 38 16 16* **Fax** *04-93 68 29 57* **Rooms** *24*

This 19th-century building is very close to la Croisette, Cannes' sea-front esplanade, with bright and comfortable rooms and balconies overlooking an attractive garden where breakfast is served. Good value and very much in demand – book well in advance. **www.hotel-moliere.com**

CANNES Carlton Inter-Continental

58 la Croisette, 06400 **Tel** *04-93 06 40 06* **Fax** *04-93 06 40 25* **Rooms** *374*

The grandest of the grand, this is where the stars come to stay. During the film festival, there is a long waiting list for reservations. Art Deco surroundings, with discreetly luxurious facilities in the rooms and public areas, and a private beach with loungers and parasols. **www.intercontinental.com**

CARCASSONNE Hôtel de la Cité

Pl August-Pierre Pont, 11000 **Tel** *04-68 71 98 71* **Fax** *04-68 71 50 15* **Rooms** *61*

The finest hotel in the Languedoc-Roussillon region, with immaculate service, opulent rooms, a glorious pool, formal gardens, superb restaurants, and an unbeatable location within Carcassonne's medieval town, La Cité. Golf, canoeing, and white-water rafting are available nearby. **www.hoteldelacite.com**

NICE Windsor

11 rue Dalpozzo, 06000 **Tel** *04-93 88 59 35* **Fax** *04-93 88 94 57* **Rooms** *57*

The Hôtel Windsor provides a wide array of services and facilities, including a pool in an exotic palm garden, a children's play area, and a health and beauty center offering massage and a sauna. Some rooms are individually decorated by local artists. Snack bar and restaurant. **www.hotelwindsornice.com**

NICE Le Negresco

37 promenade des Anglais, 6000 **Tel** *04-93 16 64 00* **Fax** *04-93 88 35 68* **Rooms** *137*

The Negresco is the grande dame of Riviera hotels and has been a landmark on the promenade des Anglais since it opened in 1913, with a seemingly endless list of rich and famous guests. Superbly decorated and furnished with works of art, flawless service, and modern facilities. **www.hotel-negresco-nice.com**

NIMES New Hôtel la Baume

21 rue Nationale, 30000 **Tel** *04-66 76 28 42* **Fax** *04-66 76 28 45* **Rooms** *34*

Housed in an elegant 17th-century townhouse, la Baume is one of the most pleasant places to stay in Nîmes. A short step from the sights, it blends old-world charm with modern facilities. Some rooms are even listed as historic monuments. No restaurant, but a welcoming café-bar. **www.new-hotel.com**

ST JEAN CAP FERRAT La Voile d'Or

Port de St-Jean, 06230 **Tel** *04-93 01 13 13* **Fax** *04-93 76 11 17* **Rooms** *45*

Not quite the most expensive hotel in St-Jean but not far off, La Voile d'Or is worth every cent – service is superb and the rooms are immaculate. Two pools, views of the yacht harbour and the coast, and beach pavilions. Excellent restaurant in classic French culinary tradition. Closed Nov–Mar. **www.lavoiledor.fr**

ST TROPEZ La Ponche

Port des Pêcheurs, 83990 **Tel** *04-94 97 02 53* **Fax** *04-94 97 78 61* **Rooms** *18*

For those looking for a boutique hideaway in St-Tropez, this cluster of one-time fishermen's cottages may fit the bill. The bedrooms are large and artfully chic, and include two family-size rooms. Among the famous guests have been Pablo Picasso and 1950s film star Romy Schneider. **www.laponche.com**

VILLEFRANCHE SUR MER Welcome Hotel

3 Quai Amiral Courbet, 06230 **Tel** *04-93 76 27 62* **Fax** *04-93 76 27 66* **Rooms** *35*

Formerly an 18th-century convent, this hotel offers period charm and attractive views of the sea and the port. Rooms are decorated in different artistic themes: Chagall, Dufy, Matisse. Most have balconies or terraces – ask for one overlooking the bay. Artist Jean Cocteau stayed here after his partner's death in the 1920s. **www.welcomehotel.com**

Where to Eat in France

The variety of places to eat in France is enormous. Throughout the day, the ubiquitous café is ideal for a snack, while bistros and brasseries offer full menus. Restaurants encompass the whole gamut of French cooking, from simple and rustic to the very finest *haute cuisine*. Fixed-price menus are a good value option.

PRICE CATEGORIES
Price categories are for a three-course meal for one, including a half-bottle of house wine, tax and service:

€ under €30
€€ €30–€45
€€€ €45–€60
€€€€ €60–€90
€€€€€ over €90

PARIS

BEAUBOURG AND LES HALLES Au Pied du Cochon   €€
6 rue Coquillière, 75004 **Tel** *01-40 13 77 00*   **Map** *D3*

This colorfully restored brasserie was once popular with high society, who came to observe the workers in the old market and to savor the onion soup. Although touristy, this huge place is fun, and its menu has something for everyone (including excellent shellfish). Still one of the best places after a night out.

BEAUBOURG AND LES HALLES Georges   €€€€
19 rue Beaubourg, 75004 **Tel** *01-44 78 47 99*   **Map** *E3*

On the top floor of the Centre Pompidou, the Georges offers stunning views, especially from the immense terrace. Light and inspired cuisine caters to the tastes of an international clientele. Minimalist decor, with lots of steel and aluminium. In summer, request an outdoor table.

CHAILLOT AND PORTE MAILLOT Bistro Le Goupil   €€
4 rue Claude Debussy, 75017 **Tel** *01-45 74 83 25*   **Map** *A3*

This is a good bistro on the edge of Paris, frequented by local businessmen at lunch and a more fashionable set in the evenings. Simple ingredients are turned into something more special in the open kitchen. The menu includes perfectly cooked *entrecôte*, seared tuna and monkfish with artichokes.

CHAILLOT AND PORTE MAILLOT Zebra Square   €€€
3 Place Clément Ader, 75016 **Tel** *01-44 14 91 90*

Part of the Hotel Square complex, this restaurant is in a modern building and has stylish, minimalist decor, spiced up by splashes of zebra prints. The food is classic gourmet with choices such as *tartare de boeuf*, and cheesecake served with a fruit coulis. A hit with the fashion and media crowd.

CHAMPS-ELYSEES Le Bœuf sur le Toit   €€
34 rue du Colisée, 75008 **Tel** *01-53 93 65 55*   **Map** *B2*

Highly inspired by the 1930s Les Années Folles, this building was formerly a cabaret venue (The Ox on the Roof). Exemplifying the classic Paris Art Deco brasserie, its changing menu can include sole meunière, snails, *foie gras* and crème brûlée. The specialty is crêpes Suzette.

CHAMPS-ELYSEES Guy Savoy   €€€€€
18 rue Troyon, 75017 **Tel** *01-43 80 40 61*   **Map** *B2*

A handsome dining room and professional service further complement the remarkable cuisine of Guy Savoy. The three Michelin-starred menu includes whiting accompanied by a *tartare* of langoustine, grilled sea bass, and an extraordinary dessert list.

FONTAINEBLEAU Croquembouche   €€€€
43 rue de France, 77300 **Tel** *01-64 22 01 57*

Located near the Château de Fontainebleau, this warm and welcoming restaurant serves well-cooked traditional French cuisine using fresh, seasonal ingredients. There are several tasting menus, otherwise the lunchtime menu offers excellent value for money.

ILE DE LA CITE AND ILE SAINT-LOUIS La Rose de France   €€
24 pl Dauphine, 75001 **Tel** *01-43 54 10 12*   **Map** *E4*

Majestic setting overlooking a 17th-century square. Updated French classics, including traditional dishes such as *escargot*, *tarte tatin*, and an excellent duck fillet with ratatouille. A *cuisine du marché* restaurant, La Rose uses the freshest produce from the day's market. It offers good value for money, too.

INVALIDES AND EIFFEL TOWER QUARTER L'Arpège   €€€€€
84 rue de Varenne, 75007 **Tel** *01-47 05 09 06*   **Map** *C4*

Alain Passard's three-star restaurant near the Musée Rodin is one of the most highly regarded in Paris. It has striking pale-wood decor as well as excellent food. The focus here is on fish, shellfish, poultry, and vegetables, although red meat is occasionally featured on the menu. Don't miss the apple tart.

Key to Symbols *see back cover flap*

JARDIN DES PLANTES QUARTER Marty Restaurant   €€€
20 av des Gobelins, 75005 **Tel** *01-43 31 39 51*   **Map** E5

The Marty was established by E. Marty in 1913 and is still family-run. The interior is authentic Art Deco in style, but the cuisine steals the show. The menu features hearty fare, such as roast duck or rabbit casserole, and seasonal dishes, such as gazpacho. Excellent crème brûlée.

LATIN QUARTER Le Balzar   €€
49 rue des Ecoles, 75005 **Tel** *01-43 54 13 67*   **Map** E4

There's a fair choice of brasserie food here but the main attraction is the Left Bank ambiance. Traditionally dressed waiters weave their way among the hustle and bustle, providing express service, with archetypal brasserie decor to match: there are large mirrors and comfortable leather seats.

LATIN QUARTER L'Atelier Maître Albert   €€€
1 rue Maître Albert, 75005 **Tel** *01-56 81 30 01*   **Map** D4

Dishes from the rôtisserie are this restaurant's specialty, although there is always a vegetarian option. Traditional fare such as veal kidneys and mouthwatering chocolate cake are the chief attractions. Other specialties include veal, mixed salad *du moment*, and chicken livers. The antique fireplace is a nice touch. This is another Guy Savoy restaurant.

MONTMARTRE La Table d'Eugène   €€€
41 Rue Eugène-Sue, 75018 **Tel** *01-42 55 61 64*

This up-and-coming bistro is located in the heart of the Montmartre district, and the quality of the food far out-weighs the prices. Tasty, well-prepared dishes feature on the menu, such as cod served with ham and a vinaigrette of *pequillo* peppers and chives, or duck served with pear and polenta. It's advisable to book a few days in advance.

MONTPARNASSE La Coupole   €€
102 bd du Montparnasse, 75014 **Tel** *01-43 20 14 20*

This famous brasserie has been popular with the fashionistas, artists, and thinkers since its creation in 1927. Under the same ownership as Brasserie Flo, it has a similar menu: shellfish, smoked salmon, and good desserts. Lamb curry is a specialty. Open from breakfast until 2am.

OPERA QUARTER La Vaudeville   €€
29 rue Vivienne, 75002 **Tel** *01-40 20 04 62*   **Map** D2

This is one of 14 brasseries owned by Paris's reigning brasserie king, Jean-Paul Bucher. Good shellfish, Bucher's famous smoked salmon, many fish dishes as well as classic brasserie standbys like pig's trotters and *andouillette* (tripe sausage). Quick, friendly service and a noisy ambiance make it fun.

OPERA QUARTER La Fontaine Gaillon   €€€€
1 rue de la Michodière, 75002 **Tel** *01-47 42 63 22*   **Map** D2

Housed in a 17th-century mansion, Fontaine Gaillon is partly owned by legendary film actor Gérard Depardieu. The menu changes daily and showcases sautéed John Dory, Merlan Colbert with sorrel purée, confit de canard, and lamb chops. The interiors are comfortable, and there is a good wine list.

SAINT-GERMAIN-DES-PRES Procope   €€€
13 rue de l'Ancienne Comédie, 75006 **Tel** *01-40 46 79 00*   **Map** D4

Opened in 1686, Paris's oldest café welcomed literary and political figures such as Voltaire and Diderot. Nowadays, it's still a hub for the intelligentsia, who sit alongside those curious about this historical place. Coq-au-vin (chicken cooked in wine) is the specialty. Shellfish platters, too.

THE MARAIS Auberge Nicolas Flamel   €€€
51 rue de Montmorency, 75003 **Tel** *01-42 71 77 78*   **Map** E3

Located in Paris's oldest house (1407) and named after the famous alchemist who lived here, this restaurant's specialties include *tatin de foie gras poellé* (pan-fried *foie gras*) and a spectacular 7-hour lamb dish. The tour de force here, however, is the great choice of desserts.

THE MARAIS L'Ambroisie   €€€€€
9 pl des Vosges, 75004 **Tel** *01-42 78 51 45*   **Map** F4

In a former jewelry shop restored by Chef Bernard Pacaud, this is one of only nine Michelin three-star restaurants in Paris. The cuisine includes a crispy caramelized pigeon, and langoustine *feuillantine* with sesame seeds. Reservations accepted one month in advance.

TUILERIES QUARTER Le Grand Véfour   €€€€€
17 rue de Beaujolais, 75001 **Tel** *01-42 96 56 27*   **Map** D3

This 18th-century restaurant is considered by many to be Paris's most attractive. The chef Guy Martin effortlessly maintains his second Michelin star with dishes such as *foie gras* ravioli with a truffle cream, and hazelnut and milk chocolate *palet* served with caramel ice cream.

VERSAILLES Le Valmont   €€€
20 rue au Pain, 78000 **Tel** *01-39 51 39 00*

Refined cuisine is served at this bistro tucked behind the market hall. Chef Philippe Mathieu presents an ambitious menu with dishes such as veal steak with a truffle mushroom sauce, and beef tenderloin with *foie gras*, served with a rich red wine sauce. Good wines by the glass.

Map References see map of Paris pp150–51

NORTHERN FRANCE

BAYEUX La Coline d'Enzo €€

4 rue des Bouchers, 14400 Tel 02-31 92 03 01

The menu here focuses mainly on fish presented beautifully; sea bass cooked in clay is a specialty. The family-run restaurant is small, with just two rooms, but the decor is bright and charming and there is some outside seating. Popular with locals. Service is attentive but unfussy. Booking ahead is advisable.

CARNAC La Bavolette €€

9 allée du Parc, 56340 Tel 02-97 52 19 69

One of the classier eating places at the popular seaside resort of Carnac-Plage. Fish brochettes and sardine terrine are among the favorites. La Bavolette's specialties include fish soup served with a rich garlicky *aioli* and croutons, and flambéed langoustines.

EPERNAY La Table Kobus €€€

3 rue Dr Rousseau, 51200 Tel 03-26 51 53 53

An original brasserie near the center of this town that is all about champagne. Uniquely, you can bring your own bottle of champagne to drink with your meal. The menu is classic French cuisine. The home-made terrine of *foie gras* is particularly recommended.

MONT-ST-MICHEL Auberge St Pierre €€

Grande rue, 50170 Tel 02-33 60 14 03

Lamb grazed on the surrounding salt marshes, known as *agneau pré-salé*, features on the menu in this charming timbered 15th-century building. Seafood is also a house specialty. Try the favorites such as crab or salmon. Fresh local produce is used in the preparation of traditional dishes.

MONT-ST-MICHEL La Mère Poulard €€€€

Grande rue, 50170 Tel 02-33 89 68 68

A deluxe brasserie on the famous Mont St-Michel, where visitors come from all over the world to sample the famous omelette Mère Poulard, cooked in a long-handled pan over a fire. Also delicious are the *pré-salé* lamb (lamb fed on the surrounding salt marshes), and spit-roasted pig.

REIMS La Brasserie Boulingrin €

48 rue Mars, 51100 Tel 03-26 40 96 22

This famous Reims brasserie and a regular meeting place for locals has kept its Art Deco mosaics of jolly grape harvesters known as "Vendangeurs en Champagne". Good value and a lively place to dine, near the covered market. Oysters and steak tartare are specialties. There is also a large selection of champagnes.

REIMS Château les Crayères €€€€€

64 bd Vasnier, 51100 Tel 03-26 24 90 00

In the former home of the Pommery Champagne family, this gourmet retreat allows visitors to relax in sumptuous guest rooms and savor superb cuisine. The dining room is grand, with huge windows and tapestries. Try the lobster, or the *vol au vent* filled with scallops and truffles. There's an excellent choice of fine champagnes.

ROUEN La Couronne €€€

31 pl Vieux Marché, 76000 Tel 02-35 71 40 90

In the oldest auberge in France, dating from 1345, the experienced, talented chef ensures that you pass a memorable moment here with classic gourmet dishes such as pan-fried escalope of *foie gras*, roast veal, and duck à la Rouennaise. Great Normandy cheeses.

ROUEN Restaurant Gill €€€€

8–9 quai de la Bourse, 76000 Tel 02-35 71 16 14

A highly recommended restaurant on the Seine quays. For more than 20 years chef Gilles Tournadre has been creating sophisticated dishes in this elegant dining room. Specialities include crayfish salad, Pigeon *à la rouennaise* and fillet of bass with onion marmalade. Remarkable wine list.

ST-MALO Le Chalut €€€€

8 rue de la Corne de Cerf, 35400 Tel 02-99 56 71 58

One of St. Malo's best restaurants, the chef excels in fish dishes and well-chosen produce simply prepared. Fillet of red mullet with orange and saffron sauce, St-Pierre perfumed with fresh coriander, and scallops seasoned with orange-infused oil and saffron are examples of the delicious dishes on offer. Good selection of cheese, too.

STRASBOURG Au Crocodile €€€€€

10 rue Outre, 67000 Tel 03-88 32 13 02

One of the finest restaurants in France's other capital. Splendid polished woodwork, elegant decor, and the famous crocodile brought back from a campaign in Egypt by an Alsatian Captain in the French army. Super service and light original cuisine. A truly great wine list that covers the world.

Key to Price Guide *see p212* **Key to Symbols** *see back cover flap*

THE LOIRE VALLEY

BLOIS Au Rendez-vous des Pêcheurs
27 rue du Foix, 41000 **Tel** *02-54 74 67 48*

Well known regionally, this restaurant is famed for its menu focusing on seafood and fish creations like pike-perch wrapped in spinach accompanied by gnocchi, and eel mousse served on a bed of aubergine caviar with an artichoke purée. There is also Sologne game, in season, and a good selection of wines from Cheverny and Montlouis. Book ahead.

CHARTRES Le Grand Monarque
22 pl des Epars, 28000 **Tel** *02-37 18 15 15*

Within this magnificent 17th-century staging post are both a gourmet "le Georges" restaurant, and a brasserie serving traditional food. The cuisine is ambitious and flavorful, with dishes such as sea bass served with onion confit and cep mushrooms, and crayfish with beetroot *carpaccio*. Excellent desserts. First-rate wine cellar.

CHENONCEAU Auberge de Bon Laboureur
6 rue de Docteur Bretonneau, 37150 **Tel** *02-47 23 90 02*

Refined classic cuisine is served in this former coaching inn just a few minutes from the château. The produce is seasonal and vegetables come from their own vegetable patch. A typical menu could include crayfish bisque, seared langoustine, *ris de veau* (sweetbreads), and a chocolate *millefeuille*.

FONTEVRAUD-L'ABBAYE La Licorne
31 rue Robert d'Arbrissel, 49590 **Tel** *02-41 51 72 49*

Next to the splendid abbey, this popular restaurant has a pretty courtyard terrace and elegant dining room. The menu includes creations such as prawns and basil ravioli in morel sauce and, for dessert, strawberries flavored with roses. Good Saumur wines. Book ahead.

NANTES La Cigale
4 pl Graslin, 44000 **Tel** *02-51 84 94 94*

This ornate Belle Epoque brasserie dates from 1895 when it was frequented by celebrated writers and the Nantes elite. The quality of the cuisine matches the exceptional interior. Oysters, carpaccio of salmon, and beef *à la plancha* (cooked on a hot plate). Open all day. Extensive wine list.

ORLEANS La Chancellerie
27 pl Demartroi, 45000 **Tel** *02-38 53 57 54*

This lively brasserie is located in the town's main square. Formerly a bus station, the interior has high ceilings, a marble-top bar, leather banquettes, and brass trimmings. Classic bistro food is enhanced by a good wine list. There's outdoor seating too.

TOURS L'Atelier Gourmand
37 rue Etienne Marcel, 37000 **Tel** *02-47 38 59 87*

A charming small restaurant in a 15th-century building in the old part of Tours. Fabrice Bironneau presents a competitively priced, interesting menu. Authentic dishes are served, such as a hearty lamb cassoulet. Warm, homely ambiance. Book ahead.

TOURS La Roche le Roy
55 Route de St-Avertin, 37200 **Tel** *02-47 27 22 00*

Located at the edge of the city center, in an elegant 18th-century mansion house, is the Michelin-starred La Roche le Roy. Classic, quality French cuisine includes specialties such as scallops with a nut oil sauce and creamed celeriac, roast breast of squab pigeon with a sweet and spicy sauce, and civet of hare.

BURGUNDY AND THE FRENCH ALPS

BEAUNE La Ciboulette
69 rue Lorraine, 21200 **Tel** *03-80 24 70 72*

A delightful little bistro frequented by locals; always a good sign. The basic decor is in contrast with the high standard of cooking. Hearty dishes, such as steak with pungent Epoisses cheese feature on the menu. The best value in town. Local wine merchants come here to choose from the excellent wine list.

BEAUNE Hostellerie de Levernois
Route de Cobertault, Levernois, 21200 **Tel** *03-80 24 73 58*

This beautiful old mansion with formal gardens occupies an idyllic country setting. The classic restaurant serves up "serious" cuisine, such as snail and frogs' legs risotto, Charolais beef served with a Pinot Noir sauce, or salmon smoked over vine cuttings. Vast wine list. Faultless service.

DIJON Le Bistrot des Halles   🚊 🍽 P   €€
10 rue Bannelier, 21000 **Tel** *03-80 49 94 15*

At lunchtime this 1900s-style bistro is roaring. Located next to the market, it attracts food merchants and local business people with its meat pie, *jambon persillé* (ham with a parsley sauce) and *bœuf bourguignon*. Well-known Dijon chef Jean-Pierre Billoux, who has an up-market restaurant in Dijon center, oversees this bistro.

DIJON Le Pré aux Clercs   🚶 🚊 🍽   €€€€
13 pl de la Libération, 21000 **Tel** *03-80 38 05 05*

Run by Jean-Pierre Billoux, one of the most renowned chefs in Dijon. Traditional rustic ingredients with a novel modern twist result in unique dishes, such as fillet of bream served with *foie gras* flan and oyster sauce. The fixed-price menus offer classic dishes, such as a *foie gras* terrine. Charming dining area and good choice of Burgundy wines.

GRENOBLE Le Chasse-Spleen   🚊 🍽   €€€
6 pl Lavalette, 38000 **Tel** *04-38 37 03 52*

Well situated in central Grenoble, Le Chasse-Spleen is known for the quality of its cooking. Dishes are inventive, such as the red tuna baked in seaweed and served with baby artichokes, and the regional dessert baba with Chartreuse. Inside, walnut-drying racks hang from the ceiling, and Baudelaire's poems decorate the walls.

LYON Le Mercière   🚊 🍽   €€
56 rue Mercière, 69002 **Tel** *04-78 37 67 35*

Chic, lively Lyonnais brasserie with its own *traboule* (medieval passageway) crossing the dining room. Frequented by both tourists and locals, the menu includes regional specialties such as ravioli served in a truffle stock, Bobosse *andouillette* (tripe sausage), and a mouthwatering chocolate mousse. Good Rhône wines.

LYON L'Alexandrin   🍽 👤   €€€€
83 Rue Moncey, 69003 **Tel** *04-72 61 15 69*

The young, talented chef at L'Alexandrin prepares gourmet Lyonnais dishes that are cooked to perfection and ooze personality – try the free-range pigeon with cherries in a Bigarde (orange) sauce, served with sautéed mushrooms and a vegetable casserole. The same care is taken with the vegetables in such creations as *cocotte* of vegetables.

SOUTHWEST FRANCE

BAYONNE Auberge du Cheval Blanc   🚊 🚶 🍽 P   €€€
68 rue Bourgneuf, 64100 **Tel** *05-59 59 01 33*

Stray from the set menu to eat à la carte at this well-regarded hotel in the riverside Petit Bayonne quarter. The menu changes with the seasons, with local dishes, such as *xamano* (ham and mashed potatoes), fine Atlantic seafood, interesting soups and casseroles, and delicious desserts. Respectable wine list. Closed Feb–mid-Mar.

BIARRITZ Chez Albert   🚶 🚊 P   €€
Port des Pêcheurs, 64200 **Tel** *05-59 24 43 84*

From the terrace there are superb views of Biarritz's picturesque fishing harbor and surrounding cliffs and beaches, making this fine seafood restaurant popular. Arrive early for the best tables. Piled platters of seafood, freshly caught lobster, sole, sea bream, tuna, and sardines are among the treats here.

BIARRITZ Le Sissinou   🚶 🍽   €€€€
5 av Maréchal Foch, 64200 **Tel** *05-59 22 51 50*

Managed by chef Michel Cassou-Debat – a veteran of some of France's top establishments – Sissinou is one of Biarritz most talked-about restaurants. Wonderful food such as tuna carpaccio and roast monkfish. There are also authentic regional dishes such as *entrecôte Chalosse* (beef with olives and anchovies) and desserts that invite indulgence.

BORDEAUX La Tupina   🚶 🚊 👤   €€€
6 rue Porte de la Monnaie, 33800 **Tel** *05-56 91 56 37*

The heart of La Tupina is the open fire over which succulent meats are grilled and in winter a cauldron of soup bubbles away. This is an excellent place to try bordelais specialties such as lamprey in wine, grilled shad, or baby eel cooked in wine. Simple, old-fashioned desserts.

PAU Chez Pierre   🚶 🍽 P   €€
16 rue Louis Barthou, 64000 **Tel** *05-59 27 76 86*

Chez Pierre exudes 19th-century elegance and prides itself on the old-fashioned, club-like atmosphere that harks back to Pau's heyday as a British expatriate's hideaway. Classic French regional cooking along with some surprises, such as cod with sweet potato purée, and an extensive wine list.

TOULOUSE Brasserie Flo Les Beaux Arts   🚶 🚊 🍽   €€€
1 quai de la Daurade, 31000 **Tel** *05-61 21 12 12*

An authentic and bustling brasserie serving a broad range of dishes, from salads and seafood to southwestern favorites. To start, you could opt for a flavorsome dish of *tartare* of avocado with king prawns, followed by beef *carpaccio* with olive oil and parmesan, and gazpacho of red fruits and gingerbread ice cream. The menu changes regularly.

TOULOUSE Les Jardins de l'Opéra 🏃 🗐 🖺 🖳   €€€€

1 pl du Capitole, 31000 **Tel** *05-61 23 07 76*

Gourmet dining at its most refined in the restaurant of the Grand Hôtel de l'Opéra. Hushed tones and widely spaced tables create a suitably reverent atmosphere for dishes such as fricasée of lobster with a Thai curry sauce or chocolate pudding with *Espelette* pepper and mango coulis. Impeccable service.

THE SOUTH OF FRANCE

AIX-EN-PROVENCE L'Aixquis 🗐 🖳   €€€

22 rue Victor Leydet, 13100 **Tel** *04-42 27 76 16*

An up-to-date array of dishes and a good wine list have made this one of Aix's most popular eating places. L'Aixquis is located in a narrow lane in central Aix. Chef Benoît Strohm is known for excellent Provençal cooking, such as rabbit marinated in herbs. Closed Sun, Mon lunch.

AIX-EN-PROVENCE Le Clos de la Violette 🖼 🗐 🖳   €€€€€

10 av Violette, 13100 **Tel** *04-42 23 30 71*

This is an elegant address in a chic mansion standing in its own gardens: tranquil, intimate, and perfect for a romantic evening. People do dress up a little to eat here. The wine list is extensive (and very strong on local and Provençal wines) and the menu is Provençal with a modern edge. Closed Sun, Mon.

ARLES Lou Marques 🏃 🖼 🖳   €€€€

Bd Lices, 13200 **Tel** *04-90 52 52 52*

Lou Marques – the restaurant of the venerable Hôtel Jules César – is one of the best places to eat in Arles, with a central location, pleasant terrace with tables under white umbrellas, and a bill of fare that concentrates on classic Provençal dishes. Dignified surroundings. Closed Nov–Apr; Sat, Sun.

AVIGNON Hiély-Lucullus 🏃 🗐 🖳   €€€€

5 rue de la République, 84000 **Tel** *04-90 86 17 07*

Old-fashioned provincial restaurant with a long history of catering to the gourmands of Avignon. Decorated in Belle Epoque style, the restaurant has a menu concentrating on the classics revisited, such as red mullet with sliced carrots in parsley juice. On the first floor of a medieval building.

CANNES La Palme d'Or 🖔 🗐 🖩 P 🖳   €€€€€

73 la Croisette, 06400 **Tel** *04-92 98 74 14*

Children are not actually barred from this restaurant of the stars, nor is it essential to wear a tie – but diners who are not dressed to impress may feel self-conscious here. The food is imaginative and superb, with an impressive, costly wine list. Reservations required. Closed Sun, Mon.

CARCASSONNE L'Ecurie 🏃 🖼 🗐 P   €€

43 boulevard Barbes, 11000 **Tel** *04-68 72 04 04*

Housed in 18th-century stable buildings, "The Stables" is worth a visit just to sit in these elegant old-fashioned surroundings. A favorite with local people, its restaurant tends towards meat dishes, traditionally presented. There is a pretty inner courtyard with tables in the shade or in the sun.

MARSEILLE Restaurant Michel 🖔 🏃 🖼 🗐 🖳   €€€€

6 rue des Catalans, 13000 **Tel** *04-91 52 30 63*

Bouillabaisse is the specialty of the house at this fine, busy brasserie. Other fish dishes include bourride, sardines, and the always reliable catch of the day, fresh and simply grilled. Popular with locals – get there early to be sure of a table. Wine list includes names from Bandol and Cassis.

MONACO Trattoria 🖼 🗐 🖳   €€€

26 av Princesse Grace, 98000 **Tel** *00 377 98 06 71 71*

The Trattoria is the most casual of the three Alain Ducasse restaurants in Monaco. Part of the Sporting Club, the rooftop setting overlooking the harbor is perfect. Open only from mid-May to mid-September, the menu has over 20 choices of antipasti, and delicious desserts.

NICE Le Boccaccio 🖼 🗐 🖳   €€€

7 rue Massena, 06000 **Tel** *04-93 87 71 76*

One of the best places for seafood in Nice, the central Boccaccio is on a bustling car-free street. The interior design is imaginative, with stained-glass windows and tables spread over several floors, and the bill of fare features the best fish dishes – fresh, simply prepared, and with attentive service.

NIMES Lisita 🏃 🖼 🗐 🖳   €€€€

2 bd des Arènes, 30000 **Tel** *04-66 67 29 15*

Lisita is not to be missed. This is one of the most popular restaurants in Nîmes, serving cutting-edge food and an outstanding wine list. The surroundings are attractive too, with modern design set off by old stone walls in two rooms, plus an attractive terrace. Closed Sun, Mon.

BELGIUM AND LUXEMBOURG

Famed for its magnificent Flemish art and Gothic architecture, Belgium, like neighboring Luxembourg, is a melting pot of various influences including Dutch, French, and German. The histories of the two countries have long been interlinked, but culturally and linguistically they are distinct. Luxembourg, a major financial center, is one of the smallest states in Europe.

In recent times, both Belgium and Luxembourg have largely avoided the limelight, but it was here, in the Middle Ages, that the first great towns of Northern Europe were born, and where the first experiments with oil paintings were made. Today, Brussels, as the center of government for the European Union, is theoretically the capital of Europe, but its reputation remains overshadowed by those of the larger European capitals.

Perhaps more than any other country in Europe, Belgium is most aptly defined by contrasts. The division between the Flemish inhabitants of the north and the French-speaking Walloons in the south is mirrored by a geographical divide; the estuarial plains of Brabant and Flanders give way to the rolling hill-country of the Ardennes, which stretches south and east through the castle-dotted woods of Luxembourg.

HISTORY

At the start of the 12th century, commerce became the guiding force in Europe, and the centers of trade quickly grew into powerful cities. Rivers and canals were keys to the growth of the area's towns; Brussels, Ghent, Ypres, Antwerp, and Bruges became the focus of a cloth trade between Belgium, France, Germany, Italy, and England.

In 1369 Philip, Duke of Burgundy, married the daughter of the Count of Flanders, and a few years later the Low Countries and eastern France came under the couple's Burgundian rule. A century later, the death of Mary of Burgundy left her husband, the Habsburg Emperor Maximilian, ruler of Belgium. In 1488 Brussels and the rest of Flanders rebelled against this new power, but the Austrians prevailed, largely because of a plague which decimated the population in 1490.

European Parliament building rising above the trees of Parc Léopold, Brussels

◁ Detail of the façade of the Hôtel de Ville in the Grand Place, Brussels

By 1555 the Low Countries had passed into the hands of the Spanish Habsburgs, whose Catholic repression of the Protestants sparked the Dutch Revolt. In the course of the wars that led to Dutch independence (1568–1648), the predominantly Catholic southern part of the Low Countries remained under Spanish rule. In 1700 the Spanish Habsburg dynasty died out, and England, Austria, and other powers united to oppose French designs on the region in the War of the Spanish Succession. When the war came to an end in 1713, the Treaty of Utrecht transferred Belgium and Luxembourg to the Austrian Habsburgs.

King Leopold I, the first king of the Belgians, crowned in 1830

Belgium was again ruled by foreign powers between 1794 and 1830. First, by the French Republicans, and then, after Napoleon's defeat, by the Dutch. William I of Orange was appointed King of the Netherlands at the Congress of Vienna in 1815, and his autocratic style, together with a series of anti-Catholic measures, bred considerable discontent, especially among the French-speaking Walloons. An 1830 uprising ousted the Dutch and made Leopold I king of a newly independent Belgium. Nine years later Luxembourg, a Grand-Duchy since 1815, also gained independence.

Both countries' economies flourished throughout the 19th century, but all was eclipsed with the start of World War I. In 1940 the Germans invaded again, this time under Hitler's command.

Belgium's history in the latter half of the 20th century was dominated by the ongoing language debate between the Flemings and the Walloons. The constitution was redrawn, creating a federal state with three separate regions: Flanders, Wallonia, and Brussels.

KEY DATES IN THE HISTORY OF BELGIUM AND LUXEMBOURG

56 BC Julius Caesar conquers the Low Countries

963 AD Count Siegfried establishes Luxembourg

1229 Brussels granted its first charter

1430 Under Burgundian rule, Brussels becomes the major administrative center of the region

1482 The region falls under Austrian sovereignty

1519 Charles V, ruler of Burgundy, becomes Holy Roman Emperor.

1555–1794 Spanish and Austrian rule

1794 French Republican armies take over

1815 Belgium and Luxembourg pass to William I of Orange, King of the Netherlands

1830 Belgium gains independence

1839 Luxembourg gains independence

1914 Both countries invaded by Germany

1940 Nazi troops occupy both countries

1958 EEC headquarters set up in Brussels

1962 Act of Parliament divides Belgium into Dutch- and French-speaking regions

1967 NATO headquarters move to Brussels

1988 Flemish and Walloon regions of Belgium granted fiscal autonomy

2000 Grand Duke of Luxembourg abdicates in favor of his eldest son, Henri

LANGUAGE AND CULTURE

In the north of Belgium, the Flemish have their roots in the Netherlands and Germany, while the Walloons of the south are related to the French. French is one of the official languages of Luxembourg, as is German, but the indigenous language is Letzeburgesch, a dialect of German spoken by all. Artistically, Belgium is best known for its 17th-century painters (including Rubens, van Dyck, and Jordaans) and more recently for its Art Nouveau style of architecture and Surrealist artists such as Magritte. Today the country is one of the world's most popular producers of chocolate and beer.

A glass of Chimay, a popular Belgian beer

Exploring Belgium and Luxembourg

Brussels is not only the capital of Belgium but also of Europe, as the center of government for the European Union. The city lies in the center of the country on the flat, fertile Brabant plain. Today, its excellent communications make it an ideal place from which to explore the historic towns of Antwerp, Ghent, and Bruges. Toll-free motorways compare favorably with any in France, train travel is swift and competitively priced, and there are good bus services in the areas not covered by trains. Transport in Luxembourg is equally good, with the hub of communications in Luxembourg City itself.

The medieval market square, seen from the Belfort tower, Bruges

SIGHTS AT A GLANCE

Antwerp ❷

Bruges pp232–4 ❸

BRUSSELS pp222–9 ❶

Ghent ❹

Luxembourg ❻

Waterloo ❺

Picturesque Château de Vianden, Luxembourg

KEY

✈ Airport

⛴ Ferry port

— Highway

— Major road

— Railroad

▪▪▪ International border

Brussels ❶

With over one million inhabitants, the Brussels-Capital Region is made up of nineteen districts. The actual city of Brussels is much smaller and divided into two main areas. Historically the poorer area, where workers and immigrants lived, the Lower Town is centered around the splendid 17th-century Grand Place. The Upper Town, traditional home of the aristocracy, is an elegant area that encircles the city's green oasis, the Parc de Bruxelles. Some of the most striking buildings in this part of the city are the shiny postmodern structures of European institutions.

SEE ALSO

- *Where to Stay* p240
- *Where to Eat* p242

Two famous Belgians: Tintin and Snowy

SIGHTS AT A GLANCE

Cathédrale Sts-Michel
  et Gudule ⑤
Centre Belge de la
  Bande Dessinée ④
Grand Place ①
Manneken Pis ③
Musée du Costume et
  de la Dentelle ②
Musées Royaux des
  Beaux-Arts ⑥
Palais Royal ⑦
Parc du Cinquantenaire ⑩
Parliament Quarter ⑨
Place du Grand Sablon ⑧

Greater Brussels
(see inset map)
Bruparck ⑫
Musée Horta ⑪

0 meters   500
0 yards   500

GETTING AROUND

Brussels' Lower Town is well served by trams. However, many streets are pedestrianized, and usually the quickest way of getting around is on foot. In the Upper Town, the best option is to take one of the buses that run through the district. Brussels' metro stations are well placed for the main sights of interest, and the system offers a fast and efficient way of reaching the suburbs.

Revelers in colorful costume at
a festival in the Grand Place

GREATER BRUSSELS

Antwerp

A1

RO   A12   Strombeek-
Bever   ⑫   Bruxelles National
Brussel Nationaal

N1   Diegem

R21   A201   Zaventem

Jette   Evere   N2   *Liège*

Ghent   Schaerbeek   A3   Kraainem

N8   N2   Woluwe-
Saint-Lambert   RO   N227

N6   BRUSSELS   Woluwe-
Saint-Pierre   *Charleroi*

St-Gilles   Etterbeek

⑪   Ixelles

0 kilometers   3

0 miles   3

KEY

Area of main map

KEY

	Sight / Place of interest
✈	Airport
🚆	Train station
M	Metro station
🚊	Main tram stop
🚌	Main bus stop
P	Parking
i	Tourist information
✝	Church
—	Pedestrian street

Bronze statues in the Place du Petit Sablon in the Upper Town

D   E   F

Grand Place, Brussels' historic main square

Grand Place ①

Ⓜ *Bourse, Gare Centrale.* 🚌 *29,
34, 47, 48, 71 & many others.* 🚋 *3,
55, 81.* **Musée de la Ville**
Maison du Roi. **Tel** *02-279 4350.*
⏰ *10am–5pm Tue–Sun.* 🚫 *Jan 1,
May 1, Nov 1 & 11, Dec 25.* 🎨 💳
by prior arrangement.

The geographical, historical,
and commercial heart of the
city, the Grand Place is the
first port of call for most
visitors to Brussels. A market
was held on this site as early
as the 11th century. During
the first half of the 15th
century, Brussels' town hall,
the Hôtel de Ville, was built,
and city traders began to add
individual guildhalls in a
medley of styles. In 1695,
however, two days of cannon
fire by the French destroyed
all but the town hall and two
façades. Trade guilds were
urged to rebuild their halls to

La Maison du Roi, built on the site
of old bread, meat, and cloth halls

designs approved by the
town council, resulting in the
splendid Baroque ensemble
that can be seen today.

Occupying the entire southwest side of the square, the
Gothic **Hôtel de Ville** (*see
p225*) is the architectural
masterpiece of the Grand
Place. Opposite it stands
La Maison du Roi (1536).
Despite its name, no king
ever lived here; the building
was used as a temporary jail
and a tax office. Redesigned
in Gothic style in the late
19th century, it is now
home to the Musée de la
Ville, which contains
16th-century paintings
and tapestries, and a
collection of around
815 costumes created
for the Manneken Pis.

On the square's eastern
flank, the vast Neoclassical
edifice known as **La Maison
des Ducs de Brabant**
was designed by
Guillaume de Bruyn
and consists of six
former guildhalls. Facing
it are **Le Renard**, built in the
1690s for the guild of haber-
dashers, and **Le Cornet**
(1697), the boatmen's guildhall, whose gable resembles a
17th-century frigate's bow. **Le
Roy d'Espagne**, also known as
La Maison des Boulangers,
was built in the late 17th
century by the wealthy bakers'
guild. The gilt bust over the
entrance represents St. Aubert,
patron saint of bakers. Today,
the building houses one of the
Grand Place's best-loved bars,
whose first floor offers fine
views of the bustling square.

Musée du Costume et de la Dentelle ②

Rue de Violette 12. **Tel** *02-213 4450.*
Ⓜ *Gare Centrale.* 🚌 *34, 48, 95, 96.*
⏰ *10am–5pm Thu–Tue.* 🎨 💳 *on
request.* ♿ *restricted.*

Located within two 18th-
century gabled houses, this
museum is dedicated to
one of Brussels' most
successful exports, Belgian
lace, which has been made
here since the 12th century.
The ground floor has a display
of costumes on mannequins
showing how lace has
adorned fashions of every
era. Upstairs is a fine collection of antique lace from
France, Flanders, and Italy.

Manneken Pis ③

Rues de l'Etuve & du Chêne.
Ⓜ *Gare Centrale.* 🚌 *34, 48, 95, 96.*
🚋 *3, 55, 81.*

The tiny statue of a young
boy relieving himself is
Brussels' most unusual sight.
The original bronze statue
by Jérôme Duquesnoy the
Elder was first placed on
the site in 1619. After it
was stolen and damaged
by a former convict in
1817, a replica was
made and returned to
its revered site. The
inspiration for the statue
is unknown, but the
mystery only lends itself
to rumor and fable
and increases the little
boy's charm. One
theory claims that in
the 12th century the
son of a duke was caught
urinating against a tree in the
midst of a battle, and was
thus commemorated in
bronze as a symbol of the
country's military courage.
When, in 1698, a city governor
provided a set of clothes with
which to dress the statue, he
began a tradition that is still
observed today. Visiting heads
of state donate miniature
versions of their national
costume for the boy, and now
a collection of 815 outfits,
including an Elvis suit, can be
seen in the Musée de la Ville.

Manneken Pis
statue

Hôtel de Ville

The idea of erecting a town hall to reflect Brussels' growth as a major European trading center had been under consideration since the end of the 13th century, but it was not until 1401 that the first foundation stone was laid. Completed in 1459, the Hôtel de Ville emerged as the finest civic building in the country, a stature it still enjoys. Jacques van Thienen was commissioned to design the left wing, where he used ornate columns, sculptures, turrets, and arcades. Jan van Ruysbroeck's elegant spire helped seal the building's reputation. Tours are available of the interior, which contains 15th-century tapestries and works of art.

VISITORS' CHECKLIST

Grand Place. *Tel* 02-279 2343.
M Bourse, Gare Centrale. 🚌
many routes. 🚊 3, 55, 81.
◯ (for guided tours) 3:15pm
Tue & Wed (all year); 10:45am,
12:15pm Sun (Apr–Sep). ● public hols & election days. 📷 ♿

★ Council Chamber
*This room was where
the ruling council of
Brabant used to meet.
Ancient tapestries and
gilt mirrors line the
walls above an
inlaid floor.*

★ Maximilian Room
*This lavish hall, used today
by the city council, takes its
name from the portrait of
Maximilian I of Austria over
the fireplace. It contains
18th-century tapestries
depicting the history of
6th-century King Clovis.*

The tower, begun
in 1449, is 96 m (315
ft) high. It is topped by
a statue of St. Michael,
patron saint of Brussels.

The gabled roof, like
much of the town hall,
was fully restored in
1837 and cleaned
in the 1990s.

Gothic Room

**137 stone
statues** adorn
the facades.

STAR FEATURES

★ Council Chamber
★ Maximilian Room

Wedding Room
*A Neo-Gothic style dominates
this civil marriage office. Its
ornate carved timbers include
mahogany inlaid with ebony.*

Art Nouveau entrance hall of the Centre Belge de la Bande Dessinée

Centre Belge de la Bande Dessinée ④

20 Rue des Sables. **Tel** 02-219 1980. 🚌 29, 38, 58, 61, 63, 71. 🚋 25, 55 81, 90. Ⓜ Botanique, Rogier, Centrale. ◻ 10am–6pm Tue–Sun. ◻ Jan 1, Dec 25. ▨ ✔ 🍴 ⬛ ⭑

This unique museum pays tribute to the Belgian passion for comic strips, or *bandes dessinées*, and to world-famous comic strip artists from Belgium and abroad.

One of the exhibitions shows the great comic strip heroes, from Hergé's Tintin – who made his debut in 1929 – to the Smurfs and the Flemish comic strip characters Suske and Wiske. Other displays explain the stages of putting together a comic strip. There is also a series of life-size cartoon sets, of special appeal to children. The museum holds 6,000 original plates, and a valuable archive of photographs and artifacts.

The collection is housed in a beautiful building, built in 1903–6 to the design of the Belgian Art Nouveau architect Victor Horta *(see p229)*.

Cathédrale Sts-Michel et Gudule ⑤

Parvis Ste-Gudule. **Tel** 02-217 8345. 🚌 29, 60, 63, 65, 66, 71. 🚋 92, 94. Ⓜ Centrale. ◻ daily. ▨ to crypt and treasury. ⭑ call in advance. **www**.cathedralestmichel.be

Belgium's finest surviving example of Brabant Gothic architecture, the Cathédrale

Sts-Michel et Gudule is the national church of Belgium. There has been a church on this site since at least the 11th century. Work began on the Gothic cathedral in 1226 under Henry I, Duke of Brabant, and continued over a period of 300 years.

The cathedral interior is relatively bare, due to Protestant ransacking in 1579 and thefts during the French Revolution. Over the west door, however, is a magnificent 16th-century stained-glass window of the Last Judgment. Another splendid feature is the flamboyantly carved Baroque pulpit in the central aisle, by an Antwerp sculptor, Hendrik Frans Verbruggen. In the crypt are the remains of the original Romanesque church, which dates back to 1047.

Musées Royaux des Beaux-Arts ⑥

Rue de la Régence 3. **Tel** 02-508 3211. 🚌 25, 27, 38, 60, 71, 95. 🚋 92, 94. Ⓜ Parc, Centrale. ◻ 10am–5pm Tue–Sun. ◻ public hols. ▨ call in advance. ⬛ ⬛ 🍴 ⭑ **www**.fine-arts-museum.be

Six centuries of art, both Belgian and international, are displayed in the three museums that make up the Musées Royaux des Beaux-

The white limestone façade of the Cathédrale Sts-Michel et Gudule

Arts, the Musée d'Art Ancien (15th–18th centuries), the Musée d'Art Moderne (19th century–present day) and the Magritte Museum. All the museums have colored "routes," which guide the visitor through galleries representing the different schools and periods of art.

The Musée d'Art Ancien holds one of the world's finest collections of works by the Flemish Primitive School. A work of particular note is *The Annunciation* (c.1415–25) by the Master of Flémalle. The trademarks of the Flemish Primitives are a life-like vitality and a clarity of light. The greatest exponent of the style was Rogier van der Weyden (c.1400–64), the official city painter to Brussels, who has several splendid works on display at the museum.

Peter Brueghel the Elder (c.1525–69), one of the most outstanding Flemish artists, settled in Brussels in 1563. His earthy scenes of peasant life remain his best known works, and are represented here by paintings such as *The Bird Trap* (1565). Another highlight of the Musée d'Art Ancien is the world-famous collection of

The Assumption of the Virgin (c.1615) by Rubens at the Musées Royaux des Beaux Arts

works by Peter Paul Rubens
(1577–1640). *The Assumption
of the Virgin* stands out
among his religious canvases.
Other notable paintings
include van Dyck's *Portrait of
Porzia Imperial with her
daughter Maria Francesca*
(1620s) and *Three Children
with Goatcart* by Frans Hals
(c.1582–1666).

Opened in 1984, the Musée
d'Art Moderne is situated in a
unique setting: eight levels of
the building are underground.
Works in the 19th-century
section vary greatly in style
and subject matter, from
Neoclassicism, exemplified by
David, to Realism, Impressionism, and Symbolism.

The Fauvist painter Rik
Wouters' *Woman in a Blue
Dress in front of a Mirror*
(1914) is one of many works
by leading Belgian artists of
the 20th century. Foreign
artists include Matisse, Paul
Klee, and Chagall.

The Magritte Museum is
devoted to one of Belgium's
most famous artists and a
major exponent of Surrealism,
René Magritte (1898–1967).
Spread over five floors, it is
the world's largest collection
of his work and covers all
periods of his life, from the
dazzling early Cavernous
period of the late 1920s to
the renowned *Domain of
Arnhem* (1962).

Palais Royal ⑦

Place des Palais. **Tel** 02-551 2020.
🚌 21, 27, 38, 60, 71, 95, 96.
🚊 92, 94. Ⓜ Trône, Parc.
🕐 10:30am–5pm Tue–Sun.
⭕ mid-Sep–mid-Jul. 📷 ♿
www.monarchie.be

The official home of the
Belgian monarchy, this is one
of the finest 19th-century
buildings in the Upper Town.
Construction began in the
1820s on the site of the old
Coudenberg Palace. Work
continued under Léopold II
(reigned 1865–1909), when
much of the exterior was
completed. The most lavish
state reception rooms include
the Throne Room, with 28
wall-mounted chandeliers, and
the Hall of Mirrors. The latter,

The 19th-century Palais Royal

similar to the Hall of Mirrors
at Versailles *(see pp168–9)*, is
where ceremonial occasions
are held, and guests presented
to the king and queen.

Place du Grand Sablon ⑧

🚌 27, 48, 95. 🚊 92, 94. Ⓜ
Centrale, Louise, Parc.

Located on the slope of the
escarpment that divides
Brussels in two, the Place
du Grand Sablon is like a
stepping stone between the
upper and lower towns. The
name "sablon" derives from
the French "sable" (sand),
and the square is so called
because this old route down
to the city center once passed
through sandy marshes.

Terrace café in the upscale Place du
Grand Sablon

Today this is an area of
upscale antiques dealers,
fashionable restaurants, and
trendy bars, where you can
stay drinking until the early
hours of the morning.

At the far end of the square
stands the lovely church of
Notre-Dame du Sablon, built
in the Brabant Gothic style,
and boasting some
glorious stained-
glass windows.
On the
opposite side
of the road to
the church is
the **Place du
Petit Sablon**.
In contrast to
the busy café
scene of the
larger square,
these pretty
formal gardens
are a peaceful
spot to stop for
a rest. Sit and
admire the 48 bronze
statues by Art Nouveau
artist Paul Hankar, each
representing a different
medieval guild of the city. At
the back of the gardens is a
fountain, built to commemorate
Counts Egmont and Hoorn,
the martyrs who led a Dutch
uprising against the tyrannical
rule of the Spanish under
Philip II. On either side of the
fountain are 12 further statues
of prominent 15th- and 16th-
century figures, including
Gerhard Mercator, the Flemish
geographer and mapmaker.

Notre-Dame
du Sablon
window

The triumphal central archway and surrounding colonnades of the Parc du Cinquantenaire

European Parliament Quarter ⑨

🚌 21, 27, 34, 38, 54, 60, 80, 95. Ⓜ Maelbeek, Trône, Schuman.

The vast, modern steel and glass complex, located just behind the Quartier Léopold

Postmodern building known as "Les Caprices des Dieux" in Brussels' Parliament Quarter

train station, is one of three homes of the European Parliament (the other two are Strasbourg and Luxembourg). This gleaming building has its critics: the huge structure housing the hemicycle that seats the 700-plus MEPs has been dubbed "Les Caprices des Dieux" ("Whims of the Gods"), which refers both to the shape of the building, similar to a French cheese of the same name, and to its lofty aspirations. The Parc Léopold, next to the Parliament, has some notable Art Nouveau buildings and is a delightful spot for a walk or a picnic.

Parc du Cinquantenaire ⑩

Avenue de Tervuren. 🚌 27, 28, 36, 80. 🚊 81, 82. Ⓜ Schuman, Mérode. **Musées Royaux d'Art et d'Histoire** *Tel* 02-741 7211. ☐ Tue–Sun. 🔵 public hols. 🎫 📷 www.kmkg-mrah.be **Musée Royal de l'Armée et d'Histoire Militaire** *Tel* 02-737 7811. ☐ Tue–Sun. 🔵 Jan 1, Dec 25. 🎫 ♿ www.klm-mra.be **Autoworld** *Tel* 02-736 4165. ☐ 10am–6pm daily (5pm in winter). 🔵 Jan 1, Dec 25.

The finest of Léopold II's grand projects, the Parc and Palais du Cinquantenaire were built for the Golden Jubilee celebrations of Belgian independence in 1880. The park was laid out on unused marshland. The palace, at its entrance, was to comprise a triumphal arch, based on the Arc de

BRUSSELS AND THE EUROPEAN UNION

In 1958, following the signing of the Treaty of Rome in the previous year, the European Economic Community (EEC), now the European Union (EU), was born, and Brussels became its headquarters. Today, the city remains home to most of the EU's institutions. The European Commission, the EU body that formulates policies, is based in the vast Berlaymont Building. The city is also one of the seats of the European Parliament, which currently has around 736 members, known as MEPs (Members of the European Parliament). The most powerful institution is the Council of Ministers, composed of representatives of each member state. Each nation has a certain number of votes, according to its size. The Council must approve all legislation for the EU, often a difficult task to accomplish given that most Europe-wide legislation will not be to the liking of every state.

The signing of the Treaty of Rome, 1957

Triomphe in Paris *(see p165)*, and two large exhibition areas. By the time of the 1880 Art and Industry Exposition, however, only the two side exhibition areas had been completed. Further funds were found, and work continued for 50 years. The arch was completed in 1905. Until 1935, the large halls on either side of the central archway were used to hold trade fairs, before being converted into museums.

Also known as the Musée du Cinquantenaire, the excellent **Musées Royaux d'Art et d'Histoire** contain a vast array of exhibits. Sections on ancient civilizations cover Egypt, Greece, Persia, and the Near East. Other displays feature Byzantium and Islam, China and the Indian subcontinent, and the Pre-Columbian civilizations of the Americas. Decorative arts from all ages include glassware, silverware, porcelain, lace, and tapestries. There are also religious sculptures and stained glass.

The **Musée Royal de l'Armée et d'Histoire Militaire** deals with all aspects of Belgium's military history. There are new sections on both World Wars, as well as a separate hall containing historic aircraft.

Housed in the south wing of the Cinquantenaire Palace, **Autoworld** has one of the best collections of historic automobiles in the world.

Part formal gardens, part tree-lined walks, the park is popular with Brussels' Eurocrats and families at lunchtimes and weekends.

Musée Horta ⑪

Rue Américaine 23–25. *Tel* 02-543 0490. 🚌 54. 🚋 81, 82, 92. Ⓜ *Albert, Louise.* ⏲ 2–5:30pm Tue–Sun. ⏸ *public hols.* **www**.hortamuseum.be

Architect Victor Horta (1861–1947) is considered the father of Art Nouveau, and his impact on Brussels architecture is unrivaled by any other designer of his time. A museum dedicated to

Elegant Art Nouveau staircase at the Musée Horta

his unique style is today housed in his restored family home, in the St Gilles district. Horta himself designed the house, between 1898 and 1901. The airy interior of the building displays trademarks of the architect's style – iron, glass, and curves – in every detail, while retaining a functional approach. Most impressive are the dining room, with its ornate ceiling featuring scrolled metalwork, and the central staircase. Decorated with curved wrought iron, the stairs are enhanced further by mirrors and glass, bringing natural light into the house.

Bruparck ⑫

Boulevard du Centenaire. *Tel* 02-474 8383. 🚌 84, 88, 89. 🚋 51, 81. Ⓜ *Heysel.* **Mini-Europe** *Tel* 02-474 8383. ⏲ *daily.* ⏸ *Jan–Mar.* 🅿 ♿ **Kinepolis** *Tel* 02-474 2600. ⏸ *for performances only.* **Atomium** *Tel* 02-475 4775. ⏲ *daily.* 🅿 📶 🖥 🍴 **www**.bruparck.com

Located on the outskirts of the city, this theme park is popular with families. The most visited attraction is **Mini-Europe**, which has over 300 miniature reconstructions (built at a scale of 1:25) of Europe's major sights, from Athens' Acropolis to London's Houses of Parliament.

For film fans, **Kinepolis** has 29 cinemas, including an IMAX cinema.

If warmth and relaxation are what you are looking for, **Océade** is a tropically heated water park that features giant slides, wave machines, and even artificial sandy beaches.

Towering over Bruparck is Brussels' most distinctive landmark, the **Atomium**. Designed by André Waterkeyn for the 1958 World's Fair, and representing an iron crystal magnified 165 billion times, the structure has a viewing platform and restaurant at the top.

The Atomium, rising 100 m (325 ft) over the Bruparck

Bronze statue of Silvius Brabo in Antwerp's Grote Markt

Antwerp ❷

🏠 500,000. ✈ 🚉 🚌
ℹ️ 13 Grote Markt (03-232 0103).
www.antwerpen.be

In the Middle Ages Antwerp was a thriving hub of the European cloth trade, and the principal port of the Duchy of Brabant. Today, it is the main city of Flemish-speaking Belgium, and the center of the international diamond trade.

At the heart of the city's old medieval district is the Grote Markt. The Brabo Fountain, at its center, has a statue of the soldier Silvius Brabo, said to be the nephew of Julius Caesar. The square is overlooked by the ornately gabled **Stadhuis** (Town Hall), built in 1564, and the Gothic **Onze Lieve Vrouwe Kathedraal** (Cathedral of Our Lady), which dates back to 1352.

Among the paintings inside the cathedral are two triptychs by Antwerp's most famous son, Peter Paul Rubens (1577–1640).

The narrow, winding streets of the old town are lined with fine medieval guildhalls, such as the **Vleeshuis**, or Meat Hall, once occupied by the Butchers' Guild. Dating from the early 16th century, it is built in alternate stripes of stone and brick, giving it a streaky bacon-like appearance.

When Rubens died in 1640, he was buried in the family's chapel at the lovely sandstone **Sint Jacobskerk** (1491–1656), also located in the old town.

One of the most prestigious of Antwerp's many museums is the **Koninklijk Museum voor Schone Kunsten**, which houses an impressive collection of ancient and modern art. Works from the 17th century include masterpieces by the "Antwerp Trio" of van Dyck (1599–1641), Jordaens (1593–1678), and Rubens. More modern exhibits include works by the Surrealist René Magritte (1898–1967) and Rik Wouters (1882–1916). During renovations which will last until 2017, major works will be on display at various locations throughout the city.

Other museums of note are the **Diamond Museum**, housed in a large building near to the central station, and the **Museum Plantin-Moretus**, which is devoted to the early years of printing and celebrates the achievements of Antwerp's most successful printer, Christopher Plantin.

Rubenshuis was Rubens' home and studio for the last 30 years of his life. A tour takes you round his living quarters, equipped with period furniture, his studio, and the *kunst-kamer*, or art gallery, where he exhibited both his own and other artists' work, and entertained friends and wealthy patrons.

🏛 **Koninklijk Museum voor Schone Kunsten**
Leopold de Waelplaats 1–9. **Tel** 03-238 7809. 🚌 8. ⬤ for renovations until 2017.

🏛 **Rubenshuis**
Wapper 9–11. **Tel** 03-201 1555. 🚌 1, 22, 23, 25, 26, 290. 🚋 2, 3, 5, 15. ⬤ 10am– 5pm Tue–Sun. ⬤ public hols. 📷 ♿

Bruges ❸

See pp232–4.

Stone gatehouse of Ghent's medieval Het Gravensteen

Ghent ❹

🏠 240,000. 🚉 🚌 🚋
ℹ️ Botermarkt 17A, (09-266 5660).
www.visitgent.be

The heart of Ghent's historic center was built in the 13th and 14th centuries when the city prospered as a result of the cloth trade. The closure of vital canal links in 1648, however, led to a decline in the town's fortunes. In the 18th and 19th centuries Ghent flourished again as a major industrial center.

Dominating the old medieval quarter is the imposing **Het Gravensteen**, or Castle of the Counts. Parts of the castle, once the seat of the Counts of

Jacob Jordaens' joyous *As the Old Sang, the Young Play Pipes* (1638) in the Koninklijk Museum voor Schone Kunsten, Antwerp

The Pacification Hall in Ghent's Stadhuis, with its impressive tiled floor

Flanders, date back to the 12th century, although most parts, including the gatehouse, were built later.

Many of Ghent's finest historic buildings are found on Graslei, a picturesque street that borders the river Leie. The street is lined with well-preserved guildhalls dating from the Middle Ages.

The magnificent **St Baafskathedraal** has features representing every phase of the Gothic style. In a small side chapel is one of Europe's most remarkable paintings, Jan van Eyck's *Adoration of the Mystic Lamb* (1432). Opposite the cathedral stands the huge 14th-century **Belfort** (belfry). From the top of the tower you can enjoy splendid views of the city. From here it is a short walk to the **Stadhuis** (Town Hall), whose Pacification Hall was the site of the signing of the Pacification of Ghent (a declaration of the Low Countries' repudiation of Spanish rule) in 1576.

Ghent's largest collection of fine art, covering all periods up to the 20th century, is in the **Museum voor Schone Kunsten**, some 20 minutes' walk southeast of the center. There are works by Rubens and his contemporaries Jacob Jordaens and Anthony van Dyck. Occupying an elegant 18th-century townhouse, the **Design Museum Gent** is a decorative arts museum, with lavishly furnished 17th-, 18th-, and 19th-century period rooms. An extension covers modern design, from Art Nouveau to contemporary works.

♣ **Het Gravensteen**
Sint-Veerleplein. *Tel* 09-225 9306.
◯ 9am–5pm daily (to 6pm Apr–Sep). ▨

🏛 **Museum voor Schone Kunsten**
Citadelpark. *Tel* 09-240 0700.
◯ 10am–6pm Tue–Sun. ▨ 📷 ♿

Waterloo ⑤

🏚 30,000. 🚉 🚌 🛈 Chaussée de Bruxelles 218 (02-352 0910).
www.waterloo-tourisme.be

This small town is most famous for its association with the Battle of Waterloo, which saw Napoleon and his French army defeated by the Duke of Wellington's troops on June 18, 1815. The best place to start a visit here is the **Musée Wellington**, which occupies the inn where

Wellington stayed the night before the battle. Its narrow rooms are packed with curios alongside plans and models of the battlefield.

The **Musée de Cires** (Waxwork Museum) has models of soldiers dressed in period uniforms, while the **Eglise St-Joseph** contains dozens of memorial plaques to the British soldiers who died at Waterloo.

For an excellent view over the battlefield, head for the **Butte de Lion**, a 45-m (148-ft) high earthen mound, 3 km (2 miles) south of the town. Next to it is a gallery where Louis Demoulin's fascinating circular painting *Panorama de la Bataille* is displayed.

🏛 **Musée Wellington**
Chaussée de Bruxelles 147. *Tel* 02-357 2860. ◯ 10am–5pm daily. ▨

The Butte de Lion viewed from the battlefield of Waterloo

THE BATTLEFIELDS OF BELGIUM

Belgium's strategic position between France and Germany has long made it the battleground or "cockpit" of Europe. Napoleon's defeat at Waterloo was just one of many major conflicts resolved on Belgian soil. In the early 18th century French expansion under Louis XIV was thwarted here, and more recently Belgium witnessed some of the bloodiest trench warfare of World War I, including the introduction of poison gas at Ypres (Ieper). Today there are several vast graveyards, where the tens of thousands of soldiers who died on the Western Front lie buried.

Aftermath of Passchendaele (Third Battle of Ypres), 1917

Street-by-Street: Bruges ❸

Traditional organ grinder

With good reason, Bruges is one of the most popular tourist destinations in Belgium. The city owes its pre-eminent position to the beauty of its historic center, whose winding lanes and picturesque canals are lined with splendid medieval buildings. These are mostly the legacy of the town's heyday as a center of the international cloth trade, which flourished for 200 years from the 13th century. During this golden age, Bruges' merchants lavished their fortunes on fine mansions, churches, and a set of civic buildings of such extravagance that they were the wonder of northern Europe. Today, the streets are well maintained: there are no billboards or high-rises, and traffic is heavily regulated.

View of the River Dijver
A charming introduction to Bruges is provided by the boat trips along the city's canals.

Bus and train stations

Onze Lieve Vrouwekerk
Dating from 1220, the Church of Our Lady employs many styles of architecture and contains a Madonna and Child by Michelangelo.

Memling in Sint-Jan-Hospitaal Museum
This 12th-century hospital operated until 1976. It contains a well-preserved 15th-century dispensary.

0 meters	100
0 yards	100

★ The Markt
Medieval gabled houses line this 13th-century market square at the heart of Bruges, which still holds a market each Saturday.

VISITORS' CHECKLIST

117,000. Stationsplein.
Stationsplein, Markt. t'
Zand 34, inside Concertgebouw
(050-44 46 46). www.brugge.be

Oude Griffie, or Old Recorder's House

Blind Donkey Alley
This tiny alley leads from the Burg to the 18th-century Vis-markt (Fish Market).

BURG

WOLLESTRAAT

ROZENHOEDKAAI

Heilig Bloed Basiliek
(see p234)

★ Stadhuis
One of the oldest and finest town halls in Belgium, this was built between 1376 and 1420. Inside, the beautifully restored Gothic hall is noted for its 1385 vaulted ceiling.

DIJVER

Groeninge Museum
(see p234)

The Arentshuis Museum has paintings by Frank Brangwyn (1867–1956).

Gruuthuse Museum
(see p234)

The Belfort
Built in the 13th century, the Belfort, or Belfry, is a stunning octagonal tower where the city's medieval charter of rights is held.

KEY

— — — Suggested route

STAR SIGHTS

★ The Markt

★ Stadhuis

🏛 Groeninge Museum

Dijver 12. **Tel** 050-44 8711.
⏱ 9:30am–5pm Tue–Sun.
🔴 Jan 1, Dec 25. 📷

Bruges' premier fine art museum holds a superb collection of early Flemish and Dutch masters. Artists featured include Rogier van der Weyden (c.1400–1464), Jan van Eyck (d.1441), and Hans Memling (c.1430–94). Van Eyck's *Virgin and Child with Canon* (1436), a richly detailed painting noted for its realism, and Memling's *Moreel* triptych (1484) are among the museum's most outstanding exhibits. Painted in the early 16th century, the *Last Judgment* triptych is one of a number of works at the museum by Hieronymous Bosch (c.1450–1516). Peter Brueghel the Younger (1564–1638) is also well represented. Later Belgian works include paintings by Surrealists Paul Delvaux (1897–1994) and René Magritte (1898–1967).

Fifteenth-century oak-paneled chapel in the Gruuthuse Museum

🏛 Gruuthuse Museum

Dijver 17. **Tel** 050-44 8762.
⏱ 9:30am–5pm Tue–Sun. 🔴 Jan 1, Dec 25. 📷

This museum occupies a large medieval mansion close to the Dijver Canal. In the 15th century it was inhabited by a merchant (the Lord of the Gruuthuse), who had the right to levy a tax on "gruit," an imported mixture of herbs added to barley during the beer-brewing process. The mansion's labyrinthine rooms, with their ancient chimney-pieces and wooden beams, have survived intact, and today contain a collection

Panel of Hans Memling's *Moreel* triptych in the Groeninge Museum

of fine and applied arts. The exhibits range from wood carvings, tapestries, porcelain, and ceramics, to medical instruments and weaponry. The authentic kitchen and beautiful oak-paneled chapel (1472) transport visitors back to medieval times.

🔒 Heilig Bloed Basiliek

Burg 13. **Tel** 050-33 6792.
⏱ daily. **Museum** 🔴 Mon, Wed pm (in winter). 📷 (for museum).

The Basilica of the Holy Blood is Bruges' holiest church, holding one of the most sacred relics in Europe. In the upper chapel, rebuilt after it was destroyed by the French in the 1790s, is a 17th-century tabernacle, which houses a phial said to contain a few drops of blood and water washed from the body of Christ by Joseph of Arimathea.

🚽 Begijnhof

Wijngaardplein 1. **Tel** 050-36 01 40.
⏱ daily. 📷 (for Begijn House).

Béguines were members of a lay sisterhood founded in 1245, who did not take vows, but led a devout life. The *begijnhof*, or *béguinage*, is the walled complex in a town that housed the Béguines. In Bruges this is an area of quiet tree-lined canals edged by white, gabled houses. Visitors can enjoy a stroll here and visit the simple church, built in 1602. One of the houses, now occupied by Benedictine nuns, is open to the public.

🏛 Houishbrouwerij de Halve Maan

Walplein 26. **Tel** 050-44 4222.
⏱ 11am–4pm daily (to 5pm Sat).
📷 compulsory, every hour. 📷
www.halvemaan.be

Before World War I there were 31 breweries in Bruges. This one has been producing Straffe Hendrik since 1856. Here you can follow the beer-making process, from the first hops to a taste of the finished product in the small bar. There are also good views of Bruges from the oast room at the top of the building.

🏛 Museum voor Volkskunde

Balstraat 43. **Tel** 050-44 8764.
⏱ 9:30am–5pm Tue–Sun.

This excellent folk museum occupies an attractive terrace of brick almshouses in the northeast of the town. Each of the houses is dedicated to a different aspect of traditional Flemish life. Several crafts are represented, and visitors are shown a series of typical historical domestic interiors.

Pretty 17th-century almshouses, home to the Museum voor Volkskunde

For hotels and restaurants in this region see pp240–41 and pp242–3

Luxembourg ⑥

One of Europe's smallest sovereign states, the Grand Duchy of Luxembourg is often overlooked by travelers in Europe. The capital, Luxembourg City, is well known as a world center of international finance, but behind the modern face of the city lies a rich history stretching back over 1,000 years. The northern half of the country boasts some spectacular scenery, especially the Ardennes, a region of dense forests, deep valleys, and hilltop castles. Historic towns such as Vianden and Echternach are good bases for exploring the countryside and offer plenty of opportunities for outdoor activities.

View of Luxembourg City with its aqueduct and hilltop historic center

Luxembourg City

🏠 82,000. ✈ 6 km (4 miles) E.
🚆 🚍 ℹ 30 Place Guillaume II (22 28 09). www.lcto.lu

Luxembourg City enjoys a dramatic location, set atop hills and cliffs rising above the Alzette and Pétrusse valleys. The town grew up around a castle, built on a rocky promontory known as the Rocher du Bock in AD 963. The castle was destroyed in the late 19th century by the city's inhabitants, but some of the fortifications have been preserved, most famously the Bock and Pétrusse **Casemates**. These huge networks of under-ground defensive galleries, which date back to the 17th century, not only provided shelter for thousands of soldiers, but also housed workshops, kitchens, bakeries, and slaughterhouses. The **Crypte Archéologique du Bock**, has displays and an audiovisual presentation on the history of the city's fortifications.

Luxembourg City's **Palais Grand Ducal** has been the official royal residence since 1890. The oldest parts of the building, which used to be the town hall, date from the latter half of the 16th century. Nearby, the **Cathédrale Notre-Dame** was begun in 1613. Inside is a fine Baroque organ gallery by Daniel Muller.

Two museums worth visiting are the **Musée National d'Art et d'Histoire**, which has a good archaeological section and a collection of ancient and modern sculpture and paintings, and the **Musée de l'Histoire de la Ville de Luxembourg**, which focuses on the city's historical past.

⚓ **Casemates**
Bock Casemates Montée de Clausen. ◐ Mar–Oct: 10am–5pm.
🗝 **Pétrusse Casemates** Place de la Constitution. ◐ Easter, Whitsun, & end May–mid-Sep: 11am–4pm. 🗝

🏛 **Musée National d'Art et d'Histoire**
Place Marché aux Poissons. **Tel** 47 93 301. ◐ 10am–6pm Tue–Sun. 🗝 🗝 🚻

Vianden

🏠 1,600. 🚍 ℹ 1a Rue du Vieux Marché (83 42 571). **Château de Vianden Tel** 83 41 08. ◐ Apr–Sep: 10am–6pm; Oct, Mar: 10am–5pm; Nov–Feb: 10am–4pm. ● Jan 1, Dec 25. 🗝 🗝

Surrounded by medieval ramparts, Vianden, in the Luxembourg Ardennes, is a popular tourist destination. The main attraction is the 11th-century **Château de Vianden**. Its rooms feature a range of architectural styles, from the Romanesque to the Renaissance. A cable car takes visitors to the top of a nearby hill, giving superb views of the castle.

Echternach

🏠 4,000. 🚍 ℹ 9–10 Parvis de la Basilique (72 02 30). **Abbey Basilica** ◐ daily. **Abbey Museum** ◐ Apr, May & Oct: 10am–noon, 2–5pm daily; Jun & Sep: 10am–noon, 2–6pm daily; Jul & Aug: 10am–6pm daily. 🗝 www.echternach-tourist.lu

Located in Petite Suisse (Little Switzerland), a picturesque region of wooded hills north-east of the capital, Echternach is dotted with fine medieval buildings, including the 15th-century turreted **Town Hall**. The star sight, however, is the **Benedictine abbey**, founded by St. Willibrord in the 7th century. The crypt of the abbey basilica (c.900) contains some glorious frescoes. There are good walks and cycle routes in the surrounding countryside.

Medieval Town Hall in the Place du Marché, Echternach

Practical & Travel Information

Visitors to Belgium and Luxembourg can expect high levels of service and comfort in all aspects of their stay. Public transportation is clean and efficient, and there are abundant tourist information facilities, in addition to all the other modern conveniences one expects of a highly developed country. Brussels and Luxembourg City are among the safest capital cities in Europe and, due to their small size, can be easily explored on foot.

TOURIST INFORMATION

In Belgium, the **Tourist and Information Office of Brussels** publishes maps and guides, and also offers a Brussels Card. This "tourist passport" includes one-, two- or three-day passes to all public transport in the Brussels region, combined with unlimited access to 30 museums. A similar scheme operates in Bruges, Antwerp, and Ghent.

Luxembourg's **National Tourist Office** is located in the train station in the capital. It sells the Luxembourg Card, which gives unlimited travel on public transport nationwide, as well as admission to over 30 sites of interest, and reductions on many others. The card, which is valid for one, two, or three days between Easter and October, can also be bought at hotels, campsites, youth hostels, and train and bus stations.

Local tourist information offices can be found in most towns and villages throughout Belgium and Luxembourg.

OPENING HOURS

Most shops and businesses in Belgium and Luxembourg are open from 10am until 5 or 6pm Monday to Saturday, with some local shops closing for an hour at lunch. Some stores open at noon on Mondays. In the major cities and towns many shops are open on Sundays and until later in the evening.

In both countries most museums are closed on Mondays. Outside the high season (April to September), be prepared to find many sights of interest closed.

VISA REQUIREMENTS

Citizens of the EU, US, Australia, New Zealand, and Canada do not require a visa to enter either Belgium or Luxembourg, but must present a valid passport and hold proof of onward passage (EU citizens need a valid ID document). Bear in mind that in Belgium it is a legal requirement to carry ID on one's person at all times.

SAFETY AND EMERGENCIES

Belgium and Luxembourg are safe countries, with street crime against visitors relatively rare occurrence.

However, in Brussels it is inadvisable to wander alone at night in the poorer areas to the west and north of the city center, and in the city's parks, especially at Botanique.

In case of emergencies, the numbers to call are listed in the Directory opposite.

LANGUAGE

The two principal languages of Belgium are Dutch, spoken in Flanders, and French, the language of the Wallonians. There is also a German-speaking enclave in the far east of the country. In the capital both languages are used on all street signs and in place names.

Luxembourg has three official languages: French, German, and Letzeburgesch, or Luxembourgeois. In both Belgium and Luxembourg, especially in the capital cities, many people speak very good English.

BANKING AND CURRENCY

The currency in Belgium and Luxembourg is the euro (*see p15*). All euro notes and coins are exchangeable in each of the participating Eurozone countries.

Banking hours are generally from 9am to 4pm Monday to Friday in Belgium and 9am to 4:30pm weekdays in Luxembourg. In both countries most of the banks close for an hour at lunch-time, and some of the city branches open on Saturday mornings.

COMMUNICATIONS

Belgian post offices are open from 9am to 5pm Monday to Friday. In Luxembourg the hours are 9am to noon and 1:30pm to 5pm Monday to Friday. Some larger branches open on Saturday mornings.

Many public payphones in Belgium and Luxembourg accept only phonecards, available at newsagents and post offices. In Brussels you can use cash in the phone booths in metro stations. There are no local area codes in Luxembourg.

THE CLIMATE OF BELGIUM AND LUXEMBOURG

Belgium and Luxembourg have a temperate climate, characterized by constant low rainfall throughout the year. Winters are usually chilly and damp, and rain may turn to snow or sleet. Summers are warmer and much brighter, but the evenings can still be cool. Spring is the driest season.

BRUSSELS				
°C/F		23/73		
	14/57	11/52	15/60	
0°C	5/41		6/43	4/39
32°F				0/32
☀	4.5 hrs	5.5 hrs	3.5 hrs	1.5 hrs
☂	57 mm	94 mm	82 mm	67 mm
month	Apr	Jul	Oct	Jan

ARRIVING BY AIR

Belgium's principal airport is Brussels National Airport, known locally as Zaventem. Flights into Luxembourg arrive at Findel Airport, which is 6 km (4 miles) east of Luxembourg City.

Airlines flying to Belgium and Luxembourg include **Brussels Airlines** (Belgium) and **Luxair** (Luxembourg), British Airways, BMI British Midlands, American Airlines, KLM, and Lufthansa. Brussels is also served by Air Canada and Delta Air Lines. Most flights from Canada and the US go via another European city. Ryanair has low-cost flights between Brussels and various European cities.

ARRIVING BY SEA

Belgium can be easily reached by ferry from Britain several times daily. **Norfolkline** has a number of crossings every day between Dover and Dunkirk. **P&O Ferries** also operates regular ferry crossings from Dover to Calais (France) and from Hull to Zeebrugge.

RAIL TRAVEL

Belgium is at the heart of Europe's high-speed train networks. **Eurostar** services between Brussels' Gare du Midi and London's Waterloo station take just under 2 hours. The **Thalys** network links Brussels with Amsterdam, Paris, and Cologne.

Within Belgium train services are operated by **Belgian National Railways** (Société Nationale de Chemins de Fer Belges/Belgische Spoorwegen). The network is modern and efficient, and usually the best way to travel between major cities and towns. Luxembourg's rail system is run by **Chemins de Fer Luxembourgeois (CFL)**. In both countries a variety of rail passes is available. The Benelux Tourrail pass allows unlimited travel on any five days within a month's period in Belgium, Luxembourg, and the Netherlands.

TRAVELING BY BUS

In Belgium the two main long-distance bus operators are **De Lijn**, which covers routes in Flanders, and **TEC**, which provides services in Wallonia. Bus terminuses are usually close to train stations.

Luxembourg benefits from an extensive bus network, which compensates for the more limited rail system. One-day passes are available, and can be used on both long-distance and inner-city buses from the time of purchase until 8am the next day. Benelux Tourrail passes are valid on buses operated by Chemins de Fer Luxembourgeois.

TRAVELING BY CAR

Drivers from the UK can reach mainland Europe by the car train service offered by Eurotunnel. Within Belgium and Luxembourg the freeways and main roads are well-maintained and fast. Variations between the French and Flemish spellings of town names can be confusing for visitor drivers in Belgium; it is advisable to find out both names of your destination before beginning your journey. All the major car rental firms are represented in Belgium and Luxembourg, but renting a vehicle is fairly expensive.

DIRECTORY

TOURIST OFFICES

Belgium
Grand Place 1,
1000 Brussels.
Tel 02-513 8940.
www.visitbelgium.com

Luxembourg
Gare Centrale,
Luxembourg City.
Tel 42 82 82 20.
www.ont.lu

UK
Belgian Tourist Office,
217 March Wall,
London E14 9FJ.
Tel 020-7537 1132.
Tel 0800-954 5245.
www.belgium
theplaceto.be
Luxembourg Tourist Office,
Sicilian House, Sicilian Ave,
London WC1A 2QR.
Tel 020-7434 2800.
www.luxembourg.co.uk

US

Belgian Tourist Office,
220 East 42nd St,
Suite 3402, New York, NY
10017. Tel 212-758 8130.
Luxembourg Tourist Office,
17 Beekman Place, New
York, NY 10022.
Tel 212-935 8888.
www.visitluxembourg.com

EMBASSIES

UK (Belgium)
Ave d'Auderghem 10,
B-1040 Brussels.
Tel 02-287 6211.

UK (Luxembourg)
5 Blvd Joseph II,
L-1840 Luxembourg City.
Tel 22 98 64.

US (Belgium)
Blvd du Régent 27, B-1000
Brussels. Tel 02-811 4000.

US (Luxembourg)
22 Blvd Emmanuel Servais,
L-2535 Luxembourg City.
Tel 46 01 23.

EMERGENCY NUMBERS

Belgium
Police Tel 101.
Ambulance and
fire services Tel 100.

Luxembourg
Police Tel 113.
All other services Tel 112.

AIRLINES

Brussels Airlines
Tel 090-251 600 (Belgium).
Tel 0905-609 5609 (UK).
Tel 516-296 9500 (US).
www.brusselsairlines.com

Luxair
Tel 0352-2456 4242
(Luxembourg).
www.luxair.lu

FERRY COMPANIES

Norfolkline
Tel 0871-574 7235 (UK).
www.norfolkline.com

P&O Ferries
Tel 08716-642 121 (UK).
www.poferries.com

RAIL TRAVEL

Belgian National Railways
Tel 02-528 2828.
www.b-rail.be

Chemins de Fer Luxembourgeois
Tel 24 89 24 89.
www.cfl.lu

Eurostar
Tel 08432-186 186 (UK).
Tel 02-528 2828 (Belgium).
www.eurostar.com

Thalys
Tel 02-528 2828 (Belgium).
www.thalys.com

BUSES

De Lijn
Tel 070-220 200.

TEC
Tel 01-023 5353.

Shopping & Entertainment

Belgium is an ideal place to shop for luxury goods, from fine chocolates and cutting-edge fashion to mounted diamonds. As a virtually duty-free zone, Luxembourg attracts tourists in search of cheap cigarettes and alcohol. For relatively small cities, Brussels and Luxembourg City offer a wide range of cultural events. Those who prefer outdoor activities will find plenty to entertain them. The flat Flanders region in Belgium is ideal cycling country, while the hilly Ardennes and the Petite Suisse area of Luxembourg are popular with hikers.

WHERE TO SHOP

For luxury items and gifts, one of Brussels' best shopping arcades is the **Galéries Saint-Hubert**. It houses several jewelry stores, the Belgian leather bag maker Delvaux, fine chocolate shops, and smart boutiques, including women's fashion designer Kaat Tilley. The **Galéries d'Ixelles** is full of tiny ethnic shops and cafés, while the quaint **Galérie Bortier** is the place to shop for antiquarian books and maps.

Top fashion designers are well represented in Brussels. Their outlets can be found on Avenue Louise and Boulevard de Waterloo. For the original creations of the Antwerp Six and of new wave designers, try Rue Antoine Dansaert.

Less expensive, mainstream stores, including Belgium's only department store Inno, are located in the Rue Neuve. Inno is not spectacular by British or American standards.

The principal shopping areas in Luxembourg City are the Grand Rue and its side streets, and the Auchan shopping center which is found on Kirchberg.

WHAT TO BUY

Belgian chocolate is considered by many to be the finest in the world. Among the internationally renowned *"grandes maisons de chocolat"* with stores in Brussels are **Godiva** and **Wittamer**. The sweet-toothed will also be tempted by the edible chocolate sculptures produced by **Pierre Marcolini** and by the wares of fine biscuit specialist **Dandoy**.

Another famous Belgian export is lace, though a fall in the number of people entering the trade in recent years has resulted in a shortage of authentic, handmade goods. Before purchasing an item, make sure it has not been manufactured in the Far East. Places to shop for authentic Belgian lace include **Maison F. Rubbrecht** in Brussels and the **Kant Centrum** in Bruges. The latter also has a museum of lace-making.

Specialty Belgian beers can be bought at Brussels' **Beer Mania**, while **Little Nemo** and **La Bande des Six Nez** specialize in comic-strip memorabilia. If you plan to invest in diamonds, or simply wish to gaze and admire, **Diamondland** in Antwerp is a good place to start.

Among the best buys in Luxembourg are fuel, tobacco, and alcohol, due to the low rate of duty imposed on such goods. One of the country's most famous manufacturing names is **Villeroy & Boch**, makers of fine porcelain and tableware. Their flagship store is in the Rue du Fossé in the capital. There is also a factory outlet northwest of the city center where you can buy seconds at 20 percent discount.

MARKETS

From 9am on Saturdays and Sundays, Brussels' Place du Grand Sablon is the site of a fine antiques market. Also worth visiting is the huge, vibrant market around the Gare du Midi (Sundays, 6am to 1pm), with its mix of North African and home-grown delicacies, including oils, spices, and exotic herbs. Brussells' famous Marché aux Puces is held daily on the Place du Jeu de Balle, though the biggest assortment of items can be found on Sundays.

BOOKSTORES

In Brussels, **Waterstone's** sells English-language magazines and books. For international newspapers, go to the **Librairie de Rome**.

English-language books and newspapers can be bought in Luxembourg City at the **Magasin Anglais**.

ENTERTAINMENT LISTINGS

The principal source of entertainment information in Belgium is *Brussels Weekly,* published weekly in English, and available from news-stands throughout the country.

Details of events in Luxembourg are published in the "Culture" section of *L'Agenda du Luxembourg,* available from the National Tourist Office.

OPERA, CLASSICAL MUSIC, AND DANCE

Brussels' Opera House, **La Monnaie**, is among Europe's finest venues for opera. The season runs from September through to June, and most productions are sold out many months in advance.

Designed by Victor Horta in 1928, the **Palais des Beaux-Arts** is home to the Belgian National Orchestra and boasts the city's largest auditorium for classical music. The main concert season lasts from September to June.

Regular performances of contemporary dance take place at the Art Deco **Kaaitheater** and the **Halles de Schaerbeek**.

Luxembourg's Printemps Musical is a festival of classical music concerts and ballet that takes place in the capital throughout April and May. Principal venues include the **Conservatoire de Musique de la Ville de Luxembourg** and the **Théâtre Municipal**. The City Tourist Information Office on the Place d'Armes is able to provide more information and assist with ticket reservations.

JAZZ, ROCK, AND BLUES

One of the best places to catch good jazz acts in Brussels is **Sounds**, a large venue featuring some of Belgium's top artists. The club also has Blues nights. On Saturday and Sunday afternoons, it is worth stopping at **L'Archiduc**, a refurbished Art Deco bar in the center of town, where you can listen to jazz in a relaxed atmosphere. **Ancienne Belgique** hosts up-and-coming guitar bands, folk, Latin, and techno acts.

CINEMA

At Brussels' Bruparck (see p229), the 29-screen Kinepolis cinema complex shows Hollywood blockbusters and major British and French releases. Real movie fans should not miss a visit to the Musée du Cinéma in the Palais des Beaux-Arts complex. The museum shows classic films, from Chaplin to Tarantino, with nightly programs of silent movies sometimes with a live piano accompaniment.

OUTDOOR ACTIVITIES

Belgium and Luxembourg have extensive networks of cycle tracks, and you can rent bicycles easily from a number of outlets, including many train stations. For route details the best source of information is the local tourist information office. The US-based **CBT** Tours organizes cycle tours in Belgium.

Tourist offices in Belgium and Luxembourg also offer walking guides and maps. To arrange hiking tours in the Ardennes area, contact Belgium-based **Europ'Aventure**.

In Echternach, the lake at Echternach offers plenty of opportunities for swimming, sailing, and windsurfing, while the rivers of the Ardennes region are fine territory for canoeing and kayaking. To obtain further information on the latter, contact the **Fédération Luxembourgeoise de Canoë-Kayak**. For information on the whole range of sporting activities available contact the **City Tourist Office**.

DIRECTORY

SHOPPING ARCADES

Galérie Bortier
Rue de la Madeleine 17–19, Brussels.

Galéries d'Ixelles
Chaussée d'Ixelles, Brussels.

Galéries Saint-Hubert
Rue des Bouchers, Brussels.

SPECIALTY ITEMS

La Bande des Six Nez
Chaussée de Wavre 179, Brussels.
Tel 02-513 7258.

Beer Mania
Chaussée de Wavre 174–176, Brussels.
Tel 02-512 1788.

Dandoy
Rue au Beurre 31, Brussels.
Tel 02-511 0326.

Diamondland
Appelmansstraat 33A, Antwerp.
Tel 03-229 2990.

Godiva
Grand Place 22, Brussels.
Tel 02-511 2537.

Kant Centrum
Peperstraat 3A, Bruges.
Tel 050-33 00 72.

Little Nemo
Boulevard Lemmonier 25, Brussels.
Tel 02-514 6804.

Maison F. Rubbrecht
Grand Place 23, Brussels.
Tel 02-512 0218.

Pierre Marcolini
Rue des Minimes 1, Brussels.
Tel 02-514 1206.

Villeroy & Boch
2 Rue du Fossé, Luxembourg City.
Tel 46 82 12 78.

330 Rue Rollingergrund, Luxembourg City.
Tel 46 82 11.

Wittamer
Place du Grand Sablon 6, 12–13 Brussels.
Tel 02-512 3742.
www.wittamer.com

BOOKSTORES

Librairie de Rome
16A Rue Jean Stas, Brussels.
Tel 02-511 7937.

Magasin Anglais
16 Avenue Victor Hugo, Luxembourg City.
Tel 22 49 25.

Waterstone's
Boulevard Adolphe Max 71, Brussels.
Tel 02-219 2708.

OPERA, CLASSICAL MUSIC & DANCE

Conservatoire de Musique de la Ville de Luxembourg
33 Rue Charles Martel, Luxembourg City.
Tel 47 96 55 55.

Halles de Schaerbeek
Rue Royale Sainte-Marie 22a, Brussels.
Tel 02-218 2107.
www.halles.be

Kaaitheater
Square Sainteclette 20, Brussels. *Tel 01-201 5959.*
www.kaaitheater.be

La Monnaie
Place de la Monnaie, Brussels.
Tel 07-023 3939.
www.lamonnaie.be

Palais des Beaux-Arts
Rue Ravenstein 23, Brussels.
Tel 02-507 8200.
www.bozar.be

Théâtre Municipal
1 Rond-Point Robert Schuman, Luxembourg City.
Tel 47 96 39 00.

JAZZ, ROCK & BLUES

Ancienne Belgique
Boulevard Anspach 110, Brussels.
Tel 02-548 2484.
www.abconcerts.be

L'Archiduc
Rue Antoine Dansaert 6, Brussels.
Tel 02-512 0652.
www.archiduc.net

Sounds
Rue de la Tulipe 28, Brussels.
Tel 02-512 9250.
www.soundsjazzclub.be

OUTDOOR ACTIVITIES

CBT Tours
Tel 800-575 1540 (US).
www.cbttours.com

Europ'Aventure
Tel 061-688 611 (Belgium).
www.europaventure.be

Fédération Luxembourgeoise de Canoë-Kayak
3 Route d'Arlon, L-8009, Strassen.
Tel 75 03 79.
www.flck.lu

Luxembourg City Tourist Office
Tel 22 28 09.
www.lcto.lu

Where to Stay in Belgium & Luxembourg

In both countries, top end hotels offer exceptional standards of comfort to their largely corporate clients, and their prices reflect this. However, some offer substantial weekend or summer discounts, and there are also plenty of mid-range and lower budget hotel options.

PRICE CATEGORIES:
Price categories are for a standard double room per night, including tax and service. Breakfast is not included unless specified.

€ Under €80
€€ €80–€130
€€€ €130–€180
€€€€ €180–€260
€€€€€ Over €260

BRUSSELS

LOWER TOWN Aristote
€€   Map B3

Avenue de Stalingrad 7, 1000 Brussels **Tel** *02-513 1310* **Fax** *02-513 8070* **Rooms** *25*

Located in a striking-looking building between the Grand Place and the central station, Hotel Aristote occupies a renovated 19th-century townhouse with small, but elegant bedrooms and a popular pizzeria (decorated in medieval style). Staff are friendly and offer plenty of sightseeing tips and advice. **www.aristote-hotel.be**

LOWER TOWN Mozart
€€   Map C3

Rue du Marché-aux-Fromages 23, 1000 Brussels **Tel** *02-502 6661* **Fax** *02-502 7758* **Rooms** *50*

A three-star budget hotel in a fabulous location, Hotel Mozart is a great choice for young travelers looking to stay in the thick of the action. The hotel is fantastically decorated with a luxurious reception and plenty of personal touches in each of the 50 rooms. Book early to avoid disappointment. **www.hotel-mozart.be**

LOWER TOWN Hotel Metropole
€€€   Map C2

Place de Brouckère 31, 1000 Brussels **Tel** *02-217 2300* **Fax** *02-218 0220* **Rooms** *298*

Built in 1895, this plush hotel boasts striking architecture and a mix of French Renaissance, Empire, and Art Deco styles. Most rooms are decorated in period style and there are high ceilings, stained-glass, and crystal chandeliers in the lobby, bar, and gourmet restaurant. Complimentary breakfast. **www.metropolehotel.com**

LOWER TOWN Radisson Blu Royal Hotel
€€€€   Map C2

Rue du Fosse-aux-Loups 47, 1000 Brussels **Tel** *02-219 2828* **Fax** *02-219 6262* **Rooms** *281*

A fabulous five-star hotel behind a glorious Art Deco facade (designed by famed Belgian designer, Michel Haspers), Radisson is one of the best places to stay in the city. Stunning garden and gourmet 2-star Michelin hotel restaurant. The hotel will organize city tours. **www.radissonblu.com**

LOWER TOWN Amigo
€€€€€   Map C3

Rue de l'Amigo 1–3, 1000 Brussels **Tel** *02-547 4747* **Fax** *02-513 5277* **Rooms** *174*

This five-star hotel in the Rocco Forte Hotel chain provides an elegant setting and great location just near the Grand Place. Rooms have king-size beds and marble bathrooms. Family suites are available and there is an award-winning restaurant. Meeting room, spa, and fitness facilities. **www.hotelamigo.com**

LOWER TOWN Le Plaza
€€€€€   Map C2

Boulevard Adolphe Maxlaan 118–126, 1000 Brussels **Tel** *02-278 0100* **Fax** *02-278 0101* **Rooms** *190*   Map C2

An opulent five-star hotel which regularly provides accommodation to visiting stars and gentry, Le Plaza even has its own theater. The building itself dates back to 1930 when it was built to model Paris' famous George V hotel. Rooms were renovated in 1996 to provide modern facilities. Business- and tourist-friendly. **www.leplaza-brussels.be**

UPPER TOWN Les Bluets
€   Map C4

Rue Berckmans 124, 1060 Brussels **Tel** *02-534 3983* **Fax** *02-543 0970* **Rooms** *10*

Charming, family-run, non-smoking hotel in a 19th-century bourgeois townhouse. The 10 rooms are decorated with a laidback mix of antique furnishings, objets d'art, and modern facilities. An interesting place to stay for its characterful approach to hotellery. Small plant-covered annex. Breakfast is included. **www.bluets.be**

UPPER TOWN Hotel Eurostars Sablon
€€€   Map C3

Rue de la Paille 2–8, 1000 Brussels **Tel** *02-513 6040* **Fax** *02-511 8141* **Rooms** *32*

A friendly boutique hotel with sauna and relaxation center, the Sablon boasts a fantastic location beside the city's main art galleries and is within walking distance of the characterful cafés on Place du Grand Sablon. Rooms are large with split-level suites and plenty of facilities. The staff are particularly helpful. **www.eurostarssablon.com**

UPPER TOWN Stanhope
€€€€€   Map D3

Rue du Commerce 9, 1000 Brussels **Tel** *02-506 9111* **Fax** *02-512 1708* **Rooms** *125*

Providing deluxe Belgian hospitality in three converted townhouses, the five-star boutique Hotel Stanhope is decorated in English country style and delivers old-fashioned service that even stretches to chauffeur-driven cars. Elegant rooms, beautiful interior garden, and gourmet restaurant. Conference facilities. **www.stanhope.be**

Key to Symbols *see back cover flap* **Map References** *see map of Brussels pp222–3*

REST OF BELGIUM

ANTWERP 't Sandt   📋 P W   €€€

Zand 13–19, 2000 Antwerp **Tel** *03-232 9390* **Fax** *03-232 5613* **Rooms** *29*

A cosy hotel in Antwerp's historical center, 't Sandt occupies a protected Neo-Rococo building from the mid-17th century that was the site of the city's first customs duty office. The 27 rooms and two apartments are individually decorated. The Cathedral Penthouse has one of the city's best views. Breakfast is included. **www.hotel-sandt.be**

ANTWERP Antwerp Hilton   📶 ⅲ 📺 P 🔓 W   €€€€

Groenplaats, 2000 Antwerp **Tel** *03-204 1212* **Fax** *03-204 8688* **Rooms** *211*

Well-located next to the historical cathedral, the Antwerp Hilton has some great views over the city's sights. An architectural landmark (it sits behind a listed Baroque facade), the hotel occupies part of the former Grand Bazar department store. Rooms are business-friendly with Wi-Fi Internet connections. **www.hilton.com**

BRUGES Bourgoensch Hof   📶 ⅲ P W   €€

Wollestraat 39, 8000 Bruges **Tel** *050-33 1645* **Fax** *050-34 6378* **Rooms** *17*

Situated in Bruges' historical center near the central market, the three-star Hotel Bourgoensch Hof boasts some fabulous canal-side views. Rooms are simple, but well presented; most visitors to both the hotel and its bistro come for the views. Hotel bistro with outdoor terrace. Paid parking available on request. **www.hotel-bourgoensch-hof.be**

BRUGES Hotel de Tuilerieën   🏊 P W   €€€€

Dyver 7, 8000 Bruges **Tel** *050-34 3691* **Fax** *050-34 0400* **Rooms** *45*

A luxurious four-star hotel with indoor pool, the Hotel de Tuilerieën offers a deluxe break in the heart of Bruges' medieval center. Rooms are spacious and elegantly decorated with four-poster beds and antique furnishings. Stately breakfast dining room with banquet tables and crystal chandeliers. **www.hoteltuilerieen.com**

GHENT The Boatel   🏊 P W   €€

Voorhoutkaai 44, 9000 Ghent **Tel** *09-267 1030* **Fax** *09-267 1039* **Rooms** *5*

The two-star Boatel is a floating hotel constructed from a converted canal boat. Moored in Portus Ganda, a short walk from the center of town, its five cosy rooms (three standard and two luxury) are carefully-decorated in various styles. Great river views! **www.theboatel.com**

GHENT Ghent River Hotel   📶 📺 W   €€€

Waaistraat 5+, 9000 Ghent **Tel** *09-266 1010* **Fax** *09-266 1015* **Rooms** *77*

This four-star riverside hotel occupies a mid-19th century rice mill on the banks of the River Leie. Although the entrance is modern, the rooms are more in keeping with the building's rich history, including wood-beamed ceilings and wooden floors. Fitness room with sauna. Bicycles are for rent at a nearby shop. **www.ghent-river-hotel.be**

LUXEMBOURG

LUXEMBOURG CITY Hotel Français   📶 ⅲ 🏊 📋 🔓 W   €€

14, pl d'Armes, L-1136 Luxembourg **Tel** *47 45 34* **Fax** *46 42 74* **Rooms** *24*

Friendly hotel in a fantastic location on the pedestrianized Place d'Armes in the heart of Luxembourg's old city (no access by car, but two garages nearby). Large rooms with modern bathrooms. Ask for a room on a high floor to avoid crowd noise on weekends. Gourmet restaurant with great views over the city. **www.hotelfrancais.lu**

LUXEMBOURG CITY Hôtel Le Châtelet   ⅲ 📺 📋 P W   €€

2, bd de la Pétrusse, L-2320 Luxembourg **Tel** *40 21 01* **Fax** *40 36 66* **Rooms** *40*

Small and welcoming three-star hotel in a peaceful location at the entrance to Petrusse Valley, within walking distance of the old city and the financial district. Rooms are split between two traditional old Luxembourg houses. All are cosy and clean. Small, rustic restaurant. Excellent breakfast. Free Internet corner. **www.chatelet.lu**

LUXEMBOURG CITY Hotel Le Royal Luxembourg   📶 ⅲ 🏊 📺 📋 P 🔓 W   €€€€€

12, bd Royal, L-2449 Luxembourg **Tel** *241 61 67 56* **Fax** *22 59 48* **Rooms** *210*

Elegant hotel in a fabulous location, the five-star Le Royal is one of Luxembourg's most exclusive hotels; particularly its 'Royal Club Wing' with superior rooms and suites. There is Wi-Fi in public areas and two top restaurants with outside dining. Ask for a room overlooking the park. Rated as one of the world's leading hotels. **www.hotelroyal.lu**

LUXEMBOURG CITY Parc Beaux-Arts Hotel Luxembourg   ⅲ 📋 P 🔓 W   €€€€€

1, rue Sigefroi, L-2536 Luxembourg **Tel** *26 86 76 1* **Fax** *26 86 76 36* **Rooms** *10*

First-class hotel in a fantastic location in the heart of the old city, the Parc Beaux-Arts occupies a beautifully-restored and stylishly-decorated 250-year-old building. Spacious and well-appointed rooms with views over the Grand-Ducal Palace. Generous breakfast. Children under 12 stay for free. **www.parcbeauxarts.lu**

Where to Eat in Belgium & Luxembourg

Belgians love food, and their cooking reflects this. Choose from the plethora of top gastronomic restaurants concentrated in Brussels or opt for one of the many unpretentious eateries serving local specialties. Luxembourg has its fair share of haute-cuisine restaurants with good value set lunches available.

PRICE CATEGORIES:
Price categories are for a three-course meal for one, including a half-bottle of house wine, tax, and service:
€ Under €25
€€ €25–€40
€€€ €40–€50
€€€€ €50–€65
€€€€€ Over €65

BRUSSELS

LOWER TOWN Aux Armes de Bruxelles   €

Rue des Bouchers 13, 1000 **Tel** *02-511 5550*   **Map** *C3*

One of the better establishments in the often-busy restaurant alley next to the Grand Place, this Art Deco institution has been frequented by local luminaries such as Jacques Brel. It's especially known for classic fish and seafood dishes, such as *anguilles au vert* (eel in a green herb sauce), *waterzooi* (fish stew), and *croquettes de crevettes* (shrimp croquettes).

LOWER TOWN 't Kelderke   €€

Grand Place 15, 1000 **Tel** *02-513 7344*   **Map** *B3*

On the Grand Place, this cellar restaurant is as busy as you may expect but the feel is decidedly genuine. Moules-frites (mussels and French fries) are served in their traditional, huge black pails at a fast and furious pace. Expect to wait for a table, but not for too long.

LOWER TOWN L'Achepot   €€

Place Ste-Catherine 1, 1000 **Tel** *02-511 6221*   **Map** *B2*

This small, family-run Brussels tavern off the Vismarkt (fish market) serves fish simply but very well. Apart from the seafood, try the traditional *stoemp* (a coarse mash with vegetables) and *chèvre* (goat's cheese) salad; if you're feelin more adventurous, there is a wide range of offal dishes, including kidneys, brain, tripe, and liver.

LOWER TOWN In 't Spinnekopke   €€€

1 Place du Jardin aux Fleurs, 1000 **Tel** *02-511 8695*   **Map** *B3*

A superb example of quality Belgian food can be found in this intimate former 17th-century coaching inn. In 't Spinnekopke (In the Spider's Head) has a strong range of unusual local beers and items on the menu that are cooke in them. Friendly service and a wonderful terrace in an area that's off the beaten track. **www.spinnekopke.be**

LOWER TOWN L'Ogenblik   €€€€

Galeries des Princes 1, 1000 **Tel** *02-511 6151*   **Map** *C3*

In the center of the stunning Saint Hubert's Galleries, this thirty-year-old Parisian-style bistro with a relaxed ambiance is a gastronomic wonder. Dishes such as duck magret carpaccio with parmesan cuttings, or sea bass fillet with aubergine (eggplant) caviar are a gourmand's delight. Closed Sun. **www.ogenblik.be**

LOWER TOWN Comme Chez Soi   €€€€€

Place Rouppe 23, 1000 **Tel** *02-512 2921*   **Map** *B3*

Widely regarded as the city's best restaurant, Comme Chez Soi, with its two Michelin stars, is particularly strong in the game department. A mahogany bar and over-stuffed leather couches all feature in the lounge area. If the *Mi-cuit au Chocolat Belge Grand Cru*, a hot chocolate dessert, is on the menu be sure to try it. Book well in advance

UPPER TOWN Au Vieux Saint-Martin   €

Grand Sablon 38, 1210 **Tel** *02-512 6476*   **Map** *D2*

The walls here are lined with Belgian artworks and the menu is packed with Belgian specialties, such as *pied de porc à la Bruxelloise* (pig's trotters) and *waterzooi de poulet de ferme gantoise* (chicken stew). This smart, popular restaurant at the heart of the Sablon gives a rich flavor of Brussels' twin passions: food and art.

UPPER TOWN La Tortue du Zoute   €€€€

Rue de Rollebeek 31, 1000 **Tel** *02-513 1062*   **Map** *C3*

While the menu at the Tortue is solidly based around the lobster – for which the chefs offer ten different prepara-tions – other wonders of the sea receive no less consideration. The bistro is located on a delightful, descending cobbled pedestrian street filled with boutiques and other restaurants.

UPPER TOWN L'Idiot du Village   €€€€

Rue Notre-Seigneur 19, 1000 **Tel** *02-502 5582*   **Map** *B4*

The Village Idiot is reportedly a favored establishment of foreign ministers and even Belgian royalty. No wonder, with such intriguing concoctions as the escalope of hot *foie gras*, pepper and vanilla, served on earthy crockery of a more rustic era. Reservations are recommended at this extremely popular eatery.

Key to Symbols *see back cover flap* **Map References** *see map of Brussels pp222–3*

REST OF BELGIUM

ANTWERP Rooden Hoed
Oude Koornmarkt 25, 2000 **Tel** *03-233 2844*

As the oldest restaurant in Antwerp – it first served food back in 1750 – the Rooden Hoed is one of the city's most renowned eateries. It specializes in seafood, especially mussels, of which there are at least half a dozen ways of having them cooked. You can have a pre-dinner drink in the restaurant's medieval cellar.

ANTWERP P. Preud'Homme
Suikerrui 28, 2000 **Tel** *03-233 4200*

Providing a memorable dining experience in the grand surroundings of a beautiful Art Nouveau building, P. Preud'Homme is one of Antwerp's finest restaurants. Its menu includes fine fare such as lobster, game, terrine, and scallops, and the wine list to accompany it is of suitably high quality.

BRUGES De Stove
Kleine Sint-Amandsstraat 4, 8000 **Tel** *050-337835*

The very intimate De Stove has room for just 20 patrons, so with its simple furnishings and eponymous iron stove, is the perfect place for a romantic evening. The *foie gras* and duck are exceptional, but be sure not to miss the fresh North Sea fish, supplied daily – particularly the breaded cod in butter sauce. Closed Wed & Thu.

BRUGES De Visscherie
Vismarkt 8, 8000 **Tel** *050-330212*

In 1976, Mr and Mrs Tillo Declercq opened De Visscherie, a seafood restaurant overlooking the centuries-old Vismarkt (fish market). The house's signature dish is the monkfish waterzooi with saffron, but try any of the turbot variations. The establishment is a popular destination for locals, so book ahead.

BRUGES De Karmeliet
Langestraat 19, 8000 **Tel** *050-338259*

Regarded as the best restaurant in Bruges. In 1996 chef Geert Van Hecke became the first Flemish chef to be awarded three Michelin stars. The servings are substantial, as is common in Flanders. Many dishes are made with Belgian jenever (a type of schnapps).

GHENT Coeur d'Artichaut
Onderbergen 6, 9000 **Tel** *09-225 3318*

A renowned restaurant in the centre of Ghent, Coeur d'Artichaut has a menu that changes every month. Featuring classic European dishes with a twist in addition to inventive Asian selections, it is housed in an impressive mansion building that also incorporates a patio area. A lunch menu is also available. Closed on Sundays and Mondays.

GHENT Georges
Donkersteeg 23–27, 9000 **Tel** *09-225 1918*

A Ghent institution, this friendly seafood restaurant is now over eighty years old, having remained in the same family the whole time. Georges, a father-and-son operation, is one of Ghent's pricier addresses, but offers superior, far from indifferent service. The oysters, crab and mussels of Lélande are the main attraction here.

LUXEMBOURG

LUXEMBOURG CITY Le Bouquet Garni
32, rue de l'Eau, L-1449 Luxembourg **Tel** *26 20 06 20*

Charming French restaurant in a beautifully restored 18th-century mansion in heart of the old city. Chefs Lysiane and Thierry Duhr delight customers with delicious, but well-priced set menus and original one-off mains using locally-caught game. Sister bistro, Salon Saint-Michel, can be found on the ground floor. Closed Sun & Mon.

LUXEMBOURG CITY Restaurant Speltz
8, rue Chimay, L-1333 Luxembourg **Tel** *47 49 50*

Stylish and welcoming restaurant located a stone's throw from the Grand-Ducal Palace, Speltz has built its reputation on its contemporary blend of local produce from France and Luxembourg. Popular mains include roast saddle of veal in Savoy cabbage and pike-perch fillet with potato scales. Good choice of vegetarian dishes.

LUXEMBOURG CITY Clairefontaine
Place de Clairefontaine 9, L-1341 Luxembourg **Tel** *46 22 11*

Elegant French restaurant decorated with old wood paneling and expensive silverware. Meet on the private terrace for pre-meal aperitifs to enjoy views of Place Clairefontaine and the cathedral. Impressive set menus, as well as mouthwatering à la carte dining. Advance booking recommended. Closed Sun & Mon.

THE NETHERLANDS

*S*ituated at the mouth of the River Rhine, the Netherlands is a man-made country that owes its life to the sea: much of the land once lay under water, and a maritime trading tradition was the principal source of the nation's wealth, most notably in the 17th century. The Netherlands is also one of the world's most liberal countries, with a long history of cultural and racial tolerance.

The shape of the Netherlands (or Holland, as it is also known) has changed dramatically over the last 2,000 years. Medieval maps show nearly half of the country under water, but since then large areas have been reclaimed from the sea; the current shoreline is maintained by a drainage system of windmills, dykes, and canals.

With just under 17 million people in just 41,547 sq km (16,041 sq miles) of land, it is the third most densely populated country in Europe (after Monaco and Malta), but this is barely perceptible to the visitor. Only when arriving by plane do you see how much of the area is still covered with water, and how little precious land remains. The orderly Dutch cities and towns never seem overcrowded, but homes are often small, with steep, narrow staircases and modest gardens. Given the fragility of their environment, it is understandable that the Dutch are so good at preserving it.

The three biggest cities – Amsterdam, the capital, Rotterdam, the industrial hub, and the Hague, the seat of government all in the west of the country, part of the urban conglomeration known as the Randstad.

HISTORY

Between the 4th and 8th centuries AD, after the collapse of the Roman Empire, the area corresponding to present-day Holland was conquered by the Franks. As with all the Low Countries, it was later ruled by the House of Burgundy, before passing into the hands of the Habsburgs. When the Habsburg Empire was divided in 1555, the region came under the control of the Spanish branch of the family, which caused the Dutch Revolt of 1568, led by William I of Orange. The Dutch Republic was finally established in 1579, with the Treaty of Utrecht, but it took until 1648 for the Spanish officially to recognize its sovereignty.

Skating on a frozen Dutch river, flanked by drainage windmills

◁ Boats anchored at the canalside in Amsterdam

The battle for independence and the need for wealth to fight the Spanish armies stimulated trading success overseas. The Dutch colonized much of Indonesia and established a profitable empire based on spice. The Dutch East India Company thrived, and in the New World Holland briefly ruled over large parts of Brazil. Tulip bulbs were imported from Turkey and cultivated behind the dunes, thus beginning a lucrative flower industry that still flourishes today. However, war with England radically trimmed Dutch sea-power by the end of the 17th century, and from then on the country's fortunes waned. In 1795 French troops ousted William V of Orange, and in 1813, with the retreat of Napoleon, the Netherlands united with Belgium, its neighbor, an arrangement which lasted for 17 years.

William I of Orange (1533–84), leader of the Dutch Revolt

The Netherlands remained neutral in both World Wars, and although it escaped occupation in 1914, the Nazi invasion of 1940 left lasting scars on the nation.

In the 1960s the country became a haven for the hippy counter-culture, an influence which is still visible today.

LANGUAGE AND CULTURE

Dutch, or Netherlandic, is a Germanic language which derives from the speech of the Western Franks. A number of dialects are spoken, and in Friesland the dialect (Fries) shows Celtic influences. Nevertheless, as in so many European countries, the dialects are disappearing due to the popularity of national television stations on which a standardized version of Dutch is usually spoken.

Culturally, Holland has a huge amount to offer. Its rich history is reflected in countless old buildings and its large number of fine museum collections. The compact size of the city centers makes it easy to stroll along a canal admiring gabled houses, and step into a museum for an hour or two, before ending the day at a nearby café or pub. The Dutch also have much to boast in the realm of the performing arts, so visitors should find time to enjoy one of the world-famous orchestras or modern dance companies, or attend an organ concert in an old church, or simply spend an evening in one of Amsterdam's jazz clubs or rock and pop venues.

A fiercely independent people, the Dutch have long been champions of freedom, and have a traditional tolerance of minorities. Jews have been welcome for centuries, and although Catholicism was banned after independence, the authorities turned a blind eye to its practice. Today that tolerance is extended to asylum seekers, gays and lesbians, and people of different backgrounds. A respect for the right to live one's own life underlies the liberal laws on prostitution and drugs.

KEY DATES IN DUTCH HISTORY

300–700 Region ruled by the Franks

1419 Philip the Good of Burgundy begins to unify the Low Countries

1482 The Netherlands pass by marriage to the Austrian Habsburgs

1555 Philip II of Spain inherits the Netherlands

1568 The Dutch Revolt ends Spanish rule

1579 The northern districts unite, forming the Republic of the United Netherlands

1602 The Dutch East India Company founded

1606–69 Life of Rembrandt

1648 Spain recognizes Dutch independence

1794–1813 The Napoleonic era brings the Netherlands under French control

1914–18 Holland is neutral during World War I

1940–45 The country is occupied by Germany throughout most of World War II

1949 The Dutch East Indies gain independence, becoming Indonesia

1957 The Netherlands signs the Treaty of Rome, and joins European Community

1980 Princess Beatrix becomes Queen

2000 Parliament legalizes controlled euthanasia

2002 The euro replaces the Dutch guilder

2010 Rise of right-wing politician Geert Wilders

Exploring the Netherlands

Although the Netherlands' seat of government is at The Hague, Amsterdam is the nominal capital, and it is here that the main cultural attractions can be found. The folkloric villages of Marken and Volendam are only a short drive away, as are the towns of Alkmaar, famous for its traditional cheese market, Haarlem, with its nearby bulbfields, and Utrecht, with its medieval churches. The port of Rotterdam, the pottery center of Delft, and the university town of Leiden lie to the south and west.

THE NETHERLANDS

See main map

NETHERLANDS

Groningen

AMSTERDAM
The Hague Rotterdam Enschede

GERMANY

Eindhoven

Antwerp Cologne

BELGIUM

0 km 90

0 miles 90

SIGHTS AT A GLANCE

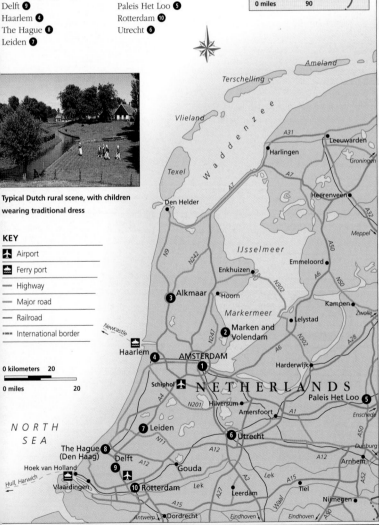

Typical Dutch rural scene, with children wearing traditional dress

KEY

✈ Airport

⛴ Ferry port

— Highway

— Major road

— Railroad

▪▪▪ International border

0 kilometers 20

0 miles 20

Amsterdam ❶

Amsterdam was founded around 1200 as a small
fishing village on marshland at the mouth of the
Amstel river. The young township grew to become
the chief trading city of northern Europe, and, in
the 17th century, the center of a massive
empire. With a population of around 770,000,
today Amsterdam is a place where beauty and
serenity coexist happily with a slightly seamy
side. From the seedy nightspots of the Red
Light District, to the grace and elegance of
the city's 17th-century canal houses and the
rich cultural heritage of its museums,
Amsterdam boasts a variety of attractions.

SIGHTS AT A GLANCE

Amsterdams Museum ⑧
Anne Frank Huis ⑩
Begijnhof ⑨
Golden Bend ⑫
Hermitage Amsterdam ⑯
Joods Historisch Museum ⑤
Jordaan ⑪
Koninklijk Paleis ⑦
Museum Het Rembrandthuis ④
Museum Ons' Lieve Heer op
  Solder ②
Nederlands
  Scheepvaartmuseum ⑭
Nemo ⑬
Nieuwe Kerk ⑥
Oude Kerk ①
Plantage ⑮
Red Light District ③
Rijksmuseum pp256–7 ⑰
Stedelijk Museum ⑲
Van Gogh Museum ⑱

**18th-century Torah mantle,
Joods Historisch Museum**

SEE ALSO

GETTING AROUND

The most useful tram routes for tourists are lines 1, 2, 4, 5, 9, and 16, which go south from Centraal Station and branch out to all the main sights. Lines 13, 14, and 17 lead west to Jordaan. Buses 22, 42, and 43 serve Nemo and the Scheepvaartmuseum, which you cannot reach by tram. A canal-bus service runs from the Singelgracht to Centraal Station, stopping at the major landmarks.

Stained glass at the Amsterdams Museum

KEY

▨	Sight / Place of interest
🚉	Train station
🚌	Bus station
🚊	Main tram stop
⛴	Canalbus boarding point
⛴	Tour boat boarding point
P	Parking
ℹ	Tourist information
✝	Church
✡	Synagogue
	Pedestrian street

0 meters 500

0 yards 500

Houseboats on Prinsengracht, in Amsterdam's western canal ring

The Oude Kerk, a calm and peaceful haven
at the heart of the Red Light District

Oude Kerk ①

Oudekerksplein (entrance at south
side). **Tel** 020-625 8284. 🚋 4, 9, 16,
24, 25. ◻ daily (Sun: pm only). ●
Jan 1, Apr 30, Dec 25. ✝ 11am Sun.
🖼 ♿ www.oudekerk.nl

The origins of the Oude Kerk
(Old Church) go back to the
early 13th century, when a
wooden church was built on
a burial ground on a sand
bank. The present Gothic
structure is 14th century, and
has grown from a single-
aisled church into a basilica.
As it expanded, the building
became a gathering place for
traders and a refuge for the
poor. Though many of its

paintings and statues
were destroyed
following the
Alteration in 1578,
the delicate 15th-
century vault
paintings on the
gilded ceiling
escaped damage. In
1755 the paintings
were hidden with
layers of blue paint
and were not
revealed until 200
years later in 1955.
The Oude Kerk's
beautiful stained-
glass windows were
also undamaged in
the ransackings of
the late 16th century.
The Lady Chapel,
which dates from
1552, contains some
of the best stained
glass. The magnificent
oak-encased Great
Organ, the work of Christian
Vater, was added to the
church in 1724.

Museum Ons' Lieve Heer op Solder ②

Oudezijds Voorburgwal 40. **Tel** 020-
624 6604. 🚋 4, 9, 16, 24, 25.
◻ daily (Sun and public hols: pm
only). ● Jan 1, Apr 30. 🖼 📷
www.opsolder.nl

Tucked away on the edge
of the Red Light District
is a restored 17th-century
canal house, with two smaller
houses to the rear. The
combined upper floors
conceal a Catholic church,

An opulent 17th-century parlor at the
Museum Ons' Lieve Heer op Solder

known as Ons' Lieve Heer
op Solder (Our Lord in the
Attic). After the Alteration,
when Amsterdam officially
became Protestant, many such
hidden churches sprang up
around the city. Built in 1663,
the one here served the Catholic community until 1887,
when the nearby St. Nicolaas-
kerk was completed. Above
the mock marble altar is Jacob
de Wit's glorious painting *The
Baptism of Christ* (1716). The
tiny box bedroom where the
resident priest slept is hidden
off a bend in the stairs.
  The building became a
museum in 1888, and today
contains elegantly refurbished
rooms, as well as a fine
collection of church silver,
religious artifacts, and paintings. Restored to its former
opulence, the parlor, with its
magnificent fireplace, is a
splendid example of a living
room in the Dutch Classical
style of the 17th century.

Red Light District ③

🚋 4, 9, 14, 16, 24, 25.

Prostitution in Amsterdam
dates back to the city's
emergence as a port in the
13th century. By 1478 it had
become so widespread that
attempts were made to
contain it. Prostitutes straying
outside their designated area
were marched back to the
sound of pipe and drum. A
century later the Calvinists
tried to outlaw the practice,

The Death of the Virgin Mary by Dirk Crabeth, one of three restored
stained-glass windows in the Oude Kerk's Lady Chapel

but their attempts were half-hearted, and by the mid-17th century prostitution was openly tolerated. In 1850 Amsterdam had a population of 200,000 and a total of 200 brothels, most of which catered for rich clients.

Today, the Red Light District, known locally as de Walletjes (the little walls), is centered around the Oude Kerk. The area is criss-crossed by a network of tiny lanes lined with garish sex shops and seedy clubs. At night the little alleys assume a sinister aspect, and it is not wise to wander around alone, but by day hordes of visitors generate a festive atmosphere, and there are interesting restaurants, bars, and cafés, and beautiful canalside houses. The council is now campaigning to make the area safer and culturally more attractive.

Museum Het Rembrandthuis ④

Jodenbreestraat 4. *Tel* 020-520 0400. Ⓜ *Nieuwmarkt.* 🚊 *9, 14.* 🔲 *daily.* ● *Jan 1.* 🖾 🖺 🖸 🖺
www.rembrandthuis.nl

Born in Leiden, Rembrandt (1606–69) worked and taught in this house from 1639 until 1656. He lived in the ground-floor rooms with his wife, Saskia, who died here in 1642, leaving the artist with a baby son, Titus. Many of the artist's most famous paintings were created in the first-floor studio, which, along with the other rooms in the house, has been restored and refurbished to show exactly how it looked in the 17th century. On display is an excellent selection of Rembrandt's etchings and drawings, including various self-portraits showing the artist in different moods and guises. There are also landscapes, nude studies, and religious pieces, as well as temporary exhibitions of other artists' works.

Interior of the Grote Synagoge, part of the Joods Historisch Museum

Joods Historisch Museum ⑤

Nieuwe Amstelstraat 1. *Tel* 020-531 0310. Ⓜ *Waterlooplein.* 🚊 *9, 14.* 🚌 *Muziektheater.* 🔲 *daily.* ● *Yom Kippur and Jewish New Year.* 🖾 🖸 on request. 🖢 **www**.jhm.nl

This complex of four synagogues was built in the 17th and 18th centuries by the Ashkenazi Jews, who arrived in Amsterdam from eastern Europe in the 1630s.

The house where Rembrandt lived and worked in the mid-17th century

At first restricted to working in certain trades, the Ashkenazi Jews were granted full civil equality in 1796. Their synagogues were central to Jewish life in Amsterdam until the devastation caused by the Nazi occupation of World War II, which left them empty. The buildings were restored in the 1980s and connected by internal walkways. In 1987 they opened as a museum dedicated to Jewish culture and the history of Judaism in the Netherlands.

The impressive Grote Synagoge, with its bright and airy interior, was designed by Elias Bouman and first opened in 1671. Next door is the Nieuwe Synagoge (New Synagogue), built in 1752. It is dominated by the wooden Holy Ark (1791), which came from a synagogue in Enkhuizen.

Religious art and artifacts on display include Hanukah lamps, Torah mantles, and scroll finials. The buildings were renovated in 2006; a print room was created in the basement and a children's museum on the upper floor in the former Obbene Shul.

18th-century Torah scroll finial

Nieuwe Kerk ⑥

Dam. **Tel** 020-638 6909. 🚇 1, 2, 4, 5 & many others. ☐ daily. 📷 ♿ 🚻 🏠 www.nieuwekerk.nl

Dating from the late 14th century, Amsterdam's second parish church was built as the population outgrew the Oude Kerk (see p250). During its turbulent history, the Nieuwe Kerk (New Church) has been destroyed by fire, rebuilt, and then stripped of its treasures after the Alteration of 1578, when the Calvinists took civil power. It eventually reached its present size in the 1650s.

Albert Vinckenbrinck's flamboyant carved pulpit (1664) is the focal point of the church interior, reflecting the Protestant belief that the sermon is central to worship. Other notable features include Jacob van Campen's ornate Great Organ (1645) and, in the apse, the tomb of the famous 17th-century commander-in-chief of the Dutch Navy, Admiral de Ruyter (1607–76), by Rombout Verhulst.

Rombout Verhulst's memorial to Michiel de Ruyter in the apse of the Nieuwe Kerk

Koninklijk Paleis ⑦

Dam. **Tel** 020-624 8698. 🚇 1, 2, 4, 5 & many others. ☐ for exhibitions during the summer & autumn; phone for details or consult website. ● public hols and when Queen in residence. 📷 📷 check website. ♿ www.koninklijkhuis.nl

The Koninklijk Paleis, still used occasionally by the Dutch royal family for official functions, was built as the Stadhuis (Town Hall). Work began on this vast sandstone edifice in 1648, after the end of the 80 Years' War with Spain. It dominated its surroundings, and more than 13,600 piles were driven into

The splendid Classical facade of the 17th-century Koninklijk Paleis

the ground for the foundations. The Classically inspired design by Jacob van Campen (1595–1657) reflects the city's mood of confidence after the Dutch victory. Civic pride is also shown in the allegorical sculptures by Artus Quellin (1609–68), which decorate the pediments, and in François Hemony's statues and carillon.

Inside, the full magnificence of the architecture is best appreciated in the huge Burgerzaal (Citizens' Hall). Based on the assembly halls of ancient Rome, this 29-m (95-ft) high room runs the length of the building, and boasts a superb marble floor, as well as epic sculptures by Quellien. Most of the furniture on display dates from 1808, when Louis Bonaparte took over the building as his royal palace.

Amsterdams Museum ⑧

Kalverstraat 92, Nieuwezijds Voorburgwal 357, St. Luciensteeg 27. **Tel** 020-523 1822. 🚇 1, 2, 4, 5, 9 & many others. ☐ daily. ● Jan 1, Apr 30, Dec 25. 📷 📷 ♿ 🚻 🏠 www.ahm.nl

The convent of St. Lucien was turned into a civic orphanage in the latter half of the 16th century. The

original red-brick convent was enlarged over the years, and in 1975 it opened as the city's historical museum. Today, some of the museum's exhibitions also focus on contemporary Amsterdam.

Clear signposting allows the visitor either to concentrate on a specific period – The Young City, The Mighty City, or The Modern City – or to take a grand tour through the entire history of Amsterdam.

The museum's largest section, The Mighty City, focuses on trade, commerce, and culture during the period of Amsterdam's Golden Age. Items on display range from a globe belonging to the famous cartographer Willem Blaeu to a late 18th-century model of an East Indiaman.

Amsterdam's wealth from trade attracted great artists, who chronicled the era in extraordinary detail. There are views of the city and the port, and portraits of prominent and ordinary citizens. Some works, such as Jacob de Wit's Maid of Amsterdam (1741), celebrate the glory of the city in heroic, allegorical style. Others give a realistic picture of the life of the paupers and orphans. The paintings of anatomy lessons include one by Rembrandt, The Anatomy Lesson of Dr. Jan Deijman (1656). This shows the dissection of "Black Jan," a convicted criminal who had been hanged.

In the Civic Guards' Gallery hangs a series of group portraits of the various militia companies charged with defending law and order in the city in the 16th and 17th centuries. Paintings by Rembrandt and Cornelis Anthonisz stand out among lesser-known works.

One of the museum's most extraordinary exhibits is the 17th-century 5.30-m (17-ft) statue of Goliath that stands in the restaurant.

Statue of Goliath (c.1650) in the Amsterdams Historisch Museum

Begijnhof ⑨

Spui (entrance at Gedempte Begijnensloot). 🚋 1, 2, 5, 9, 14, 16, 24, 25. **Tel** 020-623 3565. ⬜ daily. **www**.begijnhofamsterdam.nl

The Begijnhof was built in 1346 as a sanctuary for the Begijntjes, a lay Catholic sisterhood who lived like nuns, although they took no monastic vows. In return for lodgings within the complex, these worthy women undertook to educate the poor and look after the sick. Although none of the earliest dwellings survives, the rows of beautiful houses that over-look the Begijnhof's well-kept green include Amsterdam's oldest surviving house, Het Houten Huis, at No. 34. Dating from around 1420, it is one of only two wooden-fronted houses in the city, since timber buildings were banned in 1521 after a series of catastrophic fires. On a wall directly behind No. 34 is a collection of fascinating stone plaques, illustrating biblical themes.

The southern side of the square is dominated by the Engelse Kerk (English Church), which dates from the 15th century and retains its original medieval tower. The church was confiscated after the Alteration and rented to a group of English and Scottish Presbyterians in 1607. Directly opposite is the Begijnhof Chapel (Nos. 29–30), a well-preserved hidden church, where the Begijntjes worshipped in secret until religious tolerance was restored in 1795. Tour groups are not permitted in the Begijnhof and the occupants request that noise should be kept to a minimum.

Family photograph of Anne Frank (1929–45)

Anne Frank Huis ⑩

Prinsengracht 267. **Tel** 020-556 7105. 🚋 13, 14, 17. 🚊 Prinsengracht. ⬜ daily (Jan 1 & Dec 25: pm only). ● Yom Kippur. 🖼 **www**.annefrank.org

For two years during World War II, the Frank and Van Daan families, both Jewish, hid here until their betrayal to the Nazis. The 13-year-old Anne began her famous diary in July 1942. First published in 1947 as *Het Achterhuis (The Annex)*, and since translated into dozens of languages, the journal gives a moving account of growing up under persecution, and of life in confinement. Anne made her last entry in August 1944, three days before her family was arrested.

Visitors climb to the second floor where an introductory video is shown. You then enter the annex where the families hid via the revolving bookcase that concealed its entrance. The rooms are now empty, except for the posters in Anne's room and Otto Frank's model of the annex as it was during the occupation. The house also has exhibitions on World War II and anti-Semitism. Try to arrive early or late in the day as the museum gets very crowded. Buy tickets via the internet to avoid the queues.

Attractive gabled houses and central green of Amsterdam's Begijnhof, which is still occupied by single women

The Westerkerk, designed by Hendrick de Keyser, overlooking Prinsengracht in Jordaan

Jordaan ⑪

🚊 13, 14, 17.

The Jordaan grew up at the same time that Amsterdam's Grachtengordel (Canal Ring) was being developed in the first half of the 17th century. The marshy area to the west of the more fashionable canals was set aside as an area for workers whose industries were banned from the town center. Its network of narrow streets and waterways followed the course of old paths and drainage ditches. Immigrants fleeing religious persecution also settled here. It is thought that Huguenot refugees called the district *jardin* (garden), later corrupted to "Jordaan."

Flowing through the heart of the district are the tranquil tree-lined canals known as the Egelantiersgracht and the Bloemgracht. The canalside residences of the Egelantiersgracht were originally settled by artisans, while the Bloemgracht was a center for dye and paint manufacture. One of the most charming spots along the Egelantiersgracht is **St. Andrieshofje** at Nos. 107–114. This *hofje*

(almshouse) was built in 1617 and the passage that leads to its courtyard is decorated with splendid blue and white tiles.

The 85-m (272-ft) high tower of the **Westerkerk** soars above Jordaan's streets, and gives panoramic views of the city. Begun in 1620, the church has the largest nave of any Dutch Protestant church.

Historically a poor area, the Jordaan now has a trendy and bohemian air. Among the old workers' houses are quirky shops selling anything from designer clothes to old sinks, numerous art galleries, and lively brown cafés and bars, which spill onto the sidewalks during the summer.

Golden Bend ⑫

🚊 1, 2, 4, 5, 9, 14 & many others.
Kattenkabinet Tel 020-626 5378.
◯ 10am–4pm Tue–Fri; pm Sat & Sun. ◉ public hols.

The most impressive canalside architecture in the city can be seen along the section of the Herengracht between Leidestraat and Vijzelstraat.

This stretch of canal is known as the Golden Bend because of the great wealth of the shipbuilders, merchants, and politicians who began building houses here in the 1660s. Most of the opulent mansions have been turned into offices or banks, but their elegance gives an insight into the lifestyle of the earliest residents.

Two of the finest and best-preserved buildings are No. 412, designed by Philips Vingboons in 1664, and No. 475, with its two sculpted female figures over the front door. Built in 1730, the latter is an example of the Louis XIV style, which became popular in the 18th century. The **Kattenkabinet** (Cat Museum), at No. 497, is one of the few houses on the Golden Bend accessible to the public. It is well worth visiting for its rather unusual collection of feline artifacts. Also on view here are some splendid paintings by Jacob de Wit (1695–1754) and an attractive formal garden.

Ornate capital from the façade of a building on the Golden Bend

THE GRACHTENGORDEL

Faced with a rapidly growing population, at the beginning of the 17th century Amsterdam's town planner, Hendrick Staets, formed an ambitious project to quadruple the size of the city. In 1614, work began

on cutting three new residential canals, collectively known as the Grachtengordel (Canal Ring), to encircle the existing city. Built for the wealthiest citizens, the grand houses along the Keizersgracht (Emperor's Canal), Herengracht (Gentleman's Canal), and Prinsengracht (Prince's Canal) represent Amsterdam's finest architecture, and are a testimony to the city's Golden Age.

Seeing the world through a soap bubble at Nemo

Nemo ⑬

Oosterdok 2. **Tel** 020-531 3233. 🚌 22, 42, 43. ◐ 10am–5pm Tue–Sun. ● Jan 1, Apr 30, Dec 25. 📷 ♿ www.e-nemo.nl

In June 1997 Holland's national science center moved to this curved building that protrudes 30 m (99 ft) over the water. Divided into five themed zones (Inter-activity, Technology, Energy, Science, and Humanity), which are updated every three years, the center presents techno-logical innovations in a way that allows visitors' creativity full expression. You can inter-act with virtual reality, operate the latest industrial equipment under expert supervision, harness science to produce a work of art, participate in countless games, experiments, demonstrations, and work-shops, and take in a variety of lectures and films.

Nederlands Scheep-vaartmuseum ⑭

Kattenburgerplein 1. **Tel** 020-523 2222. 🚌 22, 42, 43. ⛴ Oosterdok, Kattenburgergracht. ◐ Tue–Sun (mid-Jun–mid-Sep: daily). ● Jan 1, Apr 30, Dec 25. 📷 ♿ www.scheepvaartmuseum.nl

Once the arsenal of the Dutch Navy, this vast Classical sand-stone edifice was built in 1656. It is supported by 18,000 piles driven into the bed of the Oosterdok. The Navy stayed here until 1973, when the building was converted into the National Maritime Museum, holding the largest collection of boats in the world.

One of the museum's finest exhibits is a 17-m (54-ft) long gilded barge, made in 1818 for King William I. Another major attraction is a full-size model of a Dutch East Indiaman, the *Amsterdam*. During the 16th century the Dutch East India Company used such vessels to sail as far as China, Japan, and Indo-nesia. The museum has a court with a magnificent high glass ceiling.

Plantage ⑮

🚊 6, 9, 14. **Artis** Plantage Kerklaan 30–40. **Tel** 020-523 3400. ◐ daily. 📷 📹 ♿ **Hortus Botanicus Amsterdam** Plantage Middenlaan 2. **Tel** 020-625 8411. ◐ daily. ● Jan 1, Dec 25. 📷 📹 ♿ **Hollandsche Schouwburg** Plantage Middenlaan 24. **Tel** 020-531 0340. ◐ daily. ● Yom Kippur. ♿

Seals basking in a pool at the Artis zoological complex in Plantage

The name Plantage dates from the time when it was an area of green parkland beyond the city wall, where 17th-century Amsterdammers spent their leisure time. Though much of the greenery has gone, there is still a lot to see and do here.

The area is dominated by **Artis**, a zoological complex founded in 1838, which has more than 5,000 animal species, a planetarium, and an excellent aquarium.

Nearby, the **Hortus Botanicus Amsterdam** began as a small apothecaries' herb garden in 1682 and now contains one of the world's largest botanical collections.

Plantage has a strong Jewish tradition, and many monu-ments commemorate Jewish history in Amsterdam. The **Hollandsche Schouwburg** is a somber memorial to the 104,000 Dutch Jewish victims of World War II.

Hermitage Amsterdam ⑯

Amstel 51. **Tel** 020-530 8751. 🚊 4, 9. ◐ daily. 📷 📹 ♿ www.hermitage.nl

This branch of the State Hermitage Museum in St. Petersburg is housed in the vast Amstelhof, a former old-people's home. Opened in 2004, this satellite museum displays temporary exhibi-tions drawn from the rich St. Petersburg's collections. The venue is now one of Amster-dam's major museums.

William I's royal barge on display at the Nederlands Scheepvaartmuseum

Rijksmuseum ⑰

The Rijksmuseum is a familiar Amsterdam landmark and possesses an unrivaled collection of Dutch art, begun in the early 19th century. The museum opened in 1885 to bitter criticism from Amsterdam's Protestant community for its Neo-Gothic style. The main building is closed for extensive renovation until late 2012, during which time the most famous treasures from the Dutch Golden Age will be on view in the Philips Wing.

Second floor

Winter Landscape with Skaters *(1618)*
Mute painter Hendrick Avercamp specialized in intricate icy winter scenes.

The Gothic facade of Cuypers' building is red brick with elaborate decoration, including colored tiles.

★ **The Kitchen Maid** *(1658)*
The light falling through the window and the stillness of this domestic scene are typical of Jan Vermeer's style.

Entrance

KEY TO FLOORPLAN

- Dutch history
- Dutch painting
- European painting
- Sculpture and decorative art
- Prints and drawings
- Asiatic art
- Temporary exhibitions
- Non-exhibition space

STAR PAINTINGS

★ The Night Watch by Rembrandt

★ St. Elizabeth's Day Flood

★ The Kitchen Maid by Vermeer

★ **St. Elizabeth's Day Flood** *(1500)*
An unknown artist painted this altarpiece, which shows a disastrous flood in 1421. The dykes protecting Dordrecht were breached, and 22 villages were swept away by the flood water.

Entrance

Study collections

VISITORS' CHECKLIST

Philips Wing, Jan Luykenstr. 1.
Tel 020-674 7047. 🚊 2, 3, 5,
7, 10, 12. 🚊 Stadhouderskade.
🕐 9am–6pm daily (Philips Wing
only). 🔴 Jan 1. 🎫 📷 ♿

★ **The Night Watch** *(1642)*
*The showpiece of Dutch
17th-century art, this vast
canvas by Rembrandt was
commissioned as a group
portrait of an Amsterdam
militia company.*

Philips Wing

GALLERY GUIDE

*There are entrances on either
side of the driveway under the
building – the left leads into
the Dutch history section, the
right to prints and drawings,
sculpture and applied art,
and then continues on up the
stairs. On the first floor is a
huge antechamber, with a
shop and information desk.
The entrance on the left begins
with early Dutch painting,
leading to the acclaimed
17th-century collection.*

**First
floor**

St. Catherine *(c.1465)*
*This sculpture by the Master of
Koudewater shows the saint stamp-
ing on Emperor Maxentius, who
allegedly killed her with his sword.*

**Philips
Wing**

GENRE PAINTING

For the contemporaries of Jan
Steen (1625–79), this cosy
everyday scene was full of
symbols that are obscure to
the modern viewer. The dog
on the pillow may represent
fidelity, and the red stockings
the woman's sexuality; she is
probably a prostitute. Such
genre paintings were often
raunchy, but nearly always
had a moral twist – domestic
scenes by artists such as ter
Borch and Honthorst were
symbolic of brothels, while
other works illustrated prov-
erbs. Symbols like candles
or skulls indicated mortality.

Jan Steen's symbolic *Woman at her Toilet***,
painted in about 1660**

**Ground
Floor**

Exploring the Rijksmuseum

The Rijksmuseum is too vast to be seen in a single visit, though the key pieces can be seen in the Philips Wing. If time is short, start with the incomparable 17th-century Dutch paintings, taking in Rembrandt, Frans Hals, Vermeer, and many other Old Masters. The collection of Asiatic artifacts and the sculpture and applied arts departments are equally wonderful, while the Dutch history section also provides a rewarding experience.

The heavily ornamented Neo-Gothic facade of the Rijksmuseum

EARLY PAINTING AND FOREIGN SCHOOLS

Alongside Flemish and Italian art are religious works by Netherlandish painters, such as *The Seven Works of Charity* (1504) by the Master of Alkmaar, Jan van Scorel's *Mary Magdalene* (1528), and Lucas van Leyden's triptych, *Adoration of the Golden Calf* (1530).

DUTCH PAINTING OF THE GOLDEN AGE

The 17th century was a golden age for Dutch art. By this time, religious themes had been replaced by secular subjects, such as realistic portraiture, landscapes, still lifes, seascapes, domestic interiors, and animal portraits.

The most famous artist of this era is Rembrandt, whose works here include *Portrait of Titus in a Monk's Habit* (1660), *Self-Portrait as the Apostle Paul* (1661), and *The Jewish Bride* (1663), as well as the brilliant *The Night Watch (see p257)*.

Also not to be missed are Jan Vermeer's (1632–75) serenely light-filled interiors, such as *The Kitchen Maid (see p257)* and *The Woman Reading a Letter* (1662). Of several portraits by Frans Hals (1580–1666) the best-known are *The Wedding Portrait* and *The Merry Drinker* (1630). *The Windmill at Wijk* by Jacob van Ruisdael (1628–82) is a great landscape by an artist at the height of his career. Other artists whose works contribute to this unforgettable collection include Pieter Saenredam (1597–1665), Jan van de Capelle (c.1624–79), and Jan Steen *(see p257)*.

LATER DUTCH PAINTING

Portraiture and still lifes continued to dominate 18th-century Dutch painting. The evocative *Still Life with Flowers and Fruit* by Jan van Huysum (1682–1749) stands out among works on display here. Other 18th-century artists represented are Adriaan van der Werff (1659–1722) and Cornelis Troost (1696–1750).

The 19th-century collection features works by the Hague School, a group of Dutch artists who came together around 1870 in Den Haag. Their landscape work captures the atmospheric quality of subdued Dutch sunlight. Look out for Anton Mauve's *Morning Ride on the Beach* (1876) and the beautiful Polder landscape, *View near the Geestbrug*, by Hendrik Weissenbruch (1824–1903).

SCULPTURE AND APPLIED ARTS

Exhibits in this section span several centuries, ranging from religious medieval sculpture to Art Nouveau glass. Highlights that capture the wealth of the Golden Age include an exquisite display of glassware, Delftware, and diamond-encrusted jewelry.

ASIATIC ART

Rewards of the Dutch imperial trading past are on show in this section. Some of the earliest artifacts are the most unusual: tiny bronze Tang-dynasty figurines from 7th-century China, and granite rock carvings from Java (c.8th century). Later exhibits include Chinese parchment paintings, inlaid Korean boxes, and decorative Vietnamese dishes.

The Jewish Bride by Dutch Master, Rembrandt (1606–69)

The Bedroom, painted during van Gogh's stay in Arles, France

Van Gogh Museum ⑱

Paulus Potterstraat 7. *Tel* 020-570 5200. 🚋 *2, 3, 5, 12, 16, 24.* ⬜ *daily.* ⬤ *from end Sep 2012–summer 2013; Jan 1.* ♿ www.vangoghmuseum.com

Vincent van Gogh in 1871

Vincent Van Gogh (1853–90), born in Zundert, began painting in 1880. He worked in the Netherlands for five years, before moving to Paris, and then settling at Arles (*see pp192–3*) in the south of France in February 1888. There he painted over 200 canvases in 15 months. During his time in France, however, van Gogh suffered recurrent nervous crises, hallucinations, and depression. After a fierce argument with the French artist Gauguin, he cut off part of his own ear and his mental instability forced him into an asylum. Van Gogh's final years were characterized by tremendous bursts of activity. During the last 70 days of his life he painted 70 canvases. In July 1890 he shot himself and died two days later. He was on the verge of being acclaimed.

Van Gogh's younger brother Theo, an art dealer, amassed a collection of 200 of his paintings and 500 drawings. These, together with around 850 letters written by the artist to Theo, form the core of the museum's collection. Famous works include *The Potato Eaters* (1885), from the artist's Dutch period, *The Bedroom* (1888), painted to celebrate his achievement of domestic stability in the Yellow House in Arles, and *Vase with Sunflowers* (1889). One of van Gogh's last paintings is the dramatic *Wheatfield and Crows* (1890). The menacing crows and violence of the sky show the depth of the artist's mental anguish in the last few weeks before his death. The museum is closed for renovation from the end of September 2012 until summer 2013. During this time the most famous works will be on view at the Hermitage Museum (*see p255*).

Stedelijk Museum ⑲

Paulus Potterstraat 13. *Tel* 020-573 2911. 🚋 *2, 3, 5, 12.* ⬜ *10am–6pm daily (closed until late 2012; check website for up-to-date information).* ⬤ *Jan 1.* ♿ www.stedelijk.nl

The Stedelijk Museum was designed to hold a personal collection bequeathed to the city in 1890 by art connoisseur Sophia de Bruyn. It is housed in a late 19th-century Neoclassical building, adorned with statues of famous artists and architects. In 1938, the museum became the national museum of modern art, showing works by well-known names such as Picasso, Matisse, Chagall, and Monet. Constantly changing exhibitions reflect the latest developments not only in painting and sculpture, but also in printing, drawing, photography, video, and industrial design.

Among the museum's best collections are works by the Dutch painter Mondriaan (1872–1944). One of the founding members of De Stijl (The Style) – an artistic movement which espoused clarity and simplicity – Mondriaan went on to produce many abstract geometrical compositions, such as *Composition in Red, Black, Blue, Yellow, and Grey*.

Other artists represented in the exhibitions include the American photographer Man Ray (1890–1977), the Russian Kazimir Malevich (1878–1935), founder of the abstract movement Suprematism, and the Swiss sculptor Jean Tinguely (1925–91), who created humorous sculptures from junk and recycled metal.

The museum reopens in late 2012 following complete renovation of the existing building and the addition of an extension, showcasing contemporary art. This has been nicknamed "the bathtub" for its visual similarities.

Statue of 16th-century artist Pieter Aertsen on the Stedelijk's facade

A typical 17th-century gabled timber house in Marken

Marken and Volendam ②

Marken 🏠 2,000. 🚌 🚢
Volendam 🏠 21,000. 🚌 🏨
Zeestraat 37 (0299-363747). 🚢 Sat.
www.vvv-volendam.nl

Located on the shores of the Marker Meer, and less than an hour's drive from Amsterdam, Marken and Volendam are extremely popular with tourists, who are drawn to their old-world character. In spite of the crowds, it is worth spending a few hours exploring their narrow streets and canals, lined, as they are, with attractive 17th-century gabled timber houses. You may even spot the local inhabitants wearing traditional dress.

Places to look out for include the **Marker Museum** in Marken, which consists of six historical houses. One of the houses is furnished as a traditional fisherman's dwelling. Volendam's

Spaander Hotel at No. 15 Haven is also worth a visit. The walls of the hotel's café are covered with works by late 19th-century artists who came here to paint the town.

Alkmaar ③

🏠 94,000. 🚉 🏨 Waaggebouw,
Waagplein 2–3 (072-5114 284).
🚢 cheese market: Apr–Sep: 10am–
12:30pm Fri. www.vvvalkmaar.nl

Alkmaar is one of the few Dutch towns to maintain its traditional cheese market, which has been held here since medieval times. Every Friday morning in summer local producers lay out Gouda and Edam cheeses in the Waagplein, and from here porters sporting colorful straw hats take them off on sledges for weighing at the **Waagge-bouw** (Weigh House). This imposing building, altered in 1582 from a 14th-century chapel, also houses the **Het Hollands Kaasmuseum**, where local cheese-making techniques are explained.

Alkmaar's massive Gothic church, the **Grote Kerk**, was completed in 1520 and contains the tomb of Floris V, Count of Holland. The nave is dominated by the 17th-century organ, built by Jacob van Campen and painted by Cesar van Everdingen.

🏛 Het Hollands Kaasmuseum
Waaggebouw, Waagplein 2. **Tel** 072-5155 516. ☐ Apr–Oct: Mon–Sat. 🎦 🔥 www.kaasmuseum.nl

The soaring pipes of the famous organ in Haarlem's Grote Kerk

Haarlem ④

🏠 147,000. 🚉 🏨 Stationsplein 1
(0900-616 1600). 🚢 Mon, Fri & Sat.
🎦 Haarlem Jazz Festival (mid-Aug).

Haarlem is the center of the Dutch printing, pharma-ceutical, and bulb-growing industries. Most of the city's main attractions are within easy walking distance of the Grote Markt, a lively square overlooked by the Gothic **Grote Kerk**. Also known as Sint Bavo's, this huge church was built between 1400 and 1550. Its highly decorative organ (1735) has been played by both Handel and Mozart. Also on the Grote Markt, the **Stadhuis** (Town Hall) dates from 1250 and displays a mixture of architectural styles. The oldest part of the building is the beamed medieval banqueting hall of the counts of Holland.

The **Amsterdamse Poort**, the medieval gateway that once formed part of the city's defenses, was built in 1355.

Haarlem is well known for its *hofjes* (almshouses), which began to appear in the 16th century. Established in 1610, **St. Elisabeth's Gasthuis** now houses a historical museum. The **Frans Hals Museum** occupies the almshouse where the famous artist (1582–1666) supposedly lived out his last years. In addition to a superb collection of paintings by Hals himself, there is a selection of

Porters carrying cheeses on sledges at Alkmaar's traditional market

For hotels and restaurants in this region see pp268–9 and pp270–71

Dutch paintings and applied art dating from the 16th and 17th centuries.

🏛 Frans Hals Museum
Groot Heiligland 62. **Tel** 023-5115 775. ⏰ Tue–Sat, pm Sun. ⬤ Jan 1, Easter, Dec 25. 📷 📹 ♿ 🏠

Paleis Het Loo ❺

Koninklijk Park 1, Apeldoorn.
Tel 055-577 2400. 🚉 to Apeldoorn, then bus 102. ⏰ Tue–Sun. ⬤ Jan 1.
📷 📹 ♿ 🍴 www.paleishetloo.nl

Stadholder William III built Het Loo in 1686 as a royal hunting lodge. Generations of the House of Orange used the lodge as a summer palace, which came to be regarded as the "Versailles of the Netherlands." The building's Classical facade belies the opulence of the interior. Among the most lavish apartments are the Royal Bedroom of William III (1713), with its wall coverings and draperies of rich orange damask and blue silk, and the Old Dining Room (1686). In the latter half of the 20th century, old prints, records, and plans were used to carefully recreate Het Loo's beautiful formal gardens.

The sumptuously decorated Royal Bedroom of Stadholder William III

Utrecht ❻

🏯 234,000. 🚉 🚌 🛈 Domplein 9 (0900-128 8732). ⬤ Wed & Sat.

Utrecht was founded by the Romans in AD 47 to protect a strategic river crossing on the Rhine. The town was one of

---

BULBFIELDS OF THE NETHERLANDS

Bulb species cultivated in the Netherlands include lilies, gladioli, daffodils, hyacinths, irises, crocuses, and dahlias. The most famous bulb of all, however, is the tulip. Originally

from Turkey, it was first grown in Dutch soil by Carolus Clusius in 1593. Occupying a 30-km (19-mile) strip between Haarlem and Leiden, the Bloembollen-streek is the most important bulb-growing area in the country. From late January the polders bloom with a succession of brightly colored bulbs, building to a climax in mid-April when the tulips flower. If you do not have a car, there are plenty of organized tours that visit the bulbfields, or you can rent a bicycle from Haarlem train station.

A blanket of color formed by tulips in the Bloembollenstreek

---

the first places in the Netherlands to embrace Christianity, and in the Middle Ages it grew into an important religious center. The city retains many of its medieval churches and monasteries. The **Domkerk**, Utrecht's cathedral, was begun in 1254. Today, only the north and south transepts, two chapels, and the choir remain, along with the 15th-century cloisters and a chapterhouse. The **Domtoren**, which stands apart from the cathedral, is one of the tallest towers in the Netherlands, at 112 m (367 ft). Completed in 1382, on the site of the small 8th-century church of St. Willibrord, it affords magnificent views of the city.

Among Utrecht's many museums are the **Museum Catharijneconvent**, which deals with the troubled history of religion in the Netherlands and owns an award-winning collection of medieval art, and the **Nederlands Spoorweg-museum**, a superb railway museum, housed in the fully restored 19th-century Maliebaan station. At the heart of the collection at the **Centraal Museum** is a series of portraits by artist Jan van Scorel (1495–1562), known as the "Utrecht Caravaggisti". There is also an impressive collection of modern and contemporary

art, with works by Van Gogh, Courbet and Damien Hirst, as well as sculpture, costume and furniture collections.

🏛 Museum Catharijneconvent
Lange Nieuwstraat 38. **Tel** 030-2313 835. ⏰ Tue–Sun. ⬤ Jan 1, Apr 30. 📷 📧 ♿ 🏠
www.catharijneconvent.nl

🏛 Centraal Museum
Nicolaaskerkhof 10. **Tel** 030-2362 362. ⏰ Tue–Sun. ⬤ Jan 1, Apr 30, Dec 25. 📷 🏠 🏠
www.centraalmuseum.nl

Utrecht's massive Gothic Domtoren, which dominates the city

Leiden ❼

🏠 *119,000.* 🚉 🚌 ℹ️ *Stationsweg 2d (071-516 600).* 🔄 *Wed, Sat.*

Leiden is a prosperous town that dates back to Roman times. Its famous university is the oldest in the Netherlands, founded in 1575 by William of Orange. Created in 1587, the university's botanical garden, the **Hortus Botanicus der Rijksuniversiteit Leiden**, is still open to the public.

One of Leiden's biggest attractions is the **Rijksmuseum van Oudheden** (National Museum of Antiquities). Established in 1818, the museum houses an outstanding collection of Egyptian artifacts, including the 1st-century AD Temple of Taffeh. There are also displays of textiles, musical instruments, Etruscan bronzework, and fragments of Roman mosaics and frescoes.

The magnificent Gothic **Pieterskerk** was built in the 15th century. Its interior is rather austere, but there is a splendid organ (1642), enclosed in gilded woodwork.

Dating back to 1640, the old Lakenhal (Cloth Hall) now houses the **Stedelijk Museum De Lakenhal**, with exhibitions of art and furniture from the 16th century onward. The pride of the collection is Lucas van Leyden's Renaissance triptych, *The Last Judgment* (1526–7). Leiden also has an excellent ethnological museum, the **Museum Volkenkunde**, which has exhibits from many countries and hosts events themed on traditions, rituals, and practices of other cultures.

Hortus Botanicus, the tranquil botanical gardens of Leiden University

🏛 **Rijksmuseum van Oudheden**
Rapenburg 28. *Tel 071-5163 163.*
🕐 *Tue–Sun.* 🔴 *Jan 1, Oct 3, Dec 25.* 🎟️ 🚻 📷 📖 www.rmo.nl

🏛 **Museum Volkenkunde**
Steenstraat 1. *Tel 071-5168 800.*
🕐 *Tue–Sun.* 🔴 *Jan 1, Oct 3, Dec 25.* 🎟️ 🚻
www.mv.nl

The Hague ❽

🏠 *446,000.* 🚉 🚌 ℹ️ *Hofweg 1 (0900-34 3505).* 🔄 *Mon, Wed, Fri, Sat.* www.denhaag.com

The political capital of the Netherlands, The Hague (Den Haag or 's-Gravenhage) is home to prestigious institutions, such as the Dutch parliament and the International Court of Justice.

When The Hague became the seat of government in 1586, it was a small town built around the castle of the counts of Holland. That same castle, much rebuilt, stands at the heart of the city, and forms part of the Binnenhof, where today's parliament sits.

The fairy-tale, double-turreted Gothic **Ridderzaal** (Hall of the Knights), the 13th-century dining hall of Count Floris V, is open to the public when parliament is not in session.

An outstanding collection of works by Dutch Masters Rembrandt, Jan Vermeer, and Jan Steen is assembled in the Royal Picture Gallery at the **Mauritshuis**. More Dutch Golden Age paintings are on view at the **Museum Bredius** and the **Galerij Prins Willem V**.

The **Haags Gemeentemuseum** has an applied arts section that includes the world's largest collection of paintings by De Stijl (*see p259*) artist Piet Mondrian.

Formerly called Het Oude Hof (the Old Court), the **Paleis Noordeinde** is a splendid 17th-century palace built in the Classical style. It is used as a temporary residence by Queen Beatrix.

🏛 **Ridderzaal**
Binnenhof 8a. *Tel 070-364 6144.*
🕐 *Mon–Fri (call in advance).*
🔴 *public hols.* 🎟️ 📷 *obligatory.*

🏛 **Mauritshuis**
Korte Vijverberg 8. *Tel 070-302 3456.* 🕐 *Tue–Sun (daily Apr–Aug).*
🔴 *Jan 1, Dec 25.* 🎟️ 📷 🚻

🏛 **Galerij Prins Willem V**
Buitenhof 35. *Tel 070-302 3456.*
🕐 *Tue–Sun (daily Apr–Aug).* 🎟️

Environs
Only a 15-minute tram ride from the center of Den Haag, **Scheveningen** has clean, sandy beaches and good seafood restaurants. The resort also has a Sea Life Center and Muzee, a small museum of marine biology and local history exhibits.

The Binnenhof, home of the Dutch parliament, in The Hague

Delft ❾

🏛 95,000. 🚉 🚌 🛈 Hippolytus-
buurt 4 (0900-5151 555). 🕑 Thu, Sat.

The charming town of Delft
is most famous for its blue-
and-white pottery, known
as Delftware, which was
introduced to the Netherlands
by immigrant Italian potters
in the 16th century. **De
Porceleyne Fles** is one of
two Delftware potteries still
in operation, and is open for
guided tours.

Delft is also the resting
place of William of Orange
(1533–84), who commanded
the Dutch Revolt against
Spanish rule from his
headquarters in the town.
His richly-decorated tomb
lies in the **Nieuwe Kerk**, built
between 1383 and 1510, but
subsequently restored

**Hand-painted
17th-century
Delft tiles**

following damage
caused by fire and
explosion. The
former convent
that William used
as his military
headquarters, and
where he was
assassinated by
order of Philip II
of Spain, is now
home to the
**Stedelijk Museum
Het Prinsenhof**.

The museum contains a rare
collection of antique Delftware, as well as tapestries,
silverware, medieval sculpture,
and portraits of the Dutch
royal family.

Other sites of interest are
the **Volkenkundig Museum
Nusantara**, an ethnological
museum, whose exhibits
were brought back from
Indonesia by traders working
for the Dutch East India
Company, and the **Oude
Kerk**, which dates from the
13th century. The church
holds the tomb of one of the
town's most famous sons, the
artist Jan Vermeer (1632–75).

🛈 Nieuwe Kerk
Markt. **Tel** 015-2123 025. 🕑 Mon–
Sat. 🌐 www.nieuwekerk-delft.nl

**🏛 Stedelijk Museum
Het Prinsenhof**
St. Agathaplein 1. **Tel** 015-2602 358.
🕑 Tue–Sat, Sun pm. ● Jan 1, Dec
25. 🌐 www.prinsenhof-delft.nl

**Delft's Nieuwe Kerk, with its
soaring 100-m (328-ft) high tower**

Rotterdam ❿

🏛 585,000. ✈ 6 km (4 miles) NW.
🚉 🚌 🛈 Coolsingel 195 (0900-403
4065). 🕑 Tue, Fri, Sat, Sun.

Rotterdam occupies a
strategic position where
the Rhine meets the North
Sea. Barges from the city
transport goods deep into
the continent, and ocean-
going ships carry European
exports around the world.

Following damage during
World War II, the Oudehaven,
Rotterdam's old harbor area,
has been rebuilt in daring and
avant-garde styles. The pencil-
shaped **Gemeente Bibliotheek**
(Public Library) is similar to
the Pompidou Center in Paris
(see p153), while Piet Blom's
Kijk-Kubus (Cube Houses) of
1982 are extraordinary

apartments set on a series
of concrete stilts.

The excellent **Museum
Boijmans-van Beuningen**
holds Netherlandish and
Dutch art, from the medieval
paintings of Jan van Eyck to
modern works using laser
technology. Among its
most famous exhibits are a
number of paintings by Peter
Brueghel and Rembrandt.

Other museums of note
are the **Historisch Museum
Rotterdam**, the city's main
historical museum, the **Wereldmuseum Rotterdam**, with its
superb ethnological collection,
and the **Maritiem Museum
Rotterdam**, devoted to the
history of shipping, whose
highlight is an iron-clad warship, De Buffel, built in 1868.

For a spectacular view of
the city, take the elevator up
the 185-m (600-ft) high **Euro-
mast**. Built in 1960, it is the
tallest construction in the
country, and has a restaurant
and an exhibition area.

**🏛 Museum Boijmans-van
Beuningen**
Museumpark 18–20. **Tel** 010-441
9400. 🕑 Tue–Sun. ● Jan 1,
Apr 30, Dec 25. 🌐 ♿

**🏛 Historisch Museum
Rotterdam**
Korte Hoogstraat 31. **Tel** 010-217
6717. 🕑 Tue–Sun. ● Jan 1,
Apr 30, Dec 25. 🌐 ♿

**🏛 Wereldmuseum
Rotterdam**
Willemskade 25. **Tel** 010-270 7172.
🕑 daily. 🌐 🛈 🖥 ♿

**Peter Brueghel the Elder's The Tower of Babel (c.1553) in the Museum
Boijmans-van Beuningen in Rotterdam**

Practical & Travel Information

The Netherlands is a straightforward country to travel in, and visitors should find its citizens, who are often multilingual, helpful and friendly. One of the joys of a visit to Amsterdam is the relatively car-free environment. Trams, bicycles, and pedestrians are given a higher priority in the center than motor vehicles. Outside the capital, the Dutch public transportation network is one of the most highly developed in Europe.

TOURIST INFORMATION

The NBTC (**Netherlands Board of Tourism and Conventions**) has offices in many cities world-wide. Within the Netherlands, the state-run tourist information organization is the Vereniging Voor Vreemdelingenverkeer, known as the **VVV**. They have around 450 offices throughout the country. Courteous and friendly staff provide information on sights, transportation, and events, and will also change money and reserve hotel rooms.

The Museum Card (*Museumkaart*), available from branches of the VVV, is valid for a year, and allows admission to over 400 museums and galleries throughout the country.

VISA REQUIREMENTS AND CUSTOMS

Citizens of the EU, Australia, New Zealand, the US, and Canada need only a valid passport to enter the Netherlands. Those visitors coming from non-EU states can reclaim VAT on certain goods. Call the freephone customs information line (0800-0143) for further details.

SAFETY AND EMERGENCIES

Amsterdam is much safer than many North American and European cities. Drugs-related crime is still a problem, but tourists should not be affected by this, as long as they act sensibly, and avoid certain areas after dark, in particular the Zeedijk district.

In case of emergencies, the appropriate number to call is listed in the directory opposite.

HEALTH ISSUES

Minor health problems can be dealt with by a chemist (*drogist*), who stocks non-prescription drugs. If you need prescription medicines, go to a pharmacy (*apotheek*), open from 8:30am to 5:30pm Monday to Friday.

Attracted by the canals, mosquitoes can be an irritant in Amsterdam, so bring plenty of repellent sprays and antihistamine creams with you.

MUSEUM OPENING TIMES

Many state-run museums are closed on Mondays, and open from 10am to 5pm, Tuesday to Saturday, and from 1 to 5pm on Sunday. Most museums adopt Sunday hours for national holidays, apart from New Year's Day, when they are always closed.

BANKING AND CURRENCY

The Dutch unit of currency is the euro (*see p15*). Banks open from 9 or 10am to 4 or 5pm, Monday to Friday. Some city branches close at 7pm on Thursdays and open on Saturday mornings. Banks are usually the best place to change money, but official bureaux de change, the GWK (*grenswissel-kantoor-bureaus*), also have reasonable exchange rates. Credit cards are not as widely accepted in the Netherlands as in other European countries.

COMMUNICATIONS

Most public telephones have been removed due to the use of cell phones but you can still find some in stations and tourist areas. The majority of phone booths only accept cards, which can be bought at post offices, tobacconists, and train stations, but it might be easier and cheaper to buy a local SIM card for your phone.

Main post offices are open Monday to Friday from 9am to 5pm. Most small local post offices have been replaced by post office agencies in supermarkets and bookshops. Stamps can be bought at post offices, tobacconists or souvenir shops.

FLYING TO THE NETHERLANDS

Carriers operating non-stop flights from the US to the Netherlands include charter operator **Martinair**, **Delta Air Lines**, **United Airlines** and **KLM**. Seven airlines fly direct from the UK to the Netherlands, among them **British Airways** and low-cost airlines including **Ryanair**, **easyJet**, and **Transavia**. The least expensive way to get from Amsterdam's Schiphol Airport to the city center is by the airport rail service. Trains leave for Central Station seven times each hour

THE CLIMATE OF THE NETHERLANDS

The Netherlands has a temperate climate. Winters are frequently freezing, and spring and autumn can be chilly. July and August are the warmest months, but North Sea winds often make it seem cooler. You should expect rainfall all year round, but spring is generally the driest season. The heaviest rainfall occurs in the autumn, especially in November.

AMSTERDAM

	Apr	Jul	Oct	Jan
°C/F (high)	13/55	22/72 / 12/54	14/58	5/51
°C/F (low)	0°C 4/39 / 32°F		7/45	1/34
☀ hrs	5 hrs	6.5 hrs	3 hrs	1.5 hrs
☂ mm	35 mm	57 mm	70 mm	56 mm

between 5:40am and 1am, after which they run hourly. The journey takes 20 minutes. Schiphol Airport station is also connected to other cities in the Netherlands.

ARRIVING BY SEA

Ferry companies offering car and passenger services from the UK to the Netherlands include **P&O North Sea Ferries**, with daily sailings from Hull to Rotterdam and **Stena Line**, which sails from Harwich to Hook of Holland.

P&O also operates regular crossings from Hull to Zeebrugge in Belgium. **DFDS Seaways** runs an overnight service from Newcastle to Ijmuiden.

RAIL TRAVEL

International rail routes provide a fast and efficient link between Amsterdam and many other European cities. From Centraal Station high-speed **Thalys** trains run to Brussels in 2 hours 30 minutes, and to Paris in about 4 hours. In both Paris and Brussels,

passengers can change to the **Eurostar** for an onward connection to London. Stena Line offers a train and ferry combination ticket from London to Amsterdam.

The Dutch rail system, operated by Nederlandse Spoorwegen, is one of the most modern and efficient in Europe, with an extensive route network. The **OVR** (Openbaar Vervoer Reisinformatie) has information on rail trips for tourists, plus details of special fares. It does not, however, issue tickets, which you buy at the ticket office. If you need to arrange rail travel abroad, visit the offices of **NS Hispeed**, located in Amsterdam's Centraal Station.

TRAVELING BY BUS

Long-distance bus travel is an inexpensive, if tiring, way to reach the Netherlands. **Eurolines** has at least two daily services from the UK to Amsterdam, via the Channel Tunnel.

Buses in the Netherlands are reliable and efficient. The old *strippenkaart* (ticket strip)

system has now been replaced by the *OV Chipkaart*. This is a card the size of a credit card which can be loaded with credit at machines (found at bus and train stations) and used on all means of public transport. The card is held against a card-reader in the bus, train, or tram, and debited depending on the distance traveled. You can buy a *Chipkaart* at train and bus stations.

TRAVELING BY CAR

An ever-expanding highway system makes it easy to travel to the Netherlands from anywhere in Europe. Major roads (marked N) are generally well-maintained, but Dutch highways (labeled A) have narrow lanes, traffic lights, and sometimes no hard shoulder. When driving in towns, especially in Amsterdam, be careful of cyclists and trams.

Most of the principal international car rental firms have offices in Amsterdam and at Schiphol Airport, but local companies are cheaper.

DIRECTORY

NETHERLANDS BOARD OF TOURISM AND CONVENTIONS

UK

PO Box 30783,
London, WC2B 6DH.
Tel 020-7539 7950.
Fax 020-7539 7953.
www.holland.com/uk

US

355 Lexington Avenue,
New York, NY 10017.
Tel 212-370 7360.
Fax 212-370 9507.
www.holland.com/us

TOURIST OFFICES IN THE NETHERLANDS

VVV Centraal Station

Centraal Station,
Stationsplein, Amsterdam.
Tel 0900-400 4040.

EMBASSIES

Australia

Carnegielaan 4,
2517 KH Den Haag.
Tel 070-310 8200.

Canada

Sophialaan 7,
2514 JP Den Haag.
Tel 070-311 1600.

Ireland

Scheveningseweg 12,
2584 AE Den Haag.
Tel 070-363 0993.

UK

Lange Voorhout 10,
2514 ED Den Haag.
Tel 070-427 0427.

US

Museumplein 19, 1071 DJ
Amsterdam.
Tel 020-575 5309.

EMERGENCIES

Ambulance, Fire, and Police

Tel 112.

AIRLINES

British Airways

Tel 0844-493 0787 (UK).
Tel 020-346 9559
(Netherlands).

Delta Air Lines

Tel 800-241 4141 (US).

easyJet

Tel 0871-244 2366 (UK).
www.easyjet.com

KLM

Tel 0871-222 7474 (UK).
Tel 020-474 7747
(Netherlands).

Martinair

Tel 800-627 8462 (US).

Ryanair

Tel 0871-246 0000 (UK).
www.ryanair.com

Transavia

Tel 0906-680 0065 (UK).
Tel 0900-0737.

United Airlines

Tel 800-538 2929 (US).

FERRY COMPANIES

DFDS Seaways

Tel 0871-522 9955 (UK).

P&O European

Tel 08716-645 645 (UK).

Stena Line

Tel 08705-455 455 (UK).

RAIL TRAVEL

NI Hispeed

Tel 0900-9296.

OVR

Tel 0900-9292.
www.9292ov.nl
www.ov-chipkaart.nl

Thalys

Tel 0900-9296.

BUSES

Eurolines UK Ltd

Tel 08717-818 177 or
08717-818 181.

Shopping & Entertainment

The Netherlands is justly famous for its cheeses, beers, and flowers, available at specialist stores and super-markets across the country. Amsterdam is a cosmopolitan city, so it is also easy to find a selection of foreign and ethnic goods, from Indonesian beads to French designer wear. The famous brown cafés and coffee shops are an important part of Dutch social life, and visitors to the Netherlands should not miss the chance to try one.

OPENING HOURS

Stores in the Netherlands are usually open from 9 or 10am to 6pm Tuesday to Saturday, and from 1 to 6pm on Monday. In the larger cities, many shops stay open until 9pm on Thursdays and Sundays.

WHERE TO SHOP

Most of Amsterdam's large department and clothing stores are located in the Nieuwe Zijde, along Kalver-straat. The city's best-known department stores are **De Bijenkorf**, often described as the Dutch Harrods, **Metz & Co**, and **Maison de Bonneterie**. Less expensive ones include Vroom & Dreesman and Hema. For luxury fashion, PC Hooft-straat and Van Baerlestraat are lined with chic designer boutiques, such as Gucci, Chanel, and Louis Vuitton.

The streets crossing Amster-dam's Canal Ring, such as Herenstraat and Hartenstraat, contain many specialist stores, selling everything from ethnic fabrics to handmade dolls.

WHAT TO BUY

One famous Dutch export is Delftware, the blue-and-white pottery from Delft *(see p263)*. Only two factories still make it, though imitation pieces are found in tourist stores all over the country. A certification stamp indicates that an article is genuine. In Amsterdam, the **Galleria d'Arte Rinascimento** and **Jorrit Heinen** both stock authentic Delftware.

The Dutch are keen beer drinkers. As well as brand names like Heineken, Grolsch, and Amstel, there are many local specialties, such as Zatte, a rare, bottle-fermented beer, and Wieckse Witte, a

white beer. Specialist store **De Bierkoning** offers the widest choice and best advice.

You can usually buy a good selection of Dutch cheeses at supermarkets, including any branch of **Albert Heijn**, street markets, or specialist food stores. Instead of buying the ubiquitous Edam, try one of the many varieties of Gouda. Mature Gouda has a rich, salty taste and crumbly texture, while young Gouda is fresh and curdy.

Other items for which the Netherlands is famous are flowers, which you can buy at street stalls, markets, and shops, and diamonds. For the latter, visit the diamond-cut-ting center **Gassan Diamonds**.

MARKETS

The Dutch love street trading and almost every town has at least one open-air market. In Amsterdam, the best-known are the Albert Cuypmarkt in Albert Cuypstraat, with a mix of Dutch and ethnic food, cheap clothes, and flowers, and the Waterlooplein flea market, in Oude Zijde. The Looier Kunst en Antiekcen-trum, at No. 109 Elandsgracht, is a covered market boasting the largest collection of art and antiques in the Netherlands. For flowers, visit the market along the Singel, between Konigsplein and Vizelstraat.

ENTERTAINMENT LISTINGS AND TICKETS

For up-to-date listings of events and concerts, the capital's official tourist website www. iamsterdam.com, in English, is a good starting point. *Time Out Amsterdam*, a monthly magazine in English, carries extensive listings and restau-rant reviews. The magazine is

available from most newsagents in the city center.

The main reservations office for entertainment and cultural activities in Amsterdam is the **AUB** (Amsterdam Uitburo). The VVV and Dutch Tourist Information Office will also book tickets for some venues.

ENTERTAINMENT VENUES

Among Amsterdam's many theater venues are the **Theater Bellevue**, the **Stads-schouwburg**, and the **Felix Meritis**. For experimental theater, head for **De Brakke Grond** and other venues located along the street known as the Nes. The **Koninklijk Theater Carré** hosts long-running international musicals.

Dance is an important aspect of cultural life in the Netherlands. The Dutch National Ballet is housed in Amsterdam's large-capacity **Muziektheater**, while experimental dance can be enjoyed at **De Meervaart** and the **Stadsschouwburg**. The **Muziektheater** is also home to the Dutch National Opera.

The focus for Amsterdam's classical music scene is the **Concertgebouw**, home to the celebrated Royal Concertgebouw Orchestra.

The Netherlands has a huge number of jazz venues. In Amsterdam the internationally renowned **Bimhuis**, the **Muziekgebouw aan 't IJ**, and the **Alto Jazz Café** are worth visiting. The North Sea Jazz Festival, held in Rotter-dam in July, attracts some of the biggest names in jazz.

Amsterdammers equate rock and pop with two venues, **Paradiso** and **De Melkweg**, which offer a varied program. Big-name bands also play at Rotterdam's Ahoy and Amsterdam's **Heineken Music Hall** stadiums.

BROWN CAFES AND COFFEE SHOPS

The traditional Dutch "local pub," the brown café, is characterized by dark wooden furnishings, low ceilings, dim lights, and until the ban on smoking in public places was introduced in 2008, a fog of tobacco smoke. It is a friendly place, and often a social focus for the local neighborhood. There are hundreds in Amsterdam, but one of the best is the tiny and characterful **'t Doktertje**.

For many visitors, a stay in the Netherlands is incomplete without a trip to a smoking coffee shop, where cannabis is openly sold and, since the smoking ban was introduced, smoked in designated areas. Though technically illegal, the sale of soft drugs is tolerated by the authorities if it remains discreet. **Siberië** is one of the smaller, more relaxed places in Amsterdam, while **The Bulldog** is more tourist-filled.

CANAL TOURS

There are many operators in Amsterdam offering canal tours. In addition to the daytime sightseeing trips, there are night cruises, which often feature cheese-and-wine refreshments, a stop at a pub, or a romantic candlelit dinner. **Lovers** cruises are the most reasonably-priced, while **P. Kooij** are more upscale.

CYCLING

It is claimed that there are more bicycles in the Netherlands than inhabitants. The endlessly flat landscape and thousands of miles of well-maintained cycle tracks make cycling an extremely popular activity, even within cities. **Yellow Bike** organizes excursions in and around Amsterdam between April and October, while the US-based **Euro-Bike and Walking Tours** arranges week-long tours around the whole country. **Cycletours Holland** has a number of "bike-and-boat" itineraries covering the main regions of interest. For those who wish to do things independently, bicycles can be rented easily from many outlets across the country, and at over 100 train stations. The VVV are able to supply detailed route maps.

DIRECTORY

DEPARTMENT STORES

De Bijenkorf
Dam 1, Amsterdam.
Tel 0900-0919.
Wagenstraat 32, Den Haag.
Tel 0900-0919.
Coolsingel 105, Rotterdam.
Tel 0900-0919.

Maison de Bonneterie
Rokin 140–142,
Amsterdam.
Tel 020-531 3400.
Gravenstraat 2, Den Haag.
Tel 070-330 5300.

Metz & Co
Leidsestraat 34–36,
Amsterdam.
Tel 020-520 7020.

SPECIALIST ITEMS

Albert Heijn
Jodenbreestraat 21,
Amsterdam.
Tel 020-624 1249.

De Bierkoning
Paleisstraat 125,
Amsterdam.
Tel 020-625 2336.

Galleria d'Arte Rinascimento
Prinsengracht 170,
Amsterdam.
Tel 020-622 7509.

Gassan Diamonds
Nieuwe Uilenburgerstraat 173, Amsterdam.
Tel 020-622 5333.

Jorrit Heinen
Muntplein 12, Amsterdam.
Tel 020-623 2271.

ENTERTAINMENT TICKETS

AUB
Leidseplein 26, Amsterdam.
Tel 0900-0191.

ENTERTAINMENT VENUES

Alto Jazz Café
Korte Leidsedwarsstraat
115, Amsterdam.
Tel 020-626 3249.

Bimhuis
Piet Heinkade 3,
Amsterdam.
Tel 020-788 2188.

De Brakke Grond
Vlaams Cultureel Centrum,
Nes 45, Amsterdam.
Tel 020-626 6866.

Concertgebouw
Concertgebouwplein 2–6,
Amsterdam.
Tel 020-671 8345.

Felix Meritis
Keizersgracht 324,
Amsterdam.
Tel 020-623 1311.

Heineken Music Hall & Arena
Boulevard 590,
Amsterdam Zuid Oost.
Tel 0900-6874 242.

Koninklijk Theater Carré
Amstel 115–125,
Amsterdam.
Tel 0900-252 5255.

De Meervaart
Meer en Vaart 300,
Amsterdam.
Tel 020-410 7700.

De Melkweg
Lijnbaansgracht 234a,
Amsterdam.
Tel 020-531 8181.

Muziekgebouw aan 't IJ
Piet Heinkade 1,
Amsterdam.
Tel 020-788 2000.

Het Muziektheater
Amstel 3, Amsterdam.
Tel 020-625 5455.

Paradiso
Weteringschans 6–8,
Amsterdam.
Tel 020-626 4521.

Stadsschouwburg
Leidseplein 26, Amsterdam.
Tel 020-624 2311.

Theater Bellevue
Leidsekade 90,
Amsterdam.
Tel 020-530 5301.

BROWN CAFES & COFFEE SHOPS

't Doktertje
Rozenboomsteeg 4,
Amsterdam.
Tel 020-626 4427.

Siberië
Brouwersgracht 11,
Amsterdam.
Tel 020-623 5909.

The Bulldog
Leidseplein 15, Amsterdam.
Tel 020-627 1908.

CANAL TOURS

Lovers
Opposite Prins Hendrikkade
26, Amsterdam.
Tel 020-530 1090.
www.lovers.nl

P. Kooij
Opposite Rokin 125,
Amsterdam.
Tel 020-623 3810.

CYCLING

Cycletours Holland
Buiksloterweg 7a,
Amsterdam.
Tel 020-521 8490.

Euro-Bike and Walking Tours
PO Box 81025, Billings
MT 59108, USA.
Tel 1-800-321 6060.

Yellow Bike
Nieuwezijds Kolk 29,
Amsterdam.
Tel 020-620 6940.

Where to Stay in the Netherlands

Accommodations in Amsterdam range from luxurious five-star hotels to cheap hostels for those on a budget. In between are scores of B&Bs (bed and breakfasts), many in pretty canal houses, whose interiors are often maintained in period style. Elsewhere in the Netherlands, standards of accommodations are generally high.

PRICE CATEGORIES
The following prices are for a standard double room per night, including breakfast, tax and service.

€ Under €120
€€ €120–€170
€€€ €170–€220
€€€€ €220–€270
€€€€€ Over €270

AMSTERDAM

CENTRAL CANAL RING Dikker & Thijs Fenice Hotel 　　🛗 🍴 ♿ W　　€€€

Prinsengracht 444, 1017 KE **Tel** *020-620 1212* **Fax** *020-625 8986* **Rooms** *42*　　**Map** *C3*

Owned by a publisher, this hotel is proud of its literary connections and the authors who stay here. The 18th-century warehouse building is magnificent, and the decor is smart. Although just moments from Leidseplein, the atmosphere here is resolutely upmarket. All the sights are within walking distance. **www.dtfh.nl**

CENTRAL CANAL RING Ambassade Hotel 　　🛗 🍴 W　　€€€€

Herengracht 341, 1016 AZ **Tel** *020-555 0222* **Fax** *020-555 0277* **Rooms** *58*　　**Map** *C3*

With its long literary associations, this is the bookworm's choice of lodgings: the library is lined with signed copies from the numerous authors who have stayed here. Arranged across ten buildings, rooms are furnished in an unfussy classic way, and bathrooms, though small, are marbled. Staff are discreet and attentive. **www.ambassade-hotel.n**

EASTERN CANAL RING NH Schiller 　　🛗 🍴 ♿ W　　€€€

Rembrandtplein 26–36, 1017 CV **Tel** *020-554 0700* **Fax** *020-624 0098* **Rooms** *92*　　**Map** *D3*

Fun-seekers should look no further than this hotel, with its commanding view over Rembrandtplein. The rooms at the back are not so noisy, and all are decorated with smart furnishings. Brasserie Schiller is very cosy, while the eponymous next-door bar has Art Deco fittings and attracts a media crowd. **www.nh-hotels.com**

MUSEUM QUARTER Stayokay City Hostel Vondelpark 　　🛗 🍴 W　　€

Zandpad 5, 1054 GA **Tel** *020-589 8996* **Fax** *020-589 8955* **Rooms** *150*　　**Map** *B4*

The second Amsterdam outpost of a worthy organization, this hostel on the edge of the Vondelpark is ideal for families and nature lovers. Accommodations range from double rooms to 20-bed dorms, and it is all non-smoking. There is a TV room, and Brasserie Backpackers has a lovely terrace looking onto the park. **www.stayokay.com**

MUSEUM QUARTER De Filosoof 　　🛗 P W　　€€

Anna van den Vondelstraat 6, 1054 GZ **Tel** *020-683 3013* **Fax** *020-685 3750* **Rooms** *38*　　**Map** *A4*

A much-loved hotel on a street off the Vondelpark. Every room here is individually decorated according to a different philosopher or treatise. There is Passion, Wittgenstein or local boy Spinoza, for example. It is a favorite of brooding intellectuals, who make use of the lovely garden and, of course, the library. **www.hotelfilosoof.nl**

NIEUWE ZIJDE Rho Hotel 　　🛗 P W　　€€

Nes 5–23, 1012 KC **Tel** *020-620 7371* **Fax** *020-620 7826* **Rooms** *170*　　**Map** *C3*

Just steps from bustling Dam Square, though tucked down a backstreet bristling with interesting bars, restaurants, and theaters, this hotel is well placed and good value. Its glory days as a gold merchants' office are visible in the beautiful Art Nouveau lobby. Though plain, the rooms are neat and tidy. **www.rhohotel.nl**

NIEUWE ZIJDE NH Barbizon Palace 　　🛗 P 🍴 🛗 W　　€€€

Prins Hendrikkade 59–72, 1012 AD **Tel** *020-556 4564* **Fax** *020-624 3353* **Rooms** *274*　　**Map** *D2*

The jewel in the NH crown, this hotel's public area has sleek black-and-white décor. Facilities are outstanding and include excellent breakfasts, the gourmet Restaurant Vermeer, and a 14th-century chapel serving as one of eight conference rooms. **www.nh-hotels.com**

NIEUWE ZIJDE Grand Hotel Krasnapolsky 　　🛗 P 🍴 ♿ 🛗 W　　€€€€

Dam 9, 1012 JS **Tel** *020-554 9111* **Fax** *020-622 8607* **Rooms** *468*　　**Map** *C2*

The location of this hotel – on Dam Square, overlooking the Koninklijk Paleis – is great. Accommodations range from utter luxury in the Tower Suite to compact rooms at the back. Facilities are top-notch and include restaurants, a café and a cocktail bar. The Winter Garden is where weekend brunches are enjoyed. **www.nh-hotels.com**

OUDE ZIJDE Grand Hôtel Amrâth Amsterdam 　　🍴 ♿ 🖥 🛗 🛗 ♿ W　　€€€€€

Prins Hendrikkade 108–114, 1011 AK **Tel** *020-552 0000* **Fax** *020-552 0900* **Rooms** *163*　　**Map** *D2*

Overlooking the old harbor, this luxury hotel occupies the 1913 Sheepvaarthuis, one of the landmark Amsterdam School buildings. The hotel offers spacious rooms equipped with every comfort. The Seven Seas restaurant serves fine French/international cuisine and a splendid high tea. **www.amrathamsterdam.com**

Key to Symbols *see back cover flap*

PLANTAGE Rembrandt ⓘ Ⓦ €

Plantage Middenlaan 17, 1018 DA **Tel** *020-627 2714* **Fax** *020-638 0293* **Rooms** *17* **Map** *E3*

One of the few cheaper options in this area, this hotel is good for families intent on visiting nearby Artis zoo. Public spaces are covered in flamboyant murals that recall the hotel's namesake, and have dark, wooden furniture. The bedrooms, meanwhile, are brighter and more modern, and all are en suite. **www.hotelrembrandt.nl**

WESTERN CANAL RING Truelove Antiek and Guesthouse Ⓦ €

Prinsenstraat 4, 1015 DC **Tel** *020-320 2500* **Fax** *0847-114 950* **Rooms** *2* **Map** *C2*

A small, two-roomed, romantic bolt hole in the heart of Amsterdam's most interesting shopping area. It is non-smoking, simple and stylish; although there is no breakfast (you are spoiled for choice nearby), there are considerate touches like wine, water, and fresh flowers in the rooms. **www.truelove.be**

WESTERN CANAL RING The Toren ⓘ Ⓦ €€€€

Keizersgracht 164, 1015 CZ **Tel** *020-622 6352* **Fax** *020-626 9705* **Rooms** *37* **Map** *C2*

A stylish place decorated in golds and baroque reds. The Toren boasts a fascinating history: it has been a merchant's house and a university, and it was also used to hide Jews during World War II. On the downside, standard rooms are small, so spend a little extra on a superior: you get extra leg room and a spa bath. **www.thetoren.nl**

REST OF THE NETHERLANDS

APELDOORN Bilderberg Hotel De Keizerskroon ⓘ Ⓟ Ⓤ ⓢ Ⓜ ⓘ Ⓦ €€

Koningstraat 7, 7315 HR **Tel** *055-521 7744* **Fax** *055-521 4737* **Rooms** *93*

A large, popular hotel with good facilities, pleasingly situated on the edge of a park near the Paleis Het Loo. Rooms are spacious, and decorated in trendy citrus and brown shades, with big comfortable beds; the largest rooms have sofas. There's a smart restaurant, a snug bar, and a small swimming pool. **www.bilderberg.nl**

DELFT Hotel de Ark ⓘ Ⓦ €€

Koornmarkt 65, 2611 EC **Tel** *015-215 7999* **Fax** *015-214 4997* **Rooms** *38*

Arranged across four houses beside a bustling canal, De Ark is convenient for the station and city center. Rooms, in bright, fresh colors are well-sized (as are bathrooms), with lovely touches like Delft-tiled fireplaces. The bridal suites boast two-person baths and saunas, and there are also apartments for longer stays. **www.deark.nl**

THE HAGUE Hotel des Indes ⓘ Ⓟ Ⓤ ⓢ Ⓜ ⓘ Ⓦ €€€€

Lange Voorhout 54-56, 2514 EG **Tel** *070-361 2345* **Fax** *070-361 2350* **Rooms** *92*

One of the most famous – and best – in the whole country, this monumental hotel is a luxurious base for exploring the city. Decor references the colonial period with dark heavy wood, swathes of marble and potted palms. Rooms are spacious and well-equipped. **www.hoteldesindes.nl**

HAARLEM Haarlem Hotelsuites Ⓦ €€

Kleine Houtstraat 13, 2011 DD **Tel** *023-540 7146* **Fax** *023-551 8923* **Rooms** *4*

On a restaurant-lined street at the heart of the city, the apartments here are spacious and stylish. They have large living rooms with squashy sofas and bedrooms have comfy big beds; some apartments have private roof terraces. Breakfast is served in the nearby Boulangerie café, or delivered to the apartment. **www.haarlem-hotelsuites.nl**

LEIDEN Pension De Witte Singel Ⓦ €

Witte Singel 80, 2311 BP **Tel** *071-512 4592* **Rooms** *7*

This simple, unpretentious little guesthouse occupies a lovely town house overlooking a canal. There are just seven rooms; the ones at the back have views over the trees in the garden, while the front-facing ones overlook the water. Rooms are clean and tidy, with either private or shared facilities. **www.pension-ws.demon.nl**

ROTTERDAM Hotel New York ⓘ Ⓤ ⓘ Ⓦ €€€

Koninginnenhoofd 1, 3072 AD **Tel** *010-439 0500* **Fax** *010-484 2701* **Rooms** *72*

This monumental hotel in a former shipping-line HQ feels gloriously isolated, though it's near the center. Most rooms are decorated in bold modern designs with lovely bathrooms; the more expensive ones, in the directors' boardrooms, remain untouched, with wood-paneling and chandeliers. **www.hotelnewyork.nl**

UTRECHT Grand Hotel Karel V ⓘ Ⓟ Ⓤ Ⓜ ⓘ Ⓦ €€€

Geertebolwerk 1, 3511 XA **Tel** *030-233 7555* **Fax** *030-233 7500* **Rooms** *121*

The best hotel in the city is housed in a former military building filled with historical detail. The luxurious rooms and suites have great bathrooms, and are arranged across different wings. Amenities are tip-top: a Michelin-starred restaurant, a brasserie, a wine bar, and huge gardens. Breakfasts are excellent. **www.karelv.nl**

VOLENDAM Hotel Restaurant Van den Hogen Ⓟ Ⓤ €

Haven 106, 1131 EV **Tel** *0299-363 775* **Fax** *0299-369 498* **Rooms** *5*

This small hotel is right on the waterfront, close to all the fishing boats, and near the bars and restaurants. Most rooms have views over the IJsselmeer, and are clean and tidy, though decorated in plain, functional style, and all are en suite. There's a cosy, traditional fish restaurant downstairs. **www.hogen.nl**

Map References see map of Amsterdam pp248–9

Where to Eat in the Netherlands

Although the Netherlands does not boast the gastronomic reputation of France or Italy, the chance of finding good food at a reasonable price is high. As well as Dutch restaurants, there are plenty of other establishments serving culinary delights from around the world. Amsterdam, in particular, is full of ethnic restaurants.

PRICE CATEGORIES
The following price ranges are for a three-course meal for one, including half a bottle of wine, plus all unavoidable extra charges, such as cover, service and tax.
€ Under €30
€€ €30–€40
€€€ €40–€50
€€€€ Over €50

AMSTERDAM

CENTRAL CANAL RING Los Pilones
€€

Kerkstraat 63, 1017 GC **Tel** *020-320 4651*   **Map** *C3*

A small cantina run by two Mexican brothers who serve authentic dishes. Los Pilones offers some of the best Mexican food in the whole of Amsterdam. Expect the occasional unusual combination such as *enchiladas* with a chocolate sauce. The pièce de résistance is their huge range of tequilas (around 35). Closed lunch; Mon.

CENTRAL CANAL RING Proeverij 274
€€€

Prinsengracht 274, 1016 HH **Tel** *020-421 1848*   **Map** *B3*

Popular with both locals and visitors to the city, this warm and romantic two-floored restaurant serves classic international dishes made with organic ingredients. Book the round table by the door for a delightful view over the canal. Groups of up to 25 people can be catered for in the downstairs basement. Closed lunch.

EASTERN CANAL RING Bouchon du Centre
€€

Falckstraat 3, 1017 VV **Tel** *020-330 1128*   **Map** *D4*

You will feel like you are having dinner at a friend's house at Bouchon du Centre. Hostess-chef Hanneke van den Bergh creates a fixed three-course meal using produce she has bought fresh from the market and specialist shops. The cuisine is traditional French. Organic wines are chosen to match the food. Closed lunch; Sun–Tue.

EASTERN CANAL RING Beddington's
€€€€

Utrechtsedwarsstraat 141, 1017 WE **Tel** *020-620 7393*   **Map** *D4*

One for discerning taste buds and those in search of slow-paced dining in sober, stylish surroundings. From the open kitchen, British owner/chef Jean Beddington produces seamless French and Asian fusion, with a sprinkling of British sensibility. Delightful desserts and friendly service. Closed lunch; Mon, Sun.

MUSEUM QUARTER Brasserie van Baerle
€€€€

Van Baerlestraat 158, 1071 BG **Tel** *020-679 1532*   **Map** *B4*

This French-style brasserie is particularly popular with Dutch celebrities, especially for lunch and Sunday brunch (when it opens at 10am). Mouth-watering dishes include sea bass with prawn risotto and langoustine cream. Exceptional wine list and gorgeous garden terrace. Booking recommended. Closed Sat lunch.

NIEUWE ZIJDE Brasserie Harkema
€€

Nes 67, 1012 KD **Tel** *020-428 2222*   **Map** *C3*

A classic Parisian brasserie with a stylish New York sensibility, Harkema serves haute cuisine at affordable prices. It is immensely popular, especially in the evenings, so it is wise to book ahead. Feast on delights such as sautéed sole with pinot blanc, lemon and parsley, followed by apple tarte tatin.

NIEUWE ZIJDE De Waaghals
€€

Frans Halsstraat 29, 1012 VA **Tel** *020-679 9609*   **Map** *C3*

Innovative, sophisticated vegetarian dishes are served in an attractive setting; ask for an outside table. There are a number of tasting menus, and the menus change twice a month. Wines are organic and some of the beers are locally brewed. Booking recommended. Closed lunch; Mon.

NIEUWE ZIJDE Kapitein Zeppos
€€€

Gebed Zonder End 5, 1012 HS **Tel** *020-624 2057*   **Map** *C3*

Tucked down a tiny alley, lit by fairy-lights, this bar-restaurant (with Belgian ceramic-tile tables and eclectic ornaments) was once a coach stable, then a cigar factory. The kitchen turns out delicious French-Mediterranean cuisine, with Italian, Moroccan and Spanish influences. Ideal for a romantic evening. Closed Mon.

NIEUWE ZIJDE Supperclub
€€€€

Jonge Roelensteeg 21, 1012 PL **Tel** *020-344 6400*   **Map** *C3*

Remove your shoes and recline on cushioned beds at this restaurant-club. DJs spin upbeat lounge music as you graze on culinary delights from the open kitchen – all spread out over five courses. Fine wines, video art, massage, and offbeat performances complete this assault on the senses. There is also a lounge bar downstairs. Closed lunch.

Key to Symbols *see back cover flap*

OUDE ZIJDE Bridges (The Grand Hotel) 🔥🖼️ €€€€

Oudezijds Voorburgwal 197, 1012 EX **Tel** *020-555 3560* **Map** *C3*

If you can afford it, dine in style at the acclaimed Bridges restaurant. It's Amsterdam's finest seafood spot, and hugely popular with gastronomes. Chef Aurélien Poirot creates innovative Dutch cuisine using fresh, organic ingredients. The wine list is also excellent. Closed lunch.

PLANTAGE La Rive (Amstel Hotel) 🔥 €€€€

Professor Tulpplein 1, 1018 GX **Tel** *020-520 3264* **Map** *D4*

This Michelin-starred restaurant within the Amstel Hotel is one for connoisseurs. Outstanding cuisine from its modern French-Mediterranean kitchen is matched by an excellent wine list. Reserve the chef's table in the kitchen (four to eight people) for an unusual twist to your dining experience. Dress code is elegant. Closed Sat lunch, Sun.

REST OF THE NETHERLANDS

ALKMAAR Roses €

Fnidsen 107, 1811 NE **Tel** *072-515 2606*

Brightly colored Mexican restaurant that offers a reasonably priced and filling menu full of the classics. Alongside favorites like *tacos, enchiladas* and *fajitas*, there are burgers and more refined dishes such as blackened fish and duck breast with tamarind. To accompany, there is a varied menu of cocktails and Mexican beers. Closed lunch.

DELFT Le Vieux Jean 🧍 €€€€

Heilige Geestkerkhof 3, 2611 HP **Tel** *015-213 0433*

This lovely, understated little place near the Nieuwe Kerk looks – and tastes – like a real French restaurant. Polished wood, white linen table cloths, and fine crockery are a fitting setting to show off classics like *coquilles St. Jacques* and lamb chops in butter, rounded off with cheese and a glass of 20-year-old port. Closed Sat lunch; Mon, Sun.

HAARLEM Lambermon's Brasserie En Suites €€

Korte Veerstraat 1, 2011 CL **Tel** *023-542 7804*

Chef Michel Lambermon has created a culinary palace on two floors of a townhouse. In the brasserie diners enjoy platters laden with seafood and charcuterie. The first-floor restaurant has an à la carte menu. The top floor offers ten luxury suites for diners to stay the night. Restaurant closed lunch, Mon & Sun; brasserie closed Mon, lunch Tue.

THE HAGUE Dayang 📋 €

Prinsestraat 65, 2513CB **Tel** *070-364 9979*

This tiny "toko" is thought by many to have some of the best Indonesian food in the The Hague – a real accolade, as the city is famed for that country's cuisine. The authentic food is cheap, but nothing is sacrificed to quality: meat and fish are juicy, and anything served with the spicy peanut sauce is recommended. Closed Mon.

THE HAGUE Bistro Mer 🖼️ €€€€

Javastraat 9, 2585 AB **Tel** *070-360 7389*

Fish, lobster and oysters are the specialty at this restaurant in The Hague's refined embassy district. An abundance of mirrors and the airy conservatory overlooking the courtyard (with outside seating) enhance the experience of the French-influenced food. For dessert, the *crêpes suzettes* with ginger are recommended. Open for lunch Tue–Fri.

LEIDEN City Hall 🧍🔥🖼️ €€

Stadshuisplein 3, 2311 EJ **Tel** *071-514 4055*

A well-priced staple in the basement of the town hall, attracting a cross-section of Leiden's population, from students to businesspeople. The interior is slick, white and space age, and food imaginative Mediterranean: swordfish carpaccio, *mesclun* and goat's cheese salad, giant profiterole with nutty ice cream. Also popular for breakfast and lunch.

ROTTERDAM Kade 4 🧍🖼️ €€

Spaansekade 4, 3011 ML **Tel** *010-270 9001*

On the water's edge in the beautiful Old Harbour in the shadow of the expressionist cube houses, "Quay 4" comes into its own in summer when diners can eat on the water's edge (and it's also pleasant inside). Lunch offers light wraps and salads, while evening meals offer anything from pasta to fish and burgers.

UTRECHT Le Bibelot 🧍🖼️ €€

Oudegracht 181, 3511 NE **Tel** *030-231 3353*

Traditional French food served in the unpretentious surroundings of a friendly, cosy restaurant with canal views in the city center. All the favorites are present, from onion soup to delicious *crêpes suzettes*, and unusually for this kind of restaurant, there is a good choice for vegetarians. The three-course set dinner is excellent value. Closed lunch; Mon.

UTRECHT Goesting 🔥🖼️ €€€€

Veeartsenijpad 150, 3572 DH **Tel** *030-273 3346*

This building was a stable, but is now an upmarket restaurant, with low ceilings and tables nestled in arches. The short menu shows off the kitchen's skills in innovating around formal dishes such as *confit de canard*, grilled lobster, and lamb casserole, using the best ingredients. Closed lunch; Mon, Sun.

Map References *see map of Amsterdam pp248–9*

THE IBERIAN
PENINSULA

The Iberian Peninsula at a Glance

A wonderful, warm climate and superb beaches have made the Iberian Peninsula a popular package-tour destination, drawing millions of visitors to well-known areas such as the Algarve in Portugal, and the Costa del Sol in Spain. But there are also tranquil fishing villages, first-class museums and galleries, and a wealth of splendid architecture, from the grand monuments left by the region's Moorish rulers to ultramodern, 20th-century designs. The Catholic faith has deep roots in Portugal and Spain. As well as spectacular cathedrals, there are many colorful religious festivals that take place all year round, making a visit all the more enjoyable.

0 km 75
0 miles 75

Toledo (see pp296–8) *has one of the largest cathedrals in Christendom, a massive Gothic structure that soars above the rooftops of the perfectly preserved medieval town.*

Oviedo

Lugo

Santiago de Compostela

León

Valladolid

Oporto

Salamanca

PORTUGAL
(See pp352–381)

LISBON

Ciu

Lisbon (see pp356–65) *rises above the estuary of the Tagus on a series of a hills. The oldest part of the city is crowned by the restored battlements of the Castelo de São Jorge.*

Córdob

Seville

Málaga

Seville (see pp328–31) *is regarded as the soul of Andalusia. The city's famous bullring is arguably the finest in the whole of Spain and a perfect venue for a first experience of the corrida, or bullfight.*

◁ The rocky coast of Galicia, northwestern Spain

Madrid (see pp282–92) *is home to some of Europe's greatest art galleries. The Museo del Prado has outstanding collections of paintings by Veláz-quez and Goya, whose statue stands outside the main entrance.*

LOCATOR MAP

• Bilbao
  (Bilbo)

• Pamplona
  (Iruña)

• Zaragoza

• Teruel

SPAIN
(See pp276–351)

• Valencia

• Albacete

• Barcelona

Barcelona (see pp306–15) *is famous for its Modernist buildings, which include Gaudí's unfinished master-piece, the Sagrada Família.*

Maó •

• Palma de
  Mallorca

Ibiza •
(Eivissa)

• Alicante
  (Alacant)

Granada (see pp320 and 322–3), *in the foothills of the snowcapped Sierra Nevada, is unmissable for its Moorish heritage. Its greatest monument is the stunning Alhambra palace.*

The Balearic Islands (see p319) *are often associated with mass tourism, but away from the busy resorts, there are hundreds of unspoiled coastal villages and beautiful coves to be discovered.*

SPAIN

The familiar images of Spain – flamenco dancing, bullfighting, tapas bars, and solemn Easter processions – do no more than hint at the diversity of this country. Spain has four official languages, two major cities of almost equal importance, and a greater range of landscapes than any other European country. These contrasts make Spain an endlessly fascinating place to visit.

Separated from the rest of Europe by the Pyrenees, Spain reaches south to the coast of North Africa, and has both Atlantic and Mediterranean coastlines. The country's climate and scenery vary dramatically, from the snow-capped peaks of the Pyrenees, through the green meadows of Galicia and the orange groves of Valencia, to the dry, barren regions in the south.

Madrid, Spain's capital, lies geographically in the center of the country. The *madrileños* – as the city's inhabitants are known – have an individualistic spirit and a sardonic sense of humor that set them apart from other Spaniards. Madrid may be the nominal capital, but it is rivaled in commerce, sport, and the arts by Barcelona, the main city of Catalonia.

In the last 50 years Spain has undergone more social change than anywhere else in western Europe. In the first half of the 20th century, it was largely a poor, rural country. Gradually people flooded into the cities, leaving the rural areas depopulated. The 1960s saw the beginning of spectacular economic growth, partly due to a burgeoning tourist industry. Since then Spain has become a major player in European and world affairs.

HISTORY

From the 11th century BC the coastal regions of the Iberian Peninsula were colonized by sophisticated eastern Mediterranean civilizations, starting with the Phoenicians, then the Greeks and the Carthaginians. Celts mixed with native Iberian tribes, forming the Celtiberians. The Romans arrived in 218 BC to take possession of the peninsula's huge mineral wealth. The fall of the Roman Empire in the 5th century AD left Spain in the hands of the Visigoths, invaders from the north. Their poor political organization,

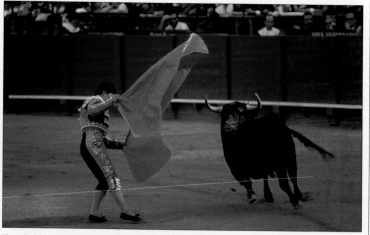

The colorful art of bullfighting, still a strong tradition all over Spain

◁ View from a typical hilltop Castilian town across the vast plains of central Spain

The Moor Boabdil surrendering Granada to the Catholic Monarchs

however, meant they were easily conquered by the Moors, who arrived from North Africa around 711.

Within a few years the Moors controlled almost the entire peninsula. Europe's only major Muslim territory, the civilization of Al Andalus excelled in mathematics, geography, astronomy, and poetry, and by the 9th century Córdoba was Europe's leading city.

In the 11th century, northern Christian kingdoms initiated a military reconquest of Al Andalus. The marriage, in 1469, of Fernando of Aragón and Isabel of Castile – the so-called Catholic Monarchs – led to Spanish unity. They took Granada, the last Moorish stronghold, in 1492. In the same year Columbus discovered the Americas, and the conquistadors began plundering the civilizations of the New World.

The 17th century was a golden age for Spain – a time of outstanding artistic and literary output. This brilliance occurred, however, against a backdrop of economic deterioration and ruinous wars with France and the Low Countries. Spain's misfortunes continued in the 19th century, with an invasion by Napoleon's troops, leading to the War of Independence (Peninsular War). In the course of this century, Spain also lost all her South and Central American colonies.

The late 19th century was a time of national decline, with anarchism developing as a response to rampant political corruption. Political instability led to

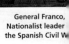

General Franco, Nationalist leader the Spanish Civil W

dictatorship in the 1920s and, a decade later, the Spanish Civil War. The victor, the Nationalist General Franco, ruled by repression until his death in 1975. Since then Spain has been a democratic state.

KEY DATES IN SPANISH HISTORY

1100 BC Arrival of Phoenicians, first in a wave of settlers from across the Mediterranean

218–202 BC Romans oust Carthaginians from southeastern Spain

5th century AD Visigoths take control of Spain

711 Moors invade Spain and defeat Visigoths

756 Independent emirate established at Córdoba; Moorish civilization flourishes

11th century Christian kingdoms begin reconquest of Moorish territories

1492 Catholic Monarchs capture Granada, last Moorish stronghold. Columbus reaches America

1561 Madrid becomes capital of Spain

17th century Spain's Golden Age

1808–14 Spanish War of Independence

1898 Spain loses her last American colony, Cuba

1936–9 Spanish Civil War; Nationalist General Franco emerges victor

1975 Death of Franco; restoration of Bourbon monarchy as Juan Carlos I is proclaimed king

1986 Spain joins the EC (now EU)

1992 Barcelona hosts the Olympic Games

2000 Spain celebrates 25 years of democracy

2004 Nearly 200 people die in terrorist bomb attacks on trains in Madrid

DEVELOPMENT AND DIPLOMACY

After the death of the dictator General Franco in 1975, Spain became a constitutional monarchy under King Juan Carlos I. The post-Franco era, up until the mid-1990s, was dominated by the Socialist Prime Minister Felipe González, whose party, PSOE, was responsible for major improvements in roads, education, and health services. Spain's entry to the European Community in 1986 triggered a spectacular increase in the country's prosperity. Its international reputation was given a further boost in 1992 when Barcelona hosted the Olympic Games and Seville was the site of Expo '92.

With the establishment of democracy, the 17 autonomous regions of Spain have acquired considerable powers. A significant number of Basques favor independence for the Basque Country. The Basque terrorist group ETA, and its campaign of violence, has been one of the major problems facing the government, headed by José Luis Rodríguez Zapatero of the Socialist Workers' Party.

RELIGION, LANGUAGE, AND CULTURE

Following the Christian Reconquest in the Middle Ages, a succession of rulers tried to impose a common culture, but today Spain remains a culturally diverse nation. Several regions have maintained a strong sense of their own identities. Catalonia, the Basque Country, Valencia, the Balearic Islands, and Galicia have their own languages, which are in everyday use, and, in some cases, have supplanted Castilian as the first language of the region.

During the Middle Ages Spain gained a reputation for religious intolerance. The Inquisition, established by the Catholic Monarchs, saw thousands of non-Catholics tortured, executed, or expelled from the country. Today, Spain enjoys complete religious freedom. Catholicism is becoming a less powerful influence in society but saints' days and other important events in the Christian calendar are still marked by many traditional ceremonies, enthusiastically maintained in towns and villages throughout modern Spain.

Religious procession in a Seville street during *Semana Santa* (Holy Week)

THE SPANISH WAY OF LIFE

The Spanish are known for their natural sociability and zest for living. They commonly put as much energy into enjoying life as they do into their work. The stereotypical "mañana" ("leave it until tomorrow") is a myth, but many people fit their work around the demands of their social life, rather than be ruled by the clock. The day is long in Spain, and the Spanish have a word, *madrugada*, for the time between midnight and dawn, when city streets are often still full of revelers enjoying themselves. Eating out is an important social activity, with friends and family often meeting up in a pavement café or restaurant for a chat and a meal.

Underpinning Spanish society is the extended family. In the past, a lack of efficient public services has forced the Spanish to rely on close relatives, rather than institutions, to find work or seek assistance in a crisis. It is not uncommon for three generations to live under one roof, and even life-long city dwellers refer fondly to their *pueblo* – the town or village where their family comes from, and which they return to as often as they can.

Spaniards socializing over drinks and a meal at a sidewalk café

Exploring Spain

Although many visitors to Spain come for the beaches alone, increasingly tourists are drawn by the country's rich cultural heritage. The most popular destinations are Madrid and Barcelona, which boast world-class museums and a wealth of medieval and modern architecture. For those with time to travel further afield, Seville, Granada, and Córdoba in the far south are the best places to see relics of Spain's Moorish past. Spain is Europe's third largest country, so getting around can be time-consuming. However, there is a reliable network of trains, as well as good highways and bus services.

Ciutadella harbor, on the island of Menorca, at twilight

DISTANCE CHART

Distance in kilometers
Distance in miles

MADRID								
621 / 388	BARCELONA							
397 / 248	**620** / 388	BILBAO						
400 / 250	**908** / 568	**795** / 497	CÓRDOBA					
544 / 340	**997** / 623	**939** / 587	**187** / 117	MALAGA				
623 / 389	**1129** / 706	**707** / 442	**977** / 611	**1153** / 721	PONTEVEDRA			
538 / 336	**1046** / 654	**933** / 583	**138** / 86	**219** / 137	**922** / 576	SEVILLE		
352 / 220	**349** / 218	**633** / 396	**545** / 341	**648** / 405	**975** / 609	**697** / 436	VALENCIA	
325 / 203	**296** / 185	**324** / 203	**725** / 453	**869** / 543	**833** / 521	**863** / 539	**326** / 204	ZARAGOZA

The Giralda in Seville, a legacy of Spain's Moorish rulers

KEY

- ✈ Airport
- ⛴ Ferry port
- — Highway
- — Major road
- — Railroad
- -·- International border

0 kilometers 80
0 miles 80

Madrid ❶

Spain's capital, a city of over three million people, is situated close to the geographical center of the country, at the hub of both road and rail networks. The origins of the city date back to AD 852, when the Moors built a fortress near the Manzanares river and a small community grew up around it. It was not until 1561, however, that the city became the capital of a newly formed nation-state. In the following centuries, under the Habsburgs and then the Bourbons, the city acquired some of its most notable landmarks, including the splendid Plaza Mayor and the Palacio Real. At the same time, the blossoming city attracted some of Spain's most outstanding artists, such as court painters Velázquez and Goya, whose works can be admired in the world-famous Museo del Prado.

19th-century *taberna* (taverna), one of the few left in Madrid today

KEY

- 🟩 Sight / Place of interest
- ✈ Airport
- 🚆 Train station
- Ⓜ Metro station
- 🚌 Main bus stop
- 🅿 Parking
- ℹ Tourist information
- ✝ Church
- — Pedestrian street

GETTING AROUND

The Metro is the most efficient way of getting around. Lines 1, 2, 3, 5, and 10 serve the main sights; lines 1 and 2 are good for getting to the museums around the Paseo del Prado. Line 8 links Nuevos Ministerios and the airport. Useful buses include the 50, 51, 52, 53, and 150 to the Puerta del Sol, and 2, 8, 14, 15, 27, 74, and 146 to the Plaza de Cibeles. Buses to Barajas airport depart the terminal below Plaza de Colón.

SEE ALSO

- *Where to Stay* pp340–41
- *Where to Eat* pp346–7

GREATER MADRID

KEY

■ Area of main map

SIGHTS AT A GLANCE

Centro de Arte
Reina Sofía ⑨
Gran Vía ④
Monasterio de las
Descalzas Reales ③
Museo Arqueológico
Nacional ⑪
Museo del Prado
pp288–90 ⑦
Museo Thyssen-
Bornemisza ⑧
Palacio Real ⑤
Parque del Retiro ⑩
Plaza Mayor ②
Puerta del Sol ①
El Rastro ⑥

Greater Madrid
(see inset map)
Museo de América ⑫
Plaza de Toros de
las Ventas ⑬

The beautiful 17th-century Plaza
Mayor, at the heart of Old Madrid

Old Madrid

When Felipe II chose Madrid as his capital in 1561, it was a small Castilian town of little importance. In the following years, it was to grow into the nerve center of a mighty empire. During the reign of the Habsburg dynasty, many royal monasteries, churches, and private palaces were built. In the 17th century the Plaza Mayor was added, and the Puerta del Sol became the spiritual and geographical heart not only of Madrid but of all Spain. Old Madrid's splendid Bourbon palace, the Palacio Real, was built under Felipe V in the first half of the 18th century.

Bear and strawberry tree, the symbol of Madrid, Puerta del Sol

Puerta del Sol ①

Ⓜ *Sol.*

With its many shops and cafés, the Puerta del Sol ("Gateway of the Sun") is one of Madrid's liveliest areas attracting huge crowds. The square marks the site of the original eastern entrance to the city, once occupied by a gatehouse and a castle.

A statue of Carlos III (reigned 1759–88) stands at the center of the square. On its southern edge is the austere Casa de Correos, dating from the 1760s. Originally the city's post office, it later became the headquarters of the Ministry of the Interior. During the Franco regime, the police cells below the building were the site of human rights abuses. Outside the building, a symbol on the ground marks Kilometer Zero, considered the center of Spain's road network.

On the opposite side of the square is a bronze statue of the symbol of Madrid – a bear reaching for the fruit of a *madroño* (strawberry tree).

The Puerta del Sol has witnessed many important historical events. On May 2, 1808 the uprising against the occupying French forces began in the square, and in 1912 the liberal prime minister José Canalejas was assassinated here.

Plaza Mayor ②

Ⓜ *Sol.*

For hundreds of years this beautiful 17th-century square was a center of activity, with bullfights, executions, pageants, and trials by the Inquisition taking place here.

The first great public event was the beatification of the city's patron, St. Isidore, in 1621. Perhaps the greatest occasion, however, was the arrival from Italy of Carlos III (Carlos VII of Naples) in 1760. He became king of Spain after his half-brother, Fernando VI, died without an heir.

Facade of the Casa de la Panadería on the Plaza Mayor

Designed by architect Juan Gómez de Mora, the square was started in 1617 and built in just two years. At its center is an equestrian statue of Felipe III, who ordered the square's construction.

The elegant arcades that line the Plaza Mayor are today filled with cafés and craft shops. One of the more interesting buildings is the Casa de la Panadería, whose facade is decorated with splendid allegorical paintings.

On Sundays the square is the venue for a collectors' market, with stalls selling coins, stamps, books, and other items.

Decorated chapel, Monasterio de las Descalzas Reales

Monasterio de las Descalzas Reales ③

Plaza de las Descalzas 3. **Tel** 91-454 88 03. Ⓜ *Sol, Callao.* ⏰ *10:30am–1:30pm, 4–6:30pm Tue–Thu & Sat, 10:30am–1:30pm Fri, 11am–2:30pm Sun & public hols.* ⏰ *Jan 1 & 6, 3 days after Easter, May 1 & 15, Sep 9, Nov 9, Dec 24, 25 & 31.* 🎟 *(except Wed for EU residents).* 📷 **www**.*patrimonionacional.es*

This religious building is a rare surviving example of 16th-century architecture in Madrid. Around 1560, Felipe II's sister, Doña Juana, decided to convert a medieval palace on this site into a convent.

Doña Juana's rank accounts for the massive store of art amassed by the Descalzas Reales (Royal Barefoot Sisters) which includes a fresco of

The vast Palacio Real, Madrid's 18th-century Bourbon palace

Felipe IV's family and, above the main staircase, a ceiling by Claudio Coello. The Sala de Tapices contains stunning tapestries, while paintings on display include works by Brueghel the Elder, Titian, Zurbarán, Murillo, and Ribera.

Gran Vía ④

Ⓜ *Plaza de España, Santo Domingo, Callao, Gran Vía.*

A main traffic artery of the modern city, the Gran Vía was inaugurated in 1910.

Lined with cinemas, tourist shops, hotels, and restaurants, this grand avenue also has many buildings of architectural interest. At the Alcalá end of the street, the French-inspired Edificio Metrópolis and the Edificio la Estrella (No. 10) are both worth seeing. The latter is a good example of the eclectic mix of Neoclassical design and ornamental detail

One of the many 1930s Art Deco buildings lining the Gran Vía

that was fashionable when the street was first developed. Look out for some interesting carved stone decoration, such as the striking gargoyle-like caryatids at No. 12.

Further along the Gran Vía, around the Plaza del Callao, are a number of Art Deco buildings, including the well-known Capitol cinema and bingo hall, built in the 1930s.

Palacio Real ⑤

Calle de Bailén. ***Tel*** 91-454 88 00.
www.patrimonionacional.es
Ⓜ *Ópera, Plaza de España.* 🚌 *3, 25, 33, 39, 148.* ⬜ *Apr–Sep: 9am–7pm Mon–Sat, 9am–4pm Sun & hols; Oct–Mar: 10am–6pm Mon–Sat, 10am–4pm Sun & hols.* ⬤ *Jan 1 & 6, May 1 & 15, Sep 9, Dec 24, 25 & 31.* 🎟 *(except Wed & Thu pm for EU residents.)* 🗺 ⌂ ♿ ▯

Madrid's vast and lavish Palacio Real (Royal Palace) was commissioned by Felipe V after the royal fortress that had occupied the site for centuries was ravaged by fire in 1734. The palace was the home of Spanish royalty until the abdication of Alfonso XIII in 1931. Today it is used by the present king for state occasions only.

The exuberant decor of the interior reflects the tastes of the Bourbon kings, Carlos III and Carlos IV. The walls and ceiling of the Porcelain Room, commissioned by the former, are covered in green and white royal porcelain, which is embossed with cherubs and wreaths. Named after its Neapolitan designer, the

Gasparini Room is equally lavishly decorated. In the adjacent antechamber hangs a portrait of Carlos IV by Goya. Other star attractions are the Dining Room, with its fine ceiling paintings and superb Flemish tapestries, and the 18th-century Throne Room.

Shoppers browsing around the Rastro flea market

El Rastro ⑥

Calle de la Ribera de Curtidores.
Ⓜ *La Latina, Embajadores.*
⬜ *10am–2pm Sun & public hols.*

Madrid's famous flea market was established in the Middle Ages. Its heyday came in the 19th century, but today there are still plenty of locals, as well as tourists, who come to the Calle de la Ribera de Curtidores to browse around the many stalls selling a huge range of wares – from new furniture to second-hand clothes. The market's other main street is the Calle de Embajadores, which runs down past the dusty Baroque facade of the Iglesia de San Cayetano.

Street-by-Street: Paseo del Prado

Banco de España sculpture

In the late 18th century, before the museums and lavish hotels of Bourbon Madrid took shape, the Paseo del Prado was laid out and soon became a fashionable spot for strolling. Today the Paseo's main attraction lies in its museums and art galleries. Most notable are the Museo del Prado (just south of the Plaza Cánovas del Castillo) and the Museo Thyssen-Bornemisza, both displaying world-famous collections of paintings. Among the monuments built under Carlos III are the Puerta de Alcalá, the Fuente de Neptuno, and the Fuente de Cibeles, which stand in the middle of busy roundabouts.

Paseo del Prado
Based on the Piazza Navona in Rome, the Paseo was built by Ca III as a center for the arts and sciences in Madrid.

Banco de España
Spain's central reserve bank is housed in this massive building with three facades at the Plaza de Cibeles.

Banco de España

★ Museo Thyssen-Bornemisza
Petrus Christus's Our Lady of the Dry Tree *(c.1450) is one of many early Flemish works in this excellent art collection* (see p291).

Tourist information ↓

The Congreso de los Diputados, home of the Spanish parliament, witnessed the country's transition from dictatorship to democracy.

The Plaza de Neptuno is dominated by a sculpted fountain of the god Neptune in his chariot.

STAR SIGHTS

* ★ Museo Thyssen-Bornemisza
* ★ Puerta de Alcalá
* ★ Plaza de Cibeles

Hotel Palace

Muse del Prad

0 meters	100
0 yards	100

Palacio de Linares
This grandly decorated late 19th-century palace now houses the Casa de América, an organization that promotes Latin American culture.

Palacio de Comunicaciones

★ Puerta de Alcalá
Sculpted from granite, this former gateway into the city is especially beautiful when floodlit at night.

CALLE DE ALCALÁ

PLAZA DE LA

INDEPENDENCIA

CALLE DE ALFONSO XI

CALLE DE MONTALBAN

★ Plaza de Cibeles
A fountain with a statue of the Roman goddess Cybele stands in this square.

The Museo Nacional de Artes Decorativas was founded in 1912 as a showcase for Spanish ceramics and interior design.

CALLE ANTONIO MAURA

→ **Parque del Retiro**

A DE LA LEALTAD

RUIZ DE ALARCON

ALLE FELIPE IV

The Hotel Ritz, with its *belle-époque* interior, is one of the most elegant hotels in the whole of Spain.

The Monumento del Dos de Mayo commemorates the War of Independence against the French.

KEY

 Suggested route

Salón de Reinos
This part of the old Retiro Palace has some halls decorated by Velázquez. It is now part of the Prado Museum.

Museo del Prado ⑦

The Prado Museum houses the world's greatest assembly of Spanish paintings from the 12th to the 19th centuries, including major works by Velázquez and Goya. It also houses impressive foreign collections, particularly of Italian and Flemish works. The Neoclassical building was designed in 1785 by Juan de Villanueva on the orders of Carlos III. In 2006, a fully refurbished Casón del Buen Retiro and a new building in the cloisters on San Jéronimo's church opened to the public. In 2009 the former army museum (Salón de Reinos) also became part of the Prado.

★ Velázquez Collection
The Triumph of Bacchus *(1629), Velázquez's first portrayal of a mythological subject, shows the god of wine (Bacchus) with a group of drunkards.*

The Martyrdom of St. Philip
(c.1639)
The Valencian José de Ribera moved to Naples as a young man. He was influenced by Caravaggio's use of light and shadow, known as chiaroscuro, as seen in this work.

The Garden of Delights *(c.1505)*
Hieronymus Bosch, known as El Bosco in Spanish, was one of Felipe II's favorite artists, and is especially well represented in the Prado. This enigmatic painting is part of a triptych depicting paradise and hell.

Main entrance

STAR EXHIBITS

★ Velázquez Collection

★ Goya Collection

The museum's facade, dating from the 18th century, illustrates the Neoclassical move towards dignity away from the excesses of Baroque architecture.

Ticket office

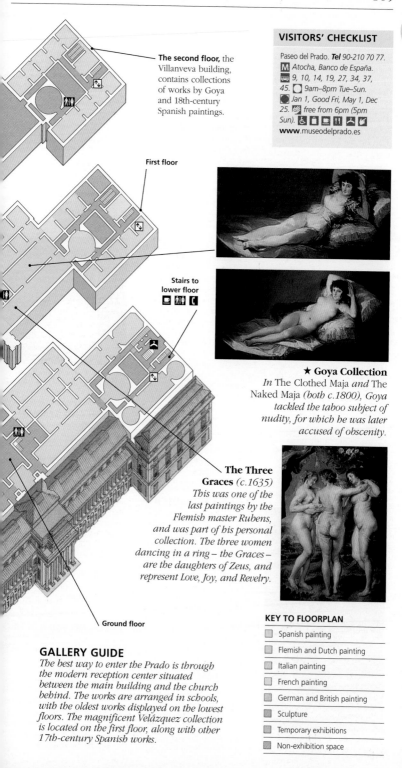

The second floor, the Villanveva building, contains collections of works by Goya and 18th-century Spanish paintings.

First floor

Stairs to lower floor

VISITORS' CHECKLIST

Paseo del Prado. *Tel* 90-210 70 77.
Ⓜ Atocha, Banco de España.
🚌 9, 10, 14, 19, 27, 34, 37, 45. 🕐 9am–8pm Tue–Sun.
🕐 Jan 1, Good Fri, May 1, Dec 25. 🎫 free from 6pm (5pm Sun). ♿📷📖🍴🎨🎁
www.museodelprado.es

★ **Goya Collection**
In The Clothed Maja *and* The Naked Maja *(both c.1800), Goya tackled the taboo subject of nudity, for which he was later accused of obscenity.*

The Three Graces *(c.1635)*
This was one of the last paintings by the Flemish master Rubens, and was part of his personal collection. The three women dancing in a ring – the Graces – are the daughters of Zeus, and represent Love, Joy, and Revelry.

Ground floor

GALLERY GUIDE
The best way to enter the Prado is through the modern reception center situated between the main building and the church behind. The works are arranged in schools, with the oldest works displayed on the lowest floors. The magnificent Velázquez collection is located on the first floor, along with other 17th-century Spanish works.

KEY TO FLOORPLAN

- Spanish painting
- Flemish and Dutch painting
- Italian painting
- French painting
- German and British painting
- Sculpture
- Temporary exhibitions
- Non-exhibition space

Exploring the Prado's Collection

The importance of the Prado is founded on its royal collections. The wealth of foreign art, including many of Europe's finest works, reflects the historical power of the Spanish crown. The Low Countries and parts of Italy were under Spanish rule for hundreds of years. The 18th century was an era of French influence, following the Bourbon accession to the Spanish throne. The Prado is worthy of repeated visits, but if you go only once, see the Spanish works of the 17th century.

SPANISH PAINTING

Right up to the 19th century, Spanish painting focused on religious and royal themes. There are a few examples of Spain's early medieval art in the Prado, such as the anonymous mural paintings from the Holy Cross hermitage in Maderuelo. Spanish Gothic art can be seen in the works of Bartolomé Bermejo and Fernando Gallego.

Renaissance features began to emerge in the paintings of Pedro de Berruguete and Fernando Yáñez de la Alme-dina, whose work shows the influence of Leonardo da Vinci. Among examples of 16th-century Mannerism are paintings by Pedro Machuca and Luis de Morales "the Divine". One of the great masters of this period was the Cretan-born artist El Greco, who made his home in Toledo. The distortion of the human figure, typical of the Mannerist style, is carried to extreme in his painting *The Adoration of the Shepherds* (1612–14).

The Golden Age of the 17th century produced such great artists as José de Ribera and Francisco de Zurbarán. Works by both are on display in the Prado. This period, however, is best represented by the work of Diego Velázquez, Spain's leading court painter. Examples of his royal portraits and religious and mythological paintings are displayed, including his masterpiece *Las Meninas* (1656), a portrait of the Infanta Margarita surrounded by her courtiers.

Another great Spanish painter, Francisco de Goya, revived Spanish art in the 18th century. His later work embraces the horrors of war, as seen in *The 3rd of May* (1814), and culminated in a somber series known as *The Black Paintings*.

FLEMISH AND DUTCH PAINTING

Exceptional Flemish works of art include Rogier van der Weyden's masterpiece, *The Deposition* (c.1430), and some of Hieronymus Bosch's major paintings, such as the *Temptation of St. Anthony* (c.1500) and *The Haywain* (c.1485–90). Among the 16th-century paintings is the superb *Triumph of Death* (1562) by Brueghel the Elder. There are nearly 100 canvases by the 17th-century Flemish painter Peter Paul Rubens, of which the greatest is *The Adoration of the Magi*. The two most notable Dutch paintings on display are both by Rembrandt: *Artemisia* (c.1500) and a fine self-portrait.

The Adoration of the Shepherds (1612–14) by El Greco

ITALIAN PAINTING

The most remarkable Italian paintings are Botticelli's dramatic wooden panels that depict *The Story of Nastagio degli Onesti*, Raphael's *Christ Falls on the Way to Calvary* (1516), and *Christ Washing the Disciples' Feet* (c.1547) by Tintoretto. Venetian masters Titian – Charles V's court painter – and Veronese are equally well represented. Also on display are works by Giordano, Fra Angelico, Caravaggio, and Tiepolo, master of Italian Rococo.

Fra Angelico's *The Annunciation* (c.1430), from the Early Renaissance

FRENCH AND GERMAN PAINTING

Marriages between French and Spanish royalty in the 17th century brought French art to Spain. This section contains a selection of works by Poussin, Jean Ranc, Claude Lorrain, and Antoine Watteau.

German art is represented by Albrecht Dürer's lively *Self-Portrait* (1498), as well as by the works of Lucas Cranach and the late 18th-century court painter Anton Raffael Mengs.

CASON DEL BUEN RETIRO

The Casón is a study center, housing restoration studios, a specialist school, and an art library. On weekends there are guided visits of the dome painted by Luca Giordano. You will need to ask for permission to use the art library, as it is otherwise closed to the public.

Spacious interior of the Museo Thyssen-Bornemisza

influential artists as Picasso, Salvador Dalí, Joan Miró, and Eduardo Chillida. There is also space dedicated to post-World War II movements, such as Abstract, Pop, and Minimal Art.

The highlight of the collection is Picasso's *Guernica* (1937). This Civil War protest painting was inspired by the mass air attack in 1937 on the Basque village of Gernika by German pilots flying for the Nationalist air force.

Museo Thyssen-Bornemisza ⑧

Paseo del Prado 8. **Tel** 90-276 05 11.
Ⓜ *Banco de España, Sevilla.* 🚌 *1, 2, 5, 9, 14, 15, 20.* 🕐 *10am–7pm Tue–Sun (to 11pm on Sat for temporary exhibitions).* 🌑 *Jan 1, May 1, Dec 25.* 🌐 www.museothyssen.org

This magnificent museum houses a collection of art assembled by Baron Heinrich Thyssen-Bornemisza and his son, Hans Heinrich. From its beginnings in the 1920s, the collection was intended to illustrate the history of Western art, from the 14th to the 20th century. Among the museum's exhibits are masterpieces by Titian, Goya, and Van Gogh.

The series of Dutch and Flemish works is a strong point of the collection. Highlights include Jan van Eyck's *The Annunciation* (c.1435–41), Petrus Christus's *Our Lady of the Dry Tree* (c.1450), and *The Toilet of Venus* (c.1629)

by Peter Paul Rubens. On the ground floor are two temporary exhibition galleries, with free access. There is also a café/restaurant.

An extension has joined the museum to two adjacent buildings in order to better display its collection of Impressionist works, mainly from the 19th century.

Centro de Arte Reina Sofía ⑨

Calle Santa Isabel 52. **Tel** 91-774 10 00. Ⓜ *Atocha.* 🚌 *6, 8, 10, 14, 19, 27, 45, 55, 60, 78.* 🕐 *10am–9pm Mon, Wed–Sat, 10am–2:30pm Sun.* 🌑 *Tue, main public hols.* 🌐 *(free from 7pm weekdays, Sat pm & Sun).* www.museoreinasofia.es

Housed in an 18th-century former general hospital with three additional modern glass buildings, this superb museum traces art through the 20th-century. It houses major works by such

Parque del Retiro ⑩

Ⓜ *Retiro, Ibiza, Atocha.* 🕐 *daily.* www.parquedelretiro.es

The Retiro Park formed part of Felipe IV's royal palace complex. All that remains of the palace is the Casón del Buen Retiro (now part of the Prado museum) and the Salón de Reinos (the former army museum). In 2008 the latter moved to the Alcázar in Toledo *(see p298)*.

First fully opened to the public in 1869, the Retiro remains a popular place for relaxing in Madrid. The park has a pleasure lake, where rowing boats can be hired. On one side of the lake, in front of a half-moon colonnade, stands an equestrian statue of Alfonso XII.

To the south of the lake are two attractive palaces. The Neoclassical Palacio de Velázquez and the Palacio de Cristal (Crystal Palace) were built by Velázquez Bosco in 1887 as exhibition venues.

Colonnade and statue of Alfonso XII (1901) overlooking the Parque del Retiro's boating lake

For hotels and restaurants in this region see pp340–41 and pp346–7

Roman floor mosaic in the Museo Arqueológico Nacional

Museo Arqueológico Nacional ⑪

Calle Serrano 13. **Tel** 91-577 79 12.
Ⓜ Serrano, Retiro. 🚌 1, 9, 19, 51, 74.
◯ 9:30am–8pm (6:30pm Jul & Aug)
Tue–Sat, 9:30am–3pm Sun. ◉ main
public hols. 📷 ♿ http://man.mcu.es

Founded by Isabel II in 1867, Madrid's National Archaeological Museum has hundreds of fascinating exhibits, ranging from the pre-historic era to the 19th century.

One of the highlights of the prehistoric section is the exhibition on the ancient civilization of El Argar (1800–1100 BC) – an advanced agrarian society that flourished in southeast Spain. There is also a display of jewelry uncovered at the Roman settlement of Numantia, near Soria, and a 5th-century BC bust of *La Dama de Elche*.

The museum's ground floor is largely devoted to the period between Roman and Mudéjar Spain, and contains some impressive Roman mosaics.

Outstanding pieces from the Visigothic period include a collection of 7th-century gold votive crowns from Toledo province, known as the Treasure of Guarrazar.

Also on show are examples of Andalusian pottery from the Islamic era and various Romanesque exhibits, among them an ivory crucifix carved in 1063 for King Fernando I. Steps outside the museum's entrance lead underground to

an exact replica of the Altamira caves in Cantabria – complete with their Paleolithic paintings. The earliest engravings and drawings date back to around 18,000 BC. The boldly colored bison paintings date from around 13,000 BC.

Museo de América ⑫

Avenida de los Reyes Católicos 6.
Tel 91-549 26 41. Ⓜ Moncloa.
◯ 10am–8:30pm Tue–Sat,
10am–3pm Sun. ◉ some public
hols. 📷 (free on Sun). ♿
http://museodeamerica.mcu.es

This fine museum houses a collection of artifacts relating to Spain's colonization of the Americas. Many of the exhibits, which date back to prehistoric times, were brought to Europe by the early explorers of the New World. The collection is arranged thematically, with individual rooms on, for

example, society, religion, and communication. One of the highlights of the museum is the rare Mayan *Códice Tro-cortesiano* (AD 1250–1500) from Mexico – a hieroglyphic parchment illustrated with scenes of everyday life. Also worth seeing are the Treasure of the Quimbayas, pre-Columbian gold and silver items dating from AD 500–1000, and the display of contemporary folk art from some of Spain's former American colonies.

Plaza de Toros de las Ventas ⑬

Calle Alcalá 237. **Tel** 91-356 22 00.
Ⓜ Ventas. ◯ for bullfights & guided visits only. **Museo Taurino**
Tel 91-725 18 57. ◯ 9:30am–2:30pm Tue–Fri, 10am–1pm Sun
(Nov–Feb: 9:30am–2:30pm Mon–Fri).
📷 daily (91-556 9237). ♿
www.las-ventas.com

Las Ventas is undoubtedly one of the most beautiful bullrings in Spain. Built in 1929 in Neo-Mudéjar style, it replaced the city's original bullring which stood near the Puerta de Alcalá. Outside the bullring are monuments to two famous bullfighters: Antonio Bienvenida and José Cubero.

Adjoining the building, the **Museo Taurino** contains bullfighting memorabilia, such as portraits and sculptures of famous matadors. There is also a display of the tools of the bullfighter's trade, including capes and *banderillas* – sharp darts used to wound the bull *(see opposite)*.

Plaza de Toros de Las Ventas, Madrid's magnificent bullring

The Art of Bullfighting

Bullfighting is a sacrificial ritual in which men (and a few women) pit themselves against an animal bred for the ring. In this "authentic religious drama," as the poet Federico García Lorca described it, the spectator experiences the same intensity of fear and exaltation as the matador. There are three stages, or *tercios*, in the *corrida* (bullfight). The first two, which involve a team of men both on horseback and

Poster for a bullfight

on foot, are aimed at progressively weakening the bull. In the third, the matador moves in for the kill. Despite opposition on the grounds of cruelty, bullfighting is still very popular. For many Spaniards, the *toreo*, the art of bullfighting, is a noble part of their heritage. However, fights today are often debased by practises designed to disadvantage the bull, in particular shaving its horns to make them blunt.

The *toro bravo* (fighting bull), *bred for courage and aggression, enjoys a full life prior to its time in the ring. Bulls must be at least four years old before they can fight.*

Manolete *is regarded by most followers of bullfighting as one of Spain's greatest matadors ever. He was finally gored to death by the bull Islero at Linares, Jaén, in 1947.*

The matador wears a *traje de luces* (suit of lights), a colorful silk outfit embroidered with gold sequins.

Joselito *was a leading matador, famous for his purist style. He displayed superb skill with the* capote *(red cape) and the* muleta *(matador's stick). Following a short retirement, he has returned to the* ruedos *(bullring).*

Banderillas, barbed darts, are thrust into the bull's back muscles to weaken them.

THE BULLRING

The audience at a bullfight is seated in the *tendidos* (stalls) or in the *palcos* (balcony), where the *presidencia* (president's box) is situated. Opposite are the *puerta de cuadrillas*, through which the matador and team arrive, and the *arrastre de toros* (exit for bulls). Before entering the ring, the matadors wait in a *callejón* (corridor) behind *barreras* and *burladeros* (barriers). Horses are kept in the *patio de caballos* and the bulls in the *corrales*.

Plan of a typical bullring

KEY

- Tendidos
- Palcos
- Presidencia
- Puerta de cuadrillas
- Arrastre de toros
- Callejón
- Barreras
- Burladeros
- Patio de caballos
- Corrales

Central Spain

Much of Spain's vast central plateau, the *meseta*, is covered with wheat fields or dry, dusty plains, but there are many attractive places to explore. Spain's largest region, Castilla y León, has a rich history. It boasts some of the country's most splendid architecture, from Segovia's famous Roman aqueduct, to the Gothic cathedrals of Burgos and Léon and the Renaissance grandeur of Salamanca's monuments. Ávila's medieval city walls are a legacy of the long struggles between the Christians and the Moors. Dotted with windmills and medieval castles, Castilla-La Mancha is home to the historic town of Toledo, another popular destination.

The Library at El Escorial, with its 16th-century frescoed ceiling

El Escorial ❷

El Escorial. **Tel** 91-890 59 03. 🚉 from Atocha or Chamartin, Madrid. 🚌 661, 664 from Moncloa, Madrid. ⏰ 10am–7pm Tue–Sun (to 6pm Oct–Mar). 🔴 public hols. 🎫 (except Wed & Thu pm for EU residents). 📷

Felipe II's imposing palace of San Lorenzo de El Escorial was built in 1563–84 in honor of St. Lawrence. The austere, unornamented building set a new architectural style – known as "Herreriano" after the palace's architect, Juan de Herrera. Its interior was conceived as a mausoleum and contemplative retreat rather than a splendid residence.

Among the most impressive parts is the **Library**, with a collection of over 40,000 books and manuscripts. Its ceiling is decorated with 16th-century frescoes by Tibaldi. The **Royal Pantheon**, a mausoleum made in marble, contains the funerary urns of Spanish monarchs.

Some of the most important works of the royal Habsburg collections, including Flemish, Italian, and Spanish paintings, are housed in the **Museum of Art**, located on the first floor. Other fine works of art can be found in the chapter houses, with their fresco-adorned ceilings, and in the basilica.

In contrast to the artistic wealth of other parts of the palace, the royal apartments are remarkably humble.

Toledo ❸

See pp296–8.

Segovia ❹

Segovia. 🏛 56,000. 🚉 🚌 ℹ Plaza Mayor 10 (921-46 03 34).

Segovia is one of the most spectacularly sited cities in Spain. The old town is set high on a rocky spur, surrounded by the Eresma and Clamores

rivers. With its cathedral, aqueduct, and castle dominating the skyline, the view of the town from the valley below at sunset is magical.

Perched on a rocky outcrop at the city's western end is the **Alcázar**, a fairytale castle with gabled roofs, turrets, and crenellations. Begun in the 12th century, the castle assumed its present form between 1410 and 1455, though it had to be largely rebuilt following a fire in 1862. The castle contains a museum of weaponry and several sumptuous apartments.

Dating from 1525, Segovia's **cathedral** was the last great Gothic church to be built in Spain. It replaced the old cathedral, destroyed in 1520 when the Castilian towns revolted against King Carlos I. Other churches in the old town include the Romanesque **San Juan de los Caballeros**, which has an outstanding sculpted portico, **San Esteban**, and **San Martín**.

Segovia's Roman **aqueduct** was built in the 1st century AD and remained in use until the late 19th century.

🏰 **Alcázar**
Plaza de la Reina Victoria Eugenia. **Tel** 921-46 07 59. ⏰ daily. 🔴 Jan 1 & 6, Dec 25. 🎫 📷 (by appt and for fee). ♿

Environs
The palace of **Riofrío**, 11 km (7 miles) southwest of the city, was built as a hunting lodge for Felipe V's widow, Isabel Farnese, in 1752. Today, it houses a hunting museum.

Segovia's distinctive Alcázar, perched high above the city

Section of Ávila's 12th-century city walls

Ávila ⑤

Ávila. 🏠 58,000. 🚉 🚌 🛈 *Calle San Segundo 17 (920-21 13 87)*.

The perfectly preserved medieval walls that encircle this historic city were built in the 12th century by Christian forces as a defense against the Moors. Of the nine gateways in the walls, the most impressive is the **Puerta de San Vicente**. Ávila's **cathedral**, whose unusual exterior is carved with beasts and scaly wild men, also forms part of the city walls.

Ávila is the birthplace of St. Teresa (1515–82), one of the Catholic Church's greatest mystics and reformers. The **Convento de Santa Teresa** occupies the site of the home of this saint, who also lived for many years in the **Monasterio de la Encarnación**.

Among the city's finest churches are the 12th-century **Iglesia de San Vicente** and the Romanesque-Gothic **Iglesia de San Pedro**.

Beyond the town center, the beautiful **Real Monasterio de Santo Tomás** contains the tomb of Tomás de Torquemada (1420–98), the notorious head of the Spanish Inquisition.

Salamanca ⑥

Salamanca. 🏠 155,000. ✈ 15 km (9 miles) E. 🚉 🚌 🛈 *Plaza Mayor 32 (923-21 83 42).* **www**.salamanca.es

Home to one of the oldest universities in Europe, Salamanca is also Spain's best showcase of Renaissance and Plateresque architecture.

The city's famous **university** was founded by Alfonso IX of León in 1218. The 16th-century facade of the main building on the Patio de las Escuelas is a splendid example of the Plateresque style. This form of early Spanish Renaissance architecture is so called because of its fine detail, which resembles ornate silverwork – *platero* in Spanish means silversmith.

The 16th-century, mainly Gothic, **new cathedral** and the 12th- to 13th-century Romanesque **old cathedral** stand side by side. A highlight of the old cathedral is the richly colored altarpiece (1445) by Nicolás Florentino.

The magnificent **Plaza Mayor** was built by Felipe V in the 18th century to thank the city for its support during the War of the Spanish Succession. Among the arcaded buildings lining the square are the Baroque town hall and the Royal Pavilion, from where the royal family used to watch events in the square.

Other fine monuments located in the heart of the city include the 16th-century **Iglesia-Convento de San Esteban**, with its lovely ornamented facade, and the **Convento de las Dueñas**, which preserves Moorish and Renaissance features.

The **Museo Art Nouveau y Art Deco** holds an important collection of 19th- and 20th-century paintings, jewelry, ceramics, and stained glass.

On the city outskirts, the 1st-century AD Roman bridge, the **Puente Romano**, offers a good view over the entire city.

🏛 **Universidad**
Calle Libreros. **Tel** 923-29 44 00.
◯ daily. ● Dec 25. 🎟 (except Mon am).

🏛 **Museo Art Nouveau y Art Deco**
Calle El Expolio. **Tel** 923-12 14 25.
◯ Tue–Sun. 🎟 (free Thu am). ♿ 🛈

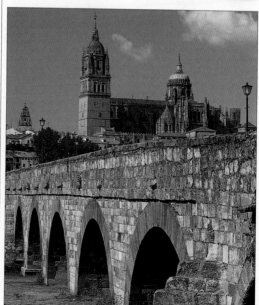

View of Salamanca's twin cathedrals from the Puente Romano

Street-by-Street: Toledo ❸

Picturesquely sited on a hill above the River
Tagus is the historic center of Toledo. Behind
the old walls lies much evidence of the city's
rich history. The Romans built a fortress on
the site of the present-day Alcázar. In the 6th
century AD the Visigoths made Toledo their
capital, and left behind many churches. After
it was captured from the Moors by Alfonso VI
in 1085, the city became the capital of the
Christian kingdom of Castile. During the
Middle Ages, Toledo was a melting pot of
Christian, Muslim, and Jewish cultures, and it
was during this period that the city's most
outstanding monument – its cathedral – was
built. In the 16th century the painter El Greco
came to live in Toledo, and today the city is
home to many of his works.

Puerta de Valmardón

Iglesia de San Román
This church contains a museum relating the city's past under the Visigoths.

CARDENAL LORENZANA
CALLE DE SAN ROMÁN
CALLE DE ALFONSO XII
CALLE DE LA TRINIDAD

0 meters 100
0 yards 100

★ Iglesia de Santo Tomé
This church, with a beautiful Mudéjar tower, houses El Greco's masterpiece, The Burial of the Count of Orgaz.

Sinagoga del Tránsito and Casa-Museo de El Greco

Archbishop's Palace

Taller del Moro
This Mudéjar palace houses a museum of Mudéjar ceramics and tiles. It is, however, closed for renovation with no confirmation of an end date.

STAR SIGHTS

★ Iglesia de Santo Tomé

★ Museo de Santa Cruz

★ Cathedral

he Puerta del
has a double
rish arch and
, two towers.

Ermita del Cristo de la Luz

This small mosque, the city's only remaining Muslim building, dates from around AD 1000.

VISITORS' CHECKLIST

Toledo. 🏘 82,000. 🚉 Paseo de la Rosa (902-24 02 02). 🚌 Avenida de Castilla-La Mancha (925-21 58 50). 🛈 Plaza del Consistorio 1 (925-25 40 30). 🛒 Tue. 🎉 Corpus Christi (May/Jun), Virgen del Sagrario, (Aug 15). **Iglesia de San Román** ◯ Tue–Sun. **Taller del Moro** ⬤ for renovation. 🌐

Tourist information, bus and train stations

The Plaza de Zocodover is named after the market which was held here in Moorish times. It is still the city's main square, with many cafés and shops.

PLAZA DE ZOCODOVER

CUESTA DE CARLOS V

ERITOS

CALLE DEL COMERCIO

SIXTO RAMÓN PARRO

★ **Museo de Santa Cruz**
The city's main fine arts collection includes several tapestries from Flanders. Among them is this 15th-century zodiac tapestry, with well-preserved rich colors.

KEY

– – – Suggested route

★ **Cathedral**
Built on the site of a Visigothic cathedral and a mosque, this impressive structure is one of the largest cathedrals in Christendom (see p298). The beautiful Gothic high altar reredos (1504) is the work of several artists.

Alcázar
In the central patio of the fortress is a replica of the statue Carlos V y el Furor. The original is housed in Madrid's Museo del Prado.

Exploring Toledo

Easily reached from Madrid by rail, bus or car, Toledo is best explored on foot. To visit all the main sights you need at least two days, but it is possible to walk around the medieval and Jewish quarters in a long morning. To avoid the heavy crowds, go midweek and stay for a night, when the city is at its most atmospheric.

Toledo cathedral rising above the rooftops of the medieval quarter

🔒 Cathedral

Calle Cardenal Cisneros 1. **Tel** 925-22 22 41. **Choir, Treasury, Chapterhouse, and Sacristy** ☐ Mon–Sat, Sun pm. 🖼 📷 ♿

The splendor of Toledo's cathedral reflects its history as the spiritual heart of the Spanish church and the seat of the Primate of all Spain. The present cathedral stands on the site of a 7th-century church. Work began in 1226, but the last vaults were not completed until 1493. This long period of construction explains the cathedral's mixture of styles: the exterior is pure French Gothic, while inside, Spanish decorative styles, such as Mudéjar – a hybrid Christian-Islamic style – and Plateresque, are used.

Among the cathedral's most outstanding features are the polychrome reredos of the high altar (1504) and the choir. In the treasury is a 16th-century Gothic silver monstrance, over 3 m (10 ft) high. The monstrance is carried through the streets of Toledo during the Corpus Christi celebrations. Standing out from the mainly Gothic interior, the Transparente is a stunning Baroque altarpiece of marble, jasper, and bronze, sculpted by Narciso Tomé.

🏛 Museo de Santa Cruz

Calle Cervantes 3. **Tel** 925-22 10 36. ☐ daily. 📷 Jan 1, May 1, Dec 25.
This museum of fine arts has a superb collection of medieval and Renaissance tapestries, paintings, and sculptures. There are also works by the Cretan artist El Greco, as well as examples of two typical Toledan crafts: armor and damascened swords, the latter made by inlaying blackened steel with gold wire. The museum is housed in a fine renovated Renaissance building and has an elegant courtyard.

The Assumption (1613) by El Greco, in the Museo de Santa Cruz

🔒 Iglesia de Santo Tomé

Calle Santo Tomé s/n. **Tel** 925-25 60 98. ☐ daily. 📷 except Wed pm for EU residents.
Visitors come to this church mainly to admire El Greco's masterpiece, *The Burial of the Count of Orgaz*. The church is thought to date back to the 12th century, and its tower is one of the best examples of Mudéjar architecture in Toledo.

🏰 Alcázar

Cuesta de Carlos V. **Tel** 925-23 88 00. ☐ 10am–7pm Tue–Sat (to 9pm Jun–Sep), 10am–3pm Sun. 📷 (free Sun).
Charles V's fortified palace stands on the site of former Roman, Visigothic, and Muslim fortresses. In 1936 it was almost completely destroyed during a 70-day siege by the Republicans. The restored building houses the Museo del Ejército (National Army Museum) and a private library, which holds a valuable collection of books and manuscripts dating back to the 11th century.

🔒 Sinagoga del Tránsito

Calle Samuel Leví. **Tel** 925-22 36 65. ☐ Tue–Sun. 📷 (free Sat pm & Sun).
A wonderfully elaborate Mudéjar interior is hidden behind the humble facade of this 14th-century former synagogue. Next door is a museum dedicated to the Sephardic (Spanish Jewish) culture.

🏛 Casa-Museo de El Greco

Paseo del Tránsito. **Tel** 925-22 36 65. ☐ Tue–Sun. 📷
It is uncertain whether El Greco actually lived in or simply near to this house, now a museum containing a collection of his works. Canvases include the superb series *Christ and the Apostles*. On the ground floor is a chapel with a fine Mudéjar ceiling and works of art by painters of the Toledan School, such as Luis Tristán, a student of El Greco.

🚪 Puerta Antigua de Bisagra

When Alfonso VI of Castile conquered Toledo in 1085, he entered it through this gateway – the only one in the city to have kept its original 10th-century military architecture. The towers are topped by a 12th-century Arab gatehouse.

The Arco de Santa María in Burgos, adorned with statues and turrets

Burgos ⑦

Burgos. 🏠 *178,000.* 🚊 🚌 🛈 *Plaza de Alonso Martínez 7 (947-20 31 25).*

Founded in 884, Burgos was the capital of the united kingdoms of Castile and León from 1073 until 1492. A few hundred years later, Franco chose Burgos as his head-quarters during the Civil War.

Approaching the city via the bridge called the Puente de Santa María, you enter the old town through the grand **Arco de Santa María**. The other main route into Burgos is the Puente de San Pablo, where a statue commemorates local hero El Cid (1043–99). Born Rodrigo Díaz de Vivar, this great warrior fought for both the Moors and the Christians in the Reconquest, and for his heroism was named El Cid, from the Arabic *Sidi* (Lord). He is immortalized in the anonymous poem, *El Cantar del Mío Cid* (1180).

Not far from the statue of El Cid stands the **Casa del Cordón**, a 15th-century former palace (now a bank). It was here that the Catholic Monarchs welcomed Columbus on his return, in 1497, from the second of his voyages to the Americas.

Burgos's **cathedral** *(see pp300–301)* is a UNESCO World Heritage site and the city's most prominent landmark. Nearby, the **Iglesia de San Nicolás** boasts a fine 16th-century altarpiece, while the **Iglesia de San Lorenzo** has a splendid Baroque ceiling. The **Museo de Burgos** contains archaeological and fine art collections. West of the city is the 12th-century **Real Monasterio de Huelgas**, a former convent that houses a textile museum.

Statue of El Cid, Burgos's most famous son

🏛 Museo de Burgos
Calle Calera 25. *Tel 947-26 58 75.* ◯ *Tue–Sun.* 🕮 *(except Sat & Sun).* 🗲

⛪ Real Monasterio de Huelgas
Calle de los Compases. *Tel 947-20 16 30.* ◯ *10am–2pm, 3:45–6:30pm Tue–Sat, 10:30am–3pm Sun & public hols.* ● *Jan 1 & 6, Good Fri, May 1, May 30, Dec 24, 25, & 31.* 🗲 ♿ 🕮 *(except Wed for EU residents).*

León ⑧

León. 🏠 *134,000.* 🚊 🚌 🛈 *Plaza de la Regla 4 (987-23 70 82).*

Founded as a camp for the Romans' Seventh Legion, León became the capital of the kingdom of León in the Middle Ages and played a central role in the early years of the Reconquest.

The city's Gothic **cathedral**, on Plaza de la Regla, dates from the mid-13th century. As well as some glorious stained glass, it has a splendid west front, decorated with a series of 13th-century carvings. The **Colegiata de San Isidoro** is built into the Roman walls encircling the city. The Roman-esque **Panteón Real** (Royal Pantheon) is decorated with carved capitals and 12th-century frescoes. León's old quarter is a maze of narrow alleyways, lined with bars, cafés, churches, and old mansions. The **Hostal de San Marcos** was founded in the 12th century as a monastery for pilgrims on route to Santiago *(see p302)*. A gem of Spanish Renaissance archite-cture, the present building was begun in 1513 for the Knights of Santiago. Today it houses a luxurious hotel and the **Museo de León**.

🏛 Museo de León
Plaza Santo Domingo. *Tel 987-23 64 05.* ◯ *Tue–Sun.* ● *main public hols.* 🕮 *(free Sat & Sun).*

Environs
To the east of León, the 10th-century **Iglesia de San Miguel de Escalada** is one of the finest surviving churches built by the Mozarabs – Christians influenced by the Moors.

Detail from a 13th-century carving decorating the west front of León's cathedral

Burgos Cathedral

Spain's third-largest cathedral was founded in 1221 under Fernando III and was named a UNESCO World Heritage site in 1984. The groundplan – a Latin cross – measures 84 m (276 ft) by 59 m (194 ft). Its construction was carried out in several stages over three centuries, involving artists and architects from across Europe. The style is almost entirely Gothic, with influences from Germany, France, and the Low Countries. In the Middle Ages the cathedral was a main stopping point for pilgrims on the road to Santiago *(see p302)*. Burgos's most celebrated son, the medieval hero of the Reconquest, El Cid, is buried in the cathedral, as is his wife.

Christ at the Column, by Diego de Siloé

West Front
The lacy, steel-grey spires soar above a sculpted balustrade depicting Castile's early kings.

Lantern

Tomb of El Cid

★ Golden Staircase
Diego de Siloé's elegant Renaissance staircase (1519–22) links the nave with the Gothic Coroneria Gate (kept locked) at street level.

STAR FEATURES

★ Golden Staircase

★ Constable's Chapel

★ Crossing

Capilla de Santa Tecla

Puerta de Santa María (main entrance)

Capilla de Santa Ana
The altarpiece (1490) in this chapel is by the sculptor Gil de Siloé. The central panel shows the Virgin with St. Joachim.

The Capilla de la Presentación (1519–24) is a funerary chapel with a star-shaped, traceried vault.

Ambulatory
Several of the reliefs around the chancel were carved by Philippe de Bigarny. This expressive scene, which was completed in 1499, depicts the road to Calvary.

VISITORS' CHECKLIST

Plaza de Santa María. *Tel* 947-27 39 50. ☐ mid-Mar–Oct: 9:30am–7:30pm daily; Nov–mid-Mar: 10am–7pm. ✝ 9am, 10am, 11am, 7:30pm daily; Sun also: noon (sung), 1pm, 2pm. ☒ ☒ ☒

Capilla de San Juan Bautista and museum

★ **Constable's Chapel**
The tomb of the High Constable of Castile and his wife lies beneath the openwork vault of this chapel of 1496.

Sacristy *(1765)*
The sacristy was rebuilt in Baroque style, with an exuberant plasterwork vault and Rococo altars.

Capilla de la Visitación

Puerta de la Coronería
The tympanum of this portal of 1240 shows Christ flanked by the Evangelists. Statues of the apostles sit below.

Capilla del Santísimo Cristo

★ **Crossing**
The star-ribbed central dome, begun in 1539, is supported by four huge pillars. It is decorated with effigies of prophets and saints. Beneath it is the tomb of El Cid and his wife.

Northern Spain

Northern Spain encompasses a variety of landscapes and cultures. In the far northwest of the peninsula, the Galicians are fiercely proud of their customs and language. Spain's greenest region, Galicia boasts some of the most attractive stretches of Atlantic coast, as well as the beautiful city of Santiago de Compostela. Popular with hikers and naturalists, the spectacular Picos de Europa massif sits astride the border between Asturias and Cantabria. The Basque Country is a unique part of Spain whose main attractions include superb cuisine, fashionable seaside resorts, and the cultural center of Bilbao, with its famous Guggenheim Museum.

Santiago de Compostela's grand cathedral towering over the city

Santiago de Compostela **9**

A Coruña. 🏃 95,000. ✈ 10 km (6 miles) N. 🚉 🚌 **i** Calle Rúa do Villar 63 (981-55 51 29). 🎉 Fiesta (Jul 25). www.santiagoturismo.com

In the Middle Ages this fine city was Christendom's third most important place of pilgrimage after Jerusalem and Rome. In 813 the body of Christ's apostle James was supposedly discovered here, and in the following centuries pilgrims from all over Europe flocked to the city.

On the Praza do Obradoiro stands the city's **cathedral**, built in honor of St. James. The present structure dates from the 11th–13th centuries, but the Baroque west facade was added in the 18th century. The square's northern edge is flanked by the grand **Hostal de los Reyes Católicos**, built by the Catholic Monarchs (see p278) as a resting place for

sick pilgrims. It is now a parador hotel. Nearby are the 9th-century **Convento de San Paio de Antealtares**, one of the city's oldest monasteries, and the **Convento de San Martiño Pinario**, whose Baroque church has a wonderfully ornate Plateresque facade.

The **Convento de Santo Domingo de Bonaval**, east of the center, is also worth visiting. Part of the monastery now houses a Galician folk museum. There is also the

Centro Gallego de Arte Contemporáneo, with works by leading Galician artists.

🏛 **Centro Gallego de Arte Contemporáneo**
Calle Valle Inclán s/n. **Tel** 981-54 66 19. ⏱ Tue–Sun. 📷 by prior appointment (call 981-54 66 23). ♿

Rías Baixas **10**

Pontevedra. 🚉 🚌 Pontevedra. **i** Calle General Gutierrez Mellado 1, Pontevedra (986-85 08 14).

The southern part of Galicia's west coast consists of four large rías, or inlets, between pine-covered hills. Known as the Rías Baixas (Rías Bajas), they offer fine beaches, safe bathing, and lovely scenery.

The main town on the coast is lively **Pontevedra**, which has many historic monuments, such as the Gothic Convento de Santo Domingo, and an excellent provincial museum.

Many areas along the coast have become popular holiday resorts, such as **Sanxenxo**, west of Pontevedra. To the south, **Baiona** and **Panxón** both have good beaches, as well as sailing and a variety of water sports. In spite of tourism, much of the coastline, particularly the quieter northernmost part, remains unspoiled. Here you can visit many small fishing ports and watch the locals harvesting mussels and clams.

While in Rías Baixas look out for bórreos – traditional stone-built granaries raised on stilts. The waterfront of picturesque **Combarro** is lined with these buildings, typical of the whole of Galicia.

The tranquil fishing village of Combarro in the Rías Baixas

For hotels and restaurants in this region see pp340–45 and pp346–51

Santa María del Naranco, a Pre-Romanesque church in Oviedo

Oviedo ⓫

Asturias. 🏚 225,000. 🚉 🚌
🛈 Marqués de Santa Cruz 1 (985-22 75 86). www.ayto-oviedo.es

Oviedo, the cultural and commercial capital of Asturias, is best known for its Pre-Romanesque buildings. This style flourished in the 8th–10th centuries and was confined to a small area of the kingdom of Asturias, one of the few areas of Spain that escaped invasion by the Moors.

With its huge barrel-vaulted hall and arcaded galleries, the church of **Santa María del Naranco**, in the north of the city, was built as a summer palace for Ramiro I in the 9th century. Equally impressive are the church of **San Miguel de Lillo** and the 9th-century church of **San Julián de los Prados**, with its frescoes.

In the center of Oviedo, the Flamboyant Gothic **cathedral** and the 9th-century **Iglesia de San Tirso** are both worth taking some time to see.

The city has two museums of note: the **Museo Arque-ológico**, which contains local prehistoric, Roman, and Romanesque treasures, and the **Museo de Bellas Artes** (Museum of Fine Arts).

🏛 **Museo Arqueológico**
Calle San Vicente 5. *Tel* 985-20 89 77. ◯ Wed–Sun. ♿

🏛 **Museo de Bellas Artes**
Calle Santa Ana 1. *Tel* 985-21 30 61. ◯ Tue–Sun. ♿

Picos de Europa ⓬

Asturias, Cantabria, and Castilla y León. 🚌 Oviedo to Cangas de Onís.
🛈 Cangas de Onís (985-84 86 14).
Fuente Dé cable car *Tel* 942-73 66 10. ◯ daily. ⬤ Jan 8–Feb 20.

This beautiful mountain range – christened "Peaks of Europe" by returning sailors as this was often the first sight of their homeland – offers superb upland hiking and supports a diversity of wildlife.

The two main gateways to the Picos are **Cangas de Onís**, northwest of the park, and **Potes**, on the eastern side. About 8 km (5 miles) southeast of the former, **Covadonga** is where, in 722, the Visigoth Pelayo is said to have defeated a Moorish army, inspiring Christians to reconquer the peninsula. The road south from Cangas de Onís follows the spectacular gorge known as the Desfiladero de los Beyes.

The Fuente Dé cable car, in the heart of the park, climbs 900 m (2,950 ft) to a rocky plateau, offering magnificent panoramic views.

Santander ⓭

Cantabria. 🏚 182,000. ✈ 🚢 🚉 🚌
🛈 Jardines de Pereda (942-203 000).
🎭 International Festival (Jul–Aug).

Cantabria's capital, Santander, is a busy port that enjoys a splendid site on a deep bay on Spain's north Atlantic coast.

The early 20th-century Palacio de la Magdalena in Santander

The **cathedral** was rebuilt in Gothic style, following a fire in 1941 that destroyed the entire town. The 12th-century crypt has been preserved. Nearby, the **Museo de Bellas Artes** has works by Goya and Zurbarán, while the **Museo de Prehistoria y Arqueología** displays local finds, including Neolithic axe heads, Roman coins, pottery, and figurines.

On the Península de la Magdalena stands the **Palacio de la Magdalena**, built for Alfonso XIII in 1912. The upscale seaside resort of **El Sardinero**, to the north, has a long beach, chic cafés, and a majestic white casino.

🏛 **Museo de Bellas Artes**
Calle Rubio 6. *Tel* 942-20 31 20. ◯ Mon–Sat. 📷

🏛 **Museo de Prehistoria y Arqueología**
Calle Casimiro Saenz 4. *Tel* 942-20 71 09. ◯ Tue–Sun. ♿ 📷

19th-century Neo-Romanesque basilica in Covadonga, Picos de Europa

Frank Gehry's ultramodern Museo Guggenheim building in Bilbao

Bilbao 🕙

Vizcaya. 🏠 354,000. ✈ 🚢 🚉
🚌 🚏 Pl Ensanche 11 (944-79 57
60). 🎭 Fiesta (third week Aug).

Bilbao (Bilbo) is the center of Basque industry and Spain's leading commercial port, yet it has many cultural attractions worth visiting. In the city's medieval quarter – the *Casco Viejo* – the **Museo Arqueológico, Etnográfico e Histórico Vasco** displays Basque art and folk artifacts, while in the newer town, the **Museo de Bellas Artes** is one of Spain's best art museums.

The jewel in Bilbao's cultural crown, however, is the **Museo Guggenheim Bilbao**, which has a superb collection of Modern and contemporary art. It is just one of the city's many pieces of modern architecture, which also include the striking **Palacio de la Música y Congresos Euskalduna**.

🏛 **Museo Guggenheim**
Avenida Abandoibarra. *Tel* 944-35
90 00. ⏰ 10am–8pm. ● Sep–Jun:
Mon; public hols. 📷 🍴 ♿ 🅿 🎧
www.guggenheim-bilbao.es

San Sebastián 🕙

Guipúzcoa. 🏠 185,000. 🚉 🚌
🚏 Boulevard 8 (943-48 11 66).
🎬 International Film Festival (late Sep).

Popular with the aristocracy, San Sebastián (Donostia) became a fashionable seaside resort in the late 19th century.

At the heart of the old town are the handsome Plaza de la Constitución and the church of **Santa María del Coro**, with its Baroque portal. Behind the old town, Monte Urgull is worth climbing for the superb views from its summit. At the foot of the hill, the **Museo de San Telmo** holds exhibits ranging from Basque funerary columns to works by El Greco.

A short bus ride from the Calle Oquendo takes you to **Chillida-Leku**, a display of works by renowned Basque sculptor, Eduardo Chillida.

Between the city's two main beaches – the Playa de la Concha and the Playa de Ondarreta – is the **Palacio Miramar** (1889), built for Queen María Cristina.

🏛 **Museo de San Telmo**
Plaza Zuloaga. *Tel* 943-48 15 80.
⏰ 10am–8pm Tue–Sun. 📷 ♿ 🎧

Mural by Josep Maria Sert in the Museo de San Telmo, San Sebastián

Bulls scattering the runners during Sanfermines in Pamplona

Pamplona 🕙

Navarra. 🏠 198,000. ✈ 🚉 🚌
🚏 Avenida Roncesvalles 4 (848-420
420). 🎭 Sanfermines (Jul 6–14).

Supposedly founded by the Roman general, Pompey, Pamplona is most famous for the fiesta of Los Sanfermines, with its daredevil bull running.

West of the city's mainly Gothic **cathedral** lies the old Jewish quarter, with the Neo-Classic **Palacio del Gobierno de Navarra** and the medieval **Iglesia de San Saturnino**.

The **Museo de Navarra** is a museum of regional history, archaeology, and art.

Southeast of the center is Felipe II's massive **citadel**, erected in the 16th century.

🏛 **Museo de Navarra**
Calle Santo Domingo. *Tel* 848-42
64 92. ⏰ Tue–Sun. 📷 free Sat
pm, Sun. ♿ 🎧 by appointment.

BASQUE CULTURE

Possibly Europe's oldest race, the Basques are thought to be descended from Cro-Magnon people, who lived in the Pyrenees 40,000 years ago. Long isolated in their mountain villages, the Basques preserved their unique language (Euskera), myths, and art for millennia, almost untouched by other influences. Many families still live in the stone *caseríos*, or farmhouses, built by their forebears. The *fueros*, or ancient Basque laws, were suppressed under General Franco, but since 1975 the Basque region (Euskadi) has had its own parliament. Nevertheless, there is still a strong separatist movement seeking to sever links with the government in Madrid.

The Ikurriña, the flag of the Basque region

Catalonia

A nation-within-a-nation, Catalonia has its own semi-autonomous regional government, and its own language. Spoken by more than eight million people, Catalan has supplanted Castilian Spanish as the first language of the region, and is used on road signs and in place names everywhere. Barcelona is the region's capital, rivaling Madrid in economic and cultural importance. Catalonia offers a variety of attractions. The flower-filled valleys of the Pyrenees offer a paradise for naturalists and walkers, while inland are medieval towns, Roman ruins, and spectacular monasteries, such as Montserrat.

Parc Nacional d'Aigüestortes ⑰

Lleida. 🚍 La Pobla de Segur. 🚌 El Pont de Suert, La Pobla de Segur. 🛈 Boí (973-69 61 89).

The pristine mountain scenery of Catalonia's only national park is among the most spectacular in the Pyrenees. The main village in the area is the mountain settlement of Espot, on the park's eastern edge. Dotted around the park are waterfalls and more than a hundred lakes and tarns.

The most beautiful scenery is around Sant Maurici lake, from where several walks lead north to the towering peaks of Agulles d'Amitges. The park is home to an impressive variety of wildlife: chamois, beavers, otters, and golden eagles have all found a habitat here.

Barcelona ⑱

See pp306–15.

Monestir de Montserrat ⑲

See pp316–17.

Poblet ⑳

Off N240, 10 km (6 miles) from Montblanc. **Tel** 977-87 02 54. 🚍 to L'Espluga de Francolí, then taxi. 🚌 ⬤ 10am–12:45pm, 3–5:30pm daily. ⬤ Jan 1, Dec 25 & 26. 🖼

Santa Maria de Poblet was the first and most important of three medieval monasteries, known as the "Cistercian triangle." In 1835, during the

The superb high altar piece at Santa Maria de Poblet

Carlist upheavals, the abbey sustained serious damage. Restoration began in 1930, and monks returned a decade later.

Poblet is enclosed by fortified walls that have hardly changed since the Middle Ages. Its evocative, vaulted cloisters were built in the 12th and 13th centuries. Beautiful, carved scrollwork decorates the capitals. Behind the stone altar, an impressive alabaster reredos, carved by Damià Forment in 1527, fills the apse. Other highlights include the Royal Tombs, where many Spanish monarchs are buried. Begun in 1359, they were reconstructed by Marès in 1950.

Tarragona ㉑

Tarragona. 🚶 140,000. ✈ 🚉 🚍 🛈 Carrer Major 39 (977-25 07 95).

Now a major industrial port, Tarragona preserves many remnants of its Roman past, when it was the capital of the Roman province, Tarraconensis.

Among the extensive ruins are the **Anfiteatro Romano** (Roman Amphitheater) and the Praetorium, a Roman tower that was later converted into a medieval palace. Also known as the Castell de Pilato (after Pontius Pilate), the tower houses the **Museu de la Romanitat**, which contains Roman and medieval finds and gives access to the cavernous passageways of the 1st-century AD Roman circus. In the adjacent building is the **Museu Nacional Arqueològic**, which holds the most important collection of Roman artifacts in Catalonia, including some beautiful frescoes. An archaeological walk follows part of the Roman city wall.

Tarragona's 12th-century **cathedral** was built on the site of a Roman temple and an Arab mosque, and exhibits a harmonious blend of styles.

🏛 Museu Nacional Arqueològic de Tarragona
Plaça del Rei 5. **Tel** 977-23 62 09. ⬤ Jun–Sep: 9:30am–8:30pm Tue–Sat; Oct–May: 9:30am–6pm Tue–Sat, 10am–2pm Sun all year. 🖼 ♿

View across the Roman amphitheater at Tarragona to the sea

Barcelona ⑱

Barcelona, one of the Mediterranean's busiest ports, is more than the capital of Catalonia. In culture, commerce, and sport, it rivals not only Madrid, but also many of Europe's greatest cities. The success of the 1992 Olympic Games, staged in the Parc de Montjuïc, confirmed this to the world. Although there are many historical monuments in the Old Town, the city is best known for the scores of superb buildings left behind by the artistic explosion of Modernisme in the decades around 1900. Today, Barcelona still sizzles with creativity; its bars and public parks speak more of bold contemporary design than of tradition.

GREATER BARCELONA

0 km   2
0 miles

KEY

Area of main map

SIGHTS AT A GLANCE

Barcelona Cathedral ①
Basílica de Santa
   Maria del Mar ④
Fundació Joan Miró ⑩
Montjuïc ⑨
Museu d'Història de la
   Ciutat – Conjunt
   Monumental de la
   Plaça del Rei ②
Museu Nacional d'Art
   de Catalunya ⑪
Museu Picasso ⑤
Quadrat d'Or ⑧
La Rambla ③
Sagrada Família
   pp312–13 ⑦
Vila Olímpica ⑥

Greater Barcelona
(see inset map)
Parc Güell ⑫
Tibidabo ⑬

KEY

▪	Sight / Place of interest
✈	Airport
▤	Train station
Ⓜ	Metro station
🚍	Main bus stop
🚊	Tram stop
🚠	Cable car station
🚡	Funicular station
P	Parking
ℹ	Tourist information
✝	Church
▬	Pedestrian street

Pedestrian swing bridge in Port Vell, at the end of La Rambla

A   B   C

1

2

3

4

GETTING AROUND

The Old Town is well served by Metro lines 1, 3, and 4. Jaume I metro station is in the heart of the Barri Gòtic, and many buses pass through the Plaça de Catalunya on the edge of the district. Metro line 5 takes you to the Sagrada Família, a long walk from other sights. Set atop a steep hill, most of Montjuïc's attractions can be reached by buses 13, 50, and 61 from the Plaça d'Espanya, or by funicular and cable car from Metro Paral·lel.

5

D   **E**   **F**

Street-by-Street: Barri Gòtic

The Barri Gòtic (Gothic Quarter) is the true heart of Barcelona. This site was chosen by the Romans in the reign of Augustus (27 BC–AD 14) to found a new *colonia* (town), and has been the location of the city's administrative buildings ever since. The Roman forum was on the Plaça de Sant Jaume, where the medieval Palau de la Generalitat, Catalonia's parliament, and the Casa de la Ciutat, the town hall, now stand. Nearby are the Gothic cathedral and royal palace, where Columbus was received by the Catholic Monarchs on his return from the New World in 1492.

The Casa de l'Ardiaca (Archdeacon's House), a Gothic-Renaissance building on the Roman city wall, now houses Barcelona's historical archives.

Roman city wall

Plaça de Catalunya

★ **Cathedral**
The façade and spire are 19th-century additions to the original building. The cathedral's treasures include medieval Catalan paintings.

Palau de la Generalitat
The superb Gothic features of the Catalan Parliament include the chapel and a stone staircase rising to an arcaded gallery.

CARRER DEL BISBE

SANT SEVER

CARRER DE SANT HONORAT

PLAÇA DE SANT JAUME

CARRER DE FARRAN

La Rambla ←

CARRER DE LA CIUTAT

CARRER D

Casa de la Ciutat
Barcelona's town hall was built in the 14th and 15th centuries. The façade is a Neoclassical addition. In the entrance hall stands Three Gypsy Boys *by Joan Rebull (1899–1981), a 1976 copy of a sculpture he originally created in 1946.*

The Centre Excursionista de Catalunya, housed in a medieval mansion, displays Roman columns from the Temple of Augustus, whose site is marked by a millstone in the street outside.

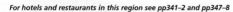

Museu Frederic Marès
This medieval doorway is from an extensive display of Spanish sculpture – the mainstay of this museum's extraordinarily eclectic and high-quality collections.

★ Conjunt Monumental de la Plaça del Rei
The 14th-century Capella Reial de Santa Àgata, with its 1466 altarpiece, is one of the best-preserved sections of the palace.

Capella Reial de Santa Àgata

Plaça del Rei

Palau del Lloctinent

Museu d'Història de la Ciutat – Conjunt Monumental de la Plaça del Rei
Housed in a 14th-century mansion are the most extensive subterranean Roman ruins in the world. Visitors can see the streets of Roman Barcelona and an exhibition on the city's 13th- and 14th-century growth.

VIA LAIETANA

 Jaume I

KEY

--- Suggested route

STAR SIGHTS

★ Cathedral

★ Palau Reial

0 meters 100
0 yards 100

Barcelona Cathedral ①

Plaça de la Seu. *Tel* 93-310 71 95.
M *Jaume I.* 17, 19, 45. 8am–7:30pm daily. (lunchtime).

Begun in 1298 under Jaime II, on the foundations of a site dating back to Visigothic times, this compact Gothic cathedral was not finished until the late 19th century. The interior has beautiful Gothic cloisters and carved 15th-century choir stalls with painted coats of arms. Beneath the main altar, the crypt houses the sarcophagus of St. Eulalia, martyred in the 4th century AD. The nave has 28 side chapels, and a vaulted ceiling that rises to 26 m (85 ft).

The wide Catalan Gothic nave of Barcelona Cathedral

Museu d'Història de la Ciutat – Conjunt Monumental de la Plaça del Rei ②

Plaça del Rei. *Tel* 93-256 21 00.
M *Jaume I.* 10am–7pm Tue–Sat (Nov–Mar: to 5pm), 10am–8pm Sun.
Jan 1, May 1, Jun 24, Dec 25.
by appt.

The Royal Palace, founded in the 13th century, was the residence of the count-kings of Barcelona. The complex includes the Gothic Saló del Tinell and the Capella de Santa Àgata, with a painted wood ceiling by Jaume Huguet. Entire streets of old Barcino are accessible via walkways suspended over the ruins.

Las Ramblas ③

Ⓜ *Drassanes, Liceu, Catalunya.*

Busy around the clock, this is one of the most famous streets in Spain. A stroll down its tree-shaded, central walkway to the seafront, taking in the mansions, shops, and cafés, makes a perfect introduction to Barcelona life.

The name (Les Rambles in Catalan) comes from the Arabic *ramla*, meaning the dried-up bed of a seasonal river. Barcelona's 13th-century city wall followed the left bank of one such river. During the 16th century, convents, monasteries, and a university were built on the opposite bank. Later demolished, they have left their legacy in the names of the five sections of the street. Today Las Ramblas is thronged by street vendors, tarot readers, musicians, and mime artists.

Among its many famous buildings is the **Palau Güell**, a Neo-Gothic mansion that established the international reputation of Catalan architect Antoni Gaudí for outstanding,

The Gothic interior of the Basílica de Santa Maria del Mar

original architecture. Built in 1889, this fascinating work of art is located on a narrow street just off Las Ramblas. Nearby, the **Gran Teatre del Liceu**, the city's fine opera house, has been restored twice after fires in 1861 and 1994. Further along is the huge **Mercat de Sant Josep**, a colorful food market popularly known as "La Boqueria."

On the opposite side of Las Ramblas, midway between the Drassanes and Liceu metro stations, the **Plaça Reial** is Barcelona's liveliest square and dates from the 1850s. Also worth visiting, the **Museu de Cera** (wax-work museum) is housed in an atmospheric 19th-century building, and holds around 300 exhibits.

🏛 **Palau Güell**
Carrer Nou de la Rambla 3–5. **Tel** 93-472 57 75. Ⓜ *Drassanes, Liceu.* 🕙 *10am–8pm Tue–Sun (Oct–Mar: to 5:30pm).* 🎫 📷 ♿

Basílica de Santa Maria del Mar ④

Plaza Sta Maria 1. **Tel** 93-310 23 90. Ⓜ *Jaume I.* 🕙 *9am–1:30pm, 4:30–8pm daily (from 10am Sun).*

This beautiful building, the city's favorite church, has superb acoustics for concerts. It is also the only surviving example of an entirely Catalan Gothic-style church.

The church took just 55 years to build. The speed of its construction – unrivaled in the Middle Ages – gave it a unity of style both inside and out. The west front has a 15th-century rose window of the Coronation of the Virgin. More stained glass, dating from the 15th to the 18th centuries, lights the wide nave and high aisles.

The choir and furnishings were destroyed during the Spanish Civil War (1936–9), which only serves to enhance the sense of space and simplicity.

Monument to Columbus at the southern end of the tree-lined Ramblas

For hotels and restaurants in this region see pp341–2 and pp347–8

Museu Picasso ⑤

Carrer Montcada 15–23. **Tel** 93-256 30 00. M *Jaume I.* ☐ 10am–8pm Tue–Sun. ☐ Jan 1, May 1, Jun 24, Dec 25 & 26. ☒ *(free Sun pm & first Sun of month).* ☐ ☐ **www**.museupicasso.bcn.es

One of Barcelona's most popular attractions, the Picasso Museum is housed in five adjoining palaces on the Carrer Montcada. It was founded in 1963, displaying works donated by Jaime Sabartes, a great friend of Picasso. Later, Picasso himself donated paintings, including some graphic works left in his will. Several ceramic pieces were given to the museum by his widow, Jacqueline.

The strength of the 3,000-piece collection is Picasso's early drawings and paintings, such as *The First Communion* (1896), produced when he was still an adolescent. The most famous work on show is the series *Las Meninas*, based on Velázquez's 1656 masterpiece *(see p290).*

Yachts in the marina at the Port Olímpic, overlooked by skyscrapers

Vila Olímpica ⑥

M *Ciutadella-Vila Olímpica.*

The most dramatic rebuilding for the 1992 Olympics was the demolition of the old industrial waterfront and the laying out of 4 km (2 miles) of promenade and pristine sandy beaches. Suddenly Barcelona seemed like a seaside resort, with a new estate of 2,000 apartments and parks called Nova Icària. The area is still popularly known as the Vila Olímpica because the buildings once housed Olympic athletes.

On the seafront there are twin 44-floor towers – Spain's tallest skyscrapers. They stand beside the Port Olímpic, also built for the Olympics. Two levels of restaurants, shops, and nightclubs around the marina attract business people at lunchtimes and pleasure seekers at weekends.

Sagrada Família ⑦

See pp312–13.

Quadrat d'Or ⑧

M *Diagonal, Passeig de Gracia.*

Called the "Golden Square" because it contains so many of the city's best Modernista buildings, the Quadrat d'Or is made up of around a hundred city blocks centering on the Passeig de Gràcia. The wealthy bourgeoisie, who favored this area of the Eixample, embraced the new artistic and architectural style, both

The rippled facade of Gaudí's Casa Milà "La Pedrera" in the Quadrat d'Or

for their homes and offices. Many interiors are open to the public, revealing a feast of stained glass, ceramics, and ironwork.

The most remarkable single block is the **Illa de la Discòrdia**, where four of Barcelona's most famous Modernista houses – all built between 1900 and 1910 – vie for attention. Nearby, the late 19th-century **Fundació Tàpies**, by Domènech i Montaner, houses paintings, sculptures, and graphics, and is topped by Tàpies' wire sculpture, *Cloud and Chair*.

Gaudí's famous **Casa Milà "La Pedrera"** has a wave-like facade and a roofscape of chimneys and vents resembling abstract sculptures. The Palau Baró de Quadras, designed by Puig i Cadalfalch in 1904, is now home to the Casa Asia, which holds occasional exhibitions dedicated to Asian art and culture.

Carving of a coiled beast on the doorway of the Casa Asia, Quadrat d'Or

Sagrada Família ⑦

Europe's most unconventional church, the Temple Expiatori de la Sagrada Família is an emblem of a city that likes to think of itself as individualistic. Full of symbolism inspired by nature and striving for originality, it is the greatest work of Catalan architect Antoni Gaudí (1852–1926). In 1883, a year after work began on a Neo-Gothic church on the site, he was given the task of completing it. Gaudí changed everything, extemporizing as he went along. It became his life's work and he lived like a recluse on the site for the last few years of his life. He is buried in the crypt. By the time of his death only one tower on the Nativity facade had been completed, but several more have since been finished to his original plans. After the Civil War, work resumed and continues today, financed by public subscription.

Bell Towers
Eight of the 12 spires, one for each apostle, have been built. Each is topped by Venetian mosaics.

THE FINISHED CHURCH

Gaudí's initial ambitions have been scaled down over the years, but the design for the building's completion remains impressive. Still to come is the central tower, which is to be encircled by four large towers representing the Evangelists. Four towers on the Glory (south) facade will match the existing four on the Passion (west) and four on the Nativity (east) facades. An ambulatory – like an inside-out cloister – will run round the outside of the building.

Tower with elevator

The apse was the first part of the church Gaudí completed. Stairs lead down from here to the crypt below.

Entrance to Crypt

The altar canopy, designed by Gaudí, is still waiting for the altar.

Main entrance

★ **Passion Facade**
This bleak facade was completed from 1986 to 2000 by artist Josep Maria Subirachs. A controversial work, its sculpted figures are angular and often sinister.

For hotels and restaurants in this region see pp341–2 and pp347–8

Spiral Staircases
The stone steps
tured are not open
e public, but there
n elevator instead.
There are majestic
ws from the towers
nd upper galleries.

Tower
with
elevator

VISITORS' CHECKLIST

Calle Mallorca 401. *Tel* 93-208
04 14. M Sagrada Familia.
19, 33, 34, 43, 44, 50, 51,
54. 9am–8pm (Oct–Mar: to
6pm). Jan 1 & 6, Dec 25 & 26
(from 2pm). 9am, 8:15pm
Mon–Sat, 9am, 10:30am,
11:45am, 1pm, 8:15pm Sun.
ground floor.
www.sagradafamilia.org

★ **Nativity Facade**
The most complete part of
Gaudí's church has doorways
representing Faith, Hope, and
Charity. Scenes of the Nativity
and Christ's childhood contain
imagery, such as doves, which
symbolize the congregation.

★ **Crypt**
The crypt, where Gaudí is buried
and services are currently held,
was begun by the original architect,
Francesc de Paula Villar i Lozano,
in 1882. A small museum traces
the careers of both architects and
the church's complicated history.

Nave
In the nave, a forest of fluted
pillars support five galleries
above the side aisles, while
skylights let in natural light.

STAR FEATURES

★ Passion Facade

★ Nativity Facade

★ Crypt

Pretty whitewashed houses in Poble Espanyol, Montjuïc

Montjuïc ⑨

M Espanya, Poble Sec, Paral·lel.
🚌 13, 50 from Plaça Espanya.

The hill of Montjuic, rising to 213 m (699 ft) above the commercial port on the south side of the city, is Barcelona's biggest recreation area. Its museums, art galleries, funfair, and nightclubs make it popular night and day. The hill is also a spectacular vantage point from which to view the city.

There was probably a Celtiberian settlement here before the Romans built a temple to Jupiter on their Mons Jovis, which may have given Montjuïc its name. Another theory suggests that a Jewish cemetery on the hill inspired the name Mount of the Jews. Many buildings were erected in 1929, when an International Exhibition was held here, and later for the 1992 Olympics. On

the western edge is the **Poble Espanyol** – a "village" of streets and squares, created in 1929 to showcase different Spanish architectural styles. The **Museu Arqueològic** holds important finds from prehistoric cultures in Catalonia and the Balearic Islands. The **Museu Etnològic** houses artifacts from Oceania, Africa, Asia, and Latin America.

The summit of Montjuïc is occupied by the huge 18th-century **Castell de Montjuïc**, built for the Bourbon family. The castle is being converted into an International Peace Center, with exhibitions on the history of the castle and the Montjuïc Mountain. Renovations will last until 2013.

⚜ Castell de Montjuïc
Parc de Montjuïc. **Tel** 93-329 86 13.
M Paral·lel, then funicular & cable car. **Museum** ☐ Sat & Sun. ● Jan 1, Good Fri, May 1, Dec 25 & 26.

🏛 Museu Arqueològic
Passeig Santa Madrona 39.
Tel 93-423 21 49. **M** Espanya, Poble Sec. ☐ Tue–Sat, Sun am & public hols. ● Jan 1, Dec 25 & 26.
📷 ♿ www.mac.es

Fundació Joan Miró ⑩

Parc de Montjuïc. **Tel** 93-443 94 70.
www.fundaciomiro-bcn.org
M Espanya or Paral·lel, then bus 50 or 55. ☐ Tue–Sat, Sun am & public hols. ● Jan 1, Dec 25 & 26. 📷 ♿

Housed in a boldly modern building designed in 1975 by Josep Lluís Sert, this collection of paintings, sculptures, and tapestries by Catalan artist Joan Miró (1893–1983) is lit by natural light.

An admirer of primitive Catalan art and Gaudí's Modernism, Miró developed a Surrealistic style, with vivid colors and fantastical forms that suggested dreamlike situations. Miró himself donated the works displayed here. Some of the best pieces at the museum include his *Barcelona Series* (1939–44), a set of 50 black-and-white lithographs. Temporary exhibitions of other artists' work are also held here.

The Palau Nacional, home of the Museu Nacional d'Art de Catalunya

Museu Nacional d'Art de Catalunya ⑪

Palau Nacional, Parc de Montjuïc.
Tel 93-622 03 76. **M** Espanya.
☐ Tue–Sat, Sun am & public hols.
● Jan 1, May 1, Dec 25. 📷 📷 call 93-622 03 75 in advance. ♿

Originally built for the 1929 International Exhibition, since 1934 the austere Palau Nacional (National Palace) has been used to house the city's most important art collection.

The museum contains one of the greatest displays of Romanesque art in the world, its centerpiece being a series of magnificent 12th-century frescoes. These have been peeled from Catalan Pyrenean churches (to save them from the ravages of pollution and time) and pasted on to replicas of the original vaulted ceilings

A section of the 18th-century castle on the summit of Montjuïc

and apses they adorned. The most remarkable are the wall paintings from the churches of Santa Maria de Taüll and Sant Climent de Taüll in Vall de Boí.

The museum's superb Gothic collection covers the whole of Spain, but is particularly good on Catalonia. Several outstanding works by El Greco, Velázquez, and Zurbarán are on display in the Renaissance and Baroque section.

Parc Güell ⑫

Carrer d'Olot. **Tel** 93-413 24 00. Ⓜ Lesseps. ◯ daily. 🖼 ♿ **Casa-Museu Gaudí Tel** 93-219 38 11. ◯ daily. ⬤ Jan 1 & 6, Dec 25 & 26 (am). 🖼

Designated a World Heritage Site by UNESCO, the Parc Güell is Gaudí's most colorful creation. He was commissioned in the 1890s by Count Eusebi Güell to design a garden city on 20 hectares (50 acres) of family estate. Little of Gaudí's grand plan for decorative buildings among landscaped gardens became reality. What we see today was completed between 1910 and 1914.

Most atmospheric is the Room of a Hundred Columns, a cavernous hall of 84 crooked pillars, which is brightened by glass and ceramic mosaics. Above it, reached by a flight of steps flanked by ceramic animals, is the Gran Plaça Circular, an

Mosaic-encrusted chimney by Gaudí at the entrance of the Parc Güell

open space with a snaking balcony of colored mosaics, said to have the longest bench in the world. It was executed by Josep Jujol, one of Gaudí's chief collaborators.

The two mosaic-decorated pavilions at the entrance are by Gaudí, but the **Casa-Museu Gaudí**, a gingerbread-style house where he lived from 1906–26, was built by Francesc Berenguer. The drawings and furniture inside are all by Gaudí.

Tibidabo ⑬

Plaça del Tibidabo 3–4. **Tel** 93-211 79 42. Ⓜ Avda Tibidabo, then Tramvia Blau & funicular, or TibiBus from Plaça Catalunya. **Funfair** ◯ call to check. ⬤ Oct–Apr: Mon–Fri. ♿ **Temple del Sagrat Cor Tel** 93-417 56 86. ◯ daily. www.tibidabo.cat

The heights of Tibidabo are reached by Barcelona's last surviving tram, the Tramvia Blau, and a funicular railway.

An ornate merry-go-round at the Parc d'Atraccions, Tibidabo

The name, inspired by Tibidabo's views of the city, comes from the Latin *tibi dabo* (I shall give you) – a reference to the Temptation of Christ, who was taken up a mountain by Satan and offered the world spread at his feet.

The hugely popular funfair at **Parc d'Atraccions** first opened in 1908. The rides were completely renovated in the 1980s. While the old ones retain their charm, the newer ones provide the latest in vertiginous experiences. Their hilltop location at 517 m (1,696 ft) adds to the thrill. Also in the park is the **Museu d'Automates**, which displays automated toys, jukeboxes, and gaming machines.

Tibidabo is crowned by the **Temple Expiatori del Sagrat Cor** (Church of the Sacred Heart), built with religious zeal but little taste by Enric Sagnier between 1902 and 1911. Inside one of its towers, an elevator takes you up to an enormous statue of Christ.

Monestir de Montserrat ⑲

Its highest peak rising to 1,236 m (4,055 ft), the "Serrated Mountain" *(mont serrat)* is a magnificent setting for Catalonia's holiest place, the Monastery of Montserrat, which is surrounded by chapels and hermits' caves. The earliest record of a chapel on this site is from the 9th century. The monastery was founded in the 11th century. In 1811, when the French attacked Catalonia in the War of Independence, the monastery was destroyed and the monks killed. Rebuilt and repopulated in 1844, it was a beacon of Catalan culture in the Franco years. Today Benedictine monks live here. Visitors can hear the famous male choir singing the *Salve Regina i Virolai* (the Montserrat hymn) at 1pm Monday to Friday, and noon and 6:45pm Sunday except in July and August, and from December 26 to January 8.

A Benedictine monk

Plaça de Santa Maria
The focal points of the square are two wings of the Gothic cloister built in 1477. The modern monastery facade is by Françesc Folguera.

Gothic cloister

Funicular to the holy site of Santa Cova

Information Office

The Museum holds 19th- and 20th-century Catalan paintings and many archaeological exhibits from West Asia.

The Way of the Cross
This path passes 14 statues representing the Stations of the Cross. It begins near the Plaça de l'Abat Oliba.

STAR FEATURES

★ Basilica Facade

★ Black Virgin

View of Montserrat
The complex includes cafés and a hotel. A second funicular railway takes visitors to nature trails above the monastery.

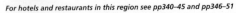

★ Basilica Façade
Agapit and Venanci Vallmitjana sculpted Christ and the apostles on the basilica's Neo-Renaissance facade. It was built in 1900 to replace the Renaissance facade of the original church, consecrated in 1592.

★ Black Virgin
La Moreneta looks down from behind the altar, protected behind glass. Her wooden orb protrudes for pilgrims to touch.

VISITORS' CHECKLIST

Montserrat (Barcelona province). **Tel** 93-877 77 77. 🚠 to Aeri de Montserrat (from Barcelona via Monistrol), then cable car. 🚂 from Barcelona. **Basilica** ◯ 7:30am–7:30pm daily (Jul–Sep: to 8:30pm). ✝ from 9am Mon–Sat, from 9:30am Sun & religious hols. 📷 **Museum** ◯ 10am–5:45pm Mon–Fri, 10am–6:45pm Sat & Sun. 📷🎥♿ www.abadiamontserrat.net

Basilica Interior
The sanctuary in the domed basilica is adorned by a richly enameled altar and paintings by Catalan artists.

The rack railway follows the course of a historic rail line built in 1880.

Terminal for cable car from Aeri de Montserrat train station

THE VIRGIN OF MONTSERRAT

The small wooden statue of La Moreneta ("the dark one") is the soul of Montserrat. It is said to have been made by St. Luke and brought here by St. Peter in AD 50. Centuries later, the statue is believed to have been hidden from the Moors in the nearby Santa Cova (Holy Cave). Carbon dating suggests, however, that the statue was carved around the 12th century. In 1881 Montserrat's Black Virgin became patroness of Catalonia.

The Black Virgin of Montserrat

Inner Courtyard
On one side of the courtyard is the baptistry (1902), with sculptures by Charles Collet. Pilgrims may approach the Virgin through a door to the right.

Eastern Spain and the Balearic Islands

Eastern Spain covers an extraordinary range of climates and landscapes, from the snowbound peaks of the Pyrenees in Aragón to the beaches of the Costa Blanca. The region has many historical sights, including the striking Mudéjar churches of Zaragoza and the great cathedral of Valencia. The coastal resorts of Eastern Spain are a popular destination, as are the Balearic Islands. Mallorca is the most culturally rich of the islands, while Menorca is dotted with prehistoric sites. Ibiza is chiefly known for its exuberant nightlife, but Formentera remains largely unspoiled. A dialect of the Catalan language, brought by 13th-century settlers, is still widely spoken on the islands.

Cupolas of the Basílica de Nuestra Señora del Pilar in Zaragoza

Zaragoza ㉒

Zaragoza. 675,000. Plaza del Pilar (902-14 20 08). Wed, Sun.

The Roman settlement of Caesaraugusta gave Zaragoza its name. Located on the fertile banks of the Río Ebro, it grew to become Spain's fifth largest city, and the capital of Aragón.

Badly damaged during the early 19th-century War of Independence, the old center nevertheless retains several fine monuments. Overlooking the vast Plaza del Pilar is the **Basílica de Nuestra Señora del Pilar**. With its 11 brightly tiled cupolas, it is one of the city's most impressive sights.

Also on the square are the Gothic-Plateresque **Lonja** (commodities exchange), the **Palacio Episcopal**, and Zaragoza's cathedral, **La Seo**, which displays a great mix of styles. Part of the exterior is faced with typical Mudéjar brick and ceramic decoration, while inside are a fine Gothic reredos and splendid Flemish tapestries. Nearby is the flamboyant Mudéjar bell tower of the **Iglesia de la Magdalena**, and remains of the Roman forum.

Parts of the Roman walls can be seen on the opposite side of the Plaza del Pilar near the **Mercado de Lanuza**, a market with sinuous ironwork in Art Nouveau style. The **Museo Camón Aznar** houses the eclectic collection of an art historian, whose special interest was the locally-born artist Goya.

The **Alfajería**, a beautiful 11th-century Moorish palace with gardens and a mosque, lies on the main road to Bilbao.

🏛 **Museo Camón Aznar**
Calle Espoz y Mina 23. **Tel** 976-39 73 28. Tue–Sun.

Valencia ㉓

Valencia. 810,000. 8 km (5 miles) SW. Plaza de la Reina 19 (963-15 39 31). Las Fallas (Mar 15–19). www.turisvalencia.es

Valencia, Spain's third largest city, is famous for its ceramics, and for the spectacular fiesta of Las Fallas, marked by the erection and burning of elaborate papier-mâché monuments (*fallas*).

Among the city's finest buildings are **La Lonja**, an exquisite Late Gothic hall built between 1482 and 1498, and the **cathedral** (1262) on Plaza de la Reina. Other monuments worth visiting include the Gothic **Palau de la Generalitat**, with its splendidly decorated first-floor chambers, and the 17th-century **Basílica de la Virgen de los Desamparados**.

Beyond the city center is the **Torres de Serranos** gateway, erected in 1391.

Valencia has a number of fine museums. The **Museo de Bellas Artes** holds 2,000 paintings and statues dating from antiquity to the 19th century, including six paintings by Goya, while the **Museo Domingo Fletcher** has a unique collection of local Stone Age engravings. Valencia's metro system takes tourists to the extensive beaches of El Cabañal and La Malvarrosa, east of the city.

🏛 **La Lonja**
Plaza del Mercado s/n. **Tel** 96-352 54 78 (ext. 4153). Tue–Sun.

Effigy burning in Valencia during the annual fiesta of Las Fallas

The mountain village of Castell de Guadalest, Costa Blanca

🏛 Palau de la Generalitat
Plaza des Manises. **Tel** 96-386 34 61. ⬜ *by prior appointment only.*

🏛 Museo de Bellas Artes
Calle San Pio V 9. **Tel** 96-387 03 00. ⬜ *10am–8pm Tue–Sun.* ● *Jan 1, Good Friday, Dec 25.* ⬜ *(by appt only, 963-870 320).* ♿

Costa Blanca 24

🏖 🏖 🚉 🚌 *Alicante.* ℹ️ *Calle Portugal 17, Alicante (96-592 98 02).* **www**.comunidadvalenciana.com

The Costa Blanca occupies a prime stretch of Spain's Mediterranean coastline. The main city, **Alicante** (Alacant), has an 18th-century Baroque town hall and a 16th-century castle, the Castillo de Santa Bárbara. The nearest beach to the city center is the popular Postiguet; slightly farther afield are the vast beaches of La Albufereta and Sant Joan.

The massive, rocky outcrop of the **Penyal d'Ifach** towers over Calp harbor, and is one of the Costa Blanca's most dramatic sights. Its summit offers spectacular views. A short drive inland, **Castell de Guadalest** is a pretty mountain village with castle ruins and a distinctive belfry perched precariously on top of a rock.

Also worth visiting are the whitewashed hilltop town of **Altea, Denia**, which has good snorkeling, and the cliffs and coves around **Xabia**. South of Alicante, **Guardamar del Segura** has a quiet beach bordered by aromatic pine woods, while **Torrevieja** is a highly-developed resort with sweeping, sandy shores.

Mallorca and the Balearic Islands 25

✈ 🚢 🚌 *Palma, Mallorca; Maó, Menorca.* ℹ️ *Passeig des Born 27, Palma, Mallorca (902-10 23 65).*

The largest of the Balearic islands, Mallorca has a varied landscape and a rich cultural heritage. A massive Gothic cathedral is poised high on the sea wall of **Palma**, its capital. Completed in 1587 and known locally as Sa Seu, the cathedral is one of Spain's most breathtaking buildings. The interior was remodeled by Antoni Gaudí and a highlight is the Baldachino, his bizarre wrought-iron canopy above the altar.

Also worth visiting in Palma are the Basílica de Sant Francesc, the Moorish Palau de l'Almudaina, and the Fundació Pilar i Joan Miró – a stunning modern building housing Miró's studio and a collection of the artist's work.

Around the island, **Andratx** is a chic and affluent town with yachts moored along its harbor, while **Pollença** is a popular tourist resort which has remained relatively unspoiled. The 18th-century family home, **La Granja**, and **Alfàbia**, which exudes a Moorish atmosphere, are aristocratic estates open to the public. The **Monasteri de Lluc**, in the remote mountain village of the same name, incorporates a guesthouse, a museum, and a church.

Menorca
Menorca's capital, **Maó**, has one of the finest harbors in the Mediterranean, an 18th-century Carmelite church, and a museum, the Collecció Hernández Mora, housing Menorcan art and antiques. The town of **Ciutadella** boasts an impressive main square and a delightful Art Nouveau market. Menorca's many Bronze Age villages – to which there is usually free access – are mostly the work of the "talaiotic" people, who lived from 2000–1000 BC.

Ibiza and Formentera
A popular package-tour destination, Ibiza has some of the wildest nightclubs in Europe. An hour's boat ride from Ibiza harbor are the tranquil shores of Formentera. The capital, **Sant Francesc**, has a pretty 18th-century church and a folk museum.

View across the marina at Palma, Mallorca to the spectacular cathedral

Southern Spain

One large region – Andalusia – extends across the south of Spain. It was here that the Moors lingered longest and left their greatest monuments in the cities of Granada, Córdoba, Málaga, and Seville. The eight southern provinces span a wide range of landscapes, with deserts in the east, sandy beaches along the Costa del Sol, and sherry-producing vineyards around Jerez. From flamingoes in the wetland Doñana National Park to flamenco – the uniquely Andalusian art form – the region has something to interest every visitor.

Antonio Palamino's cupola in the Monasterio de la Cartuja, Granada

Granada ㉖

Granada. 239,000. 12 km (7 miles) SW. Plaza Mariana Pineda (958-24 71 28). Corpus Christi (May–Jun). www.turismodegranada.org

The ancient city of Granada, founded by the Iberians, was for 250 years the capital of a Moorish kingdom. The Nasrid dynasty, who ruled from 1238 until 1492 when Granada fell to the Catholic Monarchs, left some outstanding examples of Moorish architecture here. The greatest legacy of their rule is the spectacular palace complex of the Alhambra (see pp322–3). Under the Nasrids the city enjoyed a golden age, acquiring an international reputation as a major cultural center. Later, under Christian rule, the city became a focus for the Renaissance.

Granada's 16th-century Gothic **cathedral** has a Renaissance facade and a Baroque west front. Nearby, the **Capilla Real** (Royal Chapel), built between 1505 and 1507, houses Carrara marble figures of the Catholic Monarchs, whose bodies lie in the crypt. Equally impressive are the **Museo Casa de los Tiros**, a fortress-like palace built in Mudéjar style, and the **Monasterio de la Cartuja**, both dating from the 16th century. Founded by a Christian warrior, the latter has a dazzling cupola by Antonio Palomino.

Relics of the Moorish era in the old town include the **Corral del Carbón**, a former storehouse and inn for merchants, and the **Palacio de la Madraza**. Originally an Arab university, the palace has a splendid Moorish hall with a finely decorated *mihrab* (prayer niche). The palace holds temporary art exhibitions.

Granada's Moorish ancestry is most evident in the hillside Albaicín district, which faces the Alhambra. Along its cobbled alleys stand *cármenes* – villas with Moorish decor and gardens – and **El Bañuelo**, the 11th-century brick-vaulted Arab baths. The churches here were mostly built on the sites of mosques. The most beautiful of these, the **Iglesia de Santa Ana**, has an elegant Plateresque portal. The **Real Chancillería**, or Royal Chancery (1530), boasts a beautiful Renaissance facade.

Also worth visiting in the Albaicín district is the **Museo Arqueológico**, with Iberian, Phoenician, and Roman finds.

From one end of the district, a road leads up to **Sacromonte**. Granada's gypsies once lived in the caves lining this hillside. Their legacy lives on in the flamenco shows performed here in the evenings.

From the northern side of the Alhambra, a footpath leads to the **Generalife** (see pp322–3), the country estate of the Nasrid kings. The gardens, begun in the 13th century, originally contained orchards and pastures. Today, their lush greenery, pools, and graceful water fountains provide a magical setting for the many events staged each year between mid-June and early July on the occasion of the city's international music and dance festival.

Museo Casa de los Tiros
Calle Pavaneras. *Tel* 958-57 54 66. Tue–Sun. main public hols.

Palacio de la Madraza
Calle Oficios 14. *Tel* 958-24 34 84. 9am–2pm, 5–8pm Mon–Fri.

Museo Arqueológico
Carrera del Darro 43. *Tel* 958-57 54 08. closed for renovations until 2013.

Entrance to the Moorish *mihrab* in the Palacio de la Madraza, Granada

The main facade of Málaga's unusual cathedral, consecrated in 1588

Málaga ㉗

Málaga. 🏛 570,000. ✈ ⛴ 🚉 🚌
ℹ️ *Av. Cervantes 1 (95-220 96 03).*

Málaga, the second largest city in Andalusia, was a thriving port under Phoenician, Roman, and Moorish rule. It also flourished during the 19th century, when sweet Málaga wine was one of Europe's most popular drinks. At the heart of the old town is the **cathedral**, begun in 1528 by Diego de Siloé. The half-built second tower, abandoned in 1765 when funds ran out, gave the cathedral its nickname: La Manquita ("the one-armed one").

The **Casa Natal de Picasso**, where the painter spent his early years, is now the headquarters of the international Picasso Foundation. Málaga's old Museo de Bellas Artes is being moved to the Palacio de la Aduana, where it will open in 2014. Temporary exhibitions are held at the Palacio Episcopal.

The city's vast fortress – the **Alcazaba** – was built between the 8th and 11th centuries. Its major attractions are the display of Phoenician, Roman, and Moorish artifacts, as well as a Roman theater. The ruined **Castillo de Gibralfaro**, a 14th-century Moorish castle, lies behind the Alcazaba.

🏰 **Alcazaba**
Calle Alcazabilla. **Tel** 95-222 72 30.
⏰ 9:30am–8pm Tue–Sun.

MOORISH SPAIN

Typical Moorish *alcazaba*, dating from the 10th century

In the 8th century, the Iberian Peninsula came almost entirely under Moorish rule. The Muslim settlers called Spain "Al Andalus." A powerful caliphate was established in Córdoba, which became the center of one of the most brilliant civilizations of early medieval Europe. The Moors erected *alcazabas* (castles built into city ramparts) and palaces surrounded by patios, pools, and gardens, making lavish use of arches, stucco work, glazed wall tiles *(azulejos)*, and ornamental calligraphy. They also introduced new crops to Spain, such as oranges and rice. By the 11th century the caliphate had collapsed into 30 *taifas* (splinter states) and the northern Christian kingdoms were reconquering parts of Moorish Spain. In 1492 the Catholic Monarchs took Granada, its last stronghold. Though many Muslims were expelled from Spain following the Reconquest, some were employed to build new churches and palaces for the Christian rulers. Known as Mudéjares (the name literally means "those permitted to stay"), these craftsmen developed a hybrid Christian-Islamic style that survived into the 18th century.

Costa del Sol ㉘

✈ ⛴ 🚉 🚌 Málaga. ℹ️ Avenida Cervantes 1, Málaga (95-220 96 03).

With its year-round sunshine and varied coastline, the Costa del Sol attracts crowds of vacationers every year and also has half a million foreign residents.

Its most stylish resort is **Marbella**, frequented by royalty and film stars, who spend their summers here in the smart villas or luxury hotels overlooking the area's 28 beaches. Puerto Banús is its ostentatious marina. In winter the major attraction is golf: 30 of Europe's finest golf courses lie just inland.

Among the highlights of Marbella's old town is the Museo de Grabado Contemporáneo, which displays some of Picasso's least-known work, the peaceful Iglesia de Nuestra Señora de la Encarnación, and the town hall, with its exquisite, panelled Mudéjar ceiling.

Sotogrande, to the west of Marbella, is an exclusive resort of luxury villas. The marina is fronted by good seafood restaurants. In spite of tourism, **Estepona** preserves its Spanish character, with pretty tree-filled squares and inexpensive tapas bars.

To the east are the package-holiday resorts of **Fuengirola** and **Torremolinos**. Once the brash haunt of young northern European tourists, they are now more family-oriented.

Player on a green at one of Marbella's high-profile golf courses

Granada: the Alhambra

A magical use of space, light, water, and decoration characterizes this most sensual piece of architecture. It was built under Ismail I, Yusuf I, and Muhammad V, caliphs when the Nasrid dynasty (1238–1492) ruled Granada. Seeking to belie an image of waning power, they created their idea of paradise on earth. Modest materials were used (plaster, timber, and tiles), but they were superbly worked. Although the Alhambra suffered decay and pillage, including an attempt by Napoleon's troops to blow it up, it has been restored and its delicate craftsmanship still dazzles the eye.

★ Salón de Embajadores
The ceiling of this sumptuous throne room, built between 1334 and 1354, represents the seven heavens of the Muslim cosmos.

Sala de la Barca

★ Patio de Arrayanes
This pool, set amid myrtle hedges and graceful arcades, reflects light into the surrounding halls.

Patio de Machuca

Entrance

Patio del Mexuar
This council chamber, completed in 1365, was where the reigning sultan listened to the petitions of his subjects and held meetings with his ministers.

PLAN OF THE ALHAMBRA

To the Generalife

Main gate

The Alhambra complex includes the Casas Reales, the 13th-century Alcazaba, the 16th-century Palace of Charles V, and the Generalife (*see p320*), which is located just off the map.

KEY

- Casas Reales (shown above)
- Palace of Charles V
- Alcazaba (fortress)
- Gardens
- Iglesia de Santa María
- Other buildings

Palacio del Partal

A pavilion with an arched portico and a tower is all that remains of this palace, the oldest building in the Alhambra.

Washington Irving's apartments

Baños Reales

Jardín de Lindaraja

VISITORS' CHECKLIST

For the Alhambra and Generalife. **Tel** 902-88 80 01. 2. ☐ 8:30am–8pm daily (mid-Oct–mid-Mar: to 6pm). **Night visits:** mid-Mar–mid-Oct: 10–11:30pm Tue–Sat; mid-Oct–mid-Mar: 8–9:30pm Fri & Sat. (reservations are essential). **www**.alhambra-patronato.es or **www**.alhambra-tickets.es

The Sala de las Dos Hermanas, with its honeycomb dome, is regarded as a splendid example of Spanish-Islamic architecture.

Sala de los Reyes

This great banqueting hall was used to hold extravagant parties and feasts. Beautiful leather ceiling paintings, from the 14th century, depict tales of hunting and chivalry.

Puerta de la Rawda

★ Sala de los Abencerrajes

This hall takes its name from a noble family – rivals of the last Nasrid ruler, Boabdil. Legend claims he had the family massacred while they attended a banquet here. The geometrical ceiling was inspired by Pythagoras' theorem.

The Palace of Charles V (1526) houses a collection of Spanish-Islamic art, whose highlight is the Alhambra vase.

★ Patio de los Leones

Built by Muhammad V, this patio is lined with arcades supported by 124 slender marble columns. At its center, a fountain rests on 12 stocky marble lions.

STAR FEATURES

- ★ Salón de Embajadores
- ★ Patio de Arrayanes
- ★ Sala de los Abencerrajes
- ★ Patio de los Leones

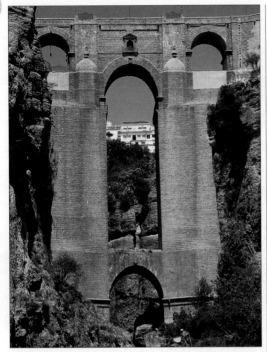

The Puente Nuevo, spanning the deep Tajo gorge at Ronda

Ronda ㉙

Málaga. 👥 37,000. 🚊 🚌
ℹ️ Plaza de España 9 (95-287 12 72).

Ronda sits on a massive, rocky outcrop, straddling a precipitous limestone cleft. Because of its impregnable position, it was one of the last Moorish bastions, finally falling to the Christians in 1485.

On the south side perches a classic *pueblo blanco* – a white town – so-called because the houses are whitewashed in the Moorish tradition.

Among Ronda's historic buildings is the **Palacio Mondragón**, adorned with original Moorish mosaics. The facade of the 18th-century **Palacio del Marqués de Salvatierra** is decorated with images of South American Indians. From the **Casa del Rey Moro**, built on the site of a Moorish palace, 365 steps lead down to the river.

Across the **Puente Nuevo** or "New Bridge," which spans the deep Tajo gorge, is the modern town, and the site of one of Spain's oldest bullrings.

Inaugurated in 1785, the **Plaza de Toros** and its bull-fighting museum, the **Museo Taurino**, attract aficionados from all over the country.

🐂 **Plaza de Toros & Museo Taurino**
Calle Virgen de la Paz. **Tel** 952-87 41 32. ☐ daily. 🎫 ♿

Córdoba ㉚

Córdoba. 👥 328,000. 🚊 🚌
ℹ️ Calle Campo Santo de los Martires (in front of Alcázar (902-20 17 74).

With its glorious mosque and pretty Moorish patios, Córdoba is northern Andalusia's star attraction. In the 10th century the city enjoyed a golden age as the western capital of the Islamic empire.

Córdoba's most impressive Moorish monument is the mighty Mezquita *(see pp326–7)*. To the west of its towering walls, the **Alcázar de los Reyes Cristianos**, in the old Jewish quarter, is a stunning 14th-century palace-fortress built

by Alfonso XI. The Catholic Monarchs stayed here during their campaign to wrest Granada from Moorish rule.

The small Mudéjar-style **synagogue** (c.1315) has decorative plasterwork with Hebrew script. Nearby, the **Museo Taurino**, a bullfighting museum, contains a replica of the tomb of Manolete, a famous matador, and the hide of the bull that killed him.

A Roman bridge, spanning the Río Guadalquivir, links the old town to the 14th-century **Torre de la Calahorra**. This defensive tower houses a small museum depicting life in 10th-century Córdoba.

In the newer part of the city, the **Museo Arqueológico** displays Roman and Moorish artifacts. The **Museo de Bellas Artes** contains sculptures by local artist Mateo Inurria (1867–1924) and paintings by Murillo and Zurbarán. Other notable buildings are the beautiful 17th-century **Palacio de Viana**, filled with works of art, and the handsome arcades of the **Plaza de la Corredera**.

🏰 **Alcázar de los Reyes Cristianos**
Calle Caballerizas Reales s/n. **Tel** 957-42 01 51. ☐ mid-Jun–mid-Sep: 8:30am–2:30pm Tue–Sat, 9:30am–1:30pm Sun; mid-Sep–mid-Jun: 8:30am–7:30pm Tue–Fri, 9:30am–4:30pm Sat, 9:30am–2:30pm Sun. ● Jan 1, Dec 25. 🎫 (free on Wed).

Seville ㉛

See pp328–31.

Water gardens at the Alcázar de los Reyes Cristianos, Córdoba

Marshes and sand dunes of the Parque Nacional de Doñana

Parque Nacional de Doñana 🟢

Huelva & Sevilla. **i** 959-43 96 29.
Park interior ⬜ summer: Mon–Sat;
winter: Tue–Sun. **Tel** 959-43 04 32
for reservations.

Doñana National Park is
ranked among Europe's
greatest wetlands, comprising
more than 185,000 acres of
marshes and sand dunes. The
area, officially protected since
1969, was once a ducal
hunting ground (coto).

A road runs through part
of the park, with information
points located along it. There
are also several self-guided
walks on the park outskirts, but
the interior can be visited on
official guided day tours only.

Doñana is home to wild
cattle, fallow and red deer, and
the lynx – one of Europe's
rarest mammals. The greater
flamingo and the rare imperial
eagle can also be seen. It
is also a stopping place for
thousands of migratory birds.

Jerez de la Frontera 🟢

Cádiz. 🚹 209,000. ✈ 🚌
i Alameda Cristina 7 (956-33
88 74). **www.**turismojerez.com

Jerez is the capital of sherry
production and many
bodegas (cellars) can be
visited. Among the well-known
names are **González Byass**
and **Pedro Domecq**.

The city is also famous for
its **Real Escuela Andaluza
de Arte Ecuestre**, a school

of equestrian skills. Public
dressage displays are
held on Thursdays. On
the Plaza de San Juan,
the 18th-century **Palacio
de Penmartín** houses
the Centro Andaluz
de Flamenco, with
exhibitions on this music
and dance tradition. The
11th-century **Alcázar**
encompasses a
well-preserved mosque,
now a church.
Just to the north
is the **cathedral**.
Its most famous
treasure, *The
Sleeping Girl*
by Zurbarán.

**Golden chalice from the
treasury of Cádiz cathedral**

🍷 Sherry Bodegas
González Byass Calle Manuel María
González 12, Jerez. **Tel** 902-44 00
77. **Pedro Domecq** Calle
San Ildefonso 3, Jerez. **Tel** 956-15
15 00. ⬜ Mon–Sat.

Cádiz 🟢

Cádiz. 🚹 126,000. 🚌 **i** Paseo
de Canalejas (956-24 10 01) or Avda
Ramón de Carranza (956-20 31 92).

Surrounded almost entirely by
water, Cádiz lays claim to
being Europe's oldest city.
After the Catholic reconquest,
the city prospered on wealth
brought from the New World.

Modern Cádiz is a busy
port, with a pleasant waterfront, while the old town has
narrow alleys and lively
markets. The Baroque and
Neoclassical **cathedral**, with
its dome of golden yellow
tiles, is one of Spain's
largest. The **Museo de
Cádiz** has one of the
largest art collections
in Andalusia, and arch-
aeological exhibits chart
the history of the city.

The 18th-century
**Oratorio de San Felipe
Neri** has been a shrine
to liberalism since 1812
when a provisional
government
assembled in
the church to
try to establish
Spain's first
constitutional
monarchy. The
Torre Tavira, an 18th-century
watchtower, offers spectacular
views of the city.

🏛 Museo de Cádiz
Plaza de Mina. **Tel** 956-20 33 71.
⬜ Tue–Sun. ⚫ public hols.

TAPAS

The light snacks known as tapas – and sometimes as
pinchos – originated in Andalusia in the 19th century as an
accompaniment to sherry. The name derives
from a bartender's practice of covering a
glass with a saucer or *tapa* (cover) to keep
out flies. The custom progressed to a
chunk of cheese, or a few olives,
placed on a platter to serve
with a drink. Today tapas
range from cold snacks to
elaborately prepared hot
dishes, generally eaten
standing at the bar rather
than sitting at a table.
Almost every village in
Spain has a tapas bar.
In the larger towns it is
customary to move from bar to bar,
sampling the specialties of each.

Olives

**Jamón serrano
(salt-cured ham)**

**Patatas bravas (potatoes
in spicy tomato sauce)**

Córdoba: the Mezquita

Córdoba's great mosque, dating back 12
centuries, embodied the power of Islam
on the Iberian Peninsula. Abd al
Rahman I built the original mosque
between 785 and 787. The building
evolved over the centuries, blending
many architectural forms. In the
10th century al Hakam II made
some of the most lavish additions,
including the elaborate *mihrab*
(prayer niche) and the *maqsura*
(caliph's enclosure). During the
16th century a cathedral was built
in the heart of the mosque, part
of which was destroyed.

Patio de los Naranjos
*Orange trees grow in the courtyard
where the faithful washed
before prayer.*

Torre del Alminar
*This bell tower, 93 m (305 ft)
high, is built on the site of
the original minaret. Steep
steps lead to the top for a
fine view of the city.*

**The Puerta del
Perdón** is a Mudéjar-
style entrance gate, built
during Christian rule in
1377. Penitents were
pardoned here.

**The Puerta de
San Esteban** is
set in a section of
wall from an earlier
Visigothic church.

EXPANSION OF THE MEZQUITA

Abd al Rahman I built the
original mosque. Extensions
were added by Abd al Rahman
II, al Hakam II, and al Mansur.

KEY TO ADDITIONS

☐ Original mosque (785–787)
☐ Added by Abd al Rahman II (833)
☐ Added by al Hakam II (c.961)
☐ Added by al Mansur (c.987–90)
☐ Patio de los Naranjos

STAR FEATURES

★ Arches and Pillars

★ Mihrab

★ Capilla de Villaviciosa

Cathedral

Part of the mosque was destroyed to accommodate the cathedral, begun in 1523. Featuring an Italianate dome, it was designed chiefly by members of the Hernán Ruiz family.

VISITORS' CHECKLIST

Calle Cardenal Herrero 1.
Tel 957-47 05 12. ☐ 8:30am–7pm Mon–Sat, 8:30–10am, 2–7pm Sun (winter: to 6pm). ▨ (free 8:30–10am Mon–Sat). ✝ 11am & 1pm daily. ♿

The cathedral choir has Churrigueresque – excessive Baroque-style – stalls carved by Pedro Duque Cornejo in 1758.

Capilla Mayor

Capilla Real

★ Arches and Pillars

More than 850 columns of granite, jasper, and marble support the roof, creating a dazzling visual effect. Many were taken from Roman and Visigothic buildings.

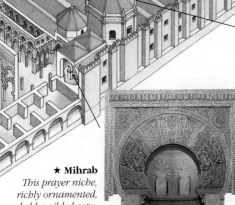

★ Mihrab

This prayer niche, richly ornamented, held a gilded copy of the Koran. The worn flagstones indicate where pilgrims circled it seven times on their knees.

★ Capilla de Villaviciosa

The first Christian chapel was built in the mosque in 1371 by Mudéjar crafts-men (see p321). Its multi-lobed arches are stunning.

Street-by-Street: Seville ㉛

The maze of narrow streets that makes up the Barrio de Santa Cruz represents Seville at its most romantic and compact. This is a good place to begin an exploration of the city, since many of the best-known sights are located here. As well as the expected souvenir shops, tapas bars, and strolling guitarists, there are plenty of picturesque alleys, hidden plazas, and flower-decked patios to reward the casual wanderer. Once a Jewish ghetto, its restored buildings, with characteristic window grilles, are now a harmonious mix of upscale residences and tourist accommodations. Good restaurants and bars make the area well worth an evening visit.

Plaza Virgen de los Reyes
This delightful square, which is often lined with horse-drawn carriages, has an early 20th-century fountain by José Lafita

Palacio Arzobispal, the 18th-century Archbishop's Palace, is still used by Seville's clergy.

Bus station

★ Cathedral and La Giralda
This huge Gothic cathedral and its Moorish bell tower are Seville's most popular sights (see p330).

Convento de la Encarnación (1591)

Archivo de Indias
Built in the 16th century as a merchants' exchange, the Archive of the Indies now houses documents and maps relating to the Spanish colonization of the Americas.

Plaza del Triunfo
The square was built to celebrate the city's survival of the great earthquake of 1755. In the center is a modern statue the Virgin Ma

Calle Mateos Gago
This street is filled with souvenir shops and tapas bars. Bar Giralda at No.2, whose vaults are the remains of a Moorish bath, is popular for its wide variety of tapas.

VISITORS' CHECKLIST

Sevilla. 704,000. 4 km (2.5 miles) NE. Santa Justa, Avda de Kansas City. Plaza de Armas, Calle de Arjona. Avda de la Constitución 21 (95-478 75 78), Plaza del Triunfo (95-421 00 05). **Archivo de Indias Tel** 95-450 05 28.

Train station

The Plaza Santa Cruz is adorned by an ornate iron cross from 1692.

MESON DEL MORO

SANTA TERESA

XIMENEZ ENCISO

RODRIGO CARO

TAMERDANA

LOPE DE RUEDA

REINOSO

PLAZA STA CRUZ

GLORIA

JUSTINO DE NEVE

PL DOÑA ELVIRA

SUSONA

PIMIENTA

CALLEJÓN DEL AGUA

VIDA

Hospital de los Venerables
The 17th-century home for elderly priests has a splendidly restored Baroque church (see p330).

Callejón del Agua
This whitewashed alley-way offers glimpses of enchanting plant-filled patios, such as the one pictured here.

★ Real Alcázar
Seville's Royal Palace is a rewarding combination of exquisite Mudéjar (see p321) craftsmanship, regal grandeur, and landscaped gardens (see p330).

| 0 meters | 50 |
| 0 yards | 50 |

STAR SIGHTS

★ Cathedral and La Giralda

★ Real Alcázar

KEY

– – – – Suggested route

The mighty Giralda bell tower rising above the Gothic cathedral

🏛 Cathedral and La Giralda

Avenida de la Constitución. *Tel 954-21 49 71.* ◻ 11am–5pm Mon–Sat (Jul & Aug: 9:30am–4pm), Sun pm only. 🖼 🛇 except Giralda tower.

Seville's cathedral occupies the site of a great mosque, built by the Almohads in the late 12th century. La Giralda, its huge bell tower, and the beautiful Patio de los Naranjos, which is filled with orange trees, are a legacy of this Moorish structure. Work on the Christian cathedral began in 1401. The bronze spheres on the original Moorish minaret were replaced by Christian symbols, though the Giralda did not assume its present appearance until 1568. Today it is crowned by a bronze sculpture portraying Faith. This weathervane *(giraldillo)* has given the tower its name. Visitors can climb La Giralda for superb views of the city.

The cathedral houses many fine works of art, including the stunning high altar reredos with its 44 gilded reliefs, carved by Spanish and Flemish sculptors in 1482–1564.

🏛 Real Alcázar

Patio de Banderas. *Tel 95-450 23 24.* ◻ 9:30am–7pm daily (Oct–Mar: to 5pm); Jul & Aug: also open at night for concerts, tel 902-45 99 54 for details. 🖼 www.patronato-alcazarsevilla.es

In 1364 Pedro I of Castile ordered the construction of a royal residence within the palaces that had been built in the 12th century by the Moors. Craftsmen from Granada and Toledo created a stunning complex of Mudéjar patios and halls, the Palacio Pedro I, now at the heart of Seville's Real Alcázar. Successive monarchs added their own distinguishing marks: Isabel I dispatched navigators to explore the New World from her Casa de Contratación, while Carlos I (the Holy Roman Emperor Charles V) had grandiose, richly decorated apartments built.

A star feature of the palace is the Salón de Embajadores (Ambassadors' Hall), with its dazzling dome of carved and gilded, interlaced wood. The hall overlooks the Patio de las Doncellas (Patio of the Maidens), which boasts some exquisite plasterwork and has been restored to its function as a "floating garden," as it was during Pedro I's reign.

Laid out with terraces, fountains, and pavilions, the gardens of the Real Alcázar provide a delightful refuge from the bustle of Seville.

🏛 Hospital de los Venerables

Plaza de los Venerables 8. *Tel 95-456 26 96.* ◻ 10am–2pm, 4–8pm daily. ● Jan 1, Good Friday, Dec 25. 🖼 (free Sun pm). 🛇 🛇

This late 17th-century home for elderly priests has been restored as a cultural center, its upper floors, cellar, and infirmary serving as exhibition galleries. The Hospital church is a showcase of Baroque splendors, with frescoes by both Juan de Valdés Leal and his son Lucas Valdés. There are also fine sculptures by Pedro Roldán.

🏛 Torre del Oro

Paseo de Cristóbal Colón. *Tel 95-422 24 19.* ◻ 10am–2pm Tue–Fri, 11am–2pm Sat & Sun. ● Aug. 🖼 except Tue.

The Moors built Seville's Torre del Oro (Tower of Gold) as a defensive lookout in 1220. Its turret was not added until 1760. The gold in the tower's name may refer to the gilded *azulejos* (ceramic tiles) that once clad its walls, or to treasures from

Fresco by Juan de Valdés Leal in the Hospital de los Venerables

Arcaded arena of the Plaza de Toros de la Maestranza, begun in 1761

the Americas unloaded here. It now houses the **Museo Marítimo**, which exhibits maritime maps and antiques.

🏛 Plaza de Toros de la Maestranza
Paseo de Cristóbal Colón 12. **Tel** 95-421 03 15. ◯ daily. ● for bullfights. 🎫 🎥

Built between 1761 and 1881, Seville's famous bullring seats up to 14,000 spectators.

Visitors who take a guided tour of this enormous building are shown many interesting features, including a chapel where the matadors pray for success, and the stables where the horses of the *picadores* (lance-carrying horsemen) are kept. There is also a small museum.

Between Easter Sunday and October, *corridas* (bullfights) take place every Sunday evening. Tickets can be bought from the *taquilla* (ticket office) at the bullring.

🏛 Museo de Bellas Artes
Plaza del Museo 9. **Tel** 95-478 65 00. ◯ 9am–8:30pm Tue–Sat, 9am–2:30pm Sun. 🎫 ♿

The magnificently restored Convento de la Merced Calzada houses one of Spain's best art museums. Delightful tree-filled patios, colorful *azulejos*, and a church with a beautiful Baroque painted ceiling make this a wonderful setting for the fine works of art.

The museum's collection of Spanish art and sculpture – which covers all periods from the medieval to the modern – focuses on the work of the Seville School artists. Among the star attractions are masterpieces by Murillo, Juan de Valdés Leal, and Zurbarán.

🌿 Parque María Luisa
In 1893 Princess María Luisa donated part of the grounds of the Palacio San Telmo to the city for this park. Its most extravagant feature is the semicircular Plaza de España, designed by Aníbal González for the 1929 Ibero-American Exposition. At the center of the park, the Pabellón Mudéjar houses the **Museo de Artes y Costumbres Populares**, with displays of traditional Andalusian folk arts. Nearby, located in the grand Neo-Renaissance Pabellón de Bellas Artes, is the provincial **Museo Arqueológico** (Archaeological Museum).

⛪ Monasterio de Santa María de las Cuevas
Calle Americo Vespucio 2, Isla de la Cartuja. **Tel** 95-503 70 70. ◯ Tue–Sat, Sun am. 🎫 🎥 by prior appointment only. ♿

This 15th-century Carthusian monastery was inhabited by monks until 1836. Columbus lay buried in the crypt of its church between 1507 and 1542.

FLAMENCO
More than just a dance, flamenco is an artistic expression of the joys and sorrows of life. A uniquely Andalusian art, its origins are hard to trace. Gypsies may have been the main creators of the art, mixing their own Indian-influenced culture with existing Moorish and Andalusian folklore, and with Jewish and Christian music. Gypsies were already living in Andalusia by the early Middle Ages, but only in the 18th century did flamenco begin to develop into its present form. There are many styles of *cante* (song) from different parts of Andalusia, but no strict choreography – dancers *(bailaores)* improvise from basic movements, following the rhythm of the guitar and their feelings.

Flamenco dancer (bailaora)

The monastery stands at the heart of the Isla de Cartuja, the site of Expo '92, and also houses the **Museo de Arte Contemporáneo**, with its collection of Spanish and international art. The **Isla Mágica** theme park is also nearby.

Seville's dazzling Plaza de España in the Parque María Luisa

Practical Information

Spain's tourist information service is efficient and extensive, with offices in most towns providing advice on lodgings, restaurants, and local events. In August, many businesses close and roads are busy. It is worth finding out whether local fiestas will coincide with your visit, as while these are enjoyable, they may also cause closures. Public telephones are widely available, but international call charges are high. When changing money, credit cards often offer the best exchange rate and can be used in cash dispensers. The Spanish lunch hour extends from 2pm to 5pm.

WHEN TO VISIT

August is Spain's busiest vacation month. Spanish holidaymakers and millions of foreign tourists flock to the coast. Easter is a good time to visit: temperatures are more bearable, especially in the south, the countryside is in bloom, and some of the country's most important fiestas take place. In the mountains the ski season is from mid-December until March/April.

TOURIST INFORMATION

All major cities and towns have a tourist information office (*oficina de turismo*), which will provide town plans, lists of hotels and restaurants, and details of local activities. There is a **Spanish National Tourist Office** in several large cities worldwide.

OPENING HOURS

Most monuments and museums in Spain close on Mondays. On other days they are generally open from 10am to 2pm, and, usually, reopen from 5pm to 8pm. The main museums stay open through lunch. Most charge for entry. Some churches may only be opened for services.

In smaller towns, churches, castles, and other sights are often kept locked. The key, available on request, will be lodged in a neighboring house, in the town hall, or perhaps with the local bar owners.

VISA REQUIREMENTS AND CUSTOMS

Citizens of the EU, Switzerland, Iceland, and Norway do not require a visa for entry to Spain. A list of entry requirements – available from Spanish embassies – specifies other countries, including the US, Canada, Australia, and New Zealand, whose nationals do not need a visa for visits of less than 90 days.

Non-EU residents can reclaim IVA (sales tax) on some single items. You pay the full price and ask the sales assistant for a *formulario* (tax exemption form). On leaving Spain, you must ask customs to stamp your *formulario* (this must be within six months of the purchase). You receive the refund by mail or on your credit card account.

PERSONAL SECURITY

Violent crime is rare in Spain. Petty theft is the main problem in the cities, especially Madrid, Barcelona, and Seville, where visitors should be extra vigilant. Men may make complimentary remarks (*piropos*) to women in the street. This is customary and not intended to be intimidating.

POLICE

There are essentially three types of police force in Spain. The *Guardia Civil* (National Guard) mainly police rural areas and impose fines for traffic offenses. The *Policía Nacional* operate in larger towns. They are replaced by a regional force, the *Ertzaintza*, in the Basque country, and by the *Mossos d'Esquadra* in Catalonia. The *Policía Local*, also called *Policía Municipal* or *Guardia Urbana*, operate independently in each town and have a branch for city traffic control.

All three services will direct you to the relevant authority in the event of an incident requiring police help.

EMERGENCY SERVICES

Only the *Policía Nacional* operates a nationwide emergency phone number (*see Directory*). Telephone

MADRID

°C/F	Apr	Jul	Oct	Jan
	17/63	32/90	20/68	10/50
0°C / 32°F	5/41	16/61	8/46	0/32
☀ hrs	8	12	6.5	5
☂ mm	48	11	53	39

SEVILLE

°C/F	Apr	Jul	Oct	Jan
	21/70	35/95	25/77	16/61
0°C / 32°F	10/50	18/64	13/55	5/41
☀ hrs	6	8	4.5	2
☂ mm	50	58	55	55

directories list local emergency numbers under *Servicios de Urgencia*. For emergency medical treatment call the Cruz Roja (Red Cross), look under *Ambulancias* in the phone book, or go to a hospital emergency room (*Urgencias*).

HEALTH ISSUES

Spanish pharmacists have wide responsibilities. They can advise and, in certain cases, prescribe without consulting a doctor (antibiotics not included). In a non-emergency, a *farmacéutico* is a good person to see first. It is usually easy to find one who speaks English.

The pharmacy (*farmacia*) sign is a green or red illuminated cross. Those open at night are listed in the windows of all the local pharmacies.

FACILITIES FOR THE DISABLED

Spain's national association for the disabled, the Confederación Coordinadora Estatal de Minusválidos Físicos de España (**COCEMFE**), has a tour company, Servi-COCEMFE, which publishes guides to facilities in Spain and will help plan a vacation to individual requirements. A Spanish travel agency, **Viajes 2000**, specializes in vacations for disabled people.

LANGUAGE AND ETIQUETTE

The Spanish commonly greet and say goodbye to strangers at bus stops and in stores and other public places. People shake hands when introduced and whenever they meet. In Catalonia and the Basque country, regional languages are as much in use as the national tongue, which is Castilian Spanish.

BANKING AND CURRENCY

The Spanish unit of currency is the euro (*see p15*). Generally, banks are open from 8am to 2pm Monday to Friday. Some branches are also open on Thursday afternoon. Most have a foreign exchange desk with the sign *Cambio* or *Extranjero*. Take some form of ID when changing money. Bureaux de change charge higher rates of commission but are open longer hours. The best rate is to be found by withdrawing cash from an ATM or paying by credit card. Visa and Mastercard are accepted in most places.

COMMUNICATIONS

As well as public telephone booths (*cabinas*), there are nearly always pay phones in bars. Most take coins, but some take tokens. Phonecards can be bought at newsstands and *estancos* (tobacconists). At public telephone offices, which are called *locutorios*, you can make a call and pay for it afterwards. Telefónica run the official ones, which are less expensive than private offices.

The Spanish postal service, Correos, is rather slow: a national or international delivery may take more than a week. Send important mail by *urgente* (express) or *certificado* (registered) mail. The main Correos offices open from 8:30am to 9:30pm from Monday to Friday and from 9am to 2pm on Saturday. Conveniently, you will find that stamps for letters and postcards can also be bought from an *estanco*.

DIRECTORY

SPANISH NATIONAL TOURIST OFFICES ABROAD

Canada
2 Bloor West, 34th floor, Toronto, ON, M4W 3E2.
Tel 416-961 31 31.

United Kingdom
79 New Cavendish Street, London W1W 6XB (by prior appointment only).
Tel 020-7486 8077.
www.spain.info

United States
60 East 42nd St, Suite 5300 (53rd floor), New York, NY 10165-0039.
Tel 212-265 8822.
www.spain.info

TOURIST OFFICES IN SPAIN

Barcelona
Plaça de Catalunya 17–S, 08002 Barcelona.
Tel 93-285 38 34.

Madrid
Calle Duque de Medinaceli 2, 28014 Madrid.
Tel 91-429 49 51.

Seville
Avenida de la Constitución 21b, 41004 Seville.
Tel 95-478 75 78.

EMBASSIES

Australia
Torre Espacio, Paseo de la Castellana 259D, 24th Floor, 28046 Madrid.
Tel 91-353 66 00.

Canada
Calle de Núñez de Balboa 35, 28001 Madrid.
Tel 91-423 32 50.

UK
Torre Espacio, Paseo de la Castellana 259D, 28046 Madrid.
Tel 90-210 93 56.
Tel 91-334 21 94.

US
Calle Serrano 75, 28006 Madrid.
Tel 91-587 22 00.

EMERGENCY NUMBERS

Emergency: all services
Tel 112 (most large cities).

Police
Tel 091 (nationwide).

Ambulance
(Red Cross, Cruz Roja).
Tel 112 or 90-222 22 92.

Fire Brigade (Bomberos)
Tel 080 (in most large cities).

FACILITIES FOR THE DISABLED

COCEMFE
Calle de Luis Cabrera 63, 28002 Madrid.
Tel 91-744 36 00.

Viajes 2000
Paseo de la Castellana 228–230, 28046 Madrid.
Tel 91-323 10 29.
www.viajes2000.com

Travel Information

Spain has an increasingly efficient transportation system. All the major cities and islands have airports, and flights from around the globe arrive at those of Madrid and Barcelona. Both the road and rail networks were greatly improved during the 1980s and in the run-up to the Barcelona Olympics in 1992. Intercity rail services are reliable, but buses are a faster and more frequent option between smaller towns. In much of rural Spain, however, public transportation is limited and a car is the most practical solution for getting around. Ferries connect mainland Spain with the Balearic Islands, Morocco, and ports in the UK.

FLYING TO SPAIN

Of the several US airlines serving Spain, **American Airlines** flies to Madrid, while **Continental Airlines** and **Delta Air Lines** fly to both Madrid and Barcelona. **Iberia**, the Spanish national airline, has direct flights to Madrid from New York, Miami, and Los Angeles.

Iberia also offers scheduled flights daily to Madrid and Barcelona from all Western European capitals, including Dublin, which is served by the affiliated Air Nostrum. Its partner **British Airways** has scheduled flights to Madrid and Barcelona and several other cities daily from London Heathrow or Gatwick.

From Australasia the best connections to Spain are via Athens, Bangkok, Frankfurt, and London.

CHARTERS AND PACKAGE DEALS

Charter flights from the UK serve airports such as Málaga, Alicante, and Girona. These can be inexpensive, but are less reliable and have limited schedules. Make sure your agent is ABTA bonded before booking. Special deals are often offered in the winter and may include accommodation. Low-cost airline **easyJet** serves Madrid, Barcelona, Mallorca, Málaga, Alicante, and Ibiza from London Luton, Stansted, and Gatwick airports, Liverpool, and Bristol, while **bmibaby** and **Ryanair** fly from London Stansted and other UK regional airports to mainland and island Spain.

DOMESTIC FLIGHTS

Most of Spain's domestic flights have traditionally been operated by **Iberia**, however this monopoly has been broken to encourage competition. The two main alternative Spanish carriers are **Air Europa** and **Spanair**.

The most frequent shuttle service is the Puente Aéreo, run between Barcelona and Madrid by Iberia. Flights leave every 15 minutes at peak business times. A ticket machine allows passengers to buy tickets up to 15 minutes before departure. The journey usually takes 50 minutes.

Air Europa and Spanair services between Madrid and the regional capitals are not as frequent as the Puente Aéreo. Air services within the Canary Islands are run by **Binter**, which is affiliated to Iberia Airlines. The low-cost company **Vueling** serves many destinations in Spain.

GETTING AROUND MADRID AND BARCELONA

The metro is the quickest and least expensive way to travel around Madrid. It is open from 6am to 1:30am and consists of 11 color-coded lines, plus the Ópera-Príncipe Pío link and a service to the airport. Day buses run from 6am until midnight; night buses continue operating until 6am and leave from the Plaza de Cibeles. A *Metro-bus* ticket, valid for ten trips on the buses and metro, can be bought at any metro station, as well as from newsstands and *estancos* (tobacconists). Sightseeing bus tours are run by **City Discovery**.

Barcelona's metro system generally runs from 5am to midnight; on Fridays it stays open until 2am, and all night on Saturdays. There are various types of travelcard available, valid for bus, metro, and the FGC *(Ferrocarrils de la Generalitat de Catalunya)* suburban train network. The city buses in Barcelona are usually colored white and red. The *Nitbus* (night bus) runs from around 10pm to 5am; and the *Aerobús* provides an excellent service between the Plaça de Catalunya and the two terminals of the airport.

Sightseeing tours in Barcelona are operated by Bus Turístic on three routes from Plaça de Catalunya.

RAIL TRAVEL

Spain offers many options for users of the state railroad **RENFE**. The high-speed services are the intercity TALGO trains and the AVE service between Madrid, Seville, and Málaga via Córdoba; from Madrid to Barcelona via Zaragoza and Lleida; and from Barcelona to Seville or Málaga. Tickets for these are the most expensive and may be bought at train stations from the *taquilla* (ticket office), obtained from travel agents, or ordered via the Renfe website or telephone booking line.

The *largo recorrido* (long-distance trains) and *regionales y cercanías* (regional and local) services are frequent, inexpensive, but slower. Tickets for local travel may be purchased from machines at the station.

In Madrid the major stations for long-distance trains are Atocha and Chamartín. Barcelona's two principal train stations are Sants and Francia.

Regional rail companies operate in three areas of Spain. Catalonia and Valencia each has its own *Ferrocarrils de la Generalitat*, known respectively as the **FGC** and the **FGV**. The Basque country has the **ET** *(Eusko*

Trenbideale). **Iberrail** holidays offer rail-plus-hotel deals for traveling between Spanish cities. Two services similar to the Orient Express are also operated by Iberrail. The El Expreso de la Robla has two routes, one around Bilbao and the other from Gijon to Galicia. The Transcantábrico, run by **FEVE** *(Ferrocarriles de Vía Estrecha)* leaves San Sebastián to travel the length of Spain's north coast, ending its journey in Santiago de Compostela. Passengers travel in style in 14 restored period carriages that date from between 1900–30.

LONG-DISTANCE BUSES

Spain has no national long-distance bus company. The largest private company, **Alsa**, offers a variety of bus tours and sightseeing trips throughout Spain. Other companies operate in particular regions. Tickets and information for long-distance travel are available at main bus stations and from travel agents.

TRAVELING BY ROAD

Spain's fastest roads are its *autopistas.* They are normally dual carriageways subject to *peajes* (tolls). *Autovías* are similar but have no tolls. Smaller roads are less well kept but are a more relaxed way to see rural Spain.

As well as the international car rental companies, a few Spanish companies, such as **Atesa**, operate nationwide. The best deals with international companies are accessed through the companies' websites. There are also fly-drive package deals, which include car rental. *Gasolina* (gas) is priced by the liter. Spanish law requires drivers to carry at all times valid insurance and registration documents, a driver's license, and ID.

FERRY SERVICES

Two car ferry routes link the Spanish mainland with the UK. **Brittany Ferries** sails between Plymouth in the UK and Santander in Cantabria; **P&O European Ferries** sails from Portsmouth to Bilbao. The crossings take over 24 hours. Advance reservations are essential in the summer.

Trasmediterránea runs car ferry services from Barcelona and Valencia on the Spanish mainland to the Balearic Islands. The crossing takes about eight hours. The same company also operates frequent inter-island services.

DIRECTORY

IBERIA AND AFFILIATES

International and domestic flights
Tel 902-400 500 (Spain).
Tel 0870-609 0500 (UK).
Tel 800-772 4642 (US).
www.iberia.com

OTHER AIRLINES

Air Europa
Tel 902-401 501 (Spain).
www.aireuropa.com

American Airlines
Tel 902-115 570 (Spain).
Tel 800-433 7300 (US).
www.aa.com

bmibaby
www.bmibaby.com

British Airways
Tel 902-111 333 (Spain).
Tel 08444-930 787 (UK).
Tel 800-247 92 97 (US).
www.britishairways.com

Continental Airlines
www.continental.com

Delta Air Lines
Tel 900-800 743 (Spain).
Tel 800-241 41 41 (US).
www.delta.com

easyJet
www.easyjet.com

Ryanair
www.ryanair.com

Spanair
Tel 902-13 14 15 (Spain).
www.spanair.com

Vueling
Tel 807-001 717 (Spain).
www.vueling.com

MADRID TOURS

City Discovery
www.city-discovery.com/madrid

RAIL TRAVEL

ET
Tel 902-54 32 10.
www.euskotren.es

FEVE
Tel 985-98 23 81.
www.feve.es

FGC
Tel 93-205 15 15.
www.fgc.cat

FGV
Tel 96-526 27 31.
www.fgv.es

Iberrail
Tel 902-10 80 23.
www.iberrail.es

RENFE
Tel 902-32 03 20.
www.renfe.es

BUS COMPANIES

Alsa
Tel 90-242 22 42 (Spain).
www.alsa.es

Eurolines
Tel 90-240 50 40 (Spain).
Tel 0871-781 81 81 (UK).
www.eurolines.es
www.eurolines.com

BUS STATIONS

Madrid
Estación Sur
(for whole of Spain).
Tel 91-468 42 00.

Intercambiador des Autobuses
(for northern Spain).
Tel 902-42 22 42.

Terminal Auto Res
(for Valencia, Extremadura, Andalusia).
Tel 90-202 09 99.

Barcelona
Estació del Nord.
Tel 90-226 06 06.

Seville
Estación Plaza de Armas.
Tel 90-245 05 50.

CAR RENTAL

Atesa
Tel 902-10 01 01 (Spain).
www.atesa.com

Avis
Tel 90-218 08 54 (Spain).
Tel 0844-54 45 566 (UK).
www.avis.com

Europcar
Tel 902-10 50 30 (Spain).
Tel 08457-222 525 (UK).
www.europcar.com

Hertz
Tel 901-10 10 01 (Spain).
Tel 0870-844 8844 (UK).
www.hertz.es
www.hertz.co.uk

FERRY SERVICES

Brittany Ferries
Tel 942-36 06 11 (Spain).
Tel 0871-244 0744 (UK).
www.brittany-ferries.com

P&O European Ferries
Tel 90-202 0461 (Spain).
Tel 0871-664 5645 (UK).
www.poferries.com

Trasmediterránea
Tel 90-245 46 45 (Spain).
Tel 0870-499 1305 (UK).
www. trasmediterranea.es

Shopping

Shopping in Spain is a pleasurable activity, particularly if you approach it in a leisurely way, punctuating it with frequent breaks for coffee. In small, family-run shops especially, people will go out of their way to fulfill your smallest request. Markets sell the freshest of produce and quality wines can be found at almost any grocer. Leatherwork is still highly regarded among Spain's many traditional crafts. Spanish design has come to the forefront in both fashion and decor.

OPENING HOURS

Shops usually open at 10am, close at 2pm, and reopen from 5pm to 8pm. Bakeries generally open early, at around 8am. Supermarkets and department stores stay open over lunchtime.

Rural markets are held in the morning only. In some regions Sunday trading is just limited to the bakeries, *pastelerías* (pastry shops), and newspaper kiosks, but in many tourist resorts stores open on Sunday.

LARGER STORES

The *hipermercados* (super-stores) are sited outside towns and can often be found by following signs to the *centro comercial*. The best known are Carrefour, Alcampo, and Hipercor.

Spain's leading department store is **El Corte Inglés**. It has branches in all cities and in the larger regional towns.

Major seasonal sales are advertised by the word *Rebajas* displayed in store windows.

CLOTHING STORES

The larger cities naturally offer the widest selection of clothing stores, but Spanish designer labels can be found even in the smaller towns.

The Calle de Serrano and Calle de José Ortega y Gasset are the main streets for fashionwear in Madrid, while the work of young designers is mostly located in the Chueca district. **Adolfo Domínguez** is the doyen of Madrid's minimalist look. The adventurous will appreciate the designs of **Agatha Ruiz de la Prada**.

In Barcelona, international fashion labels and clothes by young designers can be found in and around the Passeig de Gràcia, including **Armand Basi**, vendors of quality leisure and sportswear.

Victorio & Lucchino in Seville sells clothes with a distinctly Andalusian style.

LEATHER GOODS

Leather accessories and shoes are a popular purchase and there is a wide range in terms of quality and price. It is the practice in mid-range stores for customers to choose from the selection in the window and give the sales assistant the code number indicated and the *talla* (size) required. If you want an all-leather shoe, look for *cuero*, the hide label mark. **Calçats Sole** in Barcelona is well known for its classic hand-made shoes and boots.

Leather clothes and bags of all kinds are usually of good quality and well designed. The prestigious **Loewe** hand-bags are sold in retail outlets in Madrid and other major Spanish cities. Madrid's **Piamonte** also offers stylish bags at affordable prices.

SPECIALTY STORES

Specialty stores are often run by generations of the same family. *Panaderías* (also called *hornos*) are bakeries selling bread and *bollos* (sweet buns). Cakes and pastries are sold in *pastelerías*.

Fresh meat can be bought in a *carnicería*, but a *char-cutería* will have the best selection of cold, cooked meats, and also sells a wide selection of cheeses.

Pescaderías sell fish and shell-fish, although the best fish is often to be found on the local market stands.

For fruit and vegetables, a *frutería* or *verdulería* will have better produce, because they stock only what is in season.

Hardware stores are called *ferreterías*. *Librerías* are in fact bookshops, not libraries, and *papelerías* are stationers. Anything you buy as a *regalo* (gift) will be gift-wrapped on request. When you buy flowers from a *floristería*, the assistant will expect to arrange them.

MARKETS

Every large town has a daily market *(mercado)*, open from 9am to 2pm, and from 5pm to 8pm. Small towns have one or more market days a week.

Markets usually have the best fresh produce, but they sell all types of food, including *frutos secos* (dried fruits) and seasonal produce, such as mushrooms, soft fruit, and game. There are also usually other types of goods on sale, such as flowers, hardware, and clothes.

Flea markets *(rastros)* are held everywhere in Spain, but the largest – known as El Rastro – is in Madrid, and is held on Sundays and public holidays. Prices on the clothes, records, antiques, and other items sold here can be bargained down. Madrid also has a coin, stamp and postcard market held on Sundays in the Plaza Mayor.

The **Encants Vells**, the flea market in Barcelona, is held on Mondays, Wednesdays, Fridays, and Saturdays. The food market, **La Boqueria**, is open daily on La Rambla.

FOOD AND DRINK

Spanish regional specialties are often better value when bought where they are made. Each region produces its own type of sausage. In Burgos, for example, *morcilla* (blood sausage) is made, while a fiery red *chorizo* comes from Guijuelo, Extremadura. Andalusia is renowned for olives and olive oil, and Galicia for its cheeses.

Among the preserves and sweets of Spain, Seville marmalade is famous. The delicious almond-based nougat, called *turrón*, is eaten at Christmas but can be bought all year from food stores around the country.

Wine can be bought by the liter at a *bodega* (local wine shop). It can also be purchased directly from vineyards (also called *bodegas*), but you may need an appointment.

Spain's most famous vine-growing regions are La Rioja and Navarra, Penedés, home of *cava* (sparkling wine), Valdepeñas, Ribera del Duero, and Jerez, the sherry region.

TRADITIONAL CRAFTS

Authentic items such as guitars, fans, castanets, and flamenco shoes are sold in major cities. Madrid's **Moda y Ole** has a good selection of hand-painted fans. **Guitarrería F. Manzanero** sells handmade guitars. Some traditional crafts originated with the Moors, such as Toledo's filigree metalwork and the *azulejos* (ceramic tiles) of Andalusia. **Cántaro**, near the Plaza de España in Madrid, **La Caixa de Fang** in Barcelona, and **Azulejos Santa Isabel** in Seville all sell ceramics.

Catalan-style espadrilles are another popular buy. **La Manual Alpargatera** in Barcelona makes them by hand on the premises and sells them in a wide range of colors.

Lace from the villages of the Sierra de Gata in Extremadura and Galicia's Costa da Morte is prized. Spanish linen and silk shawls can be purchased from **Borca**, off the Puerta del Sol in Madrid. In Barcelona, **L'Arca de l'Avia** sells antique silk and lace. One of the most celebrated traditional hat makers in Spain is the **Sombrerería Herederos de J. Russi** in Córdoba.

HOUSEHOLD AND KITCHEN GOODS

Department stores have a good selection of household goods, but the *ferreterías* (small hardware shops) often have the more authentic selection. Traditional pottery, such as red clay *cazuelas* (dishes) that can be used in the oven and on the hob are inexpensive. Paella pans have always been made of iron or enamel, but now come in stainless steel or with non-stick finishes. Table linen is often a bargain on market stands. Spanish lighting design is widely admired and sold in *lampisterías*. Traditional wrought-iron goods, such as candlesticks and door hardware, are always popular.

DIRECTORY

DEPARTMENT STORES

El Corte Inglés
Calle de Preciados 1–3,
Madrid.
Tel 90-112 21 22.
www.elcorteingles.es
Plaça Catalunya 14,
Barcelona.
Tel 93-306 38 00.
Plaza Duque de la Victoria 10, Seville.
Tel 95-459 70 00.

CLOTHING STORES

Adolfo Domínguez
Calle de Serrano 18,
Madrid.
Tel 91-577 82 80.
Passeig de Gràcia 89,
Barcelona.
Tel 93-215 13 39.

Armand Basi
Passeig de Gràcia 49,
Barcelona.
Tel 93-215 14 21.
www.armandbasi.com

Agatha Ruiz de la Prada
Calle de Serrano 27,
Madrid.
Tel 91-781 10 74.

Victorio & Lucchino
Calle de las Sierpes 87,
Seville.
Tel 95-422 79 51.

LEATHER GOODS

Calçats Sole
Carrer Ample 7,
Barcelona.
Tel 93-301 69 84.

Loewe
Calle de Serrano 26,
Madrid.
Tel 91-426 35 88.
Plaza Nueva 12,
Seville.
Tel 91-577 60 56.

Piamonte
Calle del Marqués de Monasterio 5,
Madrid.
Tel 91-575 55 20.

MARKETS

La Boqueria
Las Ramblas 100,
Barcelona.

Encants Vells
Plaça de les Glòries Catalanes,
Barcelona.

El Rastro
Calle de la Ribera de Curtidores,
Madrid.

TRADITIONAL CRAFTS

L'Arca de l'Avia
Carrer dels Banys Nous 20, Barcelona.
Tel 93-302 15 98.

Azulejos Santa Isabel
Calle Alfarería 12,
Triana, Seville.
Tel 95-434 46 08.

Borca
Calle del Marqués Viudo de Pontejos 2,
Madrid.
Tel 91-532 61 53.

La Caixa de Fang
Calle Freneria 1,
Barcelona.
Tel 93-315 17 04.

Cántaro
Calle de la Flor Baja 8,
Madrid.
Tel 91-547 95 14.

Guitarrería F. Manzanero
Calle de Santa Ana 12,
Madrid.
Tel 91-366 00 47.

La Manual Alpargatera
Calle d'Avinyó 7,
Barcelona.
Tel 93-301 01 72.

Moda y Ole
Plaza Mayor 12,
Madrid.
Tel 91-354 04 03.

Sombrerería Herederos de J. Russi
Cde Cardenas 1,
Córdoba.
Tel 957-47 79 53.

Entertainment

The Spanish take particular pride in their cultural heritage. As well as the traditional art form of flamenco dance and the three-act drama of the bullfight (corrida), the theaters and opera houses of Spanish cities provide one of the best ways of sharing the experience of Spain. Many activities begin well after midnight and taking full advantage of the afternoon siesta is a good way to prepare for the evening ahead. Spain's mountain ranges, woodlands, and extensive coast offer great potential for scenic tours and sports vacations as alternatives to lounging on the beach.

ENTERTAINMENT LISTINGS

For Spanish speakers, the most complete guide to what's going on in Madrid and Barcelona can be found in the weekly Guía del Ocio (published on Fridays). Daily newspapers such as El País, El Mundo, and ABC have weekly entertainment supplements. The free monthly English-language publication, In Madrid, can be found in bookshops and Irish bars.

SEASONS AND TICKETS

The main concert and theater season in Spain runs from September to June.

In Madrid, the easiest ways to acquire tickets for the theater, concerts, and opera are by telephone or online. Entradas.com and Telentrada both accept credit card payment. Other agencies are El Corte Inglés and FNAC.

In Barcelona, theater tickets can be bought from ATMS at branches of the Catalunya Caixa and from Ticket Ramblas at the Palau de la Virreina, which also has last-minute reduced price tickets. Tickets for special events can be bought from tourist offices.

In other parts of Spain, your hotel or local tourist office will provide details of events and where to purchase tickets.

Tickets for bullfights, generally held between mid-March and mid-October, are sold at the reservations office (taquilla) of the bullring. The TEYCI agency sells tickets for bullfights, but charges up to 20 percent commission.

OPERA AND ZARZUELA

A visit to the Spanish capital would not be complete without spending a night at the zarzuela, Madrid's own variety of comic opera. The best productions are those staged at the Teatro de la Zarzuela. Other venues include Los Teatros del Canal and the Teatro Príncipe – Palacio de las Variedades. Several other theaters offer zarzuela productions throughout the summer.

The best place to see national and international opera, including Madrid's own opera company, is the Teatro Real de Madrid. The Teatro Calderón also hosts excellent classical and modern opera productions. Barcelona's opera house, the Gran Teatre del Liceu, is now fully operational following a fire in 1994.

THEATER

Madrid's most prestigious theaters are the Teatro de la Comedia (closed for renovations until 2013) and the Teatro María Guerre-ro. The former stages classic works by Spanish playwrights, while the latter hosts foreign productions and modern Spanish drama. The Teatro Muñoz Seca and Teatro Reina Victoria put on comedy productions. Madrid's autumn festival of classical and modern drama (Festival de Otoño) takes place between mid-September and mid-November.

In Barcelona, the Teatre Nacional de Catalunya is a fine showcase for Catalan drama.

CLASSICAL MUSIC

In Madrid, the two concert halls of the Auditorio Nacional de Música host international classical music performances, and the Orquesta Nacional de España plays here regularly. The Teatro Real de Madrid also hosts important classical music concerts.

Barcelona's Modernista Palau de la Música Catalana is one of the world's most beautiful concert halls, with world-renowned acoustics.

BULLFIGHTING

Bullfighting continues to be a popular spectacle throughout the country, but it is not for the squeamish. The Plaza de Toros de Las Ventas in Madrid is the most famous bullring in the world. It holds corridas every Sunday during the bullfighting season. During the May Fiestas de San Isidro fights are held every day. Some of Spain's most important fights are held at the Maestranza bullring in Seville during the Feria de Abril (a spring fair held during the fortnight after Easter). Since 2012, bullfights have been banned in Catalonia. Most towns in Andalusia have their own bullrings: Ronda, Córdoba, and Granada are among the best-known venues.

FLAMENCO

A spontaneous musical art form, flamenco has its roots in the gypsy culture of Andalusia. However, many of the best exponents are now based in the capital.

In Madrid, Casa Patas is still the best place to catch the raw power of genuine flamenco guitar and cante singing. Both music and dance can be enjoyed at Café de Chinitas.

Flamenco is performed late at night with most venues offering dinner and a show. In Andalusia, visitors can enjoy top-quality performances in the tablaos (flamenco bars of the Barrio de Santa Cruz, in Seville, and listen to soul-stirring songs in the bars of another of the city's districts

Triana. One of the best-known flamenco venues in Granada is in the gypsy caves of Sacromonte (see p320).

SPECIAL INTEREST VACATIONS

All tourist offices in Spain can provide details of special interest vacations. Cookery, wine, and painting courses, as well as history and archaeology tours, are popular. Nature lovers and hikers head for Spain's many national parks.

Information about Spanish language courses is provided by **Canning House** in London and the **Instituto Cervantes**.

OUTDOOR ACTIVITIES

For information on horseback riding and pony trekking in most regions, contact the **Real Federación Hípica Española** or local Spanish tourist offices.

Picturesque minor roads in many parts of Spain are excellent for cycle-touring. Walking tours are also popular. The **Federación Española de Montaña y Escalada** can provide information about climbing and many other mountain sports.

Spain's most popular resorts for downhill skiing are the Vall d'Aran in Catalonia and the Sierra Nevada, near Granada.

As well as white-water rafting and canoeing, a wide variety of water sports is possible in Spain. Jet skis and windsurfing equipment are available to rent in many coastal resorts. Information about sailing can be obtained from the **Real Federación Española de Vela**.

Spain has an abundance of top-quality golf courses. The **Real Federación Española de Golf** will give locations and more detailed information. In most tourist areas there are tennis courts for rental by the hour. Travel agents arrange tennis holidays for enthusiasts. More information is available from the **Real Federación Española de Tenis**.

DIRECTORY

TICKETS

Entradas.com
Tel 902-48 84 88
(Madrid).

El Corte Inglés
Tel 902-40 02 22
(Madrid).
www.elcorteingles.es

Telentrada
Tel 902-10 12 12 (Madrid).
www.telentrada.com

TEYCI
Madrid.
www.ticketstoros.com

Ticket Ramblas
La Rambla 99, Barcelona.

OPERA AND ZARZUELA

Gran Teatre del Liceu
La Rambla 51, Barcelona.
Tel 93-485 99 00.

Los Teatros del Canal
Calle Cea Bermúdez 1,
Madrid.
Tel 902-48 84 88.

Teatro Príncipe – Palacio de las Variedades
Calle de las Tres Cruces 8,
Madrid.
Tel 91-521 83 81.

Teatro Real de Madrid
Plaza de Oriente, Madrid.
Tel 90-224 48 48.

Teatro de la Zarzuela
Calle de Jovellanos 4,
Madrid.
Tel 91-524 54 00.

THEATER

Teatre Nacional de Catalunya
Plaça de les Arts 1,
Barcelona.
Tel 93-306 57 00.

Teatro de la Comedia
Calle del Príncipe 14,
Madrid.
Tel 91-532 79 28.

Teatro María Guerrero
Calle de Tamayo y Baus 4,
Madrid.
Tel 91-310 29 49.

Teatro Muñoz Seca
Plaza del Carmen 1,
Madrid.
Tel 91-523 21 28.

Teatro Reina Victoria
Carrera de San
Jerónimo 24, Madrid.
Tel 91-369 22 88.

CLASSICAL MUSIC

Auditorio Nacional de Música
Calle del Príncipe de
Vergara 146, Madrid.
Tel 91-337 01 40.

Palau de la Música Catalana
Carrer de Palau de la
Musica 4–6, Barcelona.
Tel 90-244 28 82.

BULLFIGHTING

Plaza de Toros de la Maestranza
Paseo de Cristóbal
Cólon 12, Seville.
Tel 90-222 35 06.

Plaza de Toros de las Ventas
Calle de Alcalá 237,
Madrid.
Tel 91-356 22 00.

FLAMENCO

Café de Chinitas
Calle de Torija 7, Madrid.
Tel 91-547 15 02.

Casa Patas
Calle de Cañizares 10,
Madrid.
Tel 91-369 04 96.

SPECIAL INTEREST VACATIONS

Canning House
2 Belgrave Square,
London SW1X 8PJ.
Tel 020-7235 2303.

Instituto Cervantes (Spain)
Calle Libreros 23, 28801
Alcalá de Henares, Madrid.
Tel 91-436 75 70.

Instituto Cervantes (UK)
102 Eaton Square,
London
SW1W 9AN.
Tel 020-7235 0353.

OUTDOOR ACTIVITIES

Federación Española de Montaña y Escalada
Calle Floridablanca 84,
08015 Barcelona.
Tel 93-426 42 67.
www.fedme.es

Real Federación Hípica Española
Calle Monte Esquinza
28 3°, 28010 Madrid.
Tel 91-575 07 70.

Real Federación Española de Golf
Paseo Joaquin Rodrigo 4,
letra 1, 28224 Pozuelo
de Alarcón, Madrid.
Tel 90-220 00 52.
www.golfspain
federacion.com

Real Federación Española de Tenis
Passeig Olimpic 17, 08038
Barcelona. Tel 93-200 53
55. www.rfet.es

Real Federación Española de Vela
Calle Luis Salazar 9,
28002 Madrid.
Tel 91-519 50 08.
www.rfev.es

Where to Stay in Spain

Visitors to Spain have a wide variety of accommodations to choose from, at a range of prices. At the top of the scale are elegant suites in converted medieval castles or royal palaces – many of these are paradors, luxurious state-run hotels. Then there are stylish beach hotels and villas or family-run guesthouses for the budget traveler.

PRICE CATEGORIES
Price categories are for a
standard double room per night
during the high season, including
tax and service:
€ Under €85
€€ €85–€125
€€€ €125–€175
€€€€ €175–€225
€€€€€ Over €225

MADRID

OLD MADRID Hostal Madrid
€
C/ Esparteros 6–2°, 28012 **Tel** 915-22 00 60 **Fax** 915-32 35 10 **Rooms** 15
Map C4

One of the best budget options in Madrid, this hotel is set in the heart of the old city. Offers both rooms and apartments decorated in a mixture of traditional and modern styles, with amenities such as Wi-Fi. The staff are friendly, and the city's sights, restaurants, bars, and nightlife are right on the doorstep. **www.hostal-madrid.info**

OLD MADRID Carlos V
€€
C/ Maestro Victoria 5, 28013 **Tel** 915-31 41 00 **Fax** 915-31 37 61 **Rooms** 67
Map C4

A city-center hotel in a pedestrian street beside the Puerta del Sol. This family-run hotel has interconnecting bedrooms as well as family rooms. Some of the rooms also have balconies and sun terraces. A generous buffet breakfast is served in the café bar, and the staff are friendly and helpful. **www.hotelcarlosv.com**

OLD MADRID Hotel Plaza Mayor
€€
C/ Atocha 2, 28012 **Tel** 913-60 06 06 **Fax** 913-60 06 10 **Rooms** 34
Map D5

Just around the corner of Madrid's central square, this popular hotel fills up fast, so book well in advance. Rooms vary in size and decor, but are spotless and brightly painted. The attic suite is more expensive, but offers fine views from its private terrace. Also has a reading room. Free wireless Internet in cafeteria. **www.h-plazamayor.com**

OLD MADRID Tryp Gran Via
€€
Gran Via 25, 28013 **Tel** 915-22 11 21 **Fax** 915-21 24 24 **Rooms** 175
Map B3

This expansive hotel is situated in an old building between the Plaza del Callao and the Plaza de España, close to a large public car park. It has spacious public rooms and well-equipped bedrooms, each with its own safe. Offers good value for money considering the central location and reasonable amenities. **www.solmelia.com**

OLD MADRID Casa de Madrid
€€€€€
C/ Arrieta 2, 28013 **Tel** 915-59 57 91 **Fax** 915-40 11 00 **Rooms** 7
Map B4

Housed in an 18th-century palace, this stylish little hotel is ideal for a romantic getaway. The seven rooms – two of which are suites – are exquisitely decorated with antiques. The breakfast includes freshly squeezed juice and home-made marmalade. Highly recommended. **www.casademadrid.com**

BOURBON MADRID Hostal Gonzalo
€
C/ Cervantes 34, 28014 **Tel** 914-29 27 14 **Fax** 914-20 20 07 **Rooms** 15
Map D4

A family-run hostal, which often fills up well in advance. Provides good facilities, immaculate bedrooms, free Wi-Fi, and excellent value for money. The multi-lingual owners are hospitable and offer helpful information regarding nearby attractions. Several restaurants can be found within walking distance. **www.hostalgonzalo.com**

BOURBON MADRID Mora
€
Paseo del Prado 32, 28014 **Tel** 914-20 15 69 **Fax** 914-20 05 64 **Rooms** 62
Map D4

A 1930s hotel with an attractive entrance and a lobby with an original glass skylight. Rooms are modern, functional, and brightly furnished. Located close to the main museums, the hotel offers very good value for money. Families can request an extra bed in the room for a small surcharge. **www.hotelmora.com**

BOURBON MADRID Hotel Liabeny
€€€
C/ Salud 3, 28013 **Tel** 915-31 90 00 **Fax** 915-32 74 21 **Rooms** 220
Map C4

An elegant, modern hotel, located just a short walk from the main sights, yet away from the hubbub of the city center. The extensively renovated hotel features traditionally decorated rooms and suites with every modern amenity, a good restaurant, and excellent service. The private parking and disabled access is a plus. **www.liabeny.es**

BOURBON MADRID Villa Real
€€€€
Plaza de las Cortes 10, 28014 **Tel** 914-20 37 67 **Fax** 914-20 25 47 **Rooms** 115
Map D4

Close to the Prado and the Retiro gardens, this stylish hotel is based in an opulent, early 19th-century building. One of Madrid's smartest hotels, the spacious rooms and suites are decorated in a tasteful mixture of traditional and contemporary styles, and scattered with ancient Roman art. Some suites even have a Jacuzzi. **www.derbyhotels.es**

Key to Symbols see back cover flap

BOURBON MADRID Ritz
🛏 🍴 🎿 📺 🗒 🚻 🅿 W €€€€€

Plaza de la Lealtad 5, 28014 **Tel** *917-01 67 67* **Fax** *917-01 67 76* **Rooms** *167*   **Map** D4

Inaugurated in 1910 as a hotel for aristocrats, the Ritz is still one of Spain's most elegant hotels. Close to the Prado, the hotel has an ornate, circular foyer, and a terraced garden, and serves tea and brunch along with live music. Rooms are luxurious and offer every imaginable comfort. There are good offers if you book through the website. **www.ritz.es**

FARTHER AFIELD NH Alcalá
🛏 🍴 🎿 🗒 🚻 🅿 W €€€

C/ de Alcalá 66, 28009 **Tel** *914-35 10 60* **Fax** *914-35 11 05* **Rooms** *146*   **Map** E3

A large, chain hotel close to the lovely Retiro gardens. Features spacious, well-equipped rooms with amenities that include Wi-Fi and Internet access. This reasonably priced hotel also has a café, a bar, and private car park. It is within walking distance to the upmarket shopping district in Salamanca, and three museums. **www.nh-hotels.com**

FARTHER AFIELD Santo Mauro
🛏 🍴 🎿 📺 🗒 🚻 🅿 W €€€€€

C/ Zurbano 36, 28010 **Tel** *913-19 69 00* **Fax** *913-08 54 77* **Rooms** *50*

This palace, built in 1894 on one of Madrid's most elegant streets, is surrounded by beautiful wooded gardens. The rooms and suites are stylishly decorated, and the two fine restaurants offer romantic outdoor dining in summer. Also houses a swimming pool in the vaulted cellars. **www.ac-hotels.com**

BARCELONA

EIXAMPLE The Praktik
🛏 🎿 🗒 🚻 W €€

Diputació 325, 08009 **Tel** *934-67 3115* **Fax** *934-67 3110* **Rooms** *43*   **Map** D2

Situated near the Plaça de Catalunya is this new concept of a modern hostel, with limited services but clean, elegant rooms, extra-large beds, and huge showers. Some rooms have balconies. There are also apartments. Breakfast is served in a nearby restaurant and a late check-out is possible for a small fee. **www.praktikhotels.com**

EIXAMPLE Actual
🛏 🗒 🚻 W €€€

Carrer Rosselló 238, 08008 **Tel** *935-52 05 50* **Fax** *935-52 05 55* **Rooms** *38*   **Map** F2

This modern hotel is fashionably decorated in sleek minimalist style. It has a superb location on the same block as Gaudí's La Pedrera, and the upmarket boutiques of the Passeig de Gràcia are on the doorstep. Like many hotels in this area, it is geared toward business travelers, which means good weekend deals. **www.hotelactual.com**

EIXAMPLE Condes de Barcelona
🛏 🍴 🎿 📺 🗒 🚻 W €€€€

Passeig de Gràcia 73–75, 08008 **Tel** *934-45 00 00* **Fax** *934-45 32 32* **Rooms** *235*   **Map** D2

This hotel is located in two handsomely renovated Modernista palaces, with marble lobbies and creamy facades. The rooms in both locations are cool and contemporary, and some have Jacuzzis. Choose a room with a terrace to admire Gaudí's La Pedrera building directly across the street. **www.condesdebarcelona.com**

EIXAMPLE El Palace
🛏 🍴 🎿 📺 🗒 🚻 W €€€€€

Gran Via de les Corts Catalanes 668, 08010 **Tel** *935-10 11 30* **Fax** *933-18 01 48* **Rooms** *125*   **Map** E2

El Palace is the most elegant of Barcelona's grand hotels. The large, luxurious bedrooms are decorated in classical style and boast huge marble bathrooms. Contains a health club and a beauty parlor. Famous guests have included the Spanish royal family and Frank Sinatra. It also has a Michelin-starred restaurant. **www.hotelpalacebarcelona.com**

OLD TOWN Fontanella
🛏 W €

Via Laietana 71–2°, 08003 **Tel** *933-17 59 43* **Fax** *933-17 59 43* **Rooms** *11*   **Map** D3

Fontanella is a simple, family-run hostal where the owners do their best to make visitors feel at home. There is a wonderful antique lift, which creaks up to a knick-knack filled lobby. The basic rooms are made cozy and welcoming with flowery prints and lots of goodies in the bathrooms, some of which are shared. **www.hostalfontanella.com**

OLD TOWN Peninsular
🛏 🗒 W €

Carrer de Sant Pau 34, 08001 **Tel** *933-02 31 38* **Fax** *934-12 36 99* **Rooms** *59*   **Map** D3

Rooms are truly basic, but of good value in this former Carmelite convent. Just off La Rambla behind the Liceu opera house, this hotel's charms lie in its luminous, plant-filled inner courtyard and friendly staff. Breakfast is served in an old-fashioned dining room with a high ceiling, but there is no restaurant. **www.hotelpeninsular.net**

OLD TOWN Jardí
🛏 🗒 €€

Plaça Sant Josep Oriol 1, 08002 **Tel** *933-01 59 00* **Fax** *933-42 57 33* **Rooms** *42*   **Map** D3

A popular hostal overlooking a pretty leafy square in the Barri Gòtic quarter. Some bedrooms have been renovated and have good views of the square and the handsome Gothic church of Santa María del Pi; others are cheaper but not as atmospheric. The location is perfect for nightowls. **www.eljardi-barcelona.com**

OLD TOWN Montecarlo
🛏 🍴 🎿 🗒 🚻 🅿 W €€

La Rambla 124, 08002 **Tel** *934-12 04 04* **Fax** *933-18 73 23* **Rooms** *76*   **Map** D3

This beautiful hotel right on La Rambla in the center of Barcelona occupies a former 19th-century palace. The lobby is a gorgeous whirl of gilt and marble, while the rooms are smart and modern. Staff are particularly helpful here, and there are fantastic deals available on the website. **www.montecarlobcn.com**

Map References *see maps of Madrid pp282–3 and Barcelona pp306–7*

OLD TOWN Colón

€€€

Avda de la Catedral 7, 08002 **Tel** 933-01 14 04 **Fax** 933-17 29 15 **Rooms** 141   Map D3

A classic in Barcelona, this traditional, rather formal hotel has a fabulous location opposite the Gothic cathedral. The best rooms have terraces overlooking the square, where guests can watch the Sardana, the traditional Catalan folk dance, performed in the Plaça de Catedral on Sunday mornings. **www.hotelcolon.es**

OLD TOWN Jazz Hotel

€€€

Carrer Pelai 3, 08001 **Tel** 935-52 96 96 **Fax** 935-52 96 97 **Rooms** 108   Map D3

A glassy ultra-modern hotel, close to the Plaça de Catalunya, Jazz offers better facilities than its three-star rating would suggest. There is a rooftop pool with sun deck, and the rooms (all soundproofed) are stylishly decorated with contemporary furniture and fabrics. **www.hoteljazz.com**

OLD TOWN Arts

€€€€€

Carrer de Marina 19–21, 08005 **Tel** 932-21 10 00 **Fax** 932-21 10 70 **Rooms** 455   Map F4

Set in a soaring tower overlooking the Port Olímpic, Arts is one of the most luxurious and glamorous hotels in Europe. Huge rooms boast spectacular views along with a stunning collection of contemporary Spanish art. There are gorgeous suites on the upper floors for those with very deep pockets. **www.hotelartsbarcelona.com**

NORTHERN SPAIN

BAIONA, RIAS BAIXAS Parador de Baiona

€€€€

Castillo Monterreal, 36300 (Pontevedra) **Tel** 986-35 50 00 **Fax** 986-35 50 76 **Rooms** 122

This parador, built in an old Galician *pazo* (manor house) style, is located within the walls of Monterreal castle. The restaurant serves seafood accompanied by the local Ribeiro wine. Some rooms have four-poster beds and offer sea views, while others look out on to the gardens. **www.parador.es**

BILBAO (BILBO) Mirohotel

€€€

Alameda Mazarredo 77, 48009 (Vicaya) **Tel** 946-61 18 80 **Fax** 944-25 51 82 **Rooms** 50

This glass-fronted boutique hotel designed by Antonio Miró is located between the Guggenheim and Fine Arts Museums. Facilities include a library, a gym, and a spa. The bar, which hosts jazz or other live music some evenings, acts as a meeting point for art lovers. **www.mirohotelbilbao.com**

CANGAS DE ONIS Parador de Cangas de Onis

€€€

Villanueva (km 2 from Cangas), 33550 (Asturias) **Tel** 985-84 94 02 **Fax** 985-84 95 20 **Rooms** 64

A restored 12th-century Benedictine monastery with magnificent cloisters, located on the bank of the Río Sellar just outside the town of Cangas de Onis. The rooms are spacious and comfortable, and the restaurant serves regional dishes. Includes facilities such as meeting rooms. **www.parador.es**

OVIEDO Hotel de la Reconquista

€€€€€

C/ Gil de Jaz 16, 33004 (Asturias) **Tel** 985-24 11 00 **Fax** 985-24 60 11 **Rooms** 142

A luxury hotel in a magnificent 18th-century building, originally an orphanage, with a massive stone coat of arms above the main entrance. Its name commemorates the Reconquest of Spain which was launched from Asturias. The public rooms are arranged around several courtyards. **www.hoteldelareconquista.com**

PAMPLONA (IRUNA) Ciudad de Pamplona

€€

Iturrama 21, 31007 (Navarra) **Tel** 948-26 60 11 **Fax** 948-17 36 26 **Rooms** 108

An ultra-modern luxury hotel, decorated in warm tones and scattered with avant-garde furniture. It has four sitting rooms and ample facilities for business people. The hotel is at some distance from the old part of Pamplona, in one of the streets behind the Ciudadela fortress. The restaurant serves classic Navarran dishes. **www.ac-hotels.com**

PONTEVEDRA Parador de Pontevedra

€€€

Rua del Barón 19, 36002 **Tel** 986-85 58 00 **Fax** 986-85 21 95 **Rooms** 47

A parador in a 16th–18th-century Renaissance palace, which was once a school, granary, masonic lodge, and an aristocratic residence. The decor incorporates antiques, gilt mirrors, chandeliers, and tapestries. Some rooms are in a new wing. The restaurant specializes in seafood of the Rías Baixas. **www.parador.es**

SAN SEBASTIAN (DONOSTIA) María Cristina

€€€€€

Paseo República Argentina 4, 20004 (Guipúzcoa) **Tel** 943-43 76 00 **Fax** 943-43 76 76 **Rooms** 136

Built in 1912 and named after Queen Maria Cristina, this is a landmark of the city and one of the most historic hotels in Spain. It was designed by the architect of the London and Paris Ritz hotels and is decorated in belle époque style. It is also the venue of the San Sebastián film festival. **www.mariacristina.es**

SANTANDER Las Brisas

€€

La Braña 14, El Sardinero, 39005 (Cantabria) **Tel** 942-27 50 11 **Fax** 942-28 11 73 **Rooms** 13

A homely hotel in a 19th-century white turret-shaped villa, close to the popular Sardinero beach. Each room is different with floral fabrics predominating. Breakfast, included in the price, can be served on a seaside terrace. The hotel also has five self-catering apartments. Closed 22 Dec–15 Jan. **www.hotellasbrisas.net**

ANTIAGO DE COMPOSTELA Parador Hostal Dos Reis Catolicos 🔲🍴🧊🍴🅿️🆆 €€€€€

raza do Obradoiro 1, 15705 (A Coruña) **Tel** 981-58 22 00 **Fax** 981-56 30 94 **Rooms** 127

uilt under the Catholic monarchs as a hospice for poor pilgrims, this luxurious 16th-century parador, on the same quare as Santiago de Compostela's famous cathedral, is one of the world's grandest hotels. It is built around four rcaded courtyards with fountains. The public rooms have regal touches such as hanging tapestries. **www.parador.es**

CATALONIA & EASTERN SPAIN

LICANTE (ALACANT) Gravina Cinco 🔲🚶🧊🆆 €

/Gravina 5, 03540 (Alicante) **Tel** 965-14 73 17 **Fax** 902-93 43 05 **Rooms** 22

his modern and warm small hotel is perfectly located at the heart of Alicante, and very close to the Postiquet beach nd the marina. Comfortable, bright rooms are nicely decorated. Free coffee and tea is available 24 hours in the reakfast room. **http://hotelgravinacinco.es**

ENIA Rosa 🔲🍴🏊🧊🅿️🆆 €

/ Congre 3, Las Marinas, 03700 (Alicante) **Tel** 965-78 15 73 **Fax** 966-42 47 74 **Rooms** 40

, modern, white villa with a perfect location close to the beach. It was built and is run by a hospitable Parisian expat ho has several repeat customers. Comfortable rooms have sun-trapping, Florentine-style balconies. Guests can also pt for one of the garden bungalows. The family-friendly pool has a section for toddlers. **www.hotelrosadenia.com**

IGUERES Hotel Durán 🔲🍴🧊🅿️🆆 €

arrer de Lausaca 5, 17600 (Girona) **Tel** 972-50 12 50 **Fax** 972-50 26 09 **Rooms** 65

stablished in 1855, this ochre-and-pink hotel is set above one of the finest restaurants in the region. It is still owned y the same family, who are warm and friendly. Rooms are attractively, if simply, furnished, and many have pretty vrought-iron balconies overlooking the street below. **www.hotelduran.com**

ARRAGONA Imperial Tarraco 🔲🍴🏊🧊🅿️🆆 €€

asseig Les Palmeres s/n, 43003 (Tarragona) **Tel** 977-23 30 40 **Fax** 977-21 65 66 **Rooms** 170

he plushest option in Tarragona, this large, modern hotel has a panoramic location right on the balcón del Mediterrani he balcony of the Mediterranean). Many of the spacious, elegant rooms and suites have large terraces. There's a pool nd tennis courts. The hotel is conveniently close to the historic center of the city. **www.hotelhusaimperialtarraco.com**

VALENCIA Meliá Inglés 🔲🍴🧊 €€

/ Marqués de Dos Aguas 6, 46002 (Valencia) **Tel** 963-51 64 26 **Fax** 963-94 02 51 **Rooms** 63

his convenient and stylish city-center hotel is in the old palace of the Dukes of Cardona, next to the National eramics Museum. The rooms and suites overlook the street, and are equipped with amenities such as Internet ccess, a TV, a minibar, and a safe. The restaurant serves regional specialties. **www.hotelinglesboutique.com**

ABIA (JAVEA) Parador de Jávea 🔲🍴🏊🅿️🧊🆆 €€€€

laya del Arenal, Avda Mediterráneo 233, 03730 (Alicante) **Tel** 965-79 02 00 **Fax** 965-79 03 08 **Rooms** 70

large, modern parador surrounded by lush gardens right on the beach. The rooms are bright and spacious and most all have balconies overlooking the sea. Offers a wide range of sports facilities, including horseback riding, iving, sailing, and golf. The restaurant serves regional cuisine. Lunch or dinner included Jul–Sep. **www.parador.es**

ARAGOZA Palafox 🔲🍴🏊🎣🆆🅿️🧊 €€€

/Marqués de Casa Jimenez s/n, 50004 **Tel** 976-23 77 00 **Fax** 976-23 47 05 **Rooms** 179

he Spanish architect Pascua Ortega went to town on his design for this luxurious hotel. The grand entrance is anked by full-scale representations of the old gates to the city. The rooms, on the other hand, are tasteful and ninimalist. In terms of location and facilities this is one of the best places in the city. **www.palafoxhoteles.com**

CENTRAL SPAIN

AVILA Parador de Ávila 🔲🍴🧊🅿️🆆 €€€

/ Marqués Canales de Chozas 2, 05001 **Tel** 920-21 13 40 **Fax** 920-22 61 66 **Rooms** 61

eal for history lovers, this hotel is set in a 16th-century palace, next to the walls that surround Ávila's old town. efurbished with stone and adobe, the hotel is furnished with many antiques. It also boasts a covered interior patio nd a garden replete with archaeological remains. **www.parador.es**

URGOS Hotel Velada 🔲🍴🧊🆆 €€

/Fernán González 6-10, 09003 **Tel** 947-25 76 80 **Fax** 947-25 76 81 **Rooms** 64

charming hotel at the heart of Burgos old town, five minutes from the Cathedral and the Plaza Mayor. Large rooms vith modern decoration have original stone walls. The hotel living rooms have fireplaces, and most rooms have their wn living room with sofabed. **www.veladahoteles.es**

Key to Symbols *see back cover flap*

LEON Parador de San Marcos 🔊 🍴 🗐 🕭 🅿 🗏 €€€€
Plaza de San Marcos 7, 24001 **Tel** *987-23 73 00* **Fax** *987-23 34 58* **Rooms** *226*

The dramatic Renaissance facade of this former San Marcos monastery gives way to an interior full of stone work and wooden masterpieces by medieval maestros. The rooms are comfortable and luxurious. A stay at this museum-like hotel is an experience in itself. **www.parador.es**

SALAMANCA AC Palacio de San Esteban 🔊 🍴 📺 🗐 🅿 🗏 €€€
Arroyo de Santo Domingo 3, 37001 **Tel** *923-26 22 96* **Fax** *923-26 88 72* **Rooms** *51*

The AC hotel chain took over this 16th-century convent in 2002 and converted it into one of the city's finest hotels. The original character of the building has been kept alive within the context of a modern hotel. The vaulted ceilings and stone walls breathe history, while the comfortable rooms do not lack any amenities. **www.ac-hotels.com**

SAN LORENZO DE EL ESCORIAL Botánico 🔊 🍴 🗐 🅿 €€
C/ Timoteo Padrós 16, 28200 **Tel** *918-90 78 79* **Fax** *918-90 81 58* **Rooms** *20*

An appealing hotel, housed in a handsome, whitewashed country mansion. A stone's throw from the vast El Escorial monastery, it is surrounded by beautiful gardens and is situated opposite the golf course. The bedrooms are decorated with modern furnishings, and offer great views. Breakfast included. **www.botanicohotel.com**

SEGOVIA Parador de Segovia 🔊 🍴 ♨ 🗐 🗐 🅿 🕭 🗏 €€€
Ctra de Valadolid s/n, 40003 **Tel** *921-44 37 37* **Fax** *921-43 73 62* **Rooms** *113*

This country house is just a short distance from the aqueduct and offers magnificent views of Segovia. The abstract art in the large lobby forms a nice contrast to the sober lines of the classical interior. The restaurant is one of the best places to sample the city's favorite dish, *cochinillo* (suckling pig). **www.parador.es**

TOLEDO Pintor El Greco 🔊 🗐 🕭 🗏 €€
C/ Alamillos del Tránsito 13, 45002 (Toledo) **Tel** *925-28 51 91* **Fax** *925-21 58 19* **Rooms** *60*

A 17th-century bakery in Toledo's former Jewish quarter has been discreetly extended behind the original facade and patio. Wrought iron, traditional ceramics, and lots of flowering plants add character to the hotel. The bedrooms are modern, yet in keeping with the historic surroundings. **www.hotel-pintorelgreco.com**

SOUTHERN SPAIN

ARCOS DE LA FRONTERA Parador de Arcos de Frontera 🗐 🗏 €€€
Plaza del Cabildo s/n, 11630 (Cádiz) **Tel** *956-70 05 00* **Fax** *956-70 11 16* **Rooms** *24*

Formerly a magistrate's house, this mansion perched on a cliff above the old city is now a smart parador. A huge terrace offers great views of ancient spires and rooftops below, and the rooms are set around a series of beautifully tiled patios with wells and fountains. Rooms are plush and comfortable and some have Jacuzzis. **www.parador.es**

CORDOBA Casa de los Azulejos 🍴 🗐 🕭 🗏 €€
C/ Fernando Colón 5, 14002 (Córdoba) **Tel** *957-47 00 00* **Fax** *957-47 54 96* **Rooms** *9*

The "House of the Tiles" is an enchanting 17th-century mansion set around a typical patio with exquisite local tiles, pretty wrought iron, and lush greenery. The pretty rooms are cool and modern, with extras such as Internet. A terrific restaurant offers traditional Andalusian cuisine and tapas. **www.casadelosazulejos.com**

GRANADA Posada del Toro 🔊 🍴 🎎 🗐 🕭 €€
C/ Elvira 25, 18010 (Granada) **Tel** *958-22 73 33* **Fax** *958-21 62 18* **Rooms** *15*

Rustic charm and a historic ambiance are combined with modern comforts in this welcoming hotel which is located close to Albaicín, Plaza Nueva, and the cathedral. There is an attractive central courtyard where guests can relax. Internet is available by cable. **www.posadadeltoro.com**

GRANADA Parador de Granada 🔊 🍴 🗐 🅿 🗏 €€€€€
C/ Real de la Alhambra, 18009 (Granada) **Tel** *958-22 14 40* **Fax** *958-22 22 64* **Rooms** *40*

This elegant parador in the jasmine-scented gardens of the Alhambra was once a convent, and the cloister has been transformed into a tree-filled oasis filled with flowers. From the elegant bedrooms, you can hear the fountains of the Generalife and enjoy blissful views of the city and the ancient palace. Book well in advance. **www.parador.es**

MALAGA Don Curro 🔊 🍴 🗐 🅿 🗏 €
C/ Sancha de Lara 7, 29015 (Málaga) **Tel** *952-22 72 00* **Fax** *952-21 59 46* **Rooms** *118*

The exterior may not be attractive, but this hotel's interior is charming and comfortable, with a welcoming ambiance. Rooms are tastefully furnished with dark wood and marble, and they offer some thoughtful extras, including a valet parking service. Houses a simple bar-restaurant and is popular with business travelers. **www.hoteldoncurro.com**

MARBELLA El Fuerte 🔊 🍴 ♨ 🎣 🗐 🗐 🕭 🅿 🗏 €€€
Av El Fuerte, 29600 (Málaga) **Tel** *952-92 00 00* **Fax** *952-82 44 11* **Rooms** *263*

El Fuerte was the first purpose-built hotel in Marbella and is still one of the best. It is unmissable – a big pink building surrounded by tropical gardens. Some rooms have mountain views but the best look out to sea. Next to the beachfront, it has a heated, glassed-in pool, an outdoor pool, and a health and beauty center. **www.fuertehoteles.com**

RONDA Parador de Ronda

Plaza España, 29400 (Málaga) **Tel** *952-87 75 00* **Fax** *952-87 81 88* **Rooms** *79*

€€€€

Edging up to Ronda's famous cliff, yet close to the town center, this modern, purpose-built parador has stunning views over the gorge, especially from the top-floor suites. The bedrooms are full of light and stylishly decorated. The parador is surrounded by huge gardens with an outdoor pool right on the cliff edge. **www.parador.es**

SEVILLE Vincci la Rabida

C/ Castelar 24, 41001 **Tel** *954-50 12 80* **Fax** *954-21 66 00* **Rooms** *81*

€€

Located in El Arenal district, close to shops, restaurants, and a bullring, this 18th-century palace has a traditional Andalusian patio. The guest rooms combine warm, earthy tones with dark furnishings and wrought-iron beds. Some rooms have views of the central courtyard. **www.vinccihoteles.com**

SEVILLE La Casa del Maestro

C/ Niño Ricardo 5, 41003 **Tel** *954-50 00 07* **Fax** *954-50 00 06* **Rooms** *11*

€€€

Once the home of celebrated flamenco guitarist Niño Ricardo, this charming yellow-and-ochre painted townhouse is built around a patio bursting with plants and flowers. Rooms are on the small side, but full of thoughtful touches such as a jug of iced water and chocolates placed by the bed. Has a lovely roof terrace. **www.lacasadelmaestro.com**

SEVILLE Casa Numero Siete

C/ Virgenes 7, 41004 **Tel** *954-22 15 81* **Fax** *954-21 45 27* **Rooms** *6*

€€€€€

One of the loveliest and most romantic hotels in Seville. This elegant guesthouse occupies a mansion and features just a handful of rooms. The decor includes a range of antiques and family heirlooms. Also has an opulent sitting room with a bar. The breakfasts here are delicious. **www.casanumero7.com**

TORREMOLINOS Hotel Miami

C/ Aladino 14, 29620 (Málaga) **Tel** *952-38 52 55* **Fax** *952-37 85 08* **Rooms** *26*

€

The Miami offers welcome respite from the Costa del Sol's modern growth. It has whitewashed walls, tiles, balconies, and potted plants. Rooms are simple, and vary in terms of size and amenities, but they are all comfortable and the staff are friendly and helpful. The pool is an added bonus. **www.residencia-miami.com**

THE BALEARIC ISLANDS

FORMENTERA, ES PUJOLS Sa Volta

C/ Miramar 94, 07871 (Formentera) **Tel** *971-32 81 25* **Fax** *971-32 81 43* **Rooms** *25*

€€€

A family-run hostal in a modern block close to the beach in one of Formentera's main resorts. The standard rooms are simple, but comfortable. It is worth splashing out on one of the three semi-suites, which have plush modern decor, including canopied beds and spacious private terraces. Charming staff. Open Mar–Dec. **www.savolta.com**

IBIZA, IBIZA TOWN Hostal La Marina

C/ Barcelona 7, 07800 (Formentera) **Tel** *971-31 01 72* **Fax** *971-31 48 94* **Rooms** *26*

€€

A classic on the seafront, Hostal La Marina is located in a modernized 19th-century building, which retains some charming original details. Rooms are brightly painted in Mediterranean colors and the best have sea views. In high season, it is a little overpriced, but a good deal otherwise. Minimum four-night stay. **www.hostal-lamarina.com**

MALLORCA, PALMA DE MALLORCA Born

C/ Sant Jaume 3, 07012 (Mallorca) **Tel** *971-71 29 42* **Fax** *971-71 86 18* **Rooms** *30*

€

The Marquis of Ferrandell's town mansion, built in the 16th century and restored in the 18th, makes a splendid little hotel. The simple but comfortable bedrooms are set around a typical Mallorcan courtyard with palms and a grand staircase. A few have tiny balconies overlooking the courtyard. One of the best budget options. **www.hotelborn.com**

MALLORCA, PORT DE POLLENCA Formentor

Playa de Formentor, 07470 (Mallorca) **Tel** *971-89 91 00* **Fax** *971-86 51 55* **Rooms** *122*

€€€€€

Writers, opera singers, film stars, and the Dalai Lama have stayed at this luxury hotel on the island's northwest tip. No longer quite the celebrity haunt that it was, it still remains an elegant retreat. The rooms are traditionally decorated. Superb sports facilities and the beach is on the doorstep. **www.barceloformentor.com**

MENORCA, CIUTADELLA Patricia

Paseo San Nicolás 90–92, 07760 (Menorca) **Tel** *971-38 55 11* **Fax** *971-48 11 20* **Rooms** *44*

€€€

A modern, cream-colored chain hotel with white bay windows near the harbor. Rooms are spacious and blandly furnished. Geared toward business travelers, it has conference facilities and a business center. The convenient location and efficient staff make it a good bet for tourists. Low prices in the off-season. **www.hesperia-patricia.com**

MENORCA, MAO Port Mahón

Avenida Port de Maó, 07701 (Menorca) **Tel** *971-36 26 00* **Fax** *971-35 10 50* **Rooms** *82*

€€€

Housed in an attractive red and white colonial-style building, this hotel – probably the most luxurious in the city – overlooks Maó harbor. Its grounds include wide terraces and a curving swimming pool surrounded by lawns. The best rooms, comfortably furnished in chain-hotel style, have private terraces. **www.sethotels.com**

Where to Eat in Spain

The quickest and best-value places to eat in Spain are bars that serve tapas, small appetizers traditionally eaten standing at the bar *(see p325)*. Family-run *posadas* or *mesones* serve reasonably priced, sit-down meals. Spain also has many top-quality restaurants, notably in the Basque Country, Galicia, Madrid, and Barcelona.

MADRID

OLD MADRID Casa Patas
Tapas   €
C/ Cañizares 10, 28012 **Tel** *913-69 04 96*   Map C4

Casa Patas is primarily known for its flamenco shows in the evenings, which are among the best in the city. It is also an original place to eat in the heart of Old Madrid, with a well-stocked tapas bar and an unbeatable fixed-price lunch menu. Wheelchair-users must call in advance for assistance. The admission charge includes one drink. Closed Sun.

OLD MADRID Delic
Tapas   €
Plaza de la Paja 8, 28005 **Tel** *913-64 54 50*   Map B4

Stylish Delic is a popular café-bar, doubling as a hip local drinking hole. It serves everything from delicious breakfasts, to light snacks and more substantial cuisine with an exotic touch. With a perfect location on the trendy Plaza de la Paja, the terrace is a good place to watch a smart crowd of locals hang out on summer nights. Closed until 8pm Mon.

OLD MADRID El Estragón
€
Plaza de la Paja 10, 28005 **Tel** *913-65 89 82*   Map B4

El Estragón is located in a pretty spot, overlooking one of Madrid's loveliest and most fashionable squares. *Madrileño* cuisine is decidedly meaty, but this long-standing vegetarian restaurant provides a welcome break for veggies. The menu features a variety of delectable vegetable- and soy-based dishes. Note that there are two sittings for dinner.

OLD MADRID Taberna Bilbao
Tapas   €€
C/ Costanilla de San Andrés 8, 28005 **Tel** *913-65 61 25*   Map B4

A hugely popular Basque tavern, Taberna Bilbao serves home-made specialties such as *bacalao* (cod) cooked in a range of styles. The *chipirones* (baby squid), prepared in their own ink, are excellent. Try the house *txakolí*, a light, tart, and very refreshing Basque wine. Reservations are highly recommended. Closed Mon.

OLD MADRID Botín
€€€
C/ de Cuchilleros 17, 28011 **Tel** *913-66 42 17*   Map B4

Dating back to 1725, Botín is reputedly the oldest restaurant in the world. With its brick-lined vaults and heavy wooden beams, it has changed little since. Even the original wood-burning oven is still used to cook the traditional roast lamb and suckling pig. There is a reasonable fixed-price lunch menu. Book well in advance.

OLD MADRID Casa Lucio
Tapas   €€€€
C/ Cava Baja 35, 28005 **Tel** *913-65 82 17*   Map B4

Casa Lucio is a historic tavern serving Castillian specialties. The *huevos estrellados* (fried eggs with potatoes) are so exquisite that they have even made it into a celebrated Spanish poem. The typical *Madrileño* tripe and rice pudding are equally renowned. The wine list has some fine wines from around Spain. Closed Sat lunch & Aug.

BOURBON MADRID Café Gijón
Tapas   €
Paseo Recoletos 21, 28007 **Tel** *915-21 54 25*   Map D3

A legendary café, established in 1888 and still decorated with original Art Nouveau furnishings, Café Gijón is perfect for breakfast, a fixed-price lunch, or afternoon tea with cakes. Specialties include hake with cider and seafood *paella*. There is an elegant terrace, frequented by the well-heeled. Prices in the restaurant are more expensive.

BOURBON MADRID Casa Labra
Tapas   €
C/ Tetuán 12, 28013 **Tel** *915-31 00 81*   Map C4

Founded in 1860, Casa Labra is one of Madrid's most atmospheric tapas bars. It is tucked away on a small street close to the Puerta del Sol, and retains its gleaming wood panels and pretty tiles. In the same family since 1947, the restaurant is renowned for its *bacalao* (cod). Closed Jan 1.

BOURBON MADRID Le Café
€€
C/ Recoletas 13, 28001 **Tel** *917-81 15 86*   Map E3

A block away from the famous Retiro park, this stylish, cosmopolitan restaurant serves international food based on quality Mediterranean fare. Specialties include red tuna fillet with black pepper and guacamole, ox *carpaccio*, and wild mushroom risotto with white truffle. Closed Sun.

Key to Symbols *see back cover flap*

BOURBON MADRID Teatriz

Tapas 🚻▤ €€€€

C/ Hermosilla 15, 28001 **Tel** *915-77 53 79* **Map** *E3*

Formerly a theater, Teatriz was completely transformed by French designer Philippe Starck in 1989 and now houses a chic restaurant and a stylish tapas bar. In the restaurant, you can dine on fresh Mediterranean cuisine with Italian influences, while the tapas bar offers gourmet tapas. Prices reflect the glamorous setting.

BOURBON MADRID Viridiana

▤🍷 €€€€

C/ Juan de Mena 14, 28014 **Tel** *915-23 44 78* **Map** *E4*

Innovative Spanish cuisine, complemented by an encyclopedic wine list, is offered in this restaurant decorated with stills from Luís Buñuel's film, Viridiana. The creative menu changes frequently, and features elaborate creations prepared with the best seasonal produce. Leave some room for dessert, as they serve amazing pannacotta. Closed Sun, Easter.

BARCELONA

EIXAMPLE Tapaç 24

Tapas 🌐🚶▤🍷 €€

C/ Diputació 269, 08007 **Tel** *934-88 09 77* **Map** *D2*

With 1960s tapas bar-style decor, Tapaç 24 serves both traditional and more creative tapas made with local produce and fresh fish from the market. It opens at 8am for breakfasts with a choice of eggs cooked how you want them, then serves tapas all day long. Try the *bravas* (spicy potatoes) or the hot Iberian ham and truffle sandwich. Closed Sun.

EIXAMPLE Casa Calvet

🚻▤🍴🍷 €€€€

C/ Casp 48, 08010 **Tel** *934-12 40 12* **Map** *D2*

A beautiful restaurant that was originally designed by Gaudí as a private home and offices for a wealthy textile merchant. The cozy seating booths, formal table settings, and old-school service set the ambiance. There is a seasonal menu that changes according to what is available. Closed Sun & public hols.

EIXAMPLE Igueldo

🚻▤🍷 €€€€

C/ Rosselló 186, 08008 **Tel** *934-52 25 55* **Map** *D2*

This elegant and stylish restaurant is very popular among the city's artists and writers. It serves mainly Basque dishes; especially outstanding is the grilled *chuleton* (T-bone steak). The wine selection and the desserts are also excellent. A fixed-price menu is served at the bar for lunch. Closed Sun.

OLD TOWN Bodega La Palma

Tapas 🚶▤🍷 €

C/ Palma de Sant Just 7, 08002 **Tel** *933-15 06 56* **Map** *D3*

An authentic old cellar hidden in the heart of the Gothic quarter and decorated with antique marble tables and wooden barrels, Bodega La Palma serves its own wines to accompany a delicious selection of tapas, cold meats, local cheeses, and salads. The *patatas bravas* (spicy potatoes) are unmissable. Closed Sun, 2 weeks in Aug.

OLD TOWN Kiosko Universal

Tapas 🚻🌐🚶 €

Mercat Sant Josep 691, 08002 **Tel** *933-17 82 86* **Map** *D3*

This is a lively and popular bar inside the Bouqueria market (at the left corner as you enter from the Ramblas). Simple but superb dishes are made with ultra-fresh seafood and vegetables, such as mixed grilled wild mushrooms in season, grilled calamari or clams. Closed Sun.

OLD TOWN Las Fernández

🚻🚶▤🍷 €€

C/ Carretas 11, 08001 **Tel** *934-43 20 43* **Map** *C3*

At the heart of the El Raval neighborhood is this friendly restaurant with a warm red decor and recycled furniture. It is run by three sisters from the Bierzo region, who serve home-town specialties with a Mediterranean touch, together with their own creations and delicious desserts. Reservations are recommended. Closed lunch, Mon, two weeks Aug.

OLD TOWN 7 Portes

🚻▤🍷 €€€

Passeig Isabel II 14, 08003 **Tel** *933-19 30 33* **Map** *E3*

A long-standing Barcelona institution since 1836, with a who's who of past guests, including Winston Churchill and Che Guevara. It is famed for its classic marble tiles and wood-paneled dining room, and most of all for *paella*, which comes in 10 different varieties. They serve a different *paella* every day of the week. Open 1pm–1am daily.

OLD TOWN Cal Pep

Tapas ▤🍷 €€€

Plaça de les Olles 8, 08003 **Tel** *933-10 79 61* **Map** *E3*

Arguably the best bar in town for fresh fish and seafood, right off the boats. Cal Pep has an excellent selection of tapas as well. The long, narrow, standing bar means it gets crowded at peak times. Arrive early for one of five tables out back. Closed Sat dinner, Sun, Mon lunch, & Aug.

OLD TOWN Taxidermista

🚻🌐▤🍷 €€€

Plaça Reial 8, 08002 **Tel** *934-12 45 36* **Map** *D3*

Soft color schemes and high ceilings give this trendy restaurant an edge over the touristy competition on the bustling Plaça Reial. Inventive market cooking offers a wide range of dishes from around the Mediterranean Rim, including *baba ghanoush* (Lebanese eggplant purée), sardine tarts, and duck confit. Closed Mon & two weeks Jan.

Map References see maps of Madrid pp282–3 and Barcelona pp306–7

FURTHER AFIELD Hofmann
€€€€

La Granada del Penedés 14–16, 08006 **Tel** *932-18 71 65*

This Michelin-starred restaurant-cum-cookery school in the Gracia area produces high-quality cuisine in a sophisticated locale with attentive service. Daily specials are always a good bet. Do not miss the desserts as they are highly elaborate and artistic. Closed Sat & Sun, Easter, Aug, & Christmas.

NORTHERN SPAIN

BAIONA, RIAS BAIXAS Moscón
€€

C/ Alférez Barreiro 2, 36300 (Pontevedra) **Tel** *986-35 50 08*

This restaurant in Baiona serves mainly Galician cuisine with fish stews predominating on the menu. These include a tasty fish *caldeirada* (casserole) spiced with paprika. There is also seafood from the estuary; all complemented by a good selection of Galician wines. The harbor view makes for a pleasant dining experience. Outside tables in summer.

BILBAO (BILBO) Zortziko
€€€€

C/ Alameda Mazarredo 17, 48001 (Vizcaya) **Tel** *944-23 97 43*

Contemporary haute cuisine served in a beautiful building, not far from the Guggenheim Museum. The menu is seasonal with creative Basque touches. Among the specialties are local turbot and hake, *foie gras*, and a delicious tiramisu. Closed Sun, Mon, & mid-Aug–mid-Sep.

CANGAS DE ONIS El Molín de la Pedrera
Tapas €

C/ Río Güeña 2, 33550 (Asturias) **Tel** *985-84 91 09*

A stylish *sidrería* (cider house) with a rustic air. It serves original combinations such as *crujiente de cabrales con avellanas* (Cabrales cheese from the Picos de Europa with hazelnuts) and more traditional dishes. Prices are higher in the restaurant. There's a gluten-free menu. Closed Wed except in summer & Jan.

OVIEDO Casa Fermín
€€€

C/ San Francisco 8, 33003 (Asturias) **Tel** *985-21 64 52*

The cozy Casa Fermín is one of Oviedo's most classic restaurants offering a combination of traditional and modern, seasonal cuisine. Try the *Cantabrico* anchovies with goats' cheese or the hake in green sauce with cockles. For dessert, try the *arroz con leche requemado* (burned rice pudding). Closed Sun.

PAMPLONA (IRUNA) Europa
€€€€

C/ Espoz y Mina 11, 31002 (Navarra) **Tel** *948-22 18 00*

Located in the Hotel Europa, in the old part of the city near the cathedral, this Michelin-starred restaurant is one of Pamplona's best places to eat. It offers a range of creative dishes based on Navarrese cuisine such as *menestra de verduras* (vegetable stew), creamy rice with artichokes, and sugared suckling pig. Closed Sun.

PONTEVEDRA, RIAS BAIXAS Alameda 10
€€€€

C/ Alameda 10, 36001 **Tel** *986-85 74 12*

Alameda 10 offers regional cuisine in a refined and beautiful setting overlooking a lovely tree-lined avenue. Monkfish salad, marinated sea bass salad, and *mero al vapor* (grouper) with vegetables and olive oil are favorites. The shellfish dishes are popular too. Closed Sun.

SAN SEBASTIAN (DONOSTIA) Arzak
€€€€

Av Alcalde Elósegui 273, 20015 (Guipúzcoa) **Tel** *943-27 84 65*

Celebrity chef Juan Mari Arzak has earned a reputation beyond Spain for his perfectly presented, creative dishes, which have earned him three Michelin stars. His daughter Elena works here as well. They even run a "laboratory" where a team of cooks experiment. Closed Sun, Mon, & two weeks in Jun & Nov.

SANTANDER El Serbal
€€€€

C/ Andrés del Río, 39004 **Tel** *942-22 25 15*

Holder of a Michelin star since 2003, this elegant, cosmopolitan restaurant near Puerto Chico offers modern cuisine based on traditional Cantabrian recipes and fresh local produce in such dishes as white beans with oxtail or *bacalao al pil-pil* (cod with parsley sauce). Try a range of dishes on the tasting menu. Exquisite service. Closed Mon & Sun dinner.

SANTIAGO DE COMPOSTELA Casa Marcelo
€€€€

Rua Hortas 1, 15705 **Tel** *981-55 85 80*

Close to the cathedral, in an 18th-century stone building, is Marcelo Tejedor's Michelin-starred restaurant. Inside, the decor is modern and the open kitchen in the center of the dining room turns out creative Galician cuisine based on fresh, local produce. The menu consists of a tasting menu that changes daily. Closed Sun & Mon.

VILAGARCIA DE AROUSA, RIAS BAIXAS Casa Bóveda
€€€€

C/ La Marina 2, Carril, 36610 (Pontevedra) **Tel** *986-51 12 04*

It is better to book in advance to eat in this busy restaurant situated on Carril harbor, a short way from Vilagarcía de Arousa. It specializes in fish and shellfish from the Rias Baixas and also prepares excellent *guisos* (stews) and rice dishes. Closed Sun evenings & Mon (except Aug) and Dec 20–Jan 20.

Key to Price Guide *see p346* **Map References** *see map of Barcelona pp306–7*

CATALONIA & EASTERN SPAIN

ALICANTE (ALACANT) Nou Manolín

Tapas 🔖📋🍷　€€€€

C/ Villegas 3, 03001 (Alicante) **Tel** *965-20 03 68*

An Alicantino favorite, this attractive restaurant is tucked away in the old quarter in the former home of local author Gabriel Miró. There is an excellent tapas bar downstairs, while upstairs you can dine in an elegant brick-lined salon on classic Valencian seafood and rice dishes, accompanied by an extensive wine list.

ALTEA, COSTA BLANCA Racó de Toni

Tapas 🔖📋🍷　€

C/ de la Mar 127, 03590 (Alicante) **Tel** *965-84 17 63*

An old-fashioned charmer, this cozy, traditional *mesón* serves good regional specialties including excellent rice dishes and locally caught fish. Specialties include rice with salt cod and vegetables, and peppers stuffed with anchovies. There's a good-value *menú del día* and tapas in the lively bar. Closed Sun evenings, Nov 20–30.

TARRAGONA Grotta

Tapas 🔖📶👥📋🍷　€€

Plaza Sedassos 28, 43003 (Tarragona) **Tel** *977-25 18 87*

Located near the Roman circus in the old town, in a modern interior that resembles a cave, is this restaurant and lounge bar. It offers an excellent fixed-price lunch menu of home-style market cooking each day and creative, international tapas at night. There's a young clientele at weekends when it stays open late for music and drinks.

VALENCIA Ca Sento

🔖📶📋🍷　€€€€

C/ Méndez Nuñez 17, 46024 (Valencia) **Tel** *963-30 17 75*

Raúl Aleixandre is one of the most outstanding chefs in Spain. He prepares traditional but developed Valencian recipes, from *arroz en perol* (rice in the pot), learned from his mother, to more creative dishes, mostly based on seafood. The fish stew is highly recommended but can only be ordered in advance.

ZARAGOZA La Rinconada de Lorenzo

Tapas 🔖📶👥📋🍷　€€€

C/ La Salle 3, 50006 **Tel** *976-55 51 08*

Traditional Aragonese dishes are combined with a large selection of Aragonese wines. Two large dining rooms decorated with still-life paintings and beautiful Muel tiles are the setting for such specialties as *sopa de pastor* (meat and vegetable soup) and a rabbit and snail stew. Delicious tapas too. Closed Sun evenings and Mon in Jul & Aug.

CENTRAL SPAIN

AVILA El Almacén

🔖📶📋🍷　€€€€

Crta Salamanca 6, 05002 **Tel** *920-25 44 55*

This restaurant, located in an old warehouse, is generally regarded as one of the best in all of Castilla, and is particularly noted for its wine cellar. It offers creative cooking with prime-quality local produce, all cooked to perfection. There are views of Ávila's famous wall from the dining room. Closed Sun evenings, Mon, & Sep.

BURGOS Mesón del Cid

🔖📋　€€€

Plaza Santa María 8, 09003 **Tel** *947-20 87 15*

In a 15th-century edifice located in front of the cathedral, this rustic place is named after Spain's most notorious conqueror. A favorite among locals, it is celebrated for its home-style cooking. The menu features traditional fare such as roast lamb, garlic soup, and cod cooked with garlic. There is an excellent house wine. Closed Sun evenings.

LEON Vivaldi

🔖👥📋🍷　€€€€

MUSAC, Avda de los Reyes Leoneses 24, 24003 **Tel** *987-26 07 60*

Located in the MUSAC museum (Museo de Arte Contemporáneo), this modern restaurant serves Spanish *haute cuisine* inspired by local traditions. There is a fixed-price miniature tasting menu with 12 small dishes, or *à la carte* dining. Closed Sun, Mon & Tue eve.

SALAMANCA El Río de la Plata

Tapas 📋🍷　€€€

Plaza del Peso 1, 37001 **Tel** *923-21 90 05*

Located in the heart of the old town, this traditional restaurant, run by the locally celebrated Andrés brothers, serves slow-cooked lamb, pork and veal stews, and suckling pig. Lighter eaters may wish to stick to the excellent selection of tapas. Among the tasty desserts is apple baked in a secret sauce! Closed Mon & 15–20 days in Feb & Jul.

SAN LORENZO DE EL ESCORIAL Taberna La Cueva

Tapas 📶🍷　€€€

C/ San Antón 4, 28200 **Tel** *918-90 15 16*

Juan de Villanueva, architect of the Prado, designed this 18th-century inn whose specialties include the *heuvos a la cueva* (fried eggs and ham served in a nest of straw potatoes). A cool stone house, it is cozy in winter and cool in summer, when you can also tuck into tapas out on the terrace. A good range of local wines. Closed Mon.

Key to Symbols *see back cover flap*

SEGOVIA José Maria
Tapas €€€€

C/ Cronista Lecea 11, 40001 **Tel** 921-46 11 11

This well-known restaurant, located in the heart of the old town, offers traditional elaborate Castillian cuisine, such as an outstanding roast suckling pig. The perfect side dishes are the roast red peppers and the *judiones* (butter beans). On weekends there are two sittings for lunch, at 1:30pm and 3pm.

TOLEDO Hostal del Cardenal
€€€

Paseo de Recadero 24, 45004 (Toledo) **Tel** 925-22 08 62

Once the summer residence of Cardinal Lorenzana, this 18th-century palace retains its beautiful Arabic-style gardens, enclosed by the city walls. It serves suckling pig, traditionally roasted in a brick oven, along with game (particularly pheasant) in season. Desserts always feature the famous Toledo *mazapán* (marzipan).

SOUTHERN SPAIN

CADIZ El Faro
Tapas €€€

C/ San Félix 15, 11011 (Cádiz) **Tel** 956-21 10 68

El Faro restaurant has a warm atmosphere in the old fishermen's barrio of Cádiz. The menu, a wonderful blend of modern and traditional, changes daily but always features local seafood, such as the *tortillitas de camarones* (fritters of tiny shrimps), or the rice dishes flavored with shellfish from the bay. There is a popular tapas bar, too.

CORDOBA Casa Pepe de la Judería
Tapas €€

C/ Romero 1, 14003 (Córdoba) **Tel** 957-20 07 44

This has been one of Córdoba's most appealing restaurants since it opened in 1928. Dine on a lovely Córdoban patio blazing with flowers, or sit in the dining rooms festooned with photos of notable customers. Try the *flamenquín* (fried rolls of veal and ham), or the unusual cherry gazpacho flavored with mint. Closed Dec 24–31.

ESTEPONA La Alcaría de Ramos
€€

Ctra de Cádiz, km 167, Urb El Paraíso, 29680 (Málaga) **Tel** 952-88 61 78

Located in an old country manor overlooking the Mediterranean, the food here is mostly Spanish with international touches. Among its star dishes are the house paté with Cumberland sauce, salmon, *millefeuille* with king prawns, or the roast duck with apple purée. Closed Sun, Dec 1–15.

FUENGIROLA Portofino
€€

Edificio Perla 1, Paseo Marítimo 29, 29640 (Málaga) **Tel** 952-47 06 43

This seafront restaurant is popular for its friendly service and good international food, such as the fish brochette or delicious pastas with rich sauces. It also prepares traditional Andalusian dishes, all served in generous portions. The terrace has views over the glossy, yacht-filled port. Closed Mon, 2 weeks in Jul & Dec.

GRANADA Mirador de Morayma
€€€

C/ Pianista Garcia Carrillo 2, 18010 (Granada) **Tel** 958-22 82 90

Situated in the Albaícin with views of the Alhambra, this charming patio-restaurant specializes in typical dishes of Granada, such as *remojón* (a salad of oranges and codfish) and lamb sautéed with garlic. The wine list includes organic wines produced on the restaurant's estate. Flamenco on Mon & Wed, call to confirm times. Closed Sun pm and Sun in Jul & Aug.

GRANADA Carmen de San Miguel
€€€€

Plaza Torres Bermejas 3, 18009 (Granada) **Tel** 958-22 67 23

The Andalusian specialties at this pretty restaurant with Moorish-style decor include the seabass with aubergine (eggplant) and the *foie gras* pastry with mango chutney. Everything is fresh and prepared with imagination by a talented young chef. There are wonderful views of the whitewashed maze of the Albaícin from the terrace. Closed Sun.

JEREZ DE LA FRONTERA La Mesa Redonda
€€€€

C/ Manuel de la Quintana 3, 11402 (Cádiz) **Tel** 956-34 00 69

A charming, family-run restaurant, which remains a favorite with locals for the quality and excellence of its cuisine. The creative menu changes with the seasons offering seafood, meat dishes, and game. Try the *mojama* (cured tuna) as a starter, and do not miss the spectacular beef *salteado* (sautéed with black sausage). Closed Sun, mid-Jul–mid-Aug.

MALAGA Mesón Astorga
Tapas €€€

C/ Gerona 11, 29006 (Málaga) **Tel** 952-34 25 63

Using Málaga's superb local produce with flair makes this classically decorated and typically Andalusian restaurant popular. Try the fried aubergine (eggplant) drizzled with molasses or the salad of fresh tuna with sherry vinegar dressing. At the lively tapas bar, you can join the locals tucking into generous *raciones*. Closed Sun.

MARBELLA Santiago
Tapas €€€€

Avda Duque de Ahumada 5, 29600 (Málaga) **Tel** 952-77 00 78

This is probably the best place for seafood on the Costa del Sol. On any day, there might be 40 or 50 fish and shellfish dishes, all very fresh. Famous for more than 50 years, it's essential to book your table well in advance. Tapas are served at the bar, but there is a huge variety (more than 500) on offer at the adjoining Taberna de Santiago.

Key to Price Guide see p346 **Key to Symbols** see back cover flap

RONDA Del Escudero

⏸️🏠📋🍷 €€

Paseo de Blás Infante 1, 29400 (Málaga) Tel 952-87 13 67

With an incomparable garden setting near Ronda's famous bullring, this elegant restaurant offers spectacular views over the valley to go with its traditional Andalusian cuisine. Go for the good-value fixed-price lunch menu which you can enjoy on the panoramic garden terrace. Closed Sun evenings.

SEVILLE La Azotea

Tapas ⏸️🏃📋🍷 €

C/ Jesús del Gran Poder 31, 41002 Tel 955-11 67 48

La Azotea is considered one of the best tapas bars in town. Creative touches are added to traditional tapas, using top quality ingredients. Try the ox sirloin, sausage with caramelized onions, or the fried quail eggs, and the delicious desserts. Go early, as there are only six tables and bookings are not accepted.

SEVILLE El Cabildo

🏠📋🍷 €€€

Plaza del Cabildo, 41001 (Seville) Tel 954-22 79 70

Part of the ancient Arabic walls have been conserved in this classic and delightfully old-fashioned restaurant. All the traditional Andalusian favorites are on the menu, excellently cooked with fresh local ingredients. Try a platter of fresh fried fish, Sevillian *revueltos* (scrambled eggs with different fillings) accompanied by sturdy local wine.

SEVILLE Corral del Agua

🏠📋 €€€€

Callejón del Agua 6, 41004 Tel 954-22 48 41

Dine on the cool patio of the Reales Alcázares gardens, with plants trailing romantically around wrought-iron grilles and a marble fountain burbling quietly. Antique furniture and paintings adorn the dining room, and the menu emphasizes seasonal specialties, traditionally prepared. Closed Sun.

TORREMOLINOS Frutos

Tapas ⏸️🏠📋🍷 €€€€

Urb Los Álamos, Av de la Riviera 80, 29620 (Málaga) Tel 952-38 14 50

The grande dame of Costa del Sol restaurants, serving superb meat and fish. There is a terrace, and two classy dining areas where you can enjoy suckling pig, followed by *arroz con leche* (rice pudding). The remarkable wine cellar in the basement can be visited. An informal tapas bar at the entrance serves lighter meals. Closed Sun evenings.

THE BALEARIC ISLANDS

FORMENTERA, ES PUJOLS Sa Palmera

⏸️🏠📋🍷 €€

Playa Es Pujols, C/Aguadulce 15–31, 07871 (Formentera) Tel 971-32 83 58

Freshly caught seafood is served at this classic seafront restaurant, which specializes in traditionally prepared regional cuisine. Try the mixed fish *paella* or the *zarzuela de mariscos* (shellfish casserole), although you will also find a few meat dishes on the menu. You can eat out on the breezy terrace and enjoy great sea views. Closed Nov–Feb & Mon.

IBIZA, IBIZA TOWN La Masía d'en Sort

⏸️🏠📋P €€€

Ctra San Miguel km 1, 07814 (Ibiza) Tel 971-31 02 28

A sturdy Ibizan *masia* (farmhouse) set in orange groves is home to this elegant restaurant, with stylish dining rooms which double as art galleries. The food is no less artistic, and features reinventions of classic Balearic cuisine prepared with fresh local ingredients. Try the refreshing langoustine salad. Closed lunch, Mon (except Aug); Nov–Mar.

MALLORCA Es Baluard

🏠📋🍷 €€€€

Pl Puerta de Santa Catalina 9 (Palma), 07012 (Mallorca) Tel 971-71 96 09

The chef was one of the pioneers of the "new Mallorcan cuisine", creatively developing traditional local recipes. The result is just delicious, as the cod supreme *au gratin* with smoked eggplant or the slow-cooked pork cheeks attest. Ask for a table on the quiet terrace overlooking the square. Closed Sun.

MALLORCA, PORT DE POLLENCA Stay

⏸️🏠📋🍷 €€€€

C/ Muelle Nuevo s/n, 07470 (Mallorca) Tel 971-86 40 13

With tables right on the bay, this popular local restaurant serves tasty regional cuisine with emphasis on fish and seafood. Try the *salsa de eneldo* (fillets of white fish grilled with vegetables and served with a dill sauce). They also have a cheap and cheerful snack bar (for sandwiches and burgers), good for families coming off the beaches.

MENORCA, CIUTADELLA Café Balear

Tapas ⏸️🏠📋 €€€€

Pla de Sant Joan 15, 07760 (Menorca) Tel 971-38 00 05

A legendary restaurant right on the port, Café Balear specializes in fish and seafood including *caldera de langosta* (lobster casserole) and *fritada de gambas* (fried prawns). The fish arrives on the restaurant's own boat, and is prepared with the minimum of fuss to better appreciate its freshness. Reservations essential. Closed Sun evenings.

MENORCA, MAO Jágaro

⏸️🏠📋🍷 €€€€

Moll de Levant 334, 07701 (Menorca) Tel 971-36 23 90

A classic restaurant right on the harbor, with a cozy dining room filled with knick knacks and a popular breezy terrace. It serves fine Mediterranean seafood dishes, including the Menorcan specialty *caldereta de langosta* (lobster stew). There are over 100 wines on their wine list. Closed Sun–Thu evenings in winter.

PORTUGAL

*M*ost visitors to Portugal head for the sandy coves, pretty fishing villages, and manicured golf courses of the Algarve. But beyond the south coast resorts lies the least explored corner of Western Europe: a country of rugged landscapes, ancient cities with proud traditions, and quiet rural backwaters.

Portugal appears to have no obvious geographical claim to nationhood, yet the country has existed within borders virtually unchanged for nearly 800 years, making it one of the oldest nation states in Europe. Its ten million people are proudly independent from, and distrustful of, neighboring Spain.

For a small country, the regions of Portugal are immensely varied. The rural Minho and Trás-os-Montes in the north are the most traditional – some might say backward. Over the last few decades many inhabitants of these neglected regions have been forced to emigrate in search of work. At the same time, the Algarve, with its beautiful sandy beaches and warm Mediterranean climate, has become a vacation playground for North Europeans as well as the Portuguese themselves. Lisbon, the capital, at the mouth of the Tagus, is a cosmopolitan metropolis with a rich cultural life. Oporto is a serious rival, especially in terms of commerce and industry, and is the center for the production and export of Portugal's most famous product – port wine, grown on steeply terraced vineyards hewn out of mountainsides in the wild upper reaches of the Douro valley.

HISTORY

The Romans, who arrived in 216 BC, called the whole peninsula Hispania, but the region between the Douro and Tagus rivers was named Lusitania after the Celtiberian tribe that lived there. After the collapse of the Roman Empire in the 5th century, Hispania was overrun first by Germanic tribes, then by Moors from North Africa in 711.

Reconquest by the Christian kingdoms of the north began in earnest in the 11th century. In the process Portucale, a small county of the kingdom of León and Castile, was declared an independent kingdom by its ruler, Afonso Henriques, in 1139. With the aid of English crusaders, he succeeded in recapturing Lisbon in 1147.

Fishing boats on the beach at the popular Algarve resort of Albufeira

◁ Nave of the Manueline church of Santa Maria in the Jerónimos monastery, Belém, Lisbon

The kingdom expanded south to the Algarve, and Portuguese sailors began to explore the African coast and the Atlantic. Portugal's golden age reached its zenith in the reign of Manuel I, with Vasco da Gama's voyage to India in 1498 and the discovery of Brazil in 1500. The era also produced the one uniquely Portuguese style of architecture: the Manueline. Trade with the East brought incredible wealth, but military defeat in Morocco meant that the prosperity was short-lived. Spain invaded in 1580 and ruled Portugal for the next 60 years.

Manuel I (reigned 1495–1521), who made vast profits from Portugal's spice trade

After Portugal regained independence, its fortunes were restored by gold from Brazil. In the late 18th century, the chief minister, the Marquês de Pombal, began to modernize the country. However, Napoleon's invasion in 1807 and the loss of Brazil in 1825 left Portugal impoverished and divided. Absolutists and Constitutionalists struggled for power, until, in 1910, a republican revolution overthrew the monarchy.

The weakness of the economy led to a military coup in 1926 and a long period of dictatorship. António Salazar, who held power from 1928 to 1968, rid the country of its debts, but poverty was widespread and all opposition banned. The country was a virtual recluse in the world community, the prime concern of foreign policy being the defense of its African and Asian colonies. The bloodless Carnation Revolution ended the dictatorship in 1974, and full democracy was restored in 1976. Since its entry into the European Community in 1986, Portugal has enjoyed rapid economic growth and assumed the self-confident attitude of a modern Western European state.

KEY DATES IN PORTUGUESE HISTORY

139 BC Romans subdue the Lusitani

415 AD Visigoths invade Iberian Peninsula

711 Muslim army conquers Visigothic kingdom

1139 Afonso Henriques declares himself king

1147 Afonso Henriques takes Lisbon

1249 Conquest of Algarve complete

1385 João I defeats Castilians at Aljubarrota

1418 Prince Henry the Navigator made governor of Algarve; sponsors expeditions to Africa

1498 Vasco da Gama reaches India

1578 King Sebastião killed on ill-fated expedition to Morocco

1580 Philip II of Spain becomes king of Portugal

1640 Restoration; Duke of Bragança crowned João IV; start of war of independence

1668 Spain recognizes Portugal's independence

1755 Lisbon earthquake

1807 French invade; royal family flees to Brazil

1910 Revolution; Manuel II abdicates and flees to England; republic proclaimed

1932 António Salazar becomes prime minister

1974 Carnation Revolution

2000 Portugal joins European single currency

2005 Socialists win first outright majority in parliament since democracy began in 1974

LANGUAGE AND CULTURE

The family is the hub of Portuguese daily life and Catholicism remains a powerful force in rural communities. But the country has come a long way since the repression and self-censorship of the Salazar era. Urban Portugal, in particular, presents a fairly emancipated and eagerly consumerist face to the world.

The national psyche encapsulates this dualism in its struggle between a forward-looking, realistic approach to life and the dreamy, inward-looking side that finds expression in the Portuguese notion of *saudade*, a melancholy yearning for something lost or unattainable.

The Portuguese language is a source of national pride, and visitors should not assume that it is interchangeable with Spanish. Portuguese people are also often eager to speak English. Pride, too, is taken in *fado*, the native musical tradition that expresses *saudade*.

Exploring Portugal

Portugal is a small country and there are fast road
and train links between the country's three great cities,
Lisbon, Coimbra, and Oporto. Many of the most
famous sights, such as the royal palaces at Sintra and
the monastery of Alcobaça, make a good day's outing
from Lisbon. In the south, the great attractions are the
sandy beaches of the Algarve. Arriving from the north
is quite easy on the Lisbon-Algarve motorway, but
most visitors fly direct to Faro airport and once there,
traveling between the various resorts is no problem.

Sintra, dominated by the conical
chimneys of the old royal palace

KEY

✈ Airport

⛴ Ferry port

— Highway

— Major road

— Railroad

••• International border

SIGHTS AT A GLANCE

Albufeira **⑪**   Tomar **④**

Alcobaça **⑤**

Batalha **⑥**   **The Lisbon Coast**

Coimbra **⑦**   *(see inset map)*

Évora **⑨**   Cascais **②**

Faro **⑩**   *LISBON pp356–65* **①**

Lagos **⑬**   *Sintra p.366,*

Oporto **⑧**   *pp368–9* **③**

Portimão **⑫**

Lisbon ❶

The capital of Portugal occupies a hilly site on the estuary of the Tagus. Over the centuries, the city expanded along the coast to Belém, the starting point for the voyages of discovery in the 15th century, and even to the other side of the river, known as the Outra Banda. It has now spread far inland, making the population of Greater Lisbon nearly two million. The historic center (the Baixa) is a small, low-lying area, pinned between the heights of the Alfama to the east and the Bairro Alto to the west. The city underwent a great cleanup for the Expo '98 exhibition, especially in the old docks and industrial areas along the waterfront.

Portugal's coat of arms in the treasury of the Sé (cathedral)

SIGHTS AT A GLANCE

Alfama ④
Bairro Alto ⑨
Baixa ⑧
Castelo de São Jorge ⑤
Museu Nacional de Arte Antiga ⑪
Praça do Comércio ⑦
São Vicente de Fora ③
Sé ⑥

Greater Lisbon
(see inset map)
Museu Calouste Gulbenkian ⑩
Museu Nacional do Azulejo ②
Oceanário de Lisboa ①

Belém *(see inset map)*
Monument to the Discoveries ⑬
Mosteiro dos Jerónimos pp364–5 ⑭
Museu da Marinha ⑮
Museu Nacional dos Coches ⑫
Torre de Belém ⑯

Mosteiro dos Jerónimos overlooking Praça do Império

GETTING AROUND

Lisbon's limited metro system links the north of the city with sights in the center around Rossio square. Buses cover the whole city and are the most common form of public transportation. Take the Santa Justa lift to reach the Bairro Alto district and the 28 tram to climb the steep hill up to the Alfama. Belém is served by tram, train, and bus. Taxis are inexpensive, but a taxi ride can be alarming, as can any experience of driving in Lisbon.

SEE ALSO

Where to Stay p378

Where to Eat p380

GREATER LISBON

Vila Franca

Lisbon Airport

Olivais

Oriente

Amadora

Pontinha

Campo Grande

Benfica

PARQUE FLORESTAL DE MONSANTO

Estefânia

Xabregas

Graça

Carnaxide

Cascais

Alcântara

Belém

Montijo

Barreiro

Tejo

Cacilhas

Almada

Porto Brandão Trafaria

Setúbal

Seixal

0 km 2

0 mile 2

KEY

Area of main map

GRAÇA

Martim Moniz

Restauradores

Rossio

ROSSIO (PRAÇA DOM PEDRO IV)

São Roque

Igreja do Carmo

RUA GARRETT

Chiado

Teatro de São Carlos

Museu do Chiado

RUA DO ARSENAL

ALFAMA

BAIXA

ALCANTARA

Santa Engrácia

Santa Apolónia

Museu Militar

AVENIDA INFANTE DOM HENRIQUE

RUA DE SÃO JULIÃO

RUA DO COMÉRCIO

RUA DOS BACALHOEIROS

Estação Fluvial Terreiro do Paço

Terreiro do Paço

AVENIDA DA RIBEIRA DAS NAUS

Tejo

0 meters 500

0 yards 500

KEY

- Sight / Place of interest
- ✈ Airport
- ⚓ Ferry boarding point
- 🚆 Train station
- Ⓜ Metro station
- Funicular station
- P Parking
- ℹ Tourist information
- ✝ Church
- Pedestrian street

BELÉM

ESTÁDIO MUNICIPAL DO RESTELO

BELÉM

AJUDA

Centro Cultural de Belém

PRAÇA DO IMPÉRIO

RUA DE BELÉM

Belém

Estação Fluvial de Belém

AVENIDA DA ÍNDIA

AVENIDA DE BRASÍLIA

Tejo

0 meters 250

0 yards 250

D

E

F

Oceanário de Lisboa ①

Esplanada dom Carlos I, Parque das Nações. **Tel** 218-917 002. **M** Oriente. 🚌 5, 21, 28, 44, 750, 208 (night). 🚉 Gare do Oriente. ⬜ daily. 🅿 ♿

This huge oceanarium, on the banks of the Tagus, is the second largest in the world. It was designed for Expo '98 by the American architect, Peter Chermayeff, to illustrate the environmental theme of "The Oceans: A Heritage for the Future."

The central feature is a gigantic aquarium, the "Open Tank," with enough water to fill four Olympic swimming pools. Representing the open ocean, this contains fauna of the high seas, from sea bream to sharks. Around the main tank four smaller aquariums reconstruct the ecosystems of the Atlantic, Antarctic, Pacific, and Indian oceans.

Museu Nacional do Azulejo ②

Rua da Madre de Deus 4. **Tel** 218-100 340. 🚌 28, 718, 742, 759, 794. ⬜ Tue pm–Sun. ⬤ Jan 1, Easter, May 1, Dec 25. 🖥 🍴 🎫 http://mnazulejo.imc-ip.pt

The idea of decorative tiles was a legacy of the Moors. From the 16th century onward, Portugal started producing its own painted ceramic tiles (azulejos). The blue-and-white tiles of the Baroque era are considered by many to be the finest.

The National Tile Museum is housed in the Convento da Madre de Deus, founded by Dona Leonor (widow of João II) in 1509. The interior of the church has striking Baroque decoration, added by João V.

An important surviving feature of the original convent is the Manueline cloister. Along with the larger Renaissance cloister, it provides a stunning setting for the museum. Decorative panels, individual tiles, and photographs trace tile-making from its introduction, through Spanish influence and

Statue of woman praying beside tomb of Carlos I in São Vicente de Fora

the development of Portugal's own styles, to today. Panels from churches, monasteries, and other sites around Portugal have been reassembled here. Highlights include a blue-and-white, 18th-century panorama showing Lisbon before the earthquake, and the colorful 17th-century carpet tiles (so-called because they imitated the patterns of Moorish rugs).

Detail from 16th-century altarpiece in the Museu Nacional do Azulejo

São Vicente de Fora ③

Largo de São Vicente. **Tel** 218-810 500. 🚌 28. 🚋 12, 34. ⬜ Tue–Sun. ⬤ public hols. 🎫 to cloisters.

St. Vincent was proclaimed Lisbon's patron saint in 1173, when his relics were brought

to a church on this site. The present church was completed in 1627. The Italianate facade has statues of Saints Vincent, Augustine, and Sebastian over the entrance. The church has reopened after extensive renovation.

Behind the church is the old refectory, transformed into the Bragança Pantheon in 1885. The tombs of almost every Bragança king and queen are here, from João IV, who died in 1656, to Manuel II, last king of Portugal. Only Maria I and Pedro IV are not buried here. A stone mourner kneels at the tomb of Carlos I and his son Luís Felipe, assassinated in Praça do Comércio (see p360) in 1908.

Alfama ④

🚌 37. 🚋 12, 28.

A fascinating quarter at any time of day, the Alfama comes to life in the late afternoon and early evening, when the small restaurants and bars start to fill and music, often fado, can be heard in the alleyways. It is hard to believe that this, the oldest part of Lisbon, was once the most desirable quarter of the city. In the Middle Ages wealthy residents started to move away, fearing earthquakes, leaving the quarter to fishermen and paupers. Ironically, the Alfama was spared by the earthquake of 1755. Today, the area is a varren of narrow streets and mall, picturesque houses clinging to the hillside below he Castelo de São Jorge.

The least strenuous way to see this area is to start at the castle at the top and work your way down. Attractions on the way include the **Museu de Artes Decorativas** (Museum of Decorative Arts), which has its own workshops, and the sweeping views from the terrace of the **Miradouro de Santa Luzia**. You could also visit, on a Tuesday or Saturday, the colorful **Feira da Ladra** (Thieves' Market) in Campo de Santa Clara to the east of the castle or the early morning fish market in Rua de São Pedro.

Castelo de São Jorge ⑤

Porta de S. Jorge, Rua do Chão da Feira. **Tel** 218-800 620. 🚌 37. 🚋 28. ◯ daily. 📷

Following the recapture of Lisbon from the Moors in 1147, King Afonso Henriques transformed their citadel – which crowned Lisbon's eastern hill – into the residence of the Portuguese kings. In 1511 Manuel I built a more lavish palace beside the river (see p360). In the centuries that followed the Castelo de São Jorge was used variously as a theater, a prison, and an arms depot. After the 1755 earthquake, the ramparts lay in

ruins until 1938 when the castle was completely rebuilt. It was restored again, along with parts of the Santa Cruz district, in 2006.

The castle gardens and narrow streets of the old Santa Cruz district, which lies within the walls, are a pleasant place for a stroll, and the views are the finest in Lisbon. Visitors can climb the towers, one of which has a camera obscura, walk along the reconstructed ramparts, or stand on the shaded observation terrace.

The Sé, Lisbon's austere 12th-century cathedral

Sé ⑥

Largo da Sé. **Tel** 218-866 752. 🚌 37. 🚋 12, 28. ◯ daily. **Cloister & treasury** ◯ daily. 📷

In 1150, Afonso Henriques built a cathedral for the first bishop of Lisbon (Gilbert of Hastings) on the site of the Moorish mosque. Sé denotes the seat of a bishop.

Though much renovated over the centuries, the Sé has kept its solid Romanesque facade. The Capela de Santo

Ildefonso, one of nine Gothic chapels in the ambulatory behind the altar, contains two fine 14th-century tombs and in the Franciscan chapel by the entrance stands the font where St. Antony of Padua was baptized in 1195. In the Gothic cloister behind the Sé, excavations have unearthed Roman and other remains.

The treasury, located in one of the towers, has a splendid collection of exhibits, including the relics of St. Vincent. Legend has it that his remains were watched over by two ravens on their journey to Lisbon in 1173, hence the raven on the city's coat of arms.

View of the Castelo de São Jorge across the Baixa, Lisbon's lower town

Praça do Comércio, a grand entrance to the city of Lisbon

Praça do Comércio ⑦

🚌 702, 714, 740, 745, & many others. 🚊 15, 18.

More commonly known as *Terreiro do Paço* (Palace Square), this was the site of the royal palace for 400 years. Manuel I transferred the royal residence here, from the Castelo de São Jorge, in 1511. The first palace, together with its library and 70,000 books, was destroyed in the 1755 earthquake. Its replacement was built around three sides of the square. After the 1910 revolution it became government administrative offices.

The south side looks across the Tagus and was once the finest gateway to Lisbon – used by royalty and ambassadors – with marble steps up from the river. In the center of the square is an equestrian statue of José I (1775) by Machado de Castro, leading Portuguese sculptor of the 18th century.

The impressive triumphal arch on the north side, decorated with statues of historical figures, leads into Rua Augusta and the Baixa.

On February 1, 1908, King Carlos and his son, Luís Felipe, were assassinated in the square. In 1974 it witnessed the first uprising of the Armed Forces Movement, which overthrew the Caetano regime in a bloodless coup that became known as the Carnation Revolution.

Baixa ⑧

🚌 36, 702, 709, 714, 740, 746, & many others. 🚊 15, 18. Ⓜ *Rossio, Restauradores, Terreiro do Paço.*

Following the 1755 earthquake, the Marquês de Pombal created an entirely new city center, one of Europe's first examples of town planning. Using a grid layout of streets, the Praça do Comércio was linked with the busy central square of Rossio. The streets were flanked by splendid Neoclassical buildings.

The Baixa (lower town) is still the commercial hub of the city, housing banks, offices, and stores. The streets are crowded by day, especially the central Rua Augusta, but less so after dark.

By the Restauradores metro station is the **Palácio Foz**, an 18th-century palace. Tourists are naturally drawn to Rossio, an elegant square and social focal point with cafés and *pastelarias*. The **National Theater** stands on the north side. Just to the east of Rossio is the less attractive Praça da Figueira, the city's main marketplace in Pombal's time. Rua das Portas de Santo Antão, north of the two squares, is a lively pedestrian street full of restaurants.

Bairro Alto ⑨

🚌 7, 706, 709, 727, 732, 758, & many others. 🚊 28 (also Elevador da Glória & Elevador da Santa Justa). Ⓜ *Baixa-Chiado.*

The hilltop Bairro Alto quarter, dating from the 16th century, is one of Lisbon's most picturesque districts. Its narrow, cobbled streets house a traditional, close-knit community, with small workshops and family-run *tascas* (cheap restaurants). This predominantly residential area has become fashionable at night for its bars, night clubs, and *fado* houses (see p377).

Rossio Square and the Neoclassical National Theater in the Baixa

For hotels and restaurants in this region see p378 and p380

THE EARTHQUAKE OF 1755

The first tremor of the devastating earthquake was felt at 9:30am on November 1. It was followed by a second, far more violent, shock a few minutes later, which reduced over half the city to rubble. A third shock was followed by fires which quickly spread. An hour later huge waves came rolling in from the Tagus, flooding the lower part of the city. Most of Portugal suffered damage, but Lisbon was the worst affected: an estimated 15,000 people died in the city. Sebastião José de Carvalho e Melo, chief minister to King José I, later Marquês de Pombal, restored order and began a progressive town-planning scheme. His cool efficiency gained him almost total political control.

Marquês de Pombal

Portrait of an Old Man. Other major artists exhibited include Ghirlandaio, Rubens, Guardi, Gainsborough, Turner, Manet, and Renoir. The collection also includes sculpture, jewelry, textiles, manuscripts, porcelain, and a variety of decorative arts.

Museu Nacional de Arte Antiga ⑪

Rua das Janelas Verdes. **Tel** 213-912 800. 🚌 727, 751, 760. 🚋 15, 18. 🕐 Tue–Sun (Tue: pm only). 🔴 public hols. 🎟 ♿ 📷 🍴 http://mnaa.imc-ip.pt

The national art collection, housed in a 17th-century palace, was inaugurated in 1770. In 1940 a modern annex (including the main facade) was added. This was built on the site of a monastery, largely destroyed in the 1755 earthquake. Its only surviving feature, the chapel, has been integrated into the museum.

The second floor houses 14th–19th-century European paintings, decorative arts, and furniture. Artists exhibited include Piero della Francesca, Hans Holbein the Elder, Raphael, Lucas Cranach the Elder, Hieronymus Bosch, and Albrecht Dürer. Oriental and African art, Chinese ceramics, and the gold, silver, and jewelry collection are on the second floor. The top floor houses Portuguese works.

The pride of the Portuguese collection is the *Panels of St. Vincent* (c.1467–70), attributed to Nuno Gonçalves. It is an altarpiece painted on six panels, featuring portraits of a wide range of contemporary figures, from beggars and sailors to bishops and princes, including Henry the Navigator and the future João II, all paying homage to the saint. Another fascinating aspect of the Age of Exploration is recorded in the 16th-century Japanese screens, which show Portuguese traders arriving in Japan.

The Elevador de Santa Justa, which links the Baixa to the Carmo district

Very different in character is the neighboring, elegant, commercial district known as the Chiado, where affluent Lisboetas shop. On the main street, Rua Garrett, the Café Brasileira – once frequented by writers and intellectuals – remains popular. The Chiado was devastated by fire in 1988, but has been painstakingly renovated.

The best way to reach the Bairro Alto from the Baixa is via the Carmo district and the **Elevador de Santa Justa**, a Neo-Gothic elevator dating from 1901–2. Tourist attractions include the richly decorated **São Roque** church, the ruined **Igreja do Carmo**, once the largest church in Lisbon, and the **Museu do Chiado**, which houses art from 1850–1950.

Museu Calouste Gulbenkian ⑩

Avenida de Berna 45. **Tel** 217-823 000. Ⓜ Praça de Espanha, São Sebastião. 🚌 31, 716, 756, 726, 746. 🕐 Tue–Sun. 🔴 Mon & public hols. 🎟 (free Sun). 🍴 📷 ♿ www.museu.gulbenkian.pt

Thanks to wealthy Armenian oil magnate, Calouste Gulbenkian, Portugal owns one of the finest personal art collections assembled during the 20th century. Gulbenkian moved to Portugal in World War II, because of the country's neutral status. This museum was inaugurated in 1969, as part of the charitable institution bequeathed to the nation. The building was devised to create the best layout for the founder's varied collection: the exhibits span over 4,000 years, from ancient Egypt and China, through an extensive collection of Islamic ceramics and carpets, to Art Nouveau. Gulbenkian was a friend of René Lalique, the great glassware and jewelry maker and one room is filled with his work.

Highlights of the European art collection include Van der Weyden's *St. Catherine* and Rembrandt's

Statue of the founder at Gulbenkian Museum

Belém

At the mouth of the Tagus, where the Portuguese mariners set sail on their voyages of discovery, Manuel I commissioned two grand monuments in the exuberant Manueline style of architecture: the Mosteiro dos Jerónimos and the Torre de Belém. Today Belém is a spacious, relatively green suburb with museums and gardens, including the vast Praça do Império, a formal square with a central fountain in front of the monastery. The area enjoys an attractive riverside setting with cafés and a promenade; on sunny days it has a distinct seaside feel. In Rua de Belém is the Antiga Confeitaria de Belém, a 19th-century café that sells the local specialty: *pastéis de Belém*, rich flaky-pastry custard tarts.

The neighboring gallery includes pony-drawn chaises. There is also a 19th-century Lisbon cab, painted black and green, the colors of taxis right up to the 1990s. The 18th-century Eyeglass Chaise has a black leather hood pierced with sinister eyelike windows. It dates from the era of Pombal *(see p361)*, when lavish decoration was discouraged.

Museu Nacional dos Coches ⑫

Praça Afonso de Albuquerque (from 2012 the museum will move to Avenida da India 123). *Tel* 213-610 850. 🚌 28, 714, 727, 729, 751. 🚊 15. 🚆 Belém. ⬛ Tue–Sun. ⬤ Jan 1, Easter, May 1, Dec 25. 🎟 (free 10am–2pm Sun). ♿ **www**.museudoscoches.pt

The National Coach Museum was established in 1905 by King Carlos's wife, Dona Amélia, whose pink riding cloak can be seen on display. It occupies the former riding school of the Palace of Belém. The rest of the elegant pink palace is now the residence of the president of Portugal.

The coaches on display span three centuries and range from the practical to the preposterous. The main gallery, in Louis XVI style with a splendid painted ceiling, is the setting for two rows of coaches created for Portuguese royalty. The oldest is the comparatively plain 16th-century red leather and wood coach of Philip II of Spain. The coaches become increasingly sumptuous, interiors lined with red velvet and gold, exteriors carved with allegorical figures. The most extravagant of all are three Baroque coaches made in Rome for the Portuguese ambassador to the Vatican in the early 18th century.

Baroque coach in the Museu Nacional dos Coches

Monument to the Discoveries ⑬

Padrão dos Descobrimentos, Avenida de Brasília. *Tel* 213-031 950. 🚌 28, 727, 729, 751. 🚊 15. ⬛ Tue–Sun. ⬤ public hols. 🎟 **www**.padraodosdescobrimentos.egeac.pt

Standing prominently on the Belém waterfront, the Padrão dos Descobrimentos was built in 1960 to mark the 500th anniversary of the death of Henry the Navigator *(see p354)*. The 52-m- (170-ft-) high monument resembles a caravel – the small, lateen-rigged ship used by Portuguese sailors to explore the coast of

EASTERN FACE OF THE MONUMENT TO THE DISCOVERIES

Afonso V (1432–81)

Henry the Navigator (1394–1460), patron of the first explorers

Pedro Álvares Cabral (1467–1520), discoverer of Brazil

Vasco da Gama (1460–1524)

Fernão Magalhães (Magellan), who crossed the Pacific in 1520–21

Padrão erected by Diogo Cão in the Congo in 1482

Africa – with Portugal's coat of arms on the sides. Henry the Navigator stands at the prow with a caravel in hand. In two sloping lines either side of the monument are heroes linked with the Discoveries.

In front of the monument is a huge mariner's compass cut into the paving. The central map, dotted with galleons and mermaids, shows the routes of the discoverers in the 15th and 16th centuries. Inside the monument, an elevator whisks you to the sixth floor where steps lead to the top for a splendid panorama.

Mosteiro dos Jerónimos ⑭

See pp364–5.

Museu de Marinha ⑮

Praça do Império. *Tel 213-620 019.* 🚌 28, 727, 729, 751. 🚊 15. ⏰ Tue–Sun. ⏰ public hols. 🎟 *(free on Sun).* ♿ **http://**museu.marinha.pt

The Maritime Museum was inaugurated in 1962 in the west wing of the Jerónimos monastery. A hall devoted to the Discoveries illustrates the rapid progress in ship design from the mid-15th century. Small replicas show the transition from the bark to the lateen-rigged caravel, through the faster square-rigged caravel, to the Portuguese *nau* or great ship. There is also a display of astrolabes and navigational instruments, and replicas of 16th-century maps. The pillars carved with the Cross of the Order of Christ are replicas of various kinds of *padrão*, a stone marker set up to denote sovereignty over the new lands discovered.

Beyond the Hall of Discoveries are models of modern Portuguese ships and the Royal Quarters, housing the exquisitely furnished wood-paneled cabin of King Carlos and Queen Amélia from the royal yacht *Amélia*, built in Scotland in 1900. The modern pavilion opposite houses original royal barges and a display of seaplanes.

The Torre de Belém, a landmark for sailors returning to Lisbon

Torre de Belém ⑯

Avenida da India. *Tel 213-620 034.* 🚌 28, 727, 729, 751. 🚊 15. 🚉 Belém. ⏰ Tue–Sun. ⏰ Jan 1, Easter Sun, May 1, Dec 25. 🎟 *(free 10am–2pm Sun; public hols).* ♿ *ground floor only.* **www.**torrebelem.pt

Commissioned by Manuel I, the tower was built as a fortress in the middle of the Tagus in 1515–21. Before nearby land was reclaimed in the 19th century, the tower stood much further from the shore than it does today. As the starting point for the navigators who set out to discover the trade routes to the east, this Manueline gem became a symbol of Portugal's great era of expansion. On the terrace,

Royal coat of arms on the Torre de Belém

facing the sea, stands a statue of Our Lady of Safe Homecoming, watching over the lives of Portugal's sailors.

The beauty of the tower lies in the exterior decoration: Manueline ropework carved in stone, openwork balconies, and Moorish-style watchtowers. The distinctive battlements are in the shape of shields, decorated with the squared cross of the Order of Christ, the emblem that also adorned the sails of Portuguese ships.

The space below the terrace, which served as a store-room and a prison, is very austere, but the private quarters in the tower are worth visiting for the elegant arcaded Renaissance loggia and the wonderful panorama.

VASCO DA GAMA (C.1460–1524)

In 1498 Vasco da Gama sailed around the Cape of Good Hope and opened the sea route to India. Although the Hindu ruler of Calicut, who received him wearing diamond and ruby rings, was not impressed by his humble offerings of cloth and wash basins, da Gama returned to Portugal with a valuable cargo of spices. In 1502 he sailed again to India, establishing Portuguese trade routes in the Indian Ocean. João III nominated him Viceroy of India in 1524, but he died of a fever soon after.

Portrait of Vasco da Gama, painted in India

Mosteiro dos Jerónimos ⑭

Armillary sphere in the cloister

A monument to the wealth of Portugal's Age of Discovery, the monastery is the culmination of the Manueline style of architecture. Commissioned by Manuel I around 1501, soon after Vasco da Gama's return from his historic voyage, it was funded largely by "pepper money," taxes on spices, precious stones, and gold. Various masterbuilders worked on the building, the most notable being Diogo Boitac, replaced by João de Castilho in 1517. The monastery was entrusted to the Order of St. Jerome (Hieronymites) until 1834, when all religious orders were disbanded.

Tomb of Vasco da Gama
The 19th-century tomb of the explorer (see p361) is carved with ropes, armillary spheres, and other seafaring symbols

The fountain is in the shape of a lion, the heraldic animal of St. Jerome.

Refectory
The walls of the refectory are tiled with 18th-century azulejos. The panel at the northern end depicts the Feeding of the Five Thousand.

The modern wing, built in 1850 in Neo-Manueline style, houses the National Museum of Archaeology and part of the Maritime Museum *(see p361).*

Entrance to church and cloister

Gallery

View of the Monastery
The facade of the monastery church is dominated by the magnificent South Portal. This makes dramatic use of the Manueline style of architecture, essentially a Portuguese variant of Late Gothic.

The West Portal was designed by the French sculptor Nicolau Chanterène. One of the niches holds a sculpture of the kneeling figure of King Manuel I.

STAR FEATURES

★ South Portal

★ Cloister

★ Cloister
*João de Castilho's pure
Manueline creation
was completed in 1544.
Delicate tracery and
richly carved images
decorate the arches
and balustrades.*

VISITORS' CHECKLIST

Praça do Império. *Tel* 213-620
034. 🚌 28, 714, 727, 729, 751.
🚃 15. ⏰ 10am–6pm (6:30pm
May–Sep) Tue–Sun (last adm: 30
mins before closing). ⬤ public
hols. 🎟 (free am Sun). ♿ cloister. **www**.mosteirojeronimos.pt

Nave
*The spectacular vault-
ing in the church
of Santa Maria
is held aloft by
slender octagonal
pillars. These rise
like palm trees to
the roof creating
a feeling of space
and harmony.*

The chapter house holds the
tomb of Alexandre Herculano
(1810–77), historian
and first mayor
of Belém.

The chancel
was commis-
sioned in1572
by Dona
Catarina,
wife of
João III.

The tombs
of Manuel I,
his wife
Dona Maria,
João III and
Catarina are
supported
by elephants.

★ South Portal
*The strict geometrical
architecture of the portal
is almost obscured by the
exuberant decoration.
João de Castilho unites
religious themes, such as
this image of St. Jerome,
with the secular, exalting
the kings of Portugal.*

Tomb of King Sebastião
*The tomb of the "longed for"
Dom Sebastião stands empty.
The young king never returned
from battle in 1578 (see p354).*

Beach at Estoril, east of Cascais

Cascais ❷

🏛 33,000. 🚉 🚌 **i** Rua Visconde da Luz 14 (214-868 204). 🗓 first and third Sundays in month.

A harbor since prehistoric times, Cascais became a fashionable resort in the 1870s, when Luís I's summer palace was sited here. Today it is a bustling cosmopolitan resort, with many upscale shops in the pedestrian streets of the old town and a new marina complex. Fishing is still an important activity, and the day's catch is auctioned near the harbor in the afternoon.

Environs
Along the coast, 3 km (2 miles) to the east, the resort of **Estoril** has been home to exiled European royalty. It has retained its sense of place with grand villas and hotels lining the coast.

Guincho, 10 km (6 miles) west of Cascais, has a magnificent sandy beach. Its Atlantic breakers make it popular with surfers. Further north is **Cabo da Roca**, the most westerly point of mainland Europe.

Sintra ❸

🏛 25,000. 🚉 🚌 **i** Praça da República 23 (219-231 157). 🗓 2nd and 4th Sun of month in São Pedro. 🎭 Sintra Festival (Jun–Jul).

Sintra's setting among wooded ravines and fresh water springs made it a favorite summer retreat for the kings of Portugal, who built the fabulous **Palácio Nacional de Sintra** (see pp368–9) here.

Designated a UNESCO World Heritage Site in 1995, the town draws thousands of visitors, yet there are many tranquil walks in the surrounding hills.

Present-day Sintra is a maze of winding roads, and exploring the town on foot involves much walking and climbing; for a more leisurely tour, take a horse and carriage ride. The **Mira-douro da Vigia** in São Pedro offers impressive views, as does the cozy **Casa de Sapa** café, where you can sample *queijadas*, cheese tarts spiced with cinnamon.

High above the town is the **Castelo dos Mouros**, an 8th-century Moorish castle. On a nearby hilltop stands the **Palácio da Pena**, built in the 19th century for Ferdinand, King Consort of Maria II, in a bizarre medley of architectural styles. A magnificent park surrounds the fairy-tale castle.

🏰 **Castelo dos Mouros**
Estrada da Pena, 5 km (3 miles) S. **Tel** 219-237 300. 🚌 or taxi from Sintra. ⏰ daily. ⬤ Jan 1, Dec 25.

🏛 **Palácio da Pena**
Estrada da Pena, 5 km (3 miles) S. **Tel** 219-105 340. 🚌 or taxi from Sintra. ⏰ Tue–Sun. ⬤ Jan 1, May 1, Jun 29, Dec 25. 🎟 www.parquesdesintra.pt

Tomar ❹

🏛 43,000. 🚉 🚌 **i** Avenida Dr. Cândido Madureira (249-322 427). 🗓 Fri. 🎭 Festa dos Tabuleiros (Jul, every 4 years, next one will be 2015).

Founded in 1157 by Gualdim Pais, the first Grand Master of the Order of the Templars in Portugal, Tomar is dominated by the castle containing the **Convento de Cristo**. It was begun in 1162, built on land given to the Templars for services in battle, and preserves many traces of its founders and the inheritors of their mantle, the Order of Christ. The nucleus of the castle is the 12th-century Charola, the Templars' octag-onal oratory. In 1356, Tomar became the headquarters of the Order of Christ.

Manueline window at Tomar's monastery

Cloisters were built in the time of Henry the Navigator, but it was in the reigns of Manuel I (1495–1521) and his successor, João III (1521–57), that the greatest changes were made, with the addition of the Manueline church and Renaissance cloisters. The church window (c.1510), commissioned by Manuel I, is probably the best-known single example of the Manueline style of architecture.

Other fascinating features include the Terrace of Wax, where honeycombs were left to dry, and the "bread" cloister, where loaves were handed out to the poor.

The town of Tomar is the site of the curious Festa dos Tabuleiros, in which young girls carry towering structures made of 30 loaves of bread on their heads. They parade

Palácio da Pena in Sintra, the hilltop retreat of the last kings of Portugal

through the main square, Praça da República. The square's focal point is the 15th-century Gothic church of **São João Baptista**. Tomar is also home to one of Portugal's oldest synagogues, now the **Museu Luso-Hebraico de Abraham Zacuto**, a Jewish museum.

🛡 **Convento de Cristo**
Tel 249-313 481. ☐ daily.
🌑 Jan 1, Easter, May 1, Dec 25. 🖼

The Convento de Cristo, Tomar

Alcobaça ❺

Praça 25 de Abril, Alcobaça.
Tel 262-505 120. 🚌 from Lisbon or Coimbra. ☐ daily. 🌑 Jan 1, Easter, May 1, Dec 25. 🖼

The Mosteiro de Santa Maria de Alcobaça is Portugal's largest church and a UNESCO World Heritage site. Founded in 1153, the abbey is closely linked to the arrival of the Cistercian order in Portugal in 1138 as well as to the birth of the nation. In March 1147, Afonso Henriques conquered the Moorish stronghold of

Santarém. To commemorate the victory, he gave land and money to build a church to the Cistercians. Completed in 1223, the church is a beautiful building of austere simplicity. Portugal's rulers continued to endow the monastery, notably King Dinis (1279–1325), who added the main cloister, known as the Cloister of Silence. In the Sala dos Reis, 18th-century tiles depict the founding of the abbey, and statues of Portuguese kings adorn the walls.

Among those buried here are the tragic lovers King Pedro (1357–67) and his murdered mistress, Inês de Castro (d.1355), whose tombs face each other across the transept of the abbey church. Inês' death was ordered by Pedro's father, Afonso IV (1325–57). After Afonso's death, Pedro had two of Inês' murderers killed brutally. He then had her body exhumed and reburied.

One of Alcobaça's most popular features is the vast kitchen. Here whole oxen could be roasted on a spit inside the fireplace and a specially diverted stream provided a constant water supply.

Batalha ❻

Mosteiro de Santa Maria da Vitória, Batalha. *Tel* 244-765 497. 🚌 from Lisbon, Leiria, Porto de Mós, & Fátima. ☐ daily. 🌑 Jan 1, Easter, May 1, Dec 25. 🖼 (free 9am–2pm Sun).

The Dominican Abbey of Santa Maria da Vitória at Batalha is a masterpiece of Portuguese Gothic architecture and a UNESCO World Heritage site.

Manueline portal leading to the Unfinished Chapels at Batalha

The pale limestone monastery was built to celebrate João I's historic victory at Aljubarrota in 1385. Today, the abbey still has military significance: two unknown soldiers from World War I lie in the chapter house. João I, his English wife, Philippa of Lancaster, and their son, Henry the Navigator, are also buried here, in the Founder's Chapel.

The abbey was begun in 1388 and work continued for the next two centuries. King Duarte, João's son, began an octagonal mausoleum for the royal house of Avis. The project was taken up again but then abandoned by Manuel I. It is now known as the Unfinished Chapels. Much of the decoration of the abbey is in the Manueline style.

The magnificent Gothic tomb of Pedro I in the transept of the monastery church at Alcobaça

Palácio Nacional de Sintra ❶

Swan panel, Sala dos Cisnes

At the heart of the old town of Sintra (Sintra Vila), a pair of strange conical chimneys rises high above the Royal Palace. The main part of the palace, including the central block with its plain Gothic facade and the large kitchens beneath the chimneys, was built by João I in the late 14th century, on a site once occupied by the Moorish rulers. The Paço Real, as it is also known, became the favorite summer retreat for the court and continued as a residence for Portuguese royalty until the 1880s. Additions to the building by the wealthy Manuel I, in the early 16th century, echo the Moorish style. Gradual rebuilding of the palace has resulted in a fascinating amalgamation of various different styles.

★ Sala das Pegas
It is said that King João I had the ceiling panels painted as a rebuke to the court women for indulging in idle gossip like chattering magpies (pegas).

The Torre da Meca has dovecotes below the cornice decorated with armillary spheres and nautical rope.

The Sala das Galés (galleons) houses temporary exhibitions.

★ Sala dos Brasões
The domed ceiling of this majestic room is decorated with stags holding the coats of arms (brasões) of 72 noble Portuguese families. The lower walls are lined with 18th-century Delft-like tiled panels.

Jardim da Preta, a walled garden

Sala de Dom Sebastião, the audience chamber

AZULEJOS – PAINTED CERAMIC TILES

Spanish-made, Moorish-style tiles from the palace chapel (1510)

The Palácio Nacional de Sintra contains *azulejos* from the 16th–18th centuries, many painted with Moorish-influenced designs. In the early 16th century, tiles were produced by compartmental techniques, using raised and depressed areas to prevent the tin-glaze colors from running. The maiolica technique appeared in the mid-16th century. This allowed artists to paint directly onto prepared flat tiles using several colors, as these did not run in the firing process.
By the 18th century, no other European country was producing as many decorative tiles as Portugal, and there are many examples of 18th-century blue-and-white *azulejos* in the palace at Sintra, notably in the Sala dos Brasões.

★ Sala dos Cisnes
The magnificent ceiling of the former banqueting hall, painted in the 17th century, is divided into octagonal panels decorated with swans (cisnes).

The Sala dos Árabes is decorated with fine *azulejos*.

Sala das Sereias
Intricate Arabesque designs on 16th-century tiles frame the door of the Room of the Sirens.

VISITORS' CHECKLIST

Largo Rainha Dona Amélia. *Tel* 219-106 840. 9:30am–5:30pm Thu–Tue (last adm: 30 mins before closing). Jan 1, Easter, May 1, Jun 29, Dec 25. (free 9:30am–2pm Sun).

The kitchens, beneath the huge conical chimneys, have spits and utensils once used for preparing royal banquets.

Entrance

Sala dos Archeiros, the entrance hall

Manuel I added the *ajimene* windows, a distinctive Moorish design with a slender column dividing two arches.

Chapel
Symmetrical Moorish patterns decorate the original 15th-century chestnut and oak ceiling and the mosaic floor of the private chapel.

STAR FEATURES

★ Sala dos Brasões

★ Sala dos Cisnes

★ Sala das Pegas

18th-century library of Coimbra University

Coimbra ⑦

🏠 144,000. 🚇 🚍 ⓘ Edifício da Bibloteca Geral da Universidade de Coimbra (239-834 158); Largo da Portajem (239-834 038). 🚢 Mon–Sat. 🎭 Queima das Fitas (early May).

Afonso Henriques chose Coimbra as his capital in 1139, an honor it retained until 1256. Today, the city on the Mondego is famous as the home of Portugal's oldest university. Most sights are within walking distance of each other, so Coimbra is best explored on foot, despite the steep hill on which it is built.

Coimbra's two cathedrals, the **Sé Velha** ("old") and **Sé Nova** ("new"), lie in the shadow of the hilltop University. The Sé Velha, begun in 1064, is seen as the finest Romanesque building in Portugal. The Sé Nova was founded in 1598 by the Jesuits.

The **University**, a short walk away, was founded in 1290 by King Dinis. Originally its location alternated between Lisbon and Coimbra, but it was finally installed in Coimbra's royal palace in 1537. Its oldest buildings are grouped around the Pátio das Escolas. The **belltower** (1733) can be seen from all over the city. The **Library** was a gift of João V (1706–50). Its rooms, of gilt and exotic wood, are lined with 300,000 books. Nearby is the similarly ornate **Capela de**

São Miguel. Each May, at the end of the academic year, the Queima das Fitas takes place, at which students hold a ceremonial burning of their faculty ribbons, a tradition that dates back 700 years.

Another fascinating site is the **Museu Nacional Machado de Castro**, which holds some of Portugal's finest 15th- to 20th-century paintings and sculpture set among the elegant 16th-century loggias and courtyards of the former bishops' palace.

After visiting this area (the "upper town"), head to the "lower town." Largo da Portagem is a useful starting point, and river trips depart from nearby. In the Praça do Comércio, alongside coffee shops and bars, is the restored 12th-century church of **São Tiago**. North of this is **Santa Cruz**, founded in 1131, where Portugal's first two kings are buried.

In the southeast of the city is the **Jardim Botânico**. The gardens, which are Portugal's largest, were created in 1772 and house 1,200 plant species.

On the opposite bank of the Mondego are the two convents of **Santa Clara**; these have ties with Santa Isabel, the widow of King Dinis

Student in May celebrations

(1279–1325), and Inês de Castro, stabbed to death here in 1355 (see p367). Nearby is a fun place for those with children: the **Portugal dos Pequenitos** theme park.

🏛 **University**
Paço das Escolas. **Tel** 239-859 884.
◻ daily. ⬤ Dec 25. 🎫
♿ Library only. **www**.uc.pt

🏛 **Museu Nacional Machado de Castro**
Largo Dr. José Rodrigues. **Tel** 239-823 727. ◻ Tue–Sun. 🎫

🎡 **Portugal dos Pequenitos**
Santa Clara. **Tel** 239-801 170.
◻ daily. ⬤ Dec 25. 🎫 ♿

Environs
Buçaco National Forest, 16 km (10 miles) north of Coimbra, was once the retreat of Carmelite monks. Part ancient woodland and part arboretum, it is dotted with chapels and fountains. It also houses the splendid Palace Hotel Bussaco, built in Neo-Manueline style as a royal hunting lodge in 1907. Buçaco was also the site of a crucial battle (1810) in the Peninsular War.

The Roman town of **Conímbriga** lay south of modern Coimbra. Portugal's largest Roman site, it has some opulent villas with fine floor mosaics, and an excellent museum.

♙ **Conímbriga**
2 km (1 mile) S of Condeixa-a-Nova.
🚌 from Coimbra. **Site** ◻ daily.
⬤ public hols. **Museum Tel** 239-941 177. ◻ daily. 🎫 ♿ museum.

The Palace Hotel Bussaco in its enchanting woodland setting

The river Douro and old city of Oporto, with the Ponte de Dom Luís I and modern metro line in the foreground

Oporto ⑧

🗺 245,000. ✈ 10 km (6 miles) N.
🚉 🚌 ℹ Rua Clube dos Fenianos
25 (223-393 472); Rua Infante Dom
Henrique 63 (222-060 412); Praça
Dom João I 43 (222-057 514);
Terreiro de Sé (223-325 174).
🎉 São João do Porto (Jun 23–24).

Ever since the Romans built a
fort here, at the mouth of the
Douro, Oporto (Porto in
Portuguese) has prospered
from commerce. Today it is
Portugal's second city and a
thriving industrial center.

The commercial center of
the city and the Baixa ("lower")
district attract fashionable
shoppers. Also in the Baixa is
the colorful Bolhão market.
Most of the tourist sights,
however, are to be found in
the older riverside quarters.

High above the river, on
Penaventosa Hill, stands
Oporto's cathedral, or **Sé**,
originally a fortress church.
A noteworthy 13th-century
feature is the rose window,
while the upper level of the
beautiful 14th-century cloister
affords splendid views.

Nearby are the Renaissance
church of **Santa Clara**, and
São Bento Station, completed
in 1916, decorated with
spectacular azulejo panels.

Below the Sé is the hillside
Barredo quarter, seemingly
unchanged since medieval
days. This leads down to the
riverside quarter, the **Ribeira**,
its houses decorated with tiled
or pastel-painted facades.
The district is being restored,
attracting restaurants and clubs.

Sights close to the river
include the **Palácio da Bolsa**,

the city's stock exchange,
built in 1842. Its highlight is
the Arabian Room decorated
in the style of the Alhambra.
Close by is the 14th-century
São Francisco church. Its
interior is richly covered in
carved and gilded wood.

In the Cordoaria district, west
of the Sé, stands the 18th-
century **Igreja dos Clérigos**.
The church tower, at 75 m
(246 ft), offers superb views.

Situated in the lovely
Serralves park, the **Fundação
de Serralves** is dedicated to
contemporary art. It presents
temporary exhibitions in the
Art Deco Casa de Serralves,
and its art collection, from the
1960s to the present, in the
Modernist Museu de Arte
Contemporânea, designed by

Alvaro Siza Vieira.

The oldest of the five bridges spanning the Douro are
the Dona Maria Pia rail bridge
(1877), designed by Gustave
Eiffel, and the two-tiered
Ponte de Dom Luís I (1886),
by one of Eiffel's assistants.

Across the river is the town
of **Vila Nova de Gaia**, the
center of port production,
housing the lodges (armazéns)
of over 50 companies. Many
offer guided tours.

🏛 Fundação Serralves
Rua Dom João de Castro 210. **Tel**
808-200 543. ⏰ 10am–5pm Tue–
Fri, 10am–7pm Sat, Sun, & public
hols (to 8pm in summer). 🌙 Jan 1,
Dec 25. 🎟 (free 10am–2pm Sun).
♿ 📷 🛒 www.serralves.pt

THE STORY OF PORT

Port comes only from a demarcated
region of the upper Douro valley.
Its "discovery" dates from the 17th
century, when British merchants
added brandy to Douro wine to
stop it turning sour in transit. Over
the years, methods of maturing
and blending were refined and
continue today in the port lodges
of Vila Nova de Gaia. Much of the
trade is still in British control.

A classic after-dinner drink, port
is rich and usually full-bodied. The
tawnies are lighter in color than
ruby or vintage, but can be more
complex. All ports are blended
from several wines, selected from
scores of samples. White port,
unlike the other styles, is drunk chilled as an aperitif.

Traditionally the wine was shipped down the Douro from
the wine-growing estates (quintas) to the port lodges on
narrow sailing barges called barcos rabelos. Some of these
can still be seen moored along the quay at Vila Nova de Gaia.

**Tiled panel of a barco
rabelo on the Douro**

Southern Portugal

Southern Portugal encompasses the Alentejo and the Algarve, which are separated by ranges of hills. The Alentejo, nearly one-third of Portugal, stretches south from the Tagus. It is typified by vast rolling plains of olive trees, cork oaks, or wheat, as well as whitewashed villages, castles, and a sense of space and tranquility. The Algarve is very different from the rest of Portugal in climate, culture, and scenery. Its stunning coastline and year-round mild weather make it a popular vacation resort.

Renaissance fountain in Évora's main square, Praça do Giraldo

Carved figures of the Apostles on the portal of the Sé, Évora

Évora ❾

🏛 55,000. 🚌 🚌 ℹ Praça do Giraldo (266-777 071). 🚤 Sat & 2nd Tue of month. 🎪 Festa de São João (Jun).

Rising dramatically out of the Alentejo plain, the enchanting city of Évora is set in Roman, medieval, and 17th-century walls. In 1986, UNESCO declared it a World Heritage Site.

The fortresslike cathedral, the **Sé**, on the Largo do Marquês de Marialva, was begun in 1186. The portal is flanked by a pair of unmatched towers. Inside, a glittering treasury houses sacred art. Beside it stands a 16th-century palace that houses the newly renovated **Museu de Évora**, which has exhibits on the history of the city from Roman columns to modern sculpture. Opposite the museum is a **Roman temple** – erected in the 2nd or 3rd century AD – believed to have been dedicated to Diana.

Walk from the Sé past the craft shops of Rua 5 de Outubro to reach Praça do Giraldo, the main square, with its Moorish arcades and central fountain (1571). In 1573 the square was the site of an Inquisitional burning.

Just outside the city's Roman walls stands the **University**, founded by the Jesuits in 1559. It was closed in 1759 by the Marquês de Pombal *(see p361)*. The building, with its graceful cloister and notable *azulejos*, forms part of the present-day university and the 18th-century Baroque chapel is used for graduation ceremonies.

Évora has over 20 churches and monasteries, including the 15th-century **São Francisco**. The church's gruesome 17th-century **Capela dos Ossos** was created from the bones of 5,000 monks.

Northwest of the city stands the remaining 9 km (5 miles) of Évora's aqueduct, the **Aqueduto da Água de Prata**, (1531–37), which was damaged in the 17th century, during the Restoration War with Spain.

🏛 **Museu de Évora**
Largo do Conde de Vila Flor.
Tel 266-702 604. ⬜ Tue–Sun.
🔴 some public hols. 🎫

🏫 **University**
Largo dos Colegiais. **Tel** 266-740 875. ⬜ Mon–Sat am.
🔴 public hols.

Faro ❿

🏛 55,000. ✈ 🚌 🚌 ℹ Av. 5 de Outubro 18 (289-803 604). 🚤 daily. 🎪 Dia da Cidade (Sep 7).

Faro has been the capital of the Algarve since 1756. It was damaged by the 1755 earthquake and, although some parts of the ancient city walls remain, most of the buildings date from the 18th or 19th centuries.

The old city is easy to explore on foot. At its heart is the Largo da Sé, lined with orange trees and flanked by the 18th-century bishops' palace, the **Paço Episcopal**, which is still in use today.

The **Sé** itself is a mixture of Baroque and Renaissance styles and has a fine 18th-century organ. Next to the Sé is the **Museu Municpal**, which contains local Roman, medieval, and Manueline archeological finds from all over the region.

On the other side of the Old City wall is the impressive 18th-century church of **São Francisco**.

Orange trees in front of the Bishops' Palace in the old city of Faro

For hotels and restaurants in this region see pp378–9 and pp380–81

The lively center of modern Faro, along the Rua de Santo António, is stylish and pedestrianized, full of shops, bars, and restaurants. A little to the north is Faro's parish church, the Baroque and Italianate **São Pedro**. In the nearby Largo do Carmo is the impressive **Igreja do Carmo**. Its magnificent facade and richly decorated interior are in sharp contrast to its somber **Capela dos Ossos** (Chapel of Bones), built in 1816.

At the far northeast corner of the town is the **Cemitério dos Judeus**. The Jewish cemetery served from 1838 until 1932; there is no Jewish community in Faro today.

🏛 Museu Municipal
Largo Dom Afonso III. *Tel* 289-897 400. ☐ *Tue–Sun.* ● *public hols.* 🗯

Yachts and power boats at the Vilamoura marina, near Albufeira

Albufeira ⓫

🏙 *31,000.* 🚉 🚌 ▌ *Rua 5 de Outubro (289-585 279).* 🕙 *1st & 3rd Tue of month.*

This charming fishing port has become the tourist capital of the Algarve. The Romans built a castle here and under the Arabs the town prospered from trade with North Africa. The oldest part of the town, around Rua da Igreja Velha, retains some original Moorish arches.

Environs
From **Praia de São Rafael**, 1 mile (2 km) west of Albufeira, to **Praia da Oura** due east, the area is punctuated by small sandy coves set between eroded ocher rocks.

Ocher sandstone rocks sheltering the Praia de Dona Ana beach, Lagos

East of Albufeira, **Vilamoura** is set to become Europe's largest leisure complex. It has a large marina with lively cafés, shops, and restaurants.

Portimão ⓬

🏙 *40,000.* 🚉 🚌 ▌ *Avenida Tomás Cabreira, Praia da Rocha (282-419 132).* 🕙 *first Mon of month.*

The Romans were attracted to Portimão by its natural harbor. It is still a flourishing fishing port and one of the largest towns in the Algarve.

The town center, around the pedestrianized Rua Vasco da Gama, dates mainly from the 18th century, since it was rebuilt after the 1755 earthquake. The 14th-century origins of the church of Nossa Senhora da Conceição are revealed in its portico. The interior contains 17th- and 18th-century *azulejo* panels.

Environs
Just 3 km (2 miles) south of Portimão is **Praia da Rocha**, a series of fabulous sandy coves. At its east end is the 16th-century castle, Fortaleza de Santa Catarina, with a superb view of the beach and cliffs – and a swathe of high-rise hotels. Inland from Portimão is the town of **Silves**, once the Moorish capital, Xelb. It has an impressive castle and picturesque groves of orange and lemon trees.

Lagos ⓭

🏙 *16,000.* 🚉 🚌 ▌ *Sítio de São João (282-763 031).* 🕙 *first Sat of month.*

Lagos is set on one of the Algarve's largest bays; it was the region's capital from 1576–1756. The town suffered badly in the 1755 earthquake, so as a result most of the buildings date from the late 18th and 19th centuries.

In the 15th century Lagos became an important naval center, unfortunately also becoming the site of the first slave market in Europe.

Lagos's parish church is the 16th-century **Santa Maria**. The 18th-century **Santo António** is worth a visit for its Baroque *azulejos* and carving. The statue of St. Anthony, kept in the church, accompanied the local regiment during the Peninsular War (1807–11).

Environs
The promontory, **Ponta da Piedade**, shelters the bay of Lagos and should not be missed. **Praia de Dona Ana** beach is 25 minutes' walk from the town center, but **Praia do Camilo** may be less crowded. **Meia Praia**, east of Lagos, stretches for 4 km (2 miles).

Lying 10 km (6 miles) north is the peaceful **Barragem de Bravura** reservoir. Another popular excursion is southwest to **Sagres** and the rocky headland of **Cabo de São Vicente**.

Practical & Travel Information

The Portuguese are a hospitable people and in Lisbon, Oporto and the Algarve the choice of hotels, restaurants and entertainment is vast, and English is widely spoken. Elsewhere, visitors will usually find help easily available, with locals keen to show off their region.

Travel and communication networks in Portugal have improved greatly in recent years. For national travel there are efficient rail and bus services. Cities have buses and trams, and Lisbon has a metro as well.

TOURIST INFORMATION

The country is divided into tourist regions, separate from its administrative districts. All cities and large towns have a *Posto de Turismo* (tourist office), where you can obtain information about the region, lists of hotels, and details of regional events. Visitors can also consult Portuguese tourist offices abroad.

Most state museums open from 10am to 5pm and are usually closed on Mondays. Many museums and sights also close for lunch for one, or even two hours.

In Lisbon, the convenient Lisboa Card entitles visitors to free public transportation and free or reduced entry to museums. It can be bought at the airport, the city's tourist offices, and some hotels, travel agents, and major sights. It is valid for up to three days.

VISA REQUIREMENTS

There are currently no visa requirements for American, Canadian, Australian, and New Zealand nationals for stays up to 90 days. It is worth checking with the nearest Portuguese

embassy or consulate as this may change. Citizens of the EU need only a valid passport to enter Portugal.

PERSONAL SECURITY

Violent crime is rare, but sensible precautions should be taken after dark, especially in Lisbon, Oporto, and the Algarve. To report a crime, contact the nearest police station. Ask for an interpreter if necessary. Theft of documents, such as a passport, should also be reported to your consulate or embassy. Remember that many travel insurance companies insist on policy holders reporting thefts within 24 hours to substantiate any subsequent claim.

EMERGENCY SERVICES

The number to call in an emergency is 112. Ask for either *polícia* (the police), *ambulância* (an ambulance), or *bombeiros* (the fire brigade). For emergency medical treatment you should go to the emergency room *(serviço de urgência)* of the nearest main hospital.

HEALTH ISSUES

For non-emergency medical treatment, details of how to contact an English-speaking doctor can be found in English-language newspapers, such as *Algarve Resident*.

Pharmacies *(farmâcias)* can dispense a range of drugs that would require a prescription in many other countries. They open from 9am to 1pm and 3pm to 7pm (not Sat) and carry a sign with a green illuminated cross. No vaccinations are needed for Portugal, although a typhoid shot and polio booster are recommended.

FACILITIES FOR THE DISABLED

These are limited, although the situation is improving. Wheelchairs and adapted restrooms are available at airports and major stations, and ramps, reserved parking, and elevators are becoming more common. Lisbon has a special taxi service, but you have to book well in advance.

LANGUAGE AND ETIQUETTE

Written Portuguese looks similar to Spanish, but its pronunciation is very different. The Portuguese do not take kindly to being spoken to in Spanish, so it is useful to learn a few basic phrases before you go. It is polite to address strangers as *senhor* or *senhora* and, when introduced to someone, to shake their hand.

Although dress is generally relaxed, especially in the more tourist-oriented areas, when visiting religious buildings arms and knees should be kept covered.

BANKING AND CURRENCY

The currency in Portugal is the euro *(see p15)*. Money can be changed at most banks, hotels, and bureaux de change *(câmbio)*. Banks tend to offer a good rate of exchange. Traveler's checks can often be expensive to cash although they are a safe way of carrying money. Most major

THE CLIMATE OF PORTUGAL

In the south, especially along the sheltered coast of the Algarve, winters are very mild, but July and August can be extremely hot. Between April and October, the north is pleasantly warm, though rain is not unusual. Winters in the north can be very cold, especially in the mountainous inland regions. The best times to visit are spring and fall.

LISBON

°C/F	Apr	Jul	Oct	Jan
	19/67	28/82	23/73	
	12/53	17/63	14/57	14/57
				8/46
☀	9 hrs	12.5 hrs	7.5 hrs	5 hrs
☂	47.5 mm	0 mm	65 mm	95 mm
month	Apr	Jul	Oct	Jan

0°C / 32°F

credit cards can be used to make withdrawals from ATMs.

COMMUNICATIONS

The postal service is known as *Correios*. First-class mail *(correio azul)* and overseas letters are posted in blue mailboxes; second-class mail *(normal)* is posted in red mailboxes. Public payphones take either coins or cards (including credit cards), although there are less payphones now due to widespread use of mobile phones. You can also make calls from post offices.

FLYING TO PORTUGAL

The only direct flight from New York (Newark) to Lisbon is operated by **TAP Air Portugal**. Once in Lisbon, passengers can change for Faro or Oporto. Internal flights are operated by **SATA**.

Many airlines operate flights from the US to European hubs, such as London, Paris, or Madrid, where passengers can change for Lisbon.

There are no direct flights to Portugal from Australia or New Zealand; visitors from these countries should fly via London or Madrid. Regular flights go from many European cities direct to Lisbon, Faro, and Oporto in Portugal.

RAIL TRAVEL

Direct trains to Portugal go from Paris and Madrid. Once in Portugal, you can reach many places by rail, but services vary enormously. The high-speed Alfa service from Lisbon to Oporto via Coimbra is good, but local trains can be slow and infrequent. Fares are cheap compared to other parts of Europe and tourist tickets, valid for five days within one zone, are available. It is best to book in advance.

Lisbon can be confusing for visitors as there are five main stations. **Santa Apolónia** and **Oriente** (on the same line) serve international routes and the north; for the Alentejo, you must take a ferry to Barreiro on the south bank of the Tagus. Trains to the Algarve depart from Oriente. Trains from Rossio go to Sintra and a few destinations on the coast; trains from Cais do Sodré serve Estoril and Cascais.

LONG-DISTANCE BUSES

Some long-distance bus services – Lisbon to Évora for example – are quicker and more comfortable than going by train. There are no central bus stations because companies are private and operate separately, but tourist offices and travel agencies offer information.

TRAVELING BY CAR

Portugal's highway network is expanding, but many older roads are in need of repair and minor roads can be treacherous. Driving can be a hair-raising experience – the country has one of the highest accident rates in Europe and traffic jams are a problem in and near cities. Beware of reckless drivers and do not drive in the rush hour if you can possibly avoid it.

If renting a car, check its condition and insurance very carefully. Always carry your passport, car insurance, license, and rental contract with you (or you may incur a fine).

Traffic drives on the right hand side and Continental European regulations apply. Seat belts must be worn. Speed limits are 50 kph (31 mph) in towns, 90 kph (55 mph) on other roads, and 120 kph (74 mph) on highways. Tolls are payable on highways and some bridges. Do not use the *Via Verde* (green lane) at tolls; this is for the use of drivers who have paid automatically. If you are involved in a car accident on a highway or a main road, use one of the orange SOS telephones to call for help.

Gas stations can be scarce in remote areas, so always fill up your car before leaving a town.

DIRECTORY

TOURIST OFFICES

Lisbon
Lisboa Welcome Center,
Rua do Arsenal 15.
Tel *210-312 700.*

Oporto
Rua Clube dos Fenianos
25. **Tel** *223-393 472.*
www.visitporto.travel

UK
11 Belgrave Square,
London SW1X 8PP.
Tel *020-7201 6666.*

US
590 Fifth Ave, 3rd floor,
New York, NY 10036.
Tel *646-723 0200.*
www.visitportugal.com

EMBASSIES

Australia
Av. de Liberdade 196–200,
2° (Edifício Victoria),
1269-121 Lisbon.
Tel *213-101 500.*

Canada
Av. de Liberdade
196–200, 3° (Edifício
Victoria), 1269-121 Lisbon.
Tel *213-164 600.*

Ireland
Rua da Imprensa à Estrela
1, 4°, 1200-685 Lisbon.
Tel *213-929 440.*

UK
Rua de São Bernardo 33,
1249-082 Lisbon.
Tel *213-924 000.*

US
Avenida das Forças
Armadas, 1600-081 Lisbon.
Tel *217-273 300.*

EMERGENCIES

**Ambulance, Police,
and Fire services**
Tel *112.*

AIRLINES

SATA
Tel *707-227 282.*

TAP Air Portugal
Tel *707-205 700 (Portugal).*
Tel *0845-601 0932 (UK).*
Tel *800-221 73 70 (US).*
www.flytap.com

TRAIN INFORMATION

Tel *808-208 208.*
www.cp.pt

CAR RENTAL

Auto Jardim, Faro
Tel *289-818 491.*
www.auto-jardim.com

Budget, Oporto
Tel *226-076 970.*
www.budget.com

Europcar, Faro
Tel *289-891 650.*

Hertz, Lisbon
Tel *213-812 430.*
www.hertz.com

Sixt, Lisbon
Tel *217-998 701.*
www.sixt.com

Shopping & Entertainment

Traditional arts and crafts flourish in Portugal. A wide range of interesting pottery can be found in all parts of the country, while in the north embroidery, lace, and gold filigree jewelry from the Minho region make unusual presents. Many visitors come to Portugal for the sporting facilities, principally the golf courses of the Algarve. Water sports, both in the Algarve and on the wilder west coast, are another great attraction. Tourists are usually encouraged to sample *fado*, Lisbon's native folk music, and there are also classical cultural events to be enjoyed in the big cities and at annual festivals.

WHERE TO SHOP

Although it is not difficult to find shops that seem a little behind the times when compared with other European countries, modern shopping malls are now a common feature of most cities. In Lisbon, **Amoreiras** shopping center led the way, with 247 shops, underground parking, cinemas, and restaurants. **Colombo** followed, and is Portugal's largest mall. **Cascaishopping**, between Sintra and Estoril, is similar in style. Opening times for shopping centers are usually from 10am until 11pm daily (including Sunday). Ordinary stores open at 9am or 10am and close at 7pm, though smaller stores and those in quieter areas usually close for lunch between 1pm and 3pm.

RECLAIMING TAX

Value Added Tax (IVA) can be reclaimed by non-EU residents who stay for less than 180 days. Ask for an *Isenção de IVA* form or invoice in triplicate, describing the goods, quantity, value, and buyer's identity (best done where you see the "Global Refund Portugal" signs). Present the forms at customs on departure.

WHAT TO BUY

Portugal is not expensive when compared with the rest of Europe, and prices are very reasonable for traditional crafts, especially away from the big cities and tourist centers. The Portuguese are well known for their delicate embroidery and fine lace. Some of the finest examples come from towns in the Minho such as Viana do Castelo, also famous for its brightly printed shawls. Embroidered bedspreads are made in Castelo Branco in the Beira Baixa, and colorful carpets are sold in the Alentejo.

Filigree jewelry *(filigrana)* from the Minho is typically worn at local festivals. Gold and silver threads are worked into intricate brooches, earrings, and pendants.

Woven baskets, produced throughout the country, make delightful souvenirs. Cork from the Alentejo is used to make articles such as mats and ice buckets.

CERAMICS

In most cities you can buy as well as commission ceramic tiles and panels. Portugal has a long-standing tradition in ceramics, both for decorative purposes and for home use. Styles range from elegant Vista Alegre porcelain to simple glazed brown earthenware, plain or painted with simple patterns. Antique *azulejos* are highly sought after and very expensive, but you can buy reproductions of well-known historic designs at places such as Lisbon's Museu Nacional do Azulejo *(see p358)*.

MARKETS

A social and commercial occasion, the street market is integral to Portuguese life. It is usually held in the town's main square. Most markets sell a wide range of goods, from food to household items and clothes, but you will also see sites devoted to antiques, pottery, lace, rugs, clothes, and local crafts. Most markets are held in the morning only, but in tourist areas they may go on until late afternoon.

FOOD AND DRINK

Some visitors may want to buy regional produce such as Serra cheese from the Serra da Estrela mountains. However, more are likely to bring back a bottle as a souvenir – most probably of port. It is not especially cheap, but you will never have the opportunity to sample so many styles and vintages as you will on a tour of the port lodges of Vila Nova de Gaia *(see p371)*. Of table wines you might enjoy the young, slightly sparkling *vinho verde* from Douro in the north, an aged red Dão, or one of the new southern wines from the Alentejo.

ENTERTAINMENT LISTINGS AND TICKETS

Tickets for almost all events in Lisbon can be bought in **FNAC** stores, or be reserved by visiting or phoning the Agência de Bilhetes para Espectáculos **(ABEP)**. Pay in cash when you collect them from the kiosk. Some cinemas and theaters take phone or credit card reservations.

Previews of forthcoming events and listings of bars and clubs appear in several magazines in Lisbon. English-language publications include the monthly *Follow Me Lisboa*, which is available free from tourist offices.

CLASSICAL MUSIC, OPERA, AND DANCE

Lisbon's top cultural centers are the **Fundação Calouste Gulbenkian** and the vast **Centro Cultural de Belém**. These host national and international events including ballet, opera, and concerts. The Portuguese national opera house is the **Teatro Nacional de São Carlos**.

Classical music festivals are also held in many areas. One of the best is the summer festival in Sintra *(see p366)*.

THEATER AND CINEMA

In Lisbon theater-lovers can enjoy performances of Portuguese and foreign-language plays at the **Teatro Nacional Dona Maria II**.

Cult movies and international arthouse films can be seen at the **Cinemateca Portuguesa**, which has a comprehensive monthly film calendar.

In Portugal movies are almost always shown in the original language version with Portuguese subtitles.

FADO

Fado is an expression of longing and sorrow. Literally meaning "fate," the term may be applied to an individual song as well as the genre itself. The dominant emotion is *saudade* – a longing for what has been lost or has never been attained. It is sung as often by women as men, accompanied by the *guitarra* (a flat-backed instrument shaped like a mandolin, with paired strings) and the *viola* (acoustic Spanish guitar).

The traditional way to enjoy *fado* is with a meal at a *fado* house. It can be an expensive night out, so make sure you like *fado* before you go. The best establishments are run by the *fadistas* themselves, for example the **Parreirinha de Alfama**, which is now run by the legendary performer, Argentina Santos.

OUTDOOR ACTIVITIES

Although a small country, Portugal offers a great variety of terrain, with sports and activities to match. Water sports are extremely popular along its 500 miles of coast. The best beach for surfing is the world-famous Guincho, near Cascais *(see p366)*. However, the ocean breakers there are only suitable for experienced surfers. In fact, all along the Atlantic coast conditions can be dangerous for swimming and water sports, hence the appeal of the sheltered bays of the Algarve. These are well-equipped for all kinds of activities. Windsurfing boards and small sailboats can be rented at most resorts and lessons are easily arranged. The marinas at Lagos and the giant vacation complex of Vilamoura are the most important yachting centers.

Many parts of Portugal's rugged interior are excellent for hiking, cycling, and horseback riding.

GOLF AND TENNIS

Most of Portugal's best golf courses are concentrated in the Algarve, which has gained a reputation as one of Europe's prime destinations for golfing vacations. The mild climate ensures that a game can be enjoyed all year round and many courses have been designed by top professionals. Some of the best courses insist that players show a reasonable degree of proficiency, while others welcome golfers of any ability and provide excellent coaching. Serious golfers might consider booking a specialist golf vacation. For information on golfing activities and vacations, contact the **Federação Portuguesa de Golfe**.

Tennis courts are found virtually all over Portugal, especially alongside tourist facilities. Some of the larger Algarve resorts offer tennis coaching vacations. Based in London, **Jonathan Markson Tennis** organizes special vacation packages at resorts in Portugal for tennis enthusiasts.

BULLFIGHTING

Portuguese bullfighting differs from the Spanish version in many ways. The bull is not killed in the ring and the star of the show is the horseman *(cavaleiro)*. An added attraction is the *pega*, in which a team of men, the *forcados*, attempts to topple the bull and immobilize it with their bare hands.

The traditional center for bullfighting is the Ribatejo, but Lisbon has a splendid Neo-Moorish arena at Campo Pequeno, which now has a modern retractable ceiling.

DIRECTORY

SHOPPING MALLS

Amoreiras
Avenida Eng. Duarte Pacheco. *Tel 213-810 240.*

Cascaishopping
Estrada Nacional 9, Alcabideche - Estoril.
Tel 210-121 628.

Colombo
Avenida Lusíada, Lisbon.
Tel 217-113 600.

ENTERTAINMENT TICKETS

ABEP
Praça dos Restauradores, Lisbon.
Tel 213-425 360.

CLASSICAL MUSIC, OPERA, & DANCE

Centro Cultural de Belém
Praça do Império, Belém, Lisbon.
Tel 707-303 000.

Fundação Calouste Gulbenkian
Avenida de Berna 45, Lisbon.
Tel 217-823 700 (tickets).

Teatro Nacional de São Carlos
Rua Serpa Pinto 9, Lisbon.
Tel 213-253 000.

THEATER

Cinemateca Portuguesa
Rua Barata Salgueiro 39, Lisbon.
Tel 213-596 200.

Teatro Nacional Dona Maria II
Praça Dom Pedro IV, Lisbon.
Tel 213-250 800.

FADO

Parreirinha de Alfama
Beco do Espírito Santo 1, Lisbon.
Tel 218-868 209.

GOLF AND TENNIS

Federação Portuguesa de Golfe
Avenida das Túlipas 6, Edifício Miraflores, 17º, 1495-161 Algés.
Tel 214-123 780.

Jonathan Markson Tennis
Springside House, 84 North End Road, London W14 9ES, UK.
Tel 020-7603 2422.

Where to Stay in Portugal

Hotels in Portugal vary enormously in quality, price, and facilities – from huge resort villages in the Algarve to the simple *pensão*, or guesthouse. In Lisbon and the Algarve, there are hotels to suit every budget. Many hotels have great character, especially the *pousadas*, or state-run inns, which are often housed in converted historic buildings.

PRICE CATEGORIES
Price categories are for a standard double room per night, including breakfast:

€ Under €60
€€ €60–€90
€€€ €90–€140
€€€€ €140–€200
€€€€€ Over €200

LISBON

AVENIDA Lisboa Plaza
€€€€€   Map C2
Travessa do Salitre 7, 1269-066 **Tel** *213-218 218* **Fax** *213-471 630* **Rooms** *112*

Built in 1953, and situated off Praça da Alegria and Av. da Liberdade, this boutique hotel possesses an air of informal good taste and understated charm. The decor is by the Portuguese interior designer Graça Viterbo, and her characteristic color-coordinated fabrics and furnishings are carried through the entire property. **www.heritage.pt**

AVENIDA Tivoli Lisboa
€€€€€   Map D2
Avenida da Liberdade 185, 1269-050 **Tel** *213-198 900* **Fax** *213-198 950* **Rooms** *308*

One of Lisbon's most emblematic hotels, the Tivoli holds court over Avenida da Liberdade and is renowned for its high levels of service and personal attention. The 329 rooms are fully insulated and sound proofed, and the rooftop Terrace Grill is a gourmet hotspot. The property regularly hosts VIP conferences. **www.tivolihotels.com**

BAIXA Duas Nações
€€   Map D3
Rua da Vitória 41, 1100-618 **Tel** *213-460 710* **Fax** *213-470 206* **Rooms** *54*

The "Two Nations" is a rather grand building straddling the corner of Rua Augusta and Rua da Vitória, both pedestrianized. The property is fashioned as a traditional Lisbon boarding house with rooms that are well appointed and have private bathroom facilities. Those overlooking Rua Augusta can be noisy at times. **www.duasnacoes.com**

CASTELO Ninho das Águias
€   Map E3
Costa do Castelo 74, 1100-179 **Tel** *218-854 070* **Rooms** *16*

Easily identified by its rooftop turret, the unusual "Eagle's Nest" *pensão* perches under the castle walls. A huge stuffed eagle greets visitors at reception. The bright and sometimes breezy rooms are very popular so it's wise to book ahead. The terraced flower garden offers peace and solitude. No breakfast.

CHIADO Hotel do Chiado
€€€€€   Map D4
Rua Nova do Almada 114, 1200-290 **Tel** *213-256 100* **Fax** *213-256 161* **Rooms** *40*

Japanese silk-screen prints adorn the lobby of this prestigious boutique hotel in Lisbon's most fashionable district. It was designed by Portuguese architect Álvaro Siza Vieira who has cleverly blended Oriental and colonial Portuguese influences with a modern and stylish functionality. Some rooms offer outstanding views.

LAPA York House
€€€€   Map B4
Rua das Janelas Verdes 32, 1200-691 **Tel** *213-962 435* **Fax** *213-972 793* **Rooms** *32*

Behind the rose-pink walls of this enchanting 17th-century *pensão* are luxurious rooms with wooden or terra-cotta floors, and elegant antique furniture. There is a charming, plant-filled courtyard and the atmosphere is one of peace and serenity. Wholly inviting. **www.yorkhouselisboa.com**

MARQUES DE POMBAL Jorge V
€€€
Rua Mouzinho da Silveira 3, 1250-165 **Tel** *213-562 525* **Fax** *213-150 319* **Rooms** *49*

Considering the central location, this pleasant, comfortable hotel offers good value for money. Roughly half the rooms have balconies, so request one when checking in. There are also six suites. The downstairs bar is a good place to mingle with fellow guests, and there are Internet facilities in the lobby. **www.hoteljorgev.com**

MARQUES DE POMBAL Ritz Four Seasons
€€€€€
Rua Rodrigo da Fonseca 88, 1099-039 **Tel** *213-811 400* **Fax** *213-831 783* **Rooms** *282*

Hospitality at the legendary Ritz combines luxury and elegance in a grand style. The hotel is a prominent landmark and a stunning locale from which to experience the city. A major draw is the spa. Designed in marble and rich oak, the facility offers a wealth of treatments and therapies. **www.fourseasons.com/lisbon**

ROSSIO Métropole
€€€€   Map D3
Praça Dom Pedro IV 30, 1100-200 **Tel** *213-219 030* **Fax** *213-469 166* **Rooms** *36*

Inaugurated in 1917, this hotel was a favorite haunt of spies and double agents during World War II. The individually styled and elegant rooms are partly furnished with original pieces from the 1920s, and the whole building exudes a distinctly retro atmosphere. The balcony views across Rossio are picture-postcard. **www.almeidahotels.com**

REST OF PORTUGAL

ALBUFERA Falésia

Praia da Falésia, 8201-911 **Tel** 289-501 237 **Fax** 289-501 270 **Rooms** 172

€€€

Located near Falésia beach and surrounded by umbrella pine, this smart hotel has brightly furnished, airy rooms that enjoy either pool or garden views. A huge, marble floor atrium decorated with hanging plants is a central feature. A piano bar provides nightly entertainment, and reception can arrange various outdoor activities. **www.falesia.com**

CASCAIS Albatroz

Rua Frederico Arouca 100, 2750-353 **Tel** 214-847 380 **Fax** 214-844 827 **Rooms** 59

€€€€€

Built in the 19th century as a retreat for the Portuguese royal family, the Albatroz sits perched on the rocks directly overlooking the ocean. Notable for its traditional style of luxury and exceptional design, the service is first class and discreet. The hotel has its own outdoor salt-water swimming pool. **www.albatrozhotels.com**

COIMBRA Astória

Avenida Emidio Navarro 21, 3000-150 **Tel** 239-853 020 **Fax** 239-822 057 **Rooms** 62

€€€

One of Coimbra's best-known hotels, the Astória has preserved its Art Deco heritage and 1920s ambiance while modernizing its extensive facilities. Stylish rooms offer fine views across the River Mondego, especially those in the turret facade. The bar, Bar 21, is popular. **www.almeidahotels.com**

COIMBRA Quinta das Lágrimas

Rua António Augusto Gonçalves, 3041-901 **Tel** 239-802 380 **Fax** 239-441 695 **Rooms** 52

€€€€

The renowned Quinta das Lágrimas offers three accommodation options: the palace, the garden, and spa guest rooms. The beautiful 18th-century manor house, forever linked with lovers Pedro and Inês, is complemented by a modern hotel wing with guest rooms and a luxury spa. The restaurant is Michelin starred. **www.quintadaslagrimas.pt**

ÉVORA Pousada dos Lóios

Largo Conde Vila Flor, 7000-804 **Tel** 266-730 070 **Fax** 266-707 248 **Rooms** 33

€€€€€

Originally a 15th-century monastery, the decorative public spaces in this elegant pousada contrast with the simple but characterful rooms that were converted from the monks' cells. An intricately embroidered carpet hangs from the wall skirting the marble staircase. The delightful swimming pool is sunk into an inner courtyard. **www.pousadas.pt**

FARO Alnacir

Estrada Senhor da Saúde 24, 8000-500 **Tel** 289-803 678 **Fax** 289-803 548 **Rooms** 53

€

A tidy, modern hotel located on a quiet street close to the center of the Algarve's regional capital. Pleasantly decorated throughout, two of the double rooms have a panoramic terrace overlooking the Ria Formosa Natural Park. Breakfast is served in a light, airy dining room. A laundry service is available. **www.alnacir.netfirms.com**

LAGOS Hotel Tivoli Lagos

Rua António Crisógono Santos, 8600-678 **Tel** 282-790 079 **Fax** 282-790 345 **Rooms** 324

€€€€

Built to exude the charm and character of a small village, this pleasant complex has five restaurants, a health club, and swimming pool surrounded by trim gardens. The hotel operates its own beach club and barbecues are organized for hotel guests during the summer. A free shuttle service is also provided. **www.tivolihotels.com**

OPORTO Malaposta

Rua da Conceição 80, 4050-214 **Tel** 223-391 920 **Fax** 223-391 929 **Rooms** 37

€

Tucked away on a quiet side street, the attractive and modern Malaposta is a friendly, good-value hotel and benefits from its city-center location. Within walking distance are some of Oporto's best-known historical monuments. Guests can use the nearby car park, free from 8pm-8am, and on weekends and bank holidays. **www.hotelmalaposta.com**

OPORTO Pestana Porto

Praça da Ribeira 1, 4050-513 **Tel** 223-402 300 **Fax** 223-402 400 **Rooms** 48

€€€€

One of the most desirable hotels in the city, this charming boutique property is located on the Praça da Ribeira, in a block of carefully restored riverfront buildings. The rooms are contemporary in style and fashionable in taste and offer gracious living and fabulous views. The romantic setting makes advance booking advisable. **www.pestana.com**

PORTIMÃO Bela Vista

Avenida Tomas Cabreira, Praia da Rocha, 8500-802 **Tel** 282-450 480 **Fax** 282-415 369 **Rooms** 21

€€€

This delightful hotel is housed in one of the few surviving examples of early 19th-century manor houses that once lined this stretch of coast. The interior maintains much of the original decoration, including in some rooms and public spaces, dazzling azulejo tiles, and ceilings fashioned out of Brazilian wood. **www.hotelbelavista.net**

SINTRA Tivoli Palácio de Seteais

Avenida Barbosa do Bocage 8, 2710-517 **Tel** 219-233 200 **Fax** 219-234 277 **Rooms** 30

€€€€€

One of the most cherished and romantic hotels in the country, this splendid property is a magnificent example of 18th-century architecture, with rooms that dazzle in the classical style of the era. Rare period furniture graces the public areas and guests are free to wander the beautifully landscaped topiary gardens. **www.tivolihotels.com**

Where to Eat in Portugal

Many restaurants in Lisbon and the Algarve serve international cuisine, but the Portuguese like to stick to their culinary traditions, so salted cod *(bacalhau)* and unusual combinations such as pork and clams are often on the menu. Marvelous fish dishes are available all along the coast, but choices for vegetarians are limited.

PRICE CATEGORIES
Price categories are for a three-course meal for one, including a half-bottle of house wine, tax and service:

€ Under €20
€€ €20–€25
€€€ €25–€30
€€€€ €30–€35
€€€€€ Over €35

LISBON

ALFAMA Lautasco

€

Beco do Azinhal 7a (off Rua de São Pedro), 1100-067 **Tel** *218-860 173*　　Map E3

Rustically decorated with wooden paneling and wagon-wheel chandeliers, Lautasco specializes in typical Portuguese cuisine that can be enjoyed on the outside terrace. Decorative streamers and colorful spotlights enhance an already atmospheric setting and the restaurant is extremely popular in summer. Reservations recommended. Closed Sun.

BAIRRO ALTO Buenos Aires

€

Calçada Escadinhas do Duque 31b, 1200-155 **Tel** *213-420 739*　　Map D3

The generous cuts of Argentine beef served with potatoes and a crispy green salad are the obvious choice at this decorative eatery that draws a young, attractive crowd. Cozy and intimate, the walls are festooned with colorful cards and posters. The menu features some truly memorable chocolate desserts. Reservations recommended. Closed Sun.

BAIRRO ALTO Casonostra

€

Travessa do Poço da Cidade 60, 1200-334 **Tel** *213-425 931*　　Map D3

A favorite haunt of Lisbon's artistic and intellectual set, this Italian restaurant is renowned for its creative six-page menu. Popular choices include *penne all'arrabbiata* (pasta with bacon smothered in spicy tomato and garlic sauce). The wine list has been carefully chosen to complement each dish. Closed Sat lunch.

BAIRRO ALTO Pap'Açorda

€€€€€

Rua da Atalaia 57, 1200-037 **Tel** *213-464 811*　　Map D3

One of Lisbon's great gastronomic landmarks, this establishment was one of the first to modernize Portuguese food and remains one of the most successful restaurants in the city. Both locals and tourists come here for the delicious *açorda de mariscos* (bread stew and seafood). Comprehensive wine list. Reservations essential. Closed Sun & Mon.

BAIXA Terreiro do Paço

€€€€€

Pátio da Galé, Praça do Comércio, 1100-148 **Tel** *210-995 679*　　Map D4

Tucked under a colonnaded building overlooking Praça do Comércio, this is a wonderful example of how 18th-century elegance can be enriched by 21st-century style. There are two restaurants – downstairs for light dishes, upstairs for an à la carte menu paying homage to Portugal's great culinary traditions. Excellent wine list. Snacks only on Sun.

BELEM No Solo Itália

€€

Avenida Brasilia 202, 1400-038 **Tel** *213-015 969*

Set right beside the river, facing the Discoveries monument, No Solo Itália offers an extensive selection of pizzas, ice cream, and other traditional Italian cuisine, along with a dozen freshly prepared salads. A large outdoor terrace offers splendid views of the Tagus estuary.

LAPA Sua Excelência

€€€

Rua do Conde 34, 1200-637 **Tel** *213-903 614*　　Map B4

At Sua Excelência, in Lisbon's diplomatic quarter, the food is classic Portuguese, with the *cogumelos salteados em manteiga com natas e vinho da Madeira* (fried mushrooms in a butter, cream, and Madeira wine sauce) just one example of the chef's creativity. Booking advised. Closed Sat lunch & Sun.

RESTAURADORES Casa do Alentejo

€

Rua das Portas de Santo Antão 58, 1150-268 **Tel** *213-405 140*　　Map D3

Visitors to this extraordinary 19th-century house are in for a surprise. Behind the unremarkable facade is a Moorish-style courtyard decorated with tiles inlaid with intricate Arabic calligraphy. Art exhibitions regularly take place here, as do choral recitals. The food is standard regional fare, but the exuberant surroundings more than compensate.

RESTAURADORES Gambrinus

€€€€€

Rua das Portas de Santo Antão 23, 1150-264 **Tel** *213-421 466*　　Map D3

One of the best seafood restaurants in the country, Gambrinus is exclusive and expensive. It is not only shellfish that attracts visitors, the menu lists Iranian Beluga caviar and truffle *foie gras*, among the starters. Fresh fish is the mainstay, however, with a carefully selected choice available. The extensive wine list includes an array of vintage ports.

Key to Symbols *see back cover flap* **Map References** *see map of Lisbon pp356–7*

REST OF PORTUGAL

ALBUFEIRA Evaristo 🏃 🗐 🅿 €€

Praia do Evaristo, 8200-903 **Tel** *289-591 666*

This contemporary beachfront restaurant enjoys fabulous views over Praia do Evaristo, west of Albufeira. The fish and seafood is first class and the menu features *lagosta na grelha* (broiled lobster), *lulas grelhadas em olho* (grilled squid with garlic) and an array of fresh fish. Meat choices include entrecôte steak. Closed Jan, Feb 1–14, Sun & Mon dinner in winter.

BATALHA Vintage 🏃 🚌 🗐 🅿 €

Largo Mestre Afonso Domingues, 2440-102 **Tel** *244-765 260*

This centrally located restaurant, found in the Mestre Afonso Domingues hotel, serves such regional delights as fried pork with turnip tops and bream fillet with spinach. The terrace offers a superb view of the 14th-century monument and the whole experience is infused with a palatable sense of history.

CASCAIS O Pescador 🏃 🚌 🗐 €€€€

Rua das Flores 10b, 2750-348 **Tel** *214-832 054*

This well-established seafood restaurant has lured Mick Jagger and Julio Iglesias, among many other famous personalities. It is decorated with quirky maritime artifacts. An ocean of choice leaps from the menu, with lobster soup, rose shrimp cocktail, spidercrab platter, swordfish steak, and codfish *cataplana*. Closed Sun in winter and Mon lunch in summer.

COIMBRA Arcadas da Capela 🗐 🅿 €€€€€

Quinta das Lágrimas, Rua António Augusto Gonçalves, 3041-901 **Tel** *239-802 380*

A luxury gourmet restaurant, dining here is a Michelin-starred treat. Executive chef Albano Lourenço changes the menu four times a year. One dish is themed around Portugal's enduring love story – that of the doomed, 14th-century affair between Pedro and Inês de Castro. The kitchen celebrates the couple's lives with a Pedro & Inês four-course dinner.

EVORA Fialho 🗐 €€€€

Travessa das Mascarenhas 16, 7000-557 **Tel** *266-703 079*

Arguably the best restaurant in the Alentejo, and highly regarded throughout Portugal, Fialho has collected many awards for its inventive cuisine, such as *atum grelhado e amêijoas na cataplana* (grilled tuna and cockle *cataplana*) and *medalhões de porco preto* (medallions of black pork). Reservations essential. Closed Mon; Sep 1–24.

FARO O Estaminé 🚌 €€

Ilha Deserta, 8000-138 **Tel** *917-811 856*

Reachable only by boat or water taxi, this shanty-style beach restaurant is located on a deserted island (Ilha Deserta) off the coast near Faro, and promises a very different kind of dining experience. Fresh fish, not surprisingly, dominates the menu, along with seafood caught in the nearby Ria Formosa nature reserve. The sunsets are breathtaking.

LAGOS No Pátio 🏃 🚌 🗐 €€€

Rua Lançarote de Freitas 46, 8600-605 **Tel** *282-763 777*

The creative, British-run kitchen serves international-themed cuisine exemplified by dishes like pea risotto. Good wine selection from Portuguese, Australian, and US labels. There is a charming rear patio for secluded dining. Open for lunch Sun (except Jul & Aug), & dinner Thu–Sat (Tue–Sat from Apr–Oct).

OPORTO Restaurante Casa da Música ♿ 🗐 €€€

Casa da Música, Avenida da Boavista, 4100-111 **Tel** *220-107 160*

On the 7th floor of the city's Casa da Musica building, this stark, angular restaurant is named after Dutch architect Rem Koolhaas. The menu is haute cuisine at accessible prices. Choices include poached eggs with warm Brie cheese, Savoy cabbage and bacon, and grilled lamb cutlets with country parsley sauce with baby potatoes. Closed Sun.

OPORTO Dom Tonho 🚌 🗐 €€€€

Cais da Ribeira, 4050-509 **Tel** *222-004 307*

Located in a refurbished 17th-century warehouse on the historic *ribeira* (quayside) in the shadow of the Dom Luís bridge, the menu here respects the culinary traditions of northern Portugal. Dishes like *arroz de pato à moda antiga* (duck rice-traditional style) are served in a contemporary space under soft spotlight. Good wine list.

PORTIMAO Marisqueira O Mané 🚌 🗐 €€

Largo Dr. Bastos 1–3, 8500-600 **Tel** *282-423 496*

Situated close to Portimáo's harbor, Marisqueira O Mané is one of the town's many fish restaurants. It is a traditional Portuguese restaurant specializing in seafood, such as crab, lobster, and prawns, and offers an excellent choice of very fresh fish caught locally. Try the sardines, simply served with bread, salad, and potatoes. Closed Sun dinner & Mon.

SINTRA Tulhas 🏃 🗐 €

Rua Gil Vicente 4–6, 2710-568 **Tel** *219-232 378*

The mysterious hole near the entrance is the last vestige of a series of medieval granaries that once stood here (the Portuguese word for granary is Tulhas). Small and down-to-earth, the home-made food is wholesome and great value. The veal steak in Madeira wine is particularly flavorsome, but leave room for the cheesecake. Closed Wed.

ITALY AND GREECE

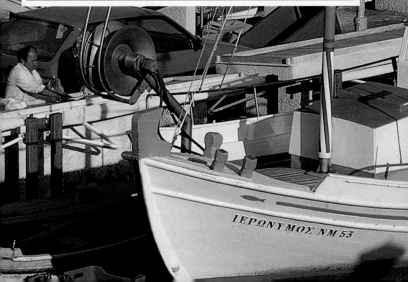

Italy and Greece at a Glance

The appeal of Italy and Greece is both cultural and hedonistic. As the cradles of Europe's two great Classical civilizations, both countries are famous for their ancient temples and monuments, concentrated principally in the cities of Rome and Athens. Located in the southern half of Europe, Italy and Greece share a sunny Mediterranean climate and a correspondingly laid-back way of life. Away from the main cultural sights, the peaceful countryside, beautiful beaches, and warm seas guarantee a relaxed vacation.

Venice (see pp432–41) *is a city quite unlike any other: a fabulous treasure house of art and architecture, built on a series of islands, where there are no cars and the streets are canals.*

ITALY
(See pp386–

Milan
Verona
Venice
Turin
Genoa
Bologna
Florence
Siena
ROME
Naples
Sardinia
Cagliari
Reggio di Cal
Palermo
Sicily

Florence (see pp412–25) *embodies the Renaissance of art and learning in the 15th century. Familiar masterpieces of the period, such as this copy of Michelangelo's* David, *adorn the streets.*

Rome (see pp392–405) *owes its grandest monuments to the era of papal rule. The vast colonnaded square in front of St. Peter's and the Vatican was created by Bernini in the 17th century.*

◁ Fishermen unloading their catch on the island of Mýkonos in the Cyclades, Greece

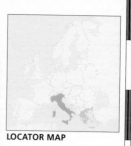

LOCATOR MAP

The Peloponnese (see pp490–93), *a large peninsula, connected to the rest of the Greek mainland by the Corinth isthmus, abounds in ancient and medieval ruins. The heavily fortified sea port of Monemvasía, in the southeastern corner, has many well-preserved Byzantine and Venetian buildings.*

Athens (see pp474–81) *is renowned for its unrivaled collection of Classical antiquities. The world-famous Acropolis is dominated by the 2,500-year-old Parthenon, built as an expression of the glory of ancient Greece.*

- Brindisi

- Thessaloníki

- Neápoli

Corfu

- Metéora

GREECE
(See pp468–517)

- ATHENS

Ancient Olympia -

- Náfplio

0 km   100

0 miles   100

- Monemvasía

Rhodes Town -

Rhodes

- Irákleio

Crete

Crete (see pp500–501), *the largest and most southerly of the Greek islands, boasts clear blue seas and fine sandy beaches. Inland there are ancient Minoan palaces and dramatic mountainous landscapes.*

ITALY

*I*taly has drawn people in search of culture and romance for centuries. Few countries can compete with its Classical origins, its art, architecture, musical, and literary traditions, its scenery, or its food and wine. Since World War II Italy has climbed into the top ten world economies, yet at its heart it retains many of the customs, traditions, and regional allegiances of its agricultural heritage.

Italy has no single cultural identity. Between the snowy peaks of the Alps and the rugged shores of Sicily lies a whole series of regions, each with its own distinctive dialect, architecture, and cuisine. There is also a larger regional division. People speak of two Italies: the rich industrial north and the poorer agricultural south, known as *Il Mezzogiorno* (Land of the Midday Sun).

The north is directly responsible for Italy's place among the world's top industrial nations, a success achieved by names such as Fiat, Pirelli, Olivetti, Zanussi, Alessi, and Armani. The south, in contrast, has high unemployment, many areas in the grip of organized crime, and regions that rank among the most depressed in Europe.

History and geography have both contributed to the division. The north is closer both in location and spirit to Germany and France while the south has suffered a succession of invasions from foreign powers: Carthaginians and Greeks in ancient times, Saracens and Normans in the Middle Ages and until the middle of the last century, the Bourbons from Spain held sway.

HISTORY

Italy is a young country: it did not exist as a unified nation state until 1861. The idea of Italy as a geographic entity goes back to the time of the Etruscans, but prior to the 19th century, the only time the peninsula was united was under the Romans, who by the 2nd century BC had subdued the other Italian tribes and the Greek colonies around the coast. Rome became the capital of a huge empire, introducing its language, laws, and calendar to most of Europe before falling to Germanic invaders in the 5th century AD.

A timeless view and way of life: peaceful old age amid the hills of Tuscany

◁ Piazza Navona, a Baroque fantasy created in papal Rome in the 17th century

The ostentatious Victor Emmanuel Monument in Rome, built to commemorate the completion of the unification of Italy in 1870

Another important legacy of the Roman Empire was Christianity, with the pope as head of the Catholic church throughout western Europe. The medieval papacy summoned the Franks to drive out the Lombards from Italy and, in AD 800, crowned the Frankish king Charlemagne Holy Roman Emperor. Unfortunately, for five centuries popes and emperors fought to decide which of them should be in charge of their nebulous empire.

KEY DATES IN ITALIAN HISTORY

c.800 BC First Greek colonists reach Italy

c.700 BC Rise of the Etruscans

509 BC Foundation of Roman Republic

202 BC Victory over Carthaginians makes Rome dominant power in the Mediterranean

27 BC Augustus establishes Roman Empire

AD 476 Collapse of Western Roman Empire

564 Lombards invade northern Italy

878 Saracens gain control of Sicily

1061 Start of Norman conquest of Sicily

11th–13th century Constant struggles between rival supporters of popes and emperors

1321 Dante writes *The Divine Comedy*

15th century Medici rule Florence; Renaissance

1527 Sack of Rome by Emperor's troops puts end to political ambitions of the papacy

1713 Much of the north passes to Austria

1735 Bourbon dynasty become rulers of Naples and Sicily (Kingdom of the Two Sicilies)

1860 Garibaldi and the Thousand capture Kingdom of the Two Sicilies

1861 Unification of most of Italy under House of Savoy, rulers of Piedmont and Sardinia

1870 Rome becomes capital of modern Italy

1922 Fascists come to power under Mussolini

1946 Foundation of modern Italian republic

2002 Italy joins European single currency

2005 Pope John Paul II dies

2006 Italy wins World Cup in Germany

Meanwhile, a succession of foreign invaders – Normans, Angevins, and Aragonese – conquered Sicily and the south. The north, in contrast, saw a growth of independent city states, the most powerful being Venice, fabulously wealthy from trade with the East. Northern Italy became the most prosperous and cultured region in western Europe and it was the artists and scholars of 15th-century Florence who inspired the Renaissance. Small, fragmented states, however, could not compete with great powers. In the 16th century Italy's petty kingdoms fell prey to a foreign invader, this time to Spain. The north subsequently came under the control of Austria, while the papacy ruled a small region in the center.

One small kingdom that remained independent was Piedmont and in the 19th century it became the focus for a movement towards a united Italy, a goal that was achieved in 1870, thanks largely to the heroic military exploits of Garibaldi. In the 1920s, the Fascists seized power and, in 1946, the monarchy was abandoned for today's republic.

Governments in the postwar era have consistently been short-lived coalitions, dominated by the Christian Democrats. Investigations in Milan in 1992 revealed an organized network of corruption which exposed a huge number of politicians and businessmen. Silvio Berlusconi, Prime Minister from 2001–2006, was succeeded by Romano Prodi, but then re-elected in 2008.

TRADITION AND PROGRESS

Variations between Italy's regions have much to do with the mountainous landscape and inaccessible valleys. Throughout the country, ancient techniques of husbandry endure and many livelihoods are linked to the land and the seasons. Main crops include wheat, olives, and grapes. Although some of the north's postwar economic prosperity can be attributed to industry (especially car production in Turin), much of it has grown from the expansion of family-owned artisan businesses exporting handmade goods abroad. The clothes chain, Benetton, is a typical example of Italian design flair capturing a large slice of the global market.

LANGUAGE AND CULTURE

A tradition of literary Italian was established back in the 14th century by the poets Dante and Petrarch, who wrote in a cultured Florentine dialect. Yet, even today, with national television and radio stations, Italy's regional dialects show an astonishing resilience and northerners have great difficulty understanding a Neapolitan or Sicilian.

The arts in Italy have enjoyed a long and glorious history and Italians are very proud of this. Given the fact that Italy has some 100,000 monuments of major historical significance, it is not surprising that there is a shortage of funds to keep them in good repair. However, with tourism accounting for 3 percent of Italy's GDP, efforts are being made to put as many great buildings and art collections on show as possible.

The performing arts are also underfunded, yet there are spectacular cultural festivals. In the land of Verdi and Rossini, opera is naturally well supported, with almost every town of any size having its own opera house. Cinema is another art form that flourishes, keeping alive the tradition of great directors of the second half of the 20th century, such as Federico Fellini, Vittorio de Sica, and Luchino Visconti.

Children on their way to take First Communion in the Basilica di Monte Berico in Vicenza

Alessi kettle, an icon of modern Italian design

MODERN LIFE

The number of practising Catholics in Italy has been in decline for years. In spite of this, Italian society is still highly traditional, and Italians can be very formal. Italian chic decrees that whatever clothes you wear should give the impression of wealth. If people wear similar outfits, it is because Italians are conformists in fashion as in many other aspects of daily life.

The emphasis on conformity and a commitment to the family remain key factors in Italian society despite the country's low, and falling, birth rate. Grandparents, children and grandchildren still live in family units, although this is becoming less common. All children are pampered but the most cherished ones are, usually, male. Attitudes to women in the workplace have changed, particularly in the cities. However, the idea that men should help with housework is still a fairly foreign notion to the older generation.

Food and football are the great constants; Italians live for both. Much time is spent on preparing food and eating. The Italian diet, particularly in the south, is among the healthiest in the world. Football is a national passion and inspires massive public interest.

Despite the political upheaval and corruption scandals of the 1990s, Italy appears little changed to foreign visitors, maintaining its regional identities and traditional values. The cost of living has soared, however, since the introduction of the Euro in 2002, leading to increased poverty for some.

The Italian football team, Euro 2000 winners

Exploring Italy

Italy's elongated shape means travel can take up a fair proportion of your visit. Rome, Florence, and Venice are naturally the main tourist destinations, but there are many other attractive historic towns and cities that merit a detour of a couple of days or more. Visitors with time to explore often choose to tour a particular region, such as Tuscany, the Veneto, or the island of Sicily. Road and rail connections are generally better in the north, where Milan, Bologna, and Verona are the key transport hubs.

SIGHTS AT A GLANCE

Agrigento 32
Amalfi Coast 27
Assisi pp406–7 2
Bologna 22
Ferrara 21
Florence pp412–25 6
Genoa 10
Lake Como 14
Lake Garda 15
Lake Maggiore 13
Lucca 8
Mantua 16
Milan 12
Mount Etna 30
Naples 25
Padua 19

Palermo 28
Perugia 3
Pisa 7
Pompei 26
Portofino Peninsula 9
Ravenna 23
ROME pp392–405 1
San Gimignano 5
Siena 408–10 4
Syracuse 31
Taormina 29
Turin 11
Urbino 24
Venice pp432–41 20
Verona 17
Vicenza 18

SEE ALSO

- *Practical Information* pp448–9
- *Travel Information* pp450–51
- *Shopping* pp452–3
- *Entertainment* pp454–5
- *Where to Stay* pp456–61
- *Where to Eat* pp462–7

0 kilometers   80

0 miles   8

Rome ❶

From its early days as a settlement of shepherds on the Palatine hill, Rome grew to rule a vast empire stretching beyond western Europe. Later, after the fall of the Roman empire, Rome became the center of the Christian world. The legacy of this history can be seen all over the city. The Pope, head of the Roman Catholic Church, still resides in the Vatican City, an independent enclave at the heart of Rome. In 1870 Rome became the capital of a newly unified Italy, and now has over 2.8 million inhabitants. In summer, many of the grand Baroque piazzas and narrow medieval streets are crammed with attractive sidewalk bars and restaurants.

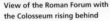

View of the Roman Forum with the Colosseum rising behind

SIGHTS AT A GLANCE

GETTING AROUND

Rome has a subway system known as *la metropolitana* (metro for short). Line A crosses the city from northwest to southeast, Line B from southwest to northeast. The two lines meet at Stazione Termini, the city's central station, which is also the starting point for many bus routes covering most of the city. Official taxis are white or yellow. Walking is preferable to driving in the city's narrow streets.

GREATER ROME

Tivoli

Civitavecchia

VATICAN CITY

Leonardo da Vinci (Fiumicino)

Ciampino

Tevere (Tiber)

Lido di Ostia

0 km 4

0 miles 4

KEY

Area of main map

Fontana della Barcaccia at the foot of the Spanish Steps

KEY

▦	Sight / Place of interest
✈	Airport
🚆	Train station
Ⓜ	Metro station
🚌	Main bus stop
🚊	Tram stop
🛈	Tourist information
✝	Church
—	City walls
—	Pedestrian street

SEE ALSO

0 meters 750

0 yards 750

St. Peter's ①

Catholicism's most sacred shrine, the vast, marble-encrusted basilica draws pilgrims and tourists from all over the world. A shrine was erected on the site of St. Peter's tomb in the 2nd century and the first basilica was commissioned by Constantine. Centuries later, in 1506, Pope Julius II laid the first stone of a new church while the original basilica was still in use. The present basilica, 187 m (615 ft) long, took more than a century to build and all the great architects of the Roman Renaissance and Baroque had a hand in its design. The dominant tone of the interior is set by Bernini, creator of the *baldacchino* below Michelangelo's magnificent dome.

★ Dome
The 137-m (448-ft) dome, designed by Michelangelo, was not completed until 1590, long after his death.

The apse is dominated by Bernini's spectacular bronze monument containing the Throne of St. Peter in Glory.

Baldacchino
Commissioned by Urban VIII in 1624, Bernini's extravagant Baroque canopy stands above the Papal Altar, a plain slab of marble, at which only the pope may say mass. The altar is sited directly above the tomb of St. Peter in the Grottoes below.

Monument to Pope Alexander VII
Bernini's last work in St. Peter's was finished in 1678 and shows the pope surrounded by the allegorical figures of Truth, Justice, Charity, and Prudence.

The Treasury is reached via the Sacristy. It houses ecclesiastical treasures, including reliquaries, tombs, and vestments.

The Grottoes
A fragment of this 13th-century mosaic by Giotto, salvaged from the old basilica, is now in the Grottoes, where many popes are buried.

STAR FEATURES

★ Statue of St. Peter

★ Michelangelo's Pietà

★ Dome

★ **Statue of St. Peter**
This 13th-century bronze is thought to be by Arnolfo di Cambio. The foot of the statue has worn thin from the kisses of millions of pilgrims over the centuries.

Two minor cupolas by Vignola (1507–73)

Michelangelo's Pietà
Protected by glass since an attack in 1972, the Pietà stands in the first side chapel on the right. It was created in 1499 when Michelangelo was only 25.

The facade (1614) is by Carlo Maderno, who lengthened the basilica to create its Latin-cross floorplan.

From this window, the pope blesses the faithful gathered in the piazza below.

Filarete Door
This bronze door, decorated with reliefs by Filarete (1439–45), was one of the doors of the old St. Peter's.

Entrance for stairs to dome

Main entrance

The nave floor has markings that show the lengths of other churches compared with St. Peter's.

Piazza San Pietro
The piazza in front of St. Peter's is enclosed by a vast pincer-shaped colonnade by Bernini. It is topped by statues of saints.

Vatican Museums ②

Four centuries of papal patronage and connoisseurship have resulted in one of the world's great collections of Classical and Renaissance art. The Vatican houses many of the great archaeological finds of central Italy, including the *Laocoön* group and the *Apollo del Belvedere*. The museums are housed in palaces originally built for wealthy Renaissance popes such as Innocent VIII, Sixtus IV, and Julius II. Parts of these were decorated with wonderful frescoes by the finest painters of the age – most notably the Borgia Apartment, the Raphael Rooms and the Sistine Chapel *(see p398)*.

Gallery of the Candelabra
Once an open loggia, this gallery of Greek and Roman sculpture has a fine view of the Vatican Gardens.

Room of the Biga (a two-horse chariot)

Gallery of Tapestries

Etruscan Museum

Gallery of Maps
The gallery is an important record of 16th-century cartography and history. This painting shows the Turkish siege of Malta in 1565.

The Raphael Loggia contains Raphael frescoes, but special permis sion is needed to visit it.

Upper floor

Sistine Chapel

Raphael Rooms
This detail from the Expulsion of Heliodorus from the Temple *contains a portrait of Julius II. It is one of a series of frescoes painted by Raphael for the pope's private apartments (see p398).*

The Cortile del Belvedere was designed by Bramante in 1506.

The Borgia Apartment, frescoed by Pinturicchio in a highly decorative style in the 1490s, also houses a collection of modern religious art.

Pio-Christian Museum

Gregorian Profane Museum

Room of the Animals

Roman mosaics, like these ducks, decorate the walls and floor of this room of animal sculptures.

Entrance

Round Room

acoteca

Greek Cross Room

Simonetti Staircase

Egyptian Museum

Braccio Nuovo

Gallery of the Statues

The Room of the Busts contains portraits of emperors and other notable Romans.

Chiaramonti Museum

Lower floor

Cortile della Pigna

This huge bronze pine cone, part of an ancient Roman fountain, once stood in the courtyard of old St. Peter's. Its niche was designed by Pirro Ligorio.

Lapidary Gallery

Apollo del Belvedere

This Roman copy of a Greek statue of the sun god Apollo perfectly embodies the ideals of Classical beauty.

VISITORS' CHECKLIST

Città del Vaticano (entrance in Viale Vaticano). *Tel* 06-69 88 49 47. **www**.vatican.va
M Ottaviano S. Pietro, Cipro Musei Vaticani. 49 to entrance, 23, 81, 492, 990.
9am–6pm (last adm: 4pm) Mon–Sat, 8:30am–2:30pm (last adm: 12:30pm) last Sun of month – check website.
religious and public hols. Special permit required for Vatican Library, Lapidary Gallery, & Vatican Archives. free last Sun of month. special routes.

GALLERY GUIDE

Visitors have to follow a one-way system. It is best to concentrate on a single collection or to choose one of the suggested itineraries. These are color-coded so that you can follow them throughout the museums. They vary in length from 90 minutes to five hours. If you are planning a long visit, make sure you allow plenty of time for resting. Conserve your stamina for the Sistine Chapel and the Raphael Rooms; they are 20–30 minutes' walk from the entrance, without allowing for any viewing time along the way.

KEY TO FLOORPLAN

- Egyptian and Assyrian art
- Greek and Roman art
- Etruscan and Italic art
- Early Christian and medieval art
- 15th- to 19th-century art
- Modern religious art
- Non-exhibition space
- Open by special permit only

Exploring the Vatican's Collections

The Vatican's greatest treasures are its Greek and
Roman antiquities, which have been on display since
the 18th century. The 19th century saw the addition of
exciting discoveries from Etruscan tombs and
excavations in Egypt. Then there are works by many of
Italy's greatest Renaissance artists housed in the
Pinacoteca (art gallery) and decorating the walls of
chapels and papal apartments.

The *Laocoön*, a Roman copy of a Greek
original, excavated in Rome in 1506

ANCIENT ART

The Egyptian collection
contains finds from 19th-
and 20th-century excavations,
as well as items brought to
Rome in Imperial times. There
are also Roman imitations of
Egyptian art. Genuine Egyptian
works include the tomb of Iri,
guardian of the Pyramid of
Cheops (22nd century BC).
   Prize Greek and Roman art
in the Pio-Clementine
Museum includes Roman
copies of the 4th-century BC
Greek statues *Apoxyomenos*
and the *Apollo del Belvedere*,
and a splendid *Laocoön* from
the 1st century AD.
   The Chiaramonti Museum is
lined with ancient busts, and
its extension, the Braccio
Nuovo, has a 1st-century BC
statue of Emperor Augustus.
   The Etruscan Museum
houses a superb collection,
including the bronze throne,
bed, and funeral cart, found
in the 650 BC Regolini-Galassi
tomb in Cerveteri.
   In the Vatican Library is the
Aldobrandini Wedding, a
beautiful Roman fresco from
the 1st century AD.

CHRISTIAN ART

The Pio-Christian Museum
has Early Christian art, such
as inscriptions and
sculpture from catacombs
and basilicas. The first
two rooms of the Pinacoteca
house medieval art, including
Giotto's *Stefaneschi Triptych*
(c.1300), which decorated
the main altar of the old
St. Peter's. Other rooms in
the Pinacoteca contain
Renaissance works. 15th-
century highlights are a
Pietà by Giovanni Bellini
and Leonardo da Vinci's
unfinished *St. Jerome*.
Exceptional 16th-century
pieces include an altarpiece
by Titian, a *Deposition* by
Caravaggio, *St. Helen* by
Paolo Veronese, and a whole
room devoted to Raphael.

THE SISTINE CHAPEL

The Sistine Chapel takes its
name from Pope Sixtus IV: it
was built in 1473 at his
request. The walls were
frescoed by some of the finest
artists of the age, including
Signorelli, Botticelli, Roselli,
Ghirlandaio, and Perugino
(who is credited with having
overseen the project). There
are 12 frescoes on the side

walls, painted between 1481
and 1483. Their subjects are
parallel episodes in the lives
of Moses and Christ.
   In 1508–12, at the request
of Pope Julius II, Michelangelo
created what has become his
most famous work, the chapel
ceiling. The main panels chart
the *Creation of the World* and
Fall of Man. They are
surrounded by subjects from
the Old and New Testaments.
   In 1534–41 Michelangelo
completed the chapel walls,
painting *The Last Judgment*
on the altar wall. It depicts the
souls of the dead rising up to
face the wrath of God and the
damned being hurled down
to hell. The artist's own
tormented attitude to his faith
is seen in his self-portrait,
painted on the skin held by
the martyr, St. Bartholomew.

RAPHAEL ROOMS

Pope Julius II chose Raphael
(1483–1520) to redecorate
four rooms (*stanze*) of his
apartments. The frescoes in
the Room of the Segnatura
(1508–11) include the famous
School of Athens, which centers
on a debate between Plato
and Aristotle. Raphael depicted
Leonardo da Vinci and
Michelangelo as philosophers.
The decoration of the Room
of Heliodorus (1512–4)
incorporates a famous portrait
of Julius II, whereas the
Room of the Fire in the Borgo
(1514–7) was painted during
the reign of Pope Leo X,
Julius II's successor. All the
frescoes here exalt the new
pope or his earlier namesakes.
   The Hall of Constantine
(1517–25) was largely the
work of Raphael's pupils.

Original Sin, from Michelangelo's fresco on the Sistine Chapel ceiling

View across the Tiber to Castel Sant'Angelo, crowned by the figure of the angel that gave it its name

Castel Sant'Angelo ③

Lungotevere Castello 50. **Tel** 06-681 91 11. 🚌 23, 34, 40, 280. ⏰ Tue–Sun. 🔘 public hols. 🎟️ 👤 **www.** castelsantangelo.com

This massive cylindrical fortress takes its name from the vision of the Archangel Michael, experienced by Pope Gregory the Great in the 6th century, as he led a procession across the bridge, fervently praying for the end of the plague.

The castle began life in AD 139 as the Emperor Hadrian's mausoleum. Since then it has been a bridgehead in the Emperor Aurelian's city wall, a medieval citadel and prison, and a place of safety for popes during times of war or political unrest.

Visitors are given a glimpse into all aspects of the castle's history – from its dank prison cells to the lavish apartments of Renaissance popes.

Villa Farnesina ④

Via della Lungara 230. **Tel** 06-68 02 73 97. 🚌 H, 280, 780. ⏰ Mon–Sat. 🔘 public hols. 🎟️

The fabulously wealthy Sienese banker, Agostino Chigi, commissioned this villa in 1508 from his fellow Sienese, Baldassare Peruzzi. Chigi's main home was across the Tiber – the villa was just for extravagant banquets.

Chigi also used it for sojourns with the courtesan Imperia, who allegedly inspired one of the *Three Graces* painted by Raphael in the Loggia of Cupid and Psyche.

The simple, harmonious design of the Farnesina, with a central block and projecting wings, made it one of the first true villas of the Renaissance. Peruzzi decorated some of the interiors himself, such as the Sala della Prospettiva upstairs, in which illusionistic frescoes create the impression of looking out over Rome through a marble colonnade.

The painted vault of the main hall, the Sala di Galatea, shows the position of the stars at the time of Chigi's birth. After his death the banking business collapsed, and in 1577 the villa was sold to the Farnese family.

Trompe l'oeil view in the Sala della Prospettiva, Villa Farnesina

Santa Maria in Trastevere ⑤

Piazza Santa Maria in Trastevere. **Tel** 06-581 94 43. 🚌 H, 23, 280, 630, 780. ⏰ daily. 👤

Trastevere, the area "across the Tiber," is one of the city's most attractive quarters: a maze of narrow, cobbled alleys. Once home to the city's poor, it has witnessed a proliferation of fashionable clubs, restaurants, and boutiques.

At the heart of Trastevere, overlooking an attractive traffic-free square stands the Basilica of Santa Maria – probably the first official place of Christian worship in Rome. It was founded by Pope Callixtus I in the 3rd century, when Christianity was still a minority cult. According to legend, it was built on the site where a fountain of oil had sprung up miraculously on the day that Christ was born.

The basilica became the focus of devotion to the Madonna. Mary and Christ are among the figures depicted in the facade mosaics (c.12th century). In the apse is a stylized 12th-century mosaic *Coronation of the Virgin*, and below it, a series of realistic mosaic scenes from the life of Mary by the 13th-century artist Pietro Cavallini. The oldest image of the Virgin is a 7th-century icon, which depicts her as a Byzantine empress flanked by a guard of angels.

Piazza Navona ⑥

40, 46, 62, 64, 81, 87, 116, 492, 628.

Rome's most spectactular Baroque piazza follows the shape of a 1st-century AD stadium, built by Domitian and used for athletic contests (agones), chariot races, and other sports. The foundations of the surrounding buildings come from the ruined stadium, traces of which are visible below the church of Sant' Agnese in Agone. The church, created by the architects Girolamo and Carlo Rainaldi and Francesco Borromini, is dedicated to the virgin martyr, St. Agnes. When she was stripped naked to force her to renounce her faith, her hair grew miraculously long, concealing her body.

The piazza began to take on its present appearance in the 17th century, when Pope Innocent X commissioned a new church, palace, and fountain. The fountain, the Fontana dei Quattro Fiumi, is Bernini's most magnificent,

with statues of four gods personifying the world's greatest known rivers at the time – the Nile, the Plate, the Ganges, and the Danube – sitting on rocks below an obelisk. Bernini also sculpted the muscle-bound Moor in the Fontana del Moro, though the present statue is a copy.

The Pantheon, a place of worship since the 2nd century AD

Pantheon ⑦

Piazza della Rotonda. **Tel** 06-68 30 02 30. 116 & many others. daily. Jan 1, May 1, Dec 25.

The Pantheon, the Roman "temple of all the gods," is the most extraordinary and best preserved ancient building in Rome. The first temple on the site is thought to have been a conventional rectangular affair erected by Agrippa between 27 and 25 BC.

The present structure was built, and possibly designed, by Emperor Hadrian in AD 118.

The temple is fronted by a massive pedimented portico, screening what appears to be a cylinder fused to a shallow dome. Only from the inside can the true scale and beauty of the temple be appreciated: a vast hemispherical dome equal in radius to the height of the cylinder gives perfectly harmonious proportions to the building. A circular opening in the center of the coffered dome, the oculus, lets in the only light.

In the 7th century, Christians claimed that they were being plagued by demons as they passed by, and permission was given to turn the Pantheon into a church. Today it is lined with tombs, ranging from the restrained monument to Raphael to the huge marble and porphyry sarcophagi holding the bodies of Italian monarchs.

Palazzo Doria Pamphilj ⑧

Via del Corso 305. **Tel** 06-679 73 23. 64, 70, 81, 85, 117, 119, 492. daily. Jan 1, Easter Sun, May 1, Aug 15, Dec 25. **www. doriapamphilj.it**

Palazzo Doria Pamphilj is a vast stone edifice, whose oldest parts date from 1435. It was owned by the della Rovere family and then by the Aldobrandini family, before the Pamphilj family took possession of it in 1647. The Pamphilj added a new wing, a splendid chapel, and a theater.

Personification of the Ganges, Fontana dei Quattro Fiumi, Piazza Navona

The family art collection has over 400 paintings dating from the 15th to the 18th century, including a portrait of Pope Innocent X by Velázquez and works by Caravaggio, Titian, Guercino, and Claude Lorrain. The opulent rooms of the private apartments retain many of their original furnishings, including Brussels and Gobelins tapestries, Murano chandeliers, and a gilded crib.

In the first half of the 18th century, Gabriele Valvassori created the gallery above the courtyard and a new facade along the Corso, using the highly decorative style of the period, known as the *barocchetto*, which now dominates the building.

Triumph of Faith over Heresy by
Pierre Legros in the Gesù

Gesù ⑨

Piazza del Gesù. **Tel** 06-69 70 01.
🚌 many routes. ⬜ daily.

The Gesù, built between 1568 and 1584, was Rome's first Jesuit church. The Jesuit order was founded in Rome in 1537 by a Basque soldier, Ignatius Loyola, who became a Christian after he was wounded in battle. The order was intellectual, austere, and heavily engaged in teaching and missionary activities.

The much-imitated design of the Gesù typifies Counter Reformation architecture: a large nave with side pulpits for preaching to crowds, and a main altar as the centerpiece for the mass. The illusionistic decoration that covers the nave ceiling and the dome was added by Il Baciccia during

the 17th century. The painting in the nave depicts the *Triumph of the Name of Jesus* and its message is clear: faithful, Catholic worshippers will be joyfully uplifted to heaven while Protestants and heretics are flung into the fires of hell. The message is reiterated in the Cappella di Sant'Ignazio, a rich display of lapis lazuli, serpentine, silver, and gold. The Baroque marble by Pierre Legros, *Triumph of Faith over Idolatry*, shows a female "Religion" trampling on the head of the serpent "Idolatry."

Capitoline Museums ⑩

Musei Capitolini, Piazza del Campidoglio. **Tel** 06-06 08.
🚌 63, 64, 70, 75 & many others.
⬜ Tue–Sun. ⬛ Jan 1, May 1,
Dec 25. 🎫 📷 🚻
www.museicapitolini.org

When Emperor Charles V announced he was to visit Rome in 1536, Pope Paul III asked Michelangelo to give the Capitol, formerly the citadel of Ancient Rome, a facelift. He redesigned the piazza, renovated the facades of its palaces and built a new staircase, the Cordonata. This gently rising ramp is now crowned with the massive Classical statues of Castor and Pollux.

The Capitoline Museums – the Palazzo Nuovo and the Palazzo dei Conservatori – stand on opposite sides of the impressive Piazza del Campidoglio. Since 2000, they have been connected via a subterranean passage. In the center of the piazza is an equestrian statue of Marcus Aurelius (it is a copy; the original bronze is in the Palazzo Nuovo).

The facade of the Palazzo Nuovo was designed by Michelangelo, but the work was finished in 1655 by the brothers Carlo and Girolamo Rainaldi.

Statue of Marcus Aurelius in the center of Piazza del Campidoglio

The Palazzo dei Conservatori had been the seat of the city's magistrates during the late Middle Ages. Its frescoed halls are still used occasionally for political meetings and the ground floor houses the municipal registry office. The current building was begun in 1536, built by Giacomo della Porta, who also carried out Michelangelo's other designs for Piazza del Campidoglio.

A collection of Classical statues has been kept on the Capitoline Hill since the Renaissance. When the Palazzo Nuovo was completed, some of the statues were transferred there. In 1734 Pope Clement XII decreed that the building be turned into the world's first public museum.

The museum is still devoted chiefly to sculpture. Most of its finest works, such as *The Dying Galatian*, are Roman copies of Greek masterpieces. There are also two collections of busts, assembled in the 18th century, of the philosophers and poets of ancient Greece and the rulers of ancient Rome.

Although much of the museum is given over to sculpture, it also houses a collection of porcelain, and its art galleries contain various works by Veronese, Titian, Caravaggio, Rubens, van Dyck, and Tintoretto.

Esquiline Venus, Capitoline Museums

Ancient Rome

Traces of ancient Rome are visible all over the city, occasionally a whole building, often just a column from a temple or an arch of an aqueduct recycled in a later construction. The major archaeological sites are to be found along Via dei Fori Imperiali, which runs from Piazza Venezia to the Colosseum. On the north side lie Trajan's Markets and the forums of various emperors; on the south side are the Roman Forum and the Palatine Hill. Many museums hold extensive collections of antiquities excavated in the city.

Romans fortifying a town in a detail from Trajan's Column

Trajan's Markets ⑪

Via IV Novembre 94. *Tel 06-69 78 05 32.* 🚌 *40, 60, 171.* ⭕ *Tue–Sun.* ● *public hols.* 🈺

Originally considered among the wonders of the Classical world, Trajan's Markets now show only a hint of their former splendor.

Emperor Trajan and his architect, Apollodorus of Damascus, built this visionary complex of 150 shops and offices in the early 2nd century AD. The Markets sold everything from Middle Eastern silks and spices to fresh fish, fruit, and flowers. It was also the place where the corn dole was administered: a free ration for Roman men.

Shops opened early and closed about noon. Almost all the shopping was done by men and the traders were almost exclusively male.

The **Forum of Trajan** (AD 107–13) was built in front of the market complex. It was a vast colonnaded open space with a huge basilica, and included two libraries.

Dominating the ruins today is **Trajan's Column**. Spiralling up its 30-m- (98-ft-) high stem are minutely detailed scenes showing episodes from Trajan's successful campaigns in Dacia (present-day Romania).

Roman Forum ⑫

Entrances: Via di San Gregorio and Via della Salara Vecchia 56. *Tel 06-39 96 77 00.* Ⓜ *Colosseo.* 🚌 *60, 75, 85, 87, 117, 175, 186, 810, 850.* ⭕ *daily.* ● *Jan 1, May 1, Dec 25.* 🈺 *(includes entry to the Colosseum and Palatine).*

The Forum was the center of political, commercial, and judicial life in ancient Rome. As Rome's population grew, however, this ancient Forum became too small, so Julius Caesar built a new one (46 BC). This move was emulated by successive emperors. The newer forums are known as the "Imperial Fora."

The ruins of the Roman Forum date from many eras and the layout is confusing. It is a good idea to view them from the vantage point of the Capitoline Hill, before walking around. From there you can make out the Via Sacra, the route of religious and triumphal processions.

The best preserved monuments are two triumphal arches. The **Arch of Titus** commemorates the crushing of the Jewish Revolt by Titus in AD 70. The later **Arch of Septimius Severus** (AD 203) records the emperor's victories over the Parthians.

Most of the other ruins are temples or basilicas. The latter were huge public buildings, which served as law courts and places of business. At the western end of the forum are the scant remains of the **Basilica Julia**, named after Julius Caesar, and the earlier **Basilica Aemilia**. Close to the latter stands the reconstructed **Curia**, where the Roman Senate once met.

The eastern end of the Forum is dominated by the shell of the **Basilica of Constantine and Maxentius** (4th century AD). The adjacent **Temple of Romulus** is now part of a church. Cross the Via Sacra from here to see the partly reconstructed **Temple of Vesta** and the **House of the Vestal Virgins**.

Further east past the Arch of Titus are the extensive ruins of the **Temple of Venus and Rome**, built in AD 121 by Hadrian. Attached to the ruined temple is the church of **Santa Francesca Romana** – patron saint of motorists. On March 9, drivers bring their cars here to have them blessed.

Central garden of the House of the Vestal Virgins in the Roman Forum

Ruins of oval fountain in the Domus Flavia on the Palatine

Palatine ⑬

Entrances: Via di San Gregorio and near the Arch of Titus on Via Sacra. **Tel** 06-39 96 77 00. M Colosseo. 60, 75, 81, 160, 175 & many others. 3. ☐ daily. ● public hols. (includes entry to the Colosseum and Forum).

The Palatine, the hill where the Roman aristocracy lived and emperors built their palaces, is the most pleasant and relaxing of the city's ancient sites. Shaded by pines and carpeted with wild flowers in the spring, it is dominated by the imposing ruins of the **Domus Augustana** and the **Domus Flavia**, two parts of Domitian's huge palace (1st century AD).

Other remains here include the **House of Augustus** and the **House of Livia**, where the Emperor Augustus lived with his wife Livia; and the **Cryptoporticus**, a long underground gallery built by Nero.

The **Huts of Romulus**, not far from the House of Augustus, are Iron Age huts (10th century BC), which provide archaeological support for the area's legendary links with the founding of Rome. According to legend Romulus and Remus grew up on this hill in the 8th century BC.

After admiring the ancient sights, visit the **Farnese Gardens**, created in the mid-16th century by Cardinal Alessandro Farnese, with tree-lined avenues, rose gardens, and glorious views.

Colosseum ⑭

Piazza del Colosseo. **Tel** 06-3996 77 00. M Colosseo. 75, 81, 85, 87, 117, 175, 673, 810. 3. ☐ daily. ● Jan 1, May 1, Dec 25. (includes entry to the Palatine and Forum). limited.

Rome's great amphitheater, commissioned by the Emperor Vespasian in AD 72, was built on the marshy site of a lake in the grounds of Nero's palace.

It is likely that the arena took its name, not from its own size, but from that of an enormous statue, the Colossus of Nero, that stood nearby.

The Colosseum was the site of deadly gladiatorial combats and wild animal fights, staged free of charge by the emperor and wealthy citizens. It was built to a very practical design, its 80 entrances allowing easy access for 55,000 spectators. Excavations in the 19th century exposed a network of rooms under the arena, from which animals could be released.

The four tiers of the outside walls were built in differing styles. The lower three are arched: the bottom with Doric columns, the next with Ionic, and the third with Corinthian. The top level supported a huge awning, used to shade spectators from the sun.

Beside the Colosseum stands the **Arch of Constantine**, commemorating Constantine's victory in AD 312 over his co-emperor Maxentius. Most of the medallions, reliefs, and statues were scavenged from earlier monuments. Inside the arch are reliefs showing one of Trajan's victories.

ANCIENT ROMAN SITES AND MUSEUMS

Baths of Caracalla

Viale delle Terme di Caracalla 52. **Tel** 06-39 96 77 00. M Circo Massimo. 160, 628. 3. ☐ Tue–Sun & Mon am. Extensive ruins of bath complex built in AD 217.

Theatre of Marcellus

Via del Teatro di Marcello. 30, 44, 63, 81, 95, 130, 160, 170, 271, 628, 630, 715, 716, 780, 781. ☐ daily. An Imperial theater, which later housed a number of medieval shops.

Museo Nazionale Romano

Palazzo Massimo, Largo di Villa Peretti 1. **Tel** 06-39 36 77 00. M Repubblica, Termini. 36, 38, 64, 86, 110, 170, 175, H, and many others to Piazza dei Cinquecento. ☐ Tue–Sun. Sculpture, mosaics, wall-paintings, and a Roman mummy. Another branch of the museum is at the Baths of Diocletian across the road.

Palazzo Altemps

Piazza Sant'Apollinare 44. **Tel** 06-39 36 77 00. 70, 81, 115, 116, 280, 492, 628. ☐ Tue–Sun. Fine collection of Classical statuary in beautiful Renaissance palazzo.

Temples of the Forum Boarium

Piazza della Bocca della Verità. 44, 81, 95, 160, 170, 280, 628, 715, 716. Two miraculously preserved Republican-era temples.

The Colosseum, a majestic sight despite centuries of damage and neglect

Santa Maria Maggiore ⑮

Piazza di Santa Maria Maggiore.
Tel 06-69 88 68 00. Ⓜ *Termini,
Cavour.* 🚌 *16, 70, 71, 714.* 🚊 *14.*
☐ *daily.* 🎫

Of all the great Roman
basilicas, Santa Maria has the
most successful blend of
different architectural styles.
Its colonnaded triple nave is
part of the original 5th-century
building; the marble floor and
Romanesque bell tower, with
its blue ceramic roundels, are
medieval; the Renaissance saw
a new coffered ceiling; and
the Baroque gave the church
twin domes and its imposing
front and rear facades.

Santa Maria is most famous
for its mosaics. Those in the
nave and on the triumphal
arch date from the 5th century.
Medieval mosaics include a
13th-century enthroned Christ
in the loggia and Jacopo
Torriti's *Coronation of the
Virgin* (1295) in the apse.

The gilded ceiling was a gift
of Alexander VI, the Borgia
pope. The gold used is said
to be the first brought back
from America by Columbus.

Trevi Fountain ⑯

Piazza di Trevi. 🚌 *52, 53, 61, 62, 63,
71, 80, 95, 116, 119 & many others.*

Most visitors gathering around
the coin-filled fountain
assume that it has always
been there, but by the
standards of the Eternal City,
the Trevi is a fairly recent
creation. Nicola Salvi's

The Spanish Steps, with the church of Trinità dei Monti above

theatrical design for Rome's
largest and most famous
fountain was completed only
in 1762. The central figure is
Neptune, flanked by two
Tritons. One Triton struggles
to master a very unruly "sea-
horse," the other leads a far
more docile animal. These
symbolize the two contrasting
moods of the sea.

The site was originally the
terminal of the Aqua Virgo
aqueduct (19 BC). A relief
shows the legendary virgin,
after whom the aqueduct was
named, pointing to the spring
from which the water flows.

Spanish Steps ⑰

Scalinata della Trinità dei Monti,
Piazza di Spagna. Ⓜ *Spagna.*
🚌 *116, 117, 119, 590.*

The steps, which link the
church of Trinità dei Monti
with Piazza di Spagna below,
were completed in 1726.
They combine straight
sections, curves, and terraces
to create one of the city's
most dramatic and distinctive
landmarks. To the right as
you look at the steps from the
square is the **Keats-Shelley
Memorial House**, a small
museum in the house where
the poet John Keats died of
consumption in 1821.

In the 19th century the
steps were a meeting place
for artists' models; today they
are filled with people sitting,
writing postcards, taking
photos, flirting, busking, or
just watching the passers-by.
Eating here is not allowed.

The steps overlook Via
Condotti and the surrounding
streets. In the 18th century
this area was full of hotels for
foreigners doing the Grand
Tour. It now contains the
smartest shops in Rome.

The Trevi Fountain, the most famous of Rome's Baroque landmarks

For hotels and restaurants in this region see pp456–7 and pp462–3

Santa Maria del Popolo ⑱

Piazza del Popolo 12. **Tel** 06-361 08 36. Ⓜ Flaminio. 🚌 95, 117, 119, 120, 150, 491. ◯ daily.

Santa Maria del Popolo was commissioned by Sixtus IV in 1472. After his death in 1484, the pope's family chapel, the Della Rovere Chapel (first on the right), was frescoed by Pinturicchio.

In 1503 Sixtus IV's nephew Giuliano became Pope Julius II and had Bramante build a new apse. Pinturicchio was called in again to paint its vaults with Sibyls and Apostles framed by freakish beasts.

In 1513 Raphael created the Chigi Chapel (second on the left) – a Renaissance fusion of the sacred and profane – for the banker Agostino Chigi. Bernini later added the statues of Daniel and Habakkuk. In the Cerasi Chapel, left of the altar, are two Caravaggios: *The Crucifixion of St Peter* and *The Conversion of St Paul*.

The Chigi Chapel in Santa Maria del Popolo, designed by Raphael

Museo e Galleria Borghese ⑲

Piazzale Scipione Borghese 5. **Tel** 06-328 10 (reservations). 🚌 52, 53, 910. 🚋 3, 19. ◯ Tue–Sun (reservations obligatory). ● Jan 1, May 1, Dec 25. 🈂 www.galleriaborghese.it

The Villa Borghese and its park were designed in 1605 for Cardinal Scipione Borghese, nephew of Pope

Detail from Bernini's *Rape of Proserpine* in the Museo Borghese

Paul V. The park was the first of its kind in Rome. It was laid out with 400 pine trees, sculpture by Bernini, and dramatic water features.

The villa was used for entertaining and displaying the cardinal's impressive collection of paintings and sculpture. Unfortunately, between 1801 and 1809 Prince Camillo Borghese, husband to Napoleon's sister Pauline, sold many of these to his brother-in-law, and swapped 200 of Scipione's Classical statues for an estate in Piedmont. The statues are still in the Louvre. However, some Classical treasures remain, including fragments of a 3rd-century AD mosaic of gladiators fighting wild animals.

The highlights of the remaining collection are the sculptures by the young Bernini. *Apollo and Daphne* (1624), shows the nymph Daphne being transformed into a laurel tree to escape being abducted by Apollo. Other striking works are *The Rape of Proserpine* and a *David*, whose face is said to be a self-portrait of Bernini.

The most notorious work is a sculpture by Canova of Pauline Borghese as *Venus Victrix* (1805), in which the semi-naked Pauline reclines on a chaise longue.

The Galleria Borghese, on the upper floor, houses some fine Renaissance and Baroque paintings. These include Raphael's *Deposition*, along with works by Pinturicchio, Correggio, Caravaggio, Rubens, and Titian.

Within the Villa Borghese park are other museums and galleries, foreign academies, a zoo, schools of archaeology, an artificial lake, and an array of fountains and follies.

Villa Giulia ⑳

Piazzale di Villa Giulia 9. **Tel** 06-322 65 71. 🚌 52, 926, 88, 95, 490, 495. 🚋 3, 19. ◯ Tue–Sun. ● Jan 1, May 1, Dec 25. 🈂 🎧 audio. ♿

Villa Giulia was built as a country retreat for Pope Julius III. Today it houses a world-famous collection of Etruscan and other pre-Roman remains. There are fascinating pieces of jewelry, bronzes, mirrors, and a marvelous terra-cotta sarcophagus of a husband and wife from Cerveteri.

The delightful villa was the work of architects Vasari and Vignola, and the sculptor Ammannati. Michelangelo also contributed. At the center of the garden is a *nympheum* – a sunken courtyard decorated with mosaics, statues, and fountains, built in imitation of ancient Roman models.

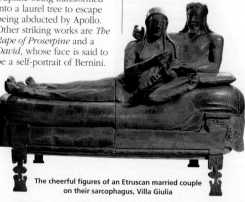

The cheerful figures of an Etruscan married couple on their sarcophagus, Villa Giulia

Assisi: Basilica di San Francesco

The burial place of St. Francis, this basilica was begun in 1228, two years after the saint's death. Over the next century its Upper and Lower Churches were decorated by the foremost artists of their day, among them Cimabue, Simone Martini, Pietro Lorenzetti, and Giotto, whose frescoes of the *Life of St. Francis* are some of the most renowned in Italy. Many of the basilica's frescoes were badly damaged in the earthquake that hit Assisi in 1997, but all have been restored. The basilica, which dominates Assisi, is one of the great Christian shrines and receives vast numbers of pilgrims throughout the year.

★ Frescoes by Giotto
The Ecstasy of St. Francis is one of 28 panels that make up Giotto's cycle on the Life of St. Francis *(c.1290–95).*

St. Francis
Cimabue's simple painting (c.1280) captures the humility of the revered saint, who stood for poverty, chastity, and obedience.

Faded paintings
by Roman artists line the walls above Giotto's *Life of St. Francis.*

The choir
(1501) features a 13th-century stone papal throne.

The vaulting of the Lower Church is covered almost entirely in frescoes.

Steps to the Treasury

A Renaissance portico shelters the original Gothic portal of the Lower Church.

The crypt contains the tomb of St. Francis.

★ Frescoes by Lorenzetti
The bold composition of Pietro Lorenzetti's fresco, entitled The Deposition *(1323), is based around the truncated Cross, focusing attention on the twisted figure of Christ.*

★ Cappella di San Martino
The frescoes in this chapel on the life of St. Martin (1315) are by the Sienese painter Simone Martini. This panel shows the death of the Saint. Martini was also responsible for the fine stained glass in the chapel.

The Upper Church has soaring Gothic vaulting painted with a starry sky, symbolizing the heavenly glory of St. Francis. Its style influenced that of many later Franciscan churches.

The rose window is framed by the carved symbols of the four Evangelists.

Entrance to Upper Church

The facade and its rose window are early examples of Italian Gothic.

STAR FEATURES

★ Frescoes by Giotto

★ Frescoes by Lorenzetti

★ Cappella di San Martino

The ancient Tempio di Minerva in the Piazza del Comune, Assisi

Assisi ❷

🏛 25,000. 🚊 🚌 🚹 Piazza del Comune 22 (075-813 86 80). 🚃 Sat. **www**.assisi.regioneumbria.eu

This beautiful medieval town, with its geranium-hung streets, lovely views, and fountain-splashed piazzas, is heir to the legacy of St. Francis (c.1181–1226), who is buried in the **Basilica di San Francesco**.

Piazza del Comune, Assisi's main square, is dominated by the columns of the **Tempio di Minerva**, a Roman temple-front from the Augustan age. The Palazzo Comunale, opposite, houses an art gallery the **Pinacoteca Comunale**.

The town has many other interesting churches. On Corso Mazzini is the **Basilica di Santa Chiara**. Here, St. Clare – Francis's companion and the founder of the Poor Clares (an order of nuns) – is buried. The **Duomo** has a superb Romanesque facade. **San Pietro** is a simple, well-restored Romanesque church, while the nearby **Oratorio dei Pellegrini**, a 15th-century pilgrims' hospice, contains well-preserved frescoes by Matteo da Gualdo.

Perugia ❸

🏛 160,000. 🚊 🚌 🚹 Piazza Matteotti 19, Loggia dei Lanari (075-572 33 27). 🚃 Tue, Thu, Sat.

Perugia's old center hinges around Corso Vannucci, named after the local painter Pietro Vannucci (Perugino). It is dominated by Umbria's finest building and former town hall, the monumental **Palazzo dei Priori**. Among its richly decorated rooms is the Sala dei Notari or Lawyers' Hall (c.1295), vividly frescoed with scenes from the Old Testament. Superlative frescoes (1498–1500) by Perugino cover the walls of the Collegio del Cambio, Perugia's medieval money exchange. The **Galleria Nazionale dell'Umbria** on the third floor displays a fine collection of paintings.

The Cappella del Santo Anello in Perugia's 15th-century **Duomo** houses the Virgin's agate "wedding ring," said to change color according to the character of its wearer. The Renaissance *Madonna delle Grazie* by Gian Nicola di Paolo hangs in the nave.

On Piazza San Francesco the **Oratorio di San Bernardino** (1457–61), has a colorful façade by Agostino di Duccio. Beyond the old city walls, the 10th-century **San Pietro** is Perugia's most extravagantly decorated church. **San Domenico** (1305–1632), on Piazza Giordano Bruno, is Umbria's largest church. It houses the tomb of Pope Benedict XI (c.1304) and the **Museo Archeologico Nazionale dell'Umbria**, a collection of prehistoric, Etruscan, and Roman artifacts.

🏛 **Galleria Nazionale dell'Umbria**
Corso Vannucci 19. **Tel** 075-572 10 09. ⭕ Tue–Sun. ⭕ Jan 1, May 1, Dec 25. 🎫 🚻

Palazzo dei Priori, Perugia's imposing medieval town hall

Street-by-Street: Siena ❹

Unicorn
contrada

Siena's principal sights cluster in the maze of narrow streets and alleys around the fan-shaped Piazza del Campo. One of Europe's greatest medieval squares, the piazza sits at the heart of the city's 17 *contrade*, the historic districts whose ancient rivalries are still acted out in the twice-yearly Palio (*see p410*). Loyalty to the *contrada* of one's birth is fierce, and as you wander the streets you will see the parishes' animal symbols repeated on flags, plaques, and carvings.

The Duomo dominating Siena's skyline

Bus station ↑

Train station

Via della Galluzza leads to the house of St. Catherine, Siena's patron saint (*see p410*).

The Baptistry has fine frescoes and a font with reliefs by Donatello, Jacopo della Quercia, and Ghiberti.

★ **Duomo**
Striped black and white marble pillars, surmounted by a carved frieze of the popes, support the Duomo's vaulted ceiling, painted blue with gold stars to resemble the night sky (see p410).

Each tier of the Duomo's bell tower has one more window than the floor below.

Cafés and shops fill the streets around Piazza del Duomo.

VIA D. GALLUZZA

PIAZZA INDIPENDENZA

VIA DI FONTEBRANDA

VIA DI DIACCETO

VIA DEI PELLEGRINI

VIA FRANCIOSA

PIAZZA SAN GIOVANNI

VIA DEL POGGIO

VIA DI CITTA

PIAZZA DEL DUOMO

VIA DEL CAPITANO

Museo dell'Opera del Duomo
The museum (see p410) houses weathered sculptures from the cathedral, including this battered she-wolf suckling Romulus and Remus.

KEY

- - - Suggested route

| 0 meters | 300 |
| 0 yards | 300 |

Loggia della Mercanzia
This graceful arcade (1417)
was used by Siena's medieval
merchants and money dealers.

Tourist
information

Palazzo Piccolomini,
built in 1460, now
holds the Sienese state
archives. Many of the
original painted
wooden bindings
are on display.

★ Palazzo Pubblico
The graceful Gothic town
hall was completed in
1342. At 102 m (330 ft),
the bell tower, the Torre
del Mangia, is the second
highest medieval tower
ever built in Italy.

Fonte Gaia
The reliefs on the fountain
are 19th-century copies of
the 15th-century originals
by Jacopo della Quercia.

🏛 Palazzo Pubblico
Piazza del Campo 1. *Tel 0577-22 62
30*. **Museo Civico & Torre del
Mangia** ◯ daily. ● Dec 25. 🎫
Although the Palazzo Pubblico
(1297–1342) continues in its
ancient role as Siena's town
hall, the **Museo Civico** is also
housed here. Many of the
medieval rooms, some decorated with paintings of the
Sienese School, are open to
the public. They include the
main council chamber, or Sala
del Mappamondo, named
after a map of the world
painted here by Ambrogio
Lorenzetti in the early 14th
century. One wall is covered
by Simone Martini's fresco
Maestà (1315), which depicts
the Virgin in Majesty. The Sala
della Pace houses the famous
*Allegory of Good and Bad
Government*, a pair of frescoes
by Lorenzetti finished in 1338.
  In the palace courtyard is
the magnificent **Torre del
Mangia** bell tower, which
offers superb views of the city.

🏛 Piazza del Campo
Italy's loveliest piazza
occupies the site of the old
Roman forum, and for much
of Siena's early history was
the city's principal marketplace. The Council of Nine,
Siena's ruling body, gave the
order for work to start on the
piazza in 1293. The red brick
paving was finished in 1349.
It is divided into nine sections,
representing not only the
authority of the council, but
also the protective folds of
the Madonna's cloak. The
piazza has been the focus of
city life ever since, a setting
for executions, bullfights, and
the drama of the Palio. Cafés,
restaurants, and fine medieval
palazzi now line the square,
which is dominated by the
Palazzo Pubblico and the
Torre del Mangia.

**Piazza del Campo, viewed from the
top of the Torre del Mangia**

Exploring Siena

Once a capital to rival Florence, Siena is still unspoiled and endowed with the grandeur of the age in which it was at its peak (1260–1348). The magnificent Duomo is one of Italy's greatest cathedrals. The best place to begin an exploration of the historic city center is Piazza del Campo and the surrounding maze of medieval streets. Siena's hilly position means that walks through the city are rewarded with countless sudden views of the surrounding countryside.

Massacre of the Innocents, a detail from the Duomo's marble floor

Richly decorated facade of Siena's Duomo

including a tondo (circular relief) of a Madonna and Child, probably by Donatello. The highlight is Duccio's huge altarpiece, *Maestà* (1308–11), which depicts the *Madonna and Child* on one side, and *Scenes from the Life of Christ* on the other.

🏛 Pinacoteca Nazionale
Via San Pietro 29. **Tel** 0577-28 11 61. ☐ daily. ● Sun & Mon pm, Jan 1, May 1, Dec 25. 🖾 ᬓ
Housed in the Palazzo Buonsignori, this gallery contains an unsurpassed collection of paintings by artists of the Sienese School. Highlights include Duccio's *Madonna dei Francescani* (1285) and Simone Martini's *The Blessed Agostino Novello and Four of his Miracles* (c.1330).

🏠 San Domenico
Piazza San Domenico. ☐ daily.
The preserved head of the city's patroness, St. Catherine of Siena (1347–80), can be seen in a gilded tabernacle on the altar of a chapel dedicated to her in

this huge, barn-like Gothic church. Built in 1460, the chapel is dominated by Sodoma's frescoes (1526), which show Catherine in states of religious fervor. The church has the only portrait of St. Catherine considered authentic, painted by her friend Andrea Vanni.

St. Catherine's house, the **Casa di Santa Caterina**, is also a popular shrine for visitors to Siena.

♣ Fortezza Medicea
Viale Maccari. **Fortezza** ☐ daily. **Enoteca Italiana** Via Camollia 72. **Tel** 0577-22 88 11. ☐ noon–1am Mon–Sat. 🖾
This huge red-brick fortress was built by Cosimo I in 1560 following Siena's defeat by Florence in the 1554–5 war. After an 18-month siege, during which more than 8,000 Sienese died, the town's banking and wool industries were suppressed by the Florentines.

The fortress now houses the **Enoteca Italiana**, where you can taste and buy Italian wines.

🏠 Duomo
Piazza del Duomo. **Tel** 0577-28 30 48. ☐ daily. ● Sun am. **Museo dell'Opera del Duomo Tel** 0577-28 30 48. ☐ early–mid-Mar: 9:30am–7:30pm daily; mid-Mar–Sep: 9:30am–8pm daily; Nov–Feb: 10am–5pm daily. ● Jan 1, Dec 25. 🖾
Siena's cathedral (1136–1382) is a spectacular example of Pisan-influenced Romanesque-Gothic architecture. Had the 14th-century plan to create a new nave come to fruition, it would have become the largest church in Christendom, but the idea was abandoned when the Black Death of 1348 virtually halved the city's population. Among the Duomo's treasures are sculptural masterpieces by Nicola Pisano, Donatello, and Michelangelo, a fine inlaid marble floor, and a magnificent fresco cycle by Pinturicchio.

In the side aisle of the unfinished nave, which has been roofed over, is the **Museo dell'Opera del Duomo**. The museum is devoted mainly to sculpture removed from the exterior of the Duomo,

---

THE PALIO

The Palio is Tuscany's most celebrated festival and it occurs in the Campo each year on July 2 and August 16. This bareback horse race was first recorded in 1283, but it may have had its origins in Roman military training. The jockeys represent Siena's 17 *contrade* (districts) and the horses are chosen by the drawing of lots. Preceded by days of colorful pageantry and heavy betting, the races themselves last only 90 seconds each, the winner being rewarded with a silk *palio* (banner).

Drummer taking part in the Palio's noisy pre-race pageant

The skyline of San Gimignano, bristling with medieval towers

San Gimignano ❺

Siena. 🏛 7,000. 🚌 ℹ Piazza del Duomo 1 (0577-94 00 08). 🎪 Thu. 🎭 San Gimignano (Jan 31).

The thirteen towers that dominate San Gimignano's skyline were built by rival noble families in the 12th and 13th centuries, when the town's position on the main pilgrim route to Rome brought it great prosperity. The plague of 1348, and later the diversion of the pilgrim route, led to its economic decline and its miraculous preservation.

Full of good restaurants and shops, the town is also home to many fine works of art. The **Museo Civico** holds works by Pinturicchio, Benozzo Gozzoli, and Filippino Lippi, while the church of **Sant'Agostino** has a Baroque interior by Vanvitelli (c.1740) and a fresco cycle on *The Life of St. Augustine* by Benozzo Gozzoli (1465).

Florence ❻

See pp412–25.

Pisa ❼

🏛 90,000. ✈ Galileo Galilei, 5 km (3 miles) S. 🚉 🚌 ℹ Piazza Vittorio Emanuele 13 (050-42 291). 🎪 Wed & Sat. **www**.pisaunicaterra.it

In the Middle Ages, Pisa's navy dominated the western Mediterranean. Trade with Spain and North Africa brought vast wealth, reflected in the city's splendid buildings. The **Duomo**, begun in 1064, is a magnificent example of Pisan-Romanesque architecture, its four-tiered facade an intricate medley of creamy colonnades and blind arcades. Inside, highlights include a pulpit (1302–11) by Giovanni Pisano and a mosaic of *Christ in Majesty* by Cimabue (1302).

Begun in 1173 on sandy silt subsoil, the famous **Leaning Tower** (Torre Pendente) was completed in 1350. The tower has attracted many visitors over the centuries, including Galileo, who came here to conduct experiments on falling objects. Recent engineering work has reduced the tower's tilt to approximately 4.12 m (13.5 ft).

The graceful **Baptistry** was begun in 1152 and finished a century later by Nicola and Giovanni Pisano.

The **Museo Nazionale di San Matteo** holds Pisan and Florentine art from the 12th to the 17th centuries. Major 15th-century works include Masaccio's *St. Paul*, Gentile da Fabriano's radiant *Madonna of Humility*, and Donatello's reliquary bust of *San Rossore*.

🏛 **Museo Nazionale di San Matteo**
Piazza San Matteo 1. **Tel** 050-54 18 65. ◐ Tue–Sun. ● Sun pm. 🎫

Lucca ❽

🏛 85,000. 🚉 🚌 ℹ Piazza Santa Maria 35 (0583-91 99 31). 🎪 Wed, Sat, 3rd Sun of month (antiques).

The city of Lucca is still enclosed within its 17th-century walls, and visitors can stroll along the ramparts, which were converted into a public park in the early 19th century. Within the walls, narrow lanes wind among dark medieval buildings, opening suddenly to reveal stunning churches and piazzas, including the vast Piazza del Anfiteatro, which traces the outline of the old Roman amphitheater. The finest of the churches are all Romanesque: **San Martino**, the 11th-century cathedral, **San Michele in Foro**, built on the sight of the old Roman forum, and **San Frediano**.

The Baptistry in front of Pisa's Duomo, with the Leaning Tower behind

Florence ❻

Florence is a monument to the Renaissance, the
artistic and cultural reawakening of the 15th century.
The buildings of Brunelleschi and the paintings and
sculptures of artists such as Botticelli and
Michelangelo turned the city into one of the world's
greatest artistic capitals. During this time Florence
was at the cultural and intellectual heart of Europe,
its cosmopolitan atmosphere and wealthy patrons,
such as the Medici, providing the impetus for a
period of unparalleled artistic growth. The legacy of
the Renaissance draws many visitors to the city
today, with its numerous museums, galleries,
churches, and monuments the major attractions.
Florence's best sights are encompassed within
such a compact area that the city seems to reveal
its treasures at every step.

SIGHTS AT A GLANCE

Bargello ⑥
Boboli Gardens ⑭
Duomo pp416–17 ①
Galleria dell'Accademia ④
Museo di Storia
 della Scienza ⑩
Palazzo Pitti ⑬
Palazzo Vecchio ⑨
Piazza della Signoria ⑧
Ponte Vecchio ⑫
San Lorenzo ②
San Marco ⑤
Santa Croce ⑦
Santa Maria Novella ③
Uffizi pp422–4 ⑪

Michelangelo's *David* in
the Galleria dell'Accademia

VIA PIER ANTONIO MICHELI

VIA GIORGIO LA PIRA

GIARDINO DEI SEMPLICI

⑤

VIA DEGLI ARAZZIERI

PIAZZA DI SAN MARCO

Convento di Sant' Apollonia

VIA CAVOUR

VIA CESARE BATTISTI

VIA GINO CAPPONI

VIA GIUSEPPE GIUSTI

Santissima Annunziata

④

PIAZZA DELLA SANTISSIMA ANNUNZIATA

Museo Archeologico

VIA DELLA COLONNA

alazzo edici cardi

V. DE' MARTELLI

VIA

DEGLI

VIA DEI SERVI

Palazzo Pucci

PIAZZA FILIPPO BRUNELLESCHI

Spedale degli Innocenti

BORGO PINTI

ALFANI

VIA DE' PUCCI

VIA MAURIZIO BUFALINI

VIA DELL'ORIUOLO

V.S. EGIDIO

①

PIAZZA DEL DUOMO

Museo di Firenze com'era

VIA DELL'OCHE

VIA DEL PROCONSOLO

Palazzo Nonfinito

VIA DEL CORSO

BORGO DEGLI ALBIZI

PIAZZA GAETANO SALVEMINI

VIA DEI TAVOLINI

V. DANTE ALIGHIERI

V. D. CONDOTTA

⑥

PIAZZA DI SAN FIRENZE

VIA GIUSEPPE VERDI

Casa Buonarroti

GHIBELLINA

AZZA DELLA SIGNORIA

⑨

VIA DE' BENCI

PIAZZA DI SANTA CROCE

L-GO PIERO BARGELLINI

VIA DEL CASTELLANI

⑪

⑩

PIAZZA DE' PERUZZI

PIAZZA DI S. REMIGIO

⑦

V. D. S. GIUSEPPE

PIAZZA MENTANA

LUNG. GEN. DIAZ

Arno

PIAZZA DEI CAVALLEGGERI

LUNG. DELLE GRAZIE

Ponte alle Grazie

LUNG. TORRIGIANI

ARDI

LUNG. SERRISTORI

PIAZZA DE' MOZZI

PIAZZA DEMIDOFF

V. D. S. NICCOLÒ

PORTA SAN NICCOLO

GIORGIO

Palazzo de' Mozzi

PIAZZA GIUSEPPE POGGI

The dome of the cathedral, or Duomo, Florence's greatest landmark

KEY

▢ Sight / Place of interest

🚇 Train station

🚏 Bus stop

🚊 Tram stop

🅿 Parking

ℹ Tourist information

✛ Church

▬ Pedestrian street

▬ City walls

SEE ALSO

• *Where to Stay* pp457–8

• *Where to Eat* pp463–4

0 meters   300

0 yards   300

GETTING AROUND

Buses in Florence are bright orange; most can be picked up at Santa Maria Novella station. Lines run until at least 9:30pm, the most popular until midnight or 1am. Information about routes can be found on www.ataf.net. Official taxis are white, and are generally costly. What with one-way systems, erratic drivers, and limited traffic zones – where only authorized vehicles are permitted to go – driving is not recommended. Walking is easily the most enjoyable way to get around the city.

Duomo ①

See pp416–17.

San Lorenzo ②

Piazza di San Lorenzo. 🚌 *many routes.*
Basilica *Tel* 055-21 40 42. 🕐 *Mon–*
Sat. ● *religious hols.* 📷 **Biblioteca**
Tel 055-21 07 60. 🕐 *am Mon–Sat.*
● *public hols.* **Cappelle Medicee**
Piazza di Madonna degli Aldobrandini.
Tel 055-238 86 02. 🕐 *daily (to*
4:20pm). ● *alternate Mon & Sun of*
month, Jan 1, May 1 & Dec 25. 📷 &

San Lorenzo was the parish
church of the Medici family,
who lavished their wealth on
its adornment. Rebuilt in
Renaissance Classical style in
1419, the outer facade was
never completed.

The inner facade of the
Basilica was designed by
Michelangelo. Cosimo il
Vecchio, founder of the Medici
dynasty, is buried under a
stone slab before the High
Altar. The bronze pulpits in
the nave are Donatello's last
works. Opposite is Bronzino's
vast fresco of the human form
in various poses (1659).

The **Biblioteca Mediceo-
Laurenzia**, which housed the
family's manuscripts, has an
elaborate sandstone staircase,
desks, and ceilings designed
by Michelangelo in 1524.

The **Cappelle Medicee**
incorporate three sacristies
which epitomize different
periods of art. Donatello's
decoration of the Old
Sacristy contrasts
with the design
of the New
Sacristy

Detail from Donatello pulpit, San Lorenzo

Facade of Santa Maria Novella, redesigned by Alberti in 1456–70

by Michelangelo. The latter's
funerary figures (1520–34)
around its walls are among
his greatest works. The
Chapel of the Princes (1604)
is opulently decorated with
inlaid semiprecious stones
and bright frescoes. Six Grand
Dukes of the Medici family
are buried here.

Santa Maria Novella ③

Piazza di Santa Maria Novella. 🚌
many routes. & **Church** *Tel* 055-21
92 57. 🕐 *daily (pm only Fri–Sun &*
religious hols). 📷 **Museum** *Tel* 055-
28 21 87. 🕐 *9am–5pm Mon–Thu, Sat.*
● *Jan 1, Easter Sun, May 1.* 📷 &

The Gothic church of Santa
Maria Novella, built by the
Dominicans between 1279 and
1357, contains some of the
most important works of art in
Florence. The interior displays
a number of superb
frescoes, including
Masaccio's *Trinity*
(c.1428), which is
renowned as a master-
piece of perspective
and portraiture. The
close spacing of the
nave piers at the east
end accentuates the
illusion of length. The
Tornabuoni Chapel
contains Ghirlandaio's
famous fresco cycle,
*The Life of John the
Baptist* (1485). In the
Filippo Strozzi Chapel,
Lippi's dramatic frescoes

show St. John raising Drusiana
from the dead and St. Philip
slaying a dragon. Boccaccio
set the beginning of *The
Decameron* in this chapel.
The Strozzi Tomb (1493)
is by Florentine sculptor
Benedetto da Maiano.

The 14th-century frescoes
in the Strozzi Chapel are by
two brothers (Nardo di Cione
and Andrea Orcagna) and
were inspired by Dante's
Divine Comedy.

Beside the church is a
walled cemetery with grave
niches. The cloisters on the
other side of the church form
a museum. The Green
Cloister's name derives from
the green tinge to Uccello's
Noah and the Flood frescoes,
damaged by the 1966 floods.
The adjoining Spanish
Chapel contains frescoes
on the theme of salvation
and damnation.

Galleria dell'Accademia ④

Via Ricasoli 60. 🚌 *many routes.*
Tel 055-29 48 83 *(bookings).*
🕐 *Tue–Sun.* ● *Mon & public hols.*
📷 & www.polomuseale.firenze.it

The Academy of Fine Arts in
Florence, founded in 1563,
was the first school in Europe
set up to teach drawing,
painting, and sculpture.

Since 1873, many of Michelangelo's most important works
have been in the Accademia.
Perhaps the most famous of

all dominates the collection: Michelangelo's *David* (1504). This colossal nude depicts the biblical hero who killed the giant Goliath; it established Michelangelo, then aged 29, as the foremost sculptor of his time. The statue was moved here from the Palazzo Vecchio in 1873 to protect it from the elements.

Michelangelo's other masterpieces include a statue of St. Matthew finished in 1508, and the *Quattro Prigioni* (four prisons), sculpted between 1521 and 1523. The muscular figures struggling to free themselves from the stone are among the most dramatic of his works.

The gallery contains an important collection of paintings by 15th- and 16th-century Florentine artists, and many major works including the *Madonna del Mare* attributed to Botticelli (1445–1510), Pacino di Bonaguida's *Tree of Life* (1310), and *Venus and Cupid* by Jacopo Pontormo (1494–1556). Also on display is an elaborately painted wooden chest, the *Cassone Adimari* (c.1440) by Lo Scheggia. It was originally used as part of a bride's trousseau, and is covered with details of Florentine daily life, clothing, and architecture.

The Salone della Toscana (Tuscany Room) exhibits more modest 19th-century sculpture and paintings by members of the Accademia.

Fra Angelico's *Annunciation*, in the monastery of San Marco

San Marco ⑤

Piazza di San Marco. 🚌 *many routes.*
🚾 *partial.* **Church** ◯ *daily.*
Museum Tel *055-23 88 608.*
◯ *Mon–Fri: am only, Sat: am & pm.*
⬤ *Jan 1, May 1, Dec 25, 2nd & 4th Mon and 1st, 3rd, & 5th Sun each month.* 🎟 🚾

The church of San Marco, and the monastery built around it, date from the 13th century. Following the transfer of the site to the Dominicans of Fiesole by Pope Eugene IV in 1436, Cosimo il Vecchio paid a considerable sum for its reconstruction, overseen by his favorite architect, Michelozzo. The single-naved church holds valuable works of art, and the funerary chapel of St. Anthony is considered Giambologna's main work of architecture.

To the right of the church, the oldest part of the monastery is now a museum. It contains a remarkable series of devotional frescoes by Fra Angelico. The former Pilgrims' Hospice houses *The Deposition* (1435–40), a poignant scene of the dead Christ; his *Crucifixion* (1441–2) can be seen in the Chapter House.

There are over 40 cells adorned with frescoes by Fra Angelico. *The Annunciation* (c.1445) demonstrates his mastery of perspective. Relics of the fiery orator Savonarola (1452–98), dragged from here and executed in Piazza della Signoria, are also on display.

The monastery houses Europe's first public library, designed by Michelozzo in a light and airy colonnaded hall. Valuable manuscripts and bibles are held here.

A scene from Lo Scheggia's *Cassone Adimari* in the Galleria dell'Accademia

Duomo ①

Set in the heart of Florence, Santa Maria del Fiore – the Duomo, or cathedral, of Florence – dominates the city with its enormous dome. Its sheer size was typical of Florentine determination to lead in all things, and to this day, no other building stands taller in the city. The Baptistry, with its celebrated doors, is one of Florence's oldest buildings, dating perhaps from the 4th century. In his capacity as city architect, Giotto designed the Campanile in 1334; it was completed in 1359, 22 years after his death.

★ Campanile
At 85 m (276 ft), the Campanile is 6 m (20 ft) shorter than the dome. It is clad in white, green and pink Tuscan marble. The first-floor reliefs are by Andrea Pisano.

Gothic windows

The Neo-Gothic marble façade echoes the style of Giotto's campanile, but was only added in 1871–87.

★ Baptistry
Colorful 13th-century mosaics illustrating The Last Judgment *decorate the ceiling above the large octagonal font where many famous Florentines, including Dante, were baptized.*

The Baptistry doors demonstrate the artistic ideas that led to the Renaissance.

Main entrance

The east doors known as the "Gate of Paradise" (1424–52) were made by Ghiberti. The originals are in the Duomo museum.

STAR FEATURES

- ★ Dome
- ★ Baptistry
- ★ Campanile

South Door Panels
This scene from the south doors of the Baptistry, completed by the sculptor Andrea Pisano in 1336, depicts The Baptism of St. John the Baptist.

For hotels and restaurants in this region see pp457–8 and pp463–4

★ **Dome**
*Brunelleschi's revolutionary
achievement was to build the
largest dome of its time without
scaffolding. As you climb the
463 steps to the top, you can
see how an inner shell provides a platform for the
timbers that support
the outer shell.*

**he top of the
ome** offers
pectacular views
ver the city.

Last Judgment
**frescoes by
Vasari**

Bricks of varying size
were set in a self-
supporting herringbone
pattern – a technique
Brunelleschi copied
from the Pantheon
in Rome.

VISITORS' CHECKLIST

Piazza del Duomo. **Tel** 055-230
28 85. 🚌 1, 6, 14, 17, 23.
🔵 Mon– Sat, Sun pm. 🔵
religious hols. 🔵 **Crypt** 🔵
Mon–Sat. 🈂 **Dome** 🔵
Mon–Sat. 🈂 **Campanile**
🔵 daily. 🈂 **Baptistry** 🔵 pm
Mon–Sat; Sun am. All buildings
🔵 Jan 1 & religious hols. 🈂
www.duomofirenze.it

Chapels at the East End
*The three apses each house
five chapels and are
crowned by a miniature
copy of the dome. The
15th-century stained glass
is by Lorenzo Ghiberti
and other artists.*

**The octagonal marble
sanctuary** around the
High Altar was decorated
by Baccio Bandinelli.

**Entrance
to steps to
the dome**

Marble Pavement
*As you climb up to the dome,
you can see that the 16th-century
marble pavement, designed in part by
Baccio d'Agnelo, is laid out as a maze.*

Steps to Santa Reparata
*The crypt contains the remains of the church
of Santa Reparata, built in the 4th century,
and demolished in 1296 to make way for a
cathedral which would more fittingly represent
Florence and rival those of Siena and Pisa.*

Bargello ⑥

Via del Proconsolo 4. **Tel** 055-29 48
83. 🚌 A, 14. 🕒 8:15am–6:50pm
daily. 🔴 1st, 3rd & 5th Sun and 2nd
& 4th Mon of each month, Jan 1,
May 1, Dec 25. 🎫 ♿

Florence's second-ranking
museum after the Uffizi, the
Bargello houses Italy's finest
collection of Renaissance
sculpture and some superb
Mannerist bronzes. Begun in
1255, the fortress-like building
was initially the town hall but
later home to the chief of
police (the *Bargello*). The
renovated building opened as
one of Italy's first national
museums in 1865.

The key exhibits range over
three floors, beginning with
the Michelangelo Room. Here
visitors can admire *Bacchus*
(1497), the sculptor's first
large free-standing work, a
delicate circular relief
depicting the
*Madonna and
Child* (1503–5),
and *Brutus*
(1539–40), his
only known
portrait bust.
Among other
sculptors' works
in the same room is
Mercury (1564),
Giambologna's
famous bronze.
Across the
courtyard, two
more rooms
contain exterior
sculptures
removed from
sites around
the city and
an external
staircase leads to a first-floor
collection of bronze birds by
Giambologna. To the right,
the Salone del Consiglio
Generale contains the cream
of the museum's Early Renaissance sculpture, including
Donatello's heroic *St George*
(1416) and his androgynous
David (c.1430). Restored in
2008, it is famous as the first
free-standing nude by a
Western artist since antiquity.

Beyond the Salone, the
Bargello's emphasis shifts to
the applied arts, with room
after room devoted to rugs,
ceramics, silverware, and

Gaddi's night scene fresco in the
Baroncelli Chapel, Santa Croce

other *objets d'art*. The Salone
del Camino on the second
floor holds the finest collection
of small bronzes in Italy.
Benvenuto Cellini (1500–71)
is among the artists featured.

Santa Croce ⑦

Piazza di Santa Croce. **Tel** 055-246
61 05. 🚌 C, 14, 23. 🕒 daily (Sun:
pm only). 🎫 ♿

The Gothic church of Santa
Croce (1294) contains the
tombs and monuments of
many famous Florentines,
among them Galileo,
Michelangelo, and
Machiavelli, as well as
radiant early 14th-
century frescoes by
Giotto and his gifted
pupil, Taddeo Gaddi.
In 1842 the Neo-Gothic
campanile of Santa
Croce was added,
and the facade in 1863.

In the Basilica,
Rossellino's effigy
(1447) of Leonardo
Bruni, the great
Humanist depicted in
serene old age, is a
triumph of realistic
portraiture. Close by it
is the 15th-century
Annunciation by
Donatello. The
remainder of the
monastic buildings
scattered around the
cloister form a museum
of religious painting
and sculpture.

The museum houses
Cimabue's *Crucifixion*, a
13th-century masterpiece
damaged in the flood of 1966,
and Gaddi's magnificent *Last
Supper* (c.1355–60).

Of the church's many
chapels, the most famous is
the Bardi Chapel, decorated
by Giotto with frescoes of the
life of St. Francis (1315–23).
The Peruzzi Chapel houses
further Giotto frescoes. Gaddi's
1338 fresco in the Baroncelli
Chapel of an angel appearing
to sleeping shepherds is
notable as the first true night
scene in Western art.

In the cloister alongside
the church is Brunelleschi's
Cappella de' Pazzi (Pazzi
Chapel), a masterpiece of
Renaissance architecture. The
delicate gray stonework of
the domed chapel is set off
by white plaster, which is
inset with terra-cotta roundels
of the Evangelists by Luca
della Robbia.

Piazza della Signoria ⑧

🚌 A, B.

Piazza della Signoria has been
at the heart of Florence's
political and social life for
centuries. Citizens were once
summoned to public meetings
here, and the square's statues

Statue of Cosimo I in Piazza della Signoria

**Donatello's
statue of *David*
in the Bargello**

celebrate events in the city's
history. That of Grand Duke
Cosimo I (1595) by
Giambologna commemorates
the man who subjugated all
Tuscany, while Ammannati's
Neptune Fountain honors
Tuscan naval victories.
Michelangelo's original *David*
stood here until 1873, when it
was replaced by a copy.
Donatello's original statue of
the heraldic lion of Florence,
known as the *Marzocco*, is
now in the Bargello.

Other notable statues
include Cellini's bronze
Perseus, and *The Rape of the
Sabine Women* by
Giambologna, carved from a
single block of marble.

Painting of Penelope in Eleonora's rooms in the Palazzo Vecchio

The Putto fountain in Vasari's
courtyard, at the Palazzo Vecchio

Palazzo Vecchio ⑨

Piazza della Signoria. **Tel** 055-276 82
24. 🚌 A, B. 🔲 daily (Thu: am only).
🗓 ♿

Palazzo Vecchio, completed
in 1322, has retained its
external medieval appearance,
and its imposing bell tower
dominates the square. The
"Old Palace" still fulfils its
original role as Florence's
own hall. Much of the interior
was remodeled for Duke
Cosimo I in the mid-16th
century by Vasari, whose work
includes several frescoes that
laud the Duke's achievements.

The palazzo is entered via
a courtyard, in which stands
Verrochio's *Putto* fountain.
A staircase leads to the Salone
dei Cinquecento, which is
graced by Michelangelo's
Victory statue (1525), and

to the tiny Studiolo decorated
by 30 of Florence's leading
Mannerist painters.

Eleonora of Toledo, wife of
Cosimo I, had a suite of rooms
in the palace, decorated with
scenes of virtuous women.
Highlights of the palace include
the paintings by Il Bronzino in
the Cappella di Eleonora and
the loggia, which has wonderful
views over the city. The Sala
dei Gigli (Room of Lilies),
contains frescoes of Roman
heroes and Donatello's *Judith
and Holofernes*.

There is also a Children's
Museum, with story-telling
sessions and tours in various
languages. One tour takes in
formerly secret stairways,
hidden passages, and attics.

Museo di Storia
della Scienza ⑩

Piazza de' Giudici 1. **Tel** 055-26 53
11. 🔲 9:30am–6pm Mon–Sat (to
1pm Tue). ● public hols. 🎫
www.imss.fi.it

This lively museum
devotes numerous
rooms on two floors
to different scientific
themes, illustrat-
ing each with fine
displays and beau-
tifully made early
scientific instru-
ments. It is also
something of a shrine
to the Pisa-born
scientist, Galileo Galilei
(1564–1642), and features
two of his telescopes as
well as large-scale
reconstructions of his
experiments into motion,
weight, velocity, and

acceleration. These are
sometimes demonstrated by
the attendants. Other exhibits
come from the Accademia
del Cimento (Academy for
Experimentation), founded in
memory of Galileo by Grand
Duke Ferdinand II in 1657.

Some of the finest exhibits
include early maps, antique
microscopes, astrolabes, and
barometers. Of equal interest
are the huge 16th- and 17th-
century globes illustrating the
motion of the planets and
stars. Be sure to see Lopo
Homem's 16th-century map of
the world, showing the newly
charted coasts of the Americas,
and the nautical instruments
invented by Sir Robert Dudley,
an Elizabethan marine engineer
employed by the Medicis.

The second-floor rooms
display fine old clocks,
calculators, a horrifying
collection of 19th-century
surgical instruments, weights
and measures, and graphic
anatomical models.

Armillary sphere, Museo di
Storia della Scienza

The Florentine Renaissance

Fifteenth-century Italy saw a flowering of the arts and scholarship unmatched in Europe since Ancient Greek and Roman times. It was in wealthy Florence that this artistic and intellectual activity, later dubbed the Renaissance, was at its most intense. The patronage of the rich banking dynasty, the Medici, rulers of Florence from 1434, was lavished on the city, especially under Lorenzo the Magnificent (1469–92), and the city aspired to become the new Rome. Architects turned to Classical models for inspiration, while the art world, with a new understanding of perspective and anatomy, produced a series of painters and sculptors that included such giants as Donatello, Botticelli, Leonardo da Vinci, and Michelangelo.

ITALY IN 1492

☐ *Republic of Florence*

☐ *Papal States*

☐ *Aragonese possessions*

THE PROCESSION OF THE MAGI

Benozzo Gozzoli's fresco (1459) in the Palazzo Medici-Riccardi, Florence, depicts members of the Medici family and other contemporary notables. It contains references to the church council held in Florence in 1439, which, it was hoped, would effect a reconciliation between the Church of Rome and the Eastern Church.

Giuliano was the younger son of Piero de' Medici.

Piero de' Medici, Lorenzo' father, was given the nickname "the Gouty."

Self-portrait of the artist

Pope Leo X
There were two Medici popes: Giovanni, who reigned as Leo X (1513–21), and Giulio, who took his place as Clement VII (1521–34). Corruption in the church under Leo inspired Luther and the growth of Protestantism.

TIMELINE

1420 Martin V re-establishes papacy in Rome

1434 Cosimo de' Medici comes to power in Florence

Cosimo de' Medici

1435 Publication of *On Painting* by Alberti, which contains the first system for the use of linear perspective

1436 Brunelleschi completes dome of Florence cathedral

1425

1452 Birth of Leonardo da Vinci

1453 Fall of Constantinople

1450

1464 Death of Cosimo il Vecchio

1469 Lore the Magnifi becomes r of Flore

Michelangelo's Sculpture

The Quattro Prigioni *(see p415), unfinished works intended for the tomb of Pope Julius II, illustrate Michelangelo's ideal of liberating "the figure imprisoned in the marble."*

Filippo Brunelleschi

In order to realize his design for the dome of Florence's cathedral, Brunelleschi devised engineering techniques decades ahead of their time.

Lorenzo de' Medici (the Magnificent) is depicted as one of the three kings traveling to Bethlehem.

The Medici emblem of seven balls appears on the trappings of Lorenzo's horse.

RENAISSANCE ARCHITECTURE

In place of the spectacular Gothic style, Renaissance architects favored the rational, orderly, human scale of Greek and Roman buildings. The various stories of a palazzo were designed according to Classical proportions and there was a widespread revival in the use of Roman arches and the Doric, Ionic, and Corinthian orders of columns.

Palazzo Strozzi *(1489–1536) is a typical Florentine building of the period. Rusticated stonework gives an impression of great strength. Decorative detail is largely on the upper stories above the fortress-like ground floor.*

The Spedale degli Innocenti, *an orphanage, was one of Brunelleschi's first buildings in Florence. Slender Corinthian columns support a delicate arcade.*

Humanism

Carpaccio's painting St. Augustine in his Study *(1502) is thought to show Cardinal Bessarion (c.1395–1472), one of the scholars who revived interest in Classical philosophy, especially Plato.*

1498 Savonarola executed; Machiavelli crowned secretary to ruling Council in Florence

1513 Giovanni de' Medici crowned Pope Leo X

1532 Machiavelli's book *The Prince* is published, five years after his death

1530 Medici restored as rulers of Florence

1500   **1525**

1494 Italy invaded by Charles VIII of France. Florence declared republic under leadership of the religious fanatic Savonarola

1512 Michelangelo completes Sistine Chapel ceiling

5 Birth of ...elangelo

1483 Birth of Raphael

Niccolò Machiavelli

Uffizi ⑪

The Uffizi was built in 1560–80 as a suite of offices *(uffici)* for Duke Cosimo I's new Tuscan administration. The architect, Vasari, used iron reinforcement to create an almost continuous wall of glass on the upper story. From 1581 Cosimo's heirs, beginning with Francesco I, used this well-lit space to display the Medici family art treasures, thus creating what is now the oldest art gallery in the world.

The Vasari Corridor leads to the Palaz Vecchio.

Main staircase

Entrance Hall

Entrance

The café terrace merits a visit for its unusual views of Piazza della Signoria *(see pp418–19).*

Bar

Corridor ceilings are frescoed in the "grotesque" style of the 1580s, inspired by Roman grottoes.

GALLERY GUIDE

The Uffizi art collection is housed on the top floor. Ancient Greek and Roman sculptures are displayed in the corridor running round the inner side of the building. The paintings are hung in a series of rooms off the main corridor, in chronological order, to reveal the development of Florentine art from Gothic to High Renaissance and beyond. Most of the best-known paintings are grouped in rooms 7–18. To avoid the long queues, book your visiting time in advance.

The Ognissanti Madonna
Giotto's grasp of spatial depth in this altarpiece (1310) was a milestone in the mastery of perspective.

Buontalenti staircase

Entrance to the Vasari Corridor

STAR PAINTINGS

* ★ The Duke and Duchess of Urbino by Piero della Francesca

* ★ The Birth of Venus by Botticelli

* ★ The Holy Family by Michelangelo

* ★ The Venus of Urbino by Titian

★ The Venus of Urbino *(1538)*
Titian's sensuous nude was condemned for portraying the goddess in such an immodest pose.

★ **The Duke and Duchess of Urbino** *(1460)*
*Piero della Francesca's panels are among the first
true Renaissance portraits. He even recorded the
Duke's hooked nose – broken by a sword blow.*

VISITORS' CHECKLIST

Piazzale degli Uffizi 6.
Tel 055-29 48 83). B, 23.
8:15am–6:50pm Tue–Sun
(last adm: 45 mins before
closing). Jan 1, May 1, Dec
25. (partial)
www.polomuseale.firenze.it

KEY

☐ East Corridor

☐ West Corridor

☐ Arno Corridor

☐ Gallery Rooms 1–45

☐ Non-exhibition space

The Tribune,
decorated in
red and gold,
contains the
works that
the Medici
valued most.

★ **The Birth of Venus** *(1485)*
*Botticelli's captivating image shows the Roman
goddess of love, born in a storm in the Aegean sea.
She is blown ashore by the winds and greeted by
nymphs, ready to wrap her in a cloak.*

**Adoration of the
Magi** *(c.1481)*
*Although Leonardo
da Vinci did not
finish this painting
of the wise men
worshipping the
baby Jesus, it is
considered to be one
of his most important
early works.*

**Vasari's
Classical
Arno
facade**

★ **The Holy Family** *(1507)*
*Michelangelo's painting, the first to break
with the convention of showing Christ on
the Virgin's lap, inspired subsequent
Mannerist artists through its expressive
handling of color and posture.*

Exploring the Uffizi's Collection

The Uffizi houses some of the greatest art of the Renaissance. Accumulated over the centuries by the Medici, the collection was first housed in the Uffizi in 1581, and eventually bequeathed to the people of Florence by Anna Maria Lodovica, the last of the Medici (1667–1743). Roman statues collected by the Medici are on display in the Arno Corridor, but the pride of the gallery is its matchless collection of paintings.

GOTHIC ART

Following the collection of statues and antiquities in room 1, the gallery's next six rooms are devoted to Tuscan art from the 12th to the 14th centuries, notably works by Cimabue, Duccio, and Giotto, the three greatest artists of this period. Giotto (1266–1337) introduced a degree of naturalism new to Tuscan art. This is apparent in the range of emotions expressed by the angels and saints in his *Ognissanti Madonna* (1310). There are also fine works by Ambrogio and Pietro Lorenzetti, and Simone Martini of the Sienese School.

EARLY RENAISSANCE

A better understanding of geometry and perspective allowed Renaissance artists to create an illusion of space and depth in their works. No artist was more obsessed with perspective than Paolo Uccello

(1397–1475), whose *Battle of San Romano* is displayed in room 7. Portraits include two panels by Piero della Francesca (1410–92), depicting the Duke and Duchess of Urbino, while Fra Filippo Lippi's *Madonna and Child with Angels* (1455–66) is a work of great warmth and humanity.

For most visitors, however, the famous Botticellis in rooms 10–14 are the highlight of the gallery. In *The Birth of Venus*, Botticelli replaces the Virgin with the Classical goddess of love, while in *Primavera* (1480), he breaks with Christian religious painting to depict the pagan rite of spring.

HIGH RENAISSANCE AND MANNERISM

Room 15 contains works attributed to the young Leonardo da Vinci. The evolution of his masterly style can be traced in *The Annunciation* (1472–5) and his unfinished *Adoration of the Magi* (1481). The octagonal Tribune (room 18) displays some of the best-loved pieces of the Medici collection, including the 1st century BC *Medici Venus*, considered the most erotic of ancient statues. There are also paintings of family members, including Bronzino's fine portrait of Eleonora of Toledo, Cosimo I's wife (1545).

Rooms 19 to 23 illustrate the spread of Renaissance ideas and techniques beyond Florence to other parts of Italy and beyond. The Umbrian artist Perugino (1446–1523)

Madonna of the Long Neck by Parmigianino (c.1534)

and northern European painters such as Dürer (1471–1528) are well represented.

Michelangelo's *Holy Family* (1507), in Room 25, is striking for its vibrant colors and the curious twisted pose of the Virgin. This painting had great influence on the next generation of Tuscan painters, notably Bronzino (1503–72), Pontormo (1494–1556), and Parmigianino (1503–40), whose *Madonna of the Long Neck* with its contorted anatomy and unusual colors is a classic example of what came to be known as Mannerism.

Sublime examples of High Renaissance art located nearby include Raphael's *Madonna of the Goldfinch* and Titian's notorious *Venus of Urbino* (1538), considered by many to be the most beautiful nude ever painted.

LATER PAINTINGS

Rooms 41–45 of the Uffizi hold paintings acquired by the Medici in the 17th and 18th centuries. These include works by Rubens (1577–1640). Three paintings by Caravaggio – *Bacchus* (c.1589), *The Sacrifice of Isaac* (c.1590), and *Medusa* (1596–8) are in the Sala del Caravaggio. Room 44 is dedicated to northern European painting, and features *Portrait of an Old Man* (1665) by Rembrandt.

Madonna of the Goldfinch (1506) by Raphael

Ponte Vecchio ⑫

🚌 *many routes.*

The Ponte Vecchio, the oldest surviving bridge in the city, was designed by Taddeo Gaddi, and built in 1345. The three-arched bridge rests on two stout piers with boat-shaped cutwaters. Its picturesque shops were originally occupied by black-smiths, butchers, and tanners (who used the river as a convenient garbage dump). They were evicted in 1593 by Duke Ferdinando I and replaced by jewelers and goldsmiths who were able to pay higher rents. A bust of the most famous of Florence's goldsmiths, Benvenuto Cellini (1500–71), is located in the middle of the bridge.

The elevated Vasari Corridor runs along the eastern side of the bridge, above the shops. It was designed in 1565 to allow the Medici to move from the Palazzo Vecchio to Palazzo Pitti via the Uffizi, without having to mix with the public. The Mannelli family refused to demolish their tower to make way for the corridor, and it stands there defiantly to this day. The corridor passes around it, supported on brackets.

The "Old Bridge," at its most attractive when viewed at sunset, was the only one to escape destruction during World War II. Visitors today come to admire the views and to browse among the antiques and specialized jewelry shops.

The massive Renaissance Palazzo Pitti, home to several museums

Palazzo Pitti ⑬

Piazza Pitti. 🚌 *D, 11, 36, 37.* **Tel** *055-29 48 83.* ⏰ *8:15am–6:50pm Tue–Sun.* 🚫 *public hols.* 📷 ♿

Palazzo Pitti was originally built for the banker Luca Pitti, but his attempt to outrival the Medici backfired when costs of the building, begun in 1457, bankrupted his heirs. The Medici moved in and subsequent rulers of the city lived here. Today the richly decorated rooms exhibit many treasures from the Medici collections.

The Palatine Gallery contains numerous works of art and ceiling frescoes glorifying the Medici. Raphael's *Madonna della Seggiola* (c.1515) and Titian's *Portrait of a Gentleman* (1540) are among the exhibits.

On the first floor of the south wing, the royal apartments – Appartamenti Reali – are opulently decorated with ornate gold and white stuccoed ceilings. The rooms are hung with portraits of the Medici family and decorated with beautiful frescoes and Gobelins tapestries.

Other collections at the Palazzo include the Galleria d'Arte Moderna, with mainly 19th-century works of art, the Galleria del Costume, opened in 1983, which reflects changing taste in courtly fashions, and the Museo degli Argenti which displays the family's lavish tastes in silverware and furniture.

L'Isolotto with Giambologna's *Oceanus Fountain*, **Boboli Gardens**

Boboli Gardens ⑭

Piazza de' Pitti. 🚌 *D, 11, 36, 37.* ⏰ *daily.* 🚫 *1st & last Mon of month, Jan 1, May 1, Dec 25.* 📷 ♿

Laid out behind the Palazzo Pitti, the Boboli Gardens are an excellent example of highly stylized Renaissance gardening. Formal box hedges lead to peaceful groves of holly and cypress trees, inter-spersed with Classical statues.

Highlights include the stone amphitheater where early opera performances were staged and L'Isolotto (Little Island), with its statues of dancing peasants around a moated garden. The Grotta Grande is a Mannerist folly, which houses several statues including *Venus Bathing* (1565) by Giambologna and Vincenzo de' Rossi's *Paris with Helen of Troy* (1560).

View of the Ponte Vecchio and the Arno at sunset

For hotels and restaurants in this region see pp457–8 and pp463–4

Portofino Peninsula ❾

🏠 🚆 ℹ️ *Via Roma 35, Portofino (0185-26 90 24).*
www.terrediportofino.eu

Portofino is the most exclusive harbor and resort town in Italy, crammed with the yachts of the wealthy. Cars are not allowed in the village but boats run regularly between here and the resort of **Santa Margherita Ligure**. Boats also run to the **Abbazia di San Fruttuoso**, an 11th-century abbey situated on the other side of the peninsula.

Further west along the coast is **Punta Chiappa**, a rocky promontory famous for the changing colors of the sea. Other attractive resorts along the Ligurian coast include the fishing village of **Camogli**, **Rapallo** and its patrician villas, and romantic **Portovenere**.

Genoa ❿

🏙️ *660,000.* ✈️ *Cristoforo Colombo 6 km (4 miles) W.* 🚉 🚇 🚌 ℹ️ *Via Garibaldi (010-557 29 03).* 📅 *Mon, Wed, & Thu.* 🎭 *International Ballet Festival (Jul); Fiera Nautica (Oct).*
www.turismoinliguria.it

The most important commercial port in Italy, Genoa (Genova in Italian) also possesses palaces, paintings,

Gothic facade of San Lorenzo, Genoa

and sculptures dotted around the city, which are among the finest in northwestern Italy.

The austere-looking **Palazzo Reale**, one-time residence of the Kings of Savoy, has a highly ornate Rococo interior, a collection of paintings including works by Parodi and van Dyck, and an attractive garden. Opposite the palace is the old **University** (1634), built on four levels and designed by the architect Bartolomeo Bianco.

Palazzo Bianco, on the **Via Garibaldi**, contains the city's prime collection of paintings, including works by Lippi, van Dyck, and Rubens. Across the

street, **Palazzo Rosso** houses works by Dürer and Caravaggio, and 17th-century frescoes by local artists.

Once the seat of the doges of Genoa and now an arts and cultural center, the **Palazzo Ducale** is located between **San Lorenzo** cathedral with its attached museum, and **Il Gesù**, a Baroque church.

All that remains of the Gothic church of **Sant' Agostino**, bombed in World War II, is the bell tower, which is decorated with colored tiles.

Two surviving cloisters of its surrounding monastery have been turned into the **Museo di Sant' Agostino**, which contains the city's collection of sculptural and architectural fragments.

🏛️ **Palazzo Reale**
Via Balbi 10. **Tel** 010-271 02 36.
🕐 Tue–Sun (Tue & Wed am only).
🔴 Jan 1, Apr 25, May 1, Dec 25.
📷 ♿ www.palazzorealegenova.it

🏛️ **Palazzo Bianco**
Via Garibaldi 11. **Tel** 010-557 2193.
🕐 Tue–Sun. 📷 **Palazzo Rosso**
Tel 010-557 49 72. 🕐 Tue–Sun. 📷

🏛️ **Museo di Sant' Agostino**
Piazza Sarzano 35R. **Tel** 010-251 12 63. 🕐 Tue–Sun. 🔴 public hols.
📷 ♿ www.museosantagostino.it

Portofino's famous harbor, showing the large yachts moored here

The Dome of San Lorenzo in Turin

Turin ⓫

🏛 940,000. ✈ Caselle 15 km (9 miles) N. 🚆 🚌 🛈 Piazza Castello (011-53 51 81). 🛍 Sat. 🎉 Festa di San Giovanni (Jun 24).

Home of the Fiat car company, the famous Shroud, and the Juventus football team, Turin (Torino to the Italians) is also a town of grace and charm, with superb Baroque architecture.

Many of Turin's monuments were erected by the House of Savoy (rulers of Piedmont and Sardinia) from their capital here, before Italian unification in 1861 made the head of the House of Savoy King of Italy.

The **Museo Egizio** – one of the world's great collections of Egyptian artifacts – was amassed by Bernardo Drovetti, Napoleon's Consul General in Egypt. Wall and tomb paintings, papyri, sculptures, and a reconstruction of the 15th-century BC **Rock Temple of Ellessya** are among its marvels.

The **Galleria Sabauda**, in the same building, was the House of Savoy's main painting collection, and houses a stunning array of works by Italian, French, Flemish, and Dutch masters.

Other notable buildings include **San Lorenzo**, the former Royal Chapel designed by Guarino Guarini (1624–83), which boasts an extraordinary geometric dome. The **Palazzo Reale**, seat of the Savoys, holds a vast arms collection.

The **Duomo** (1497–8), Turin's cathedral dedicated to St. John the Baptist, is the only example of Renaissance architecture in the city. Inside, the **Cappella della Sacra Sindone**, also designed by Guarini, houses the famous Turin Shroud.

Inside the **Palazzo Madama**, the **Museo Civico d'Arte Antica** contains a variety of Classical and antique treasures. Turin's symbol, the 167-m (547-ft) Mole Antonelliana, hosts the excellent **Museo Nazionale del Cinema**.

🏛 **Museo Egizio**
Via Accademia delle Scienze 6. *Tel* 011-561 77 76. ⭕ Tue–Sun. ⬤ Jan 1, Dec 25. 🔲 ♿ 🅿 www.museoegizio.it

🏛 **Palazzo Reale**
Piazzetta Reale 1. *Tel* 011-436 14 55. ⭕ Tue–Sun. ⬤ Jan 1, May 1, Dec 25. 🔲 🔲 ♿ 🅿

🏛 **Museo Nazionale del Cinema**
Via Montebello 20. *Tel* 011-813 85 60. ⭕ Tue–Sun. ⬤ Jan 1, Dec 25. 🔲 🔲 🅿 www.museocinema.it

The imposing facade of the Baroque Basilica di Superga

Environs

In the countryside near Turin, two superb monuments to the House of Savoy are worth visiting. About 9 km (5 miles) southwest of Turin, **Stupinigi** is a magnificent hunting lodge, sumptuously decorated with frescoes and paintings. It has a vast collection of 17th- and 18th-century furniture.

The Baroque **Basilica di Superga**, on a hill to the east of Turin, offers good views of the city. Its mausoleum commemorates kings of Sardinia and other royals.

🏛 **Stupinigi**
Piazza Principe Amedeo 7. *Tel* 011-358 12 20. 🚌 41. ⬤ closed for restoration until at least 2013. 🔲 ♿

⛪ **Basilica di Superga**
Strada Basilica di Superga 73. *Tel* 011-899 74 56. 🚋 Historic tram from Sassi. ⭕ daily. **Tombs** 🔲 www.basilicadisuperga.com

---

THE TURIN SHROUD

The most famous – and most dubious – holy relic of them all is kept in Turin's Duomo. The shroud, said to be the sheet in which the body of Christ was wrapped after the Crucifixion, bears the imprint of a man with a side wound, and bruises, possibly from a crown of thorns.

The shroud's early history is unclear, but the House of Savoy was in possession of it around 1450, and displayed it in Guarini's chapel in the Duomo from 1694. The shroud sits in a silver casket inside an iron box within a marble coffer. This has been placed inside an urn on the chapel altar. A replica shroud is on view. Tests done in 1988 claiming the shroud to be only a 12th-century relic were discredited by a US scientist in 2005. The shroud may be 1,300–3,000 years old, pending further tests.

The supposed face of Christ imprinted on the Turin Shroud

The giant Gothic Duomo in central Milan, crowned with spires

Milan ⑫

🏃 1,350,000. ✈ Malpensa 55 km (34 miles) NW; Linate 8 km (5 miles) E. 🚉 🚌 ℹ Piazza Duomo 19A (02-77 40 43 43). 🛍 daily, major market Sat. 🎭 Sant'Ambrogio (Dec 7). www.provincia.milano.it/turismo

Center of fashion and business, Milan (Milano in Italian) also has a wealth of impressive sights reflecting its long and checkered history.

An important trading center since it was founded by the Romans in 222 BC, Milan's central position made it a favored location for the empire's rulers. It was here that Emperor Constantine declared that Christianity was officially recognized, following his own conversion (known as the Edict of Milan, AD 313).

By the Middle Ages Milan was one of many cities in Lombardy which opposed the power of the Holy Roman Emperor. A period of local dynastic rule followed the fall of the region to the Visconti family in 1277. They were succeeded by the Sforzas during the Renaissance.

These dynasties became great patrons of the arts, with the result that Milan has acquired a host of artistic treasures. Today this chic, bustling, and prosperous metropolis also offers opportunities for designer shopping and gastronomic pleasures.

Situated at the very heart of Milan, the giant **Duomo** is one of the largest Gothic churches in the world. The roof is extraordinary with 135 spires and innumerable statues and gargoyles. Inside, there are remarkable stained-glass

windows, bas-reliefs, and a medieval treasury. More religious artifacts can usually be seen in the **Museo del Duomo** located in the Palazzo Reale, but it is closed for renovations until 2012.

An ornate shopping arcade completed in 1878, the **Galleria Vittorio Emanuele II** links the Piazza del Duomo with the Piazza della Scala. It boasts a superb metal and glass roof crowned with a central dome, has mosaic floors, and houses stylish shops and restaurants.

The Neo-Classical **Teatro alla Scala** opened in 1778 and is among the most prestigious opera houses in the world. Its stage is one of the largest in Europe. The adjoining **Museo Teatrale** displays past sets and costumes and offers a glimpse of the auditorium.

The **Castello Sforzesco**, a symbol of Milan, was initially the palace of the Visconti family. Francesco Sforza, who became lord of Milan in 1450, embellished it, turning it into a magnificent Renaissance residence. The building has a forbidding exterior, a delightful interior, and contains an impressive collection of furniture, antiquities, and paintings. Michelangelo's unfinished sculpture, known as the *Rondanini Pietà*, can also be seen here.

Milan's finest art collection is held in the imposing 17th-century Palazzo di Brera. Major works of Italian Renaissance and Baroque painters including *The Marriage of the Virgin* by Raphael, and Mantegna's

The glass dome of the Galleria Vittorio Emanuele II in Milan

For hotels and restaurants in this region see pp456–61 and pp462–7

ead Christ, hang in the 38 ooms of the **Pinacoteca di rera**. Works by some of aly's 20th-century artists are so on display.

The beautiful 15th-century enaissance convent of **Santa Maria delle Grazie**, in the outhwest of the city, is a ust-see because it contains ne of the key images of estern civilization: the *Last Supper* (or *Cenacolo*) of eonardo da Vinci. The large all painting has deteriorated adly but remains an iconic ork of great subtlety.

Sant'Ambrogio is a mainly 0th-century Romanesque asilica dedicated to the atron saint of Milan whose omb lies in the crypt. The th-century church of **San orenzo** holds an important ollection of Roman and early hristian remains.

Duomo
azza del Duomo. 🖼 for roof. ♿
Museo del Duomo Tel 02-86 03 58 2. 🔴 for renovation until end 2012.

Castello Sforzesco
azza Castello.
el 02-88 46 37 00. 🔴 Tue–Sun.
🔴 public hols. ♿ limited.

Pinacoteca di Brera
a Brera 28. **Tel** 02-92 80 03 61.
🔴 Tue–Sun. 🔴 Jan 1, May 1, Dec
5. 🖼 🖾 ♿ 📷

Santa Maria delle Grazie
azza Santa Maria delle Grazie 2.
enacolo Tel 02-92 80 03 60.
🔴 Mon–Sat (booking compulsory).
🔴 public hols. 🖼 ♿

ake Maggiore ⑬

🚆 to Stresa and Laveno. 🚌
🚢 Navigazione Lago Maggiore
322-23 32 00). 🏠 Piazza Marconi
, Stresa (0323-301 50).

ke Maggiore is a long
xpanse of water that nestles
ght against the mountains
d stretches away into Alpine
witzerland. In the center lie
e exquisite Borromean
ands named after the chief
atron of the lake, St. Carlo
orromeo, of whom there is a
ant statue in **Arona**.
Further up the western
ast of the lake is **Stresa**, the
ief resort and main
mping-off point for visits to
e islands. From here **Monte**

Statue of Carlo Borromeo, patron saint of Lake Maggiore, in Arona

Mottarone, a snow-capped peak offering spectacular panoramic views, can be reached by cable car.

Lake Como ⑭

🚆 to Como and Lecco. 🚌 🚢
Navigazione Lago di Como (031-57
92 11). 🏠 Piazza Cavour 17, Como
(031-240 111).

Set in an idyllic landscape, Como has long attracted visitors who come to walk in the hills or to go boating. The long, narrow lake, also known as Lario, is shaped like an upside-down Y, and offers fine views of the Alps.

In the heart of the town of **Como** lies the elegant Piazza Cavour. The beautiful 14th-century **Duomo** nearby has 15th- and 16th-century reliefs and paintings, and fine tombs.

Bellagio, at the junction of the "Y," has spectacular views, and is one of the most popular spots on Lake Como.

In the lakeside town of **Tremezzo**, the 18th-century **Villa Carlotta** is adorned with sculptures and celebrated for its terraced gardens.

Lake Garda ⑮

🚆 to Desenzano and Orta San
Giulio. 🚌 🚢 Navigazione Lago di
Garda (030-914 95 11). 🏠 Viale
Marconi 2, Sirmione (030-91 61 14).

Garda, the largest of the northern lakes, borders the three regions of Trentino, Lombardy, and Veneto.

Hydrofoils and catamarans ply the lake, offering stops at **Sirmione**, site of a medieval castle, **Gardone** with the curiosity-filled **Villa il Vittoriale**, and **Salò** where Mussolini established a short-lived Republic in 1943.

Lake Como, one of the most attractive summer resorts of northern Italy

The Arena, Verona's Roman amphitheater – the setting for spectacular summer opera performances

Mantua 🖲

🏠 55,000. 🚇 🚌 ℹ️ *Piazza Andrea Mantegna 6 (0376-43 24 32).* 🗓 *Thu.*

A striking if stern-looking city of fine squares and aristocratic architecture, Mantua (Mantova in Italian) is bordered on three sides by lakes. It was the birthplace of the poet Virgil and playground for three centuries of the Gonzaga dukes. Mantua was also the setting for Verdi's opera *Rigoletto*, and is mentioned in Shakespeare's *Romeo and Juliet*. These theatrical connections are celebrated in local street-names and monuments and are reinforced by the presence in the town of the 18th-century **Teatro Scientifico Bibiena**, a masterpiece of late Baroque theater architecture.

Mantua is focused on three attractive main squares. Piazza Sordello is the site of the **Palazzo Ducale**, the vast former home of the Gonzaga family which also incorporates

a 14th-century fortress and a basilica. The frescoes by Mantegna in the **Camera degli Sposi** (1465–74), are a highlight. They portray the Gonzaga family and court, and the room is completed by a light-hearted *trompe l'oeil* ceiling. The nearby **Duomo** has an 18th-century façade and fine interior stuccoes by Giulio Romano (c.1492–1546).

Piazza dell'Erbe is dominated by the Basilica di Sant' Andrea (15th century), designed largely by the early Renaissance architect and theorist, Alberti.

Across town is the early 16th-century Palazzo del Tè, designed as the Gonzaga family's summer retreat. This extraordinary palace is decorated with frescoes by Giulio Romano and has rooms lavishly painted with horses and signs of the zodiac.

🏛 **Palazzo Ducale**
Piazza Sordello 40. *Tel 0376-22 48 32.* 🕐 *Tue–Sun.* ● *Jan 1, May 1, Dec 25.* 📷 🎫 *(audio).* ♿ **Camera degli Sposi** *Tel 041-241 18 97.* 🕐 *by appointment only.*

Verona 🖲

🏠 261,000. ✈️ *Villafranca 12 km (7 miles) SW.* 🚇 🚌 ℹ️ *Via degli Alpini 9 (045-806 86 80).* 🗓 *daily.* 🎭 *Estate Teatrale Veronese (Jun–Aug); Opera Festival (Jul–Sep).*

Verona, a large and prosperous city of the Veneto region, boasts magnificent Roman ruins, second only to those of Rome itself, as well as some important medieval monuments.

The Arena, Verona's Roman amphitheater completed in AD 30, is the third largest in the world. Concerts, plays, and opera productions are staged here. Other Roman sites include the Roman Theater, and artifacts from Roman times can be seen in the Museo Archeologico.

The tragic story of Romeo and Juliet, first set here by Luigi da Porto in the 1520s and immortalized by Shakespeare, has inspired local monuments such as Romeo's House and the so-called Tomb of Juliet. Verona focal point is Piazza Erbe, scene of colorful markets for 2,000 years.

The ornate tombs of members of the Scaglieri family, who ruled the city for 127 years from 1263, are situated beside the entrance to the church of Santa Maria Antica. Another legacy of the family is Castelvecchio, an impressive castle built by Cangrande II between 1355 and 1375. There is a fine art gallery in the castle, which has a collection of 15th-century late Renaissance Madonnas.

The 13th-century facade of the Palazzo Ducale in Mantua

Built in 1125–35 to house the shrine of Verona's patron saint, **San Zeno Maggiore** is the most ornate Romanesque church in northern Italy, famous for its unusual medieval bronze door panels.

The **Duomo** also dates from the 12th century and displays Titian's *Assumption*. Other notable medieval churches in Verona are **San Fermo Maggiore** with many interior frescoes including the *Annunciation* by Pisanello (1377–1455), and **Sant'Anastasia**, which houses 15th-century frescoes and holy water stoups supported by figures of beggars known locally as *i gobbi*.

The Basilica di Sant'Antonio in Padua, with its Byzantine domes

Arena
Piazza Brà. *Tel 045-800 32 04.*
☐ daily (Mon: pm only). ● Jan 1, Dec 25–26.

Castelvecchio
Corso Castelvecchio 2. *Tel 045-806 26 11.* ☐ daily (Mon: pm only). 🎫 🖼 (audio).

Vicenza ⓭

116,000. 🚊 🚌 🛈 Piazza Matteotti 12 (0444-32 08 54). ● Tue & Thu. 🎵 Concert season (May–Jun).

Vicenza is celebrated for its splendid, varied architecture. Known as the city of Andrea Palladio (1508–80), stonemason turned architect, it offers a unique opportunity to study the evolution of his distinctive style.

Piazza dei Signori at the heart of Vicenza is dominated by the Palazzo della Ragione, known also as the **Basilica**. Palladio's first public

The illusionistic stage set of the Teatro Olimpico in Vicenza

commission, it has a roof like an upturned boat, and a balustrade bristling with statues. Beside it stands the 12th-century **Torre di Piazza**.

The **Loggia del Capitaniato**, to the northwest, was built by Palladio in 1571. Its upper rooms contain the city's council chamber.

Europe's oldest surviving indoor theater, the **Teatro Olimpico** was begun by Palladio in 1579 and completed by his pupil, Vincenzo Scamozzi. It was Scamozzi who created the permanent stage, built largely of wood and plaster and painted to look like marble. It represents Thebes, a Greek city, and uses perspective to create an illusion of depth.

Palladio was also responsible for the design of **Palazzo Chiericati** which houses the **Museo Civico**, but the epitome of his work can be seen in the villa known as **La Rotonda**, located in the countryside to the south of Vicenza.

Memorial to Andrea Palladio in Vicenza

Piazza dei Signori
Basilica *Tel 0444-32 21 96.* ● for restoration until late 2012. 🎫

Teatro Olimpico
Piazza Matteotti. *Tel 0444-32 08 54.* ☐ Tue–Sun. ● Jan 1, Dec 25. 🎫 ♿

La Rotonda
Via Rotonda 45. *Tel 0444-3217 93.* Villa ☐ Mar–Nov: Wed. 🎫 Garden ☐ Tue–Sun. 🎫 ♿

Padua ⓭

220,000. 🚊 🚌 🛈 Vicolo Pedrocchi (049-876 79 27). ● Mon–Sat at Piazza delle Erbe.

Padua is an old university town with an illustrious academic history. The city (Padova in Italian) has two major attractions – the **Basilica di Sant' Antonio**, one of the most popular sites of pilgrimage in Italy, and the **Cappella degli Scrovegni**, a beautifully decorated chapel. The exotic Basilica was built from 1232 to house the remains of the great Franciscan preacher, St. Anthony of Padua.

The chapel (1303) features a series of frescoes depicting the life of Christ, painted by Giotto. The **Museo Civico Eremitani** on the same site has a rich coin collection and an art gallery.

Other attractions include the **Duomo** and **Baptistry**, which contains one of Italy's most complete medieval fresco cycles (painted by Giusto de'Menabuoi in 1378), and the **Palazzo della Ragione**, built in 1218 to serve as Padua's law court and council chamber.

Cappella degli Scrovegni
Piazza Eremitani. *Tel 049-201 00 20.* ☐ daily (advance booking necessary). ● public hols. 🎫 ♿

Venice ⑳

Created on a series of mud banks in a lagoon, with canals in place of roads, Venice can truly claim to be unique. Originally a province of the Byzantine Empire, by the 12th century Venice was an independent city-state and, through its control of the spice and silk trade from the East, the richest trading nation in Europe. The banks of its canals are lined with magnificent palaces dating from this period up until the 18th century. By then Venice's power and influence were waning. It finally lost its independence in 1797, since when this astonishing city has remained more or less frozen in time.

Ponte della Paglia beside the Doge's Palace

SIGHTS AT A GLANCE

Accademia ⑪
Doge's Palace pp436–7 ②
Grand Canal ⑥
Museo Correr ③
Peggy Guggenheim
  Collection ⑩
St. Mark's pp434–5 ①
Santa Maria Gloriosa
  dei Frari ⑤
Santa Maria della Salute ⑨
Santi Giovanni e Paolo ⑦
Scuola di San Giorgio
  degli Schiavoni ⑧
Scuola Grande di
  San Rocco ④

The Lagoon (see inset map)
Murano ⑫

GETTING AROUND

On land, the only way to get around Venice is by foot, and strolling through the city's narrow streets is one its greatest pleasures. By water, the *vaporetto (see p450)* water bus plies the canals of the city and links it to the various lagoon islands. More exotic craft include gondolas, which are very expensive, and the more reasonable *traghetti* (gondola ferries). The speediest means of travel is water taxi.

SEE ALSO

• *Where to Stay* p458

• *Where to Eat* p464

VENICE: THE LAGOON

Treviso
S Dona
Marco Polo
Torcello
Burano
Mestre
Padua
Veneta
Laguna
VENICE
La Giudecca
Lido
0 km 4
0 miles 4

KEY

Area of main map

-- Vaporetto route

Madonna dell'Orto
CAMPIELLO PIAVE
Fondamente Nuove
Ca' Pésaro
Ca' d'Oro
CAMPO S FELICE
Murano, Burano
Fondamente Nuove
CAMPO SANT'ANTONIO
CAMPO DEI GESUITI
CPLO D. PIETA
Ospedale
Ca' d'Oro
CAMPO DEI SANTI APOSTOLI
CPLO DEL CASON
CAMPIELLO WIDMAN
CAMPO S MARIA NOVA
CPLO SANTA MARIA NOVA
Pescheria
CAMPO SAN CASSIANO
Canal Grande
Ponte di Rialto
Fondaco dei Tedeschi
CAMPO SAN MARINA
R di San Marina
CAMPO SAN ZANIPOLO
CAMPO S GIUSTINA
CAMPO DELLA CONFRATERNITA
Rialto
CAMPO SAN SILVESTRO
San Silvestro
CAMPO SAN BARTOLOMEO
CAMPO SAN LIO
CAMPO S MARIA FORMOSA
CAMPO SAN LORENZO
CASTELLO
CORTE TEATRO
CAMPO SAN LUCA
CAMPO D. GUERRA
CAMPO SAN MARINA
SAN MARCO
CAMPO SAN BENETO
CAMPO MANIN
CAMPO SAN PROVOLO
CAMPO SAN ZACCARIA
CAMPO BANDIERA E MORO
CPLO D. PIOVAN
CAMPO SAN ANZOLO
PIAZZA SAN MARCO
CAMPIELLO CALEGHERI
CAMPO SAN MOISE
San Marco Giardinetti
San Zaccaria
CAMPO SAN MAURIZIO
CAMPO DEL TRAGHETTO
San Marco Vallaresso
Santa Maria del Giglio
Salute
Canale di San Marco
Canale di San Marco

KEY

Sight / Place of interest

Airport

Train station

Vaporetto / ferry boarding point

Traghetto crossing

Gondola waiting point

Tourist information

Church

Synagogue

0 meters 300
0 yards 300

St. Mark's ①

The basilica blends architectural and decorative styles from East and West to create one of Europe's greatest buildings. Built on a Greek-cross plan and crowned with five huge domes, it is the third church to stand on this site. The first, built to enshrine the body of St. Mark in the 9th century, was destroyed by fire. The second was pulled down in the 11th century to make way for a truly spectacular edifice, reflecting the growing power of the Republic and its links with Byzantium. The dark interior is clad in wonderful mosaics, gleaming with gold. Many treasures – statues, icons, and the famous horses – were brought to St. Mark's after the 4th Crusade had plundered Constantinople in 1204.

★ Pentecost Mosaic
The interior of the dome above the nave is decorated with a 12th-century mosaic of the Holy Spirit descending on the Apostles in tongues of fire.

St. Mark flanked by Angels
The statues crowning the central arch were added in the early 15th century.

The atrium, or narthex, contains many fine mosaics, notably those of the Genesis Cupola showing the Creation.

The central arch features 13th-century carvings of the Labours of the Months.

★ Horses of St. Mark
The four horses are replicas of the gilded bronze originals, kept in the Museo Marciano, reached from the atrium.

Main entrance

★ Facade Mosaics
These are either heavily restored or replacements of the originals. This 17th-century work shows the body of St. Mark being smuggled out of Alexandria.

The Ascension Dome features a magnificent 13th-century mosaic of Christ surrounded by angels, the 12 Apostles, and the Virgin Mary.

★ **Pala d'Oro**
The greatest treasure of St. Mark's is kept behind the high altar. The magnificent altarpiece, created originally in the 10th century, is made up of 250 gold panels, adorned with enamels and precious stones.

VISITORS' CHECKLIST

Piazza San Marco. *Tel* 041-270 83 11. San Marco. Apr–Sep: 9:45am–5pm Mon–Sat, 2–5pm Sun; Nov–Mar: 9:45am–5pm Mon–Sat, 2–4pm Sun. sight-seeing limited during services. strict dress code applies in the church.

The altar canopy, or baldacchino, has alabaster columns carved with New Testament scenes.

St. Mark's body, thought to have been lost in the fire of 976, reappeared when the new church was consecrated in 1094. The remains are housed below the altar.

★ **Treasury**
This contains many treasures looted from Constantinople by the Venetians in 1204. This 11th-century silver-gilt reliquary is in the shape of a domed basilica.

Allegorical mosaics decorate the floor of the south transept.

Baptistry

The Tetrarchs
This porphyry sculptural group (4th-century Egyptian) may represent Diocletian, Maximian, Constantius, and Valerian – the four joint rulers of the Roman Empire c.AD 300, known as the tetrarchs.

STAR FEATURES

★ Mosaics

★ Horses of St. Mark

★ Pala d'Oro

★ Treasury

Doge's Palace ②

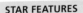

The official residence of the Venetian ruler (doge) was founded in the 9th century. The present palace owes its external appearance to the building work of the 14th and early 15th centuries. To create their airy Gothic masterpiece, the Venetians broke with tradition by perching the bulk of the palace (built of pink Veronese marble) on top of an apparent fretwork of loggias and arcades (built of white Istrian stone). A tour of the palace leads through a succession of richly decorated chambers and halls, ending with the Bridge of Sighs and the prisons.

Mars by Sansovino

In the Sala del Collegio the doge would receive ambassadors. The ceiling is decorated with 11 paintings by Veronese.

The Sala del Senato was the home of the senate, which had some 200 members.

Anticollegio

Arco Foscari

★ Porta della Carta
This 15th-century Gothic gate was the principal entrance to the palace. From it, a vaulted passageway leads to the Arco Foscari and the internal courtyard.

Exit

STAR FEATURES

★ Giants' Staircase

★ Porta della Carta

★ Sala del Maggior Consiglio

The balcony on the west facade was added in 1536 to mirror the early 15th-century balcony looking onto the quay.

★ Giants' Staircase
Statues by Sansovino of Neptune and Mars at the top of this late 15th-century staircase symbolize Venice's power at sea and on land. Doges were crowned with the glittering zogia or ducal cap on the landing.

Torture Chamber
Suspects under interrogation were hung on the walls of this room by cords tied around their wrists.

VISITORS' CHECKLIST

Piazza San Marco 1. **Tel** 041-271 59 42. 🚤 San Marco. ⏰ Apr–Oct: 8:30am–7pm daily; Nov–Mar: 8:30am–5:30pm daily. ⬤ Jan 1, Dec 25. 🎫 📷 🛍 ✍ (audio). ♿ limited.

The Sala del **Consiglio dei Dieci** was once the meeting place of the powerful Council of Ten.

Sala della Bussola (Compass Room)

Bridge of Sighs
The bridge was built in 1600 to link the palace with the state prisons. It reputedly acquired its name from the sighs of prisoners being led across it to face trial.

Drunkenness of Noah
This early 15th-century sculpture, symbolic of the frailty of man, is set on the corner of the palace.

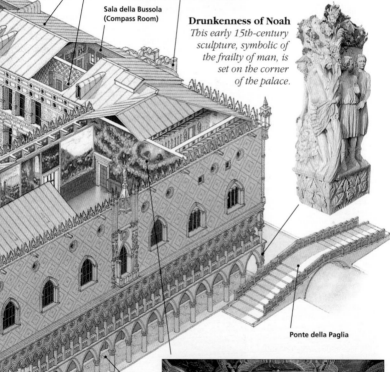

Ponte della Paglia

Main entrance

★ **Sala del Maggior Consiglio**
This vast chamber was the meeting hall of Venice's Great Council. By the 16th century this had over 2,000 members. The entire end wall is taken up by Tintoretto's Paradise *(1588–92).*

Portrait of a Young Man in a Red Hat (anonymous), Museo Correr

Museo Correr ③

Piazza San Marco (entrance in Ala Napoleonica). *Tel* 041-271 59 42. 🚏 *San Marco.* 🔘 *daily.* 🌑 *Jan 1, Dec 25.* 📷 🏛 🚻 🛗 **www.** museicivicivenezioni.it

Teodoro Correr bequeathed his extensive collection of works of art to Venice in 1830, thus forming the core of the city's fine civic museum.

Its first rooms form a suitably Neoclassical backdrop for early statues by Antonio Canova (1757–1822). The rest of the floor covers the history of the Venetian Republic, with maps, coins, armor, and a host of doge-related exhibits.

The second floor contains the picture gallery. Works are hung chronologically, enabling one to trace the evolution of Venetian painting. The most famous include the *Portrait of a Young Man in a Red Hat* (c.1490), once attributed to Carpaccio, now thought to be by an artist from the Ferrara/ Bologna area, and Carpaccio's *Two Venetian Ladies* (c.1507).

Scuola Grande di San Rocco ④

Campo San Rocco. *Tel* 041-523 48 64. 🚏 *San Tomà.* 🔘 *daily.* 🌑 *Jan 1, Easter, Dec 25.* 📷 🛗 🏛 🎧 (audio).

Founded in honor of San Rocco (St. Roch), a saint who dedicated his life to helping the sick, the Scuola started out as a charitable confraternity.

Construction began in 1515. The work was financed by donations from Venetians keen to invoke San Rocco's protection, and the Scuola quickly became one of the wealthiest in Venice. In 1564 its members decided to commission Tintoretto to decorate its walls and ceilings. His earliest paintings, the first of over 50 works he eventually created for the Scuola, fill the small Sala dell'Albergo off the Upper Hall. His later paintings are in the Ground Floor Hall, just inside the entrance.

The ground floor cycle was executed in 1583–7, when Tintoretto was in his sixties, and consists of eight episodes from the life of Mary. They are remarkable for the tranquil serenity of paintings such as *The Flight into Egypt* and *St. Mary of Egypt*.

Scarpagnino's great staircase (1544–6), leads to the Upper Hall, which was decorated by Tintoretto in 1575–81. The ceiling is painted with scenes from the Old Testament. The three large square paintings in the center show episodes from the Book of Exodus, all alluding to the charitable aims of the Scuola in alleviating thirst, sickness, and hunger. The vast wall paintings feature episodes from the New Testament, linking with the ceiling paintings. Two of the most striking are *The Temptation of Christ*, which shows a handsome young Satan offering Christ two loaves of bread, and *The Adoration of the Shepherds*.

The carvings below the paintings were added in the 17th century by sculptor Francesco Pianta. They include (near the altar) a caricature of Tintoretto with his palette and brushes.

The Sala dell'Albergo contains perhaps the most breathtaking of all Tintoretto's masterpieces – the *Crucifixion* (1565). Henry James once remarked of this painting: "no single picture contains more of human life; there is everything in it, including the most exquisite beauty."

Santa Maria Gloriosa dei Frari ⑤

Campo dei Frari. *Tel* 041-272 86 18. 🚏 *San Tomà.* 🔘 *Mon–Sat & Sun pm.* 🌑 *Jan 1, Jan 6, Easter, Dec 25.* 📷 *unless attending mass.* 📷

More commonly known as the Frari (a corruption of Frati, meaning brothers), this vast Gothic church dwarfs the eastern area of San Polo. Its 83-m (272-ft) campanile is the tallest in the city after that of San Marco. The first church on the site was built by the Franciscans in 1250–1338, but was replaced by a larger building completed in the mid-15th century. The airy interior is striking for its sheer size and for the quality of its works of art, including master-pieces by Titian and Giovanni Bellini, a statue by Donatello, and several grandiose tombs.

The sacristy altarpiece *The Madonna and Child* (1488)

Detail from Tintoretto's *Flight into Egypt*, Scuola Grande di San Rocco

by Bellini, with its sublime use of color, is one of Venice's most beautiful Renaissance paintings. The main altarpiece is *The Assumption of the Virgin*, a spectacular, glowing work by Titian (1518), which draws the eye through the Renaissance rood screen to the altar. Between the altar and the screen is the Monks' Choir (1468), its three-tiered stalls lavishly carved with saints and Venetian city scenes.

The Tomb of Canova, a marble, pyramid-shaped tomb, was built after Canova's death in 1822 by his pupils. It is similar to a design Canova himself had planned for a memorial for Titian. The Titian monument in the shape of a triumphal arch that stands opposite was built by two of Canova's pupils in 1853.

View across the Grand Canal to the Pescheria (fishmarket)

High altar of the Frari church with Titian's *Assumption of the Virgin*

Grand Canal ⑥

🚤 1 from Ferrovia and many others.

The best way to view the Grand Canal as it winds through the heart of the city is from a *vaporetto*, or water bus. Several lines travel the length of the canal. The palaces lining the waterway were built over a span of five centuries and present a panoramic survey of the city's history, almost all bearing the name of some once-great Venetian family.

Nearly 4 km (2.5 miles) long, the canal varies in width from 30 to 70 m (100 to 230 ft) and is spanned by three bridges, the Scalzi, the Rialto, and the Accademia. After passing the Rialto, the canal doubles back on itself along a stretch known as La Volta (the bend). It then widens out and the views become more spectacular approaching San Marco. Facades may have faded and foundations rotted, yet the canal remains, in the words of the French ambassador in 1495, "the most beautiful street in the world."

Santi Giovanni e Paolo ⑦

Campo Santi Giovanni e Paolo (also signposted San Zanipolo). *Tel* 041-523 59 13. 🚤 Fondamenta Nuove or Ospedale Civile. ⭕ daily. 🔵 Sun am for mass. 🚹 🏛

Known colloquially as San Zanipolo, Santi Giovanni e Paolo vies with the Frari as the city's greatest Gothic church. Built by the Dominicans in the 14th century, it is striking for its vast scale and architectural austerity. Known as the Pantheon of Venice, it houses monuments to no fewer than 25 doges. Among these are several fine works of art, executed by the Lombardi family and other leading sculptors. Pietro Lombardo created the magnificent tombs of the doges Nicolò Marcello (died 1474) and Pietro Mocenigo (died 1476). His masterpiece, the Tomb of Andrea Vendramin (died 1478), takes the form of a Roman triumphal arch.

The main doorway, which is decorated with Byzantine reliefs and carvings, is one of Venice's earliest Renaissance architectural works. On the right as you enter the church is a polyptych by Giovanni Bellini (c.1465) showing St. Vincent Ferrer, a Spanish cleric, flanked by St. Sebastian and St. Christopher.

THE GONDOLAS OF VENICE

The gondola has been a part of Venice since the 11th century. With its slim hull and flat underside, the craft is perfectly adapted to negotiating narrow, shallow canals. There is a slight leftward curve to the prow, which counteracts the force of the oar, preventing the gondola from going around in circles.

In 1562 it was decreed that all gondolas should be black to stop people making an ostentatious show of their wealth. For special occasions they were decorated with flowers. Today, gondola rides are expensive and usually taken by tourists.

Gondolas moored in a Venice canal

Scuola di San Giorgio degli Schiavoni ⑧

Calle Furlani. **Tel** 041-522 88 28.
🚊 San Zaccaria. ⬜ daily. ⬤ Mon
am, Sun pm. 📷

Within this small Scuola, established in 1451 and rebuilt in 1551, are some of the finest paintings of Vittore Carpaccio (c.1460–1525). Commissioned by the Schiavoni, or Dalmatian Slav trading community in Venice, Carpaccio's exquisite frieze (1502–08) shows scenes from the lives of three saints: St. George, St. Tryphon, and St. Jerome. Each episode of the narrative cycle is remarkable for its vivid coloring and minutely observed detail of Venetian life. *St. George Slaying the Dragon* and *The Vision of St. Jerome* are both outstanding.

Santa Maria della Salute ⑨

Campo della Salute. **Tel** 041-274 39
28. 🚊 Salute. ⬜ daily. 📷 to sacristy.

The great Baroque church of Santa Maria della Salute, standing at the entrance of the Grand Canal, is an imposing

The single-story palazzo housing the Peggy Guggenheim Collection

architectural landmark of Venice. Construction of the church, begun in 1630 by Baldassare Longhena, was not completed until 1687, five years after his death.

The comparatively sober interior of Santa Maria della Salute consists of a large octagonal space below the cupola and six chapels radiating from the ambulatory. The sculptural group around the grandiose high altar is by Giusto Le Corte and represents the Virgin and Child protecting the city of Venice from the plague.

In the sacristy to the left of the altar, Titian's early altarpiece *St. Mark Enthroned with St. Cosmas, St. Damian, St. Roch and St. Sebastian* (1511–12) and his dramatic ceiling paintings of *David and Goliath*, *Cain and Abel*, and *The Sacrifice of Isaac* (1540–9) are considered the finest paintings in the church. *The Wedding at Cana* (1551) on the wall opposite the entrance, is a major work by Jacopo Tintoretto.

The church was named *Salute*, which means both "health" and "salvation," in thanksgiving for the deliverance of the city from the plague epidemic of 1630. Each November, in a moving ceremony of remembrance, worshipers light candles and approach the church across a bridge of boats which spans the mouth of the Grand Canal.

The Baroque church of Santa Maria della Salute, viewed from the other side of the Grand Canal

Peggy Guggenheim Collection ⑩

Palazzo Venier dei Leoni. **Tel** 041-240
54 11. 🚊 Accademia. ⬜ Wed–Mon.
⬤ Dec 25. 📷 🎧 (audio). 🔲 🔲
www.guggenheim-venice.it

Intended as a four-story palace, the 18th-century Palazzo Venier dei Leoni in fact never rose beyond the ground floor – hence its nickname "The Unfinished Palace." In 1949 the building was bought by Peggy Guggenheim (1898–1979), an American collector, dealer, and patron of the arts. One of the most visited sights of Venice, the palace is the best place in the city to see modern art. The light-filled rooms and modern canvases are in striking contrast to the majority of the art on display in Venice.

Her collection consists of 200 fine paintings and sculptures, representing the 20th century's most influential modern art movements. The dining room has notable Cubist works of art, including *The Poet* by Pablo Picasso, and an entire room is devoted to Jackson Pollock, who was "discovered" by Guggenheim. There are also works by Braque, Chagall, Dalí, Klee, Mondrian, and Magritte, whose Surreal *Empire of Light* (1953–4) shows a night scene of a darkened house with bright daylight above.

The sculpture collection, which includes Constantin Brancusi's elegant *Bird in Space* (c.1923), is laid out in the house and the garden.

Perhaps the most provocative piece, on the canal terrace, is Marino Marini's *Angelo della Città* (1948). It shows a man sitting on a horse, erect in all respects.

Accademia ⑪

Campo della Carità. **Tel** 041-520 03
15 (bookings). 🚤 Accademia.
⬜ daily (Mon: am only). ◯ Jan 1,
May 1, Dec 25. 🎫 🎧 (audio). 📷
www.gallerieaccademia.org

Spanning five centuries,
the matchless collection of
paintings in the Accademia
provides a complete spectrum
of the Venetian school, from
the Byzantine period through
the Renaissance to the
Baroque and later.

Housed in three former
religious buildings, the basis
of the collection was the
Accademia di Belle Arti,
founded in 1750 by the
painter Giovanni Battista
Piazzetta. In 1807 Napoleon
moved the academy to its
present premises, greatly
enlarging the collection with
artworks from churches and
monasteries he suppressed.

The gallery is currently
being enlarged and some
rooms may be closed.

A highlight of the Byzantine
and Gothic section is Paolo
Veneziano's *Coronation of the
Virgin* (1325), which contrasts
with the delicate naturalism of
Giambono's painting of the
same name (1448).

The Bellini family played a
dominant role in the early
Venetian Renaissance, and
outstanding examples of their
work include Giovanni
Bellini's *Madonna and Child
between St. John the Baptist
and a Saint* (c.1504), and
other paintings of his
Madonna collection in room
13. One of Bellini's students,
Giorgione, painted the

The colonnaded apse of Murano's Basilica dei Santi Maria e Donato

atmospheric *Tempest* (c.1507).
Among Renaissance works on
display are *Feast in the House
of Levi* (1573) by Veronese,
and *The Miracle of the Slave*
(1548) which made the reputation of Jacopo Tintoretto.

The long gallery of Baroque,
genre, and landscape paintings
alongside Palladio's inner
courtyard (1561) features
works by Giambattista Tiepolo,
the greatest Venetian painter
of the 18th century, and a view
of Venice (1763) by Canaletto.

Rooms 20 and 21 contain
two cycles of paintings portraying Venetian settings: *The
Stories of the Cross*, and *Scenes
from the Legend of St. Ursula*,
painted by Carpaccio (1490s).

Murano ⑫

🚤 LN, 41 and 42 from Fondamenta
Nuove; DM from Ferrovia and
Piazzale Roma.

Like the city of Venice,
Murano consists of a cluster of
small islands, connected by
bridges. In the 15th and 16th
centuries Murano was the
principal glass-producing
center in Europe and today
most tourists visit to tour the
furnaces and buy traditionally
designed glass from the
manufacturers' showrooms.

The **Museo del Vetro** in the
Palazzo Giustinian houses a
fine collection of antique
pieces. The prize exhibit is
the dark blue wedding cup
(1470–80) with enamel
work by Angelo Barovier.

The architectural highlight
of the island is the 12th-
century **Basilica dei Santi
Maria e Donato** with its
lovely colonnaded apse. Of
particular note are the Gothic
ship's-keel roof, the mosaic
Madonna in the apse, and the
beautiful medieval mosaic
floor, which dates from 1140.

🏛 **Museo del Vetro**
Fondamenta Giustinian 8. **Tel** 041-
73 95 86. ◯ daily. ◯ Jan 1, May
1, Dec 25. 🎫 📷

⛪ **Basilica dei Santi Maria
e Donato**
Campo San Donato. **Tel** 041-73 90
56. ◯ daily (Sun: pm only).

Veronese's painting of Christ's Last Supper, retitled *The Feast in the House of Levi* (1573), in the Accademia

Ferrara ㉑

🏛 *140,000.* 🚉 🚌 ℹ️ *Castello Estense, Piazza Castello (0532-20 93 70).* 🗓 *Mon & Fri.*

The D'este Dynasty has left an indelible mark on Ferrara, one of the Emilia-Romagna region's greatest walled towns. The noble family took control of the town under Nicolò II in the late 13th century, holding power until 1598. **Castello Estense**, the family's formidable dynastic seat, with its moats, towers, and battlements, looms over the town center.

Bronze statues of Nicolò III and Borso d'Este, one of Nicolò's reputed 27 children, adorn the medieval **Palazzo del Comune**. The d'Este summer retreat was the **Palazzo Schifanoia**. Begun in 1385, it is famous for its Salone dei Mesi, whose walls are covered with murals by Cosmè Tura and other Ferrarese painters.

Ferrara's **cathedral** has an excellent museum, which contains marble reliefs of the *Labours of the Months* (late 12th century), two painted organ shutters (1469) of *St. George* and the *Annunciation* by Tura, and the *Madonna of the Pomegranate* (1408) by Sienese sculptor Jacopo della Quercia (c.1374–1438).

🏛 **Castello Estense**
Piazza Castello. **Tel** *0532-29 92 33.* ☐ *Tue–Sun.* ⬤ *Dec 25.* 📷 ♿

🏛 **Palazzo Schifanoia**
Via Scandiana 23. **Tel** *0532-24 49 49.* ☐ *Tue–Sun.* ⬤ *public hols.* 📷

The medieval Castello Estense and surrounding moat in Ferrara

Flagged medieval street with shady, arcaded buildings, typical of central Bologna

Bologna ㉒

🏛 *385,000.* ✈️ *Marconi 9 km (5 miles) NW.* 🚉 🚌 ℹ️ *Piazza Maggiore 1/e (051-23 96 60).* 🗓 *Fri & Sat.* 🎭 *Bologna Estate (Jun–Sep).*

Capital of Emilia-Romagna and one of Italy's most prosperous cities, Bologna has a rich cultural heritage, ranging from medieval palaces and churches to leaning towers. Celebrated in the Middle Ages for its university – believed to be the oldest in Europe – Bologna came under papal rule in 1506 and a large part of the city was given over to monasteries and convents. After the arrival of Napoleon's occupying force in 1797, the university was moved from its Catholic cradle in the **Archiginnasio** to a science building where Marconi later studied. After unification the old city walls were demolished and an era of prosperity was ushered in.

The two central squares of the city, Piazza Maggiore and Piazza del Nettuno, are bordered to the south by the churches of **San Petronio** and **San Domenico**. The former ranks among the greatest of Italy's brick-built medieval buildings. Founded in 1390, its construction was halted halfway due to financial constraints, and the planned central row of columns became the eastern flank. Twenty-two chapels open off the nave of the Gothic interior, many with fine works of art.

San Domenico is the most important of Italy's many Dominican churches, housing, as it does, the tomb of St. Dominic himself. A magnificent composite work, the tomb features statues and reliefs by Nicola Pisano, while the figures of angels and saints are early works by Michelangelo.

The **Torri degli Asinelli e Garisenda** are among the few surviving towers of the 200 that once formed the skyline of Bologna. Both were begun in the 12th century. The Garisenda tower (closed to the public) leans some 3 m (10 ft), while the Asinelli tower has a 500-step ascent and offers fine views.

The Romanesque-Gothic church of **San Giacomo Maggiore**, begun in 1267 but altered substantially since, is visited mainly for the superb Bentivoglio family chapel, decorated with frescoes by Lorenzo Costa (1460–1535). The Bentivoglio tomb is among the last works of Jacopo della Quercia.

Bologna's main art gallery, the **Pinacoteca Nazionale**, stands on the edge of the university district. Its two highlights are Perugino's *Madonna in Glory* (c.1491) and Raphael's famous *Ecstasy of St. Cecilia*, painted around 1515.

The cuisine of Bologna is among the finest in Italy. To try the famous Bolognese meat sauce you should order *tagliatelle al ragù.*

🏛 **Torri degli Asinelli e Garisenda**
Piazza di Porta Ravegnana. ☐ *daily.* 📷

🏛 **Pinacoteca Nazionale**
Via delle Belle Arti 56. **Tel** *051-420 94 11.* ☐ *Tue–Sun.* ⬤ *May 1, Aug 16.* 📷 ♿
www.pinacotecabologna.it

Ravenna ❷❸

🏛 140,000. 🚇 🚌 🛈 Via Salara
8–12 (0544-354 04). 🔄 Wed & Sat.

Ravenna rose to power in the
1st century BC when Emperor
Augustus built a port and
naval base nearby, but gained
further prominence after
becoming the administrative
capital of the Byzantine
Empire in AD 402.

Most people visit the city
for its superb early Christian
mosaics. Spanning the years
of Roman and Byzantine rule,
they can be seen in many of
Ravenna's 5th- and 6th-century
buildings. In the church of
San Vitale, apse mosaics
(526–547) show the saint
being handed a martyr's
crown. Another mosaic
depicts Emperor Justinian,
who ruled from 527 to 565,
and members of his court.
Next door, the tiny **Mausoleo
di Galla Placidia** is adorned
with a mosaic of *The Good*

**Apse of San Vitale, Ravenna,
showing 6th-century mosaics**

Shepherd. Galla Placidia ran
the Western Empire for 20
years after the death of her
husband, the Visigothic King
Altauf. The 6th-century church
of **Sant'Apollinare Nuovo**
is dominated by two rows
of mosaics which depict
processions of martyrs and
virgins bearing gifts.

Travelers in Ravenna can
also visit **Dante's Tomb** – the
great writer died here in 1321
– and the **Museo Nazionale**,
which houses icons, paintings,
and archaeological displays.
The best place to relax and
take a break from sightseeing
is among the lovely ensemble
of medieval buildings in the
Piazza del Popolo.

🛐 **San Vitale & Mausoleo di
Galla Placidia**
Via Fiandrini. **Tel** 800-30 39 99.
◻ daily. ◼ Jan 1, Dec 25. 🎫 ♿
🛐 **Sant'Apollinare Nuovo**
Via di Roma. **Tel** 0544-54 16 88.
◻ daily. ◼ Jan 1, Dec 25. 🎫 ♿

BYZANTINE ITALY

By the 5th century AD
the Roman Empire was
split into two. Rome
and the Western
Empire could not
stem the tide of
Germanic invaders
as they migrated
southwards
and Italy fell
to the Goths.
In the years after
535 AD,
however, the
Eastern Empire
reconquered
most of Italy.
Its stronghold,
Ravenna,
became the
richest, most
powerful
Italian city.

**Byzantine
Emperor
Justinian**

Most of the
peninsula was
subsequently
lost to the Lombards who
invaded in 564, but
Ravenna, protected by
marshes and lagoons, was
able to hold out until
752 when the Lombard
King Aistulf finally
recaptured the city.

Urbino ❷❹

🏛 16,000. 🚌 🛈 Piazza
Rinascimento 1 (0722-26 13). 🔄 Sat.

Urbino traces its origins to the
Umbrians, centuries before
Christ, and became a Roman
municipality in the 3rd
century BC. The city's zenith,
however, came in the 15th
century under the rule of the
philosopher-warrior Federico
da Montefeltro, who
commissioned the building of
the **Palazzo Ducale** in 1444.
This beautiful Renaissance
palace has an extensive
library, hanging gardens, and
numerous fine paintings. Two
great 15th-century works,
The Flagellation by Piero
della Francesca, and *Ideal
City* attributed to Luciano
Laurana, are notable for their
use of perspective.

Of special interest in the
Neoclassical **Duomo**, built
in 1789, is the painting of
the *Last Supper* by Federico
Barocci (c.1535–1612). The
Museo Diocesano contains
a collection of ceramics, glass,
and religious artifacts.

The **Casa Natale di
Raffaello**, home of Urbino's
famous son, the painter
Raphael (1483–1520), is also
open to visitors.

🏛 **Palazzo Ducale**
Piazza Duca Federico 13. **Tel** 0722-
32 26 25. ◻ 8:30am–7:15pm
Tue–Sun, 8:30am–2pm Mon.
◼ Jan 1, Dec 25. 🎫 📷 ♿
🏛 **Casa Natale di Raffaello**
Via di Raffaello 57. **Tel** 0722-32 01
05. ◻ daily (Nov–Feb: am only).
◼ Jan 1, Dec 25. 🎫

The Palazzo Ducale, rising above the rooftops of Urbino

View across the Bay of Naples to the slopes of Mount Vesuvius

Naples ㉕

🏙 1,100,000. ✈ Capodichino 4 km (2.5 miles) NW. 🚢 🚉 🚌 🛈 Piazza del Gesù Nuovo (081-552 33 28). 🛒 daily. 🎪 Maggio dei Monumenti (May), San Gennaro (Sep 19).

The chaotic yet spectacular city of Naples (Napoli) sprawls around the edge of a beautiful bay in the shadow of Mount Vesuvius.

Originally a Greek city named Neapolis, founded in 600 BC, Naples became an "allied city" of Rome two centuries later. It has since had many foreign rulers. The French House of Anjou controled Naples between 1266 and 1421, when power passed to Alfonso V of Aragón. A colony of Spain by 1503, in 1707 Naples was ceded to Austria, and in 1734 Charles III of Bourbon took over. In 1860, Naples became part of the new kingdom of Italy. The centuries of occupation have left Naples with a rich store of ancient ruins, churches, and palaces, many of which can be seen in the compact center of the old city. The **Museo Archeologico Nazionale** holds treasures from Pompeii and Herculaneum, including a bust of Seneca, fine glassware, frescoes, mosaics, and the fabulous Farnese Classical sculptures. Nearby, the church of **San Giovanni a Carbonara** houses some glorious medieval works of art, such as the tomb of King Ladislas of Naples (1386–1414). The French Gothic **Duomo** holds the relics of San Gennaro, martyred in 305 AD. Next to it is one of Italy's finest Renaissance gateways, the **Porta Capuana**, completed in 1490.

Also worth visiting, the **Monte della Misericordia**, a 17th-century octagonal church, houses Caravaggio's huge *Seven Acts of Mercy* (1607).

Central Naples is particularly rich in 14th- and 15th-century churches. **San Domenico Maggiore** contains some fine Renaissance sculpture while **Santa Chiara** houses the tombs of the Angevin monarchs and a museum whose exhibits include the ruins of a Roman bathhouse. Southeast Naples is home to the city's castles and the royal palace of **Castel Nuovo**, built for Charles of Anjou in 1279–82. Another star sight, the **Palazzo Reale** was designed for the viceroy Ruiz de Castro, and has a superb library, richly adorned royal apartments, and a court theater. Begun in 1600, the palace was not completed until 1843.

The Palazzo Reale di Capodimonte, once a hunting lodge, now houses the **Museo di Capodimonte**, with its magnificent collection of Italian paintings, including works by Titian, Botticelli, and Raphael. This part of Naples is also known for its "Spanish Quarter," or **Quartieri Spagnoli**, a neighborhood of narrow, cobbled alleys often used to represent the archetypal Neapolitan street scene.

Environs
A trip by funicular railway up **Vomero** hill brings you to the **Certosa di San Martino**. This 14th-century charterhouse has been lavishly redecorated over the centuries. The Church and the Prior's Residence are particularly impressive. Just behind the Certosa lies the **Castel Sant Elmo**, which offers fine views.

Farnese Hercules, Museo Archeologico Nazionale

Boat excursions can be taken along the Posillipo coast, and to the islands of **Capri, Ischia**, and **Procida**. Inland, **Caserta** has its own **Palazzo Reale**, which boasts over 1,000 sumptuously decorated rooms. The town of **Santa Maria Capua Vetere** has a Roman amphitheater and a Mithraeum.

🏛 **Museo Archeologico Nazionale**
Piazza Museo Nazionale 19. **Tel** 081-44 22 149. Ⓜ Museo. ⬤ Thu–Wed. ⬤ May 1, Dec 25. 📷

🏛 **Museo di Capodimonte**
Parco di Capodimonte. **Tel** 081-749 91 11. ⬤ Thu–Tue. 📷 ♿

Tomb of King Ladislas of Naples in San Giovanni a Carbonara

A breathtaking view of the steep village of Positano on the Amalfi Coast

Pompeii ㉖

Porta Marina. **Tel** 081-857 53 47. 🔲
🚉 ⬤ daily. ⬤ Jan 1, May 1, Dec 25.
📷 ♿ ✔

Ancient Pompeii, destroyed in AD 79 by an eruption of Vesuvius, lay buried under rock and ash until the 18th century. When excavations began in 1748, a city frozen in time was revealed. Many buildings survived, some complete with paintings and sculptures. The villa of the wealthy patrician Casii is known as House of the Faun after its bronze statuette. The House of the Vettii, named after its owners, contains rich wall decorations.

The original layout of the city can be clearly seen. The Forum was the center of public life, with administrative and religious institutions grouped around it. Theaters, the marketplace, temples, stores, and even brothels can be visited. Around 2,000 people died at Pompeii and casts of numerous recumbent figures have been made.

Much of our knowledge of the daily lives of the ancient Romans has been derived from the excavations at Pompeii and nearby Herculaneum. The baths were divided into separate sections for men and women, but the citizens of Pompeii were not prudish – graphic frescoes reveal the services offered by male and female prostitutes in the *lupanares*, or brothels.

Many works of art, domestic items, and other artifacts were preserved by the mud and ash are on permanent display in the Museo Archeologico Nazionale in Naples.

Amalfi Coast ㉗

🛥 🚉 Amalfi. ℹ Via delle Repubbliche Marinare 19–21, Amalfi (089-87 11 07).

The most enchanting and most visited route in Campania skirts the southern flank of Sorrento's peninsula: the Amalfi Coast (Costiera Amalfitana).

Among the popular pleasures here are dining on locally caught grilled fish and sipping icy Lacrima Christi from Vesuvian vineyards, interspersed with beach-hopping.

From **Sorrento**, a well-developed holiday resort, the road winds down to **Positano**, a village clambering down a vertiginous slope to the sea. Further on, **Praiano** is another fashionable resort.

Amalfi – the coast's largest town – was a maritime power before it was subdued in 1131 by King Roger of Naples. Its most illustrious citizens were buried in the 13th-century Chiostro del Paradiso, flanking the 9th-century Duomo. Above Amalfi, **Ravello** offers peace and quiet and superb views of the coast.

Sacrarium of the Lares, shrine of Pompeii's guardian deities

Sicily

Located at a crossroads in the Mediterranean, Sicily was a magnet for colonists and invaders from half the ancient civilized world. As Greek, Arab, and Norman conquerors came and went, they left behind a rich and varied cultural heritage. This has evolved into a colorful mixture of language, customs, and cuisine, and is reflected in the diverse art and architecture of the island. Sicily has magnificent beaches, remote hilltowns, flower-covered mountain ranges, and an active volcano whose lava flows over the centuries have created a fertile land of walnut trees, citrus groves, and vineyards.

Front facade of the Norman Duomo (cathedral) in Palermo

Palermo ㉘

🏛 700,000. ✈ Punta Raisi 32 km (20 miles) W. ⛴ 🚌 🚃 ℹ Piazza Castelnuovo 35 (091-605 81 11) and railway station. 🛒 Mon–Sat. 🎉 U Festinu for Santa Rosalia (Jul 10–15).

Capital of Sicily and situated along the bay at the foot of Monte Pellegrino, Palermo was originally called Panormos, or "port" by the Phoenicians. A prosperous Roman town, Palermo's golden age came later, while under Arab domination. The Baroque period (17th–18th centuries) has also left a lasting mark on the city's civic and religious buildings.

Palermo suffered heavy bombardment by the Allies in World War II, but, despite chaotic rebuilding, the city remains an exotic mix of the oriental and the European.

The old Arab quarter can be found in North Palermo, typified by **Vucciria**, one of the city's lively markets. On Piazza Marina, the focal point of North Palermo, the Palazzo Abatellis houses the **Galleria Regionale di Sicilia**, which has a fine collection of sculptures, medieval crucifixes, frescoes, and paintings.

On the Piazza della Vittoria in South Palermo, the **Palazzo Reale** – a focus of power since Byzantine rule – is now home to Sicily's regional government. Its splendid **Cappella Palatina** is adorned with mosaics. The **Duomo**, founded in 1184, has a Catalan Gothic portico (1430) and a cupola in Baroque style.

The **Museo Regionale Salinas** is considered one of Italy's most important archaeology museums.

🏛 **Galleria Regionale di Sicilia**
Via Alloro 4. **Tel** 091-623 00 11.
◯ am daily, pm Tue–Thu. 📷

🏛 **Palazzo Reale & Cappella Palatina**
Piazza Indipendenza. **Tel** 091-626 28 33. ◯ daily. 📷

🏛 **Museo Regionale Salinas**
Piazza Olivella 24. **Tel** 091-611 68 05. ◯ Tue–Sun (am only Sat, Sun & hols). 📷

Environs

A few miles inland from Palermo, the cathedral at **Monreale**, founded in 1172, is one of the great sights of Norman Sicily. The glittering mosaics and Saracenic-style cloisters, represent Norman artistry at its peak.

🏰 **Monreale**
Piazza Vittorio Emanuele. 🚌 📷
Cloister Tel 091-640 44 13.
◯ daily (am only Sun & hols). 📷 for treasury & terrace.

Taormina ㉙

Messina. 🏛 10,000. 🚌 🚃 ℹ Palazzo Corvaja, Piazza Santa Caterina (0942 232 43). 🛒 Wed.

Sicily's most popular tourist resort has sandy beaches and numerous restaurants.

The most illustrious relic of the past is the 3rd-century BC **Theater**, begun by the Greeks, and rebuilt by the Romans. Among other Classical ruins are the **Odeon** (a musical theater) and the **Naumachia** (a man-made lake for mock battles).

The 14th-century **Palazzo Corvaia** and the 13th-century **Duomo**, renovated in 1636, are also worth visiting.

Taormina's Greek theater with Mount Etna in the background

Fishing boats moored in the picturesque harbor of Syracuse

Mount Etna ㉚

🗺 Catania. 🚉 to Linguaglossa or
Randazzo; Circumetnea (095-541 250).
🚌 to Nicolosi. 🛈 Via G Garibaldi
63, Nicolosi (095-91 44 88).

One of the world's largest
active volcanoes, Mount
Etna was thought by the
Romans to have been the forge
of Vulcan, the god of fire. To
view it in comfort, take the
Circumetnea railway, which
runs around the base from
Catania to Riposto.

Now a protected area,
about 58 sq km (22 sq miles)
in size, Etna offers numerous
opportunities for excursions.
One of the most popular is
from Zafferana to the Valle
del Bove. Guided hikes can
also be taken up to the large
craters at the summit.

Syracuse ㉛

🗺 118,000. ✈ 🚉 🚌 🛈 Via Maestranza 33 (0931-464 255). 🛒 Wed.

The most important and
powerful Greek city from 400
to 211 BC when it fell to the
Romans, Syracuse (Siracusa in
Italian) was also regarded as
the most beautiful.

The peninsula of Ortigia is
the hub of the old city. A
highlight is the 18th-century
Duomo. Its Baroque facade
masks the **Temple of Athena**
(5th century BC), which has
been absorbed into it. Nearby
is the **Palazzo Beneventano
del Bosco** (1778–88) where

Admiral Nelson once stayed.
At Ortigia's farthest point is the
Castello Maniace, built by
Frederick II around 1239, and
the **Galleria Regionale di
Palazzo Bellomo**, where
Caravaggio's *Burial of St.
Lucy* (1608) may be seen.

One of the most important
examples of ancient theater
architecture, the 5th-century
BC **Greek Theater** has a 67-
tier auditorium or *cavea*. The
great Greek playwrights
staged their works here.

At Tyche, north of Syracuse,
the **Museo Archeologico
Regionale Paolo Orsi** houses
an important collection of
artifacts excavated from local
digs, which date from the
Paleolithic to the Byzantine era.

🏛 **Galleria Regionale di
Palazzo Bellomo**
Palazzo Bellomo, Via Capodieci 16.
Tel 0931-695 11. ⬭ Tue–Sat, Sun am.

🏛 **Museo Archeologico
Regionale Paolo Orsi**
Viale Teocrito 66. **Tel** 0931-46 40
22. ⬭ Tue–Sat, Sun am.

Agrigento ㉜

🗺 57,000. ✈ 🚉 🚌 🛈 Via
Empedocle 73 (0922-203 91). 🛒 Fri.

Modern Agrigento occupies
the site of Akragas, an
important city of the ancient
Greeks. Following the Roman
conquest of 210 BC, Agrigento
was renamed and successively
occupied by Byzantines,
Arabs, and Normans. The
historic medieval core of the

city focuses on the Via
Atenea. The 13th-century
abbey complex of **Santo
Spirito** houses stuccoes by
Giacomo Serpotta (1695).

Environs
South of Agrigento, the **Valley
of Temples** is the principal
sacred site of ancient Akragas.
The mainly 5th- and 6th-
century ruins rank among the
most impressive complexes of
ancient Greek buildings outside Greece. **Museo Regionale
Archeologico** houses
outstanding artifacts from
the temples and the city.

🏛 **Museo Regionale
Archeologico**
Contrada San Nicola, Viale
Panoramica. **Tel** 0922-62 16 11.
⬭ daily.

**The Temple of Concord (c.430 BC)
in the Valley of Temples, Agrigento**

Practical Information

Italy's charm and allure help to mask an idiosyncratic public sector in which delays and long lines are common. Be prepared to wait in offices and banks, and to persevere when seeking information. However, communications – other than the post office – are good, and banking and exchange facilities are widely available. Italy is generally safe for visitors and there is a visible police presence should a crisis arise. Personal belongings should nevertheless be watched at all times. Many shops and offices close at lunch for the siesta, reopening in the late afternoon. Pharmacies are a useful first stop for health advice.

WHEN TO VISIT

Italy's towns and historic sites are extremely popular attractions and it is worth considering this when planning your trip. Rome, Florence, and Venice are all crowded from spring to October and it is advisable to reserve a hotel well in advance. In August the cities are generally slightly less busy, and the seaside resorts fill up. June and September can be as hot as midsummer, but the beaches are less crowded. The skiing season runs from December to Easter.

TOURIST INFORMATION

The national tourist board, **ENIT**, has branches in capital cities worldwide and offers general information on Italy. Locally, there are two types of tourist office: an EPT (*Ente Provinciale di Turismo*) has information on its town and surrounding province, whereas an **APT** (*Azienda di Promozione Turistica*)

deals exclusively with an individual town. Both can help with practical issues such as hotel reservations and local tour guides. They also provide free maps and guidebooks in several languages.

OPENING HOURS

Italian museums are gradually conforming to new regulations, particularly in the north, opening daily from about 9am to 7pm, but some still close on Mondays. In summer, many museums stay open longer at weekends. In winter, opening times are more limited. It is advisable to check beforehand. Archaeological sites usually open from 9am to an hour before sunset, Tuesday to Sunday. Churches are open from about 7am to 12:30pm and 4 to 7pm, but they often prefer not to admit tourists during services.

Visits to some of the more popular tourist sights, such as Leonardo da Vinci's painting of *The Last Supper* in Milan, must be organized in advance.

VISA REQUIREMENTS

Citizens of the European Union (EU), US, Canada, Australia, and New Zealand do not require a visa for stays of up to three months. Most European Union visitors need only a valid identity document to enter Italy. Citizens from other countries should contact their Italian consulate for visa information.

PERSONAL SECURITY

Although petty crime in the cities is frequent, violent crime in Italy is rare. However, it is common for people to raise their voices aggressively during an argument. Usually, remaining calm and being polite will help to defuse the situation. Unofficial tour guides, taxi drivers, or strangers who try to advise you on accommodations may expect money in return.

Women traveling alone in Italy are likely to meet with a lot of attention, although this is often more of an irritation than a danger. Staff at hotels and restaurants generally treat their single female customers with extra care and attention.

POLICE

There are several different police forces in Italy and each one fulfills a particular role. Both the state police, the *polizia* and the *carabinieri*, deal with crime in general and they also conduct random security checks. The *vigili urbani*, the municipal traffic police, issue fines for traffic

THE CLIMATE OF ITALY

The Italian peninsula has a varied climate falling into three distinct geographical regions. Cold Alpine winters and warm, increasingly wet summers characterize the northern regions. In the extensive Po Valley, arid summers contrast with freezing, damp winters. The rest of Italy has long, and often very hot, summers and mild, sunny winters.

ROME			
°C/F	29/84		
	18/64 19/66	22/72	
	9/48	13/55	12/54
0°C			4/40
32°F			
	6 hrs	10 hrs	7 hrs	5 hrs
	51 mm	21 mm	95 mm	87 mm
month	Apr	Jul	Oct	Jan

VENICE			
°C/F	28/82		
	17/63 18/64	18/64	
	7/44	9/48	7/44
0°C			0/32
32°F			
	7 hrs	9 hrs	4 hrs	2 hrs
	112 mm	108 mm	134 mm	90 mm
month	Apr	Jul	Oct	Jan

nd parking offences. If you ave anything stolen, you hould go to the nearest olice station and file a eport *(denuncia)*.

MERGENCY SERVICES

n case of emergencies while on vacation the appropriate numbers to call are listed in he directory below.

HEALTH ISSUES

No inoculations are needed or Italy, but it is advisable to arry mosquito repellent in he summer months. If mergency medical treatment becomes necessary, you hould go to the *Pronto Soccorso* (emergency room) of the nearest hospital.

Various medical products, including homeopathic medicines, are available in ny pharmacy *(farmacia)*, but a prescription may be required. Thanks to a night rota *(servizio notturno)* – listed in the local pages of daily newspapers and on pharmacy doors – there is always a pharmacy open in all cities and most towns.

LANGUAGE AND ETIQUETTE

People in Italy are very dress-conscious and unusual or risqué clothes get noticed. Strict dress codes are enforced in many places of worship, where your torso, knees, and upper arms should be covered.

Forms of address are still governed by traditional social formalities. *Ciao* should only be used as a greeting for famil-iar friends, otherwise *piacere* (pleased to meet you), *buon giorno* (good day), or *buona sera* (good evening) are polite greetings. Say *arrivederci* on parting. Kissing on the cheeks is common among friends, but shake hands with strangers.

Tipping of taxi drivers and waiting staff in restaurants is not common practice among Italians. However, when a service charge is added to a restaurant bill it is non-negotiable. Hotel porters expect a reasonable tip if they have been helpful.

FACILITIES FOR THE DISABLED

Public awareness of the needs of the disabled is improving quickly in Italy. **CO.IN.Sociale** (Consorzio Cooperative Integrate) provides information on facilities for the disabled.

BANKING AND CURRENCY

Italy has used the euro since 2002 *(see p15)*. Banks open between about 8:30am and 1:30pm Monday to Friday. Most also open from 2:15 to 3pm or 2:30 to 3:30pm.

Electronic exchange machines, with multilingual instructions, are located at all major airports, train stations, and banks. Bureaux de change can be found in main

towns, and are usually open all day, and also into the evening in resorts. However, they quite often tend to have less favorable exchange rates and charge a higher commission than banks. Post offices usually have the lowest charges.

COMMUNICATIONS

Post offices open from about 8am to 2pm weekdays, and from 8am to noon on Saturday. Main post offices are usually open from 8am to 6pm or 7pm non-stop. The red mailboxes (blue in the Vatican City) usually have two slots labeled *per la città* (for the city only) and *tutte le altre destinazioni* (for all other destinations). The Italian post-al service was once renowned for its unreliability, but has improved in recent years. The standard mail service is called *prioritaria*.

The few public telephones remaining are generally card-operated. A telephone card *(scheda telefonica)* can be purchased from bars, newspaper kiosks, post offices, and tobacconists *(tabacchi)*. A corner of the card must be broken off before use. Alternatively, many towns have telephone offices *(Telefoni)* with low rates for long-distance calls. Here you are assigned a booth and pay-after calls are completed. Credit cards can only be used to make calls at major airports.

DIRECTORY

TOURIST OFFICES

APT Florence
Via Cavour 1R.
Tel 055-29 08 32.

APT Milan
Piazza Duomo 19A.
Tel 02-77 40 43 43.

APT Rome
Via Parigi 5.
Tel 06-488 992 12.

APT Venice
Castello 5050.
Tel 041-529 87 11.

ENIT Rome
Via Marghera 2.
Tel 06-497 11.
www.enit.it

ENIT UK
1 Princes St, London W1.
Tel 020-7408 1254.
www.italiantourist
board.co.uk

ENIT US
630 Fifth Ave, New York,
NY 10111.
Tel 212-245 5618.
www.italiantourism.com

EMBASSIES

Australia
Via A. Bosio 5, Rome.
Tel 06-85 27 21. www.
italy.embassy.gov.au

Canada
Via Zara 30, Rome.
Tel 06-854 44 29 11.
www.canada.it

UK
Via XX Settembre 80,
Rome. *Tel 06-42 20 00
01.* www.britain.it

US
Via Veneto 121, Rome.
Tel 06-467 41.
www.usembassy.it

EMERGENCY NUMBERS

General Emergency
Tel 113.

Medical Emergency
Tel 118.

Police (Carabinieri)
Tel 112.

FACILITIES FOR THE DISABLED

CO.IN.Sociale
Via Enrico Giglioli 54A,
Rome.
Tel 06-712 9011.

Travel Information

Italy has transportation systems of varying efficiency, from the modern road, bus, and rail networks of the north to the slower and more antiquated systems of the south. Numerous airlines operate flights to the country's major airports. Highways are good, but busy at weekends and peak periods, and delays are common at Alpine passes. Train travel is inexpensive and services generally frequent, although they can be overcrowded during local holidays. The major Italian cities have a number of transportation options and that most suited to the tourist varies from place to place: the bus is more practical in Rome and the metro in Milan.

FLYING TO ITALY

Flight destinations and routes change frequently, but **United Airlines**, **Delta**, and **American Airlines** all operate regular flights to Italy from the United States. **Air Canada** flies from several Canadian airports, and **Qantas** has flights from various Australian airports to Rome.

Alitalia offers regular services to the United States and Europe. It may be more convenient and less expensive for long-haul passengers to take a budget flight to London, Frankfurt, Paris, or Amsterdam before continuing their journey to Italy from there. **Meridiana** also has direct flights to Italy from New York.

Low-cost airlines **easyJet** and **Ryanair** offer flights from various UK airports to numerous Italian destinations according to the season.

Rome's Leonardo da Vinci (Fiumicino) and Milan's Malpensa are the key airports for long-haul flights into Italy. Milan's Linate airport handles European flights.

CHARTERS AND PACKAGE DEALS

Package holidays to Italy are usually less costly than traveling independently, unless you are on a tight budget and are prepared to make use of youth hostels and campsites. Rome, Florence, and Venice are often offered as separate or linked package deals, and many operators have packages to Tuscany and Umbria, the Lakes, the Riviera, Naples, Sicily, and the Amalfi Coast. Several firms organize fly-drive packages. In winter, ski packages to many Alpine resorts are available. Specialty walking, gastronomy, and art tours are increasingly common.

DOMESTIC FLIGHTS

Alitalia, **Air One**, and **Ryanair** run regular services between many Italian cities. Long-haul passengers can transfer to domestic flights in Rome and Milan.

As internal flights can be expensive, and busy at peak periods, trains are a good alternative. Flights to airports in the north can be disrupted by fog in the winter.

TRAVELING IN CITIES

Milan and Rome both have a metro system known as *la metropolitana* (*metro* for short). Rome's network amounts to just two lines – A and B – which converge at Stazione Termini, the city's central train station. Several stations are useful for key sights but the system is designed for commuters and carriages are usually stiflingly hot in summer. A third metro line is under construction, with the first stretch due to open in 2013.

Milan has three principal lines – MM1 (the red line), MM2 (green), and MM3 (yellow) – that give easy access to the city's main sights.

Cars are a liability in all city centers and many, including Florence, have a large limited-traffic zone. Walking is usually the easiest and most enjoyable way to negotiate the narrow streets of historic town centers. Trams still run in some cities such as Milan and Rome. Taxis must be met at official taxi stands or reserved by telephone; in theory, you cannot hail a taxi in the street.

Most Italian cities and towns have a bus system which is inexpensive, comprehensive, and as efficient as traffic will allow. Bus stops are known as *fermate*, and buses (*autobus*) usually run from about 6am to midnight. Train stations are invariably linked to the city centers by shuttle buses. Tickets (*biglietti*) must usually be bought before boarding the bus, and are available from kiosks, bars, and *tabacchi* (tobacconists). Buses are boarded via the front and rear doors and exited via the central doors. Tickets are validated by being punched in machines on board.

GETTING AROUND VENICE

The water buses (*vaporetti*) are an entertaining form of public transportation in Venice, although most journeys within the city can easily be covered on foot. The main route for the water buses is the Grand Canal. They also link the city to the islands in the lagoon. Tickets can be purchased from kiosks at each stop, and the main routes run every 10 to 20 minutes until early evening. For general inquiries, contact the **ACTV Information Office**.

Gondolas are a luxury form of transportation. Sharing can make it cheaper. Before boarding, agree on a price with the gondolier. *Traghetti* (gondola ferries), on the other hand, are an inexpensive, convenient way of crossing the Grand Canal.

For those with sufficient funds, the most practical means of traveling around Venice is by water taxi. These motorboats run from 16 water taxi ranks and can reach the airport in 20 minutes. Extra charges are made for luggage, waiting, night service, and calling out a taxi.

RAIL TRAVEL

The bulk of Italy's rail network is an integrated partially privatized system operated by the **Ferrovie dello Stato** (FS). Train journeys into Italy from other parts of Europe wind through the Alps and are an exciting way to travel. **Alta Velocità** (high-speed trains) and **Eurostar**, which operate on main lines to the coast or between cities, require pre-booking of seats. These and intercity (IC) trains only stop at main stations and require the payment of a supplement *(supplemento)*. *Regionale* trains make more stops and require no supplement.

The most useful pass for visitors is the Interrail One Country, which gives unlimited travel for 3–8 consecutive or non-consecutive days over a one-month period, with special rates for those under 26. This pass can be purchased at most mainline stations and various agencies outside Italy. It is available only to non-residents.

Before traveling, all tickets need to be validated in one of the yellow machines found on the platform.

TRAVELING BY BUS

Long-distance buses *(pullman* or *corriere)* operate between towns and can be less expensive and more frequent than the trains. Tickets can be purchased on board, and services usually depart from a town's train station or main square. Buses in some areas may be run by several companies *(see Directory below)*.

TRAVELING BY ROAD

A car is invaluable for touring the Italian countryside. Drivers should take into account high gas *(benzina)* prices, the difficulty of parking in towns, and the Italians' often erratic approach to driving. Italy has a good network of highways, but most have tollbooths, often leading to congestion. Care should be taken at night when many traffic lights switch to flashing amber. Car theft is rife in Italy and valuables should not be left unattended.

Car rental *(autonoleggio)* is expensive in Italy, and should be organized beforehand through fly-drive deals or prebooked with firms that have branches in Italy. Local firms may be less expensive than the international firms. Most airports have rental offices on site *(see Directory below)*. Visitors from outside the EU need an international license, but in practice not all rental firms insist on this.

FERRY SERVICES

Italy's large number of off-shore islands means that it has a well-developed network of ferries. Boats of various kinds also operate on the Italian Lakes.

Ferries depart for Sicily from Naples and Reggio di Calabria. They also run from the mainland and from Sicily to surrounding islands and archipelagoes, for example from Naples to Capri and Ischia. Boats for Sardinia leave from Civitavecchia near Rome, Livorno, and Genoa. There are car ferry services from Brindisi to Corfu and Patras in Greece. In summer, these ferries can get very crowded, so make sure you reserve well in advance.

DIRECTORY

AIRLINES

Air Canada
Tel 1-888 247 2262
(Canada).
www.aircanada.com

Air One
Tel 199-207 080 (Italy).
www.flyairone.it

Alitalia
Tel 06-22 22 (Italy).
Tel 800-223 5730 (US).
Tel 08714 241 424 (UK).
www.alitalia.com

American Airlines
Tel 199-257 300 (Italy).
Tel 800-433 7300 (US).
www.aa.com

British Airways
Tel 199-71 22 66 (Italy).
Tel 0844-493 0787 (UK).
www.ba.com

Delta
Tel 800-221 1212 (US).
Tel 02-38 59 10 87 (Italy).
www.delta.com

easyJet
www.easyjet.com

Meridiana
Tel 892-892 898 (Italy).
www.meridiana.it

Qantas
Tel 848-35 00 10
(Italy).
Tel 13 13 13 (Australia).
www.qantas.com

Ryanair
www.ryanair.com

United Airlines
Tel 02-69 63 37 07 (Italy).
Tel 1-800-589 55 82 (US).
www.united.com

GETTING AROUND VENICE

ACTV Information Office
Piazzale Roma, Venice.
Tel 041-24 24.
www.actv.it

Consorzio Motoscafi Rialto (Water Taxis)
Tel 041-522 23 03.

RAIL TRAVEL

Alta Velocità
www.trenitalia.com

Eurostar
www.raileurope.com (US)
www.eurostar.com (UK).

Ferrovie dello Stato
Toll-free number;
information and inquiries.
Tel 89-20 21.
www.trenitalia.com

BUS COMPANIES

Cotral
Rome: *Tel 800-17 44 71.*
www.cotralspa.it

Lazzi
Tel 055-36 30 41
(Florence).
www.lazzi.it

Sita
Tel 055-47 821.
www.sitabus.it

CAR RENTAL

Avis
Tel 199-10 01 33
(Italy).
www.avisautonoleggio.it

Europcar
Tel 199-30 70 30
(Italy).
www.europcar.it

Hertz
Tel 199-11 22 11
(Italy).
www.hertz.it

Maggiore
Tel 199-15 11 20
(Rome).
www.maggiore.it

Sixt
Tel 199-10 06 66 (Italy).
www.sixt.it

Shopping

Italy is known for its quality designer goods, ranging from chic clothing and sleek cars to stylish household items. There is a strong tradition of craftsmanship, often from family-run businesses, and there are numerous markets selling regional specialties. Apart from the town markets, it is not a country for bargains, but the joys of window-shopping will offer plenty of compensation.

OPENING HOURS

Opening times for shops are usually 9:30am–1pm, and 3:30 or 5–8pm. In many places, stores are traditionally closed on Monday mornings, but shopkeepers are increasingly working more flexible hours.

DEPARTMENT STORES

Department stores are often open without a lunchbreak (*orario continuato*) from 9am until 8pm Monday to Saturday. **La Rinascente** stores are good for ready-to-wear clothes, haberdashery, and perfumes.

DESIGNER FASHION

Italy is famous worldwide for its fashion industry. Milan, its designer capital, is stormed each year by Italians and foreigners alike in search of the latest catwalk novelty. **Giò Moretti**, in Via della Spiga, features articles by the top names, as well as pieces by up-and-coming designers.

Retail outlets of famous designers can be found in most Italian city centers. In Venice, **Armani** and others have stylish shops just off the Piazza San Marco. Rome's most famous designer is **Valentino**. His and other top fashion names dominate Rome's Via Condotti, Via de' Tornabuoni in Florence, and the Chiaia district of Naples.

CLOTHING STORES

Less expensive clothes are available in high-street stores, where the styles tend to be more conventional and classical. Sales, *saldi*, are held during summer and winter. The rare secondhand shops may seem expensive, but the quality of the clothes is good.

JEWELRY

Glitzy gold jewelry is very popular in Italy and every *gioielleria* (jewelry shop) will offer a wide selection of items. Elegant, classic jewelry can be purchased at **Cusi** in Milan, while Venice's smartest jewelers are **Missiaglia** and **Nardi** in Piazza San Marco. **Bulgari**, known for its beautiful jewelry and watches, has a number of retail outlets, as does **Buccellati**, famous for its delicately engraved designs inspired by the Italian Renaissance. For reasonably priced jewelry try **Gioie** in Rome. Naples has several jewelers' and goldsmiths' shops where traditional engraving and cameo work can still be seen. Unusual and original items can often be found in artisan shops (*oreficeria*).

ACCESSORIES

Stylish Italian leather shoes and handbags have an international market, and are a popular purchase of visitors to all parts of the country. **Ferragamo**, the well-known Italian designer, has stores in most Italian cities, offering elegant, classic shoes. Leather bags and luggage are available at **Gatti Francesco**, and **Mandarina Duck** bags are sold in boutiques throughout Italy. **Ottica Nuova di Malizia Michela** sells trendy sunglasses, and **Borsalino** is the place for top-quality classic hats.

One-off pieces by local designers can also be found. In Naples, **Marinella** has a store selling her famous ties worn by many celebrities.

HOUSEHOLD ITEMS

Household stores in cities and towns throughout the country sell the well-designed utensils for which Italy is famous.

Stainless steel and copper kitchenware is a favorite buy with visitors.

REGIONAL CRAFTS

Traditional crafts are still practised in Italy and range from delicate lacework and glassware in Venice to leatherwork, jewelry, and marbled paper in Florence. Elaborate Tuscan pottery, hand-painted dishes from around Amalfi, and De Simone's stylized designer plates from Sicily are among many ceramic styles available.

Among the best craft workshops in Rome is **Spazio Artigiano**, which specializes in original, handmade wood, glass, and terra-cotta items. Naples' **Il Cantuccio della Ceramica** is the place to go for ceramics.

In Venice, the best place to buy local blue- and claret-colored glass is the island of Murano. Here, **Barovier e Toso** produces original designs. Some of the most expensive glass in Venice can be bought from **Venini**. Carnival masks, available from **Tragicomica**, and traditional Burano lace are also popular buys.

The Etruscan art of working alabaster is best seen in Volterra. Handmade perfumes and toiletries, and hand-painted majolica are favorite purchases in Tuscany. Sicily is well known for its ceramics, and for traditional puppets. The latter, now rare, can still be found in antique shops.

GOURMET FOODS

Many of Italy's regional food specialties are world-famous: Parma ham, Chianti wine, olive oil, and grappa. Regional sweets, including Sienese *panforte* and Sicilian marzipan, are also well-known, as are cheeses such as Gorgonzola from Lombardy and Parmesan from Emilia-Romagna. Other delicacies include truffles from Piedmont and Umbria. The Lombardy region produces the famous *panettone* cake, and *amaretto* biscuits are made in the Veneto. *Vesuvio* chocolate with rum from Naples is also delicious.

To make the most of Italian food, try to buy what is in season. Mushrooms and grapes are best in the fall, whereas spring is the season for asparagus, strawberries, and artichokes. In winter, cauliflower and broccoli are at their best, as are lemons from Amalfi and Sicilian blood oranges. Summer is the time for plums, pears, and cherries, as well as zucchini, eggplant, tomatoes, and melon.

FOOD STORES

Specialty stores are the most interesting way to shop for food in Italy. A *fornaio* has the best bread and a *macellaio* has the finest meat (go to a *norcineria* for pork products). Vegetables are freshest from market stands or the *fruttivendolo*. You can buy cakes at the *pasticceria*, milk at the *latteria*, and pasta, ham, and cheese at the well-stocked *alimentari* and delicatessens.

To buy wine, head for the *enoteca*, *vineria*, or *vinaio*, where you can sometimes taste the products first. Italy is a major wine producer and stores stock a wide range of labels, from the prized Barolo and Barbaresco vintages to the inexpensive but palatable local *vino da tavola*.

MARKETS

All Italian towns have at least one market a week. Large towns have small, daily markets in addition to a weekly flea market, usually held on a Sunday. Traders set up early and usually start to clear away at about 1:30pm. Bargaining is not usual when buying food, but it is worth asking for a discount *(sconto)* for clothes and other items.

Larger markets have stands piled high with secondhand clothes, and many markets sell fake Ray-Ban sunglasses, Lacoste T-shirts, and Levi's jeans. Popular gifts from Italy include the ceramics and wooden kitchen items sold in most markets.

Specialty markets can be found in many cities. Milan's antique market, the Mercatone dell'Antiquariato, is held on the last Sunday of the month, and the Via Sannio and Porta Portese markets of Rome are a mecca for secondhand clothes. The fish market by the Rialto Bridge in Venice is an interesting place to visit.

DIRECTORY

DEPARTMENT STORES

La Rinascente
Galleria Alberto Sordi, Piazza Colonna, Rome.
Tel *06-679 01 09.*
Piazza Fiume, Rome.
Tel *06-884 12 31.*
Piazza della Repubblica 1, Florence.
Tel *055-21 91 13.*
Piazza Duomo, Milan.
Tel *02-885 21.*

DESIGNER FASHION

Armani
Via Condotti 77, Rome.
Tel *06-699 14 60.*
Via de Tornabuoni 48r, Florence.
Tel *055-21 90 41.*
Via Manzoni 31, Milan.
Tel *02-7231 86 00.*
Piazza Martiri 61, Naples.
Tel *081-40 63 63.*
San Marco 4412, Venice.
Tel *041-523 47 58.*

Giò Moretti
Via della Spiga 4, Milan.
Tel *02-76 00 73 27.*

Valentino
Via Bocca di Leone 16, Rome.
Tel *06-667 83 656.*
Via dei Tosinghi 52r, Florence.
Tel *055-29 31 42.*

JEWELRY

Buccellati
Via Condotti 31, Rome.
Tel *06-679 03 29.*
Via della Vigna Nuova 73R, Florence.
Tel *055-239 65 79.*
Via Monte Napoleone 23, Milan.
Tel *02-79 50 59.*

Bulgari
Via Condotti 10, Rome.
Tel *06-679 38 76.*
Via della Spiga 6, Milan.
Tel *02-76 01 34 48.*

Cusi
Via Monte Napoleone 21a, Milan.
Tel *02-76 01 43 23.*

Gioie
Via di Grotta Rossa 126, Rome.
Tel *06-33 26 03 51.*

Missiaglia
Procuratie Vecchie Piazza, San Marco 125, Venice.
Tel *041-522 44 64.*

Nardi
Procuratie Nuove, Piazza San Marco 69, Venice.
Tel *041-522 57 33.*

ACCESSORIES

Borsalino
Piazza del Popolo 20, Rome.
Tel *06-32 60 92 56.*
Galleria Vittorio Emanuele II 92, Milan.
Tel *02-890 15 436.*

Ferragamo
Via Condotti 73, Rome.
Tel *06-679 15 65.*
Via de' Tornabuoni 16r, Florence.
Tel *055-29 21 23.*
Via Montenapoleone 3, Milan.
Tel *02-76 00 00 54.*

Gatti Francesco
Via di Propaganda 19, Rome.
Tel *06-679 39 58.*

Mandarina Duck
Via dei due Macelli 59, Rome. **Tel** *06-67 86 414.*

Marinella
Riviera di Chiaia 287A, Naples.
Tel *081-764 42 14.*

Ottica Nuova di Malizia Michela
Via P. Rossi 38, Milan.
Tel *02-648 03 10.*

REGIONAL CRAFTS

Barovier e Toso
Fondamenta Vetrai 28, Murano.
Tel *041-73 90 49.*

Il Cantuccio della Ceramica
Via Benedetto Croce 38, Naples.
Tel *081-552 58 57.*

Spazio Artigiano
Vicolo dei Serpenti 13, Rome.
Tel *06-47 82 48 60.*

Tragicomica
Calle dei Nomboli, San Polo 2800, Venice.
Tel *041-72 11 02.*

Venini
Piazzetta dei Leoncini San Marco 314, Venice.
Tel *041-522 40 45.*

Entertainment

With world-class sporting and a host of cultural events, Italy has something to offer everyone. The cities boast a varied and lively nightlife, while its Riviera resorts, hill villages, and classical sites are ideal for the avid sightseer or walker. Skiing in the Alps, water sports of all kinds on the coast, and pony trekking in the countryside, are tourist favorites. The open-air theater and music performances in summer are world-famous. Or simply join the Italians in their traditional evening stroll, the *passeggiata*, followed by a drink at a bar or café in a picturesque piazza.

ENTERTAINMENT LISTINGS

Information about what's on in Rome can be found in *Trovaroma*, the weekly Thursday supplement to the *La Repubblica* newspaper. There is also a weekly listings publication, *Roma C'è*, which has a section in English.

In Florence, the monthly magazine *Firenze Spettacolo* has restaurant and café guides, as well as details of concerts, exhibitions, and sporting events. *Milano Mese* is a free brochure listing concerts and other cultural events held in and around the city.

Un Ospite di Venezia (A Guest in Venice), produced by the Hotels' Association, comes out fortnightly in summer and monthly in winter and is free.

If you can read Italian, regional newspapers are also a good source of information about current events. Local tourist offices display posters advertising forthcoming events.

TICKETS

Making advance reservations for concerts is not the custom in Italy, where decisions are often made on the spur of the moment. To guarantee a seat you may have to visit the box office in person, although online agencies such as **Ticketone** (www.ticketone.it) and **Listicket** (www.listicket.it) sell tickets for many events. You may have to pay an advance booking supplement, or *prevendita,* which is generally about 10 percent of the ticket price.

Tickets for popular music concerts are normally sold through record and music shops, whose names are displayed on the publicity material distributed.

Whereas tickets for classical concerts are sold on the spot for same-day performances, opera tickets are purchased months in advance. Prices vary significantly according to the artists scheduled to perform and the type of venue.

ENTERTAINMENT VENUES

Rome's city churches and the **Parco della Musica** are favorite venues for classical music lovers. Venice also makes good use of its most magnificent churches as concert halls. **La Pietà** was Vivaldi's own church and is still used for classical music performances. In Milan, by contrast, the **San Siro** football stadium is often used as a concert venue along with the 5,400-capacity **Pala AJ** and the even larger **Palasharp**.

OPEN-AIR VENUES

During the summer, Italy's historic buildings and classical ruins become dramatic settings for open-air events. Concerts are held in the grounds of Rome's Villa Celimontana and Villa Ada, while Greek and Roman plays are staged in the restored theater of **Ostia Antica**, southwest of Rome.

In Venice the gardens of the Baroque palace, **Ca'Rezzonico,** and the ornate, enclosed courtyard of the Doge's Palace *(see pp436–7)* are used as outdoor concert venues. The 1st-century Teatro Romano *(see pp430–31)* in Verona also stages open-air concerts.

OPERA

Opera is one of the great cultural delights of Italy, whether experienced in the magnificent opera houses of **La Scala** in Milan or Venice's **Teatro La Fenice,** or in a spectacular open-air venue like Verona's superb **Arena**. The opera house of Naples, **San Carlo,** also boasts world-class performers. The **Teatro dell'Opera** in Rome has a late winter season and an open-air summer festival in the Terme di Caracalla archaeological park.

The opera season at the Verona Arena runs from the first week in July until the beginning of September, and every year features a lavish production of Verdi's *Aida*.

CLUBS AND DISCOS

Cities and resorts in Italy are packed with trendy discos, and upscale night-clubs. **Gilda,** with its two elegant restaurants and large dancefloor, is a favorite with Rome's jet set. A younger crowd frequents **Alien**. In the summer months the nightlife shifts to the Roman seaside resort of Fregene.

Currently attracting the fashion crowd of Milan is the **Hollywood** club. Venice's historic casino **Casinò di Venezia** draws well-dressed gamblers from far and wide. There are a number of discos at Mestre on the mainland.

ITALIAN FESTIVALS

The distinctive regionalism which has survived in modern Italy is marked by the diverse local festivals celebrated each year. For example, on April 25 Venetians commemorate St. Mark with a gondola race, and on June 24 Florence relives its past with a procession of people in 16th-century costumes. The Sienese celebrate the Palio – a bareback horse race dating from 1283 – on July 2 and August 16 each year. Traditional dress is worn in the processions and pre-race pageants. Other *festas* celebrate the harvesting of local produce: the wine festivals held in September and October in Chianti, Tuscany, and the Castelli Romani south of Rome, are popular with visitors.

Many events have an international flavor, such as the film festivals held in Venice (Aug–Sep), Taormina, (Jul–Aug), and Rome (Oct). From May to June Florence hosts an arts festival and Syracuse celebrates Greek drama. Ravello, near Naples, hosts an international festival of music each May.

Masked Venetians spill onto the streets during Carnival in February, and on summer evenings throughout Italy tourists can join in street dancing at local *festas*.

SPECIAL INTEREST VACATIONS

Culinary holidays run by English-speaking experts in Italian cooking are very popular. **Tasting Places**, for example, organizes wine tours and week-long courses in Italian cuisine. The course locations include the Veneto, Sicily, Tuscany, and Umbria.

The **Società Dante Alighieri** provides courses in the Italian language, literature, history of art, and culture. There are both full- and part-time courses available, for every level of ability.

The **Gruppo Archeologico Romano** runs digs in various regions. There are summer and winter trips for both adults and children.

For those with an interest in more energetic activities, the **Federazione Arrampicata Sportiva Italiana** has a list of mountain-climbing schools that organize climbs for people of all abilities. Ski holidays are best arranged with agents offering package deals. Trekking excursions can be organized with **Club Alpino Italiano (CAI)**. Nature walks and bird-watching trips are run by the **Italian Birds Protection League (LIPU)**. Cyclists will find miles of flat and scenic cycling routes in the Po Delta.

WATER SPORTS

Most lakeside towns and many seaside resorts in Italy rent out sailboats, canoes, and windsurfing equipment and lessons are often available. Longer courses in a variety of water sports are organized by clubs, which usually require membership.

The **Federazione Italiana Attività Subacquee** runs underwater diving courses. Most travel agents have a selection of sailing vacations.

Swimming pools are expensive in Italy, but it is cheaper if you pay for a certain number of sessions or for a short membership. Water parks are popular and provide pools, slides, wave machines, and games.

DIRECTORY

ENTERTAINMENT VENUES

Ca'Rezzonico
Fondamenta Rezzonico 3136, Venice.
Tel *041-241 01 00.*

La Pietà
Calle della Pietà, Venice.
Tel *041-522 21 71.*

Ostia Antica
Viale dei Romagnoli 717, Rome.
Tel *06-56 35 28 30.*

Palasharp
Via San Elia 33, Milan.
Tel *02-33 40 05 51.*

Parco della Musica
Viale de Coubertin, Rome.
Tel *06-80 24 12 81.*

San Siro
Via dei Piccolomini 5, Milan. **Tel** *02-48 71 37 13.*

OPERA

Teatro alla Scala
Via Filodrammatici 2, Milan.
Tel *02-88 791.*
www.teatroallascala.org

Teatro dell'Opera
Piazza Beniamino Gigli 7, Rome.
Tel *06-48 16 01.*
www.operaroma.it

Teatro La Fenice
San Marco Campo, San Fantin 1965, Venice.
Tel *041-24 24.*

Teatro San Carlo
Via San Carlo 98/f, Naples.
Tel *081-797 23 31.*

Verona Arena
Via Dietro Anfiteatro 6/b, Verona.
Tel *045-59 65 17.*

CLUBS AND DISCOS

Alien
Via Velletri 13, Rome.
Tel *06-841 22 12.*

Casinò di Venezia
Cannaregio 2040.
Tel *041-529 71 11.*

Gilda
Via Mario de' Fiori 97, Rome.
Tel *06-67 84 838.*

Hollywood
Corso Como 15, Milan.
Tel *328-15 19 288.*

Pala AJ
Piazza Carlo Stuparich 1, Milan.

SPECIAL INTEREST VACATIONS

Club Alpino Italiano
Via Galvani 10, 00153 Rome.
Tel *06-57 28 71 43.*
www.cairoma.it

Federazione Arrampicata Sportiva Italiana
Via del Terrapieno 27, Bologna.
Tel *051-601 48 90.*
www.federclimb.it

Gruppo Archeologico Romano
Via Baldo degli Ubaldi 168, Rome.
Tel *06-638 52 56.* **www**. gruppoarcheologico.it

Italian Birds Protection League
Via Trento 49, 43100 Parma.
Tel *0521-27 30 43.*
www.lipu.it

Società Dante Alighieri
Piazza Firenze 27, 00186 Rome.
Tel *06-687 36 94.*
www.ladante.it

Tasting Places
PO Box 38174, London W10 5ZP, England.
Tel *0208-964 5333.*
www.tastingplaces.com

WATER SPORTS

Federazione Italiana Attività Subacquee
Via A. Dona 8, 20124 Milan. **Tel** *02-670 50 05.*
www.fias.it

Where to Stay in Italy

Accommodations in Italy range from the family-run *pensione* to the Renaissance palazzo, and prices vary accordingly. Top hotels in Venice and Florence are very expensive. Italian lodgings tend to have fewer facilities, but you can find excellent value in all price ranges. Book early, especially if you want a room with a view.

PRICE CATEGORIES
Price categories are for a standard double room per night, including tax and service charges but not breakfast.

€ Under €85
€€ €85–€150
€€€ €150–€250
€€€€ €250–€350
€€€€€ Over €350

ROME

AVENTINE Sant'Anselmo
€€€ — Map D4

Piazza di Sant'Anselmo 2, 00153 **Tel** *06-570 057* **Fax** *06-578 36 04* **Rooms** *45*

This pretty villa is on a peaceful square halfway up the Aventine hill. The entrance hall is stenciled with flowers; there are chandeliers and corridors with floors of inlaid marble. The lounge looks onto the hotel's garden. Many of the rooms have terraces. The staff provide a warm service. **www.aventinohotels.com**

CAMPO DE' FIORI Teatro di Pompeo
€€€ — Map C3

Largo del Pallaro 8, 00186 **Tel** *06-687 28 12* **Fax** *06-68 80 55 31* **Rooms** *12*

A lovely little hotel built on the remains of the ancient theater of the same name, where Julius Caesar is said to have met his destiny. Rooms are large and comfortable with wooden beams and dark wooden furniture. Breakfast is served in the basement under a Roman vault. **www.hotelteatrodipompeo.it**

FORUM Lancelot
€€€ — Map E4

Via Capo d'Africa 47, 00184 **Tel** *06-70 45 06 15* **Fax** *06-70 45 06 40* **Rooms** *60*

A popular place to stay near the Colosseum with very friendly, helpful staff. Rooms are spacious and charming. Some have private terraces with views, and two are specially adapted for guests with disabilities. A half-board option is available and a hearty breakfast is served in the patio garden. **www.lancelothotel.com**

PANTHEON Grand Hotel de la Minerve
€€€€€ — Map C3

Piazza della Minerva 69, 00186 **Tel** *06-69 52 01* **Fax** *06-679 41 65* **Rooms** *135*

Favored by Italy's first Grand Tourists, with generations following ever since, the charismatic Minerve is a fusion of Old-World elegance and contemporary styling. Marble and chandeliers abound, as do wonderful frescoes, tastefully blended with cutting-edge design. Excellent rooftop bar and restaurant. **www.grandhoteldelaminerve.com**

PIAZZA DI SPAGNA Panda
€€ — Map C2

Via della Croce 35, 00187 **Tel** *06-678 01 79* **Fax** *06-69 94 21 51* **Rooms** *28*

Panda is an appealing little hotel with a faithful clientele, offering unpretentious, cheap accommodations in one of Rome's most expensive areas. Clean rooms with or without bathrooms, but all with air-conditioning, telephone, and Internet access. A couple of the rooms feature original 19th-century frescoes. **www.hotelpanda.it**

PIAZZA DI SPAGNA Hassler
€€€€€ — Map D2

Piazza Trinità dei Monti 6, 00187 **Tel** *06-69 93 40* **Fax** *06-678 99 91* **Rooms** *98*

At the top of the Spanish Steps, this is the glitterati's choice and the grande dame of Rome's hotels. Service is impeccable and the public spaces are luxurious with marble, chandeliers, and wood paneling. Bedrooms and suites are plush, styled individually, and most have views. Legendary roof restaurant. **www.hotelhasslerroma.com**

PIAZZA NAVONA Raphael
€€€€€ — Map C3

Largo Febo 2, 00186 **Tel** *06-68 28 31* **Fax** *06-687 89 93* **Rooms** *59*

A lovely burnt sienna palazzo, strewn with ivy and fairy lights just off the piazza, Raphael is romantic and stylish. There are breathtaking views from its roof terrace, where meals are served in summer. Rooms are well appointed, if fairly small. The lobby is filled with art, including a Picasso porcelain collection. **www.raphaelhotelrome.com**

TERMINI Hotel Columbia
€€€ — Map C3

Via del Viminale 15, 00184 **Tel** *06-488 35 09* **Fax** *06-474 02 09* **Rooms** *45*

A quiet gem of a hotel in one of Rome's busiest neighbourhoods. Dark wood and light colored fabrics give the rooms (some with balconies) an airy, Mediterranean feel. The extensive buffet breakfast can be enjoyed on the pretty roof terrace. **www.hotelcolumbia.com**

TRASTEVERE San Francesco
€€€ — Map C4

Via Jacopa de' Settesoli 7, 00153 **Tel** *06-58 30 00 51* **Fax** *06-58 33 34 13* **Rooms** *24*

A lovely little hotel, away from the crowds, with the perfect roof terrace. Very stylish, modern rooms in a converted Franciscan convent. Professional and friendly staff. A tiny shuttle bus on the adjacent square takes you to the heart of Trastevere and a tram takes you across the river to the centre. **www.hotelsanfrancesco.net**

Key to Symbols *see back cover flap*

ATICAN Hilton Cavalieri
☐ Ⅱ ☆ ≋ ⅶ 🏠 🅿 Ⅷ   €€€€€

*ia Cadlolo 101, 00136 **Tel** 06-350 91 **Fax** 06-35 09 22 41 **Rooms** 370*
Map B2

lthough a 15-minute drive from the centre of Rome, Hilton Cavalieri is one of the city's top hotels, with the finest estaurant, La Pergola. Set in large, lush gardens, it has a huge pool and a sumptuous spa. Rooms are beautifully ecorated and some have spectacular views over Rome. Extras are expensive. **www.romecavalieri.it**

IA VENETO Westin Excelsior
☐ Ⅱ ☆ ≋ ⅶ 🏠 🅿 Ⅷ   €€€€€

*ia Veneto 125, 00187 **Tel** 06-470 81 **Fax** 06-482 62 05 **Rooms** 317*
Map D2

xotically sculpted balconies with caryatid figures announce the presence of this extravagant hotel on Via Veneto. nside are boutiques, a wonderful new spa with pool, excellent panoramic restaurants and bar, and even a children's lub. The rooms are classically sumptuous throughout. **http://excelsior.hotelinroma.com**

ILLA BORGHESE Villa Mangili
🏠 🗐 🅿 Ⅷ   €€€

*ia G Mangili 31, 00197 **Tel** 06-321 71 30 **Fax** 06-322 43 13 **Rooms** 12*
Map D1

n a pleasant, quiet part of Parioli, Villa Mangili is close to the Villa Borghese park near the auditorium and the Villa iiulia. Although small, it has spacious and beautifully decorated rooms with wooden parquet floors. Breakfast is erved in a lovely garden. The hotel exhibits and sells the works of new artists. **www.hotelvillamangili.it**

FLORENCE

ITY CENTER Hermitage
🏠 🗐 Ⅷ   €€

*icolo Marzio 1, 50122 **Tel** 055-28 72 16 **Fax** 055-21 22 08 **Rooms** 28*
Map D4

his hotel is on four floors of a medieval tower: the reception and common areas are on the fifth floor; the roof-arden on the sixth offers a panoramic view of the Vasari Corridor, the Ponte Vecchio, the Arno and beyond. Rooms acing the Duomo are quieter. Wi-Fi is in the common areas of the hotel only. **www.hermitagehotel.com**

ITY CENTER Grand Hotel Minerva
🏠 Ⅱ ≋ 🗐 Ⅷ   €€€

*iazza Santa Maria Novella 16, 50123 **Tel** 055-272 30 **Fax** 055-26 82 81 **Rooms** 102*
Map C2

he only hotel in Florence to have a rooftop swimming pool. Watching the sunset from here or from the adjacent bar s a totally memorable experience. Many of the rooms have views over the adjacent Maria Novella church and clois-ers. Famous guests have included the likes of Henry James. **www.grandhotelminerva.com**

ITY CENTER Loggiato dei Serviti
🏠 🗐 Ⅷ   €€€

*iazza Santissima Annunziata 3, 50122 **Tel** 055-28 95 92 **Fax** 055-28 95 95 **Rooms** 39*
Map D3

uilt in the 16th century by the Padri Serviti order to house traveling prelates. A mirror-image of Brunelleschi's pedale degli Innocenti across the square. All the rooms are different. Rooms overlook either the piazza or the arden of the Accademia delle Belle Arti. Advanced booking essential. **www.loggiatodeiservitihotel.it**

ITY CENTER Palazzo Niccolini al Duomo
🏠 Ⅱ 🗐 Ⅷ   €€€

*ia dei Servi 2, 50122 **Tel** 055-28 24 12 **Fax** 055-29 09 79 **Rooms** 10*
Map D4

n a prime location directly facing the Duomo, this 16th-century palazzo is run by descendants of the original owners. eception and guestrooms are on the second floor. Public areas have paintings and antiques. Rooms have marble athrooms. The living room of the suite has a unique view of Brunelleschi's dome. **www.niccolinidomepalace.com**

ITY CENTER Porta Rossa
🏠 🗐 Ⅷ   €€€

*ia Porta Rossa 19, 50123 **Tel** 055-27 10 911 **Fax** 055-27 10 901 **Rooms** 78*
Map D2

ocated between the Ponte Vecchio and Piazza Santa Trinità. While the current building dates from 1500, documents onfirm that a house stood here as early as 1386. The hotel's vaulted entrance hall is decorated in the Italian Art louveau style known as Liberty. Wi-Fi in the lobby only. **www.nh-hoteles.com**

ITY CENTER Excelsior
🏠 Ⅱ ⅶ 🗐 Ⅷ   €€€€€

*iazza Ognissanti 3, 50123 **Tel** 055-271 51 **Fax** 055-21 02 78 **Rooms** 171*
Map B3

he Excelsior excels. Marble floor and columns, grand staircases, stained-glass windows, statues, and period aintings. The rooms are equally opulent, and the service impeccable. The restaurant Orvm serves contemporary Mediterranean cuisine; the ground-floor terrace provides splendid views. **www.starwoodhotels.com/westin**

ITY CENTER Savoy
🏠 Ⅱ ⅶ 🗐 Ⅷ   €€€€€

*iazza della Repubblica 7, 50123 **Tel** 055-273 51 **Fax** 055-273 58 88 **Rooms** 102*
Map B2

rchitecturally magnificent, lavish interiors, elegantly appointed rooms with 14 suites (two of which have a ammam). The sixth-floor gym has spectacular views of the Duomo and Giotto's *campanile*. The L'Incontro bar on he piazza is a rendezvous point for the Florentines. Wi-Fi in public areas only. **www.hotelsavoy.it**

OUTH OF THE ARNO Silla
🏠 🗐 Ⅷ   €€€

*ia de' Renai 5, 50126 **Tel** 055-234 28 88 **Fax** 055-234 14 37 **Rooms** 35*
Map E4

ocated in a 16th-century building, this family-run hotel on the Oltrarno side of the river is reached through an legant courtyard. A grand staircase leads to the entrance of this hotel (also lift). Breakfast is served on the terrace in he summer, overlooking the river and the city. **www.hotelsilla.it**

Map References *see maps of Rome pp392–3 and Florence pp412–3*

VENICE

CANNAREGIO Continental
€€€
Map C2

Lista di Spagna 166, 30121 **Tel** *041-71 51 22* **Fax** *041-524 24 32* **Rooms** *93*

This sizeable modern hotel caters mainly to large groups. It boasts a restaurant with panoramic views next to the Grand Canal. Many rooms have views of the canals, while others overlook a shady square. The hotel's location is especially handy for one of the city's main tourist shopping districts. **www.hotelcontinentalvenice.com**

CASTELLO Paganelli
€€€
Map F4

Riva degli Schiavoni 4182, 30122 **Tel** *041-522 43 24* **Fax** *041-523 92 67* **Rooms** *21*

This hotel has an excellent location on the San Marco waterfront, close to ferry services, with wonderful views from the front rooms, which are furnished in an old style and cozy. The accommodations in the annexe (*dipendenza*) are quieter but less attractive. Babysitting can be arranged with prior notice. **www.hotelpaganelli.com**

CASTELLO Londra Palace
€€€€€
Map F4

Riva degli Schiavoni 4171, 30122 **Tel** *041-520 05 33* **Fax** *041-522 50 32* **Rooms** *53*

Elegance, excellent service, and spacious rooms characterize this top hotel. Located close to the monument to King Vittorio Emanuele on the broad bustling Riva a short stroll from the Piazza, it has splendid views over the water. It was here that Tchaikovsky composed his Fourth Symphony. **www.hotellondra.it**

DORSODURO Ca' Pisani
€€€€
Map C5

Dorsoduro 979a, 30123 **Tel** *041-240 14 11* **Fax** *041-277 10 61* **Rooms** *29*

This converted 15th-century palace is very handily located for the Accademia galleries and the Peggy Guggenheim Collection. The atmosphere is compounded by stunning modern design, a roof terrace, and a relaxing steam bath. There is an onsite restaurant, and a wine and cheese bar in the summer months. **www.capisanihotel.it**

LIDO DI VENEZIA Villa Mabapa
€€€

Riviera San Nicolò 16, 30126 **Tel** *041-526 05 90* **Fax** *041-526 94 41* **Rooms** *70*

This 1930s villa, originally built as a private residence, has been converted into a comfortable guesthouse. An attractive shady garden welcomes guests back from sightseeing expeditions. Close to the *vaporetto* landing stages, it stands on a promenade overlooking the lagoon. **www.villamabapa.com**

LIDO DI VENEZIA Excelsior
€€€€€
Lungomare Marconi 41, 30126 **Tel** *041-526 02 01* **Fax** *041-526 72 76* **Rooms** *178*

Some find the decor a little dated, but others revel in the nostalgia of the sumptuous 1950s Moorish furnishings. Some rooms face the Adriatic, and others have a spectacular view of the lagoon, with Venice on the horizon. There's a private beach just across the road. **www.ho10.net**

RIALTO Rialto
€€€
Map D3

Riva di Ferro 5149, 30124 **Tel** *041-520 91 66* **Fax** *041-523 89 58* **Rooms** *79*

This rambling establishment has good family rooms, excellent facilities, and a canalside restaurant in the summer months. The marvelous position at the foot of the Rialto bridge ensures spectacular views from many of its rooms, and the *vaporetto* is very convenient. The Wi-Fi is in common areas only. **www.rialtohotel.com**

SAN MARCO Flora
€€€
Map D4

Via XXII Marzo 2283a, 30124 **Tel** *041-520 58 44* **Fax** *041-522 82 17* **Rooms** *43*

This tiny hotel is squeezed in a narrow alley just off a major fashion shopping street, close to Piazza San Marco and the *vaporetto* landing stages. The rooms are a little cramped, but furnished with antiques. A small but pleasant garden can be enjoyed when the weather is fine. It is advisable to reserve in advance. **www.hotelflora.it**

SAN MARCO Danieli
€€€€€
Map D4

Riva degli Schiavoni 4196, 30124 **Tel** *041-522 64 80* **Fax** *041-520 02 08* **Rooms** *225*

Located next to Piazza San Marco, this is one of Venice's most luxurious hotels, perfect for a honeymoon or other romantic stay. Three palazzos from the 14th, 19th, and 20th centuries are furnished with antiques and handmade chandeliers from Murano and embody the splendour of Venice. **www.starwoodhotels.com**

SAN MARCO Europa & Regina
€€€€€
Map D4

San Marco 2159, 30124 **Tel** *041-520 04 77* **Fax** *041-523 15 33* **Rooms** *185*

This splendid establishment was the home of 18th-century artist Tiepolo. In an inspiring position on the Grand Canal close to Piazza San Marco, it has beautifully decorated spacious rooms and sumptuous public areas. The excellent alfresco waterside restaurant is recommended. **http://europa.hotelinvenice.com**

SANTA CROCE Al Sole
€€
Map C4

Fondamenta Minotto 136, 30135 **Tel** *041-244 03 28* **Fax** *041-72 22 87* **Rooms** *51*

Book well in advance to stay in this lovely 14th-century palace, with its marble-floored reception area and photogenic facade. Its courtyard is a blaze of scented blooms in summer. Handy for Piazzale Roma for buses and vaporetti. The inviting rooms have views over the canal or private garden. **www.alsolehotels.com**

Key to Price Guide *see p456* **Map References** *see map of venice pp432–3*

NORTHERN ITALY

GENOA Torre Cambiaso
🏨 🏃 🏊 P W   €€

Via Scarpanto 49, 16157 **Tel** *010-698 06 36* **Fax** *010-697 30 22* **Rooms** *42*

A unique noble villa with romantic tower, orchards, formal gardens, and a tree-lined avenue leading up to the entrance. Rooms with swathes of fabric and period furniture are located in the villa or the elegantly restored lodge. Guests can enjoy the hotel's heated outdoor pool and the restaurant's Ligurian cuisine. **www.torre-cambiaso.com**

LAKE COMO Hotel du Lac
🛏 🗐 P W   €€€

Via del Prestino 11, 23829 **Tel** *0341-83 02 38* **Fax** *0341-83 10 81* **Rooms** *17*

A peaceful hotel at the water's edge with enchanting views from the lake-facing bedrooms. The breakfast room looks out over the water, too. Charming features include marble columns, wrought-iron balustrades and floral names for every room. Tranquil and relaxing. Closed mid-Nov–mid-Feb. **www.albergodulac.com**

LAKE GARDA Locanda San Vigilio
🏨 🏃 🗐 P W   €€€€€

Punta San Vigilio, 37016 **Tel** *045-725 66 88* **Fax** *045-627 81 82* **Rooms** *14*

One of the loveliest, most exclusive hotels on Lake Garda, exuding old-world charm. Set in tranquil grounds with a small church dedicated to Saint Vigilio. Comfort and service live up to all expectations and there is a private beach and free mooring for waterborne guests. Closed Dec–mid-Mar. **www.locanda-sanvigilio.it**

LAKE MAGGIORE Giardino
🛏 🗐 W   €€

Corso Repubblica 1, 28041 **Tel** *0322-459 94* **Fax** *0322-24 94 01* **Rooms** *56*

The Giardino Hotel is in the centre of town and faces the lake. It is comfortable but sparsely decorated, with a light airy feel. Some rooms have a Jacuzzi. There's a garden and large terrace with views across Lake Maggiore, as well as a small bar. **www.giardinoarona.com**

MANTUA Rechigi
🛏 P W   €€

Via Pier Fortunato Calvi 30, 46100 **Tel** *0376-32 07 81* **Fax** *0376-22 02 91* **Rooms** *60*

A bright, contemporary hotel in the historic center of Mantua with a spacious, modern entrance hall, gleaming in white marble. Innovative art is displayed on the ground floor and the hotel boasts a lovely little indoor garden. Close to the great monuments and restaurants of the town. **www.rechigi.com**

MILAN Antica Locanda Leonardo
🛏 🗐 P W   €€

Corso Magenta 78, 20123 **Tel** *02-48 01 41 97* **Fax** *02-48 01 90 12* **Rooms** *20*

A chic family-run guesthouse with bar and dining room, and a wonderful terraced garden at the back. This 19th-century palazzo has antiques mixed with more contemporary decor, and is close to Leonardo da Vinci's Last Supper. Wi-Fi Internet connection in every room. Closed 3 weeks Aug. **www.anticalocandaleonardo.com**

MILAN Park Hyatt Milano
🛏 🏨 🏊 🗐 W   €€€€€

Via Tommaso Grossi 1, 20121 **Tel** *02-88 21 12 34* **Fax** *02-88 21 12 35* **Rooms** *117*

Housed in an old bank, this relaxed hotel is an elegant modern addition to Milan's more traditional hotels. You can't get more central: from the front doors you step into the beautiful domed Galleria, Milan's central walkway of shops alongside the Duomo cathedral. Excellent restaurant, facilities, and service. **www.milan.park.hyatt.com**

PADUA Plaza
🏨 🖥 🗐 P W   €€€

Corso Milano 40, 35139 **Tel** *049-65 68 22* **Fax** *049-66 11 17* **Rooms** *139*

An established and efficiently run hotel with a deservedly good reputation. Though its 1970s exterior appears somewhat unattractive, inside it offers up-to-date technology and modern comforts. It provides a full range of services and a thoroughly warm welcome. **www.plazapadova.it**

PORTOFINO Splendido
🛏 🏨 🏊 🖥 P W   €€€€€

Salita Baratta 16, 16034 **Tel** *0185-26 78 01* **Fax** *0185-26 78 06* **Rooms** *64*

Positioned on a series of terraces and housed in a former monastery overlooking Italy's luxurious fishing village resort of Portofino, this is a truly magnificent place to stay. Service is impeccable and the views from all rooms are unforgettable. Closed mid-Nov–end-Mar. **www.hotelsplendido.com**

TURIN Golden Palace
🛏 🏨 🏃 🖥 P W   €€€€

Via Dell'Arcivescovado 14, 10121 **Tel** *011-551 21 11* **Fax** *011-561 28 00* **Rooms** *195*

This hotel, located in Turin's historic city center, was built in the 1960s and consists of two geometric buildings, Golden One and Golden Two. The furnishings are modern, with ivory, brown, and black colours, and brass and lacquer accents. There's a large spa for relaxing after a day out and about. **www.thi.it**

VERONA Giulietta e Romeo
🛏 🏃 🗐 P W   €€

Vicolo Tre Marchetti 3, 37121 **Tel** *045-800 35 54* **Fax** *045-801 08 62* **Rooms** *30*

This prettily named hotel is situated in a quiet street just behind the Arena, which is just a few minutes' walk away. The city's main attractions are also nearby. The bedrooms are bright and comfortable with modern furnishings. Breakfast is served in the bar. The hotel also offers free bike hire. **www.giuliettaeromeo.com**

Key to Symbols *see back cover flap*

VERONA Due Torri Hotel

🔲 👖 🛎 👖 P W   €€€€

Piazza Sant'Anastasia 4, 37121 **Tel** *045-59 50 44* **Fax** *045-800 41 30* **Rooms** *90*

Standing alongside a beautiful church in the heart of medieval Verona, this sumptuous 14th-century building is one of Italy's most eccentric hotels. Each bedroom is decorated and furnished in the style of a different era and the public areas are equally opulent. Personal shopper available by arrangement. **www.duetorrihotels.com**

VICENZA Campo Marzio

🔲 👖 🗐 P W   €€

Viale Roma 27, 36100 **Tel** *0444-54 57 00* **Fax** *0444-32 04 95* **Rooms** *35*

A stylish boutique hotel with good facilities, just a short stroll from the city center and the principal Palladian sites. The bedrooms are large and beautifully furnished – each room with its own individual decor and Wi-Fi connection. It is situated in a peaceful location. **www.hotelcampomarzio.com**

CENTRAL ITALY

ASSISI Hotel Umbra

🔲 👖 🗐 W   €€

Via degli Archi 6 (Piazza del Comune), 06081 **Tel** *075-81 22 40* **Fax** *075-81 36 53* **Rooms** *25*

Tucked away on a small street, not far from the town hall, this is a very popular little hotel and restaurant with a courtyard garden offering alfresco dining in summer. Quiet and family run, it has tiled floors and antiques throughout. Bedrooms are airy and elegantly decorated. **www.hotelumbra.it**

BOLOGNA De Commercianti

🔲 🗐 P W   €€€

Via De'Pignattari 11, 40124 **Tel** *051-745 75 11* **Fax** *051-745 75 22* **Rooms** *36*

Just off Piazza Maggiore, this historic building dates from the 12th century. Delightful bedrooms and suites, some with wooden beams or frescoes, others with a private terrace overlooking the church of San Petronio. Prices surge during the trade fairs. Bicycles and Internet access available. **www.bolognaarthotels.it**

FERRARA Duchessa Isabella

🔲 👖 🗐 P W   €€€€

Via Palestro 70, 44100 **Tel** *0532-20 21 21* **Fax** *0532-20 26 38* **Rooms** *27*

A Relais & Chateaux hotel in a delightful 16th-century palazzo. Bedrooms are named after flowers, with plasma-screen televisions and lovely bathrooms. The hotel offers its horse and carriage for glamorous rides around Ferrara. Bicycles for hire. Relaxing grounds and excellent restaurant. **www.duchessaisabella.it**

LUCCA Piccolo Hotel Puccini

W   €€

Via di Poggio 9, 55100 **Tel** *0583-554 21* **Fax** *0583-534 87* **Rooms** *14*

A small, friendly hotel in an attractive stone building in the very heart of Lucca, just over the road from the house in which Giacomo Puccini was born (now a museum) and the busy central square of San Michele. The rooms are small but well priced for the location. **www.hotelpuccini.com**

PERUGIA Albergo Brufani Palace

🔲 👖 🏊 👖 🗐 P W   €€€

Piazza Italia 12, 06100 **Tel** *075-573 25 41* **Fax** *075-572 02 10* **Rooms** *94*

A four-storey luxury hotel on a hill in central Perugia with lovely views over the valleys below. High, frescoed ceilings, parquet floors, stone fireplaces, chandeliers and antiques abound; bedrooms are sumptuous. The swimming pool has a glass floor above Etruscan ruins. There's also a hammam, a gym, and a fine restaurant. **www.brufanipalace.com**

PISA Royal Victoria Hotel

🔲 🗐 P W   €€

Lungarno Pacinotti 12, 56126 **Tel** *050-94 01 11* **Fax** *050-94 01 80* **Rooms** *48*

The Royal Victoria occupies a 10th-century tower built to house the Winemaker's Guild. It became Pisa's first hotel in 1837, combining several medieval tower houses in the process. Run by the welcoming Piegaja family, the rooms are charming in their size and decor. Bike rental and private garage. **www.royalvictoria.it**

RAVENNA Albergo Cappello

🔲 👖 👖 🗐 P W   €€

Via IV Novembre 41, 48100 **Tel** *0544-21 98 13* **Fax** *0544-21 98 14* **Rooms** *7*

Extremely central, on a pedestrianized street, this small boutique hotel is Ravenna's prettiest, though bedrooms are fairly small. Each bedroom has been individually styled and furnished with antiques. The hotel's restaurant and wine bar are renowned. Wi-Fi is in common areas only. **www.albergocappello.it**

SIENA Pensione Palazzo Ravizza

👖 🗐 W   €€€

Pian dei Mantellini 34, 53100 **Tel** *0577-28 04 62* **Fax** *0577-22 15 97* **Rooms** *30*

A *pensione* in a quiet, Renaissance palace in the historical center of Siena. Rooms have original terra-cotta floors, frescoed ceilings, carved wooden doorways, and antique furnishings. Suites have their own lounge areas. Gourmet evening restaurant and a garden terrace overlooking the Tuscan hills. Wi-Fi is in common areas only. **www.palazzoravizza.**

URBINO Hotel Bonconte

🔲 👖 🗐 W   €€

Via delle Mura 28, 61029 **Tel** *0722-24 63* **Fax** *0722-47 82* **Rooms** *23*

A short walk away from the centro storico, just within the city walls, this hotel has lovely views of the countryside around Urbino. This elegant old villa below the town is filled with antiques and set in a garden oasis, where breakfast is served in summer (not included in room rate). Good restaurant. **www.viphotels.it**

Key to Price Guide *see p456* **Key to Symbols** *see back cover flap*

NAPLES AND THE SOUTH

AMALFI Hotel Santa Caterina
🗓 🍴 👥 🎡 📺 🗎 🅿 🅦   €€€€€

S Amalfitana 9, 84011 **Tel** *089-87 10 12* **Fax** *089-87 13 51* **Rooms** *66*

Run by the same family since 1880, this luxury hotel is one of the Amalfi Coast's finest. High over Amalfi, perched on a promontory tumbling down to the sea, it has extensive gardens and terraces. Rooms and suites are lavish, all with antiques, *majolica* floor tiles, and balconies or terraces. Spa and excellent restaurant. **www.hotelsantacaterina.it**

CAPRI Hotel La Minerva
🗓 🗎 🅦   €€€

Via Occhio Marino 8, 80073 **Tel** *081-837 03 74* **Fax** *081-837 52 21* **Rooms** *18*

A pretty five-story hotel with flower-filled terraces, in a quiet, picturesque spot not far from the center of Capri town. *Majolica* tile floors, antiques, and sea views. Superior rooms have a terrace, deluxe rooms have whirlpool bathtubs and sea-facing terraces, while standard rooms are much cheaper. **www.laminervacapri.com**

NAPLES Hotel Chiaja de Charme
🗎 🅦   €€

Via Chiaia 216, 81021 **Tel** *081-41 55 55* **Fax** *081-42 23 44* **Rooms** *27*

A lovely intimate hotel with reception on the first floor of a noble palazzo on the pedestrian street of Via Chiaia, two minutes' walk from Piazza Plebescito. All the rooms are soundproofed and individually furnished with antiques. Some of the bathrooms have whirlpool bathtubs. Charming, professional staff. **www.hotelchiaia.it**

NAPLES Grand Hotel Vesuvio
🗓 🍴 👥 🎡 📺 🗎 🅿 🅦   €€€

Via Partenope 45, 81021 **Tel** *081-764 00 44* **Fax** *081-764 44 83* **Rooms** *143*

In Santa Lucia, the Vesuvio is unarguably Naples' most luxurious hotel, with a spectacular penthouse. All bedrooms and suites are extremely comfortable, furnished with antiques, and have a terrace or balcony with sea or street views. Spa and gym, terrace restaurant, and babysitting room. **www.vesuvio.it**

POSITANO Palazzo Murat
🍴 👥 🗎 🅿 🅦   €€€€

Via dei Mulini 23, 84017 **Tel** *089-87 51 77* **Fax** *089-81 14 19* **Rooms** *30*

This genteel palazzo was once the summer residence of Napoleon's brother-in-law, Murat. Set in an enchanting courtyard with an excellent restaurant, the bedrooms are in the 18th-century wing – and are complete with stucco, beams, and frescoes – or in the elegant modern annex. Guests can use the private boat. **www.palazzomurat.it**

SICILY

AGRIGENTO Park Hotel Colleverde
🗓 🍴 👥 🎡 📺 🗎 🅿 🅦   €€

Via dei Templi, 92100 **Tel** *0922-295 55* **Fax** *0922-290 12* **Rooms** *48*

A modern hotel with a fine view of the Valley of the Temples from its landscaped gardens. The bedrooms are comfortable and nicely furnished: deluxe rooms have wonderful views. Close to Agrigento's center and train station. The restaurant has a terrace. Two rooms have disabled facilities. **www.colleverdehotel.it**

CATANIA Hotel Katane Palace
🗓 🍴 🗎 🅿 🅦   €€

Via Finocchiaro Aprile 110, 95129 **Tel** *095-747 07 02* **Fax** *095-747 01 72* **Rooms** *58*

In a central position, convenient for the port, railway station, and visiting the old quarter. Bedrooms are spacious, elegantly furnished and soundproofed; the en suite bathrooms are very smart. Cuciniere, the hotel's restaurant, is critically renowned and an annual series of music concerts is held here. **www.katanepalace.it**

PALERMO Massimo Plaza Hotel
🗎 👥 🅿 🅦   €€€

Via Maqueda 437, 90133 **Tel** *091-32 56 57* **Fax** *091-32 57 11* **Rooms** *15*

In an extremely central position, opposite the Teatro Massimo, this lovingly restored palazzo has stylish decor and an air of calm. Bedrooms are large and fresh, with soundproofing – some have prime views over the elegant square. There is a welcoming bar and lounge area, and service is excellent. **www.massimoplazahotel.com**

PALERMO Grand Hotel Villa Igiea
🗓 🍴 👥 🎡 📺 🗎 🅿 🅦   €€€€

Salita Belmonte 43, 90142 **Tel** *091-631 21 11* **Fax** *091-631 24 64* **Rooms** *110*

A romantic Hilton hotel outside Palermo, with jasmine-scented gardens overlooking the sea. Built in 1908 by Ernesto Basile, a key proponent of the Italian Art Nouveau style, there are exquisite frescoes in the public areas and original furniture. Elegant bedrooms with garden views or private sea-facing terraces. **www.villa-igiea-palermo.com**

TAORMINA Villa Belvedere
🗓 🍴 🎡 🗎 🅿 🅦   €€

Via Bagnoli Croce 79, 98039 **Tel** *0942-237 91* **Fax** *0942-62 58 30* **Rooms** *47*

A pretty, yellow Liberty style villa in a garden of orange and lemon trees surrounding a pool facing the sea. Five minutes from both the old quarter and the funicular down to the beach. Its public rooms are cool and welcoming and the bedrooms are generally airy and light, most with a balcony or terrace. **www.villabelvedere.it**

Where to Eat in Italy

Each region has its own distinctive cuisine, using local, seasonal ingredients, although national favorites, such as classic pasta dishes, pizzas, and desserts are produced all over the country. Among the countless delights of Italian food, look out for Sicilian fish, game and steaks in Tuscany, and the rich cuisine of Emilia-Romagna.

PRICE CATEGORIES
Price categories are for a three-course meal for one, including half a bottle of house wine, tax, and service.
€ Under €25
€€ €25–€35
€€€ €35–€45
€€€€ €45–€55
€€€€€ Over €55

ROME

CAMPO DE' FIORI Al Pompiere
€€
Via S. M. dei Calderari 38, 00186 **Tel** *06-686 83 77*
Map C3

On the first floor of Palazzo Cenci, in the Ghetto, Al Pompiere has an attractive dining room with frescoes and wooden beams. The Roman-Jewish menu features specialties such as *carciofi alla giudia* (fried artichokes) and beef stew. Fresh fish arrives daily. Desserts are all home-made.

CAMPO DE' FIORI Camponeschi
€€€€€
Piazza Farnese 50, 00186 **Tel** *06-687 49 27*
Map C3

One of Rome's finest restaurants, Camponeschi offers wonderful views of the Piazza Farnese. Its cuisine, a fusion of Italian, Mediterranean and French, is extremely refined. Superb fish and meat dishes. Its *cantina* contains over 400 wines, including its own prestigious label from the family vineyard. Open in evenings only.

CAMPO DE' FIORI Piperno
€€€€€
Monte de' Cenci 9, 00186 **Tel** *06-68 80 66 29*
Map C3

A restaurant has been here since the mid-1800s, though the original Piperno has long gone. His name still carries great kudos, though as one of the finest in Roman-Jewish cooking. The pasta is handmade every day; the fish arrive daily. The house wine is a delicious Frascati. Don't miss the *carciofi alla giudia* (fried artichokes). Book ahead.

PANTHEON Da Gino
€€
Vicolo Rosini 4, 00186 **Tel** *06-687 34 34*
Map C2

Da Gino is a friendly restaurant packed to the gills with politicans and journalists. The frescoed, old-fashioned interior is charming. Classic Roman dishes include *spaghetti alla carbonara*, *abbacchio alla cacciatora* (a lamb dish), *seppie con piselli* (cuttlefish with peas), and rabbit.

PANTHEON El Toulà
€€€€€
Via della Lupa 29B, 00186 **Tel** *06-687 34 98*
Map C2

Justly renowned as one of Rome's most exclusive and luxurious restaurants, El Toulà serves creative versions of traditional Mediterranean dishes. The elegant vaulted dining room and excellent service are perfect for a special lunch or dinner. The wine list contains around 400 labels.

PIAZZA DI SPAGNA Margutta Vegetariana
€€
Via Margutta 118, 00187 **Tel** *06-32 65 05 77*
Map C2

A colorful, plant-filled dining room with modern art in profusion and a jazz soundtrack, this is Rome's first and finest vegetarian eatery. It offers an excellent-value daily brunch and a fantastic menu of creative vegetarian dishes. There's also a separate vegan menu.

PIAZZA NAVONA L'Osteria de Memmo
€€
Via dei Soldati 22–23, 00186 **Tel** *06-68 13 51 12*
Map C2

On the ground floor of the Museo Napoleonico in Palazzo Primoli, this family-run trattoria serves good traditional Roman home cooking. The main specialty is *amatriciana* pasta (with a spicy sauce). Other typical dishes include *ossobuco* (veal shanks) and *saltimbocca alla romana* (veal cutlets with prosciutto and sage). Fresh fish too.

QUIRINAL Al Presidente
€€€€
Via in Arcione 95, 00187 **Tel** *06-679 73 42*
Map D3

One of the city's best restaurants, with wonderful, modern Roman cuisine, elegant decor, and fine wine – ideal for intimate chats. Only a short walk from the Trevi Fountain, it also has a great outdoor terrace. Ingredients, particularly fish and meat, are well researched, with the menu changing accordingly. Four taster menus are available at dinner.

TRASTEVERE Ripa 12
€€€
Via di San Francesco a Ripa 12, 00153 **Tel** *06-580 9093*
Map C4

In Southern Trastevere, far from the tourist trail, Ripa 12 serves excellent seafood. The specialty is the house starter which includes at least ten types of fish *carpaccio* (raw and marinated). The restaurant's oyster and champagne bar a great location for apéritifs. Very much a locals' favorite.

Key to Symbols *see back cover flap*

VATICANO Dal Toscano

€€€€

Via Germanico 56, 00192 **Tel** *06-39 72 57 17*   **Map** *B2*

A popular and ever-reliable restaurant, Dal Toscano has outside tables in summer and a wood-paneled dining room. Roman and Tuscan specialties include exquisitely cooked meat dishes and excellent red wines. Try *Pappardelle alla lepre* (pasta in a hare sauce), fettuccine with porcini mushrooms, or *bistecca alla Fiorentina* (steak on the bone).

VIA VENETO Papà Baccus

€€€€

Via Toscana 36, 00187 **Tel** *06-42 74 28 08*   **Map** *D2*

One of the best addresses in the city for bona fide Tuscan cuisine. From the classic ribollita (a soup of beans, vegetables, and bread) to the various cuts of Chianina beef, every option here is a good one. The restaurant's own farm rears prestigious Cinta Senese pigs – don't miss the exquisite hams, salamis, and grilled meats.

VILLA BORGHESE Baby

€€€€€

Via Ulisse Aldrovandi 15, 00197 **Tel** *06-321 61 26*   **Map** *D1*

Baby is run by the renowned chef behind Don Alfonso (one of Italy's finest restaurants) on the Amalfi Coast. Out-standing Neapolitan-inspired cuisine is served in a delightful dining room, at the poolside, and on the garden terrace at one of Rome's top hotels, the Aldrovandi Palace.

FLORENCE

CITY CENTER Coquinarius

€€

Via delle Oche 15r, 50122 **Tel** *055-230 21 53*   **Map** *D3*

A convenient, cozy little wine bar, just behind the Duomo, where you can eat at almost any time of the day or evening. There are some delicious pasta dishes and the platters of cheeses and cured meats should not be missed. Salads and sandwiches are also available. There are excellent wines by the glass and bottle too.

CITY CENTER Il Santo Bevitore

€€

Via Santo Spirito 64/66r, 50125 **Tel** *055-21 12 64*   **Map** *D4*

Housed in an ex-stable, this relaxed restaurant/wine bar features innovative dishes. The menu changes each month, but there is always a selection of soups and home-made pastas, fish, and grilled meat. The excellent cheeses and cured meats are also on sale at the restaurant's own deli down the road at No. 60r.

CITY CENTER Ristorante Ricchi

€€

Piazza Santo Spirito 8/9r, 50125 **Tel** *055-28 08 30*   **Map** *B4*

With elegant, modern decor and a lovely terrace, this small fish restaurant is situated on one of Florence's most beautiful squares. The pasta and desserts are all home-made. House specialties include ravioli filled with squid, and fillet of red tuna. There's a limited choice for carnivores too.

CITY CENTER Frescobaldi Wine Bar

€€€

Via dei Magazzini 2/4r, 50122 **Tel** *055-28 47 24*   **Map** *B4*

This wine bar and restaurant is owned by one of Tuscany's foremost wine producers. Lunch is a casual affair, while dinner is a little more formal, with white tablecloths and gleaming crystal. Creative, elegant food is accompanied by some fine in-house wines; if you just want a snack and a glass, pop into Frescobaldino next door.

CITY CENTER Il Latini

€€€

Via dei Palchetti 6r, 50123 **Tel** *055-21 09 16*   **Map** *C3*

There is always a crowd of both foreigners and locals clamoring for a table outside this large, noisy *trattoria* where huge hams hang from the ceiling. The food is traditional and the portions are enormous. Try the succulent grilled and roasted meats; *bistecca alla fiorentina* (T-bone steak) is an experience.

CITY CENTER Targa Bistrot

€€€

Lungarno C Colombo 7, 50136 (east of city centre) **Tel** *055-67 73 77*

Background jazz and a warm wood-and-glass interior, softened by lots of greenery, make for a relaxed setting in this bistro on the Arno. The menu changes monthly and includes simple, well-prepared dishes using local ingredients. Great care is taken over desserts such as hot chocolate soufflé. Fantastic wine list.

CITY CENTER Borgo San Jacopo

€€€€€

Borgo San Jacopo 62r, 50125 **Tel** *055-28 16 61*   **Map** *C4*

San Jacopo enjoys a fabulous setting on the south bank of the Arno. Book ahead and ask for one of the coveted tables on the tiny terrace. The chic and breezy atmosphere suits the unpretentious but beautifully served food very well. Fish fans should try the *brodetto* (fish soup), an Adriatic specialty.

CITY CENTER Enoteca Pinchiorri

€€€€€

Via Ghibellina 87, 50122 **Tel** *055-24 27 57*   **Map** *E4*

Pinchiorri is frequently described as Italy's finest restaurant and it has one of Europe's best-stocked cellars, boasting over 80,000 bottles. On the ground floor of a 15th-century palazzo, the ambience is very special too, but the food (ultra-refined Tuscan/French) and the fussy service will not please all.

Map References *see maps of Rome pp392–3 and Florence pp412–3*

VENICE

BURANO Da Romano
☴ ⛓ 🗐 €€€€

Via Galuppi 221, 30012 **Tel** *041-73 00 30*

It is advisable to book ahead to avoid disappointment since this is the leading restaurant on the island of Burano. A wide range of fish is served in traditional Venetian fashion, under the watchful eye of a descendant of the original 19th-century owner. Closed Sun dinner, Tue; mid-Dec–Jan.

CANNAREGIO Vini Da Gigio
🗐 €€€€

Fondamenta San Felice 3628A, 30121 **Tel** *041-528 51 40*   **Map** *E2*

Smart yet rustic decor and refined dishes that use seasonal produce. Risotto with prawns or grilled cuttlefish often feature on the menu, or delicious duck and local artichokes. There is also a vast wine list. Advance booking is advisable. Closed Mon, Tue; 2 wks Jan, 2 wks Aug.

CASTELLO La Corte Sconta
⛓ 🗐 €€€€€

Calle del Pestrin 3886, 30122 **Tel** *041-522 70 24*   **Map** *D4*

Tricky to find, but worth the effort, this simple, laid-back eatery rates among the city's best restaurants. The fresh fish and home-made pasta are superb, and desserts such as *pincia* (a traditional Venetian cake) round off the meal. Closed Sun, Mon; Jan, Aug 1–15.

DORSODURO La Rivista
☴ ⛓ 🗐 €€€

Rio Terrà Foscarini 979/A, 30123 **Tel** *041-240 14 25*   **Map** *C4*

A modern, welcoming establishment close to the Accademia, La Rivista does light salads and cold platters for lunch. Imaginative versions of traditional Venetian dishes are also on offer, and there are divine desserts such as wild-berry cream. The creative menu changes on a monthly basis. Closed Mon.

GIUDECCA Hotel Cipriani
☴ ⛓ 🍸 🗐 €€€€€

Giudecca 10, 30133 **Tel** *041-520 77 44*

A 24-hour courtesy launch ferries guests from the San Marco waterfront to this exclusive island hotel/restaurant for an unforgettable meal. The views are stunning, from the sumptuous Fortuny Restaurant, the more informal Cip's Club restaurant, and the lunchtime Pool Restaurant (open from spring to autumn). Closed Nov–Mar.

SAN MARCO Da Raffaele
☴ ⛓ 🗐 €€€€€

Ponte delle Ostreghe 2347, 30124 **Tel** *041-523 23 17*   **Map** *D4*

This well-established bustling restaurant offers a vast range of regional dishes in an especially romantic setting. Dishes worth trying include *granseola* (spider crab) as an antipasto, risotto with scampi and radicchio, and turbot as a main course. Closed Thu; Dec–early Feb.

SAN MARCO Harry's Bar
🗐 €€€€€

Calle Vallaresso 1323, 30124 **Tel** *041-528 57 77*   **Map** *D4*

Known the world over as Ernest Hemingway's favorite watering hole in Venice, Harry's Bar is a hallowed institution as well as a cozy café. Coffee and toasted sandwiches can be ordered, or a Bellini cocktail. The renowned food on the menu includes *carpaccio* (raw marinated beef), a dish invented by the owner.

SAN POLO Da Fiore
⛓ 🗐 €€€€€

Calle del Scaleter 2202, 30125 **Tel** *041-72 13 08*   **Map** *C3*

An exclusive establishment hidden behind Campo San Polo, Da Fiore is probably the city's best restaurant. Seasonal produce is the rule. Gourmet diners appreciate the sea bass with balsamic vinegar, tuna with rosemary, and *molecche* (soft-shelled crabs). Leave room for a delicate fruit sorbet. Closed Sun, Mon; 3 wks Aug, early Jan.

NORTHERN ITALY

GENOA Da Genio
☴ €€

Salita San Leonardo 61r, 16128 **Tel** *010-58 84 63*

One of Genoa's best-loved *trattorias*, with a loyal clientele, situated in the old quarter. The menu includes well-prepared fish dishes, such as fresh swordfish and stuffed anchovies, but the most famous is the local favorite *trenett al pesto* (pasta with pesto sauce). Closed Sun.

LAKE COMO Albergo Ristorante Silvio
⛓ €€€

Via Carcano 12, 22021 **Tel** *031-95 03 22*

Silvio and Cristian Ponzini, the owner and his son, are the professional fishermen providing an abundant catch of fine freshwater fish for their restaurant. Visitors can even arrange a fishing trip with them, or stay at the self-catering apart-ments. The views over Lake Como are enchanting, especially from the vine-clad terrace. Closed Jan & weekends in Feb

Key to Price Guide *see p462* **Map References** *see map of venice pp432–3*

LAKE GARDA Capriccio

☐ ☐ ⓔⓔⓔⓔⓔ

Piazza S. Bernardo 6, 25080 **Tel** *0365-55 11 24*

This refined establishment with views of Lake Garda offers high-quality cuisine such as *taglioni con lastice* (pasta with lobster) and baked sea bass. The wine bar next door, Il Gusto, offers equally good food and wines in a more informal environment. Closed Tue; Jan–Feb.

MANTUA Il Cigno Trattoria dei Martini

☐ ⓔⓔⓔⓔⓔ

Piazza Carlo d'Arco 1, 46100 **Tel** *0376-32 71 01*

Il Cigno Trattoria dei Martini is a forerunner of the new Mantuan cuisine that simplified traditional heavy dishes and reduced prices. Its signature dish, *cappone in agrodolce* (sweet-and-sour capon) still survives. The fine Mantuan fare is complemented by a good wine list. Closed Mon, Tue; first wk Jan, Aug.

MILAN Trattoria Milanese

☐ ⓔⓔⓔⓔ

Via Santa Marta 11, 20123 **Tel** *02-86 45 19 91*

This trattoria is a Milan institution. Set in a 14th-century palazzo, it has served genuine Milanese food near the Stock Exchange for generations. Classics include *ossobuco* (veal shank), great saffron risotto, and *carpione* (cold mini-cutlets in onion and vinegar dressing). Closed Sat, Sun; mid-Jul–Sep 1, Christmas–Jan 10.

MILAN Da Giacomo

☐ ⓔⓔⓔⓔⓔ

Via Sottocorno 6, corner Via Cellini, 20129 **Tel** *02-76 02 33 13*

A stylish family-run establishment, and an insider address for the well-heeled and fashionable Milanese. House specialties are fish such as sea bass *alla Giacomo* (with herbs and olives). The wine list offers quality vintages. The adjacent bistro is ideal for an apéritif or dinner in a more informal setting. Closed 2 wks Aug, 1 wk Christmas.

PADUA San Pietro

☐ ⓔⓔ

Via San Pietro 95, 35100 **Tel** *049-876 03 30*

The perfect place for regional dishes such as risotto with radicchio cooked with fresh, local ingredients. This traditional Paduan restaurant offers attentive service in an informal atmosphere. Many dishes come from the Lombardy region of Italy. Closed Sun; summer Sat and Sun; Jul.

PORTOFINO Da Puny

☐ ☐ ⓔⓔⓔⓔⓔ

Piazza Martiri dell'Olivetta 5, 16034 **Tel** *0185-26 90 37*

One of the best restaurants lining the tiny harbor square. The proprietor is a gregarious character, happy to recount anecdotes and flatter his guests. Fresh fish, pasta in *pesto corto* (the rich basil, cheese and pine nut sauce lifted with a dash of tomato) and home antipasti are excellent. Closed Thu; mid-Dec–mid-Feb.

TURIN Porto di Savona

☐ ☐ ⓔⓔ

Piazza Vittorio Veneto 2, 10100 **Tel** *011-817 35 00*

This restaurant is housed in an 18th-century building near the River Po. It offers regional dishes such as gnocchi with gorgonzola cheese, local pasta varieties *tajarin* and *agnolotti*, *vitello tonnato* (thin slices of veal in tuna and caper sauce), and other specialties, some using Barolo wine.

VERONA Il Desco

☐ ⓔⓔⓔⓔⓔ

Via Dietro San Sebastiano 5–7, 37121 **Tel** *045-59 53 58*

One of Italy's finest restaurants, set in a 15th-century palazzo, Il Desco truly deserves its two Michelin stars. It is both romantic and understated. Dishes include pumpkin and Amarone wine risotto and the famous aubergine (eggplant) ravioli. A gourmet menu offers a staggering seven courses. Closed Mon; 2 wks Christmas, 2 wks Jun.

VICENZA Taverna Aeolia

☐ ☐ ☐ ⓔⓔ

Piazza Conte da Schio 1, Costozza di Longare, 36023 **Tel** *0444-55 50 36*

This restaurant is housed in an elegant villa with a beautiful frescoed ceiling. The menu changes monthly but specializes in creative meat dishes, such as kangaroo and bison. More traditional dishes and a children's menu are also available. Closed Tue; Nov 1–15.

CENTRAL ITALY

ASSISI Medioevo

☐ ☐ ⓔⓔⓔ

Via Arco dei Priori 4B, 06081 **Tel** *075-81 30 68*

An elegant restaurant set under the medieval stone vaults of an ancient palazzo in the centre of Assisi. Try the home-made pastas (featuring local truffles in season). Meat, such as *agnello al tartufo* (lamb with truffles), is cooked to traditional recipes and they work wonders with steak. Great home-made desserts.

BOLOGNA Antica Trattoria Spiga

☐ ⓔⓔ

Via Broccaindosso 21a, 40125 **Tel** *051-23 00 63*

Cozy, old-fashioned trattoria popular with the locals for its authentic and immaculately prepared traditional cuisine. Among the specialties: lasagne, *tagliatelle al ragù*, *pasta e fagioli* (pasta and bean soup), pasta filled with pumpkin, and a variety of game dishes.

Key to Symbols *see back cover flap*

BOLOGNA Pappagallo

Piazza Mercanzia 3, 40125 **Tel** *051-23 28 07*

Since 1919, princes, artists, and actors have left signed photos to line the walls of this elegant restaurant housed in a 14th-century palazzo practically underneath Bologna's twin towers. The cuisine is traditional Bolognese, including tortellini (in broth), lasagne, and *tagliatelle al ragù*.

FERRARA Al Brindisi

Via Adelardi 11, 44100 **Tel** *0532-47 12 25*

Dating from 1435, this ancient wine bar and restaurant is tucked away down a narrow lane next to the cathedral. Atmospheric and cozy, it offers tasty local dishes such as *cappellacci di zucca* (pasta filled with butternut squash) and *salama da sugo* (richly flavored sausage meat served with mashed potato).

LUCCA Buca di Sant'Antonio

Via della Cervia 3, 55100 **Tel** *0583-558 81*

This carefully restored 19th-century tavern, with an excellent location, serves classic local fare with the occasional innovative touch. The stuffed rabbit en croute with porcini mushrooms is excellent. In winter, several dishes feature locally grown chestnuts. Try *buccellato*, the tasty local pudding. Interesting wines.

PERUGIA Giò Arte e Vini

Via Ruggero d'Andreotto 19, 06124 **Tel** *075-573 11 00*

This modern hotel restaurant and wine bar on the outskirts of town is famous for its spectacular selection of wines (some 1,200 choices). The traditional restaurant serves well-chosen regional dishes prepared with special touches. The pumpkin ravioli and the *trecciola di agnello* (lamb) are particularly good.

PISA Ristorante V. Beni

Piazza Chiara Gambacorti 22, 56125 **Tel** *050-25 067*

In a building dating back to the 14th century, this restaurant is situated a 15-minute walk from the Leaning Tower of Pisa, meaning that it is relatively off the tourist trail. Even so, it is enormously popular with the locals, and it is best to book in advance. Fish-based dishes are a specialty. Closed Sun.

RAVENNA Ca' de' Vén

Via C. Ricci 24, 48100 **Tel** *0544-301 63*

They say Dante stayed at a boarding house on this site, now occupied by a 16th-century palazzo next to the poet's tomb. Its brick vaulted rooms are lined with prestigious wine bottles, hence the name, which means "House of Wines." The specialty is *piadina*, the local flatbread, topped with meat, cheeses, or vegetables.

SAN GIMGNANO Dorandò

Vicolo dell'Oro 2, 53037 **Tel** *0577-94 18 62*

This restaurant is small and very select, so booking is advised. Impressive wine list, and a seasonal menu of delicious local dishes to go with it. Meats include guinea fowl, venison, and prestigious Cinta Senese pork. Take your time to savor it all while enjoying the work of local artists hanging on the walls.

SIENA Osteria Le Logge

Via del Porrione 33, 53100 **Tel** *0577-480 13*

Siena's prettiest, and often full, restaurant has a dark wood and marble interior. The tables are laid with crisp linen cloths and decorated with plants. Home-produced oils and Montalcino wines accompany dishes that wander slightly from mainstream Tuscan cooking. The stuffed guinea fowl is delicious.

URBINO Vecchia Urbino

Via dei Vasari 3–5, 61029 **Tel** *0722-44 47*

An elegantly rustic restaurant in a 16th-century structure serving simply prepared traditional dishes, including *vincisgrassi* (the local lasagne of chicken, ham, and veal), *raviolone al tartufo* (a giant pasta parcel stuffed with ricotta and dressed in black truffles), rabbit, and polenta with mushrooms.

NAPLES AND THE SOUTH

AMALFI La Marinella

Lungomare dei Cavalieri di San Giovanni di Gerusalemme 1, 84011 **Tel** *089-87 10 43*

A lively, friendly restaurant overlooking the Amalfi Coast with a terrace over the sea. Much fish is served, as well as traditional local specialties such as *scialatelli ai frutti di mare* (home-made pasta with seafood and crustaceans). Open for lunch only, except in high season.

CAPRI La Savardina da Eduardo

Via Lo Capo 8, 80073 **Tel** *081-837 63 00*

This is one of the most traditional restaurants on Capri, with an outdoor pergola, orange trees, sea views, and tasty regional specialties such as *ravioli alla caprese* (cheese ravioli in a tomato and mozzarella sauce), *linguini al limone* (pasta with a lemon sauce), and *coniglio alla Poppea* (stewed rabbit).

NAPLES Da Ettore

€€

Via Santa Lucia 56, 80123 **Tel** *081-76 404 98*

Unpretentious neighborhood *trattoria* and pizzeria serving typical Neapolitan cuisine. Good pizzas and excellent seafood pasta with mussels or clams. Also sample the *parmigiana di melanzane* (a baked casserole of aubergines/eggplant, mozzarella and tomatoes). Excellent buffalo mozzarella antipasto.

NAPLES Renzo e Lucia

€€€

Via Tito Angelini 33, 80129 **Tel** *081-191 71 022*

This modern, minimalist restaurant is a great spot for a romantic dinner as well as a more informal get-together. The menu is varied and includes pizzas as well as meat and fish dishes, but the real attraction is the view over Naples from the terrace.

NAPLES La Cantinella

€€€€€

Via Cuma 42/Lungomare di Santa Lucia, 80132 **Tel** *081-764 86 84*

One of Naples's most famous restaurants, this place has a distinctly colonial feel. Diners are attracted by the sea views, the impeccable service, and a reputation for carefully and successfully prepared regional and international cuisine based around seafood and traditional dishes.

POMPEII Il Principe

€€€€

Piazza B. Longo 8, 80045 **Tel** *081-850 55 66*

This airy, refined restaurant with a seasonally changing menu is close to the excavations. The cuisine is based on fish, including fish-filled ravioli, and turbot with vegetables. Dishes may be inspired by 17th-century Neapolitan or ancient Roman recipes. The *cassata di Oplontis* (a dessert of ricotta, honey, and dried fruit) is pictured in Pompeii frescoes.

POSITANO La Sponda

€€€€€

Via Colombo 30, 84017 **Tel** *089-87 50 66*

A sumptuous restaurant in one of Italy's most elegant hotels, where guests are treated like wealthy family friends. A tempting range of traditional regional dishes based on fresh fish and seasonal ingredients is on offer. The locally produced *paccheri* pasta from Gragnano is delicious.

SICILY

AGRIGENTO Trattoria il Pescatore

€€€

Lungomare Falcone e Borsellino 20, Località Lido di San Leone, 92100 **Tel** *0922-41 43 42*

The chef chooses the fish daily and uses it, sometimes raw, in simple but delicious dishes – often just grilling it, and drizzling on some olive oil and lemon juice. The pasta specialties include spaghetti served with a lobster or crab sauce and gramigna pasta with chunks of swordfish, aubergines, and fresh basil.

PALERMO Trattoria Sympaty

€€€

Via Piano Gallo 18, Località Mondello, 90151 **Tel** *091-45 44 70*

The dining room has good views over the bay of Mondello – Palermo's most popular beach resort – and the menu is, appropriately, almost exclusively fish-based. Try the *fettuccine all'aragosta* (pasta with lobster), *buccatini alle sarde* (with sardines), *spaghetti al ricci* (with sea urchins), octopus or squid.

PALERMO La Scuderia

€€€€€

Viale del Fante 9, 90146 **Tel** *091-52 03 23*

This elegant restaurant set in the Parco della Favorita sticks to traditional Sicilian cuisine, carefully and deliciously prepared. Try the *merluzzetti alla ghiotta* (whiting stewed with capers, potatoes, saffron, and cherry tomatoes) or the house specialty *sformatino di melanzane* (aubergine/eggplant bake).

SYRACUSE Jonico 'a Rutta 'e Ciauli

€€€

Riviera Dionisio il Grande 194, 96100 **Tel** *0931-655 40*

This refined restaurant has walls covered in Sicilian ceramics and agricultural artifacts, plus terrace tables just above the waves. Regional cuisine on a menu written mostly in Sicilian dialect; try the *cernia alla mattalotta* (grouper in white wine, onions, olives, capers, and tomatoes). Pizzas are served only in the evening.

TAORMINA Al Duomo

€€€

Vico degli Ebrei 11, 98039 **Tel** *0942-62 56 56*

A typical Sicilian restaurant with an outdoor terrace. Dishes make good use of Sicily's twin fish specialties: tuna and swordfish. But the chef's signature dish is *pasta ca 'nocca* (home-made macaroni with fresh anchovies, breadcrumbs, and wild fennel), followed by grilled *agnello* (lamb).

TAORMINA La Giara

€€€€€

Vico La Floresta 1, 98039 **Tel** *0942-233 60*

A striking restaurant of columns and arches with beautiful views over the bay from tables out on the terrace. The carefully planned menu offers a good range of creative dishes that make imaginative use of local ingredients and varies according to the freshest produce available. It also has a piano bar/club. Closed lunch.

GREECE

Greece is one of the most visited countries in Europe, yet remains one of the least known. Although most visitors will be familiar with the images of Ancient Greece, the modern Greek state dates only from 1830. Situated at a geographical crossroads, Greece combines cultural elements of the Balkans, the Middle East, and the Mediterranean.

For a small country, Greece possesses marked regional differences. Nearly three-quarters of the land is mountainous, uninhabited, or uncultivated. On the mainland, fertile agricultural land supports tobacco farming in the northeast, with orchard fruits and vegetables grown farther south. A third of the population lives in the capital, Athens, the cultural, financial, and political center, where ancient and modern stand side by side. Of the myriad islands, only about a hundred are today inhabited.

For centuries a large number of Greeks have lived abroad. Currently there are over half as many Greeks outside the country as in, although recent years have seen reverse immigration, with expatriates returning home, especially to the islands.

Rural and urban life in contemporary Greece has been transformed since the start of the 20th century, despite foreign occupation and civil war. Until the 1960s, the country remained underdeveloped, with many rural areas lacking basic amenities. Since then, a number of improvements, including the growth of tourism, the country's largest hard-currency earner, have helped Greece develop into a relatively wealthy, modern state.

HISTORY

Early Greek history is marked by a series of internal struggles, from the Mycenaean and Minoan cultures of the Bronze Age to the competing city-states of the 1st millennium BC. In spite of warfare, the 4th and 5th centuries BC were the high point of ancient Greek civilization, a golden age of exceptional creativity in philosophy and the arts.

In 338 BC the Greeks were conquered by Philip II of Macedonia at Chaironeia, and Greece soon became absorbed into Alexander the Great's vast empire. With the defeat of

Whitewashed stone windmills, a common feature of the Cyclades and the Dodecanese islands

◁ The awe-inspiring rock "towers" of Metéora in central Greece, first settled by hermits in the 10th century the Macedonians by the Romans in 168 BC, Greece was made a province of Rome. As part of the Eastern Empire, it was ruled from Constantinople and became a powerful element within the Orthodox Christian, Byzantine world.

Following the Ottomans' momentous capture of Constantinople in 1453, the Greek mainland was ruled by the Turks for the next 350 years. Crete and the Ionian islands were seized for long periods by the Venetians. Eventually the Greeks rebelled and, in 1821, the Greek War of Independence began. In 1832 the Great Powers that dominated Europe established a protectorate over Greece, marking the end of Ottoman rule. During the 19th century the Greeks expanded their national territory, reasserting Greek sovereignty over many of the islands.

Almost a century of significant territorial gains came to a disastrous end in 1922, when millions of Greeks were expelled from Smyrna in Turkish Anatolia, bringing to a close thousands of years of Greek presence in Asia

19th-century lithograph celebrating the Greek War of Independence

Minor. The ensuing years were a time of hardship and instability. The Metaxás dictatorship was followed by Italian, German, and Bulgarian occupation during World War II, and then a bitter civil war. The present boundaries of the Greek state date from 1948, when the Dodecanese were finally returned by the Italians. Today, Greece is a stable democracy and has been a member of the European Union since 1981.

KEY DATES IN GREEK HISTORY

3000–1200 BC Bronze Age; Cycladic, Minoan, and Mycenaean cultures flourish

800 Emergence of city-states

5th century Classical period; high point of Athenian culture under Perikles

431–404 Peloponnesian Wars; defeat of the Athenians by the city-state of Sparta

338 Greek army conquered by Philip II of Macedonia

333 Alexander the Great declares himself king of Asia; Greece absorbed into his vast empire

168 Greece becomes province of Rome

AD 49–54 St. Paul preaches Christianity in Greece

395 Greece becomes part of the new Eastern Roman Empire, ruled from Constantinople

1453 Constantinople falls to the Ottoman Turks

1821 Start of the Greek War of Independence

1832 Great Powers establish protectorate over Greece, and appoint Otto of Bavaria king

1922 Greeks fail to capture Smyrna from Turks

1946–9 Civil war leaves thousands dead or homeless

1981 Admission to the European Union

2002 Euro becomes legal currency

2004 Greece hosts Olympic Games and wins the football European Cup

2010 Greece narrowly avoids bankruptcy after taking a €110 billion loan from the EU and IMF

RELIGION, LANGUAGE, AND CULTURE

During Venetian and Ottoman domination, the Greek Orthodox church succeeded in preserving the Greek language and identity. Today, the Orthodox church is still a powerful force. Great importance is placed on baptisms and church weddings, although civil marriages are valid in law. Sunday mass is very popular with women, for whom church is a meeting place for socializing, just as the *kafeneía* (cafés) are for men.

The Greek language was for a long time a field of conflict between *katharévousa*, an artificial form devised around the time of independence, and the slowly evolved everyday speech, or *dimotikí*. Today's prevalence of *dimotikí* was perhaps a foregone conclusion in an oral culture. The art of storytelling is as prized now as it was in Homer's time, with conversation pursued for its own sake in *kafeneía* and at dinner tables. Singers, writers, and poet-lyricists have all kept *dimotikí* alive until the present day.

DEVELOPMENT AND DIPLOMACY

Greece remains one of the poorer members of the European Union. It still bears the hallmarks of a developing economy, with agriculture and the service sector accounting for two-thirds of the GNP. Nevertheless, with a nominally capitalist orientation, it has overcome its resemblance to pre-1989 Eastern Europe. However, unemployment remains high. Tourism has compensated for the decline in other industries, such as world shipping.

Typical scene at a Greek taverna, a popular place for friends and family to socialize

The fact that the Greek state is less than 200 years old, combined with recent periods of political instability, means that there is little faith in government institutions. Life operates on networks of personal friendships and official contacts. In the political sphere, the years following World War II were largely shaped by the influence of two men: Andréas Papandréou of the Panhellenic Socialist Movement (PASOK) and Conservative Konstantínos Karamanlís, who between them held office for the most part of the 1980s and 1990s.

The late Andréas Papandréou, three times Greek premier

The conservative New Democracy Party led by Costas Karamanlís (nephew of Konstantínos) took over from PASOK after a convincing election win in 2004. PASOK were back in power by autumn 2009. In spring 2010 it was revealed that the Greek state was close to bankruptcy and a €110 billion loan from the EU and IMF was agreed.

HOME LIFE

The family is still the basic Greek social unit. Traditionally, one family would farm its own land independently, and today family-run businesses are common in urban settings. Family life and social life are usually one and the same, and tend to revolve around eating out. Arranged marriages and dowries, though officially banned, persist. Most single young adults live with their parents and outside the largest cities, few unmarried couples dare to cohabit. Despite the previous generations' love of children, Greece has one of the lowest birth rates in Europe. Recently, the status of urban Greek women has greatly improved. They are now better represented in medicine and law, and many women run their own firms. However, in the country macho attitudes still exist, women often sacrificing a career to look after the house and children. New imported attitudes have crept in, but generally the Greek traditional way of life remains resolutely strong.

Fishermen mending their nets on one of the Greek islands

Exploring Greece

From beaches to ancient archaeological sites, Greece boasts a wide range of attractions. The nation's greatest ancient monuments are located in the capital, Athens, but relics of the Mycenaean, Minoan, Classical, and Byzantine civilizations can be found all over. The Greek islands attract thousands of tourists, many of whom come simply to enjoy the sun and sand and the relaxed pace of life. Ferries link the different island groups to the mainland, and "island-hopping" is a popular way to explore the many archipelagos.

SIGHTS AT A GLANCE

Ancient Corinth ⑫
Ancient Delphi ⑤
Ancient Olympia ⑳
Ancient Pélla ⑨
ATHENS pp474–81 ①
Corfu and the Ionian
  Islands ㉑
Epidaurus ⑭
Loúsios Gorge ⑲
Máni Peninsula ⑰
Metéora pp486–7 ⑦
Monastery of Dafní ③
Monastery of
  Osios Loukás ④
Monemvasía ⑯
Mount Athos ⑩
Mount Olympos ⑪
Mycenae ⑬
Mystrás ⑱
Náfplio ⑮
Pílio ⑥
Soúnio ②
Thessaloníki ⑧

**Islands South of the
Mainland (see inset map)**
Crete ㉔
Cyclades ㉒
Rhodes and the
  Dodecanese ㉓

SEE ALSO

- *Practical Information* pp502–3
- *Travel Information* pp504–5
- *Shopping & Entertainment* pp506–7
- *Where to Stay* pp508–13
- *Where to Eat* pp514–17

BULGARIA

Kastaniés
Orestiáda
Istanbul

Sidirókastro
Dráma
Sérres
Néa
Zíchni
Xánthi
Komotiní
Soufli
Amfípoli
Kavála
Keramotí
Alexandroúpoli
Istanbul
Thásos

THRACIAN   SEA

Moudaniá
Ouranoúpoli
10 Mount Athos

Samothráki

Imvros

Limnos

Ténedos

TURKEY

Agios
Efstrátios

Athos
Alónnisos
Gioúra
Kyrá Panagiá
Peristerá
Skópelos

Lésvos

Skýros

AEGEAN

Kými
Chalkída

SEA

Psará
Oinoússes
Chíos

Marathónas
ATHENS
Marmari
Kárystos
Andros

Sámos

Aígina
Makrónisos
Soúnio
Kéa
Gyáros
Tínos

Póros

Kýthnos
Sýros

Sérifos
Antiparos
Páros
Sifnos

Mílos
Kímolos
Sikinos
Polýaigos
Foleíandros

KEY

✈	Airport
⛴	Ferry port
—	Highway
—	Major road
—	Railroad
···	International boundary

ISLANDS SOUTH OF THE MAINLAND

TURKEY

ATHENS
Chíos
Andros
Sámos
Kéa
Tínos
Ikaría
Pátmos
Kýthnos
Sýros
Mýkonos
Délos
Kálymnos
Kos
Sérifos
Páros
Náxos
The Cyclades 22
Amorgós
Astypálaia
Mílos
Íos
Santoríni
Anáfi
Rhodes
Town
**Rhodes and
the Dodecanese 23**
Lindos
Rhodes
Kárpathos
MEDITERRANEAN
SEA
Kásos

Chaniá
Sea of Crete
Irákleio
Crete 24
Agios
Nikólaos

0 kilometers   50
0 miles   50

0 km   50
0 miles   50

Athens ❶

Athens has been inhabited for 7,000 years. The city's greatest glory was during the Classical period (4th and 5th centuries BC) of ancient Greece, from which so many buildings and artifacts survive. The city is dominated by the world-famous Acropolis and its theaters and temples, including the Parthenon, erected by Perikles as part of his grand building plan in the mid-5th century BC. Within the Byzantine Empire and under Ottoman rule, Athens played only a minor role. It returned to prominence in 1834, when King Otto made it capital of Greece. When the king's architects planned the new, European-style city, they included many splendid Neoclassical public buildings, which today provide elegant homes for some of Athens' best museums and galleries.

Marble figurine from the Museum of Cycladic Art

METSOV

AFTOKRATOROS IRAM

PATISION

STOURNARA

KANINGOS SOLOMOU

KAPODISTRIOU

PLATEIA KANINGOS

VERANZEROU

GLADSTONOS NIKITARA

AKADIMI

PANEPISTIMIOU

M **Omónoia**

OMONOIA

PEIRAIOS

ANAXAGORA

GERANIOU KLEISTHENOUS

LYKOURGOUU

EVPOLIDOS

PLATEIA KOTZIA

SOFOKLEOUS

ATHINAS

STADIOU

ARSAKI

Town Hall

PLATEIA THEATROU

Theatrou

SOFOKLEOUS

Panepistin P

PLATEIA KLAFTHMONOS

City of Athens M

Central Market

EVRIPIDOU AGIOI THEODOROI

ARISTEIDOU

P

KORAI

National Historical Museum

Monastiraki M

ERMOU ②

Thiseio M

PLATEIA AVISSYNIAS

PLATEIA MONASTIRAKIOU

Kapnikaréa

MONASTIRAKI S Y E R

Kyriazopoulos Folk Ceramic Museum

Hephaisteion

Stoa of Attalos ③

ADRIANOU

Mitrópoli

Panagía Gorgoepikoos

AERIDES

Tower of the Winds

Kanellopoulos Museum

ANAFIOTIKA

Agios Nikólaos Ragavás

⑤ BLAK

Propylaia ④ *Parthenon*

Temple of Athena Nike

Monument of Lysikrates

PLATEIA LYSIKRATOUS

Theater of Herodes Atticus

Theater of Dionysos

APOSTOLOU PAVLOU

DIONYSIOU AREOPAGITOU

Acropolis Museum 220 yards (200m)

Akropoli M

SIGHTS AT A GLANCE

Acropolis pp478–80 ④
Ancient Agora ③
Benáki Museum ⑦
Monastiráki ②
Museum of Cycladic Art ⑧
National Archaeological
  Museum ①
National Gallery of Art ⑨
Pláka ⑤
Temple of Olympian Zeus ⑥

SEE ALSO

The 1st-century BC Tower of the
Winds in Monastiráki, central Athens

GETTING AROUND

The sights of Athens' city center are closely packed,
and often the best way of getting around is on
foot, especially with the appalling traffic. There
are about 20 bus and trolley bus routes that
crisscross the city. The metro system is most
useful for crossing the city, getting to the port of
Piraeus and to the airport.

KEY

▢	Sight / Place of interest
🚋	Tram stop
🚎	Trolleybus
Ⓜ	Metro station
Ⓟ	Parking
ⓘ	Tourist information
✝	Church
▦	Pedestrian street

0 meters   300

0 yards   300

Neoclassical entrance to the National Archaeological Museum

National Archaeological Museum ①

Patission 44, Exárcheia. **Tel** 210-821 7717. **M** Omónoia. ⬛ summer: 8am–7pm daily; winter 1–7:30pm Mon, 8:30am–3pm Tue–Sun. 🖼️ 📷 ♿ www.namuseum.gr

When it was opened in 1891, this museum brought together antiquities that had previously been stored in different places all over the city. New wings were added in 1939, but during World War II the museum's priceless exhibits were dispersed and buried underground to protect them from possible damage. The museum reopened in 1946, but it has taken another 50 or so years of renovation and reorganization to finally do justice to its formidable collection. With the combination of such unique exhibits as the Mycenaean gold, and an unrivaled assembly of sculpture, pottery, and jewelry, it can definitely be claimed as one of the finest museums in the world. It is a good idea to plan ahead and be selective when visiting the museum and not attempt to cover everything in one visit.

The museum's exhibits can be divided into seven main collections: Neolithic and Cycladic, Mycenaean, Geometric and Archaic sculpture, Classical sculpture, Roman and Hellenistic sculpture, the pottery collections, and the Thíra frescoes. There are also other smaller collections that are well worth seeing. These include the stunning Eléni Stathátou jewelry collection and the Egyptian rooms.

High points of the museum include the unique finds from the grave circle at Mycenae (see p490), in particular the gold Mask of Agamemnon. Also not to be missed are the Archaic *kouroi* statues and the unrivaled collection of Classical and Hellenistic statues. Two of the most important and finest of the bronzes are the *Horse with the Little Jockey* and *Poseidon*. One of the world's largest collections of ancient ceramics can also be found here, comprising a vast array of elegant red- and black-figure vases from the 6th and 5th centuries BC and some Geometric funerary vases that date back as far as 1000 BC.

Monastiráki ②

M Monastiráki. **Market** ⬜ daily.

This lively and atmospheric area, which is named after the little monastery in Plateía Monastirakíou, is synonymous with Athens' famous flea market. Located next to the ancient Agora, it is bounded by Sari in the west and Aiólou in the east. The streets of Pandrósou, Ifaístou, and Areos leading off Plateía Monastirakíou are full of shops, selling a range of goods from expensive antiques, leather, and silver to tourist trinkets.

The heart of the flea market is in Plateía Avyssinías, west of Plateía Monastirakíou, where every morning junk dealers arrive with pieces of furniture and various odds and ends. During the week the shops and stalls are filled with antiques, second-hand books, rugs, leatherware, taverna chairs, army surplus gear, and tools.

On Sunday mornings, when the shops are closed, the market itself still flourishes along Adrianoú and in Plateía Agíou Filíppou. There are always numerous bargains to be had. Items particularly worth investing in include some of the brightly colored woven and embroidered cloths and an abundance of good silver jewelry.

Shoppers browsing in Athens' lively Monastiráki market

For hotels and restaurants in this region see pp508–9 and pp514–15

View across the Agora, showing the reconstructed Stoa of Attalos on the right

Ancient Agora ③

Main entrance at Adrianoú,
Monastiráki. **Tel** 210-321 0185.
Ⓜ Thiseío, Monastiráki. **Museum
and site** ◯ 8am–7:30pm daily
(winter: to 3pm). ● main public
hols. ⊠ ♿ limited.

The American School of
Archaeology commenced
excavations of the Ancient
Agora in the 1930s, and since
then a complex array of public
buildings and temples has been
revealed. The democratically
governed Agora was the
political and religious heart of
ancient Athens. Also the center
of commercial and daily life,
it abounded with schools and
elegant stoas, or roofed
arcades, filled with shops.
The state prison was here, as
was the city's mint. Even the
remains of an olive oil mill
have been found.

The main building standing
today is the impressive two-
story Stoa of Attalos. This was
rebuilt in the 1950s on the
original foundations and
using ancient building
materials. Founded by King
Attalos of Pergamon (ruled
159–138 BC), it dominated
the eastern quarter of the
Agora until it was destroyed
in AD 267. It is used today as
a museum, exhibiting the
finds from the Agora. These
include a *klepsydra* (a water
clock that was used for timing
plaintiffs' speeches), bronze
ballots, and items from
everyday life such as some
terra-cotta toys and leather
sandals. The best-preserved
ruins on the site are the

Odeion of Agrippa, a covered
theater, and the Hephaisteion,
a temple to Hephaistos, also
known as the Theseion.

Acropolis ④

See pp478–80.

Pláka ⑤

Ⓜ Monastiráki, Acropolis. 🚇 1, 2,
4, 5, and many others.

The area of Plaka is the
historic heart of Athens. Even
though only a few buildings
date back farther than the
Ottoman period, it remains
the oldest continually
inhabited area in the city.
One probable explanation of
its name comes from the
word used by Albanian
soldiers in the service of the
Turks who settled here in the
16th century – *pliaka* (old)
was how they used to
describe the area. Despite the

constant swarm of tourists
and Athenians, who come to
eat in old-fashioned tavernas
or browse in the antique and
icon shops, Pláka still retains
the atmosphere of a traditional neighborhood. The
Lysikrates Monument in
Plateía Lysikrátous is one of a
number of monuments that
were built to commemorate
the victors at the annual
choral and dramatic festival
at the Theater of Dionysos.
Taking its name from the
sponsor of the winning team,
it is the only such monument
still intact in Athens.

Many churches are worth a
visit: the 11th-century **Agios
Nikólaos Ragavás** has ancient
columns built into the walls.

The **Tower of the Winds**, in
the far west of Pláka, lies in
the grounds of the Roman
Agora. It was built by a Syrian
astronomer in the 2nd century
BC as a weather vane and
water clock. The name comes
from external friezes depicting
the eight mythological winds.

The Byzantine church of Agios Nikólaos Ragavás in Pláka

Acropolis ④

In the mid-5th century BC, Perikles persuaded the Athenians to begin a grand program of new building work. The resulting transformation has come to embody the political and cultural achievements of ancient Greece. Three contrasting temples were built on the Acropolis, together with a monumental gateway. The Theater of Dionysos and the Theater of Herodes Atticus were added later, in the 4th century BC and the 2nd century AD respectively.

LOCATOR MAP

★ Porch of the Caryatids
These statues of women were used in place of columns on the south porch of the Erechtheion. The originals, four of which can be seen in the Acropolis Museum, have been replaced by casts.

An olive tree now grows where Athena first planted her tree in a competition against Poseidon.

The Propylaia was built in 437–432 BC to form a new entrance to the Acropolis.

★ Temple of Athena Nike
This temple to Athena of Victory is on the west side of the Propylaia. It was built in 426–421 BC.

The Beulé Gate was the first entrance to the Acropolis.

Pathway to Acropolis from ticket office

STAR SIGHTS

- ★ Parthenon
- ★ Porch of the Caryatids
- ★ Temple of Athena Nike

Theater of Herodes Atticus
Also known as the Odeion of Herodes Atticus, this superb theater was originally built in AD 161. It was restored in 1955 and is used today for outdoor concerts.

★ Parthenon
Although few sculptures are left on this famous temple to Athena, some can still be admired, such as this one from the east pediment (see p480).

VISITORS' CHECKLIST

Dionysíou Areopagítou (main entrance), Pláka. *Tel* 210-321 0219. M Acropolis. 230, 231. **Site** Apr–Oct: 8am–7:30pm daily; Nov–Mar: 8am–5pm daily. Jan 1, Mar 25, Easter Sun, May 1, 25 & 26 Dec. **New Acropolis Museum** *Tel* 210-321 4172. 8am–8pm Tue–Sun. Jan 1, Mar 25, Easter Sun, May 1, Dec 25 & 26. www.acropolisofathens.gr

Two Corinthian columns are the remains of choregic monuments erected by sponsors of successful dramatic performances.

Panagía Spilótissa is a chapel set up in a cave in the Acropolis rock.

Theater of Dionysos
This figure of the comic satyr, Silenus, can be seen here. The theater visible today was built by Lykourgos in 342–326 BC.

Shrine of Asklepios

Stoa of Eumenes

The Acropolis rock was an easily defended site. It has been in use for nearly 5,000 years.

THE ELGIN MARBLES

These famous sculptures, also called the Parthenon Marbles, are held in the British Museum in London. They were acquired from the occupying Turkish authorities by Lord Elgin in 1801–3. He sold them to the British nation for £35,000 in 1816. There is great controversy surrounding the Marbles. While some argue that they are more carefully preserved in the British Museum, the Greek government does not accept the legality of the sale and believes they belong in Athens.

The newly arrived Elgin Marbles at the British Museum, in a painting by A. Archer

Exploring the Acropolis

Once you are through the Propylaia, the grand entrance to the site, the Parthenon exerts an overwhelming fascination. The other fine temples on "the Rock" include the Erechtheion and the Temple of Athena Nike. Since 1975, access to all the temple precincts has been banned. However, it is a miracle that anything remains at all. The ravages of war, the removal of treasures, and pollution have all taken their irrevocable toll on the Acropolis.

View of the Parthenon from the southwest at sunrise

The Parthenon

One of the world's most famous monuments, the Parthenon was commissioned by Perikles as part of his rebuilding plan. Work began in 447 BC, when the sculptor Pheidias was entrusted with supervising the building of a new Doric temple to Athena, the patron goddess of the city. Built on the site of earlier Archaic temples, it was designed primarily to house the *Parthenos*, Pheidias's impressive cult statue of Athena.

Taking just nine years to complete, the temple was dedicated to the goddess in the course of the Great Panathenaia festival of 438 BC. Designed and constructed in Pentelic marble by the architects Kallikrates and Iktinos, the Parthenon replaces straight lines with slight curves. It is thought that this complex architectural style was used to create an illusion of perfection (*see pp482–3*).

For the pediments and the friezes that ran all the way around the temple, an army of sculptors and painters was employed. Agorakritos and Alkamenes, both pupils of Pheidias, are two of the sculptors who worked on the frieze, which depicted the people and horses in the Panathenaic procession.

Despite much damage and alterations made to adapt it to various uses, which have included a church, a mosque, and even an arsenal, the Parthenon remains a majestic sight today.

New Acropolis Museum

Dionysiou Areopagitou 15, Makrigianni. **Tel** 210-900 0900. ☐ 8am–8pm Tue–Sun. ◉ public hols. **www**.theacropolismuseum.gr

Located a short walk from the Acropolis, this ultra-modern glass, steel, and concrete building, built by the Swiss architect Bernard Tschumi, exhibits finds from the Acropolis site.

The ground floor is made of partially reinforced glass, which exposes 4th century BC archaeological excavations below the building. Cases set in the walls display finds from early sanctuaries on the Acropolis, including votive offerings such as jewelry, figurines, and female protomes (busts) symbolizing fertility.

The Archaic Gallery showcases statues of young men, women, and horses, while the entire top floor is devoted to a reconstruction of a marble frieze that once ran around the top of the Parthenon. The original bas-reliefs are combined with crude white plaster copies of the so-called Elgin Marbles, removed by Lord Elgin in 1801 and now displayed in the British Museum in London.

Around the Acropolis

The area around the Acropolis was the center of public life in Athens. In addition to the Agora in the north (*see p477*), there were two theaters on the southern slope, the Theater of Herodes Atticus and the Theater of Dionysos. Political life was largely centered on the Areopagos and the Pynx Hills to the west of the Acropolis: the *Ekklesia* (citizens' assembly) met on the latter, while the former was the seat of the Supreme Judicial Court. Filopáppos Hill has always played an important defensive role in the city's history – an important fort was built here overlooking the strategic Piraeus road in 294 BC. On the tree-clad Hill of the Nymphs, the 19th-century Danish-built Asteroskopeíon (Observatory) occupies the site of an old sanctuary dedicated to nymphs associated with childbirth.

The Asteroskopeíon (Observatory) on the Hill of the Nymphs

mple of ympian Zeus ⑥

ner of Amalias & Vasilíssis Olgas,
a. **Tel** 210-922 6330. 🚇 2, 4,
🕐 summer: 8am–7:30pm daily;
ter: 8am–3pm daily. 🅿 main
lic hols. 🚫 ♿ limited.

s vast temple is the largest
Greece, exceeding even
Parthenon in size. The
nt Peisístratos allegedly
iated the building of the
ıple in the 6th century BC
gain public favor. It was not
npleted until 650 years later.
 AD 132 the Roman
peror Hadrian dedicated
 temple to Zeus Olympios
 set up a statue of the god
de, a copy of the original
Pheidias at Olympia (see
93). Next to it he placed a
ge statue of himself. Both
ues have since been lost.
nly 15 of the original 104
ımns remain, but enough
give a sense of the once
rmous size of this temple
pproximately 96 m (315 ft)
g and 40 m (130 ft) wide.
nan-style Corinthian capitals
re added to the original
ric columns in 174 BC.
he temple lies next to
drian's Arch, built in AD
 and marking the boundary
ween the ancient city and
 new Athens of Hadrian.

The remains of the Temple of Olympian Zeus

náki Museum ⑦

ner of Koumpári & Vasilíssis Sofías,
náki. **Tel** 210-367 1000. 🚇 3, 7,
3. 🕐 daily. 🅿 public hols.
 except Thu. ♿ limited.
w.benaki.gr

is museum contains a
erb collection of Greek
 and crafts, jewelry,
ional costumes, and
litical memorabilia from
 Neolithic era to the 20th
ntury. It was founded by
tónios Benákis (1873–1954),
o was interested in Greek,
rsian, Egyptian, and
oman art from an early
 e and started collecting
ile living in Alexandria.
 moving to Athens in 1926,
donated his collection to
 Greek state. The family
me, an elegant 19th-century

Neoclassical mansion, was
used as a museum and opened
to the public in 1931.

A major part of the Benáki
collection consists of gold
jewelry dating from as far
back as 3000 BC. Also on
display are icons, liturgical
silverware, Egyptian artifacts,
and Greek embroideries.

Museum of Cycladic Art ⑧

Neofýtou Doúka 4 (new wing at
Irodótou 1), Kolonáki. **Tel** 210-722
8321. 🚇 3, 7, 8, 13. 🕐 daily.
🅿 main public hols. 🚫 ♿
www.cycladic.gr

A magnificent selection of
ancient Greek art, including
the world's most important
collection of Cycladic
figurines, is on view at this
modern museum.

The displays start on the first
floor, with the Cycladic

collection. Dating
back to the 3rd
millennium BC,
the Cycladic
figurines were
found mostly in
graves, although
their exact
usage remains
a mystery.
Ancient Greek
art is exhibited
on the second
floor and the
Charles Polítis
collection of
Classical and
Prehistoric art on
the fourth floor.
The third floor
displays some
excellent
ancient
Cypriot art.
A new wing, which opened
in the adjoining Stathátos
Mansion in 1992, contains
the Greek Art Collection of
the Athens Academy.

National Gallery of Art ⑨

Vasiléos Konstantínou 50, Ilísia.
Tel 210-723 5937. 🚇 3, 13.
🕐 9am–3pm Mon, Wed–Sat, 10am–
2pm Sun. 🅿 main public hols. 🚫 ♿

This modern building holds a
permanent collection of
European and Greek art.
European exhibits include
various works by van Dyck,
Cézanne, Dürer, Rembrandt,
Picasso, and Caravaggio. The
majority of the collection,
however, is made up of Greek
art from the 18th to 20th
centuries, and includes
paintings of the Greek War of
Independence, seascapes, and
some excellent portraits.

Modern sculpture outside the National Gallery of Art

Temple Architecture

Temples were the most important public buildings in ancient Greece, largely because religion was a central part of everyday life. Often placed in prominent positions, temples were also statements about political and divine power. The earliest temples, in the 8th century BC, were built of wood and sun-dried bricks. Many of their features were copied in marble buildings from the 6th century BC onward.

The Parthenon on the Acropolis in Athens

TEMPLE CONSTRUCTION

This drawing is of an idealized Doric temple, showing how it was both built and used.

The cella, or inner sanctum, housed the cult statue.

The pediment, triangular in shape, often held sculpture.

The cult statue was of the god or goddess to whom the temple was dedicated.

Fluting columns was car situ, guided by that top and bottom

The column drums were initially carved with bosses for lifting them into place.

A ramp led up to the temple entrance.

The stepped platform was built on a stone foundation.

THE ILLUSION OF PERFECTION

Every aspect of the Parthenon was built on a 9:4 ratio to make the temple completely symmetrical. The sculptors also used visual trickery to counteract the laws of perspective. The illustration *(right)* is exaggerated to show the techniques they employed.

The base of the temple is higher in the middle than at the edges.

Entasis (a bulge in the middle) makes each column look straight.

Each column leans slightly inward.

The gable ends of the roof were surmounted by statues, known as *akroteria*, in this case of a Nike or "Winged Victory". Almost no upper portions of Greek temples survive.

The roof was supported on wooden beams and covered in rows of terra-cotta tiles, each ending in an upright antefix.

Stone blocks were smoothly fitted together and held by metal clamps and dowels: no mortar was used in the temple's construction.

The ground plan was derived from the megaron of the Mycenaean house: a rectangular hall with a front porch that was supported by columns.

Caryatids, *or figures of women, were used instead of columns in the Erechtheion at Athens' Acropolis. In Athens' Agora (see p477), tritons (half-fish, half-human creatures) were used.*

THE DEVELOPMENT OF TEMPLE ARCHITECTURE

Greek temple architecture is divided into three styles, which evolved chronologically, and are most easily distinguished by the column capitals.

Doric *temples were surrounded by sturdy columns with plain capitals and no bases. As the earliest style of stone buildings, they recall wooden prototypes.*

Triangular pediment filled with sculpture

Guttae imitated the pegs for fastening the wooden roof beams.

Triglyphs resembled the ends of cross beams.

Metopes could contain sculpture.

Doric capital

Ionic *temples differed from Doric in their tendency to have more columns, of a different form. The capital has a pair of volutes, like rams' horns, front and back.*

Akroteria, at the roof corners, could look Persian in style.

The frieze was a continuous band of decoration.

The Ionic architrave was subdivided into projecting bands.

The Ionic frieze took the place of Doric *triglyphs* and *metopes.*

Ionic capital

Corinthian *temples in Greece were built under the Romans and only in Athens. They feature columns with slender shafts and elaborate capitals decorated with acanthus leaves.*

Akroterion in the shape of a griffin

The cella entrance was at the east end.

The entablature was everything above the capitals.

The pediment was decorated with a variety of moldings.

Acanthus leaf capital

Central Greece

Beyond the endless urban sprawl of Athens, the vast expanse of central Greece has a little of everything for the visitor, from sandy beaches and fishing ports, to one of the country's most important archaeological sites, Ancient Delphi. Not to be missed is the Byzantine splendor of the monasteries of Dafní and Osios Loúkas, while the extraordinary mountain-top monasteries of Metéora are another of the region's principal attractions. The beautiful wooded mountain slopes of the Pílio offer some of the best scenery on the mainland.

The Temple of Poseidon on the cape at Soúnio

Soúnio ❷

9 km (5.5 miles) S of Lávrio, Attica. **Tel** 22920-39363. ▦ to Lávrio. ◯ 9:30am–sunset daily. ▨

The temple of Poseidon, situated at the top of sheer cliffs tumbling into the Aegean Sea at Soúnio (Cape Sounion), was ideally located as a place to worship the powerful god of the sea. Its brilliant white marble columns have been a landmark for ancient and modern mariners alike.

The present temple, built in 444 BC, stands on the site of older ruins. An Ionic frieze, made from 13 slabs of Parian marble, is located on the east side of the temple's main approach path. It is very eroded, but is known to have depicted scenes from mythological battles, as well as the adventures of the hero Theseus, said in some legends to be the son of Poseidon.

Local marble from the quarries at Agriléza was used for the temple's 34 slender Doric columns, of which 15 survive today. In 1810, the British Romantic poet, Lord

Byron, carved his name on one of the columns, setting an unfortunate precedent of vandalism at the temple.

Monastery of Dafní ❸

10 km (6 miles) NW of Athens, Attica. **Tel** 210-581 1558. ▦ ◯ 8:30am–3pm daily. ♿ limited.

Founded in the 5th century AD, the Monastery of Dafní is named after the laurels (dáfnes) that once grew here. It was built with the remains

The 5th-century Byzantine Monastery of Dafní near Athens

of an ancient sanctuary of Apollo, which had occupied the site until it was destroyed in AD 395. In the early 13th century, Otto de la Roche, the first Frankish Duke of Athens, bequeathed it to Cistercian monks in Burgundy. Greek Orthodox monks took the site in the 16th century, erecting the elegant cloisters just south of the church. The monastery is presently closed for restoration, due to an earthquake which hit in the year 2000.

Among the monastery's principal attractions are the beautiful gold-leaf Byzantine mosaics in the *katholikón* (main church). Byzantine church architecture was concerned almost exclusively with decoration. Mosaics and frescoes portraying the whole body of the Church, from Christ downward, had a dual purpose: they gave inspiration to worshipers and represented windows to the spiritual world. The most impressive mosaics at Dafní are the Esonarthex Mosaics, which include the *Last Supper*, the *Washing of the Feet,* and the *Betrayal of Judas.* Equally magnificent, the *Christ Pantokrátor* is a mosaic of Christ in judgment that fills the church's huge dome.

Monastery of Osios Loúkas ❹

8 km (5 miles) E of Dístomo, Stereá Elláda. **Tel** 22670-22797. ▦ ◯ 8am–5pm daily. ▨

Dedicated to a local hermit and healer, Osios Loúkas ("Holy Luke"), who lived in the 10th century, this splendid monastery was one of medieval Greece's most important buildings architecturally. It was built around AD 1011 by the Emperor Romanós, who extended an earlier church dating from 944. The octagonal style of the main church, the *katholikón*, became a hallmark of late Byzantine church design, while the mosaics inside lifted Byzantine art into its final great period.

Among the most impressive features of the monastery are the 10th-century crypt, which

Detail from an 11th-century mosaic in the Monastery of Osios Loúkas

is from the original church and contains the sarcophagus of Holy Luke, and a mosaic entitled *Washing of the Apostles' Feet*. This 11th-century work, based on a style dating back to the 6th century, is the finest of a number of mosaics found in the narthex, the western entrance hall. The monastery's main dome is decorated with an imposing mural of Christ, painted in the 16th century to replace fallen mosaics.

Ancient Delphi ❺

Mount Parnassus, Stereá Elláda.
Tel 22650-82312. 🚌 🚋 *8:30am–7:30pm daily (winter: to 3pm).*
🌐 *main public hols.* 🎫 ♿

In ancient times Delphi was believed to be the center of the earth. The site was renowned as a dwelling place of Apollo, and from the late 8th century BC people came here to worship and seek advice from the god. With the political rise of Delphi in the 6th century BC, and the establishment of the Pythian Games – a cultural, religious, and athletic festival – the site entered a golden age that lasted until the arrival of the Romans in 191 BC. The Delphic Oracle was abolished in AD 393 after Christianity was introduced as the state religion.

The Sanctuary of Apollo, also known as the Sacred Precinct, forms the heart of the complex, and one of its most impressive sights is the **Temple of Apollo**. A temple has stood on this spot since the 6th century BC, but the

remains visible today date from the 4th century BC. Leading from the sanctuary entrance to the Temple of Apollo is the **Sacred Way**, once lined with some 3,000 statues and treasuries. Also worth seeing is the well-preserved **Stadium**. The present structure dates from Roman times, and most of the seating is still intact.

The Marmaria Precinct, or marble quarry, is where the **Sanctuary of Athena Pronaia** is found. Here, the most remarkable monument is the *tholos*, which dates from the 4th century BC. The purpose of this circular structure, originally surrounded by 20 columns, remains a mystery.

The museum at Ancient Delphi houses an impressive collection of sculptures and architectural remains.

Pílio ❻

Thessaly. 🚌 *Vólos.* 🚉 🛈 *Plateía Riga Feraíou, Vólos (24210-23500).*

The Pílio Peninsula is one of the most beautiful areas of the mainland. The mountain air is sweet with the scent of herbs, which in ancient times were renowned for their healing properties. The area became populated in the 13th century by Greeks retreating

Traditional-style guesthouses in the Pílio village of Vyzítsa

from the Ottomans. After centuries of protecting its culture, the Pílio is known for its strong local cuisine.

The main town on the peninsula is **Vólos**, which has an excellent Archaeological Museum. From here you can make a tour of the many traditional hillside villages and fishing ports. Worth visiting are **Miliés**, with its Folk Museum and fresco-adorned church, and picturesque **Vyzítsa**. **Argalastí** has a busy market, though its tavernas and cafés retain a peaceful atmosphere. For fine sandy beaches and excellent seafood, visit the popular coastal resorts of **Plataniá** or **Agios Ioánnis**.

The *tholos* beside the Sanctuary of Athena Pronaia at Ancient Delphi

Metéora 🟑

The extraordinary sandstone towers of Metéora (or "suspended rocks") were formed by the action of the sea that covered the plain of Thessaly around 30 million years ago. The huge columns of rock were first used as a religious retreat in AD 985, when a hermit named Barnabas occupied a cave here. In the mid-14th century Neílos, the Prior of Stagai convent, built a small church. A few years later, in 1382, the monk Athanásios, from Mount Athos, founded the huge monastery of Megálo Metéoro on one of the many pinnacles. A further 23 monasteries were built, though most had fallen into ruin by the 19th century. In the 1920s stairs were cut in the rock faces to make the remaining six monasteries more accessible, and today a religious revival has seen the return of a number of monks and nuns.

Monastic cells

Outer walls

LOCATION OF MONASTERIES OF METEORA

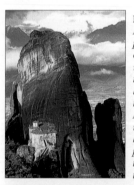

Rousánou

Moní Rousánou, perched precariously on the very tip of a narrow spire of rock, is the most spectacularly located of all the monasteries. Its church of the Metamórfosis (1545) is renowned for its harrowing frescoes, painted in 1560 by the iconographers of the Cretan school.

VARLAAM

Founded in 1518, the monastery of Varlaám is named after the first hermit to live on this rock in 1350. The *katholikón* (main church) was built in 1542 and contains frescoes by the Theban iconographer Frágkos Katelános.

Megálo Metéoro

Also known as the Great Meteoron, this was the first and, at 623 m (2,045 ft), highest monastery to be founded. By the entrance is a cave in which Athanásios first lived. His body is buried in the main church.

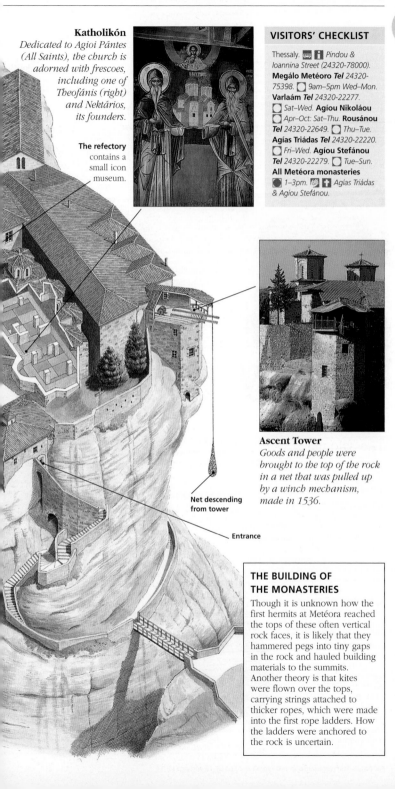

Katholikón
Dedicated to Agioi Pántes (All Saints), the church is adorned with frescoes, including one of Theofánis (right) and Nektários, its founders.

The refectory contains a small icon museum.

VISITORS' CHECKLIST

Thessaly. 🚌 🛈 *Pindou & Ioannina Street (24320-78000).*
Megálo Metéoro *Tel 24320-75398.* ⬜ *9am–5pm Wed–Mon.*
Varlaám *Tel 24320-22277.* ⬜ *Sat–Wed.* **Agíou Nikoláou** ⬜ *Apr–Oct: Sat–Thu.* **Rousánou** *Tel 24320-22649.* ⬜ *Thu–Tue.*
Agías Triádas *Tel 24320-22220.* ⬜ *Fri–Wed.* **Agíou Stefánou** *Tel 24320-22279.* ⬜ *Tue–Sun.*
All Metéora monasteries ⬤ *1–3pm.* 🚫 🛈 *Agías Triádas & Agíou Stefánou.*

Ascent Tower
Goods and people were brought to the top of the rock in a net that was pulled up by a winch mechanism, made in 1536.

Net descending from tower

Entrance

THE BUILDING OF THE MONASTERIES

Though it is unknown how the first hermits at Metéora reached the tops of these often vertical rock faces, it is likely that they hammered pegs into tiny gaps in the rock and hauled building materials to the summits. Another theory is that kites were flown over the tops, carrying strings attached to thicker ropes, which were made into the first rope ladders. How the ladders were anchored to the rock is uncertain.

Northern Greece

Northern Greece offers an appealing combination of comparatively unexplored natural beauty and a rich cultural heritage. The stunning scenery of places like Mount Olympos holds special appeal to walking enthusiasts, while of historical interest in the region are several ancient archaeological sites, including Pélla, the birthplace of Alexander the Great. Many of northern Greece's finest examples of Byzantine architecture and art are to be found on the Athos Peninsula and in the bustling city of Thessaloníki.

The 15th-century White Tower on the waterfront in Thessaloníki

The **Arch of Galerius** was built in AD 303 by the Emperor Galerius to celebrate victory over the Persians, and is the principal architectural legacy of Roman rule. Standing north of the arch is the **Rotónda**, believed to have been constructed as a mausoleum for Galerius. Now closed, it has been used in the past as both a church and a mosque.

Thessaloníki has a number of museums, including the **Museum of Byzantine Culture** and the **Museum of the Macedonian Struggle**, which focuses on the centuries of Turkish domination. The star attractions at the city's newly refurbished **Archaeological Museum** are the Roman floor

Thessaloníki ❽

🏙 1,000,000. ✈ 25 km (15 miles) SE. 🚢 🚆 🚌 ℹ 136 Tsimiski (2310-221100).

Thessaloniki, also known as Salonica, is Greece's second city, and was founded by King Kassandros in 315 BC. The capital of the Roman province of Macedonia Prima from 146 BC, it later became part of the Byzantine Empire. In 1430 it was captured by the Turks, who held it until 1912. Today Thessaloníki is a bustling cosmopolitan city and a major religious center.

On the *paralía*, the city's attractive waterfront, stands one of Thessaloníki's most famous sights, the **White Tower**. Built in 1430, this is one of three towers that were added to the city walls by the Turks. Today it houses a permanent exhibition tracing the city's history.

mosaics, and the splendid Dervéni Krater, a 4th-century BC bronze wine-mixing bowl. You should also make time to see the museum's stunning collection of Macedonian gold.

Visitors should not miss the city's rich array of UNESCO-listed Byzantine churches, which include the 5th-century **Agios Dimitrios** – the largest church in Greece. Dating from the mid-8th century, **Agía Sofía** is an important building, both for its mosaics and for its role in influencing future architectural development, while the 14th-century **Agios Nikólaos Orfanós** contains the best-preserved collection of late Byzantine frescoes in the city.

🏛 **Archaeological Museum**
Manóli Andrónikou & Leof Stratoú.
Tel 2310-830538. 🚌 3. 🕐 daily (Mon: pm only). 🌑 main public hols.
📷 🚻 www.amth.gr

Ancient Pélla ❾

38 km (24 miles) NW of Thessaloníki. *Tel* 23820-33094. 🚌
🕐 Tue–Fri). 🌑 main public hols.
📷 🚻

This small site was once the flourishing capital of Macedonia. The court was moved here from Aigai (near modern Vergína) in 410 BC

THE MACEDONIAN ROYAL FAMILY

The gold burial casket found at Vergína is emblazoned with the Macedonian Sun, the symbol of the king. Philip II was from a long line of Macedonian kings that began in about 640 BC with Perdiccas I. Philip was the first ruler to unite the whole of Greece as it existed at that time. Much of Greece's pride in the symbol lies in the fact that Alexander the Great used it throughout his empire. He was just 20 when his father was assassinated in 336 BC. He inherited his father's already large empire and also his ambition to conquer the Persians. In 334 BC Alexander crossed the Dardanelles with 40,000 men and defeated the Persians in three different battles, advancing as far as the Indus Valley before he died at the age of 33. With his death the Macedonian empire divided.

Gold burial casket from the Royal Tombs at Vergína

Russian Orthodox monastery, Agíou Panteleímonos, on Mount Athos

by King Archelaos, who ruled from 413 to 399 BC. It is here that Alexander the Great was born in 356 BC, and was later tutored by the philosopher Aristotle. Some sense of the existence of a city can be gained from a plan of the site, which shows where the main street and stores were located. The palace, believed to have been north of the main site, is still being excavated.

At the site, and in the museum, are some of the best-preserved pebble mosaics in Greece. Dating from about 300 BC, the mosaics depict vivid hunting scenes. One of the most famous is of Dionysos riding a panther; it is housed in the now-covered, 4th-century BC House of the Lion Hunt. Originally comprising 12 rooms around three open courtyards, this building was constructed at the end of the 4th century BC.

Mount Athos ⓾

Athos Peninsula. 🚢 Dáfni (boat trips from Ouranoúpoli & Thessaloníki for the west coast, or from Ierissós for the east coast). 🚌 to Karyés. 🎫 donation.

Also known as the Holy Mountain, Mount Athos is the highest point on the Athos Peninsula – an autonomous republic, ruled by the 1,700 monks who live in its 20 monasteries. Only adult males may visit the peninsula, but it is possible to see many of the monasteries from a boat trip along the coast. They include some fine

examples of Byzantine architecture and provide a fascinating insight into Orthodox monastic life.

For the monks who live here, the day begins at 3 or 4am with morning services and prayers. They eat two meals a day, which consist mainly of food they grow themselves. There are 159 fasting days in the year. Between meals the monks spend their time working, resting, and praying.

Ouranoúpoli is the main town on Athos and where the boat trips for the peninsula's west coast start. Among the monasteries that can be viewed are the 10th-century **Docheiaríou, Agíou Panteleímonos**, an 11th-century Russian Orthodox monastery, and **Moní Agíou Pávlou**. On the east coast, **Megístis Lávras** was the first monastery to be founded on Athos, while 10th-century **Moní Vatopedíou**, farther north, is one of the largest and best-preserved buildings.

Mount Olympos ⓫

17 km (10 miles) W of Litóchoro. 🚆 Litóchoro. 🛈 EOS: Evángelou Karavákou 20, Litóchoro (23520-83100).

The name Mount Olympos refers to a whole range of mountains, 20 km (12 miles) across. The highest peak in the range is Mytikas, at 2,917 m (9,570 ft). The entire area constitutes the Olympos National Park, an area of outstanding natural beauty that attracts naturalists and walkers alike. The park's rich flora and fauna include 1,700 plant species, in addition to chamois, boars, and roe deer. From **Litóchoro**, which has several hotels and tavernas, walkers can follow a series of trails.

A short distance from Litóchoro is **Ancient Díon**, considered a holy city by the ancient Macedonians. The flat plains were used as a military camp by King Philip II of Macedon in the 4th century BC. The ruins visible today – which include mosaics, baths, and a theater – date mainly from the Roman era. A museum shows finds from the site.

The peaks of the Mount Olympos range rising above Litóchoro

The Peloponnese

One of the primary strongholds and battlefields of the 1821–31 Revolution, the Peloponnese is the kernel from which the modern Greek state grew. The region boasts a wealth of ancient and medieval ruins, from Bronze Age Mycenae to the Byzantine town of Mystrás. As popular as its vast array of historical sites is the Peloponnese's spectacularly varied landscape. The breathtaking scenery of places like the Loúsios Gorge attracts walkers and naturalists in their thousands.

The ruins of Acrocorinth, south of Ancient Corinth

Ancient Corinth ⑫

7 km (4 miles) SW of modern Corinth. **Tel** 27410-31207. 🚌 ⭘ 8am–8pm daily (winter: to 3pm). ⬤ main public hols. 🎟 ♿ limited.

A settlement since Neolithic times, Ancient Corinth was razed in 146 BC by the Romans, who rebuilt it a century later. Attaining a population of 750,000 under the patronage of the Roman emperors, the town gained a reputation for licentious living, which St. Paul attacked when he came here in AD 52. Excavations have revealed the vast extent of the ancient city, which was destroyed by earthquakes in Byzantine times. The ruins constitute the largest Roman township in Greece.

Among the most impressive remains are the **Lechaion Way**, the marble-paved road that linked the nearby port of Lechaion with the city, and the **Temple of Apollo**, with its striking Doric columns.

The temple was one of the few buildings preserved by the Romans when they rebuilt the city in 44 BC. Of the **Temple of Octavia**, once dedicated to the sister of Emperor Augustus, three ornate Corinthian columns, overarched by a restored architrave, are all that remain. The **Odeion** is one of several buildings endowed to the city by Herodes Atticus, the wealthy Athenian and friend of the Emperor Hadrian.

Close to the Odeion, the **Museum** houses a collection of exhibits representing all periods of the town's history. The Roman gallery is particularly rich, containing some spectacular 2nd-century AD mosaics lifted from the floors of nearby villas.

Just 4 km (2 miles) south of Ancient Corinth is the bastion of **Acrocorinth**, to which there is access between 8:30am and 3pm each day. Held and refortified by every occupying power in Greece from Roman times onward, it was one of the country's most important fortresses in medieval times. The ruins show evidence of Byzantine, Turkish, Frankish, and Venetian occupation. The summit of Acrocorinth affords one of the most sweeping views in the whole of Greece.

RECONSTRUCTION OF ANCIENT CORINTH (C.AD 100)

- Northwest stoa
- Temple of Octavia
- Agora
- Odeion
- South stoa
- Theater
- Basilica
- Temple of Apollo
- Lechaion Way

Interior of the tomb known as the Treasury of Atreus, at Mycenae

Mycenae ⓭

2 km (1 mile) N of Mykines. **Tel** 27510-76585. ▭ to Mykines. ▢ daily. ● main public hols. ▨ &. Treasury of Atreus and museum only.

Discovered in 1874, the fortified palace complex of Mycenae is an early example of sophisticated citadel architecture. The Mycenaeans were a Bronze Age culture that existed between 1700 and 1100 BC. Only the ruling class inhabited the palace, with artisans and merchants living outside the city walls. The citadel was abandoned in 1100 BC after much disruption in the region.

The tombs at Mycenae are one of the most famous attractions of the site. The city's nobles were entombed in shaft graves, such as those at **Grave Circle A**, or, later, in *tholos* ("beehive") tombs, so-called because of their shape. The *tholos* tombs, found outside the palace walls, were buried under an earth mound, the only entrance being via a *dromos*, or open-air corridor. The 14th-century BC **Treasury of Atreus** is the most outstanding of the *tholos* tombs. Here a Mycenaean king was buried with his weapons and enough food and drink for his journey to the underworld. The so-called **Tomb of Klytemnestra** is equally well preserved.

Also of interest at the site are the remains of the **Royal Palace**, the **Secret Stairway**, which leads down to a cistern deep beneath the citadel, and the 13th-century BC **Lion Gate**, the grand entrance to Mycenae.

Epidaurus ⓮

30 km (19 miles) E of Náfplio. **Tel** 27530-22009. ▭ ▢ daily. ● main public hols. ▨ & limited. 📷

Active from the 6th century BC until at least the 2nd century AD, the Sanctuary of Epidaurus was an extensive therapeutic and religious center, dedicated to the healing god Asklepios.

The site is most renowned for its magnificent **Theater**, whose *cavea* (cavity) is 114 m (374 ft) across and surrounds a 20-m (66-ft) diameter *orchestra* (stage). Designed in the late 4th century BC, the theater is well known for near-perfect acoustics, and has the only circular *orchestra* to have survived from antiquity. Today, it is the venue for an annual summer festival of ancient drama.

Most of the **Asklepieion**, or Sanctuary of Asklepios, is currently being re-excavated. Accessible remains include the *propylaia*, or monumental gateway, a late Classical stadium, and the *tholos* – a circular building, thought to have been used either as a pit for sacred serpents, or as the setting for religious rites. Of Asklepios's temple, to the east of the *tholos*, only the foundations have survived.

Náfplio ⓯

🏚 12,000. ▢ ▭ 🛈 Ikosispémptis Martíou 24 (27520-24444).

One of the most elegant towns in mainland Greece, Náfplio emerged in the 13th century and later endured many sieges during the struggles between the Turks and the Venetians for the ports of the Peloponnese. From 1829 to 1834, it was the first capital of liberated Greece.

A number of fortifications testify to the town's checkered history. The island fortress of **Boúrtzi** is a legacy of the second Venetian occupation (1686–1715). **Akronafplía**, also known as Its Kale ("Inner Castle" in Turkish), was the site of the Byzantine and early medieval town, while the Venetian citadel of **Palamídi** was built between 1711 and 1714.

The Plateía Syntágmatos, the hub of public life, looks much as it did three centuries ago, when two mosques were built by the victorious Ottomans. These are now the cathedral, **Agios Geórgios**, and the **Catholic church**.

The town has two museums of note: the award-winning **Folk Art Museum**, and the **Archaeological Museum**, which houses mainly local pre-Mycenaean artifacts.

Located 4 km (2 miles) outside Náfplio, the 12th-century convent of **Agía Moní** is worth visiting.

🏛 **Archaeological Museum**
Plateía Syntágmatos. **Tel** 27520-27502. ▢ summer: 8am–8pm Tue–Sun (Mon pm only); winter: 8:30am–3pm Tue–Sun. ● main public hols.

The fortified isle of Boúrtzi, north of Náfplio harbor

The cliff-top church of Agía Sofía, Monemvasía upper town

Monemvasía ⓰

🏛 800. ⛴ 🚌 🛈 27320-61210.

This fortified town is built on two levels on a rock rising 350 m (1,150 ft) above the sea. A town of 50,000 in its 15th-century halcyon days, Monemvasía was for centuries a semi-autonomous city-state, which prospered thanks to its strategic position astride the sea lanes from Italy to the Black Sea. After a long and protracted siege, the town was finally surrendered by the Turks in 1821 during the War of Independence.

In the restored lower town, enclosed by the formidable 16th-century walls, are a number of mosques and churches. They include the 18th-century **Panagía Myrtidióssa** and the 13th-century cathedral, **Christós Elkómenos**, with its Venetian belfry. Also found in the lower town is **Giánnis Rítsos's House**, where this prominent 20th-century Greek poet and communist was born.

The upper town, which lies largely in ruins, has been uninhabited since 1911. It was first fortified in the 6th century, and is the oldest part of Monemvasía. Here, the most impressive sight is the still-intact, cliff-top church of **Agía Sofía**, founded by Emperor Andronikos II (1282–1328) and modeled on the Monastery of Dafní (see p484). Visitors can also see the remains of a 13th-century fortress.

Máni Peninsula ⓱

🚢 Gýtheio. 🚌 Kalamáta (Outer Máni), Areópoli (Inner Máni). 🛈 Vasiléos Georgiou 20, Gýtheio (27330-24484).

The harsh and remote Máni Peninsula is divided into two areas, Outer Máni and Inner Máni, separated by a ravine at Oítylo. The area is most famous for its history of internal feuding, which led to the building of many fine tower houses. From the 15th century, rival clansmen, fighting over the inadequate land, used the towers to shoot at their opponents. After years of bloodshed, the clans finally united, instigating the Greek Independence uprising in 1821.

The main places of interest in more fertile Outer Máni are **Oítylo**, with its elegant 19th-century mansions, and **Kardamýli**, the lair of the Troupákis family, one of the most important Maniot clans. In the environs of Kardamýli are the stunning **Vyrós Gorge**, and **Stoúpa**, popular for its two sandy bays. **Mount Taÿgetos** is one of the area's beauty spots, and can offer several days of wilderness trekking to experienced, well-equipped mountaineers.

In Inner Máni, bustling **Gýtheio** is one of the most attractive coastal towns in the southern Peloponnese. Its 18th-century fortress houses the Museum of the Máni. **Areópoli**, "the city of Ares" (god of war), was where the Maniot uprising against the Turks was proclaimed by Pétros Mavromichális. Nearby

Fishing boats moored in Gýtheio harbor in Inner Máni

is the 17th-century Ottoman **Kelefá Castle**. Visitors to Inner Máni should also see the **Pýrgos Diroú** cave system, and the many Byzantine churches scattered along the west coast. Built between the 10th and 14th centuries, the finest churches include **Taxiarchón**, at Charoúda, **Agios Theódoros**, at Vámvaka, and, near Ano Mpoulárioi village, **Agios Panteleímon** contains 10th-century frescoes. Overlooking the sea and Cape Taínaro, **Vátheia** is one of the most dramatically located of the villages in the Máni. It is worth visiting just to see its collection of tower houses.

Ruins of the Despots' Palace in the Byzantine town of Mystrás

Mystrás ⓲

5 km (3 miles) W of Spárti. **Tel** 27310-83377. 🚌 to Néos Mystrás. ⬭ daily. ⬤ main public hols. 🎟

Majestic Mystras occupies a panoramic site on a spur of the severe Taÿgetos range. Founded by the Franks in 1249, the town soon passed to the Byzantines, under whom it attained a population of 20,000 and, after 1348, became the seat of the Despots of Morea. The despotate acted semi-independently and, by the 15th century, Mystrás had become the last major Byzantine cultural center, attracting scholars and artists from Italy, Constantinople, and Serbia. One result was the uniquely cosmopolitan decoration of Mystrás's churches, whose pastel-colored frescoes, crowded with detail, reflect Italian Renaissance influence.

Now in ruins, Mystrás consists of an upper and lower town, with a wealth of churches, monasteries, palaces, and houses lining its narrow, winding streets. Among the churches and monasteries worth visiting are **Mitrópoli** – the oldest church in Mystrás, dating from 1291 – **Moní Perivléptou**, and **Moní Pantánassas**. The **Vrontóchion**, a 13th-century monastic complex, was the cultural heart of medieval Mystrás. Visitors can also explore the ruins of the **Despots' Palace**, and the **Kástro**, an impressive fortification that crowns the summit of the upper town, and affords magnificent views of the entire site.

Loúsios Gorge ⑲

🚌 *Dimitsána.* **All monasteries**
⭕ *dawn to dusk daily.*
Moní Aimyalón 🌙 *2–5pm.*

Although merely a tributary of the Alfeiós River, the Loúsios stream boasts one of the most impressive canyons in Greece. Scarcely 5 km (3 miles) long, the Loúsios Gorge is nearly 300 m (985 ft) deep at its narrowest section.

Moní Agíou Ioánnou Prodrómou in the Loúsios Gorge

Remains of the Palaestra, or training center, at Ancient Olympia

A number of hiking trails connect the area's highlights, which include several churches and monasteries clinging to the steep cliffs of the gorge. Of these, the most impressive are **Moní Aimyalón**, founded in 1605 and containing some magnificent frescoes, the 17th-century **Néa Moní Filosófou**, and the 10th-century **Moní Agíou Ioánnou Prodrómou**, wedged into the canyon's east flank. Occupying a sunken excavation on the stream's west bank is the Asklepieíon, or therapeutic center, of **Ancient Gortys**. On this site lie the foundations of a 4th-century BC temple to Asklepios, the god of healing.

Overlooking the gorge, the beautiful hillside towns of **Dimitsána** and **Stemnítsa** make a good base from which to explore the area.

🏛 **Ancient Gortys**
⭕ *daily.* 🌑 *main public hols.*

Ancient Olympia ⑳

Tel 26240-22517. 🚌 🚍 ⭕ *daily*
(winter: Mon–Tue). 🌑 *main public hols.* 📷

The sanctuary of Olympia enjoyed over 1,000 years of renown as a religious and athletics center. Though it flourished in Mycenaean times, its historic importance dates to the coming of the Dorians, at the beginning of the first millennium BC. They brought the worship of Zeus, after whose abode on Mount Olympos the site was named. Olympia reached its zenith in the 5th century BC, but by the end of the reign of Roman Emperor Hadrian (AD 117–38), it had begun to have less religious and political significance. The first Olympian Games, the forerunner of the Olympic Games, took place here in 776 BC, but were banned in AD 393 by Emperor Theodosius I, who took a dim view of the pagan festival.

The most important ruins include the 5th-century BC Doric **Temple of Zeus**, of which only column bases and tumbled sections remain, and the partly reconstructed **Palaestra**, which was a training center for athletes. In **Pheidias's Workshop**, a huge statue of Zeus was sculpted in the 5th century BC.

Also not to be missed is the **Archaeological Museum**, one of the richest museums in Greece, with exhibits from prehistory, through to the Classical period and the Roman era. The central hall houses the pediment and metope sculpture from the Temple of Zeus. There is also a small museum dedicated to the Olympic Games.

🏛 **Archaeological Museum**
Tel 26240-22742. ⭕ *daily (winter: Mon–Sat).* 🌑 *main public hols, May–mid-Oct.* 📷 📷 ♿

Corfu and the Ionian Islands ㉑

The Ionian Islands are the greenest and most fertile of all the island groups. Lying off the west coast of mainland Greece, they have been greatly influenced by Western Europe. Periods of rule by the Venetians, French, and British have left their mark on many of the islands, especially in the mixed architecture of places like Corfu town. The Ionians first became a holiday destination during the Roman era, and today their beaches remain one of their most popular attractions.

LOCATOR MAP

The elegant parade of cafés known as the Liston in Corfu town

Corfu

🏙 100,000. ✈ 3 km (1.5 miles) S of Corfu town. 🚢 Xenofóntos Stratigoú, Corfu town. 🚌 ⓘ Evangelistrias 4 (26610-37520).

Corfu offers the diverse attractions of secluded coves, bustling resorts, and traditional hill villages. Between 229 BC and AD 337 it was part of the Roman empire. It remained under Byzantine rule until the 14th century, when the Venetians took control. French and British occupation followed, before unification with Greece in 1864. Though the island is most popular for its beaches, inland there are many places where you can still observe the traditional lifestyle of the Corfiot people.

Corfu Town

The checkered history of the island is reflected in Corfu town's varied architecture. With its grand French-style colonnades, elegant Italianate buildings, and famous cricket pitch, the town is a delightful blend of European influences.

The **Palace of St. Michael and St. George** was built by the British between 1819 and 1824 to serve as the residence of a high commissioner. Used for a short time by the Greek royal family after the British left the island, the palace is now home to the **Museum of Asiatic Art**.

The palace overlooks the Esplanade, or Spianáda, a mixture of park and town square, and the site of the cricket ground. Once a Venetian firing range, the cricket pitch was developed by the British, and local teams play here regularly. Nearby, the Enosis Monument commemorates the 1864 union of the Ionian Islands with the rest of Greece. The **Liston**, a parade of cafés that was built in 1807 as a copy of the Rue de Rivoli in Paris, lines one side of the square.

Another of the town's most famous sights, the distinctive red-domed belfry of **Agios Spyrídon** is the tallest belfry on Corfu. The church was built in 1589 and dedicated to the island's patron saint.

Also worth seeing are the Town Hall – a grand Venetian building located in the Plateía Dimarcheíou – the **Byzantine Museum**, and the fascinating **Archaeological Museum**. The latter's centerpiece is a stunning Gorgon frieze.

On the town's eastern side stands the 16th-century Venetian-built **Old Fortress**, which affords magnificent views of the town and along the island's east coast. The **New Fortress** was built shortly after the old one to strengthen the town's defenses.

🏛 **Palace of St. Michael and St. George**
Plateía Spianáda. **Tel** 26610-30443.
🕐 Tue–Sun. 🔴 main public hols.

Northern Corfu

Northern Corfu, in particular the northeast coast, is a busy vacation destination, which boasts a whole host of popular resorts and beaches.

The multiple picturesque bays of Palaiokastrítsa in northern Corfu

For hotels and restaurants in this region see pp510–13 and pp514–17

Vacation apartments at Fiskárdo on the island of Kefalloniá

Set around a fishing harbor, **Kassiópi** has retained its character in spite of the influx of tourists. Nearby are the ruins of a 13th-century castle, and the church of Kassiopítissa, which occupies the site of a former temple of Jupiter.

The bustling vacation center of **Sidári** is famous for its sandy beaches and unusual rock formations, while picturesque **Palaiokastrítsa** has safe swimming and water sports, as well as boat trips to nearby grottoes. Vacationers wanting a diversion from the busy resort atmosphere can visit the 17th-century monastery, **Moní Theotókou**.

Mount Pantokrátor, a short drive north of Corfu town, is popular with walkers and naturalists. The highest point on Corfu, it offers fine views of the whole island.

Southern Corfu
More varied than the north, southern Corfu offers other attractions apart from beaches. Tranquil hillside villages, such as **Vátos** and **Pélekas**, contrast with noisy resorts like **Benítses**, offering a more traditional image of Greece.

Among the more peaceful spots in the south is the **Korisíon Lagoon**, a 5-km (3-mile) stretch of water, separated from the sea by some of the most beautiful dunes and beaches on Corfu. The area provides a habitat for many species of birds and wild flowers.

A popular day trip from any of Corfu's resorts is to the **Achílleion Palace**, built between 1890 and 1891 as a personal retreat for the Empress Elizabeth of Austria (1837–98). After a tour of the palace and its gardens, visit the Vasilákis Tastery opposite, and sample this local distiller's products.

> **🏛 Achílleion Palace**
> 19 km (12 miles) SW of Corfu town.
> 📞 **Tel** 26610-56210. ⬭ daily.

Kefalloniá

> 🏚 31,000. ✈ 9 km (6 miles) S of Argostóli. ⛴ Argostóli, Fiskárdo. 🚌 Ioánnou Metaxá, Argostóli. 🛈 Waterfront, Argostóli (26710-22248).

The largest island in the Ionians, Kefalloniá has a range of attractions, from busy beach resorts to areas of outstanding natural beauty.

The capital, **Argostóli**, is a busy town located by a bay. Of interest are the Historical and Folk Museum and the Archaeological Museum.

Around the island the liveliest places are **Lássi** and the south-coast resorts, but elsewhere there are quiet villages and stunning scenery.

Mount Aínos and the **Mount Aínos National Park**, in the south, and the haunting, subterranean **Melissaní Cave-Lake** are sights not to be missed. **Fiskárdo**, with its 18th-century Venetian houses clustered by the harbor, is Kefalloniá's prettiest village. From here ferry services are available to the islands of **Ithaca** and **Lefkáda**.

Zákynthos

> 🏚 30,000. ✈ 4 km (2.5 miles) S of Zákynthos town. ⛴ Zákynthos town, Agios Nikólaos. 🚌 Zákynthos town. 🛈 Molos Ag Dionysios, Zákynthos town (26950-25428).

Zákynthos is an attractive and green island, with good beaches and beautiful scenery to be enjoyed.

Zákynthos town is the point of arrival on the island. Here, the impressive church of Agios Dionéysios, and the Byzantine Museum, which houses a breathtaking array of frescoes, both deserve a visit.

The growth of tourism on Zákynthos has been heavily concentrated in **Laganás** and its 14-km (9-mile) sweep of soft sand. The town's hectic nightlife continues until dawn. Alternatively, visitors can head to the island's north coast for the beach resorts of **Tsiliví** and **Alykés**, the latter being especially good for windsurfing. At the northern-most tip of the island are the unusual and spectacular **Blue Caves**. The caves can be visited by boat from the resort of **Agios Nikólaos**.

The Blue Caves of Zákynthos at the northern tip of the island

Cyclades ㉒

The most visited island group, the Cyclades are everyone's Greek island ideal, with their whitewashed, cliff-top villages, blue-domed churches, and stunning beaches. The islands vary greatly, from the quiet and traditional to the more nightlife-oriented. The cradle of the Cycladic civilization (3000–1000 BC), they also offer a rich ancient history. Important archaeological sites, such as those on Delos and Santoríni, provide a fascinating insight into the past.

LOCATOR MAP

Working 16th-century windmill, part of the Folk Museum in Mýkonos town

Mýkonos

🏠 4,500. ✈ 3 km (1.5 miles) SE of Mýkonos town. ⛴ Mýkonos town. 🚌 Polykandrióti, Mýkonos town (for north of island); on road to Ornós, Mýkonos town (for south of island). 🛈 Harborfront, Mýkonos town (22890-25250).

Sandy beaches and dynamic nightlife combine to make Mýkonos one of the most popular islands in the Cyclades. Visited by intellectuals in the early days of tourism, today it thrives on its reputation as the glitziest island in Greece. In addition to offering sun, sea, and sand, the island is a good base from which to visit the ancient archaeological site on Delos.

Mýkonos Town
The supreme example of a Cycladic town, Mýkonos town (or Chóra) is a tangle of dazzling white alleys and cube-shaped houses. It has a bustling port, from where taxi boats for the island of **Delos** leave. To the south, the **Archaeological Museum** has a fine collection of exhibits, including finds from the excavations of the ruins on Delos.

In the Kástro, the oldest part of town, is the excellent **Folk Museum**. The 16th-century Voní's Windmill, still in working order, is part of the museum. Nearby, the most famous church on the island is **Panagía Paraportianí**, which dates back to 1425. From Kástro, the lanes run down into picturesque Venetía, or Little Venice, the artists' quarter. Also worth visiting are the **Maritime Museum of the Aegean** and the **Municipal Art Gallery**.

🏛 Archaeological Museum
Harborfront. **Tel** 22890-22325.
🕐 Tue–Sun. 🔴 main public hols. 🖼

Around the Island
Mýkonos is popular primarily for its beaches and one of the best is stylish **Platýs Gialós**, 3.5 km (2 miles) south of Mýkonos town. There are also several nudist beaches, including quiet **Parága** and the more lively **Paradise**, **Super Paradise**, and **Eliá**.

Inland, the traditional village of **Ano Merá** remains largely unspoiled by tourism. The main attraction here is the 16th-century monastery **Panagía i Tourlianí**.

⛩ Delos
2.5 km (1 mile) SW of Mýkonos town. **Tel** 22890-22259. ⛴ 8–10am daily from Mýkonos town returning noon–2pm. 🕐 Tue–Sun. 🔴 main public hols. 🖼 🎫

The tiny, uninhabited island of Delos is one of the most important archaeological sites in Greece. The legendary birthplace of Artemis and Apollo, from 1000 BC it was home to the annual Delian Festival, held in honor of the god Apollo. By 700 BC it had become a major religious center and place of pilgrimage. In addition to some impressive 2nd-century BC mosaics and temple ruins, the most important remains on Delos are the magnificent 7th-century BC **Lion Terrace**, the **Theater**, built in 300 BC to hold 5,500 people, and the **Theater Quarter**.

Lions carved from Naxian marble along the Lion Terrace on Delos

Whitewashed buildings lining the cliff top in Firá, Santoríni

Santoríni

🏘 12,500. ✈ 5 km (3 miles) SE of Firá. ⛴ Skála Firón. 🚌 50 m (160 ft) S of main square, Firá. 🚹 Firá (22860-27199).

Colonized by the Minoans in 3000 BC, this volcanic island erupted in 1450 BC, forming Santoríni's distinct crescent shape. A popular tourist destination, it is a stunning island, as famous for its ancient archaeological sites as for its white-washed villages, volcanic cliffs, and black sand beaches.

Firá

Founded in the late 18th century, Firá was destroyed by an earthquake in 1956 and rebuilt along terraces on the volcanic cliffs. Packed with hotels, bars, and restaurants, its streets enjoy magnificent views out to sea. The tiny port of Skála Firón, 270 m (890 ft) below, is connected to the town by cable car or by mule up 580 steps.

Among Firá's most interesting sights are the **Archaeological Museum**, with finds from Ancient Thíra and Minoan Akrotíri, and the 18th-century church of **Agíos Minás**. The pretty ocher chapel of **Agios Stylianós** is also worth a visit on the way to the Frangika, or Frankish quarter, with its maze of arcaded streets.

🏛 Archaeological Museum
Opposite cable car station.
Tel 22860-22217. ◯ 8:30am–3pm Tue–Sun. ◯ main public hols. 🈹

Around the Island

Within easy reach of Firá, on the headland of Mésa Vounó, the ruins of the Dorian town of **Ancient Thíra** are not to be missed. Most of the ruins date from the Ptolemies, who built temples to the Egyptian gods in the 4th and 3rd centuries BC. There are also Hellenistic and Roman remains. Below the site are the popular beaches of **Períssa** and **Kamári**.

A donkey ride in Firá, Santoríni

Another of the Cyclades' most inspiring archaeological sites, the Minoan settlement of **Akrotíri** was unearthed in 1967, still wonderfully preserved after some 3,500 years of burial under volcanic ash. Some of the frescoes discovered here are now on display in the National Archaeological Museum in Athens (*see p476*).

🔭 Ancient Thira
11 km (7 miles) SW of Firá.
Tel 22860-23217. 🚌 to Kamári.
◯ Tue–Sun. ◯ main public hols.

Náxos

🏘 20,000. ✈ 2 km (1 mile) S of Náxos town. ⛴ 🚌 Harborfront, Náxos town. 🚹 Harborfront, Náxos town (22850-25201).

The largest of the Cyclades, Náxos was a major center of the Cycladic civilization. The Venetians, who arrived in the 13th century, built many fortifications that still stand on the island today. History and superb beaches make Náxos an ideal vacation destination.

Náxos Town

Overlooking Náxos town's bustling harbor is the huge, marble, 6th-century BC Portára gateway, built as the entrance to the unfinished Temple of Apollo. To the south, **Agios Geórgios** is the main tourist center, with a wealth of hotels, apartments, and restaurants. The old town divides into the Kástro – the 13th-century Venetian fortifications – and the medieval Bourg. The fine 18th-century Orthodox cathedral, the **Mitrópoli Zoödóchou Pigís**, stands in the Bourg, which also has a busy market area. In the Kástro, the **Archaeological Museum**, in the Palace of Sanoúdo, has one of the best collections of Cycladic marble figurines in the Greek islands.

🏛 Archaeological Museum
Palace of Sanoúdo. **Tel** 22850-22725.
◯ Tue–Sun. ◯ main public hols. 🈹

Around the Island

South of Náxos town are many fine beaches, including **Agía Anna** and **Kastráki** – both good for water sports – and tranquil **Pláka**.

Inland the Tragaía Valley is a walkers' paradise. It is dotted with picturesque villages, such as **Chalkí**, with its Byzantine and Venetian architecture, and **Filóti**, which sits on the slopes of 1,000-m (3,300-ft) Mount Zas.

The Portára gateway that overlooks Náxos town's harbor

Rhodes and the Dodecanese ⑳

The Dodecanese offer a wide range of landscapes and activities. Their hot climate and fine beaches attract many visitors, but the islands also boast lush, fertile valleys and wooded mountains. The Dodecanese have been subject to several invasions, with periods of occupation by the medieval Knights of St. John, the Ottomans, and the Italians. This checkered history is still apparent in the islands' impressively varied architecture and wealth of historical sites.

LOCATOR MAP

The Palace of the Grand Masters in Rhodes town

Rhodes

🏛 100,000. ✈ 25 km (15 miles) SW of Rhodes town. ⛴ Commercial harbor, Rhodes town. 🚌 Mandráki, Rhodes town. ℹ Archiepiskopou Makariou 1, Rhodes town (22410-44330).

An important center from the 5th to 3rd centuries BC, Rhodes was later part of both the Roman and Byzantine empires before being conquered by the Knights of St. John, the order founded in the 11th century to tend Christian pilgrims in Jerusalem. They occupied the island from 1306 to 1522, and their medieval walled city still dominates Rhodes town. Ottoman and Italian rulers followed, leaving their own traces of occupation. Rhodes' rich and varied history, sandy beaches, and lively nightlife attract tens of thousands of tourists each year.

Rhodes Old Town

The town of Rhodes has been inhabited for over 2,400 years. A city was first built here in 408 BC, and when the Knights of St. John arrived in

1306 they built their citadel over these ancient remains. Surrounded by moats and 3 km (2 miles) of walls, the Knights' medieval citadel forms the center of the Old Town, which is divided into the Collachium and the Bourg. The Collachium was the Knights' quarter, while the Bourg was home to the rest of the population.

Dominating the Old Town is the 14th-century **Palace of the Grand Masters**, the seat of 19 Grand Masters of the Knights during two centuries of occupation. The palace houses several priceless mosaics from sites in Kos, as well as two permanent exhibitions about ancient and medieval Rhodes.

The medieval **Street of the Knights** is lined with the Inns of the Tongues of the Order of St. John. The Inns – there was one for each of the seven Tongues, or nationalities, into which the Order was

divided – were used as meeting places for the Knights. Begun in the 14th century in Gothic style, they were restored by the Italians in the early 20th century.

The **Archaeological Museum** and the **Byzantine Museum**, both located in the Collachium, contain many fine exhibits from different periods in Rhodes' history.

In the Bourg area, the **Mosque of Suleiman the Magnificent** was built to commemorate the Sultan's victory over the Knights in 1522. The **Library of Ahmet Havuz**, which houses the chronicle of the Turks' siege of Rhodes, and the **Hammam**, the public baths, provide further reminders of the town's Turkish past.

🏰 Palace of the Grand Masters
Ippotón. **Tel** 22410-25500.
🕐 Tue–Sun. 🔴 main public hols.
🅿 ♿ limited.

Rhodes New Town
Beyond the original citadel walls, the new town of Rhodes is made up of a number of areas. These include **Néa Agora**, with its Moorish domes and lively market, and **Mandráki harbor** in the eastern half of town. Close to the harbor are the mock Venetian Gothic **Government House** – a legacy of the Italian occupation of the 1920s – and the **Mosque of Murad Reis**, with its graceful minaret. The west side of town is a busy tourist center, with lively streets and a packed beach.

The minaret of the Mosque of Murad Reis

The acropolis overlooking Líndos town on Rhodes

Western Rhodes

A short distance southwest of Rhodes town, set on the beautiful green and wooded hillsides of Filérimos, is **Moní Filerímou**. A place of worship for 2,000 years, this monastery has layers of history and tradition, from Phoenician to Byzantine, Orthodox, and Catholic.

A few kilometers farther southwest, **Ancient Kámeiros** is one of the best-preserved Classical Greek cities. Its remains include a 3rd-century BC Doric temple. Also worth visiting are the wine-making village of **Émponas**, and **Petaloúdes**, or Butterfly Valley. Popular with walkers, this valley teems with Jersey tiger moths from June to September.

🏛 Ancient Kámeiros
36 km (22 miles) SW of Rhodes town.
⬜ Tue–Sun. 🔴 main public hols. 🈯
♿ to lower sections only

Eastern Rhodes

Halfway along Rhodes' sheltered east coast, **Líndos** is one of the island's most popular resorts. A magnet for tourists seeking sun, sea, and sand, it is also famous for its cliff-top acropolis overlooking the bay. This temple site, crowned by the 4th-century BC Temple of Lindian Athena, was one of the most sacred spots in the ancient world.

Located in the Valley of Áthona, between Líndos and Rhodes town, **Archángelos** is famous for its pottery, hand-woven rugs and leather boots. Above the town are the ruins of the Crusader Castle, built in 1467 by the Knights of St. John as a defense against the Turks.

🏛 Acropolis at Líndos
1 km (0.5 miles) E of Líndos village.
Tel 22440-31258. ⬜ Jul–Sep:
daily; Oct–Jun: Tue–Sun. 🔴 main
public hols. 🈯

Kos

🏛 27,000. ✈ 27 km (16 miles) W of
Kos town. ⛴ 🚌 Aktí Koudouriótou,
Kos town. 🚶 Vasiléos Georgíou 1,
Kos town (22420-29910).

Mainly flat and fertile, Kos is known as the "Floating Garden." It has a wealth of archaeological sites, Hellenistic and Roman ruins, and Byzantine and Venetian castles, many of which can be found in **Kos town**. Here, the 16th-century Castle of the Knights, the Ancient Agora, and the Roman remains should not be missed.

Most visitors to Kos come for the sandy beaches. The best of these are easily reached from the resort of **Kamári** on the island's southwest coast. **Kardámaina** is Kos's biggest and noisiest resort, while the northwest bays, such as **Tigkáki**, are ideal for water sports. In spite of tourist development, inland you can still see remnants of Kos's traditional lifestyle.

Kos is a good base from which to explore the more northerly islands of the Dodecanese, including **Pátmos**, home to the 11th-century Monastery of St. John.

Kárpathos

🏛 5,000. ✈ 17 km (11 miles) S of
Kárpathos town. 🚌 corner of 28
Oktovríou & Dimokratías, Kárpathos
town. ⛴ Kárpathos town, Diáfani.
🚶 Kárpathos town (22450-22222).

Despite an increase in tourism from the late 1990s onwards, wild and rugged Kárpathos remains largely unspoiled. Its capital, **Kárpathos town**, is a busy center, with hotels, cafés, and restaurants around its bay. Nearby is the main resort of **Amoopí**, with its sweep of sandy shore. In addition to some magnificent beaches on the west coast, including **Lefkós** and **Apélla**, the island has places of archaeological and historical interest. **Vroukoúnda** is the site of a 6th-century BC city, while in the village of **Olympos** traditional Greek life and customs can still be observed.

Windmills in the traditional village of Olympos on Kárpathos

Crete ㉔

Rugged mountains, sparkling seas, and ancient history combine with the Cretans' relaxed nature to make this island an idyllic vacation destination. The center of the Minoan civilization over 3,000 years ago, Crete has also been occupied by Romans, Byzantines, Venetians, and Turks. Historic towns such as Irákleio, Chaniá, and Réthymno, and the famous Minoan palaces at Knossos and Phaestos, give a fascinating insight into some of the most important periods in Cretan history.

LOCATOR MAP

Irákleio's boat-lined harbor, dominated by the vast Venetian fortress

Irákleio

116,000. ✈ 5 km (3 miles) E. 🚢 🚌 🛈 *Xanthoudídou 1 (2810-246299).*

A busy, sprawling town of concrete buildings, Irákleio nevertheless has much of interest to the visitor. Four centuries of Venetian rule have left a rich architectural legacy, evident in the imposing 16th-century **fortress** overlooking the harbor, and the elegantly-restored 17th-century **Loggia**, a former meeting place for the island's nobility. Among Irákleio's many churches, **Agios Márkos**, built by the Venetians in 1239, and 16th-century **Agios Títos** deserve a visit. Also not to be missed are the Archaeological Museum (*see below*) and the **Historical Museum**, which traces the history of Crete from early Christian times. The heart of the town is the Plateía Eleftheríou Venizélou, a bustling pedestrianized zone of cafés and shops.

Those interested in the beaches should head to the package-tour resorts of **Mália** and **Chersónisos**, just a short drive east of the town.

🏛 Irákleio Archaeological Museum

Corner of Xanthoudídou & Mpofór, Plateía Eleftherías. *Tel 2810-279086/279000.* 🔴 *currently closed for restoration.* 📷

This impressive museum displays Minoan artifacts from all over Crete. Its most magnificent exhibits include the famous Minoan frescoes from Knossos, and the Phaestos Disk, which was discovered at the site of the palace of Phaestos in 1903. Inscribed with pictorial symbols, the disk's meaning and origin remain a mystery. Among the museum's many other treasures are the Snake Goddesses, two figurines dating from around 1600 BC.

♙ Palace of Knossos

5 km (3 miles) S of Irákleio. *Tel 2810-231 940.* 🚌 🔴 *daily.* 🔴 *main public hols.* 📷 📷

The capital of Minoan Crete, Knossos was the largest and most sophisticated of the Minoan palaces on the island. Built around 1900 BC, the first palace of Knossos was destroyed by an earthquake in about 1700 BC and was soon completely rebuilt. The ruins visible today are almost entirely from this second palace. They were restored by Sir Arthur Evans in the early 20th century; although the subject of academic controversy, his reconstructions give one of the best impressions of life in Minoan Crete to be found anywhere on the island.

Highlights of a tour of the site – the focal point of which is the vast Central Court – include the replica of the Priest-King Fresco, the Giant Pithoi, one of over 100 *pithoi* (storage jars) unearthed at Knossos, the Throne Room, believed to have served as a shrine, and the Royal Apartments. The original frescoes from the palace are now housed in Irákleio's Archaeological Museum.

The South Propylon (entrance) of the Palace of Knossos

Phaestos

5 km (40 miles) SW of Irákleio.
el 28920-42315. ☐ 8am–8pm
aily (winter: 8:30am–3pm).
☐ *main public hols.*

Phaestos was one of the most
nportant Minoan palaces on
Crete. In 1900 Italian-led
xcavations unearthed two
alaces. Remains of the first
alace, constructed around
900 BC and destroyed by an
arthquake in 1700 BC, are still
isible. Most of the present
uins, however, are of the
econd palace. Phaestos was
nally destroyed in the 2nd
entury BC by the ancient
ity-state of Górtys.

The most impressive
emains are the Grand
taircase, which was the main
ntrance to the palace, and
he Central Court.

A few kilometers northeast
f Phaestos, the archaeological
emains of ancient **Górtys**
date from about 1000 BC to
he late 7th century AD.

Agios Nikólaos

🏛 10,000. ✈ ⛴ 🚌 ℹ Koundoúrou
1 (28410-22357). 🛒 Wed.

The main transport hub for the
e east of the island,
lelightful Agios Nikólaos is
a thriving vacation center
with an attractive harbor and
ine beaches, as well as an
nteresting **Folk Museum** and
an **Archaeological Museum**.

A few kilometers north is
he well-established resort of
Eloúnda, boasting attractive
sandy coves and a good
range of accommodations.

Chaniá

🏛 50,000. ✈ 16 km (10 miles) E.
⛴ 🚌 ℹ Kriári 40 (28210-92943).

One of Crete's most
appealing cities, Chánia
was ruled by the Venetians
from 1204 to 1669, and is
dotted with elegant houses,
churches, and fortifications
dating from this period. Many
of these can be found in the
Venetian quarter around the
harbor, and in the picturesque
Splántzia district. The
Mosque of the Janissaries,
on one side of the harbor,
dates back to the arrival of
the Turks in 1645, and is the
oldest Ottoman building on
Crete. The lively covered
market, with its many shops
and fresh produce stalls, is an
area worth exploring. Nearby
the **Archaeological Museum**
is housed in the Venetian
church of San Francesco.

A short walk west of Chaniá
is the relatively undisturbed
beach of **Agioi Apóstoloi**.

Samariá Gorge

44 km (27 miles) S of Chaniá. 🚌 *to*
Xylóskalo. ⛴ *Agía Rouméli to Sfakia*
or Palaiochóra (via Soúgia); last boat
back leaves at 5pm. ☐ *May–mid-*
Oct: 6am–4pm daily; Apr 10–30 &
Oct 16–31: if weather permits.

Crete's most spectacular
scenery lies along the
Samariá Gorge, the longest
ravine in Europe. When it
became a national park, the
inhabitants of the village of
Samariá moved elsewhere,
leaving behind the ruined
buildings and chapels seen
here today. Starting from the
Xylóskalo (Wooden Stairs), an
18-km (11-mile) trail leads to
the seaside village of Agía
Rouméli. A truly impressive
sight along the route is the
Sideróportes, or Iron Gates,
where the path squeezes
between two towering walls
of rock, only 3 m (9 ft) apart.
Upon reaching Agía Rouméli
walkers can take a boat to
Sfakia, Soúgia, or Palaiochóra
to join the road and buses
back to Chaniá.

The narrow defile known as the
Iron Gates in the Samariá Gorge

Réthymno

🏛 24,000. ⛴ 🚌 ℹ Sofokli
Venizélou (28310-29148).
🍷 Wine Festival (mid-Jul).

Despite tourism and modern
development, Réthymno has
retained much of its charm.
The old quarter is rich in
well-preserved Venetian and
Ottoman architecture,
including the elegant 16th-
century Venetian **Lótzia**
(Loggia) and the **Nerantzés
Mosque**, converted from a
church by the Turks in 1675.
The huge **Fortétsa** was built
by the Venetians in the 16th
century to defend the port
against both pirates and the
Turks. Below it is a pretty
harbor, lined with cafés and
restaurants. Also worth
visiting in the town is the
Archaeological Museum.

East of Réthymno there are
several resorts, while to the
west lies a 20-km (12-mile)
stretch of uncrowded beach.

Tavernas and bars along Réthymno's waterfront

Practical Information

Tourism is one of Greece's most important industries, and as a consequence, visitors to the country are well catered for: transportation networks are relatively efficient, there are banks and exchange facilities in all the major resorts, and telecommunications have improved dramatically in recent years. The country's hot climate, together with the easy-going outlook of its people, are conducive to a relaxed vacation, and it is usually best to adopt the philosophy *sigá, sigá* (slowly, slowly). In summer, almost everything closes for a few hours after lunch, reopening later in the day when the air cools and Greece comes to life again.

WHEN TO VISIT

Tourist season in Greece – late June to early September – is the hottest and most expensive time to visit, as well as being very crowded. December to March are the coldest and wettest months, with reduced public transportation facilities, and many hotels and restaurants closed for the winter. Spring is a good time to visit; there are fewer tourists, and the weather and the countryside are at their best.

TOURIST INFORMATION

Tourist information is available in many towns and villages throughout Greece, from government-run **EOT** offices (Ellinikós Organismós Tourismoú), municipally run tourist offices, the local tourist police, or privately owned travel agencies. However, visitors should be aware that not all of the information published by the EOT is reliable or up-to-date.

OPENING HOURS

Opening hours tend to be vague in Greece, varying from day to day, season to season, and place to place. To avoid disappointment, visitors are advised to confirm the opening times of sites covered in this chapter once they arrive in the country.

All post offices and banks, and most stores, offices, state-run museums, and archaeological sites close on public holidays. Some facilities may also be closed on local festival days.

The main public holidays in Greece are as follows: January 1, March 25, Good Friday, Easter Sunday, May 1, December 25 and 26.

VISA REQUIREMENTS AND CUSTOMS

Visitors from EU countries, the US, Canada, Australia, and New Zealand need only a valid passport for entry to Greece (no visa is required), and can stay for up to 90 days.

The unauthorized export of antiquities and archaeological artifacts from Greece is treated as a serious offence, incurring hefty fines or even a prison sentence.

Prescription drugs brought into the country should be accompanied by a prescription note for the purposes of the customs authorities.

PERSONAL SECURITY

The crime rate in Greece is low compared with other European countries, but it is worth taking a few sensible precautions, such as keeping all personal possessions secure. Parts of Athens, such as Omonia, can be dangerous after midnight. If you have anything stolen, you should contact either the police or the tourist police.

Foreign women traveling alone in Greece are usually treated with respect, especially if they are dressed modestly. However, hitchhiking alone is not advisable.

POLICE

Greece's police are split into three forces: the regular police, the port police, and the tourist police. The tourist police provide advice to vacationers in addition to carrying out normal police duties. Should you suffer a theft, lose your passport, or have cause to complain about shops, restaurants, tour guides, or taxi drivers, you should contact them first. Every tourist police office claims to have at least one English speaker. Their offices also offer maps, brochures, and useful advice on finding accommodations in Greece.

EMERGENCY SERVICES

In the unlikely event of an emergency while on vacation, the appropriate numbers to call are listed in the Directory opposite.

HEALTH ISSUES

No inoculations are required for visitors to Greece, though tetanus and typhoid boosters may be

THE CLIMATE OF GREECE

On the mainland, summers are very hot, while spring and autumn generally bring milder but wetter weather. In winter, rainfall is at its greatest everywhere. Mountainous regions usually get heavy snow, but around Athens, temperatures rarely drop below freezing. Throughout the islands, the tendency is for long, dry summers and mild but rainy winters.

ATHENS

°C/F			
	31/88		
	22/72	22/72	
18/64		15/59	12/54
11/52			6/43
0°C / 32°F			
8 hrs	12 hrs	7 hrs	4 hrs
23 mm	6 mm	51 mm	62 mm
month	Apr	Jul	Oct	Jan

recommended by your doctor. Tap water in Greece is generally safe to drink, but in remote communities it is a good precaution to check with the locals.

Jellyfish, sea urchins, and weaver fish are potential hazards on beach holidays.

PHARMACIES

Greek pharmacies, *farmakeía,* are open from 8:30am to 2pm Monday to Friday, but are usually closed in the afternoon and all day on Saturdays. In larger towns there is often a rota system to maintain a service from 7:30am to 2pm and from 5:30 to 10pm. Details are posted in pharmacy windows, in both Greek and English.

FACILITIES FOR THE DISABLED

There are few facilities in Greece for assisting the disabled, so careful, advance planning is essential.

ETIQUETTE

Though formal attire is rarely needed, modest clothing (trousers for men and skirts and covered shoulders for women) should be worn

when visiting churches and monasteries. In restaurants, the service charge is always included in the check, but tips are still appreciated – the custom is to leave between 10 and 15 percent. Public restroom attendants should also be tipped. Taxi drivers, hotel porters, and chambermaids do not expect a tip, but are not averse to them either.

PHOTOGRAPHY

Taking photographs inside churches and monasteries is officially forbidden in Greece. Inside museums, photography is usually permitted, although flashes and tripods are often not. Wherever you go, it is best to gain permission before using a camera, as rules vary.

BANKING AND CURRENCY

The Greek unit of currency was the drachma, but since January 2002 it has been replaced by the euro *(see p15).*

Greek banks open from 8am to 2pm Monday to Thursday, and 8am to 1:30pm on Friday. In major cities and resorts, at least one bank usually opens its exchange desk for a few hours on weekday evenings and on Saturday mornings in summer.

Exchange facilities are also available at post offices, travel agents, hotels, tourist offices, and car rental agencies. Take your passport with you when cashing traveler's checks. Cash point machines (ATMs) operate 24 hours a day.

COMMUNICATIONS

Public telephones can be found in hotel lobbies and street kiosks, although they are becoming less and less easy to find with the advent of the mobile phone. Before you leave your home country, make sure your phone has international roaming, although this can prove to be very expensive. A better option is to buy a pay-as-you-go SIM card, particularly as the first €10 of calls are free with Vodafone (Greece), which will cover a few calls and texts.

Greek post offices *(tachydromeía)* are generally open from 7:30am to 2pm Monday to Friday; some main branches close as late as 8pm and occasionally open for a few hours at weekends. All post offices are closed on public holidays. Those displaying an "Exchange" sign will change money in addition to offering the usual services.

DIRECTORY

Travel Information

During the tourist season (late June–early September), there are countless international flights bringing millions of vacationers to the shores of Greece, especially from the colder parts of northern Europe and North America. Traveling within Greece is easy enough. While many of the larger islands can be reached from the mainland by plane, there are ferry routes to even the remotest destinations. Greece's extensive bus network serves virtually everywhere, from the largest city to the tiniest community. Renting a car or motorcycle is another popular way of exploring the country.

FLYING TO GREECE

There are around 20 international airports in Greece that can be reached directly from Europe. Only Crete, Rhodes, and Corfu among the islands, and Athens and Thessaloníki on the mainland, handle both charter and scheduled flights. The other international airports can only be reached directly by charter flights.

Direct scheduled flights from London to Athens and Thessaloníki are operated by **Aegean Airlines**, British Airways, and easyJet (Athens only). From outside Europe, all scheduled flights to Greece arrive in Athens, and only a few airlines offer direct flights. Continental Airlines and Delta Air Lines operate direct flights daily from New York.

Flights from Southeast Asia with connections to Australia are run by Singapore Airlines and Thai Airways.

Athens' international airport, Eléfthérios Venizélos, opened in 2001 and is located 27 km (17 miles) north-east of the center. There are two 24-hour bus services from the city to the airport: the E95 from the Plateía Syntágmatos takes approximately 1 hour; the E96 departs from Piraeus and takes 1 hour and 20 minutes. Metro line 3 now runs from Syntagma to the airport.

CHARTERS AND PACKAGE DEALS

Charter flights to Greece are nearly all from within Europe, and mostly operate between May and October.

Tickets are sold by travel agencies either as part of an all-inclusive package tour or as a flight-only deal.

DOMESTIC FLIGHTS

Most internal flights in Greece and the Greek Islands are operated by **Olympic Air**. Olympic Air operates direct flights from Athens and Thessaloníki to many of the islands. In addition, there are a number of inter-island services available throughout the year. Private companies, such as **Aegean Airlines** and **Athens Airways** also provide services between Athens and some of the major mainland and island destinations. Fares for domestic flights are at least double the equivalent bus journey or deck-class ferry trip.

GETTING AROUND ATHENS

Athens has a network of buses, trolley buses, and trams, in addition to a metro system. Buses are inexpensive, but can be very slow, as well as crowded. Tickets for buses and trams must be purchased in advance from a *períptero* (street kiosk), a transport booth, or certain other designated places. A brown, red, and white logo, with the words *eisitíria edó*, indicates where you can buy them. Each ticket is valid for one journey only, regardless of the distance traveled.

Since most of the major sights in the city center are within walking distance of one another, you can avoid using public transportation.

RAIL TRAVEL

Greece's rail network is operated by the state-owned **OSE** (Organismós Sidirodrómon Elládos). Limited to the mainland, it is fairly skeletal by European standards. First- and second-class tickets are less expensive than the equivalent bus journey, but services tend to be slower. Though more costly, tickets for intercity express trains are worth it for the time they save. A Greek Rail Pass allows the user three or five days of unlimited rail travel in one month on first- and second-class services, anywhere in Greece.

TRAVELING BY BUS

International buses connect Greece with eastern Europe, though during the tourist season fares are more expensive than charter flights.

Within Greece, the long-distance bus network is extensive, with buses stopping at least once a day at even the remotest destinations, and frequent express services on all the major routes.

From Athens there are regular departures to all the larger mainland towns, apart from those in Thrace, which are served by buses from Thessaloníki. Athens' Terminal A serves Epirus, Macedonia, the Peloponnese, and the Ionian islands of Corfu, Kefalloniá, Lefkáda, and Zákynthos. Terminal B serves most destinations in central Greece, including Delphi.

TRAVELING BY CAR

On the mainland there are express highways between Athens, Thessaloníki, Vólos, and Pátra. These roads are very fast, but tolls are charged for their use. There has been much upgrading of the roads on the islands, but they are still often poorly surfaced, particularly in more remote areas.

Car rental agencies are found in every tourist resort and major town. International companies such as **Budget**, **Avis**, **Hertz**, and **Europcar** tend to be more expensive than their local counterparts. The car rental agency should have an agreement with an emergency recovery company, such as Express, Hellas, or the InterAmerican Towing Company, in the event of a vehicle breakdown. Mopeds and motorcycles are also available for rent in many tourist resorts.

Greece has one of the highest road traffic accident rates in Europe; visitors are advised to take extra care when driving around.

FERRY SERVICES

There are regular, year-round ferry crossings from Italy, Israel, and Turkey to the Greek mainland and islands.

Piraeus, the port of Athens, is Greece's busiest port, with ferry routes to international destinations, as well as to scores of locations on the mainland and islands. A number of companies run the ferry services, each with their own ticket agency on the dockside. All fares except first class are set by the Ministry of Transport, so a journey should cost you the same, regardless of which shipping company you choose.

Ferry tickets can be purchased from the shipping line office on the dockside, or any authorized travel agency. Advance reservations are essential in peak season, which runs from June to August. In off season, services may be reduced or suspended altogether. Check local sources – such as the Greek tourist office or a travel agency – for the latest information before you travel. The port police, who have an office at Piraeus, are also a good source of reliable, up-to-date information.

In addition to the large ferries, there are smaller vessels that make inter-island crossings in summer.

HYDROFOILS AND CATAMARANS

The main operator of hydrofoil and catamaran services between the mainland and the islands is **Flying Dolphin** (run by Hellenic Seaways). However, all hydrofoils, regardless of which company they are operated by, are known locally as "Flying Dolphins." They are twice as fast as ferries, but twice as expensive. Most vessels function only in the summer months and are often cancelled in bad weather.

DIRECTORY

OLYMPIC AIR
Tel 210-355 0500.
www.olympicair.com

DOMESTIC AIRLINES

Aegean Airlines
Viltanoti 31,
14561 Athens.
Tel 80-11 12 00 00 (in Greece).
Tel 30-210 355 0500 (outside Greece).
www.aegeanair.com

Athens Airways
Tel 210-669 6000 (in Greece).
www.athensairways.com

TRAVEL AGENCIES IN GREECE

National Travel Information.
Tel 14541 (boat, train, coach times).

American Express Travel Services
Messogion Ave 318,
15341 Athens.
Tel 210-659 0700.

Sunisle Travel
Eslin 4,
Athens.
Tel 210-641 0881.
www.sunisle.gr

Superfast Ferries
Syngrou 123-4,
11745 Athens.
Tel 210-891 9130.
www.superfast.com

RAIL TRAVEL

OSE (Information & Reservations)
Sína 6, Athens.
Tel 1110.
www.trainose.gr

Rail Europe
Tel 08708-371 371 (UK).
www.raileurope.co.uk

Train Stations in Athens
Laríssis station (for northern Greece).
Tel 210-529 7777.

BUSES

Bus Terminals in Athens
Terminal A:
Kifisoú 100.
Tel 210-512 4910.
Terminal B:
Liosíon 260.
Tel 210-832 9585.

CAR RENTAL AGENCIES

Avis
Leofóros Amalías 48,
10558 Athens.
Tel 210-322 4951.
www.avis.com

Budget
Syngroú 8,
11742 Athens.
Tel 210-921 4771.
www.budget.com

Europcar
Syngroú 25,
11742 Athens.
Tel 210-921 1444.
www.europcar.com

Hertz
Syngroú 12,
11742 Athens.
Tel 210-922 0102.
www.hertz.gr

PIRAEUS PORT
Tel 210-422 6000 (port police).
Tel 14541 (ferry timetable).

HYDROFOIL AND CATAMARAN SERVICES

Flying Dolphin
Hellenic Seaways.
www.hellenicseaways.gr
Tel 210-419 9000.

Shopping & Entertainment

The choice of places to shop in Greece ranges from colorful, bustling street markets, found in almost every town and village, through traditional arts and crafts shops, to the designer fashion boutiques of Athens. Entertainment is as varied; visitors can try an open-air concert in the atmospheric setting of an ancient theater, or enjoy some late-night dining in a local taverna before heading for a bar or disco. With its dry, sunny climate and clear, warm seas, Greece offers countless opportunities for outdoor activities, from snorkeling to windsurfing, sailing, and hiking.

WHAT TO BUY

Traditional handicrafts, though often expensive, are the most genuinely Greek souvenirs. In Athens, Monastiráki and Pláka are the best places to purchase such items. There are also many unusual shops offering unique services, such as that of self-styled poet, **Stávros Melissinós**, who makes a wide variety of sturdy sandals and leather items. An excellent selection of goods, including tapestries and rugs, is available at **Olkotexnia**, while at the fascinating **Center of Hellenic Tradition** you can buy, among other things, finely crafted ceramics.

Some of the country's best ceramics can be found in the markets and shops of Athens' northern suburb Maroúsi, and on the island of Crete.

Brightly colored embroidery and wall-hangings are produced in many Greek villages. Colorful *flokáti* rugs, which are handwoven from sheep or goat's wool, are made mainly in the Píndos mountains, but can also be found in other parts of the mainland and on the islands.

Sold throughout Greece, leather goods are particularly noted on Crete, where the town of Chaniá hosts a huge leather market.

Well-crafted copies of ancient and Byzantine Greek art can be found in museum shops in many of the major cities. In Pláka in Athens, **Orféas** offers good quality marble and pottery copies of Classical Greek works, in addition to glittering Byzantine icons.

For jewelry, Athens is the best place to shop. Exclusive names include **Vourákis** and **Anagnostópoulos**, on Voukourestíou. The **Ilías Lalaoúnis Jewelry Museum** has over 3,000 designs, inspired by Classical and other archaeological sources.

MARKETS

Most towns in Greece have a weekly street market *(laïkí agorá)*, where fresh produce is sold alongside shoes, fabrics, and sundry household items. In Athens, the one on Xenokrátous in centrally located Kolonáki takes place every Friday. The busy Central Market is excellent for food, while the famous Sunday-morning flea market in Monastiráki should not be missed.

FOOD AND DRINK

Culinary delights to look for in Greece include honey, olives, olive oil, pistachios, and cheeses, such as the salty feta. Also worth trying are ouzo (an anise-flavored liquor), retsina (wine flavored with pine resin), and the fire-water *tsípouro*.

ENTERTAINMENT LISTINGS AND TICKETS

For detailed information on entertainment in Athens, try the weekly *Athinorama*, (in Greek only), or the English-language *Athens News*.

Most theaters and music clubs in the capital sell tickets at the door on the day of the performance. However, tickets for the summer Athens Festival and for concerts at the Mousikís Mégaron Concert Hall should be purchased in advance; there is a central ticket office, open daily from 10am to 4pm, located near the Plateía Syntágmatos.

Elsewhere, your nearest tourist office should be able to provide information on what is happening locally.

ENTERTAINMENT VENUES

The main entertainment venues in Athens host a wide variety of events. As well as excellent productions of 19th-century Greek and European plays, the **National Theater** puts on opera, ballet, and contemporary dance. The **Mousikís Mégaron Concert Hall** is a first-class classical concert venue, while the Olýmpia Theater is home to the **Lyrikí Skini** (National Opera). At the **Dóra Strátou Dance Theater** there is traditional regional Greek dancing nightly between May and September.

OPEN-AIR CINEMAS AND THEATERS

Found in towns and cities all over Greece, the outdoor cinema is extremely popular with Greeks and an experience not to be missed by anyone visiting the country in summer. Most movies are in English with Greek subtitles.

Open-air performances of Classical and modern drama, held at famous ancient archaeological sites, are an equally popular form of entertainment. The **Herodes Atticus Theater** hosts plays, as well as opera, ballet, and classical music concerts, during the annual Athens Festival (mid-June to mid-September). The theater at **Epidaurus** in the Peloponnese is another well-known venue.

TRADITIONAL GREEK MUSIC

To hear traditional Greek music in Athens head for **Diogénis Studio** or **Rex**. At **Taksími** and **Rempétiki Istoría** you can hear genuine *bouzouki* (Greek mandolin) music. In smaller towns and resorts around the country, the local taverna is often a good place to see traditional musicians perform while you dine.

SPECIAL INTEREST VACATIONS

Companies offering special interest vacations include **Inntravel** and **Ramblers Holidays**, which organize archaeological tours, and **Andante Travels**. Inntravel also runs courses on creative writing, drawing, and painting in Greece.

For specialist wildlife tours contact **Naturetrek**, **Limosa Holidays**, or the **Hellenic Ornithological Society**.

OUTDOOR ACTIVITIES

With miles of coastline, and crystal clear seas, Greece is the perfect place to pursue water sports. Windsurfing, water-skiing, jet-skiing, and parasailing are all available in the larger resorts. Snorkeling and scuba diving are also popular, although the latter is restricted. A list of places where it is permissible to dive with oxygen equipment can be obtained from the EOT (Greek Tourist Office) *(see p502)*.

For information on sailing vacations and chartering yachts, contact the **Hellenic Yachting Federation**. Cruises on luxury liners can be booked through **Swan Hellenic Cruises**, while inexpensive mini-cruises and boat trips are best arranged at a local travel agent on the spot.

Those wishing to simply relax on the beach should look for one with a Blue Flag; this indicates that the water is regularly tested for purity, and that the beach meets over a dozen other environmental criteria for both cleanliness and safety.

Inland the range of leisure opportunities is very varied, ranging from kayaking, white-water rafting, and canoeing, to hiking. **Trekking Hellas** organizes vacations based on these and other activities.

DIRECTORY

ART AND CRAFTS

Center of Hellenic Tradition
Mitropóleos 59 (Arcade) – Pandrósou 36,
Monastiráki, Athens.
Tel 210-321 3023.

Olkotexnia
Filenninon 14,
Syntagma, Athens.
Tel 210-325 0240.

Stávros Melissinós
Ag. Theklas 2,
Psyrri, Athens.
Tel 210-321 9247.

MUSEUM COPIES

Orféas
Pandrósou 28, Pláka,
Athens.
Tel 210-324 5034.

JEWELRY

Anagnostópoulos
Voukourestíou 6,
Kolonáki,
Athens.
Tel 210-360 4426.

Ilías Lalaoúnis Jewelry Museum
Karyatidon 4a,
Pláka, Athens.
Tel 210-922 1044.

Vourákis
Voukourestíou 8, Kolonáki,
Athens.
Tel 210-322 1600.

THEATERS

Dóra Strátou Dance Theater
Filopáppou Hill,
Filopáppou, Athens.
Tel 210-324 4395.

National Theater
Agíou Konstantínou 22,
Omónoia, Athens.
Tel 210-528 8100.

CLASSICAL MUSIC AND OPERA

Lyrikí Skiní, Olympia Theater
Akadimías 59,
Omónoia, Athens.
Tel 210-361 2461.

Mousikís Mégaron Concert Hall
V Sofías & Kókkali,
Stégi Patrídos, Athens.
Tel 210-728 2333.

OPEN-AIR THEATERS

Herodes Atticus Theater
Dionysíou Areopagítou,
Acropolis, Athens.
Tel 210-327 2000.

TRADITIONAL GREEK MUSIC

Diogénis Studio
Leof A Syngroú 259,
N. Smyrni, Athens.
Tel 210-942 5754.

Rempétiki Istoría
Ippokrátous 181,
Neápoli, Athens.
Tel 210-642 4937.

Rex
Panepistimíou 48,
Omonoia, Athens.
Tel 210-381 4591.

Taksími
C Trikoúpi & Isávron 29,
Neápoli, Athens.
Tel 210-363 9919.

SPECIAL INTEREST VACATIONS

Andante Travels
The Old Barn, Old Road,
Alderbury, Salisbury SP5 3AR, England. *Tel 01722-713 800.* www.andante travels.co.uk

Hellenic Ornithological Society
Vasileos Irakleion 24,
10682 Athens.
Tel 210-822 7937.

Inntravel
Castle Howard, York,
YO60 7JU, England.
Tel 01653-617 755.
www.inntravel.co.uk

Limosa Holidays
West End Farmhouse,
Chapel Field, Stalham,
Norfolk NR12 9EJ, UK.
Tel 01692-580 623.
www.limosaholidays.co.uk

Naturetrek
Cheriton Mill, Cheriton,
Alresford, Hants
SO24 0NG,
England.
Tel 01962-733 051.
www.naturetrek.co.uk

Ramblers Holidays
Box 43, Welwyn Garden City, Herts AL8 6PQ,
England.
Tel 01707-331 133.
www.ramblers holidays.co.uk

OUTDOOR ACTIVITIES

Hellenic Yachting Federation
Akti Possidónas 51,
Moschato, Athens,
Greece.
Tel 210-940 4825.

Swan Hellenic Cruises
Lynnem House, Victoria Way, Burgess Hill, West Sussex, RH15 9NF, UK.
Tel 0844-871 4603.
www.swanhellenic.com

Trekking Hellas
Saripoulou 10, 10682
Athens. *Tel 210-331 0323.* www.trekking.gr

Where to Stay in Greece

In a country so heavily dependent on tourism, accommodations are always easily found, and are very inexpensive compared with those in most other European destinations. Visitors to Greece can choose to stay in a range of surroundings, from modern luxury chain hotels to restored historic buildings.

PRICE CATEGORIES
The following price ranges are for a standard double room with tax per night during the high season. Breakfast is not included, unless specified:

€ Under €50
€€ €50–€90
€€€ €90–€130
€€€€ €130–€200
€€€€€ Over €200

ATHENS

EXARCHEIA Exarchion   🔲 ♿   €€
Themistokléous 55, 106 83 **Tel** *210-38 00731* **Fax** *210-38 03296* **Rooms** *58*   **Map** D1

The dated rooms of this 1960s high-rise, with their linoleum floors and dark furniture, are ready for a facelift, but they do have fridges, air-conditioning and TVs; given the price and the location in the heart of the district's nightlife scene, you can't complain. The mezzanine breakfast room is cheerful enough. **www.exarchion.com**

EXARCHEIA Best Western Museum   🔲🔲🔲 P ♿ 🔲   €€€
Mpoumpoulinas 16, 106 82 **Tel** *210-38 05611* **Fax** *210-38 00507* **Rooms** *90*   **Map** C1

This hotel takes its name from the National Archaeological Museum at the front, and is popular with academic visitors. The rooms are up to the standards of the Best Western chain without being especially distinctive. There are also triples and quads for families. **www.bestwestern.gr**

ILISIA Hilton   🔲🔲🔲🔲 P ♿ 🔲   €€€€€
Vassilísis Sofías 46, 115 28 **Tel** *210-72 81000* **Fax** *210-72 81111* **Rooms** *306*   **Map** F3

For years the only five-star hotel in the city center, the Hilton's pre-Olympics overhaul has vaulted back into the top rank, with the rooms retaining their large balconies. The hotel's three restaurants and huge outdoor pool (open to the public for a fee) are still major meeting points. **www.athens.hilton.com**

KOLONAKI St. George Lycabettus   🔲🔲🔲🔲 P ♿ 🔲   €€€€
Kleoménous 2, 106 75 **Tel** *210-72 90711* **Fax** *210-72 90439* **Rooms** *154*   **Map** E3

Situated just off Platía Dexamenís halfway up Lykavittós Hill, the St. George offers a rooftop pool, two well-regarded restaurants, and a summer bar that's a popular local hangout. The rooms are a mix of retro and modern minimalist; try to get a south-facing one with a view over the city. **www.sglycabettus.gr**

KOUKAKI Marble House   🔲 🔲   €
Alley off Anastasíou Zínni 35, 11741 **Tel** *210-92 28294* **Fax** *210-92 26461* **Rooms** *16*   **Map** B5

The helpful Nikoloulias family's pension has an enviable location on a quiet cul-de-sac. The simple but tidy rooms upstairs, most with bath and balcony, are complete with wrought-iron beds. There are two slightly larger ground floor studios. Very popular in season, so book well in advance. **www.marblehouse.gr**

MAKRYGIANNI Herodion   🔲🔲 🔲   €€€
Rovértou Gkálli 4, 117 42 **Tel** *210-92 36832* **Fax** *210-92 11650* **Rooms** *90*   **Map** B5

The Herodion has lovely common areas: the café-restaurant with patio seating shaded by wild pistachios, and the roof garden with two Jacuzzi tubs and the Acropolis a stone's throw away. Functional but fair-sized rooms, some with disabled-friendly baths and Acropolis views, have coco-fiber mattresses. **www.herodion.gr**

MAKRYGIANNI Divani Palace Acropolis   🔲🔲🔲🔲 P 🔲   €€€€
Parthenónos 19–25, 117 42 **Tel** *210-92 80100* **Fax** *210-92 14993* **Rooms** *250*   **Map** B5

This popular business and conference hotel has vast common facilities, though the underground restaurant is gloomily lit. Equally subterranean are exhibited sections of the Themistoklean Long Walls, discovered when the hotel was built. Rooms are a good size; there's also a small pool area and summer rooftop garden. **www.divanis.gr**

MONASTIRAKI Cecil   🔲 🔲   €€
Athinás 39, 105 54 **Tel** *210-32 17079* **Fax** *210-32 19606* **Rooms** *40*   **Map** B3

One of the oldest buildings in central Athens, dating from the 1850s, has been restored as a good-value character hotel with soundproofed, tastefully decorated, en suite rooms. Breakfast (charged separately) is abundant, featuring homemade jams, plus there's a roof terrace. **www.cecilhotel.gr**

OMONOIA Art Athens Hotel   🔲🔲 🔲   €€€
Márnis 27/Aristotélous 16, 104 32 **Tel** *210-52 40501* **Fax** *210-52 43384* **Rooms** *30*   **Map** B1

Boutique hotels are now ten a penny in Athens, but this one – occupying a converted Neoclassical mansion – offers good value for money. Light cream tones characterize the wood-floored rooms, accented by colorful original artwork. Everything is hi-tech, from lighting to individual thermostats. Service is excellent. Wi-Fi in lobby only. **www.arthotelathens.gr**

Key to Symbols *see back cover flap*

PLAKA Phaedra
🅿️ 🟦 W ⓔ

Chairefontos 16, corner of Adrianoú, 105 58 **Tel** *210-32 38461* **Fax** *210-32 27795* **Rooms** *21*   **Map** C5

Located at the intersection of two pedestrian lanes, the Phaedra had a thorough makeover before the Olympics and offers the best budget value in the area. Although not all tiled-floor rooms are en suite, each has an allocated bathroom and TV, while some have balconies. Pleasant ground-floor breakfast room. **www.hotelphaedra.com**

PLAKA Central
🍽️ 🟦 P   ⓔⓔⓔ

Apóllonos 21, 105 57 **Tel** *210-32 34357* **Fax** *210-32 25244* **Rooms** *84*   **Map** C4

Italian designer furniture, marble-clad bathrooms, and wooden flooring set the tone for this revamped hotel, with warm-toned soft furnishings in the comfortable, soundproofed rooms, some of which interconnect. There are four conference rooms, and a rooftop bar with a small Jacuzzi and view of the Acropolis. **www.centralhotel.gr**

PLAKA Hotel Philippos
🟦 W   ⓔⓔⓔ

Mitseon 3, Makrigianni 117 42 **Tel** *210-92 23611* **Rooms** *50*   **Map** B2

Hotel Philippos offers excellent value for money and is located in a peaceful residential area just a five-minute walk from the New Acropolis Museum. Some rooms have balconies with views of the Acropolis. There's a generous buffet breakfast, and a choice of restaurants nearby. Staff can arrange day trips. Wi-fi access in the lobby. **www.philipposhotel.gr**

PLAKA Plaka
🍽️ 🟦   ⓔⓔⓔ

Kapnikaréa 7, corner of Mitropóleos, 105 66 **Tel** *210-32 22706* **Fax** *210-32 11800* **Rooms** *67*   **Map** C4

A sister hotel to the Hermes, the Plaka is located five minutes' walk from Syntagma Square. From the leather sofas in the lobby to the striking color schemes in the wood-floored rooms, the place is sleek and tasteful. Many nearby hotels boast of roof gardens; the Plaka's is one of the best. **www.plakahotel.gr**

PLAKA Electra Palace
🍽️ 🏊 🟦 P   ⓔⓔⓔⓔⓔ

Navárchou Nikodhímou 18–20, 105 57 **Tel** *210-33 70000* **Fax** *210-33 41875* **Rooms** *155*   **Map** C4

The only de luxe hotel in Pláka attracts attention with its Neoclassical façade. The interior lives up to this promise, with plush rooms, antique and mock-antique decor, a wellness centre, plus a rooftop pool and restaurant. Rooms facing the garden are quieter. It's worth paying extra for a suite. **www.electrahotels.gr**

PSYRRI Fresh
🍽️ 🏊 🟦 W   ⓔⓔⓔⓔ

Sofokléous 26 & Kleisthénous, 105 52 **Tel** *210-52 48511* **Fax** *210-52 48517* **Rooms** *133*   **Map** B3

The closest design hotel to the town centre, Fresh combines minimalist chic with shockingly vibrant colors, right down to the balcony partitions. Rooms are small but cleverly designed – you can control the blinds from your bed to reveal views of the interior rock gardens. Stylish rooftop pool and bar. Wi-Fi access. **www.freshhotel.gr**

PSYRRI Ochre & Brown
🍽️ 🟦 W   ⓔⓔⓔⓔ

Leokoriou 7, 105 54 **Tel** *210-33 12940* **Fax** *210-52 39564* **Rooms** *22*   **Map** B2

This stylish, welcoming boutique hotel lies within walking distance of both the Acropolis and the Gazi nightlife district. Rooms have comfortable beds and good showers, and children are well catered for. The all-day bar-restaurant serves a delectable cooked-to-order breakfast and creative Mediterranean fare. **www.oandbhotel.com**

STATHMOS LARÍSSIS Oscar
🍽️ 🏊 🟦 P   ⓔⓔⓔ

Filadélfias 25, 104 39 **Tel** *210-88 34215* **Fax** *210-82 16368* **Rooms** *162*

The Oscar's main advantage is its position opposite the main Athens train station – ideal for late-night arrivals or early-morning departures to/from the airport or the north mainland. The common facilities, including a rooftop pool, are more than you would expect for this price, though rooms are a little dull and the area a little seedy. **www.oscar.gr**

SYNTAGMA Metropolis
🅿️ 🟦 P W   ⓔⓔ

Mitrópoleos 46, 105 63 **Tel** *210-32 17469* **Fax** *210-32 17871* **Rooms** *25*   **Map** C4

This small, five-story hotel enjoys views over its namesake, the Mitrópoli (Cathedral), and on to the Acropolis from the upper rooms. Rooms are basic, with vinyl floors and balconies, though the staff are friendly and the price is reasonable. There are no common areas, and breakfast is not provided. **www.hotelmetropolis.gr**

SYNTAGMA Athens Cypria
🟦 W   ⓔⓔⓔ

Diomeías 5, 105 63 **Tel** *210-32 38034* **Fax** *210-32 48792* **Rooms** *71*   **Map** C4

The exterior of this hotel just off pedestrianized Ermoú is deceptively bland. Inside, earth-toned rooms with small balconies are matched by the color scheme and stone dressing in the lobby. There is an all-day bar serving drinks and snacks. **www.athenscypria.com**

SYNTAGMA Grande Bretagne
🍽️ 🏊 🟦 ♿ W   ⓔⓔⓔⓔⓔ

Vassiléos Georgíou 1, Plateía Syntágmatos, 105 63 **Tel** *210-33 30000* **Fax** *210-32 28034* **Rooms** *321*   **Map** D4

Originally built in 1842 for King Otto, the Grande Bretagne has always been Athens' most exclusive hotel. Its restaurants and bars stand out in their own right: Alexander's Bar has an 18th-century tapestry of Alexander the Great, and the brasserie and rooftop restaurant are justifiably busy. **www.grandebretagne.gr**

SYNTAGMA King George Palace
🍽️ 🏊 🟦 ♿ W   ⓔⓔⓔⓔⓔ

Vassiléos Georgíou 3, Plateía Syntágmatos, 105 64 **Tel** *210-32 22210* **Fax** *210-32 50504* **Rooms** *102*   **Map** D4

The 1936-founded King George is more intimate and personal than other luxury hotels in the immediate vicinity, but boasts similar antique Belle Époque decor, a small pool in the fitness center, and a rooftop restaurant. Rooms are a good size, all unique, with handmade furniture in Second Empire style, and all mod cons. **www.classicalhotels.com**

Map References *see map of Athens pp474–5*

REST OF MAINLAND GREECE

ÁGIOS IOANNIS Sofoklis

Seafront, north end, 370 12 **Tel** *24260-31230* **Fax** *24260-31021* **Rooms** *20*

This professionally run hotel tries a bit harder than the competition at this beach resort. There is a century-old stone-walled ground floor lounge, oblique or direct sea views from most rooms, a tasteful breakfast terrace, and an attractive pool. Unusually for this area, it's open all year. www.sofokleshotel.com

AREOPOLI Xenonas Londas

Off Plateía Taxiarchón, 23062 **Tel** *27330-51360* **Fax** *27330-51012* **Rooms** *4*

This tower-mansion has been sympathetically converted into a small, sophisticated inn by Iakovos, painter and chef, and Han Jakob. The colorful textiles and wall tones are in the best of taste. Local honey and Iakovos' marmalade is served at breakfast. www.londas.com

DELPHI Pan

Pávlou ké Fredherikis 53, 330 54 **Tel** *22650-82294* **Fax** *22650-83244* **Rooms** *15*

Most rooms here have fine views of the gulf. The best rooms sleep four and are in the attic. Immediately across the street is a slightly pricier annex, with larger rooms and bathrooms, including bathtubs, but without the views of the older building. www.panartemis.gr

DIMITSANA Xenonas Kazakou

Near the top of the village, 220 07 **Tel** *27950-31660* **Fax** *27950-31660* **Rooms** *5*

Externally austere, this tastefully restored, stone and wood mansion is discreetly comfortable inside – with central heating for the chilly mountain winters. It is very quiet, apart from the Sunday church-bells. A rich traditional breakfast, including *loukomádes*, is served in the vaulted cellar. Wi-Fi in lobby only. www.xenonaskazakou.gr

GYTHEIO Githio

Vassiléos Pávlou 33, 232 00 **Tel** *27330-23452* **Fax** *27330-23523* **Rooms** *7*

This fine Neoclassical building from 1864 was formerly a gentleman's club; it's now a stylishly refurbished hotel above an ice cream parlor, overlooking the seafront and harbor. Elegant, high-ceilinged rooms sleep two or three; two four-bed apartments have kitchen facilities. Breakfast served in an area carved out of the natural rock. www.gythionhotel.gr

KALAMPAKA Alsos House

Kanári 5, 422 00 **Tel** *24320-24097* **Fax** *24320-79191* **Rooms** *6*

This small inn at the heart of Kalampáka's oldest quarter offers a mix of doubles, triples, and a four-bed family suite, all with balconies and sharing a well-equipped communal kitchen. The multilingual proprietor is a mine of information on the surrounding area. www.alsoshouse.gr

KARDAMYLI Cardamili Beach

Northern end of Ritsia beach, 240 22 **Tel** *27210-73180* **Fax** *27210-73184* **Rooms** *34*

Situated in a large orchard on the beachfront, and a short distance from the village, the hotel has rooms in the main building and a number of garden bungalows; some of the latter have kitchen facilities. All rooms have a fridge and views of the sea or mountains. Taverna and swimming pool on site. Open Apr–Oct. www.cardamilibeach.com

LITOCHORO Villa Drosos

Archeláou 20, Ágios Geórgios district, 602 00 **Tel** *23520-84561* **Fax** *23520-84563* **Rooms** *13*

The Villa Drosos may not have the unimpeded mountain views of the central-square hotels, but it does offer excellent standards in its small but balconied rooms, the best of which overlook the swimming pool and a small wood. The breakfast room has a fireplace, and the restaurant serves good grills. Open all year.

MONEMVASIA Malvasia

Inside the Kástro, 230 70 **Tel** *27320-63007* **Fax** *27320-63009* **Rooms** *34*

Named after the malmsey wine historically grown in the area and spread over three sites in the old city, Malvasia offers sympathetically restored rooms, each different, with traditional, low-key furnishings and antique furniture, some with wooden floors, fireplaces, and kitchenette facilities. Most rooms have terraces or sea views. Competitively priced

MYKINES Belle Helene

Tsoúnta 15, 212 00 **Tel** *27510-76225* **Fax** *27510-76179* **Rooms** *5*

This historical building (built in 1862) is where Heinrich Schliemann stayed for some of his excavations in the 1870s – his bed is still in use. Later visitors included Agatha Christie and Virginia Woolf. The ambience is still almost Victorian and bathrooms are not en suite, but the restaurant and hospitality are excellent.

MYSTRAS Hotel Pyrgos

Manousaki 3, 231 00 **Tel** *27310-20770* **Rooms** *7*

In a restored mansion dating from 1850, set in a garden with orange trees and in the shadow of Mount Taygetos, this small boutique hotel offers five rooms and two suites, all furnished with antiques. The welcoming and helpful staff serve a generous home-made breakfast on a stone patio. www.pyrgomystra.com

Key to Price Guide *see p508* **Key to Symbols** *see back cover flap*

NAFPLIO Byron
目 W   €€

Plátonos 2, 211 00 **Tel** *27520-22351* **Fax** *27520-26338* **Rooms** *18*

An elegant hotel with antique furniture, in a tastefully restored mansion above Ágios Spyrídon church. Rooms are modestly decorated in a simple but charming style, with wooden floors and rugs. Some rooms have a view or balcony. Breakfast can be taken on the patio. Internet facilities are available. **www.byronhotel.gr**

NAFPLIO King Othon 1 & 2
目 P W   €€

Farmakopoúlou 4/Spiliádou 5, 211 00 **Tel** *27520-27585* **Fax** *27520-27595* **Rooms** *20*

This restored mansion, originally the Ionian Bank and retaining its spectacular curving wooden staircase, is near the old town center. Rooms vary, some having balconies, but bathrooms are small. Breakfast is served in a flowery courtyard. Othon 2, nearby, has slightly larger rooms and suites. **www.kingothon.gr**

NAFPLIO Grande Bretagne
¶¶ 目 W   €€€€

Plateía Filellínon, 211 00 **Tel** *27520-96200* **Fax** *27520-96209* **Rooms** *20*

This three-storey Neoclassical building on the seafront has been transformed into an elegant hotel. All rooms feature dark hardwood furniture, high ceilings and marble-trimmed bathrooms; a few lucky ones have balconies. The restaurant here serves international cuisine. **www.grandebretagne.com.gr**

NEOS MYSTRAS Byzantion
🔲 🏊 目 P   €

Village center, 231 00 **Tel** *27310-83309* **Fax** *27310-20019* **Rooms** *22*

Ideally situated for exploration of the nearby Mystras site or walking in the foothills of Taygetos, the Byzantion offers quiet, spacious rooms with castle views and a pleasant pool-garden. The hotel has a bar and café, and tavernas are a few minutes' stroll away. Popular with groups, so book early. **www.byzantionhotel.com**

OLYMPIA Pelops
¶¶ 目 P ♿ W   €€

Varelás 2, 270 65 **Tel** *26240-22543* **Fax** *26240-22213* **Rooms** *18*

Stylishly refurbished in 2004 by friendly Greek-Australian owners Theodore and Susanna, the well-equipped rooms all have balconies, and Wi-Fi is available. The hotel, where the Olympics Committee stays, is within easy walking distance of the archaeological sites. Cooking and art courses are offered. Open Mar–Oct. **www.hotelpelops.gr**

THESSALONIKI Tourist
🔲 目 W   €€

Mitropóleos 21, 546 24 **Tel** *2310-270501* **Fax** *2310-226865* **Rooms** *37*

One of the few surviving interwar buildings in this area, the Tourist features parquet-floored lounges, a breakfast room accessed by a period lift, and irregularly shaped rooms with en suite. It's been featured in many publications on the city and has a staunchly loyal word-of-mouth clientele, so reservations are mandatory. **www.touristhotel.gr**

THESSALONIKI Le Palace
¶¶ 目 W   €€€

Tsimiskí 12, 546 24 **Tel** *2310-257400* **Fax** *2310-256589* **Rooms** *54*

The city's first boutique hotel is located in a 1926 Art Deco building, transformed from 1998–2002. The large, double-glazed rooms have contemporary bathrooms, while the common areas preserve some interwar touches. There's a mezzanine lounge and restaurant, which serves an outstanding buffet breakfast, and a café. **www.lepalace.gr**

THESSALONIKI Electra Palace
¶¶ 🏊 🏋 目 ♿ W   €€€€€

Plateía Aristotélous 9, 546 24 **Tel** *2310-294000* **Fax** *2310-294001* **Rooms** *131*

This landmark semicircular building has common areas palatially fitted with walnut and marble trim as well as chandeliers, while the wood-trimmed rooms – with every conceivable gadget – have ochre and red decor. Rooftop pool, fitness center, English-themed bar, and two restaurants. **www.electrahotels.gr**

CORFU AND THE IONIAN ISLANDS

CORFU Bella Venezia
目 🍸 W   €€€

N. Zambéli 4, Corfu Town, 49100 **Tel** *26610-46500* **Fax** *26610-20708* **Rooms** *32*

Close to the center of Corfu town, this dignified Neoclassical mansion has been restored and converted into a pleasant boutique hotel. High-ceilinged rooms are comfortable and tasteful without being extravagant. Hospitable, friendly staff. Public areas and some rooms are wheelchair-accessible. **www.bellaveneziahotel.com**

CORFU Akrotiri Beach
🔲 🏊 🏋 目 🍸   €€€€

Desýlla 155, Palaiokastrítsa, 49100 **Tel** *26630-41237* **Fax** *26630-41277* **Rooms** *127*

Largest and best of the hotels around popular Palaiokastrítsa. The hotel offers a plethora of facilities including two pools, a restaurant, three bars, live entertainment, and water sports including scuba diving nearby. Comfortable, well-equipped rooms with balconies and some of Corfu's best views. Closed Oct–Apr. **www.akrotiri-beach.com**

CORFU Corfu Palace
🔲 🏊 🏋 目 🍸 W   €€€€

Dimokratías 2, Corfu Town, 49100 **Tel** *26610-39485* **Fax** *26610-31749* **Rooms** *115*

The "grande dame" of Corfu hotels, built in 1954 and still the best place to stay in Corfu town. The marble bathrooms, cheerfully decorated rooms and suites, and grand public areas lend a touch of class. The rooms at the front have fine sea views. Large pool with shaded terrace. **www.corfupalace.com**

KEFALLONIA Linardos

Asos, 28085 **Tel** *26740-51563* **Fax** *26740-51563* **Rooms** *12*

Located in the center of the pretty village of Asos, Linardos offers rooms with fine views across the bay to the ruins of the Venetian castle. A choice of doubles, triples, twins, and family rooms, each with a well-equipped mini-kitchen. Hire a motor boat at the harbor to explore the nearby coast. Closed Oct–May. **www.linardosapartments.gr**

KEFALLONIA Emelisse Art Hotel

Eblisi, Fiskárdo, 28084 **Tel** *26740-41200* **Fax** *26740-41026* **Rooms** *65*

Fourteen traditional-style stone houses with stylish rooms boasting four-poster beds and private terraces. Facilities include a poolside bar and restaurant, breakfast terrace, tennis court, gym, and billiards. Mountain bikes are also available for guests to use. Good views over bay area. Closed Oct–Apr. **www.arthotel.gr**

ZAKYNTHOS Leedas Village

Lithákia, Agios Sóstis, 29092 **Tel** *26950-51305* **Fax** *26950-29934* **Rooms** *20*

Self-catering apartments for two–nine people in five attractive stone villas, all with terraces. Apartments are plain and cool, with terra-cotta paved floors and fully equipped kitchens. The villas are set in pretty, flower-filled gardens and are a short walk from the beach. Children's playground. Closed Nov–Apr. **www.leedas-village.com**

THE CYCLADES

MYKONOS Cavo Tagoo

Thesi Tagkou, Mýkonos, 84600 **Tel** *22890-20100* **Fax** *22890-20150* **Rooms** *80*

Located on a hillside about 2 km (1 mile) from the center of Mýkonos Town, Cavo Tagoo stands in splendid isolation away from the bustle of the island capital, but within a short drive of its shops, restaurants and nightlife. Built in village style, with white walls and blue woodwork. Shady eucalyptus trees and fine views. Closed Nov–Mar. **www.cavotagoo.gr**

MYKONOS Princess of Mýkonos

Agios Stéfanos, 84600 **Tel** *22890-23806* **Fax** *22890-23031* **Rooms** *38*

Situated on one of the island's most exclusive beaches, 4 km (2.5 miles) from Mýkonos town, this hotel is chic and stylish. Its small size allows for personal, attentive service and, like most Mýkonos hotels, it is designed in mock-Cycladic style. The pool is on the small side, but the beach is nearby. Closed Nov–Mar. **www.princessofmykonos.gr**

NAXOS Kavos

Agios Prokopios, 84300 **Tel** *22850-23355* **Fax** *22850-26031* **Rooms** *15*

Located on one of the best beaches in the Aegean, Kavos offers a collection of excellent-value studios, apartments, and suites with self-catering facilities. Rooms are in simple white cottages, surrounded by greenery, and each has painted furniture and galleried bed spaces. Closed Nov–Mar. **www.kavos-naxos.com**

SANTORINI Keti

Thira, 84700 **Tel** *22860-22324* **Fax** *22860-22380* **Rooms** *9*

Just off the steep steps that lead from Thira Town to the harbor below, Hotel Keti shares the same stunning crater view as the much more costly boutique hotels elsewhere on the island. The whitewashed rooms have arched ceilings and marble floors, and are simply furnished and decorated. Closed Oct–Apr. **www.hotelketi.gr**

SANTORINI Katikies

Oia, Santoríni, 84700 **Tel** *22860-71401* **Fax** *22860-71129* **Rooms** *27*

Stunning views from the horizon pool make this the best hotel on Santoríni. The elegantly appointed, traditional cave-rooms are whitewashed, each has a private terrace, some terraces also have whirlpools. Fine restaurant and attentive service. Closed Nov–Apr. **www.katikieshotelsantorini.com**

RHODES AND THE DODECANESE

KOS Afendoulis

Evripidou 1, Kos Town, 85300 **Tel** *22420-25321* **Fax** *22420-25797* **Rooms** *23*

A small, family hotel in the center of Kos town with friendly, English-speaking management and comfortable, simple rooms. Fairly quiet (by Kos Town standards) and a short walk from the good town beach. Breakfast and drinks are served in a lovely garden filled with jasmine and bougainvillea. Closed Nov–Apr. **www.afendoulishotel.com**

KOS Porto Bello Beach

Kardámaina, 85302 **Tel** *22420-91217* **Fax** *22420-91168* **Rooms** *295*

Billed as an "ultra all-inclusive" resort, the luxury Porto Bello is located on a 5-km- (3-mile-) long beach, 2 km (1 mile) from Kardámaina. Rate includes buffet breakfast, lunch and dinner, snacks, drinks, non-motorized water sports, a wide range of land sports, and live entertainment. Closed Nov–Apr. **www.portobellohotels.gr**

Key to Price Guide *see p508* **Key to Symbols** *see back cover flap*

KOS Grecotel Kos Royal Park

🄽🏊🚶🍽🍸 €€€€€

Agios Geórgios, Marmári, 85300 **Tel** *22420-41488* **Fax** *22420-41373* **Rooms** *236*

This well-appointed and well-located luxury resort on sandy Marmári beach, offers all-inclusive packages as well as standard rates. Facilities and activities include pools for adults and children, windsurfing, pedaloes, canoes, beach sports, and live entertainment. Bicycle rental and horseback riding are available nearby. Closed Nov–Apr. **www.grecotel.gr**

RHODES Apollo

🗒 €€

Omirou 28, 85100 **Tel** *22410-32003* **Rooms** *6*

This restored old house has bright, breezy rooms with four-poster beds – spend a bit extra for the more expensive top-floor rooms at the front which have wonderful Old Town views. Set in a quieter part of the Old Town with a pretty inner courtyard. Short walk to sights and shopping. Closed Dec–Feb. **www.apollo-touristhouse.com**

RHODES San Nikolis Hotel

🗒🍸 €€€

Ipodamou, Rhodes Old Town, 85100 **Tel** *22410-34561* **Fax** *22410-32034* **Rooms** *18*

Nestling under the walls of the Old Town is this charming, small hotel housed in an old Rhodian townhouse with stone walls covered with ivy and bougainvillea. Rooms are very comfortable, with antique furnishings, and some with balconies. Excellent views from the rooftop terrace. Closed Nov–Apr. **www.s-nikolis.gr**

RHODES Lindos Blu

🄽🏊🚶🗒🍸Ⓦ €€€€€

Lindos, 85107 **Tel** *22440-32110* **Fax** *22440-32111* **Rooms** *70*

Built into the hillside above the coast with amazing sea views, 2 km (1 mile) from Lindos, the romantic Lindos Blu has a choice of rooms, villas, and maisonettes, the latter with their own private pools. There are two restaurants, two bars, a spa, gym, tennis court, and a beach with water-sports facilities. **www.lindosblu.gr**

CRETE

AGIOS NIKOLAOS St Nicolas Bay

🏊🚶🗒🍸 €€€€€

Agios Nikólaos, 72100 **Tel** *28410-90200* **Fax** *28410-24556* **Rooms** *108*

Magnificent complex of bungalows and luxury suites – some with private pool – on an enviable seaside site just outside Agios Nikólaos. Landscaped gardens full of citrus and olive trees surround the buildings and the hotel has its own virtually private beach. Water sports and choice of eight restaurants and bars. Closed Nov–Mar. **www.stnicolasbay.gr**

CHANIA Amphora

🗒Ⓦ €€€

Parodos Theotokopoulou 20, 73131 **Tel** *28210-93224* **Fax** *28210-93226* **Rooms** *21*

This 13th-century Venetian mansion has tastefully appointed rooms and a charming roof terrace overlooking Chaniá's picturesque harbor. Situated in the heart of Chaniá's old quarter, on a mostly traffic-free street just a few steps from the waterfront with its numerous restaurants, shops, and bars. **www.amphora.gr**

CHANIA Villa Andromeda

🏊Ⓦ €€€€€

Venizelou 150, 73133 **Tel** *28210-28300* **Fax** *28210-28303* **Rooms** *8*

Oozing period dignity, this 19th-century building was once the German consulate. There are eight plainly furnished suites. The grand sitting rooms, by contrast, glow with yellow stucco. Large pool and terrace outside. Located 2 km (1 mile) from the harbor front. Closed Nov–Mar. **www.villandromeda.gr**

ELOUNTA Eloúnda Beach Hotel

🄽🏊🚶🗒🍸Ⓦ €€€€€

Eloúnta, 72053 **Tel** *28410-63000* **Fax** *28410-41373* **Rooms** *258*

The "grande dame" of Greek resorts, the Eloúnda Beach offers luxurious villas – some with private pools – scattered around a picturesque headland and a private beach. Excellent water sports, spa, fine dining, very attentive service. Closed Nov–Mar. **www.eloundabeach.gr**

IRAKLEIO Lato Hotel

🗒🍸Ⓦ €€€€

Epimenidou 15, 71202 **Tel** *28102-28103* **Fax** *28102-40350* **Rooms** *58*

Formerly comfortable but undistinguished, the Lato – in the center of the old town – has been reborn as Irákleio's first boutique hotel. Its rooms are stylish with balconies, terraces or glassed-in mini-conservatories, satellite TV and Internet access. There is also a roof garden, mini-gym, and sauna. **www.lato.gr**

IRAKLEIO Out of the Blue Capsis Elite Resort

🄽🏊🚶🗒🍸Ⓦ €€€€€

Agía Pelagía, 71000 **Tel** *28108-11112* **Fax** *28018-11314* **Rooms** *420*

This huge, self-contained luxury complex stands on its own promontory and combines two hotels and a conference center. The complex offers a full range of water sports and other facilities and activities, including its own zoo. Rooms range from standard doubles to large suites with private pool, butler and maid service. Private beach. **www.capsis.gr**

RETHYMNO Palazzo Vecchio

🗒🍸Ⓦ €€€

Iroon Polytechniou/Melissinou, 74100 **Tel** *28310-35351* **Fax** *28310-25479* **Rooms** *23*

New meets old in this 15th-century townhouse which has been converted into a stylishly grand modern hotel with in-room facilities including satellite TV, mini-kitchen, and full-sized bathrooms (a rarity in most historic hotels in Réthymno). Pleasant courtyard bar with fountain, attentive service, central location. Closed Nov–Mar. **www.palazzovecchio.gr**

Where to Eat in Greece

Eating out is an important part of Greek social life, enjoyed by rich and poor, old and young alike. As a result, the country boasts a vast array of eating places. With a host of stylish restaurants serving international fare, friendly tavernas offering traditional, local cooking, and lively cafés and bars, Greece caters for all tastes.

PRICE CATEGORIES
The following price ranges are for a three-course meal for one, including a half bottle of house wine, tax and service:
€ Under €15
€€ €15–€25
€€€ €25–€35
€€€€ €35–€45
€€€€€ Over €45

ATHENS

EXARCHEIA Mparmpa Giannis
€
Map C2
Emmanouíl Mpenáki 94, 106 81 **Tel** *210-38 24138*

A favorite that hasn't changed much in decades, this place dishes up consistently good *mageireftá* (baked dishes) and a handful of grills. On any given day there might be *giouvarláki* (rice & meat balls in *avgolémono*), stewed okra or baked *pérka* fish. The tables in pedestrianized Derveníon fill first in summer. Closed Sun dinner; Aug.

GAZI Mamacas
€€€
Persefónis 41, 104 35 **Tel** *210-34 64984*

The original new-wave taverna that kick-started the gentrification of Gázi, Mamacas is still steaming along after its 1998 opening. The fare is wholesome, updated Greek like Cretan *dákos* salad (rusks, tomato, cheese, oregano) and cuttlefish with greens. The decor is trendy and the clientele equally so. After midnight DJ sounds predominate.

KOLONAKI Ouzadiko
€€€
Map E3
Karneádou 25–29, 106 76 **Tel** *210-72 95484*

This *ouzerí* claims to offer more varieties of *ouzo* and *tsípouro* (wine spirit) to wash down *lakérda* (white-fleshed marinated bonito) and *hortópitta* than anywhere else in town. Always crowded and convivial, it's a popular hangout for politicians and journalists. Closed Aug.

KOLONAKI Orizontes Lykavittou
€€€€€
Map E3
Lykavittós Hill, 106 75 **Tel** *210-72 27065*

The views are sky-high and so are the prices (for dishes like sea bass in sauce with tagliatelle) at this spot near the summit of the hill, accessible only by the funicular or a long hike up through the pines. Seating is either in a conservatory or on a terrace.

MONASTIRAKI Thanassis
€
Map B4
Mitropóleos 69, 105 55 **Tel** *210-32 44705*

Perennial candidate for best purveyor of *souvláki* and *yíros* in town, Thanassis is always packed with Athenians queuing for a take-out or waiting for a table (you can't book ahead). It's frenetic and there's pressure to give up your seat quickly, but for a quick bite you can't beat it. The side dish of peppers is delicious.

MONASTIRAKI Café Avissynia
€€€
Map B4
Kynéttou 7, off Plateía Avissynías, 105 55 **Tel** *210-32 17047*

Tables indoors and out are always packed at weekend lunchtimes and Friday evenings when entertainment is provided by an accordionist and singer. The food – Macedonian staples, mussel *pilaf*, baked feta – is rich and the clientele verging on the bohemian. Closed Sun dinner, Mon; summer.

OMONOIA Ideal
€€€
Map C2
Panepistimíou 46, 106 78 **Tel** *210-33 03000*

A city-center institution since 1922, serving international cuisine (*schnitzel* and chops) along with more exciting, and more Hellenic dishes of the day such as milk-fed veal with aubergine (eggplant) and stuffed courgettes (zucchini). Locals love both the consistent food quality and the Art Nouveau interior. Closed Sun.

PLAKA O Platanos
€€
Map C4
Diogénous 4, 105 57 **Tel** *210-32 20666*

Taking its name from the *plátanos* (plane) tree outside, this 1932-founded taverna emphasizes meat-based stews and *laderá* (cooked vegetable dishes) in its repertoire. Their exceptionally good barrelled *retsina* has been profiled in Niko Manesi's *The Greek Wine Guide*. Closed Sun in winter.

PSYRRI Zeideron
€€€
Map B3
Taki 10–12, 105 52 **Tel** *210-32 15368*

Gazi has now taken over from Psyrri as Athens' favorite night time playground, but Zeideron remains a fine place to kick off the evening. Diners feast on modern taverna fare in an old stone building with a light and airy upper-level glass extension. There are also several highly coveted tables outside on the street. Closed Mon in winter.

Key to Symbols *see back cover flap* **Map References** *see map of Athens pp474–5*

SYNTAGMA Avocado

Nikis 30, 105 57 **Tel** *210-32 37878*

⊟ ©©

Map *D3*

This bright and breezy little vegetarian restaurant offers a fine selection of soups, salads, sandwiches, and hot cooked dishes such as pizzas, as well as smoothies and organic wine and beer. There are some vegan dishes, too. Although the food is fresh and healthy, with no artificial ingredients or preservatives, the desserts are wonderfully indulgent.

THISEIO Kuzina

Adrianou 9, 105 55 **Tel** *210-32 40133*

⊞⊟ ©©©©

Map *A4*

The big draw here is the roof terrace, with views of the Acropolis, although if that doesn't suffice there are also tables out front overlooking the Ancient Agora. The set menu offers creative Mediterranean cuisine and there are daily specials for those looking for a less expensive lunch.

REST OF MAINLAND GREECE

ANCIENT CORINTH Archontikó

Paralía Lechaíou, 200 06 **Tel** *27410-27968*

⧉⊞⊟ ©©

Overlooking the coastal road, about 3.5 km (2 miles) west of town, near the Lechaion archaeological site, this taverna offers well-prepared meat dishes and *mezédes*. Specialties include *kokkinistó Archontiko*, a wine-based meat stew with mushrooms, and cockerel *kokkinistó* with pasta. Popular with locals, so book ahead.

GYTHEIO Saga

Odós Tzanetáki, opposite Marathonísi, 232 00 **Tel** *27330-23220*

⧉⧏⊞ ©©

From ground floor premises under the eponymous French-Greek-owned pension, this restaurant spreads tables across the narrow pavement and along the sea wall opposite. Excellent for fresh fish, with a wide choice in the chiller cabinet – including several types of sea bream – plus fish soup and charcoal-grilled octopus.

KALAMPAKA Meteora

Oikonomou 4, 422 00 **Tel** *24320-22316*

⊞⊟ ©

This restaurant is easy to find, as it's located on the main square. It's friendly and family-run and has been serving up traditional Greek home-made food since 1925. Guests can enter the kitchen to see what's cooking and choose from favorites such as moussaka. There are tables on a vineyard terrace out front.

LITOCHORO Gastrodromeío en Olympo

Kentrikí Plateía, 602 00 **Tel** *23520-21300*

⧉⊞ ©©©

Most tavernas in Litóchoro, used to a stream of visitors heading quickly through town en route to the mountain, don't make a special effort; Gastrodromeío does, with good renditions of suckling pig and rabbit stew, plus a decent wine list – at a price.

MONEMVASIA Skorpiós

South coast road, Géfyra district, 230 70 **Tel** *27320-62090*

⧉⧏⊞ ©©

South of the bridge linking the mainland with the rock of Monemvasiá is Skorpios, with seating outside and unimpeded views towards the rock. Good *mezédes* like *tzatziki* and *tyrokafteri* (spicy cheese dip) and simple small fish like marinated *gávros* and *atherína* are served. Good wine.

NAFPLIO Ta Fanária

Staïkopoulou 13 corner Soútsou, 211 00 **Tel** *27520-27141*

⊞ ©©

This long-running restaurant offers outdoor seating under climbing vines; indoor seating is limited and for winter only. Ta Fanária is best for lunch when *maghireftá* (baked dishes) such as *moussakás* and *soutzoukákia* (minced lamb and tomato dish) emerge fresh from the oven. There's good bulk *retsina* from Mégara to wash it all down.

OLYMPIA Aegean

Off the main pedestrian street, 270 65 **Tel** *26240-22540*

⊞ ©©©

This place serves Greek taverna food with a twist. The menu features dishes such as roast pork with artichoke hearts and fresh dill, and a salad of lettuce, rocket, fennel, and pomegranate seeds. Friendly and reasonably priced, it's popular with both visitors and locals alike.

THESSALONIKI Kamares

Plateía Agíou Georgíou 11 **Tel** *23102-19686*

⧉⊞ ©©

Located close to the Roman-Byzantine *Rotónda*, this neighborhood favorite offers the usual range of salads, attractively priced seafood and a few meat grills, accompanied by white wine from Límnos. In summer Kamares has seating beside the little park.

THESSALONIKI Ta Nisiá

Proxénou Koromilá 13, 546 23 **Tel** *23102-85991*

©©©

Open since 1981, this upscale restaurant purveys a balanced mix of fish, shellfish, and meat recipes. Typical platters include *kakaviá* (fish soup), stewed octopus, roast pork in wine sauce, and creative desserts. The wine list is unusually comprehensive. Pleasant interior, with island colors and decor. Closed Sun dinner.

CORFU AND THE IONIAN ISLANDS

CORFU Rex

€€

Kapodistriou 66, Corfu Town **Tel** *26610-39649*

Housed in a mid-19th-century building, one block behind the arcades and cafés of the Spianádha, the Rex is a Corfu institution – a truly traditional Greek restaurant serving genuine Corfiot food. Specialties include swordfish *bourthéto* (a spicy fish stew with tomatoes, peppers, and potatoes). Good, attentive service.

CORFU Rouvas

€€

St. Desillas 13, Corfu Town **Tel** *26610-31182*

One of the most affordable traditional eating places in Corfu Town, with a well-established reputation for some of the best Greek and Corfiot dishes. Located in the center of town, near the main produce market, so the ingredients are usually very fresh. Closed dinner; Sun.

KEFALLONIA Patsouras

€

Ioannou Metaxas 40, Argostóli **Tel** *26710-22779*

Surprisingly cheap taverna in the center of Kefalloniá's island capital. Patsouras is family-run, and its menu includes all the traditional taverna favorites plus Kefallonian island specialties such as *kreatópita* (meat pie) and *krasáto* (pork in wine sauce). Enjoy lunch or dinner in a pleasant garden setting.

KEFALLONIA Tassia

€€€€

Limáni Fiskardou **Tel** *26740-41205*

This internationally acclaimed restaurant sits right on the harbor and features a good wine list which emphasizes some of Kefalloniá's own vintages, recognized as among the best in Greece. The menu includes fine seafood, simply but well prepared, as well as pasta dishes, salads, appetizers, and desserts. Closed Oct–Apr.

ZAKYNTHOS Zakanthi

€€€

Kalamáki **Tel** *26950-43586*

This lively restaurant and bar is a good place to spend the evening whether you are looking for a light snack with drinks or something more substantial. The menu is eclectic, with a reasonable selection of Greek favorites along with pasta, burgers, and other international dishes.

THE CYCLADES

MYKONOS Bakalo

€€€

Lakka, Mykonos Town **Tel** *22890-781 21*

Bakalo serves classic Greek home-cooking including dishes such as *keftedes* (meatballs), *horta* (wild greens), and moussaka. The stylish interior is inspired by a 1950s-style grocery store, with an old tile floor and an open-plan kitchen, and there are whitewashed tables out front.

MYKONOS Sea Satin Market Caprice

€€€€

Mýloi, Mýkonos Town **Tel** *22890-24676*

This lively fish restaurant and traditional grill is located by the sea with open-air tables below the village's famous windmills and with views of Little Venice. The restaurant is a delight for seafood lovers and carnivores alike, this is one of the few places you can get a really good steak. Closed lunch; Nov–Apr.

NAXOS Manolis

€

Bourgos, Náxos Town **Tel** *22850-25168*

This garden taverna, in the heart of the old town, serves traditional Greek cuisine in very pleasant surroundings. Dishes on offer include *melitzánes* (fried aubergines), *skordaliá* (potato and garlic purée) and other well-known favorites at prices to suit even smaller budgets. Closed lunch; Nov–Mar.

SANTORINI Iliovasilema

€€€

Ammoudi, Oía **Tel** *22860-71614*

A delightfully simple quayside restaurant where the fish comes straight off the boat and onto the grill. The menu here mainly depends on the catch of the day which can be enjoyed at rickety wooden tables beside a tiny pebbly beach. Extremely good value. Closed Nov–Apr.

SANTORINI 1800

€€€€€

Main street, Oía **Tel** *22860-71485*

Book ahead for an evening at Oía's swankiest restaurant where the sophisticated menu blends Greek and European influences. There is an extensive wine list with a good sampling of Santorini's more interesting labels and vintages. Not too formal, but not ideal for children. Closed lunch; Oct–Apr.

Key to Price Guide *see p514* **Key to Symbols** *see back cover flap*

THE DODECANESE

KARPATHOS The Olive Garden
Kira Beach, Kira Panagia **Tel** *22450-23663*

Above the beach, and with fantastic sea views, this friendly informal eatery serves traditional Greek fare, including fresh fish caught by the owner and Italian pasta dishes. It's especially romantic at night, when the tables are candlelit, and best of all, when there's a full moon.

KOS O Makis
Mastichári **Tel** *22420-59061*

One of the best little fish tavernas on the island, O Makis is located next to an attractive little fishing harbor from which comes most of the seafood that it serves. Expect sea-fresh *tsipoura* and *fagri* as well as prawns, squid, octopus, and – for special occasions, and worth ordering a couple of days in advance – langouste. Closed lunch.

KOS Plátanos
Plateía Platanou **Tel** *22420-28991*

Located on the square beside the Castle of Knights, this café-restaurant overlooks the ancient agora. More peaceful than Kos Town's parade of harbor-side restaurants, it serves light meals, snacks, and drinks, and is reasonably priced compared with many eating places in town. Closed Nov–May.

RHODES Meltemi
Akti Koundourioti **Tel** *22410-30480*

This unpretentious family-run restaurant is right on the beach, near the marina. The simple menu has a good choice of hot and cold appetizers, grills, and fish dishes – a basket of fresh hot bread is served with every meal. Its terrace with sea views makes it an ideal spot for lunch. Closed Nov–Mar.

RHODES Alexis
Sokratous 18, Old Town **Tel** *22410-29347*

This wonderful restaurant in the heart of the picturesque Old Town has been specializing in seafood since it opened in 1957. A host of celebrity guests have come to enjoy the perfectly grilled fresh fish, good wines, and professional but friendly service. Choice of tables on two floors and sunny terrace. Better for dinner than lunch. Closed Nov–Mar.

CRETE

AGIOS NIKOLAOS The Ferryman
Seafront, Elounda **Tel** *28410-41230*

With a position right on the waterfront and with amazing views of the island of Spinalonga, this friendly family-run eatery serves excellent fresh fish and slow-cooked lamb. It's named after the 1977 BBC series, *Who Pays the Ferryman*, which was filmed here.

CHANIA To Pigadi tou Tourkou (The Well of the Turk)
1–3 Kallinikou Sarpaki, Splantzia, 73100 **Tel** *28210-54547*

This cozy restaurant is housed in the arched stone cellar of an ancient Chaniá mansion, with candle-lit tables and Cretan and Levantine background music. The menu is more imaginative than most – try the aubergine meatballs, or the spicy stuffed squid – and uses local produce. Closed lunch; Wed; mid-Nov–Feb.

IRAKLEIO O Kyriákos
Leofóros Dimokratías 53 **Tel** *28102-22464*

You will be beckoned into the kitchen of this old-fashioned restaurant to choose your meal from bubbling pots or glass cases filled with fish, vegetables, and cuts of meat. O Kyriákos is an Irákleio institution, unpretentious and catering to a loyal local following. Wine from the barrel.

IRAKLEIO Loukoulos
Korai 5 **Tel** *28102-24435*

A mainly Mediterranean menu in upmarket surroundings – with white linen tablecloths, candles in the evening, and a dining room decorated with antique prints and paintings. With its excellent food, Loukoulos has been regarded for years as one of the best restaurants in Irákleio.

RETHYMNO Avlí
22 Xanthoudidou, 74100 **Tel** *28310-26213*

This charming restaurant offers dining in vaulted rooms or in the courtyard of an old mansion. The menu consists mainly of grilled and roast meat and there is an extensive wine list featuring some of the best Greek wines. Attentive service and spotless interior.

GERMANY, AUSTRIA, AND SWITZERLAND

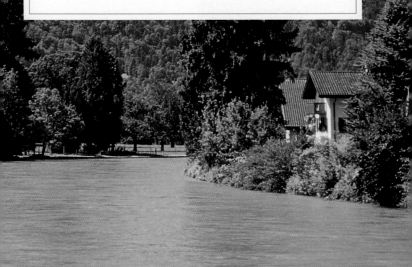

Germany, Austria, and Switzerland at a Glance

Europe's three main German-speaking countries occupy a broad swathe of Europe stretching from the Alps to the North Sea and the Baltic. Germany has many great cities, the former capitals of the small states that made up Germany under the Holy Roman Empire. It also has beautiful countryside, rivers, and forests. Austria's main attractions are the former imperial capital Vienna, the river Danube, and its mountains. More than half of Switzerland, which also has important French- and Italian-speaking regions, is mountainous, dominated by its permanently snow-capped Alpine peaks.

Lübe

Hamburg

Bremen

Hanover

Münster

GERMANY
(See pp520–585)

Düsseldorf

Cologne

Kassel

Bonn

Frankfurt
am Main

Trier

Mainz

Würzburg

Stuttgart

Freiburg
im Breisgau

Basel

Zürich

BERN

SWITZERLAND
(See pp612–633)

Geneva

The Rhine Valley (see pp558–9) *attracts hordes of visitors in summer, drawn by the beautiful scenery, medieval and mock-medieval castles, and Germany's finest white wines. You can either tour by car or take a river cruise from cities such as Mainz and Koblenz.*

The Swiss Alps (see pp619–24) *are a popular destination all year round: in winter for the skiing and other winter sports, in summer for the excellent walking or simply for the crisp, clean air and unrivaled scenery.*

Salzburg (see pp602–3) *trades on the legacy of Mozart, its most famous son, and stages one of the world's great music festivals. It also boasts a rich architectural heritage from the prince-archbishops who ruled the city from 1278 to 1816.*

◁ **Swiss lakeland scene, Interlaken**

Berlin (see pp528–41), *since 1990 once more the capital of a united Germany, combines relics of its imperial past, such as the Berliner Dom, with modern landmarks such as the towering Fernsehturm.*

LOCATOR MAP

Munich (see pp546–54) *is the cultural capital of southern Germany. It owes many of its great buildings and art collections to the kings of Bavaria. The city is also remarkable for its 18th-century churches, such as the astonishingly ornate Asamkirche.*

• Rostock

• BERLIN

Magdeburg

• Leipzig

• Dresden

berg

• Linz

VIENNA •

• Munich

• Salzburg

AUSTRIA
(See pp586–611)

nsbruck

• Graz

0 kilometers   100

0 miles   100

Vienna (see pp590–99) *was largely the the creation of the 18th- and 19th- century Habsburg emperors. More modern landmarks include the ferris wheel in the Prater funfair, immortalized in* The Third Man, *the 1949 film starring Orson Welles.*

GERMANY

*B*y reputation the Germans are a hard-working, efficient, competitive people and this is borne out by their recent economic success. However, Germany's turbulent, divided past and the centuries when it was a patchwork of many tiny states mean that there are profound regional differences, apparent in a wealth of fascinating historical sights and colorful local traditions.

Thanks initially to American aid, industry and commerce boomed in West Germany following World War II. This so-called *Wirtschaftswunder* (economic miracle) made West Germany a dominant member of the European Economic Community (now the European Union). Demand for labor led to reliance on migrant workers or *Gastarbeiter* (guest workers). As a result, over 7 million immigrants now live in Germany, the largest number coming from Turkey, but many too from Italy, Greece, and increasingly the former Yugoslavia. In the manufacturing city of Stuttgart one inhabitant in three is an immigrant.

Despite its many industrial cities and a population of over 80 million, Germany is large enough to also possess a great variety of attractive rural landscapes. For many the Rhine epitomizes Germany, especially the romantic stretch between Mainz and Cologne. However, the country has much more to offer in the way of scenery, especially its forests, heaths, and mountains. In the far south the Alps are the major attraction, especially around Lake Constance (the Bodensee), the large lake that borders Austria and Switzerland.

HISTORY

Germanic tribes became established in the region sometime during the 1st millennium BC. They clashed with the Romans, defeating them in AD 9 at the Teutoburger forest. Thereafter the Romans fixed their frontier along the Rhine and the Danube. Although relations were often hostile, the Goths and other Germanic tribes traded and made alliances with Rome, and as the Roman Empire collapsed, these peoples carved out kingdoms of their own.

The dome of Berlin's Reichstag – home to the Bundestag (Federal Parliament)

◁ Neuschwanstein, King Ludwig II's theatrical castle in the Bavarian Alps

The people who eventually inherited the largest kingdom were the Franks, who conquered France and in the early 9th century, under Charlemagne, subdued most of the German tribes, including the Saxons, Swabians, and Bavarians. The pope gave his blessing to Charlemagne's overlordship, thus creating the Holy Roman Empire.

**Frederick II (the Great),
King of Prussia (1740–86)**

After Charlemagne, the German kingdom became separated from the rest of the empire. The next strong German ruler was the Saxon Otto I, who increased his power further after his defeat of the Magyars in 955.

The Middle Ages saw the development of a complicated feudal system with hundreds of dukedoms, counties, and ecclesiastical estates owing allegiance to the German emperor, as well as free "imperial cities." In the 11th and 12th centuries popes and emperors joined in a fierce struggle over who should grant lands, appoint bishops, and collect revenues. Each would try to bribe the Electors (*Kurfürsten*) – princes and bishops who chose the emperor. The role of the Electors was clarified in the Golden Bull issued by Emperor Charles IV in 1356, but by the 16th century the position had become the more or less hereditary right of the Austrian Habsburgs.

The power of the church created many problems and it was no surprise that the Reformation began in Germany in 1517 with Martin Luther's *95 Theses* pointing out the abuses of the clergy. In the ensuing wars of religion, princes saw a chance to increase their lands at the expense of the Church. The Peace of Augsburg in 1555 established the principle *cuius regio eius religio* – each state followed the religion of its ruler. In the 17th century religious differences were again a major factor in the Thirty Years' War. Other countries, such as France and Sweden, joined the conflict, which laid waste most of Germany.

In the 17th and 18th centuries Germany remained a patchwork of small states, theoretically still part of the Habsburg Empire. However, Prussia gradually became a power to rival the Habsburgs. During the Enlightenment and Romantic periods German literature found its voice, especially in the dramas of Goethe and Schiller, and Napoleon's invasion of Germany sparked ideas of nationalism. In the mid-19th century it was Prussia that assumed the leadership of Germany through the skilful politics of Otto von Bismarck, the Prussian chancellor. After the Prussians had defeated the Austrians in 1866 and the French in 1870, the Second German Reich was declared with the Prussian King as Kaiser Wilhelm I.

Wilhelm's grandson Wilhelm II had great ambitions for the new empire and rivalry with Britain, France, and Russia plunged Europe into World War I. The humiliation of defeat and the terms of the Treaty of Versailles (1919) left

KEY DATES IN GERMAN HISTORY

5th century AD Germanic peoples overrun large parts of Roman Empire

c.750 Mission of St. Boniface to Germany

843 Charlemagne's empire divided; Louis the German rules lands east of the Rhine

962 Otto I crowned emperor

1077 Pope Gregory VII and Emperor Heinrich IV clash over investiture of bishops

1155 Frederick Barbarossa crowned Emperor

13th century North German Hanseatic League starts to dominate trade in Baltic region

1356 Golden Bull establishes role of Electors

1517 Martin Luther attaches his *95 Theses to* the door of a church in Wittenberg

1555 Peace of Augsburg ends religious wars

1618–48 Germany ravaged by Thirty Years' War

1740–86 Reign of Frederick the Great

1806 Napoleon abolishes Holy Roman Empire

1871 German Empire proclaimed

1914–18 World War I

1933 End of Weimar Republic; Hitler comes to power

1939–45 World War II; after Germany's defeat country divided into West and East

1990 Reunification of Germany

2002 Germany joins single European currency

Germany in economic chaos. The Weimar Republic struggled on until 1933 when Hitler seized power. His nationalist policies appealed to a demoralized people, but his territorial ambitions led the country into World War II and a second defeat.

Despite the atrocities committed by the Nazis, the Germans were soon forgiven by both America and Russia as they divided the country in such a way that it became the theater for the Cold War between East and West. The Berlin Wall erected in 1961 to stop East Germans fleeing to the West became the symbol of an era. Its fall in 1989 was the start of the process of reunification.

Modern Germany, the Bundesrepublik, is a federal country, with each *Land* (state) electing its own parliament. Regional differences due to Germany's checkered history are still much in evidence, the Catholic south being much more conservative than the north. Differences between the former West Germany and the old DDR (East Germany) are also very visible. The East suffers from high unemployment and its people tend to be suspicious of the motives of the West Germans, despite all the money poured into the region to equalize living standards.

CULTURE AND THE ARTS

Germany is rich in legends and sagas, such as the tale of Siegfried told in the epic poem the *Nibelungenlied*, written down around 1200. It has been reworked many times, notably in Richard Wagner's great *Ring* opera cycle.

Celebrating the fall of the Berlin Wall in 1989

Of all the arts it is to classical music that Germany has made the greatest contribution, Johann Sebastian Bach from the Baroque period and Ludwig van Beethoven from the Classical period being perhaps the two most influential figures. In the 19th century poems by Goethe, Schiller, and others were set to music by composers Robert Schumann, Johannes Brahms, and Hugo Wolf.

Germany has also produced many of the world's most influential philosophers: from Immanuel Kant (1724–1804), father of modern philosophy, to Karl Marx (1818–83), founder of the 20th century's most potent political ideology.

MODERN LIFE

The German economy tends to be dominated by long-established giants such as Siemens in the electrical and electronic sectors, Volkswagen and BMW in cars, and BASF in chemicals. Despite the continuing success of German industry and banking, and the people's reputation for hard work, the Germans actually enjoy longer annual holidays and spend more money on foreign travel than any other European nation. When at home they are enthusiastic participants in many sports, and have enjoyed great success in recent years at football, motor racing, and tennis. They also enjoy gregarious public merrymaking, for example at *Fasching* (carnival) and the Oktoberfest, Munich's annual beer festival.

Munich's Olympic Stadium, created for the 1972 Olympic Games

Exploring Germany

Visitors in search of classical German landscapes flock to the Black Forest, the Rhine Valley, and the Bavarian Alps. The attractive German countryside is easily accessed thanks to the best road network in Europe. Of the cities, the most popular destinations are the capital Berlin, a vibrant metropolis in a state of transition since reunification in 1990, and Munich, the historic former capital of the Kingdom of Bavaria. East Germany, now open for tourism, has many attractions to draw visitors – particularly the city of Dresden, rebuilt after World War II.

SIGHTS AT A GLANCE

Thickly wooded landscape of the Black Forest region

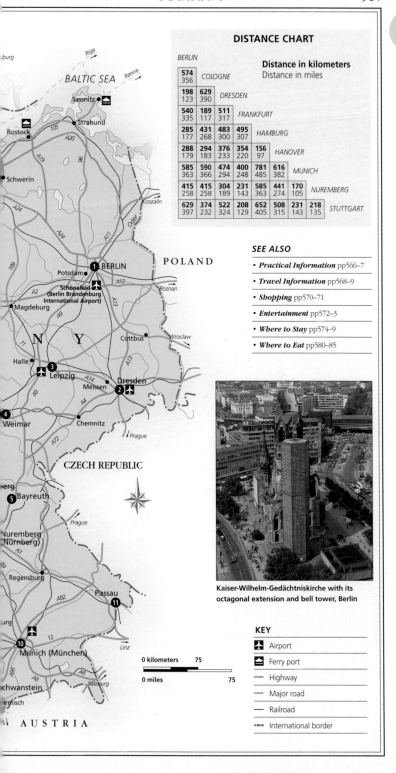

DISTANCE CHART

Distance in kilometers
Distance in miles

BERLIN								
574 356	COLOGNE							
198 123	**629** 390	DRESDEN						
540 335	**189** 117	**511** 317	FRANKFURT					
285 177	**431** 268	**483** 300	**495** 307	HAMBURG				
288 179	**294** 183	**376** 233	**354** 220	**156** 97	HANOVER			
585 363	**590** 366	**474** 294	**400** 248	**781** 485	**616** 382	MUNICH		
415 258	**415** 258	**304** 189	**231** 143	**585** 363	**441** 274	**170** 105	NUREMBERG	
629 397	**374** 232	**522** 324	**208** 129	**652** 405	**508** 315	**231** 143	**218** 135	STUTTGART

SEE ALSO

- *Practical Information* pp566–7
- *Travel Information* pp568–9
- *Shopping* pp570–71
- *Entertainment* pp572–3
- *Where to Stay* pp574–9
- *Where to Eat* pp580–85

Kaiser-Wilhelm-Gedächtniskirche with its octagonal extension and bell tower, Berlin

KEY

- ✈ Airport
- ⛴ Ferry port
- — Highway
- — Major road
- — Railroad
- --- International border

0 kilometers 75

0 miles 75

Berlin ❶

Since becoming the capital of the Federal
Republic of Germany following reunification
in 1990, Berlin has become an ever popular
destination for visitors. The historic heart of
the city is located around the wide avenue
Unter den Linden and on Museum Island,
which takes its name from the fine museums
built there in the 19th and early 20th
centuries. South of Unter den Linden is
Checkpoint Charlie, a legacy of Berlin's status
as a divided city during the Cold War. To the
west are the green open spaces of Tiergarten
and Kurfürstendamm, the center of the
former West Berlin. Farther afield, the
splendid palaces of Potsdam, now almost a
suburb of Berlin, are not to be missed.

**The grand approach to the 18th-century
Rococo Schloss Sanssouci in Potsdam**

SIGHTS AT A GLANCE

GETTING AROUND

Berlin's U- and S-Bahn trains are the quickest way of getting around the city. They also serve outlying areas, such as Grunewald, Dahlem, and Potsdam. Buses are reliable, but slow, especially during rush hour, owing to congestion. Trams are another option in the east of the city, and accept the same tickets as the buses and S-Bahn lines.

GREATER BERLIN

0 km 3

0 miles 3

Hamburg
Reinickendorf
Pankow
Spandau
Wedding
Hamburg
Tiergarten
Havel
Wilmersdorf
(19) Grunewald Schöneberg
Hannover
(20)
Schönefeld (Berlin Brandenburg International Airport)
Steglitz
Zehlendorf
Mariendorf
(21) Potsdam
Lankwitz
Leipzig

KEY

Area of main map

Bahnhof
Friedric H.-List-Ufer
MOABIT
INVALIDENSTRASSE HANNOVERSCHE STR. TORSTRASSE ALTER JÜDISCHER FRIEDHOF TORSTR.
CHAUSSEESTR.
LUISENSTRASSE
WILHELMSTRASSE
FRIEDRICHSTR.
Oranienburger Str. (5)(10)
ORANIENBURGER STR.
Oranienburger Str.
Hackescher Markt (S)
ROSENTHALER STR.
Rosa Luxemburg Platz
LATE SCHÖNHAUSER STR.
MÖLLSTR.
Weinmeisterstr.
WEINMEISTERSTR.
MITTE
Friedrichstrasse (S)(U)
Spree
DOROTHEENSTR.
Humboldt Universität
Zeughaus
(8)
BODESTRASSE
(9) (7)
KARL-LIEBKNECHT-STR.
Marienkirche
Alexanderplatz (S)(R)(U)
KARL-MARX-ALLEE
(11)
(12)
GRUNERSTR.
Kloster str.
(U)
-DULLES-ALLEE
SCHEIDEMANNSTR.
(2)
(1)
PARISER PLATZ
(3) UNTER DEN LINDEN
Franz-ösische
str.
FRIEDRICHSTR.
FRANZÖSISCHE STR.
WERDERSTR.
RATHAUSSTR.
BREITE
STRALAUER STR.
STRASSE DES 17. JUNI
Brandenburger Tor
EBERTSTRASSE
Stadtmitte (U)
Mohren-straße (U)
Hausvogteiplatz
GERTRAUDEN
MÜHLENDAMM
Jannowitzbrücke (U)
BRÜCKENSTR.
ARTEN
LENNÉ STR.
Potsdamer Platz (S)
LEIPZIGER STRASSE
WALLSTR.
Märkisches Museum
N. ROSS STR.
RTENSTRASSE (S)
SIGISMUNDSTR.
(4) Potsdamer Platz (U)
STRESEMANNSTRASSE
WILHELMSTRASSE
Spittel-markt (U)
Heinrich-Heine-Str. (U)
HEINRICH-HEINE-STR.
ETSCHUFER
POTSDAMER STR.
Mendelssohn-Bartholdy-Park
SCHÖNEBERGER UFER
Checkpoint Charlie (13) ZIMMERSTR.
RUDI- DUTSCHKE STR.
Kochstr. (U)
FRIEDRICHSTR.
ORANIENSTRASSE
KREUZBERG
Moritzplatz (U)
ürsten-e
STR.
Lapidarium
SCHÖNEBERGER STR.
Anhalter Bahnhof (S)
HALLESCHES UFER
Möckern-brücke (U)
LINDENSTRASSE
Berlin-Museum
Jüdisches Museum
Prinzen-straße (U)
PRINZENSTRASSE
Gleis-dreieck (U)
TEMPELHOFER UFER
MEHRINGDAMM
Hallesches Tor (U)
MEHRING PLATZ
GITSCHINER STR.
BLÜCHERSTR.
Yorckstraße (U) Yorckstraße
GROSSBEERENSTR.
Mehringdamm (U)
URBANSTR.
ZOSSENER STR.
Gneisenau-straße (U)
BAERWALDSTR.
YORCKSTRASSE
Yorckstraße (S)
YORCKSTR.
MEHRINGDAMM
GNEISENAUSTRASSE
KREUZBERGSTRASSE

KEY

	Sight / Place of interest
✈	Airport
🚆	Train station
Ⓢ	S-Bahn station
Ⓤ	U-Bahn station
🚌	Bus stop
🚊	Tram stop
ℹ	Tourist information
✝	Church
✡	Synagogue
	Pedestrian street

0 meters 750

0 yards 750

The imposing Brandenburg Gate at Pariser Platz, at the western end of Unter den Linden

Brandenburg Gate ①

Pariser Platz. Ⓢ Unter den Linden.
🚌 100.

The Brandenburg Gate is the quintessential symbol of Berlin. This magnificent Neo-classical structure was designed by Carl Gotthard Langhans and modeled on the Propylaia of the Acropolis in Athens (see p478). It was erected between 1788 and 1791, although the sculptural decorations were not completed until 1795. Pavilions frame its simple Doric colonnade, and bas-reliefs on the entablature above the columns depict scenes from Greek myth. The structure is crowned by the famous sculpture of a quadriga – a chariot drawn by four horses – designed by Johann Gottfried Schadow.

The Brandenburg Gate has witnessed many important historical events. Military parades and demonstrating workers have marched under its arches, and it was the site of celebrations marking the birth of the Deutsches Reich in 1871. It was here, too, that the Soviet flag was raised in 1945.

Restored between 1956 and 1958, for the next 30 years the gate stood watch over the divided city, until the fall of the Berlin Wall in 1989. It was renovated once again in 2002.

Reichstag ②

Platz der Republik. Ⓢ Unter den Linden. 🚌 U85, 100.
Tel 030-2273 2152. **Dome & Assembly Hall** ⬜ daily. ⬤ Dec 24, Dec 31. 🎫

Built to house the German Parliament, the Reichstag was intended as a symbol of national unity and to showcase the aspirations of the new German Empire, declared in 1871. Constructed between 1884 and 1894, the Neo-Renaissance building by Paul Wallot captured the prevailing spirit of German optimism. On the night of February 27, 1933, a fire destroyed the main hall. Rebuilding work undertaken between 1957 and 1972 removed the dome and most of the ornamentation on the façades. On December 2, 1990, the Reichstag was the first meeting place of a newly-elected Bundestag following German reunification.

The latest rebuilding project, completed in 1999 to a design by Sir Norman Foster, transformed the Reichstag into a modern meeting hall crowned by an elliptical glass dome.

Unter den Linden ③

🚉 Unter den Linden. 🚌 100, TXL.

One of the most famous streets in Berlin, Unter den Linden was once the route to the royal hunting grounds that were transformed into the Tiergarten. In the 17th century it was planted with lime trees, to which it owes its name.

In the 18th century, Unter den Linden became the main street of the westward-growing city. It gradually filled with prestigious buildings, such as the Baroque **Zeughaus**, home of the Deutsches Historisches Museum, and the **Humboldt Universität** (1753). Next door, the **Neue Wache** (1816–1818) commemorates the victims of war and dictatorship.

Since reunification, many buildings have been restored and Unter den Linden has acquired several cafés and restaurants, as well as smart new shops. The street is also the venue for outdoor events.

The Reichstag, crowned by a dome designed by Sir Norman Foster

For hotels and restaurants in this region see pp574–5 and pp580–81

Potsdamer Platz ④

(S) *Potsdamer Platz.*

Before the onset of World War II, Potsdamer Platz was one of the busiest and most densely built-up areas of Berlin. Most of the area's landmarks ceased to exist after the bombing of 1945, and the destruction was completed when the burned-out ruins were finally pulled down to build the Berlin Wall. Since the mid-1990s a new financial and business district has sprung up on this empty wasteland, which once divided East and West Berlin. The huge complex comprises not only office buildings, but also a concert hall, a multi-screen cinema, and the Arkaden shopping mall. The first finished structure was the Daimler-Benz-Areal office block, designed by Renzo Piano and Christoph Kohlbecker. To the north lies the impressive Sony-Center complex, by Helmut Jahn.

Silver and ivory tankard from the Kunstgewerbemuseum

Kulturforum ⑤

(S) *Potsdamer Platz.* **Tel** 030-266 3666. **Kunstgewerbemuseum** Tue–Sun. first Tue after Easter, Whitsun, Oct 1, Dec 24, 25 & 31. **Gemäldegalerie** Tue–Sun. 1st Tue after Easter, Whitsun, May 1, Dec 24, 25 & 31. **Neue Nationalgalerie** Tue–Sun.

The idea of creating a new cultural center in West Berlin was first mooted in 1956. The first building to go up was the

Philharmonie (Berlin Philharmonic concert hall), built to an innovative design by Hans Scharoun in 1961. Most of the other plans for the Kulturforum were realized between 1961 and 1987. With many museums and galleries, the area attracts millions of visitors every year.

The **Kunstgewerbemuseum** (Museum of Arts and Crafts) holds a rich collection of decorative art and crafts dating from the early Middle Ages to the modern day. Goldwork is very well represented, and the museum takes great pride in its late Gothic and Renaissance silver.

The **Gemäldegalerie** fine art collection is in a modern building designed by Heinz Hilmer and Christopher Sattler. Works by German Renaissance artists, including Albrecht Dürer and Hans Holbein, dominate the exhibition space, but there are also pieces by van Dyck, Rembrandt, Raphael, Velázquez, and Caravaggio.

Housed in a striking building with a flat steel roof over a glass hall, the **Neue Nationalgalerie** contains mainly 20th-century art, but begins with artists of the late 19th century, such as Edvard Munch and Ferdinand Hodler. Paintings from the *Die Brücke* movement include pieces by Ernst Ludwig Kirchner and Karl Schmidt-Rottluff. Also on display are works by Picasso, Léger, Dalí, Magritte, and Max Ernst.

A tranquil stretch of water in Berlin's 19th-century Tiergarten

Tiergarten ⑥

(S) *Tiergarten, Bellevue.* 100, 200.

The Tiergarten is the largest park in Berlin. Situated at the geographical center of the city, it occupies a 210-ha (520-acre) area. Once the Elector's hunting reserve, the forest was transformed into a landscaped park by Peter Joseph Lenné in the 1830s. A triumphal avenue was built at the end of the 19th century, lined with statues of the nation's rulers and statesmen.

World War II inflicted huge damage on the Tiergarten, including the destruction of the triumphal avenue, many of whose surviving monuments can now be seen in the Lapidarium in Kreuzberg. Replanting has restored the Tiergarten, and many of its avenues are now lined with statues of national celebrities, including Goethe and Wagner.

The Philharmonie, with the later addition of the Kammermusiksaal (1984–7) in front, at Kulturforum

Mosaic from Hadrian's Villa (2nd century AD), at the Altes Museum

Altes Museum ⑦

Am Lustgarten. **Tel** 030-266 3660.
Ⓢ Hackescher Markt. 🚊 M1, M4,
M5, M6. 🚌 100, 200. ⬜ daily. 🖼

The Altes Museum, designed by Karl Friedrich Schinkel, is one of the world's finest Neo-classical structures, with an impressive 87-m- (285-ft-) high portico supported by Ionic columns. The stately rotunda is decorated with sculptures and ringed by a colonnade.

Officially opened in 1830, this was one of the first purpose-built museums in Europe, designed to house the royal collection of paintings and antiquities. Following World War II, the building was used to display temporary exhibitions. Since 1998 the Altes Museum has housed a portion of the Antikensammlung, a magnificent collection of Greek and Roman antiquities. Among the highlights of the collection are a colorful floor mosaic from Hadrian's Villa near Tivoli, and Perikles' Head, a Roman copy of the sculpture by Kresilas that stood at the entrance to the Acropolis in Athens.

Pergamon-museum ⑧

Bodestraße 1–3 (entrance from Am Kupfergraben). **Tel** 030-266 3666.
Ⓢ Hackescher Markt, Friedrich-strasse. 🚌 100, 200, TXL. ⬜ daily.
🔴 Jan 1, first Tue after Easter and Pentecost, Dec 24, 25 & 31. 🖼 ♿
📷 (no flash).

Built between 1912 and 1930 to a design by Alfred Messel and Ludwig Hoffmann, the Pergamonmuseum is one of Berlin's major attractions. Its three large independent collections, the result of extensive archaeological excavations, form one of Europe's most famous archives of antiquities.

The highlight of Berlin's collection of Greek and Roman antiquities (Antikensammlung) is the huge Pergamon Altar from the acropolis of ancient Pergamon in Asia Minor. This magnificently restored altar, which gives the museum its name, is thought to have been commissioned by King Eumenes in 160 BC. Roman architecture is represented by the market gate from the Roman city of Miletus, which dates from the 2nd century BC.

Major excavations begun in the 1820s form the basis of a royal collection at the Museum of Near Eastern Antiquities (Vorderasiatisches Museum). One striking exhibit is the splendid Ishtar Gate, built during the reign of Nebuchadnezzar II (604–562 BC) in ancient Babylon. Also on display are pieces from the neighboring regions of Persia, Syria, and Pales-tine, including a basalt sculpture of a bird from Tel Halaf and a glazed wall relief of a spear-bearer from Artaxerxes II's palace in Susa, capital of the Persian Empire.

Persian relief, Pergamon-museum

The history of the Museum of Islamic Art (Museum für Islamische Kunst) begins in 1904 when Wilhelm von Bode donated his extensive collection of carpets. He also brought to Berlin a 45-m (150-ft) long section of the facade of a Jordanian desert palace, dating from the Omayyad period (AD 661–750). Another fascinating exhibit is a beautiful 13th-century *mihrab* (Islamic prayer niche). Made in the Iranian town of Kashan, the *mihrab* is covered in lustrous metallic glazed tiles. The collection's many carpets come from as far afield as Iran, Asia Minor, Egypt, and the Caucasus.

Berliner Dom ⑨

See pp534–5.

Relief carving of Athena from the Pergamon Altar, Pergamonmuseum

For hotels and restaurants in this region see pp574–5 and pp580–81

the splendidly reconstructed gilded domes of the Neue Synagoge

Centrum Judaicum & Neue Synagoge ⑩

Oranienburger Straße 28 & 30.
Tel 030-8802 8316 (Centrum Judaicum). Ⓢ Oranienburger Straße.
🚃 1, M1, M6. ◯ Sun–Thu, ri am. ◯ Jewish festivals.

Occupying the former premises of the Jewish community council, the Centrum Judaicum contains an extensive library, archives, and a research center all devoted to the history and cultural heritage of Berlin's Jews. Next door, the restored rooms of the Neue Synagoge are used as a museum, exhibiting material relating to the local Jewish community.

The building of the New Synagogue was started in 1859 and completed in 1866, when it was opened in the presence of Chancellor Otto von Bismarck. The narrow facade is flanked by a pair of towers and crowned with a dome that sparkles with gold and contains a round vestibule.

This fascinating structure was Berlin's largest synagogue. However, on November 9, 1938, it was partially destroyed during the infamous "*Kristallnacht*" ("Night of the Broken Glass"), when thousands of synagogues, cemeteries, and Jewish homes and shops all over Germany were looted and burned. The building was damaged further by Allied bombing in 1943, and was finally demolished in 1958. Reconstruction began in 1988 and was completed in 1995.

Fernsehturm ⑪

Panoramastraße. Ⓤ Ⓢ Alexanderplatz. 🚃 M4, M6, M8. 🚌 100, 200, 248. ◯ daily.

Known as the *Telespargel*, or toothpick, by the locals, this 368-m (1,206-ft) high television mast soars above the massive Alexanderplatz. It is the third tallest structure in Germany and one of the tallest in Europe.

The concrete shaft contains elevators that carry passengers to the viewing platform. Situated inside a steel-clad giant sphere, this platform is 203 m (666 ft) above the ground. Visitors can enjoy a bird's-eye view of the whole city while sipping a cup of coffee in the revolving café. Visibility can reach up to 40 km (25 miles).

Nikolaiviertel ⑫

Ⓤ Alexanderplatz, Klosterstraße. Ⓢ Alexanderplatz. 🚃 M48. 🚌 100, 143, 200, 248, TXL.

This small area on the bank of the Spree, known as the Nikolaiviertel (St. Nicholas Quarter), is a favorite strolling ground for both Berliners and tourists. Some of Berlin's oldest houses stood here until they were destroyed in World War II. The redevelopment of the area, carried out between

Berlin's massive Fernsehturm, towering over the city

1979 and 1987, proved to be an interesting, if somewhat controversial, attempt at recreating a medieval village.

Today the area consists mostly of newly built replicas of historic buildings. The narrow streets are filled with small shops, cafés, bars, and restaurants, among them the popular Zum Nussbaum, a historical inn that was once located on Fischer Island. Dating from 1507, the original building was destroyed, and subsequently reconstructed at the junction of Am Nussbaum and Propststraße.

Riverside buildings of the Nikolaiviertel

Berliner Dom ⑨

Royal crest of Friedrich III

This Protestant cathedral was built by Jan Boumann between 1747 and 1750 on the site of a Dominican church. It incorporated the crypt of the Hohenzollern dynasty, which ruled the city for nearly 500 years, and is one of the largest of its kind in Europe. The present Neo-Baroque structure is the work of Julius Raschdorff and dates from 1894–1905. The central copper dome reaches 98 m (322 ft), with an inner cupola which is 70 m (230 ft) high. Following severe damage sustained in World War II, the building has been restored in a simplified form, including the dismantling of the Hohenzollern memorial chapel, which originally adjoined the northern wall.

Figures of the Apostles

Philipp der Großmütige
At the base of the arcade stand statues of church reformers and princes who supported the Reformation. The statue of Philip the Magnanimous, Landgrave of Hesse (1509–67) is the work of Walter Schott.

★ Church Interior
The impressive, richly-decorated interior was designed by Julius Raschdorff at the turn of the 20th century.

Sauer's Organ
The organ, the work of Wilhelm Sauer, has an exquisitely carved case. The instrument contains some 7,200 pipes.

Main entrance

★ Hohenzollern Sarcophagi
The imperial Hohenzollern family crypt, hidden beneath the floor of the cathedral, contains 100 richly decorated sarcophagi, including that of Prince Friedrich Ludwig.

The Four Evangelists
Mosaics depicting the Four Evangelists decorate the ceilings of the smaller niches in the cathedral. They were designed by Woldemar Friedrich.

VISITORS' CHECKLIST

Am Lustgarten. *Tel* 030-20 26 91 19. Ⓢ Hackescher Markt. 🚌 100, 200. ◯ 9am–8pm Mon–Sat, noon–8pm Sun (Oct–Mar: until 7pm). ♿ ✝ 10am & 6pm Sun.

The Resurrection
The stained glass in the windows of the apses, designed by Anton von Werner, shows scenes from the life of Jesus.

The main altar, saved from the previous cathedral, is the work of Friedrich August Stüler and dates from 1850.

Pulpit
This elaborate Neo-Baroque pulpit is part of the cathedral's ornate decor dating from the early 20th century.

★ **Sarcophagi of Friedrich I and his Wife**
Both of these were designed by Andreas Schlüter. The sculpture on Sophie Charlotte's sarcophagus depicts death.

STAR FEATURES

★ Hohenzollern Sarcophagi

★ Church Interior

★ Sarcophagi of Friedrich I and his Wife

Kreuzberg ⑬

Checkpoint Charlie Friedrichstraße 43–45. **Tel** 030-253 7250. Ⓤ *Kochstraße.* 🚌 *M29.* 🕐 9am–10pm daily. 🖼 **Jüdisches Museum** Lindenstraße 14. Ⓤ *Hallesches Tor, Kochstraße.* 🚌 *248.* **Tel** 030-2599 3300. 🕐 10am–10pm Mon, 10am–8pm Tue–Sun.

Kreuzberg is an area of contrasts, with luxury apartments next to dilapidated buildings. The district's attractions are its wealth of restaurants and Turkish bazaars, as well as a wide selection of theaters, cinemas, and galleries.

Checkpoint Charlie was once the notorious border crossing between the Soviet and American sectors, and witness to a number of dramatic events during the Cold War. The museum close by, Haus am Checkpoint Charlie, houses exhibits connected with the ingenious attempts by East Germans to escape to the West.

The imaginative architecture of the **Jüdisches Museum**, dedicated to Jewish history and art, conveys something of the tragic history of the millions of Jews who lost their lives in the Holocaust. The zigzag layout recalls a torn Star of David, while the interior arrangement is dominated by a long empty area, which symbolizes the void left in Europe by the exile and murder of countless thousands of Jews.

Berlin Wall sculpture at entrance to Haus am Checkpoint Charlie

Zoologischer Garten, home to over 1,400 animal species

Zoologischer Garten ⑭

Hardenbergplatz 8 or Budapester Straße 34. **Tel** 030-254 010. Ⓤ Ⓢ *Zoologischer Garten.* 🚌 *100, 204, 249 & many others.* 🕐 daily. 🖼

The Zoological Garden forms part of the Tiergarten and dates from 1844, making it the oldest zoo in Germany. It offers a number of attractions, including the monkey house, which contains a family of gorillas, and a specially darkened pavilion for observing nocturnal animals. The hippopotamus pool has a glazed wall that enables visitors to watch these enormous creatures moving through the water. The aquarium, one of the largest in Europe, contains sharks, piranhas, and unusual animals from coral reefs. There is also a huge terrarium with an overgrown jungle that is home to a group of crocodiles.

Kaiser-Wilhelm-Gedächtniskirche ⑮

Breitscheidplatz. **Tel** 030-218 5023. Ⓤ *Zoologischer Garten, Kurfürsten-straße.* Ⓢ *Zoologischer Garten.* 🚌 *100, 200, X9.* **Gedenkhalle** 🕐 Mon–Sat, Sun pm. 🖼

The damaged roof of this former church has become one of the best-known symbols of postwar Berlin. The vast Neo-Romanesque building was consecrated in 1895, but was destroyed by bombs in 1943. After World War II the ruins were removed, leaving only the massive front tower, at the base of which the Gedenkhalle (Memorial Hall) is situated. This hall documents the history of the church and contains some of the original ceiling mosaics, marble reliefs, and liturgical objects. The latter include the Coventry Crucifix, a modest cross fashioned from nails found in the ashes of Coventry Cathedral, England, which was destroyed in the bombing raids of the 1940s.

In 1963, Egon Eiermann designed a new octagonal church in blue glass. His hexagonal bell tower stands on the site of the former nave of the destroyed church.

New and old bell towers of the Kaiser-Wilhelm-Gedächtniskirche

A bustling outdoor café on the Kurfürstendamm

Kurfürstendamm ⑯

U Kurfürstendamm. 🚌 204, 249, M0, M19, M29, M46, X10.

This wide avenue was established in the 1880s on the site of a former track that led to the Grunewald forest (*see p538*). It quickly acquired many imposing buildings and grand hotels. In the 20 years between World Wars I and II, the Ku'damm, as it is popularly called, was renowned for its cafés, visited by famous film directors, writers, and painters.

After World War II, new buildings replaced the damaged houses, but this did not change the character of the street. Elegant shops and pretty cafés still attract a chic crowd. Not far from here is the city's newest photography museum, the **Newton-Sammlung**.

Sammlung Berggruen ⑰

Schlossstraße 1. **Tel** 030-326 9580. U Richard-Wagner-Platz, Sophie-Charlotte-Platz. Ⓢ Westend. 🚌 109, 309, M45. ◯ 10am–6pm Tue–Sun. 🎧 ♿

Heinz Berggruen assembled this tasteful collection of art dating from the late 19th and first half of the 20th centuries. The museum is well-known for its impressive array of paintings, drawings, and gouaches by Pablo Picasso. There is also a display of more than 20 works by Paul Klee and paintings by Van Gogh, Braque, and Cézanne. The exhibition is supplemented by some excellent sculptures.

Schloss Charlottenburg ⑱

Spandauer Damm. **Tel** 030-3209 1440. U Richard-Wagner-Platz, Sophie-Charlotte-Platz. Ⓢ Westend. 🚌 109, 309, M45. ◯ Tue–Sun. 🎧 compulsory on ground floor. 📷

The palace in Charlottenburg was intended as a summer residence for Sophie Charlotte, Elector Friedrich III's wife. Construction began in 1695 to a design by Johann Arnold Nering. Between 1701 and 1713 the palace was enlarged, and a Baroque cupola and an orangery were added. Subsequent extensions were undertaken by Frederick the Great (King Friedrich II), who added the Neuer Flügel (New Wing) between 1740 and 1746.

Restored to its former elegance after World War II, the palace's richly decorated interior is unequalled in Berlin. In the central section of the palace, the mirrored gallery of the Porzellankabinett has walls lined with fine Japanese and Chinese porcelain.

The Neuer Flügel, the new wing of the palace, used to house the Galerie der Romantik. The former private apartment of Friedrik the Great, it now has displays of the king's exquisite furniture. The Neuer Flügel and the upper floor can be visited independently.

The Orangery was originally used to protect rare plants during the winter, but in the summer months was used as a scene for festivities by the court. It has been reconstructed and is now a restaurant.

The park surrounding the palace is one of the most picturesque places in Berlin. Among the many fine monuments dotted around the grounds are the charming Neoclassical **Neuer Pavillion** (New Pavilion), whose interior is furnished in period style, and the **Belvedere** (1788), housing a large collection of porcelain.

Central tower and 18th-century cupola of Schloss Charlottenburg

Restaurant in the Forsthaus Paulsborn in the Grunewald

Grunewald ⑲

Ⓢ *Grunewald.* 🚌 *115.* **Jagdschloss Grunewald.** *Tel 030-813 3597.* ⏱ *10am–6pm Tue–Sun.*

Just a short S-Bahn ride from central Berlin lie the vast forests of the Grunewald, bordering some of the city's most elegant suburbs. Once the haunt of politicians, wealthy industrialists, and renowned artists, some of the villas here now serve as the headquarters of Berlin's academic institutes.

On the shore of the picturesque Grunewaldsee is the **Jagdschloss Grunewald**, one of the oldest civic buildings in Berlin. Built by Elector Joachim II in 1542, it was rebuilt in the Baroque style around 1700. Inside the small palace is Berlin's only surviving Renaissance hall, which houses canvases by Rubens and van Dyck among others. Opposite the Jagdschloss, the **Jagdzeugmagazin** (Hunting Museum) holds displays of historic hunting equipment. Just 4 km (2 miles) away is the Waldmuseum, the only museum devoted to forest life in the Berlin area.

To the southwest of the Grunewaldsee is **Forsthaus Paulsborn**. This rather picturesque hunting lodge, which nowadays houses a very good restaurant, was constructed in 1905.

Dahlem ⑳

Ⓤ *Dahlem Dorf.* 🚌 *101, 110, X11, X83.* **Museumszentrum** *Tel 030-266 424242.* ⏱ *Tue–Sun.*

First mentioned in 1275, by the 19th century Dahlem had grown from a small village into an affluent, tranquil city suburb. At the beginning of the 20th century, a number of museums, designed by Bruno Paul, were built. They were extended considerably in the 1960s, when the **Museumszentrum** was created to rival East Berlin's Museum Island *(see pp532–4).*

Highlights from this cluster of museums include bronzes from Benin in West Africa and gold Inca jewelry from South America at the Ethnologisches Museum (Museum of Ethnography). The other collections range from the Museum für Indische Kunst (Museum of Indian Art) and the Museum für Ostasiatische Kunst (Museum of Far Eastern Art), now known together as the Museum of Asian Art, to the Nordamerica Ausstellung (Exhibition of Native North American Cultures).

Not far from the Museumszentrum, the **Museum Europäischer Kulturen** specializes in European folk art and culture. Among the exhibits you can expect to see are earthenware items, costumes, jewelry, toys, and tools.

Domäne Dahlem is a rare oasis of country life in the Berlin suburbs. Part of the Stadtmuseum Berlin (Museum of the City of Berlin), the Baroque manor house (c.1680) boasts splendid period interiors, while the 19th-century farm buildings hold a collection of agricultural tools.

The elegant Functionalist building occupied by the **Brücke-Museum** was built by Werner Düttmann in 1966–7. The museum houses German Expressionist paintings by members of the artistic group known as *Die Brücke.*

The combined museum and working farm of Domäne Dahlem

Potsdam and Park Sanssouci ㉑

An independent city close to Berlin, Potsdam has almost 150,000 inhabitants and is the capital of Brandenburg. The first documented reference to the town dates from AD 993; it was later granted municipal rights in 1317. The town blossomed in the 1600s, during the era of the Great Elector, and then again in the 18th century, when the splendid summer palace, Schloss Sanssouci, was built for Frederick the Great. Potsdam suffered badly in World War II, particularly on April 14 and 15, 1945, when the Allies bombed the town's center.

VISITORS' CHECKLIST

Brandenburg. 🏙 150,000.
🚉 from Bahnhof Zoo, Berlin
to Potsdam-Stadt. Ⓢ 🚌 🚋
🛈 Brandenburger Straße 3
(0331-27 55 80).
www.potsdam.de

A Russian-style wooden house in the charming Alexandrowka district

Exploring Potsdam

Despite its wartime losses, today Potsdam is one of Germany's most attractive towns. Tourists flock to see the magnificent royal estate, Park Sanssouci *(see pp540–41)*, to stroll in the Neuer Garten, which boasts its own grand palaces, and to see the pretty Alexandrowka district and the historic Dutch quarter.

🏛 Marmorpalais

Am Ufer des Heiligen Sees (Neuer Garten). **Tel** 0331-969 4550.
🚌 692, 695. ◯ May–Oct 31: Tue–Sun; Nov 1–Apr: Sat & Sun.
The Marmorpalais (Marble Palace) is located on the edge of the lake in the Neuer Garten, a park northeast of Potsdam's center. Completed in 1791, the grand Neoclassical building owes its name to the Silesian marble that decorates its facade. The rooms in the main part of the palace contain Neoclassical furnishings from the late 18th century, including Wedgwood porcelain and furniture from the workshops of Roentgen. The concert hall in the right wing, whose interior dates from the 1840s, is particularly impressive.

🏛 Schloss Cecilienhof

Am Neuen Garten. **Tel** 0331-969 4244. 🚌 692, 695. ◯ Tue–Sun.
Schloss Cecilienhof was built for the Hohenzollern family between 1914 and 1917. In July 1945 the palace played an important role in history, when it served as the venue for the Potsdam Conference – an event that played a major part in establishing the political balance of power in Europe following the end of World War II. Today it is a museum as well as a hotel.

🏛 Alexandrowka

Russische Kolonie Allee/ Puschkinallee. 🚌 604, 609, 638, 639. 🚋 92.
A trip to Alexandrowka, in the northeast of the city, takes the visitor into the world of Pushkin's fairy tales. Wooden log cabins, set in their own gardens, form a charming residential estate. The houses were built in 1826 for singers in a Russian choir established to entertain military troops. Peter Joseph Lenné was responsible for the overall appearance of the estate, named after the Tsarina, the Prussian Princess Charlotte.

🏛 Holländisches Viertel

Friedrich-Ebertstraße/ Kurfürsten-straße/ Hebbelstraße/ Gutenberg-straße. 🚌 138, 601, 602, 603, 604 & many others.
The Dutch Quarter attracts crowds of tourists, with numerous stores, galleries, cafés, and beer cellars, especially along Mittelstraße. The area was built up in the first half of the 18th century, when Dutch workers, invited by Friedrich Wilhelm I, began to settle in Potsdam. Today, you can still see the pretty red-brick, gabled houses that were built for them.

🏛 Filmpark Babelsberg

Großbeerenstraße. **Tel** 0331-721 2750. ◯ mid-Apr–Oct: daily ⬤ Mon in May & Sep. 🎦
This amazing film park was laid out on the site of the film studios where Germany's first movies were made in 1912. From 1917, the studios belonged to Universum-Film-AG, which produced some of the most renowned movies of the silent era, such as Fritz Lang's futuristic *Metropolis* (1927) and films starring Marlene Dietrich and Greta Garbo. Later, Nazi propaganda films were also made here. The studio is still in operation today, but part of the complex is open to the public. Visitors can see old film sets, exciting special effects demonstrations, and stuntmen in action.

Original film prop on display at the Filmpark Babelsberg

Park Sanssouci

The enormous Park Sanssouci, covering an area of
287 hectares (709 acres), is among the most beautiful
palace complexes in Europe. The first building to be
constructed, Frederick the Great's Schloss Sanssouci, was
built on the site of an orchard in 1745–7. Its name –
sans souci is French for "without a care" – gives an indication
of the building's flamboyant character. Over the years, the
park has been enriched by other palaces and pavilions.
Today, the park is made up of small gardens dating
from different eras, all maintained in their original style.

Communs (1766–9)
*This house for the palace staff
has an unusually elegant
character, and is situated
next to a pretty courtyard.*

★ Neues Palais
*The monumental New Palace,
constructed in 1763–1769, is
crowned by a massive dome.
Bas-reliefs on the triangular
tympanum depict figures
from Greek mythology.*

0 meters   200

0 yards   200

Schloss Charlottenhof
*The most interesting interior of
this Neoclassical palace is the
Humboldt Room, also called
the Tent Room due to its
resemblance to a marquee.*

The Lustgarten
(pleasure garden) has
a symmetrical layout
lined with rose beds.

STAR SIGHTS

★ Schloss Sanssouci

★ Neues Palais

The Römische Bäder
(Roman Baths) date from
1829 and include a mock-
Renaissance villa and a
suite of Roman-style rooms.

The Chinesisches Teehaus
(Chinese Teahouse) features
an exhibition of exquisite
Oriental porcelain.

Orangerie

*This Neo-Renaissance palace,
the largest in the park, was
built in the mid-19th
century to house
foreign royalty
and guests.*

Neue
Kammern

Bildergalerie
(art gallery)

🏛 Neues Palais

Am Neuen Palais. **Tel** 0331-969 4202.
🚌 605, 606, 695. ◯ Wed–Mon.
📷 🎫
This imposing Baroque palace
was begun at the request of
Frederick the Great in 1763.
Decorated with hundreds of
sculptures, the vast two-story
building contains more than
200 richly adorned rooms.
Especially unusual is the
Grottensaal (Grotto Salon),
where man-made stalactites
hang from the ceiling.

🏛 Schloss Sanssouci

Zur Historischen Mühle.
Tel 0331-969 4202. 🚌 612, 614,
695. 🚋 94, 96. ◯ Tue–Sun. 📷 🎫
Schloss Sanssouci is an enchanting Rococo palace, built in
1745–7. Frederick the Great
made the original sketches for
the building. The walls of the
Konzertzimmer (Concert Hall)
are lined with paintings by
Antoine Pesne. The greatest
treasures are the paintings of
fêtes galantes by Antoine
Watteau (1684–1721), a favorite
artist of Frederick the Great.

🏛 Orangerie

Maulbeerallee (Nordischer Garten).
Tel 0331-969 4200. 🚌 695. ◯ Apr:
Sat & Sun; May–Oct: Tue–Sun.
The highlight of this guest
house is the Raphael Hall,
which is decorated with copies
of works by the great Italian
Renaissance artist. The view
from the observation terrace
extends over Potsdam.

🏛 Schloss Charlottenhof

Geschwister-Scholl-Strasse. **Tel** 0331-
969 4202. 🚌 606. 🚋 94, 96.
◯ May–Oct: Tue–Sun.
This small Neoclassical
palace was designed by
Friedrich Schinkel and

**The elegant Baroque exterior
of the Neue Kammern**

Ludwig Persius in 1829, in the
style of a Roman villa. The
rear of the palace has a portico that opens out onto the
garden terrace. Some of the
wall paintings, produced by
Schinkel, are still in place.

🏛 Neue Kammern

Zur Historischen Mühle (Lustgarten).
Tel 0331-969 4202. 🚌 612, 614,
695. ◯ Nov–Apr: Wed–Mon; May–
Oct: Tue–Sun. 📷 🎫
Originally built as an orangery
for Schloss Sanssouci in 1747,
the Neue Kammern (New
Chambers) was remodeled
as guest accommodations in
1777. The most impressive
of the building's four elegant
Rococo halls is the Ovidsaal,
with its rich reliefs and
marble floors.

🏛 Bildergalerie

Zur Historischen Mühle.
Tel 0331-969 4202. 🚌 612, 614,
695. ◯ May–Oct: Tue–Sun. 📷
Constructed between 1755
and 1764 to a design by
J.G. Buring, the Bildergalerie
holds an exhibition of paintings
once owned by Frederick
the Great. Highlights include
Caravaggio's *Doubting
Thomas* (1597), and Guido
Reni's *Cleopatra's Death* (1626),
as well as a number of works
by Rubens and van Dyck.

★ **Schloss Sanssouci**
*The oldest building in
the complex, this palace
contains the imposing
Marmorsaal (Marble
Hall), decorated with
pairs of columns made
from Carrara marble.
Frederick the Great
wanted the room to be
based on the Pantheon
in Rome (see p400).*

Eastern Germany

Closed to the West for over 40 years of Communist rule, Eastern Germany is now fast rebuilding its reputation as an attractive tourist destination. The powerful duchy of Saxony, whose rulers were also Electors and, in the early 18th century, kings of Poland, has left behind a rich cultural heritage for visitors to explore. After Berlin, the area's main attractions are Dresden, the ancient capital of Saxony, the old university town of Leipzig, and the important cultural center of Weimar in Thuringia.

Vermeer's *Girl Reading a Letter*, Gemäldegalerie Alte Meister

Dresden ❷

Saxony. 🏛 480,000. ✈ 15 km (9 miles) N. 🚉 🚌 🚊 ⓘ Schloßstr. 2 (0351-501 601 60). **www**.dresden.de

One of Germany's most beautiful cities, Dresden blossomed during the 18th century, when it became a cultural center and acquired many magnificent buildings. Almost all of these, however, were completely destroyed during World War II, when Allied air forces mounted vast carpet-bombing raids on the city.

Today, meticulous restoration work is in progress to return the city to its former glory.

The most celebrated building in Dresden is the **Frauenkirche**. The landmark Church of Our Lady (1726–43) was left in ruins during the communist era to serve as a reminder of World War II damage but reconstruction began after reunification. The church was finally reconsecrated in 2005, and now serves as a symbol of reconciliation between former warring nations.

The **Zwinger** is an imposing Baroque building constructed in

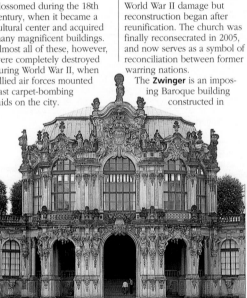

The Baroque Wallpavilion, part of the Zwinger building in Dresden

1709–32 with a spacious courtyard surrounded on all sides by galleries housing several museums, including the **Gemäldegalerie Alte Meister**. This contains one of Europe's finest art collections, with works by Antoine Watteau, Rembrandt, van Eyck, Velázquez, Vermeer, Raphael, Titian, and Albrecht Dürer.

The 19th-century **Sächsische Staatsoper** (Saxon State Opera) has been the venue for many world premieres, including *The Flying Dutchman* and *Tannhäuser* by Wagner, as well as works by Richard Strauss.

Dresden's **Residenzschloss** was built in stages from the late 15th to the 17th centuries. The palace now houses some of the most beautiful art collections in Eastern Germany. The Verkehrsmuseum has been a museum of transportation since 1956. The Residenzschloss also houses the famous **Grünes Gewölbe**, a vast royal treasury

Once part of the town's fortifications, the **Brühlsche Terrasse** was subsequently transformed into magnificent

REBUILT FROM THE ASHES

Once known as the "Florence of the north," Dresden was one of the most beautiful cities in Europe. Then, on the night of February 13, 1945, 800 British aircraft launched the first of five massive firebomb raids on the city made by Allied air forces. The raids completely destroyed the greater part of the city, killing over 35,000 people, many of whom were refugees. The rebuilding of Dresden began soon after the war, when it was decided to restore the Zwinger and other historic buildings, and create a new city of modern developments on the levelled land around the old city center. Much of Dresden has now been reconstructed, though some reminders of the city's destruction remain.

The center of Dresden after Allied carpet-bombing

ardens by Heinrich von Brühl. Offering splendid views over the Elbe river, it is known as the balcony of Europe." The **Albertinum** houses several magnificent collections, including the **Gemäldegalerie Neue Meister**, which holds paintings from the 19th and 20th centuries. These include landscapes by Caspar David Friedrich, canvases by the Nazarene group of painters, and works by Degas, van Gogh, Manet, and Monet.

On the banks of the Elbe stands **Schloss Pillnitz**, the charming summer residence of Augustus the Strong. The main attraction is the park, laid out in English and Chinese styles.

🏛 Gemäldegalerie Alte Meister
Theaterplatz 1. **Tel** 0351-4914 2000. ◯ 10am–6pm Tue–Sun. 🖼

Environs

Meissen, 19 km (12 miles) northwest of Dresden, is famous for its porcelain manufacture. The **Albrechtsburg** is a vast fortified hilltop complex with a cathedral and a palace once used by the electors. Europe's first porcelain factory was set up in the palace in 1710 but moved to premises in Talstrasse in 1865. Documents relating to the history of the factory and examples of its products are on display in the palace rooms.

⚜ Albrechtsburg
Domplatz 1. **Tel** 03521-470 70. ◯ daily. 🖼

Leipzig ❸

Saxony. 🏠 493,000. ✈ 🚉 🚌
🛈 Katharinenstr. 8 (0341-710 42 60).

Leipzig is not only one of Germany's leading commercial towns, but also a center of culture and learning. Most of the interesting sights can be found in the old town, including Europe's biggest train station, the **Hauptbahnhof**.

Lovers of Johann Sebastian Bach's music can visit the **Thomaskirche** (1482–96), where he was choirmaster from 1723. It now contains

The lofty Neoclassical interior of the Nikolaikirche, Leipzig

his tomb. The **Bacharchive und Bachmuseum** houses items relating to the composer.

The 16th-century **Nikolaikirche** (Church of St. Nicholas) was redecorated in Neoclassical style in 1784–97. The grand Renaissance **Altes Rathaus** (Old Town Hall), built in only nine months in 1556, is now the municipal museum. The **Museum der Bildenden Künste** has an excellent collection of German masters, including works by Caspar David Friedrich and Lucas Cranach the Elder, as well as van Eyck, Rubens, and Rodin.

The **Grassimuseum** complex houses three collections: a museum of ethnography, a museum of applied arts, and a large collection of musical instruments.

🏛 Museum der Bildenden Künste
Katharinenstr. 10. **Tel** 0341-216 9914. ◯ Tue–Sun (Wed: noon–8pm).

Weimar ❹

Thuringia. 🏠 62,000. 🚉 🚌
🛈 Markt 10 (03643-19433).
www.weimar.de

Weimar rose to prominence due to the enlightened sponsorship of its rulers, particularly Duke Carl Augustus and his wife Anna Amalia in the 18th century. Former residents include Goethe, Schiller, and Nietzsche, as well as the designers of the Bauhaus School, founded here in 1919.

Weimar is relatively small, and most of its museums are in the town center. To the north stands the **Neues Museum**, which holds a large collection of modern art. The nearby **Stadtmuseum** (currently closed for renovation) is devoted to Weimar's history, while the **Goethe-Museum** displays items associated with the famous writer.

The Neoclassical **Deutsches Nationaltheater**, built in 1906–7, was the venue for the world premiere of Wagner's *Lohengrin*. In 1919 the National Congress sat here to pass the new constitution for the Weimar Republic.

The vast ducal castle, **Weimar Schloss**, has original interiors and fine paintings by Peter Paul Rubens. Also known as the Grünes Schloss (Green Castle), the **Herzogin-Anna-Amalia Bibliothek** was converted into the duchess' library in 1761–6. It has a splendid Rococo interior.

Set in attractive Belvedere Park, the ducal summer residence of **Schloss Belvedere** (1761–6) has fine collections of Rococo decorative art and vintage vehicles.

⚜ Weimar Schloss
Burgplatz 4. **Tel** 03643-54 59 60. ◯ Tue–Sun. 🖼

Weimar Schloss in Burgplatz, with its tall Renaissance tower

Bavaria

Bavaria is the largest state in the Federal Republic of Germany. Ruled by the Wittelsbach dynasty from 1180, the duchy of Bavaria was elevated to the status of a kingdom in 1806. In addition to historic cities, fairy-tale castles, and exquisite Baroque and Renaissance palaces, the region has more than its fair share of glorious Alpine scenery, beer halls, and colorful festivals.

The auditorium of Bayreuth's Markgräfliches Opernhaus

Bayreuth ❺

🏛 75,000. 🚉 ℹ Luitpoldplatz 9 (0921-885 88). 🎭 Richard-Wagner-Festspiele (Jul–Aug).

Music lovers associate this city with the German composer Richard Wagner (1813–83), who took up residence here in 1872. The **Villa Wahnfried** was built for Wagner by Carl Wölfel and today houses a museum dedicated to the famous musician. Nearby, the **Franz-Liszt-Museum** occupies the house where the Hungarian composer died in 1886.

Other sights of interest in Bayreuth include the **Markgräfliches Opernhaus**, the lavish Baroque opera house, which dates from the mid-18th century, and the **Neues Schloss**. Built for Margravine Wilhelmine in the 18th century, the palace retains its splendid Baroque and Rococo interiors, and its English-style gardens.

Bamberg ❻

🏛 71,000. 🚉 ℹ Geyerswörth-straße 3 (0951-297 62 00).

Bamberg's most interesting historical monuments are clustered around Domplatz, including the magnificent **Cathedral of St. Peter and St. George**. Begun around 1211, the cathedral combines the

late Romanesque and early French-Gothic styles. The eastern choir contains the famous equestrian statue of the "Bamberg Rider" (1225–30), whose identity remains a mystery to this day.

The west side of Domplatz is flanked by the **Alte Hofhaltung**, the former bishop's residence. Built in the 15th and 16th centuries, it houses a museum of local history. The more recent Baroque **Bishop's Palace** (1763) stands behind the cathedral.

Also on Dom-platz is the **Neue Residenz** (1695–1704), with its richly decorated apartments. Inside, the Staatsgalerie has a collection of old German masters.

On the east side of the town, the **Altes Rathaus** was originally Gothic in style, but was remodeled in 1744–56 by Jakob Michael Küchel.

Bamberger Reiter (Bamberg Rider) in the city's cathedral

🏛 **Neue Residenz**
Domplatz 8. **Tel** 0951-519 390.
◯ daily. 📷

Neumann's stunning Treppenhaus (staircase) at Würzburg's Residenz

Würzburg ❼

🏛 130,000. 🚉 ℹ Marktplatz, Am Falkenhaus (0931-37 23 35).

Located on the bank of the Main river, Würzburg is an important cultural and commercial center, and home of the excellent Franconian wine.

The city's most impressive landmark is the **Residenz**, where Würzburg's prince-bishops lived from 1744. A highlight of this lavish Baroque palace is the huge Treppenhaus (staircase), by Balthasar Neumann (1687–1753). Above it is a glorious ceiling fresco by the Venetian artist, Giovanni Battista Tiepolo.

Before the Residenz was built, the city's prince-bishops resided in the fortress known as the **Festung Marienberg**, which has stood on a hill overlooking the river since 1210. The Mainfränkisches Museum, housed inside the fortress, illustrates the history of the town and holds a number of works by the renowned German sculptor Tilman Riemen-schneider (1460–1531).

Würzburg's cathedral, the **Dom St. Kilian**, dates from 1045 and is one of Germany's largest Romanesque churches. North of it is the 11th-century basilica **Neumünster**. Its imposing Baroque dome and sandstone facade are 18th-century additions. Dating from the 13th century, the picturesque **Rathaus** (Town Hall) has a late-Renaissance tower, added 1660.

🏛 **Residenz**
Residenzplatz 2. **Tel** 0931-35 51 70. ◯ daily. 📷

⛰ **Festung Marienberg**
📷 Apr–Oct: 11am, 2pm, 3pm, 4pm Tue–Fri, 10am, 11am, 1pm, 2pm, 3pm, 4pm Sat & Sun. 📷
Mainfränkisches Museum
Tel 0931-205 940.
◯ Tue–Sun. 📷

Rothenburg ob der Tauber ⑧

🏠 12,000. 🚇 ℹ️ *Marktplatz 2 (09861-40 48 00).*

Encircled by ramparts, Rothenburg is a perfectly preserved medieval town in a picturesque setting on the banks of the Tauber river.

At the heart of the town is Marktplatz, whose focal point is the **Rathaus** (Town Hall), combining Renaissance and Gothic styles. Off the main square, **St. Jakobs Kirche** (1373–1464) and the **Franziskanerkirche** both contain many historical treasures.

Two museums of note are the **Reichsstadtmuseum**, devoted to the town's history, and the **Mittelalterliches Museum**, which contains a large collection of medieval instruments of torture.

Through the Burgtor, a gateway in the city walls, you arrive at the **Burggarten** – pretty gardens giving views over the town and river.

Rothenburg's Rathaus (Town Hall), begun in the 14th century

Nuremberg ⑨

🏠 490,000. ✈️ 🚇 ℹ️ *Königstraße 93 (0911-233 60).*

The largest town in Bavaria after Munich, Nuremberg (Nürnberg) flourished in the 15th and 16th centuries, when many prominent artists, craftsmen, and intellectuals worked here, making it a leading European cultural center. The city is divided in two by the Pegnitz river. In the southern half, the mighty **Frauentor** is one of several gateways in the massive 15th and 16th-century ramparts. A short walk away is the **Germanisches Nationalmuseum**. Founded in 1853, the museum houses a superb collection of antiquities from the German-speaking world, including masterworks by Tilman Riemenschneider, Lucas Cranach the Elder (1472–1553), and Albrecht Dürer (1471–1528).

Overlooking the bustling Lorenzer Platz, the Gothic **St. Lorenz-Kirche** is one of the city's most important churches. Begun in 1270, it boasts some glorious stained-glass windows.

As you cross over the Pegnitz to the north side of town, look out for the **Heilig-Geist-Spital** (Hospital of the Holy Spirit), which dates from 1332 and spans the river.

A major landmark north of the river is the **Frauenkirche**, commissioned by the Holy Roman Emperor Charles IV in the mid-14th century. Also of importance is the **Albrecht-Dürer-Haus**, where the celebrated Renaissance painter lived in 1509–28. Copies of a wide selection of his works are on display here.

A climb up Burgstraße brings you to the **Kaiserburg**, the imperial castle complex. The oldest surviving part is a pentagonal tower, the **Fünfeckturm**, which dates from 1040. At its foot is the Kaiserstallung (Imperial Stables), now a youth hostel.

At the Christkindlmarkt, the lively Christmas fair held during Advent in the Hauptmarkt, you can warm yourself with a glass of hot red wine spiced with cloves and buy locally made crafts.

🏛 **Germanisches Nationalmuseum**
Kartäusergasse 1. *Tel 0911-13 310.* ⏰ Tue–Sun. 🌐

🏛 **Albrecht-Dürer-Haus**
Albrecht–Dürer-Straße 39. *Tel 0911-231 25 68.* ⏰ Tue–Sun (Jul–Sep: daily). 🌐 📷

The half-timbered buildings of Nuremberg's Kaiserburg at the top of Burgstraße

Munich

Founded in 1158, Munich became the capital of Bavaria in the 16th century. The town rapidly overshadowed once powerful neighbors, such as Augsburg and Nuremberg, to become southern Germany's main metropolis. The period of greatest growth was in the 19th century, when the city was developed along Neoclassical lines. Many of the grand buildings around Königsplatz and along Ludwigstrasse date from this time. As well as historic monuments, Munich has first-class museums and excellent shopping. It also hosts the world-famous annual beer festival, the Oktoberfest.

SIGHTS AT A GLANCE

Alte Pinakothek ⑦
Asamkirche ⑤
Bayerisches Nationalmuseum ⑪
Deutsches Museum ⑩
Englischer Garten ⑫
Frauenkirche ②
Glyptothek ⑥
Marienplatz ③
Neue Pinakothek ⑧
Pinakothek der Moderne ⑨
Residenz pp548–9 ①
Stadtmuseum ④

Greater Munich
(see inset map)
Nymphenburg ⑭
Olympiapark ⑬

KEY

▨	Sight / Place of interest
✈	Airport
🚊	Train station
🚊	Tram stop
Ⓢ	S-Bahn station
Ⓤ	U-Bahn station
🚌	Bus stop
🅿	Parking
ℹ	Tourist information
✝	Church
—	Pedestrian street

GETTING AROUND

Most of the main sights of interest can be reached by Munich's efficient U- and S-Bahn train networks, including sights located farther afield, such as Olympia-park and Nymphenburg. Buses and trams also serve many of the main tourist spots. There is a large pedestrianized zone at the heart of the city making walking a pleasant alternative to public transportation.

GREATER MUNICH

Nuremberg   *Freimann*

Munich Airport

Moosach

Obermenzing   304

Gern   (13)

Nymphenburg   (14)   Schwabing   Bogenhausen

Neuhsn.

Hauptbahnhof

Laim   2R   94

Haidhausen   Berg am Laim

Landsberg   96

0 km   3

0 mile   3   Giesing   *Salzburg*

KEY

Area of main map

VETERINÄRSTR.

gskirche

KAULBACHSTRASSE

KÖNIGINSTRASSE

ELDSTRASSE

sche ibliothek

ENGLISCHER GARTEN

(12)

LERCHENFELDSTRASSE

OETTINGENSTRASSE

ROSENBUSCHSTR.

Haus der Kunst P

Prähistorische Staatssammlung

REITMORSTRASSE AM GRIES

PRINZREGENTENSTRASSE

P   (11)

Schackgalerie

Staatskanzlei

STRAUSS-RING

PILOTYSTR.

SEITZSTRASSE

BRUDERSTRASSE

UNSÖLDSTRASSE

WAGMÜLLER STRASSE

ALEXANDRASTR.

Luitpoldbr.

SEE ALSO

• *Where to Stay* pp575–6

• *Where to Eat* p582

ST. LIEBIGSTRASSE

ST.-ANNA-PLATZ

LIEBIGSTRASSE

REITMORSTR.

ST.-ANNA-STRASSE

Anna-kirche

Anna Klosterkirche

BÜRKLEINSTRASSE

U Lehel

R.-KOCH-STR.

TATTENBACH-

GRANDMÜHL-STRASSE

THIERSCH-TRIFTSTRASSE

STERNSTRASSE

WIDENMAYERSTRASSE

Isar

SCHARNAGL-RING

stall

P

Regierung von Oberbayern

TH. WIMMER-RING

XIMILIANSTRASSE

ammerspiele

RDSTRASSE

Völkerkunde-museum

KNÖBELSTRASSE

KNÖBELSTRASSE

ADELGUNDEN STRASSE

Maximiliansbr.

PRATER-INSEL

MANNHARDT-STRASSE

THIERSCHSTRASSE

Mariannenbr.

Kabelsteg

STEINSDORFSTRASSE

AUF DER INSEL

PRATERINSEL

WEINSTEG

OR S Isartor

THIERSCHSTR.

ZWEIBRÜCKENSTR.

DTSTRASSE

Ludwigsbr.

MUSEUMSINSEL

oschr.

(10)

Zenneckbr.

0 meters   400

0 yards   400

St. Mary's column and the Neo-Gothic Neues Rathaus towering over Marienplatz

E   F

Residenz ①

The origins of Munich's grand Residenz – the former residence of Bavarian kings – go back to the 14th century, when a castle was built here for the Wittelsbach dynasty. In the following centuries the fortress was replaced by a palace complex, which in turn was gradually modified and extended. Major work in the 17th century included the construction of two chapels, the Reiche Kapelle and the Hofkapelle. The Königsbau, containing the superb Nibelungensäle, was added by Leo von Klenze in the first half of the 19th century. Since 1920 the palace has been open to the public as a museum, displaying a wealth of magnificent treasures. In addition to the collections of the Residenzmuseum and the Schatzkammer (Treasury), there is an interesting museum of Egyptian art, the Staatliches Museum Ägyptischer Kunst.

Hofkapelle
This imposing chapel, which dates from the early 17th century, was modeled on nearby St. Michael's Church.

Kaiser Hof (Emperor's Court) is housed in this wing of the Residenz.

Patrona Boiariae
The Renaissance facade features two magnificent portals, and a statue of the Holy Virgin as Patroness of Bavaria (Patrona Boiariae).

The Reiche Kapelle, built for Maximilian I, contains lavish furnishings.

Grottenhof (Grotto Court)

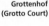

★ **Nibelungensäle**
The Nibelungensäle (Halls of the Nibelungs), a series of five rooms in the Königsbau, take their name from the wall paintings depicting scenes from the great German epic, the Nibelungenlied.

STAR FEATURES

★ Nibelungensäle

★ Schatzkammer

★ Antiquarium

★ Antiquarium
This magnificent vaulted chamber, with its stunning frescoes, was begun in the second half of the 16th century to house the royal collection of antiquities.

VISITORS' CHECKLIST

Residenzmuseum & Schatzkammer Max-Joseph-Platz 3. *Tel* 089-29 06 71.
U *Odeonsplatz.* ◯ *Apr 1–Oct 15: 9am–6pm daily; Oct 16–Mar 31: 10am–5pm daily.*
▨ **Staatliches Museum Ägyptischer Kunst**
Hofgartenstraße 1. *Tel* 089-29 85 46. U *Odeonsplatz.*
◯ *9am–5pm Tue–Fri, 10am–5pm Sat & Sun.* ▨ **Cuvilliés-Theater**
Residenzstraße 1. *Tel* 089-29 06 71. ◯ *phone to check.* ▨
www.residenz-muenchen.de

Cuvilliés-Theater
Designed in 1751–3 by François de Cuvilliés, this is Europe's finest surviving Rococo theater and is still in use today.

Main entrance

The Brunnenhof has as its centerpiece an elaborately decorated fountain dedicated to the Wittelsbachs.

★ Schatzkammer
The rooms of the treasury hold many priceless artifacts, including liturgical objects, jewelry, and items of gold. The highlight of Room V is the Bavarian crown jewels.

Frauenkirche ②

Frauenkirche 1. **U** or **S** Karlsplatz,
Marienplatz. 🚋 19. **Tower**
◻ Apr–Oct: Mon–Sat. 🦽

The site of the Frauenkirche
was originally occupied by a
small chapel dedicated to the
Virgin Mary, built in the 13th
century. Some 200 years later,
a new, much larger church
was built here by the
architects Jörg von Halspach
and Lukas Rottaler. The new
Frauenkirche (or Dom) was
completed in 1488, although
the distinctive copper onion
domes were not added to its
towers until 1525. The church
is one of southern Germany's
largest Gothic structures.
Over 100-m- (330-ft-) long
and 40-m- (130-ft-) wide, it can
accommodate a congregation
of about 2,000 people. The
vast triple-naved hall has no
transept. There are long rows
of side chapels and a gallery
surrounding the choir. For a
good view of central Munich,
you can take an elevator to
the top of one of the towers.

Partly demolished in 1944–5,
the church was rebuilt after
World War II. Church treasures
that escaped destruction
include a painting of the
Virgin by Jan Polack (c.1500),
the altar of St. Andrew in the
Chapel of St. Sebastian, and
the huge monumental tomb of
Ludwig IV the Bavarian, the
first member of the house of
Wittelsbach to be elected Holy
Roman Emperor (c.1283–1347).
The monument was the work
of Hans Krumpper (1619–22).

Altes Rathaus and the Talbruktor on
Marienplatz

Marienplatz ③

U or **S** Marienplatz.
Spielzeugmuseum *Tel* 089-29 40 01.
◻ daily. 🦽

In medieval times Marienplatz
was Munich's salt- and corn-
market. In the center stands a
column with a statue of the
Virgin Mary dating from 1623.
The square is dominated by
the Neo-Gothic **Neues
Rathaus** (New Town Hall),
built in 1867–1909. Its walls
are adorned with statues of
Bavarian rulers, mythological
figures, saints, and monstrous
gargoyles. At 11am and 5pm
the center of attention is the
clocktower. The bells ring out
a carillon, while figures of
knights fight a tournament
and a crowd dances. The
dance is the "Coopers'
Dance," first performed in
1517 to raise citizens' morale
during a plague epidemic.

At the eastern end of the
square stands the **Altes
Rathaus** (Old Town Hall).
Originally built in the late
15th century, it has been
rebuilt many times since. The
high tower, above the old city
gate beside the town hall,
was rebuilt in 1975 to a
design based on pictures
dating from 1493. Since 1983
the tower has been the
home of the city's **Spielzeugmuseum** (toy museum).

Stadtmuseum ④

St. Jakobsplatz 1. *Tel* 089-23 32 23
70. **U** or **S** Marienplatz.
U Sendlinger Tor. ◻ Tue–Sun. 🦽

The collection of the city
museum has been housed
since 1880 in this former
arsenal. Exhibits illustrate daily
life in Munich throughout the
ages. One of the greatest treasures is the "Dancing Moors"
by Erasmus Grasser (1480).
Originally there were 18 highly
expressive limewood carvings
of dancing figures surrounding
the figure of a woman, but
only ten survive.

The Waffenhalle has a fine
collection of arms and armor.
There are also displays of
furniture, paintings, prints,
photographs, dolls, and musical instruments. The vast doll
collection includes paper dolls
from India and China, as well
as automata and puppets.

Also located in the square is
the Judisches Zentrum Jakobsplatz (the Jewish Center),
housed in a cube-shaped,
freestanding building. Three
floors of exhibitions, a library,
and a learning center offer
extensive information on
Jewish culture and history, and
highlight important aspects of
contemporary Jewish life.

Asamkirche ⑤

Sendlinger Straße 32. **U** Sendlinger
Tor. 🚋 16, 17, 18, 27. 🚌 52, 152.
◻ daily.

This extraordinary Rococo
church is dedicated to St.
John Nepomuk, but is known
as the Asamkirche after the
brothers Cosmas Damian and

The distinctive onion domes of the Frauenkirche rising above the city

Egid Quirin Asam, who built it as a private family church. Completed in 1746, the tiny church is a riot of decoration with a dynamically shaped single nave, where no surface is left unembellished. The eye is drawn to the altar, and its sculptural group of the Holy Trinity. The house next door to the church was the residence of Egid Quirin Asam, who was a stuccoist and sculptor. From one of the windows of his house he could see the altar.

Temple of Aphaia on the Greek island of Aegina. The museum's imposing facade, with the portico of an Ionic temple at the center, is part of a kind of Neoclassical forum created in the first half of the 19th century to house the archaeological finds acquired by King Ludwig I of Bavaria. On the opposite side of the square, the **Staatliche Antikensammlung** houses smaller treasures, in particular a vast array of Greek vases.

Four Apostles (1526) by Albrecht Dürer, in the Alte Pinakothek

Alte Pinakothek ⑦

Barer Straße 27. **Tel** 089-23 80 52 16. Ⓤ Königsplatz. 🚊 27. 🚌 100. ☐ Tue–Sun. 🖼 ♿

This magnificent gallery is filled with masterpieces of European art from the Middle Ages to the mid-18th century. Many of the Wittelsbach rulers of Bavaria were great collectors, the first being Wilhelm IV the Steadfast, who ruled from 1508 to 1550. The Alte Pinakothek (Old Picture Gallery) was built for Ludwig I by Leo von Klenze in 1826–36 in the form of a Florentine Renaissance palazzo. The ground floor is devoted to the works of German and Flemish Old Masters from the 16th and 17th centuries. On the first floor are works by Dutch, Flemish, French, German, Italian, and Spanish artists.

Of the German works, pride of place goes to Albrecht Dürer's famous *Self-Portrait* (1500) and two panels of an altarpiece showing *Four Apostles*. Among the other German artists represented are Lucas Cranach the Elder and Grünewald. Early Flemish

masterpieces include *St. Luke Painting the Madonna* by Rogier van der Weyden, and works by Hans Memling and Pieter Brueghel the Elder.

Of later artists, the one with most works on display is the prolific Rubens. There are also interesting works by El Greco, Rembrandt, Raphael, Titian, and Tintoretto.

Neue Pinakothek ⑧

Barer Straße 29. **Tel** 089-23 80 51 95. Ⓤ Theresienstraße. 🚊 27. 🚌 100. ☐ Wed–Mon. 🖼

Bavaria's collection of late 18th- and 19th-century European painting and sculpture occupies a purpose-built gallery completed in 1981. German painting of every artistic movement of the 19th century, including Romanticism, the "Nazarenes," German and Austrian Biedermeier, and Impressionism is well represented. There are also works by French Realists, Impressionists, and Symbolists purchased when the gallery's director was the art historian Hugo von Tschudi.

The open space between the Neue and Alte Pinakothek has been turned into a sculpture park.

The richly decorated altar of the Rococo Asamkirche

Glyptothek ⑥

Königsplatz 3. **Tel** 089-28 61 00. Ⓤ Königsplatz. ☐ Tue–Sun. 🖼
Staatliche Antikensammlung
Königsplatz 1. **Tel** 089-59 98 88 30. ☐ Tue–Sun. 🖼

On the northern side of Königsplatz stands the Glyptothek, a collection of Greek and Roman sculpture, notably statues from the

Neoclassical facade of the Glyptothek, which houses a collection of Greek and Roman sculpture

Pinakothek der Moderne ⑨

Barer Straße 40. **Tel** 089-23 80 53 60. Ⓤ Königsplatz. 27. 100. ☐ 10am–6pm Tue–Sun (to 8pm Thu). except Sun. www.pinakothek-der-moderne.de

Designed by the German architect Stephan Braunfels, this new museum brings together the worlds of art, design, graphics, and architecture under one roof. The collections of four previously separate museums, including the Staatliche Graphische Sammlung, the design collection of Die Neue Sammlung, and the models, drawings, and objects of the Architekturmuseum, are now housed here. As well as the individual permanent displays, there are also temporary and mixed exhibitions.

Deutsches Museum ⑩

Museuminsel 1. **Tel** 089-217 91. Ⓢ Isartor. 18. 52, 56. ☐ daily. www.deutsches-museum.de

Reputed to be the largest science and technology museum in the world, the Deutsches Museum is also the most popular museum in Germany. Founded in 1904, the vast collection features more than 18,000 exhibits across a wide range of subject areas, from agriculture to telecommunications.

In the basement and on the ground floor are some of the museum's largest exhibits. The aeronautics section holds an aeroplane that belonged to the Wright brothers and a 1936

Neapolitan crib in the Bayerisches Nationalmuseum

Messerschmitt ME 109. A hall charting the history of seafaring houses a 14th-century cog, a trading ship used by the Hanseatic League, and a 19th-century fishing vessel.

The museums's superb collection of automobiles and other exhibits related to land travel is now largely on display in the Deutsches Museum Verkehrszentrum at Theresienhöhe 14a, in the west of the city.

Temporary exhibitions are regularly held at the museum, which also has an excellent library archive and a range of multimedia facilities.

Bayerisches Nationalmuseum ⑪

Prinzregentenstraße 3. **Tel** 089-211 24 01. 17. 100. ☐ Tue–Sun.

Founded in 1855 by King Maximilian II, the Bavarian National Museum holds a superb collection of fine and applied arts and historical artifacts. Since 1900 the museum has occupied an impressive building on Prinzregentenstrasse. designed

by Gabriel von Seidl. The ground floor contains works from the Romanesque, Gothic, Renaissance, Baroque, and Neoclassical periods. Star exhibits are German sculptor Conrat Meit's *Judith* (1515) and a beautiful sculpture of the Madonna by Tilman Riemenschneider (c.1460–1531). The first-floor collections include German porcelain, clocks, glassware, ivory carvings, textiles, and items of gold.

In the basement rooms, the Christmas nativity scenes by Bavarian and Italian artists are especially worth seeing.

Englischer Garten ⑫

Ⓤ Giselastraße. 54.

The idea of creating a park in the heart of the city open to all Munich's citizens came from the American-born Count von Rumford, who lived in Bavaria from 1784. In 1789, taking advantage of his position as Bavaria's Minister of War, he persuaded Elector Karl Theodor to put his plans into action. Opened in 1808, the Karl-Theodor-Park is today simply known as the Englischer Garten (English Garden). The park covers an area of 3.7 sq km (914 acres), and has become a popular place for walking, jogging, or simply relaxing.

Several interesting buildings dotted about the gardens include the Monopteros, a Neoclassical temple (1837) by Leo von Klenze, and the Chinese Tower (1789–90), similar to the pagoda in

Benz's tricycle, the first petrol-driven car, on display at the Deutsches Museum

For hotels and restaurants in this region see pp575–6 and p582

London's Kew Gardens *(see p63)*. In the delightful Japanese Teahouse, demonstrations on the art of tea brewing are held. Within Englischer Garten are three beer gardens, where locals and tourists alike come to drink and listen to live music. Visitors can also take out rowing boats on the park's lake, the Kleinhesseloher See.

The late 18th-century Chinese Tower in the Englischer Garten

Olympiapark ⑬

Tel 089-30 67 24 14. Ⓤ *Olympiazentrum.* 🚋 *20, 21, 27.* **Pavilion** ⭘ *daily.*

Built for the 1972 Olympic Games, the Olympiapark is visible from almost anywhere in Munich, identifiable by the 290-m (950-ft) high television tower, the Olympiaturm. The site has three main facilities: the Olympic stadium, which seats over 60,000 spectators, the Olympic Hall, and the Swimming Hall. All three are covered by a vast transparent canopy, stretched between several tall masts to form an irregular-shaped pavilion. Also within the complex are an indoor skating rink, a cycle racing track, and tennis courts.

As well as sporting occasions, the Olympiapark hosts many popular cultural events, such as fireworks displays and open-air rock and pop concerts during the summer months.

Schloss Nymphenburg ⑭

Tel 089-17 90 80. Ⓤ *Rotkreuzplatz.* 🚌 *668.* ⭘ *daily.* 🖼
Botanischer Garten ⭘ *daily.* 🖼

Located northwest of the city center, the stunning Schloss Nymphenburg grew up around an Italianate villa, built in 1663–4 for Electress Henrietta-Adelaide. The Electress dedicated the palace, which became the summer residence of the Wittelsbachs, to the pastoral pleasures of the goddess Flora and her nymphs, hence the name. Several additions were made in the following century, including the construction of four pavilions, connected to the original villa by arcaded passageways.

The palace's interior boasts some magnificent examples of the Rococo style. One of the most impressive rooms is the **Festsaal** – a sumptuous ballroom, designed by father and son, Johann Baptiste and Franz Zimmermann. Equally impressive is the **Schönheitengalerie** (Gallery of Beauties). Hanging here are 38 portraits of beautiful women – favorites of King Ludwig I. The palace also houses a small natural history and science museum. The old stables are now home to the **Marstallmuseum**, a collection of wonderfully ornate carriages that once belonged to Bavarian rulers.

Interior of the Amalienburg, in the grounds of Schloss Nymphenburg

The approach to the palace is dominated by a broad canal, bordered by immaculately presented gardens. On the edge of the gardens is the Porcelain Factory, established in 1741, and one of the oldest factories of its type in Europe.

Behind the palace stretches the **Schlosspark**, an English-style country park dotted with lakes and various royal lodges. The most notable of these is François de Cuvilliés' **Amalienburg**, a hunting lodge with a lavish Rococo interior. Its highlight is the splendid Spiegelsaal (Hall of Mirrors). Joseph Effner, the principal architect of the palace's extensions, was also responsible for designing the **Pagodenburg**, used for entertaining, and the Baroque bathing house, the **Badenburg**. Also in the park is the **Magdalenenklause**, built as a hermitage for Maximilian Emmanuel, but not completed until after the Elector's death in 1725.

North of the palace, the **Botanischer Garten** (Botanical Garden) holds many rare and exotic species.

Facade of the splendid Schloss Nymphenburg, begun in the 17th century

The Beers of Germany

Although Germany produces many fine wines, it is for its beer that the country has won worldwide renown. Nowhere is the business of brewing and beer drinking taken so seriously as in Munich. Bavarians are probably the world's greatest consumers of beer, with an annual average intake of 240 liters per head. However, this figure is possibly inflated by the vast

Logo of the Paulaner brewery in Munich

quantities downed at the annual Oktoberfest, during which some 7 million lovers of beer converge on Munich for 16 days of revelry lasting from late September to early October. When traveling in Germany, make a point of trying the specialties of the local brewery, in a *Bierkeller* (beer cellar) or *Bierstube* (pub) in winter, and in summer in a *Biergarten* (beer garden).

The tankard *known as a* Mass *(measure) holds one liter, although German beer is always served with a considerable head on it. Waitresses at the Oktoberfest have no difficulty carrying eight or nine of these at once.*

PILSENER

The most widely drunk beer in Germany is Pils (short for Pilsener), a light lager-style beer produced by bottom-fermentation. This method was perfected in Pilsen (Plzeň in the Czech Republic) in the 19th century. Fermentation occurs at low temperatures, so takes longer than with other beers. The essential ingredients are barley, hops, and crystal-clear water. Two of the main breweries producing this kind of beer in Munich are Löwenbräu and Paulaner.

Munich's Oktoberfest *attracts so many visitors, a great tented village, with stalls, a funfair, and loud music, is set up on Theresienwiese, just to the west of the city center. This open space was where the marriage of King Ludwig was celebrated in 1810.*

OTHER GERMAN BEERS

Germany produces many varieties of beer, some of which are brewed only at certain times of year. Of these seasonal beers, it is worth trying spring beers such as the strong *Maibock*. Other interesting beers include dark styles – known as *Dunkelbier* or *Schwarzbier* – and *Weizenbier*, a beer made from wheat rather than barley. The Berlin version of the latter, *Berliner Weisse* (white beer), is served with fruit juice. Many local breweries have their own specialties. Bamberg is famous for its *Rauchbier*, which has a light smokiness. In the lower Rhine valley, *Altbier* is still produced; this is a top-fermented beer, prepared by traditional methods.

Berliner Weisse (wheat beer)

Dunkel-bier

Oktoberfest beer

St. Stephans Dom, Passau's imposing Baroque cathedral

Passau ⑪

🏛 50,000. 🚆 🚌 ⓘ Rathausplatz 3 (0851-95 59 80).

Passau lies on a peninsula between the Danube and the Inn, near the Austrian border. In 739 the Irish monk St. Boniface founded a major bishopric here. After two destructive fires in 1662 and 1680, the town was rebuilt by Italian architects, who left many fine Baroque buildings, including the cathedral, **St. Stephans Dom**. However, the town retains a medieval feel in its narrow alleys and archways. The Gothic town hall dates from the 14th and 15th centuries. Opposite it is the **Passauer Glasmuseum**, which has a fine collection of Bohemian, Austrian, and Bavarian glass. High above the Inn stands a pretty Baroque pilgrimage church, the **Wallfahrtskirche Mariahilf**.

Neuschwanstein ⑫

🚌 to Schwangau. **Tel** 08362-93 98 80. ◯ Oct–Mar: 10am–4pm daily; Apr–Sep: 9am–6pm daily. 🎟 📷 🚻 (limited access).

Set amid magnificent mountain scenery on the shores of the Alpsee, this fairy-tale castle was built in 1869–86 for the eccentric Bavarian King Ludwig II, to a design by the theater designer Christian Jank. Its pinnacled turrets have provided the inspiration for countless models, book illustrations, and film sets.

The walls of the vestibule and other rooms in the castle are lavishly covered with paintings depicting scenes from German myths and legends. The gilded interior of the throne room is reminiscent of a Byzantine basilica, while the dining room has intricately carved panels and fabulous pictures and furniture. The pale grey granite castle, which draws on a variety of historical styles, is a 20-minute walk from the village of Schwangau.

In the village itself is another castle, **Schloss Hohenschwangau**, built in 1832 by Maximilian, heir to the throne of Bavaria, over the ruins of a medieval castle. A tour of the Neo-Gothic castle gives a fascinating insight into the history of the Wittelsbach family, rulers of Bavaria from 1180 to 1918. There are also some fine 19th-century furnishings and the castle's terraced gardens afford magnificent views.

Gilded apse of the throne room, Neuschwanstein

🏰 **Schloss Hohenschwangau**
Tel 08362-819 80. ◯ daily.
◉ Dec 24. 🎟 📷

Lake Constance ⑬

🚉 Konstanz. 🚌 ⓘ Bahnhofsplatz 13, Konstanz (07531-13 30 30).

Lake Constance (in German, the Bodensee) lies on the borders of Germany, Austria, and Switzerland. The area surrounding the lake is one of the most attractive in Germany, in terms of both natural beauty and cultural heritage. The best time to visit is summer, when local fishermen stage colorful festivals and there are plenty of opportunities for water sports and cruises on the lake.

Konstanz (Constance) is the largest town in the region, and its main attraction is the magnificent 11th-century Romanesque cathedral. The town is in two parts: the old town (Altstadt) is a German enclave in Switzerland on the southern shore, while the newer part stands on a peninsula between the two main arms of the lake.

The many romantic old towns and beautiful islands of Lake Constance attract hordes of visitors every summer. The exquisite little town of **Meersburg** opposite Konstanz is a very popular destination. So too is **Mainau**, the "Island of Flowers." The most beautiful gardens on the island are in the park of the Baroque palace, built in 1739–46. At the northeastern (Bavarian) end of the lake, the medieval island town of **Lindau** is the major draw.

Lake Constance, with the Swiss Alps rising above the southern shore

Baden-Württemberg

Baden-Württemberg, which includes territories of the former Grand Duchy of Baden, is one of Germany's most popular tourist destinations. Its magnificent castles, luxurious resorts, and the beautiful recreation areas of the Black Forest guarantee a memorable vacation, while the region's long and turbulent history has given it a rich cultural and religious diversity. Germany's oldest university, Heidelberg, is also located in the region.

The Kaufhaus, Freiburg's historic merchants' meeting hall

Freiburg im Breisgau 🄸

🄸 197,000. 🚆 🚌 🄸 *Rotteckring 14 (0761-388 18 80).* 🎭 *Fasnet (end of carnival), Weintage (Jun).*

Freiburg is a natural gateway to the Black Forest. The counts von Zähringen first established the town in 1120, and since 1805 it has been part of Baden. From the Middle Ages, fast-flowing canals, or *bächle*, have run through the town, providing water to help extinguish the once frequent fires.

The **cathedral** was built in the 13th century in Gothic style. Münsterplatz, the picturesque cathedral square, is lined with houses from various architectural periods.

Completed in 1520, with ground-floor arcades and richly adorned gables, the **Kaufhaus** was used by merchants for meetings and conferences.

Black Forest 🄸

🚆 *to Freiburg.* 🚌 *to all towns.* 🄸 *Wehratalstraße 19, Todtmoos (07674- 906 00).* **www**.todtmoos.de

Densely planted with tall firs and spruces, the Black Forest (Schwarzwald) is one of Germany's most picturesque

regions. The area is famous for *Schwarzwälder Kirschtorte* (Black Forest gateau) and *Kirschwasser* (schnapps), as well as for its therapeutic spring waters.

Todtnau is a popular sports center and a base for hikers. Nearby, Hangloch-Wasserfall is one of the most magnificent waterfalls in the region.

The heart of the resort of **Todtmoos** is the Baroque pilgrimage church, which dates from the 17th–18th centuries. Popular dog-sled races are held annually in the town.

In the health resort of **St. Blasien** stands a Benedictine Abbey, founded in the 9th century. Its church (1783) is an excellent example of early Neoclassical style.

The main attraction of **Furtwangen** is its clock museum (Uhrenmuseum), which houses a collection of more than 4,000 chronometers.

In the open-air museum near the small town of **Gutach** visitors can see the Black Forest's oldest house – the 16th-century Vogtsbauernhof.

Rembrandt's *St. Paul in Prison* **(1627), Staatsgalerie, Stuttgart**

Stuttgart 🄸

🄸 586,000. ✈ 🚆 🚌
🄸 *Königstraße 1A (0711-222 820).*

Stuttgart grew from humble beginnings as a stud farm to become the ducal and royal capital of Württemberg. It is now one of the largest and most important towns of the Federal Republic. Beautifully situated among picturesque hills, the town is a major industrial and cultural center, with a world-famous ballet company, chamber orchestra, and splendid art collections.

When Württemberg castle burned down in 1311, the family seat was moved to Stuttgart. The ducal residence, the **Altes Schloss**, was given its present square layout in 1553–78. The palace now houses the Württembergisches Landesmuseum, which holds vast collections of decorative art and jewelry.

The Vogtsbauernhof in Gutach, the oldest house in the Black Forest

For hotels and restaurants in this region see pp574–9 and pp580–85

On the east side of Stuttgart's main square is a huge palace complex, the **Neues Schloss**, built in 1746–1807. The palace gardens have maintained much of their original charm, with neat avenues and impressive sculptures.

The **Staatsgalerie** grew from a fine art museum containing King Wilhelm I of Württemberg's private collection. Among the Old Masters on display are Rembrandt and Bellini, while modern artists include Monet, Picasso, and Modigliani.

A building exhibition held in 1927 left behind a complete housing estate, the **Weißenhofsiedlung**, which contains houses by Mies van der Rohe, Le Corbusier, Peter Behrens, and Hans Scharoun. Another must for all lovers of modern architecture, the **Liederhalle** congress center is a successful synthesis of tradition and modernism.

The **Linden Museum** is one of Germany's finest ethnology museums, containing exhibits from all over the world. Figures from the Indonesian theater of shadows and a 6th–8th-century mask from Peru are among the eclectic items on display.

To the east of the center is the famous **Mercedes-Benz-Museum**. Its splendid collection illustrates the development of the automobile with over 70 historic vehicles, all in immaculate condition. Stuttgart's other famous car manufacturer has created the **Porsche-Museum**, which includes around 50 examples of these high-speed, expensive vehicles.

Once an independent health resort, **Bad Cannstatt** is now a district of Stuttgart. Set in a beautiful park, it has a late-Gothic church, a Neoclassical town hall, and a *kursaal* (spa-house). One of its main attractions is the Neoclassical Schloss Rosenstein (1824–9).

🏛 **Staatsgalerie**
Konrad-Adenauer-Straße 30–32.
Tel 0711-470 400. ⬜ *Tue–Sun.*
🈂

🏛 **Mercedes-Benz-Museum**
Mercedesstraße 100. *Tel* 0711-173 00 00. ⬜ *Tue–Sun.*

Classic cars on display in the Mercedes-Benz-Museum, Stuttgart

Heidelberg ⓱

🏨 *139,000.* 🚉 🚌 ℹ️ *Willy-Brandt-Platz 1 (06221-194 33).*

Situated on the banks of the Neckar river, Heidelberg is one of Germany's most beautiful towns. For centuries it was a center of political power, with a lively and influential cultural life. In 1386, Germany's first university was established here by the Elector Ruprecht I. The construction of the town's palace began during his reign, continuing until the mid-17th century. However,

French incursions in the late 17th century totally destroyed medieval Heidelberg. The town was subsequently rebuilt in the 18th-century in Baroque style.

Towering over the town, the **Heidelberger Schloss** is a vast residential complex that was built and repeatedly extended between the 13th and 17th centuries. Originally a supremely well-fortified Gothic castle, it is now mostly in ruins.

The **Universitätsbibliothek** (University Library), erected in 1901–5, has one of the largest book collections in Germany, with over two million volumes.

The French Count Charles de Graimberg built up an extensive collection of fine drawings, paintings, arms, and other curios. His collection forms the core of the **Kurpfälzisches Museum**, which also has a fascinating archaeology section.

The Baroque domes of the **Heiliggeistkirche** are city landmarks. Former canons of the college were university scholars, and the church aisle features extensive galleries of books.

🏛 **Kurpfälzisches Museum**
Hauptstraße 97. *Tel* 06221-583 40 20. ⬜ *Tue–Sun (Wed: 10am–6pm).* 🈂

Heidelberger Schloss rising above Heidelberg's Alte Brücke (Old Bridge)

The Rhine and Mosel Valleys

The Rhine and Mosel Valleys offer a series of fairy-tale landscapes – spectacular gorges, rocky crags topped by romantic castles, and picturesque villages surrounded by vineyards producing excellent white wines. After flowing into Germany from France, the Mosel meanders between steep-sided banks to join the Rhine at Koblenz. South of Koblenz lies one of the most stunning stretches of the Rhine, which is also the birthplace of German myths such as the Lorelei and the *Nibelungenlied*, the great medieval epic poem of vengeance and honor.

The colorful portal of Trier's Kurfürstliches Schloss

Trier ⓲

Rhineland-Palatinate. 🏙 99,000.
🚉 🚌 🚹 *An der Porta Nigra (0651-97 80 80).* **www**.trier.de

Germany's oldest town, Trier was founded by the Emperor Augustus in 16 BC. Its monumental Roman gateway, the **Porta Nigra**, was built in the 3rd century AD. Among the city's other Roman relics are the **Aula Palatina**, a vast, austere building that served as the throne hall of Roman emperors and also as a church, the **Basilika und Kurfürstliches Schloss**. The basilica was built for Emperor Constantine around AD 305. In the 16th century part of it was incorporated into a Renaissance castle, later transformed into a Baroque palace for the archbishop-electors of Trier. The 4th-century **Kaisarthermen** (Imperial Baths) are also in the same building. A superb collection of Roman artifacts is held in the **Rheinisches Landesmuseum** close by.

🏛 **Rheinisches Landesmuseum**
Weimarer Allee 1. **Tel** 0651-977 40.
🕐 9:30am–5:30pm Tue–Sun. 🖼

Mosel Valley ⓳

🚹 *Am Gestade 6, Bernkastel-Kues (06531-50 01 90).* 🚌 *Hans Michels (06531-8222); Gebrüder Kolb, Briedern (02673-1515).*

On the stretch of the Mosel between Trier and Koblenz, romantic castles tower above extensive vineyards. Between May and October river trips are available all along the river – either short daytrips or longer cruises. However, progress can be slow because of the number of locks. A tour by car or bus is an attractive alternative. Two of the most popular excursions are from Trier to Bernkastel-Kues and from Koblenz to Cochem. Wine-tasting and eating play a big part in visitors' enjoyment of the region. Of the many castles that line the river be sure to visit **Burg Eltz** – the core of which has survived more or less intact since it was built in the 12th century – a short walk from the town of Wierschem.

⚓ **Burg Eltz**
🚌 *to Wierschem.* 🕐 *Apr–Oct: daily.* 🖼

Mainz ⓴

Rhineland-Palatinate. 🏙 190,000.
🚉 🚌 🚹 *Im Brückenturm am Rathaus (06131-28 62 10).*

Mainz enjoyed power and influence under the Holy Roman Empire, as the city's Archbishop was one of the Electors. The **Kaiserdom**, the Romanesque cathedral, dates back to the 11th century. Like others from this period it has a choir at each end – one for the emperor and one for the clergy. The nave is

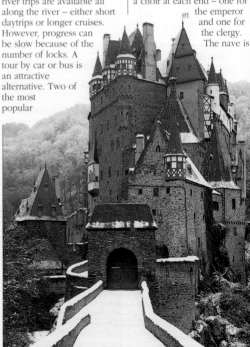

Burg Eltz, the most authentic and evocative castle in the Mosel Valley

pretty town on the left bank, and the striking white-walled island castle of **Pfalzgrafen-stein**, which levied tolls on passing ships until the mid-19th century. Past the town of Kaub on the right bank is the rock of the **Lorelei**, a legendary siren who lured sailors to their deaths with her song and her beauty. A modern statue marks the spot. Across the river is the town of **St. Goar**, dominated by the ruined Burg Rheinfels, blown up by French troops in 1797. **Burg Katz** offers one of the best-known views of the Rhine valley. At **Boppard** the attractions include the 13th-century Church of St. Severus and more spectacular views of the Rhine. Just south of Koblenz stands **Schloss Stolzenfels**, created in the early 19th century for King Friedrich Wilhelm IV. There are no bridges on this stretch of the river, but if you are exploring by car, there are ferries at various points along the route. However, the best way to enjoy the Rhine's magnificent scenery is by boat.

two rivers, stands a huge equestrian statue of Emperor Wilhelm I.

Florinsmarkt takes its name from the Romanesque-Gothic **Church of St. Florin**, which dates from the 12th century. Nestling among the square's historic buildings is the **Mittelrheinisches Museum**, with medieval art and archaeological collections.

The present appearance of the ruined **Alte Burg**, with its fine Renaissance facade, dates from the 17th century, but a fortress has stood on this site since the early Middle Ages.

Other sights of interest are the **Liebfrauenkirche**, which has a beautiful Gothic choir, the **Kurfürstliches Schloss** (the Electors' palace), and **Festung Ehrenbreitstein**, where the archbishops of Trier resided from 1648–1786.

Detail on tomb of Heinrich II, Maria Laach

Environs

Northwest of Koblenz, the Benedictine abbey of **Maria Laach** is a masterpiece of Romanesque architecture. It was begun in 1093 on the orders of Count Palatine Heinrich II, who lies buried here. The Paradise courtyard, meant to symbolize the Garden of Eden, resembles the Alhambra in Granada (see pp322–3).

🏛 Maria Laach
Off A61, 25 km (16 miles) NW of Koblenz. **Tel** 02652-590. 🚌 from Andernach or Niedermendig. ☐ daily.

The apse and towers at the east end of the Kaiserdom, Mainz

filled with the splendid tombs of the archbishops, ranging in date from the 13th to the 19th century. The **St. Gotthard-Kapelle** beside the cathedral was the private chapel of the archbishops. It has a fine 12th-century arcaded loggia.

Other attractions include the well-preserved old half-timbered houses of the **Kirschgarten** area and the Baroque **Kurfürstliches Schloss**, now a museum of Roman and other relics.

Mainz is also famous for the development in the 1440s by Johannes Gutenberg of printing with movable metal type. The **Gutenberg Museum** has a recreation of his studio and a copy of his famous 42-line Bible.

🏛 Gutenberg Museum
Liebfrauenplatz 5. **Tel** 06131-12 26 40. ☐ Tue–Sun. ● public hols.

Rhine Valley ㉑

🛈 Bahnhofplatz 17, Koblenz (0261-313 04). 🚢 K-D Linie, Konrad-Adenauer-Ufer, Koblenz (0261-310 30).

Cruises on the Rhine are available along much of its length, but the most scenic and popular stretch is the Rhine Gorge between Mainz and Bonn. The gorge starts at Bingen, where the Nahe joins the Rhine on its 1,320-km (825-mile) journey from Switzerland to the North Sea. Popular sights along the route include **Bacharach**, a

Koblenz ㉒

Rhineland-Palatinate. 🚶 109,300. 🚉 🛈 Bahnhofplatz 17 (0261-313 04), Jesuitenplatz (0261-13 09 20).

Koblenz stands at the confluence of the Mosel and Rhine rivers. On the **Deutsches Eck**, the spur of land between the

Burg Katz above the town of St. Goarhausen in the Rhine Gorge

Frankfurt's skyscraper district, nicknamed "Mainhattan"

Frankfurt am Main ㉓

Hesse. 🏛 660,000. ✈ 🚉 🚌 🚢
ℹ *Hauptbahnhof (069-21 23 88 00).*

Frankfurt am Main is one of the main economic and cultural centers of Europe. The headquarters of many major banks and newspaper publishers are based here, and the city's International Book Fair is the world's largest event of its kind.

Since 1878, the **Städelsches Kunstinstitut** has occupied a Neo-Renaissance building on Schaumainkai, the picturesque "museum embankment." The ground floor houses a collection of Dutch and German prints and drawings, the first floor

is devoted to 19th- and 20th-century art, and the second floor displays works by Old Masters such as Botticelli, van Eyck, Vermeer, and Rembrandt.

Another interesting museum in the Schaumainkai complex is the **Deutsches Architektur-museum**, which concentrates mainly on developments in 20th-century architecture.

Nearby is the **Deutsches Filmmuseum**, which holds documents and objects relating to the art of filmmaking and the development of film technology. The museum has its own cinema, which shows old and often long-forgotten films.

The great German poet, novelist, and dramatist Johann Wolfgang von Goethe was born at the **Goethehaus** in 1749. The house was totally destroyed in World War II, but later lovingly restored, its interior reconstructed in typical 18th-century style. The desk at which Goethe wrote his early works, such as *The Sorrows of Young Werther* (1774), remains.

Located in the center of the old town, the **Römer** is a collection of 15th- to 18th-century houses, including the Altes Rathaus (Old Town Hall), rebuilt after World War II. Opposite is a group of half-timbered houses, known as the **Ostzeile**.

On the banks of the Main stands **St. Leonhardkirche**, a fine example of Gothic and Romanesque architecture.

Built in stages in the 13th and 15th centuries, the church contains many treasures, including a copy of Leonardo da Vinci's *Last Supper* by Hans Holbein the Elder, from 1501.

The **Historisches Museum** has an interesting display of items relating to Frankfurt's history, including a fascinating model of the medieval town, a collection of local prehistoric finds, and several decorative fragments from buildings destroyed during World War II.

The twin-naved **Alte Nikolaikirche**, or Church of St. Nicholas, is popular with visitors for its fine statues of St. Nicholas and the 40-bell carillon, which plays German folk songs twice a day.

The **Kaiserdom**, an imperial cathedral, was built between the 13th and 15th centuries. It has several priceless masterpieces of Gothic artwork, including the 15th-century Maria-Schlaf-Altar.

Portrait of a Woman (c.1480) by Botticelli, Städelsches Kunstinstitut

The collection at the **Museum für Moderne Kunst** (Museum of Modern Art) represents all the major artistic trends from the 1960s until the present day, with works by Roy Lichtenstein and Andy Warhol.

The **Liebieghaus**, a museum of sculpture, has works ranging from antiquity through to Mannerism and Rococo. There are some superb examples of ancient Egyptian and Far Eastern art, as well as splendid works from the Middle Ages and the Renaissance.

🏛 **Städelsches Kunstinstitut**
Schaumainkai 63. *Tel* 069-605 09 80. ⭘ Tue–Sun. 🎨 📷

🏛 **Museum für Moderne Kunst**
Domstraße 10. *Tel* 069-21 23 04 47. ⭘ Tue–Sun. 🎨

Environs
Hanau, 30 km (19 miles) east of Frankfurt, is the birthplace of the brothers Wilhelm and Jakob Grimm. There is an exhibition devoted to their lives and work at the local historical museum.

The Ostzeile on the Römerberg, one of the symbols of Frankfurt

The Baroque Elector's palace, housing Bonn University

Bonn ㉔

North Rhine-Westphalia.
310,000.
Windeckstraße 1 (0228-77 50 00).

There has been a crossing over the Rhine at Bonn since pre-Roman times, but the settlement first rose to prominence under the Archbishops of Cologne in the 13th century. Bonn was the capital of the Federal Republic of Germany between 1949 and 1991.

The central market square is surrounded by a mixture of modern and Baroque architecture, including the late-Baroque **Rathaus** (Town Hall), built in 1737–8. Just north of the market square stands the 18th-century Baroque house where Beethoven was born. The **Beethovenhaus** is now a museum housing an impressive collection of memorabilia.

Bonn has many fine museums. The **Rheinisches Landesmuseum** has a vast collection of archaeological exhibits dating back to Roman times, as well as medieval and modern art. A Neanderthal skull is also exhibited here. The **Kunstmuseum Bonn**, a museum of modern art, has a superb display of Expressionist paintings.

Cologne ㉕

North Rhine-Westphalia.
1,005,000.
Fettenhennen 19 (0221-22 13 04 00).

Originally founded by the Romans, Cologne (Köln) is one of the oldest settlements in Germany. Present-day Cologne is an important ecclesiastical and cultural center, boasting 12 Romanesque churches and the famous cathedral (see pp562–3), as well as several excellent museums, historic buildings, and superb galleries.

The **Wallraf-Richartz-Museum** contains 14th- to 19th-century paintings organized by the schools of art they represent. Featured artists include Rubens, Dürer, Munch, and Max Liebermann.

Housing archaeological finds from Cologne and the Rhine Valley, the modern **Römisch-Germanisches Museum** displays Roman weapons, tools, and decorative objects, as well as the superb Dionysus mosaic from around 250 BC.

The **Museum Ludwig** boasts one of Europe's best collections of modern art. German Expressionists, Surrealists, and American Pop Artists are all represented.

The Romans built a sports arena on the site now occupied by the 12th-century **Groß St. Martin**. Remains of the baths have been uncovered underneath the crypt.

Cologne's **Rathaus** (Town Hall) is an irregular-shaped building, the result of successive modifications after 1330. Under a glass pyramid at the front are the remains of 12th-century Jewish baths.

Highlights of the late-Gothic **Church of St. Peter**, built in 1515–39, are its stained-glass windows and the magnificent *Crucifixion of St. Peter* (c.1637) by Peter Paul Rubens.

The southern chamber of the **Church of St. Ursula** is lined with many shrines. According to legend, they hold the remains of St. Ursula and 11,000 virgins, reputedly killed by the Huns.

🏛 **Wallraf-Richartz-Museum**
Obenmarspforten. *Tel* 0221-22 12 11 19. ⬜ *Tue–Sun.*

Skyline of Cologne, dominated by the spires of the Rathaus, Gross St. Martin, and the cathedral

Cologne Cathedral

The history of Germany's greatest Gothic cathedral is long and complicated. The foundation stone was laid on August 15, 1248, the chancel was consecrated in 1322, and building work continued until about 1520. The cathedral then stood unfinished until the 19th century, when the original Gothic designs were rediscovered. It was finally completed in 1842–80. Precious works of art include the fabulous Shrine of the Three Kings, the Altar of the Magi, and an early-Gothic carving of the Virgin Mary (c.1290) known as the Mailänder (Milanese) Madonna.

Mailänder Madonna

The north tower, at 157.38 m (516 ft), is slightly higher than the south tower.

Elaborately decorated pinnacles top the supporting pillars.

Main entrance

Buttresses support the entire bulk of the cathedral.

Cathedral Interior
The chancel, the ambulatory, and the chapels retain a large number of Gothic, mainly early 14th-century, stained-glass windows.

The Petrusportal is the only entrance built in the Middle Ages. Of the figures flanking the doorway, five were original Gothic statues, but these have been replaced by copies.

Englebert Reliquary (c.1630)
The treasury on the north side of the cathedral is famous for its large collection of gold objects, vestments, and the beautifully decorated liturgical books.

★ **Choir**
The massive oak stalls were built in 1308–11. They are backed by beautiful painted walls.

VISITORS' CHECKLIST

Kölner Dom. ◯ 6am–7:30pm daily. 🅿 **Domforum (Visitors' Center)** *Tel* 0221-92 58 47 30. **Treasury** Domkloster 4. *Tel* 0221-92 58 47 30. ◯ 10am–6pm daily. 🎟 🅿 **Tower** ◯ May–Sep: 9am–6pm; Oct–Apr 9am–4pm. 🎟

★ **Shrine of the Three Kings**
This huge Romanesque reliquary was made by Nikolaus von Verdun in 1181–1220, to hold the relics of the Three Kings. These were brought to Cologne from Italy in 1164 by Emperor Friedrich 1 Barbarossa.

High Altar
The Gothic altar dates back to the consecration of the chancel. The frieze depicts the Coronation of the Virgin Mary, flanked by the twelve Apostles.

★ **Altar of the City Patrons**
This magnificent altarpiece (c.1442) by Stephan Lochner depicts The Adoration of the Magi. *When the panels are closed, it shows* The Annunciation.

STAR FEATURES

★ Choir

★ Shrine of the Three Kings

★ Altar of the City Patrons

Northern Germany

Three federal states – Lower Saxony and the city-states of Hamburg and Bremen – occupy a huge swathe of northern Germany. Lower Saxony's capital, Hanover, has splendid architecture and fine museums. Hamburg and Bremen were wealthy Hanseatic trading towns, and today their ports still play an important role in city life. The region's other main attractions are the well-preserved medieval towns of Münster, in North Rhine-Westphalia, and Lübeck in Schleswig-Holstein.

The beautifully restored facade of Münster's Gothic Rathaus

Münster 26

🏛 280,000. ✈ 🚉 🛈 *Heinrich-Brüning-Straße 9 (0251-492 27 10).*

Münster's main sights of interest are located in the Altstadt, the historic heart of the city. The imposing Gothic **Rathaus** (Town Hall), carefully restored following damage during World War II, dates from the late 12th century. In 1648 the Treaty of Westphalia was signed here, ending the Thirty Years' War.

Münster's great cathedral, the **Dom St. Paulus**, on Domplatz, was built in 1225–65. Its best-known treasure is the astronomical clock (1540). Also on the square is the **Westfälisches Landes-museum**, which specializes in Gothic art. Nearby, the **Lambertikirche** (1375–1450) is a fine example of the hall-churches typical of Westphalia.

West of the center stands the **Residenzschloss**. Built in 1767–87, the splendid Baroque palace, now the headquarters of Münster's university, overlooks pleasant gardens.

Hanover 27

🏛 522,000. 🚉 🛈 *Ernst-August-Platz 8 (0511-12 34 51 11).*
🎡 *Schützenfest (Jun–Jul).*

Hanover (Hannover) is the capital of Lower Saxony, and for more than a century, from 1714 to 1837, shared a succession of rulers with Britain. Heavily bombed during World War II, the city has been largely rebuilt.

Among the city's finest landmarks are the grand **Opernhaus** (Opera House), built in Neoclassical style in 1845–57, and, on Tramm-platz, the **Neues Rathaus** (Town Hall), which dates from 1901–13 and combines Neo-Gothic and Secessionist detail. The latter's massive central dome offers fine views of the city.

On Marktplatz, in the old town, are many restored, 15th-century, half-timbered houses, as well as the **Markt-kirche St. Georg und St. Jacobus** with its 14th-century nave and fine Gothic altar.

One of Europe's best museums of modern art, the **Sprengel-Museum** holds works by Munch, Chagall, Picasso, and Christo. Also worth visiting is the **Niedersächsisches Landesmuseum**, whose picture gallery has German medieval and Renaissance paintings, Dutch and Flemish works by Rubens, Rembrandt, and van Dyck, and 19th- and 20th-century German art.

West of the city center, the **Herrenhauser Gärten** are among the most beautiful Baroque gardens in Germany.

🏛 **Sprengel Museum**
Kurt-Schwitters-Platz. **Tel** *0511-16 84 38 75.* ⏰ *Tue–Sun.* 📷
🏛 **Niedersächsisches Landesmuseum**
Willy-Brandt-Allee 5.
Tel *0511-980 7686.* ⏰ *Tue–Sun.*

Bremen 28

🏛 556,000. ✈ 🚉 🛈 *Am Bahnhofplatz 15 (0421-308 000).*

A member of the Hanseatic League from 1358, in the Middle Ages Bremen was a thriving seaport, trading in grain, wine, and salt. Today, the independent city-state still prospers from its port, Germany's second-largest.

Bremen's **Rathaus** (Town Hall), on Marktplatz, was built in 1405–10 and boasts a fine Renaissance facade, added to the original Gothic structure 200 years later. Opposite is the 11th-century Romanesque

Hanover's medieval quarter, with the Church of St. George and St. Jacobus

For hotels and restaurants in this region see pp574–9 and pp580–85

Attractive gabled houses and the statue of Roland in Bremen's Marktplatz

Dom, which contains some fine bas-reliefs. In Marktplatz itself stand a tall statue of Charlemagne's knight Roland (1404) and a sculpture of the *Musicians of Bremen* (1953), recalling the Grimm fairy tale.

Two museums of note are the **Kunsthalle**, with European art dating from the Middle Ages to the 20th century, and the **Focke Museum**, a museum of local history and decorative arts.

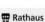

Rathaus
Marktplatz. ☐ for guided tours only (11am, noon, 3pm, 4pm) book at ℹ️ 🎧 🎥

Kunsthalle
Am Wall 207. **Tel** 0421-32 90 80. ☐ 10am–9pm Tue, 10am–6pm Wed–Sun.

Hamburg ㉙

🏛 1,700,000. ✈ 🚢 🚆 ℹ️ Hauptbahnhof, Kirchenallee (040-30 05 12 00).

For many years Hamburg, Germany's second largest city, was a leading member of the Hanseatic League and an independent trading town. In 1945 it became a city-state of the Federal Republic.

Hamburg sustained considerable damage during World War II, and little of the old town remains. The ruined tower of the Neo-Gothic **Nikolai-kirche** serves as a monument to the tragic consequences of war. Nearby, the **Jakobikirche** (1340) has been rebuilt in its original style. Inside is a massive 17th-century Baroque organ by Arp Schnitger. Another fine church is the Baroque **Michaeliskirche**, whose 132-m (433-ft) tower gives splendid views of the city.

Hamburg's Neo-Renaissance town hall, on the Rathausmarkt, is the fifth in the city's history. Just north of it is a large recreational lake, the Binnenalster. Also nearby, the prestigious **Kunsthalle** traces the history of European art from medieval times to the 20th century. The section devoted to the 19th-century German Romantics is especially good.

The best-known example of the city's collection of Expressionist buildings is Fritz Höger's **Chilehaus** (1922–4) in Kontorhausviertel.

Hamburg is the second largest port in Europe after Rotterdam, and a tour is

Triptych adorning the main altar in Hamburg's Jakobikirche

highly recommended. There are two museum ships moored here: the freighter *Cap San Diego* and the sailing boat *Rickmer Rickmers* (1896).

Kunsthalle
Glockengießerwall. **Tel** 040-428 13 12 00. ☐ Tue–Sun.

Port
Ⓤ Baumwall or St-Pauli-Landungsbrücken. **Cap San Diego Tel** 040-36 42 09. ☐ daily. **Rickmer Rickmers Tel** 040-319 59 59. ☐ daily.

Lübeck's 15th-century Holstentor, on the western edge of the town

Lübeck ㉚

🏛 215,000. 🚆 ℹ️ Holstentorplatz 1 (0451-409 1950).

The most important town in the Baltic basin at the end of the Middle Ages, Lübeck is known for its wealth of superb medieval architecture.

The city's 13th-century **Marienkirche** (St. Mary's Church), boasts the highest vaulted brick nave in the world. A short walk away, the turreted **Rathaus** (Town Hall) dates from 1226 and is a fine example of Lübeck's distinctive Gothic brick architecture. The Gothic **Dom** (Cathedral) was begun in 1173. Nearby, the **St.-Annen-Museum** has historical artifacts dating from the 13th to the 18th centuries. Another famous monument is the **Holstentor** (1466–78), the western gateway to the city.

The **Buddenbrook-Haus** is a museum devoted to the great writers Thomas and Heinrich Mann, whose family lived here in 1841–91.

Buddenbrook-Haus
Heinrich-und-Thomas-Mann-Zentrum, Mengstrasse 4. **Tel** 0451-122 4192. ☐ daily. ● Dec 24, 25 & 31. 🎥

Practical Information

Germany is renowned as a safe, clean, and efficient country to visit. Travelers will find that every town has a helpful tourist information center offering advice on restaurants, attractions, and activities. Larger cities also have Internet web sites which give up-to-the-minute information. Hotels are plentiful but may be busy during the festivals and fairs which occur throughout the year in different parts of the country.

WHEN TO VISIT

The climate in Germany is pleasantly temperate. Cities and historic monuments are best visited in spring or early fall, particularly in the south of the country where it can be very warm. July and August are ideal months for a restful holiday by the sea, in the lake districts or in the mountains. In Bavaria during the second half of September and early October the Oktoberfest takes place. This is an annual beer-drinking event which is open to all visitors. In December everybody is preoccupied with Christmas shopping, while during winter, skiing is a popular pursuit in the Black Forest, the Alps, and the Harz Mountains. The roads are busiest during the school holidays, dates of which vary from state to state, and during the "long weekends" at Easter, Whitsun, and other national public holidays.

VISA REQUIREMENTS AND CUSTOMS

Citizens of countries that are members of the EU, as well as citizens from the US, Canada, Australia, and New Zealand, do not need a visa to visit Germany, so long as their stay does not exceed three months. Visitors from South Africa must have a visa. Visitors from EU countries do not require a passport to enter Germany, as long as they have a national ID card.

Drugs, animals, animal products, such as cured meats, and exotic plants under special protection are totally prohibited from importation into Germany. Regulations also restrict the importation of cigarettes and wine.

PERSONAL SECURITY

As in other countries, visitors are far safer in small towns and villages than in big cities, where extra care must be taken against street theft – particularly when traveling on public transport during the rush hour. Pickpockets tend to frequent popular tourist sights and any events where large groups of people gather. It is worth using a money belt to conceal your money and documents. Also keep cameras and audio equipment out of sight. Better still, leave valuable items in the hotel safe.

POLICE

German police uniforms and signs are mostly blue (they are green in Bavaria and the Saarland, but otherwise blue). Look out for motorized police units, the *Verkehrspolizei*, which are concerned with safety on the streets, roads, and highways, and are distinguished by their white caps. Certain town police have navy-blue uniforms and their job is to catch motorists for parking offences for which they can impose an on-the-spot fine. Remember that you should carry ID such as a passport, driving license or student card with you at all times.

PHARMACIES

Look out for the stylized letter "A" (*Apotheke*) which indicates a pharmacy. They are usually open from 8am to 6pm; in small towns they close between 1 and 3pm. In larger towns there is always a rota and this is displayed in the window of each pharmacy with a note of addresses. Information on rota pharmacies may also be obtained from tourist offices.

ACCIDENTS AND EMERGENCIES

If you have an accident or a serious breakdown on the motorway, it is best to use one of the special telephones that are situated at regular intervals along the hard shoulder. Throughout the country a special emergency

THE CLIMATE OF GERMANY

Germany lies in a temperate climatic zone. In the north, with marine influences predominating, summers tend to be quite cool and winters mild, with relatively high rainfall. In the eastern part of the country, however, the climate is more continental and this produces harsher winters and hotter summers. Germany's highest rainfall and lowest temperatures are recorded in the Alps.

BERLIN

	Apr	Jul	Oct	Jan
°C/F		23/73		
	13/56	12/54	14/57	
0°C 32°F	3/37		3/37	1/34
				-5/23
☀	6 hrs	8 hrs	4 hrs	2 hrs
☂	24 mm	60 mm	41 mm	31 mm
month	Apr	Jul	Oct	Jan

MUNICH

	Apr	Jul	Oct	Jan
°C/F		23/73		
	14/57	11/53	13/56	
0°C 32°F	3/37		3/37	2/36
				-5/23
☀	5 hrs	8 hrs	5 hrs	2 hrs
☂	56 mm	99 mm	48 mm	46 mm
month	Apr	Jul	Oct	Jan

number, 110, is answered by an operator who will inform the appropriate emergency services. This number is free on all telephones, including mobiles. If you lose your passport, you should go to your consulate.

TOURIST INFORMATION

A well-developed network of tourist information centers exists in Germany. These are usually run by the city or regional tourist authorities, *Verkehrsamt*. They provide advice on accommodations, addresses, and opening hours of monuments, museums, tours, and excursions, as well as brochures covering the most important tourist attractions. They may also be able to find and book you a hotel room.

OPENING HOURS

The opening hours of stores, offices, and most other businesses depend to a great extent on the size of the town. In larger cities, office hours are usually from 9am until 6pm, and larger shops are open from 9am to 8pm weekdays, and until 6pm on Saturday. Banks operate shorter hours: 9am–3:30pm Monday–Friday, with a lunchbreak between noon and 1pm. They usually stay open later one evening a week until 6pm. Some new shopping malls are open on Sundays. In smaller towns, not much tends to open before 10am, and many businesses close from 1–2pm for lunch, on Saturday afternoons, Sundays and public holidays.

DISABLED TRAVELERS

There are ramps or lifts for people confined to wheelchairs at large museums and major historical sites. Banks are also accessible by wheelchair and there are lifts at railroad stations and larger underground stations. Some public transport is adapted to take wheelchairs. Most higher grade hotels have suitably equipped bedrooms. Public restroom facilities in parking lots, train stations, and airports usually have suitable cubicles. For information contact **Bundesverband Selbsthilfe Körperbehinderter (BSK)**.

COMMUNICATIONS

As everywhere in Europe, the introduction of mobile phones has brought about a revolution in telephone usage. Visitors wishing to use their mobile phone in Germany should contact their service provider for information. The number of payphones taking coins is constantly dwindling, and a telephone card gives better value for money. They can be bought at post offices and most newsagents. Other phones are operated by credit card only. These phones have their own phone number, so you can arrange to be called back.

Post offices are usually open from 6am–8pm on weekdays and from 8am–noon on Saturdays. Stamps can be bought at post offices as well as stamp machines, and are sometimes sold along with postcards.

BANKING AND CURRENCY

Germany has used the euro since 2002 *(see p15)*. Foreign currency can be changed at banks, most hotels, or bureau de change *(Wechselstube)*.

DIRECTORY

TOURIST INFORMATION

German National Tourist Office
Tel 069-97 46 40.
www.germany-tourism.de

Berlin
Am Karlsbad 11, 10785 Berlin.
Tel 030-25 00 25.
www.visitberlin.de

Frankfurt am Main
Hauptbahnhof Empfangshalle,
60329 Frankfurt am Main.
Tel 069-21 23 88 00.
www.frankfurt-tourismus.de

Munich
Marienplatz, Rathaus,
80331 Munich.
Tel 089-2339 6500.
www.muenchen-tourist.de

Stuttgart
Königstraße 1a,
70173 Stuttgart.
Tel 0711-222 80.
www.stuttgart-tourist.de

EMBASSIES

Australia
Wallstraße 76–79,
10179 Berlin.
Tel 030-880 08 80.
Fax 030-88 00 88 210.
www.australian-embassy.de

Canada
Leipziger Platz 17, 10117 Berlin. *Tel 030-20 31 20.*
Fax 030-20 31 25 90.
www.kanada-info.de

New Zealand
Friedrichstraße 60,
10117 Berlin.
Tel 030-20 62 10.
Fax 030-20 62 11 14.
www.nzembassy.com/germany

South Africa
Tiergartenstraße 18,
12683 Berlin.
Tel 030-22 07 30.
Fax 030-22 07 31 90.
www.suedafrika.org

UNITED KINGDOM

Embassy
Wilhelmstraße 70,
10117 Berlin.
Tel 030-20 45 70.
Fax 030-20 45 75 74.
www.britischebotschaft.de

Consulate
Neuer Jungfernstieg 20,
20354 Hamburg.
Tel 040-448 32 30.
Fax 040-343 122.

UNITED STATES

Embassy
Clayallee 170,
14195 Berlin.
Tel 030-83050.
Fax 030-8305 2050.
www.usembassy.de

Consulate
Königinstraße 5,
80539 Munich.
Tel 089-288 80.
Fax 089-280 99 98.

EMERGENCY NUMBERS

Police and Fire services
Tel 110 or 112.

Ambulance
Tel 19222 or 112.

DISABLED TRAVELERS

Mobility International
North America.
Tel 541-343 1284.

Bundesverband Selbsthilfe Körper-behinderter (BSK)
Postfach 20,
74238 Krautheim.
Tel 06294-42810.
www.bsk-ev.org

Travel Information

Traveling to and around Germany is fast and easy. In every large city there is an airport, and most of these offer international connections. The whole of Germany is linked by a dense network of highways, while the main roads are of a high standard and well signposted. Train travel throughout the country is comfortable and reliable; for longer journeys it is worth taking advantage of the fast connections offered by InterCityExpress (ICE). Buses are also comfortable and efficient and can be essential in rural areas that cannot be reached by train. Large cities have tram, bus, and sometimes subway services.

ARRIVING BY AIR

Germany's most important airports are Berlin, Frankfurt am Main, Munich and Düsseldorf. You can get connecting flights from these to other cities such as Hamburg and Stuttgart. The country's national airline is **Lufthansa**, which flies between Germany and most of the world's major destinations. From the UK, flights are operated by **BA** and **BMI**. **Ryanair**, **Air Berlin**, and **easyJet** all offer cheaper alternatives as well.

There are frequent flights from the US to Germany, mainly to Munich and Frankfurt, which is Germany's largest airport and one of the busiest in Europe. Direct flights are available from many major US cities.

Although Canada does not have many direct flights to Germany, **Air Canada** operates a regular flight from Toronto to Frankfurt and its subsidiary Canadian Airlines flies from Vancouver to Frankfurt.

DOMESTIC FLIGHTS

In addition to Lufthansa, there are a number of smaller airlines in Germany including **Air Berlin**, which may offer cheaper fares than Lufthansa on internal routes, as well as providing air links with small airports, such as Augsburg, Dortmund, and Erfurt.

BORDER CROSSINGS

There are many crossings into Germany and provided that you carry the necessary documents and your car does not look disreputable, you should experience a minimum of delay and formalities at the border. There are limits on the amount of duty-free items that can be brought in by non-EU citizens (see p13).

TRAVELING BY CAR

The fastest and most comfortable way to travel around the country is by road. Germany's excellent network of toll-free highway routes guarantees fast journeys over long distances, while a well-maintained system of good smaller roads means that many interesting places throughout the country are within easy reach. On smaller roads and in remote areas, filling stations may be few and far between.

The German *Autobahn* (highway) network is extensive. An *Autobahn* is indicated by the letter "A" followed by a number – some also have a letter "E" and a number, denoting that the road crosses the German border. They are all toll-free and have regularly spaced filling stations, as well as parking lots with restrooms, restaurants, and motels. A *Bundesstraße* (main road) has the letter "B" and a number.

In the event of an accident on an *Autobahn*, or if sudden traffic congestion means you have to brake hard, drivers should turn on their flashing emergency lights to warn drivers behind of the danger. Along the hard shoulder there are yellow poles with emergency buttons, which can be used to call for help if you have a breakdown or an accident. The two automobile associations **Allgemeiner Deutscher Automobil Club (ADAC)** and **Automobilclub von Deutschland (AvD)** offer roadside assistance.

RULES OF THE ROAD

In Germany, the same road traffic regulations apply as in most European countries. The car must carry a plate indicating country of origin, and be equipped with a red warning triangle for use in case of breakdown.

The wearing of seatbelts is compulsory and children under 12 must sit in the back, with babies and toddlers secured in child-seats.

Driving after drinking a small amount of alcohol is allowed, but if you have an accident, the consequences will be more severe if a breathalyzer shows alcohol in your blood.

In built-up areas the speed limit is 50 km/h (31 mph); beyond this it is 100 km/h (62 mph), and on highways there is no limit, of which many drivers take full advantage. When traveling with a caravan or camping trailer outside built-up areas, drivers should not exceed 70 km/h (44 mph), and on highways 100 km/h (62 mph). Road traffic police are strict about imposing fines for speeding. Drivers can also be fined for driving too close to the vehicle in front and for parking in prohibited areas.

PARKING IN TOWNS

Finding a place to park is not easy: it is often best to use a multi-level parking lot, which is indicated by *"Parkhaus"*; a sign with the word *"Frei"* indicates that spaces are available. It is never worth leaving your car in a prohibited area. If you do risk it, a traffic warden may find your car, immediately impose a fine and arrange for the car to be towed away. Retrieving your car is then expensive and difficult.

Cars left in a parking zone must either display a parking ticket or be at a meter.

TRAVELING BY TRAIN

Traveling around Germany by train is not the cheapest form of transport, but it is undoubtedly one of the most efficient. Trains operated by **Deutsche Bahn**, the German rail company, are renowned for their punctuality, safety, and cleanliness. The fastest are InterCityExpress (ICE) trains; these are aerodynamically designed, painted white, with air-conditioning in the coaches and airline-style seats. Unfortunately, there is not much room for luggage. These trains can travel at more than 200 km/h (125 mph), which means that a journey from Hamburg to Munich takes just under six hours. ICE trains operate on just a few routes linking the largest cities. The InterCity (IC) trains, which stop only at certain stations, are cheaper but still offer an express service. For short distances, it is best to take the Regional Express (RE) trains. The S-Bahn (short for *Schnellbahn*) is a fast commuter rail network which operates in some of the major German cities.

TRAIN FARES

Train fares in Germany are quite expensive and there is a compulsory surcharge (*Zuschlag*) for express train travel. It is not usually necessary to reserve seats, but in the high season this is a good idea and it does not cost a lot. If you are staying for some time and want to use trains frequently, one way to travel more cheaply is to buy a *BahnCard*. After an initial hefty outlay, this gives you a 50 percent discount on rail tickets for a whole year.

CITY TRANSPORT

Several major cities in Germany, including Berlin, Hamburg, Munich, and Nuremberg, have a network of fast connections by subway (*U-Bahn*). *U-Bahn* stations are indicated by square signs with a white "U" on a dark blue background, while *S-Bahn* stations have round signs with a white "S" on a green background. The *U-Bahn* offers very frequent services – at peak hours trains normally run every 3–5 minutes – and stations are only a short distance from each other. The *S-Bahn* trains are less frequent and the stations are farther apart.

In some cities (especially in eastern Germany) trams are the most common method of travel; in some cities they also have underground sections. Trams are ideal urban transport because they do not get stuck in traffic jams. You can use the same tickets as on buses and the *S-Bahn*. When they are above ground, remember that trams have right of way.

Various types of ticket can be bought from machines located by the entrance to stations. Children under six travel free while those under 14 get a reduced rate.

TRAVELING BY BUS

There is a good network of inter-city bus services in Germany, though journeys are generally no cheaper than traveling by train. Most towns have a *Zentraler Omnibus Bahnhof* (ZOB) close to the train station. Most bus services originate here and you can also get timetables and buy your tickets here.

CYCLING TOURS

Cycling is a slow but environmentally friendly means of getting around. It also enables you to combine sightseeing with physical exercise. It is easy to rent bikes in some tourist areas, particularly at main train stations from April to October. Bikes can be taken on trains, on the *U-Bahn*, and the *S-Bahn*. For cycling routes, you will find that many newsstands, bookstores, and tourist offices have excellent maps.

DIRECTORY

AIRLINES

Air Berlin
www.airberlin.com

Air Canada
Tel 069-27 11 51 11.
www.aircanada.ca

American Airlines
US: *Tel 800-433 7300.*
Frankfurt: *Tel 069-5098 5070.* www.AA.com

BMI
www.flybmi.com

British Airways
UK: *Tel 0844-493 0787.*
Frankfurt: *Tel 01805-26 65 22.* www. britishairways.com

Delta Air Lines
US: *Tel 800-221 12 12.*
Berlin: *Tel 030-230 9400.*
www.delta.com

easyJet
www.easyjet.com

Lufthansa
US: *Tel 800-645 3880.*
Berlin: *Tel 01805-83 84 26.*
www.lufthansa.com

Qantas
Frankfurt: *Tel 01805-25 06 20.* www.qantas.com

Ryanair
www.ryanair.com

United Airlines
US: *Tel 800-241 6522.*
Frankfurt: *Tel 069-50 07 03 87.* www. unitedairlines.de

AIRPORT INFORMATION

Berlin Schönefeld
Tel 0180-500 01 86.

Frankfurt am Main
Tel 0180-53 72 46 36.

Munich
Tel 089-97 52 13 13.

CAR RENTAL

Avis
Tel 01805-21 77 02.
www.avis.com

Hertz
Tel 0180-533 35 35.
www.hertz.com

Sixt Rent-a-Car
Tel 0180-525 25 25.
www.sixt.com

EMERGENCY SERVICES

ADAC
Tel 01802-222 222.

AvD
Tel 069-660 60.

TRAIN TRAVEL

Deutsche Bahn
National Rail Inquiries:
Tel 0180 599 6633.

Shopping

Stores in Germany are generally of high quality but many products are not cheap. In Berlin almost anything can be bought, so long as you know where to look; outside Berlin, you'll discover that in many areas of the country the tradition of producing handicrafts and various types of folk art continues. A visit to a local market could give you the chance to buy a regional specialty to take home as a souvenir. The vast shopping malls that are springing up in every large city offer a wide choice of stores and top-quality brands.

MARKETS

A weekly market, known as a *Wochenmarkt*, is held in many towns throughout Germany. In smaller towns, stalls are set up in the market square, while in larger towns and cities markets may be held in specially designated squares in different neighborhoods. At these markets, you can buy fresh fruit and vegetables, cheeses, and many everyday items. Specialist fairs are often held at weekends – for example *Blumenmärkte*, where flowers are sold, or *Kunstmärkte*, where artists and craftsmen display their work for sale.

Every large town also has its *Flohmarkt* (fleamarket) where, among the masses of junk, pieces of amusing kitsch and genuine antiques can sometimes be found. In Berlin the **Antik-und Trödelmarkt** is worth a visit.

In Munich there is a famous market specializing in crafts, antiques, and hardware called **Auer Dult**. This is held during the last weeks of April, July, and October.

REGIONAL SPECIALTIES

Almost every state in Germany produces its own regional specialty and although you might not be able to take certain fresh foods back home, you could try them while you are visiting. For example, Lübeck is known for marzipan, while Nuremberg is synonymous with gingerbread. The Spreewald region is known for its pickled cucumbers, while you'll find the cherry jam produced in the Black Forest region is excellent. In Friesland and Schleswig in the north, marinated herrings and excellent cheeses are worth trying. The hams of Westphalia have a well-deserved reputation, as do sausages from Braunschweig (Brunswick).

GIFTS AND SOUVENIRS

Just about every region of Germany has something special to offer. You could buy a beer stein from a beer hall, or a cuckoo clock from the Black Forest, for instance. If you are keen on dressing up, traditional clothes such as lederhosen and dirndl skirts can be found in Bavaria. For children, handmade puppets and marionettes are good gifts, while in Nuremberg there is a wide selection of toys. Don't forget that German optical items such as cameras, binoculars, and lenses are top quality and may be cheaper than at home.

ALCOHOLIC DRINKS

Renowned German beers are best drunk straight from the barrel, but it is also worth looking out for the bottled beers that are rarely seen outside Germany.

There are a number of fine German wines, especially those from vineyards in the Mosel and Rhine valleys. Excellent wines are also produced in Bavaria and Baden-Württemberg.

Various types of spirits, as well as herbal and root-flavored liqueurs and bitters, are produced on a large scale. If you visit a monastery you may be able to buy a bottle of a herbal infusion or a liqueur that is made to a centuries-old recipe.

SHOPPING IN BERLIN

Although German cities all boast shopping malls and every town has a shopping district popular with local residents, Berlin stands out with its choice and quality of shops. If it is luxury you want, you must head for the large stores on the Kurfürstendamm, Friedrichstraße, and Potsdamer Platz, where all the major fashion houses and perfume makers have their stores. Alternatively, if you want to explore the smaller boutiques of lesser-known designers, make your way to Berlin's Hackescher Markt in the Mitte district, or to Prenzlauer Berg.

Kaufhaus des Westens, better known as **KaDeWe** in Wittenbergplatz, is the biggest and the best department store in Berlin. Only products of the highest quality are sold in these luxurious halls, where virtually everything you need is on sale – from unusual perfumes and elegant underwear to *haute couture*, all sold in a system of stores-within-stores. The food hall on the sixth floor is legendary for its restaurant overlooking Tauentzienstrasse.

Galeries Lafayette on Friedrichstraße is nothing less than a slice of Paris placed in the heart of Berlin. Its perfumes, household items, and clothing attract an enormous clientele, many of whom also visit the food counter, which offers a wide range of French specialties. An extraordinary glass cone rises through the middle of the store, reflecting the interiors of the stores.

Another very popular store is **Karstadt** on the Kurfürstendamm. Although its range of goods is not as broad as that at Galeries Lafayette, there is still an enormous choice and its top-floor restaurant offers excellent views over the city.

New shopping malls are being opened all the time, usually situated conveniently close to S-Bahn stations. *Passagen* (arcades) are massive three-level structures, resembling huge arcaded passageways, which contain an enormous number of stores, ranging from supermarkets and pharmacies to bars, fashion outlets, and bookstores. Like most of the stores in Berlin, they stay open until 8pm during the week and are open on Sundays.

One of the newest shopping malls is the **Potsdamer Platz Arkaden**. Built in October 1998 this is now very popular both as a shopping mall and a meeting place for Berliners and visitors.

The **Gesundbrunnen-Center** is the biggest shopping arcade in Berlin, and has countless stalls and tables offering every kind of bargain. A large number of bars also makes this a popular place to meet friends for a beer or a coffee.

SHOPPING IN OTHER CITIES

Most shoppers in Munich make a beeline for the pedestrian precinct in the old town center between Karlsplatz and Marienplatz. Here you will find many big department stores such as **Ludwig Beck am Rathauseck** and chain stores where you can buy fashion and shoes as well as jewelry, souvenirs, and music.

For haute couture in Munich, the big-name stores are concentrated in these streets: Maximilianstrasse, Theatinerstrasse, Residenzstrasse, and Briennerstrasse.

The place to shop for food in Munich is the colorful **Viktualienmarkt** near Marienplatz. This has been the city's main food market for over 200 years.

The largest and most interesting shopping area in Frankfurt is the Zeil, while in Hamburg it is the Alsterhaus. Hamburg also prides itself on its many fine shopping arcades, several of which are covered and heated, making them ideal for window shopping.

CERAMICS AND GLASS

Porcelain made by Meissen is among the most sought-after in the world but it is expensive. Meissen porcelain can be found in the town itself at the **Staatliche Porzellan-Manufaktur** *(see p543)* or in several shops situated along the popular Kurfürstendamm in Berlin. Munich's **Porzellan Manufaktur Nymphenburg**, which has a factory and a shop in the grounds of Schloss Nymphenburg *(see*

p553), produces china of similarly exquisite quality. Berlin's **KPM** (Königliche Porzellan-Manufaktur), which has been in operation for over 250 years, also makes excellent porcelain.

German glassware is renowned. Old glassworks in Saxony and Bavaria still make glassware by traditional techniques: for example, beautifully cut and polished crystal tableware and ruby-colored glassware.

Some porcelain and glass-ware factories operate retail outlets with showrooms. Visitors can arrange to have purchases sent to their home.

BOOKSTORES

When you need a book in English or an American newspaper, **Buchexpress** is the place to go in Berlin. In Munich, look for the **Words'Worth** and **Geobuch** for good maps and guides. In Frankfurt try the **British Bookshop**.

The **Bücherbogen** chain offers a huge choice of books and has several outlets in Berlin and elsewhere; the one under the S-Bahn bridge near Savignyplatz in Berlin has the largest stock.

DIRECTORY

MARKETS

Antik-und Trödelmarkt
Ostbahnhof, Erich-Steinfurth-Straße, Berlin.
◯ *9am–5pm Sun.*

Auer Dult
Mariahilfplatz, Munich.
◯ *last weeks of Apr, Jul & Oct.*

SHOPPING IN BERLIN

Galeries Lafayette
Französische Straße 23, Berlin.
Tel *030-20 94 80.*

Gesundbrunnen-Center
Badstraße 4, Berlin.
Tel *030-493 00 00.*

KaDeWe
Tauentzienstraße 21–24, Berlin. **Tel** *030-212 10.*

Karstadt
Kurfürstendamm 231, Berlin.
Tel *030-88 00 33 00.*

Potsdamer Platz Arkaden
Alte Potsdamer Straße 7, Berlin. **Tel** *030-255 92 70.*

SHOPPING IN OTHER CITIES

Ludwig Beck am Rathauseck
Am Marienplatz 11, Munich.
Tel *089-23 69 10.*

Viktualienmarkt
Peterplatz–Frauenstraße, Munich. ◯ *Mon–Sat.*

CERAMICS AND GLASS

KPM
Wegelystraße 1, Berlin.
Tel *030-39 00 90.*

Porzellan Manufaktur Nymphenburg
Schloss Nymphenburg, Nördliches Schloßrondell 8, Munich.
Tel *089-179 19 70.*

Odeonsplatz 1, Munich.
Tel *089-28 24 28.*

Staatliche Porzellan-Manufaktur
Talstraße 9, Meissen.
Showroom ◯ *9am–6pm (Nov–Apr: to 5pm).*
Tel *03521-4680.*

BOOKSTORES

British Bookshop
Börsenstraße 17, Frankfurt am Main.
Tel *069-28 04 92.*

Bücherbogen
Savignyplatz, Berlin.
Tel *030-31 86 95 11.*

Buchexpress
Unter den Eichen 57, Berlin.
Tel *030-831 40 04.*

Geobuch
Rosental 6, Munich.
Tel *089-26 50 30.*

Words'Worth
Schellingstraße 3, Munich.
Tel *089-280 9141.*

Entertainment

With so much on offer in Germany, it is possible to indulge just about any taste, whether you are looking for avant-garde theater and performance art, atmospheric clubs, or prestigious music festivals. Outside Berlin the larger cosmopolitan cities, such as Munich and Frankfurt, also offer a wide range of entertainment, from classical drama to eclectic nightclubs, from grand opera to discos.

ENTERTAINMENT LISTINGS

Tourist information centers offer basic information in every city and town, but the most comprehensive guides are in the local press and listings magazines. In Berlin there are *Tip* and *Zitty*, which are published every other Wednesday. The daily *Berliner Morgenpost* publishes its supplement *bm Live* on Fridays, while *Ticket* comes out on Wednesdays, together with *Tagesspiegel*.

Useful listing magazines in Munich are *In München* and *Münchener Stadtmagazin*. There is also a monthly review in English called *Munich Found*, available from the Tourist Office. You can get a monthly jazz magazine called *Münchener Jazz-Zeitung* in music shops and at jazz cafés and clubs.

In Frankfurt a magazine detailing events called *Prinz* is on sale from news kiosks. There are also free publications such as *Fritz*, while the *Frankfurter Woche* is available for the tourist office for a small sum.

BOOKING TICKETS

Theater and concert tickets can usually be booked up to two weeks in advance, and you can buy directly at the box office or by telephone. Reserved tickets must be picked up and paid for at least half an hour before the performance. For many performances in Berlin you can also pre-book tickets at **Ticket Online**.

One Berlin agency that specializes in last-minute ticket purchase is **Hekticket Theaterkassen** on Hardenbergstraße, where you

can get tickets on the day, even up to as little as an hour before a show. These tickets are usually sold at a 50 percent discount.

Students, senior citizens, and the disabled are entitled to a 50 percent discount on tickets, for which they must present proof of their status.

THEATER

As you would expect in the land of Goethe and Schiller, theatrical traditions are very strong in Germany. Almost every large town has a good local theater. Berlin's most famous theater is the magnificent **Berliner Ensemble**, which was once managed by Bertold Brecht. The **Deutsches Theater** offers an ambitious program, while the **Volksbühne** stages works by young playwrights. Munich has many theaters, with most of the productions in German. A venerable venue is the **Cuvilliéstheater** in the Residenz (*see pp548–9*), while the **Deutsches Theater** offers some foreign plays. The **Kammerspiele** is dedicated to contemporary works.

Frankfurt has a theater that offers productions in English, aptly called the **English Theatre**. You will find a range of old and new plays put on at the city's main theater, the **Schauspiel Frankfurt**.

CLASSICAL MUSIC AND DANCE

Berlin has one of the finest orchestras in the world — the Berlin Philharmonic Orchestra, whose home, the **Philharmonie**, is also one of the world's most beautiful concert halls. The city boasts three opera houses: the **Staatsoper Unter den Linden**

and the **Komische Oper** are in the eastern part of city, while the **Deutsche Oper Berlin** is in the west. The three opera houses have ballet programs built into their repertoires and these are performed largely by resident dance companies.

Munich has two opera houses and several distinguished resident orchestras. A visit to the **Bayerische Staatsoper** is a must if you appreciate grand opera and ballet. The **Gasteig** is a modern complex offering a range of classical concerts, large and small. Munich's **Prinzregententheater** is the main venue for ballet and other musical performances.

Frankfurt has a wide choice of musical events. At the **Alte Oper**, there are three halls for orchestral and vocal performances, while the **Jahrhunderthalle** also offers classical recitals and concerts.

JAZZ, ROCK, AND POP

Berlin is always a popular destination for world-famous musicians, whose concerts are often held in the **Waldbühne**. Numerous music clubs offer daily opportunities to hear good music. Favorite venues are **Quasimodo** in the western part of the city center, **Schlot** in Prenzlauer Berg and **Junction Bar** in Kreuzberg. Good traditional jazz can be heard at Berlin's annual Jazzfest in the first week of November. At the same time experimental modern works are performed at the Total Music Meeting.

In Munich in the late evening you could drop into a small, hip club like **Atomic Café** or go to hear blues, rock, or jazz at **Feierwerk**. Dixieland jazz is played at the **Alabamahalle** and traditional jazz at **Jazzclub Unterfahrt**. There are often free rock concerts in Munich in summer at the Theatron in Olympiapark. Frankfurt has an enthusiastic jazz scene which is centered around *Jazzgasse* (Jazz Alley) or Kleine Bockenheimer Straße. Here you will find the city's top jazz venue, **Jazzkeller**, in a cellar. If you like to listen to different kinds of live music such as African, Asian, and salsa, try **Brotfabrik**, which also has a café.

Discos in Munich and Frankfurt mainly cater, naturally enough, for a young crowd and play music of all kinds: from chart hits, funk, and techno to heavy metal. Some have a dress policy.

FESTIVALS AND FAIRS

Germans love festivals and fairs and this country probably has more than most other European countries. The most famous is the *Oktoberfest* in Munich *(see p554)*, which is a huge event that celebrates beer with two weeks of drinking, from the last week in September. Not to be outdone, wine-drinkers can enjoy a wine festival *(Weinfest)* in August in the Rhine-Mosel area and in October in the Rhineland.

Germany has produced many of the world's foremost musicians, so classical music festivals are popular and take place in many German towns. To give a few examples, there is a Bach Festival in May in Leipzig *(see p543)*, while Bonn *(see p561)* is the venue for the International Beethoven Festival from late September. Beginning in late July, Bayreuth *(see p540)* hosts the annual *Opernfest* of Richard Wagner's *Ring Cycle*. However, be aware that you cannot just turn up for a performance here – you will have to book tickets at least a year in advance or else get them with a package holiday.

December brings a rush of fairs. Many towns and cities, including Berlin and Munich, stage a Christmas market *(Christkindlmarkt)*, but the one in Nuremberg is considered to be the most impressive.

OUTDOOR ACTIVITIES

Germany is the ideal destination for a range of outdoor activities, including hiking, cycling, fishing, and sailing. It also has a number of winter-sports resorts with first-class ski slopes, the best being in the Bavarian Alps, which lie only an hour's drive from Munich.

There is a tradition of great horsemanship in Germany. Keen riders will find excellent facilities in many areas, as well as the chance to attend international competitions.

Tennis is the second most popular sport (after soccer) and there are several annual professional tournaments. You can play on the many public courts, or find a hotel with its own facilities. Golfers with the appropriate handicap can play on most golf courses simply by paying a green fee.

DIRECTORY

BOOKING TICKETS

Hekticket Theaterkassen
Hardenbergstraße 29d,
Berlin.
Tel 030-23 09 930.

Ticket Online
Tel 01805-447 0111.
www.ticketonline.de

THEATER

Berliner Ensemble
Bertolt-Brecht-Platz 1,
Berlin.
Tel 030-28 40 80.

Cuvilliéstheater
Residenzstraße 1,
Munich.
Tel 089-21 85 19 40.

Deutsches Theater
Schumannstraße 13a,
Berlin.
Tel 030-28 44 12 25.

Deutsches Theater
Werner-Heisenberg-Allee 1,
Munich.
Tel 089-55 23 44 44.

English Theatre
Kaiserstraße 34,
Frankfurt.
Tel 069-24 23 16 20.

Kammerspiele
Maximillianstraße 28,
Munich.

Schauspiel Frankfurt
Neue Mainzer Straße 17,
Frankfurt.
Tel 069-212 494 94.

Volksbühne
Rosa-Luxemburg-Platz,
Berlin.
Tel 030-247 7694.

CLASSICAL MUSIC AND DANCE

Alte Oper
Opernplatz, Frankfurt.
Tel 069-134 04 00.

Bayerische Staatsoper
Max-Joseph-Platz 2,
Munich.
Tel 089-21 85 19 20.

Deutsche Oper
Bismarckstraße 35,
Berlin.
Tel 030-343 84 01.

Gasteig
Rosenheimer Straße 5,
Munich.
Tel 089-480 980.

Jahrhunderthalle
Pffafenwiese,
Frankfurt.
Tel 069-360 12 36.

Komische Oper
Behrenstraße 55–57,
Berlin.
Tel 030-47 99 74 00.

Philharmonie
Herbert-von-Karajan-Straße 1, Berlin.
Tel 030-25 48 89 99.

Prinzregenten-theater
Prinzregentenplatz 12,
Munich.
Tel 089-21 85 02.

Staatsoper
Unter den Linden 7,
Berlin.
Tel 030-20 35 45 55.

JAZZ, ROCK, AND POP

Alabamahalle
Domagkstraße 33,
Munich.
Tel 089-368 14 50.

Atomic Café
Neuturmstraße 5,
Munich.
Tel 089-548 181 81.

Brotfabrik
Bachmannstraße 2–4,
Frankfurt.
Tel 069-247 90 800.

Feierwerk
Hansastraße 39, Munich.
Tel 089-72 48 80.

Jazzclub Unterfahrt
Einsteinstraße 42, Munich.
Tel 089-448 2794.

Jazzkeller
Kleine Bockenheimer Straße 18a, Frankfurt.
Tel 069-28 85 37.

Junction Bar
Gneisenaustraße 18,
Berlin.
Tel 030-694 66 02.

Quasimodo
Kantstraße 12a,
Berlin.
Tel 030-312 80 86.

Schlot
Chausseestraße 18,
Berlin.
Tel 030-448 21 60.

Waldbühne
Am Glockenturm,
Berlin.
Tel 030-23 09 93 33.

Where to Stay in Germany

Most German cities have several deluxe and international chain hotels offering a high level of comfort. Finding less expensive accommodations can be difficult, unless you stay outside the center. Away from the cities, high prices generally apply to hotels in historic or peaceful locations; a room in a pension or private home is usually cheaper.

PRICE CATEGORIES
Price categories are for a standard double room for one night in peak season, including tax, service charges, and breakfast:
€ Under €75
€€ €75–€125
€€€ €125–€175
€€€€ €175–€225
€€€€€ Over €225

BERLIN

EAST OF CENTER Alexander Plaza Berlin
€€€

Rosenstraße 1, 10178 **Tel** *030-240 010* **Fax** *030-240 017 77* **Rooms** *92* Map F3

This top-quality hotel, opened in 1997, is located near the S-Bahn station Hackescher Markt. Rooms in the late 19th-century building, an intriguing mixture of stucco ceilings, glass and steel, are large, comfortable, and full of light, with soundproofed windows. There is a nice lobby bar and café. **www.hotel-alexander-plaza.de**

EAST OF CENTER Art'otel Berlin Mitte
€€€

Wallstraße 70–73, 10179 **Tel** *030-240 620* **Fax** *030-240 622 22* **Rooms** *109* Map F3

Overlooking the Spree river, this upmarket hotel is well priced and one of the most popular establishments in Mitte. Inside, it is modern with simple and elegant furniture. In summer there is a café on a riverboat tied to the riverbank. The hotel is popular with young, culture-oriented guests. **www.artotel.de**

EAST OF CENTER Derag Residenz Hotel Henriette
€€€

Neue Rosstraße 13, 10179 **Tel** *030-246 009 00* **Fax** *030-246 009 40* **Rooms** *54* Map F3/4

The small and intimate Henriette is the nicest – and the most unknown – of the many Derag hotels in town. Although built in 2000, it exudes an incredibly elegant, historic flair, with oak furniture, precious carpets and beds. The hotel provides excellent service. **www.deraghotels.de**

EAST OF CENTER Hotel Gendarm
€€€

Charlottenstraße 61, 10117 **Tel** *030-206 06 60* **Fax** *030-206 066 66* **Rooms** *31* Map E4

The Gendarm's reputation as one of the best and most popular smaller hotels in Berlin is more than justified. An excellent service, a great location off Gendarmenmarkt and traditional, elegantly furnished rooms make this a serious competitor of the big five-star hotels nearby. **www.hotel-gendarm-berlin.de**

EAST OF CENTER Hotel de Rome
€€€€€

Behrenstraße 37, 10117 **Tel** *030-460 60 90* **Fax** *030-460 60 92 000* **Rooms** *146* Map E3

Hidden behind the classicist facade of a former 19th-century bank, this is a new shining star among the city's first-class hotels. The interior design is very modern, with subdued colors complementing the historic setting. The service is impeccable and the fairly large rooms offer wonderful views of Opernplatz. **www.hotelderome.com**

EAST OF CENTER Sofitel am Gendarmenmarkt
€€€€€

Charlottenstraße 50–52, 10117 **Tel** *030-203 750* **Fax** *030-203 751 00* **Rooms** *92* Map E4

This luxury hotel offers well-furnished rooms and excellent service. It is conveniently located near the Gendarmenmarkt, not far from Unter den Linden and sights such as the Brandenburg Gate and the Reichstag. The Aigner restaurant downstairs specializes in good Austrian food. **www.sofitel.com**

WEST OF CENTER Arte Luise Kunsthotel
€€

Luisenstraße 19, 10117 **Tel** *030-284 480* **Fax** *030-284 484 48* **Rooms** *50* Map E3

An authentic Berlin artist's hotel, the Künstlerheim (literally "home for artists") welcomes the artsy crowd into individually designed rooms, created by various German artists, in an early 19th-century house. It is steps away from the Scheunenviertel and offers great service. **www.arte-luise.com**

WEST OF CENTER Ellington Hotel
€€

Nürnberger Straße 50–55, 10789 **Tel** *030-683 150* **Fax** *030-683 155 555* **Rooms** *285* Map C4

An oasis of modern design behind the stunning facade of a 1920s Bauhaus-style office building, the Ellington is an affordable stylish alternative to other central hotels. The bright colors, perfect service, and great location more than make up for the small rooms, with many thoughtful touches ensuring a comfortable stay. **www.ellington-hotel.com**

WEST OF CENTER Hotel Brandenburger Hof
€€€€€

Eislebener Straße 14, 10789 **Tel** *030-214 050* **Fax** *030-214 051 00* **Rooms** *72* Map B4

An intimate family atmosphere, impeccable service and quiet luxurious rooms make this one of the most desirable top-notch hotels in Berlin. The enchanting building has been restored and rooms feature Bauhaus furniture. The Michelin-awarded restaurant, Die Quadriga, is a must. **www.brandenburger-hof.com**

Key to Symbols *see back cover flap*

WEST OF CENTER Hotel Concorde Berlin

🖕 🍴 🛗 📺 📖 🅆 €€€€€

Augsburger Straße 41, 10789 **Tel** *030-800 999 0* **Fax** *030-800 999 99* **Rooms** *311* Map C4

Offering sophisticated charm, this modern hotel is decorated in minimalist style, with a lot of glass, warm lights, and wooden paneling. The large, comfortable rooms, impeccable service, and French restaurant, Faubourg, all contribute to its appeal, as do the views of bustling street life on Kurfürstendamm. **www.berlin.concorde-hotels.com**

FARTHER AFIELD Hotel-Pension Kastanienhof

🖕 🅆 €€

Kastanienallee 65, 10119 **Tel** *030-44 30 50* **Fax** *030-443 051 11* **Rooms** *35*

The Kastanienhof is a budget *Pension* hidden in a fully restored, typical Berlin tenement house. Its location is perfect for exploring the clubbing scene in Prenzlauer Berg. The rooms are surprisingly nice and come equipped with a hairdryer, mini bar and safe. **www.kastanienhof.de**

FARTHER AFIELD Honigmond

🖕 🍴 🅆 €€

Tieckstraße 11, 10115 **Tel** *030-284 45 50* **Fax** *030-284 455 11* **Rooms** *60*

The Honigmond is great for exploring the Mitte and Prenzlauer Berg arts scenes. Originally a traditional 19th-century tenement house with a courtyard, it has individually designed rooms, some of which feature four-poster beds and parquet floors, while other rooms entice you with their summerhouse feel. **www.honigmond.de**

EASTERN GERMANY

DRESDEN Romantik Hotel Pattis

🖕 🍴 🛗 🅆 €€€

Merbitzer Straße 53, 1157 **Tel** *0351-42 55 0* **Fax** *0351-42 55 25 5* **Rooms** *46*

This is very much a family-run hotel (pictures, birth dates, and other family information are given on the website) and offers a rather effective mix of business-class standards and personal touches that will make you feel both important and relaxed at the same time. **www.pattis.de**

DRESDEN Steigenberger Hotel de Saxe

🖕 🍴 🛗 📺 📖 🅆 €€€

Neumarkt 9, 1067 **Tel** *0351-43 86 0* **Fax** *0351-43 86 88 8* **Rooms** *185*

Even the simple rooms are vast and elegant and offer Internet, satellite television, safes, and the usual list of comforts and conveniences. There is a definite sense of sparkle and fresh opulence in the dining areas. This is a very refined establishment. **www.desaxe-dresden.steigenberger.de**

LEIPZIG Alt-Connewitz Hotel-Restaurant

🖕 🍴 🛗 🅆 €€

Meusdorfer Straße 47a, 4277 **Tel** *0341-30 13 77 0* **Fax** *0341-30 13 80 0* **Rooms** *35*

A simple and straightforward hotel with very reasonable prices. The comfortable guest rooms have a fresh, clean decor and include Internet access and TV. They also have a good restaurant with a fine selection of wines, as well as a sauna. **www.alt-connewitz.de**

LEIPZIG Hotel Fürstenhof

🖕 🍴 🏊 🛗 📺 📖 🅆 €€€€

Tröndlinring 8, 4105 **Tel** *0341-14 00* **Fax** *0341-14 03 70 0* **Rooms** *92*

A hotel with a bright and confident classiness. Its rooms are colorfully decorated and furnished, and tall slim windows offer plenty of light and a feeling of space. All rooms have a mini bar and satellite television, but the ones that overlook the courtyard are worth requesting. A bold and luxurious hotel. **www.luxurycollection.com/fuerstenhof**

WEIMAR Hotel Elephant

🖕 🍴 🛗 🅆 €€€

Markt 19, 99423 **Tel** *03643-80 20* **Fax** *03643-80 26 10* **Rooms** *99*

Despite the hotel's name, the style here is very refined and stately. Everything is squared-off, neat, respectable, and comfortable. All rooms also have original artworks, and the hotel has a tradition of being a meeting place for artists, poets, and intellectuals. **www.luxurycollection.com/elephant**

MUNICH

CENTRAL MUNICH Cosmopolitan Hotel

🖕 🅆 €€

Hohenzollernstraße 5, 80801 **Tel** *089-383810* **Fax** *089-38381-111* **Rooms** *71* Map 2 C1

A contemporary hotel in a quieter side street in the fashionable Schwabing district. There is a modern design feel throughout and rooms have Ligne Roset furniture. Enjoy breakfast on the outdoor terrace in warmer weather. It is located just a short walk from the English Garden. **www.geisel-privathotels.de**

CENTRAL MUNICH Gästehaus Englischer Garten

🅆 €€

Liebergesellstraße 8, 80802 **Tel** *089-3839410* **Fax** *089-38394-133* **Rooms** *25*

A cozy little guesthouse with pleasant, if small, rooms. The hotel is quiet and family run. Longer-stay apartments are also available, offering more space and a balcony. Once a watermill, the now-listed building has a lovely garden where you can sit out and enjoy breakfast. **www.hotelenglischergarten.de**

Map References *see maps of Berlin pp528–9 and Munich pp546–7*

CENTRAL MUNICH Insel Mühle

🔳 Ⓦ   €€€

Von-Kahr-Straße 87, 80999 **Tel** *089-810 10* **Fax** *089-812 05 71* **Rooms** *38*

This hotel has a dreamy romantic setting in an old mill with beautiful gardens by a small river. The style is simple, rustic, and comfortable. There is also an excellent restaurant, beer garden, wine cellar, and bar. Choose tables in shady spots, under trees, or simply relax and wander around the grounds. **www.insel-muehle.com**

CENTRAL MUNICH Novotel Muenchen City

🔳 Ⓜ ⌹ ⴹ Ⓜ 🔳 Ⓦ   €€€

Hochstraße 11, 81669 **Tel** *089-661 070* **Fax** *089-66 10 79 99* **Rooms** *307*

A very contemporary four-star hotel with simple, sleek, bright decor. The welcoming breakfast room has large floral photographs. There is also a spacious pool and relaxation room plus fitness area. Its central location means that you can walk to Marienplatz, the Gasteig cultural center or museums. **www.novotel.com**

CENTRAL MUNICH Bayerischer Hof

🔳 Ⓜ ⌹ ⴹ Ⓜ 🔳 Ⓦ   €€€€€

Promenadeplatz 2–6, 80333 **Tel** *089-212 00* **Fax** *089-212 09 06* **Rooms** *373*   **Map** *2 A3*

A large luxurious hotel in a prominent central location near the best shops, museums, opera house, theaters, and restaurants. Elegant rooms with swathes of fabrics mixing plaids and florals in a country-house style. It also has a spa, three restaurants, including the Garden Restaurant, and a great bar. **www.bayerischerhof.de**

CENTRAL MUNICH Kempinski Hotel Vier Jahreszeiten

🔳 Ⓜ ⌹ ⴹ Ⓜ 🔳 Ⓦ   €€€€€

Maximilianstraße 17, 80539 **Tel** *089-212 50* **Fax** *089-21 25 20 00* **Rooms** *308*   **Map** *2 C4*

The top address in Munich (built for King Maximilian II in 1858) nestled among the designer stores on Maximilian-straße. Excellent service, gastronomy, and bars. A stunning entrance hall in rich gold and reds sets the tone. The pool and wellness floor are excellent. **www.kempinski-vierjahreszeiten.de**

SOUTHERN GERMANY

BAMBERG Alt Ringlein

🔳 Ⓜ ⴹ Ⓦ   €€

Dominikanerstraße 9, 96049 **Tel** *0951-953 20* **Fax** *0951-953 25 00* **Rooms** *33*

A pleasant and comfortable hotel in Bamberg's center. Enjoy the choice of Franconian meals in its restaurant of the same name and try one of several local beers, including their own home-brewed one. In the wing dating back to 1296 they have Franconian-styled rooms. Make sure you spend time in the nice beer garden. **www.alt-ringlein.com**

BAMBERG Welcome Hotel Residenzschloss

🔳 Ⓜ ⴹ Ⓜ 🔳 Ⓦ   €€€

Untere Sandstraße 32, 96049 **Tel** *0951-609 10* **Fax** *0951-609 17 01* **Rooms** *184*

This hotel has classic rooms in a listed building on the banks of the river Regnitz. Now a spa and conference hotel, it began life as a hospital back in 1789. Guests can choose between two restaurants, and there is also a piano bar and small chapel, which sometimes holds classical concerts. **www.residenzschloss.com**

FREIBURG IM BREISGAU Zum Roten Bären

🔳 Ⓜ Ⓦ   €€€

Oberlinden 12, 79098 **Tel** *0761-387 870* **Rooms** *25*

Situated in a building that dates back to the 12th century, just minutes from the center of Freiburg, this hotel also has a lovely traditional *Stube*, a tavern-style restaurant serving regional seasonal food. The guest rooms are comfortable and there is also a peaceful courtyard. **www.roter-baeren.de**

HEIDELBERG Holländer Hof

🔳 Ⓦ   €€€

Neckarstaden 66, 69117 **Tel** *06221-605 00* **Rooms** *39*

An old house in the center of town with a pretty facade and classic, elegant rooms, this hotel is within easy reach of the famous castle and not far from the shops, restaurants, churches, and pedestrianized area of Heidelberg. It is also close to where boat rides are run up and down the Neckar. **www.hollaender-hof.de**

HEIDELBERG Europäischer Hof Hotel Europa

🔳 Ⓜ ⌹ ⴹ Ⓜ 🔳 Ⓦ   €€€€€

Friedrich-Ebert-Anlage 1, 69117 **Tel** *06221-515 0* **Rooms** *118*

The best in the area this hotel has luxurious suites, high-quality rooms, courteous and helpful staff, à la carte dinners in the Kurfürstenstube, a terrace overlooking a garden, a shopping arcade, and the Panorama spa and fitness club. There is everything you could possibly want to make it a memorable stay. **www.europaeischerhof.com**

LINDAU Bayerischer Hof

🔳 Ⓜ ⌹ Ⓜ 🔳 Ⓦ   €€€

Seepromenade, 88131 **Tel** *08382-9150* **Fax** *08382-915 591* **Rooms** *97*

A luxurious Neoclassical building dating back to 1854, located on the harbor front, which has spacious rooms and suites, good service and excellent fitness, pool, sauna, and wellbeing facilities. Enjoy the international cuisine in the restaurant of the same name and unforgettable lake views from the bar. **www.bayerischerhof-lindau.de**

NUREMBERG Romantik Hotel am Josephplatz

🔳 Ⓜ 🔳 Ⓦ   €€

Josephsplatz 30–32, 90403 **Tel** *0911-214 470* **Fax** *0911-21 44 72 00* **Rooms** *36*

A romantic hotel dating back to 1675, located within walking distance of Nuremburg's old center. There are small apartments which would suit a family. Enjoy the good breakfast buffet, roof terrace, sauna, solarium, fitness room, and winter garden. There are also several restaurants close by. **www.hotel-am-josephsplatz.de**

Key to Price Guide *see p574* **Map References** *see map of Munich pp546–7*

NUREMBERG Burghotel
🛏️ 🏛️ Ⓦ   €€€

Lammgasse 3, 90403 **Tel** *0911-238 890* **Fax** *0911-2388 9100* **Rooms** *58*

Charming simple rooms filled with light offer some great views over the roofs of the old town. Burghotel has traces of ancient castle life, such as armour and coats-of-arms. There is also a lounge with an open fire, rustic bar, sun terrace, and sauna. **www.altstadthotels-nuernberg.com**

NUREMBERG Maritim Hotel Nürnberg
🛏️ 🍽️ 🏛️ ♿ 🎿 Ⓦ   €€€€

Frauentorgraben 11, 90443 **Tel** *0911-236 30* **Fax** *0911-236 38 23* **Rooms** *316*

The Maritim has a slightly corporate feel (it is run by a large German chain), but has an excellent central location opposite the ancient city wall. There are good swimming and wellbeing facilities plus a choice of restaurants – Stube for international cuisine, the Blauer Salon café, or the piano bar. **www.maritim.de**

PASSAU Passauer Wolf
🛏️ Ⓦ   €€€

Rindermarkt 6–8, 94032 **Tel** *0851-931 510* **Fax** *0851-931 5150* **Rooms** *39*

This hotel is located in the old town of Passau, next to the pedestrian precinct and on the banks of the Danube. The St. Stephan cathedral and several museums and unique sights are within walking distance. Choose between rooms with a view over the river, the old town or the courtyard. **www.hotel-passauer-wolf.de**

ROTHENBURG OB DER TAUBER Prinzhotel
🛏️ 🍽️ Ⓦ   €€

An der Hofstett 3, 91541 **Tel** *09861-9750* **Fax** *09861-97575* **Rooms** *52*

Within the old town walls, this historic hotel is in a very quiet location surrounded by the town's medieval history. All the sights are within walking distance. The hotel's restaurant serves Franconian-Italian cuisine. Parking is available in front of the hotel. **www.prinzhotel.rothenburg.de**

STUTTGART Hansa Hotel
🛏️ Ⓦ   €

Silberburgstraße 114–116, 70176 **Tel** *0711-656 7800* **Fax** *0711-617 349* **Rooms** *75*

This is located near the pedestrianized area, so it is a good central base for exploring the Swabian capital of Stuttgart. It is also close to shops, restaurants, the station, and museums. There is Internet access, bike hire, a restaurant, Petrarca, offering Mediterranean specials, and a beer garden. **www.hansa-stuttgart.de**

STUTTGART Kronen Hotel
🛏️ 📋 Ⓦ   €€€

Kronenstraße 48, 70174 **Tel** *0711-225 10* **Rooms** *80*

Located in a quiet spot, but still with easy access to the railway station, this hotel has a nice garden with terrace. Enjoy the great breakfast buffet in the modern breakfast room, looking out onto a palmed terrace. Guests can also take drinks at the little lobby bar or use the hotel sauna. **www.kronenhotel-stuttgart.de**

WÜRZBURG/HOCHBERG Minotel Zum Lamm
🛏️ 🍽️ Ⓦ   €€

Hauptstraße 76, 97204 **Tel** *0931-304 5630* **Fax** *0931-408 973* **Rooms** *37*

The hotel lies in Höchberg, outside the Baroque center of Würzburg and offers guests a typical Franconian hospitality and great gourmet food. It also boasts a lovely courtyard and garden. Guests are spoiled with great food and wine, and it is popular with cyclists, motorcyclists, and hikers touring the area. **www.lamm-hoechberg.de**

WESTERN GERMANY

BONN Schlosshotel Kommende Ramersdorf
🍽️ Ⓦ   €€

Oberkasslerstraße 10, 53227 **Tel** *0228-440 734* **Fax** *0228-444 400* **Rooms** *20*

Situated in a fairy-tale castle, the rooms and hallways here are filled with antiques and works of art that help set it apart from other hotels. There is a medieval feel to the hotel, and each room is individual. The restaurant is also worth a visit. **www.schlosshotel-kommende-ramersdorf.de**

BONN Kaiser Karl
🛏️ 🍽️ Ⓦ   €€€

Vorgebirgsstraße 56, 53119 **Tel** *0228-985 570* **Fax** *0228-985 5777* **Rooms** *42*

Exquisitely decorated rooms and a keen eye for detail make this hotel a welcome oasis of leisure and pleasure. All rooms cater to those with allergies. Many famous guests have passed through the doors, and more than a few have tinkled the keys of the piano in the old-fashioned and dignified bar. **www.kaiser-karl-hotel-bonn.de**

BONN Dorint Sofitel Venusberg
🛏️ 🍽️ 🎿 📋 Ⓦ   €€€€€

An der Casselsruhe 1, 53127 **Tel** *0228-2880* **Fax** *0228-288 288* **Rooms** *85*

This hotel sits on the banks of the Rhine and has colorful and decadent rooms that overlook the surrounding forest. There are a number of sporting facilities in the area, such as golf and tennis, and there is a jogging track inside the hotel for fitness fans. **www.dorint.com**

COLOGNE Hotel Leonardo
🛏️ 🍽️ 🏛️ 🎿 📋 Ⓦ   €€

Waldecker Straße 11–15, 51065 **Tel** *0221-67090* **Fax** *0221-6709321* **Rooms** *161*

Set in an otherwise dull area this hotel is an oasis of comfort and hospitality. The air-conditioned rooms are spacious and well equipped. The hotel is still family run and great care has gone into retaining its charm. They have a large pool and good fitness facilities. It attracts mostly business guests for trade fairs. **www.leonardo-hotels.com**

Key to Symbols *see back cover flap*

COLOGNE Hyatt Regency
Kennedy-Ufer 2a, 50679 **Tel** *0221-828 12 34* **Fax** *0221-828 1370* **Rooms** *306*

One of the best hotels in Germany, this Hyatt has a prime location perfect both for crossing the bridge into the Old Town and visiting the trade fairs. All tastes are catered for and the view over the Rhine and the Old Town is unparalleled. **www.cologne.regency.hyatt.com**

COLOGNE Jolly Hotel MediaPark
Im MediaPark 8b, 50670 **Tel** *0221-271 50* **Fax** *0221-271 59 99* **Rooms** *217*

Part of an Italian chain of hotels, this one displays the subtle and refined styling that serves them well. There are luxurious and comfortable rooms and facilities, situated in the MediaPark, next to the tall tower. There are excellent fitness and wellness facilities, and guests receive discounts at the nearby Holmes gym. **www.jollyhotels.de**

COLOGNE Hotel im Wasserturm
Kaygaße 2, 50676 **Tel** *0221-200 80* **Fax** *0221-200 88 88* **Rooms** *88*

Integrated into a historic water tower in the heart of Cologne, this top class hotel is one of the most distinctive in the city. The building's shape has spawned oddly shaped rooms, some with two levels. On the 11th floor is an opulent restaurant, La Vision, that has been awarded a Michelin star. **www.hotel-im-wasserturm.de**

FRANKFURT AM MAIN Hotel Borger
Triebstraße 51, 60388 **Tel** *06109-309 00* **Fax** *06109-309 030* **Rooms** *36*

A family-styled hotel with a comfortable atmosphere and a convenient location, the rooms here offer the basic amenities, and the hotel is the perfect base for exploring the city and surrounding areas. The villa has been in the family for over a hundred years and was renovated late in the 20th century. **www.hotel-borger.de**

FRANKFURT AM MAIN Frankfurt Hotel Savoy
Wiesenhüttenstraße 42, 60329 **Tel** *069-273 960* **Fax** *069-273 967 95* **Rooms** *144*

This hotel has a classy attitude. Situated in a convenient location for trade fairs and with good access to the airport, guests will find the hotel itself a charming place to explore. There is a swimming pool on the top floor, which offers a rare and beautiful skyline view of Frankfurt am Main. **www.savoyhotel.de**

FRANKFURT AM MAIN Hessischer Hof
Friedrich Ebert Anlage 40, 60325 **Tel** *069-754 00* **Fax** *069-754 029 24* **Rooms** *117*

An exquisitely styled hotel with a sense of class. The rooms are styled either in a modern manner or with more of an antique feel about them, with some of the suites furnished with pieces from the Prince of Hesse. The restaurant and bar complement each other well. **www.hessischer-hof.de**

FRANKFURT AM MAIN Steigenberger Frankfurter Hof
Am Kaiserplatz, 60311 **Tel** *069-215 02* **Fax** *069-215 09 00* **Rooms** *321*

A very large and comprehensive hotel where everything you desire is catered for and is done in style. The rooms are impeccable and the restaurants are among the best in the city. It is situated less than a kilometer away from the main station and has very helpful and friendly staff. **www.frankfurter-hof.steigenberger.de**

KOBLENZ Top Hotel Krämer Garni
Kardinal-Krementz-Straße 12, 56073 **Tel** *0261-406 200* **Fax** *0261-413 40* **Rooms** *23*

A comfortable hotel, with a touch of the traditional German style. The rooms have a modern feel about them, and fresh flowers are a colorful touch which contrast well with the somewhat minimalist decor. The service is friendly and enhances the personal atmosphere of the hotel. **www.tophotel-k.de**

KOBLENZ Mercure
Julius-Wegeler-Straße 6, 56068 **Tel** *0261-136 0* **Fax** *0261-1361199* **Rooms** *168*

There is a home-like feeling to the colorful and comfortable rooms, which also offer nice views. The hotel has an elegant restaurant and a stylish lounge bar. There is also a good view from the higher floors of the hotel looking over Koblenz and the surrounding district. **www.mercure.com**

MAINZ Favorite Parkhotel
Karl-Weiser-Straße 1, 55131 **Tel** *06131-801 50* **Fax** *06131-801 54 20* **Rooms** *122*

There is a pleasant surprise around every door here. Apart from the ultra-comfortable rooms and suites, there is a greenhouse with different varieties of palms, a gourmet restaurant, and a beer garden that is a favorite meeting place for locals as well as guests. **www.favorite-mainz.de**

MAINZ Novotel Mainz
Augustusstraße 6, 55131 **Tel** *06131-954 0* **Fax** *06131-954 100* **Rooms** *217*

The bright and well-equipped rooms are very comfortable, and there is a spacious and relaxing pool area. Their restaurant offers elegant dining and a must-see wine bar, Kasematten, which is situated in a 17th-century vaulted cellar, providing a distinctive atmosphere for wine tastings. **www.novotel.com**

TRIER Römischer Kaiser
Porta-Nigra-Platz 6, 54292 **Tel** *0651-977 0100* **Fax** *0651-977 019 99* **Rooms** *43*

This hotel is housed in part of a historic building in the illustrious Porta Nigra Square. First mentioned in 1885, the hotel has a great central location and offers a decadent retreat in the heart of Trier. The rooms are tastefully furnished and spacious. It has a highly recommended restaurant of the same name. **www.friedrich-hotels.de**

Key to Price Guide *see p574* **Key to Symbols** *see back cover flap*

NORTHERN GERMANY

BREMEN Landhaus Radler Garni

Kastanienweg 17, 27404 **Tel** *04281-988 20* **Fax** *04281-988 210* **Rooms** *16*

A family-owned and managed hotel, this place is a little distant from the center of Bremen, but offers a peaceful atmosphere that is appreciated by families. There is a playground for children and the surrounding area is perfect for cycling and exploring on foot. Nestled in the rear is a well-maintained little garden. **www.landhaus-radler.de**

BREMEN Park Hotel

Im Bürgerpark, 28209 **Tel** *0421-340 80* **Fax** *0421-340 86 02* **Rooms** *177*

Opulent and expansive, the Park Hotel brings to life all your dreams of luxury and comfort. The grounds are well sculpted and spectacular, as are the rooms which are guaranteed to make you feel relaxed. There are several restaurants, bars, and bistros, so take your pick. **www.park-hotel-bremen.de**

HAMBURG Le Royal Méridien

An Der Alster 52–56, 20099 **Tel** *040-210 00* **Fax** *040-210 011 11* **Rooms** *284*

Situated on the banks of Alster lake, this modern, luxury hotel offers some of the best views Hamburg has to offer. Rooms are sparsely furnished but offer all the amenities of a first-class hotel. The Meridien spa and fitness club is considered to be one of the best designed in Germany. **www.leroyalmeridien-hamburg.com**

HAMBURG Side Hotel Hamburg

Drehbahn 49, 20354 **Tel** *040-309 990* **Fax** *040-309 993 99* **Rooms** *178*

This five-star dream of a hotel is a comfortable and centrally located alternative to the more classic top hotels in the downtown area. The architecture and interior design is cutting edge; rooms are decorated in soft, shiny beige and white colors. For a little extra you can book an Executive room with a kitchenette. **www.side-hamburg.de**

HAMBURG Park Hyatt

Bugenhagenstraße 8, 20095 **Tel** *040-333 212 34* **Fax** *040-333 212 35* **Rooms** *252*

The Park Hyatt is located in the heart of historic Hamburg and off Mönckebergstrasse – the city's main shopping pedestrian zone. Rooms are modern and feature large-screen TVs and moveable bathroom doors. The breakfast buffet offers a huge range of international and German dishes. **www.hamburg.park.hyatt.com**

HANNOVER Best Western Parkhotel Kronsberg

Gut Kronsberg 1, 30539 **Tel** *0511-874 00* **Fax** *0511-867 112* **Rooms** *200*

Conveniently located opposite the fairground, the hotel has become a favorite with business guests. With lots of light and space, the lobby is crowned with a glass dome. There is a mixture of room styles which are all comfortable and spacious. The restaurants and bistros offer character and good food. **www.parkhotel-kronsberg.de**

HANNOVER Hotel Kaiserhof

Ernst-August-Platz 4, 30159 **Tel** *0511-368 30* **Fax** *0511-368 31 14* **Rooms** *78*

Housed in a historic building constructed in 1915, this hotel has been well preserved. There is a subtle French style to the tastefully detailed rooms. It is located opposite the main train station and close to the city center. The restaurant is highly acclaimed, and serves trout that they raise themselves in a courtyard fountain. **www.centralhotel.de**

HANNOVER Novotel Hannover

Podbielskistraße 21–23, 30163 **Tel** *0511-390 40* **Fax** *0511-390 41 00* **Rooms** *206*

Housed in an old biscuit factory, this hotel has luxurious amenities and guest rooms, with a playground for children, as well as a babysitting service if required. It also has extensive conference facilities, indeed one conference room still retains some old machinery from the factory days. **www.novotel.de**

LÜBECK Kaiserhof

Kronsforder Allee 11–13, 23560 **Tel** *0451-703 301* **Fax** *0451-795 083* **Rooms** *58*

Sitting in the middle of the "island," you could not ask for a better location. Close to historic attractions and museums, some guest rooms here have a balcony. Their restaurant focuses on fish and there is an elegant banquet hall which is often used for weddings and other functions. **www.kaiserhof-luebeck.de**

LÜBECK Radisson SAS Senator Hotel

Willy-Brandt-Allee 6, 23554 **Tel** *0451-14 20* **Fax** *0451-142 22 22* **Rooms** *224*

Overlooking the river and close to the center, the rooms here are very comfortable and bright. There are many facilities to keep children occupied and when accompanied by parents they eat in the restaurant for free. Along with the restaurant, there is a cocktail bar, a café, and a tavern with adjoining beer garden. **www.senatorhotel.de**

MÜNSTER Schloss Wilkinghege

Steinfurter Straße 374, 48159 **Tel** *0251-144 270* **Fax** *0251-212 898* **Rooms** *35*

A successful blend of modern comfort and historic charm, the top suite here has been furnished with antiques, and the bathroom adorned with Philippe Starck fixtures. The restaurant serves refined cuisine with a subtle French flair. Next door there is a golf course and tennis courts. **www.schloss-wilkinghege.de**

Where to Eat in Germany

German cuisine does not enjoy the same reputation as that of some European countries. Nevertheless you can eat very well here with many restaurants specializing in appetizing, if somewhat heavy, regional dishes. In the past few years, some fine restaurants have opened serving excellent international cuisine.

BERLIN

EAST OF CENTER Historische Weinstuben
€€

Poststraße 23, 10178 **Tel** *030-242 41 07*   **Map 5 E2**

This popular wine bar is housed in one of the most decorative buildings of the Nicolaiviertel. Traditional dishes from Berlin, such as *Kohl* or *Rinderrouladen* (rolled and roasted stuffed beef), can be accompanied by a drink from a small but exquisite wine list of 50 mostly German vintages.

EAST OF CENTER Zum Nussbaum
€€€

Am Nussbaum 3, 10178 **Tel** *030-242 30 95*   **Map 5 E2**

Situated in an alley in the Nicolaiviertel, this is a reconstruction of a 16th-century country inn, serving traditional Berlin cuisine, with tender pork knuckle, rollmops or *Berliner Boulette*, a spicy hamburger patty without a bun. In summer, dine in its garden and enjoy the various brands of local beer.

EAST OF CENTER Lutter & Wegner
€€€€

Charlottenstraße 56, 10117 **Tel** *030-202 954 17*   **Map 4 C3**

The first restaurant to start the revitalization of the gourmet scene in the historic center of Eastern Berlin. Formerly know as a fine German champagne brand, it now serves delicious German–Austrian food. The huge *Wiener Schnitzel* with potato salad, best served lukewarm, is a delight, as are the duck and goose specialties in winter.

EAST OF CENTER Vau
€€€€€

Jägerstraße 54–55, 10117 **Tel** *030-202 97 30*   **Map 4 B2**

This restaurant stands out with its elegant and unpretentious interior. The excellent and imaginative Austrian- and French-based dishes are created by Berlin's star chef, Kolja Kleeberg. The service is welcoming and there is a selection of good wines. The small courtyard is used during lunch. Closed Sun.

WEST OF CENTER Francucci's
€€€

Kurfürstendamm 90, 10711 **Tel** *030-323 33 18*   **Map 4 B1**

One of Berlin's best-kept secrets and a favorite among locals is this upscale neighborhood restaurant offering hearty but supreme Tuscan country cooking. Specialties include the home-made pasta dishes and meat recipes as well as Berlin classics such as their signature pizza, served by the slice.

WEST OF CENTER Ganymed
€€€

Schiffbauerdamm 5, 10117 **Tel** *030-285 990 46*   **Map 4 B1**

A good-quality brasserie restaurant in charming surroundings with a small garden and views of the Spree river. The chef favors fish dishes, including Berlin fish specialties, but also offers traditional French fare such as steak tartare, fresh scallops sauteéd in white wine, and a good cheese selection.

WEST OF CENTER Nolle
€€€

Georgenstraße 203, 10117 **Tel** *030-208 26 55*   **Map 4 C1**

The Nolle is a pleasantly decorated, 1920s-style Berlin restaurant tucked way under the S-Bahn tracks. The lush greenery around the place, the elegantly appointed tables, and candlelight make a perfect setting for its international and German dishes. The *Schnitzel* selection is impressive.

WEST OF CENTER Desbrosses
€€€€

Potsdamer Platz 3, 10785 **Tel** *030-337 776 341*   **Map 4 A3**

Desbrosses has the most authentic French brasserie interior in all of Berlin. Dark wood-paneled walls, comfortable, plush leather bistro chairs, an open show kitchen, and recordings of Piaf all make for a real French experience. A must here is the seafood platter.

WEST OF CENTER Hugos
€€€€€

Budapester Straße 2, 10787 **Tel** *030-260 212 63*   **Map 2 C4**

This elegant restaurant, in the Inter-Continental Hotel, is one of the best in Berlin. Unusual French and international dishes are prepared with a German influence. The fish and seafood dishes are proof of the chef's real mastery. An attraction is the restaurant's rooftop location with great views. Reservations necessary. Closed Sun.

Key to Symbols *see back cover flap*

POTSDAM Restaurant Juliette
                                    €€€€€

Jägerstraße 39, 14467 **Tel** *0331-270 17 91*

A French restaurant with all the romantic trimmings you would expect – candles, white tablecloths, and a lit fireplace. French food traditionalists beware, the decorated and imaginative chef serves up both traditional and experimental cuisine. Try the ever-popular *crème brûlée* for dessert. There are vegetarian options on the menu.

FARTHER AFIELD Mutter
                                    €€

Hohenstaufenstraße 4, 10781 **Tel** *030-219 15 100*

True to its name, Mutter (German for "mother") serves generous portions to its patrons. A fixture of the bustling Winterfeldplatz nightlife scene, it offers cool Caribbean drinks and an eclectic mix of some traditional German, Italian, and Asian dishes, with an emphasis on sushi and Thai food.

FARTHER AFIELD Remise im Schloss Klein-Glienicke
                           €€€€€

Königstraße 36, 14109 **Tel** *030-805 40 00*

This is the ideal place for an elegant meal on the outskirts of Berlin. Now run by Anja Raneberger, the restaurant offers excellent German cuisine, with perch, crayfish, and game, all prepared with a dose of imagination. The restaurant is also a good choice for lunch. Closed Mon–Tue.

EASTERN GERMANY

DRESDEN Sophienkeller
                              €€

Taschenberg 3, 0-1067 **Tel** *0351-49 72 60*

One of the most popular and lively restaurants in Dresden. It is one of three eateries located in the Taschenbergpalais. Come here for the re-created rustic atmosphere of an 18th-century beer cellar. They have authentic regional cuisine on the menu. The staff wear period costumes. Ask to sit at the indoor carousel table.

DRESDEN Intermezzo
                              €€€

Taschenberg 3, 0-1067 **Tel** *0351-491 27 72*

This restaurant in the Kempinski Taschenbergpalais serves unconventional dishes with a touch of the Mediterranean. Try one of the delicious salads or soups for lunch. Desserts are also worth noting as is the extensive wine list. The dining area of the hotel also includes an American-style bar, a café, and other dining options.

DRESDEN Das Caroussel
                         €€€€€

Königstr. 14, 0-1097 **Tel** *0351-800 30*

The hotel and restaurant are located in the Bülow Palais, in the historic city center, which dates from 1730. Famed in the region as one of the best restaurants in Saxony, dine on Mediterranean cuisine while sipping one of the first-class wines. Truly spectacular. There's also a less elaborate but excellent bistro.

LEIPZIG Zest
                                      €

Bornaische Str. 54, 4277 **Tel** *0341-231 91 26*

A fresh and creative take on meatless international fusion food. Try one of the wildly imaginative and intriguing vegetarian dishes, such as spinach risotto balls with a cashew nut crust and coconut crème. The rosemary lemon cake is also tempting and worth sampling. An extensive wine list. Open daily at 11am.

LEIPZIG La Mirabelle
                                  €€

Gohliserstraße 11, 4105 **Tel** *0341-590 29 81*

A typical French restaurant with lots of goat's cheese and wine on the menu. Ask for the seasonal or special dishes during dinner. A refined and stylish place, reservations are not required but recommended. Open for lunch Monday to Friday from 11:30am and for dinner every evening from 6pm.

MEISSEN Mercure Grandhotel Meissen
                                  €€

Hafenstr. 27–31, 1662 **Tel** *03521-722 50*

This classy hotel-restaurant, based in a large Art Nouveau villa on the bank of the Elbe, serves regional and international food. Look for a wide selection of fish dishes on the menu. Their wine list is superb. Guests can also dine in the café, which has a terrace, or in the intimate hotel bar.

WEIMAR Brasserie Central
                                  €€

Rollplatz 8a, 99423 **Tel** *03643-85 27 74*

Typical French provincial cuisine with some international influences, mostly German and Italian. Sweet or savory crêpes are made to order. The menu changes constantly, so check with the staff for current offerings. They have a vast wine list, so it is a great place to try a new wine or enjoy an old favorite.

WEIMAR Anna Amalia
                         €€€€€

Markt 19, 99423 **Tel** *03643-80 20*

This restaurant has a venerable tradition, with famous customers such as Richard Wagner and Thomas Mann, and remains popular to this day. You will enjoy some of the finest Italian cooking in all of Thuringia, with an ever-evolving menu. The interior is decorated in Art Deco style. Service is first class.

Map References *see map of Berlin pp528–9*

MUNICH

CENTRAL MUNICH Zum Franziskaner
€€

Residenzstraße 9, Perusastraße 5, 80331 **Tel** *089-2318120*   **Map** *2 B4*

Rich in tradition and one of the best places to head for typical Bavarian specials. Their home-made white sausage, *Weisswurst*, is famous in Munich. Also, try the Bavarian meatloaf with mustard, fillet of ox, plus a variety of salads and vegetarian dishes. Being the brewery's restaurant, you must try the Franziskaner beer, originally brewed by monks.

CENTRAL MUNICH Dallmayr
€€€

Dienerstraße 14–15, 80331 **Tel** *089-2135100*   **Map** *2 B4*

Dallmayr is a Munich institution, famous for its coffee house and café. The elegant restaurant offers delicious treats such as courgette (zucchini) flowers with lobster on a bed of ratatouille in curry sauce, plus a selection of superb wines. Very popular with locals and tourists for its high level of service, patisserie, and cuisine.

CENTRAL MUNICH Ederer
€€€€

Kardinal-Faulhaber-Straße 10, 80333 **Tel** *089-24231310*   **Map** *2 B3*

A first-floor restaurant within the Fünf Höfe building opposite a large bank. Excellent fish and seafood is available, such as terrine of sardines and sweet peppers or pea soup and gambas, all fresh from the market. Also, over 500 great wines from their cellar. Diners can enjoy the courtyard terrace in summer.

CENTRAL MUNICH Käfer Schänke
€€€€€

Prinzregentenstraße 73, 81675 **Tel** *089-4168247*

Michael Käfer's renowned gourmet restaurant attracts a mix of politicians and artsy and business types. Open all day from 11am for lunch and dinner whenever you want. There are cozy, intimate dining rooms in a contemporary chic style, as well as a traditional Bavarian hunting room, opera room, and a lounge with an open fire.

CENTRAL MUNICH Tantris
€€€€€

Johann-Fichte Straße 7, 80805 **Tel** *089-3619590*

A classic establishment and a Munich institution for over 30 years. Designed in a 1970s style it offers gourmet menus, a high standard of luxury and also has two Michelin stars, a garden, and a terrace. Booking is essential. Try the specials, aubergine (eggplant) and sardine terrine with pesto, or salmon with leek purée and brown butter.

BAVARIA

BAMBERG St Nepomuk
€€

Obere Mühlbrücke 9, 96049 **Tel** *0951-98420*

Dine in a traditional restaurant which has been a staple in the community for centuries. Good selection of game and fish dishes as well as accompanying local wines and beers. The cuisine is generally international. Part of a former mill, it has a charming atmosphere and great views across the river and the town.

BAYREUTH Oskar
€€

Maximilianstraße 33, 95444 **Tel** *0921-5160553*

A traditional institution in Beyreuth, this popular spot draws the crowds for its lively bar which often hosts comedy shows. Fine old dining rooms serve a good selection of regional Franconian food at reasonable prices. A great atmosphere and friendly young staff. Housed in the former town hall right on the marketplace in the heart of town.

BAYREUTH Schlossgaststätte Eremitage
€€€

Eremitage 6, 95448 **Tel** *0921-799970*

An incredibly beautiful setting in the castle where there is also a terrace for alfresco summer dining, an orangerie for the afternoon or apéritifs, and a café. Excellent cuisine, service, and international wines. Highly recommended is the fine perch, or steak in balsamic and shallot sauce with rocket roast potatoes. The desserts are also exquisite.

FREIBURG Enoteca
€€€€

Gerberau 21, 79098 **Tel** *0761-3899130*

With 20 years of experience, Enoteca is one of Freiburg's leading restaurants. It offers a high level of light but classic Italian dishes, where the emphasis is on simplicity and wonderful fresh produce. There are several menus to choose from: the fish menu, the daily menu, or à la carte. The dining room is stylish and understated.

HEIDELBERG Zur Herrenmühle
€€€

Hauptstraße 237–9, 69117 **Tel** *06221-602909*

Located in a 17th-century former grain mill with oak ceiling beams, this romantic restaurant offers the warm welcome of a typical Gashaus. The menu is a mix of top quality French and local cuisine, with an emphasis on fresh fish like *loup de mer* (sea bass) or *dorade* (John Dory), as well as free-range game and lamb. Closed lunch & Sun.

HEIDELBERG Simplicissimus

Ingrimstraße 16, 69117 **Tel** *06221-183336*

Owing to the busy central location in Heidelberg's old town, booking is recommended. Tourists and locals flock here for the simple but outstanding cuisine, combining fresh produce, French flavors, and good wines. Sit in the intimate dining room or in the flower-filled courtyard. Wine-tasting events take place every first Friday of the month. Closed Sun & Mon.

NUREMBERG Sebald

Weinmarkt 14, 90403 **Tel** *0911-381303*

A smart contemporary restaurant in the center of the old town. The chef combines his global experience to serve appetizing dishes with a German and Italian predominance, from *vitello tonnato* (chilled veal in a tuna sauce) to clear oxtail soup, scallops, and *Wiener Schnitzel*. The cuisine does not disappoint. It is very popular, so be sure to book.

NUREMBERG Essigbrätlein

Weinmarkt 3, 90403 **Tel** *0911-225131*

Just a stroll away from the main market square, this small intimate restaurant only has 20 tables so booking ahead is essential. Tightly packed, cozy, and familiar, there is excellent food, staff, and wines. You can choose from the daily changing menu or let the head waiter and sommelier advise you. Delicious fish dishes plus exquisite desserts. Closed Sun & Mon.

PASSAU Gasthaus zur Blauen Donau

Höllgasse 14, 94032 **Tel** *0851-4908660*

Located just below the cathedral and the old town, this long-time favorite in Passau is a cozy Gasthaus with a typically warm German atmosphere. The hearty, traditional Bavarian food is delicious, freshly made, and a far cry from regular pub fare. The upstairs dining room offers a good view of the Danube. Closed Sun–Mon.

PASSAU Heilig-Geist-Stift Stiftskeller

Heilig-Geist-Gasse 4, 94032 **Tel** *0851-2607*

Dark wood panelling throughout with a historical feel and old tiled stoves. Dinner is served in the hunting room or bishop's room, where coats of arms, hunting trophies and old prints adorn the walls. This rustic restaurant and wine bar specialize in Bavarian food. Try the locally caught freshwater fish. Closed Wednesday.

ROTHENBURG OB DER TAUBER Gerberhaus Cafe

Spitalgasse 25, 91541 **Tel** *09861-94900*

Try a local Franconian specialty such as *Nürnberger Bratwürstl mit Sauerkraut* (Nuremberg sausages with Sauerkraut) in the lovely beer garden of the Hotel Gerberhaus, below the city wall. The popular café offers great pastries and cappuccino. Other light meals are served accompanied by local wine from the Tauber valley. Closed Mon.

STUTTGART Hotel Traube

Brabandtgasse 2, 70599 **Tel** *0711-458920*

Steeped in history, the Traube is a half-timbered, small hotel in Plieningen, a village just outside Stuttgart. From its antique furniture to old doors, cobblestones, and gabled roof, it exudes a romantic charm. The wood-paneled dining room is cozy indoors and the summer terrace is a pretty alternative. Good Swabian game and fish. Closed Sun.

STUTTGART Wielandshöhe

Alte Weinsteige 71, 70597 **Tel** *0711-6408848*

At one of Stuttgart's leading restaurants, with a Michelin star to prove it, chef Vincent Klink serves gourmet cuisine in a relaxed setting. The menu offers regional, mainly Alsatian and French-influenced, dishes based on local, organic produce. Signature dishes include lamb, veal kidneys, lobster, and for dessert, *Tarte Tatin*. Closed Sun–Mon.

STUTTGART Cube

Kleiner Schlossplatz 1, 70173 **Tel** *0711-2804441*

A gastronomic delight within Stuttgart's modern art museum. The vast glass cube houses this excellent restaurant for cultured dining on the fourth floor. Minimal, stylish, and cosmopolitan, the Pacific Rim cuisine in the evenings offers fusion dishes such as honey-and-soya-glazed duck breast on chilli-vanilla cabbage.

WÜRZBURG Schloss Steinburg

Auf dem Steinberg, 97080 **Tel** *0931-97020*

The romantic Steinburg castle provides the attractive setting for this hotel and restaurant. It boasts fabulous views over the town from the garden terrace in fine weather. Steeped in history the castle was first mentioned in 1236. Enjoy German gourmet specialties with excellent service. Perhaps book a romantic candlelit dinner for two.

WESTERN GERMANY

BONN Zur Lindenwirtin Aennchen

Aennchenplatz 2, 53173 **Tel** *0228-312051*

The interior is very ornate and the stylish setting creates an intimate and romantic atmosphere. The kitchen produces international dishes with a leaning towards France. Their carefully chosen wine list encompasses great wines from nine different countries. The service is impeccable and polite. Closed Sun.

Map References *see map of Munich pp546–7*

BONN-BAD GODESBERG Halbedel's Gasthaus
Rheinallee 47, 53173 **Tel** *0228-354253*

A stone's throw from the Rhine in an exclusive part of town in a nondescript villa. The chef concocts fantastic and interesting international cuisine and is constantly inventing new dishes. They cater to the serious wine lover, too, with more than 700 different wines. The service is first rate.

COLOGNE Restaurant Pöttgen
Landmannstraße 19, 50825 **Tel** *0221-555246*

This traditional and cheerful restaurant has been in the Pöttgen family for four generations and is still going strong. The history of the restaurant and family can be seen in the charming decor. The food is always very tasty and is fantastic value. The chef has kept some dishes from the menus of his ancestors.

COLOGNE Il Carpaccio
Lindenstraße 5, 50674 **Tel** *0221-236487*

This is one of the best-known Italian restaurants in Cologne. One of their secrets is the top-quality ingredients they use – always fresh and authentic. Their home-made pasta is quite simply fantastic. Every Friday and Saturday there is live music. Stylish decor, great food, and a good wine selection.

COLOGNE Landhaus Kuckuck
Olympiaweg 2, 50933 **Tel** *0221-485360*

This restaurant is located in a quiet part of Cologne and has a reputation for its fine cuisine as well as its very extensive wine cellar. The menu is changed frequently and the chef makes good use of seasonal produce. The outside seating area has a very pleasant ambience.

FRANKFURT AM MAIN Zum Schwarzen Stern
Römerberg 6, 60311 **Tel** *069-291979*

A restaurant serving traditional fare as well as international dishes. There is a specific menu section called "Grandmother's recipes," which caters to the taste for regional cuisine. It is located next to the cathedral in a very old building and there are references to it dating back to 1453.

FRANKFURT AM MAIN Tigerpalast
Heiligkreuzgasse 16–20, 60313 **Tel** *069-92002225*

This rare find combines Michelin-starred dining with a variety show. Light Mediterranean dishes are served with flair and passion. The walls are adorned with show posters from all over the world. It is common for guests to combine dining in the restaurant with watching the show.

KOBLENZ Da Vinci
Firmungstraße 32b, 56068 **Tel** *0261-9215444*

An Italian restaurant with a sophisticated atmosphere and superb cuisine. There are often functions held here, such as wine tastings and fashion shows. The walls are covered with paintings and there is often soft music playing. The fresh ingredients and traditional Italian dishes have made this restaurant popular amongst the locals.

KOBLENZ Finesse
Julius-Wegeler-Straße 6, 56068 **Tel** *0261-1360*

This contemporary restaurant in the Mercure Hotel Koblenz offers international and regional specialties. The historic city center is within walking distance, and during the summer you can eat out on the terrace with a gorgeous view of the Rhine. Open evenings only.

MAINZ Der Halbe Mond
In der Witz 12, 55252 **Tel** *06134-23913*

A tiny restaurant offering some very special creations. Because there are only five tables it is a good idea to make reservations first. The dishes have a refined flavor and a French influence. The night is not complete without sampling their white and dark chocolate mousse with caramelized hazelnuts.

MARIA LAACH Seespiegel-Seehotel Maria Laach
Orsteil Maria Laach, 56653 **Tel** *02652-584512*

This unique and well-respected restaurant is located in a hotel close to an 11th-century monastery, which provides the kitchen with fresh produce. Seafood has a starring role on the menu, although their lamb fillet salad is tempting and seductive. The chef is sympathetic to vegetarians and provides them with fantastic fare.

TRIER Pfeffermühle
Zurlaubener Ufer 76, 54292 **Tel** *0651-26133*

This restaurant overlooks the Mosel river and has a great view that can be enjoyed from their terrace in the warmer months. The building dates back to the 19th century and provides an intimate location to enjoy their international cuisine. The terrace is a little more sociable, as there are more tables outside. Closed Sun & Mon.

TRIER Römischer Kaiser-Taverne
Porta-Nigra-Platz 6, 54292 **Tel** *0651-9770100*

This restaurant is inside the Römischer Kaiser hotel, which is located at the edge of a scenic square in Trier. The specials are often interesting and tasty, especially the game dishes. There is an extensive wine list that has a number of international wines, as well as a good selection of German wines. It is best to book on weekends.

NORTHERN GERMANY

BREMEN Ratskeller

       ♿ 🍷   €€€

Am Markt, 28195 **Tel** *0421-321676*

Ratskeller is housed in the oldest operating wine cellar in Germany, established in the 15th century. There is a wine bar which offers over 600 different wines. The restaurant serves great international food in a truly magnificent dining area, complete with wood-paneled walls, chandeliers, and wall paintings.

BREMEN Meierei im Bürgerpark

       🍴 🍷   €€€€€

Im Bürgerpark, 28209 **Tel** *0421-3408619*

This restaurant first opened in 1881. There is a Mediterranean flavor running through the menu, however, one should not overlook their fabulous rabbit *ragout*. The inside is inviting with a warm fireplace in the dining area which is dominated by earth tones. There is a large wine selection, mainly Italian.

HAMBURG Au Quai

       🍴   €€

Grosse Elbstraße 145 B-D, 22767 **Tel** *040-38037730*

Housed in a refurbished cold storage depot, the conversion has resulted in a fantastic place to try the best of Hamburg's seafood. Operated by a brother and sister, the kitchen reflects their heritage with great Mediterranean dishes and a subtle French influence that works well with the delicate fish-dominated menu. Closed Sun.

HAMBURG Fischereihafen-Restaurant

       ♿ 🍴 🍷   €€€€

Grosse Elbstraße 143, 22767 **Tel** *040-381816*

This is the place to go for fresh, delicious seafood (though other dishes are offered). The large menu is changed often to suit the seasons. The terrace overlooks the water and has one of the best views of the harbor. The list of famous guests is longer than the extensive wine list and reflects the great food and outstanding service.

HAMBURG Jacobs Restaurant

       🍴   €€€€€

Elbchaussee 401–403, 22609 **Tel** *040-822550*

This restaurant, situated in the beautiful Hotel Louis C. Jacob, is among the best in the city. The cuisine is international with a definite French infusion. There is also a wine cellar that keeps connoisseurs happily occupied for hours, with the help of the master sommelier. There is an adjacent wine bar and a terrace. Closed Mon & Tue.

HANNOVER Die Insel

       🍴   €€€

Rudolf-von-Bennigsen-Ufer 81, 30519 **Tel** *0511-831214*

There is a picturesque view of nearby Lake Masch from the dining area. This restaurant attracts customers from the music industry to politics. The cuisine is hard to pin down, with some great regional dishes as well as some well-executed oriental creations. The food is matched by the equally impressive wine selection.

HANNOVER Gallo Nero

       🍴   €€€

Gross-Buchholzer Kirchweg 72b, 30655 **Tel** *0511-5463434*

The "Black Rooster" offers top-quality Italian cuisine, ranging from basic flavors and produce to more refined sauces and spices. The interior of the restaurant resembles a Tuscan art gallery, which gives a very intimate and unique atmosphere to enjoy their unpretentious food. They have a large selection of Italian wines. Closed Sun.

HANNOVER Le Chalet

       🍴   €€€€€

Isernhagener Straße 21, 30161 **Tel** *0511-344837*

An intimate dining experience in an elegant part of town. The French cuisine has won popularity amongst patrons with their rich sauces and exquisite salads. The staff blend into the background until they are needed, at which time they seem to materialize out of thin air. This is particularly helpful when selecting wines, as they are experts.

LÜBECK Historischer Weinkeller

       🍴   €€

Koberg 6–8, 23552 **Tel** *0451-76234*

This unique restaurant is located in a 13th-century wine cellar under a historic hospital. There is a medieval tone to the restaurant, which has retained the ambience of its heritage, while at the same time creating a light and friendly atmosphere. Their game dishes have won the hearts of locals and tourists.

LÜBECK Wullenwever

       🍴   €€€€€

Beckergrube 71, 23552 **Tel** *0451-704333*

A very elegant restaurant that offers a number of unique rooms and dining areas, the chef is liberal with his creations, happily giving out recipes to interested patrons. The set menus have been artfully chosen to give a perfect balance of tastes, and there are wine suggestions for each dish. It is well-known, so book ahead. Closed Sun & Mon.

MÜNSTER Landhaus Eggert

       ♿ 🍷   €€€

Zur Haskenau 81, 48157 **Tel** *0251-328040*

The hotel and restaurant are family-owned and run, and there is a personal approach to the service. The chef produces fantastic and varied menus, exploring international cuisine while also showcasing the region's best dishes. The setting is a peaceful country area and the hotel was once a farm.

AUSTRIA

ustria has existed as a country for less than 100 years but, despite inauspicious beginnings, has thrived thanks to its position at the heart of Europe. Visitors are attracted by the glories of its Imperial Habsburg past, especially in the capital, Vienna. Austria also has a strong musical tradition and great natural beauty, especially in the Alps and the valley of the Danube.

Present-day Austria emerged in 1919, when the lands of its former empire were granted independence, as a curiously shaped, landlocked country. It is bordered by Switzerland and Germany to the west and north. Along the rest of its border lie the former lands of the old Habsburg Empire, the Czech Republic, Slovakia, Hungary, Slovenia, and the South Tyrol. The regions of the west, the Vorarlberg and the Tyrol, are mountainous, dominated by the eastern Alps. This is where you will find the most familiar images of Austria: well-appointed skiing resorts, snow-capped peaks, and beautiful valleys cloaked in forest.

The Alps are not the traditional heart of Austria – this lies in the regions of Upper and Lower Austria in the northeast, where the Danube (Donau) flows eastwards across the country for 360 km (225 miles). Vienna stands at a point just beyond where the great river emerges from the mountains to flow into the Hungarian plain. The east of the country is more populous, with more agriculture and industry.

HISTORY

In the 1st millennium BC, settlements in the region of present-day Austria prospered from mining iron and salt. One settlement, Hallstatt, has given its name to an important Iron Age culture that spread across Europe. It was iron that first drew the Romans to occupy the region, where they established the provinces of Rhaetia, Noricum, and Pannonia, making the Danube the frontier of their empire. When the Romans withdrew, the region was settled by Germanic tribes, such as the Alemanni and the Bavarians, and Slavs, but it was the German-speaking peoples who prevailed.

Ruined castle of Aggstein overlooking the Danube in the Wachau region

◁ **The magnificent staircase at the entrance to the Vienna State Opera House**

The geographical kernel of Austria (Österreich) was the Ostmark (eastern march or border county) established by Charlemagne in the 9th century to protect the frontier of his empire. In the 10th century, the Babenbergs acquired the county, which was elevated to a dukedom in 1156. Their dynasty died out in the 13th century and their lands were fought over until they came under the control of Rudolf of Habsburg, who was elected Holy Roman Emperor in 1273.

The Central, one of the grandest of Vienna's coffee houses

Over the next three centuries the Habsburg domains grew, occasionally by conquest, but usually by means of marriages and inheritances. In time it became a matter of course that they were elected as Holy Roman Emperors.

From the 15th century, Turkish invasions threatened the Habsburg lands. In 1683 the Turks laid siege to Vienna, but they were dispersed by a relieving army. This marked the start of many successful campaigns in the Balkans. In the 18th century Austria was a major power, although the rise of Prussia and Napoleon's occupation of Vienna in 1809 dented Habsburg pride.

The Austrian empire was considerably weakened in the 19th century by the growth of nationalist movements, but Vienna enjoyed its heyday as a great cosmopolitan European capital.

After World War I, the defeated Austrian Empire was dismembered and countries such as Czechoslovakia and Hungary gained their independence. There followed bitter struggles between Right and Left for control of the new Austrian republic. The country was annexed by Germany in 1938 and then, following Hitler's defeat in 1945, came under Allied control until 1955, when it

Exploring Austria

Austria's main attractions are the alpine resorts in the west of the country around Innsbruck and the capital, Vienna, in the east. In between there are many other sights worth seeking out: ancient monasteries and castles, well-preserved medieval cities, such as Salzburg and Graz, the picturesque lakes of the Salzkammergut region, and the scenic stretch of the Danube known as the Wachau. Road and rail communications along the main axis of the country between Vienna, Linz, Salzburg, and Innsbruck are very good.

SIGHTS AT A GLANCE

Skiing at the fashionable resort of Kitzbühel in the Austrian Alps

0 kilometers   50

0 miles   50

Munich

Ulm   Ulm   Munich   GERMAN

Bregenz
St Gallen   Dornbirn   Jenbach   Kitzb
Zürich   Feldkirch   Inn   ✈ Innsbruck 165
LIECHTENSTEIN   St Anton   Landeck   Mayrho
Milan
SWITZERLAND   ITALY
Bolzano   Bolzano

became a sovereign state once more. As a keen member of the EU, Austria has flourished economically, but the old political divisions have arisen. The far-right FPÖ (then led by Jörg Haider), were part of government coalitions from 2000 – resulting in international outrage – until the Social Democratic party (SPÖ) took over in 2006. Elections in 2008 showed a large increase in votes for both far-right parties: the FPÖ, led by H.C. Strache, and Jörg Haider's BZÖ/Alliance for the Future of Austria. Following weeks of negotiations, the SPÖ and conservative People's Party (ÖVP) formed a coalition.

LANGUAGE AND CULTURE

Austria is linguistically homogenous, with 98 percent of the population speaking German. There are, however, considerable differences in dialect between the various regions.

Culturally, Austria is synonymous with music, the long list of great Austrian composers including Mozart, Haydn, Schubert, and Mahler, not forgetting the Strausses, father and son, and their famous waltzes. Vienna's intellectual

KEY DATES IN AUSTRIAN HISTORY

c.800 BC Rise of Hallstatt culture

15 BC Noricum occupied by Romans

AD 976–1246 Babenberg dynasty rules Eastern March of the Holy Roman Empire

1276 Rudolf of Habsburg ruler of Austria

1519 Charles V is elected Holy Roman Emperor

1618–48 Thirty Years' War

1683 Siege of Vienna

1740–80 Reign of Maria Theresa

1805 Napoleon defeats Austrians at Austerlitz

1815 Congress of Vienna

1848 Revolutions throughout Habsburg Empire

1918 Defeat in World War I brings Habsburg rule to an end – Austria declared republic

1938 Anschluss – Austria absorbed by Germany

1945–55 Vienna occupied by Allies

1994 Austria joins EU

2004 Elfriede Jelinek receives Nobel Prize for Literature

2006 After FPÖ party splits in 2005, Social Democrats defeat conservatives in elections

2008 Coalition between Social Democratic Party (SPÖ) and People's Party (ÖVP). Jörg Haider dies

2009 200th anniversary of the death of composer, Joseph Haydn

and artistic life enjoyed an extraordinary flowering in the late 19th and early 20th century with the Secession movement in painting, architecture, and design. It was also the period of Sigmund Freud's investigations, which laid the foundations of modern psychology.

KEY

Symbol	Description
✈	Airport
—	Highway
—	Major road
—	Railroad
▪▪▪	International border

Vienna ❶

Greater Vienna has a population of 1.6 million, but the Austrian capital is a compact city with many of the important sights, especially those that date from the Habsburg era, clustered around the Hofburg, the former imperial court. In the mid-19th century the city's old defenses were pulled down and a wide circular boulevard, the Ringstrasse, was built linking new political and cultural institutions, such as Vienna's great art gallery, the Kunsthistorisches Museum. Completed in the 1880s, the Ringstrasse still defines the Innere Stadt or heart of the city. The Danube (Donau) river flows through the east of the city, where it has been canalized to prevent flooding.

SIGHTS AT A GLANCE

Albertina ⑫
Burgtheater ②
Freud Museum ⑧
Hofburg pp592–4 ①
Karlskirche ⑪
Kunsthistorisches Museum ⑥
Museum of Applied Arts ⑨
MuseumsQuartier Wien ⑦
Naturhistorisches Museum ⑤
Secession Building ⑩
Staatsoper ④
Stephansdom ③

Greater Vienna *(see inset map)*
Belvedere ⑭
Prater ⑬
Schönbrunn Palace
and Gardens ⑮

GETTING AROUND

The center of the city is easily explored on foot. Trams 1 and 2 take you along parts of the Ringstrasse past many of the main sights. To see these in old-world style, but at great expense, hire a horse-drawn *Fiaker*. The suburbs are served by the U-bahn (subway) and S-bahn services, although the latter is of more use to locals.

Lipizzaner stallion at the Spanish Riding School in the Hofburg

SEE ALSO

• *Where to Stay* pp608–9

• *Where to Eat* pp610–11

A   B   C

GREATER VIENNA

Stockerau / Brno

Währing

Herrnals

Penzing

Franz-Josefs-Bahnhof

Josefstadt

Westbahnhof

Linz
Melk

Hietzing

Meidling

Favoriten

Graz
Wiener Neustadt

Eisenstadt

Alte Donau

Donaustadt

Praterstern-Wien Nord
13

Landstrasse
14

Ostbahnhof

Simmering

Schwechat
Airport

Bratislava

0 km 2

0 miles 2

KEY

Area of main map

ROSSAUER

NGERGASSE

ASSE

MERGASSE

Rossauer
Lände

HANGASSE

BERGGASSE

RASSE
HÖRLGASSE

SCHLICK-
PLATZ

Schottenring

CHOTTENRING

EBESIENSTRASSE

HOHENSTAUFENG.

FRANZ-JOSEFS-KAI

GONZAGAG.

NEUTORG.

BÖRSEGASSE

WERDERTORG.

CONCORDIA-
PLATZ
Altes
Rathaus

HEINRICHSG.

RUDOLFS-
PLATZ

MORZIN-
PLATZ

SALZGRIES

WIPPLINGER STRASSE

SALVATORG.

MAC-AUREL-STR.

Schweden
platz

FRANZ-JOSEFS-KAI

JULIUS-RAAB-
PLATZ

INNERE

STADT

FREYUNG

TIEFER
GRABEN

AM
HOF

NAGLERGASSE

HERRENGASSE

WALLNERSTR.

REITSCHUL.

WALLNERSTR.

JUDEN-
PLATZ

TUCHLAUBEN

BRANDSTÄTTE

BAUERNMARKT

ROTENTURMSTRASSE

FLEISCHMARKT

POSTGASSE

DOMINIKANERBASTEI

BIBERSTRASSE

STUBENRING

P

P

P

Stephans
platz

KOHLMARKT

GRABEN

HAELER-
PLATZ

JOSEFS-
PLATZ

DOROTHERG.

SPIEGELGASSE

STEPHANS-
PLATZ

3

SCHULERSTRASSE

WOLLZEILE

SINGERSTR.

SCHULERSTRASSE

Stubentor

9

1

AUGUSTINERSTR.

Lobkowitz
Palais

12

KÄRNTNERSTRASSE

WEIHBURG.

HIMMELPFORT.

SEILERSTÄTTE

STUBENBASTEI

GASSE

PARKRING

Winter Palace
of Prince
Eugene

HEGELGASSE

SCHWARZENBERGSTR.

SCHUBERTRING

JRGGARTEN

ALBERTINA-
PLATZ

OPERNRING

4

MAHLERSTR.

ELISABETHSTRASSE
LATZ

NIBELUNGENGASSE

Akademie
der Bildenden
Künste

10

KÄRNTNER RING

BÖSENDORFERSTR.

WIENZEILE

WIEDNER HAUPTSTRASSE

Karlsplatz

LOTHRINGERSTR.

KARLS-
PLATZ

11

SCHWARZEN-
BERGPLATZ

PANIGLG.

KARLSG.

GUSSHAUSSTRASSE

PAULANERG.

MOZART-
PLATZ

0 meters 500

0 yards 500

KEY

	Sight / Place of interest
✈	Airport
🚉	Train station
Ⓤ	U-Bahn station
🅿	Parking
ℹ	Tourist information
✝	Church
✡	Synagogue
—	Pedestrian street

D E F

Hofburg ①

What began as a small fortress in 1275 grew over the centuries into a vast palace, the Hofburg. It was the seat of Austrian power for over six centuries, and successive rulers were all anxious to leave their mark. The various buildings range in style from Gothic to late 19th-century Neo-Renaissance. The complex was still expanding up until a few years before the Habsburgs fell from power in 1918. The presence of the imperial court had a profound effect on the surrounding area, with noble families competing to site their palaces as close as possible to the Hofburg.

Burggarten

The Albertina houses a collection of Old Master drawings and prints.

Statue of Joseph II (1806) in Josefsplatz

★ Augustinerkirche
The former parish church of the Habsburgs houses the spectacular late 18th-century tomb of Maria Christina, Maria Theresa's favorite daughter, by Antonio Canova.

Prunksaal
The showpiece of the Austrian National Library (1722–35) is the grand, wood-paneled Prunksaal, or Hall of Honor.

Stallburg

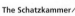

The Schatzkammer (treasuries) are housed in the Alte Burg, the core of the old palace.

The Michaelertor is the gate through which visitors reach the older parts of the palace.

★ Spanish Riding School
The white Lipizzaner horses are stabled in the Stallburg opposite the Riding School itself, where they are trained and give performances.

STAR FEATURES

★ State Apartments

★ Spanish Riding School

★ Augustinerkirche

Mozart Memorial *(1896)*
*Viktor Tilgner's statue of
the composer stands just
inside the Ringstrasse
entrance.*

VISITORS' CHECKLIST

Michaelerplatz 1, A-1010.
Ⓤ *Stephansplatz, Herrengasse,
Volkstheater.* 🚌 *2A, 3A.* 🚃 *D,
1, 2. For details of individual
museums, see p594.*

The Burgtor or outer
gate was built to a
design by Peter Nobile
in 1821–4.

Neue Burg
*A monument to
the great general,
Eugene of Savoy
(1663–1736), stands
in front of the newest
wing of the palace,
completed in 1913.*

Volksgarten

Heldenplatz

Schweizertor
*This 16th-century
gateway leads to the
Schweizerhof, the oldest part
of the Hofburg, originally a
stronghold with four towers.*

The Burgkapelle,
the Hofburg's
chapel, is where the
famous Vienna
Boys' Choir sings.

★ State Apartments
*The table in the state
banqueting hall is laid
as it used to be in the
latter
part of the reign of Franz
Joseph I (1848–1916).*

Exploring the Hofburg Complex

The vast Hofburg complex contains the former imperial apartments and treasuries (Schatzkammer) of the Habsburgs, several museums, a chapel, a church, the Austrian National Library, the Winter Riding School, and the President of Austria's offices. The entrance to the imperial apartments and the treasuries is through the Michaelertor on Michaelerplatz.

10th-century crown of the Holy Roman Empire, Schatzkammer

Portrait of the Empress Elisabeth by Winterhalter (1865)

Neue Burg

Heldenplatz. *Tel* 01-5252 4484. ◯ 10am–6pm Wed–Mon. 📷
The massive curved Neue Burg on Heldenplatz was added to the Hofburg in 1881–1913. Archaeological finds from Ephesus are on display in the **Ephesos Museum**, while pianos that belonged to Beethoven, Schubert, and Haydn are housed in the musical instrument museum – the **Sammlung alter Musikinstrumente**. The weapons collection in the **Hofjagd und Rüstkammer** is one of the finest in Europe. There is also an excellent ethnological collection – the **Völkerkundemuseum**, as well as collections from the Kunsthistorisches Museum (*see p596*).

Augustinerkirche

Augustinerstraße 3. *Tel* 01-533 7099. ◯ daily. **www**.hochamt.at
The church has one of the best-preserved 14th-century Gothic interiors in Vienna. In the Loreto Chapel are a series of silver urns that contain the hearts of the Habsburg family. The church is also celebrated for its music, with masses by Schubert or Haydn performed here on Sundays and holidays.

State Apartments

Michaelerkuppel-Feststiege. *Tel* 01-533 7570. ◯ 9am–5pm daily. 📷 📷
The State Apartments (Kaiserappartements) in the Reichskanzleitrakt (1726–30) and the Amalienburg (1575) include the rooms occupied by Franz Joseph from 1857 to 1916, Empress Elisabeth's apartments from 1854 to 1898, and the rooms where Czar Alexander I lived during the Congress of Vienna in 1815.

Spanish Riding School

Tel 01-533 9031. ◯ for performances & morning training Tue–Sun (except Jul). 🔴 public hols. 📷 ♿ some areas.
The Spanish Riding School is believed to have been founded in 1572 to cultivate the classic skills of *haute école* horsemanship. By breeding and training horses from Spain, the Habsburgs formed the Spanische Reitschule. Today, 80-minute shows take place in the building known as the Winter Riding School, built in 1729–35 to a design by Josef Emanuel Fischer von Erlach.

Schatzkammer

Schweizerhof. *Tel* 01-525 240. ◯ 10am–6pm Wed–Mon. 🔴 Jan 1, May 1, Nov 1, Dec 25. 📷 ♿
Sacred and secular treasures amassed during centuries of Habsburg rule are displayed in 21 rooms, known as the Schatzkammer or Treasury. They include relics of the Holy Roman Empire, the crown jewels, and liturgical objects of the imperial court. Visitors can also admire the dazzling gold, silver, and porcelain once used at state banquets.

Burgkapelle

Schweizerhof. *Tel* 01-533 9927. ◯ 11am–3pm Mon–Thu, 11am–1pm Fri. 🔴 Nov 1, Dec 8, Jan 1, Jul, Aug. 📷 **Vienna Boys' Choir** Jan–Jun & Sep–Dec: 9:15am Sun (book by phone). 📷
From the Schweizerhof, steps lead up to the Burgkapelle, originally constructed in 1296. The interior has Gothic statues in canopied niches. On Sundays, visitors can hear the Wiener Sängerknaben, the Vienna Boys' Choir (*see p607*).

Burggarten and Volksgarten

Burgring/Opernring/Dr-Karl-Renner-Ring. ◯ daily.
Some of the space left around the Hofburg after Napoleon had razed part of the city walls was transformed by the Habsburgs into gardens. The Volksgarten opened to the public in 1820, but the Burggarten remained the palace's private garden until 1918.

Ornamental pond in the Volksgarten, with Burgtheater in the background

Burgtheater ②

Dr.-Karl-Lueger-Ring 2, A-1014. *Tel* 01-51444 4145. **U** *Schottentor.* *1, 2, D.* ☐ *for performances.* ● *Good Fri, Dec 24; Jul & Aug (except for guided tours).* 🎦 & 📷 *afternoons (call 01-5144 44140).*

The Burgtheater is the most prestigious stage in the German-speaking world. The original theater, built in Maria Theresa's reign, was replaced in 1888 by today's Italian Renaissance-style building by Karl von Hasenauer and Gottfried Semper. It closed for refurbishment in 1897 after the discovery that several seats had no view of the stage. At the end of World War II a bomb devastated the building, leaving only the side wings containing the Grand Staircases intact. The restoration was so successful that today it is hard to tell the new parts from the old.

Detail from the Wiener Neustädter Altar in the Stephansdom

Stephansdom ③

Stephansplatz 3, A-1010. *Tel* 01-51552 3526. **U** *Stephansplatz.* *1A.* ☐ *daily.* &

The Stephansdom, with its magnificent glazed-tile roof, is the heart and soul of Vienna. It is no mere coincidence that the urns containing the entrails of some of the Habsburgs lie in a vault beneath its main altar.

A church has stood on the site for over 800 years, but all that remains of the original 13th-century Romanesque church are the Giants' Doorway and Heathen

Auditorium of the Staatsoper, the Vienna State Opera House

Towers. The Gothic nave, the choir, and the side chapels are the result of rebuilding in the 14th and 15th centuries, while some of the outbuildings, such as the Lower Vestry, are Baroque additions.

The lofty vaulted interior contains an impressive collection of works of art. Masterpieces of Gothic sculpture include the fabulously intricate pulpit, several of the figures of saints adorning the piers, and the canopies over many of the side altars. To the left of the High Altar is the 15th-century winged Wiener Neustädter Altar bearing the painted images of 72 saints. The altar panels open out to reveal delicate sculpture groups. The most spectacular Renaissance work is the tomb of Friedrich III, while the High Altar adds a flamboyant Baroque note.

Staatsoper ④

Opernring 2, A-1010. *Tel* 01-51444 2250. **U** *Karlsplatz.* *1, 2, D.* ☐ *for performances.* 🎦 & 📷 *by arrangement (call 51444-2613).* www.wiener-staatsoper.at

Vienna's opera house, the Staatsoper, was the first of the grand Ringstrasse buildings to be completed; it opened on May 25, 1869 to the strains of Mozart's *Don Giovanni*. Built in Neo-Renaissance style, it initially failed to impress the Viennese. Yet when it was

hit by a bomb in 1945 and largely destroyed, the event was seen as a symbolic blow to the city. With a brand new auditorium and stage, the Opera House reopened in November 1955 with a performance of Beethoven's *Fidelio*.

Naturhistorisches Museum ⑤

Burgring 7, A-1014. *Tel* 01-521 77 217. **U** *Volkstheater.* *2A, 48A.* *2, D, 46, 49.* ☐ *9am–6:30pm Thu–Mon (to 9pm Wed).* ● *Jan 1, May 1, Nov 1, Dec 25.* 🎦 📷 *Wed & Sun (rooftop).* & www.nhm-wien.ac.at

Almost the mirror image of the Kunsthistorisches Museum, the Natural History Museum was designed by the same architects, and opened in 1889. Its collections include archaeological, anthropological, mineralogical, zoological, and geological displays. There are casts of dinosaur skeletons, the world's largest display of skulls illustrating the history of man, one of Europe's most comprehensive collections of gems, prehistoric sculpture, Bronze Age items, and extinct birds and mammals. In the archaeological section look out for the celebrated Venus of Willendorf, a 25,000-year-old Palaeolithic fertility figurine, and finds from the early Iron Age settlement at Hallstatt *(see p602)*.

Venus of Willendorf, Naturhistorisches Museum

Hunters in the Snow by Peter Brueghel the Elder (1565)

Kunsthistorisches Museum ⑥

Maria-Theresien-Platz. **Tel** 01-525 4025. Ⓤ MuseumsQuartier, Volkstheater. 🚌 2A, 57A. 🚋 D, 1, 2. ◯ 10am–6pm Tue–Sun (Jun–Aug: 10am–6pm daily); picture gallery also 6–9pm Thu. ◯ Jan 1, May 1, Nov 1, Dec 25. 🎫 ♿ 🖥 📷 ✉
www.khm.at

The Museum of the History of Art attracts more than one and a half million visitors each year. Its collections are based largely on those built up over a number of centuries by the Habsburgs.

The picture gallery occupies the first floor. The collection focuses on Old Masters from the 15th to the 18th centuries. Because of the links between the Habsburgs and the Netherlands, Flemish painting is well represented. About half the surviving works of Peter Brueghel the Elder (c.1525–69) are held by the museum, including *The Tower of Babel* and most of the cycle of *The Seasons*.

The Dutch paintings range from genre scenes of great domestic charm to magnificent landscapes. All the Rembrandts on show are portraits, including the famous *Large Self-Portrait* of the artist in a plain smock (1652). The only Vermeer is the enigmatic allegorical painting, *The Artist's Studio* (1665). The

Blue ceramic hippopotamus from Egypt (around 2000 BC)

Italian galleries have a strong collection of 16th-century Venetian paintings, with a comprehensive range of Titians and great works by Giovanni Bellini and Tintoretto. Also on show are the bizarre vegetable portrait heads, representing the four seasons, made for Emperor Rudolf II by Giuseppe Arcimboldo (1527–93).

The German section is rich in 16th-century paintings. There are several works by Dürer, including his *Madonna with the Pear* (1512). The most interesting of the Spanish works are the portraits of the Spanish royal family made by Diego Velázquez (1599–1660).

On the ground floor are the Greek, Roman, Egyptian, and Near Eastern collections, with new rooms devoted specifically to Greek and Roman antiquities. Among the Egyptian and Near Eastern antiquities is an entire 5th-Dynasty tomb chapel from Giza (c.2400 BC) and a splendid bust of King Tuthmosis III (c.1460 BC).

The sculpture and decorative arts collection is closed until November 2012. It usually contains some fine, late Gothic religious statues by artists such as Tilman Riemenschneider (c.1460–1531), and curiosities owned by various Habsburg monarchs, such as automata and scientific instruments.

MuseumsQuartier Wien ⑦

Museumsplatz 1. **Tel** 01-523-5881. Ⓤ MuseumsQuartier, Volkstheater. 🚌 2a to the MuseumsQuartier, 48a to Volkstheater. 🚋 49 to Volkstheater. **Visitor Centre** ◯ 10am–7pm daily. 🎫 🖥 ♿ 🍴 📷 www.mqw.at

This museum complex is one of the largest cultural centers in the world, housed in what was once the imperial stables and carriage houses. Here you will find art museums, venues for film, theater, architecture, dance, new media, and a children's creativity center. The visitor center is a good starting point.

Among the attractions is the **Leopold Museum** which focuses on Austrian art, including many works by Egon Schiele and Gustav Klimt. The **Museum of Modern Art Ludwig Foundation Vienna** shows contemporary and modern art from around the world. **ZOOM Kinder-museum** offers a lively introduction to the world of the museum for children. **Architekturzentrum** is dedicated to 20th- and 21st-century architecture.

Freud Museum ⑧

Berggasse 19. **Tel** 01-319 1596. Ⓤ Schottentor. 🚌 40A. 🚋 D. ◯ 9am–5pm daily. 🎫

No. 19 Berggasse is very like any other 19th-century apartment in Vienna, yet it is now one of the city's most famous addresses. The father of psychoanalysis, Sigmund Freud, received patients here from 1891 to 1938. The flat housed Freud's family, too.

Beautifully restored patients' waiting room in the Freud Museum

Memorabilia on display include letters and books, furnishings, and photographs. Even his hat and cane are on show. The apartment was abandoned when the Nazis forced Freud to leave, but still preserves an intimate domestic atmosphere.

Museum of Applied Arts ⑨

Stubenring 5. **Tel** 01-711 360.
🚇 Stubentor, Landstraße. 🚌 74A.
🚊 1, 2. ⬜ 10am–midnight Tue, 10am–6pm Wed–Sun. ⬤ Jan 1, May 1, Nov 1, Dec 25. 📷 ♿ 🚻 🏛 🎁

The MAK (Museum für angewandte Kunst) was founded in 1864 as a museum for art and industry. Over the years, it also acquired objects representing new artistic movements. The museum has a fine collection of furniture, including some classical works of the German cabinet-maker David Roentgen, textiles, glass, Islamic and East Asian art, and fine Renaissance jewelry. There is also a whole room full of Biedermeier furniture. The most important Austrian artistic movement was the Secession, formed by artists who seceded from the Vienna academy in 1897. Their style, also known as Jugendstil, is represented through the many and varied productions of the Wiener Werkstätte (Viennese Workshops), a cooperative arts and crafts studio, founded in 1903.

Brass vase (1903) by Kolo Moser

Secession Building ⑩

Friedrichstraße 12. **Tel** 01-587 5307.
🚇 Karlsplatz. ⬜ 10am–6pm Tue–Sun (to 8pm Thu). 📷 ♿

Joseph Maria Olbrich designed the unusual Secession Building in *Jugendstil* style as a

Group of stone owls decorating the Secession Building

showcase for the Secession movement's artists in 1898. The almost windowless building is a squat cube with four towers. The filigree globe of entwined laurel leaves on the roof gave rise to the building's nickname: "The Golden Cabbage."

Inside, Gustav Klimt's famous *Beethoven Frieze*, designed in 1902, covers three walls and stretches 34 m (110 ft) from end to end.

Karlskirche ⑪

Karlsplatz. **Tel** 01-505 6294. 🚇 Karlsplatz. 🚌 4A. 🚊 D. ⬜ daily. 📷

During Vienna's plague epidemic of 1713, Karl VI vowed that, as soon as the city was delivered, he would build a church dedicated to St. Charles Borromeo (1538–84),

Karlskirche, with column showing scenes from the life of St. Charles Borromeo

a patron saint of the plague. Johann Bernhard Fischer von Erlach's eclectic Baroque masterpiece borrows from the architecture of ancient Greece and Rome. The interior was embellished with carvings and altarpieces by leading artists of the day.

Johann Michael Rottmayr's huge fresco in the cupola (1725–30) depicts St. Charles in heaven interceding for deliverance from the plague.

Albertina ⑫

Albertinaplatz 1. **Tel** 01-534 830.
🚇 Karlsplatz, Stephansplatz. 🚊 D, 1, 2. ⬜ 10am–6pm daily (to 9pm Wed). 📷 ♿ 🎁 🏛 🚻
www.albertina.at

Hidden away in a corner of the Hofburg is the Albertina, a palace named after Duke Albert of Sachsen-Teschen, Maria Theresa's son-in-law. Its collection includes one million prints, 65,000 watercolors and drawings, and over 70,000 photographs. The gems of the collection are by Dürer, with Michelangelo and Rubens also well represented. Picasso heads a fine 20th-century section. The Batliner Collection traces the progression from Impressionism to Modernism.

The palace has been restored to its former glory and now, for the first time in over 200 years, it is possible to visit the Habsburg State Rooms with their Neoclassical architecture and interior decoration.

Vienna: Farther Afield

For a city of 1.6 million inhabitants, Vienna is surprisingly compact. Nonetheless, some of the most interesting sights are away from the city center. At Belvedere, the palace and gardens of Prince Eugene impress with their scale and grandeur. Farther away at Schönbrunn sprawls the immense palace and gardens so loved by Empress Maria Theresa. There are also many parks and gardens around the city, the largest and most interesting of which is the Prater. A former hunting ground of the Habsburgs, it is now open to the public for numerous leisure activities.

The colorful Volksprater Funfair, Prater

Prater ⑬

Prater. **U** Praterstern. 🚋 0, 5.
Park ⬭ daily. **Ferris Wheel**
⬭ daily. 🖼 www.prater.wien.info

Originally an imperial hunting ground, this huge area of woods and meadows between the Danube and the Danube Canal was opened to the public by Joseph II in 1766. The central avenue, or Hauptallee, stretches for 5 km (3 miles) through the center of the Prater, and was for a long time the preserve of the nobility and their footmen. During the 19th century the northern end of the Prater became a massive funfair, dominated by a giant ferris wheel, one of Vienna's most famous landmarks. There is also a planetarium, an exhibition center, and a trotting stadium nearby.

The southern side of the Prater contains extensive woodland – interlaced with cycle paths, a municipal golf course, and the Freudenau Racetrack, where flat racing meetings are held from April to November.

Belvedere ⑭

Upper Belvedere Prinz-Eugen-Straße 27. **Tel** 01-795 560. 🚌 13A.
⑤ Südbahnhof. 🚋 0, 18, D, 71.
⬭ 10am–6pm daily. 🖼 ♿ 📷
Lower Belvedere Rennweg 6. **Tel** 01-795 570. 🚋 71, D. ⬭ 10am– 6pm daily. 🖼 ♿ 📷 **Gardens**
⬭ daily. ♿ www.belvedere.at

The Belvedere was built by Johann Lukas von Hildebrandt as the summer residence of Prince Eugene of Savoy, the brilliant military commander whose strategies helped vanquish the Turks in 1683. Situated on a gently sloping hill, the Belvedere consists of two palaces linked by a formal garden laid out in the French style by Dominique Girard. The huge garden is sited on three levels, linked by two elaborate cascading waterfalls. Different areas of the garden are meant to convey a complicated series of Classical allusions: the lower part of the garden represents the domain of the Four Elements, the center is Parnassus, and the upper section is Olympus.

Standing at the highest point of the garden, the Upper Belvedere has a more elaborate facade than the Lower Belvedere, with lavish stone ornamentation, statues, and balustrades. The domed copper roofs of the end pavilions were designed to resemble Turkish tents – an allusion to Prince Eugene's many victories over the Turks. In fact, the whole palace was intended to be a symbolic reflection of the prince's power and glory, and was appropriate to the grand festive occasions for which it was originally used. The many impressive interiors include the Sala Terrena, with four Herculean figures supporting the ceiling, and a grand, sweeping staircase, the ornately decorated chapel, and the opulent Marble Hall.

Sphinx from Up Belvedere gard

Imposing Baroque facade of Prince Eugene's Upper Belvedere palace

For hotels and restaurants in this region see pp608–9 and pp610–11

The Sala Terrena, the grand entrance hall of the Upper Belvedere

The building also houses the collections of 19th- and 20th-century paintings belonging to the Austrian Gallery. Many of the works are by Austrian painters, including an excellent collection by Gustav Klimt. There are also works by Ferdinand Georg Waldmüller and Van Gogh.

The Lower Belvedere was used by Prince Eugene for day-to-day living, and the building itself is less elaborate than the Upper Belvedere. Many of the rooms are just as grand, however, for example the ornate, golden Hall of Mirrors. A museum here shows temporary exhibitions. Next door to the Lower Belvedere is the handsome Orangery, originally used to shelter tender plants in winter.

Some masterpieces from the Baroque collection (formerly housed in the Lower Belvedere) can now be seen on the ground floor of the Upper Belvedere. These include the character heads by Franz Xaver Messerschmidt and sculptures by Georg Raphael Donner, as well as paintings by J. M. Rottmayr, Martino Atomonte, Daniel Gran, and Paul Troger. The ground floor of the Upper Belvedere also houses some masterpieces of Austrian Medieval Art. These include the Znaimer Altar, the seven panels painted by Rueland Frueauf the Elder (1490–94) which show the Passion taking place in an Austrian setting, and the 12th-century Romanesque Stammerberg Crucifix, one of the oldest surviving examples of Tyrolean woodcarving.

Schönbrunn Palace and Gardens ⑮

Schönbrunner Schloss Straße 147, Schönbrunn. **Tel** 01-811 13239. **U** Schönbrunn. 10A. 10, 58. daily. (gardens free).

This magnificent former summer residence of the imperial family takes its name from a "beautiful spring" that was found nearby. An earlier hunting lodge was destroyed by the Turks, so Leopold I asked Johann Bernhard Fischer von Erlach to design a grand Baroque residence here in 1695. The project was finally completed by Nikolaus Pacassi in the mid-18th century, under Empress Maria Theresa.

The strict symmetry of the architecture is complemented by the extensive formal gardens, with their neat lawns and careful planting. An array of fountains and statues is framed by trees and alleyways. The gardens also contain a huge tropical Palm House with an interesting collection of exotic plants, a small zoo, a butterfly house, an orangery, and the Gloriette – a large Neoclassical arcade which crowns the hill behind the palace. Inside the palace, the Rococo decorative schemes were devised by Nikolaus Pacassi. In the state rooms, the dominant features are white paneling, often adorned with gilded ornamental framework. The rooms vary from the extremely sumptuous – such as the Millionen-Zimmer, paneled with fig-wood inlaid with Persian miniatures – to the quite plain apartments of Franz Joseph and Empress Elisabeth. The Memorial Room contains the portrait and effigy of the Duke of Reichstadt, the son of Napoleon and Princess Maria Louisa, daughter of Austrian Emperor Franz I. A virtual prisoner in the palace after Napoleon's fall from power, the duke died here in 1832 aged 21. Alongside the palace is a museum of imperial coaches and sleighs.

The beautiful Schönbrunn Palace, as seen from the gardens

The historic center of Graz, overlooked by the thickly-wooded Schlossberg

Eisenstadt ❷

🏚 14,000. 🚆 🚌 ℹ️ Hauptstraße 35 (02682-705155).

The principal attraction of Eisenstadt is the grand residence of the Esterházy princes, the Hungarian aristocrats who claimed to be descendants of Attila. **Schloss Esterházy** was built for Prince Paul Esterházy in 1663–73. In the Haydnsaal, a huge hall of state decorated with 18th-century frescoes, the famous composer Joseph Haydn (1732–1809) conducted the family orchestra. Haydn lived on Haydngasse, and his house is now a museum. He is buried in the **Bergkirche**, west of the palace.

Until World War II, Eisenstadt had a large Jewish community, and there is a **Jewish Museum** near the palace.

Schloss Esterházy, a mix of Baroque and Neoclassical styles

🏰 **Schloss Esterházy**
Esterházyplatz. **Tel** 02682-719 3000. ◯ Apr–mid-Nov: daily; mid-Nov–Mar: Mon–Fri. 🏷

Graz ❸

🏚 254,000. ✈️ 9 km (6 miles) S. 🚆 🚌 ℹ️ Herrengasse 16 (0316-807 50).

Almost entirely surrounded by mountains, Graz is Austria's second largest city. During the Middle Ages its importance rivaled that of Vienna. In the late 14th century, the Habsburg Duke Leopold III chose Graz as his base, and in the following century the town played a vital strategic role in the war against the invading Turks.

The city is dominated by the Schlossberg, the huge hill on which the town's medieval defenses were built. During the Napoleonic Wars Graz was occupied by French troops, who blew up most of the fortifications in 1809. Among the ruins visible today are a 28-m (92-ft) high clock tower, the **Uhrturm**, dating from 1561, and the **Glockenturm** (bell tower), from 1588. The former houses the **Schlossbergmuseum**, with exhibits illustrating the history of Graz. From the summit of the hill there are splendid views.

At the foot of the Schlossberg lies the Old Town, a UNESCO World Heritage site. The medieval **Burg** (fortress) was built in several stages and

completed in 1500. To the south are the late-Gothic **Cathedral of St. Ägydius**, with its striking Baroque interior, and the **Mausoleum of Ferdinand II**, designed by the Italian Pietro de Pomis in the late 17th century.

The **Universalmuseum Joanneum** includes the Neue Galerie (New Gallery), previously housed in the Herberstein Palace, and the Natural History Museum. The **Alte Galerie** (Old Gallery) at Schloss Eggenberg (see below) houses the Archaeology Museum and a notable coin collection. Also of interest is the **Landeszeughaus**, with its impressive array of over 30,000 weapons and pieces of armor.

🏛 **Universalmuseum Joanneum**
Mariahilferstraße 2–4. **Tel** 0316-80170. ◯ 10am–6pm Tue–Sun. 🏷

Environs
A few kilometers west of the city, **Schloss Eggenberg** was built by Johann Ulrich von Eggenberg in 1625–35. Open daily, the Baroque palace houses the Alte Galerie (an archaeology museum), a collection of local prehistoric finds, coins, antiquities, and gemstones. Its rich collection of paintings includes works by Lucas Cranach the Elder (1472–1553) and Peter Brueghel the Younger (1564–1638). There are displays of stuffed animals in the Jagdmuseum (Hunting Museum).

Melk and the Wachau ❹

🚌 🚆 *Melk.* ℹ️ *Babenbergerstr., Melk (02752-5230 7410).*
Benedictine abbey ⬜ *May–Sep: 9am–5:30pm daily; Apr & Oct: 9am–4:30pm daily; winter: guided tours only (11am and 2pm daily).* 📷

Melk lies at the western end of one of the loveliest stretches of the River Danube, the Wachau, which extends some 40 km (25 miles) downstream to Krems.

Dotted with Renaissance houses and old towers, **Melk** itself is most famous for its Baroque Benedictine abbey, a treasure trove of paintings, sculptures, and decorative art. One of its most impressive rooms is the Marble Hall, with beautiful ceiling paintings depicting mythological scenes.

A boat trip is the best way to enjoy the Wachau, though for the energetic there are cycle paths along the banks of the river. Landmarks to look for traveling downstream include the picturesque castle of **Schönbühel** and the ruined medieval fortress at **Aggstein**. Though not visible from the river, nearby **Willendorf** is the site of famous prehistoric finds.

At the eastern end of the Wachau are the well-preserved medieval towns of **Dürnstein** and **Krems**. The latter's tiny hillside streets offer fine views across the Danube to the Baroque **Göttweig Abbey**.

The opulent interior of the 17th-century Church of St. Ignatius in Linz

Linz ❺

🏠 *186,000.* ✈️ *10 km (6 miles) SW.* 🚌 🚆 ℹ️ *Hauptplatz 1 (0732-7070 1777). www.linz.at*

Austria's third city, Linz has been inhabited since Roman times, when it was a port called Lentia. In the early 16th century it developed into an important trading center. Although, today, Linz is a busy industrial city, the Old Town contains many historic buildings and monuments.

The Hauptplatz, one of the largest medieval squares in Europe, is bordered by splendid Baroque facades.

Among the finest buildings is the **Town Hall**, home to the Museum Linz Genesis, which tells the history of the city. The 20-m- (66-ft-) high marble Dreifaltigkeitssäule (Trinity Column) was completed in 1723.

In the southeast corner of the square is the **Church of St. Ignatius**. Also known as the Alter Dom, it was built in the 17th century in Baroque style and boasts a wonderfully ornate pulpit and altarpiece. Nearby, the **Landhaus** is well worth seeing for its three beautiful Renaissance court-yards and loggia.

The streets west of the Hauptplatz lead up to Linz's hilltop **castle**, built for Friedrich V (Holy Roman Emperor Friedrich III) in the 15th century. The castle houses the Schlossmuseum, with paintings, sculptures, and historical artifacts.

On the other side of the river, the **Ars Electronica Center** is a superb new museum that allows visitors to experiment with the latest technological innovations. Hidden away in the Lentia 2000 shopping mall is the **Lentos Kunstmuseum**, containing a fine collection of 19th- and 20th-century Austrian art, including works by Egon Schiele (1890–1918) and Gustav Klimt (1862–1918).

For splendid views of Linz, take a ride on the Pöstling-bergbahn train, which climbs to the top of Pöstlingberg Hill.

River cruises along the Danube west to Passau, in Germany, and east to Vienna depart from the quay at the Nibelungenbrücke. On-board entertainment includes themed events, such as a "Bavarian afternoon" or an "Italian night."

🏛 **Ars Electronica Center**
Hauptstraße 2. **Tel** 0732-727 20.
⬜ *Tue–Sun.* 📷 www.aec.at

🏛 **Lentos Kunstmuseum**
Ernst-Koref-Promenade 11.
Tel 0732-7070 3600. ⬜ *Tue–Sun.*
📷 www.lentos.at

Melk's massive Benedictine abbey on the banks of the Danube

Hallstatt, an attractive lakeside village in the Salzkammergut

Salzburg ❼

🏠 150,000. ✈ 3 km (2 miles) W.
🚉 🚌 ℹ Mozartplatz 5 (0662-
8898 7330). 🎭 Salzburger Festspiele
(late Jul–Aug). www.salzburg.info

Salzburg first rose to prominence in about AD 700, when a church and a monastery were established here. Until 1816, when it became part of the Habsburg empire, the independent city-state of Salzburg was ruled by a succession of prince-archbishops. Best known as the birthplace of Wolfgang Amadeus Mozart, today the city has a thriving musical tradition. Each summer large numbers of tourists arrive for the Salzburger Festspiele, a festival of opera, classical music concerts, and theater.

Salzburg's medieval fortress, the **Festung Hohensalzburg**, looms over the city from its hilltop position. The castle dates from the 11th century, but the state apartments are an early 16th-century addition.

The **Residenz**, where Salzburg's prince-archbishops lived and held court, owes its early Baroque appearance to Archbishop Wolf Dietrich von Raiteneau, who resided here from 1587. The palace contains the Residenzgalerie, a collection of European art of the 16th to 19th centuries.

Hallstatt ❻

🏠 1,000. 🚉 🚌 🚢 ℹ Seestraße
169 (06134-8208).

This pretty village on the bank of the Hallstätter See lies in the Salzkammergut, a stunning region of lakes and mountains. The area takes its name from the rich deposits of salt (salz) that have been mined here since the 1st millennium BC. From Hallstatt, it is possible to visit a working mine, the **Salzbergwerk**, by taking the cable car from the southern end of the village up to the mine entrance on the Salzberg mountain. The **Rudolfsturm**, the tower that stands close to the station at the top, was completed in 1284 to defend the mine workings.

Hallstatt's **Prähistorisches Museum** contains Celtic Iron Age artifacts discovered near the mines. Today, the name Hallstatt is used to refer to the Celtic culture that flourished from the 9th to the 5th centuries BC.

Behind the **Pfarrkirche**, the town's late-Gothic parish church, the **Beinhaus** (Charnel House) has been used to store human remains since 1600.

🏛 **Salzbergwerk Hallstatt**
Tel 06132-200 2400. ⬜ end
Apr–Oct: daily. 🎫

🏛 **Prähistorisches Museum**
Tel 06134-828 015. ⬜ Apr–Oct:
daily; Nov–Mar: Wed–Sun. 🎫

Environs
The mountains and the crystal clear waters of the Hallstätter See offer many opportunities for swimming, water sports, scuba diving, hiking, and cycling. There are also boat trips on the lake.

At the southern end of the Hallstätter See, about 2 km (1 mile) from Hallstatt, are the **Dachstein limestone caves**, open daily from May to mid-October. A cable car from south of Obertraun climbs to the entrance of the caves, giving superb views of the lake and surrounding mountains.

WOLFGANG AMADEUS MOZART

Wolfgang Amadeus Mozart (1756–91)

Salzburg's most famous son, Wolfgang Amadeus Mozart, was born in 1756, the son of Leopold, a member of the Prince-Archbishop's chamber orchestra. He learnt to play the harpsichord at the age of 3, and by the age of 5 had already written his first compositions. From 1763 Mozart traveled widely, performing for the aristocracy across Europe. His mastery of all the musical genres of the day swiftly earned him renown at home and abroad. During his short life, his prodigious output included 56 symphonies, over 20 concertos, and 15 operas, among them *The Marriage of Figaro* and *Don Giovanni*. Mozart's aspirations to lead the kind of lifestyle enjoyed by his patrons, however, led him into financial difficulties. In his final years, the musician was continually debt-ridden and prone to depression. He died in 1791 and was buried in a common grave.

Among the city's fine religious buildings are **St. Peter's Abbey** and **Benedictine monastery**, dating from c.AD 700, and the **Cathedral** (Dom), begun in 1614 to a design by Santino Solari. The **Franziskanerkirche** boasts a magnificent Baroque altarpiece (1709) by Johann Bernhard Fischer von Erlach.

A notable museum is the **Salzburg Museum**, with its historical and fine arts collections, and the **Haus der Natur**, a museum of natural history. The **Mozarts Geburtshaus** is Mozart's birthplace, while the **Mozart Wohnhaus** features audio-visual displays telling the story of his life.

On the right bank of the Salzach, **Schloss Mirabell** was built by Archbishop Wolf Dietrich for his Jewish mistress, Salome Alt. The palace gardens house the **Barock-Museum** (Baroque Museum), with its collection of 17th-and 18th-century works of art.

♣ **Festung Hohensalzburg**
Mönchsberg 34. *Tel 0662-8424 3011.* ◯ *daily.* 🖼 ▓

🏛 **Residenz**
Residenzplatz 1. *Tel 0662-8042 2690.* ◯ *daily. (Residenzgalerie Tue–Sun ● 1st 2 weeks Nov.)* 🖼 ▓

🏛 **Salzburg Museum**
Mozartplatz 1. *Tel 0662-6208 080.* ◯ *9am–5pm Tue–Sun.* ● *Nov 1, Dec 25.*🖼

🏛 **Barockmuseum**
Mirabellplatz 3. *Tel 0662-877 432.* ◯ *Tue–Sun.* 🖼

Innsbruck's Annasäule, crowned by a statue of the Virgin Mary

Innsbruck ❽

🏠 *124,000.* ✈ *4 km (2.5 miles) W.* 🚉 ▭ ℹ *Burggraben 3 (0512-59850).* **www**.innsbruck-tourismus.com

Capital of the Tyrol region, Innsbruck grew up at the crossroads of the old trade routes between Germany and Italy, Vienna, and Switzerland.

One of the city's finest pieces of architecture is the **Goldenes Dachl** (Golden Roof), commissioned by Emperor Maximilian I, who chose Innsbruck as his imperial capital at the end of the 15th century. Made of gilded copper tiles, the roof was constructed in the 1490s to cover a balcony used by members of the court to

observe events in the square below. Beneath the balcony is the **Museum Maximilianeum**, which focuses on the life of the Habsburg emperor, who ruled from 1493 to 1519.

Innsbruck's **Hofburg** (Imperial Palace) dates from the 15th century, but was rebuilt in Rococo style in the 18th century by Empress Maria Theresa (ruled 1740–80).

Built in 1555–65, the **Hofkirche** contains the impressive mausoleum of Maximilian I, which features 28 bronze statues. The highlight of the **Domkirche St. Jakob** (1717–22) is Lucas Cranach the Elder's painting of the *Madonna and Child*, which adorns the high altar.

Innsbruck's many museums include the **Tiroler Landesmuseum Ferdinandeum**, which has European art from the 15th to the 20th centuries, and the **Tiroler Volkskunstmuseum**, with exhibitions of local folk art and crafts.

🏛 **Museum Maximilianeum**
Herzog-Friedrichstraße 15. *Tel 0512-581 111.* ◯ *Tue–Sun.* 🖼

🏛 **Hofburg**
Rennweg 1. *Tel 0512-587 186.* ◯ *daily.* 🖼

🏛 **Tiroler Landesmuseum Ferdinandeum**
Museumstraße 15. *Tel 0512-59489.* ◯ *Tue–Sun.* 🖼

🏛 **Tiroler Volkskunstmuseum**
Universitätsstraße 2. *Tel 0512-594 89510.* ◯ *daily.* 🖼

Salzburg's magnificent Baroque cathedral, dominating the skyline of the Old Town

Practical & Travel Information

Austria is well equipped for tourism in both winter and summer. The extensive winter-sports facilities mean that even in the mountainous west of the country, communications are good and most roads are kept open all year. Public transport, especially the train services between the main cities, is reliable, and banking and exchange facilities are widely available. The country is generally safe for visitors except for a few unsavory bits of Vienna. Hospitals are of a high standard and, for lesser ailments, pharmacists are highly respected.

TOURIST INFORMATION

Austria has a wide network of local and regional tourist offices and the **Austrian National Tourist Office** has branches in many countries abroad. In the busier skiing resorts in winter, local offices often stay open as late as 9pm. In Vienna, **Wiener Tourismusverband** is a very helpful organization, especially with regard to forthcoming events and booking accommodations.

VISA REQUIREMENTS

Citizens of the US, Canada, Australia, and New Zealand need just a passport to visit Austria. No visa is required for stays of up to three months. Most European Union (EU) visitors need only a valid identity card to enter the country.

PERSONAL SECURITY

Although crime in the cities is rare, there are a few parts of Vienna that are best avoided at night, especially around the Karlsplatz station. Fights and pickpocketing are quite common at the Prater funfair at night.

In case of emergencies while on vacation, the appropriate services to call are listed in the Directory opposite.

HEALTH ISSUES

It is best to take out full health insurance which also covers flights home for medical reasons. This is true even for visitors from EU countries such as Great Britain. There is a reciprocal arrangement with Austria whereby emergency hospital treatment is free upon presentation of a British passport, but obtaining free treatment can involve rather a lot of bureaucracy.

In the case of a medical emergency, call an ambulance *(Rettungsdienst)* or the local **Doctor on Call**. For minor ailments or injuries, visit an *Apotheke* (pharmacy). All pharmacies display a distinctive red "A" sign. When closed, they give the address of the nearest open pharmacy.

FACILITIES FOR THE DISABLED

Public awareness of the needs of the disabled is growing in Austria. Wiener Tourismusverband has a good online information service with details of the ease of wheelchair access at tourist sights, hotels, and public restrooms.

ETIQUETTE

Austrians on the whole are a conservative people and formal in their modes of address. Waiters are summoned with a deferential "Herr Ober," and greetings in the street are accompanied by the use of titles, such as "Herr Doktor," and much handshaking.

BANKING AND CURRENCY

The euro became the unit of currency in Austria in January 2002 *(see p15)*.

Banks are usually the best places to change money. Most are open Monday to Friday from 8am to 12:30pm and from 1:30pm to 3pm (5:30pm on Thursdays). Some banks, generally those at main train stations and at airports, stay open longer and do not close for lunch. Though major credit cards are accepted at most large stores, hotels, and restaurants, they are not used as frequently as, for instance, in the UK or France, so it is a good idea to carry some cash with you. Alternatively, payment by debit card is widely accepted.

COMMUNICATIONS

The Austrian telecommunications network is run by Telekom Austria. Calls are among the most expensive in Europe. Public phones are coin- or card-operated, and you can buy phonecards from post offices and newsagents. Lower-rate calling times from Vienna are from 6pm to 8am Monday to Friday, and all day on Saturday and Sunday. Numbers starting in 05-can be dialled from anywhere in Austria at a local call rate. The postal service is reliable, verging on the pedantic, and

THE CLIMATE OF AUSTRIA

Altitude obviously plays an important role in the climate of Austria, the Alpine part of the country experiencing lower temperatures and receiving more rain and snow than Vienna and the east. Snow cover in the Alps lasts from November to May. Daytime temperatures in summer can be high, but the evenings are cool. There is a risk of thunderstorms from June to August.

VIENNA			
°C/F	25/77		
	13/55	15/59	13/55
0°C 5/41		6/43	2/36
32°F			-2/28
☀ 5.5 hrs	8 hrs	4.5 hrs	1.5 hrs
☂ 51 mm	74 mm	40 mm	38 mm
month	Apr	Jul	Oct	Jan

posting a letter can take some time. Each letter is carefully weighed and every size and shape coded separately.

Most post offices are open between 8am and noon and 2pm and 6pm from Monday to Friday. You can also buy stamps at newsagents.

FLYING TO AUSTRIA

If you fly from the United States, there are direct flights with **Delta Air Lines** from New York and Orlando to Vienna's Schwechat airport. **Austrian Airlines** flies from New York, Washington, and Chicago and **Lauda Air** has flights from Miami. Direct flights from Australia are run by **Emirates Airlines** and British Airways, which both operate services from Sydney and Melbourne.

Connections to all of the major European cities are good. There are several flights a day from London's Gatwick and Heathrow airports. British Airways is the main British airline with regular flights to Vienna, and the main Austrian carrier is Austrian Airlines. Ryanair also offers regular services at low prices.

You can get APEX tickets if you book two weeks in advance, and charters are available at very competitive prices. Weekend package deals, including the price of two nights at a good Viennese hotel, can be excellent value, sometimes costing less than the economy-class ticket price.

RAIL TRAVEL

Austria's rail network is run by the state-owned Österreichische Bundesbahnen (ÖBB). Hauptbahnhof Wien station will handle all international routes by 2015 and is located at Südtirolerplatz, with connections to the U1 subway line and the Schnellbahn as well as several bus and tram routes. The Westbahnhof still handles trains from the west, with frequent services to Innsbruck and Salzburg, and is served by the U6 and U3 subway lines. Eventually the Westbahnhof will run regional routes only. Trains to southern and eastern areas are temporarily served by Meidling Hauptbahnhof, which is linked to the U6 subway, Schnellbahn, and tram lines. Trains to Neusiedl/See, Marchegg, Bratislava, and Brno leave from the temporary Ostbahnhof located near the former Südbahnhof. The Franz-Josefs-Bahnhof, which runs services from the north, is served by the U4 and U6 subway lines, the Schnellbahn, and the cross-city D tram, which goes directly to Ringstrasse.

The travel agency (Verkehrsverein) at Westbahnhof, open from 8am to 9pm daily, provides rail information and also helps book hotels. In Vienna there is a telephone number for obtaining railway information in English (see below).

TRAVELING BY BUS

Austria's long-distance buses serve those parts of the country that are not reached by train. Bus and train timetables are well integrated. In most towns, buses leave from the train station or the post office.

TRAVELING BY CAR

Even in winter, Austrian road conditions are good and autobahns (highways) link all the major cities. There are also convenient routes into Austria from neighboring countries. Highways are subject to a toll, which is paid by buying a windshield sticker valid for a certain period of time. Stickers can be bought at the border or at post offices, gas stations, and tobacconists throughout the country. Tolls are also payable on certain mountain roads and tunnels. All drivers in Austria must carry their driver's license, car registration documents, and insurance documents.

DIRECTORY

TOURIST OFFICES

Austrian National Tourist Office
www.austria.info

In Australia:
36 Carrington Street, 1st floor, Sydney, NSW 2000.
Tel 02-9299 3621.

In Canada:
2 Bloor Street West, 400 Toronto, Ontario M4W. 3E2. *Tel 416-967 4867.*

In the UK:
9–11 Richmond Bldgs, London W1D 3HF.
Tel 020-7440 3830.

In the US:
120 West 45th St, 9th floor, New York, NY 10036.
Tel 212-944 6885.

Wiener Tourismusverband
Corner of Albertinaplatz/ Tegethoffstraße/ Meysedergaße, Vienna.
Tel 01-24555.
www.wien.info

EMBASSIES

Australia
Mattiellistraße 2–4, A-1010 Vienna.
Tel 01-506740.

Canada
Laurenzerberg 2, A-1010 Vienna.
Tel 01-5313 83000.

UK
Jaurèsgasse 12, A-1030 Vienna.
Tel 01-716130.

US
Boltzmanngasse 16, A-1090 Vienna.
Tel 01-31339.

EMERGENCY NUMBERS

Ambulance
Tel 144.

Doctor on Call
Tel 141.

Fire
Tel 122.

Police
Tel 133.

AIRLINES

Austrian Airlines
Tel 05-1766 1000 (Aust).
Tel 800-843 0002 (US).
www.aua.com

Delta Air Lines
Tel 01-79567 023 (Vienna).
Tel 800-221 1212 (US).
www.delta.com

Emirates Airlines
Tel 800-777 3999 (US).
Tel 01-532 6028 (Austria).
www.emirates.com

Lauda Air
Tel 0820-320 321 (Vienna).
Tel 800-588 8399 (US).

Ryanair
Tel 0871-246 0000 (UK).
www.ryanair.com

RAIL INFORMATION

Tel 05-1717.
www.oebb.at

Shopping and Entertainment

Shopping in Austria can be expensive, but it is a good place to buy certain high-quality traditional goods, such as Loden coats, porcelain, and glass. Famous for its coffee shops, Christmas markets, world-class opera, and orchestras, Vienna is the center of entertainment in Austria, although some important music festivals are held across the country. Outside the city, such rural pleasures as skiing and hiking are available in the west of the country, in the Tyrol, Salzburger Land, and Salzkammergut regions.

OPENING HOURS

Stores usually open at 8:30 or 9am and close at 6 or 7pm. Smaller ones may close for an hour at lunch. Most shops stay open all day on Saturday, especially in larger towns. In rural areas, however, they may close around noon on Saturday. Shops are still closed on Sundays and public holidays, but you can buy items such as groceries, flowers, books, camera film, and newspapers at major train stations.

FOOD AND DRINK

Austria is justly famous for its cakes and pastries, and in Vienna and large towns a good *Café-Konditorei* (cake shop and café) will mail cakes back home for you. Buy a prettily-packaged *Sachertorte*, the world-famous Viennese chocolate cake. In November and December try the buttery Advent *Stollen*, stuffed with fruit and nuts and dusted with icing sugar, available from **Meinl am Graben** delicatessen or any good baker. Specialist chocolate shops, such as **Altmann & Kühne**, are also worth a visit, both for the unusual packaging and the chocolates themselves.

Sweet *Eiswein* (so-called because the grapes are left on the vines until the first frosts) is an unusual and delicious white dessert wine. **Zum Schwarzen Kameel** in Vienna also sells the rarer red variety.

LUXURY GOODS

Desirable Austrian goods include clothes made of *Loden*, a felt-like woollen fabric, custom-made sheets, and high-quality down pillows and duvets. Petit point embroidery, which adorns handbags, powder compacts, and similar articles, is a Viennese specialty. A wide range is available at **Petit Point** and **Maria Stransky**.

Trachten (Austrian costume) shops are fun, selling a wide selection of hats, children's dresses, jackets, and blouses.

Glassware – including superb chandeliers – and Augarten porcelain come in highly original designs, but are very expensive. **Ostovics** is a good glass and porcelain shop for such items. The **Schloss Augarten** porcelain factory is open to visitors.

BOOKING TICKETS

You can buy tickets direct from the appropriate box office or reserve them by phone. Agencies are reliable; try the **Reisebüro Mondial**. Vienna's four state theaters, the Burgtheater, Akademietheater, Opera House, and Volksoper have a central booking office, the **Bundestheaterkassen**. In most cases tickets go on sale one month before the performance. Written applications for tickets must reach the Österreichische Bundestheater Verband (address as Bundestheaterkassen) at least three weeks in advance for opera tickets, and 10 days ahead for the theaters. Standing-room tickets (over 500 at the Opera House) are sold at the evening box office one hour before the start of the performance.

THEATER

Viennese theater enjoys a high reputation and the Burgtheater *(see p595)* is the most prestigious venue.

Classic and modern plays are performed here and at the associated Akademietheater.

The **Volkstheater** offers more modern plays as well as the occasional classic and some operetta performances.

The **Raimund Theater** and the **Ronacher** are part of the Vereinigte Bühnen Wien, the city's own theaters. Both specialize in lavish musicals.

The Wiener Festwochen, held in May and June, features theater, including musical theater, at various venues.

Vienna has a wide range of fringe theater from one-man shows to *Kabarett* – satirical shows not cabarets – but fairly fluent German is needed to appreciate them.

OPERA AND OPERETTA

The opera season runs from September to June. The historic **Theater an der Wien** is a full-time venue for opera and other forms of classical music. At the Staatsoper in Vienna, operas are usually performed in the original language. At the **Wiener Volksoper**, where the repertoire includes light opera by Mozart and Puccini and operettas by Strauss and Lehár, they are sung in German. The same singers often appear at the two venues. The New Year's Eve performance at the Opera House is always Johan Strauss the Younger's *Die Fledermaus*, and famous guests sometimes make surprise appearances during the second act.

A wonderful smaller opera house is the **Wiener Kammeroper**. Here you can expect anything from Rossini and classic operetta to rock versions of familiar operas and opera parodies. July sees opera performances in the Kaiserhof courtyard of the palatial religious foundation at **Klosterneuburg**, a short way north of Vienna.

CLASSICAL MUSIC

The principal venues for classical music concerts are the **Musikverein** (including the restored Brahms-Saal) and the concert halls of the **Konzerthaus**. Performances are also held in many other halls and historic palaces around Vienna.

The New Year's Concert is televised live from the Grosser Musikvereinsaal in the Musikverein every year. You can apply for tickets by writing direct to the **Wiener Philharmoniker**. Applications must be received on January 2 (not before, not after) for the next year's concert. You can order from abroad by telegram.

The city supports two great orchestras, the Wiener Philharmoniker and the Wiener Symphoniker. There are also a number of chamber music ensembles and church music is often of concert quality. The world-famous Vienna Boys' Choir can be heard during mass at the Burgkapelle in the Hofburg complex *(see p594)* every Sunday and religious holiday at 9:15am except from July to about mid-September (the box office is open the Friday before). You can also hear them at the Konzerthaus every Friday at 3:30pm in May, June, September, and October. Tickets are available from hotel porters and from Reisebüro Mondial.

MUSIC FESTIVALS

Seasonal events in Vienna include the Vienna Festival in May and June, and **Wien Modern**, a festival of post-1945 and contemporary classical music, with an emphasis on the avant-garde.

Inaugurated in 1920, the **Salzburg Festival** of opera, drama, and music claims to be the largest of its kind in the world. It is held annually in late July and August, attracting the world's finest conductors, soloists, and opera and theater companies. The spectacular venues include the Felsenreitschule, the riding school of the prince-archbishops of Salzburg. There is always a strong emphasis on Mozart, the city's most famous son, but the festival has also won acclaim for its contemporary music and innovative productions of classic and modern drama.

Another smaller festival is the **Haydn Festspiele**, held at the magnificent Schloss Esterházy in Eisenstadt *(see p600)*. The festival itself is in September, but Haydn concerts are given in the palace throughout the summer.

COFFEE HOUSES AND HEURIGE

The Viennese coffee house is a throwback to a more leisured age, serving coffee in a bewildering range of styles and allowing patrons to sit and read newspapers at their leisure. The *Heuriger* is a uniquely Austrian establishment. Its literal meaning is "this year's," and it refers both to the youngest available local wine and to venues that sell it. The most famous are in villages to the north and west of Vienna, such as Heiligenstadt and Grinzing. A sign reading *Eigenbau* means that the wine is from the owner's vineyards.

WINTER SPORTS

Austria's facilities for winter sports are second only to Switzerland's. Ski resorts vary from fashionable Kitzbühel and St. Anton to small family resorts with less demanding slopes. Package tours are available from many countries around the world. Information on 800 resorts can be found on the **Austria Tourism** website, along with snow reports and other useful information.

DIRECTORY

FOOD AND DRINK

Altmann & Kühne
Graben 30, Vienna.
Tel 01-533 0927.

Meinl am Graben
Graben 19, Vienna.
Tel 01-532 3334.

Zum Schwarzen Kameel
Bognergasse 5, Vienna.
Tel 01-533 8125.

LUXURY GOODS

Maria Stransky
Hofburg Passage 2,
Vienna.
Tel 01-533 6098.

Ostovics
Stephansplatz 9, Vienna.
Tel 01-533 1411.

Petit Point
Kärntner Straße 16,
Vienna. *Tel 01-512 4886.*

Schloss Augarten
Obere Augartenstraße 1,
Vienna. *Tel 01-211 24123.*

BOOKING TICKETS

Bundestheater-kassen
Opernring 2, Vienna.
Tel 01-514 440.

Reisebüro Mondial
Operngasse 206, Vienna.
Tel 01-5880 4150.

THEATER

Raimund Theater
Wallgasse 18, Vienna.
Tel 01-599 770.

Ronacher
Seilerstätte 9, Vienna.
Tel 01-58885.

Volkstheater
Neustiftgasse 1, Vienna.
Tel 01-521 110.

OPERA AND OPERETTA

Oper Klosterneuburg
Kaiserhof Stift,
Klosterneuburg.
Tel 02243-444 424.

Theater an der Wien
Linke Wienzeile 6, Vienna.
Tel 01-58885.

Wiener Kammeroper
Fleischmarkt 24, Vienna.
Tel 01-512 010077.

Wiener Volksoper
Währinger Straße 78,
Vienna. *Tel 01-514 4430.*

CLASSICAL MUSIC

Konzerthaus
Lothringerstraße 20,
Vienna.
Tel 01-242 002.

Musikverein
Bösendorferstraße 12,
Vienna.
Tel 01-505 8190.

Wiener Philharmoniker
Bösendorferstraße 12,
Vienna.
Tel 01-505 8190.

MUSIC FESTIVALS

Haydn Festspiele
Schloss Esterházy,
A-7000 Eisenstadt.
Tel 02682-618 66.

Salzburg Festival
Hofstallgasse 1, Postfach
140, A-5100 Salzburg.
Tel 0662-804 5579.

WINTER SPORTS

Austria Tourism
www.austria.info

Where to Stay in Austria

Accommodations in Austria range from large, well-equipped, five-star hotels to simple pensions, and generally you can expect a high standard of comfort and cleanliness everywhere. Room rates in Vienna are disproportionately high compared to other costs. Save money by staying in a hotel outside the Ringstraße.

PRICE CATEGORIES
Price categories for a standard double room per night, including tax, service and breakfast:

€ Under €90
€€ €90–€140
€€€ €140–€180
€€€€ €180–€260
€€€€€ Over €260

VIENNA

CENTRAL VIENNA Hotel Pension Neuer Markt €
Seilergasse 9, 1010 **Tel** *01-512 23 16* **Fax** *01-513 9105* **Rooms** *37*   Map D4

A pension has existed on this site since the 1920s, and the Neuer Markt continues the tradition in true Viennese style. Plenty of dusty-rose colored furnishings. Friendly, personal service. For those staying longer than seven nights, a pick-up service upon arrival at the airport or train stations is provided free of charge. **www.hotelpension.at**

CENTRAL VIENNA Aviano €€
Marco d'Avianogasse 1, 1010 **Tel** *01-512 83 30* **Fax** *01-512 83 30 6* **Rooms** *17*   Map D4

Located only one minute from the Opera House, this four-star pension offers a friendly, welcoming atmosphere with very personalized service. The staff can help organize sight-seeing tours and tickets to concerts. Cheerful, well-decorated rooms. Good value for money. **www.secrethomes.at**

CENTRAL VIENNA Alma Boutique-Hotel €€€
Hafnersteig 7, 1010 **Tel** *01-533 29 61* **Fax** *01-533 29 61 81* **Rooms** *26*   Map E3

The once-modest Pension Christina has undergone a makeover and surprises the guest with its stylish ambiance in shades of gold, red, and brown. The hotel is located in the heart of Vienna, and all the famous landmarks are within walking distance. Rooms are a little small, however. **www.hotel-alma.com**

CENTRAL VIENNA Arenberg €€€€
Stubenring 2, 1010 **Tel** *01-512 52 91* **Fax** *01-513 93 56* **Rooms** *22*   Map E3, F3

Located directly on the Ringstraße, the Arenberg is a stylishly elegant establishment. The bedrooms reflect traditional decor and provide comfort and charm as well as sound-proofed windows. The bathrooms are modern and gleaming. Several good value weekend stay packages are available. **www.arenberg.at**

CENTRAL VIENNA Kaiserin Elisabeth €€€€
Weihburggasse 3, 1010 **Tel** *01-512 26 0* **Fax** *01-515 26 7* **Rooms** *63*   Map E4

This elegant hotel, named after the indomitable Habsburg empress, is located just off the Stephansplatz. In the 1800s, it played host to many famous musicians such as Wagner and Liszt. The *fin-de-siècle*-style bedrooms are smart, and Persian rugs lie on parquet floors in the public rooms. Pets are permitted. **www.kaiserinelisabeth.at**

CENTRAL VIENNA Mailberger Hof €€€€
Annagasse 7, 1010 **Tel** *01-512 06 41* **Fax** *01-512 06 41 10* **Rooms** *40*   Map E4

Two Gothic houses have merged to create a small Baroque palace, this building is owned by the Knights of Malta and is under landmark protection. You can dine in the striking vaulted restaurant. A wide, stone staircase leads to the spacious, tastefully furnished bedrooms. **www.mailbergerhof.at**

CENTRAL VIENNA Wandl €€€€
Peterplatz 9, 1010 **Tel** *01-534 55 0* **Fax** *01-534 55 77* **Rooms** *138*   Map D3

Located close to the Peterskirche, this charming, old-fashioned hotel has been in the same family for generations. Fine stuccoed features are in some of the bedrooms as well as in the covered courtyard that serves as a breakfast room. Other rooms are simpler, but large, and feature parquet floors. **www.hotel-wandl.com**

CENTRAL VIENNA Astoria €€€€€
Kärntner Straße 32–34, 1015 **Tel** *01-515 77* **Fax** *01-515 77 58 2* **Rooms** *118*   Map D4

A hotel since 1912, it features a paneled Jugendstil foyer leading to a grand dining room on the first floor. Some of the splendid bedrooms feature their own brass letter boxes. The spacious rooms are traditionally furnished, often with period decor. Ideally located near the Opera House. **www.austria-trend.at**

CENTRAL VIENNA Palais Coburg Hotel Residenz €€€€€
Coburgbastei 4, 1010 **Tel** *01-518 18 0* **Fax** *01-512 22 47 66* **Rooms** *35*   Map E4

This 19th-century former Saxe-Coburg-Gotha palace is now a luxury Relais & Chateaux hotel. There are 35 elegant suites, from traditional to contemporary, plus a unique rooftop spa and two fine restaurants. The wine cellar is stocked with one of Europe's finest collections. **www.coburg.at**

Map References *see map of Vienna pp590–91*

REST OF AUSTRIA

GRAZ Hotel Zum Dom
€€€

Bürgergasse 14, Graz, 8010 **Tel** *0316-82 48 00* **Fax** *0316-82 48 00 8* **Rooms** *29*

A unique boutique hotel incorporating modern luxuries within the structure of the handsome historic building. Well located in the picturesque old city and close to shopping, restaurants, and bars. Its 29 rooms and suites have striking pieces of art, decadent baths and a real sense of style. **www.domhotel.co.at**

GRAZ Erzherzog Johann
€€€€

Sackstraße 3–5, 8010 **Tel** *0316-81 16 16* **Fax** *0316-81 15 15* **Rooms** *62*

Elegant old-world hotel which was an inn since the 16th century, and a grand *palais* during the 18th century. The beautifully crafted interior iron work dates from this period. Rooms and grand suites are furnished with lovely antiques and parquet floors. There is an elegant winter garden restaurant and Viennese-style café. **www.erzherzog-johann.com**

HALLSTATT Seehotel Grüner Baum
€€€

Marktplatz 104, 4830 **Tel** *06134-82 63* **Fax** *06134-82 63 44* **Rooms** *20*

The lakeside hotel dates to at least 1700, its splendid facade dominating the quaint Hallstatt marketplace. An inviting terrace looks directly on to the lake. An impressive guest list includes Empress Elisabeth (Sissy) of Austria and Agatha Christie. Rooms are charmingly furnished with a mixture of contemporary and antique pieces. **www.gruenerbaum.cc**

INNSBRUCK Goldener Adler
€€

Herzog-Friedrich-Straße 6, 6020 **Tel** *0512-57 11 11* **Fax** *0512-58 44 09* **Rooms** *34*

Located in the heart of the old town, this is one of the first inns in Europe, built in 1390. The rooms are named after former guests, which have included emperors, kings, and Mozart himself. Several restaurants serve fine Tyrolean cuisine. The Goethe Stube is a fine place to take in living history. **www.goldeneradler.com**

INNSBRUCK Parkhotel Leipzigerhof
€€€

Defreggerstraße 13, 6020 **Tel** *0512-34 35 25* **Fax** *0512-39 43 57* **Rooms** *55*

A fully modernized, family-owned, four-star hotel in the centre of Innsbruck. Bright en suite bathrooms, an elegant traditional restaurant, plus recreation centre with sauna and solarium. Rooms are equipped with high-speed Internet and a flat-screen TV. **www.bestwestern.at**

INNSBRUCK Schlosshotel Igls
€€€€€

A-6080 Igls **Tel** *0512-377 217* **Fax** *0512-377 217 198* **Rooms** *18*

At this luxurious and discreet mountain castle every guest is treated royally. The elegant Blue Saloon serves as breakfast room, and the mahogany-paneled restaurant offers fine seasonally influenced menus. Each of the bedrooms is uniquely furnished. Combined indoor-outdoor pool, sauna, steam-bath, solarium, and massage. **www.schlosshotel-igls.com**

LINZ Arcotel Nike
€€€

Untere Donaulände 9, 4020 **Tel** *0732-76 26 0* **Fax** *0732-76 26 2* **Rooms** *176*

The River Danube makes an idyllic backdrop for this modern, efficiently appointed hotel. A five-minute walk from the old centre, its rooms are furnished in a clean, modern style. A restaurant and café as well as wellness centre with hammam, indoor pool, sauna, and steam bath are in house. Bright conference rooms. **www.arcotel.at**

LINZ Austria Trend Hotel Schillerpark
€€€

Rainerstraße 2–4, 4020 **Tel** *0732-69 50 0* **Fax** *0732-69 50 9* **Rooms** *111*

This rectangular glass and steel designed building offers functional modern rooms and suites with en suite bathrooms, air-conditioning, TV, Pay-TV, minibar, and safe. All single rooms feature double beds. Rooms located on the executive floor are more luxuriously equipped. There is a restaurant and several cafés and bars. **www.austria-trend.at**

SALZBURG Bergland
€€

Rupertgasse 15, 5020 **Tel** *0662-87 23 18 0* **Fax** *0662-87 23 18 8* **Rooms** *18*

Located in a quiet street just ten minutes' walk to the centre, this is a small family-run hotel. Bathrooms are large and stylish, and downstairs a music room with piano and small English library make a cozy spot. Bicycles are available to hire. Rooms are non-smoking and have satellite TV. **www.berglandhotel.at**

SALZBURG NH Salzburg City
€€€

Franz-Josef-Straße 26, 5020 **Tel** *0662-88 20 41* **Fax** *0662-87 42 40* **Rooms** *140*

This sleek, stylishly designed hotel serves both business and holiday travelers looking to be near the historical centre and Mirabell Gardens. The hotel offers access to Wi-Fi and concierge services. There is an underground garage as well as public parking. The train station is 2 km (1 mile) away. **www.nh-hotels.com**

SALZBURG Hotel Sacher Salzburg
€€€€€

Schwarzstraße 5–7, 5020 **Tel** *0662-88 97 7* **Fax** *0662-88 977 551* **Rooms** *118*

Residing here in five-star splendor comes with unlimited access to Sachertorte, the chocolate cake Austria is famous for. This renovated turn-of-the-century hotel offers state-of-the-art luxury paired with grand tradition. Rich red interiors, bright marble bathrooms, and splendid views of the Salzach River and the Old Town. **www.sacher.com**

Key to Symbols *see back cover flap*

Where to Eat in Austria

Austria has a range of restaurants to suit most tastes and
budgets. In the capital, the most luxurious establishments
are found in or near the Stephansdom Quarter. Some,
including those in the big hotels, offer international
menus. There are also many ethnic restaurants. In
smaller towns, most venues prepare local specialties.

PRICE CATEGORIES
Price categories for a three-course meal
for one, without drinks, including tax
and service:

€ Under €20
€€ €20–€35
€€€ €35–€45
€€€€ €45–€55
€€€€€ Over €55

VIENNA

CENTRAL VIENNA Zu den 3 Hacken
€
Singerstraße 28, 1010 **Tel** *01-810 33 09*
Map E4

Said to be the oldest tavern in Vienna, Zu den 3 Hacken is made up of four old-fashioned wood-paneled stube
dining rooms, one dedicated to the composer Schubert (a regular guest in his day). Small tasting room in the wine
cellar. This is classic Viennese cooking in a friendly ambience. **www.vinum-wien.at**

CENTRAL VIENNA Glacis Beisl
€€
Museumsquartier, Zugang Breitegasse 4, 1070 **Tel** *01-526 56 60*
Map C4

This is a moderately priced restaurant in the museum district that has a huge aquarium at the entrance. A popular
restaurant with tourists, it offers carefully chosen dishes of meats, dumplings, pasta, and fish. Shady summer garden
for fine weather as well as an enclosed winter garden. Menu in English. Open daily until 2am.

CENTRAL VIENNA Ofenloch
€€€
Kurrentgasse 8, 1010 **Tel** *01-533 88 44*
Map D3

Classic Viennese dishes are served in this historic restaurant with a traditional *Wirtshaus* (tavern) interior. The dishes
are prepared using only the very best local products, which are largely organically grown. Weather permitting, diners
can eat outside on one of Vienna's oldest streets. Closed Sun.

CENTRAL VIENNA Plachutta
€€€
Wollzeile 38, 1010 **Tel** *01-512 15 77*
Map E3

This is the flagship restaurant of the Plachutta chain and the unrivalled headquarters of Austria's famous *Taflspitz*
dish of boiled beef. The Plachutta restaurants are dedicated to keeping Viennese traditional cooking alive, using
classic ingredients and methods. Open daily until midnight.

CENTRAL VIENNA Wirtshaus im Palais Kinsky
€€€
Freyung 4, 1010 **Tel** *01-535 34 35*
Map E4

This restaurant is located in the quiet courtyard of one of the most important Baroque palaces in Vienna. The menu
features both Austrian and international cuisine, with an emphasis on seasonal specialties. Dishes include *confit* of
duck with pak choi and crunchy pickled vegetable salad, and classic beef *tartare*.

CENTRAL VIENNA Wrenkh
€€€
Bauernmarkt 10, 1010 **Tel** *01-533 15 26*
Map E3

Famous for years as Vienna's premier strictly vegetarian restaurant, Wrenkh's now serves chicken and fish as well,
though tofu still figures prominently on the menu. Its unique "happy cuisine" philosophy tries to take the seriousness
out of *haute cuisine*, and is demonstrated in cooking workshops open to the public. Menus in English. Closed Sun.

CENTRAL VIENNA Do & Co
€€€€
Stephansplatz 12, 1010 **Tel** *01-535 39 69*
Map D3

Part of a catering empire as well as a Viennese institution, Do & Co is on the 7th floor of the Haas-Haus building and
has a striking view of the Stephansdom. Excellent international and regional dishes are served, and the specialties
include kebabs. Reservations are required.

CENTRAL VIENNA Meinl am Graben
€€€€€
Graben 19, 1010 **Tel** *01-532 33 34 6000*
Map D3

Meinl is the biggest name in Austria for food. The downstairs wine bar always has 30 open wine varieties to taste.
The café with attached garden offers unlimited blends of coffee beans. The restaurant is one of the best in the country, and is applauded for its creativity and superb presentation.

FARTHER AFIELD Steman
€€
Otto/Bauer Gasse 7, 1060 **Tel** *01-597 85 09*

This is a comfortable and homely guest house, retaining many period features. Diners eat family-style at long tables
in a dining room of paneled wood and old oil paintings. The Viennese dishes produced have won favorable comment
in the local press. Closed Sat & Sun.

Map References *see map of Vienna pp590–91*

REST OF AUSTRIA

GRAZ Johan 〔symbols〕 €€€

Landhausgasse 1, 8010 **Tel** *0316-82 13 12*

One of the busiest and most popular eating spots in Graz, especially for the young and hip. One reason is the stunning architecture of the ancient Landhaus building. Squat stone columns support vaulted ceilings under which acres of white tablecloths are spread. There is also a courtyard terrace for summer dining. Eclectic cuisine. Closed Sun–Mon.

GRAZ Wintergarten 〔symbols〕 €€€

Sackstraße 3–5, 8010 **Tel** *0316-81 16 16*

This spacious and spectacular atrium restaurant is built into the old courtyard of the majestic palace hotel, Erzherzog Johann. The glass-roofed dining area is overflowing with vegetation. Classic Austrian cuisine is enlivened by Italian influences. An ideal setting for afternoon coffee and cakes. Tables are limited, so reservations advised. Closed Mon–Tue.

HALLSTATT Gasthof Zauner-Seewirt €€

Marktplatz 51, 4830 **Tel** *06134-82 46*

Don't be surprised if the food is a bit salty here, as this town boasts the world's oldest salt mine. The trademark *Salzfürstenplatte* includes both savory boar and fish. The Seewirt dates back a century, and fish has always been the main item on the menu. An all-wooden interior, and very attentive service.

LINZ Stieglbräu Zum Klosterhof 〔symbols〕 €€

Landstraße 30, 4020 **Tel** *0732-77 33 73*

Enjoy seasonal cuisine in a historic listed building close to the main shopping street; typical dishes feature mushrooms, venison, and goose. There's live music on Fridays and Saturdays. The spacious outdoor area is a particular attraction in fine weather. Smaller portions are available.

LINZ Chizuru 〔symbols〕 €€€

Untere Donaulände 21–25, 4020 **Tel** *0732-77 27 79*

An authentic Japanese restaurant in Linz with a real sushi bar, where diners sit close up to the chef slicing and dicing. The interior is somewhat spartan in decor and limited in space; however, in summer there is garden seating for an additional 60 guests. Reservations are advised, as Chizuru is very popular with local residents. Closed Sun.

INNSBRUCK Kapeller 〔symbols〕 €€

Philippine-Welser-Straße 96, 6020 **Tel** *0512-34 31 06*

The Kappeller is a tastefully appointed historic guest house in the centre of Innsbruck. The Dorfstube offers intimacy and Tyrolean traditional dishes. Most attractive is the small dining terrace, partly covered in glass, in an interior courtyard with views of the old town. Closed Sun.

INNSBRUCK Goldener Adler 〔symbols〕 €€€

Herzog-Friedrich-Straße 6, 6020 **Tel** *0512-57 11 11*

The restaurant of the Best Western Hotel Goldener Adler is one of the oldest inns in Europe, dating from 1390. Mozart is said to have eaten here. There are five dining areas, including intimate and cozy stube rooms. Outdoor dining on the pavement outside the hotel. Open daily until midnight, but kitchen closes at 10:30pm.

SALZBURG Stieglbräu 〔symbols〕 €€

Rainerstraße 14, 5020 **Tel** *0662-87 76 94*

Stieglbräu is a restaurant, beer garden, and bar in a Best Western hotel within walking distance of the train station and most tourist attractions in downtown Salzburg. The menu features typical international dishes and standard Austrian specialties. The bar is a popular meeting place. There is also a beer garden, which becomes lively in summer.

SALZBURG Die Gersberg Alm 〔symbols〕 €€€

Gersberg 37, 5020 **Tel** *0662-64 12 57*

Just outside Salzburg in an extensive park on a hill, Die Gersberg Alm offers organic beef, fresh fish, and a wide range of mouth-watering pastries. The wine list features mostly Austrian vintages and many local schnapps. One of the most enticing garden areas in which to eat in the Salzburg region. Open daily until midnight.

SALZBURG Alt Salzburg €€€€

Bürgerspitalgasse 2, 5020 **Tel** *0662-84 14 76*

In the historical centre of Salzburg, this is a popular and lively restaurant with a high reputation for good food at a reasonable price. Three dining areas, including one carved out of solid rock at the rear. The menu concentrates on standard Austrian and Salzburg favorites. No menus in English, but waiters are happy to translate. Closed Sun.

SALZBURG Hotel Sacher Salzburg 〔symbols〕 €€€€€

Schwarzstraße 5–7, 5020 **Tel** *0662-88 997*

The Hotel Sacher is no place to contemplate starting a diet. Home of the famous chocolate cake of the same name, the hotel emphasizes that nothing you eat elsewhere can compare. The recipe has remained a secret since 1832. Among three restaurants, one a grill and one for local specialties, is the opulent gourmet room, the Zirbelzimmer.

Key to Symbols *see back cover flap*

SWITZERLAND

The stereotypical images of Switzerland – cozy wooden chalets, alpine meadows, and chic skiing resorts – are easy to find. But there are many other sides to this small, diverse country that are equally accessible, from picturesque medieval towns to world-class art and fine gastronomy. Switzerland's rural retreats offer wonderful opportunities for relaxing and recharging.

Switzerland lies at the very heart of Europe, landlocked between the Alps and the Jura mountains. It is bordered to the west by France, to the north by Germany, to the east by Austria and Liechtenstein, and to the south by Italy.

Mountains make up almost a third of Switzerland's 41,285 sq km (15,949 sq miles). The St. Gotthard Massif is the source of many lakes and two major rivers, the Rhine and the Rhône. Central Switzerland has the highest concentration of picturesque Alpine peaks, although the loftiest Alps are those of the Valais in the southwest. The valleys of Graubünden in the east provide the setting for many winter resorts. In the west, the cities lining the northern shore of Lake Geneva comprise the "Swiss Riviera," while a series of high passes provides overland access from German-speaking Switzerland to the Ticino, the Italian-speaking part of the country, and to Italy.

With almost a quarter of its area comprising high Alps, lakes, and barren rock, and with no seaboard and few natural resources other than water power, the country has managed to preserve a proud and united spirit of independence.

HISTORY

Switzerland's geography has presented both opportunities and disadvantages. Its story has been of a gradual coming together, not without bloodshed, of a population of diverse cultures, religions, and languages, making what is today viewed as a haven of peace and reason.

The Jura mountains provide the earliest evidence of Switzerland's habitation, which dates to over 50,000 years ago. By the start of the Christian era, Celtic peoples were living in western Switzerland and Germanic tribes in the north and east. Many of

The snow-capped Jungfrau, one of the Alps' most famous peaks

◁ The colorful façade of a typical Swiss chalet, Interlaken

these communities were under the control of the expanding Roman Empire, whose influence spread after 58 BC.

The Germanic tribes to the north eventually broke through Roman defenses; by the 5th century AD the era of Roman rule had ended. During the so-called "Dark Ages," the Burgundian tribe controlled the west, the Alemanni the center and east. In the 5th century, both tribes came under the control of the Franks, and later the Holy Roman Empire. The 13th century saw the rise of powerful local families such as the Habsburgs and the Zähringen, who established feudal rule over the area.

In 1291 three forest cantons around Lake Lucerne – Uri, Schwyz, and Unterwalden – came together to swear an Oath of Allegiance, thus forming an independent Swiss state. Over the coming centuries, more cantons came to join the Confederation. These included lands south of the Alps known as the Ticino, and those to the west, where Charles of Burgundy was defeated by the Swiss in 1477. Switzerland was famous at this period for producing skilled mercenaries, who were paid handsomely to fight battles well beyond Swiss frontiers.

Protestantism took root in Switzerland in the 16th century, spread by the teachings of Zwingli and Calvin. Swiss cities embraced the new doctrines, whereas rural cantons remained mostly Catholic. Tensions between the two communities erupted into violence from time to time, and apart from a brief period at the turn of the 19th century when Napoleon established the Helvetic Republic, these issues were not resolved until the adoption of a federal constitution in 1848.

With stability came development – railways were built, agriculture diversified, resorts developed. A tradition

Huldrych Zwingli (1484–1531), leader of the Swiss Reformation

Exploring Switzerland

Switzerland is a small country – only 350 km (220 miles) by 220 km (140 miles) at its greatest extent. The Alps run across the southern part of the country, and in the northwest, the Jura mountains stretch along the French border. Mediterranean influences can be felt and seen in mild winters and palm-lined esplanades south of the Alps. Traveling by car is the most flexible mode of transportation, but the reliable rail network makes sightseeing by train easy and surprisingly affordable.

SIGHTS AT A GLANCE

Basel **4**
Bern **5**
Chur **10**
Geneva **1**
Interlaken and the Jungfrau **6**
Lake Geneva **2**
Lucerne **8**
Neuchâtel **3**
Swiss National Park **11**
Ticino **12**
Zermatt **7**
Zürich **9**

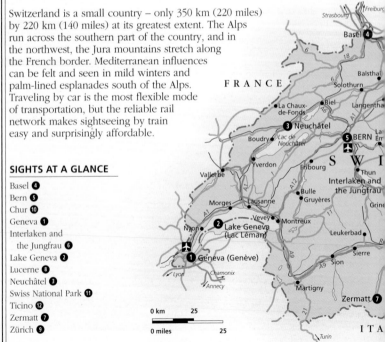

FRANCE

Strasbourg
Freiburg
Basel **4**
Balsthal
Solothurn
La Chaux-de-Fonds
Biel
Langentha
Neuchâtel **3**
Boudry
Lac de Neuchâtel
BERN **5**
Yverdon
Fribourg
Thun
Interlaken and the Jungfrau **6**
Vallorbe
Bulle
Gruyères
Grin
Morges
Lausanne
Nyon
Vevey
Montreux
Lake Geneva (Lac Léman) **2**
Leukerbad
Geneva (Genève) **1**
Sierre
Lyon
Chamonix
Sion
Annecy
Martigny
Zermatt **7**
Turin
ITA

0 km   25

0 miles   25

of humanitarianism began in the mid-19th century with the founding of the International Red Cross. In the 20th century Switzerland remained neutral during the two world wars, and concentrated on furthering its economic development, notably in the sectors of finance and pharmaceuticals.

LANGUAGE AND CULTURE

Switzerland is a quadrilingual nation. German, French, Italian, and Romansch (the language of a few valleys in the canton of Graubünden) are spoken in different parts of the country, though German is the language of the majority.

For many centuries Swiss culture had a predominantly rural tradition, and wine festivals are still a feature of village life. Great pride is taken in traditional crafts and regional specialties, such as the famous Emmental cheese. Swiss chocolate is also renowned for its high quality. Switzerland is now an outward-looking country, keen to export its expertise in finance and watchmaking worldwide.

KEY DATES IN SWISS HISTORY

58 BC–AD 400 Roman occupation

AD 400–1100 Germanic peoples – the Allemani and Burgundians – inhabit the area

12th century Holy Roman Empire extends feudal law over much of present-day Switzerland

1220 Gotthard Pass opened

1291 Oath of Allegiance marks beginning of the Swiss Confederation

1351 Zürich joins the Confederation

1477 Charles the Bold of Burgundy defeated by Swiss troops at Battle of Nancy

16th century Reformation; Protestantism takes firm hold in Swiss cities

1798 Napoleon creates the Helvetic Republic

1815 Power of cantons re-established

1830–48 Federal constitution drawn up

1864 International Red Cross set up

1914–18 & 1939–45 Switzerland remains neutral during two world wars

1946 UN offices established in Geneva

1990 Swiss women granted right to vote in every canton

2002 Switzerland declared member of the UN

2008 Switzerland joins EU Schengen Area, removing road and rail border checks

Sidewalk cafés surrounding the Place du Bourg-du-Four, Geneva

KEY

🛧 Airport

— Motorway

— Major road

— Railroad

▪▪▪ International border

Narrow, winding street in Geneva's historic old town

Geneva ❶

Geneva. 🏛 416,000. ✈ 🚉 🚌
🛈 Rue du Mont-Blanc 18 (022-909 7000). 🎭 Fêtes de Genève (early Aug). **www**.geneva-tourism.ch

Geneva is an ancient settlement with origins that go back to Roman times. The **old town**, situated on a craggy hill up above the western end of Lake Geneva, is the most attractive part of the city, with narrow, cobbled lanes and streets, fountain-filled squares, and an array of galleries, shops, and cafés.

In the heart of the old town stands the **Cathédrale St-Pierre**. Although the building dates from the 12th century it was much altered in the 16th century – the plain facade and interiors are in keeping with its Reformist heritage. A splendid 14th-century town-house close by, the **Maison Tavel**, gives a good insight into life in the developing city of Geneva through the centuries. In Rue Jean-Calvin the **Barbier-Müller Museum** displays artifacts and objects from traditional societies in Africa and the Asia-Pacific region. There is a mesmerizing array of beautiful carvings, jewelry, and textiles.

Geneva's grandest museum, however, is the **Musée d'Art et d'Histoire**, at the eastern end of the old town. The stately early 19th-century edifice houses a diverse array of Swiss and European art

and artifacts, from prehistory to the modern age. It also has a sizeable collection of Egyptian antiquities.

At the foot of the old town Geneva's main shopping street – the Rue de Rive – runs parallel to the lake shore. The quays either side of the lake are pleasant places to stroll, with the Jardin Anglais and the **Jet d'Eau** (one of the world's largest fountains) on the Left Bank, and the Quai du Mont-Blanc on the right. It is from the latter that the ferries and paddlesteamers operate pleasure cruises and regular services to towns along the lake. Farther along the Right Bank are the city's **botanic gardens**, and if you take the road bordering them you will come to the international quarter of the city. Here the **Palais des Nations** – European head-quarters of the UN – runs frequent guided tours through the day (ID documents mandatory). Opposite, the **International Red Cross and Red Crescent Museum** offers a moving testimony to the need for such an organization.

Jet d'Eau fountain, Geneva harbor

🏛 **Musée d'Art et d'Histoire**
Rue Charles-Galland 2. **Tel** 022-418 2600. 🔲 Tue–Sun. 🚫 🖾 for temporary exhibitions (free 1st Sun each month). **www**.ville-ge.ch/mah

🏛 **Palais des Nations**
Avenue de la Paix 14. **Tel** 022-917 4896. 🔲 daily. 🚩 obligatory. 🔴 Nov–Mar: Sat & Sun. 🖾 🚫 **www**.unog.ch

Lake Geneva ❷

Vaud. 🚉 🚌 ⛴ 🛈 Avenue d' Ouchy 60, Lausanne (021-613 2626). 🎭 Nyon Paléo Music Festival (Jul). **www**.region-du-leman.ch

The region skirting Lake Geneva offers a string of interesting settlements in a landscape replete with rolling hills, pretty stone-built villages, vine-clad slopes, and palm-fringed esplanades.

Coppet, 15 km (10 miles) north of Geneva, is a quaint medieval village. The 17th-century Château de Coppet was the home of Madame de Staël, whose literary soirées and opposition to Napoleon enhanced the popularity of the château in the 18th century.

Farther along the lake, **Nyon** is a charming lakeside town dating from Roman times, a heritage displayed at the excellent Roman Museum. With its fortress-like château and network of lanes, Nyon commands a fine hilltop view over the lake.

Lausanne, 60 km (38 miles) east of Geneva, is a bustling city with a fine old town, a beautiful Gothic cathedral, and excellent shopping. The city is also home to the international Olympic movement – at the lakeside district of Ouchy, the Musée Olympique (www.museum. olympic.org) is a must for all sports enthusiasts.

Wine château and vineyards near the town of Nyon

The resort of **Montreux** at the eastern end of the lake has a palm-lined promenade and a busy marina. As well as Belle Epoque hotels and health resorts, the town boasts one of Switzerland's top attractions – the **Château de Chillon**. This former bastion of the dukes of Savoy has all the accoutrements of a medieval castle – damp dungeons, weaponry, and huge banqueting halls.

About 25 km (15 miles) north of Montreux, the wonderfully preserved medieval hilltop town of **Gruyères** is also a major tourist attraction. The walled town is divided by a cobbled main street flanked by tempting restaurants. You can see the famous cheese being made in the traditional way in Moléson-sur-Gruyères.

Pit Stop (1984), sculpture in the Museum Jean Tinguely, Basel

♣ **Château de Chillon**
Avenue de Chillon 21, 1820 Veytaux.
Tel 021-966 8910. ☐ *daily.* ● *Dec 25, Jan 1.* 🎫 www.chillon.ch

Neuchâtel ❸

Neuchâtel. 🏙 *32,000.* 🚆 🚌
🛈 *Hôtel des Postes (032-889 6890).*
🎪 *Wine Festival (late Sep).*
www.neuchatel-tourisme.ch

Neuchâtel, an old religious center and university town, lies at the eastern end of Lake Neuchâtel at the base of the Jura mountains. It is a little off the beaten track, but has an extensive and attractive old town overlooked by the partly Romanesque **Collegiate Church**. Just below the church, the **Tour des Prisons** offers a stunning view of the lake and city. The market square – Place des Halles – is bounded by elegant 17th-century buildings, including the turreted **Maison des Halles**, now a restaurant. The area around Neuchâtel is known for its wines, including Perdrix Blanche.

Environs
20 km (12 miles) northwest of Neuchâtel lies **La Chaux-de-Fonds**, the largest of Switzerland's watchmaking towns. Located 992 m (3,255 ft) above sea level, it does not have the feel of a typical Swiss town. Its rigid grid pattern was adopted when the town was rebuilt after a devastating fire in the 18th century. Le Corbusier and Louis Chevrolet are famous sons, though there is little evidence of the former in the town's architecture. The **Musée International d'Horlogerie** has a wonderful collection devoted to the watch industry, and is well worth a visit.

🏛 **Musée International d'Horlogerie**
Rue des Musées 29. *Tel 032-967 6861.* ☐ *Tue–Sun.* ● *public hols.*
🎫 www.mih.ch

Enameled watch (c.1665) in the Musée International d'Horlogerie

Basel ❹

Basel. 🏙 *188,000.* ✈ 🚆 🚌
🛈 *Basel Tourismus, Stadt-Casino, Barfüsserplatz (061-268 6868).* 🎪
Fair (Oct–Nov). www.basel.com

Basel sits in the northernmost corner of Switzerland, straddling the Rhine at the farthest point that the river is navigable to sea-going vessels. It is a large commercial city, and a world center for the chemical and pharmaceutical industries. This specialization is a legacy of its liberal past, when the city offered a home to Huguenots fleeing persecution. Their traditional silk-weaving skills eventually led to the development of synthetic dyes, and to pharmaceutical processes.

The **old town** remains the heart of the city and is a maze of fine streets and squares, including Marktplatz with its daily fruit and vegetable market. The striking red painted **Rathaus** (city hall) stands here, on the southern bank of the Rhine.

The twin sandstone towers of the Gothic **cathedral** are major landmarks. This imposing 12th-century building stands in a grand square – site of the famous autumn fair that has been an annual event since the 15th century.

Basel has a modern side too, with a vibrant cultural scene and a number of interesting museums, most notably the **Kunstmuseum**, which includes an impressive range of 20th-century artists such as Picasso, and the **Beyeler Foundation**, in Baselstrasse, a collection of around 200 paintings by modern masters.

Switzerland's most famous artist, Jean Tinguely (1925–91), has a museum devoted to his outlandish mechanical sculptures – **Museum Tinguely**.

🏛 **Kunstmuseum**
St. Alban-Graben 16. *Tel 061-206 6262.* ☐ *Tue–Sun.* 🎫 ⚙ ♿

🏛 **Museum Tinguely**
Paul Sacher Anlage 1. *Tel 061-681 9320.* ☐ *Tue–Sun.* 🎫 ♿

The tall spire of Bern Cathedral rising above the city skyline

Bern ❺

Bern. 🏔 *300,000.* 🚶 ✈ 🚇
ℹ *Central Railway Station (031-328 1212).* 🎭 *Ziebelemaerit (Nov).*
www.berninfo.com

Bern is the capital of Switzerland and its most attractive city – it has the best-preserved medieval town center in the country. It is located on raised land in a bend of the Aare River. From the city's terraces there are spectacular views over the river and across to the peaks of the distant Alps.

The city was founded at the end of the 12th century by the Duke of Zähringen and allegedly named after the first animal – a bear – killed in the forests which previously covered the area. The bear has been the city's emblem ever since. Most of the center of Bern, with its many fine stone Renaissance houses and covered arcades, dates from the 16th and 17th centuries.

Since 1848 Bern has been the capital of the Confederation. The massive **Bundeshaus** (Parliament House) is the home of the Swiss Parliament, and the building is open to visitors when parliament is not in session. It is situated at the end of the city's main market squares – Bärenplatz and Bundesplatz. These linked squares are also the site of the annual onion market which takes place on the fourth Monday in November, when the local onion harvest is traditionally celebrated.

The grotesque Kindlifresser or Ogre Fountain

The attractive **old town** at the heart of Bern is a UNESCO World Heritage site, famous for its arcaded streets, which offer comprehensive protection in the event of bad weather. The main streets – Kramgasse, Spitalgasse, Marktgasse, and Gerechtigkeitsgasse – are all lined with tempting shops, galleries, and cafés.

The city's famous **clocktower** stands where Kramgasse meets Marktgasse. The clock dates from 1530, and on the hour a series of figures – including bears, a jester, and a rooster – plays out its performance. The old town is filled with magnificent fountains, each of which depicts a famous historical or legendary figure. A wander around the city center will reveal the likenesses of Moses, the Duke of Zähringen, and the gruesome child-eating ogre, the Kindlifresser.

The **cathedral** on Münstergasse was built in the 15th century and is a beautiful example of late Gothic architecture. The building's most magnificent element is

the main portal – a masterpiece of carved and painted stone, which depicts the Last Judgment. The tall spire was only added in the late 19th century. To the right of the cathedral is a delightful small park overlooking the Aare flowing far below. This makes a good picnic spot in summer.

A huge bear park is situated on the shore of the Aare just below the old **Bärengraben**, or bear pits. The park's caves, pools, and forest give the bears a more natural home than the 19th-century pits. The city's **Historical Museum** – located just south of the old town over the river across Kirchenfeldbrücke – provides a great introduction to the city's history. Among the notable exhibits are wonderful Flemish tapestries. There is also the brand-new **Paul Klee Centre**, on Monument in Fruchtland, which contains around 4,000 works by the renowned Expressionist artist, who lived in Bern for 33 years.

🏛 **Historical Museum**
Helvetiaplatz 5. *Tel 031-350 7711.*
🕐 *Tue–Sun.* 📷 ♿ ✔
www.bhm.ch

Environs

To the southeast of Bern is the **Emmental Valley**. This verdant agri-cultural region, with its lush grazing, is famous for the cheese of the same name. A drive around the region can make an ideal half-day countryside tour. Take in some of the delightful towns and villages – Burgdorf, Affoltern, or Langnau im Emmental – and the gentle rolling hills dotted with covered wooden bridges and distinctive gabled wooden farmhouses of the area.

The Last Judgment, in the tympanum of Bern Cathedral's main portal

Interlaken cruise ship moored by the banks of the Thunersee

Interlaken and the Jungfrau ➏

Bern. 🏠 *15,000.* 🚃 🚌
ℹ *Höheweg 37 (033-826 5300).*
www.interlaken.ch

Interlaken, as its name suggests, lies between two lakes – the Thunersee and the Brienzersee – in the foothills of the Alps. To the south is the classic landscape of the Jungfrau mountains – one of the first regions of Switzerland to be opened up to tourism in the middle of the 19th century. Tourism is virtually the only industry in town, which caters for skiers in winter and sightseers by the busload in summer. A **funicular**, built in 1906, takes visitors up to the summit of the Heimwehfluh (669 m/ 2,195 ft), a wonderful vantage point above Interlaken. From here you can walk along woodland paths, visit an open-air model railway, or take the bob-run all the way down to the base station in Interlaken. There is also a restaurant and a children's play area.

Environs
One of the Alps' most famous peaks, the 4,158-m (13,642-ft) **Jungfrau** lies 20 km (12 miles) to the south of Interlaken. The almost equally high **Mönch** and **Eiger** mountains are neighbors and the stretch between Interlaken and the mountains is full of pretty alpine valleys and villages. From **Wengen** and **Grindelwald** you can take

a train up to Kleine Scheidegg, and another to Jungfraujoch, at 3,454 m (11,332 ft) Europe's highest train station. Another popular viewpoint is the **Schilthorn** peak at the head of the Lauterbrunnen valley. This can be reached via **Mürren** and **Gimmelwald**, by cable car on the last stretch. The region is perfect skiing and hiking territory, with walking trails to suit all ability levels.

A few kilometers east of Brienz, the main town on Brienzersee, lies the Swiss Open Air Museum (known as the **Ballenberg**). Original buildings from all over the country have been brought to this living museum. A special bus runs from Brienz train station to the Ballenberg.

🏛 **Ballenberg**
Tel *033-952 1030.* ⏰ *Apr–Oct: daily.* 📷 ♿ 🎫 **www**.ballenberg.ch

Zermatt ➐

Valais. 🏠 *6,000.* 🚃
ℹ *Bahnhofplatz (027-966 8100).*
www.zermatt.ch

Switzerland's most famous resort, Zermatt sits directly below the **Matterhorn**, a peak of 4,478 m (14,688 ft), which has been a mountain-climbers' mecca for the best part of two centuries. In addition to mountaineering, Zermatt offers top-quality skiing and hiking. Skiing is possible all year round at this, the highest of Swiss resorts, and there are miles of well-marked trails accessible to all walkers.

The most scenic way to arrive in Zermatt is via the Glacier Express from St. Moritz, but most tourists arrive by train from Täsch, 5 km (3 miles) down the valley. Taxis from Täsch to car-free Zermatt cost about the same as the train.

Hinterdorf is the most historic part of town. The parish church and cemetery contain some poignant reminders of the dangers of the high mountains. The displays at **Atlantis**, an alpine museum near the church, reflect the importance of the region's mountaineering tradition.

Gornergrat is probably the best viewing point for the Matterhorn, and can be reached by taking a cogwheel railroad. You can carry on by cable car to the **Stockhorn** peak for more mountain views.

Cog-wheel mountain railroad, with the Matterhorn peak rising behind

The Alps

The Alps are one of the oldest mountain ranges in the world, formed 65 million years ago when the Eurasian and African tectonic plates collided. They dominate Switzerland's landscape, covering more than half its surface area, and have shaped its history and economy. Switzerland is home to many well-known, distinctive peaks – such as the Matterhorn, Jungfrau, and Eiger – which were early tourist attractions in the 18th and 19th centuries. Trade and pilgrimage routes have crossed the Alps since Roman times but it is only in the last century that this wild and beautiful landscape has become truly accessible, with the development of long road and rail tunnels, mountain railroads, and cable cars.

Peak of the Matterhorn and the Gornergrat mountain railroad

Lake Lucerne surrounded by peaks and alpine meadows

ALPINE FLORA

Deciduous trees are common on the lower slopes of the Alps, but these gradually give way to coniferous spruce and pine. Between the tree line and the snow line lie lush alpine meadows famous for their wildflowers.

The Alpine aster *is one of many beautiful, brief-flowering, alpine plants found throughout the higher slopes and pastures. It blooms from July to August.*

Androsace alpina, *or rock jasmine, grows in mats which cling to alpine rockfaces. The shoots produce pinky-white flowers between July and August.*

Edelweiss *is the country's most famous flower, a symbol of purity and everlasting love. Increasingly rare, it is now a protected species.*

ALPINE WILDLIFE

Several national parks amid the Alps ensure the preservation of the unique native fauna. Although some animals have disappeared, a few species have adapted well to the higher altitudes, such as the marmot, chamois, ibex, mountain hare, and alpine chough.

Marmots *are difficult to spot but quite easy to hear, and live in burrows high on the valley slopes. Found throughout the Alps, these mammals are particularly abundant in Graubünden and Ticino.*

Chamois *are goat-like antelopes which can be seen adeptly scaling the highest mountain ridges. In the past they were hunted for their hide, which makes a very soft leather, but hunting quotas are now imposed.*

The alpine chough, *a crow-like bird with a yellow bill, glossy blue-black plumage, and gregarious disposition, spends the summer above the tree line. They descend to the valleys and villages in winter, where they accept food from tourists.*

THE ALPS IN SUMMER

Long before skiing became popular, foreign visitors were coming to Switzerland's alpine areas for quiet, relaxing holidays full of fabulous vistas and fresh air. In general, alpine resorts are quieter in summer than during the ski season, but there are good outdoor activities provided in most areas. Some resorts, such as Verbier and Gstaad, host summer music festivals of some note. Most cable cars and mountain railroads operate throughout the summer, transporting hikers and sightseers.

Hikers and mountain bikers *are very well-catered for in summer, as Switzerland has thousands of kilometers of designated footpaths. Trails are well-marked and maintained, with regular refreshment stops en route.*

Désalpe, *a traditional Swiss festival, celebrates the return of herds of cows from the high mountain pastures at the end of summer. In alpine valleys and the Jura, lines of groomed and festooned cattle are herded down the country roads, stopping off at village cattle troughs and fountains for refreshment, on their way back to the lowland farms.*

THE ALPS IN WINTER

Switzerland has ski resorts to suit most tastes and budgets, from the chic, five-star hotels of St. Moritz, where celebrity spotting is almost as popular as skiing, to family-oriented resorts with facilities and slopes for all abilities such as Grindelwald. Some are predominantly modern – Verbier has grown from the unvisited hamlet of 50 years ago into one of the biggest ski resorts in Switzerland. Others, such as Zermatt – with its historic town center, alpine museum, and slow pace of life – are more traditional.

Davos *is the largest resort in Switzerland, attracting visitors from all over the world. The twin towns of Davos Dorf and Davos Platz offer a wide choice of activities off piste, with an indoor sports center and many bars, nightclubs, and restaurants.*

EDWARD WHYMPER

An illustrator by profession, the mountaineer Edward Whymper (1840–1911) was one of a long line of British climbers who came to the Swiss Alps in the 19th century to scale hitherto unconquered peaks. In 1865, he reached the peak of the Matterhorn at 4,478 m (14,688 ft), together with two Swiss guides. Today, despite remaining a difficult ascent, more than 2,000 climbers scale the Matterhorn in a good summer.

Winter snow *is what draws most visitors to the Alps, whether for traditional skiing or trendy snowboarding. More bizarre sports include horseboarding (like water-skiing with a horse) and "zorbing" (tumbling down the slopes strapped to the inside of a balloon).*

Breathtaking Lake Lucerne and its surrounding mountain peaks

Lucerne ❽

Lucerne. 🚶 *60,000.* 🚉 📧
ℹ️ *Zentralstrasse 5 (041-227 1717).*
🎭 *Lucerne Festival Sommer (mid-Aug–mid-Sep).* **www**.luzern.org

The city of Lucerne makes a good base for touring most of central Switzerland. The surrounding countryside is possibly the most stereotypically Swiss – crystal-clear lakes ringed with snow-capped mountains, hemmed with lush pastures in summer, and criss-crossed with cog-wheel rail-roads. This is also the heartland of the Swiss Confederation – the three forest cantons of Uri, Schwyz, and Unterwalden, which swore the original Oath of Allegiance in 1291 (*see p614*), border the shores of Lake Lucerne. Today the region remains one of the most con-servative parts of Switzerland.

The town's historic center stands on the north bank of the Reuss river, which flows out of Lake Lucerne at its westernmost corner. Stretches of the ancient city wall and its watchtowers can be clearly seen bounding a ridge that marks the northern edge of the old town. The cobbled streets and shady squares are bustling both day and night.

The **Kapellbrücke** is the city's most famous symbol. Spanning the river at the lake end, this covered wooden

bridge was built in 1333, and formed part of the city's original boundary. Much of the bridge, including its decorative paintings, had to be renovated following a destructive fire in 1993. Also nearby is the **Rosengart Collection**, with over 200 works by various classic Modernist artists such as Klee, Picasso, and Cézanne.

The Rosengart now houses the collection of the former Picasso Museum. The works include photographs of Picasso, taken during the last 20 years of his life by British photographer David Douglas Duncan – images which further illuminate the artist's character.

🏛 **Rosengart Collection**
Pilatusstrasse 10. **Tel** *041-220 1660.*
⭕ *daily.* 🎫 🚫 *Sun am.*
www.rosengart.ch

Environs

Less than 2 km (1 mile) southeast of the town center stands the **Richard Wagner Museum**, where the composer lived and worked from 1866 to 1872. There are letters, manuscripts, and photographs relating to Wagner's life, and a fine collection of 17th-, 18th-, and 19th-century instruments.

About 28 km (17 miles) east of Lucerne, **Schwyz** is the capital of one of the original three forest cantons, and has given the country its name. The charter detailing the 1291 Oath of Allegiance which marks the beginning of the Swiss Confederation is housed in the town's Bundesbriefmuseum. More interesting is the **Ital Reding Hofstatt**, a fine 17th-century mansion on the northwest side of town, built on the proceeds of one of Switzerland's first exports – mercenaries. The fighting skills of the men of Schwyz were highly prized by warring European rulers until well into the 18th century.

Pilatus and **Rigi** mountains tower over the area and both are easily accessible. Mount Rigi has the distinction of being the first mountain in Europe to have a rail line constructed to the summit. This starts at Vitznau on the lake shore. Mount Pilatus to the south is higher and gives unrivaled views of the Alps. Its peak can be reached either by cable car from Kriens or cog-wheel railroad from Alpnachstad.

🏛 **Richard Wagner Museum**
Wagnerweg 27. **Tel** *041-360 2370.*
⭕ *mid-Mar–Nov: Tue–Sun.* 🎫 🚫

The 17th-century mansion of Ital Reding Hofstatt in Schwyz

For hotels and restaurants in this region see pp630–31 and pp632–3

Zürich **9**

Zürich. 🧍 *364,000.*
✈ *10 km (6 miles) N.* 🚊 🚏
ℹ *Hauptbahnhof (044-215 4000).*
www.zuerich.com

The dominant position of Zürich in the nation's economy has long been felt – in medieval times the guilds ruled the city and, boosted by the Reformation, Zürich and its inhabitants developed a talent for hard work and accumulating wealth. The stock exchange, which is the world's ninth largest, opened in 1877, and today Swiss bankers control the purse strings of many international companies and organizations.

Despite this tradition, the city also knows how to enjoy itself, and the medieval town center, which stretches either side of the Limmat river, is a

Grossmünster and Fraumünster in Zürich, separated by the Limmat river

Lively flea market at a lakeside park in Zürich's old town

hive of cafés, bars, and hip boutiques. On the east bank the warren of streets and alleys lies close to the university, adding to the café culture of this district. Also on the east bank, the extremely austere **Grossmünster** dominates the city. This was the church from which Ulrich Zwingli launched the Reformation on the receptive burghers of Zürich in 1520. Along Limmat Quai you can see the town hall (*rathaus*) built out on supports over the river, opposite one of Zürich's grand guildhalls.

On the other side of the river there are a number of interesting sights. **Lindenhof**,

a small hill, overlooks the city and was the site chosen by the Romans to build a customs post and thus found the city. **Fraumünster** and **St. Peter's** churches are nearby; the latter, with its Romanesque cloisters and stained-glass windows created by Marc Chagall, is well worth a visit.

Augustinergasse, which leads down from St. Peter's, is a delightful street with traces of medieval storefronts. It is a world away from Zürich's main shopping street, which it meets; Bahnhofstrasse is one of the world's most famous shopping areas – a wide, tree-lined avenue with trams running along its length. There are plenty of high-priced emporia, especially towards the southern lake end, but interesting and reasonably priced shops and department stores can be found here or in the streets nearby. At No. 70, **Orell Füssli** is Switzerland's largest English-language bookshop, and nearby on Löwenplatz you will find hard-to-resist outlets of the celebrated **Confiserie Sprüngli**.

Just behind the main train station at the top of Bahnhofstrasse, housed in a suitably Schloss-like building, the **Swiss National Museum** contains a comprehensive collection of art and artifacts detailing the history and cultural diversity of the country.

🏛 **Swiss National Museum**
Museumstrasse 2.
Tel 044-218 6511. ◻ Tue–Sun.
📷 ♿ **www**.nationalmuseum.ch

Environs
Winterthur, 25 km (15 miles) northwest of Zürich, is an interesting and little visited Swiss town. Its history as an industrial center in the 19th century has left a legacy of old factory and mill architecture. It also boasts excellent museums; the best of these are the eclectic Oskar Reinhart Collection am Römerholz and the Fotomuseum.

The nucleus of medieval **Stein-am-Rhein**, 40 km (25 miles) northeast of Zürich, is unchanged since the 16th century. Rathausplatz and Understadt, at its heart, are lined with buildings covered in colorful frescoes, oriel windows, and window boxes.

Oriel window and frescoed facade of the Gasthaus zur Sonne, Stein-am-Rhein

Chur ⓾

Graubünden. 🏘 35,000. 🚉
🛈 Bahnhofplat 3 (081-252 1818).
www.churtourismus.ch

Chur, the capital of
Switzerland's largest canton
Graubünden, is a quiet,
ancient town with origins that
go back 2,000 years. It is
located on the upper reaches
of the Rhine, on an ancient
route between northern
Europe and Italy. It has long
been a religious center –
the bishop of Chur controls
dioceses as far away as Zürich
– as well as a commercial
center, and is famous
throughout the country for
the Passugger mineral water
which is bottled just outside
the town.

The pedestrianized historic
town center is a maze of
cobbled streets and small
squares, including Arcas Square
with its sunny, café-filled
corners in summer. At the
southern tip of the old town
the late-Romanesque
cathedral, set in a square,
overlooks the rest of town.
The highlight of the cathedral
is its intricately carved and
gilded 15th-century altarpiece,
depicting Christ stumbling
under the weight of the cross
and scenes from the life of
St. Catherine. Unfortunately,
lighting levels are so low
inside the building that its full
glory is hard to discern. Next

**Elaborate 15th-century gilded
altarpiece in Chur Cathedral**

to the cathedral stands the
Bishop's Palace (not open to
the public) and at the bottom
of the small flight of steps
leading up to the cathedral
square is the **Rätisches
Museum**, which focuses on
the history and culture of the
canton of Graubünden.

🏛 **Rätisches Museum**
Hofstrasse 1. **Tel** 081-254 1640.
◻ Tue–Sun. 🖳 **www.**rm.gr.ch

Environs
To the east of Chur there are
a number of world-class ski
resorts. The two best-known,
with very different characters,
are **Klosters** and **Davos**. The
former, famous as the favorite
ski destination of British

royalty, is a small traditional
resort filled with charming
chalets. Davos, on the other
hand, is a big, brash town with
plenty of diversions away from
the slopes. It has grown from a
19th-century mountain health
resort to a major sporting
center, renowned for skiing,
snowboarding, paragliding,
and tobogganing in the
winter, and hiking, running,
and cycling in the summer.

Swiss National
Park ⓫

Graubünden. 🚉 Zernez, Scuol,
S-Chanf. 🛈 National Park House,
Zernez (081-851 4141). ◻ May–Oct:
daily. 🖳 **www.**nationalpark.ch

Switzerland has many small
nature reserves but only
one national park. By
international standards it is
small, covering only 172 sq
km (66 sq miles), but it is an
area where conservation
measures have been strictly
enforced for the best part of a
century, and people always
take second place to the
natural environment.

The Ofenpass road, linking
Switzerland with Austria, cuts
through the center of the park
and affords good views of
one of the park's valleys.
Otherwise the best way to see
the park is to take some of the
80 km (50 miles) of marked
trails – walkers are not allowed
to deviate off the paths.

The landscape is one of
wooded lower slopes and
jagged scree-covered ridges,
including the park's highest
peak at 3,174 m (10,414 ft) –
Piz Pisoc. Among the
abundant wildlife you may
see are chamois, ibex,
marmots, and the glorious
bearded vultures, which are
very rare in Europe and were
reintroduced into the park in
1991. From June to August,
with the retreat of the snows
at higher altitudes, a carpet of
beautiful alpine flowers,
including edelweiss and Swiss
androsace, appears.

The park has an interesting
bear exhibition in the
Schmelzra Museum, the
former headquarters of a lead
and silver mining company.

The lively winter-sports resort of Davos, in the mountains east of Chur

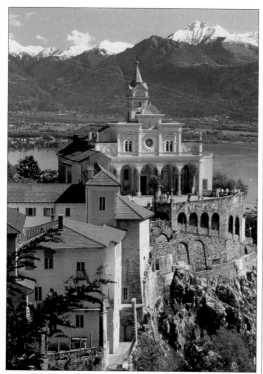

Hilltop sanctuary of Madonna del Sasso, Ticino, with its lakeside views

Ticino ⑫

🛬 Agno. 🚆 Bellinzona, Locarno, Lugano. 🛈 Via Lugano 1, Bellinzona (091-825 7056). 🎬 Locarno International Film Festival (early Aug). **www.**ticino.ch

The Ticino, Switzerland's most southerly canton, feels much more Italian than Swiss with its mild climate and Italian cuisine and language. It lies south of the Alps, bordering the Italian lakes (see p429), and is traversed by routes up the Alpine passes of St. Gotthard and San Bernardino. The three main towns of Bellinzona, Locarno, and Lugano all make attractive bases for exploring the area, with plenty of attractions, cafés and restaurants. Beyond, the valleys of the Ticino offer great sightseeing opportunities.

Bellinzona is the capital of the canton. Lying on the main north–south route between the Alps and Italy, it provides the first hint of Italian life with elegant piazzas, hilltop

fortresses, and fine Renaissance churches. The three castles of **Castelgrande**, in the town, **Montebello**, in the middle, and **Sasso Corbaro**, on top of the hill, feature on UNESCO's list of protected monuments. Castelgrande, with its imposing battlements, was the stronghold of the Visconti family in medieval times. Bellinzona is also appealing on Saturdays, when the streets of its old town are filled with tempting market stalls.

Locarno is located at the northern end of Lake Maggiore. The suitably named Piazza Grande is the heart of town, which for two weeks

in August becomes a giant open-air cinema during the **International Film Festival**. The festival aims to keep alive experimentation, discovery, eclecticism, and passion for auteur cinema. Moviegoers of all ages and nationalities gather in the square to watch a movie on one of the world's biggest screens.

Winding lanes filled with restaurants and boutiques radiate off the piazza. Above the town, easily accessible by a funicular railroad, the sanctuary of **Madonna del Sasso** is a major tourist and pilgrimage site. There has been a church here since 1480 when a vision of the Virgin Mary appeared to a local monk. The Baroque church is filled with marvelous frescoes and commands a fantastic view over the lake.

Probably the most charming of the three main centers of the region is **Lugano**, with its palm-lined lakeside location and attractive historic center of elegant piazzas. The arcaded streets are full of interesting old shops selling local produce.

Away from the main centers there are plenty of quaint villages along the Maggiore and Lugano lakes, such as **Ascona** and **Gandria**. These are now filled with waterside restaurants and arts and crafts shops. The valleys to the north offer great hiking and beautiful, peaceful scenery. Val Verzasca, north of Locarno, is one such valley, with the photogenic stone hamlet of **Corippo** clinging to the steep sides, and the pretty villages of **Brione** and **Sonogno** towards the head of the valley.

🏰 **Castelgrande**
Monte San Michele, Bellinzona. **Tel** 091-825 8145. ☐ daily. 🖼
🏛 **Madonna del Sasso**
Locarno. **Tel** 091-743 6265. ☐ daily.

Crowd gathered for Locarno's annual International Film Festival

Practical & Travel Information

Thanks to the famous Swiss efficiency, traveling around Switzerland is generally a pleasant and hassle-free experience. The country prides itself on its excellent transportation systems, with an extensive national rail network and frequent tram and bus services in the big cities. There are abundant tourist information offices and banking and communication facilities are of a high standard. Switzerland has four national languages – German, French, Italian, and Romansh – but the use of English is widespread, especially in tourist destinations.

TOURIST INFORMATION

Up-to-date information on many of Switzerland's towns and cities can be obtained from brochures and Internet sites. Most large cities have at least one centrally located tourist information office (*Verkehrsverein, Tourismus,* or *Office du Tourisme*), offering a wide range of information and facilities. Even the smallest towns and resorts have tourist offices, but the opening hours of those in ski resorts may be limited in summer. Most embassies are located in Bern, but many countries also have a consulate in Geneva.

OPENING HOURS

The 24-hour society has yet to reach Switzerland and while large stores in cities may have late-night opening (usually on a Thursday), most shops, museums, and offices close at 5 or 6pm. Many museums are closed on Mondays and village restaurants often close one or two days a week.

VISA REQUIREMENTS

Visitors to Switzerland must have a valid passport to enter the country. A visa is not required for visitors from the European Union, USA, Canada, Australia, and New Zealand for stays of up to 90 days. Border controls at road and rail frontiers have been abolished within the Schengen Area, which covers Switzerland and 24 other European countries.

SAFETY AND EMERGENCIES

Switzerland is one of the world's safest countries but you should still take all the usual precautions. Since Switzerland has no public health system, travel and health insurance are essential, especially considering the medical costs associated with skiing accidents. Hospitals have 24-hour emergency cover and in cities and towns there is always a pharmacy open. All pharmacies should post details of a 24-hour roster in their window.

Emergency services, including **helicopter rescue**, are very efficient, and there is also an **avalanche bulletin** hotline. If skiing or hiking at altitude, remember that dehydration or sunburn can cause problems.

BANKING AND CURRENCY

The unit of currency in Switzerland is the Swiss franc (CHF). Banking hours are generally 8:30am–4:30pm Monday to Friday, with some branches in tourist resorts also opening on Saturdays. Outside the big cities some banks may close for lunch between noon and 2pm. Money can be changed at banks or at bureaux de change. The latter are found in hundreds of locations, including at major train stations. Swiss francs and euros can also be withdrawn from cash machines. Credit cards are widely accepted.

COMMUNICATIONS

Even the smallest villages in Switzerland have a post office, and the bright yellow mail boxes are easy to spot. Post offices usually open from 7:30am to noon and from 1:30 to 6:30pm Monday to Friday, and from 8 to 11am on Saturday. However, times can vary from region to region, and smaller post offices often have more restricted hours. Public telephones are plentiful, and take both phonecards – available from post offices and newsagents – and credit cards. Internet facilities are found at airports and train stations, among other places.

The principal newspapers with nationwide circulation are the *Neue Zürcher Zeitung* from Zürich and *Le Temps* from Geneva. Most British newspapers are available in major centers from lunchtime.

FLYING TO SWITZERLAND

Switzerland has international airports at Zürich, Geneva, Basel, Bern, Lugano, and Sion. Among the major airlines that fly to Switzerland are Swiss International Airlines (Swiss), Qantas, American Airlines,

THE CLIMATE OF SWITZERLAND

Generally summers are sunny with temperatures frequently reaching 25° C (77° F), though thunderstorms can be a feature of summer evenings. Winters are cold with plenty of snow, but many places get a lot of winter sunshine, especially the ski resorts of the Valais. South of the Alps, in the Ticino, the climate is milder and much more Mediterranean in character.

BERN

month	Apr	Jul	Oct	Jan
°C/F max	12/54	23/73	13/55	6/43
°C/F	3/37	13/55	13/55	2/36
min	0°C 32°F			-2/38
sun (hrs)	6 hrs	8 hrs	4 hrs	2 hrs
rain (mm)	70 mm	85 mm	65 mm	75 mm

and British Airways. Low-cost airline easyJet *(see p17)* flies from London Gatwick, London Luton, and other European cities to Zürich and Geneva.

Because of the many business travelers who fly to Switzerland on a weekly basis, Monday and Friday flights can be hard to obtain, especially during the skiing season.

TRAVELING BY TRAIN

Switzerland is at the heart of Europe and rail links to major European cities are fast and efficient. The journey time from Zürich to Paris is six hours; from Geneva to Paris it is three and a half hours.

Switzerland's rail network is operated by the state-owned **Swiss Federal Railways** and private companies. It reaches all major cities and towns and even the smallest villages in the mountains. There is an integrated ticketing and fare system. When traveling to a major city, ask for a ticket that covers your destination's transportation network too – this usually costs only a small amount more. The Swiss Travel System (www. swisstravelsystem.com) offers a range of discount offers, which vary depending on how long you want to stay and where you want to go. Most popular

is the Swiss Pass, which allows unlimited travel on trains, lake ferries, and many mountain railways. Switzerland has a number of spectacular train routes. The best-known are those that pass through the Alps, such as the Glacier Express between St. Moritz and Zermatt. These services are included in the Swiss Passes and are reasonably priced.

TRAVELING BY CAR

The most direct route by car from Great Britain to Switzerland is via the Channel Tunnel and French motorways to western Switzerland. If you want to make use of the excellent motorway network you will need to buy a motorway sticker *(vignette)*, available at border crossings, tourist offices, and gas stations.

Most of the international car rental firms have offices at airports and in the major towns. Many allow you to leave the car at a destination in France, Germany, or Italy.

As in the rest of continental Europe, the Swiss drive on the right. Since most freight is moved by rail in Switzerland, the majority of country routes, main roads, and motorways are generally free of congestion. Driving around major

cities, however, can be more difficult. Road signs are generally clear, with main roads in blue and freeways in green. Historic sights are usually signposted in brown. Speed limits are strictly enforced – 120 km/h (75 mph) on freeways, 80 km/h (50 mph) on main roads, and 50 km/h (30 mph) in built-up areas. Many mountain passes are closed from November to June. A sign at the foot of the pass will indicate whether the road is open or closed.

GETTING AROUND CITIES AND TOWNS

Buses and trams are found in the major cities and they provide frequent and reliable services. Tickets can be purchased from machines at bus and tram stops. Taxis are generally very expensive, as in most major cities in Europe. Some cities such as Bern offer bicycle rental facilities, as do 80 of the major train stations. Many small villages that are not served by trains are on a "post bus" route, which usually originates at the train station of the nearest main town. Buses are timed to coincide with the arrival and departure of trains.

DIRECTORY

TOURIST INFORMATION

UK
Switzerland Tourism,
30 Bedford Street,
London WC2E 9ED.
*Tel 00800-100 200 30
(international toll free).*

US & Canada
Swiss Center, 608 Fifth
Ave, New York, NY 10020.
*Tel 00800-100 200 30
(international toll free).*

**Switzerland & all
other countries**
P.O. Box 695, 8027 Zürich.
*Tel 00800-100 200 30
(international toll free).*
**www.
myswitzerland.com**

EMBASSIES

Australia
Chemin des Fins 2,
Case Postale 172,
Geneva 1211.
Tel 012-799 9100.

Canada
Kirchenfeldstrasse 88,
3005 Bern.
Tel 031-357 3200.

Ireland
Kirchenfeldstrasse 68,
3005 Bern.
Tel 031-352 1442.

UK
Thunstrasse 50, 3000
Bern. *Tel 031-359 7700.*

US
Sulgeneckstrasse 19, 3007
Bern. *Tel 031-357 7011.*

EMERGENCY NUMBERS

Ambulance
Tel 144.

Avalanche Bulletin
Tel 187.

Fire
Tel 118.

Helicopter Rescue
Tel 1414 / 1415.

Police
Tel 117.

Weather Forecast
Tel 162.

**SWISS
INTERNATIONAL
AIRLINES**

Australia
Tel 1-800 883 199.

Ireland
Tel 01-890 200 515.

New Zealand
Tel 09-977 2238.

Switzerland
Tel 0848-852 000.
Tel 0820-040 506 (24 hrs).

UK
Tel 0845-601 0956.
www.swiss.com

US & Canada
Tel 1-877 359 7947.

TRAVELING BY TRAIN

**Swiss Federal
Railways**
Hochschulstrasse 6, 3000
Bern. *Tel 0900-300 300.*
www.sbb.ch

Shopping & Entertainment

There are plenty of high-quality Swiss-made products to take away from your trip, including, of course, watches and chocolate. Porcelain, lace, wine, and cheese are also popular purchases. Apart from major events, such as the Montreux Jazz Festival, there is entertainment on a smaller scale throughout the country. Classical and jazz concerts abound in the large cities, which also have cinemas, opera halls, and dance venues. Most regions hold a number of seasonal local events, from wine festivals to antiques and bric-a-brac fairs. Switzerland's greatest attractions, however, are its landscape and outdoor sports. The mountains welcome skiers in winter and climbers, hikers, and cyclists in summer, with all levels of ability catered for.

WHERE TO SHOP

In the large cities the old town areas usually have the most rewarding shopping – often you'll find narrow streets crammed with interesting, if often expensive, specialist stores and galleries. Bern's old town, with its arcaded streets, offers varied and sheltered shopping whatever the weather. The major department stores, such as Globus, offer a fairly standard international shopping experience. Nationwide supermarket chains such as Coop, Migros, and Denner are very competitively priced, and you can pick up some interesting items, especially when it comes to food and wine.

WHAT TO BUY

After you have stocked up with Swiss chocolate, other items you might consider taking away with you as souvenirs and gifts are linen and lace. Switzerland has a long tradition of textile-working in the northeast of the country and the quality is generally very good.

Swiss army knives are popular and incredibly useful. Victorinox is the make to look out for. Swiss porcelain and pottery can also be a good buy. Many of the designs favor strong colors and rural motifs.

Basketry and carved wooden items (such as toys) make ideal gifts, and these can sometimes be found on market stalls. A wide range of watches and jewelry is available, particularly at the top end of the market. Watches are one of Switzerland's most important exports, so the quality of Swiss watchmaking is very high.

Other places where you might find suitable gifts include any branch of **Schweizer Heimatwerk**, which is a national chain of Swiss handicraft stores. They have outlets in many large towns and cities, as well as at the airports if you leave your present-buying late.

Major museums, cheese showrooms and similar locations will often have a small store. In the major tourist destinations, such as Gruyères, there is no shortage of shops selling cheap tourist souvenirs, but you will also find knowledgeable retailers offering high-quality genuine Swiss-made items.

MARKETS

Outdoor produce and craft markets are common in Switzerland. Most towns and cities have a market on one or two mornings a week, and almost always on a Saturday morning. These are great places to try out local wines and cheeses, as well as simply to savor the lively atmosphere.

FOOD AND DRINK

Very little Swiss wine is exported, so it makes an unusual gift. Some of the Valais wines, such as *Fendant* (white) and *Dôle* (red), are among the best. Among more transportable food items are dried meats from the German parts of Switzerland, such as *Bündnerfleisch*, alpine cheeses such as Gruyère, and spicy *Leckerli* biscuits from Lucerne or Basel. Even packets of ready-made *rösti* mixture from supermarkets can make a fun gift.

ENTERTAINMENT LISTINGS AND TICKETS

A great variety of small town- and village-based concerts, festivals, and events takes place in Switzerland throughout the year. Local tourist offices can supply details of what's happening during your visit, while the Swiss Tourist Board offices abroad can provide comprehensive listings of all major sporting and cultural events taking place in Switzerland over the coming year.

Most major cities have a variety of venues dedicated to the arts, whether it be classical music, theater, cabaret, or jazz. Information about events can be found on the websites of the local tourist offices (for example, www.zuerich.com/events), on www.my switzerland.com or via the ticket office **Ticketcorner**.

ENTERTAINMENT VENUES

Many venues in Switzerland offer more than one type of entertainment. The **Reitschule** in Bern is used for live music, theater, film, and dance, while the **Théâtre de l'Usine** in Geneva hosts concerts, theater, film, and cabaret.

The Zürich Tonhalle Orchestra is based at the **Opernhaus**, a popular venue for opera and ballet. Zürich has a thriving club scene. **Rote Fabrik** by the lakeshore is inexpensive and plays alternative music. The **Widder Bar** has live jazz performances.

Cinemas in Switzerland often show films in their original language, with subtitles in French, German, Italian, or English. Zürich has more than 40 cinemas, almost all of which have regular showings of English-language films.

FESTIVALS AND PUBLIC HOLIDAYS

Across Switzerland, public holidays and religious events are celebrated in different ways. Lent and Easter are marked by masked parades, lantern processions, music concerts, and tree- and fountain-dressing in many parts of the country. Swiss National Day (August 1) commemorates the swearing of the Oath of Allegiance between the original forest cantons. Bonfires are lit and huge firework displays put on all over the country. Even the smallest village has a party with wine, food, and music.

Switzerland has many other annual festivals and themed events. Geneva's famous International Motor Show is held every year in the spring. The **Montreux International Jazz Festival** takes place in July, as does the **Paléo Music Festival**, a week-long open-air concert of world music at the town of Nyon on Lake Geneva. August brings the **Locarno International Film Festival** and Lucerne's International Music Festival. Other annual festivals include the huge

autumn fair in Basel, harvest festivals in the country's wine-growing regions, and the Combats de Reines, a form of cow fighting popular in some areas of the Valais. In spring, the animals are released from their often-cramped winter quarters. The cows butt heads in a natural fight for dominance, to see who is "Queen of the Herd." Injuries are rare.

WINTER SPORTS

Skiing and snowboarding are just a couple of the many activities that Switzerland has to offer. Despite the country's reputation for high costs, it is possible to ski inexpensively. There is a wide range of options, from small, traditional villages to large modern resorts packed with lots of additional facilities such as swimming pools and ice-skating rinks. Advice on the range and suitability of different resorts can be sought from Switzerland Tourism (see p626) or the **Ski Club of Great Britain**, which provides information, advice, and holiday and tuition packages. Cross-country skiing is very popular – some of the best places to try this are the villages of the Jura and the Lower Engadine Valley.

SUMMER SPORTS

In the summer, mountaineering and hiking take over from skiing as the most popular draw, though skiing all year round is an option at one or two high-altitude resorts, such as Zermatt. There are 60,000 km (37,200 miles) of marked hiking trails all over the country, including some long-distance ancient trade and pilgrimage routes, such as the Grand St-Bernard trail. Yellow markers indicate standard hiking trails. Higher, rougher trails have red and white markers and the very high-altitude trails are marked in blue. These should only be attempted with an experienced guide. Mountain biking is also catered for, with trails clearly indicated. Maps and information are available from the **Swiss Alpine Club** or the **Swiss Hiking Federation**.

OTHER OUTDOOR ACTIVITIES

Sailing and swimming are possible during summer at the country's clean lakes. River rafting is also a popular activity, especially along the Rhine. If slightly gentler sports – such as hot-air ballooning or horseback riding – are more your thing, tourist offices will be able to provide suggestions.

DIRECTORY

HANDICRAFTS

Schweizer Heimatwerk
www.heimatwerk.ch
Schneidergasse 2, Basel.
Tel 061-261 9178.
Airport, Geneva.
Tel 022-788 3300.
Bahnhofstrasse 2, Zürich.
Tel 044-221 0837.
Rudolf-Brun-Brücke, Zürich.
Tel 044-217 8317.

ENTERTAINMENT TICKETS

Ticketcorner
Tel 0900-800 800.
www.ticketcorner.com

ENTERTAINMENT VENUES

Opernhaus
Falkenstrasse 1, Zürich.
Tel 044-268 6400.
Fax 044-268 6401.
www.opernhaus.ch

Reitschule
Neubrückstrasse 8, Bern.
Tel 031-306 6969.
Fax 031-306 6967.
www.reitschule.ch

Rote Fabrik
Seestrasse 395, Zürich.
Tel 044-485 5858.
www.rotefabrik.ch

Théâtre de l'Usine
4 Place des Volontaires, Geneva.
Tel 022-328 0818.
Fax 022-781 4138.
www.usine.ch/theatre

Widder Bar
Widdergasse 6, Zürich.
Tel 044-224 2411.
www.widderhotel.ch

FESTIVALS

Locarno International Film Festival
www.pardo.ch

Montreux International Jazz Festival
www.montreuxjazz.com

Paléo Music Festival
www.paleo.ch

OUTDOOR ACTIVITIES

Ski Club of Great Britain
57–63 Church Road, London SW19.
Tel 020-8410 2000.
www.skiclub.co.uk

Swiss Alpine Club & Swiss Hiking Federation
Monbijoustrasse 61, Bern.
Tel 031-370 1818.

Where to Stay in Switzerland

Switzerland has always been a highly popular European tourist destination and its hoteliers are famous for their courteous enthusiasm and attention to detail. It is all too easy to think of Switzerland only as mountains and wooden chalets, but there are many smart town hotels, too, as well as spectacular lakeside accommodations.

PRICE CATEGORIES
Price categories for a standard double room with bathroom or shower, including tax and service:

(F) Under 150 CHF
(F)(F) 150–250 CHF
(F)(F)(F) 250–350 CHF
(F)(F)(F)(F) 350–500 CHF
(F)(F)(F)(F)(F) Over 500 CHF

LAKE GENEVA

GENEVA Hôtel de la Cloche
(F)(F)
6 Rue de la Cloche, 1201 **Tel** *022-732 94 81* **Fax** *022-738 16 12* **Rooms** *8*

A very popular bijou hotel in a quiet neighborhood in the center of Geneva, just behind the Quai du Mont Blanc, with the unique appeal of a 19th-century family home. Elegant stone exterior. Small but perfect rooms with parquet flooring, fireplace, and balconies with wrought-iron railings. Reserve well in advance. **www.geneva-hotel.ch/cloche**

GENEVA L'Auberge d'Hermance
(F)(F)(F)
12 Rue du Midi, Hermance, 1248 **Tel** *022-751 13 68* **Fax** *022-751 16 31* **Rooms** *6*

Intimate, elegant, and an escape from downtown Geneva. Tucked away in the picturesque hamlet of Hermance, the Auberge has just six romantic rooms, three of which are suites. Rooms feature original paintings, hand-painted furniture, open beams, stone walls, and gorgeously tiled bathrooms. Exceptional restaurant. **www.hotel-hermance.ch**

GENEVA Hôtel Beau-Rivage
(F)(F)(F)(F)(F)
13 Quai du Mont-Blanc, 1201 **Tel** *022-716 66 66* **Fax** *022-716 60 60* **Rooms** *93*

Geneva's oldest family-run hotel, poised on the edge of the lake, close to all major attractions with views of the famous *jet d'eau.* An architectural gem, with crystal chandeliers, soaring four-story interior atrium with bubbling fountain, marble walls, and Grecian columns. Exceptional concierge services and opulent rooms. Four apartments. **www.beau-rivage.ch**

GRUYERES Hostellerie des Chevaliers
(F)(F)
Route de la Cité, 1663 **Tel** *026-921 19 33* **Fax** *026-921 25 52* **Rooms** *34*

The hotel looks like a rambling old farmhouse, painted white and set by itself in the verdant pastures of the Gruyères countryside. Tranquil and evocative location, cyclists particularly welcome. Rooms range from the simply furnished to those with antiques and lavish colorful old fabrics covering beds and walls alike. **www.gruyeres-hotels.ch**

LAUSANNE Elite
(F)(F)
1 Avenue Sainte-Luce, 1003 **Tel** *021-320 23 61* **Fax** *021-320 39 63* **Rooms** *33*

Elite is a large townhouse of pink stone with white shutters and red-striped awnings, with a large garden, in the heart of downtown Lausanne between the cathedral and train station. Top rooms have views of the lake; all are non-smoking, and some have spacious wrought-iron balconies. Urban address with relaxed country ambiance. **www.elite-lausanne.ch**

LAUSANNE Lausanne Palace & Spa
(F)(F)(F)(F)(F)
7–9 Rue du Grand-Chêne, 1002 **Tel** *021-331 31 31* **Fax** *021-323 25 71* **Rooms** *154*

The epitome of the grand old Belle Époque hotel, evoking the heyday of the Swiss Riviera, with one of the most elaborately equipped spa centers in Switzerland. City center location. Rooms range in size from 30 sq m (322 sq ft) to the 95 sq m (1,020 sq ft) Presidential Suites. Black marble bathrooms. Indoor pool. **www.lausanne-palace.ch**

WESTERN SWITZERLAND

BASEL Teufelhof
(F)(F)(F)
Leonhardsgraben 47–49, 4051 **Tel** *061-261 10 10* **Fax** *061-261 10 04* **Rooms** *33*

Very special art and entertainment themed twin hotels. The Art Hotel has 8 exceptional rooms and a suite. Each room is a work of art. One room features a huge painted Bible. The Gallery Hotel's 24 rooms and suites are each given over to a specific artist to display his design sense. Superb restaurant, in-house theater. **www.teufelhof.com**

BERN Belle Époque
(F)(F)(F)
Gerechtigkeitsgasse 18, 3011 **Tel** *031-311 43 36* **Fax** *031-311 39 36* **Rooms** *17*

An oasis of art and individual design in the Old Town, this hotel lives up to its name. Each guest room is unique not only in size and ambiance, but furnished with Art Nouveau or Belle Époque antiques and paintings. One room even contains original works by the Swiss painter Ferdinand Hodler. **www.belle-epoque.ch**

Key to Symbols *see back cover flap*

GRINDELWALD Parkhotel Schoenegg

Dorfstrasse, 3818 **Tel** *033-854 18 18* **Fax** *033-854 18 18* **Rooms** *49*

Run by the same family for four generations, the Parkhotel Schoenegg is a quiet luxury hotel with top spa facilities, private garden, and cozy reading room with wood-burning stove. There is an indoor swimming pool, a whirlpool with floor to ceiling views of the Eiger and a Finnish log sauna. Well-equipped rooms. **www.parkhotelschoenegg.ch**

INTERLAKEN Victoria-Jungfrau

Höhenweg 41, 3800 **Tel** *033-828 28 28* **Fax** *033-828 28 80* **Rooms** *212*

This is one of the most majestic and impressive grand old hotels in the palace style to be found anywhere in Europe. Convenient for lake excursions, the hotel also has extensive, state-of-the-art spa, and fitness and beauty facilities. The public rooms are opulent, bedrooms generously sized and elegantly appointed. **www.victoria-jungfrau.ch**

ZERMATT Riffelalp

Riffelalp, 3920 **Tel** *027-966 05 55* **Fax** *027-966 05 50* **Rooms** *72*

Arguably the most desirable hotel in Zermatt. Tranquillity is assured, the only way up to the hotel being by train. The hotel complex dates back to 1884, but since total reconstruction in 2000 with a new spa, indoor swimming pool, and bowling alley, the hotel's rooms are among the most luxurious in the Alps. **www.riffelalp.com**

ZURICH AND LUCERNE

LUCERNE Jailhotel Löwengraben

Löwengraben 18, 6004 **Tel** *041-410 78 30* **Fax** *041-410 78 32* **Rooms** *56*

This former prison was converted in 1998, and now offers "Unplugged" rooms that resemble cells but with more comfort, modernized "Most Wanted" rooms with showers and toilet, and attractive suites (the best is the former visitors' room). The "Warden's" room has a safe, and the library suite is filled with books. **www.jailhotel.ch**

LUCERNE Art Deco Hotel Montana

Adligenswilerstrasse 22, 6002 **Tel** *041-419 00 00* **Fax** *041-419 00 01* **Rooms** *62*

This historic hotel overlooks Lake Lucerne. Each room is a unique Art Deco experience, with furniture, paint colors, and tiles chosen to complement the theme, which extends to the bathrooms. A funicular delivers guests from the lakeside right into the hotel lobby. Two towers with suites. **www.hotel-montana.ch**

ZURICH Lady's First

Mainaustrasse 24, 8008 **Tel** *044-380 80 10* **Fax** *044-380 80 20* **Rooms** *28*

Owned and operated by a team of five women, this unusual fashion hotel is aimed toward women. Although the "modern man" is welcomed, he is not permitted on the upper floors, which house a spa, recreation rooms, and terrace. The hotel occupies an elegant 19th-century townhouse with exceptional decor. Rose garden. **www.ladysfirst.ch**

ZURICH Widder

Rennweg 7, 8001 **Tel** *044-224 25 26* **Fax** *044-224 24 24* **Rooms** *49*

Unusual, wildly popular luxury hotel spread out over eight former historic townhouses in the Augustiner Quarter. Very high reputation for service. No two rooms are remotely alike. Some have old hand-carved oak furnishings and four-poster beds, others have hanging steel staircases and hip leather furniture. Latest high-tech gadgets. **www.widderhotel.ch**

GRAUBUNDEN AND TICINO

DAVOS Schatzalp

Bobbahnstrasse 23, 7270 **Tel** *081-415 51 51* **Fax** *081-415 52 52* **Rooms** *92*

Featured in Thomas Mann's *The Magic Mountain*, the Art Nouveau Schatzalp is spectacularly situated 300 m (1,000 ft) above Davos on a sunny terrace at the tree line. The only access is by private funicular. The hotel's Alpinum Schatzalp is a beautiful botanical garden with 3,000 species of alpine plants. **www.schatzalp.ch**

KLOSTERS Wynegg

Landstrasse 205, 7250 **Tel** *081-422 13 40* **Fax** *081-422 41 31* **Rooms** *20*

A charming old wooden chalet painted blue, with wooden ceilings decorated with frescoes, the hotel is famous for its food, and for being the favorite haunt of Prince Charles. Aside from royals, the clientele is almost entirely repeat customers of long standing. Rooms are cozy and comfortable rather than chic. The decor verges on kitsch.

LOCARNO Belvedere

Via ai Monti della Trinita 44, 6600 **Tel** *091-751 03 63* **Fax** *091-751 52 39* **Rooms** *81*

This luxury hotel in a former 16th-century palazzo lies on a sunny hill overlooking Locarno and Lake Maggiore. The public rooms have marble and frescoed ceilings. Large garden for dining, games, or sunbathing and an outdoor pool. Four restaurants, including an outdoor grotto. Spa with indoor pool, gym, sauna, and solarium. **www.belvedere-locarno.ch**

Where to Eat in Switzerland

There is no "national dish" in Switzerland, since menus vary from region to region. In French Switzerland, fondue is a local specialty, while in German Swiss restaurants *rösti* (hash brown potatoes) are a favorite. Pizzerias are most numerous in the Italian-speaking Ticino region. For a landlocked country, seafood is surprisingly popular.

PRICE CATEGORIES
Price categories for a three-course meal for one person, including tax and service but without wine:

(F) Under 30 CHF
(F)(F) 30–60 CHF
(F)(F)(F) 60–90 CHF
(F)(F)(F)(F) 90–120 CHF
(F)(F)(F)(F)(F) Over 120 CHF

LAKE GENEVA

GENEVA Bistrot du Bœuf Rouge
Rue Alfred-Vincent 17, 1201 **Tel** *022-732 75 37*

(F)(F)

A gastronomic restaurant at the top of its game masquerading as a small family bistro. The cooking is heavily influenced by the Lyon region of France, with savory and substantial sauces. Many Swiss wines are on the list, as are impeccable vintages from France: Louis Latour for burgundies and choice northern Rhône wines. Closed Sat and Sun.

GENEVA Café de Paris
Rue du Mont-Blanc 26, 1201 **Tel** *022-732 84 50*

(F)(F)

A short stroll from the lake, the Café de Paris is a venerable Geneva institution, famous for being written up as having only one item on the menu: entrecôte steak with chips, green salad, and the eponymous still secret butter sauce first developed in 1930. Short list of a dozen Swiss and French wines.

GENEVA L'Entrecôte Couronnée
5 rue des Pâquis, 1201 **Tel** *022-732 84 45*

(F)(F)(F)

Small, intimate bistro in downtown Geneva popular with the locals. The wine list emphasizes wines from canton Geneva and the restaurant has been awarded a certificate for its use of local meats and produce. Genuinely charming interior with retro style wooden floors and period tables. Try the steak with butter sauce. Closed Sun.

GENEVA Du Parc des Eaux-Vives
82 Quai Gustave Ador, 1211 **Tel** *022-849 75 75*

(F)(F)(F)(F)(F)

This historic château houses both a brasserie and a superbly elegant fine dining room in the grounds of a leafy park of the same name near Lake Geneva. Said to have the most beautiful summer dining terrace in Geneva. Classic French cuisine with great Simmental beef and Paulliac lamb. Two Michelin stars. Closed Sun and Mon.

LAUSANNE (OUCHY) La Croix d'Ouchy
Avenue d'Ouchy 43, 1006 **Tel** *021-616 22 33*

(F)(F)(F)

A highly regarded gourmet restaurant on the outskirts of Lausanne by the lake. The menu offers French and Italian cuisine with good vegetarian choices. Service can be slow, but the risottos are sublime and the *escalopines au miel et citron* (escalope with honey and lemon) is also superb, as is the black truffle ravioli. Sunny terrace.

MONTREUX Palais Oriental
6 Quai Ernest-Ansermet, 1820 **Tel** *021-963 12 71*

(F)(F)(F)

A Montreux landmark, the Palais Oriental is entertaining and exotic, with its ornate Islamic carpets (for sale) and metal work. It is a good spot to take afternoon tea. The meals are somewhat pricey, but there is an authentic range of Iranian, Moroccan, Lebanese, and Egyptian cuisine. The restaurant is right on the shores of Lake Geneva.

WESTERN SWITZERLAND

BASEL Goldenen Sternen
St. Alban-Rheinweg 70, 4052 **Tel** *061-272 16 66*

(F)(F)(F)

The oldest restaurant in Basel (and one of the oldest in Europe), dating from the 15th century, with old-fashioned decor and standards of service. Tables are laid with starched white linen and sterling silver. A loyal clientele of locals. Wide range of Swiss German specialties as well as international fare like grilled meats. The wine list is impressive.

BERN Kornhauskeller
Kornhausplatz 18, 3000 **Tel** *031-327 72 72*

(F)(F)(F)

A treat for the eyes as much as for the palate, the cellar dining room of the Kornhaus features dramatic, soaring vaulted arches painted with frescoes. In the past the Kornhaus fulfilled many functions, including a grain storage facility. Restored to its glory, the cellar is now immensely popular with tourists. The menu is Mediterranean.

Key to Symbols *see back cover flap*

INTERLAKEN Schuh

*Höheweg 56, 3800 **Tel** 033-888 80 50*

An Interlaken institution since the beginning of the 19th century, the "Grand Restaurant Schuh," to give its full title, is deservedly renowned for its chocolates, many of which are unique concoctions. But the dining room menu ventures into the Orient, with Japanese and Thai dishes, as well as onto Swiss-German terrain with veal *schnitzel*, Zürich style.

ZERMATT Zum See

*Zum See, 3920 **Tel** 027-967 20 45*

One of the most highly regarded mountain restaurants in the Alps, with an ever changing menu. In summer, mountain berries and vegetables from the garden right outside the old chalet add a wonderful freshness to the menu. In autumn there is game. In winter the rustic hut is filled to the rafters with skiers in the know.

ZURICH AND LUCERNE

LUCERNE World Café

*Europaplatz 1, 6405 **Tel** 041-266 71 00*

A trendy snack and wine bar that sits within the vast Culture and Congress Centre (KKL) and offers fantastic views of the lake. The decor combines cool, clean chrome with glass and walnut wood. A world theme menu includes "African muesli," Asian stir-fries, and Matcha green tea. Scrumptious desserts. Open until midnight (2am Fri & Sat).

LUCERNE Old Swiss House

*Löwenplatz 4, 6002 **Tel** 041-410 61 71*

This landmark half-timbered house in the city center near the Lion Monument has fabulous decor, with oil paintings and a wooden interior. The innovative cuisine is impeccably presented, deserving its 15 Gault Millau points. The *Wienerschnitzel* simply cannot be missed. Wine cellar with 30,000 bottles includes Château Mouton Rothschild from 1911 onwards.

ZURICH Haus zum Rüden

*Limmatquai 42, 8001 **Tel** 044-261 95 66*

The "House of the Hounds," as the name translates, has a Gothic dining hall with an 11-m- (36-ft-) high curved wooden ceiling, and dark wood wainscoting. The architecture is stunning, but the menu is even more compelling. French cuisine dominates the menu, with special attention to game, vegetables, and mushrooms as they come into season.

ZURICH Kronenhalle

*Rämistrasse 4, 8001 **Tel** 044-262 99 00*

An unmissable Zürich institution, as compelling for its interior as for its cooking. The dark-panelled walls contain original artwork from Picasso, Matisse, and Braque. The restaurant is always filled with locals, as well as tourists. Swiss German dishes vie with French classics on the menu, and portions are generous. The chocolate mousse is famous.

GRAUBUNDEN AND TICINO

BELLINZONA Ristorante Castelgrande

*Salita al Castello, 6500 **Tel** 091-826 23 53*

An outstanding restaurant with two dining options, both located in the imposing stone fortress Castlegrande. The Grotto is a relaxed dining area with a cavern-like feel where local specialties like risotto and gnocchi are served. There is also game when in season, including wild boar. The gourmet dining room, by contrast, is sleek and modern. Closed Mon.

KLOSTERS Rustico

*Landstrasse 194, 7250 **Tel** 081-410 22 88*

A rare treat, real Asian cooking with a chef from Hong Kong in the middle of Graubünden. Japanese, Chinese, Vietnamese, and Malaysian influences. Sushi and sashimi of course but also delicacies such as roe deer satay. Local Graubünden dishes are not ignored, either, and there is a good wine list. In summer Asian cooking courses are offered.

LOCARNO La Cittadella Trattoria

*Via Cittadella 18, 6600 **Tel** 091-751 58 85*

This restaurant occupies two floors in a rose-colored stone building in the heart of the Old Town in a quiet pedestrian zone. Downstairs the trattoria has a wood-burning oven, and seafood is the theme. Upstairs in a more elegant dining room, fish and shellfish are more elaborately prepared. Closed Mon.

LUGANO Al Portone

*Viale Cassarate 3, 6900 **Tel** 091-923 55 11*

A gourmet restaurant near the business district of Lugano with superb presentation. Refined and inventive Mediterranean cuisine is served in an exclusive atmosphere. The wine cellar has the best Ticino wines and a fine choice of other wines from all over the globe. The specialties include risotto and home-made pastas.

SCANDINAVIA

Scandinavia at a Glance

The Scandinavian countries – Denmark, Norway, Sweden, and Finland – are, arguably, among the least known countries in Europe. In Norway, Sweden, and Finland the majority of the population lives in the south, in affluent, modern cities, which are also rich in history and tradition. Away from the main towns and cities lie vast expanses of unspoiled, often wild terrain, from the breathtaking Norwegian fjords to the dense pine forests and clear lakes of Finland. At just over seven hours by train from Helsinki, St. Petersburg, Russia's second city, is easily accessible from eastern Scandinavia.

Oslo (see pp660–64), *Norway's capital, is an attractive city of grand Neoclassical buildings, wide boulevards, and green open spaces. In Frogner Park, one of the largest parks, is a collection of works by the eccentric Norwegian sculptor Gustav Vigeland (1869–1943).*

• Mo i Rana

Storuman

Bergen (see p666) *was the largest town and most important port in medieval Norway. Its streets are lined with fine historic monuments, including the 12th-century Mariakirken, the oldest building in the city.*

• Trondheim

NORWAY
(See pp656–671)

• Mora

Bergen •

OSLO •

• Stavanger

SWEDEN
(See pp638–655)

• Kristiansand

Gothenburg •

Aalborg •

Växjö •

Copenhagen (see pp676–81) *is a cosmopolitan city with a relaxed and welcoming atmosphere. Among the Danish capital's most visited attractions is the theme park, Tivoli Gardens, with its famous Chinese Pagoda.*

DENMARK
(See pp672–687)

COPENHAGEN Malmö •

Odense •

◁ **Pulpit Rock, giving spectacular views of the Lysefjord near Stavanger in Norway**

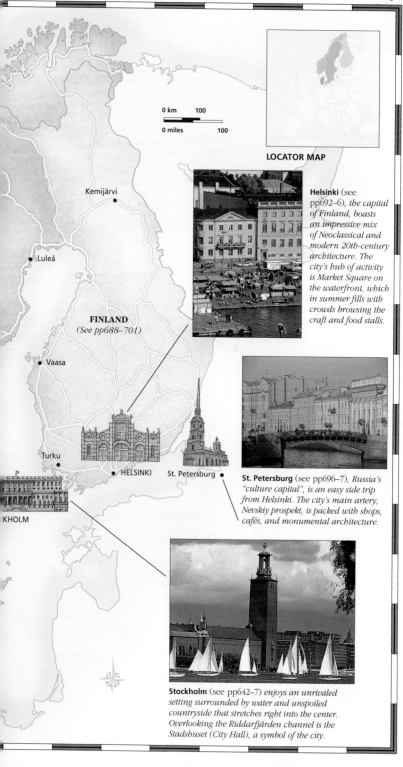

LOCATOR MAP

Kemijärvi

Luleå

FINLAND
(See pp688–701)

Vaasa

Turku

HELSINKI

St. Petersburg

KHOLM

Helsinki (see pp692–6), *the capital of Finland, boasts an impressive mix of Neoclassical and modern 20th-century architecture. The city's hub of activity is Market Square on the waterfront, which in summer fills with crowds browsing the craft and food stalls.*

St. Petersburg (see pp696–7), *Russia's "culture capital", is an easy side trip from Helsinki. The city's main artery, Nevskiy prospekt, is packed with shops, cafés, and monumental architecture.*

Stockholm (see pp642–7) *enjoys an unrivaled setting surrounded by water and unspoiled countryside that stretches right into the center. Overlooking the Riddarfjärden channel is the Stadshuset (City Hall), a symbol of the city.*

SWEDEN

The Swedes are justly proud of the natural beauty of their country. From the snow-capped mountains of the north, through rolling countryside dotted with forests and lakes, to the tiny islands of the Baltic archipelagos around Stockholm, the country is a mecca for outdoor enthusiasts. Like its people, Sweden's cities are modern and dynamic, but also rich in tradition.

Sweden is Europe's fifth-largest country, with an area about the size of California. Roughly 1,600 km (1,000 miles) lie between its southernmost and northernmost points. About 15 percent of its area lies north of the Arctic Circle, where, for a few days each summer, the sun never sets, and never rises for a similar period in winter. The Swedish climate is not severe, thanks to the warming influence of the Gulf Stream.

Only 7 percent of Sweden's area is cultivated farmland; more than half the country is covered by timberlands, consisting mainly of coniferous forests. Mountains, fells, and wetlands occupy nearly a quarter of the country. Sweden has about 100,000 lakes, which include Vänern, the third-largest body of fresh water in Europe. Norrland, the northern three-fifths of the country, is rich in natural resources, including timber, ore deposits, and rivers, whose waterfalls contribute to the national energy supply. It is here that the Sami (formerly known as the Lapps) earn their traditional livelihood herding reindeer.

HISTORY

Although the Swedish Vikings were seafaring warriors like their Danish and Norwegian cousins, they were primarily known as Sweden's first traders, opening up routes along the Russian rivers to the east as far as the Black Sea. Ruthlessly exploiting the Slav population of the area, they dealt mainly in slaves and furs. The Viking reign ended with the successful Christianization of Sweden at the end of the 11th century.

The German traders of the Hanseatic League arrived in Sweden some time during the 13th century, and dominated Swedish life for the next hundred years. In 1397, the Germans were forced out by the Union of Kalmar, which brought

Dancers in traditional folk costume in the village of Sundborn, Dalarna province

◁ View across the Strömmen in Stockholm to the dome of Katarina Kyrka on Södermalm

Scandinavia under Danish rule. This state of affairs continued until Gustav Vasa, resenting Denmark's influence, succeeded in ousting the Danes in 1523, becoming king of an independent Sweden.

The 17th and early 18th centuries were dominated by two military giants, Gustav II Adolf and Karl XII, whose conquests made Sweden for the first time more powerful than Denmark. In the 18th century, the Swedes contributed to Europe's Age of Enlightenment with advances in science and major developments in the arts, especially under the patronage of Gustav III. He opened the magnificent Royal Opera House in 1782, and was responsible for the construction of the Royal Dramatic Theater in 1788.

Karl XII of Sweden (1697–1718), the "warrior king"

By 1809, Sweden's military power had waned to such an extent that the country was forced to surrender Finland to Russia. A new constitution transferred power from the king to Parliament, marking the beginning of Sweden's democratic monarchy. In the early 19th century, Sweden was also a poor country, suffering from stagnation in agriculture and trade. In the course of the century nearly one million Swedes migrated, mostly to America. Their departure was a sobering lesson to those that remained, inspiring the philosophy of cradle-to-grave care that was put into practice in 20th-century Sweden's welfare state.

In a single century, Sweden grew from a poor rural economy to a leading industrial nation. The 1990s saw many significant changes take place. Engineering expanded rapidly, particularly in the field of telecommunications, led by the Ericsson company. Sweden joined the EU, and the church severed its role with the state after more than 400 years. In the year 2000, Malmö in Sweden and the Danish capital of Copenhagen were connected by the completion of the Öresund Bridge, symbolic of the long-standing friendship that has replaced the animosity between these once warring nations.

KEY DATES IN SWEDISH HISTORY

AD 800–1060 Era of the Swedish Vikings

13th century Hanseatic League of German merchants at height of its power in Sweden

1397 Kalmar Union links the Nordic countries

1523 Gustav Vasa becomes king of an independent Sweden

1611–32 Reign of Gustav II Adolf, "the Lion of the North," whose campaigns turn Sweden into a great European power

1718 Death of Karl XII, Sweden's last great military king, at siege of Fredriksten in Norway

1721 Sweden cedes Baltic provinces to Russia

1772 Gustav III crowned and mounts coup d'état giving the monarchy absolute power

1809 Sweden loses Finland to Russia

1814 Sweden gains Norway from Denmark

1869 Emigration to North America increases due to crop failure

1905 Parliament dissolves union with Norway

1939 Sweden declares neutrality in World War II

1995 Sweden joins European Union

2000 Öresund Bridge opens, finally connecting Sweden and Denmark

2001 EU presidency held by Sweden

2003 Single European currency rejected

2010 Crown Princess Victoria marries Daniel Westling

LANGUAGE AND CULTURE

Swedish belongs to the northern group of Germanic languages, along with Norwegian, Danish, Icelandic, and Faeroese. Various dialects are spoken, most notably in Skåne, southern Sweden, where the accent is almost Danish.

A nation of nature lovers, the Swedes are apt to retreat to their country cottages in all seasons. Deeply traditional, they love their rituals, from maypole dances at midsummer to the St. Lucia procession in December. Beneath their reserve the Swedes are a friendly people, their warmth readily unleashed with a *skål* (toast) and a round of schnapps.

Swedes are open-minded, trend-hungry, and tech-friendly. Stockholm offers the latest in design and architecture, and Sweden has become increasingly multicultural. While this new Sweden doesn't always blend easily with the old, most Swedes recognize that the country is richer for its diversity.

Exploring Sweden

The natural starting point for exploring Sweden is the capital Stockholm, built on a cluster of Baltic Sea islands. From here, visitors can explore the castles of Lake Mälaren or head north to Uppsala, a thriving university town. On the way south to Malmö or west to Gothenburg lies the Glass Kingdom, where some of the world's best-known glassmakers ply their trade. Travel throughout Sweden can be conducted quite easily by high-speed trains or by car, though the long distances involved make travel quite expensive.

SIGHTS AT A GLANCE

Dalarna **4**
Gothenburg **6**
Gotland and Visby **5**
Lake Mälaren **2**
Malmö **8**
STOCKHOLM pp642–7 **1**
Uppsala **3**
Växjö **7**

SWEDEN

0 km   250
0 miles   250

SWEDEN

NORWAY   FINLAND

See main map   Helsinki

Oslo

STOCKHOLM   ESTONIA

DENMARK   Gothenburg   LATVIA
Copenhagen   LITHUANIA

Gulf of Bothnia

Storby

Gävle

Dalarna **4**

Borlänge

Grisslehamn   Mariehamn

NORWAY

SWEDEN   Uppsala

OSLO   **3**   Kapellskär

Lake   Helsinki,
Mälaren   **2**   St Petersburg

Sandefjord   Karlstad   Örebro   **1**   STOCKHOLM

Vänern   Riga

Strömstad   Nynäshamn

Dalbosjön   Norrköping   Oxelösund

Skagerrak   Vättern

Newcastle,
Harwich   Västervik

Gothenburg   Jönköping   Visby   **5**
(Göteborg)   **6**   Borås   Gotland

Frederikshavn   Oskarshamn

Växjö   **7**   Öland

Halmstad   Kalmar

Grenå   Karlskrona

Helsingør   Helsingborg   Kristianstad   Gdansk

COPENHAGEN

Malmö   **8**   Simrishamn

Trelleborg   Ystad   Allinge

Rønne   Bornholm
(Denmark)

Rostock

0 kilometers   100
0 miles   100

KEY

✈ Airport

⛴ Ferry port

— Highway

— Major road

— Railroad

--- International border

The Göteborgsutkiken building, overlooking Gothenburg Harbor

Stockholm ❶

Stockholm was founded around 1250 on a small island in the narrow Strömmen channel between the Baltic Sea and Lake Mälaren. Today, the Swedish capital stretches across 14 islands. As well as a stunning waterside location, Stockholm boasts a rich cultural heritage. Its 750-year history has produced a wealth of beautiful buildings, such as the Royal Palace and Drottningholm – symbols of Sweden's era as a great power in the 17th and early 18th centuries. Many other impressive treasures from the past can be discovered in the city's fine museums.

The Stadshuset, Stockholm's City Hall, on the island of Kungsholmen

GETTING AROUND

Most of the main sights are served by Tunnelbana (underground train), and there are also numerous bus routes. Tram line 7 from Sergels Torg goes to the Vasamuseet, the Nordiska Museet, and Skansen, which you cannot reach by Tunnelbana. Small ferries travel between the city center and Djurgården, while archipelago boats take visitors on day trips to some of the thousands of islands in the Stockholm archipelago.

Archipelago boats sailing at Strömkajen, outside the Nationalmuseum

SIGHTS AT A GLANCE

SEE ALSO

• *Where to Stay* p654

• *Where to Eat* p655

GREATER STOCKHOLM

Uppsala

Lidingö

Sundbyberg

Bromma Airport

Solna

Ängby

Alvik

20

Lovön

Arlanda Airport

Tappström

Hägersten

276

Bredäng

E4

259

73

Norrköping, Södertälje

0 km 2

0 miles 2

KEY

■ Area of main map

ERMALM

NARVAVÄGEN

GUMSHORNSG.

STORGATAN

GREV MAGNG.

TORSTENSONSG.

BANÉRGATAN

ULRIKAGATAN

STORGATAN

STRANDVÄGEN

NOBEL-PARKEN

ANDVÄGEN

Djurgårdsbron

Ladugårdslandsviken

GALÄR-PARKEN

DJUR-GÅRDEN

DJURGÅRDSVÄGEN

SKEPPS-HOLMEN

FALKENBERGS

Kastellholms-bron

KASTELL-HOLMEN

0 meters 400

0 yards 400

KEY

■ Sights / Place of interest	T Tunnelbana station
✈ Airport	Tram stop
Long-distance ferry	P Parking
Djurgården ferry	i Tourist information
Archipelago boat	Church
Train station	Pedestrian street
Bus station	

D E

Storkyrkan ①

Trångsund 1. **Tel** 08-723 30 16.
T Gamla Stan. 2, 43, 55, 59, 76. daily. Apr–Sep.
in English: Jul–mid-Aug: 1pm.

Stockholm's 700-year-old cathedral, known as the Storkyrkan, or, literally, "big church," is of great national religious importance. From here the Swedish reformer Olaus Petri (1493–1552) spread his Lutheran message around the kingdom. The cathedral is also used for royal ceremonies.

A small church was built on this site in the 13th century, probably by the city's founder Birger Jarl. In 1306 it was replaced by a much bigger basilica, St. Nicholas.

The 15th-century Gothic interior was revealed in 1908 during restoration work. The late Baroque period provided the cathedral's so-called "royal chairs," the pews nearest the chancel, which were designed by Nicodemus Tessin the Younger (1654–1728) to be used by royal guests on special occasions. The 66-m (216-ft) high tower was added in 1743.

The cathedral houses some priceless artifacts, such as Bernt Notke's late-Gothic sculpture of *St. George and the Dragon* (1489), celebrating Sten Sture the Elder's 1471 victory over the Danes. Other prized treasures are the silver altar (1650s) and the *Parhelion Painting*, which depicts a light phenomenon observed over Stockholm in 1535. Research has proved the painting is not the original, but a copy from the 1630s.

The Italian Baroque-style façade of Stockholm's Storkyrkan

The grand facade of Stockholm's Kungliga Slottet (Royal Palace)

Royal Palace ②

Kungliga Slottet. **Tel** 08-402 61 30.
Ⓣ Gamla Stan. 🚌 2, 43, 55, 71, 76.
◯ mid-May–mid-Sep: daily; mid-
Sep–mid-May: noon–3pm Tue–Sun
(except Royal Chapel & Museum of
Antiquities). ● during official
functions of the Court. 📷 🎫 ♿
www.kungahuset.se

Completed in the mid-13th
century, the Tre Kronor
(Three Crowns) fortress was
turned into a royal residence
by the Vasa kings during the
following century. In 1697 it
was destroyed by fire. In its
place the architect Nicodemus
Tessin the Younger (1654–
1728) created a new palace
with an Italianate exterior and
a French interior that also
shows Swedish influences.
 Though the palace is no
longer the king's
residence, the **State
Apartments** are still
used for official
functions. Banquets for
visiting heads of state
are often held in the
magnificent Karl XI's
Gallery, which is
modeled on the Hall
of Mirrors at Versailles
outside Paris (see
pp168–9), and is
a fine example of
Swedish Late Baroque.
Look out for the
exquisite ivory and
silver saltcellar,
designed by Flemish
painter Rubens. The
two-story Hall of State,
designed by Tessin
and Carl Hårleman,
combines Rococo
and Classical
elements, and contains
one of the palace's most

valuable treasures, the
splendid silver coronation
throne of Queen Kristina
(reigned 1633–54).
 Below the Hall of State is
the **Treasury**, where the State
regalia are kept, including King
Erik XIV's crown, scepter, and
orb. Other priceless artifacts,
such as two crystal crowns
belonging to the present
monarchs, King Carl XVI
Gustaf and Queen Silvia, are
on view in the **Royal Chapel**.
 Within the palace are two
museums. **Gustav III's
Museum of Antiquities**
opened in 1794 in memory
of the murdered king, and
contains artifacts collected
during his journey to Italy in
1783–4. The **Tre Kronor
Museum** illustrates the palace's
1,000-year history, and has
relics rescued from the
burning palace in 1697. A

Tre Kronor (Three Crowns) symbol atop the
106-m (348-ft) tower of the Stadshuset

very popular tourist event, the
daily changing of the guard,
takes place at midday in the
palace's Outer Courtyard.

Riddarholms-
kyrkan ③

Birger Jarls Torg. **Tel** 08-402 61 30.
Ⓣ Gamla Stan. 🚌 3, 53. ◯ mid-
May–Sep: 10am–4pm daily. 📷 🎫
(call ahead for tours in English). ♿

Built on the site of the
late 13th-century Greyfriars
abbey, founded by Magnus
Ladulås, this majestic
brick church is best known
for its ornate burial vaults.
Dating back to the 16th
century, the vaults hold the
remains of all the Swedish
monarchs, from Gustav II
Adolf in the 17th century,
with two exceptions: Queen
Kristina, buried at St. Peter's
in Rome in 1689, and Gustav
VI Adolf, who was interred at
Haga, on the city outskirts, in
1973. Especially moving are
the graves of royal children,
including the many small tin
coffins that surround the
tombs of Gustav II Adolf and
his queen, Maria Eleonora.

Stadshuset ④

Hantverkargatan 1. **Tel** 08-508 290
58. Ⓣ Rådhuset. 🚌 3, 62. ◯ for
guided tours. ● Jan 1, Easter,
Dec 24–26 & 31, and during special
activities. 📷 🎫 obligatory. ♿
www.stockholm.se/cityhall

Probably Sweden's biggest
architectural project of the
20th century, the Stadshuset
(City Hall) was completed in

1923 and has become a symbol of Stockholm. It was designed by Ragnar Östberg (1866–1945) and displays influences of both the Nordic Gothic and Northern Italian schools. Many leading Swedish artists contributed to the rich interior design, including Einar Forseth (1892–1988), who created the stunning Byzantine-inspired gold-leaf wall mosaics in the Golden Room.

The building contains the Council Chamber and 250 offices for administrative staff. As well as a work place for the city's councillors, the Stadshuset also provides a venue for special events, such as the annual Nobel Prize ceremony, which takes place in the lavish Blue Hall.

Kungsträdgården, known as Stockholm's "open-air living room"

Stureplan, a popular meeting place for Stockholmers

Stureplan and Sturegallerian ⑤

ⓣ Östermalmstorg. 🚌 1, 2, 55, 56, 91. **Sturegallerian** Stureplan 4. **Tel** 08-611 46 06. ◯ daily (Sun: pm only). **Sturebadet Tel** 08-545 015 00. ◯ daily.

After a fire at the Sturebadet swimming pool in 1985, the Stureplan district was revamped and restored to its late 19th-century glory.

Part of the renovation of the area included building a stylish shopping mall, the Sture-gallerian, which boasts some 60 retail outlets. The Sturebadet public baths, within the mall, have been rebuilt according to their original late 19th-century Art Nouveau design.

Kungsträdgården ⑥

ⓣ Kungsträdgården. 🚌 2, 43, 55, 62, 65, 71, 76. **Kungliga Operan Tel** 08-791 44 00. Ticket office ◯ noon–6pm Mon–Fri, noon–3pm Sat. 🎭 by appointment. ♿

The city's oldest park, the King's Garden takes its name from when it was a royal kitchen garden in the 15th century. During the summer open-air theater, dancing, concerts, and food festivals take place here. In winter the skating rink is a popular attraction. At the center of the park is a bronze fountain (1866) by J.P. Molin, who also designed the statue of Karl XII (1868) at the park's southern end. Overlooking this part of the park is the city's royal opera house, the **Kungliga Operan** (1898), whose ornate interior includes the Gold Foyer, with ceiling paintings by Carl Larsson.

In the 16th century, the kitchen garden was transformed into a Renaissance garden. The 17th-century summer house built for Queen Kristina still stands on the park's western flank.

Nationalmuseum ⑦

Södra Blasieholmshamnen. **Tel** 08-519 543 00. ⓣ Kungsträdgården. 🚌 2, 55, 59, 62, 65, 76. ◯ Tue–Sun. ● some public hols. 🎫 ♿ 🚻 🛍 📷 🌐 www.nationalmuseum.se

The location of the National-museum, on the Strömmen channel, inspired the 19th-century German architect August Stüler to design a building in the Venetian and Florentine Renaissance styles. Completed in 1866, the museum houses some 500,000 paintings, sculptures, prints, and drawings from the 15th to the early 20th centuries. The focus of the painting and sculpture section is Swedish 18th- to early 20th-century art, but the 17th-century Dutch and Flemish, and 18th-century French schools are also well represented. Highlights include Rembrandt's *The Conspiracy of the Batavians under Claudius Civilis* (1661–62) and *The Lady with the Veil* (1769) by Swedish portrait painter Alexander Roslin. There is also a decorative arts department, which contains 30,000 works spanning the last five centuries. Among the wide range of exhibits on show is Scandinavia's largest display of porcelain, glass, silver-ware, and furniture. Another exhibit, Design 19002000, tracks the history of design to the present day.

The opulent interior of Stockholm's Nationalmuseum

The Moderna Museet's airy interior, designed by Catalan Rafael Moneo

Moderna museet ⑧

Skeppsholmen. **Tel** *08-519 552 00.* Ⓣ *Kungsträdgården.* 🚌 *65.* ◯ *Tue–Sun.* ⬤ *Jan 1 & 5, Apr 5, May 24, Jun 25, Dec 24, 25 & 31.* 🚻 ⊘ 🖥 🛈 www.modernamuseet.se

The Museum of Modern Art is an airy, contemporary building, designed by the Catalan architect Rafael Moneo in 1998. The light and spacious venue provides a perfect setting for the museum's world-class collection of international and Swedish modern art, photography, and film. Built partly underground, the museum includes a cinema and auditorium.

All the works on display date from between 1900 and the present day. Two of the star exhibits are *The Child's Brain* (1914) by Italian artist Giorgio de Chirico, widely considered a precursor to the Surrealists, and *Monogram*

(1955–59) by the late American painter and sculptor Robert Rauschenberg. Among the collection of Swedish works is Nils Dardel's Expressionistic painting, *The Dying Dandy* (1918).

Vasamuseet ⑨

Galärvarvsvägen 14, Djurgården. **Tel** *08-519 548 00.* 🚌 *44, 69.* 🚋 *7.* 🚢 *Djurgårdsfärja.* ◯ *daily.* ⬤ *Jan 1, Dec 23–25 & 31.* 🖥 ⛓ ⊘ 🛈 🖥 **Museifartygen Tel** *08-519 548 83.* ◯ *Jun 10–Aug: pm daily.* 🖥 ⊘ www.vasamuseet.se

The centerpiece of the city's most popular museum is the massive royal warship, *Vasa*, which capsized in Stockholm harbor on its maiden voyage in 1628. Rediscovered in 1956, the vessel has been painstakingly restored to 95 percent of its original appearance.

The warship is decorated with around 700 sculpted figures and carved ornaments, designed as a type of war propaganda. King Gustav II Adolf, who commissioned *Vasa*, was known as the Lion of the North, so a springing lion was the obvious choice for the figurehead on the ship's prow. It is 4 m (13 ft) long and weighs 450 kg (990 lb).

Although visitors cannot board the ship, full-scale models of *Vasa's* upper gun deck and the Admiral's cabin provide a glimpse of what life

on board was like. There is also a fascinating display of items retrieved in the salvage operation, including medical equipment, an officer's back-gammon set, and a chest still neatly packed with clothing and other personal belongings.

Moored in the dock alongside the museum are two other historic vessels, collectively referred to as the **Museifartygen**. The lightship *Finngrundet* was built in 1903 and worked for 60 years before becoming a museum. *Sankt Erik* was commissioned in 1915 and was Sweden's first sea-going icebreaker.

Midsummer celebrations at the open-air museum, Skansen

Skansen ⑩

Djurgårdsslätten 49–51. **Tel** *08-442 80 00.* 🚌 *44.* 🚋 *7.* 🚢 *Djurgårdsfärja.* ◯ *daily.* 🖥 ⊘ *Jun–Aug (call in advance).* 🍴 🛈 www.skansen.se

The world's first open-air museum opened in 1891 to show an increasingly industrialized society how people once lived. Around 150 buildings were assembled from all over Scandinavia, to portray the life of peasants and landed gentry, as well as Lapp (*Same*) culture.

In the Town Quarter are 19th-century town-houses, where glassblowers and other craftsmen demonstrate their skills. Two of Skansen's oldest "exhibits" are a 650-year-old wooden farmhouse from Dalarna, and a 14th-century storehouse from Norway.

Nordic flora and fauna can be seen, with elks, bears, and wolves in natural habitat enclosures and marine animals in an aquarium. Traditional festivals and concerts are held here throughout the year.

The restored 17th-century royal warship, *Vasa*, at the Vasamuseet

Nordiska museet ⑪

Djurgårdsvägen 6–16. **Tel** *08-519
546 00.* ⓣ *Karlaplan.* 🚌 *44, 69.*
🚊 *7.* ⛴ *Djurgårds-färja, Allmänna
Gränd.* ☐ *late Jun–Aug: daily; Sep–
mid-Jun: Tue–Sun.* ● *Jun 25, Dec
24, 25, 31.* 📷 🚫 ♿ 🎥 📋
www.nordiskamuseet.se

Housed in a Renaissance-
style building, the Nordiska
Museet's collection was
started by Artur Hazelius
(1833–1901), founder of the
Skansen open-air museum,
with the intention of
reminding future generations
of the old Nordic farming
culture. Today, the museum
has over 1.5 million exhibits
portraying everyday life in
Sweden from the 1520s to the
present day. Items on display
range from priceless jewelry,
to furniture, dolls' houses,
and replicas of period rooms,
such as the splendid 17th-
century state bedchamber
from Ulvsunda Castle. Highlights include the monumental
gilded oak statue of King
Gustav Vasa (1924), and
16 paintings by the Swedish
author and dramatist August
Strindberg (1849–1912).

**Carl Milles' huge statue of King
Gustav Vasa in the Nordiska Museet**

Historiska
museet ⑫

Narvavägen 13–17. **Tel** *08-519 556
00.* ⓣ *Karlaplan, Östermalmstorg.*
🚌 *44, 56.* ☐ *daily.* ● *Mon (Oct–
Apr); Jun 25 & 26.* 📷 ♿ 🎥

Sweden's National Historical
Museum was opened in 1943.
It originally made its name

with relics from the Viking
era, as well as its
outstanding collections from
the Middle Ages. The latter
include one of the museum's
star exhibits – a richly gilded
wooden Madonna figure,
from Sweden's early medieval
period. In the prehistoric
collection is the Alunda
Elk, a ceremonial stone
axe, discovered in 1920
at Alunda and thought
to have been made
around 2000 BC.

Since the early
1990s the museum's
priceless collection
of gold and silver,
dating from the
Bronze Age to the
Middle Ages, has
been on show in
the Guld-rummet
(Gold Room). Look
out for the stunning Elisabeth
Reliquary, an 11th-century
goblet, with a silver cover
made in 1230 to enclose the
skull of St. Elisabeth.

**Madonna figure in the
Historiska Museet**

Drottningholm ⑬

10 km (6 miles) W of Stockholm.
Tel *08-402 62 80.* ⓣ *Brommaplan,
then bus 301, 323.* 🚢 *May–Sep
from Stadshusbron.* ☐ *May–Sep:
daily; Oct–Apr: Sat & Sun. (Chinese
Pavilion: May–Sep only; Theater
Museum: May–Sep only.)* ● *public
hols.* 📷 🎥 **www**.royalcourt.se

With its sumptuous palace,
theater, park, and Chinese
pavilion, the whole of the
Drottningholm estate has
been included in UNESCO's
World Heritage list. Contemporary Italian and French

The magnificent Drottningholm palace, on the island of Lovön

architecture inspired
Nicodemus Tessin the Elder
(1615–81) in his design of the
royal palace. Begun in the
1660s on the orders of King
Karl X Gustav's widow, Queen
Hedvig Eleonora, the building
was completed by Tessin the
Younger. Today, the present
royal family still uses parts of
the palace as a private
residence. The most lavish
rooms open to the public
include Queen Lovisa
Ulrika's library, designed
by Jean Eric Rehn
(1717–93), and
Queen Hedvig
Eleonora's state
bedroom, decorated
in Baroque style.

The Baroque and
Rococo gardens and
lush parkland
surrounding the
palace are dotted with
monuments and splendid
buildings. The blue and gold
Chinese Pavilion (Kina Slott)
was built for Queen Lovisa
Ulrika in the latter half of the
18th century, and contains
many interesting artifacts from
China and Japan. The designer
of the Chinese Pavilion, Carl
Fredrik Adelcrantz, was also
responsible for the Drottningholm Court Theater
(Slottsteatern), which dates
from 1766. This simple
wooden building is the world's
oldest theater still preserved
in its original form. The
scenery, with its wooden
hand driven machinery, is still
in working order. In summer
the theater hosts opera and
ballet. There is also a
museum, which focuses on
18th-century theater.

The Renaissance Gripsholms Slott, on the shore of Lake Mälaren

Lake Mälaren ❷

Birka 🚢 May–Sep daily from
Stadshusbron, Stockholm. **Mariefred**
🚢 in summer from Stadshusbron,
Stockholm. 🚂 from
Centralstationen, Stockholm to
Läggesta, then bus or steam train.

To the west of Stockholm lies
Lake Mälaren, a vast stretch of
water, whose pretty shores
and islands offer several day
excursions from the city.

Sweden's first town, **Birka**,
was founded on the island
of Björkö in the 8th century,
although archaeological finds
indicate that trading activity
took place here at least 1,500
years ago. In the 9th and 10th
centuries Birka grew into a
busy Viking center. The
Birkamuseet has displays of
local archaeological finds and
provides a fascinating insight
into the daily lives of the
town's early inhabitants.
There are also guided tours
of ongoing excavations.

The most striking feature of
the pretty town of **Mariefred**
is the majestic **Gripsholms
Slott**, built for King Gustav
Vasa in 1537, and later modified under Gustav III in the
18th century. The palace is
known for its well-preserved

interiors, and also houses the
National Portrait Gallery, with
over 4,000 paintings spanning
some 500 years.

Mariefred itself has a lovely
17th-century church and an
18th-century timber Rådhus
(law courts' building), as well
as several specialist stores,
galleries, and antique shops.
In summer, one of the most
enjoyable ways to travel there
from Stockholm is aboard
the *Mariefred*, a historic, coal-
fired steamboat. The trip
takes around three and a half
hours and allows passengers
to enjoy the spectacular
scenery along the route.

🏛 **Birkamuseet**
Tel 08-519 180 00. ⬭ May 1–
Sep 26: daily. 🎟 📷

🏰 **Gripsholms Slott**
Tel 0159-101 94. ⬭ mid-May–mid-
Sep: daily; mid-Sep–mid-May: Sat &
Sun. ⬤ Dec 18–Jan 2. 🎟 🎟 📷

Uppsala ❸

🏙 190,000. 🚆 🚌 🚇
ℹ Fyris Torg 8 (018-727 48 00).
www.uppland.nu

One of Sweden's oldest
settlements, Uppsala,
on the banks of the Fyrisån
river, is also a lively university
town. On the last day of April,
crowds of students wearing
white caps parade through
the town for the traditional
spring season celebrations.

Dominating the town's
attractive medieval center is the
Domkyrkan, Scandinavia's
largest Gothic cathedral. Its
chapel contains the relics of
Sweden's patron saint, Saint
Erik. The onion-domed
Gustavianum, opposite the
cathedral, dates from the
1620s and houses the Uppsala
University Museum. The
museum's exhibits include a
17th-century anatomical
theater and Egyptian, Classical,
and Nordic antiquities. Just a
short walk away stands the
Carolina Rediviva, the
impressive university library.

Uppsala Slott, the town's
hilltop fortress, was built in
the 16th century by King
Gustav Vasa, although it was
later destroyed by fire. Now
restored, it also houses the
Uppsala Art Museum.

Aerial view of Uppsala, with its massive Gothic cathedral, the Domkyrkan

A short bus ride north of the town center, Gamla Uppsala is the site of the Kungshögarna, royal burial mounds believed to date from the 6th century. The **Historiskt Centrum** acquaints visitors with the history, legends, and lore surrounding the burial mounds and contains displays of local archaeological finds.

🏛 **Gustavianum**
Akademigatan 3. *Tel* 018-471 75 71. ⬜ Tue–Sun. ⬛ ⬛ ⬛ ⬛
⬛ www.gustavianum.uu.se

⚓ **Uppsala Slott**
Slottet, entrance E. *Tel* 018-727 24 82. ⬜ Wed–Sun. ⬛ ⬛ Jun–Aug.
⬛

🏛 **Historiskt Centrum**
Disavägen. *Tel* 018-23 93 00.
⬜ May–Aug: daily; at other times: call for information. ⬛ ⬛ ⬛

Dalarna ④

🚆 Falun, Mora. 🚌 Falun, Mora.
ℹ Trotzgatan 10–12 (023-640 04); Stationsväg 3, Mora (0250-59 20 20).

With its proud tradition of music, dance, and handi-crafts, Dalarna is Sweden's folklore district. The charming rural landscape, dotted with red, wooden cottages, attracts many tourists seeking a quiet country retreat in the summer. In winter, the area's mountain resorts, Sälen and Idre, are packed with skiers.

The main sights of interest are located around Lake Siljan. **Mora**, the largest of the lakeside towns, was home to one of Sweden's best-known artists, Anders Zorn (1860–1920). Open daily, the Zorn Museum, at No. 36 Vasa-gatan, holds paintings by the artist, and you can also visit his former home and studio.

Dalarna is famous for its midsummer festivals. In **Leksand** and **Rättvik** you may see traditionally dressed locals dancing and playing musical instruments or rowing on the lake in wooden longboats during the towns' colorful celebrations.

Around 15 km (9 miles) from the provincial capital and largely industrial town of

The Norderport, one of the gateways in Visby's medieval city walls

Falun is **Sundborn**, where Swedish painter Carl Larsson (1853–1919) and his wife, Karin, a textile artist, lived in the early 20th century. Their work still has a big influence on contemporary Swedish design. The couple's lakeside house is open to the public.

Gotland and Visby ⑤

🚶 60,000. ✈ 🚢 to Visby.
ℹ Skeppsbron 4–6, Visby (0498-20 17 00). www.gotland.info

The island of Gotland, Sweden's most popular holiday destination, boasts a stunning coastline, a rich cultural heritage, and a superb climate, enjoying more hours of sunshine than anywhere else in the country.

In the Viking Age, Gotland, the largest island in the Baltic Sea, was a major trading post and later its capital, Visby, became a prosperous Hanseatic port. Surrounded by one of the best-preserved city walls in the world, Visby is like a living museum, with pretty step-gabled houses and a web of narrow cobbled streets and small squares. The original Hanseatic harbor is now a park, but the **Burmeisterska Huset** (Burmeister's House), dating

Musician at a midsummer festival in Dalarna

from 1645, is a fine surviving example of the architecture of the Post-Hanseatic period. Strandgatan contains some of Visby's most attractive historic buildings, the former homes of wealthy merchants. In the same street is the excellent historical museum, **Gotlands Fornsal**, which holds a collection of artifacts spanning 8,000 years. The **Domkyrkan** (Cathedral of St. Maria) below Kyrkberget is the only medieval church still intact and in use in Visby.

Away from Visby, the rest of Gotland is dotted with many unspoilt farmhouses, old medieval churches, and secluded beaches. Among the most impressive sights are the subterranean limestone caves of **Lummelundagrottorna**, 13 km (8 miles) north of the city, and, off the northeastern tip of the island, **Fårö**. This island, known for its severe beauty, can be reached by a daily, half-hourly ferry from Fårösund. Besides old fishing hamlets such as Helgumannen, visitors can enjoy the long stretch of white sandy beach and the swimming at Suder-sands. Look out for Fårö's spectacular *raukar*. These are huge limestone rock forma-tions, rising out of the sea on the west side of the island.

🏛 **Gotlands Fornsal**
Strandgatan 14. *Tel* 0498-29 27 00.
⬜ May–mid-Sep: daily; mid-Sep–Apr: pm Tue–Sun. ⬛ in summer. ⬛

Poseidon fountain, at the end of Kungsportsavenyn in Gothenburg

Gothenburg **6**

🏛 515,000. ✈ 25 km (16 miles) E.
🚉 🚌 ⛴ 🛈 Kungsportsplatsen 2
(031-368 42 00).
www.gothenburg.com

Gothenburg (Göteborg),
Sweden's second largest city,
has a distinctive character,
with beautiful architecture,
pleasant café-lined boulevards,
a bustling harbor, and a
dynamic cultural life.

Scandinavia's largest seaport
is dominated by the **Göteborgsutkiken**, a huge lookout
tower providing stunning
panoramic views of the city
and its surroundings. A short
walk west along the quayside
are the daring, industrial-style
Göteborgsoperan (Opera
House), built in 1994, and
the **Maritiman**, reputedly the
world's largest floating ship
museum. Moored in the dock
are a dozen different types of
vessel, all open to the public.
They include a light ship, a
destroyer, and a submarine.

The pulse of the city is
Kungsportsavenyn, simply
known as Avenyn, or "The
Avenue." This 900-m (2952-ft)
long boulevard is lined with
restaurants, pubs, and cafés,
and is a favorite haunt of
street musicians and hawkers.
On a side street off Avenyn,
Röhsska Museet is Sweden's
only museum devoted to
arts, crafts, and industrial
design. At the southern end
of the avenue is Götaplatsen,
whose focal point is the
famous Poseidon fountain
by the Swedish sculptor
Carl Milles. The
square is flanked
by the fine **Konst-
museet** (Art
Museum), which
specializes
in 19th- and
20th-century
Scandinavian art.
Southeast of Göta-
platsen is **Lisebergs
Nöjespark**, the
largest amusement
park in Sweden.

🏛 **Maritiman**
Packhuskajen 8. **Tel** 031-10 59 50.
🕐 Apr & Oct: Fri–Sun; May–Sep:
daily. 🎫 🗖 🗖

🏛 **Röhsska Museet**
Vasagatan 37–39. **Tel** 031-368 31
50. 🕐 pm Tue–Sun. 🎫 🚫 🗖
🗖 www.designmuseum.se

🏛 **Konstmuseet**
Götaplatsen. **Tel** 031-368 35 00.
🕐 Tue–Sun. 🎫 🚫 🗖 🗖 🗖

Växjö **7**

🏛 83,000. 🚉 🚌 🛈 Residenset,
Stortorget-Kronoberg 7 (0470-414
10). **www**.turism.vaxjo.se

Located right at the heart of
Småland, Växjö is an ideal
base from which to explore
the Glasriket, or "Kingdom of
Glass," Sweden's world-famous
region of glassworks. The
town's main attraction is the
Smålands Museum, which tells
the story of 400 years of
glassmaking, and provides a
good introduction to a visit to
any one of the many glassworks scattered throughout
the surrounding forests.

The best-known glassworks
are at **Orrefors** and **Kosta**,
within 90 km (56 miles) of
Växjö, but other factories
worth visiting include **Åfors**
and **Strömbergshyttan**. Most
of the factories have excellent
glassblowing demonstrations,
and all have a shop where
you can choose from a wide
selection of products. In the
past, Småland's glassworks
were more than just a place
of work. Locals used to meet
here in the evenings to bake
herrings and potatoes in the
furnace, while music was
provided by a fiddler. Today
the Orrefors and Kosta glassworks arrange similar forms
of entertainment, known
as *hyttsill* evenings.

Visitors to Växjö
should not miss
the **Utvandrarnas
Hus** (House of
Emigrants). This
interesting museum
recounts the story of
the one million Swedes
who, in the face of famine
in the late 19th and early
20th centuries, left
Småland for a
better life in
America.

**Swedish glassware
from Småland**

🏛 **Smålands Museum**
Södra Järnvägsgatan 2. **Tel** 0470-
7042 00. 🕐 Jun–Aug: daily; Sep–
May: Tue–Sun. 🎫 🚫 🗖 🗖 🗖

🏛 **Kosta Glassworks**
Kosta, on route 28. **Tel** 0478-
34529. 🕐 daily. ⬤ some public
hols. 🎫 🗖

🏛 **Utvandrarnas Hus**
Vilhelm Mobergsgatan 4. **Tel** 0470-
201 20. 🕐 daily. 🎫

For hotels and restaurants in this region see p654 and p655

Malmö **8**

🏃 *300,000.* ✈ 🚢 🚉 🚌 **ℹ**
Central Station (040-34 1200).

Malmö is the capital of the province of Skåne in southwestern Sweden. In the 16th century, it was a major fishing port, competing with Copenhagen as Scandinavia's most influential city. Today the city is well-known for its busy harbor, as well as for its rich architectural heritage.

The imposing 16th-century Malmöhus was built by the Danish king Christian III, when Skåne formed part of Denmark. It contains the **Malmömuseer** (Malmö Museums), which include the Art Museum, the Museum of Natural History, the City Museum, the Science & Technology and Maritime Museum, and the Kommendants Hus (Commander's House).

The Dutch Renaissance style is evident in Malmö's impressive **Rådhuset** (Town Hall), which dates from 1546 and dominates the city's main square, Stortorget. Northeast of here is the 14th-century **St. Petri's Kyrka**, built in the Baltic Gothic style. The church's most beautiful features include the altarpiece (1611), Scandinavia's largest,

Mälmo's main square, overlooked by the Renaissance Rådhuset

and a wonderfully ornate pulpit. Amid the city's maze of café-lined pedestrianized streets is Lilla Torg (Little Square), with its cobblestones and charmingly restored houses. The square has a lively atmosphere and draws crowds of tourists and locals alike. At Möllevångstorget, you will find a part of town that reflects a diversity of cultures, especially around the square. There is a farmers' market and many small ethnic shops.

Located south of Lilla Torg is **Malmö Konsthall**, a vibrant

museum of modern art which opened in 1975. Its vast contemporary exhibition space houses an excellent collection of avant-garde and experimental art and installations, as well as photography and sculpture.

🏛 **Malmömuseer**
Malmöhus, Malmöhusvägen. *Tel* 040-34 44 37. ◗ *pm daily.* ●
Dec 24, 25 & 31, Jan 1. 🖼 📷 🗄
www.malmo.se/museer

🏛 **Malmö Konsthall**
St. Johannesgatan 7. *Tel* 040-34 12 86. ◗ *11am–5pm daily.* ● *Dec 24, 25 & 31, Jan 1.* 📷 ♿ 📷 🗄

THE ORESUND LINK

Despite a legacy of mutual warfare and rivalry, in May 2000 the close ties between Denmark and Sweden were strengthened with the inauguration of the Öresund Link. A 16-km (10-mile) long combined suspension bridge and tunnel now connects the Danish capital, Copenhagen, with the Swedish provincial capital Malmö on either side of the channel of water known as the Öresund. The bridge is the strongest cable stay bridge in the world, designed to carry the combined weight of a motorway and a dual-track railway, while the tunnel is the world's largest immersed tunnel in terms of volume. The project has been hailed as a renaissance for southern Sweden, which now seems poised to become a prospering center of trade, science, industry, and culture at the heart of the cross-border Danish-Swedish Öresund region.

The newly constructed Öresund Link, spanning the Öresund channel

Practical & Travel Information

With Sweden growing rapidly as an important tourist destination, standards in the travel industry have improved greatly. Foreign visitors will enjoy a comfortable stay in Sweden, not least because most people speak English. Sweden's infrastructure is constantly being improved – there are many new highways and the rail system has been upgraded for high-speed trains. There is also a direct link to Denmark via the Öresund Bridge. In Stockholm, public transportation on buses, subway trains, ferries, and local trains is efficient, and covers the entire city and surrounding region.

TOURIST INFORMATION

Tourist information offices are located throughout Sweden, and you can contact the **Swedish Travel & Tourism Council** for more information. Stockholm's official tourist information organization is the **Stockholm Visitors Board**. Most hotels in the capital, as well as many department stores and museums, stock the free monthly listings brochure *What's On Stockholm*.

Most museums and other sights in Sweden are open between 10 or 11am and 5 or 6pm all year round, and often have longer opening hours in the summer. They are usually closed on Monday.

VISA REQUIREMENTS

Passports are not required for visitors from most EU countries, but visitors from the US, Canada, the UK, Ireland, Australia, and New Zealand still need a valid passport. Citizens of almost all countries can enter Sweden without a visa.

PERSONAL SECURITY

Violent crime against tourists is rare in Sweden, although pickpockets are known to frequent the busier pedestrian shopping streets in the main cities. Sweden has a well-developed network of emergency services, which are efficient and reliable. Swedish police are extremely helpful and most speak good English.

HEALTH ISSUES

No special vaccinations are necessary to visit Sweden. Hygiene standards are among the highest in the world, and the tap water is safe to drink. For prescription and non-prescription medicines visit a pharmacy *(apotek)*, open during normal store hours. A 24-hour *apotek* service is also available in major cities.

CURRENCY AND BANKING

The Swedish unit of currency is the krona, abbreviated to SEK or kr. Banking hours are generally 10am–3pm Monday to Friday, though some banks stay open until 6pm at least one day a week. Traveler's checks can be changed at all banks. Bureaux de change are located throughout the main cities and airports, and normally provide a better exchange rate than banks.

All the well-known credit cards are widely accepted in Sweden. Withdrawals can be made from cash machines using all internationally accepted credit cards.

COMMUNICATIONS

Public telephone kiosks are owned by the state-run Telia company, and are usually operated by card only. Phonecards can be bought at tobacconists and newspaper kiosks, though normal credit cards or international telephone cards work just as well.

Post offices are open from 10am to 6pm on weekdays and from 10am to 1pm on Saturdays. Many of the post offices have recently been closed and postal services moved to gas stations and stores instead. Stamps can be purchased at these locations as well as at post offices, Pressbyrån kiosks, and tourist information offices.

FLYING TO SWEDEN

Most major European cities have direct flights to Stockholm. Many of the world's leading airlines serve Arlanda Airport, located about 40 km (25 miles) north of the city center. International flights also serve Gothenburg and Malmö. Services from the UK are operated by **Finnair**, **SAS** (Scandinavian Airlines), British Airways, and low-cost airline **Ryanair**. Direct flights from North America are available from SAS and Finnair, and from the US airline American.

TRAVELING BY FERRY

Ferries to Gothenburg from Fredrikshavn in Denmark (2–3 hours), and from Kiel in Germany (20–22 hours), are operated by **Stena Line**.

THE CLIMATE OF SWEDEN

Sweden's summers are usually fairly cool, although sometimes there can be heatwaves for several weeks at a time. Winter temperatures often fall below freezing, but it is rarely severely cold, except in the far north. The snow may lie until well after March in the north, but in the rest of the country some recent winters have been virtually free of snow.

STOCKHOLM

°C/F	Apr	Jul	Oct	Jan
		23/73		
		14/57	12/54	
	10/50		7/44	
0°C / 32°F	2/36			0/32
				-4/25
☀ hrs	6	8	3.5	1.5
☂ mm	21	65	48	27
month	Apr	Jul	Oct	Jan

Large passenger and car ferries sail to Stockholm from Finland; both **Viking Line** and **Silja Line** operate daily services from Helsinki (with a crossing time of about 15 hours) and Turku-Åbo (with a crossing time of about 11 hours).

Within Sweden, ferries to Visby in Gotland leave from Nynäshamn, about 75 km (47 miles) south of Stockholm. There are two crossings daily by catamaran (2 hours 50 mins) and one or two crossings daily by regular ferry (5 hours). Both services are run by **Destination Gotland**.

TRAVELING BY BUS

Travel by long-distance bus is inexpensive and hassle-free. There is an excellent network of express services, such as those run by **Swebus**, between the larger towns and cities in south and central Sweden, and between Stockholm and towns in the north.

RAIL TRAVEL

Rail travel to Sweden from mainland Europe is fast and comfortable. Journey times have been cut considerably with the opening of the Öresund Bridge; traveling from Copenhagen to Malmö now takes less than 40 minutes.

Within Sweden, the state-owned rail company Statens Järnvägar (SJ) operates many of the long-distance trains. Some routes are run by private companies – Tågkompaniet runs trains from Stockholm to Narvik, Umeå, and Luleå in the far north of Sweden.

Domestic air travel in Sweden has faced strong competition from the X 2000 high-speed trains. The journey time by train from Malmö to Stockholm is about 5 hours, and from Gothenburg to the capital takes about 3 hours.

TRAVELING BY CAR

Visitors driving from Denmark can use the spectacular Öresund toll bridge between Copenhagen and Malmö. On the Swedish side, the bridge connects with the E4, a 550-km (340-mile) highway to Stockholm.

Fines for speeding are high, and even if the limit is only slightly exceeded, you can lose your license. The maximum permitted blood alcohol level is so low that drinking is effectively banned for drivers.

When driving in the Swedish countryside, be particularly cautious, as elk and deer may appear unexpectedly in the middle of the road.

TRAVELING IN STOCKHOLM

Virtually all of Stockholm's sights and attractions can be reached by subway train or bus. Tunnelbana, the underground rail system, has 100 stations on three main routes. Travelcards are available for one-day, three-day, and monthly periods, and are also valid on bus and ferry services.

Traveling by bus is a pleasant and economical way to see the city. The best routes for sightseeing are 3, 4, 46, 62, and 69, which cover the central area and stop near many sights.

Boats and ferries provide a delightful way of getting to know the city and its environs. **Strömma Kanalbolaget** runs various hour-long excursions during the summer months.

A worthwhile purchase for any visitor is the Stockholm Card, which allows free travel on Tunnelbana trains, local buses, and local trains, free parking at official city parking areas, and free admission to more than 80 sights.

DIRECTORY

TOURIST OFFICES

Stockholm Visitors Board
Vasagatan 14, Stockholm.
Tel 08-50 82 85 00.
www.stockholmtown.com

Swedish Travel & Tourism Council
Kungsgatan 36, Stockholm.
Tel 08-789 10 00.
www.visitsweden.com
In the UK:
5 Upper Montague Street, London W1H 2AG.
Tel 0800-3080 3080.
In the US:
Grand Central Station, New York, NY 10017.
Tel 212-885 9700.

EMBASSIES

Australia
Klarabergsviadukten 63, Stockholm. *Tel 08-613 29 00.* www.sweden.embassy.gov.au

Canada
Tegelbacken 4, Stockholm.
Tel 08-453 30 00.
www.canadaemb.se

Ireland
Östermalmsgatan 97, Stockholm.
Tel 08-661 80 05.

UK
Skarpögatan 6-8, Stockholm. *Tel 08-671 30 00.* www.ukinsweden.fco.gov.uk

US
Dag Hammarskjölds Väg 31, Stockholm.
Tel 08-783 53 00.
www.usemb.se

EMERGENCY NUMBERS

Ambulance, Police and Fire
Tel 112.

AIRLINES

Finnair
Tel 0771-78 11 00
(toll-free in Sweden).
Tel 0870-241 4411 (UK).
Tel 800-950 5000 (US).
www.finnair.com

Malmö Aviation
Tel 0771-55 00 10.
www.malmoaviation.se

Ryanair
Tel 0900-100 05 00.
www.ryanair.com

SAS
Tel 0770-727 727
(toll-free in Sweden).
Tel 0870-6072 7727 (UK).
Tel 800-221 2350 (US).
www.scandinavian.net

FERRY SERVICES

Destination Gotland
Tel 0771-22 33 00.
www.destinationgotland.se

Stena Line
Tel 031-704 00 00.
www.stenaline.se

Tallink Silja Line
Tel 08-666 33 30.
www.tallinksilja.com

Viking Line
Tel 08-452 40 00.
www.vikingline.se

TRAVELING IN STOCKHOLM

Strömma Kanalbolaget
Tel 08-120 04 000.
www.strommakanalbolaget.com

Swebus
Tel 0200-21 82 18.
www.swebusexpress.se

Where to Stay in Sweden

Sweden's hotels are not usually built on the same grandiose scale as their counterparts in southern Europe, but they offer a high level of comfort and service and often have magnificent views or locations. Major hotels in the larger cities can be fairly expensive, but rooms are often available at reduced rates for weekend breaks.

PRICE CATEGORIES
The following price ranges are for a standard double room with taxes per night during the high season. Breakfast is not included, unless specified:

ⓚ Under 700 SEK
ⓚⓚ 700–1,500 SEK
ⓚⓚⓚ 1,500–2,100 SEK
ⓚⓚⓚⓚ Over 2,100 SEK

STOCKHOLM

CENTRAL STOCKHOLM Hotel Riddargatan   🅿 �𝕎   ⓚⓚⓚⓚ

Riddargatan 14, 114 35 **Tel** *08-55 57 30 00* **Fax** *08-55 57 30 11* **Rooms** *78*   **Map** *C3/D3*

This hotel retains its 1930s Art Deco styling and has a good location in Stockholm's "golden triangle", just behind the Royal Dramatic Theatre. Close to restaurants, bars, and nightlife – sometimes visiting world-famous jazz musicians stay and perform here. **www.profilhotels.se**

CENTRAL STOCKHOLM Hotel Rival   🎬 🅿 🍴 ⟨W⟩   ⓚⓚⓚⓚ

Mariatorget 3 **Tel** *08-545 789 00* **Fax** *08-545 789 24* **Rooms** *99*   **Map** *B5*

This trendy boutique hotel comes equipped with its own cinema and has a great location in the heart of Stockholm. Built in the 1930s, the owner, Benny Andersson (of Abba fame) has recaptured the glamour of the era in the hotel's design. Each of the 99 guest rooms are individually designed. **www.rival.se**

CENTRAL STOCKHOLM Radisson SAS Royal Viking Hotel   🍴 🅿 🍴 ⟨W⟩   ⓚⓚⓚⓚ

Vasagatan 1, 101 24 **Tel** *08-50 65 40 00* **Fax** *08-50 65 40 01* **Rooms** *459*   **Map** *B3*

One of Stockholm's best-known hotels, the Royal Viking offers two bars, one in the ground floor atrium and the exciting Sky Bar on the top floor, as well as the excellent Stockholm Fisk Restaurant. This hotel maintains high standards suited to both business and leisure travellers. **www.royalviking.stockholm.radissonsas.se**

SOUTHERN STOCKHOLM Tre Små Rum Hotel   ⓚⓚ

Högbergsgatan 81, 118 54 **Tel** *08-641 23 71* **Fax** *08-642 88 08* **Rooms** *7*   **Map** *C5*

This inexpensive but cozy modern hotel was started by a traveler hoping to offer an economical and friendly hotel option with a central location. All the rooms are non-smoking, and none en suite. Healthy breakfasts are created to guests' individual order. Early booking is essential. Bicycles are available for hire. **www.tresmarum.se**

WESTERN STOCKHOLM Långholmen Hotel   🅿 🍴 ⟨W⟩   ⓚⓚⓚ

Kronohäketet, Långholmen, 102 72 **Tel** *08-720 85 00* **Fax** *08-720 85 75* **Rooms** *102*

A converted prison, the Långholmen offers accommodation in modernised "cells" in the city center. There is a restaurant in the warden's residence and also a pub, wine cellar, prison museum, and even a private bathing beach. Youth hostel available from mid-June to mid-August. **www.langholmen.com**

REST OF SWEDEN

GOTHENBURG Eggers Hotell & Restaurang   🎬 🍴 ⟨W⟩   ⓚⓚⓚ

Drottningtorget, 404 24 **Tel** *031-333 44 40* **Fax** *031-333 44 49* **Rooms** *69*

A listed building and Sweden's third oldest hotel. Built on historic ground in the center of Gothenburg, this classic hotel offers a mix of early 20th-century charm and modern conveniences. No one room is the same as another, and all are tastefully furnished to reflect the historical character of the building. **www.hoteleggers.se**

MALMÖ Hotel Mäster Johan   🍴 🎬 🅿 🍴   ⓚⓚ

Mäster Johansgatan 13, 211 21 **Tel** *040-664 64 00* **Fax** *040-664 64 01* **Rooms** *69*

The first class Mäster Johan is set in a modern building in the culturally protected part of Malmö known as Gamla Väster. The interior design theme is based on natural materials such as stone, glass, and wood. All rooms have plush bathrooms, Bang & Olufsen TVs, and luxury Swedish-made beds. There is free internet but no Wi-Fi. **www.masterjohan.se**

UPPSALA First Hotel Linné   🍴 ⟨W⟩   ⓚⓚ

Skolgatan 45, 750 02 **Tel** *018-10 20 00* **Fax** *018-13 75 97* **Rooms** *116*

Well managed hotel at the edge of the impressive Linnaeus Botanical Garden. Interior design is inspired by the garden, which most rooms overlook. Less expensive doubles can be a bit cramped. The onsite restaurant, First Bistro & Bar, is popular, and there is a good breakfast buffet. **www.firsthotels.com/sv/linne**

Key to Symbols *see back cover flap*

Where to Eat in Sweden

Good Swedish restaurants tend to be small and informal. Food can be very expensive, with lunch often the best value. Some restaurants serve *smörgåsbord*, where you can eat as much as you like at a fixed price. Many menus feature *husmanskost* – traditional dishes of Swedish "home cooking" – such as Swedish meatballs.

PRICE CATEGORIES
Average price for a three-course meal for one, including half a bottle of house wine, tax, and service:

Ⓚ Under 400 SEK
ⓀⓀ 400–550 SEK
ⓀⓀⓀ 550–700 SEK
ⓀⓀⓀⓀ Over 700 SEK

STOCKHOLM

CENTRAL STOCKHOLM Bakfickan

ⒻⒻ ⓀⓀ

Kungliga Operan, Karl XII's Torg, Stockholm, 111 86 **Tel** *08-676 58 00* **Map** *C3*

A real little gem for its many regular customers, including artists from the nearby opera house, Bakfickan is ideal for those looking for a quick bite to eat. The bar menu consists of Swedish "home-cooked" specials, along with a selection of open sandwiches. More complex meals are also available. Closed Sundays.

CENTRAL STOCKHOLM Nalen

Ⓕ ⓀⓀⓀ

Regeringsgatan 74, Stockholm, 111 39 **Tel** *08-50 52 92 00* **Map** *C3*

Formerly the Grand National, this eatery now has the same name as the jazz club around the corner. The food is traditional Swedish using the best local ingredients such as reindeer, bleak roe and cloudberries. Since Mathias Nordin became the new head chef, it can be difficult to get a table, so book ahead. Closed Sundays.

CENTRAL STOCKHOLM Operakällaren

ⓅⓋ ⓀⓀⓀⓀ

Operahuset, Karl XII's Torg, Stockholm, 111 86 **Tel** *08-676 58 00* **Map** *C3*

The capital's classic temple of gastronomy. The chefs are young and creative, the dining room with its lavish 19th-century ceiling paintings and the Jugendstil bar are attractions in themselves. Café Opera has lower prices and a famous afternoon cake buffet. When it is warm you can sit outside. Closed Sundays and Mondays.

SOUTHERN STOCKHOLM Pontus by the Sea

ⓅⒻ ⓀⓀ

Tullhus 2, Skeppsbron, Stockholm, 111 30 **Tel** *08-20 20 95* **Map** *C4*

Owned by one of Stockholm's star chefs Pontus Frithiof, this restaurant offers a reasonably priced, accessible menu including a large seafood platter and cold meat platter. The food is excellent. In summer diners can sit outside and watch the ships come into port. Closed Sundays.

EASTERN STOCKHOLM Teatergrillen

ⒻⓋ ⓀⓀⓀ

Nybrogatan 3, Stockholm, 114 34 **Tel** *08-54 50 65* **Map** *C2*

Teatergrillen is one of Stockholm's oldest restaurants. The cuisine is French fine dining mixed with classical Swedish dishes. They are renowned for "Silvervagnen", the trolley that is circled around the tables serving exceptional oven-baked entrecôte. Save room for dessert. Closed Sundays.

REST OF SWEDEN

GOTHENBURG 28+

ⓅⓋ ⓀⓀⓀⓀ

Götabergsgatan 28, 411 34 **Tel** *031-20 21 61*

Regarded by many as the best restaurant in Gothenburg, 28+ offers a luxurious menu created by Swedish master chef Hans Borén. The restaurant itself is located in a cellar, and the tiled floor and antique furniture can feel a little cold, but the food is the star here. The wine cellar contains more than 800 labels and the menu changes every month.

MALMÖ Salt & Brygga

ⒻⓅⓋ ⓀⓀⓀⓀ

Sundspromenaden 7, 211 18 **Tel** *040-611 59 40*

This restaurant is located in the interesting Vastra Hamnen seaside area. The row of award plaques outside the front door pay testament to its food and service. A strong environmental philosophy runs through the entire business, with ingredients sourced locally and organic foods used whenever possible. A healthy and happy place to eat.

UPPSALA Villa Anna

ⒻⓅ ⓀⓀⓀⓀ

Odinslund 3, 753 10 **Tel** *018-58 02 000*

Villa Anna's award-winning chefs serve classic dishes with innovative touches. Traditional Swedish cuisine is also offered, and made with local produce, preferably organic. During the summer months, diners can sit outside and enjoy wonderful views. Service can be on the slow side. There's an extensive wine list.

Map References *see map of Stockholm pp642–3*

NORWAY

Norway's great attraction is the grandeur of its scenery. The landscape is one of dramatic contrasts: great mountain ranges, sheer river valleys, mighty glaciers, deep green forests, and the spectacular fjords that indent the western coast. In the far north, above the Arctic Circle, visitors can marvel at the Northern Lights and the long summer nights of the Land of the Midnight Sun.

The fjords that make the coastline of Norway one of the most jagged in the world were carved by glaciers during the last Ice Age. As the glaciers began to recede about 12,000 years ago, the sea level rose and seawater flooded back to fill the deep, eroded valleys. Norway's extraordinary geography has had a great influence on its people and development. In the past, scarcity of agricultural land led to economic dependence on the sea. In contrast, Norway today has abundant hydro-electric power as well as rich oil and gas deposits on its continental shelf.

The first settlers arrived 10,000 years ago as the Scandinavian icesheets retreated. They were hunters of reindeer, deer, bears, and fish. By the Bronze Age (1500–500 BC) rock carvings show that these early Norwegians had learnt to ski. Other inhabitants of the region were the Sami (formerly known as the Lapps), with origins in the northern regions of Russia, Finland, Sweden, and Norway, where they haved lived for thousands of years by fishing and herding reindeer. Some still follow the nomadic life of their forefathers but the majority now live and work in much the same way as Norwegians.

HISTORY

It is for the Viking Age (c.800–1050) that Norway is best known. As a result of overpopulation and clan warfare, the Norwegian Vikings traveled to find new lands. They mostly sailed west, their longships reaching the British Isles, Iceland, Greenland, and even America. The raiders soon became settlers and those who remained at home benefited both from the spoils of war and the fact that farmland was no longer in such short supply. The country was united by Harald the Fairhaired in the 9th century. This

The harbor at Bergen, the main center for tours of Norway's fjords

◁ Borgund stave church, one of the best-preserved of Norway's distinctive medieval churches

The Norwegian explorer, Roald Amundsen, checking his position after reaching the South Pole in 1911

great age of expansion, however, effectively ended in 1066, when King Harald Hardråde was defeated at the battle of Stamford Bridge in England.

The 11th and 12th centuries were marked by dynastic conflicts and the rising influence of the church. In 1217 Haakon IV came to power, ushering in a "Golden Age," when Norway flourished under strong centralized government. In 1262 both Iceland and Greenland came under Norwegian rule. However, in the following century, after suffering terrible losses in the Black Death, Norway was reduced to being the least important of the Scandinavian countries. From 1380 to 1905 it was under the rule first of Denmark and then of Sweden.

The 19th century saw the growth of a national identity and a blossoming of Norwegian culture. Most of Norway's most famous individuals were born in this century, among them the composer Edvard Grieg, dramatist Henrik Ibsen, Expressionist painter Edvard Munch, and polar explorer Roald Amundsen.

Following independence from Sweden in 1905, the government set about industrializing the country, expanding the merchant fleet, and establishing healthcare and education as the cornerstones of a welfare state.

Norway pursued a policy of neutrality in World War I and World War II. The price was high in World War I, since German submarines attacked shipping indiscriminately and Norway lost half its chartered tonnage. In World War II Germany occupied the country, but encountered a massive resistance movement. Norway's part in the war helped it gain in status and it became one of the founding members of the UN in 1945 and entered NATO in 1949.

The biggest issue of the postwar years has been whether or not to join the EU. Twice Norway has refused, but the economy thrives regardless, thanks in large part to revenues from North Sea oil.

KEY DATES IN NORWEGIAN HISTORY

AD 800–1050 Viking Age

866 Vikings control most of England

900 Norway united under hereditary rule

1030 Christianity established

1217–63 Reign of Haakon IV

1380–1814 Norway in union with Denmark

1397 Kalmar Union unites crowns of Denmark, Sweden, and Norway

1660 Modern boundaries of Norway established, through peace of Copenhagen

1814 Union with Sweden, but Norwegian parliament, the Storting, has extensive powers

1887 Norwegian Labour party is founded

1905 Norway established as a separate kingdom

1940–45 German occupation of Norway during World War II

1969 Discovery of oil and gas in North Sea

1972 Following a referendum Norway declines membership of the EU

1994 Second referendum on membership of the EU; majority again votes "no"

2011 Seventy-six people die in terror attacks

LANGUAGE AND CULTURE

There are two official Norwegian languages: *Bokmål* (book language), a modernization of old Dano-Norwegian used in the days of Danish rule, and *Nynorsk*, based on rural dialects, which was codified in the 19th century as part of the resurgence of nationalism. Despite the government's efforts to preserve the use of *Nynorsk*, it is in decline. As in other parts of Scandinavia, you don't need to speak Norwegian to get by, since most people speak English.

Perhaps because independence was so long in coming, most Norwegians are great patriots. National Independence Day (May 17) is celebrated the length and breadth of the country, with festive gatherings even at remote farms. Norwegians also have a great attachment to outdoor pursuits – fishing, hiking, walking, and skiing – and many families have a *hytte* (cottage or cabin) in the mountains or on the coast.

Exploring Norway

Norway is so long and narrow that, if Oslo remained fixed and the rest were turned upside down, it would stretch all the way to Rome. There are two main areas of attraction: Oslo, a lively, open city, particularly in summer, and Bergen and the fjords in the west. Elsewhere, up to 95 percent of the country is forested or uncultivated. Transportation (which comprises trains, buses, and coastal ferries) is reliable, though services can be cut back severely in the winter months, especially in the north.

Cruise ships moored in the Geiranger Fjord between Bergen and Trondheim

SIGHTS AT A GLANCE

Bergen and the Fjords **3**
OSLO pp660–64 **1**
Stavanger **2**
Trondheim **4**

See inset map
Tromsø **5**

KEY

- ✈ Airport
- ⛴ Ferry port
- — Highway
- — Major road
- — Railroad
- ▪▪▪ International border

Oslo ❶

Founded around 1048 by Harald Hardråde, Oslo is the oldest of the Scandinavian capital cities and occupies an enormous area, although it has only 600,000 inhabitants. The heart of the city is largely made up of late 19th- and early 20th-century Neoclassical buildings, wide avenues, and landscaped parks. The city center is compact and easy to explore on foot, and most of the city's sights are within walking distance of each other. The city is a cultural hotspot, with a large number of museums and art galleries. The Nordmarka area of forests to the north of the center gives a glimpse of the beautiful Norwegian countryside.

SIGHTS AT A GLANCE

Akershus Slott and
  Hjemmefrontmuseet ①
Frammuseet ⑨
Kongelige Slottet ④
Kon-Tiki Museum ⑩
Munch-museet ⑦
Nasjonalgalleriet ⑥
Nationaltheatret ⑤
Norsk Folkemuseum ⑫
Opera House ②
Rådhus and Aker Brygge ③
Vigelandmuseet ⑧
Vikingsskipshuset ⑪

SEE ALSO

• *Where to Stay* p670

• *Where to Eat* p671

Boats moored along the quayside, in front of the Akershus Slott

GETTING AROUND

Oslo has around 60 bus and tram routes. Most buses set out from the terminal a few hundred meters northwest of Oslo Sentralstasjon, the main train station. Route 30 goes to the museums on the Bygdøy Peninsula. From mid-March to mid-October you can also reach the peninsula by ferry from the boarding point by the Rådhus. The Tunnelbanen is most useful for reaching the city suburbs, including Nordmarka.

Busy shopping street in Oslo's city center

KEY

▨	Sight / Place of interest	🚌	Bus station
✈	Airport	🅿	Parking
⚓	Long-distance ferry	ℹ	Tourist information
⛴	Local ferry	✝	Church
🚆	Train station		Pedestrian street
Ⓣ	T-bane station		

Akershus Slott and Hjemmefront-museet ①

Festningsplassen. 🚌 12 to Christiania Torv. **Akershus Slott** Ⓣ Stortinget. **Tel** 23 09 35 53. ☐ May–Aug: daily, Sep–Apr: Sat & Sun. ● public hols. 🖼 🎫 **Hjemmefrontmuseet** **Tel** 23 09 32 80. ☐ daily. ● public hols. 🖼 🎫

Located on a knoll over-looking the Oslofjorden, the Akershus Slott (Akershus Castle) is the city's most notable memorial to medieval times. Built around 1300, the castle was besieged several times before King Christian IV of Denmark transformed it into a lavish Renaissance residence in the 1620s. He also built a new fortress around the castle. Known as the Akershus Festning, it is still in use today. Little remains of the castle's former glory, most of the rooms being relatively bare, although the tapestries in the Romerike Hall are impressive. You can also visit the royal chapel and the royal mausoleum, where members of the present Norwegian dynasty lie buried.

The most somber period in the Akershus Slott's history was during World War II, when the occupying Nazis tortured and shot members of the Norwegian resistance here. Pictorial displays at the Hjemmefrontmuseet (Resistance Museum), located by the gates of the castle, provide a moving account of the war in Norway, from occupation through resistance to liberation.

Akershus Slott, Oslo's finest surviving medieval monument

Opera House ②

Kirsten Flagstads Plass 1. *Tel* 21 42 21 21. ⓣ *Bjørvika.* ▣ 32, 34, 70, 504. ◯ 10am–11pm Mon–Fri, 11am–11pm Sat & Sun. ♿ ✎ daily (Sat & Sun in English). www.operaen.no

The home of the Norwegian National Opera and Ballet is situated right on the waterfront at Bjovika, and much of this building is positioned in or under the sea. A defining feature of the design is its sloping roof, which is covered in white marble and granite. This creates the illusion of glistening ice, like a glacier rising from the edge of Oslofjord. There are three main performance spaces for opera, ballet, and concerts, and concerts are also held in the foyer or on the roof.

Rådhus and Aker Brygge ③

Rådhuset i Oslo, Fridtjof Nansens Plass. *Tel* 23 46 16 00. ⓣ Nationaltheatret, Stortinget. ▣ 30, 31, 32, 45, 81, 83. ▤ 12, 13, 19. ◯ daily. ● public hols. ✎ (May–Sep). ♿ ▣ www.oslokommune.no

Viking warrior detail from Rådhus main doors

Inaugurated in 1950 to commemorate Oslo's 900th year, the Rådhus (City Hall) is the city's most conspicuous landmark and has become a popular symbol of civic pride. Providing a complete contrast to the exterior, the colorful murals, sculptures, and frescoes inside the building celebrate Norwegian artistic and intellectual achievements, as well as those in exploration.

The Rådhus is famous as the place where the Nobel Peace Prize is presented. All the other prizes are awarded at the Stadshuset in Stockholm *(see p644)*. Past recipients have included the Red Cross, Martin Luther King, Mother Teresa and Barack Obama.

Close by is Aker Brygge. This old shipyard is now a glass-and-chrome leisure complex with shops, restaurants,

bars, cinemas, and a theater. It is a popular place in the city to go for a beer and a meal, especially during the long Scandinavian summer evenings, when you can sit outside and enjoy the scenery of the Oslo Fjord.

Kongelige Slottet ④

Drammensveien 1. *Tel* 22 04 87 00. ⓣ Nationaltheatret. ▣ 30, 31, 32, 34, 45, 81, 83. ▤ 11, 13, 17, 18, 19. ◯ end Jun–mid-Aug: 6am–9pm daily. ✎ ✎ compulsory. ♿ ▣

The Neoclassical Royal Palace is a monument to openness, standing as it does in the freely accessible Palace gardens (Slottsparken). Without gates or walls, the gardens symbolize Norway's "open" monarchy. The palace itself was built in 1825–48 at the request of King Karl Johan. Every day at 1:30pm the ceremony of the changing of the guard takes place. On Norway's National Day on May 17, the palace becomes the focal point of celebrations when the royal family stands on the balcony to greet the processions of school children.

Oslo's Nationaltheatret, overlooking its attractive, busy piazza

Nationaltheatret ⑤

Johanne Dybwads Plass 1. *Tel* 22 00 14 00. ⓣ Nationaltheatret. ▣ 30, 31, 32, 34, 45, 81, 83. ▤ 11, 13, 17, 18, 19. ◯ Aug–mid-Jun: daily. ✎ (call in advance). ⚏ ▣

Built in 1899, Norway's National Theater is Neoclassical in style, and flanked by imposing statues of the nation's two greatest 19th-century playwrights – Henrik Johan Ibsen and Bjørnstjerne Bjørnson, who is little known outside Scandinavia these days, but was a prolific writer of plays and poetry during the 19th century. The theater has four stages, and a varied program, with all performances given in Norwegian. Visitors can make special arrangements to have a guided tour of the interior.

HENRIK JOHAN IBSEN (1828–1906)

Born in the southern town of Skien, the young Ibsen was brought up in poverty, after his timber merchant father suffered bankruptcy in 1836. Managing to escape, he lived first in Kristiania and then Bergen, where he began writing and producing his first dramas. In 1864 he left for Germany and Italy, where he spent the next 27 years. His most famous plays include *Peer Gynt* (1867), *A Doll's House* (1879), and *Hedda Gabler* (1890). Regarded as one of the founders of modern drama, Ibsen's legacy to the European stage was his introduction of themes such as the alienation of the individual from a morally bankrupt society, loss of religious faith, and women's desire to free themselves of their roles as wives and mothers – a clear departure from the unchallenging theater of the time. After returning to Norway, he died in 1906.

Playwright Henrik Johan Ibsen

Simple, red-brick facade of the Nasjonalgalleriet

Nasjonalgalleriet ⑥

Universitetsgaten 13. *Tel* 21 98 20 00. Ⓣ *Nationaltheatret.* 🚌 *11, 17, 18.* 🚋 *13, 19.* ⏺ *Tue–Sun.* ⏺ *public hols.* 🅿 ⌖
www.nasjonalmuseet.no

Norway's biggest collection of art is housed in this grand 19th-century building. It includes an impressive collection of works by the country's most famous painter, Edvard Munch, from the 1880s to 1916. The main part of the collection is housed on the second floor. There is a strong international collection including Impressionist paintings by Manet, Monet, and Degas, Post-Impressionist works by Gauguin and Cézanne, and early 20th-century paintings by Picasso and Braque. The museum also holds an important collection of Norwegian art. Among the paintings on display are some spectacular fjord and country scenes from the 19th-century National Romantic period by leading Norwegian landscape painters, notably Johan Christian Dahl. There are also works by Realist artists such as Harriet Becker, Christian Krohg, and Erik Werenskiold, as well as sculptures by Gustav Vigeland. The Munch room contains such important works as *The Sick Child* (1885) and *The Scream* (1893), the swirling forms and colours of which were to greatly inspire the growing Expressionist movement.

Munch-museet ⑦

Tøyengata 53. *Tel* 23 49 35 00. Ⓣ *Tøyen.* 🚌 *20.* ⏺ *Jun–Aug: daily; Sep–May: Tue–Sun.* ⏺ *Jan 1, May 1, May 12, Dec 24–25.* ⌖ 📷 🅿
🍴 **www**.munch.museum.no

One of Scandinavia's leading artists, Edvard Munch (1863–1944) left an amazing 1,100 paintings, 4,500 drawings, and 18,000 graphic works to the city of Oslo when he died. Most of these are housed at the Munch-museet, which opened in 1963.

Munch led a troubled life, plagued by melancholy and depression due, in part, to the untimely deaths of his favorite sister and younger brother. He nevertheless remained a highly prolific artist whose intensely psychological work remains one of the great cornerstones of early Expressionist art. Since the Munch-museet is a fairly small museum, only a fraction of his work can be shown at any one time, which prevents it from being overwhelming and means that displays are frequently changed. The core of the collection is the series of outstanding paintings from the 1890s, although other periods of his life are well represented. Munch was also a prolific graphic artist, and the print room reveals his talents using etching, lithographic, and woodcut techniques. The basement houses a permanent display of Munch's life and times, and there is also a comprehensive library.

View back towards the city across Vigelandsparken sculpture park

Vigelandsparken ⑧

Kirkeveien. *Tel* 23 49 37 00. Ⓣ *Majorstuen.* 🚌 *20, 45.* 🚋 *12.* ⏺ *daily.* 🍴 💻

Vigelandsparken lies within the larger green expanse of Frognerparken. The park takes its name from the larger-than-life sculptures of Gustav Vigeland (1869–1943), which form extraordinary tableaux of fighting, play, and love. Work on display includes a series of 58 bronzes of men, women, and infants, flanking the footbridge over the river and leading up to his most famous creation, a 17-m (56-ft) granite obelisk of no fewer than 121 intertwined figures depicting the cycle of life. One of Oslo's most visited attractions, the park is a massive artistic creation that took Vigeland 40 years to complete. Some other examples of his work can be seen at Vigelandsmuseet near the park or at the Nasjonalgalleriet.

Young Woman on the Shore (1896) by Edvard Munch, at the Munch-museet

The Bygdøy Peninsula

No trip to Oslo is complete without a visit to the Bygdøy Peninsula, which lies off the western edge of the city. The area offers beaches, walking, numerous historic sites, and fascinating museums. These include a folk museum showing traditional ways of life, the Vikingsskipshuset, which traces Norway's maritime history, and others celebrating the famous Norwegian explorers Roald Amundsen and Thor Heyerdahl.

Frammuseet ⑨

Bygdøynesveien 36. **Tel** 23 28 29 57.
🚌 30. 🚃 ◯ daily. 📷
www.fram.museum.no

Designed in 1892 by Scottish-Norwegian shipbuilder Colin Archer, the *Fram* is best known as the ship that carried Norwegian explorer Roald Amundsen on his epic journey to the South Pole in 1911. The *Fram* was an ideal vessel for this undertaking. Its sides are perfectly smooth, making it impossible for ice to get a grip on the hull. Visitors can ease themselves between the remarkable array of beams in the ship's hull and marvel at the assortment of equipment – ranging from a piano to surgical instruments – that the crew managed to take with them. A series of fascinating displays around the ship relate the history of Arctic exploration.

Kon-Tiki Museum ⑩

Bygdøynesveien 36. **Tel** 23 08 67 67.
🚌 30. 🚃 ◯ daily. ◯ public hols.
♿ 📷 www.kon-tiki.no

On display at the superb Kon-Tiki Museum are the unbelievably fragile-looking vessels used by Thor Heyerdahl to make his legendary journeys across the Pacific and Atlantic Oceans. The aim of his voyages was to prove that transoceanic contact was possible between ancient civilisations. The balsawood *Kon-Tiki* raft carried Heyerdahl and a crew from Peru to Polynesia in 1947, confirming his theory that the first Polynesian settlers could have sailed from pre-Inca Peru. In 1970 he sailed a papyrus boat, *Ra II*, from Morocco to the

Thor Heyerdahl's vessel, *Ra II*, at the Kon-Tiki Museum

Caribbean to prove that the ancient peoples of Africa or Europe might have had contact with South America. These, and other eventful sagas, are outlined in the exhibition.

Vikingskipshuset ⑪

Huk Aveny 35. **Tel** 22 13 52 80. 🚌 30.
🚃 ◯ daily. ◯ public hols. 📷 ♿
www.khm.uio.no/info/vskip_huset

Norway is best known for its Viking explorers, and this museum contains three beautifully preserved 9th-century longships. All three were unearthed from burial mounds in Norway, and funeral goods from each of the vessels are on display, including ceremonial sleighs, chests, and tapestries. Viewing platforms allow visitors to study the magnificent 22 m by 5 m (72 ft by 16 ft) Oseberg ship and the slightly larger Gokstad boat, both of which were discovered on the western side of the Oslofjord. Fragmented sections of a smaller boat, the Tune, remain much as they were when they were found on the eastern side of the fjord in 1867.

Norsk Folkemuseum ⑫

Museumsveien 10. **Tel** 22 12 37 00.
🚌 30. 🚃 ◯ daily. ◯ Jan 1,
May 17, Dec 24, 25 & 31. 📷 ♿
www.norskfolkemuseum.no

Established in 1894, this excellent attraction is devoted largely to Norwegian rural life, and visitors should set aside half a day to view the many (over 150) restored buildings. These include barns, storehouses, and a splendid stave church (c.1200) with typical steep, shingle-covered roofs and dramatic dragon finials. The indoor collections consist of displays of folk art, toys, folk dress, the playwright Ibsen's study, and a pharmacy museum. On Sundays in the summer there are displays of folk dancing, and guides demonstrate skills such as weaving tapestries or baking traditional flatbread.

A reassembled grass-roofed house at the Norsk Folkemuseum

The Vikings

From the 8th to the 11th century the Vikings, or Northmen, sailed from their overpopulated fjords in Scandinavia and made their way across Europe, plundering, looking for trade, and offering mercenary service. The Swedes (or Varangians) established themselves throughout the Baltic and controlled the overland route to the Black Sea, while the Danes invaded parts of England, Portugal, and France. The Norwegians, however, were unparalleled in their success, and their adventures became the stuff of Viking legend. After overrunning the Orkneys,

Gold and silver box brooch

the Shetlands, the Hebrides, and parts of Ireland, the Norwegians established colonies in the Faroes, Iceland, and Greenland. They even sailed to the coast of North America. The Vikings were undoubtedly the most feared Europeans of their day, and their impact on history was immense. Fear of the Viking raid unified many otherwise disparate tribes and kingdoms, and many new political states were created by the Vikings themselves. Despite profiting from the spoils of war, it was their success as settlers and traders that was the Vikings' greatest achievement.

Viking religion *was dominated by the supreme gods Odin (god of war), Thor (thunder), and Frey (fertility). Valhalla was their equivalent of heaven. Warriors were buried with whatever it was thought the afterlife required, and the rich were entombed in ships, often with their servants. Most had converted to Christianity by the late 10th century, but Sweden remained pagan well into the 11th century.*

Burial "ships" made of stone for warriors from poorer families, near Aalborg in Denmark

Frey, god of fertility

The longship *was the main vessel of the Viking raid. Longer, slimmer, and faster than the usual Viking ship, it had a large rectangular sail and between 24 and 50 oars. The sail was used in open sea and navigation was achieved by taking bearings from the stars.*

The prow, curled into a "shepherd's crook," formed a high defensive barrier.

The keel was characteristically shallow to allow for flat beach landings.

The beautifully restored Oseberg ship, unearthed in 1904, on display at the Vikingsskipshuset in Oslo

Weapons and armor *were the backbone of Viking culture, so the blacksmith's art was always in demand. Bronze and iron swords were endlessly produced, many of which followed their bearers to the grave. Arrows, axes, shields, helmets, and coats of mail were standard military gear, examples of which survive in pristine condition today.*

Gold armlet

Jewelry design *often showed Arab and eastern European influence, which illustrates the extent of the Viking trading network. Gold and silver were a sign of wealth and prestige, although many ornaments were made of bronze, pewter, colored glass, jet, and amber.*

Picture stones *were memorial blocks that celebrated the glory of dead relatives. They were carved with pictures and runic writing.*

Viking helmet with noseguard

Picture stone from Gotland

View of the waterfront at Stavanger's attractive marina

Stavanger ❷

🏛 *110,000.* ✈ 🚢 🚉 🚌
ℹ *Rosenkildetorget 1 (51 85 92 00).*
🎭 *Maijazz (May); Glamat Food Festival (Jul).*

Stavanger is best known today as Norway's major oil town, with North Sea oil having provided its prosperity since the 1970s. Earlier in its history, in the mid-19th century, the town grew rich on herring exports.

Small enough to be seen on foot, much of the center of Stavanger is modern. One exception is the cathedral, the **Stavanger Domkirke**, which dates back to the 12th century but has been restored several times since. Later 17th-century additions include a flamboyant pulpit and a number of huge, richly carved memorial tablets hanging in the aisles.

Stavanger's main attraction is Gamle Stavanger (Old Stavanger), west of the harbor. Visitors can wander down the narrow cobblestone streets of this old city quarter, amid the white-painted wooden houses, and imagine life here in the 19th century. An interesting museum in the town is the **Hermetikkmuseet** (Canning Museum) at No. 88 Øvre Strandgate, which tells the story of Stavanger's fisheries. Overlooking the harbor, the **Norsk Oljemuseum** (Norwegian Petroleum Museum) gives an insight into North Sea oil exploration.

Bergen and the Fjords ❸

🏛 *235,000.* ✈ 🚢 🚉 🚌 ℹ
Vågsallmenningen 1 (55 55 20 00). 🎭
Bergen International Festival (May–Jun).

Surrounded by no fewer than seven mountains, Norway's most westerly port offers the visitor plenty to do and see, although it rains relentlessly here. Founded in the 12th century, Bergen is one of Norway's prettiest cities, with a medieval quarter dating back to the days when the port was an important center of European trade for the all-powerful German Hanseatic League. Many of the surviving Hanseatic buildings are found on the **Bryggen** (quay), where brightly-painted old wooden warehouses – now museums, shops, and restaurants – make up an attractive harborside.

Close by the harbor is the busy Fisketorvet (Fish Market) where fresh fish, produce, and local crafts can be found. Also nearby are the 11th-century **Mariakirken** (St. Mary's Church) and the **Hanseatiske Museum** – an excellently preserved late Hansa house from the 18th century.

Around Lille Lungegårds-vann, the city's central lake, are a number of interesting art galleries. Finally, no visitor to Bergen should miss the chance to take a trip up Mount Ulriken for a panoramic view of the area. A cable car takes you from the edge of the city to the summit.

Elaborate Baroque pulpit in the Mariakirken, Bergen

Environs

Just outside the city is **Trold-haugen**, an enchanting villa filled with paintings, prints, and other memorabilia, where Norway's most famous composer Edvard Grieg (1843–1907) spent the later years of his life and composed much of his work. A short way beyond is **Fantoft Stavkirke**, a traditional, ancient wooden church, originally built in Sognefjord, but moved here.

Bergen also makes a good base for viewing the western fjord scenery, which extends from south of Bergen to distant Kristiansund in the north. Boat trips leave from Bergen throughout the summer (a few run year-round), visiting local fjords. One of the closest is **Osterfjord**, but **Hardanger-fjord**, with its majestic waterfalls, is perhaps the most spectacular. To the north,

The stunning scenery of the Sognefjord, north of Bergen

Sognefjord, at 206 km (128 miles) long and 1,308 m (4,291 ft) deep, is the deepest and longest fjord in the world.

🏛 Troldhaugen
Troldhaugveien 65, Paradis.
Tel 55 92 29 92. ☐ May–Sep: daily; Jan–Apr: Mon–Fri. 📷 ♿ 🎦
📷 🖨 **www**.troldhaugen.com

Trondheim ❹

🏛 152,000. ✈ 🚢 🚌 🚆
🛈 Munkegaten 19 (73 80 76 60).
🎪 St. Olav Festival (Jul).
www.trondheim.com

Called Nidaros (which means the mouth of the River Nid) until the 16th century, Trondheim has benefited from having a good harbor and being situated in a wide and fertile valley. Founded in AD 997, the city was for many centuries the political and religious capital of Norway, with the earliest Parliament (or *Ting*) being held here. This period saw the construction of Trondheim's most beautiful building – and one of Norway's architectural highlights – the **Nidaros Cathedral**, begun around 1077. Until the Reformation in the 16th century, the cathedral attracted pilgrims from all over Scandinavia. Notable features of this colossal building include the Gothic-style great arched nave and a magnificent stained-glass rose window above the entrance – the work of Gabriel Kjelland

Detail from the facade of Nidaros Cathedral, Trondheim

in 1930. Since 1988, the cathedral has been home to the Norwegian Crown jewels and the modest but beautiful regalia of the King, Queen, and Crown Prince, which are on display in a side chapel.

Another reminder of Trondheim's medieval past is provided by the wharves alongside the harbor and the narrow streets that wind between brightly painted warehouses. Although the buildings you see today only date back to the 18th century, the layout of the area is much as it was in earlier times when fishing and timber were the main source of the town's wealth.

Other attractions of the city include Scandinavia's largest wooden building, the **Stiftsgården**, built between 1774 and 1778 as a private home. Today it serves as the king's official residence in Trondheim. The **Nordenfjeldske Kunstindustrimuseum** (Decorative Arts Museum) houses an extensive collection of furniture, tapestries, ceramics, silver, and glassware from the 16th to the 20th century, including a fine collection of Art Nouveau pieces, plus contemporary arts, crafts, and design.

🏛 Nordenfjeldske Kunstindustrimuseum
Munkegaten 5. **Tel** 73 80 89 50.
☐ Jun–Aug: daily; Sep–May: Tue–Sun. 📷 some public hols. 📷
📷 🎦 ♿

Tromsø ❺

🏛 61,000. ✈ 🚢 🚌
🛈 Storgaten 61–63 (77 61 00 00).
🎪 Northern Lights Festival (Jan).

Situated inside the Arctic circle, Tromsø, the so-called capital of North Norway, is a lively university town. There are not many specific sights and attractions in the town itself, but its fine mountain and fjord setting makes it well worth a visit. The most spectacular time to stay in

Tromsø's modern concrete and glass Arctic Cathedral

the summer, during the period of the "midnight sun." Due to the high latitude, the sun remains above the horizon from May 21 to July 21, and the sky often glows red throughout the night. Tromsø is also a good place to view the Northern Lights.

Since Tromsø is a compact town, it is possible to stroll through the center, which sits upon a small hilly island reached by a bridge, in around 15 minutes. The major sight here is the striking white **Ishavskatedralen** (Arctic Cathedral). The cathedral is intended to represent the type of tent used by the Sami, the region's indigenous semi-nomadic people. Tromsø's **Polarmuseet** (Polar Museum) documents the history of the local economy – seal trapping played a big part until the 1950s – and polar expeditions, in particular the voyages undertaken by Norwegian explorer Roald Amundsen. Tromsø is a famous starting point for Arctic expeditions, and Amundsen made his last expedition from here to the Arctic ice cap, where he died in 1928. Visitors should not miss the opportunity to take the cable car (Fjellheisen) up the mountain behind the city to get a real sense of the setting of this polar town.

🏛 Polarmuseet
Søndre Tollbugata 11. **Tel** 77 60 66 30. ☐ daily. 📷 public hols.
🎦 📷 **www**.visitnorway.com

Practical & Travel Information

Norway has a reputation as an expensive destination, but the cost of traveling around the country is fairly reasonable. Norway's public transportation system is comprehensive and reliable, although visitors should expect a reduced service during winter. Once within the Arctic Circle, there is a period around midsummer during which the sun never sets (the "midnight sun"). Conversely, there is a "polar night" around midwinter, during which the sun never rises at all. These effects occur for longer periods the farther north you travel.

TOURIST INFORMATION

Norway has around 350 local tourist offices, as well as almost 20 regional offices. Visitors to the capital can use **Oslo Promotion Tourist Information** in the center of town. For brochures and more general information on all parts of the country, contact the **Norwegian Tourist Board** before you leave home.

As well as providing information on hiking routes and guided mountain tours, **Den Norske Turistforening** (Norwegian Mountain Touring Association) sells maps and hiking gear, and maintains more than 300 mountain huts throughout the country.

OPENING HOURS

Many museums and attractions are open all year round, although a few have seasonal opening hours. Stores are generally open from 10am to 8pm Monday to Friday, and from 10am to 6pm on Saturday. Most stores are closed on Sundays.

VISA REQUIREMENTS

Citizens of the EU, the US, Canada, Australia, and New Zealand do not require a visa for stays of less than three months. Citizens of most EU countries can use a national identity card instead of a passport for entry to Norway.

SAFETY AND EMERGENCIES

Norway is a safe country, and crime against tourists is relatively rare. Standards of healthcare are excellent. Hotels and tourist offices have lists of local doctors, or you can look in the telephone directory under doctors *(leger)*. You will have to pay a fee for a doctor's appointment and for prescriptions, but EU citizens with an E111 form will be reimbursed for part of the cost of any treatment.

BANKING AND CURRENCY

The Norwegian unit of currency is the Norwegian krone, abbreviated to NOK. Cash and traveler's checks can be changed at banks and post offices for a small commission. Outside banking hours, you can change money at hotels, some campsites, and (in Oslo) exchange booths. The greater the amount you exchange, the better rate you will get. Major credit and charge cards are accepted in most places.

Banks are open from 8:15am to 4pm Monday to Wednesday and Friday, and 8:15am to 5pm on Thursday. Between June and August, they close 30 minutes earlier.

COMMUNICATIONS

Telecommunications and postal services in Norway are very efficient and reliable. Coin-operated phone booths are gradually being phased out in favor of those that will only take phonecards (Telekort). These cards can be purchased in news kiosks.

E-mail can be collected at the country's growing number of Internet cafés (all major cities have at least a couple) or at most public libraries.

Thanks to state subsidies and loans there is a large number of newspapers in Norway. Most British and some American newspapers are sold in large towns from Narvesen newsstands.

TAX-FREE SHOPPING

Visitors to Norway can benefit from the nation's decision not to join the EU by taking advantage of the tax-free shopping scheme. This means that if you purchase goods over a certain value from any one of the 3,000 outlets that participate in the scheme you can have the VAT refunded. You will receive a tax-free voucher, which you must present upon your departure from the country. The goods must be unused for you to receive the refund.

ARRIVING BY AIR

Most international flights arrive at Oslo's airport, **Gardermoen**, 60 km (37 miles) north of the city, although some

THE CLIMATE OF NORWAY

The climate of Norway experiences intense seasonal changes. The short summer (roughly mid-June to mid-August) can be quite hot, though rain is regular and temperatures in the far north can plunge during the summer nights. Winter is long and dark, and the north is subject to sub-zero temperatures which can persist for months at a time.

OSLO			
°C/F	21/70		
		12/54	9/48
	9/48		
0°C 32°F	1/34		3/37
			0/32
			-6/21
	5 hrs	7 hrs	3 hrs	2 hrs
	48 mm	79 mm	99 mm	58 mm
month	Apr	Jul	Oct	Jan

carriers also fly to Stavanger, Bergen, Tromsø, and Kristiansand. From Britain, daily direct flights are operated by British Airways, **SAS** (Scandinavian Airline System), **Norwegian**, and Ryanair. SAS offers direct flights from other major European cities, such as Stockholm, Berlin, and Amsterdam.

Flying to Norway from North America may involve changing planes, although SAS offers a direct service from New York to Oslo.

Domestic flights can be useful if you are short on time – especially if you wish to visit the far north – and are operated by a variety of carriers, including SAS.

TRAVELING BY SEA

Ferries from Germany, Denmark, and Sweden make daily crossings to Norway. It is also possible to travel directly from Newcastle in the UK, but the journey can take as long as 27 hours. Routes are operated by **Fjord Line** and **DFDS Seaways**.

Once in Norway, you are never very far from the sea and local ferries are an invaluable means of transportation across the fjords.

Hurtigruten, the Norwegian Coastal Express service, sails from Bergen to Kirkenes, far above the Arctic Circle, putting in at 35 ports en route. It is a superb way to see Norway's dramatic coastline. Call ferry companies **OVDS** or **TFDS** to make a reservation.

RAIL TRAVEL

Many rail services link Norway with the rest of Scandinavia and mainland Europe. The major point of entry to Scandinavia from mainland Europe is Copenhagen, where trains cross the new Øresund Bridge before heading to Oslo. Within Norway, the **Norges Statsbaner** (Norwegian State Railroad) operates a more extensive network in the south than in the north, but there are routes to all the major towns.

A Norway rail pass allows unlimited travel on all trains in Norway for a specified number of days in a given period. The pass is available from rail ticket agents in Norway and abroad.

Oslo's Tunnelbanen (T-bane) consists of eight metro lines, which converge in the city center. The system runs from around 6am to 12:30am.

BUSES AND TAXIS

Buses cover the length and breadth of Norway, and are useful for getting to places the train network does not reach. Bus journeys are also reasonably priced. Most long-distance buses are operated by the national company, **NOR-WAY Bussekspress**.

Taxis are extremely expensive in the cities and towns, but in Oslo the excellent public transportation network generally means that you can avoid having to use taxis at all.

TRAVELING BY CAR

Car rental is fairly costly, although Norway's main roads are fast and extremely well maintained. All of the major international car rental companies are represented. Road regulations are strictly enforced, particularly those relating to drunken driving. Be aware that speeding in Norway can incur hefty fines, even if you are driving only a few miles above the limit. Most main roads have cameras.

Due to poor visibility and bad weather, many minor roads in Norway close during the dark winter months.

DIRECTORY

TOURIST INFORMATION

Den Norske Turistforening
Tel 40 00 18 68.
www.turistforeningen.no

Oslo Turistinformasjon
Rådhuset, Fridtjof Nansens Plass 5, 0160 Oslo.
Tel 81 53 05 55.
www.visitoslo.com

Norwegian Tourist Board
www.visitnorway.com
In Norway:
Innovasjon Norge,
Akersgate 13, Postboks 440 Sentrum, 0104 Oslo.
Tel 22 00 25 00.

In the UK:
5th Floor, Charles House, 5 Regent Street, London SW1Y 4LR.
Tel 020-7839 2650.
In the US:
655 Third Avenue, 10017 New York.
Tel 212-885 9700.

EMBASSIES

Australian Consulate
Jernbane Torget 2, Oslo.
Tel 22 47 91 70.

Canada
Wergelandsveien 7, Oslo.
Tel 22 99 53 00.

UK
Thomas Heftyes Gate 8, Oslo. *Tel 23 13 27 00.*

US
Drammensveien 18, Oslo.
Tel 22 44 85 50.

EMERGENCIES

Ambulance
Tel 113.

Fire
Tel 110.

Police
Tel 112.

AIR TRAVEL

Gardermoen Airport
Tel 815-502 50.

Norwegian
www.norwegian.no

SAS
Tel 815-20 400 (Norway).
Tel 0845-60 727 727 (UK).
Tel 800-221 2350 (US).
www.scandinavian.net

FERRY SERVICES

DFDS Seaways
Tel 22 41 90 90 (Norway).
Tel 08702 520 524 (UK).
www.dfds.co.uk

Fjord Line
Tel 55 54 87 00 (Norway).
Tel 0191-296 1313 (UK).
www.fjordline.co.uk

OVDS/TFDS
Tel 76 96 76 93 (OVDS).
Tel 77 64 82 00 (TFDS).

RAIL TRAVEL

Norges Statsbaner
Tel 81 50 08 88.

BUSES

NOR-WAY Bussekspress
Schweigaardsgata 8–10 (Visitor Centre), Oslo.
Tel 815-444 44.
www.nor-way.no

Where to Stay in Norway

Accommodations in Norway are not as expensive as might be expected for Scandinavia; almost all hotels offer weekend and summer discounts, which can reduce the cost considerably. Hotel breakfasts are huge, all-you-can-eat buffet affairs, and are normally included in the price. Guests can expect attentive service and spotless rooms.

PRICE CATEGORIES
Price categories for a standard double room (not per person) per night, including tax, service, and breakfast:

ⓚ Under 1,000 NOK
ⓚⓚ 1,000–1,400 NOK
ⓚⓚⓚ 1,400–1,800 NOK
ⓚⓚⓚⓚ Over 1,800 NOK

OSLO

CENTRAL OSLO WEST Thon Hotel Gyldenløve
Bogstadveien 20, 0355 Oslo **Tel** *23-33 23 00* **Fax** *23-33 23 03* **Rooms** *164*
Map *C2*

The Gyldenløve is superbly located in Oslo's west quarter, on one of the city's best shopping avenues. The hotel has a modern, stylish, Scandinavian feel. There is a reasonable menu at the hotel's Portofino Café and Wine Bar. **www.thonhotels.com/gyldenlove**

CENTRAL OSLO WEST Hotel Bristol
Kristian IV's gate 7, 0164 Oslo **Tel** *22-82 60 00* **Fax** *22-82 60 01* **Rooms** *251*
Map *D3*

The classy Bristol has been one of Oslo's top hotels since the 1920s and is a regular choice for visiting celebrities. Dripping in traditional elegance, the hotel's Library Bar and Wintergarden is a popular meeting point, and the Bristol Grill offers both international and Norwegian dishes. A luxurious stay is guaranteed. **www.bristol.no**

CENTRAL OSLO EAST Grand Hotel
Karl Johans Gate 31, 0159 Oslo **Tel** *23-21 20 00* **Fax** *23-21 21 00* **Rooms** *290*
Map *D3*

The Grand Hotel first opened its doors in 1874. Built in Louis XVI revival style, it is now a deluxe hotel with a hint of Nordic Art Nouveau. It has been extended and modernized over the years, and today is a superb mix of tradition and modern comfort. The hotel has a well-equipped spa and a great choice of bars and restaurants. **www.grand.no**

CENTRAL OSLO EAST Rica Oslo Hotel
Nr.1 Europarådets Plass, 0154 Oslo **Tel** *23-10 42 00* **Fax** *23-10 42 10* **Rooms** *175*

Leather furniture and marble floors decorate this hotel's lobby, while art and sculpture from prominent Norwegian artists further adds to the artistic atmosphere. Rooms are individually decorated with paintings. Buffet meals and an à la carte menu are served at the Bjorgvigen Mat & Vinhus restaurant. **www.rica-hotels.com**

WEST OSLO Clarion Collection Hotel Gabelhus
Gabelsgate 16, 0272 Oslo **Tel** *23-27 65 00* **Fax** *23-27 65 60* **Rooms** *114*
Map *C3*

The ivy-covered Gabelhus is located in an exclusive residential area with beautiful townhouses, embassies, high-class restaurants and cafés all within walking distance. This now a stylish and charming boutique hotel combines modern Scandinavian design with traditional architectural features. **www.gabelshus.no**

REST OF NORWAY

BERGEN Clarion Hotel Admiral
C. Sundtsgate 9, 5004 Bergen **Tel** *55-23 64 00* **Fax** *55-23 64 64* **Rooms** *211*

Known as "the hotel with the sea on three sides," the top-class Clarion has stunning views of the wharf, the fish market and Mt. Fløien. Built at the turn of the century as a boat warehouse, it was turned into a waterside hotel in 1987. All 211 rooms have large windows, and 40 have harbor views. **www.clarionadmiral.com**

STAVANGER Radisson Blu Atlantic Hotel
Olav V's Gate 3, 4002 Stavanger **Tel** *51-76 10 00* **Fax** *51-76 10 01* **Rooms** *354*

Overlooking Lake Breiavatnet and next to the historic Old Stavanger area, this modern, top-class hotel has 354 air-conditioned rooms spread over 13 floors. The hotel's Restaurant Ajax has a bright dining room serving breakfast, while the Antique Restaurant is a more formal eatery serving à la carte international cuisine. **www.radissonblu.com**

TRONDHEIM Britannia Hotel
Dronningensgate 5, 7011 Trondheim **Tel** *73-80 08 00* **Fax** *73-80 08 01* **Rooms** *247*

The Britannia, which opened in 1897, was Trondheim's first luxury hotel and has been synonymous with the highest standards of service, comfort, and cuisine ever since. Behind the elegant facade and stylish interior is a modern hotel offering the latest facilities, including a luxury spa, four restaurants, and a piano and cocktail bar. **www.britannia.no**

Key to Symbols *see back cover flap*

Where to Eat in Norway

Eating out, and food in general, is often expensive in Norway, especially when the price of alcohol is added to the bill. Lunchtimes are usually simple affairs, consisting of *smørbrød* (open sandwiches) and light pastries. A three-course evening meal in a Norwegian restaurant will often involve soup as a starter and fruits for dessert.

PRICE CATEGORIES
Price categories for a three-course meal for one person, including half a bottle of house wine, tax and service:

Ⓚ Under 400 NOK
ⓀⓀ 400–500 NOK
ⓀⓀⓀ 500–700 NOK
ⓀⓀⓀⓀ Over 700 NOK

OSLO

CENTRAL OSLO WEST Lofoten Fiskerestaurant
ⓀⓀⓀ
Stranden 75, 0250 Oslo **Tel** *22-83 08 08*   **Map** *C3*

This fish and seafood restaurant located next to Oslo's quay is elegantly decorated in a maritime theme and offers some of the best views of the Oslo fjord. It serves high-quality dishes with a seasonal twist such as scallop, king crab, and calamari, accompanied by a herb salad, smoked bell-pepper aioli, and croutons.

CENTRAL OSLO WEST Theatercafeen
ⓀⓀⓀ
Stortingsgata 24–26, 0161 Oslo **Tel** *22-82 40 50*   **Map** *D3*

Theatercafeen has a lively atmosphere and attracts guests from all walks of life, ranging from the rich and famous to tourists. On *The New York Times'* Top Ten list of the world's most famous cafés, there's live piano and violin music in the evenings and during the day on Saturdays. The menu is international and reservations are recommended.

CENTRAL OSLO EAST Kaffistova
Ⓚ
Rosenkrantz' Gate 8, 0159 Oslo **Tel** *23-21 42 10*   **Map** *D3*

Part of the Hotel Bondeheimen and located a stone's throw from Karl Johans Gate, the Kaffistova offers a buffet with a comprehensive choice of traditional Norwegian dishes. A popular place for Norwegian specialties such as *raspeballer* (potato dumplings), *boknafisk* (dried and salted cod) and *rømmegrøt* (sour cream porridge).

CENTRAL OSLO EAST Det Gamle Raadhus Restaurant
ⓀⓀⓀ
Nedre Slottsgate 1, 0157 Oslo **Tel** *22-42 01 07*   **Map** *D3*

Steeped in tradition, this popular restaurant close to Akershus Festning is housed in one of Oslo's oldest buildings (which was the first City Hall) dating from 1641. Today it is well known for its fish and game dishes. Their *lutefisk* platter, served just before Christmas, is one of the house specialties. There's outdoor service in the summer.

CENTRAL OSLO EAST Statholdergaarden
ⓀⓀⓀⓀ
Rådhusgaten 11, 0151 Oslo **Tel** *22-41 88 00*   **Map** *D3*

Statholdergaarden is a Norwegian gourmet restaurant where culinary world champion Bent Stiansen is in charge of the kitchen. He creates a new six-course menu every day based on the freshest ingredients inspired by European food traditions. Statholderens Krostue is the more informal restaurant in the cellar serving open sandwiches at lunchtime.

REST OF NORWAY

BERGEN Fløien Folkerestaurant
ⓀⓀⓀ
Fløifjellet 2, 5014 Bergen **Tel** *55-32 18 75*

At the top of the famous Funicular in Bergen, high above sea level, you will find Fløien Folkerestaurant. Opened in 1925, it has been completely restored and, with its distinctive architecture, prominent location and breathtaking views, is a tourist attraction in itself. On the large outdoor terrace you can gaze over Bergen while enjoying your meal.

STAVANGER Straen Fiskerestaurant
ⓀⓀⓀⓀ
Nedre Strandgate 15, 4005 Stavanger **Tel** *51-84 37 00*

Amusingly touted as being "world famous throughout Norway", this really is one of the best seafood restaurants in Stavanger. The old-fashioned interior is straight out of the 1950s and the windows open out to give fantastic views of the harbor. There is a nightclub upstairs and another restaurant downstairs that's served by the same kitchen.

TRONDHEIM Havfruen Fiskerestaurant
ⓀⓀⓀ
Kjøpmannsgata 7, 7013 Trondheim **Tel** *73-87 40 70*

One of the foremost fish restaurants in Trondheim, Havfruen offers a distinctive atmosphere in an 18th-century wharf warehouse. The menu ranges from *bouillabaisse* to fish varieties from the Norwegian coastal waters, as well as meat dishes. Instead of a standard à la carte concept there's an eight-course menu that changes each month.

Map References *see map of Oslo pp660–1*

DENMARK

*D*enmark is a peaceful and pleasant place. Its landscape is largely green, flat, and rural – with a host of half-timbered villages reminiscent of a Hans Christian Andersen fairy tale. It is an easy country to visit – not only do the majority of Danes speak English, but they are friendly and extremely hospitable. Above all, the pace of life is not as frenetic as in some European mainland countries.

Denmark consists of no fewer than 405 islands and the Jutland peninsula, which extends north from Germany. Located as it is between Scandinavia proper and mainland Europe, Denmark not surprisingly shares characteristics with both. It has the least dramatic countryside of the Scandinavian countries, yet there are also a number of important Viking sites dotted throughout the land. Zealand, the largest island, is the focal point for Denmark's 5.3 million inhabitants, a quarter of whom live in Copenhagen. Funen and Bornholm are much more tranquil islands, popular for holiday retreats. The Jutland peninsula has the most varied scenery, with marshland and desolate moors alternating with agricultural land.

HISTORY

Although nomadic hunters inhabited Jutland some 25,000 years ago, the first mention of the Danes as a distinct people is in the chronicles of Bishop Gregor of Tours from 590. Their strategic position in the north made them a central power in the Viking expansion that followed. Constant struggles for control of the North Sea with England and western Europe, for the Skagerrak – the straits between Denmark and Norway – with Norway and Sweden, and for the Baltic Sea with Germany, Poland, and Russia, ensued. But thanks to their fast ships and fearless warriors, by 1033 the Danes controlled much of England and Normandy, as well as most trading routes in the Baltic.

The next three hundred years were characterized by Denmark's attempts to maintain its power in the Baltic with the help of the German Hanseatic League. During the reign of Valdemar IV (1340–1375), Sweden, Norway, Iceland, Greenland, and the Faroe Isles came under Danish rule.

Evening illuminations in Tivoli Gardens, Copenhagen

◁ **Frederiksborg Slot, a grand Renaissance palace northwest of Copenhagen**

Valdemar's daughter Margrethe presided over this first Scandinavian federation, known as the Kalmar Union.

The next period of Danish prosperity occurred in the 16th century, when Denmark profited from the Sound dues, a levy charged to ships traversing the Øresund, the narrow channel between Denmark and Sweden. Christian IV (reigned 1588–1648), the "builder king," instigated a huge program of construction that provided Denmark with a number of architectural masterpieces, such as the Rosenborg Palace in Copenhagen (see p681).

Christian IV of Denmark (1588–1648)

By the 18th century, Denmark had discovered lucrative trading opportunities in the Far East, and consolidated its position in the Baltic. However, an alliance with the French in the Napoleonic Wars (1803–15) led to the bombardment of Copenhagen by Britain's Admiral Nelson, and King Frederik VI was forced to hand over Norway to Sweden in 1814.

The remainder of the 19th century witnessed the rise of the social democrats and the trade unions. The year 1901 saw the beginnings of parliamentary democracy and a number of social reforms, including income tax on a sliding scale and free schooling.

Denmark was neutral during both world wars, but during World War II the country was occupied by the Nazis, a move that heralded the development of a huge resistance movement. Social reforms continued after the war, and in the 1960s laws were passed allowing abortion on demand and the abolition of all forms of censorship. In 1972, Denmark became the first Scandinavian country to join the European Community, and has developed a reputation for addressing environmental issues and supporting the economies of developing nations.

As the 21st century begins, Danish citizens have a high standard of living and state-funded education and health systems, although this has been achieved through high tax bills. Nevertheless, Denmark remains one of the cheaper Scandinavian countries.

KEY DATES IN DANISH HISTORY

AD 590 First written account of the Danes in the chronicle of Bishop Gregor of Tours

960 Denmark becomes officially Christian with the baptism of King Harald "Bluetooth"

1033 Danes control much of England and Normandy and dominate trade in the Baltic

1282 Erik V forced to grant nobles a charter limiting his powers – first Danish constitution

1397 Queen Margrethe I unites Scandinavia under the Danish throne in the Kalmar Union

1814 Norway transferred from the Danish to the Swedish crown

1849 Under Frederik VII, Denmark becomes a constitutional monarchy

1890s Social reforms lay the foundations of the present welfare state

1914–18 Denmark neutral in World War I

1940–45 Despite declaring its neutrality, Denmark invaded and occupied by the Nazis

1945 Becomes a charter member of the United Nations and signs the North Atlantic Treaty

1972 Denmark joins the EC (now the EU)

2000 Danes reject euro as their currency

2002 EU presidency held by Denmark

LANGUAGE AND CULTURE

A North Germanic language, Danish is similar to Norwegian and Swedish, but there are some significant differences in word meaning ("frokost" for example, means "lunch" in Danish, but "breakfast" in Norwegian) and pronunciation. English and German are widely spoken, so visitors should have few problems in making themselves understood.

For such a small country Denmark has produced a number of world-famous writers and philosophers, including Hans Christian Andersen (see p683) and the 19th-century philosopher Søren Kierkegaard, who is claimed to have laid the foundations of modern existentialism. However, it is best known for its 20th-century design and craftsmanship, which have given the country an international reputation. The works of companies such as Georg Jensen silversmiths and Royal Copenhagen porcelain, and the furniture of architect Arne Jacobsen, enjoy a worldwide reputation.

Exploring Denmark

Copenhagen is Denmark's main attraction, a small yet lively capital with a considerable number of sights concentrated in the center. Outside the capital, the pace of life is slow, and the flat countryside is punctuated by half-timbered villages and the occasional manor house. Roads are of a high standard, and the trains and buses extremely punctual and efficient. Denmark's lack of hills makes it an excellent place for cycling.

SIGHTS AT A GLANCE

Tranquil park in Odense, the principal town of the fertile island of Funen

KEY

✈	Airport
⛴	Ferry port
—	Highway
—	Major road
—	Railroad
▪▪▪	International border

0 km   40

0 miles   40

Copenhagen ❶

Copenhagen is Denmark's largest city, with a
population of around 1.2 million. Founded in 1167
by Bishop Absalon, who built a fortress on
the island of Slotsholmen, the town grew quickly,
prospering from trade in the Baltic. In 1461 it was
declared the capital of Denmark. During the reign
of Christian IV (1588–1648), the city was endowed
with many fine Renaissance buildings, some of
which still stand today, including the splendid
Rosenborg Slot and the Børsen. As a change from
sightseeing, visitors can head for the lively,
cosmopolitan shopping area of Strøget, Europe's
longest pedestrian street, or simply relax in one of
the many restaurants and cafés of bustling Nyhavn,
with its charming, gabled townhouses.

**Cannon in the grounds of the city's
16th-century fortress, the Kastellet**

SIGHTS AT A GLANCE

Amalienborg ⑨
Børsen ⑥
Christiania ⑭
Christiansborg Palace ⑤
Kastellet and
 Frihedsmuseet ⑪
Little Mermaid ⑩
National Museum ④
Ny Carlsberg Glyptotek ②
Nyhavn ⑧
Rådhuset ③
Rosenborg Slot ⑬
Statens Museum for Kunst ⑫
Strøget ⑦
Tivoli Gardens ①

SEE ALSO

• *Where to Stay* p686

• *Where to Eat* p687

KEY

■	Sight / Place of interest
⬛	Ferry boarding point
🚉	Train station
🚌	Bus station
Ⓜ	Metro station
🅿	Parking
ℹ	Tourist information
✝	Church
✡	Synagogue
⚊	Pedestrian street

A   B   C

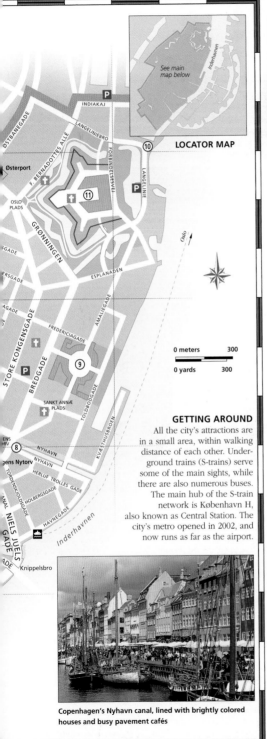

See main
map below

LOCATOR MAP

0 meters 300

0 yards 300

GETTING AROUND

All the city's attractions are
in a small area, within walking
distance of each other. Underground trains (S-trains) serve
some of the main sights, while
there are also numerous buses.
The main hub of the S-train
network is København H,
also known as Central Station. The
city's metro opened in 2002, and
now runs as far as the airport.

Copenhagen's Nyhavn canal, lined with brightly colored
houses and busy pavement cafés

The Nimb building, with its domes
and minarets, at Tivoli Gardens

Tivoli Gardens ①

Vesterbrogade 3. *Tel* 33 15 10 01.
København H. 2A, 5A, 11A, 15,
66, 2505. mid-Apr–late Sep, mid-
Oct (Halloween), & mid-Nov–late Dec:
daily. **www**.tivoli.dk

One of Copenhagen's most
famous tourist attractions, the
Tivoli Gardens opened in 1843.
This highly popular entertainment park combines all the
fun of fairground rides with
fountains and fireworks,
concerts and ballets, top-quality
restaurants and fast-food outlets. Based on the 18th-century
ornamental gardens popular in
Europe at the time, Tivoli
features Chinese-style pago-
das and Moorish pavilions, as
well as modern additions, such
as the Hanging Gardens.

Among the many fairground
rides are a traditional roller
coaster, a ferris wheel,
a "freefall" tower, and the
80-m (262-ft) Star Flyer,
which provides views over
Copenhagen. There are also
amusement arcades, shooting
galleries, and children's rides.

The gardens are at their most
enthralling after dusk, when
thousands of tiny lights
illuminate the park. At night,
open-air theaters host all
forms of entertainment, from
big bands to Friday night rock
concerts, and during the summer season, performances of
the unique Danish pantomime.

A good time to visit Tivoli is
between late November and
Christmas, when the gardens
are transformed into a
bustling Christmas fair. You
can sample traditional Danish
seasonal fare, buy many
specialty Christmas gifts, try
the toboggan run, and
generally get acquainted with
Danish Christmas traditions.

The richly decorated Neoclassical facade of Ny Carlsberg Glyptotek art gallery

Ny Carlsberg Glyptotek ②

Dantes Plads 7. *Tel* 33 41 81 41.
🚇 København H. 🚌 1A, 2A, 11A,
15. ⭕ Tue–Sun. ⭘ Jan 1, Jun 5,
Dec 24, 25. 💷 except Sun. ♿ partial.
🏠 🖥 🍴 www.glyptoteket.dk

Copenhagen's most elegant art gallery was opened in 1897 by Carl Jacobsen, son of the founder of the Carlsberg Brewery, to give more people the chance to see classical art. Housed in a magnificent Neoclassical building, the Glyptotek is best-known for its exquisite antiquities, in particular its collections of Etruscan and Roman art.

The main building's collections are completed with Egyptian, Greek, Roman, and French sculpture and works from the "Golden Age" of Danish painting (1800–1850). A modern wing, designed by acclaimed Danish architect Henning Larsen, contains Impressionist paintings by Monet, Sisley, Pissarro, Gauguin, and works by David and Bonnard. The museum also has changing exhibitions.

Rådhuset ③

Rådhuspladsen. *Tel* 33 66 33 66.
🚇 København H. 🚌 2A, 5A, 6A,
14, 26, 29 & many others. ⭕ Sun,
public hols. 💷 in English with 💷
3pm Mon–Fri, 10am & 11am Sat.
♿ 🏠

At the edge of the Indre By (city center), in the middle of a wide open square, is the Baroque-style Rådhuset or City Hall, built in the early 1900s. A statue of Copenhagen's 11th-century founder, Bishop Absalon, sits above the entrance. Climb the 300-step staircase to the top of the bell tower for a view of the city. On the way, check out the First World Clock, a super-accurate timepiece with a 570,000-year calendar designed by Jens Olsen. It took 27 years to design, and was completed in 1955.

The modern, central atrium of Denmark's National Museum

National Museum ④

Ny Vestergade 10. *Tel* 33 13 44 11.
🚇 København H. 🚌 1A, 2A, 11A,
14, 15, 26, 29. ⭕ 10am–5pm Tue–
Sun. ⭘ Dec 24–25 & 31.
♿ 🏠 🍴 www.natmus.dk

Like so many of Denmark's museums, the National Museum contains beautifully presented exhibits. The extensive ethnographic and antiquities collections detail Danish history from prehistoric to modern times, and include some fascinating exhibits of Viking life.

Many of the items on display come from the Danish isles, such as items of jewelry, bones, and even several bodies found preserved in peat bogs, as well as imposing rune stones with inscriptions dating from around AD 1000. There is also a children's museum and a host of educational activities, all housed in the restored 18th-century royal residence. Close by, and part of the museum, is a Danish home with authentic interiors from the 1890s, complete with decorated panels and elaborately carved furniture (view by guided tour at 2pm on Saturday in summer only; book in main museum).

Christiansborg Palace ⑤

Slotsholmen. *Tel* 33 92 64 92. 🚌 1A,
2A, 15, 26, 29. ⭕ May–Sep: daily;
Oct–Apr: Tue–Sun. 💷 🏠 🖥 🏠
www.slotte.dk **Teatermuseet:**
Christiansborg Ridebane 18. *Tel* 33
11 51 76. ⭕ Tue–Thu, Sat & Sun.
⭘ Dec 23–Jan 1. 💷 **Thorvaldsen's
Museum:** Bertil Thorvaldsens Plads
2. *Tel* 33 32 15 32. ⭕ Tue–Sun.
💷 🖥 🏠

Situated on the island of Slotsholmen, the **Christiansborg Palace** has been the seat of the Danish Parliament since 1918, and also houses the Royal Reception Rooms, the Queen's Library, the Supreme Court, and the Prime Minister's Office. Built on the site of a fortress constructed in 1167 by Copenhagen's founder, Bishop Absalon, the palace has twice burnt down and been rebuilt, then altered and extended. Much of this work was carried out during the 18th century under Christian VI, whose elaborate visions were realized both in the architecture and in the lavish interiors. The current palace dates mostly from the early 20th century, and it is possible to visit the Royal Reception Rooms, the Harness Room, the Stables and Coach House, and some ruins from the original fortress.

Above the riding stables is the Royal Court Theater, built by Christian VI in 1767. Now a museum, much of it has been restored to its original 18th-century appearance. Exhibits illustrate the history of Danish theater up to the present day. The auditorium, with its plush, red furnishings and small, gold side boxes, houses a wealth of memorabilia – including costumes, old theater programs, wigs, and even old make-up boxes and a reconstructed dressing room. The whole theater is dominated, however, by the grand royal box, built for King Frederik VII in 1852. Situated at the back of the auditorium, it seems almost to upstage the stage itself. Unusually, the king's wife, the former ballet dancer Louise Rasmussen, had a private box to the right of the royal box, where she sat if she was alone.

Along the north side of the palace, the **Thorvaldsen's Museum** houses the work of the country's most celebrated sculptor, Bertel Thorvaldsen (1770–1844). After completing his education in Denmark, Thorvaldsen lived for nearly 40 years in Rome, where he gained a worldwide reputation. As well as his own impressive Neoclassical sculptures, the museum houses his collection of antiquities and 19th-century Danish art. There is also a detailed account of his life.

The Børsen, Copenhagen's beautiful old stock exchange

Børsen ⑥

Børsgade. 🚌 2A, 66.
🕐 to public.

Built in 1619–40 by King Christian IV, Denmark's old stock exchange is an architectural masterpiece. The building combines tiny windows, steep roofs, and decorative gables, and is topped by a spire representing four intertwined dragon's tails. Originally a marketplace, it became a commodities and stock exchange in the 19th century. Today the building is used as offices, since the modern stock exchange has long since moved to the Strøget. It is not open to the public.

Strøget ⑦

Frederiksberggade to Østergade. 🚉 København H, Nørreport. 🚌 1A, 2A, 11A, 15, 26, 29.

Running between Rådhuspladsen (city hall square) and Kongens Nytorv (King's New Square), Strøget (pronounced "Stroll") is the world's longest pedestrian street. Located at the center of a large traffic-free zone in the heart of the city, Strøget consists of five streets – Frederiksberggade, Nygade, Vimmelskaftet, Amagertorv, and Østergade. The area is home to several exclusive stores, including top international designers Hermes and Gucci. Other stores sell the best in Danish porcelain, modern design, glass, and furnishings – all areas in which Denmark has a world-class reputation.

The best selection can be found in the Royal Copenhagen shopping mall, facing Amagertorv, which includes Royal Copenhagen, Georg Jensen, and Illums Bolighus. There are also many bustling cafés and restaurants, street performers, and musicians, making it a lively place for walking or for relaxing with a coffee. The area is extremely popular with locals and visitors, particularly on a Saturday, but it is still possible to enjoy the atmosphere and admire the many surviving 18th-century buildings.

The impressive Christiansborg Palace, once a seat of royalty and now home to the Danish Parliament

Nyhavn ⑧

Kongens Nytorv. 🚌 *1A, 11A, 15, 26, 29, 3505.* 🚢 *901, 902.*

A narrow canal flanked by a wide promenade, Nyhavn (New Harbor) was originally built 300 years ago to attract trade. It leads up to the Kongens Nytorv (King's New Square). For much of its history the district was far from inviting, being mainly frequented by sailors, but after the 1970s the area was transformed. The harbor is lined either side with brightly painted town houses, a number of which date from the 18th century. Author Hans Christian Andersen lived in three of them (numbers 18, 20, and 67). Shops, restaurants, and bars have replaced all but one of the tattoo parlors that used to be here.

The attractive buildings, as well as the dozens of old wooden sailing ships moored on the water, make Nyhavn a lively and picturesque place to spend an hour or two enjoying a meal or a beer, at least in the summer months. It is also a good starting point for seeing the city, as some boat tours of Copenhagen's canals leave from here.

Nyhavn, Copenhagen's picturesque and popular harborside promenade

Changing of Queen Margrethe's guard, Amalienborg

Amalienborg ⑨

Amaliegade. **Tel** *33 12 21 86.* 🚇 *Østerport.* 🚌 *1A, 15, 19, 26, 29.* 🚢 *901, 902.* ☐ *May–Oct: daily; Nov–Apr: Tue–Sun.* 📷 *for museum.* 📷 *call in advance.* 🎖 **Changing of the guard:** *noon daily.* **www**.ses.dk

The Amalienborg (Amalia's Castle) consists of four identical Rococo buildings arranged symmetrically around a large cobbled square with an imposing equestrian statue of Frederik V in the middle. Changing of the guard takes place every day at noon outside the palace of the present queen, Margrethe II. The buildings have housed the Danish royal family since 1874, and two of them are open to the public. Christian VII's Palace is open for guided tours on weekends from July to September, while part of the palace serves as the museum of the Danish monarchy. It is home to part of the Royal Collection, the bulk of which is housed at Rosenborg Slot, and some of the official and private rooms are open to the public. The highlights are the study of King Christian IX (1818–1906) and the drawing room of his wife, Queen Louise, which are filled with family presents, photographs, and the occasional Fabergé treasure.

There are two attractive but contrasting views from the square. On the harborside is Amaliehaven (Amalia's Garden), dating from 1983 and with a fountain in its center; in the opposite direction is Marmorkirken, a white marble church officially known as Frederikskirken, which has one of Europe's largest domes, inspired by St. Peter's in Rome. Its construction was begun in 1749 with expensive Norwegian marble, but was not completed until 150 years later (with less expensive Danish limestone) owing to the huge costs incurred. Inside, the church is decorated with many frescoes and statues.

Little Mermaid ⑩

Langelinie. 🚇 *Østerport.* 🚌 *1A, 15, 26, then a short walk.* 🚢 *901, 902.*

The subject of many Danish postcards, the Little Mermaid (Den Lille Havfrue) has become the emblem of Copenhagen and is much visited by tourists. Sitting on a stone by the promenade at Langelinie, and looking out over the Øresund, she is difficult to spot from the road and smaller than her pictures would have you believe. Sculpted by Edvard Erichsen and first unveiled in 1913, this bronze statue was inspired by the Hans Christian Andersen character, who left the sea after falling in love with a prince. The mermaid has suffered over

Copenhagen's famous Little Mermaid

the years at the hands of mischievous pranksters, even losing her head and an arm. Happily, she is currently in possession of all her "parts."

For hotels and restaurants in this region see p686 and p687

Kastellet and Frihedsmuseet ⑪

Churchillparken. **Tel** *33 13 77 14.*
🚉 Østerport. 🚌 *1A, 15, 19, 26.*
🚌 *901, 902.* **Kastellet** 🔲 *daily.*
Frihedsmuseet 🔲 *Tue–Sun.*
☑ ♿

The grassy grounds of this fortress, built by Christian IV in the 16th century (and added to by his successors), are good for strolling around or sitting quietly by the moat. Currently occupied by the Danish army, its buildings are closed to the public, but near the south entrance is the Danish Resistance Movement Museum (Frihedsmuseet). This charts the German occupation of Denmark in World War II and the growth of the organization that saved more than 7,000 Jews from the Nazis by hiding them in "safe houses" and helping them escape to neutral Sweden.

Statens Museum for Kunst ⑫

Sølvgade 48–50. **Tel** *33 74 84 94.* 🚉
Nørreport, Østerport. 🚌 *6A, 26, 184, 185, 150S.* 🔲 *Tue–Sun.* ☑ ♿ 🖥

The extensive Statens Museum for Kunst (State Art Museum) holds Danish and European art from the 14th century to the present day. Among its many paintings and sculptures are works by Titian, Rubens, Rembrandt, El Greco, Picasso, and Matisse. Danish artists are particularly well represented in the new modern art wing. There is also a vast collection of prints and drawings.

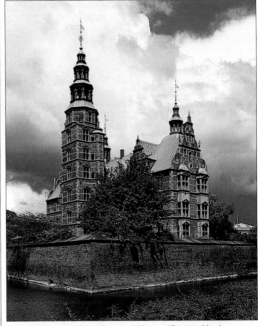

The enchanting Rosenborg Slot, set within magnificent parkland

Rosenborg Slot ⑬

Øster Voldgade 4A. **Tel** *33 15 32 86.*
🚉 Nørreport. 🚌 *11A, 6A.* 🔲 *May–Oct: daily; Nov–Apr: Tue–Sun.* ⚫ *Jan 1, end Dec.* ☑ ☑ 🖥 🏛 **www.** rosenborgcastle.dk

Originally built by Christian IV as a summer residence in 1606–7, the Rosenborg Slot was inspired by the Renaissance architecture of the Netherlands. The "builder king" continued to add to it over the next 30 years until the castle looked much as it does today – a playful version of a fortress. The interiors are particularly well preserved and its sumptuous chambers, halls, and ballrooms are full of objects including amber chandeliers, life-size silver lions, tapestries, thrones, portraits, and gilded chairs.

Two of the 24 rooms open to the public are stacked from floor to ceiling with porcelain and glass. The Porcelain Cabinet includes examples from the famous *Flora Danica* dinner service made for 100 guests, created by the Royal Copenhagen Porcelain factory between 1790 and 1803. The colorful Glass Cabinet houses nearly 1,000 examples of old Venetian glass as well as glass from the Netherlands, Bohemia, England, and most of the German glassworks.

Christiania ⑭

Bådsmandsstræde 43.
🚉 Christianshavn. 🚌 *66.*
🔲 *daily.* ☑ *for prebooked groups only.* **www**.christiania.org

Originally set up in 1971 on the site of a former military barracks, this "free town" is an enclave of an alternative lifestyle: colorful, anarchic, and self-governing. However, since 2004, there has been no open selling of drugs due to government pressure. Attractions include shops (one being the famous Christiania Bikes), a gallery, cafés, a restaurant, and a concert venue, as well as a lake.

Modern art wing of the Statens Museum for Kunst

Helsingør ❷

Zealand. 46,300.
🛈 Havnepladsen 3 (49 21 13 33).
www.visitnordsjaelland.com

Helsingør, or Elsinore, lies at the narrowest point of the Øresund, the waterway dividing Denmark and Sweden. Its attractive medieval quarter has many well-preserved merchants' and ferrymen's houses.

The town is dominated by the **Kronborg Slot** (Kronborg Castle), which stands on a spit of land overlooking the sea. Famous as the setting of *Hamlet*, the fortress actually dates from the 1500s, much later than Shakespeare's character would have lived. Highlights include the 62-m (210-ft) banqueting hall. A statue of the Viking chief Holger Danske slumbers in the castle cellars – according to legend he will awaken to defend Denmark if needed.

♣ **Kronborg Slot**
Kronborg. *Tel* 42 21 30 78. 840, 842. ☐ May–Sep: daily; Oct–Apr: Tue–Sun.

Frederiksborg Slot ❸

Hillerød, Zealand. *Tel* 48 26 04 39. to Hillerød, then bus 301, 302, 324. ☐ daily. www.frederiksborgslot.dk

One of Scandinavia's most magnificent royal castles, the Frederiksborg Slot is built across three small islands

The spires and turrets of the Kronborg Slot, Helsingør

surrounded by an artificial lake. Created as a residence for Frederik II (1559–88), the castle was rebuilt in the Dutch Renaissance style by his son, Christian IV (1588–1648).

The vaulted black marble chapel, where monarchs were once crowned, sits directly below the Great Hall, with its fine tapestries, paintings, and reliefs. The castle also houses the National History Museum.

Roskilde ❹

Zealand. 47,000.
🛈 Stændertorvet 1 (46 31 65 65).
www.visitroskilde.com

The settlement of Roskilde first came to prominence in AD 980, when a Viking king, Harald Bluetooth, built Zealand's first Christian church here. Once the center of Danish Catholicism, the town declined after the Reformation. Today it is a quiet town, except when it hosts northern Europe's largest annual music festival in the first weekend of July.

The **Roskilde Domkirke** stands on the site of Harald Bluetooth's original church. Begun by Bishop Absalon in 1170, the building is now a mix of architectural styles. The cathedral also functions as Denmark's royal mausoleum – some 39 Danish kings and queens are buried here.

Overlooking Roskilde Fjord is the **Vikingeskibsmuseet**. This Viking ship museum contains five reconstructed Viking ships, first built around AD 1000, excavated from the bottom of the fjord in 1962. In the waterside workshops Viking ship replicas are built using authentic period tools and traditional techniques.

🏛 **Vikingeskibsmuseet**
Vindeboder 12. *Tel* 46 30 02 00. ☐ daily. ⬤ Dec 24–25 & 31. in summer. ☒ call in advance.

Odense ❺

Funen. 167,600.
🛈 Rådhus, Vestergade (63 75 75 20).
www.visitodense.com

Looking like a storybook village, Odense is nevertheless Denmark's third-largest urban center. It lies at the heart of an area dubbed the "Garden of Denmark" for the variety of fruits and vegetables produced here. The town is most famous as the birthplace of Hans Christian Andersen.

Odense is easily explored on foot. The old town contains some fine museums, including three art museums, one of which is dedicated to photography. Odense's showpiece is the **Hans Christian Andersen Hus**, where the storyteller's life is detailed through drawings,

View from the outer courtyard of the Frederiksborg Slot

photographs, letters, and personal belongings. A library contains his works in more than 90 languages. The **H.C. Andersens Barndomshjem** (H.C. Andersen's Childhood Home) shows where the writer lived with his parents in a room measuring barely 2 m (6 ft) by 1.5 m (5 ft).

🏛 **Hans Christian Andersen Hus**
Bangs Boder 20. *Tel* 65 51 46 01. ⬤ mid-Jun–Aug: daily; Sep–mid-Jun: Tue–Sun. 🈺 ⬤ by prior arrangement only. **www**.odmus.dk

Half-timbered buildings at Den Gamle By outdoor museum, Århus

Århus ❻

Jutland. 👥 250,000. ✈ 44 km (27 miles) NE. 🚆 🚌 🚢 ⬤ Banegårdspladsen 20 (87 31 50 10). **www**.visitaarhus.com

Denmark's second city and Jutland's main urban center, Århus has a thriving culture scene, with a major art museum, ARoS, and an annual summer arts festival, Aarhus Festuge.

Århus divides clearly into two parts. The old town is a cluster of medieval streets with several fine churches. **Den Gamle By**, the city's open-air museum, consists of 60 or so half-timbered houses and a watermill, transported from locations all over Jutland and carefully reconstructed.

In the modern part of the city, the controversial **Rådhus** (City Hall) was built by Arne Jakobsen and Erik Møller in 1941. Its coating of pale Norwegian marble still provokes differing opinions to this day.

🏛 **Den Gamle By**
Viborgvej. *Tel* 86 12 31 88. ⬤ daily. ⬤ Jan 1, Dec 24–25 & 31. 🈺 ⬤ ⬤

Aalborg ❼

Jutland. 👥 122,000. ✈ 🚌 🚆 🚢 ⬤ Kjellerups Torv 5, Level 13 (99 31 75 00). **www**.visitaalborg.com

The port of Aalborg spreads across both sides of the Limfjord, which slices through the tip of the Jutland peninsula. Aalborg is the leading producer of the spirit aquavit, the fiery Danish national drink.

The well-preserved old town has several sights of interest, including the suitably dark and atmospheric dungeons of the town castle, the **Aalborghus Slot** (1539). The **Budolfi Domkirke**, a 16th-century Gothic cathedral, houses a collection of portraits depicting Aalborg merchants from the town's prosperous past.

The **Kunsten** (Museum of Modern Art Aalborg) houses a collection of Danish modern art, as well as works by foreign artists such as Max Ernst and Chagall.

On the edge of Aalborg is the important historical site of **Lindholm Høje**. Set on a hilltop overlooking the city, it contains more than 650 marked graves from the Iron Age and Viking Age (see p665). A museum depicting the history of the site stands nearby.

⬤ **Lindholm Høje**
Vendilavej. *Tel* 99 31 74 40. ⬤ daily. **Museum** ⬤ Apr–Oct: daily; Nov–Mar: Tue–Sun. 🈺 ⬤ ⬤ ⬤ ⬤

Legoland transportation – the colorful Lego train and monorail

Legoland ❽

Billund, Jutland. *Tel* 75 33 13 33. ✈ 🚆 to Vejle, then bus. ⬤ Apr–Oct: daily. 🈺 ⬤ ⬤ ⬤

The Legoland Billund theme park celebrates the tiny plastic blocks that have become a household name worldwide. The park opened in 1968, and more than 45 million Lego bricks were used in its construction.

Aimed primarily at 3–13 year olds, Legoland is divided into different zones. As well as Lego sculptures of animals, buildings, and landscapes, there are many rides and stage shows. Highlights include Miniland, a collection of miniature Lego towns that represent places around the world, and a driving track where children can take a safety test in a Lego car.

HANS CHRISTIAN ANDERSEN

Denmark's most internationally famous writer, Hans Christian Andersen (1805–75) was born in Odense, the son of a poor cobbler. Andersen was admitted to the University of Copenhagen in 1832, and the following year made his debut as an author with his first novel. Several plays and other novels followed but he remains best known for his children's fairy tales, published between 1835 and 1872. Andersen used everyday language, thus breaking with the literary tradition of the time. Some of his tales, such as "The Little Mermaid" (see p680), are deeply pessimistic and unhappy. A strong autobiographical element runs through these sadder tales; throughout his life Andersen saw himself as an outsider and he also suffered deeply in his closest relationships.

Statue of Hans Christian Andersen, Copenhagen

Practical & Travel Information

Visitors are always treated with courtesy and hospitality in Denmark; the Danes are one of the most tolerant nations in the world, and the Danish concept of *hygge* (coziness) makes the country a very comfortable place to stay. Denmark's travel facilities are plentiful, reliable, and easy to use. There is an extensive rail network and city public transportation services function efficiently. The capital, Copenhagen, is a compact city, which makes getting around by public transport quite straightforward. Since most Danes speak fluent English, you should have no problems with communication.

TOURIST INFORMATION

General and location-specific information on all parts of Denmark can be obtained from the **Danish Tourist Board**, which has offices in many countries worldwide, including the US and the UK. Visitors to the capital can obtain brochures, maps, and other useful information at the **Copenhagen Visitor Centre**.

OPENING HOURS

Many tourist attractions close on Mondays, and a few have seasonal opening hours. Stores are open 10am to 5:30pm Monday to Thursday, 10am to 7pm on Friday, and 9am to 2pm on Saturday, with Sunday openings becoming more frequent, especially in Copenhagen. Office hours are generally 9am to 4pm Monday to Friday.

VISA REQUIREMENTS

Visitors who are not citizens of a Scandinavian country require a valid passport to enter Denmark. Citizens of the EU may use a national identity card in lieu of their passport. No visa is required for visitors from the US, Canada, the UK, Ireland, Australia, or New Zealand.

SAFETY AND EMERGENCIES

Denmark is a peaceful country and street crime is rare, although travelers are advised to take out comprehensive travel insurance. Danish tourist offices and health offices have lists of doctors and local hospitals. For prescriptions (obtainable at a pharmacy or *apotek*) or a doctor's consultation, you will have to pay the full cost on the spot, but EU citizens can obtain a refund by taking their passport and European Health Insurance Card (EHIC) to a local health office.

BANKING AND CURRENCY

The Danish unit of currency is the krone (DKr), which is divided into 100 øre.

Danish banks usually open from 9:30am to 4pm Monday to Wednesday and Friday, and from 9:30am to 6pm on Thursday. For the most favorable exchange rates, change money and traveler's checks at a bank. Outside bank opening hours there are exchange booths at post offices, and most airports, main train stations, and ferry terminals. Major credit and charge cards are accepted in most places, and local currency can be obtained with credit or debit cards from cashpoint machines (ATMs).

COMMUNICATIONS

Public phone booths still exist, though there are far fewer than previously. Phone cards can be purchased from all post offices and kiosks.

Most post offices open from 10am to 6pm Monday to Friday, and 10am to 1pm on Saturday, although smaller branches may have restricted opening times.

Wi-Fi Internet is available in most hotels, some cafés, and on some trains (included in the price of a first-class ticket).

English-language newspapers are usually available the day after publication at train stations and many of the larger newsagents.

FLYING TO DENMARK

Most international flights arrive at Copenhagen's **Kastrup Airport**, 8 km (5 miles) from the city center. British Airways, easyJet, Norwegian, **Amber** and **SAS** (Scandinavian Airline System) operate direct flights from Britain. SAS also offers direct flights from New York; most flights from North America, however, require a stopover. Amber is the largest Danish domestic airline.

TRAVELING BY SEA

If you are considering traveling to Denmark by sea, **DFDS Seaways** operates a ferry service between Harwich in England and Esbjerg, on Denmark's west coast, three or four times a

THE CLIMATE OF DENMARK

The climate of Denmark is the least extreme of the Scandinavian countries, but the country's close proximity to the sea means that the weather can change very quickly. The summer months are generally sunny; temperatures in July can top 26° C (78° F). Winters are cold and rainy, although not severe, and there may be snow from December to February.

COPENHAGEN

°C/F	Apr	Jul	Oct	Jan
high	9/48	20/68	11/52	2/36
low	2/36	12/54	6/43	-1/30
sun (hrs)	5	8	3	1
rainfall (mm)	45	70	60	55

0°C / 32°F

week. The crossing takes around 20 hours. Special midweek offers are often available, which can cut the cost of travel considerably.

Norway and Sweden are also well connected to Denmark by sea. Ferries from Oslo call at Copenhagen, Hirtshals, and Frederikshavn, and journeys to Helsingør from Helsingborg in Sweden take just 15 minutes.

Ferries also link all the Danish islands and range in size from the car- and bus-carrying catamarans and ferries of **Mols-Linien**, which travel between Zealand and Jutland, to tiny vessels serving small settlements off the mainland and major islands.

RAIL TRAVEL

Like the rest of the public transportation system in Denmark, the trains are clean and reliable, and are by far the best way to get around. **Danish State Railways –** Danske Statsbaner (DSB) – operates an efficient network that covers most parts of the country, with the exception of Funen and northeast Jutland. In Copenhagen a local train

service, the **S-tog**, provides transportation between the city center and the surrounding areas, and as far as Hillered and Ishøj.

TRAVELING BY CAR

Car rental in Denmark is expensive. To rent a vehicle you must be at least 20 years of age, and hold an inter-national driver's license.

Driving in central Copen-hagen is not advisable due to the traffic and lack of parking.

The Danish authorities conduct random breath tests, and penalties for driving under the influence of alcohol are severe. The **Forenede Danske Motorejere (FDM)**, offers a breakdown service to Automobile Association (AA) members.

BUSES, TAXIS, AND BICYCLES

Buses are cheaper than trains, but on the whole are not com-fortable. However, they are useful for traveling to remote areas not covered by the train network. Copenhagen's **Movia Kundecenter** (customer ser-vices) has a bus information

hotline. Most taxi drivers speak English, but cabs are often expensive, especially at night and all day at weekends.

Cycling is an excellent way to enjoy Denmark's mostly flat landscape, since traffic is light on the country roads and most towns have cycle tracks. Bikes can be rented at most hotels, youth hostels, tourist offices, and bike stores, and at some train stations. In Copenhagen, **Kobenhavns Cykelbørs** is a reliable bike rental store. Contact the **Dansk Cyklist Forbund** (Danish Cycling Association) for more information.

SIGHTSEEING IN COPENHAGEN

If you plan to do a lot of sightseeing in Copenhagen, it is worth investing in a Copenhagen Card (valid for one, two, or three days). The card gives unlimited use of public transportation in the metropolitan area (including North Zealand), free or dis counted admission to many museums, as well as price reductions with certain car rental companies and on ferry crossings to Sweden.

DIRECTORY

TOURIST OFFICES

Copenhagen Visitor Centre
Vesterbrogade 4a,
Copenhagen V.
Tel 70 22 24 42.
www.visitcopenhagen.dk

Danish Tourist Board
www.visitdenmark.com

In Denmark:
Vesterbrogade 4a,
Copenhagen V.
Tel 70 22 24 42.

In the UK:
55 Sloane Street,
London SW1X 9SY.
Tel 020-7259 5959.
Fax 020-7259 5955.

In the US:
655 Third Avenue,
Suite 1810, New York.
Tel 212-885 9700.
Fax 212-885 9726.

EMBASSIES

Australia
Dampførgevej 26,
Copenhagen Ø. *Tel 70 26 36 76.* **www**.denmark.
embassy.gov.au

Canada
Kristen Bernikows Gade 1,
Copenhagen K. *Tel 33 48 32 00.* **www.**
canadainternational.gc.ca

Ireland
Østbanegade 21,
Copenhagen Ø. *Tel 35 47 32 00.* **www.**
embassyofireland.dk

UK
Kastelsvej 36–40,
Copenhagen Ø. *Tel 35 44 52 00.* **www.**
ukindenmark.fco.gov.uk

US
Dag Hammarskjölds Allé 24, Copenhagen Ø.
Tel 33 41 71 00.
http://denmark.
usembassy.gov

EMERGENCY NUMBERS

Ambulance, Fire and Police
Tel 112.

AIR TRAVEL

Kastrup Airport
Tel 32 31 32 31.
www.cph.dk

SAS
Tel 70 10 20 00 (Denmark).
Tel 0208-990 7067 (UK).
Tel 201-896-37 35 (US).
www.scandinaviaairlines.
com

FERRY SERVICES

DFDS Seaways
Tel 33 42 33 42 (Denmark).
Tel 0871-522 38 83 (UK).
www.dfdseaways.com

Mols-Linien
Tel 70 10 14 18 (Denmark).
www.mols-linien.dk

RAIL TRAVEL

Danish State Railways
Tel 70 13 14 15.
www.dsb.dk

S-tog Information
Tel 70 13 14 15.

ROAD TRAVEL

Dansk Cyklist Forbund
Tel 33 32 31 21.
www.dcf.dk

Forenede Danske Motorejere (FDM)
Tel 36 13 14 15.

Kobenhavns Cykelbørs
Gothersgade 157,
Copenhagen K.
Tel 33 14 07 17.
www.cykelboersen.dk

Where to Stay in Denmark

Although Denmark is less expensive to visit than either Sweden or Norway, a large chunk of a traveler's budget will still be spent on accommodations. However, most hotels offer discount rates for summer or weekend stays. As many Danish hotels are found in very old buildings, rooms can vary enormously, but are always clean.

PRICE CATEGORIES
Price categories are for a standard double room with bath or shower per night in high season including breakfast, tax, and service.
Ⓚ Under 750 DKr
ⓀⓀ 750–1,000 DKr
ⓀⓀⓀ 1,000–1,300 DKr
ⓀⓀⓀⓀ 1,300–1,800 DKr
ⓀⓀⓀⓀⓀ Over 1,800 DKr

COPENHAGEN

CENTRAL COPENHAGEN Danhostel Copenhagen City
H.C. Andersens Boulevard 50, 1553 **Tel** *33-11 85 85* **Fax** *33-11 85 88* **Rooms** *192*   **Map** *B4/C5*

Do not be deceived by the anonymous high-rise exterior: the interior furnishings and sleekly styled rooms would put most mid-level hotels to shame. Many of the rooms have superb views over the city. Facilities include an Internet café, comfortable TV lounge, laundry, and large kitchen. **www.danhostel.dk/copenhagencity**

CENTRAL COPENHAGEN Hotel Fox
Jarmers Plads 3, 1551 **Tel** *33-95 77 55* **Fax** *33-14 30 33* **Rooms** *61*   **Map** *B4*

Easily one of the most unusual hotels in the city, the Fox was fashioned by a group of graphic designers, street artists and illustrators. Their off-the-wall creations range from the ultra-minimalist (floor-to-ceiling white formica) to the fantastical (walls covered in outlandish murals). Friendly reception plus a sushi restaurant and cocktail bar. **www.hotelfox.dk**

CENTRAL COPENHAGEN Ibsens
Vendersgade 23, 1363 **Tel** *33-13 19 13* **Fax** *33-13 19 16* **Rooms** *118*

Set within a classic French-style apartment building, this modern boutique hotel has individually-styled rooms, ranging from modern Scandinavian to classical English, though all are modestly decorated. The hotel is hidden away in a narrow café-lined street close to Nansensgade – great for a night out. **www.ibsenshotel.dk**

CENTRAL COPENHAGEN Hotel d'Angleterre
Kongens Nytorv 34, 1050 **Tel** *33-12 00 95* **Fax** *33-12 11 18* **Rooms** *123*   **Map** *D4*

One of the most respected hotels in Copenhagen, the Angleterre has been in business for more than 250 years and remains the choice for visiting dignitaries. The rooms are very large, classic in decor, and filled with every amenity you could want. The queen's official residence is just around the corner. **www.dangleterre.dk**

CENTRAL COPENHAGEN Radisson Blu Royal Hotel
Hammerichsgade 1, 1611 **Tel** *33-42 60 00* **Fax** *33-42 61 00* **Rooms** *260*   **Map** *B4*

This is *the* original designer hotel. The entire place, inside and out, was designed in 1960 by Arne Jacobsen, including Swan and Egg chairs, a spiral staircase, and anodized doorknobs. The rooms are comfortable, up-to-date, and all have Internet access. **www.radissonblu.com/royalhotel-copenhagen**

REST OF DENMARK

AALBORG Helnan Phønix Hotel
Vesterbro 77, 9000 **Tel** *98-12 00 11* **Fax** *98-10 10 20* **Rooms** *210*

A major feature of the town, this historic hotel was built in 1783 as a palace to Brigadier William Von Halling and converted into a hotel just over 100 years later. Located in the heart of Aalborg, the hotel provides classic hospitality in an elegant setting. **www.helnan.info/helnan-phoenix-hotel**

ÅRHUS Best Western Hotel Ritz
Banegårdspladsen 12, 8000 **Tel** *86-13 44 44* **Fax** *86-13 45 87* **Rooms** *67*

Built in 1932 near to the town's Musikhuset (concert hall), theatres and restaurants, Best Western's Ritz has been redecorated and carefully refurbished in keeping with the original architecture. The hotel's steakhouse is one of the best in town. Access to the internet is available in the lobby. **www.hotelritz.dk**

ODENSE Hotel Ansgar
Østre Stationsvej 32, 5000 **Tel** *66-11 96 93* **Fax** *66-11 96 75* **Rooms** *74*

The rooms here boast plenty of classical charm thanks to their Italian-style chairs and window sashes. Catering to business and leisure travelers alike, the Ansgar's bar-restaurant offers a good dinner buffet, and there is Internet access in the lobby and rooms (Wi-Fi). **www.millinghotels.dk**

Key to Symbols *see back cover flap*

Where to Eat in Denmark

An evening meal can be expensive in Denmark, especially in the capital. Visitors are advised to have a hearty meal at lunchtime, when a few helpings of *smørrebrød* (Danish open sandwiches piled with meat, fish, cheese, and vegetables) will reduce the need for a large dinner – without reducing the size of your wallet.

PRICE CATEGORIES
The following price categories are for a three-course meal for one without alcohol or tip, but including tax:
Ⓚ Under 200 DKr
ⓀⓀ 200–250 DKr
ⓀⓀⓀ 250–350 DKr
ⓀⓀⓀⓀ 350–450 DKr
ⓀⓀⓀⓀⓀ Over 450 DKr

COPENHAGEN

CENTRAL COPENHAGEN Slotskælderen hos Gitte Kik   ⓀⓀ
Fortunstræde 4, 1065 **Tel** *33-11 15 37*   **Map** *C4*

Excellent, well-known lunch-only spot right by the Strøget that specializes in *smørrebrød*. Select what you want from behind the glass counters and they bring it to your table. Slotskælderen also serve good *frikadeller* (meatballs) and *sild* (herring). Popular with the parliamentarians who hold sessions nearby. Closed Sun, Mon.

CENTRAL COPENHAGEN Ida Davidsen   🏃 Ⓥ   ⓀⓀⓀ
Store Kongensgade 70, 1264 **Tel** *33-91 36 55*   **Map** *D3*

For a menu featuring more than 250 types of *smørrebrød*, made with the freshest ingredients by a family who have been making open sandwiches since 1888, head to Ida Davidsen's famous lunch restaurant. Book ahead because it is popular with locals and tourists alike – even Danish royals have dined here. Closed Sat, Sun; public hols & month of Jul.

CENTRAL COPENHAGEN Restaurant Cap Horn   Ⓥ   ⓀⓀⓀ
Nyhavn 21 3tv, 1051 **Tel** *33-12 85 04*   **Map** *D4*

Weathered walls, original wood floors, and an open fireplace are the setting for the Cap Horn's classic Danish menu, which focuses on regularly changing seafood and organic dishes. The organic theme extends to the beer, wine, and coffee. Service is fast and courteous and there is live jazz every Sunday along with brunch.

CENTRAL COPENHAGEN Koefoed   🏃 Ⓥ   ⓀⓀⓀⓀ
Landgreven 3, 1301 **Tel** *56-48 22 24*   **Map** *C3*

Located on a side street along from Store Kongensgade, Koefoed finds both inspiration and produce from the Danish-owned, Baltic island of Bornholm. Fresh produce sourced from the island includes meat as well as beers and wine, and the menu changes according to seasonal ingredients. Booking recommended. Closed Sun.

CENTRAL COPENHAGEN Noma   🍴 Ⓥ   ⓀⓀⓀⓀⓀ
Strandgade 93, 1401 **Tel** *32-96 32 97*

Noma is located on the waterfront in an old warehouse in Christianshavn and has created a reputation for using only seasonal, Nordic-sourced ingredients, resulting in a truly fascinating seven course menu that changes monthly. This place is booked up months in advance so reserve your table before leaving home.

REST OF DENMARK

AALBORG Duus Vinkælder   📋 🏃   ⓀⓀ
Østerågade 9, 9000 **Tel** *98-12 50 56*

Located in the cellar of the famous Jens Bang's Stenhus, this is a convivial restaurant and bar serving traditional Danish lunches and dinners. They are known for their delicious *frikadeller*, and in summer serve a wide variety of Danish *smørrebrød*. This place is full of character and makes a good stopping-off point while sightseeing.

ÅRHUS Navigator   ♿ 🏃   ⓀⓀⓀⓀ
Marselisborg Havnevej 46D, 8000 **Tel** *86-20 20 58*

A lively restaurant, decked out in cobalt blue and creamy white, serving well-cooked Danish-French staples in tune with the seasons. When the weather permits, there is an outdoor grill and salad bar. Dinner and dance evenings are on every Saturday. It is necessary to book in advance.

ODENSE Den Gamle Kro   🏃 Ⓥ   ⓀⓀⓀ
Overgade 23, 5000 **Tel** *66-12 14 33*

Set in a wonderful old building dating from 1683, this atmospheric restaurant is decorated with memorabilia from the past. Some of the more unexpected Danish dishes on the menu include smoked eel with scrambled eggs, and strawberries soaked in champagne. There are several dining rooms to choose from and a great wine cellar.

Map References see map of Copenhagen pp676–7

FINLAND

inland is perhaps the least known of the Nordic countries. Historically, geographically, and economically, the country straddles East and West, trading and maintaining links with both Western Europe and the former states of the Soviet Union. The Finnish have a strong sense of national identity, and are rightly proud of their beautiful unspoiled landscape of forest, lakes, coast, and islands.

About a third of Finland (*Suomi* in Finnish) is covered by native pine, spruce, and birch forests. Most of the rest is covered by water – an estimated 188,000 lakes, numerous rivers, and extensive areas of marshland. Finland's coastline is extremely indented and dotted with thousands of islands, most of which can be found in the archipelagos of the southwest. The land is generally flat, apart from mountainous areas in Lapland. About one third of the territory lies within the Arctic Circle, where the landscape is strikingly beautiful, if sometimes bleak.

Most of Finland's towns and cities are found in the southern coastal region, where they vie for space with extensive stretches of farmland. The lake district, at the heart of Finland, is not so populous, but industrialization of the area has been steadily increasing since the mid-20th century. Northern Finland is still fairly undeveloped, with small pockets of Finns inhabiting the south, while the Sami (the nomadic people of Lapland) are spread over the far north.

Although by nature modest and not very practised at marketing themselves, the Finns have achieved much economic success, excelling in the fields of technology and design. Nokia, the mobile phone giant, is Finland's best-known success story in global terms, although many people are unaware of the company's Finnish origins.

HISTORY

Little is known of early Finnish history, although it is believed that the ancestors of the Sami first arrived in Finland about 9,000 years ago. Another group, whose language evolved into modern Finnish, arrived some 3,000 years later. In the

A busy main street in central Helsinki

◁ Peaceful summer cottage in Finland's extensive Lakelands region

1st millennium BC the arrival of more groups, including the ancestors of the present-day Finns, forced the Sami to withdraw northwards to Lapland.

Even before the beginning of the Viking age (8th–11th century AD), Swedes had settled on the southwest coast of Finland, and in 1216 Finland became part of Sweden. Under Swedish sovereignty, the Finnish tribes gradually developed a sense of unity, which would later form the basis for a proud national identity.

From the 13th to the 18th centuries, Finland was a battleground for power struggles between Sweden and Russia. In 1809 Sweden ceded Finland to Russia, and the territory became an autonomous Grand Duchy of Russia. Helsinki was decreed the Finnish capital in 1812, and by the 1830s the transformation of this rocky fishing harbor into a major Baltic trading city was well underway.

When Czar Nicholas II unwisely removed Finland's autonomous status, a determination to achieve independence took root. This independence was finally won in 1917, aided by the maneuverings of General Carl Gustaf Emil Mannerheim (1867–1951). Mannerheim ousted the Russian soldiers still garrisoned in Finland and thus averted the immediate danger

Statue of General Mannerheim, architect of independence

that the fledging USSR might extend its Communist regime into the country. Finland's declaration of independence was finally recognized by the Soviet government on December 31, 1917.

Between the two world wars, Finland was dominated by a controversy over language. The Finns fought for the supremacy of their native tongue, and the use of Swedish declined sharply.

Despite its independent status, tensions between Finland and the Soviet Union remained throughout the early 20th century. Years of fear culminated in the 1939–40 Winter War against an invading Soviet army, swiftly followed by the "War of Continuation" (1941–44), in which Finland aided German troops against the Soviet Union. Deep suspicion of the Soviet Union continued for decades, but following the demise of the USSR in 1991, Finland reached a new agreement with Russia which pledged to end disputes between them peacefully.

In recent years, Finland has carved for itself a peace-brokering reputation, and has expanded economically through membership of the European Union and the efforts of its entrepreneurs.

LANGUAGE AND CULTURE

What began as a tentative linguistic and cultural exploration of Finnishness in the 19th century has evolved into a confident, outward-looking sense of nationhood. At the heart of Finnishness lies the notion of *sisu*, a kind of courage against the odds, but it also embraces everything in which the Finns take pride, such as the freedom to harvest berries and mushrooms in the forests.

Outdoor pursuits have an important place in the national psyche, especially cross-country skiing, swimming, boating, and cycling. Finland is also successful in some competitive sports, such as long-distance running and rally driving.

In the arts, the music of composer Jean Sibelius remains Finland's best known cultural export. Finnish architects and designers, in particular Alvar Aalto (1898–1976), are renowned worldwide.

KEY DATES IN FINNISH HISTORY

1155 First Swedish crusade to Finland

1216 Finland becomes a duchy of Sweden

1550 New market town of Helsinki established

1714 & 1721 Russia and Finland are at war

1748 Island fortress of Suomenlinna under construction to defend Finland against Russians

1809 Finland is separated from Sweden and becomes an autonomous Grand Duchy of Russia

1812 Helsinki becomes capital of Grand Duchy

1917 Declaration of independence

1939–44 Russia and Finland at war

1995 Finland joins the European Union

2000 Helsinki is European City of Culture and celebrates its 450th anniversary

2002 Finnish mark replaced by Euro

2006 Finland assumes EU presidency

2012 Helsinki is World Design Capital

Exploring Finland

After many years in the tourism wilderness, Finns are working hard to put their country on the map of world travel destinations. Wonderful natural amenities, a manageable and attractive capital city, and excellent public transportation make Finland an easy country to promote. Trains are the most convenient way to get around the country, although long-distance buses are often faster on east–west journeys. Destinations in the populous south are all easy to reach, but in the far north traveling takes more time and planning.

SIGHTS AT A GLANCE

FINLAND

NORWAY

0 km 150

0 miles 150

SWEDEN

RUSSIA

See main map

FINLAND

Turku

HELSINKI

Umeå

Kajaani

Kärsämäki

Kokkola

Iisalmi

Lieksa

Pielinen

F I N L A N D

Vaasa

Lapua

Kerele

Kuopio

Joensuu

Seinäjoki

Orivesi

Kurikka

23

Jyväskylä

Varkaus

14

Savonlinna

❸

Parkano

Jämsä

Päijänne

23

Mikkeli

R U S S I A

Pori

11

Saimaa

Lake Ladoga

Tampere

Imatra

Komemäki

12

Heinola

Rauma

Saaristomeri

Lahti

6

Lappeenranta

12

Forssa

3

25

Kouvola

St. Petersburg

❹

Åland

Salo

1

7

Kotka

Mariehamn

Turku ❷

51

HELSINKI ❶

Stockholm

Hankö

Tallinn

Gulf of Finland

St. Petersburg

Gulf of Bothnia

0 kilometers 100

0 miles 100

KEY

✈ International airport

⚓ Ferry port

━ Highway

━ Major road

━ Railroad

▪▪▪ International border

Lake Saimaa sightseeing cruise leaving Savonlinna

Helsinki ❶

Finland's capital since 1812, Helsinki is called the "White City of the North," a reference to the gleaming white Neoclassical buildings commissioned by its Russian rulers in the 19th century. It also boasts impressive modern architecture, from the copper, glass, and rock Temppeliaukio Church to the futuristic Kiasma center. The city is at its best in summer, when long days and clear light lift the mood of Finns, and the parks and waterfront cafés fill with lively crowds.

KEY

- ▢ Sight / Place of interest
- ⛴ Long-distance ferry
- ⛴ Local ferry
- 🚆 Train station
- Ⓜ Metro station
- 🚌 Bus station
- 🅿 Parking
- 🛈 Tourist information
- ✝ Church
- ✡ Synagogue
- ⸺ Pedestrian street

SIGHTS AT A GLANCE

Finlandia Hall ⑥
Helsinki Cathedral ④
Kiasma, Museum of
  Contemporary Art ⑤
Market Square ①
National Museum ⑦
Senate Square ③
Temppeliaukio Church ⑧
Uspenski Cathedral ②

Greater Helsinki
Suomenlinna Island Fortress ⑨

GETTING AROUND

The center of Helsinki is easily explored on foot. The city's efficient transportation network consists of buses, trams, and a metro system, although the latter is of limited use to tourists. Virtually all bus and tram routes converge on the streets around Helsinki Central Station. Suomenlinna Island Fortress can be reached by ferry only, from Market Square.

A   B   C

The National Museum of Finland, with its landmark tower

SEE ALSO

- *Where to Stay* p700
- *Where to Eat* p701

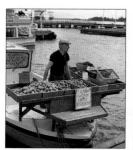

Stall holder moored alongside the quay at Helsinki's Market Square

Market Square ①

Head of South Harbor. 🚌 16. 🚊 1, 1A, 3B, 3T, 4. 🕐 6.30am–6pm Mon–Fri, 6:30am–4pm Sat, 9am–4pm Sun. ☀ Sun in winter.

In summer, a short season that must sustain a nation through a long winter, the people of Helsinki sun themselves in the cobbled Market Square (Kauppatori).

Finnish craftsmen sell handmade wares alongside fish, fruit, and vegetable stalls. Farmers will often travel for many miles by small wooden boat to sell fresh produce grown on their small holdings just like their forefathers did.

Among the fine buildings lining the square are the blue-painted **City Hall**, by Carl Ludwig Engel (1778–1840), and the 19th-century red- and yellow-brick **Old Market Hall**, containing several gourmet and specialist food shops.

Leading westward from Market Square is **Esplanadi** park, a favorite gathering place for Finns, who can be seen strolling down its wide boulevards. At the eastern end of the park is a bronze statue of a nude, *Havis Amanda* (1905) by Ville Vallgren, now a symbol of the city.

Uspenski Cathedral ②

Kanavakatu 1. *Tel* 09-634 267. 🚊 4. 🕐 Tue–Sun. ♿ ask for assistance.

With its dark red-brick exterior, this Russian Orthodox cathedral is a colorful landmark in the ubiquitous white of the historic city center. Its green

copper roof and gold "onion" domes make it highly visible on Helsinki's skyline.

Designed in the Byzantine-Russian architectural tradition by A.M. Gornostayev of St. Petersburg, the cathedral was built between 1862 and 1868. Uspenski is the biggest Russian Orthodox church in Scandinavia, and its spacious interior is resplendent in gold, silver, red, and blue. The terrace gives magnificent views over the heart of Helsinki, and the immediate area has been improved by converting old warehouses into shops and restaurants. The sheer exuberance of the building forms a sharp contrast to the Lutheran austerity of Helsinki Cathedral.

The red-brick exterior and "onion" domes of Uspenski Cathedral

Senate Square ③

🚊 1, 1A, 3B, 3T, 4, 7A, 7B. 🚌 16.

Senate Square (Senaatintori) is the masterpiece of Carl Ludwig Engel (1778–1840). It was built by Finland's Russian rulers in the early 1800s, and a statue of Czar Alexander II of Russia stands in the center.

The pleasing proportions of the square are best viewed from the top of the steps to Helsinki Cathedral. From here, the **Senate Building** lies to the left and the **University of Helsinki** to the right. Adjacent to the square is **Sederholm House** (1757), the oldest stone building in Helsinki.

The steep south-facing steps leading to the Neoclassical Helsinki Cathedral

most notable examples of Finnish National-Romantic architecture. The museum illustrates the history of Finland, from prehistory to the present day through a variety of artifacts. One of the highlights is the throne of Czar Alexander I from 1809.

The striking wall painting by Akseli Gallen-Kallela (1865–1931) in the entrance hall depicts scenes from Finland's national epic, a poem known as the *Kalevala*.

Helsinki Cathedral ④

Unioninkatu 29, Senaatintori.
Tel 09-234 0612. 🚋 1, 1A, 3B, 3T, 4, 7A, 7B. 🚌 16. ⬡ daily (Sun: pm only). ♿ call in advance.
Crypt ⬡ Jun–Aug: daily.

The five green cupolas of the gleaming white Lutheran Cathedral are a landmark on Helsinki's skyline. Designed by C.L. Engel, the Neoclassical building sits at the top of a steep flight of steps.

White Corinthian columns decorate the splendid exterior, while the inside is rather spartan. There are, however, statues of the 16th-century Protestant reformers Martin Luther, Philipp Melanchthon, the great humanist scholar, and Mikael Agricola, translator of the Bible into Finnish. Beneath the cathedral is a crypt, now used for concerts and exhibitions.

Kiasma, Museum of Contemporary Art ⑤

Mannerheiminaukio 2. *Tel* 09-173 36501. 🚌 🚋 3T & many routes.
⬡ 10am–8:30pm Wed–Fri, 10am–6pm Sat & Sun. ● public hols.
📷 ♿ 🖥 🛈 www.kiasma.fi

This glass and metal-paneled building, designed by American architect Steven Holl, was completed in 1998 at a cost of over 227 million Finnish markka. With its fluid lines and white interior, the museum is built in a curve to maximize natural light in the exhibition spaces.

Intended as an exhibition space for post-1960 art, Kiasma hosts mixed media

shows, art installations, contemporary drama, and art workshops. There is also a children's technological center.

The glass entrance to Kiasma, Museum of Contemporary Art

Finlandia Hall ⑥

Mannerheimintie 13E. *Tel* 09-402 410. 🚋 4, 7A, 7B, 10. 🚌 40. 📷 🛈 by arrangement. ♿
www.finlandiatalo.fi/en

Located in the tranquil setting of Hesperia Park, striking Finlandia Hall is one of architect Alvar Aalto's best-known works. Despite the hall's poor acoustics, it is a leading international concert venue, hosting regular performances by the Helsinki Philharmonic.

National Museum ⑦

Mannerheimintie 34. *Tel* 09-405 09 544. 🚌 40. 🚋 4, 10 & many routes.
⬡ 11am–8pm Tue, 11am–6pm Wed–Sun. ● public hols. 📷 ♿ 🛈 (by appointment). 🖥 🛈 www.nba.fi

Dating from the start of the 20th century, the National Museum is one of Helsinki's

Temppeliaukio Church ⑧

Lutherinkatu 3. *Tel* 09-234 06320. 🚋 3B, 3T. 🚌 14, 14B, 18, 24, 39, 39A. ⬡ daily. ♿

Built into a granite outcrop with walls of stone, this circular "Church in the Rock" is an astonishing piece of modern architecture. Consecrated in 1969, it is the work of architects Timo and Tuomo Suomalainen. The ceiling is an enormous, domed, copper disk, separated from the rough-surfaced rock walls by a ribbed ring of glass, which allows light to filter in from outside. The austere interior is relatively free of iconography and religious symbolism.

As well as being a major visitor attraction – some half a million people come to admire the church each year – this popular Lutheran place of worship is also used for organ concerts and choral music.

Interior of Temppeliaukio Church, with its copper and glass dome

Suomenlinna Island Fortress ⑨

🚢 from Market Square to residential area of island. **Tel** 09-684 1880. 📷 by appointment. ♿ limited. 🍴 📷

Constructed by the Swedes between 1748 and 1772, this island fortress is the biggest in Scandinavia, and is now a UNESCO World Heritage Site. Designed to defend the Finnish coast, Suomenlinna offered security to Helsinki's burghers and merchants, enabling the city to flourish. The fortress contains about 200 buildings, most of which date from the 18th century. Until the early 19th century, the fortress had more residents than Helsinki.

900 people still live on the islands which receive around 700,000 visitors a year who come to enjoy the cobbled castle courtyards and marinas. There are many eateries, galleries, and museums, including a doll and toy museum.

Turku ❷

👥 177,300. ✈ 🚉 🚌 🚢 🚢 👥 ℹ Aurakatu 4 (02-262 7444). 🎭 Medieval Market (late Jun–Jul), Music Festival (Aug). www.turkutouring.fi

Turku (Åbo in Swedish), a bustling port with a modern city center, was Finland's principal city during the sovereignty of Sweden, and remains the center of Finland's second language, Swedish.

Completed in 1300, **Turku Cathedral** is the principal place of worship for the Evangelical-Lutheran Church of Finland. The museum holds many ecclesiastical treasures.

Work on **Turku Castle** began in the late 13th century, but reached its prime in the mid-1500s with the addition of further rooms. The history of Turku and the castle are presented in the **Historical Museum of Turku**.

A double museum comprising **Aboa Vetus** and **Ars Nova** focus on life in medieval Turku and 20th-century Finnish and international art respectively.

Suomenlinna Island Fortress, the largest sea fortress in Scandinavia

Other attractions include the west bank of the River Aura and the indoor market. Archipelago steamship cruises are also available.

⛪ Turku Castle
Linnankatu 80. **Tel** 02-262 0300. ◐ Tue–Sun. ● public hols. 📷 in summer 🎭 🍴 📷 www.turunlinna.fi

🏛 Aboa Vetus and Ars Nova
Itäinen Rantakatu 4–7. **Tel** 02-250 0552. ◐ Apr–mid-Sep: daily; mid-Sep–Mar: Tue–Sun. ● public hols. 🎭 📷 ♿ (limited). www.aboavetusarsnova.fi

Environs
Just west of Turku lies **Naantali**, a popular seaside resort with cruises available from the harbor. **Moominworld**, a childrens' theme park based on Tove Jansson's creations is also here.

Moominworld
Naantali. 🚌 11, 110 from Turku. **Tel** 02-511 1111. ◐ Jun–Aug: daily; wlends for rest of Aug. 🎭 www.muumimaailma.fi

Exploring the courtyard of the late 13th-century Turku Castle

Savonlinna ❸

👥 29,000. 🚉 🚌 🚢 in summer. ℹ Puistokatu 1 (015-517 510). 🎭 International Opera Festival (Jul). www.savonlinnatravel.com

A good base from which to make excursions into the Saimaa Lakelands, Savonlinna also has charms of its own. Spread over several islands, the town boasts the castle of **Olavinlinna** (St. Olav's Castle), one of the best-preserved medieval castles in Scandinavia. The castle is home to the world-renowned Savonlinna International Opera Festival.

Founded in 1475, the castle consists of three towers and a bailey with an encircling wall reinforced by more towers. There are two museums: the **Castle Museum** illustrates the history of the castle, while the **Orthodox Museum** displays items of Russian Orthodox iconography from both Finland and Russia.

⛪ Olavinlinna
Tel 015-531 164. ◐ daily. ● some public hols. 📷 🎭 (free for children under 7). 📷

Environs
From Savonlinna harbor, steamships make excursions on Haapavesi and Pihlajavesi lakes, widely considered Finland's most beautiful scenery.

Rauhalinna Villa, in the village of Lehtiniemi, is half an hour by boat from Savonlinna. Open as a hotel-restaurant in the summer, this wooden manor house was built in 1900 by a lieutenant general of Czar Nicholas II as a wedding gift to his wife.

Side Trip to St. Petersburg ❹

Russia's second city, St. Petersburg is situated at the meeting of the Neva river and the Gulf of Finland, and is easily accessible from Helsinki by air, train, and boat. Founded in 1703 by Peter the Great and dubbed the "Venice of the North", the city comprises a bewitching mix of grand Neoclassical and Baroque architecture, sparkling waterways, and majestic bridges. Nearby, the extravagant imperial palaces of Peterhof and Czarskoe Selo offer an insight into the excesses of Czarist days.

Exploring St. Petersburg
The southern bank of the Neva is lined with stately palaces, and opposite, over the Troitskiy Most, sits the Peter and Paul Fortress. To the west lies Sennaya Ploschad, an area of pretty tree-lined canals and to the east is the Gostinyy Dvor, where shops, bars, and cafés line Nevskiy prospekt. The center is easily explored by foot but a boat trip is one of the highlights of a visit.

Nevskiy Prospekt ①

Ⓜ *Nevskiy Prospekt, Gostinyy Dvor.*

Russia's most famous street, Nevskiy prospekt, is also St. Petersburg's commercial hub. Laid out in the early days of the city, today the street teems with people late into the night.

The western stretch contains a wealth of fine buildings including the Baroque Stroganov Palace. Farther east, there are growing numbers of cafés and bars as well as three historic shopping arcades.

The Church on Spilled Blood, covered in colorful mosaics

Russian Museum ②

Inzhenernaya ulitsa 4. *Tel* 595 4248.
Ⓜ *Nevskiy Prospekt, Gostinyy Dvor.*
🚌 *3, 7, 22, K-128, K-129, K-169.*
◯ *Wed–Mon.* 🖼 ♿ *phone for details.* 🎧 *English (314 3448 to book).* **www**.rusmuseum.ru

One of Carlo Rossi's finest Neoclassical creations, the Mikhaylovskiy Palace is the splendid setting for a truly outstanding collection of Russian art, ranging from medieval icons to the latest painting, sculpture, and applied art. The palace was built in 1819–25 for Grand Duke Mikhail Pavlovich. Alexander III's plans to create a public museum were realized by his son Nicholas II when the Russian Museum opened here in 1898. The grand staircase and White Hall are original features.

Church on Spilled Blood ③

Konyushennaya ploshchad. *Tel* 315 1636. Ⓜ *Nevskiy Prospekt, Gostinyy Dvor.* ◯ *Thu–Tue.* 🖼 📷 🎧

The Church on Spilled Blood, also known as the Resurrection Church of Our Savior, was built on the spot where on March 1, 1881 Czar Alexander II was assassinated. His successor, Alexander III, launched a competition for a permanent memorial. The winning design, in the Russian Revival style, was by Alfred Parland and Ignatiy Malyshev.

A riot of color, the overall effect of the church is created by the imaginative juxtaposition of materials that are lavished on the building, including 7,000 sq m (75,300 sq ft) of mosaics.

The Hermitage ④

Dvortsovaya nab 30–8. *Tel* 710 9079. 🚌 *7, 10, T-228, K-147, K-209.* ◯ *Tue–Sun.* 🖼 ♿ 🎧 *English (571 8446 to book).*

Occupying a grand ensemble of imperial buildings including the impressive Winter Palace, the Hermitage houses one of the world's greatest collections of art and artifacts. Ranging from Egyptian mummies to a dazzling array of Old Master and Impressionist paintings, it is essential to be selective.

The golden dome of St Isaac's Cathedral, visible across the city

St. Isaac's Cathedral ⑤

Isaakievskaya ploshchad. *Tel* 315 9732. Ⓜ *Nevskiy Prospekt, Sadovaya.* 🚌 *3, 10, 22, 27, K-169, K-180, K-190, K-252, K-289.* ◯ *Thu–Tue.* 🖼 🎧

St. Isaac's, one of the world's largest cathedrals, was designed in 1818 by the then unknown architect Auguste de Montferrand. The construction of the colossal building was a major feat of engineering. Thousands of wooden piles were sunk into the marshy ground to support its 300,000 tonnes. The cathedral opened in 1858 but was designated a museum of atheism during the Soviet era. Officially still a museum today, the church is filled with hundreds of impressive 19th-century works of art.

For hotels and restaurants in this region see pp700–1

The Mariinskiy Theater, one of Russia's most important cultural institutions

Mariinskiy Theater ⑥

Teatralnaya ploshchad. *Tel 346 4141.*
📧 3, 22, 27. 🕐 daily; shows at 11:30am & 7pm. 🎭 ⁊
www.mariinsky.ru

This theater has been home to the world-famous Mariinskiy (Kirov) Opera and Ballet Company since 1860. Hidden behind its imposing façade is the sumptuous auditorium where many of Russia's greatest dancers have performed. Named in honor of Czarina Maria Alexandrovna, wife of Alexander II, the building was erected in 1860 by the architect Albert Kavos who designed the Bolshoy Theatre in Moscow.

SS Peter and Paul Fortress ⑦

Petropavlovskaya krepost.
Ⓜ Gorkovskaya. **Cathedral**
Tel 232 9454. 🕐 Thu–Tue. 🎭 ⁊ English. www.spbmuseum.ru.

The founding of the Peter and Paul Fortress on May 27, 1703, on the orders of Peter the Great, is considered to mark the founding of the city. Its history is a gruesome one, since hundreds of forced laborers died while building the fortress and its bastions were later used to guard and torture many political prisoners, including Peter's own son Aleksey. The cells where prisoners were kept are open to the public, alongside a couple of museums and the magnificent

cathedral which houses the tombs of the Romanovs.

Environs

Just a 45-minute trip by hydrofoil from the Hermitage, Peter the Great's sprawling Baroque residence, **Peterhof**, is a must-see when staying in the city for a few days. Designed by Jean Baptiste Le Blond, and built 1714–23, the palace lies at the center of a magnificent landscaped park complete with ornamental ponds and spurting fountains. Altogether, a perfect expression of imperial triumphalism.

Tsarskoe Selo, the lavish palace built for Czarina Elizabeth also lies within easy reach. Designed by Rasterelli in 1752, the 300-m (980-ft) long blue, gold, and white façade is a glitteringly striking sight.

⚓ Peterhof
Petrodvorets, 30 km (19 miles) W of St. Petersburg. *Tel 420 0073.* 🚆 from Baltic Station to Novy Petergof then bus 348, 350, and others. 🚢 board outside the Hermitage (May–Oct). 🕐 Tue–Sun. ⚫ last Tue of month. 🎭 ⚓ ⁊

⚓ Tsarskoe Selo
25 km (16 miles) S of St. Petersburg. *Tel 465 2024.* 🚆 from Vitebsk Station to Detskoe Selo, then bus 371 or 382. 🕐 Wed–Mon. ⚫ last Mon of month. 🎭 ⁊

CENTRAL ST PETERSBURG
Church on Spilled Blood ③
The Hermitage ④
Mariinskiy Theater ⑥
Nevskiy Prospekt ①
Russian Museum ②
SS Peter and Paul Fortress ⑦
St Isaac's Cathedral ⑤

0 meters 500
0 yards 500

Key to Symbols *see back flap*

Practical & Travel Information

The Finnish are a practical people, and tourists can expect the local information services to be both accurate and helpful. Finland's main cities are all served by an efficient railroad system and regular, inexpensive internal flights. Finns take pride in their public transportation systems and promote environmentally friendly modes of travel. Cycling and walking in summer and cross-country skiing in winter are an in-built part of the national psyche. The capital, Helsinki, is easy to navigate on foot, by bicycle, or using public transportation.

TOURIST INFORMATION

For general and location-specific information, get in touch with the **Finnish Tourist Board**, which has offices in major cities all over the world. The Finnish Tourist Board office in Helsinki has information about different parts of Finland in several languages. Helsinki, Turku, and Savonlinna all have a local tourist office.

The best time to visit Finland is between May and September, but winter in northern Finland has its own special, snow-laden charm. Many tourist attractions in Finland close on Mondays, and some have seasonal opening hours.

VISA REQUIREMENTS

Visitors who are not citizens of Norway, Denmark, Sweden, or Iceland must have a passport to enter Finland. Members of most EU countries may use an official EU identity card in lieu of their passport. Visas are not required for visitors from the UK, Ireland, the United States, Canada, Australia, or New Zealand. At Finnish customs, there is a blue channel for citizens of EU countries.

SAFETY AND EMERGENCIES

Finland has very low crime statistics, although drunks (largely harmless) have been a common sight in Finnish towns and cities for years. Mosquitoes are very active during the summer months near water (which is just about everywhere), but their bites do not carry disease. Tap water is safe to drink.

In case of emergencies the appropriate number to call is listed in the Directory opposite.

LANGUAGE

Finland has two official languages – Finnish, which is spoken by 94 percent of the population, and Swedish, which is spoken by 6 percent. Road signs and maps are often in both languages and there are different national newspapers for each language,

too. Younger Finns invariably speak some English, and are very eager to practise it.

BANKING AND CURRENCY

The Finnish currency unit is the euro (see p15). All euro notes and coins are exchangeable in each of the participating Eurozone countries.

Banks usually open from 9:15am to 4:15pm Monday to Friday. Most international credit cards are accepted in many places all over Finland.

COMMUNICATIONS

Post offices in Finland usually open from 9am to 6pm Monday to Friday, although the main post office in Helsinki operates longer hours. You can buy stamps from kiosks and bookstores, as well as at post offices.

Public telephones are found in thousands of locations, and are usually always well maintained. Many take phonecards, available at kiosks and post offices.

SAUNAS

Many hotels have a sauna, but they are usually electric ones. For a memorable sauna experience, seek out a wood-fired sauna – preferably close to a lake or the sea – or a traditional "smoke sauna" (savusauna). The sauna is a popular and family-friendly place in which to relax and unwind – there are over a million in Finland. Helsinki boasts the superb Kotiharjun wood-fired sauna (call 09-753 1535). The Finnish Sauna Society has two wood-fired saunas and three smoke saunas set beside the sea (call 09-686 0560 for more information).

FLYING TO FINLAND

Most international flights arrive at Helsinki's **Vantaa Airport**, which is 19 km (12 miles) north of Helsinki. **Finnair** and British Airways both operate daily scheduled services from London Heathrow to Helsinki. Some special "visit Father Christmas" winter flights

THE CLIMATE OF FINLAND

In northern Finland (beyond the Arctic Circle), the sun remains above the horizon for a month in summer. This gives Finland its sobriquet "Land of the Midnight Sun." Even in Helsinki, there are almost 20 hours of daylight in summer. In winter, the average temperature falls well below 0° C (32° F), but low humidity makes the extreme cold less raw.

HELSINKI

° C/F	Apr	Jul	Oct	Jan
	7/45	21/70	7/45	
	0/32	11/52	-2/36	-3/27
				-8/18
☀ (hrs)	9	10	8	7
☂ (mm)	38 mm	74 mm	74 mm	41 mm
month	Apr	Jul	Oct	Jan

fly direct from the UK to Rovaniemi on the Arctic Circle. KLM and SAS operate regular flights from Amsterdam and Copenhagen respectively to Helsinki. Travel from North America to Helsinki usually involves connecting flights (changing in Greenland or in Europe) but Finnair flies direct from New York to Helsinki.

ARRIVING BY SEA

The luxury ferries that ply the waters between Stockholm in Sweden and the Finnish ports of Helsinki and Turku have a reputation for offering a state-of-the-art cruising experience. The superliners – operated by **Silja Line** and **Viking Line** – take about 13 hours to make the crossing, which allows plenty of time to enjoy shopping, entertainment, and the celebrated *smörgåsbord* buffets.

RAIL TRAVEL

Finland's national rail network is run by the State Railroads of Finland (Valtion Rautatiet or VR). Finnish trains are reliable and clean. Advance reservations are recommended for long-distance, intercity (IC), and some express (EP) trains. In Helsinki, tickets can be bought either at **Helsinki Central Station** or from **TourShop**, which is located at the Helsinki City Tourist Office.

TRAVELING BY BUS

Buses in rural areas are infrequent (but reliable), while intercity buses are fast and efficient. Long-distance journeys are very time-consuming, so it is worth considering the relatively inexpensive domestic flights.

TRAVELING BY CAR

Car rental has come down in cost since Finland joined the EU. Even so, car hire using the main inter-national agencies is still pricey. **Europcar** offers some of the more reasonable rates.

Laws about driving under the influence of alcohol are strict and rigidly enforced, as are speed restrictions. Elk and reindeer are a serious road danger, so do pay attention to animal hazard signs.

GETTING AROUND HELSINKI

Helsinki is manageable on foot or by bicycle, but buses, trams, and the metro provide easy alternatives. The 3T tram circles central Helsinki, stop-ping at several important sights. Cycle tours, city walks, and cruises are all available from the TourExpert office. Taxis are an expensive way of getting around; ask the driver for an idea of the cost before you embark on your journey.

Finland's island-hopping passenger motorcruisers are a fun form of transportation, giving a real taste of relaxed Finnish summer living.

If you plan to visit several attractions, it is worth investing in a Helsinki Card (available from the Helsinki City Tourist Office and from most hotels). Valid for one, two, or three days, the Card gives unlimited travel on public transportation and on some ferries, reductions on some theater, dance, and opera tickets, and free admission to all major Helsinki sights and nearly 50 museums. Other benefits include reductions on sightseeing tours and on goods in some shops.

Another option is the Helsinki City Transport tourist ticket, which entitles you to unlimited travel on all buses, trams, the metro, and local trains in Helsinki. The ticket is valid for one, three, or five days and is available at all Helsinki City Transport (HKL) points and tourist offices.

DIRECTORY

TOURIST INFORMATION

Finnish Tourist Board
www.mek.fi
www.visitfinland.com

In Finland:
Töölönkatu 11,
FIN-00101 Helsinki.
Tel 010-605 8000.

In the UK:
PO Box 33213,
London W6 8JX.
Tel 020-7365 2512.

In the US:
PO Box 4649, Grand Central Station, New York, NY 10163.
Tel 212-885 9700.

Helsinki City Tourist Office
Pohjoisesplanadi 19,
FIN-00099 Helsinki.
Tel 09-3101 3300.
www.visithelsinki.fi

EMBASSIES

Canada
Pohjoisesplanadi 25b,
Helsinki.
Tel 09-228 530.
www.dfait-maeci.gc.ca

UK
Itäinen Puistotie 17,
Helsinki. *Tel 09-2286 5100.*
www.britishembassy.gov.uk

US
Itäinen Puistotie 14b,
Helsinki. *Tel 09-616 250.*
www.usembassy.fi

EMERGENCIES

Ambulance, Police, and Fire
Tel 112.

AIR TRAVEL

Finnair
Tel 0600-140 140 (Finland).
Tel 0870-241 4411 (UK).
Tel 800-950 5000 (US).
www.finnair.com

Vantaa Airport
Tel 0200-14636.
www.helsinkivantaa.fi

FERRY SERVICES

Tallink Silja Line
Tel 02-335 266.
www.silja.fi

Viking Line
Tel 0600-415 77.
www.vikingline.fi

RAIL TRAVEL

Helsinki Central Station
Tel 0600-41 902 or 0307-10. www.vr.fi

TourShop
Tel 09-2288 1500 (Finland).

CAR RENTAL

Avis
Tel 09-859 8333.

Budget
Tel 09-686 6500.

Europcar
Tel 040-306 2444.

Hertz
Tel 0200-11 22 33.

Where to Stay in Finland and St. Petersburg

Finns are very keen on sleek, modern hotels. As a result, Helsinki offers plenty of middle-range and upscale hotels. Prices often include a morning sauna and swim. In St. Petersburg, central hotels mainly fall into two categories: large and luxurious or smaller bed and breakfasts.

PRICE CATEGORIES
Price categories are for a standard double room per night in high season, including breakfast, tax, and service. Prices for St. Petersburg are in US dollars.

€ Under €65 (under $100)
€€ €65–€135 ($100–$175)
€€€ €135–€200 ($175–$250)
€€€€ €200–€270 ($250–$325)
€€€€€ Over €270 (over $325)

HELSINKI

CENTRAL HELSINKI Stadion Hostel

W   €

Stadiontie 4, 00250 **Tel** *09-477 8480* **Rooms** *24*   **Map** *B2*

Stadion Hostel, located right by the Olympic Stadium and National Opera, offers a low-cost way to stay in central Helsinki. The rooms are plain, but pleasant, although the larger shared dorms can be noisy. There's a shared kitchen as well as a reasonably priced breakfast buffet. **www.stadionhostel.fi**

CENTRAL HELSINKI Sokos Vaakuna

€€€

Asema-Aukio 2, 00100 **Tel** *020-1234 610* **Rooms** *270*   **Map** *C4*

Centrally located by the Central Railway Station, this lovely building, built in 1952, is one of the most stylish chain hotels in Finland. Rooms are furnished in dark woods and have very comfortable beds. The top floor restaurant, where breakfast is served, has great views of Helsinki's rooftops. **www.sokoshotels.fi**

CENTRAL HELSINKI Kämp

€€€€€

Pohjoisesplanadi 29, 00100 **Tel** *09-576 111* **Rooms** *179*   **Map** *C4*

Founded in 1887, this Belle Epoque property is one of Helsinki's most outstanding hotels, and only one of two in the city with five stars. Many of the rooms are 19th-century style but with modern amenities and opulent marble bathrooms with separate bath and walk-in shower. The breakfasts here are divine. **www.hotelkamp.fi**

REST OF FINLAND

SAVONLINNA Seurahuone

€€€

Kauppatori 4–6, 57130 **Tel** *020-7571 350* **Rooms** *84*

This modern establishment has rooms spread across two wings – one traditional, one more modern. The decor is a little bland but the hotel is reliable and the staff friendly and courteous. Rooms in the new wing have views over Lake Saimaa. Air-conditioning is only in some rooms. **www.savonlinnanseurahuone.fi**

TURKU Omena Hotelli

€

Humalistonkatu 7, 20100 **Tel** *020-7716 555* **Rooms** *75*

Finland's new chain of self-service hotels has finally arrived in Turku. This unique establishment has no receptionist: bookings are made either online or at the kiosk downstairs. The ultra-modern rooms have all the necessary amenities and very comfortable beds. Easily the best hotel deal in the city. **www.omenahotels.com**

ST. PETERSBURG

GOSTINYY DVOR Pushka Inn

$$$

Naberezhnaya reki Moyki 14 **Tel** *312 0913* **Fax** *312 1055* **Rooms** *31*

This historic building, right on the river Moyka and next door to the Pushkin Museum, has been transformed into a comfortable, modern hotel. The decor is basic but you will struggle to find anything closer to the Hermitage. There are four apartments or family suites. **www.pushkainn.ru**

PALACE EMBANKMENT Astoria

$$$$$

Isaakievskaya ploschad, Bolshaya Morskaya ulitsa 39 **Tel** *494 5757* **Fax** *495 5059* **Rooms** *223*

The Astoria retains a historic charm. Rooms at the front offer outstanding views over St. Isaac's Cathedral and Square, and along the river Moyka. Those who cannot afford to stay here can still soak up the historic surroundings by taking tea in the lounge. **www.thehotelastoria.com**

Key to Symbols *see back cover flap*

Where to Eat in Finland and St. Petersburg

Eating out used to be a prohibitively expensive experience for tourists in Finland, but a wider range of restaurants means that even city-center dining now caters for all budgets. In St. Petersburg many restaurants serve a fixed-price "business lunch" that proves good value.

PRICE CATEGORIES
Price categories are for a three-course meal for one, including a glass of house wine, tax, and service. Prices for St. Petersburg are in US dollars.

€ Under €15 (under $25)
€€ €15–€25 ($25–$40)
€€€ €25–€35 ($40–$60)
€€€€ Over €55 (over $60)

HELSINKI

CENTRAL HELSINKI Zetor €€€
Mannerheimintie 3, 00100 **Tel** *010-766 4450*   **Map** C4

Owned by Finnish icons the Kaurismäki brothers, this quirky late-night restaurant complete with a rusty tractor is typified by sawdust on the floors and a meat-and-potato centric menu. Food is served until 3:30am, along with music and a late night bar.

CENTRAL HELSINKI Romanov €€€€
Yrjönkatu 15, 00120 **Tel** *09-642 394*   **Map** C4

One of Helsinki's most respected Russian restaurants, the rooms here are decked out with portraits and photos of Csars and aristocrats. The food is rich with steak and fish dishes among the mains, as well as classic Russian dishes such as borscht and blini. A Helsinki classic well worth the price and dressing up for.

CENTRAL HELSINKI Strindberg €€€€
Pohjoisesplanadi 33, 00130 **Tel** *09-612 86900*   **Map** C4

With its Parisian bistro feel, this café-restaurant is one of the best-loved and most central cafés in the capital – a perfect place for people-watching on weekend mornings. Downstairs, the café offers tasty pastries for breakfast, as well as very good coffee. Upstairs, the upscale restaurant features reindeer, Rydberg steak, and Baltic fish dishes.

REST OF FINLAND

SAVONLINNA Hilpeä Munkki €€
Riihisaari, 57100 **Tel** *020-7291 760*

This summertime outdoor restaurant is located right next to the Olav castle, making it the perfect place to dine before or after an opera performance. The atmosphere is reminiscent of a medieval inn, with animal skins and candlelit tables. Food is traditional Finnish, with great broiled steak fillet, lamb and sausage dishes.

TURKU Viikinkiravintola Harald €€€€
Aurakatu 3, 20100 **Tel** *022-765 050*

The decor here makes this restaurant one of the most interesting places to eat in Turku. A Viking theme reigns with wooden benches and animal heads on the wall. The food consists largely of hearty meat dishes such as venison braised in wine with garlic. There is a great and inexpensive lunch buffet.

ST. PETERSBURG

GOSTINYY DVOR Kavkaz-Bar $$$
Karavannaya ulitsa 18 **Tel** *312 1665*

Caucasian (Georgian and Armenian) cuisine, and excellent Georgian wines and brandies are on offer here – at a price. Kavkaz-Bar has a superb location close to Nevskiy prospekt, and an intimate atmosphere. It also serves the best vegetarian kebabs in town. A selection of dishes is available in the less formal outer café, overlooking a quiet square.

PALACE EMBANKMENT 1913 $$
Voznesenskiy prospekt 13 **Tel** *315 5148*

Named after the last year of Russian imperial greatness, 1913 prides itself on generous portions and outstanding regional dishes such as *draniki* (potato pancakes) with bacon, and sorrel soup, as well as lobster dishes. A warm atmosphere reigns with a singer and guitarist performing Russian songs from 8pm daily. Excellent service.

Map References *see map of Helsinki pp692–3*

CENTRAL AND EASTERN EUROPE

Central and Eastern Europe at a Glance

At the geographical heart of mainland Europe, Hungary, Poland, and the Czech Republic have witnessed a huge surge in visitor numbers since the end of Communism in the late 1980s and early 1990s. Despite the widespread destruction caused by two world wars, their towns and cities retain a wealth of historic monuments, many of which have been painstakingly restored to their former glory. Fortunately, tourism has not destroyed the unique cultural identity of these once little-known countries.

Słupsk

Szczecin

Poznań

Prague
(see pp710–21), *the capital of the Czech Republic, is a vibrant city with a rich architectural and cultural heritage. The hilltop castle complex is dominated by the magnificent St. Vitus's Cathedral, whose treasures include many royal tombs.*

Wrocław

Karlsbad

PRAGUE

Kutná Hora

Plzeň

CZECH REPUBLIC
(See pp706–727)

Olomouc

Český Krumlov

Bohemia (see pp722–3) *holds the greatest appeal for most foreign visitors to the Czech Republic. The region boasts elegant spas, fairy-tale castles perched high on thickly wooded hillsides, and many perfectly preserved medieval towns, such as Český Krumlov in the far south.*

Győ

Balatonfü

Péc

Lake Balaton (see p738), *a huge freshwater lake in western Hungary, is the country's most popular summer vacation destination. Bordered by dozens of resorts, it offers beaches, safe bathing, and water sports, and also provides a habitat for a wide variety of flora and fauna.*

◁ **Charles Bridge and buildings of the Old Town in Prague, Czech Republic**

Gdańsk

Augustów •

LOCATOR MAP

• WARSAW

POLAND
(See pp744–761)

Warsaw (see pp748–53) *was largely rebuilt during the Communist era following complete destruction in World War II. Many of its grandest buildings date from the Baroque period, including the splendid Royal Castle.*

• Cracow

Cracow (see pp754–7), *in southern Poland, has historic monuments spanning hundreds of years, and has been declared a UNESCO World Heritage Site. Its skyline is dominated by dozens of churches, the most important being the Gothic St. Mary's Church in Market Square.*

• Eger

• BUDAPEST

HUNGARY
(See pp728–743)

| 0 km | 75 |
| 0 miles | 75 |

Budapest (see pp732–7) *is rich in historical treasures, from medieval ruins to late 19th- and early 20th-century Secessionist buildings. Mátyás Church preserves some of its original Gothic features, such as the glorious stone carving on the Mary Portal.*

CZECH REPUBLIC

The Czech Republic is one of Europe's youngest states. In the years after World War II, foreign visitors to what was then Czechoslovakia rarely ventured farther than the capital, Prague. Today the country's beautifully preserved medieval towns and castles are attracting an ever-increasing number of tourists.

The Czech Republic is divided into two regions, Bohemia and Moravia. Rolling plains and lush, pine-clad mountains, dotted with medieval chateaux and 19th-century spa resorts, characterize the landscape of southern and western Bohemia. In spite of the recent influx of tourists, life here still proceeds at a gentle, relaxed pace. In contrast, much of northern Bohemia has been given over to mining and other heavy industry, with devastating effects on the local environment. Moravia has orchards and vineyards in the south, and a broad industrial belt in the north of the region.

Bohemia's largest city and the capital of the Czech Republic, Prague is a thriving cultural and commercial center that bears little relation to most people's expectations of an "Eastern" European city. Its wealth of magnificent architecture, spanning over a thousand years, has withstood two world wars in the last century.

Since the early 1990s the Czech Republic has emerged as a relatively healthy democratic state. Its economy has been boosted by tourism. The country is a member of NATO and it held presidency of the EU in 2009.

HISTORY

From 500 BC the area now known as the Czech Republic was settled by Celtic tribes, who were later joined by Germanic peoples. The first Slavs, the forefathers of the Czechs, came to the region around 500 AD. Struggles for supremacy led to the emergence of a ruling dynasty, the Přemyslids, at the start of the 9th century. The Přemyslids were involved in many bloody family feuds. In 935 Prince Wenceslas was murdered by his brother, Boleslav. Later canonized, Wenceslas became Bohemia's best-known patron saint.

The reign of Holy Roman Emperor Charles IV in the 14th century heralded a Golden Age for Bohemia. Charles

Rooftops of Prague's Malá Strana (Little Quarter), covered in snow

◁ The medieval Karlstein Castle, rising above picturesque wooded valleys in Bohemia chose Prague as his imperial residence and founded many prestigious institutions there, including central Europe's first university.

In the early 15th century, central Europe shook in fear of an incredible fighting force – the Hussites, followers of the reformer Jan Hus, who preached in Prague and attacked the corrupt practices of the Catholic Church. His execution for heresy in 1415 led to the Hussite wars. The radical wing of the Hussites, the Taborites, were finally defeated at the Battle of Lipany in 1434. At the start of the 16th century the Austrian Habsburgs took over, beginning a period of rule that would last for almost 400 years. Religious turmoil led, in 1618, to the Protestant revolt and the 30 Years' War. The end of the war ushered in a period of persecution of all non-Catholics and a systematic Germanization of the country's institutions.

Engraving showing the radical cleric Jan Hus being burnt at the stake

The 19th century saw a period of Czech national revival and the burgeoning of civic pride. But, a foreign power still ruled, and it was not until 1918 and the collapse of the Habsburg Empire that the independent republic of Czechoslovakia was declared. World War II brought German occupation, followed by four decades of Communism. In 1968, a program of liberal reforms was introduced, known as the "Prague Spring"; the reforms were swiftly quashed by Soviet leaders, who sent in troops to occupy the country. The overthrow of Communism did not come until 20 years later: in November 1989 a protest rally in Prague against police brutality led to the "Velvet Revolution" – a series of mass demonstrations and strikes that resulted in the resignation of the existing regime. The most recent chapter in Czech history was closed in 1993 with the peaceful division of Czechoslovakia into two independent states – Slovakia and the Czech Republic.

KEY DATES IN CZECH HISTORY

500 BC Celts in Bohemia and Moravia. Joined by Germanic tribes in 1st century AD

AD 500–600 Slavs settle in the region

867 Dynasty of Přemyslids founded

880 Přemyslids build Prague Castle

1333 Charles IV makes Prague his home, marking the start of the city's Golden Age

1415 Jan Hus burnt at the stake for heresy; start of the Hussite Wars

1526 Habsburg rule begins with Ferdinand I

1576 Accession of Habsburg Emperor Rudolf II

1618 Protestant revolt leads to the 30 Years' War

1627 Beginning of Counter-Reformation committee in Prague

19th century Czech National Revival

1918 Foundation of Czechoslovakia

1948 Communist Party assumes power

1989 Year of the "Velvet Revolution"; Communist regime finally overthrown

1993 Czechoslovakia ceases to exist; creation of the new Czech Republic

2004 Czech Republic joins the EU

2009 Presidency of the EU

LANGUAGE AND CULTURE

Under the Habsburgs, Czech identity was largely suppressed and the Czech language became little more than a dialect, mainly spoken among the peasant population. In the 19th century, however, Austrian rule relaxed, and the Czechs began rediscovering their own culture. The first history of the Czech nation was written by the Moravian František Palacký, and Czech was re-established as an official language.

Since the Golden Age of the 14th century Prague has prided itself on its reputation as a flourishing cultural center. In the early 20th century the city had a Cubist movement to rival that of Paris. The Czech Republic has produced writers, artists, and musicians of world renown including Franz Kafka, Alfons Mucha, and Antonín Dvořák.

Exploring the Czech Republic

One of Europe's most beautiful capital cities, Prague is undoubtedly the highlight of a visit to the Czech Republic. Away from this bustling, cosmopolitan city, however, the tranquil Bohemian countryside is home to dozens of castles and historic towns, whose appearance has remained virtually unchanged for hundreds of years. Most of the main sights of interest can be visited on a day trip from Prague, and are easily reached from the capital by good public transportation and road networks. Slightly farther afield, Český Krumlov merits at least a couple of days' exploration.

Prague's Charles Bridge and the buildings of the Old Town

SIGHTS AT A GLANCE

Český Krumlov **5**
Karlsbad **4**
Karlstein **2**
Kutná Hora **3**
PRAGUE pp710–21 **1**

KEY

✈ Airport
— Highway
— Major road
— Railroad
--- International border

Prague ①

Prague, capital of the Czech Republic, has a
population of just over one million. In the late
Middle Ages, during the reign of Charles IV, Prague's
position as the crossroads of Europe aided its growth
into a magnificent city, larger than Paris or London.
In the 16th century the Austrian Habsburgs took over
and built many of the Baroque palaces and gardens
that delight visitors today. Some of these palaces
now house important museums and galleries.
Prague's Jewish Quarter has a handful of synagogues
and a cemetery, which remarkably survived the Nazi
occupation. Despite neglect under Communist rule,
the historic center of the city has been preserved.

**The Three Fiddles, an old
house sign in Nerudova Street**

KEY

⬛	Sight / Place of interest
Ⓜ	Metro station
🚊	Tram stop
🚋	Funicular station
⛴	Riverboat boarding point
🅿	Parking
ℹ	Tourist information
✚	Church
✚	Synagogue
—	Pedestrian street

SIGHTS AT A GLANCE

Charles Bridge ⑪
Church of St. Nicholas ⑨
Golden Lane ⑤
Municipal House ⑯
National Theater ⑱
Nerudova Street ⑧
Old Jewish Cemetery ⑬
Old-New Synagogue ⑫
Old Town Hall ⑮

Old Town Square ⑭
Royal Garden and Belvedere
Royal Palace ②
St. George's Convent ③
Schwarzenberg Palace ④
St. Vitus's Cathedral ①
Sternberg Palace ⑦
Wallenstein Palace ⑩
Wenceslas Square ⑰

GETTING AROUND

Prague's subway, known as the metro, is the fastest way of getting around the city. It has three lines, A, B, and C, and 57 stations. Line A covers all the main areas of the city center. Trams are the city's oldest method of public transport. There are also a number of night trams. Routes 14, 17, 18, and 22 pass many major sights on both banks of the Vltava.

SEE ALSO

- *Where to Stay* p726
- *Where to Eat* p727

Corner of Old Town Square, with the Church of St. Nicholas

NA FRANTIŠKU

Klášter sv. Anežky
St Agnes's Convent

NÁMĚSTÍ
CURIEOVÝCH

U MILOSRDNÝCH

JOSEFOV
JEWISH QUARTER

Rudolfinum

NÁMĚSTÍ JANA
PALACHA

Staroměstská

Mánesův most

Náměstí
Republiky

Masarykovo nádraží
(train station)

CELETNÁ

OVOCNÝ
TRH

MARIÁNSKÉ
NÁMĚSTÍ

MALÉ
NÁMĚSTÍ

Klementinum

KARLOVA

PLATNÉŘSKÁ

ANENSKÉ
NÁMĚSTÍ

BETLÉMSKÉ
NÁMĚSTÍ

STARÉ MĚSTO
OLD TOWN

NA PŘÍKOPĚ

NEKÁZANKA

Můstek

V CIPU

VÁCLAVSKÉ
NÁMĚSTÍ

Můstek

Můstek

Hlavní nádraží
(train station)

NÁRODNÍ

NÁRODNÍ
třída

Můstek

Národní muzeum
National Museum

VÁCLAVSKÉ
NÁMĚSTÍ

Muzeum

NOVÉ MĚSTO
NEW TOWN

Novoměstská radnice
New Town Hall

ŽITNÁ

LEGEROVA

ČELAKOVSKÉHO
SADY

SMETANOVO NÁBŘEŽÍ

MASARYKOVO NÁBŘEŽÍ

MYSLÍKOVA

0 meters 400
0 yards 400

D E F

Street-by-Street: Prague Castle

The history of Prague begins with the castle, founded by Prince Bořivoj in the 9th century. Despite periodic fires and invasions, it has retained churches, chapels, halls, and towers from every period of its history, from the Gothic splendor of St. Vitus's Cathedral to the Renaissance additions of Rudolph II, the last Habsburg to use the castle as his principal residence. The courtyards date from 1753–75, when the whole area was rebuilt in Late Baroque and Neoclassical styles. The castle became the seat of the Czechoslovak president in 1918, and the current president of the Czech Republic has an office here.

★ **Royal Palace**
The uniform exterior of the palace (see p714) conceals many fine Gothic and Renaissance halls. Coats of arms cover the walls and ceiling of the Room of the New Land Rolls.

The Powder Tower was used in the past for storing gunpowder and as a bell foundry. It is now a museum.

To Royal Garden

★ **St. Vitus's Cathedral**
This stained-glass window by Alfons Mucha is one of many 20th-century works of art added to the cathedral.

The Picture Gallery of Prague Castle, in the restored stables of the castle, has a good collection of Renaissance and Baroque paintings.

President's office

To Hradčanské náměstí (Castle Square) and Schwarzenberg Palace

KEY

– – – Suggested route

0 meters 60

0 yards 60

Matthias Gate (1614)

Church of the Holy Rood

Steps down to Little Quarter

STAR SIGHTS

★ St. Vitus's Cathedral

★ St. George's Basilica

★ Royal Palace

South Gardens
Various gardens have been laid out along the old ramparts overlooking the Little Quarter. These statues date from the 18th century.

Dalibor Tower
This grim 15th-century tower takes its name from the first man imprisoned in it, a young knight sentenced to death for harboring outlawed serfs.

Golden Lane *(see p714)*
is lined with picturesque artisans' cottages, built in the late 16th century for the Castle's guards and gunners.

White Tower

Steps down to
Malostranská
metro

The Lobkowicz Palace
dates from 1570. Some original *sgraffito* has been preserved on the façade.

St. George's Convent *(see p714)* houses a collection of 19th-century Czech art and art from Bohemia.

★ **St. George's Basilica**
The vaulted chapel of the royal Bohemian martyr St. Ludmilla is decorated with 16th-century paintings.

THE DEFENESTRATION OF 1618

On May 23, 1618, more than 100 Protestant nobles stormed the Royal Palace to protest against the succession of the Habsburg Archduke Ferdinand. The two Catholic Governors, Jaroslav Martinic and Vilém Slavata, were confronted and thrown out of the eastern window along with their secretary, Philipp Fabricius. Falling some 15 m (50 ft), they landed in a dung heap. This event signaled the beginning of the Thirty Years' War. The Catholics attributed the survival of the Governors to the intervention of angels.

St. Vitus's Cathedral ①

Prague Castle, third courtyard.
Ⓜ *Malostranská.* 🚋 22 to
Prague Castle (Pražský hrad).
◯ *daily (except during services).*
♿ **Steeple** ◯ daily. ◉ *in bad weather.* 📷 📷

Work began on the city's most distinctive landmark in 1344 on the orders of John of Luxembourg. The Gothic cathedral replaced an earlier Romanesque basilica that stood on the site of a small rotunda dating back to the time of St. Wenceslas (c.925). The first architect of the new Gothic structure was the Frenchman Matthew of Arras. After his death, the Swabian Peter Parler took over. The eastern end of the cathedral dates from this period. The original entrance was the Golden Portal on the south side of the building. The present entrance, the western end of the nave, and the façade with its twin spires were added in 1873–1929.

The chapels house many saintly relics, the Bohemian crown jewels, and a number of royal tombs. The tomb of "Good King" Wenceslas stands in the St. Wenceslas Chapel, which is decorated with Gothic frescoes. Another spectacular memorial is the huge silver tomb (1736) of St. John Nepomuk, whose cult was encouraged during the Counter-Reformation.

Spectacularly vaulted chancel of St. Vitus's Cathedral

Royal Palace ②

Prague Castle, third courtyard.
Tel *22-43 72 423.* M *Malostranská.*
🚇 *22.* ⭕ *daily.* 📷 ✔ ♿
www.hrad.cz

From the time Prague Castle
was first fortified in stone in
the 11th century, the Royal
Palace was the seat of a long
line of Bohemian kings.
  The building consists of
three different architectural
layers. A Romanesque palace,
built around 1135, forms the
basement of the present structure. Over the next 200 years,
two further palaces were built
above this – the first by
Přemysl Otakar II in 1253, and
the second by Charles IV in
1340. On the top floor is the
massive Gothic Vladislav Hall,
with its splendid rib vaulting.
Designed for King Vladislav
Jagiello, it was completed in
1502. The Riders' Staircase,
just off the hall, is a flight of
steps with a magnificent Gothic
rib-vaulted ceiling. It was
used by knights on horseback
to get to jousting contests.
  Under Habsburg rule, the
palace housed government
offices, courts, and the old
Bohemian parliament. The
Bohemian Chancellery, the
former royal offices of the
Habsburgs, is the site of the
famous 1618 defenestration
(see p713). In 1619 the Bohemian nobles deposed Emper-
or Ferdinand II as King of
Bohemia, electing in his place
Frederick of the Palatinate.
This led to the first major battle
of the Thirty Years' War.

Cannons lined up outside Schwarzenberg Palace

St. George's Convent ③

Prague Castle, Jiřské náměstí.
Tel *25–75 31 644.* M *Malostranská.*
🚇 *22.* ⭕ *daily.* 📷 ✔
www.ngprague.cz

Bohemia's first convent was
founded here in 974 by Prince
Boleslav II. Rebuilt over the
centuries, it was finally abolished in 1782 and converted
into barracks. Today, the convent holds the National Gallery's collection of 19th-century
Czech art. The collection,
chosen as an artistic mirror to
19th-century Bohemian society,
features paintings from luminaries such as Josef Navrátil,
the Mánes family, and Jakub
Schikaneder, plus sculpture
from Josef Václav Myslbek. The
collection is interspersed with
decorative art from the period.
  Adjoining the convent, **St.
George's Basilica** was founded
by Prince Vratislav in 920 and
is the best-preserved Romanesque church in Prague. The
huge twin towers and austere
interior have been restored to
give an idea of the church's
original appearance.

Schwarzenberg Palace ④

Prague Castle, Hradčanské náměstí 2.
Tel *22–48 10 758.* M *Malostranská.*
🚇 *22.* ⭕ *daily.* 📷
www.ngprague.cz

Built in the 16th century for
the Count of Lobcowicz, the
noble Schwarzenberg family

acquired the palace in 1719
by marriage. It is considered
to be one of the best preserved Renaissance buildings
in Prague. Its facades are
decorated with black and
white *scraffitto* dating back
to 1580; inside, preserved
ceilings have valuable
examples of Renaissance
figurative painting.
  The palace houses the
National Gallery permanent
exhibition, Baroque Art in
Bohemia. Sculpture and
paintings from the late Renaissance and Baroque periods
include Petr Brandl's *Simeon
and the Infant Jesus* (1725)
and works by Matyáš Bernard
Braun, Ferdinand Maximilián
Brokof, and Karel Škréta.

Golden Lane ⑤

M *Malostranská.* 🚇 *22.*
⭕ *daily.* 📷 www.hrad.cz

Named after the goldsmiths
who lived here in the 17th
century, this is one of the
most picturesque streets in
Prague. The tiny, brightly
painted houses that line one
side of it were built in the late
1500s for Rudolf II's castle
guards. A century later the
goldsmiths moved in. By the
19th century the area had
degenerated into a slum,
populated by Prague's poor
and the criminal community.
In the 1950s the area was
restored to something like its
original state, and most of the
houses were converted into
shops selling books, Bohemian
glass, and other souvenirs for
the tourists who flock here.

**The Riders' Staircase leading to the
Vladislav Hall, Royal Palace**

Golden Lane has been home to a number of well-known writers, including Franz Kafka (1883–1924), who stayed at No. 22 for a few months between 1916 and 1917.

Royal Garden and Belvedere ⑥

Prague Castle, Královský Letohrádek. M *Hradčanská, Malostranská.* 22. **Garden** ◯ *May–Oct: daily.* **Belvedere** ◯ *only for exhibitions.* www.hrad.cz

Prague's well-kept Royal Garden was created in 1535 for Ferdinand I. The garden contains some fine examples of 16th-century architecture, including the Belvedere, a beautiful arcaded summer-house with slender Ionic columns and a blue-green copper roof. Also known as the Royal Summer Palace (Královský letohrádek), the Italian Renaissance building was commissioned in the mid-16th century for Ferdinand's wife. It is now used as an art gallery. In front of it is the Singing Fountain, which owes its name to the musical sound the water makes as it hits the bronze bowl.

Also in the garden is the Ball Game Hall (Míčovna), built in 1569, and used primarily for playing a form of real tennis.

At the entrance to the garden, the Lion Court was where Rudolph II had his zoo (now a restaurant).

Artisans' cottages on Golden Lane, Prague Castle

Sternberg Palace ⑦

Hradčanské náměstí 15. **Tel** *23-30 90 570.* M *Hradčanská, Malostranská.* 22 to Brusnice or Prague Castle. ◯ *Tue–Sun.* www.ngprague.cz

Franz Josef Sternberg founded the Society of Patriotic Friends of the Arts in Bohemia in 1796. Fellow noblemen would lend their finest pictures and sculpture to the society, which had its headquarters in the early 18th-century Sternberg Palace. Since 1949 the fine Baroque building has been used to house the National Gallery's collection of European art.

The palace has an impressive array of exhibits, including some particularly fine examples of Italian medieval art, Neapolitan works of the 17th and 18th centuries, Dutch and Flemish masterpieces, and Austrian and German art of the 15th to 17th centuries. The 19th- and 20th-century exhibits, including works by Klimt, Picasso, and Miró, were moved to the Veletržní Palace, northeast of the city center, in 1996.

The palace boasts many masterpieces; among the highlights are Albrecht Dürer's *The Feast of the Rosary* (1506), *Head of Christ*, painted by El Greco in the 1590s, and Rembrandt's *Scholar in his Study* (1634).

Visitors can also see art from ancient Greece and Rome, a collection of Renaissance bronzes, as well as the fascinating Chinese Cabinet, a richly decorated chamber, which combines the Baroque style with Far Eastern motifs.

The Belvedere, Emperor Ferdinand I's summer palace in the Royal Garden beside Prague Castle

Malá Strana

Malá Strana (the Little Quarter) is the part of Prague that has been least affected by recent history. Hardly any new building has taken place here since the 18th century, and the quarter is rich in splendid Baroque palaces and churches, and old houses with attractive signs. Founded as a town in 1257, the area is built on the slopes below the castle, enjoying magnificent views across the river to the Old Town. The center of Malá Strana is Little Quarter Square, dominated by the impressive Church of St. Nicholas.

Cupola and bell tower of the Church of St. Nicholas

Sign of Jan Neruda's house, At the Two Suns, 47 Nerudova Street

Nerudova Street ⑧

Ⓜ *Malostranská.* 🚊 *12, 20, 22.*

This narrow picturesque street is named after the 19th-century writer Jan Neruda, who wrote many short stories set in this part of Prague. He lived in the house known as At the Two Suns (No. 47) between 1845 and 1857.

Before the introduction of house numbers in 1770, the city's houses were distinguished by signs. Nerudova's houses have a splendid selection of heraldic beasts and emblems. Ones to look for in particular

are the Red Eagle (No. 6), the Three Fiddles (No. 12), the Golden Horseshoe (No. 34), the Green Lobster (No. 43), and the White Swan (No. 49).

Nerudova Street also has a number of grand Baroque buildings, including the Thun-Hohenstein Palace (No. 20) – now the Italian embassy – and the Morzin Palace (No. 5) – home of the Romanian embassy. The latter has an interesting facade featuring two massive statues of Moors.

Church of St. Nicholas ⑨

Malostranské náměstí. *Tel 25 75 34 215.* Ⓜ *Malostranská.* 🚊 *12, 20, 22.* ⭕ *daily.* 🈲 🎫
www.psalterium.cz

Dominating Little Quarter Square, at the heart of Malá Strana, is the Church of St. Nicholas. Begun in 1702, it

is the acknowledged master-piece of architects Christoph and Kilian Ignaz Dientzenhofer, who were responsible for the greatest examples of Jesuit-influenced Baroque architecture in Prague. Neither lived to see the completion of the church – their work was finished in 1761 by Kilian's son-in-law, Anselmo Lurago.

Among the many works of art inside the church is Franz Palko's magnificent fresco, *The Celebration of the Holy Trinity*, which fills the 50-m (165-ft) high dome. A fresco of St. Cecilia, patron saint of music, watches over the church's splendid Baroque organ. Built in 1746, it was played by Mozart in 1787. Another star feature is the ornate 18th-century pulpit, lavishly adorned with golden cherubs. The impressive statues of the Church Fathers, which stand at the four corners of the crossing, are the work of Ignaz Platzer, as is the statue of St. Nicholas that graces the high altar.

Wallenstein Palace ⑩

Valdštejnský Palác, Valdštejnské náměstí 4. *Tel 25 70 75 707.* Ⓜ *Malostran-ská.* 🚊 *12, 18, 20, 22.* **State Rooms** ⭕ *10am–5pm Sat–Sun.* **Riding school** ⭕ *for exhibitions.* 🦽 **Garden** ⭕ *Apr–Oct: daily.*
www.senat.cz

The first large secular building of the Baroque era in Prague, this palace was commissioned by the imperial military

The superbly ornamented Baroque organ in the Church of St. Nicholas

commander Albrecht von Wallenstein (1581–1634). His victories in the 30 Years' War made him vital to Emperor Ferdinand II. Already showered with titles, Wallenstein started to covet the crown of Bohemia. He began to negotiate independently with the enemy, and in 1634 was killed on the Emperor's orders by mercenaries.

Wallenstein's intention was to overshadow even Prague Castle with his vast palace, built between 1624 and 1630. The magnificent main hall has a ceiling fresco of the commander portrayed as Mars, riding in a triumphal chariot. The palace is now used by the Czech Senate, but the State Rooms are open to the public.

Dotted with bronze statues and fountains, the gardens are laid out as they were when Wallenstein resided here. The Grotesquery is an unusual feature – an imitation of the walls of a cave, covered in stalactites. There is also a fine frescoed pavilion. The old Riding School is today used for National Gallery exhibitions.

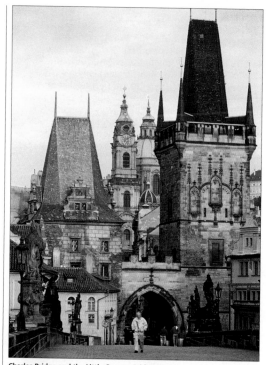

Charles Bridge and the Little Quarter Bridge Tower

Charles Bridge ⑪

Ⓜ *Staroměstská (for Old Town side).* 🚊 *12, 20, 22 to Malostranské náměstí (for Little Quarter side); 17, 18 to Staroměstská (for Old Town side).* **Little Quarter Bridge Tower** ⬜ *daily.* 🎟 **Old Town Bridge Tower** ⬜ *daily.* 🎟

One of the most familiar sights in Prague, the Charles Bridge (Karlův Most) connects the Old Town with the Little Quarter. Although it is now pedestrianized, at one time it took four carriages abreast. The bridge was commissioned by Charles IV in 1357 after the Judith Bridge was destroyed by floods.

The bridge's original decoration consisted of a simple wooden cross. In 1683 a statue of St. John Nepomuk – the first of the many Baroque statues that today line the bridge – was added. The vicar general Jan Nepomucký was arrested in 1393 by Wenceslas IV for having displeased the king. He died under torture and his body was thrown from the bridge. A number of finely worked reliefs depict the martyrdom of this saint, who was revered by the Jesuits as a rival to Jan Hus.

Between 1683 and the latter half of the 19th century several more statues were erected. Sculpted by Matthias Braun at the age of 26, the statue of St. Luitgard is regarded as one of the most artistically remarkable.

Another splendid piece of decoration, the 17th-century Crucifixion bears the Hebrew inscription "Holy, Holy, Holy Lord," paid for by a Jew as punishment for blasphemy.

At the Little Quarter end of the bridge stand two bridge towers. The shorter of these is the remains of the Judith Bridge and dates from the early 12th century. The taller pinnacled tower was built in 1464. It offers a magnificent view of the city, as does the late 14th-century Gothic tower at the Old Town end.

The vast 17th-century Wallenstein Palace and its gardens

Old-New Synagogue ⑫

Built around 1270, this is the oldest synagogue in
Europe, and one of the earliest Gothic buildings
in Prague. The synagogue has survived fires, the slum
clearances of the 19th century, and many Jewish
pogroms. Residents of the Jewish Quarter have often
had to seek refuge within its walls, and today it is still
the religious center for Prague's Jews. It was originally
called the New Synagogue, until another synagogue
was built nearby – this was later destroyed.

Right-hand Nave
*The glow from the bronze
chandeliers provides light
for worshippers using
the seats lining
the walls.*

★ Jewish Standard
*The historic banner of Prague's
Jews is decorated with a Star of
David, within which is depicted
the hat that had to be worn by
Jews in the 14th century.*

**14th-century
stepped brick
gable**

These windows
formed part of the
18th-century extension,
built to allow women
a view of the service.

Candlestick holder

★ Five-rib Vaulting
*Two massive octagonal
pillars inside the main hall
support the five-rib vaults.*

**The cantor's
platform** and
its lectern are
surrounded by
a wrought-iron
Gothic grille.

**Entrance to the
synagogue from
Červená Street**

STAR FEATURES

★ Rabbi Löw's Chair

★ Five-rib Vaulting

★ Jewish Standard

Entrance Portal
*The tympanum above
the door in the south
vestibule is carved
with a vine, which
bears 12 bunches
of grapes,
symbolizing the
tribes of Israel.*

VISITORS' CHECKLIST

Pařížská and Červená. *Tel 22 23 17 191.* Ⓜ *Staroměstská.* 🚋 *17, 18.* 🕐 *9:30am–6pm Sun–Fri. Jewish hols.* 🎫 ⭐ *8am Mon–Fri, 9am Sat.* **www**.kehilaprag.cz

The Ark is the holiest place in the synagogue and holds the sacred scrolls of the Torah. The tympanum above it is decorated with 13th-century leaf carvings.

View across the Old Jewish Cemetery towards the Klausen Synagogue

Old Jewish Cemetery ⑬

Široká 3 (main entrance). *Tel 22 23 17 191 (reservations); 22 27 49 211 (Jewish museum).* Ⓜ *Staroměstská.* 🚋 *17, 18.* 🕐 *Sun–Fri.* 🎫 *includes entry to all Jewish sites except Old-New Synagogue.* ♿

Founded in 1478, for over 300 years this was the only burial ground permitted to Jews. Because of the lack of space, people had to be buried on top of each other, up to 12 layers deep. Today you can see over 12,000 gravestones, but around 100,000 people are thought to have been buried here – the last person, Moses Beck, in 1787. The most visited grave in the cemetery is that of Rabbi Löw (1520–1609). Visitors place hundreds of pebbles and wishes on his grave as a mark of respect.

On the northern edge of the cemetery, the **Klausen Synagogue** (1694) stands on the site of a number of small Jewish schools and prayer houses, known as *klausen*. Today it is home to the **Jewish Museum**, whose exhibits trace the history of the Jews in Central Europe back to the Middle Ages. Next to the synagogue is the former ceremonial hall of the Jewish Burial Society, built in 1906. It now houses a permanent exhibition of childrens' drawings from the Terezín concentration camp.

Also bordering the cemetery, the **Pinkas Synagogue** was founded in 1479, and now serves as a memorial to all the Jewish Czechoslovak citizens who were imprisoned at Terezín. Excavations at the synagogue have turned up fascinating relics of life in the medieval ghetto, including a *mikva*, or ritual bath.

⭐ **Rabbi Löw's Chair**
A Star of David marks the chair of the Chief Rabbi, placed where the 16th-century scholar, Rabbi Löw, used to sit.

PRAGUE'S JEWISH QUARTER

In the Middle Ages Prague's Jewish community was confined in an enclosed ghetto. For centuries the Jews suffered from oppressive laws – in the 16th century they had to wear a yellow circle as a mark of shame. Discrimination was partially relaxed in 1784 by Joseph II, and the Jewish Quarter was named Josefov after him. In 1850 the area was officially incorporated as part of Prague. A few years later the city authorities razed the ghetto slums, but many synagogues, the Town Hall, and the Old Jewish Cemetery were saved.

Ten Commandments motif on the Spanish Synagogue

The Old and New Towns

The heart of the city is the Old Town (Staré Město) and its central square. In the 11th century the settlements around the castle spread to the right bank of the Vltava. A marketplace in what is now Old Town Square was first mentioned in 1091, and houses and churches quickly sprang up around it. Founded in 1348 by Charles IV, the New Town (Nové Město) was mainly inhabited by tradesmen and craftsmen. In the late 19th century, much of it was demolished and completely redeveloped, giving it the appearance it has today.

Church of Our Lady before Týn in the Old Town Square

Old Town Square ⑭

Ⓜ Staroměstská, Můstek. 🚋 17, 18.

Free of traffic, except for a handful of horse-drawn carriages, and ringed with historic buildings, Prague's enormous Old Town Square (Staroměstské náměstí) ranks among the finest public spaces of any European city.

Dominating the east side of the square is the **Church of Our Lady before Týn**, with its magnificent Gothic steeples. Begun in 1365, from the early 15th century until 1620 it was the main Hussite church in Prague.

Also on the east side of the square, the **House at the Stone Bell** has been restored to its former appearance as a Gothic town palace. The splendid 18th-century Rococo **Kinský Palace**, with its pretty pink and white stucco facade,

was designed by Kilian Ignaz Dientzenhofer. Today, it houses art exhibitions by the National Gallery.

At the northern end of the square, the **Church of St. Nicholas** stands on the site of a former church dating from the 12th century. The present building, completed by Kilian Ignaz Dientzenhofer in 1735, has a dramatic white façade, studded with statues by Antonín Braun. In summer, evening concerts are held here.

A colorful array of arcaded buildings of Romanesque or Gothic origin, with fascinating house signs, graces the south side of the square. Among the most attractive are the house called **At the Stone Ram** and the Neo-Renaissance **Štorch House**, also known as At the Stone Madonna.

At one end of the square stands the huge monument dedicated to the reformist Jan Hus, who was burnt at the stake for heresy in 1415.

In addition to historic buildings, there are also many shops, as well as restaurants and cafés, whose tables and chairs spill out onto the pavements of the square in summer.

Old Town Hall ⑮

Staroměstské náměstí 1. **Tel** 22 42 28 456. Ⓜ Staroměstská, Můstek. 🚋 17, 18. ⬜ daily. 🎫 ♿ 🛒

Standing at the southwest corner of the Old Town Square, the Old Town Hall is one of the most striking buildings in Prague.

Established in 1338 after King John of Luxemburg agreed to set up a town

council, the Town Hall grew in the course of the next few centuries, and today consists of a row of colorful Gothic and Renaissance buildings.

The Old Town Hall Tower is one of the building's star features and dates from 1364. The gallery at the top provides a magnificent view of the city. Located on the first floor is the 14th-century Oriel Chapel, with its ornate restored ceiling.

Another famous sight is the Astronomical Clock, built by the clockmaker Hanuš in 1490. The mechanism of the clock we see today was perfected by Jan Táborský between 1552 and 1572. The clock records three different kinds of time, Old Bohemian time, time as we know it, and so-called Babylonian time. It also shows the movement of the sun and moon through the 12 signs of the zodiac. Every time the clock strikes the hour, mechanical figures perform above the zodiac signs, drawing crowds of spectators. The lower section of the clock consists of the

Astronomical Clock and Calendar on the Old Town Hall Tower

Calendar. This beautifully decorated revolving dial, designed by celebrated artist Josef Mánes, dates from 1866.

Municipal House ⑯

Náměstí Republiky 5. **Tel** 22 20 02 101. Ⓜ Náměstí Republiky. 🚋 5, 8, 14, 26. **Gallery** ⬜ daily. 📷 ♿ **www.**obecnidum.cz

Prague's most prominent Art Nouveau building occupies the site of the former Royal Court palace, the king's residence between 1383 and 1484. The attractive exterior is embellished with allegorical statuary, and above the main entrance there is a mosaic entitled *Homage to Prague* by Karel Špillar.

Inside is Prague's principal concert venue, the Smetana Hall, which is also used as a ballroom. The interior is decorated with works by leading Czech artists of the early 20th century, including Alfons Mucha, one of the most successful exponents of the Art Nouveau style.

On October 28, 1918, Prague's Municipal House was the scene of the momentous proclamation of the new independent state of Czechoslovakia.

Wenceslas Square ⑰

Ⓜ Můstek, Muzeum. 🚋 3, 9, 14, 24.

Originally a medieval horse market, today Wenceslas Square remains an important commercial center, with shops, hotels, restaurants, and clubs.

At one end of the square is the **National Museum**. This grand building, with its monumental staircase and rich marbled interior, was completed in 1890 as a symbol of national prestige. The museum's collections are devoted mainly to mineralogy, archaeology, anthropology, and natural history.

View across the Vltava River to the National Theater

The huge equestrian statue of St. Wenceslas that stands in front of the National Museum was erected in 1912, the work of the 19th-century sculptor Josef Myslbek. At the foot of the pedestal there are smaller statues of Czech patron saints.

Also worth seeing are the Art Nouveau-style **Hotel Europa** (1906) and the **Church of Our Lady of the Snows**. This towering Gothic building is only part of a vast church planned in the 14th century but never completed.

Wenceslas Square has witnessed many important events in Czech history. In November 1989, a protest rally against police brutality took place here, leading to the Velvet Revolution and the overthrow of Communism.

Statue of St. Wenceslas flanked by Czech patron saints in St. Wenceslas Square

National Theater ⑱

Národní divadlo, Národní 2. **Tel** 22 49 01 448. Ⓜ Národní třída. 🚋 6, 9, 17, 18, 21, 22 to Národní divadlo. ⬜ for performances only or by arrangement (22 17 14 152). ♿ **www.**narodni-divadlo.cz

The National Theater has always been an important symbol of the Czech cultural revival. Work began on the building in 1868. The original Neo-Renaissance design was by the Czech architect Josef Zítek. After it was completely destroyed by fire – just days before the official opening – Josef Schulz was given the job of rebuilding the theater, and all the best Czech artists of the period contributed toward its lavish decoration. During the late 1970s and early 80s the theater underwent restoration work and the New Stage was built.

The theater's auditorium has an elaborately painted ceiling adorned with allegorical figures representing the arts. Equally impressive are the sumptuous gold and red stage curtain, and the ceiling fresco in the theater's lobby. The fresco is the final part of a triptych, painted by František Ženíšek in 1878, depicting the *Golden Age of Czech Art*.

The theater's vivid sky-blue roof, covered with stars, is said to symbolize the summit all artists should aim for.

Excursions in Bohemia

The sights that attract most visitors away from the capital are Bohemia's picturesque towns and castles, and its famous spa resorts. The castle at Karlstein, for example, stands in splendid isolation above wooded valleys that have changed little since Charles IV hunted here in the 14th century. Further south, the historic town of Český Krumlov retains a medieval atmosphere. Still popular as a therapeutic retreat, the spa town of Karlsbad is located in the leafy Teplá valley and offers a welcome respite from Prague's crowds.

Karlstein Castle, built by Emperor Charles IV in the 14th century

Karlstein ❷

Karlštejn, 25 km (16 miles) SW of Prague. **Tel** 274 00 81 54. 🚇 to Karlštejn (1.5 km/1 mile from castle). ◻ Mar–Nov: Tue–Sun. 🗓 🖼 obligatory. **Chapel of the Holy Rood** ◻ Jun–Oct: Tue–Sun. 🖼 obligatory and by advance reservation only. **www**.hradkarlstejn.cz

Karlstein Castle was founded by Charles IV as a country retreat and a treasury for the imperial crown jewels. The present structure is largely a 19th-century reconstruction by Josef Mocker. The original building work took place between 1348 and 1365, supervised by the French master mason Matthew of Arras, and after him by Peter Parler. You can still see the audience hall and the bed-chamber of Charles IV in the Royal Palace.

The central tower houses the Church of Our Lady, with its faded 14th-century wall paintings. A passage leads to the Chapel of St. Catherine, whose walls are adorned with semiprecious stones. The Chapel of the Holy Rood in the Great Tower, where the crown jewels were once kept, has gilded vaulting studded with glass stars. At one time the chapel held 129 panels painted by Master Theodoric (1359–67), one of the greatest painters of Charles IV's reign. Some panels have been restored and can now be seen in Prague's St. Agnes's Convent, along with other medieval art.

Kutná Hora ❸

70 km (45 miles) east of Prague. 🏯 21,000 🚊 🚌 🛈 Palackého náměstí 377 (327 51 23 78). **www**.kutnahora.cz

After deposits of silver were found here in the 13th century, Kutná Hora evolved from a small mining community into the second most important town in Bohemia after Prague. The Prague *groschen*, a silver coin that was in circulation all over Europe, was minted at the **Italian Court** (Vlašský dvůr), so-called because Florentine experts were employed to set up the mint. Strongly fortified, the Italian Court was also the ruler's seat in the town. In the late 14th century a palace was built, containing reception halls and the Chapel of St. Wenceslas and St. Ladislav. They can be visited by guided tour.

Kutná Hora's **Mining Museum**, housed in a former fort called the Hrádek, and the splendid 14th-century Gothic **Cathedral of St. Barbara** are also worth visiting.

Karlsbad ❹

Karlovy Vary, 140 km (85 miles) west of Prague. 🏯 54,000 ✈ 🚊 🚌 🛈 Lázeňská 1 (353 30 42 25). **www**.karlovyvary.cz

Legend has it that Charles IV discovered one of the sources of mineral water that would make Karlsbad's fortune when one of his staghounds fell into

The three steeples of Kutná Hora's great Cathedral of St. Barbara

For hotels and restaurants in this region see p726 and p727

The spa town of Karlsbad with its 19th-century Mill Colonnade

CZECH BEERS

Czech beer-bottle cap

The best-known Czech beer is Pilsner, which is made by the lager method: top fermented and matured at low temperatures. The word "Pils-ner" (now used as a generic name for similar lagers brewed all over the world) derives from Plzeň, a town 88 km (55 miles) southwest of Prague, where this type of beer was first brewed in 1842.

The brewery that developed the beer still makes Plzeňský prazdroj (original source), better known by its name Pilsner Urquell, as well as the very popular Gambrinus. Guided tours of the brewery include a tasting. České Budějovice is Bohemia's other famous brewing town – home to the Czech Republic's biggest selling export beer, Budweiser Budvar.

Selection of Czech beers

a hot spring. By the end of the 16th century more than 200 spa buildings had been built in the town. Today there are 13 hot mineral springs. The best-known is the Vřídlo (Sprudel), which, at 72˚C (162˚F), is also the hottest.

Among the town's historic monuments are the 18th-century Baroque parish **church of Mary Magdalene**. The elegant 19th-century **Mill Colonnade** (Mlýnská kolonáda) is by Josef Zítek, architect of the National Theater (*see p721*) in Prague.

Karlsbad is also known for its Karlovy Vary china and Moser glass, and for summer concerts and cultural events.

Environs
Around 60 km (38 miles) southwest of Karlsbad is another of Bohemia's spa towns, **Marienbad** (Mariánské Lázně). Here the cast-iron colonnade, by Josef Vylefal, is an impressive sight. There are also many pleasant walks in the local countryside, especially in the protected Slavkov Forest.

Český Krumlov ❺

180 km (112 miles) south of Prague.
👥 14,000 🚉 ℹ️ *náměstí Svornosti 2 (380 70 46 22).*
www.ckrumlov.info

Of all the Czech Republic's medieval towns, Český Krumlov must rank as the finest. Almost entirely enclosed by a bend in the River Vltava, the beautifully preserved Inner Town (Vnitřni Město) appears to have changed very little in the last few hundred years, although some buildings suffered severe flood damage in 2002. A maze of narrow cobbled streets radiates out from the main square (Náměstí Svornosti), which is lined with elegant arcaded Renaissance buildings including the former town hall. On one of these streets – Horní – is the magnificent 16th-century sgraffitoed **Jesuit College** (now a hotel) and, opposite, a **museum** explaining the town's history. **Schiele Centrum** is housed in a 15th-century former brewery. The museum has an excellent collection of works by the Austrian painter Egon Schiele.

Český Krumlov's most famous sight is its 13th-century castle – the **Krumlovský Zámek** – in the Latrán quarter. In the older, lower part of the castle complex, the splendidly restored castle tower can be climbed for superb views of the whole town. Other highlights of the castle include a Rococo chapel, a lavishly decorated ballroom – the Maškarní sál – and the ornate 18th-century Rococo theater. The castle gardens provide a tranquil spot to sit and relax, while performances of opera and ballet take place in the gardens' open-air theater in July and August.

In summer, renting a canoe from one of a number of outlets in the town is a good way to enjoy the fine views of Český Krumlov from the river.

⚓ **Krumlovský Zámek**
Latrán. ◯ *Apr–Oct: Tue–Sun.* 📷 🎟️ 📷

Český Krumlov's castle tower rising above the medieval Inner Town

Practical & Travel Information

Since 1989 the Czech Republic has become far more open to visitors. The country has responded well to the huge influx of tourists, and facilities such as communications, banks, and information centers have improved considerably. The best way to explore Prague is on foot; if you are traveling to places of interest outside the capital, buses and trains are reliable and inexpensive.

WHEN TO VISIT

The busiest months are August and September, although Prague can be very crowded in June and at Easter also. The main sights are always packed at these times, but the crowds lend a carnival atmosphere, which can make a visit all the more enjoyable. Many sights are closed between the end of October and the beginning of April.

TOURIST INFORMATION

Tourist information offices in the Czech Republic are run by several different agencies, including formerly state-owned **Čedok**. Many employ English speakers and offer a variety of English-language publications, maps, and guides. The efficient **Prague Information Service (PIS)** is the best source of tourist information for visitors to the capital. It has three offices in the city center, providing information in several languages, including English.

VISA REQUIREMENTS

Citizens of the US, EU, Australia, New Zealand, and countries of the European Free Trade Association need a valid passport to enter the Czech Republic, and can stay for up to 90 days without needing a visa.

SAFETY AND EMERGENCIES

Violent crime against tourists is rare in the Czech Republic. The main problem, especially in Prague, is petty theft from cars, hotel rooms, and pockets. At night, lone women are advised to avoid Prague's Wenceslas Square, which used to be a hangout for prostitutes.

It is an unwritten law that you should have your passport with you at all times in the Czech Republic. Although you are unlikely to be asked to produce it, having it could save a lot of problems.

In case of an emergency, the numbers to call are listed in the directory opposite.

HEALTH ISSUES

No inoculations are required for the Czech Republic. Visitors should take note that in winter sulphur dioxide levels in Prague often exceed the World Health Organization's safety levels. For prescription and non-prescription medicines, visit a pharmacy (lékárna).

FACILITIES FOR THE DISABLED

Disabled travelers seeking advice on transportation, accommodations, and sightseeing tours should contact the **Czech Association of Persons with Disabilities** or, alternatively, the **Prague Wheelchair Association**.

BANKING AND CURRENCY

The Czech unit of currency is the Czech crown (Kč). Banking hours are generally 8am to 5pm Monday to Friday, with some branches closing at lunch. Bureaux de change in tourist spots are open every day, and some offer a 24-hour service. Although they give much better exchange rates than the banks, their commission charges are huge, often as high as 12 percent. Traveler's checks can only be changed in banks. Credit cards are becoming more widely accepted in the Czech Republic, but never assume that you can pay with them.

COMMUNICATIONS

Card-operated public phone booths are found all over the Czech Republic. You can buy phone-cards (telefonní karta) from most tobacconists and news-stands. It is possible to make international calls from a public phone, a post office or a hotel, although the latter option is usually highly expensive.

Most post offices are open from 8am until 6pm, Monday to Friday, and on Saturday mornings. Stamps (známky) can be purchased at most tobacconists and newsstands, as well as from post offices.

FLYING TO THE CZECH REPUBLIC

If you are traveling from the United States, **Czech Airlines (ČSA)** is the only airline that offers direct flights to Prague. Other carriers, including **Delta Air Lines**, **KLM**, and

---

THE CLIMATE OF THE CZECH REPUBLIC

The Czech Republic enjoys long, warm days in summer, the hottest months being June, July, and August. The winter months can get bitterly cold; temperatures often drop below freezing and heavy snowfall is not uncommon. The wettest months are October and November but frequent light showers can occur in the summer months as well.

PRAGUE

° C/F	Apr	Jul	Oct	Jan
	13/55	24/75 14/57	16/61	
0°C 32°F	3/37		5/41	0/32 -5/23
☀ hrs	5.5	8.5	4	1.5
☂ mm	73	19	95	60
month	Apr	Jul	Oct	Jan

Lufthansa, operate flights from the US and Canada to the Czech Republic, via another European city.

Carriers operating direct scheduled flights daily from the UK to Prague include **British Airways** and Czech Airlines (ČSA). Low-cost **easyJet** and **Jet2.com** have flights to Prague from several UK airports.

Among a number of airlines flying from Australia and New Zealand to Prague are Lufthansa and KLM. Flights from Australasia require a stopover in Europe or Asia.

Čedaz runs an inexpensive and efficient minibus service from Prague's Ruzyně airport to the city center.

RAIL TRAVEL

Prague is connected by rail to all the major capitals of Europe, although it can be a rather slow way of getting to the Czech Republic. For example, the journey time from London to Prague is 19 hours. Many international trains arrive at and depart from Hlavní nádraží, the city's biggest and busiest station.

The Czech Republic's state-run rail company, České Dráhy (ČD), operates several types of domestic routes. Supercity trains (SC) are the fastest trains and you pay a premium to travel on them. Express trains *(rychlík)* stop only at the major towns and cities. The slow trains, or *osobní*, stop at every station.

For help with timetables and advice on fares in Prague, visit the local PIS or Information at Hlavní nádraží station.

TRAVELING BY BUS

Traveling by bus between Prague and other major European cities can be slow and tiring, but it is significantly less expensive than rail or air travel. Seats get booked up very quickly, especially in summer, so reserve well in advance. **Eurolines** is one of the main operators of international bus routes to Prague. Within the Czech Republic, long-distance buses are run by **Student Agency** and local companies. There is an extensive route network, and buses are often a less expensive way of traveling between towns than the trains. For popular routes you should buy your ticket in advance from the bus station.

The main bus terminal in Prague is Florenc, which serves all international and long-distance domestic routes.

TRAVELING BY CAR

There are now several highways in the Czech Republic, which can make car travel faster. To travel on them you must buy a tax disc *(dálniční známka)*, valid for either 7 days, one month, or a year and available at the border or from post offices and gas stations.

Most of the major car rental firms have offices in Prague and at Ruzyně airport, but renting is relatively expensive.

DIRECTORY

CZECH TOURIST OFFICES ABROAD

UK
Czech Centre, 13 Harley Street, London W1G 9QG. *Tel* 020-7307 5180. **www**.czechcentres.cz
Czech Tourism
www.czechtourism.com

US
321 East 73rd Street, New York, NY 10021. *Tel* 646-422 3383. **www**.new-york.czech centres.cz

TOURIST OFFICES IN PRAGUE

Čedok
Na příkopě 18, Prague. *Tel* 800 112 112 (toll-free). **www**.cedok.cz

Prague Information Service
Tel 12 444.
Tel 22 17 14 444 (walking tours).
www.praguewelcome.cz

EMBASSIES AND CONSULATES

Australian Consulate
Klimentská 10, Prague. *Tel* 29 65 78 350.

Canadian Embassy
Muchova 6, Prague. *Tel* 27 21 01 800.
www.canada.cz

UK Embassy
Thunovská 14, Prague. *Tel* 25 74 02 111.
www.ukinczechrepublic. fco.gov.uk

US Embassy
Tržiště 15, Prague. *Tel* 25 70 22 000.
www.czech.prague. usembassy.gov

EMERGENCY NUMBERS

Ambulance, Fire, Police
Tel 112 (English).

FACILITIES FOR THE DISABLED

Czech Association of Persons with Disabilities
Karlínské náměstí 12, Prague. *Tel* 22 18 90 411.

Prague Wheelchair Association
Benediktská 6, Prague. *Tel* 22 48 27 210.

AIRLINES

British Airways
Tel 0870-850 9850 (UK).
Tel 1-800-AIRWAYS (US).
Tel 23 90 00 299 (Czech Republic).
www.britishairways.com

Czech Airlines
Tel 207-365 9189 (UK).
Tel 23 90 07 007 (Czech Republic). **www**.csa.cz

Delta Air Lines
Tel 800-241 4141 (US).
Tel 23 30 90 933 (Czech Republic).
www.delta.com

easyJet
www.easyjet.com

Jet2.com
www.jet2.com

KLM
Tel 800-225 25 25 (US).
Tel 23 30 90 933 (Czech Republic).
www.klm.com

Lufthansa
Tel 1800-645 3880 (US).
Tel 23 40 08 234 (Czech Republic).
www.lufthansa.com

BUS COMPANIES

Eurolines
Tel 08717-818 181 (UK).
Tel 24 50 05 245 (Czech Republic).
www.eurolines.co.uk

Student Agency
www.studentagency.cz

Where to Stay in the Czech Republic

Since the "Velvet Revolution" of 1989, tourism in the Czech Republic has boomed. As such, old hotels have been revamped and new establishments have sprung up. Top-range hotels equal those in the rest of Europe for quality and price. Budget hotels are sadly scarce.

PRICE CATEGORIES
Price categories for a double room per night including taxes and breakfast:

Ⓚ Under 3000 Kč
ⓀⓀ 3000–4500 Kč
ⓀⓀⓀ 4500–6000 Kč
ⓀⓀⓀⓀ 6000–8000 Kč
ⓀⓀⓀⓀⓀ Over 8000 Kč

PRAGUE

MALA STRANA (LITTLE QUARTER) Domus Henrici
ⓀⓀ
Loretánská 11, Praha 1 **Tel** *22 05 11 369* **Fax** *22 05 11 502* **Rooms** *8*   **Map** *A3*

Part of the Hidden Places hotel group, you may have trouble finding this establishment. It's difficult to get much closer to the castle than this, so sightseers will love the location. Rooms are enormous and tastefully decorated. The terrace offers magnificent views over the old town and Petřín Gardens. **www.hidden-places.com**

MALA STRANA (LITTLE QUARTER) U Tří Pštrosů
ⓀⓀ
Drazického náměstí 12, Praha 1 **Tel** *25 72 88 888* **Fax** *25 75 33 217* **Rooms** *18*   **Map** *C3*

Just beside Charles Bridge, the hotel "At The Three Ostriches" began life as the home of Jan Fux, an ostrich-feather dealer. It is one of the best-known hotel-restaurants in Prague. Family run, it has an intimate atmosphere, and children are especially welcome. **www.utripstrosu.com**

NEW TOWN Na Zlatém Kříži
Ⓚ
Jungmannovo náměstí 2, Praha 1 **Tel** *22 22 45 419* **Fax** *22-22 45 418* **Rooms** *8*   **Map** *E4*

A challenger for the narrowest hotel in Prague award, the charming Golden Cross offers deceptively large, and rather luxurious double rooms and apartments, all with private bathrooms. A good buffet breakfast is served in the hotel's Gothic-style cellar. Transfers to and from the airport can be arranged. **www.goldencross.cz**

NEW TOWN Élite
ⓀⓀ
Ostrovní 32, 110 00 Praha 1 **Tel** *22 49 32 250* **Fax** *22 49 30 787* **Rooms** *77*   **Map** *4D*

The Élite is housed in a building which dates from the late-14th century. Its cozy atmosphere is aptly augmented by a stylish grill club on the ground floor, offering excellent Mediterranean and Argentinian cuisine, as well as a cocktail bar providing Latino music. An open atrium contains a day-bar with a small garden. **www.hotelelite.cz**

NEW TOWN Carlo IV
ⓀⓀⓀⓀ
Senovážné náměstí 13, Praha 1 **Tel** *22 45 93 090* **Fax** *22 45 93 000* **Rooms** *152*   **Map** *F3*

This magnificently decorated hotel with shimmering marble floors, intricate hand-painted frescos in a Neoclassical building, is in the heart of the city. Part of the Boscolo Group, this hotel has some wonderful features, from the Box Block restaurant to the Cigar bar, while the spa features Europe's best hotel swimming pool.

OLD TOWN Paříž
ⓀⓀⓀⓀ
U Obecního domu 1, 110 00 Praha 1 **Tel** *22 21 95 195* **Fax** *22 42 25 475* **Rooms** *86*   **Map** *F3*

Located very close to the Municipal House and Powder Gate, this Neo-Gothic building with a number of Art Nouveau elements was built by the celebrated architect Jan Vejrych, and was declared a historic monument in 1984. The rooms have been modernised in international style and everything is in pristine condition. **www.hotel-paris.cz**

REST OF THE CZECH REPUBLIC

ČESKY KRUMLOV Růže
ⓀⓀⓀⓀ
Horní 154, 381 01, Česky Krumlov **Tel** *38 07 72 100* **Fax** *38 07 13 146* **Rooms** *70*

The most luxurious hotel in Česky Krumlov. Housed in a former Jesuit monastery and furnished in Renaissance style, it also offers a superb range of facilities. The hotel hosts medieval feasts where guests can dress up in costume and sit down to a candlelit banquet accompanied by dancers, jugglers and musicians. **www.hotelruze.cz**

KARLSBAD (KARLOVY VARY) Grand Hotel Pupp
ⓀⓀⓀⓀ
Mírové náměstí 2, 360 91, Karlovy Vary **Tel** *35 31 09 111* **Rooms** *228*

One of the most famous Czech hotels, with traditions going back to the early 18th century. Luxuriously furnished rooms with minibar, safe, satellite TV, and dazzling bathrooms. The amenities include restaurant, casino, the impressive Mirror Hall with Neo-Baroque interior, and of course a fabulous spa centre. **www.pupp.cz**

Key to Symbols *see back cover flap*

Where to Eat in the Czech Republic

New restaurants are constantly opening in the Czech Republic thanks to the thriving tourist industry. Many offer international cuisine but there are also plenty of traditional eateries offering local dishes. Compared to Western Europe, eating out is relatively inexpensive.

PRICE CATEGORIES
Price categories for an average three-course meal for one, including half a bottle of wine, and all unavoidable charges:

Ⓚ under 250 Kč
ⓀⓀ 250–450 Kč
ⓀⓀⓀ 450–650 Kč
ⓀⓀⓀⓀ over 650 Kč

PRAGUE

MALA STRANA (LITTLE QUARTER) Restaurace U zlatého Preclíku   ⓀⓀⓀ
Tomášská 22, Praha 1 **Tel** *25 72 17923*   **Map** *C3*

This is a reasonably priced, romantically rustic cellar restaurant with a pleasant courtyard for outside dining. The menu features classic Bohemian dishes such as stew with two kinds of dumplings (bread and potato) and marinated beef with potato dumplings, topped with cream and cranberries. There are also pork, chicken, duck, and fish dishes.

MALA STRANA (LITTLE QUARTER) U Malířů (At the Painter's)   ⓀⓀⓀⓀ
Maltézské náměstí 11, Praha 1 **Tel** *25 75 30 318*   **Map** *C4*

There has been a restaurant on this spot since 1543. Even back then, U Malířů received high praise: King Rudolf II's foodtasters gave it three Royal stars. Today you can expect equally high quality cuisine in sumptuous surroundings. It offers Central European game dishes and some Czech wines, too.

NEW TOWN U Fleků   ⓀⓀⓀ
Křemencova 11, Praha 1 **Tel** *22 49 34 019*   **Map** *D5*

This cavernous and often raucous brewery and restaurant with its many rooms and lounges is thought to have been founded in 1499, though nobody seems to know for sure. What's certain is that there's been an onsite brewery since the early 1900s, and the food is good, reliable upmarket Czech pub fare.

NEW TOWN Céleste   ⓀⓀⓀ
Tančící Dům, Rašínovo nábřeží 80, Praha 2 **Tel** *22 19 84 160*   **Map** *D5*

Situated on the seventh floor of the Dancing House Building, with views of the Vltava and Prague Castle, this is a reasonably priced, upscale French restaurant. The wine menu is quite extensive and the knowledgeable staff can help you choose. There's a well-stocked cocktail bar with a range of trendy cocktails.

OLD TOWN Klub Architektů   ⓀⓀⓀ
Betlémské náměstí 5A, Praha 1 **Tel** *60 22 50 082*   **Map** *D4*

This hidden jewel is tucked away in a warren of tunnels and arches, reached through a discreet courtyard close to the Bethlehem Chapel. The servings are hearty, and, unusual for an inexpensive Prague dining room. The menu includes a good vegetarian selection with organic options.

OLD TOWN Chez Marcel   ⓀⓀⓀⓀ
Haštalská 12, Praha 1 **Tel** *22 23 15 676*   **Map** *E3*

Chez Marcel is a touch of real France in the centre of Prague. This is where business people and students alike come for the relaxed atmosphere, affordable French wines, and classic French dishes such as snails in garlic and duck confit with Sarladais potatoes. To finish, there's a wide selection of French desserts to choose from.

REST OF THE CZECH REPUBLIC

ČESKY KRUMLOV Pivovar Eggenberg   ⓀⓀ
Latrán 27, Česky Krumlov, 381 01 **Tel** *38 07 11 426*

Eggenberg is a brewery, and beer sets the tone in this restaurant, located in the former brewing coolrooms. There is a large, roomy restaurant with 150 seats as well as beer hall "Formanka" of 70 seats. Both offer Czech cuisine, light and dark beers on tap but you will find a good selection of Czech wine, too.

KARLSBAD (KARLOVY VARY) Lázně V.   ⓀⓀⓀ
Smetanovy sady 1145/1, Karlovy Vary, 360 01 **Tel** *60 22 66 088*

Situated on the first floor of the 19th-century Elisabethes Spa building, the restaurant offers traditional Czech as well as Mediterranean cuisine and is well renowned for its steaks. There is a wide selection of Moravian and international wines. The business lunch is good value for money.

Map References see map of Prague pp710–11

HUNGARY

Uniquely in central Europe, Hungary is peopled by descendants of the Magyars, a race from central Asia who settled here at the end of the 9th century. In more recent times the country has fought against Turkish, German, Austrian, and Russian occupiers, yet its rich indigenous culture remains intact. In 1989 Hungary became the first Soviet Bloc country to embrace Western-style democracy.

Hungary has an extremely varied landscape, with forests and mountains dominating the north and a vast plain covering the rest of the country. The Tisza river and its tributaries shape the eastern regions, while the west has Lake Balaton, one of the largest lakes in Europe. The Danube flows through the heart of the country, bisecting the capital, Budapest, where one-fifth of the population lives. Ethnically the country is 92 percent Magyar, 4 percent Romany, 2 percent German, and one percent Slovak, the final one percent being of Jewish origin.

HISTORY

In AD 100 the Romans established the town of Aquincum near modern-day Budapest, and ruled the area corresponding roughly to Hungary (then called Pannonia) for three centuries. The arrival of the Huns in the early 5th century led to the complete withdrawal of the Romans. After the death of Attila the Hun in 453, the area was ruled by the Goths, the Longobards, and the Avars. The ancestors of the modern Hungarians, the Magyars, migrated from the Urals in 896, under the leadership of Prince Árpád, whose dynasty ruled until 1301, when King András III died without leaving an heir.

The throne then passed to a series of foreign kings, including the French Angevins and the Lithuanian Jagiellos, but the country flourished, and during the reign of Mátyás Corvinus (1458–90) it became the greatest monarchy in Middle Europe. Mátyás's marriage to Beatrice, a Neapolitan princess, saw the Renaissance blossom throughout Hungary, but all was soon eclipsed by a series of Turkish invasions. The Turks won a major victory at the Battle of Mohács in 1526, then they returned in 1541 to take Buda, which

The Gellért monument in Budapest, dedicated to a martyred 11th-century bishop

◁ Neo-Gothic spires, flying buttresses, and stained-glass windows on Hungary's Parliament building became the capital of Ottoman Hungary. To quell the Turkish advance, the Austrians, under Ferdinand of Habsburg, occupied western (or "Royal") Hungary, while the central plains stayed under Ottoman control; the eastern region, including Transylvania (now in Romania), became a semi-autonomous land, feudally tied to the Turks.

Christian armies led by the Habsburgs fought to recapture Buda, and finally defeated the Turks in 1686. Economic prosperity came with Austrian rule, but nationalism was cruelly suppressed, culminating in a major uprising in 1848. After crushing the rebellion, Emperor Franz Joseph I sought to unite the two nations, and so created the Dual Monarchy of Austro-Hungary in 1867.

Mátyás Corvinus, King of Hungary (1458–90)

Following World War I, the Habsburg Empire was dismantled, and Hungary lost two-thirds of its territory to the "successor states" of Yugoslavia, Czechoslovakia, and Romania. It was to regain these territories that Hungary backed Germany in World War II, but in 1945 Budapest was taken by the Russians. The subsequent Communist rule was ruthlessly upheld, most visibly in 1956 when an attempted revolution was crushed by Soviet tanks. Nevertheless, free elections finally took place in 1989, resulting in victory for the democratic opposition. Since then, the country has invested heavily in tourism, which is now a major source of income.

LANGUAGE AND CULTURE

Modern Hungarian, like Finnish, derives from a language originally spoken by the Finno-Ugric tribes of the Urals. It differs greatly from most other European languages, although Slavic, German, Caucasian, Latin, and Turkic words have been incorporated.

Traditional peasant culture was all but destroyed in the 20th century, but folk songs and dances still survive; Christmas and Easter are the best times to witness these, particularly in the countryside.

Exploring Hungary

Budapest has a pivotal location at the heart of central Europe, and it is also the perfect base for exploring Hungary itself. Szentendre, with its Serbian religious art, and Esztergom, where Hungary's first Christian king was crowned, are both only a short drive north, while Lake Balaton lies only a little further west. Pécs, a treasure trove of European history, lies to the south, while Eger and Tokaj stand in the wine-producing area to the east; the former, with its castle and Turkish minaret, is one of Hungary's most popular towns.

SIGHTS AT A GLANCE

BUDAPEST pp422–9 ❶
Eger ❻
Esztergom ❸
Lake Balaton ❹
Pécs ❺
Szentendre ❷
Tokaj ❼

0 kilometers 50

0 miles 50

Chess-players in a bathhouse in Budapest

Musically, the country has always had much to be proud of, including composers Franz Liszt and Béla Bartók, while in literature the Communist years produced some very powerful voices, among them Tibor Déry and István Örkény. Otherwise the country is best known for its cuisine, which incorporates a wide range of wines and meat-based dishes (such as goulash), the latter invariably spiced with paprika, the country's most famous export.

KEY DATES IN HUNGARIAN HISTORY

c.AD 100 Romans establish Aquincum
c.410 Huns overrun the region
896 Magyar tribes arrive
1001 Coronation of István I, Hungary's first king
1300s Angevin rule begins
1458–90 Reign of Mátyás Corvinus
1526 Turks win the Battle of Mohács
1526–41 Turks conquer Buda on three occasions
1541 The start of Ottoman rule
1686 Christian troops enter Buda, ending Turkish rule in Hungary
1848 Hungarian Nationalist uprising
1867 Compromise with Austria gives Hungary independence in internal affairs
1873 Buda and Pest become Budapest
1918 With the break-up of the Austro-Hungarian Empire, Hungary gains independence after nearly 400 years of foreign rule
1941 Hungary enters World War II
1945 Russian army takes Budapest
1956 Russia suppresses a nationalist uprising
1989 Hungary proclaimed a democratic republic
2003 Hungary becomes a member of EU
2010 Viktor Orban is elected prime minister, introducing sweeping reforms

KEY

✈ Airport
— Highway
— Major road
— Railroad
▪▪▪ International border

Budapest ❶

Budapest was founded in 1873 after the unification of three separate towns, Buda and Óbuda on the west bank of the Danube and Pest on the east. The city dates largely from the late 19th and early 20th centuries and is very much the creation of the nationalist enthusiasm of that era. All three towns had originally grown up in the second half of the twelfth century and Buda was the seat of Hungary's rulers from 1247. Turkish rule from 1541 to 1686, when it was recaptured by the Habsburgs, left little mark, except for the city's wonderful bathhouses.

SIGHTS AT A GLANCE

Gellért Hotel and Bath Complex ③
Hungarian National Museum ⑤
Inner City Parish Church ④
Mátyás Church ②
Museum of Fine Arts ⑨
Parliament ⑧
Royal Palace ①
St. Stephen's Basilica ⑦
State Opera House ⑥
Vajdahunyad Castle ⑩

Barrel-organist playing in
the Castle district of Buda

0 meters   600

0 yards   600

GETTING AROUND

Trams are a convenient means of transportation for tourists, especially the 18, 19, and 61 on the Buda side and the 2, 4, and 6 in Pest. There are also some 200 bus routes. The three metro lines and the HÉV rail lines link the center with the suburbs. A fourth metro line opens in 2014.

Chain Bridge (Széchenyi lánchid), the first permanent bridge over the Danube, completed in 1849

KEY

▢	Sight / Place of interest
▤	Train station
Ⓜ	Metro station
▣	HÉV station
🚍	Bus station
🚋	Tram stop
🚤	River boat boarding point
▣	Parking
▮	Tourist information
✚	Church
✦	Synagogue
—	Pedestrian street

SEE ALSO

- **Where to Stay** p742

- **Where to Eat** p743

Aerial view of Castle Hill and central Budapest

Buda

In 1247, Béla IV chose Buda, on the Danube's west bank, as his capital city. Its position, at 60 m (197 ft) above the river, made it a strategic choice. Buda expanded during Angevin rule, reaching a zenith under Mátyás Corvinus (1458–90), although further development was hindered by the Turkish occupation of 1541–1686. The Habsburgs' attempts to recover the city were devastating and by the time of its liberation, the city had been largely destroyed. In the 18th and 19th centuries, the Habsburgs set about rebuilding the palace and the old town, adding some magnificent buildings, but most had to be rebuilt again after the siege of 1945.

and Baroque art, and a wonderful selection of 19th- and 20th-century Hungarian works.

Notable early works include *The Madonna of Bártfa* (1465–70), and the folding St. Anne Altarpiece (1510–20).

Among the 19th-century works, look out for the historical scenes by Bertalan Székely and the landscapes of Mihály Munkácsy (1844–1900), widely held to be Hungary's greatest artist. The 20th-century works by Tivadar Kosztka Csontváry give a unique, idiosyncratic vision of the world.

St. Anne Altarpiece, National Gallery

The rebuilt Royal Palace with the heroic statue of Eugene of Savoy

Royal Palace ①

Szinház utca. 🚌 5, 16, *Várbusz.*

King Béla IV (1235–70) built a royal castle in Buda, but its exact location is unknown. Around 1400 it was replaced by a Gothic palace, subsequently remodeled in Renaissance style by King Mátyás in 1458. Under Turkish rule, the palace was used to stable horses and store gunpowder, leading to its destruction in 1686 during the reconquest. A new palace, begun in 1719 by the Habsburgs, grew in size and grandeur under Maria Teresa, but this too was destroyed in the uprising of 1849 and had to be rebuilt in the second half of the 19th century.

When the Habsburg palace was again razed to the ground in February 1945, remains of the 15th-century Gothic palace were uncovered.

These were incorporated into the restored palace that visitors see today.

Various statues, gateways, and fountains have survived from the 19th-century palace. In the northwest courtyard stands the Mátyás Fountain (1904), depicting Mátyás Corvinus (1458–90) and his legendary love, the peasant girl, Ilonka. In front of the palace's rebuilt dome stands an equestrian statue (1900) of Prince Eugene of Savoy, victor of the Battle of Zenta against the Turks in 1697.

Today the palace houses a series of important national collections, including the Széchenyi National Library, with over five million books and manuscripts, the National Gallery, the Budapest History Museum, and the Museum of Contemporary History.

🏛 Hungarian National Gallery

Royal Palace A-B-C-D Wings, Szent György tér 2. *Tel* 20 43 97 325 or 20 43 97 331. 🚌 5, 16, *Várbusz.* ⬜ *Tue–Sun.* 🈲 🇬🇧 www.mng.hu
Established in 1957, the National Gallery has a superb collection of Hungarian art from medieval times to the 20th century. The permanent exhibits include a section of sculpture and stonework – the Lapidarium. There are also regular temporary exhibitions.

Highlights include a carved stone head of King Béla III, from c.1200, religious artifacts spanning several centuries, including many fine Gothic altarpieces, some Renaissance

🏛 Budapest History Museum

Royal Palace E Wing, Szent György tér 2. *Tel* (1) 487 8800. 🚌 5, 16, 116A, *Várbusz.* ⬜ *Tue–Sun.* 🈲 ♿ www.btm.hu
The city's history museum (*Budapesti Történeti Múzeum*), also known as the Castle Museum, illustrates the city's evolution from its origins under the Romans.

Damage to the palace in World War II led to chambers dating from the Middle Ages being uncovered in the south wing. These were recreated in the basement.

The ground floor exhibits cover the period from Roman times to the 15th century and include some Gothic statues, unearthed here in 1974. The first floor traces the history of the city from 1686 (the end of Turkish rule) to the present.

15th-century majolica floor in the Budapest History Museum

West front of the Mátyás Church, with tiled Béla Tower on the left

Mátyás Church ②

Szentháromság tér 2. **Tel** (1) 489 07 16. 🚌 5, 16, 16A, 116, Várbusz. ⏲ daily. ⬛ Sat pm, Sun am. 🎫 🖼 ♿ www.matyas-templom.hu

This church is mainly a Neo-Gothic reconstruction dating from 1874–96. Most of the original church (13th–15th centuries) was lost when the Turks turned it into their Great Mosque in 1541. The building had to be restored again after damage in World War II. The great rose window has been faithfully reproduced in its original Gothic style.

The tombs of King Béla III (13th century) and his wife can be seen in the Trinity Chapel, while the Mary Portal (near the main altar) is considered the finest example of Gothic stone carving in Hungary. Also fascinating is a Baroque statue of the Madonna: according to legend, the original was set into a wall during the Turkish occupation. When the church was virtually destroyed in 1686, the Madonna made a miraculous reappearance, which the Turks took as an omen of defeat.

Mátyás church stands in the heart of Buda's old town, which developed to the north of the Royal Palace from the 1200s onward.

In front of the church is Holy Trinity Square, with a memorial column to those who died in the plague of 1691. On the square stands the Old Town Hall, an elegant Baroque building with an onion-domed clock tower.

Gellért Hotel and Bath Complex ③

Kelenhegyi út 4. **Tel** (1) 466 61 66. 🚌 7, 86. 🚋 18, 19, 47, 49. ⏲ daily. 🖼 ♿ www.gellertbath.com

The earliest reference to the existence of healing waters at this site is found in the 13th century. In the later Middle Ages a hospital stood here and then, during the Turkish occupation, baths were built. The area takes its name from Bishop Gellért, whose monument on the hill is visible from many parts of the city. He was supposedly martyred here in 1046 by a group opposed to the introduction of Christianity. From the top of the hill one can admire a beautiful view of the whole of Budapest.

The Gellért Hotel, with its famous spa, was built between 1912 and 1918 in the Secession style, at the foot of the hill.

The men's section at the Gellért Baths

It boasts elaborate mosaics, stained-glass windows, statues, and fanciful balconies fronting the rooms. Its eastern-style towers and turrets offer superb views.

The complex houses an institute of water therapy. The baths are separated into different areas for men and women. Each has plunge pools, a sauna, and a steam bath. The facilities have been modernized, but the glorious Secession interiors remain.

There is also an outdoor swimming pool with a wave machine, installed in 1927 and still in operation. The baths and health spa, with their sun terraces, restaurants, and cafés, are open to the public as well as to hotel guests.

Baroque Madonna, Mátyás Church

OTHER MUSEUMS IN BUDAPEST

Franz Liszt Museum
Vörösmarty utca 35. **Tel** (1) 322 98 04. Ⓜ Vörösmarty utca. ⏲ Mon–Sat. 🖼 www.lisztmuseum.hu
Museum in a house built in 1877 for Liszt (1811–86).

Kodály Memorial Museum
Andrássy út 89. **Tel** (1) 352 7106. Ⓜ Kodály Körönd. ⏲ Wed–Sun. 🖼 www.kodaly-inst.hu
The house in which the composer Kodály (1882–1967) lived and worked.

Museum of Applied Arts
Üllői út 33–37. **Tel** (1) 456 51 00. Ⓜ Ferenc körút. ⏲ Tue–Sun. 🖼 ♿ www.imm.hu
Fine collection of decorative arts, especially Art Nouveau artifacts.

Museum of Contemporary Art and Ludwig Museum
Komor Marcell utca 1. **Tel** (1) 555 34 44. 🚌 15, Csepeli HÉV. 🚋 1, 2, 4, 6. ⏲ Tue–Sun. 🖼 ♿ www.ludwigmuseum.hu
A contemporary art museum with works by Warhol and Hockney.

Pest

At the end of the 17th century, much of the walled city of Pest, on the east bank of the Danube, was in ruins and few residents remained. Gradually new residential districts began to be developed, extending beyond the medieval walls, and people started to return.

After a flood in 1838, which destroyed most of the rural dwellings in the areas around Pest, redevelopment schemes introduced grand houses and apartment blocks. The area of Városliget (City Park), once an expanse of marshland, was also developed in the 19th century.

The first bridge linking Pest and Buda was built in 1766. The two cities were united as Budapest in 1873.

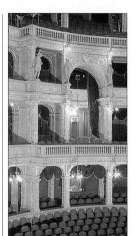

Lavish interior of the 19th-century State Opera House

The predominantly Baroque nave of the Inner City Parish Church

Inner City Parish Church ④

Március 15 tér 2. *Tel (1) 318 3108.* M *Ferenciek tere.* ◯ *daily.*

During the reign of István I (AD 1001–38), a small church stood on this site. St. Gellért was buried here after his martyrdom in 1046.

Work began on the Inner City Parish Church (*Belvárosi Plébánia templom*), adding to the existing building, in the 12th century. It is the oldest building in Pest. In the 14th century it was remodeled in Gothic style, and later used as a mosque by the Turks. After the fire of 1723, it was partly rebuilt in the Baroque style.

On the south side of the church is a Renaissance tabernacle bearing the Crest of Pest, created in the 16th century. Close to the main altar is a reminder of Turkish occupation: a *mihrab*, or prayer niche, indicating the direction of Mecca.

Hungarian National Museum ⑤

Múzeum körút 14–16. *Tel (1) 338 21 22.* ◯ *Tue–Sun.* M *Kálvin tér, Astoria.* ▭ *7, 9, 15, 173.* ▭ *47, 49.* 🏞 🅾 www.hnm.hu

The Hungarian National Museum was founded in 1802, when Count Ferenc Széchényi gave his personal collection to the nation. It is housed in an impressive Neoclassical edifice (1837–47).

In 1848, on the steps of the museum, poet Sándor Petőfi first read his *National Song*, which sparked the uprising against Habsburg rule. A re-enactment is staged each year on March 15.

The museum's eclectic exhibits span the 11th century to the present day. Items on display include an 18th-century campaign chest, decorative weapons of Transylvanian princes, and a printing press used to print nationalist propaganda in 1848.

The museum is home to the Coronation Mantle donated by St. Stephen in 1031. It is made of Byzantine silks and is one of the oldest and best-preserved textile masterpieces in Europe.

Baroque campaign chest in the National Museum

State Opera ⑥

Andrássy út 22. *Tel (1) 331 25 50.* M *Opera.* ◯ *daily.* 🏞 🅾 *3pm & 4pm obligatory.* ♿ 🏠 www.opera.hu

The State Opera (*Magyar Állami Operaház*), opened in 1884, was the life's work of architect Miklós Ybl. The facade expresses musical themes, with statues of two of Hungary's most prominent composers, Ferenc Erkel and Franz Liszt. The opulence of the foyer, with its chandeliers, murals, and vaulted ceiling, is echoed in the grandeur of the sweeping main staircase and of the three-story auditorium.

St. Stephen's Basilica ⑦

Szent István tér 1. *Tel (1) 317 28 59.* M *Deák Ferenc tér.* **Treasury** ◯ *daily.* 🏞 ♿ 🏠 *daily.* http://bazilika.biz

This Neoclassical church, dedicated to St. Stephen, or István, Hungary's first Christian king (1001–38), was built in 1851–1905 on a Greek cross floor plan. The church received the title Basilica Minor in 1938, the 900th anniversary of the king's death.

For hotels and restaurants in this region see p742 and p743

On the main altar is a marble statue of the saint; scenes from his life are depicted behind the altar. A painting to the right of the main entrance shows István dedicating Hungary to the Virgin Mary. His mummified forearm is kept in the Chapel of the Holy Right Hand.

The main entrance to the basilica is a massive door, decorated with carved heads of the 12 apostles. The dome reaches 96 m (315 ft) and is visible all over Budapest. Its interior is decorated with mosaics by Károly Lotz.

The basilica also has two distinctive towers. The one to the left of the main door houses a bell weighing 9 tons. This was funded by German Catholics to compensate for the loss of the original bell, which was looted by the Nazis in 1944.

Parliament ⑧

Kossuth Lajos tér 1–3. **Tel** (1) 441 40 00. M Kossuth tér. ▥ 70, 78. ▤ 2, 2A. ◯ daily. ◯ during ceremonies. ▨ (free for EU citizens). ▧ call (1) 441 49 04 to arrange. ▧ ▣ www.parlament.hu

The Parliament (*Országház*) is Hungary's largest building – 268 m (880 ft) long, 96 m (315 ft) high, with 691 rooms. Built between 1884 and 1902, it was based on London's Houses of Parliament (*see p45*). Although the facade is Neo-Gothic, the ground plan follows Baroque conventions, with a magnificent dome at the center. Beneath it is the Domed Hall, off which is the Gobelin Hall, with a Gobelin tapestry of Árpád

Tapestry of Árpád and Magyar chiefs in the Parliament building

(*see p729*) and fellow Magyar chiefs taking a blood oath. The greatest artists of the day decorated the interior of the building, and there are some spectacular ceiling frescoes by Károly Lotz and György Kiss.

Between the Domed Hall and the south wing is the National Assembly Hall. On the opposite side is the Congress Hall, a virtual mirror image of the National Assembly Hall. Both have public galleries.

Since 2000, the royal insignia have been displayed here.

Museum of Fine Arts ⑨

Hősök tere. **Tel** (1) 469 71 00. M Hősök tere. ▥ 20, 20E, 30, 30A 105. ▤ 72, 75, 79. ◯ Tue–Sun. ▧ ▧ www.szepmuveszeti.hu

In 1870 the state bought a magnificent collection of paintings from the Esterházy family. Enriched by donations and acquisitions, the collection moved to its present location in 1906. As well as great European paintings from

every era from the Middle Ages to the 20th century, there are Egyptian, Greek, and Roman antiquities. Renaissance pieces include a wonderful unfinished Raphael known as the *Esterházy Madonna* and a small bronze by Leonardo da Vinci of François I of France. There are also paintings by Holbein and Dürer, seven works by El Greco, and a fabulous collection of old master drawings.

French 19th-century art is also very well represented, with works by Manet, Gauguin, and Toulouse-Lautrec.

Vajdahunyad Castle ⑩

Városliget. **Tel** (1) 422 07 65. M Széchenyi Fürdő. ◯ Tue–Sun. ▨ ▧ ▧ www.mmgm.hu

This fantastical castle stands among trees at the edge of the lake in Városliget. It is in fact a complex of pavilions illustrating the evolution of Hungarian architecture. Created for the 1896 Millennium Celebrations as a temporary exhibit, it proved so popular that it was rebuilt permanently, in brick.

The pavilions are grouped in chronological order of style: Romanesque is followed by Gothic, Renaissance, Baroque, and so on, but the elements are linked to suggest a single, cohesive design. Details from more than 20 of Hungary's best-loved buildings are reproduced. The greatest emphasis is given to the medieval period, which is considered to be the most glorious in the country's history.

View across the lake of the Gothic (*left*) and Renaissance (*right*) sections of the Vajdahunyad Castle

Szentendre ❷

🚶 20,000. 🚉 🚌 🚢 from Budapest.
ℹ️ Dumtsa Jenő utca 22 **Tel** (26) 317
965. **www**.szentendreprogram.hu

Szentendre was settled by
Serbian refugees, who first
came here in the 14th century.
After the Turkish occupation
of Belgrade in 1690, more
Serbs arrived, ushering in a
period of great prosperity.

The Slavic interiors of the
town's many churches are
filled with incense, icons, and
candlelight. **Blagovestenska
Church** on Fő tér, the main
square, has a magnificent
iconostasis, while other sites
worth visiting are **Belgrade
Cathedral**, for Sunday Mass,
and the bishop's palace. Next
door, the **Museum of Serbian
Art** contains displays of icons
and other religious artifacts.

Many artists have made their
home in Szentendre, including
the Hungarian ceramic artist,
Margit Kovács (1902–77).
Her work can be seen at the
Margit Kovács Museum.

🏛 **Margit Kovács Museum**
Vastag György utca 1. **Tel** (26) 310
244. ◯ Mon–Sun. 🎫 📷

Esztergom ❸

🚶 30,000. 🚉 🚌 🚢 from Budapest.

St. István, Hungary's first
Christian king, was baptized
in Esztergom and later
crowned here on Christmas
Day in AD 1000. Dominat-
ing the city's skyline is the
huge **Catholic Cathedral**, built
in the early 19th century on
the site of a 12th-century
church. In the treasury are

The Tihany Peninsula, jutting out into Lake Balaton

religious artifacts from the
original church. The 16th-
century marble Bakócz burial
chapel, next to the southern
entrance, was built by Florentine craftsmen. South of the
cathedral, the remains of
Esztergom's **Castle** date from
the 10th century.

In the picturesque old
town, Esztergom's central
square is bordered by many
lively pavement cafés.

⚜ **Castle**
Szent István tér 1. **Tel** (33) 415 986.
◯ Tue–Sun. 🎫

Lake Balaton ❹

Siófok 🚉 🚌 🚢 to/from Balatonfüred. ℹ️ Víztorony, Pf: 75 **Tel** (84)
315 355. **Balatonfüred** 🚉 🚌
🚢 to/from Siófok and Tihany.
ℹ️ Kisfaludy u. 1 (87) 580 480.

Every summer Lake Balaton,
Europe's largest fresh-water
lake, attracts thousands of
vacationers. The southern
shore is the more developed,
with sandy beaches and a
wide choice of tourist
accommodations. The largest
resort is **Siófok**, characterized
by high-rise buildings, lively
bars, and noisy nightlife. By
day, windsurfing, sailing, and
pleasure cruises are available.

Those in search of a more
peaceful atmosphere should
head for **Balatonvilágos**, set
atop attractive wooded cliffs,
or **Balatonberény**, which
has a nudist beach. Southwest
of Balatonberény, the tiny
lake known as **Kis-Balaton**
(Little Balaton) is a protected
nature reserve, home to over
80 species of birds.

One of the most popular
destinations on Balaton's
northern shore is the spa
town of **Balatonfüred**,
whose mineral springs have
been used for curative
purposes since Roman times.
From here you can visit the
Tihany Peninsula, which
became Hungary's first
national park in 1957, and
boasts some of the most
beautiful scenery in the area.

At the far northwestern tip
of the lake, the university
town of **Keszthely** has three
beaches, as well as a number
of other attractions, including
the Balaton Museum, which
covers the history and natural
history of the region, and the
imposing Festetics Palace. A
15-minute drive from Keszthely
brings you to **Hévíz**, an old
19th-century spa resort, where
you can bathe in the world's
second largest thermal lake.

Esztergom's vast cathedral, on the banks of the Danube River

For hotels and restaurants in this region see p742 and p743

Pécs ❺

🏛 *180,000.* 🚆 🚌 ℹ️ *Széchenyi tér 9* **Tel** *(72) 213 315.*

First a Celtic, then a Roman settlement, Pécs was later ruled by the Turks from 1543 until 1686. Several monuments testify to these different periods of Pécs' history.

The city's main square, Széchenyi tér, is overlooked by the **Catholic Church**, formerly the Mosque of Gazi Kassim Pasha, built under Turkish occupation. Inside, a delicately decorated *mihrab* (prayer niche) serves as a reminder of the building's origins. Behind the church is the **Archaeological Museum**, whose exhibits date from prehistoric times to the Magyar conquest.

On Dom tér are Pécs' four-towered, Neo-Romanesque **Cathedral**, which stands on the foundations of an 11th-century basilica, and the Neo-Renaissance **Bishop's Palace** (1770). South of here, on Szent István tér, a stairway leads to the ruins of a 4th-century underground **chapel**, which contains a wonderful collection of frescoes. On nearby Apáca utca, recent excavations have unearthed a collection of **Roman tombs**. Remains of the city's **medieval walls**, erected after an invasion by the Mongols in the 13th century, include a 15th-century barbican.

Candlelit interior of Pécs' Neo-Romanesque cathedral

Pécs' museums include the **Csontváry Museum**, showing works by the artist Kosztka Tivadar Csontváry (1853–1919), and the **Vasarely Museum**, dedicated to Hungarian Op artist Victor Vasarely (1908–97).

🏛 **Archaeological Museum**
Janus Pannonius utca 1. **Tel** *(72) 310 544.* ⬜ *Tue–Sat.* 📷

🏛 **Vasarely Museum**
Káptalan utca 3. **Tel** *(72) 514 040.* ⬜ *Tue–Sun.* 📷

Eger ❻

🏛 *60,000.* 🚆 🚌 ℹ️ *Bajcsy Zsilinsky u 9* **Tel** *(36) 517 715.*

One of the most popular tourist destinations in Hungary, Eger is also famous for its world-class wines.

At the heart of the town, on Eszterházy tér, are the Neoclassical **Cathedral** (1830s) and the **Lyceum**. A highlight of the latter is the observatory, which affords stunning views of the town and surrounding vineyards.

Eger's 40-m (130-ft) **minaret** is a relic of 16th-century Turkish occupation, while the splendid Baroque **Minorite Church** on Dobó István tér dates from the 1770s.

Eger Castle was built in the 13th century following the Mongol invasion. The castle complex includes the Bishop's Palace (1470), which houses a museum of historical artifacts, and underground casemates.

⛪ **Eger Castle**
Egri Vár. **Tel** *(36) 312 744.* ⬜ *daily.* 📷

Environs
Just west of the town, in the **Szépasszony Valley**, you can sample the region's wines, including the famous dry red, Egri Bikavér, or Bull's Blood.

Tokaj ❼

🏛 *20,000.* 🚆 🚌 ℹ️ *Serház utca 1* **Tel** *(47) 352 259.*
www.tokaj-turizmus.hu

Tokaj is located at the center of one of Hungary's most important wine-growing areas. Tokaji dessert wines owe their distinctive full-bodied flavor to the volcanic soil in which the vines grow, and a type of mold peculiar to the region. The best cellars to visit for a tasting are the **Rákóczi Cellar**, run by a foreign company, and the privately owned **Hímesudvar** at No. 2 Bem utca.

Hungarian dessert wine Tokaji Aszú

Tokaj has a **synagogue** and a **Jewish cemetery**, relics of the period before World War II, when the town had a large Jewish population. The **Tokaj Museum** gives an interesting insight into the history of the town and its environs.

🍷 **Rákóczi Cellar**
Kossuth tér 15. **Tel** *(47) 352 408.* ⬜ *Apr–Oct: daily (call in advance).* 📷

Eger's Baroque Minorite church, towering over Dobó István tér

Practical & Travel Information

Tourism is an important part of the Hungarian national economy, and as a result, there have been vast improvements in communications, banking facilities, and public transportation. The biggest problem tourists face is the formidable language barrier. However, staff at many tourist offices, hotels, and other attractions, usually speak English or German.

WHEN TO VISIT

The most popular times to visit Hungary are between April and the end of June, and from the middle of August until October. July is usually extremely hot, and it is almost unbearable to stay in Budapest, although away from the capital the heat is less severe. From November until March, many museums have shorter opening hours or may close altogether.

TOURIST INFORMATION

Before leaving for Hungary, you can obtain various information leaflets and maps from the Hungarian National Tourist Office, which has branches worldwide.

Within Hungary, there are tourist information offices in most large towns. In Budapest, advice on sightseeing, accommodation, and cultural events is given by the offices of **Tourinform Budapest**. The **Vista Visitor Center** also offers these services, as well as a reduced-rate telephone center, left-luggage lockers, a bureau de change, and an internet café.

Visitors to the capital may wish to invest in the Budapest Card, which entitles card-holders, along with one child under 14, to unlimited use of the city's public transport system, discounts on entry to museums, the zoo and funfair, and on selected guided tours, and 10 to 20 percent discount on selected cultural events and at certain restaurants.

A new metro line in Budapest will run between southwest Buda and northeast Pest, and is expected to open in 2014.

VISA REQUIREMENTS

Citizens of the US, Canada, Australia, and New Zealand need only a valid passport to visit Hungary for up to 90 days. EU citizens need only an identity card.

For more information about visas and extended visits, see the Hungarian Ministry of Foreign Affairs' website (www.mfa.gov.hu).

PERSONAL SECURITY

Hungary is on the whole a safe country to travel in. As in most cities that attract large numbers of tourists, pickpockets operate in Budapest, targeting crowded metro stations, buses, and shopping malls. Rákóczi tér and Mátyás tér, in district VIII, are traditional hangouts for prostitutes; lone women should avoid these areas at night.

In the case of an emergency while on vacation, the relevant numbers to call are listed in the directory opposite.

HEALTH ISSUES

No special vaccinations are required. Allergy sufferers and people with breathing difficulties who intend to visit Budapest should take account of the summer smog conditions, which are particulary acute in Pest. Those susceptible might consider staying in the castle district, where cars are banned, or retreating to the wooded Buda hills.

For treatments for minor ailments, visit a pharmacy (Gyógyszertár or Patika). If your nearest store is closed, it should display a list of 24-hour emergency pharmacies.

People with heart conditions who wish to use Hungary's thermal baths should seek a physician's advice beforehand.

FACILITIES FOR THE DISABLED

Hungary's public transportation systems, museums, and other attractions are gradually being renovated to make them wheelchair-friendly, but people with disabilities may still encounter problems. For more detailed information contact the **Hungarian Disabled Association**.

BANKING AND CURRENCY

The Hungarian currency is the forint (HUF or Ft). If you need to change money, the best rates of exchange are offered by banks and bureaux de change. Banks open from 8am to 5pm, Monday to Friday. While all banks are closed at the weekends, bureaux de change and ATMs remain open. Credit cards are more widely accepted now than before, but their use is still not as widespread as elsewhere in Europe and you shouldn't expect to be able to use them everywhere. It's wise to carry a little extra cash.

THE CLIMATE OF HUNGARY

Hungary enjoys some of the sunniest weather in Europe, with an average of eight hours of sunshine a day in summer. June, July, and August are the hottest months. In winter, temperatures can fall well below freezing and there may also be snowfall. Hungary has comparatively low rainfall. June usually gets the most rain, while the fall is the driest season.

BUDAPEST

°C/F		26/79	
	15/59	15/59	15/59
0°C 32°F	5/41		6/43
			2/36
			-3/27
☀ 6 hrs	10 hrs	5 hrs	2 hrs
☂ 42 mm	56 mm	40 mm	40 mm
month	Apr	Jul	Oct	Jan

COMMUNICATIONS

The Hungarian telephone system used to be notoriously bad, but improvements are now slowly being made. Phonecards, which are available from tobacconists, post offices, petrol stations, and some newspaper kiosks, are the best option when using public phones, although some booths still accept coins.

Post offices open from 8am to 6pm, Monday to Friday, and on Saturday mornings. Service can be slow and there are often long lines, so be prepared to wait.

FLYING TO HUNGARY

Direct scheduled flights between New York's JFK airport and Budapest's international airport at Ferihegy are operated by many airlines. Major airlines flying from the US and Canada to Hungary include **Air France**, **British Airways**, **KLM**, and **Lufthansa**, although services entail a transfer or touch-down at another European city. British Airways

and Air France each operate three daily scheduled flights from London. Many low-cost airlines such as **Jet2.com** and **Wizz Air** also operate daily flights from London.

Budapest airport is located 16 km (10 miles) from the center of Budapest. The efficient **Airport Minibus Shuttle** will take passengers from the airport to any address in the capital. Taxis are a quick and comfortable way of getting into the city.

RAIL TRAVEL

The Hungarian national rail network is very efficient, with trains invariably departing and arriving on time. Budapest has direct international rail links with 25 other capital cities, Keleti pu station handling the majority of the international traffic. High-speed trains to Vienna, the main communications hub for western Europe, depart approximately every three hours and take around 2 hours 25 minutes. There are also car-train services from Keleti pu to Thessaloníki in Greece. Within Hungary, local trains

are categorized according to speed: "slow" (*személy*), "speedy" (*sebes*), or "fast" (*gyors*). There are also modern intercity services between Budapest and the larger cities. A number of concessionary fares are available for those planning on doing a lot of rail travel in Hungary.

TRAVELING BY BUS

International buses to all European destinations depart from Népliget station. Nationally, buses are run by Volánbusz, which operates routes to most cities and towns in Hungary.

TRAVELING BY CAR

To rent a car in Hungary you must be aged 21 years or over, and have held a full driver's license for at least a year. An international driver's license helps also. Most of the big, international firms have offices at the airport in Budapest, or you can arrange rental and travel agencies throughout the country.

DIRECTORY

Where to Stay in Hungary

Hungary offers a range of accommodations, from top-class chain hotels to family-run pensions and hostels. In Budapest, bargain hunters can benefit from substantial weekend reductions offered by many luxury hotels in the low season. During the summer, when smog can prevail, it is best to opt for an air-conditioned hotel in Pest.

PRICE CATEGORIES
Price categories are for a standard double room with bathroom per night, including breakfast, tax, and service charges:

Under 15,000 HUF
15,000–25,000 HUF
25,000–35,000 HUF
35,000–50,000 HUF
Over 50,000 HUF

BUDAPEST

BUDA Citadella
Citadella sétány, 1118 **Tel** *1-466 57 94* **Rooms** *14*   **Map** *C4*

This hostel-style hotel occupies the casements of the Citadel. It offers relatively inexpensive, neat, and clean double and multiple-occupancy rooms. A popular wine bar, restaurant, and nightclub are located in the Citadella complex, and there is also a souvenir shop and garden. **www.citadella.hu**

BUDA Danubius Hotel Gellért
Szent Gellért tér 1, 1111 **Tel** *1-889 55 00* **Rooms** *234*   **Map** *C4*

This legendary spa hotel has both indoor and outdoor pools that provide an attractive environment in which to relax. Treatments such as massage are also available. Other facilities include two restaurants, a bar, café, nightclub, and banqueting halls. The rooms have probably seen grander days. **www.danubiusgroup.com/gellert**

BUDA Hilton
Hess Andrástér 1–3, 1014 **Tel** *1-889 66 00* **Rooms** *322*   **Map** *B3*

The Hilton, one of the most luxurious hotels in Budapest, is located in a building incorporating parts of a Gothic church and Jesuit monastery. In the heart of the Castle District, with magnificent views over the Danube and the Pest cityscape, the high prices here are more than justified. **www.budapest.hilton.com**

PEST Astoria
Kossuth Lajos utca 19–21, 1053 **Tel** *1-889 6000* **Rooms** *138*   **Map** *C3*

This old hotel, designed in the Secessionist style, but with a Neo-Baroque breakfast room, has been refurbished to recreate its original interior. Even for visitors not staying at the hotel, it is worth visiting the café to see the beautiful interior. Those staying at the hotel will find the bedrooms luxurious. **www.danubiusgroup.com/astoria**

PEST Kempinski Corvinus
Erzsébet tér 7–8, 1051 **Tel** *1-429 37 77* **Rooms** *366*   **Map** *D3*

This exclusive hotel – all glass and class – often welcomes heads of state and other notable personalities among its guests. The large and luxuriously furnished rooms are relaxing, and a perfect mix of luxury with modernity. The hotel has excellent fitness facilities, a pool, two good restaurants, bars, and a pub. **www.kempinski-budapest.com**

REST OF HUNGARY

BALATONFURED Annabella
Deák Ferenc utca 25, 8230 **Tel** *87-889 400* **Fax** *87-889 412* **Rooms** *388*

Close to the lake shore in the centre of Balatonfüred, the Annabella enjoys its own private beach. It also offers a number of smaller than standard double rooms, a bargain in a resort where these are hard to find. Pets are accepted at no extra cost, though not in the restaurants. Open only May–Oct. **www.danubiushotels.com/annabella**

EGER Senator-ház
Dobó tér 11, 3300 **Tel** *36-411 711* **Fax** *36-320 466* **Rooms** *14*

One of the oldest buildings in Eger, dating from 1753, the Senator-ház has a fantastic location on Dobó square in the shadow of Eger Castle. The rooms are on the small side but most have castle views. There is a good restaurant, café, and terrace. Guests have free admission to Eger's thermal baths at weekends. **www.senatorhaz.hu**

PECS Palatinus
Király utca 5, 7621 **Tel** *72-889 400* **Fax** *72-889 438* **Rooms** *94*

A mix of Secession and Art Deco styles, the facade and lobby of this hotel are tourist attractions in themselves. In addition, the hotel boasts sumptuous rooms and a first-class location on the elegant Király utca. Sauna, solarium, and steam bath are located in the basement. **www.danubiushotels.com/palatinus**

Key to Symbols *see back cover flap*

Where to Eat in Hungary

Hungary offers a variety of eateries at prices to suit most budgets. Two of the most common types are the *étterem*, a restaurant that offers Hungarian and international dishes, and the *csárda*, a taverna serving local specialties. Many ethnic venues have also sprung up in Budapest, specializing in global cuisine.

PRICE CATEGORIES
Price categories are for an average three-course meal for one, including half a bottle of wine, and all unavoidable charges:

- Under 3,000 HUF
- 3,000–4,000 HUF
- 4,000–5,000 HUF
- 5,000–6,000 HUF
- Over 6,000 HUF

BUDAPEST

BUDA Hungarian Kitchen

Fortuna utca 21 **Tel** *1-202 21 13*   **Map** *C3*

This is one of a modern breed of restaurants breathing new life into Hungarian cuisine, using traditional recipes and flavors but with lighter ingredients. Fresh market produce is always used. The restaurant serves only Hungarian wines, including some labels not available anywhere else.

BUDA Pest Buda Vendéglô

Fortuna utca 3 **Tel** *1-212 58 80*   **Map** *B2*

This is a small, elegant restaurant with arcaded walls in a listed building. Part of the former underground cave system gives space to its popular and extensive Hungarian and international wine cellar. The menu itself is not all that long but it is interesting nevertheless, and all the dishes are excellently prepared.

BUDA Rivalda Café & Restaurant

Színház utca 5–9 **Tel** *1-489 02 36*   **Map** *B3*

Next to the Castle Theater, the Rivalda's decor is theater-inspired yet not over-the-top. Its contemporary international cuisine, with a frequently changing menu, reflects the seasons, with most dishes based on local, fresh ingredients. Many dishes are inventive, and all are superbly presented. Live jazz piano music in the evenings.

PEST Károlyi Étterem és Kávéház

Károlyi Mihály utca 16 **Tel** *1-328 02 40*   **Map** *D4*

In the lovely courtyard of the Károlyi Palace is this elegant, sophisticated restaurant. Worth trying is the *borjúpaprikás lángosban* (veal paprika stew with potato pancakes). Its attractive gardens are uncommon in the city center. At weekends it is worth booking – the restaurant is often closed for weddings in summer.

PEST Belcanto

Dalszínház utca 8 **Tel** *1-269 27 86*   **Map** *C3*

Enjoy good international and Hungarian favorites while listening to the waiters and some customers or opera professionals sing popular opera pieces in the evening at this now legendary Hungarian restaurant, as famous for its good-time atmosphere as for its super food. There is also an orchestra playing dance music to really liven things up.

REST OF HUNGARY

BALATONFURED Stefánia Vitorlás

Tagore sétány 1 **Tel** *87-343 407*

On the shore of Lake Balaton with views out to Tihany Peninsula, this restaurant is situated in the refurbished clubhouse of the Balatonfüred Rowing and Sailing Club. Serving fish and game dishes to a buzzing crowd from morning until late, it is also the perfect spot to sample great local wine.

EGER Hotel Villa Völgy

Tulipánkert út 5 **Tel** *36-321 664*

Situated in the peaceful Szépasszony valley, home of Eger wines, is this hotel with two excellent restaurants. The menus feature traditional regional Hungarian dishes, as well as international cuisine. There are large, well-tended gardens and an outdoor dining area. Wine-tasting events provide an opportunity to sample local wines.

ESZTERGOM Prímás Pince

Szent ıstván tér 4 **Tel** *33-313 495*

What has long been an Esztergom favorite has become an international one thanks to countless happy diners who come here year after year. While the cuisine is standard Hungarian and the wine list less than worthy, the setting in the cellars of the castle is legendary. Disappointingly, it closes early at 6pm, with last kitchen orders a little before.

Map References *see map of Budapest pp732–3*

POLAND

*L*ocated between Russia and Germany, Poland has always been a fiercely contested land. Released from the eastern bloc in 1989, the country is now developing rapidly, especially in the cities of Warsaw, Cracow, Gdańsk, and Wrocław. Monuments attest to a stormy history, but Poland is famed for its virtues, especially the generosity of its people and the excellence of its vodka.

Although situated on the plains of central Europe, Poland has an extremely varied landscape. Alpine scenery predominates in the Tatra Mountains to the south, while the north is dominated by lakes. Mountain lovers can make use of the well-developed infrastructure of hostels and shelters, such as those found in the Tatras. The countless lakes of Warmia and Mazuria, collectively known as the Land of a Thousand Lakes, are a haven for water-sports enthusiasts.

Poland's inhabitants, who number almost 39 million , all but constitute a single ethnic group, with minorities accounting for less than 4 percent of the population. The largest minorities are Belorussians and Ukrainians, who inhabit the east of the country, and Germans, who are concentrated mainly around the city of Opole in Silesia. The majority of Poles are Catholic, but large regions of the country, such as Cieszyn Silesia, have a substantial Protestant population. In the east there are also many Orthodox Christians. Religious denomination does not necessarily coincide with ethnic identity, although Belorussians tend to be Orthodox, while Ukrainians belong to the Greek Catholic (Uniate) Church.

HISTORY

Poland's borders have changed continually with the course of history. The origins of the Polish nation go back to the 10th century, when Slav tribes living in the area of Gniezno united under the Piast dynasty, which ruled Poland until 1370. Mieszko I converted to Christianity in 966, thus bringing his kingdom into Christian Europe, and made Poznań the seat of Poland's first bishop. The Piast dynasty ruled Poland with variable fortune and

Statue of the great 19th-century poet and patriot Adam Mickiewicz in Market Square, Cracow

◁ Altarpiece depicting the Assumption in St. Mary's Church, Cracow, carved by Veit Stoss (1447–1533)

Solidarity demonstrators staging a mass rally during a papal visit to Poland in 1987

embroiled the nation in domestic quarrels for 150 years. After this dynasty died out, the great Lithuanian prince Jagiełło took the Polish throne and founded a new dynasty. The treaty with Lithuania signed in 1385 initiated the long process of consolidation between these nations, culminating in 1569 with the signing of the Union of Lublin. Nevertheless, the so-called Republic of Two Nations *(Rzeczpospolita Obojga Narodów)* lasted until 1795. In 1572 the Jagiellonian dynasty died out, after which the Polish authorities introduced elective kings, with the nobility having the right to vote.

KEY DATES IN POLISH HISTORY

966 Adoption of Christianity under Mieszko I

1025 Coronation of Bolesław the Brave, first king of Poland

1320 The unification of the Polish state

1385 Poland and Lithuania unite under the Treaty of Krewo

1569 The Union of Lublin creates the Polish-Lithuanian Republic of Two Nations

1596 The capital moves from Cracow to Warsaw

1655 Beginning of the "Deluge" (the Swedish occupation), ending in 1660

1772–1918 Poland divided three times between Russia, Prussia, and Austria. The final partition (1795) is made after a Polish uprising led by Tadeusz Kościuszko

1918 Poland regains independence

1939 Soviet and German forces invade

1940 Auschwitz-Birkenau established; 1.5 million Poles and Jews are gassed during the war

1945 Communist government takes control

1980 Solidarity formed, led by Lech Wałęsa

1989 First free post-war elections are held. Lech Wałęsa wins the Presidency by a landslide

1999 Poland joins NATO

2004 Poland joins EU

The 17th century was dominated by wars with Sweden, Russia, and the Ottoman Empire, and although the country survived, it was considerably weakened, and its time of dominance was over. In 1795 it was partitioned by Russia, Prussia, and Austria, and was wiped off the map for more than 100 years. Attempts to wrest independence by insurrection were unsuccessful, and Poland did not regain its sovereignty until 1918. The arduous process of rebuilding and uniting the nation was still incomplete when, at the outbreak of World War II, a six-year period of German and Soviet occupation began. The price that Poland paid was very high: millions were murdered, including virtually its entire Jewish population. The country suffered devastation and there were huge territorial losses, which were only partly compensated by the Allies' decision to move the border westwards. After the war, Poland was subjugated by the Soviet Union, but the socialist economy proved ineffective. The formation of Solidarity *(Solidarność)* in 1980 accelerated the pace of change, which was completed when Poland regained its freedom after the June 1989 elections.

In 1999 Poland became a member of NATO, and in 2004 it joined the European Union.

LANGUAGE AND CULTURE

The legacy of more than 100 years of partition rule is still visible in Poland's cultural landscape. Russian, Prussian, and Austrian administrations left their mark not only on rural and urban architecture, but also on the customs and mentality of the people.

The Poles have a deep reverence for religious symbols and rituals, and the presence of the church can be seen everywhere, either in the form of lavish Baroque buildings or images of the Black Madonna. Wayside shrines are also a regular feature.

Polish is a West Slavic language closely related to Slovak and Czech. Many of its words (such as *Solidarność*) are borrowed from Latin, although German, Italian, and English words are also common.

Exploring Poland

Bordering the Baltic Sea, Poland is one of the largest countries of Central Europe, with a population of around 39 million. Warsaw, the capital, is located at the center of Poland, on the banks of the River Vistula (Wisła). Its location makes it an ideal base for visiting other cities, such as Cracow, the ancient royal capital; Gdańsk, the Hanseatic city whose shipyards gave birth to Solidarity; and Poznań, one of the oldest Polish cities. Cracow is one of the country's greatest treasures, offering excursions to the Polish mountains and the Cracow-Częstochowa Valley.

SIGHTS AT A GLANCE

Children in traditional dress on a
Polish public holiday, Cracow

The Neoclassical entrance to
Warsaw's Wilanów Palace and Park

0 kilometers 100

0 miles 100

KEY

- 🛫 Airport
- ⛴ Ferry port
- — Highway
- — Major road
- — Railroad
- ▪▪▪ International border

Warsaw ❶

Warsaw is believed to have been founded in the late 13th century, when Duke Bolesław built a castle here overlooking the Vistula. It became capital of Poland in 1596, making it one of Europe's youngest capital cities. The present castle and other grand buildings of the Old Town date largely from the Renaissance and Baroque periods. By the end of World War II, some 80 percent of the buildings had been reduced to rubble. What you see today is the product of meticulous reconstruction undertaken during the Communist era. Warsaw is rich in museums and sights and the Varsovians are immensely proud of their history of resistance to oppression. The center has been declared a UNESCO World Heritage Site.

Wilanów Palace, a 17th-century royal retreat, which stands in a magnificent park on the outskirts of the city

SIGHTS AT A GLANCE

Grand Theater ⑥
Monument to the Ghetto Heroes ⑦
Monument to those Fallen and
  Murdered in the East ⑧
National Museum ⑩
Old Town Market Square ①
Palace of Culture and
  Science ⑨
Royal Castle ③
Royal Route ⑤
St. Anna's Church ④
St. John's Cathedral ②

Greater Warsaw
(see inset map)
Łazienki Park ⑪
Wilanów Palace and Park ⑫

SEE ALSO

- *Where to Stay* p760

- *Where to Eat* p761

0 meters   350
0 yards   350

GETTING AROUND

The sights in the Old and New Town areas are easily visited on foot, since most of the streets are pedestrianized. Trams are best for short trips across the center. There is also an extensive bus service, but Warsaw's single metro line only serves suburbs to the south and is of little use to tourists. Taxis are reasonably priced, but use a reputable firm. Driving is getting more problematic, but the streets are still less crowded than in most European cities.

A B C

GREATER WARSAW

KEY

Area of main map

Congress Hall in the Palace of Culture and Science, former venue of Communist Party congresses

KEY

	Sight / Place of interest
✈	Airport
🚆	Train station
🚌	Bus station
M	Metro station
P	Parking
ℹ	Tourist information
✝	Church
✡	Synagogue
	Pedestrian street

Horse-drawn carriages in the colorful Old Town Market Square

Old Town Market Square ①

Rynek Starego Miasta. ▦ *116, 175, 180, 195, 503.* **History Museum Tel** *022-635 16 25.* ○ *Tue–Sun.*

Painstakingly restored after World War II, the Old Town Market Square was the center of Warsaw public life until the 19th century, when the focus of the growing, modern city moved. The tall, ornate, and colorful houses, which lend the square its unique character, were built by wealthy merchants in the 17th century.

The houses on one side form the **Warsaw History Museum** (Muzeum Historyczne m st Warszawy). This displays the city's history through paintings, photographs, sculpture, and archaeological finds. There is also a film show, with footage of the Nazis' systematic destruction of Warsaw in 1944. Today, café tables and stalls line the square, and horse-drawn carriages offer tours of the Old Town.

St. John's Cathedral ②

Świętojańska 8. **Tel** *022-831 02 89.* ▦ *116, 175, 178, 180, 195, 503.* ○ *daily (Sun: pm only).*

Completed in the early 15th century, St. John's Cathedral (katedra św Jana) was originally a parish church.

Gaining collegiate status in 1406, it was not until 1798 that St. John's became a cathedral. The coronation of Poland's last king, Stanisław August Poniatowski, in 1764, and the swearing of an oath by the deputies of the *Sejm* (Parliament) to uphold the 1791 Constitution took place here.

After World War II, various elaborate 19th-century additions were removed from the facade, and the cathedral was restored to its original Mazovian Gothic style. The interior features religious art, richly carved wooden stalls, and ornate tombs, including those of Gabriel Narutowicz (1865–1922), Poland's first president, assassinated two days after taking office, and Nobel prize-winning novelist Henryk Sienkiewicz (1846–1916). In a chapel founded by the Baryczka family hangs a 16th-century crucifix, which is credited with several miracles.

Royal Castle ③

Plac Zamkowy 4. **Tel** *022-355 51 70.* ▦ *116, 175, 178, 180, 195, 503.* ○ *daily (separate tickets for Royal Apartments and Parliament).* ◉ *Oct–Apr: Mon; public hols.* ▨ *(free Sun).* ▯ http://zamek-krolewski.com.pl

Warsaw's Royal Castle (Zamek Królewski) stands on the site of an original castle built here by the Mazovian dukes in the 14th century. It was transformed between 1598 and 1619 by King Zygmunt III Waza, who asked Italian architects to restyle the castle into a polygon. The king chose this castle as his royal residence in 1596, after the *Sejm* (Parliament) had moved here from Cracow in 1569. In the 18th century, King Augustus III remodeled the east wing in Baroque style and King Stanisław August Poniatowski added a library.

In 1939, the castle was burned, and then blown up by the Nazis in 1944. Reconstruction, which was funded by public donations, took from 1971 to 1988.

The castle's fascinating interiors are the result of its dual role: being a royal residence as well as the seat of parliament. Meticulously reconstructed, the castle has royal apartments, as well as the Chamber of Deputies and the Senate. Some of the woodwork and stucco is original, as are many of the furnishings and much of the art. Among the paintings are 18th-century works by Bellotto and Bacciarelli.

The opulent interior of the Marble Room in the Royal Castle

The magnificent Rococo organ loft of St. Anna's Church

St. Anna's Church ④

Krakowskie Przedmieście 68.
🚌 *116, 175, 178, 180, 195, 503.*
⬜ *daily.*

This imposing church on the Royal Route was founded by Anna, the widow of Duke Bolesław III, and built in the late 15th century, along with a Bernardine monastery. Extended between 1518 and 1533, the church was destroyed during the Swedish invasion of 1655, but later rebuilt in Baroque style. The Neoclassical facade was a subsequent addition, as was the free-standing bell tower, which dates from the 1820s.

The church has a magnificent interior, with several Rococo altars, a splendid organ, and frescoes by Walenty Żebrowski. A side chapel contains the relics of St. Władysław of Gielniów, Warsaw's patron saint. St. Anna's is a popular choice for weddings, partly due to the superstition that any marriage celebrated here will be a happy one.

Next to the church are the remains of the 16th-century Bernardine monastery, which was closed in 1864. The old cloisters in the monastery's east wing, however, have retained their original vaulted ceilings. Behind St. Anna's there is an attractive Neoclassical colonnade, known as Odwach. This is the city's best location for second-hand booksellers, and good for browsing.

Royal Route ⑤

Krakowskie Przedmieście and Nowy Świat. 🚌 *116, 180, 195, 503.*

The Royal Route (Trakt Królewski) is one of Warsaw's most historic and beautiful streets. Starting by Castle Square (Plac Zamkowy), and continuing all the way to the royal palace at Wilanów, the most interesting part of the route is along Krakowskie Przedmieście and Nowy Świat. These thoroughfares developed in the late Middle Ages, with their rural setting, by the banks of the Vistula river, attracting Warsaw's aristocracy and wealthy merchant class.

This social elite built grand summer residences and town houses here, while religious orders established lavish churches and monasteries. Krakowskie Przedmieście features many buildings from the 17th and 18th centuries, with several imposing palaces standing back from the road behind tree-lined squares and courtyards. Alongside, there are impressive town houses and some of the city's most interesting churches, including **St. Anna's**, **St. Joseph's**, and the **Church of the Assumption**. **Warsaw University** and the **Fine Arts Academy** are also located here, while various monuments pay tribute to eminent Poles.

Nowy Świat is lined with long rows of 18th- and 19th-century

Statue of Poland's most famous astronomer, Nicholas Copernicus (1473–1543), on the Royal Route

town houses. It is also one of the busiest shopping streets in the world, and full of large stores, fashionable boutiques, colorful sidewalk cafés, and a wide choice of restaurants.

Imposing Neoclassical facade of the Grand Theater

Grand Theater ⑥

Plac Teatralny. **Tel** *022-692 02 00.* 🚌 *111, 175, 410.* **Ticket office** ⬜ *daily.*

One of the city's largest buildings before World War II, the Grand Theater was built in 1825–33, to a design by Antonio Corazzi and Ludwik Kozubowski. Many renowned craftsmen also contributed to the sublime, palatial interiors. Initially the building was to be named the National Theater, but the defeat of the 1830 November Uprising forced a change of name. The two statues that stand in front of the building are of the 19th-century composer Stanisław Moniuszko, known as the father of Polish opera, and of Wojciech Bogusławski, the man who instigated the construction of the theater.

The theater currently houses the National Opera and Ballet and a small theater museum. Severely damaged during World War II, the theater retained only its impressive Neoclassical facade and a few of its rooms. Greatly enlarged in the course of reconstruction, it acquired many modern interiors and far more extensive backstage facilities.

Monument to the Ghetto Heroes ⑦

Pomnik Bohaterów Getta, Zamenhofa. 🚌 127, 111, 180.

The Nazis created the Jewish ghetto in 1940 by driving the Jewish inhabitants of Warsaw and nearby villages into an area in the northwest of the city. The ghetto initially housed around 450,000 people, but by 1942 over 300,000 had been transported to death camps, and 100,000 others had died or been killed in the ghetto. The Ghetto Uprising of 1943 was an action of heroic defiance against the Nazis, planned not as a bid for liberty, but as an honorable way to die. Built to commemorate this action, the Monument to the Ghetto Heroes stands in the center of the former ghetto. It depicts men, women, and children struggling to flee the burning ghetto, together with a procession of Jews being driven to Nazi death camps.

A **Path of Remembrance**, lined with a series of granite blocks dedicated to events or heroes of the ghetto, links the ghetto memorial to the nearby Bunker Monument – on the site from where the uprising was co-ordinated – and the Umschlagplatz Monument. Engraved with hundreds of names, it marks the place from where many Jews were deported to the death camps, and represents the cattle trucks used for transportation.

Detail from the Monument to the Ghetto Heroes

Monument to Those Fallen and Murdered in the East ⑧

ul. Muranowska. 🚌 116, 127, 178, 503. 🚋 18, 35.

This emotionally stirring monument, designed by Mirosław Biskupski and unveiled in 1995, takes the form of a typical railway wagon in which Poles were deported into the depths of the Soviet Union. It is filled with a pile of crosses symbolizing the hundreds of thousands of Poles carted off to the East in cattle vans and subsequently murdered in Soviet prison camps.

Palace of Culture and Science ⑨

Plac Defilad 1. **Tel** 022-656 76 00. **Viewing Terrace** ☐ daily. 📷

This monolithic building was a "gift" from Soviet Russia to the people of Warsaw, and intended as a monument to "the inventive spirit and social progress." Built in 1952–5 by the Russian architect, Lev Rudniev, it resembles Moscow's Socialist Realist tower blocks.

The palace still inspires extreme emotions among Varsovians, ranging from admiration to demands for its demolition. Since the end of Soviet domination, the building's role has changed. The tower itself now provides office space, and the Congress Hall, which once held Communist Party congresses, is now a venue for concerts and festivals. The palace remains a cultural center in other ways, with the Theater of Dramatic Art, a cinema, puppet theater, technology museum, and a sports complex.

The imposing Socialist Realist Palace of Culture and Science

National Museum ⑩

Aleje Jerozolimskie 3. **Tel** 022-629 30 93. 🚌 111, 117, 158, 507, 517, 521. 🚋 7, 8, 9, 22, 24, 25. ☐ noon–6pm Sat–Thu, noon–8pm Fri. ● public hols. 📷 (free Fri). **Military Museum Tel** 022-629 52 71. ☐ 10am–5pm Wed, 10am–4pm Thu–Sun. ● some public hols. 📷 (free Wed). 🎫

Originally established in 1862 as the Fine Art Museum, the National Museum (Muzeum Narodowe) was created in 1916. Its vast collection was started in 1862 with the purchase of 36 paintings. Subsequent acquisitions have turned the museum into one of the city's finest. Collections include ancient Greek, Roman, and Egyptian art, archaeological finds from Faras in present-day Sudan, and medieval Polish religious paintings, altarpieces, and sculptures.

The foreign art collection features Italian, French, Dutch, and Flemish works. There is a fine *Madonna and Child* by Sandro Botticelli. In the vast Polish art collection are works by Bernardo Bellotto (1720–80), nephew of Canaletto, who settled in Warsaw and painted fine views of the city. Of native Polish artists, Jan Matejko (1838–93) is one of the finest on display. He painted historical subjects such as *The Battle of Grunwald*. In an east wing, the **Military Museum** illustrates the history of Polish firearms and armor.

For hotels and restaurants in this region see p760 and p761

The impressive Neoclassical facade of Wilanów Palace, designed for King Jan III Sobieski

Łazienki Park ⑪

Łazienki Królewskie, Agrykola 1.
Tel 022-506 01 01. 🚌 116, 166, 180, 195. **Park** ⭘ daily until dusk.
Palace on the Water ⭘ 9am–4pm
Tue–Sun. ⬤ days after public hols. 📷

This huge park, studded with palaces, temples, and monuments, originally dates from the Middle Ages, when it belonged to the Mazovian dukes. By the early 17th century, it was owned by the Polish crown, and housed a royal menagerie. In 1674 the Grand Crown Marshal Stanisław Herakliusz Lubomirski acquired the park, and Tylman of Gameren designed its hermitage and bathing pavilion. The pavilion gave the park its name, as *łazienki* means "baths."

In the 18th century, the park was owned by King Stanisław August Poniatowski, and he commissioned Karol Agrykola, Karol Schultz, and Jan Schuch to lay it out as a formal garden. A number of new buildings were also completed during this time, and the pavilion was redesigned, by Dominik Merlini, as a royal summer residence. This became known as the **Palace on the Water**, and is one of the finest examples of Neoclassical

architecture in Poland. It now houses an architecture museum. Unfortunately the king was only able to enjoy the palace for a few years, as after the Third Partition of Poland he was forced to abdicate, and left Warsaw on January 7, 1795. The Nazis planned to blow it up but, lacking time on their withdrawal, set fire to it instead. It was rebuilt by 1965.

Solomon's Hall, reception room of Palace on the Water, Łazienki Park

Wilanów Palace and Park ⑫

S.K. Potockiego 10–16. **Tel** 022-842 25 09. 🚌 E2, 116, 117, 130, 180, 519. **Palace** ⭘ daily. ⬤ Jan, Tue (in winter). 📷 📷 **Park** ⭘ 9:30am–dusk daily. 📷 (free Thu). 📷

Although it was a royal residence, Wilanów Palace, which is set within parkland

and beautiful formal gardens, was actually designed as a private retreat for King Jan III Sobieski, who valued family life above material splendor. The original property, known as Villa Nova, was purchased in 1677 and within two years had been rebuilt as a mansion, designed by royal architect Augustyn Locci. The elaborate facades were adorned with sculptures and murals, while the interiors were decorated by Europe's finest craftsmen.

Enlarged over subsequent years by its many different owners, the palace gained two large wings, a pair of towers, and a first-floor banqueting hall. The north wing comprises 19th-century rooms, formerly used as living quarters and as a gallery. The largest room, the Great Crimson Room, is used as a venue for entertaining VIPs. The south wing includes the late Baroque Great Dining Room, designed for King August II Mocny, as well as Princess Izabela Lubomirska's apartments, which feature a bathroom dating from 1775.

The most interesting rooms in the main part of the palace are the Neoclassical Great Hall, with marble detailing and allegorical friezes, and the ornate King's Bedchamber, with its 17th-century Turkish bed canopy. There are also apartments once occupied by King Jan III Sobieski and his wife Marysieńka, which retain many of their original 17th-century features, as well as an old nursery, governesses' rooms, and a fascinating portrait gallery. Outside the palace, in the old riding school building, there is an interesting poster museum.

The enchanting Palace on the Water, Łazienki Park

Cracow **2**

Royal Castle
The Birds Hall, with its gilded coffered ceiling and marble fireplace, is one of the later 17th-century rooms in the castle's Royal Apartments.

Head in Deputies' Hall, Royal Castle

For nearly six centuries Cracow was the capital of Poland and the country's largest city. Polish rulers resided at Wawel Castle until the court and parliament moved to Warsaw in 1596. Even then Cracow continued to be regarded as the official capital and rulers were still crowned and buried in the cathedral on Wawel Hill. The city still plays an important role in preserving the national identity. The prestigious Jagiellonian University is the oldest in the country and the city is full of memorials to illustrious Poles. Perhaps Cracow's greatest attraction lies in the fact that, unlike so many Polish cities, it was scarcely damaged in World War II. In recent years many buildings and monuments have been restored to their former glory.

WAWEL HILL

In about 1038 Kazimierz the Restorer made the citadel on Wawel Hill the seat of Polish political power. In the 16th century the Jagiellonian rulers transformed the Gothic castle into a magnificent Renaissance palace and endowed the cathedral with new chapels and works of art.

Lost Wawel Exhibition

Statue of Tadeusz Kościuszko

Cathedral Museum

Fortified walls

Dragon's Lair

Cracow Cathedral
The Zygmunt Chapel with its striking gilded dome was one of many additions to the cathedral made in the early 16th century.

The foundations of medieval houses that stood within the castle walls have been excavated here. The houses were razed by the Austrians in 1805–6 to create a parade ground.

For hotels and restaurants in this region see p760 and p761

♔ Royal Castle

Wawel 5. *Tel 012-422 51 55.*
3, 6, 8, 10, 18, 40.
Royal Apartments ⬜ *daily.*
⬤ *Mon; public hols.* 🎟 *(free Mon).*
Orient in the Wawel ⬜ *Tue–Sun.*
⬤ *Mon; public hols.* 🎟 ✆
www.wawel.krakow.pl

The present Renaissance castle
was built in the first half of the
16th century. After the royal
court moved from Cracow to
Warsaw in 1596, the castle fell
into decay. At the start of the
20th century it was given to
the city of Cracow and work
began to restore it to its
former grandeur.

The richly decorated Royal
Apartments are the main
reason for visiting the castle.
Most of the rooms reflect the
tastes of the last Jagiellonian
kings. They contain Italian
paintings and furniture,
painted friezes around the
walls, and a fine collection
of Flemish tapestries. The
Hall of Deputies was where
the lower house of the Polish
parliament, the *Sejm*, met for
debates. It is also known
as the Hall of Heads
because the ceiling is
decorated with carved
heads. On the top floor
there is a suite of rooms
from the 17th century,
with portraits of the Waza
kings, including one of
Prince Władysław (later
Władysław IV) by Rubens.
The Crown Treasury and
Armory are situated on
the ground floor. The
treasury's collection of
royal jewels and regalia
includes the coronation sword
of the Polish kings.

The "Orient in the Wawel"
collection on the first and
second floors features Turkish
tents and banners seized by
the victorious Christian troops
at the Siege of Vienna in 1683.

Turkish tent in the "Orient in the Wawel" exhibition in the castle

Royal Castle with the so-called Hen's Claw Wing on the right

🏛 Lost Wawel Exhibition

Wawel Hill. *Tel 012-422 51 55.*
⬜ *daily.* ⬤ *Nov–Mar: Mon, public
hols.* 🎟 *(free Sun in winter, Mon in
summer).*

An exhibition in the basement
includes the remains of an
early church, thought to date
from the 11th century. Computer models illustrate the
development of Wawel Hill.

**Baroque silver reliquary of St. Stanisław by Peter
von der Rennen (1669–71), Cracow Cathedral**

♙ Cracow Cathedral

Wawel 3. *Tel 012-429 33 27.*
8, 18. ⬜ *daily (Sun: pm only).*
Cathedral Museum *Tel 012-429 33
21.* ⬜ *Mon–Sat.* 🎟

Originally founded in 1020,
the present cathedral is the
third to stand on this site. It
was completed in 1364 during
the reign of Kazimierz the
Great. The resting place of
many Polish kings, the cathedral has always held great
symbolic significance for the
nation. It is dedicated to St.
Stanisław, whose relics are
housed in an ornate reliquary
in the shape of a coffin
beneath an eye-catching
Baroque altar canopy in the
center of the nave.

The original Gothic cathedral
has seen many subsequent
additions, notably the Baroque
spire built in the early 18th
century and the side chapels,
which have been remodeled
many times. There are many
fine tombs of Polish rulers. The
Renaissance Zygmunt Chapel
was built in 1519–33 by the
Italian Bartolomeo Berrecci. It
contains an impressive double
monument in red marble to
Zygmunt the Old (reigned
1506–48) and his son Zygmunt
August (reigned 1548–72). Look
out too for the late Gothic
canopied sarcophagus of
Kazimierz Jagiellończyk
carved by Veit Stoss (1492)
in the Chapel of the Holy
Cross. The marble tomb of
Stefan Batory (reigned
1576–86), created by
Santi Gucci in 1595,
stands behind the altar.

The crypt is divided
into sections containing
the tombs and sarcophagi
of other Polish rulers,
leading poets, and
national heroes, including
Tadeusz Kościuszko, leader of
the failed insurrection of 1794.

The Cathedral Museum
houses a collection of sacred
art and a selection of Polish
royal regalia, including the
coronation robe of the last
Polish king, Stanisław August
Poniatowski (reigned 1764–95).

🏛 Dragon's Lair

Wawel Hill. ⬜ *Apr–Oct: daily.*
Beneath Wawel Hill is a series
of caves associated with the
legend of a dragon. In summer
part of the cave system can be
reached by a set of spiral steps.
Children take delight in the
bronze, fire-breathing statue
of a dragon at the entrance.

Cracow: the Old Quarter

In 1257 Cracow was granted a charter by Duke Bolesław the Chaste. This was of key importance to the city, ensuring local government and trade privileges and stimulating the city's future development. The charter stipulated certain conditions: a large centrally located square, surrounded by a regular grid of streets, was to become the city center. The size of each plot determined the size of the houses. Although the architecture became ever more opulent over the centuries, this urban scheme has survived almost intact. To this day the Old Quarter remains the heart of modern Cracow. Many of the streets are pedestrianized, allowing visitors to enjoy the great concentration of historic sights.

The Slacker Crucifix (1496) by Veit Stoss in St. Mary's Church

The City Hall Tower in the western corner of Market Square

🏛 Market Square

Rynek Główny.
The Market Square is said to be the largest town square in Europe. In summer nearly 30 street cafés remain open here until the early morning. Flower stalls, street musicians, and artists selling their works all contribute to the lively atmosphere. The ornate Cloth Hall virtually divides the square in two. Two other buildings stand in the square: the small green-domed Church of St. Adalbert, below which is a museum of the history of the square, and the City Hall Tower, a relic of the original Gothic town hall. There is also a monumental statue of the great Polish poet Adam Mickiewicz (1798–1855).

Buildings around the square retain elements from every era in the history of the city. Many are decorated with an emblem that gives the house its name, for example the Palace of the Rams on the west side of the square, home of a famous cabaret since 1956. Christopher Palace takes its name from a 14th-century statue of St. Christopher. The house was remodeled in 1682–5 around a beautiful arcaded courtyard. It is home to the Museum of Cracow, where paintings, gold artifacts from local workshops, documents, and memorabilia are displayed in a series of grand stuccoed rooms.

🏛 Cloth Hall

Market Square 1/3. **Tel** 012-424 46 00. ⬤ Tue–Sun. 📷 📷
The Cloth Hall (Sukiennice) in the middle of Market Square originated in medieval times as a covered market. It was rebuilt after a fire in 1555 and then remodeled entirely in 1875 with arcades along the exterior that give it a Venetian look. Most of the stalls today sell souvenirs of various kinds and there is a gallery of 19th-century Polish painting on the upper floor. The Cloth Hall also contains a number of cafés – the Noworolski Café is one of the best in Cracow.

🔒 St. Mary's Church

Mariacki Square 5. **Tel** 012-422 05 21. ⬤ daily (pm only Sun). 📷 📷
St. Mary's facade with its two impressive Gothic towers is set at an angle on the east side of Market Square. The left-hand tower is topped by a spire added in 1478. It served as the city's watch tower and still today a bugle call is played every hour. It is even broadcast on Polish radio at noon. The projecting porch between the towers was added in the Baroque period.

The church's greatest treasure is the huge altarpiece, 12-m (39-ft) high, by Veit Stoss, who lived in Cracow from 1477 to 1496. The outer panels show scenes from the lives of Christ and the Virgin. The middle shutters are opened each day at noon to reveal the huge carved centerpiece, *The Assumption of the Virgin* (see p742). There is also a fine crucifix by Veit Stoss, known as the Slacker Crucifix.

Horse-drawn cabs lined up in front of the Cloth Hall in Market Square

🏛 Czartoryski Museum

Św. Jana 19. **Tel** 012-422 55 66.
🚌 124, 152, 424, 502. 🚊 2, 3, 4,
12, 13, 14, 15, 24. 🌐 for renovations,
call to check. 📷 📹 (Sun).

The core of the museum is
the art collection assembled by
Princess Isabella Czartoryska
in the late 18th century. It
contains some magnificent
paintings, notably Leonardo
da Vinci's *Lady with an Ermine*
and Rembrandt's *Landscape
with the Good Samaritan*. The
museum also has decorative
arts from all over Europe and
a section on Polish history.

**Leonardo's *Lady with an Ermine*
in the Czartoryski Museum**

🏛 Collegium Maius

Jagiellońska 15. **Tel** 012-422 05 49.
🚌 124, 152, 424, 608, 902. 🚊 15,
18. 🌐 Mon–Sat. 📷 📹 obligatory
(call to book visit).

This is the oldest building of
the Jagiellonian University. In
the 15th century a number of
houses were amalgamated to
create lecture rooms and
housing for professors. It was
extensively remodeled in the
mid-19th century. At the heart
of the building is an attractive
Gothic cloister. The University
Museum moved here after
World War II. Visitors can see
the 16th-century Libraria and
Great Hall, rooms still used
by the Senate of the university,
and the Treasury. There is also
a Copernicus Room dedicated
to the great astronomer, who
studied here in 1491–5.

🍃 Planty

🌐 daily.

The Planty green belt follows
the outline of Cracow's
medieval walls, which were
demolished in the early 19th

century. A circuit through the
park of about 5 km (3 miles)
starting from Wawel leads
along tree-lined paths and
avenues, past fountains and
statues. Only a small stretch of
the city walls survives beside
St. Florian's Gate at the north
end of the Old Town. Nearby
stands a well-preserved round
barbican built in 1498–9,
when Turkish incursions were
a serious threat to the city.

✡ Old Synagogue

Szeroka 24. **Tel** 012-422 09 62. 🚊 9,
11, 13, 24, 29, 50. 🌐 daily. 🌐 Nov–
Mar: Tue. 📷 (free Mon).

In the late 15th century
Cracow's Jewish quarter was
established in the Kazimierz
district, east of Wawel Hill. At
the outbreak of World War II
there was a community of
some 70,000 Jews. The Nazis
moved them all to a ghetto
across the river, from where
they were eventually deported
to concentration camps.

Amazingly, a number of
Jewish sites have survived.
The Old Synagogue, carefully
restored after the war, is not
used for worship, but houses
the Jewish Museum. The
Remu'h Synagogue (c.1553),
also on Szeroka Street, still
functions. It is named after
Rabbi Moses Remu'h, a
16th-century philosopher,
whose tomb in the **Remu'h
Cemetery** attracts pilgrims
from all over the world. Most
of the graves were destroyed
by the Nazis, but fragments
from them have been piled
up to form a "wailing wall."

Hall of Prayers in Cracow's Old Synagogue

**Entrance gate to the Auschwitz
extermination camp**

Environs

Although the name Oświęcim
means little to most foreigners,
its German form **Auschwitz**
evokes fear and horror in people
all round the world. It was
here near the little town of
Oświęcim, about 55 km
(35 miles) west of Cracow,
that the Nazis established
their largest complex of concentration and extermination
camps. The Auschwitz camp
opened in June 1940, and in
March 1941 a much larger
camp was set up at nearby
Birkenau (Brzezinka in Polish).
In all, over 1,500,000 Jews and
others were murdered here.
The gas chambers, capable of
killing thousands daily, were
in use from 1942 to January
1945, when the camps were
liberated by Soviet troops.

The area has been declared
a UNESCO World Heritage
Site and the two camps are
preserved as the **Muzeum
Oświęcim-Brzezinka** – a grim
warning to future generations
of mankind's capacity for
inhumanity. Many
structures were
destroyed as the
Nazis left, but the
gate, with the
chilling words
"Arbeit macht frei"
("Work makes
free") written above
it, still stands.

🏛 Muzeum Oświęcim-Brzezinka

ul. Więźniów
Oświęcimia 20. 🚉 🚌
Tel 033-843 21 33.
🌐 daily (closing time
varies between 3pm
in winter and 7pm in
summer). 📷 **www.**
auschwitz.org.pl

Practical & Travel Information

Since the fall of Communism in 1989, tourism has greatly increased in Poland. New shops and hotels have sprung up, and the quality of service has improved, especially in banks and post offices. Nevertheless, much of Poland's economy has yet to adjust to the post-Communist era; the health service has been reformed, but it lags behind the country's many developing sectors. In general, goods in Poland are much cheaper than in Western Europe.

VISAS AND CUSTOMS INFORMATION

A valid passport is required for admittance to Poland, but you may not need a visa; contact the Polish embassy in your country for details. Personal items may be brought into the country, but limits are imposed on the import and export of alcohol, tobacco, and cigarettes. Antiques exported from the country require a special permit. Gifts worth up to €150 may be imported duty free.

PERSONAL SECURITY

Polish cities suffer from the same crime and security problems as most European capitals, so vigilance and care are needed. Security is provided by the state police, the highway police, and a number of private security organizations. The latter are often hired to protect public buildings and private houses, and to keep order at various events. In the city of Warsaw, it is advisable to avoid the Praga district after dusk, and in particular Ulica Brzeska.

MEDICAL EMERGENCIES

Citizens of the following countries are entitled to free medical treatment in Poland: EU members, Belarus, Tunisia, Ukraine, Mongolia, China, and the countries of the former Yugoslavia.

For visitors from other countries, first aid is provided free of charge at hospitals, but other types of treatment may incur a charge. Nevertheless, all visitors are advised to take out full medical insurance before arriving in Poland. Keep your policy documents with you at all times, as well as a passport for identifying yourself to hospital staff. An ambulance service is available 24 hours a day.

TOURIST INFORMATION

Information centers are generally found at train stations; these provide general regional information. For specific enquiries about accommodations, tickets, and trains, **Orbis** agencies are preferable. Hotel employees are also a good source of information.

CURRENCY AND BANKING

The official Polish currency is the złoty, each of which is divided into 100 grosze. In January 1995, four zeros were knocked off the złoty, so that 10,000 złoty became one Polish New Złoty (PLN). The old banknotes were withdrawn and replaced with new notes. Money can also be changed at bureaux de change, many of which offer better rates than banks. The majority of banks are open from 8am to 6pm.

DISABLED TRAVELERS

Poland has a poor record for providing for disabled people, but things are rapidly changing. All renovated or new public buildings have ramps or lifts built into them, and there are also special taxis available. Nevertheless, many traditional sites of interest may prove difficult to enter. For general advice or for information about specific sites, contact the **Disabled People's National Council**.

COMMUNICATIONS

Widespread use of mobile phones means there are fewer payphones than before, but phonecard-operated telephones can still be found, especially around railway stations, post offices, and the city center. Phonecards can be bought at post offices and newsagents. Charges for long-distance national calls vary according to the time of day. The highest charges are for calls made between 8am and 6pm. Local calls are cheaper from 10pm to 6am. The charges for international calls do not vary with time of day. Poland has five mobile telephone networks, which operate on two wavelengths, 900 MHz and 1,800 MHz, and cover almost all of the country.

Poczta Polska, the Polish postal service, provides a wide range of services, and its offices are open from 8am to 8pm on weekdays; the main post office in Warsaw is open 24 hours a day, seven days a week. Letters to destinations

---

THE CLIMATE OF POLAND

Poland's climate is influenced by cold polar air from Scandinavia, and subtropical air from the south. Polar-continental fronts dominate in winter, bringing crisp, frosty weather, while late summer and autumn (the most popular times to visit) enjoy plenty of warm sunny days. Winters, which always bring snow, can be very cold in the north.

WARSAW

°C/F	Apr	Jul	Oct	Jan
high	7/45	21/70	7/45	
		11/52		
low (0°C/32°F)	0/32		2/36	-3/27
				-8/18
sun (hrs)	5 hrs	7.5 hrs	3 hrs	1.5 hrs
rain (mm)	42 mm	56 mm	40 mm	40 mm

within Poland usually arrive within three or four days of posting, while international mail may take up to a week; intercontinental mail can take up to three weeks. Local correspondence (within a town) should be posted in the green post boxes, and all other mail should be posted in the red boxes. For urgent mail, Poczta Polska provides both an express service and a courier service. The international DHL and UPS courier agencies also operate in Poland.

TRAVELING BY PLANE

Poland is well connected with the rest of the world. International flights from some 90 cities in 40 countries arrive in Warsaw. The airports at Gdańsk, Katowice, Szczecin, Poznań, Wrocław, and Cracow also have international flights, linking Poland with much of Western Europe, as well as Prague, Budapest, Sofia, Bucharest, and the capitals of the former Soviet Union. Some 30 airlines, including British Airways, Air France, SAS (Scandinavia), and Lufthansa (Germany), operate from **Warsaw Okęcie** airport, which has direct connections with Canada, the US, Israel, and Thailand. **Cracow Balice**,

the second largest airport in Poland, offers a substantial number of domestic and international flights.

TRAVELING BY BUS

Most long-distance routes within Poland are served by Polish Motor Transport, Polska Komunikaja Samochodowa (PKS). A competitor is Polski Express, which offers cheaper fares, air-conditioned coaches, and pleasant staff, but the journeys tend to be longer, for the routes are rarely direct.

Local buses are sometimes the only means of getting to minor towns and villages. The services are generally punctual, although before 8am and in the afternoon they may be crowded. Tickets for these are always bought from the driver.

TRAVELING BY TRAIN

International train services run between all major European and Polish cities. The journeys by fast train from Warsaw to Prague and Berlin take just six and nine hours respectively. The main rail route runs across Poland from east to west, connecting Russia with western Europe.

Express lines connect almost all the big cities, and the trains

are fast and usually arrive on time. The most comfortable, and most expensive, are the InterCity trains, which also give passengers a snack. Euro and InterCity trains both provide compartments for mothers with children and for disabled people. Fares for ordinary and fast trains are very reasonable; express trains and sleeping cars are expensive, although not by the standards of the rest of Europe.

Suburban routes are served by electric trains, which sometimes consist of open-plan, double-decker cars.

TRAVELING BY CAR

Poland has few highways, and those that exist are generally in poor condition. An exception is the Cracow–Katowice highway, the first stretch of what promises to be a network of highways spanning the entire country.

Wherever you drive in Poland, always carry your passport, car insurance, license, green card, and rental contract with you, and if you are driving a foreign car, display the international symbol of its country of origin.

All the major international car rental companies operate in Warsaw and Cracow.

DIRECTORY

TOURIST OFFICES IN POLAND

Cracow
Rynek Główny 1–3.
Tel 012-433 73 10.

Warsaw
ul. Krakowskie Przedmieście 65.
Tel 022-635 18 81.

TOURIST OFFICES OUTSIDE POLAND

UK
First Floor, Remo House, 310–312 Regent Street, London W1B 3AX.
Tel 020-7580 8811.
www.poland.travel/en-gb

US
275 Madison Ave, New York 10016.

Tel 212-338 9412.
www.poland.travel/en-us

EMERGENCY NUMBERS

Ambulance
Tel 999.

Fire Brigade
Tel 998.

Medical Advice
Tel 94 39.

Police
Tel 997.

EMBASSIES

Australia
ul. Nowogrodzka 11, Warsaw.
Tel 022-521 34 44.

Canada
ul. Matejki 1/5, Warsaw.
Tel 022-584 31 00.
www.canada.pl

UK
ul. Kawalerii 12.
Tel 022-311 00 00.
www.ukinpoland.fco.gov.uk

US
Al Ujazdowskie 29/31, Warsaw. **Tel** 022-504 20 00. **http://**poland.usembassy.gov

FACILITIES FOR THE DISABLED

Disabled People's National Council
ul. Sapieżyńska 10a, Warsaw.
Tel 022-831 85 82.

TRAIN STATIONS

Warsaw Central
Jerozolimskie 54.
Tel 022-511 60 03.

AIRPORTS

Cracow John Paul II
Tel 012-639 00 00.

Warsaw Chopin
Tel 022-650 42 20.

CAR RENTAL

AVIS Poland
Cracow, ul. Lubicz 23.
Tel 012-639 32 89.

Warsaw Airport.
Tel 022-650 48 72.
www.avis.pl

Hertz Rent-a-Car
Cracow, al. Focha 1.
Tel 012-429 62 62.

Warsaw Airport.
Tel 022-650 28 96.
www.hertz.com.pl

Where to Stay in Poland

Poland has experienced a big improvement in hotel standards. Many new luxury hotels have been built, the majority of them part of international hotel chains. In Warsaw, good, moderately priced hotels are scarce. In central Cracow, however, a number of historic 19th-century hotels have been modernized.

PRICE CATEGORIES
Price categories are for a standard double room including breakfast, tax, and service:

ⓩ Under 270 złoty
ⓩⓩ 270–400 złoty
ⓩⓩⓩ 400–600 złoty
ⓩⓩⓩⓩ 600–800 złoty
ⓩⓩⓩⓩⓩ Over 800 złoty

WARSAW

CITY CENTER Nathan's Villa Hostel
ul. Piękna 24–26, 00-549 **Tel** 022-622 29 46 **Fax** 022-622 29 46 **Rooms** 10   **Map** C5

Warsaw's best-loved hostel boasts dormitories, modern fittings, and a quiet courtyard location. Facilities on offer include fast Internet access, a fully equipped kitchen, and daily laundry. A range of private rooms has been added for those who do not wish to share a dormitory. **www.nathansvilla.com**

CITY CENTER Radisson Blu Centrum
ul. Grzybowska 24, 00-132 **Tel** 022-321 88 88 **Fax** 022-321 88 89 **Rooms** 311   **Map** C2

Chic five-star lodgings in the heart of Warsaw's financial quarter. The hotel's modern front conceals rooms designed in three separate styles: maritime, Scandinavian, and Italian. Amenities include swimming pool and a gym, while those with less time on their hands will enjoy the addition of the "grab-and-run" breakfast. **www.radissonblu.com**

CITY CENTER InterContinental
ul. Emilii Plater 49, 00-125 **Tel** 022-328 88 88 **Fax** 022-328 88 89 **Rooms** 326   **Map** C3

A three-legged futuristic tower with a 40th-floor swimming pool that looks on to the Palace of Culture and Science. Immaculate rooms befit the hotel's ultra-modern style and offer Internet access along with cable TV. Restaurants and bars can be found on the lower floors. **www.warsaw.intercontinental.com**

CITY CENTER Le Royal Meridien-Bristol
ul. Krakowskie Przedmieście 42/44, 00-325 **Tel** 022-551 10 00 **Fax** 023-625 25 77 **Rooms** 205   **Map** D3

A sumptuous Art Nouveau building and arguably the most famous hotel in Poland: the guest list runs from regents to rock stars. Rooms combine a pre-war aesthetic with 21st-century gadgetry, and the hotel has won countless awards for excellence. The Sunday brunches are renowned across the city. **www.lemeridien-bristol.com**

FARTHER AFIELD Premiere Classe
ul. Towarowa 2, 00-811 **Tel** 022-624 08 00 **Fax** 022-620 26 29 **Rooms** 126

Basic rooms come with TVs and adjoining modern bathrooms in this building, which also houses Premiere Classe's sister hotels: the Campanile and Kyriad Prestige. The best one-star choice in Warsaw, and recommended for budget travelers who count themselves too old for hostels. Advance booking essential. **www.premiereclasse.com.pl**

CRACOW

OLD QUARTER Elektor
ul. Szpitalna 28, 31-024 **Tel** 012-423 23 17 **Fax** 012-423 23 27 **Rooms** 15

In recent years, Prince and Princess Takamodo of Japan, King Harald V of Norway, and Grand Duke Jean of Luxembourg have all stayed at this outstanding hotel, widely regarded as the city's best. Nothing is too much trouble for the staff here, who make it their mission to please all guests, royalty or otherwise. **www.hotelelektor.com.pl**

OLD QUARTER Fortuna
ul. Czapskich 5, 31-110 **Tel** 012-422 31 43 **Fax** 012-411 08 06 **Rooms** 25

A historical hotel where service always comes with a smile. Set in a charming building, it has rooms that are larger than usual for this type of building, and the bathrooms are also well sized. There is a café-restaurant, and secure parking available on site. **www.hotel-fortuna.com.pl**

OLD QUARTER Pollera
ul. Szpitalna 30, 31-024 **Tel** 012-422 10 44 **Fax** 012-422 13 89 **Rooms** 42

An Art Nouveau gem in the heart of the Old Town, the Pollera was founded in 1834 and has welcomed its guests with flair and style ever since. During World War II, the Germans fell in love with the place and forbade anyone else (except staff) from entering. Today all are welcome, though you will need to book. **www.pollera.com.pl**

Key to Symbols see back cover flap.

Where to Eat in Poland

Polish food has seen a change of image with the opening of a new generation of restaurants all over Poland. Many take pride in updating traditional specialties, such as *pierogi* (ravioli) and dumplings. Good restaurants are plentiful in Warsaw and Cracow but watch out for high prices in the more touristy areas.

PRICE CATEGORIES
Price categories for a three-course meal per person, including half a bottle of wine and all unavoidable extra charges:
㉑ Under 50 złoty
㉑㉑ 50–70 złoty
㉑㉑㉑ 70–90 złoty
㉑㉑㉑㉑ 90–110 złoty
㉑㉑㉑㉑㉑ Over 110 złoty

WARSAW

CITY CENTER Kompania Piwna Podwale 25 ㉑
ul. Podwale 25, 00-261 **Tel** 022-635 63 14 **Map** D2

This inexpensive old-town gem has a courtyard designed to resemble a Central European town square, and an interior filled with wooden benches and drinking slogans on the walls. Grilled meat and potatoes are served on wooden boards by staff dressed in traditional attire.

CITY CENTER Adler ㉑㉑㉑
ul. Mokotowska 69, 00-530 **Tel** 022-628 73 84 **Map** D5

Decked out with baskets of dried flowers and the odd *Pickelhaube* (spiked helmet), Adler embodies the atmosphere of a Bavarian beer hall, with staff in costume rushing around delivering gigantic portions of pig's neck and *Schnitzel*. The relatively high prices tend to draw in a corporate crowd, however.

CITY CENTER Papaya ㉑㉑㉑
ul. Foksal 16, 00-372 **Tel** 022-826 48 51 **Map** D4

A great addition to Warsaw's booming fusion scene, Papaya features a *tepanyaki* grill and dishes like Kobe sirloin, and tuna steak with Thai basil and shrimps. The white color scheme creates a hip, urbane atmosphere that attracts trendy young things. Expect a heavy bill at the end of your meal.

CITY CENTER U Fukiera ㉑㉑㉑㉑㉑
Rynek Starego Miasta 27, 00-272 **Tel** 022-831 10 13 **Map** D2

A main-square location and a guest list that includes world leaders and royalty speak volumes for U Fukiera's reputation – and prices. Set inside a beautiful network of chambers, it is worth a visit for the interior alone, while the menu focuses on Polish classics cooked with ingenuity. The summer courtyard represents starlit dining at its finest.

FARTHER AFIELD Dom Polski ㉑㉑㉑㉑
ul. Francuska 11, 03-906 **Tel** 022-616 24 32

Having dinner at Dom Polski has long been a vital rite of passage for holiday-makers and expats alike, and this stands out as one of the classiest treats in Warsaw. The menu is seasonal but often includes fantastic game dishes, while the interiors of this pre-war villa are redolent of a country manor.

CRACOW

OLD QUARTER Pierogarnia ㉑
ul. Sławkowska 32, 31-015 **Tel** 012-422 74 95

No visitor to Cracow should leave the city without tasting the Polish specialty of *pierogi* (ravioli), and Pierogarnia is about the best place in town to enjoy that experience. Fillings are innumerable, and these tasty treats can be eaten as a snack or as part of a larger meal. The restaurant also serves other Polish delicacies.

OLD QUARTER Farina ㉑㉑㉑㉑
ul. św. Marka 16, 31-017 **Tel** 012-422 16 80

In this simple, uncluttered restaurant, the bare, highly polished wooden floors and white-washed walls are geared towards focusing the diner's attention on the excellent menu. A successful mix of Polish and Italian dishes attracts crowds of locals and visitors. Reservations are necessary in the evenings.

OLD QUARTER Cyrano de Bergerac ㉑㉑㉑㉑㉑
ul. Sławkowska 26, 31-014 **Tel** 012-411 72 88

Prices here may be high but they do not seem to deter diners from booking weeks in advance. This is a world-class French restaurant spread over two elegant rooms, with a quiet patio used in the summer months. The food is exquisite, cooked under the auspices of masterchef Pierre Gallard. Try the *garbure soupe béarnaise* (a thick soup).

Map References see map of Warsaw pp748–9

General Index

Acknowledgments

Dorling Kindersley would like to thank the following people whose contributions and assistance have made the preparation of this book possible.

Main Contributors
Amy Brown, Nina Hathway, Vivien Stone, Kristina Woolnough.

Additional Contributors
John Ardagh, Rosemary Bailey, David Baird, Josie Barnard, Rosemary Barron, Gretel Beer, Ros Belford, Marc Bennetts, Willem de Blaauw, Kathleen Blankenship Sauret, Susie Boulton, Gerhard Bruschke, Caroline Bugler, Paula Canal, Chloe Carleton, Christopher Catling, Robin Clapp, Anthony Clark, Juliet Clough, Deidre Coffey, Dan Colwell, Marc Dubin, Paul Duncan, Sylvia Earley, Joanna Egert-Romanowska, Olivia Ercoli, Judith Fayard, Jane Foster, Stephanie Ferguson, Lisa Gerard-Sharp, Mike Gerrard, Jane Graham, Andrew Gumbel, Mark Harding, Andy Harris, Vicky Hayward, Zöe Hewetson, Sally Hogset, Adam Hopkins, Lindsay Hunt, Nick Inman, Tim Jepson, Colin Jones, Emma Jones, Marion Kaplan, Ciara Kenny, Alister Kershaw, Piotr Kozlowski, Wojciech Kozlowski, Sarah Lane, Michael Leapman, Philip Lee, Alec Lobrano, Sarah McAlister, Jerzy S. Majewski, Fred Mawer, Lynette Mitchell, Colin Nicholson, Melanie Nicholson-Hartzell, Roger Norum, Tadeusz Olsański, Małgorzata Omilanowska, Agnes Ördög, Robin Osborne, Lyn Parry, Robin Pascoe, Alice Peebles, Tim Perry, Polly Phillimore, Filip Polonsky, Paul Richardson, Anthony Roberts, Barnaby Rogerson, Zöe Ross, Doug Sager, Kaj Sandell, Jürgen Scheunemann, Jane Shaw, Barbara Sobeck-Miller, Vladimír Soukup, Solveig Steinhardt, Robert Strauss, Martin Symington, Allan Tillier, Nigel Tisdall, Roger Thomas, Tanya Tsikas, Annika Tuominen, Alison Vagen, Gerard van Vuuren, Roger Williams, Timothy Wright, Scott Alexander Young.

Illustrators
Acanto Arquitectura y Urbanismo S.L., Stephen Conlin, Gary Cross, Richard Draper, Nick Gibbard, Paul Guest, Stephen Gyapay, Studio Illibill, Kevin Jones Associates, Paweł Marczak, Maltings Partnership, Chris Orr and Associates, Otakar Pok, Robbie Polley, Jaroslav Staněk,

Paul Weston, Andrzej Wielgosz, Ann Winterbotham, John Woodcock, Martin Woodward, Piotr Zubrzycki.

Design and Editorial Assistance
Douglas Amrine, Claire Baranowski, Sonal Bhatt, Julie Bond, Emer FitzGerald, Rhiannon Furbear, Lucinda Hawksley, Matthew Ibbotson, Jacky Jackson, Laura Jones, Priya Kukadia, Michelle de Larrabeiti, Delphine Lawrance, Jude Ledger, Catherine Palmi, Helen Partington, Dave Pugh, Pete Quinlan, Marisa Renzullo, Simon Ryder, Sands Publishing Solutions, Sadie Smith, Leah Tether, Hugh Thompson, Conrad van Dyk, Karen Villabona, Simon Wilder, Dora Whitaker.

Factchecker
Jessica Hughes.

Proofreader
Stewart J. Wild.

Index
Hilary Bird.

Additional Picture Research
Marta Bescos, Nicole Kaczynski.

Additional DTP
Vinod Harish, Vincent Kurien, Azeem Siddiqui.

Additional Cartography
Uma Bhattacharya, Mohammad Hassan, Jasneet Kaur.

Production
Joanna Bull, Sarah Dodd, Marie Ingledew.

Publishing Manager
Helen Townsend.

Managing Art Editor
Jane Ewart.

Director of Publishing
Gilllian Allan.

Additional Photography
Max Alexander, Peter Anderson, Gabor Barka, Steve Bere, Clive Bournsnell, Maciej Bronarski, Demetrio Carrasco, Andrzej Chec, Krzysztof Chojnacki, Stephen Conlin, Joe Cornish, Andy Crawford, Michael Crocket, Wojciech Czerniewicz, Tim Daly, Jiří Doležal, Philip Dowell, Mike Dunning, Philip Enticknap, Jane Ewart, Foto Carfagna

+ Associati, Philip Gatward, Steve Gorton, A. Hayder, Heidi Grassley, John Heseltine, Gabriel Hilderbrandt, Roger Hilton, Rupert Horrox, Ed Ironside, Dorota Jarymowicz, Mariusz Jarymowicz, Piotr Jamski, Colin Keates, Paul Kenward, Alan Keohand, Dave King, Jiří Kopřiva, Mariusz Kowalewski, Vladimír Kozlík, Adrian Lascom, Cyril Laubscher, Neil Lukas, Eric Meacher, Wojciech Mędrzak, Neil Mersh, John Miller, John Moss, Roger Moss, David Murray, Hanna Musiał, Maciej Musiał, Tomasz Myśluk, Stephen Oliver, John Parker, Agencja "Piękna," Milan Posselt, František Přeučil, Rob Reichenfeld, Tim Ridley, Kim Sayer, Jules Selmes, Anthony Souter, Clive Streeter, Stanislav Tereba, Matthew Ward, Alan Williams, Peter Wilson, Jeremy Whitaker, Linda Whitwam, Stephen Whitehorn, Paweł Wójcik, Stephen Wooster, Francesca Yorke, Jan Zych.

Additional Assistance
Dorling Kindersley would like to give special thanks to Britt Lightbody of the Danish Tourist Board, Henrik Thierlein, International Press Officer for Wonderful Copenhagen, Petter Ree of the Norwegian Embassy in London, Riitta Balza at the Finnish Tourist Board, London, and journalist Tone Sendberg.

Photography Permissions
Dorling Kindersley would like to thank all the churches, museums, galleries, and other sights that kindly gave their permission for us to photograph their establishments and works of art.

Picture Credits
a = above; b = below/bottom; c = center; f = far; l = left; r = right; t = top.

Works of art have been reproduced with the permission of the following copyright holders:
Maman Louise Bourgeois © DACS, London/VAGA, New York 2011 59tl; *Young Woman on the Shore* Edvard Munch © Munch Museum/Munch – Ellingsen Group, BONO, Oslo/DACS, London 2011, 663bl; *Guernica* Pablo Picasso © Succession Picasso/DACS, London 2011, 31bc; Pit Stop (1984) Jean Tinguely © ADAGP, Paris and DACS, London 2011 617tr.

The publisher would like to thank the following individuals, companies, and picture libraries for permission to reproduce their photographs:

AKG London: *Cosimo de Medici* 420b, *St. Augustine* by Carpaccio 421crb, *Niccolò Machiavelli* 421br; Museo Archeologico Nazionale, *Farnese Hercules* 444c; Collection Archiv für Kunst und Geschichte, Berlin 718cla, 470t; Staatliche Kunstsammlungen, Kassel, *William I of Orange* by Anthonis Mor (1556) 246t; Museum Boijmans-van Beuningen, Rotterdam, *The Tower of Babel* (c.1525) by Peter Brueghel the Elder 263br; Naturhistorisches Museum/Eric Lessing 595brc; Niedersächsisches Landesmuseum, Hanover, *Friedrich II* by Antoine Pesne 524t; Rijksmuseum, *Winter Landscape with Skaters* (1618) by Hendrick Avercamp 256tc; San Francesco, Assisi/ Stefan Diller, *St. Francis Appears to the Monks at Arles* by Giotto (c.1295) 28br; Staatliche Kunstsammlungen, Dresden/ Gemäldegalerie Alte Meister, *Girl Reading a Letter* by Vermeer 542tr; Vatican Museums, Rome 27tl; Alamy Images: Brendan Hoffman 696bl; Ken Welsh 365tl; Alvey and Towers: 147br; Museum Amstelkring: 250tr; Amsterdams Historisch Museum: 252br, 253cl; Ancient Egypt Picture Library: The Trustees of the British Museum 24cla; Apex Photo Agency: 39t; Arenas Fotografia Artistica: 325cr; Arquivo Iconografico S.A., Barcelona: Museo del Prado, *The Triumph of Bacchus* by Velázquez 288tl; The Art Archive: The Imperial War Museum 231bl; The British Library 125bl; Art Directors & TRIP: C. Rennie 639bc, 641b, 649b; Artothek Specialarchiv für Gemäldefotografie, Peissenberg: *Four Apostles* (1526) by Albrecht Dürer 551tr; James Austin: 152b; Austrian National Tourist Board: 592bc; Avignon Tourisme: 191cr.

Basilica de la Sagrada Familia: Pep Daudé 313crb; C.H. Bastin & J. Evrard: 232bc; Bayerisches Nationalmuseum, Munich: 552t; La Belle Aurore: 193b; Berliner Dom: 534br; Bethnal Green Museum of Childhood/ Victoria & Albert Museum, London: 57b; Bildarchiv Preussischer Kulturbesitz: 532t; Kunstgewerbemuseum, Berlin 531c; Pergamon Museum, Berlin 25tl; Gérard Boullay: 155c, 155bl; The Bridgeman Art Library: Basilica di San Francesco, Assisi, *The Ecstasy of St. Francis* by Giotto 406tr;

The British Museum 52c, 53tl, *The Festival of Sekhtet* 52br, *The Young Prince with his Parents* 53c; Lauros-Giraudon/Chateau de Versailles, France, *Equestrian Portrait of Louis XIV* (c.1692) by Pierre Mignard 29tr; Crown Institute/Institute of Directors, London, UK, *Field Marshal King Leopold I of Belgium* by Nicholas Pieneman 220t; Galleria degli Uffizi, Firenze, *The Venus of Urbino* (1538) by Titian 422b, *The Duke of Urbino* (1460) by Piero della Francesca 423tr, *The Duchess of Urbino* (1460) by Piero della Francesca 423tl, *Madonna of the Gold-finch* (1506) by Raphael 424b; Kunst-historisches Museum, Vienna, *Matthias I, Hunyadi* (1440–90) 730t; Louvre, Paris, *Virgin of the Rocks* (c.1478) by Leonardo da Vinci 29bl, *The Oath of the Horatii* (1784) by Jacques-Louis David 30clb; Munch-Museet, Oslo, *Young Woman on the Shore* (1896) by Edvard Munch 663bl; Musée Carnavalet, Paris 30cla; Museo del Prado, Madrid, *The Three Graces* (1635) by Rubens 288cr, *The Clothed Maja* (c.1800) by Goya 289tr, *The Naked Maja* (c.1800) by Goya 289cra, *The Martyrdom of St. Philip* (c.1639) by José de Ribera 289cr, *The Annunciation* by Fra Angelico (c.1387–1455) 290cr, *The Santo Domingo el Antiguo Altarpiece*, depicting *The Adoration of the Shepherds*, by El Greco (1541–1614) 290bl; Museo Nacional Centro de Arte Reina Sofia, Madrid, *Guernica* (1937) by Pablo Picasso 31bc; Private Collection, *Queen Elizabeth I* by Marcus Gheeraerts the Younger 38t; Royal Holloway & Bedford New College, *Princes Edward and Richard in the Tower* by Sir John Everett Millais 61b; St. Peter's, Vatican, *Pietà* by Michelangelo 2r; THE BRITISH MUSEUM: 26br, 53br, 479br; BRITSTOCK-IFA: F. Aberham 619br; Erich Bach 623bl; S. Bohnacker 600t; Bernd Ducke 600bl; Torsten Fleer 235br; P. Graf 650t; G. Grafenhain 235cla, 601bl, 620cla, 651tr, 683br; S. Gräfenwhain 622tl; B. Moller 648b; 624bl; AP&F/Thomas Ulrich 621bc; BUDAPESTI TORTENETI MUZEUM: 734br; BUDAPESTI TURISZTIKAI HIVATAL: 735bl; INTERNATIONAL BULBFLOWER CENTRE: 261tc; MICHAEL BUSSELLE: 140–141.

CAMERA PRESS: Cecil Beaton 46cb; GIUSEPPE CARFAGNA & ASSOCIATI: 427bc; BIÈRES DE CHIMAY S.A: 220b; CHUR Tourismus: 624tc; COLLECTIONS DU MUSÉE INTERNATIONAL D'HORLOGERIE, LA CHAUX-DE-FONDS, SUISSE: Photo Institut l'homme et le Temps 617c;

COLOGNE CATHEDRAL DOMBAUARCHIV: 562tl, 562cl, 562bl, 563tl, 563cra, 563crb, 563bl; ALAN COPSON PHOTOGRAPHY: 228cl; CORBIS: Archivo Iconografico, S.A., *An Old Woman Cooking Eggs* by Velázquez 85b; Arte & Immagini srl, *The Annunciation* by Fra Angelico 415tr; Yann Arthus-Betrand 304tl; Bettman Archive 525bl, 658t; Ric Ergenbright 522; Macduff Everton 650c; Historical Picture Archive 31bl; Hulton-Deutsch Collection 331cr; JAI/Alan Copson 371tr; Bob Krist 588t; Dennis Marsico 407tc; National Gallery London *Bathers at Asnières* by Seurat 49br; Richard T. Nowitz 623tr; José F. Poblete 625tl; Michael St. Maur Sheil 757tr; Gregor Schmid 523c; Ted Spiegel 665cl; Adam Woolfitt 143crb; JOE CORNISH: 77b, 78br, 79bl, 80b, 84t, 85t, 86b, 86t, 108c, 109b, 111tr, 124tr, 124bl, 126cl, 126cr, 126bl, 127tl, 127cr, 127br, 128cl, 128cr, 128bl, 128bl, 128br, 157t, 280t, 300tr, 319br, 366c, 367tr, 367cl, 367b, 471tr, 490t, 491br, 492b, 492t, 493b, 493t, 157t, 157t, 700–701; COVER ARCHIVO: Ilenas Quim 304br; CZARTORYSKI MUSEUM, CRACOW: *Lady with an Ermine* by Leonardo da Vinci 757cl.

IL DAGHERROTIPO: Riccardo D'Errico 443t; DEAN AND CHAPTER OF WESTMINSTER: 47bl; DEUTSCHES MUSEUM, MUNICH: 552b; C.M. DIXON: Vatican Museums, Rome 25br; JURGEN DRENTH: 244c; DUCHAS, THE HERITAGE SERVICE: 122b; DEUTSCHE PRESSE-AGENTUR GMBH: 542br, 554cla.

EMPICS LTD: Tony Marshall 389bl; ENGLISH HERITAGE: by kind permission of the Provost and Fellows of King's College, Cambridge 73tr; MARY EVANS PICTURE LIBRARY: 8r, 9c, 21c, 28tr, 30tr, 33c, 75bl, 81b, 110tl, 141c, *Napoleon Bonaparte* (c.1804) by Jacques-Louis David 146t, 273c, 278cr, 383c, 579c, 602bc, 635c, 640t, 674t, 701c; EYE UBIQUITOUS: James Davis 316br.

SIGMUND FREUD MUSEUM, VIENNA: 596br. GETTY IMAGES/STONE: Hideo Kuihara 2; Panoramic Images 530t; Hugh Sitton 65t; James Strachan 704clb; GODO-FOTO: 318br; NICHOLAS P. GOULANDRIS FOUNDATION MUSEUM OF CYCLADIC AND ANCIENT GREEK ART: 474bl; MICHAEL GRYCHOWSKI: 754tr; ©FMBG GUGGENHEIM BILBAO MUSEOA: London 2001. Erica Barahona Ede (All rights reserved. Total or partial reproduction is prohibited) 31bra; GUINNESS IRELAND ARCHIVES, DUBLIN: 121c.

Sonia Halliday Photographs: 35ca; Robert Harding Picture Library: 23c, 23t, 27br, 159br, 171t, 279tr, 395b, 603tc, 620tr, 621tr, 621bla, 623cl, 637b, 649t, 682tl, 689bc, G. Hellier 603b, 739bl; K. Gillam 691b; Simon Harris 602t; John Miller 23c; The Picture Store 651b; Roy Rainford 520br; Chris Rennie 279tr; Adina Tovy 38b; Adam Woolfitt 637cla, 675t, 683cl; Gordon Henderson 81t; Historic Royal Palaces 1999 (Crown Copyright): 63t; Angelo Hornak Library: 78cla; Hulton Archive: 29tc, 30b, 146b, 228br, 253cr, 471c, 662bl, 708t; Imperial War Museum 31tl; Hungarian National Gallery: 734tr; Hungarian Tourist Board: 739tr.

Ideal Photo S.A.: T. Passios 489t; Images Colour Library: 293ca, 293cb; Impact Photos: Brian Harris 387b; Index Fototeca: 323c; Instituto Português de Museus: Museu Grão Vasco 362tr; Istituto e Museo di Storia della Scienza, Florence: 419br.

Stanisława Jabłońska: 744, 755bl; Paul Jackson 49tl; Jarrold Publishing: ©2001 His Grace Duke of Marlborough 75c; Michael Jenner Photography: 124bc; Jewish Historical Museum, Amsterdam: Liselore Kamping 251tr; Joods Historisch Museum, Amsterdam: 251tr; Jorvik, York: 79tl.

Oldrick Karasek: 706, 722b, 722t, 723tl, 723b; Kennedy PR: 114cla; Koninklijk Museum voor Schone Kunsten, Antwerp: As the Old Sang, The Young Play Pipes (1638) by Jacob Jordaen 230bl; Kunsthistorisches Museum, Vienna: 25cr, 594tr, 596c,25cr, Empress Elisabeth (1865) by Winterhalter 594tl, Hunters in the Snow (1565) by Peter Brueghel the Elder 596t.

Locarno Film Festival: 625bl; Luxembourg Tourist Office: pictures by kind permission of the Luxembourg Tourist Office, London 221b.

Tom Mackie: 32–33; Madame Tussaud's, London: 54bla; Magyar Nemzeti Muzeum: 736bc; Maria Laach Kunstverlag: 559c; MAK – Österreichische Museum für Angewandte Kunst: 597cl; Markgräfliches Opernhaus, Bayreuth: 557t; Mercedes-Benz Museum, Stuttgart: 557t; Musei Capitolini, Rome: 27bl; Musei Vaticani e Capella Sistina, Rome: 394c, 394bl, 394t, 395tl, 395cr, 395ca, 396t, 396cl, 397tc, 397cr, 397cb, 398t; Museu da Cidade, Lisbon: Portrait of Marquês de Pombal 361t; Museum Huis Lambert van Meerten, RBK: 263cl; Museum Jean Tinguely Basel: © ADAGP, Paris and DACS, London 2011 617tr; Museum of London: 58b; Museu da Marinha, Lisbon: Manuel I by Alberto Cutileiro 354t, Vasco da Gama 363br; Musée National du Château de Versailles: 168tr, 168cl, 168bl, 169tr, 169tlb, 169bc; Musées Royaux des Beaux-Arts de Belgique: 226bc; Museo Nacional del Prado, Madrid: The Garden of Delights (1505) by Hieronymus Bosch 288crb; Museo Thyssen-Bornemisza, Madrid: Our Lady of the Dry Tree (c.1450) by Petrus Christus 286bl.

National Gallery of Ireland, Dublin: The Taking of Christ (1602) by Caravaggio (Reproduction courtesy of the National Gallery of Ireland, Dublin) 117b; National Trust Photographic Library: 130b; Nick Meers 77c; Trustees of the National Museums of Scotland: 28tr; Nippon Television Network Corporation: Original Sin by Michelangelo, detail from the Sistine Chapel ceiling, Vatican, Rome 398br.

Oronoz Archivo Fotográfico: 293cla, 299c, 326c; J.A Fernandez 304tr.

PA Photos: DPA 31tr; EPA 525tr; Palace of Culture and Science, Warsaw: 749cr; Palais Het Loos: E. Boeijinga 261bl; Pictures Colour Library: 682b, 738tr; Robbie Polley: 232bla; Powerstock/Zefa Ltd: 750tl; Mauritius Gallery 598bc; Prisma Archivo Fotográfico, Barcelona: Palacio del Senado, The Fall of Granada by Francisco Pradilla 278tl.

Rex Features: 66c, 67br, 71c; Denis Cameron 325tr; Pertti Jenytin 688c; Sipa Press 196tr; Rijksmuseum Amsterdam: 257c; The Wedding Portrait (c.1622) by Frans Hals 24tr; The Kitchen Maid (1658) by Jan Vermeer 256cl; St. Elizabeth's Day Flood (1500) 256bc; The Night Watch (1642) by Rembrandt 257tl; Woman at her Toilet (1660) by Jan Steen 257br; The Jewish Bride by Rembrandt 258br; Réunion Des Musées Nationaux Agence Photographique: Louvre/Lewandowski/LeMage Mona Lisa (La Joconde) by Leonardo da Vinci 160t; Louvre/Herve Lewandowski 160c; Gilles or Pierrot (c.1717) by Watteau 24clb; The Royal Collection: ©2001 Her Majesty

Queen Elizabeth II: 60br, 60b, 61tl, 66tr, 67tl, 67tr, 67bl.

SABMiller/Pilsner Urquell: 554cr; Photo Scala, Florence: 394br, 394bla, 396b; Hermitage Museum, St. Petersburg: *After the Bath* by Edgar Degas 25cra; Basilica di San Francesco, *St. Francis* (1280) by Cimabue 406cl, *The Deposition* (1323) by Lorenzetti 406bl, *The Life of St. Martin* (1315) by Simone Martini 406br; *Pope Leo X* 420clb; Palazzo Medici Riccardi, Firenze, *The Procession of the Magi* by Gozzoli 420–421; 421tl, 421ca, 443bla; Accademia, Venice, *The Feast in the House of Levi* by Veronese 441b; Bargello, Firenze, *David* by Donatello 418cl; Galleria degli Uffizi, Firenze, *Adoration of the Magi* by Leonardo da Vinci 423cb; *The Ognissanti Madonna* (1310) by Giotto 422c, *The Birth of Venus* (1485) by Botticelli 423c, *The Holy Family* (1507) by Michelangelo, *Madonna of the Long Neck* (c.1534) by Parmigianino 424t; *The Annunciation* by Leonardo da Vinci 25crb; Galleria dell'Accademia: *Cassone Adimari* by Lo Scheggia 415b; Schlossverwaltung, Munich: 544b, 549t, 555c; Herman Scholten: 245b; Science Museum, London: 56tl, 56bl; Science Photo Library: M-SAT Ltd 10c; Scope: 186tr, 187c, 187br; Spectrum Colour Library: 8; Staatsgalerie, Stuttgart: *St. Paul in Prison* (1627) by Rembrandt 556tr; Stad Brugge Stedlijke Musea: 234tc; Städelsches Kunstinstitut und Städtische Galerie, Frankfurt am Main: *Portrait of a Woman* (1480) by Sandro Botticelli 560c; Statens Historiska Museum: 647c, 665tc, 665cr; Stiftung Preussische Schlösser und Gärten Berlin-Brandenburg: 541br; Stockphotos: David Hornback 277b; Swiss National Museum, Zürich: 614c; Swiss National Park: 620clb, 620cb, 620bl; Swiss Tourist Office: 622b.

Tate, London 2001: Marcus Lee, *Maman* (1999) by Louise Bourgeois © DACS, London/VAGA, New York 2011 59t; Topham Picturepoint: 621cr; Toros Magazine: 293cr; The Travel Library: Galleria dell'Accademia 412bl; Trinity College, Dublin: Courtesy of the Board of Trinity College, Dublin 115t, 116tl, *Portrait of St. Matthew* from *The Book of Kells* 116c, 125t; Tivoli: 673.

Van Gogh Museum, Amsterdam: Courtesy of the Vincent van Gogh Foundation 259c; *The Bedroom at Arles* by Vincent van Gogh 259t; Vasa Museum, Stockholm: Hans Hammarskiold 646bl.

Jeremy Whitaker: 75bl; Christopher Wilson: 78bl; Peter Wilson: 468; Jeppe Wikström: 20–21, 638c, 642b, 644b, 645t; Wonderful Copenhagen: 672c, 679tr, 681bl, 683tr; World Pictures: 588b.

York Castle Museum: 79c.

Zefa, Warsaw: 520cla, 555b, 556br, 561b.

Jacket:
Front – 4Corners: SIME/Giovanni Simeone; Back – Dorling Kindersley: Demetrio Carrasco clb, Alex Havret bl, Diana Jarvis tl, cla; Spine – 4Corners: SIME/Giovanni Simeone t.

All other images © Dorling Kindersley.
For further information see:
www.dkimages.com

SPECIAL EDITIONS OF DK TRAVEL GUIDES

DK Travel Guides can be purchased in bulk quantities at discounted prices for use in promotions or as premiums. We are also able to offer special editions and personalized jackets, corporate imprints, and excerpts from all of our books, tailored specifically to meet your own needs.

To find out more, please contact:
(in the United States) **SpecialSales@dk.com**
(in the UK) **travelspecialsales@uk.dk.com**
(in Canada) DK Special Sales at **general@tourmaline.ca**
(in Australia) **business.development@pearson.com.au**

Europe's Rail Network

It was in Britain that railroads were first developed in the second quarter of the 19th century, and Europe is still criss-crossed by tens of thousands of kilometers of track. Only the main routes are shown on this map. Although many lines are badly in need of modernization, the main intercity routes use high-speed, comfortable trains, making rail a quick and convenient form of transportation for many journeys both within and between countries (*see p18*). London to Paris, for example, takes just three hours, and you can travel from Paris to Marseille in the same time. Prices vary considerably from country to country. In Great Britain, for example, standard tickets are almost three times the price for equivalent journeys in Italy. Details on the rail services of individual countries are given in the *Travel Information* sections of the appropriate chapters.